CHINA

U.S. POLICY SINCE 1945

Congressional Quarterly, Inc.

Congressional Quarterly Inc., an editorial research service and publishing company, serves clients in the fields of news, education, business and government. It combines specific coverage of Congress, government and politics by Congressional Quarterly with the more general subject range of an affiliated service, Editorial Research Reports.

Congressional Quarterly was founded in 1945 by Henrietta and Nelson Poynter. Its basic periodical publication was and still is the CQ *Weekly Report,* mailed to clients every Saturday. A cumulative index is published quarterly.

The CQ *Almanac,* a compendium of legislation for one session of Congress, is published every spring. *Congress and the Nation* is published every four years as a record of government for one presidential term.

Congressional Quarterly also publishes books on public affairs. These include the twice-yearly *Guide to Current American Government* and such recent titles as *Energy Policy; The Middle East: U.S. Policy, Israel, Oil and the Arabs, Fourth Edition;* and *The Washington Lobby, Third Edition.*

CQ Direct Research is a consulting service which performs contract research and maintains a reference library and query desk for the convenience of clients.

Editorial Research Reports covers subjects beyond the specialized scope of Congressional Quarterly. It publishes reference material on foreign affairs, business, education, cultural affairs, national security, science and other topics of news interest. Service to clients includes a 6,000-word report four times a month bound and indexed semi-annually. Editorial Research Reports publishes paperback books in its fields of coverage. Founded in 1923, the service merged with Congressional Quarterly in 1956.

Editor: DuPre Jones
Major Contributor: Michael R. Gibson. **Contributors:** Renee Amrine, Alan Berlow, John Felton, Peter Harkness, Sumie Kinoshita, Bob Livernash, Buel W. Patch, Pat Towell.
Indexer: Diane Huffman
Art Director: Richard Pottern. **Staff Artist:** Robert O. Redding.
Production Manager: I. D. Fuller. **Assistant Production Manager:** Maceo Mayo.

Book Department Editor: Patricia Ann O'Connor

Copyright 1980 by Congressional Quarterly Inc.
1414 22nd Street, N.W., Washington, D.C. 20037

Cover Design: Richard Pottern
Cover Photo: Joseph Weichbrod (The photo was taken at the opening of the 30th anniversary celebration of the founding of the PRC, Oct. 1, 1979, in Peking. The Chinese characters read: "We must press ahead vigorously to create a strong modernized socialist state.")

Library of Congress Cataloging in Publication Data

Congressional Quarterly, inc.
  China: U.S. Policy since 1945.
  Bibliography: p.
  Includes index.
  1. United States — Foreign relations — China. 2. China — Foreign relations — United States. 3. China — History — 1945- 4. United States — Foreign relations — 1945- I. Title.

E183.8.C5C72   1980   327.51073   79-27840
ISBN 0-87187-188-2

Editor's Note

China: U.S. Policy Since 1945 provides a wide-ranging but concise account of China-U.S. relations since the Second World War. It follows the developing China policy of U.S. presidential administrations, Congresses and institutions — and the attitudes of the American people — toward the giant nation, as the Sinophobia of the 1950s gave way to the initiatives toward conciliation by both countries during the 1970s.

It also traces the tumultuous postwar years of China — its political, social and ideological upheavals, its shifting relations and alliances with the Western world and its emergence into the modern economic and sociopolitical family of nations.

China: U.S. Policy Since 1945 examines the events and personalities that shaped the post-war Chinese Revolution and China's entry into the global power politics of the Cold-War era; China's position in the Communist bloc; and its initial mutual hostility with the United States as China backed challenges to the U.S.-supported governments of South Korea and South Vietnam. In addition, it reports and documents China's growing rift with the Soviet Union and with China's neighbors on the border, as well as its later, increasingly friendly relations with the United States, fermented by President Nixon's trip to Peking in 1972 and culminating in President Carter's bilateral normalization of relations between the United States and the People's Republic in 1978-79.

The book is divided into four major sections:

Part 1, "U.S. Relations with China," offers a narrative account of modern Chinese history and China's relations with the United States; the steps leading to rapprochement between the two nations; congressional attitudes and legislation *vis á vis* China; the effect of China as a campaign issue in U.S. presidential elections; the opening of avenues of trade between China and the Western world; and a summary of Chinese history before World War II.

Part 2, "Chronology of Events," outlines the often day-by-day occurrences that affected China and its relations with the rest of the world between 1945 and 1980.

Part 3, "Biographies," contains profiles of both the major and minor figures who played roles in the unfolding drama of Chinese affairs since World War II.

Part 4, "Texts and Documents," reproduces significant speeches, policy statements, government documents, legislation and other data relevant to China and its relations with the United States during the past three decades.

In addition, an appendix provides a guide to modern Chinese spelling and pronunciation; a record of United Na-tions votes on Chinese representation in the U.N.; and a number of charts and tables on Chinese demographics, economy and government structure.

Spelling and Transliteration

For the most part, this book employs the new *pinyin* system by which Chinese characters are translated phonetically into the Roman alphabet. The change from the traditional system, known as Wade-Giles, came about through a decree by the Chinese government effective Jan. 1, 1979. Most publications in the Western world have since adopted this new, more accurate system of transliteration.

However, because most English texts on China until 1979 rendered Chinese names in the traditional Wade-Giles system, the editors of this book have retained that spelling in the case of frequently recurring place names and the names of important Chinese leaders now deceased. Since most literature in English spells the name of Mao Tse-tung, for example, in Wade-Giles, this book — to maintain continuity with the bulk of earlier scholarship — has kept that spelling rather than adopting Mao's name in *pinyin* (Mao Zedong).

The most prominent proper names and place names for which the older spelling was retained are:

Proper names	*Place names*
Chiang Kai-shek (not Jiang Jieshi)	China (not Zhungquo)
Chou En-lai (not Zhou Enlai)	Canton (not Guangzhou)
	Hong Kong (not Xianggang)
Confucius (not Kong Fuzi)	Macao (not Aomen)
Lin Piao (not Lin Biao)	Manchuria (not Dongbei)
Liu Shao-ch'i (not Liu Shaoqi)	Matsu (not Mazu)
	Peking (not Beijing)
Mao Tse-tung (not Mao Zedong)	Quemoy (not Jinmen)
	Tibet (not Xizang)
	Yangtze (not Changjiang)

Chinese-Americans, Nationalist Chinese and others who prefer the traditional spelling of their own names are so rendered (e.g., Sun Fo; C. K. Wang)

Elsewhere the new *pinyin* system was used, as in the case of China's top-ranking current leaders, Deng Xiaoping (Teng Hsiao-p'ing in Wade-Giles) and Hua Guofeng (Hua Kuo-feng in Wade-Giles).

A full spelling and pronunciation guide appears on pp. 361-364.

Table of Contents

Summaries and Tables (Cont.)

Maps

Appendix

Index

Introduction

The United States recognizes the Government of the People's Republic of China as the sole legal government of China.

These words — spoken by President Jimmy Carter in a Dec. 15, 1978, announcement establishing diplomatic relations between China and the United States — formally ended a turbulent 30-year era in Sino-American affairs. The statement marked the last step in a prolonged diametric reversal of American policy toward the most populous nation on earth, and signaled the emergence of China — once considered a component in the communist "monolith" — as an independent global power of immeasurable potential.

This new epoch in Chinese-Western relations was by no means an overnight phenomenon, but the culmination of three decades of transition from open hostility and ideological dialectics between the United States and China, to guarded friendship and pragmatic diplomacy. It marked, too, an evolution in the perception of China's international role by its leaders.

Significantly, the new China-U.S. rapprochement was effected just before a series of crises in the Middle East seemed to usher in a period of renewed Cold War tensions and hostilities. The Sino-American alliance had already figured in efforts early in 1980 to deter further Soviet expansion beyond Afghanistan and was sure to be a factor in global politics and territorial defense — in that area and elsewhere around the world — for some time to come.

Enmity

The split in relations between the United States and China began officially on Oct. 1, 1949, when the Communist forces led by Mao Tse-tung formally established the People's Republic of China on the mainland after defeating the U.S.-backed Nationalists led by Gen. Chiang Kai-shek.

The Nationalists fled to the nearby island of Taiwan, where they set up the Republic of China as a mainland government in exile.

Though initially reluctant to provide military aid to Chiang's new regime, the United States changed its policy after the outbreak of the Korean War in June 1950. China's entry into the war in November cemented U.S. support for Chiang.

Opposition to Peking and support for Taiwan were codified by the mutual defense treaty with the Nationalists on Dec. 2, 1954, and the Formosa Resolution of Jan. 28, 1955. *(Texts, p. 311)*

For nearly 15 years after that, U.S.-Peking relations were essentially stalemated, as America's escalating involvement in another Asian land war — this time in Vietnam — perpetuated the mutual hostility between China and the United States. Nonetheless, ambassadorial-level talks went on in Geneva and Warsaw during that period, ending only after the American invasion of Cambodia in 1970. *(Box, p. 149)*

China, meanwhile, was suffering the internal upheavals of the Great Proletarian Cultural Revolution, which began in the mid-1960s and resulted in a period of political polarization, confusion and stifling of dissent. The Cultural Revolution generated a concomitant decline in China's influence over smaller communist countries, which drifted into the Soviet orbit or into neutrality. *(Cultural Revolution, p. 170)*

Reconciliation

There were cautious moves toward reconciliation in the first two years of the Nixon administration. The U.S. government eased restrictions on American travel to China, terminated the regular U.S. naval patrol in the Taiwan Strait, and announced that all nuclear weapons on Okinawa would be removed by 1970.

Over the same period China began to reassess its relationship with the United States. The increasingly open conflict between Peking and the Soviet Union, which culminated in March 1969 in a series of armed skirmishes along the border between the two countries, and which followed the Soviet invasion of Czechoslovakia the year before, made rapprochement with the United States more attractive to Peking than it had been before.

On April 6, 1971, during the international table tennis championships in Japan, the Chinese team invited the American players to visit mainland China before returning to the United States. The invitation was accepted, and on April 10 the team — accompanied by five American journalists — entered China. It marked the first officially approved visit by Americans to the mainland since the Communists took control in 1949.

The next dramatic step came on July 15, 1971, when President Nixon announced that he would visit Peking in early 1972 "to seek the normalization of relations between the two countries."

Nixon arrived in Peking Feb. 21, 1972, for a one-week visit that included an hour-long meeting with Communist Party Chairman Mao Tse-tung. Nixon and Premier Chou En-lai issued a joint communiqué indicating agreement on the need for increased contacts between the United States and China. The communiqué included U.S. "acknowledgement" of Peking's contention that Taiwan was part of China, and included a U.S. pledge ultimately to withdraw its military forces from Taiwan.

Meanwhile, the United States announced it would "support action . . . calling for seating the People's Republic of China" in the United Nations while continuing to oppose the expulsion of Taiwan. The issue reached a climax Oct. 25, 1972, when the U.N. General Assembly voted 76-35 to adopt a resolution calling for the seating of Peking, but also expelling Taiwan.

New Principals

In 1976 the two longtime leaders of the People's Republic — Mao Tse-tung and Chou En-lai — died. Mao was succeeded by Hua Guofeng, a member of the moderate faction, and later, Chou by Deng Xiaoping, a veteran of China's internecine political wars.

And in 1978 it was a new U.S. administration — that of Democrat Jimmy Carter, who had given little hint that he planned any radical initiatives toward China — that took the final decisive step of normalizing relations with the People's Republic.

These events — the Communist victory on the Chinese mainland, the Korean and Vietnam conflicts and China's real or perceived role in them, the upheavals in Chinese leadership and policy, the Nixon and Carter diplomatic breakthroughs and the subsequent unity of the two nations in opposing Soviet expansion into Afghanistan — were but the most visible episodes in a complex, continuing and often unpredictable East-West drama of confrontation that began long before World War II and its aftermath. *(Post-revolutionary events, p. 3; earlier history, p. 19)*

U.S. RELATIONS WITH CHINA

The Reopening of China

The war with Japan, 1937-1945, had united China's two dominant political blocs — the Communist Party under Mao Tse-tung, and the Kuomintang under Chiang Kai-shek — in an uneasy alliance against the common enemy. Defeat of Japan by the allied forces on Aug. 14, 1945, immediately plunged China back into open civil war between the two indigenous forces for control of the country.

As the defeat of Chiang Kai-shek's Nationalist forces by the Communists in 1949 became a foregone conclusion, the United States and most other Western powers adopted a pragmatic, somewhat equivocal wait-and-see policy toward the emerging government of mainland China.

Despite its earlier support for the Nationalists, the United States government, in a "white paper" issued in the summer of 1949, placed the blame for Chiang's downfall on the "corruption and incompetence" of the Nationalists. A month after the Nationalists fled the mainland, President Truman said the United States did not have "any intention of utilizing its armed forces to interfere in the present situation" and would not provide military aid or advice to the Nationalists. The Communists, anticipating Soviet support, began massing a force to invade Taiwan. In response, the administration, despite some Senate opposition, decided to maintain its "hands off" policy. According to some reports, the U.S. was even moving towards recognition of the new regime in Peking.

A number of rapidly evolving developments in the late 1940s, however, soon led the United States and its allies into a policy of hostility to Communist China that would prevail for most of the next three decades. Chief among these were the growing Sino-Soviet alliance, the postwar anti-communist mood of American politics, the perceived threat to Taiwan by the communist mainland, and — the central catalyst — the Korean War.

Korea and Taiwan

Communist North Korea's invasion of South Korea in June 1950 eventually caused the United States to reverse its China policy and support Chiang's regime. President Truman stated, June 27, that in view of North Korea's action, "the occupation of Formosa [Taiwan] by Communist forces would be a direct threat to the security of the Pacific area and to the United States forces." He ordered the U.S. 7th Fleet to prevent any Communist attack on Taiwan and to see that all Nationalist air and sea operations against the mainland were halted.

Large-scale intervention of Chinese Communist forces in Korea in November 1950 cemented American support of the Nationalist regime. It also brought a resolution from the United Nations General Assembly, by a 44-7 vote, declaring Peking guilty of aggression. This declaration marked a turning point in the policy of the United States toward admitting Communist China to the United Nations.

After the fighting in Korea and the protracted negotiations over a truce, eventually signed on July 27, 1953, American support of the Nationalist regime remained strong. Late in 1954, Washington signed a mutual defense treaty with Chiang, setting up a vast program of economic and military aid. *(Text, p. 304)*

Taiwan already possessed a nascent industrial capacity, and with American aid the real income of its people was doubled. (The United States provided almost $1.5 billion in grant economic aid in the 16 years prior to termination of the economic aid program on June 30, 1965.)

Early in 1955 the United States and mainland China stood on the verge of a military showdown over the tiny islands of Quemoy and Matsu lying in the Taiwan Strait a few miles off the Chinese mainland. At President Eisenhower's request, Congress authorized the use of American forces to defend the islands which, occupied by Chiang Kai-shek's forces, had come under Communist artillery attacks from the mainland. As it turned out, American forces were not sent to the islands; by April of that year Chinese Premier Chou En-lai said "the Chinese people do not want to have war with the U.S.A." and expressed a willingness to negotiate the issue.

In the midst of the Quemoy-Matsu crisis, the Senate ratified the mutual defense treaty with Chiang's government in which the United States pledged to defend Taiwan, the Pescadores and "such other territories as may be determined by mutual agreement" against attack from China. *(Text, p. 311)* The United States regarded China as the aggressor trying to impose international communism on Asia. As recounted by Sen. Mike Mansfield, D-Mont., "It was assumed that if the endorsement of the free nations were withheld, this regime . . . would wither and eventually collapse. On this basis, recognition was not extended to Peking. The official view was that the National Government . . . [on Taiwan] continued to speak for all of China."

That view prevailed among U.S. policy-makers for some 15 years thereafter, although many observers believed that continued strained relations between the United States and Communist China bore the seeds of eventual armed conflict. The American policy of peripheral military containment of mainland China clashed with Peking's interests in two central areas: Taiwan, where U.S. support of the Nationalist government ensured the latter's existence, and in Southeast Asia, where the United States and South Vietnam were engaged in open conflict with a Chinese ally, North Vietnam. *(Details, pp. 29-35; box, p. 35)*

In the face of these conflicts, tentative efforts — by China in the mid-1950s and by the U.S. in the mid-1960s —

3

were made to improve relations between the two countries. In the latter case, senior diplomatic officials in London were reported to have said early in 1966 that the United States, during discussions between the American and Chinese ambassadors in Warsaw, had informed China that it was ready to discuss both a normalizing of relations and Peking's sought-for membership in the United Nations. The Chinese were said to have rejected the offer, insisting that U.S. forces must withdraw from Vietnam and that the United States must agree to a global disarmament treaty before the question of improving relations could be taken up.

The State Department denied that the United States had made the reported offer. But China's reaction to the publication of Secretary of State Dean Rusk's statement of March 16, 1966, was consistent with past performance. The official Xinhua news agency called it a "sham" and a "scheme to carry out infiltration in China in the vain hope" that a new generation of Chinese leaders would adopt different politics. (*Text, p. 315*)

Contacts With Peking

Although the United States and China still stood at arm's length, other Western powers expanded their diplomatic and commercial contacts with mainland China. The 49 countries which recognized the Peking regime included Denmark, Finland, France, Great Britain, the Netherlands, Norway, Sweden, and Switzerland. When France recognized Communist China, Jan. 27, 1964, it was the first Western European country to do so since 1950; the others extended recognition shortly after the Communists ousted the Nationalists late in 1949.

Opposition by the United States to recognition of Communist China and to its admission to the United Nations played a major role in delaying acceptance of the Peking regime by many other states. But commercial contacts between mainland China and the West increased despite American efforts to restrict such trade. The United States permitted no trade with Communist China by American exporters or importers. Similar total trade embargoes were imposed by Washington on Cuba, North Korea and North Vietnam, though American trade in non-strategic goods with the U.S.S.R. and the communist countries of Eastern Europe was allowed.

Seven countries — six of them allied with the United States — provided almost three-fourths of China's imports by the mid-1960s: Australia, Japan, Canada, Argentina, Cuba, the United Kingdom and France (in order of trade volume). Japan was the major supplier of products other than wheat and flour. Major purchasers of Chinese products were Hong Kong, Japan, Cuba, Malaya and Singapore. The only West European countries taking more than $50 million worth of goods from China were Great Britain and West Germany. (*China Trade, pp. 63-72*)

China and World Communism

In the late-1950s, as the Soviets failed to support Chinese plans for invading Taiwan, a Sino-Soviet rift began to develop as the two countries vied for territory and control of communist satellite states. By 1960 the two communist giants were openly criticizing each other, and by the late 1960s mutual hostility was an established geopolitical fact. (*Box, p. 158*)

In 1959, and intermittently thereafter, China skirmished with India along the border in Tibet, Kashmir,

Bhutan, Sikkim and Nepal. Its victories over India and support for Pakistan further exacerbated relations with the Soviet Union, which had vowed friendship and support for India.

In 1965 Defense Minister Lin Piao advocated protracted guerrilla wars in the emerging nations of Africa, Asia and Latin America. Espousing this theory, China encouraged leftist revolution around the globe as it sought to establish its role as the true disciple of the Marxist-Leninist world communist movement — a role abrogated by the Soviet Union, said the Chinese, by the U.S.S.R.'s "peaceful coexistence" with the capitalist Western world.

On Oct. 16, 1964, China threw a scare into the rest of the world — especially the two nuclear superpowers, the United States and the Soviet Union — when it began testing atomic weapons. It exploded its first hydrogen bomb in June 1967 and detonated a three-megaton weapon in October 1970. In April 1970 China entered the space era — and demonstrated its missile capability as well — by orbiting its first satellite. (*Box, p. 224*)

Great Proletarian Cultural Revolution

Proponents of the American policy of containment without isolation were hopeful that China's attitude toward the nations on her periphery and toward the United States might change as the old-line communist leaders relinquished control and a new leadership took over. Most of the top Chinese officials had been engaged in revolutionary warfare all their adult lives. When they were replaced, some people believed, a less belligerent Chinese government, more concerned with domestic problems and less zealous for worldwide revolution, would take charge.

Mao Tse-tung, chairman of the Communist Party's Central Committee and long the major figure among Chinese Communists, was 73 years old in 1966 and reportedly ailing. The 19 members of the ruling Politburo averaged 66 years of age.

The segment of the population that gave most concern to Chinese leaders was the group in their twenties and thirties, who were viewed by the top ranks as more interested in bourgeois pleasure and material comforts than in world revolution. The day when the younger generation would take command, however, was several decades away. And many experts believed that the immediate successors of the current leaders would be no more amenable to accommodation with the United States than was the existing regime.

But in the mid-1960s, all speculation on Mao's possible successor became meaningless, for an unexpected power struggle had developed within the party hierarchy. It soon became apparent that Mao was not enjoying full control — in fact, he found himself in the minority in his own regime. The failure of the Great Leap Forward (1958-1961) and the subsequent loss of revolutionary zeal had disenchanted the chief officials in the Communist Party apparatus.

In order to put the country's youth to a revolutionary test, and at the same time provide an instrument for purging his opponents, Mao and his heir apparent, Defense Minister Lin Piao, created the Red Guards, a militant youth group dedicated to the dissemination and preservation of "Mao's Thought." Lin Piao had impressed Mao with his ability to organize the army, which was playing an increasingly important role in running the country, since Mao could no longer rely on party officials.

Thus the Great Proletarian Cultural Revolution was created, with the Red Guards as its vanguard. Its first victims were educators, writers, journalists, intellectuals and

Korea Conflict Took Three Years, 150,000 U.S. Casualties

"Liberated" from Japan in 1945 only to become a hostage to the Cold War, Korea remained divided at the 38th parallel, its two halves occupied by American and Russian troops until 1948, when communist refusal to accept U.N.-supervised elections led to establishment of rival regimes — the Soviet-sponsored People's Republic (North) and the U.S.-backed Republic of (South) Korea. Having withdrawn all troops in 1949 — in line with a policy of disengagement — the United States was unprepared for involvement in the war that began with a massive attack on South Korea by North Korea June 24, 1950 (U.S. time) and lasted three years at a cost of more than 150,000 American casualties. The war spanned three distinct phases.

Phase I. Minus the Soviet delegate (on boycott since January 1950) the U.N. Security Council June 25, 1950, called for a cease-fire and withdrawal of North Koreans. President Truman, advised by Gen. Douglas MacArthur in Tokyo that "complete collapse" of Republic of Korea (ROK) forces was imminent, ordered him June 26 to furnish air and naval support and to place the 7th Fleet in the Taiwan Strait to discourage Chinese Communist-Nationalist hostilities. Next day the Security Council effectively endorsed Truman's initiative, calling on U.N. members to "furnish such assistance as may be necessary to repel the armed attack and to restore international peace." Asked by MacArthur June 30 to authorize use of American ground forces, Truman promptly agreed, and the United States became fully committed to repelling the aggressor. One week later MacArthur was designated U.N. Supreme Commander.

Paced by Soviet tanks, North Korean forces led by Premier Kim Il Sung quickly captured Seoul, the capital of President Syngman Rhee's ROK regime, whose demoralized troops scattered before the rapidly advancing enemy. By the end of July, however, two U.S. divisions from Japan had stopped the advance at a perimeter surrounding Pusan, southeastern port city, where buildup of U.S. troops and supplies proceeded. MacArthur then won approval of the Joint Chiefs of Staff for amphibious assault on Inchon, port of Seoul, executed successfully Sept. 15, 1950. While the 10th Corps retook Seoul, the 8th Army broke out of the Pusan perimeter and by the end of September North Koreans were in flight across the 38th parallel.

Authorized by the Joint Chiefs to move north of the parallel to attain "destruction" of North Korean forces — but forbidden to cross into Manchuria or send planes north of the border — MacArthur sent American and ROK troops into North Korea, moving up to the Yalu River by the end of October. Despite evidence of a buildup of Chinese forces on both sides of the border, MacArthur ordered a final offensive to start Nov. 25, 1950, announcing that if successful "this should for all practical purposes end the war."

Phase II. The 8th Army offensive immediately buckled under the weight of an estimated 200,000 Chinese "volunteers" massed yet undetected in North Korea, and MacArthur proclaimed the onset of an "entirely new war." With U.S. and ROK forces in full retreat and suffering heavy casualties, MacArthur urged Washing-

ton to carry the war to the Chinese mainland, through the use of strategic bombing and Nationalist forces on Taiwan. Having from the outset determined to confine the issue to Korea, and now concerned lest World War III break out in East Asia, President Truman and his advisers rejected MacArthur's proposals and ordered him to regroup his forces and hold as much of Korea as possible. Under the field command of Gen. Matthew B. Ridgway, U.S. and ROK forces pulled back to the Han River south of Seoul early in January, then began a counterattack that retook Seoul in mid-March and recrossed the 38th parallel April 3, 1951.

Reflecting the see-saw situation in Korea, the United Nations had swung from a limited objective at the outset to the restoration of a united and democratic Korea (approved by the General Assembly Oct. 7, 1950, as victory loomed) back to the limited objective of a cease-fire and the status quo ante (resolved Dec. 14 as U.N. forces retreated). On Feb. 1, 1951, the General Assembly condemned China as an aggressor but restated its limited objective. As Ridgway's forces again approached the 38th parallel in March, President Truman was readying an offer to negotiate a settlement when MacArthur issued his own call for Chinese surrender. On April 11, 1951, Truman fired MacArthur, naming Ridgway to take his place.

Phase III. After turning back a new offensive begun April 22, U.N. forces were holding positions along a line just north of the 38th parallel when, on June 23, 1951, Soviet Deputy Foreign Minister Yakov A. Malik proposed a cease-fire and armistice along the parallel. Truce talks began July 10 and continued for two years, during which heavy but limited engagements were fought with neither side mounting the forces needed for a decisive breakthrough.

By the time President Eisenhower took office Jan. 20, 1953 — having redeemed a campaign promise by flying to Korea after his election — the only remaining issue concerned repatriation of prisoners, with the United States refusing to turn over North Koreans and Chinese unwilling to return to their homelands. On March 5 Soviet Premier Joseph Stalin died; three weeks later, the Chinese agreed to the screening of prisoners by a neutral commission, and the talks moved ahead rapidly to the signing of an armistice agreement July 26.

Repatriation was completed Sept. 6, the United Nations turning over 76,000 prisoners and the communists about 13,000. Many American prisoners had died from mistreatment; others had been "brainwashed" by their captors and used to buttress communist charges that the United States had engaged in "germ warfare." When political talks that began Oct. 26 showed the communists prepared to stall indefinitely, U.S. envoy Arthur H. Dean walked out Dec. 12, 1953, and no further agreement was reached. Faced with evidence that North Korea was violating the truce terms in numerous respects, the U.N. Command announced its decision in mid-1957 "to restore the relative balance of military strength" by modernizing South Korean equipment, beginning with the delivery of F-100 jet fighters. As the 1980s began, Korea was still split into two hostile camps.

propagandists. But on June 2, 1966, it was reported that the mayor of Peking, Peng Zhen, and the army's chief of staff, Luo Reiqing, had been removed from their offices. Other major officials soon followed.

A polarization of the different factions ensued, with Mao and Lin coming out in the minority. Their main opposition centered around chief of state Liu Shao-ch'i and Deng Xiaoping, the party's secretary-general. Liu was dropped to eighth place in the party hierarchy, but, significantly, he evidently could not be dismissed altogether.

By late August 1966, the Red Guards had become uncontrollable, beating people, destroying art objects and churches, burning and plundering. But they continued to encounter resistance, forcing Peking to send orders to the Red Guards to cool off and a warning to party officials and government employees not to interfere with the activities of the youth group. By late September, however, it was clear that Mao's opposition had grown rather than diminished, as Red Guards in the provinces met armed opposition.

The civil unrest fomented by the Cultural Revolution continued apace for several years, eventually forcing the ouster not only of Liu and Deng, but many of the top leaders of the party, leaving the country in a political shambles. An element of stability began to be restored when the army intervened to stop the unrest, but trouble broke out again in 1971 after an abortive coup attempt by Lin, who was then purged himself, along with many of his supporters. After that, despite the continuing troublesome influence of oppressive radicals led by the so-called "gang of four," *(p. 285)* surviving moderates led by Chou En-lai and a subdued Mao Tse-tung began to rebuild the shattered political structure. *(Box, p. 199)*

Power Abroad Diminished

During the most violent years of the Cultural Revolution, China's influence in world affairs waned appreciably. Although China continued to pay lip service to worldwide popular revolution, it offered little real assistance to Third-World nations, and the evident confusion projected by the Cultural Revolution discouraged alliances with such an apparently unstable regime. New governments in Indonesia and Ghana, for example, turned away from China, North Korea kept its distance and North Vietnam drifted into the Soviet orbit. Sino-Soviet relations deteriorated so badly that Chinese leaders feared an armed conflict with their erstwhile ally.

According to one count, by Oct. 1, 1966, the 17th anniversary of the People's Republic, China had picked quarrels with no fewer than 32 countries. Only five foreign governments sent delegations to the Oct. 1 observances in 1967. President Lyndon Johnson said in his State of the Union message to Congress, Jan. 17, 1968: "The radical extremism of their government has isolated the Chinese people beyond their borders."

By the late-1960s the optimism and ambition generated by the 1949 revolution had turned bleak in nearly every sector of Chinese life.

Economically, the government's far-reaching plans for industrial and agricultural modernization had gone awry, leaving the country still far behind the giant nations with which it sought eventual parity.

Internationally, China — while sustaining its apparently implacable hostility toward the United States and most of the Western democracies — had alienated its powerful ally, the Soviet Union, and had lost its influence over the left-wing leaders of emerging Third-World nations.

And internally, the country was still struggling to escape from the disaster imposed upon it by the oppression and ideological rigidity of the Cultural Revolution.

China's emergence from this low point in its modern history lay not only in its own traditional resiliency, but in a dramatic and unexpected new willingness by the United States — and those allies under its sway — finally to come to terms with the new Chinese leadership.

Peaceful Overtures

Throughout the 1960s, despite the efforts of a vocal minority advocating rapprochement with Peking, the anti-communist, pro-Taiwan spokesmen dominated American political attitudes toward and dealings with the People's Republic.

Portents

That atmosphere began to change during the Lyndon Johnson years. The Senate Foreign Relations Committee held hearings in March 1966 to which a number of scholars were called to participate in a forum on "China and American attitudes toward China." The problem, as presented by A. Doak Barnett, then of Columbia University, was "how to reestablish a reasonable basis for contact and discourse between the United States and mainland China." In that year the United States eased restrictions on the travel of scholars to communist countries, and President Johnson said in a televised speech that eventual reconciliation with China was necessary. He said the United States would seek to reduce tensions between the two countries.

There is evidence to suggest that China began to reassess its position of hostility toward the United States near the end of the decade. The reassessment came at a time when the Sino-Soviet dispute over communist ideology had flared, in March 1969, into a series of armed skirmishes along the Manchurian-Siberian border, and following the Soviet invasion of Czechoslovakia in 1968. And it came after the turbulent Cultural Revolution of 1966-69 had subsided.

The Nixon administration has been credited with bringing about the first stage of a momentous diplomatic revolution in United States policy toward Communist China.

As a presidential candidate in 1960, Nixon — already famous as an anti-communist hard-liner — strongly opposed admitting China to the United Nations. In 1966, he warned of war with China "if we reward aggression in Vietnam." But as a candidate in 1968, he had begun to voice the need for a reversal in U.S. China policy:

". . . We simply cannot afford to leave China forever outside the family of nations, there to nurture its fantasies, cherish its hates and threaten its neighbors. There is no place on this small planet for a billion of its potentially most able people to live in angry isolation. . .," he said.

Stressing what was later to become the administration's Asian policy, Nixon said that "Only as the nations of non-Communist Asia become so strong — economically, politically and militarily — that they no longer furnish tempting targets for Chinese aggression, will the leaders in Peking be persuaded to turn their energies inward rather than outward. And that will be the time when the dialogue with mainland China will begin." He maintained that the world could not be safe until China changed and that the long-range goals of the United States would best be served by "pulling China back into the world community."

Speaking also in 1968 on China as a nuclear threat, Nixon said "At the end of this century, Communist China will have a billion people that will have unlimited atomic weapons and it can be exporting them all over the world, and it is essential that whoever is the next President of the United States develop policies now that will get Communist China to change so that we can open a dialogue with them."

Reaching Out to Peking

On Jan. 27, 1969, Nixon stated in his first presidential news conference, "Until some changes occur on their side . . . I see no immediate prospect of any change in our policy" toward Communist China.

Yet, by the end of the year, the administration had made several cautious overtures toward increasing U.S. contacts with the People's Republic of China, despite the fact that at first Peking showed little interest in reciprocating.

● On July 21, 1969, the State Department announced a slight easing of travel and trade restrictions. (A total embargo had been in effect since President Truman invoked the 1917 Trading with the Enemy Act against Peking in 1950.) American tourists and residents abroad were allowed to bring into the United States $100 worth of Chinese Communist-origin goods for non-commercial purposes. In addition, scholars, professors, journalists, university students, members of Congress, scientists, physicians and Red Cross representatives were automatically entitled to have their passports validated for travel to mainland China.

● In November 1969, the administration quietly ended the regular two-destroyer patrol (of the 7th Fleet) in the Taiwan Strait. The U.S. Navy had maintained a presence in the strait since June 1950.

● On Dec. 19, 1969, the government announced that subsidiaries and affiliates of U.S. firms abroad would be permitted to sell non-strategic goods to Communist China and buy Communist Chinese products for resale in foreign markets. Individuals would be able to bring Chinese products into the United States for non-commercial purposes without limit on their value. The announcement followed negotiations early in the month on resuming China-U.S. diplomatic roles in Warsaw. *(Box, p. 149)*

Chinese Moves

The unilateral U.S. initiatives at first produced little visible Chinese response. Editorials in the Peking *People's Daily* remained harshly critical of the United States, and on Feb. 18, 1969, the Chinese cancelled a meeting at Warsaw which they themselves had requested.

Within the government, however, the 1968 Soviet invasion of Czechoslovakia and the subsequent Soviet rationale for the action — the so-called "Brezhnev doctrine" of limited sovereignty — had triggered alarms. With the beginning of armed clashes all along China's 7,000-mile border with Russia in 1969, China's leaders began to review their foreign policy in earnest. They found themselves almost completely estranged from the international community in the wake of the isolationist policies of the Cultural Revolution.

Peking's first move came in March when, following the first of the border clashes, it stopped allowing the Soviet Union to ship military supplies to Vietnam using Chinese railways. In May, Peking began to resume its diplomatic representation and pick up the shattered pieces of its for-

eign relations. Later in the month, Peking began a public airing of the Sino-Soviet dispute in an obvious move to try to win world opinion to its side. It had become evident to all that the dispute was not merely a socialist ideological disagreement, but a geopolitical reality as well.

The Chinese action prompted Soviet Premier Aleksei Kosygin to travel to Peking in August 1969, but failure to negotiate an accord only hardened Chinese resolve. As border clashes continued through the year, the Chinese made their first positive response to the U.S. initiatives in January 1970, when they agreed to resume the long-suspended Warsaw talks.

On July 27, 1970, Chinese Premier Chou En-lai offered the first substantive hint of the major reworking of Chinese foreign policy which was taking place in Peking. In an interview with French journalists, Chou declared that Russia, like the United States, was a superpower that exploited and oppressed other, smaller nations. To counter this, Chou proposed a "united front" among the oppressed nations to oppose superpower domination. Peking had finally opted for *Realpolitik* over ideology.

Initiatives in 1970

Despite the official non-recognition policy, the following tentative steps toward normalization between the two nations were undertaken in 1970 by the Nixon administration:

● The U.S.-Chinese ambassadorial talks resumed in Warsaw after a two-year lapse.

● The selective licensing of goods for export to Communist China was authorized by the United States.

● The president noted that in 1970, 270 Americans had their passports validated for travel to the People's Republic of China. This brought the total number to nearly 1,000, even though only three Americans had been permitted entry.

In a foreign policy speech in early 1971, Nixon said that these unilateral efforts would continue. Although Peking had made no new overtures to the United States and had given no indication of resuming the Warsaw ambassadorial talks, again suspended in May 1970, it had moderated its tone in foreign policy and had established diplomatic relations with Canada, Italy and Chile.

The president repeated the U.S. commitment to the government of Nationalist China on Taiwan. But, he said, "The United States is prepared to see the People's Republic of China play a constructive role in the family of nations."

For the first time, the president referred to Communist China by its formal name, the People's Republic of China. Although his message to Congress and the nation did not include substantive changes in U.S.-China policy, it revealed a trend toward increased dialogue and contact with the Chinese people.

"The 22-year-old hostility between ourselves and the People's Republic of China is another unresolved problem, serious indeed in view of the fact that it determines our relationship with 750 million talented and energetic people," the president said.

He continued: "For the United States the development of a relationship with Peking embodies precisely the challenges of this decade: to deal with, and resolve vestiges of the postwar period that continue to influence our relationship and to create a balanced international structure in which all nations will have a stake. We believe that such a structure should provide full scope for the influence to which China's achievements entitle it."

热烈欢迎美国乒乓球队

Pingpong Diplomacy

Improved relations between China and the United States got off to a modest but engaging start on April 6, 1971, when the Chinese government invited a U.S. table tennis team to visit the mainland. The invitation was offered, said the Chinese, "so that we can learn from each other and elevate our standards of play. We have also extended the invitation for the sake of promoting friendship between the peoples of China and the United States."

Graham B. Steenhoven, president of the U.S. Table Tennis Association, accepted the next day, and nine players, four officials, two wives and five American newsmen arrived in China on April 10. After three days of travel, the U.S. team played — and lost — a round of exhibition matches in Peking on April 13. The next day they met with Premier Chou En-lai, who told them: "You have opened a new page in the relations between the Chinese and American people."

Despite condemnation of the breakthrough by the Nationalist ambassador to the United States, America reciprocated. A Chinese table tennis team arrived in the United States on April 12, 1972, and played a series of exhibition games in Detroit, Ann Arbor, Washington, Memphis, Los Angeles, San Francisco and at the United Nations in New York.

Athletes and Artists

Since the pingpong breakthrough, a number of athletic, cultural and educational groups have been exchanged. The United States has sent to China track and field athletes, gymnasts, swimmers and divers, tennis, volleyball, soccer (including the New York Cosmos) and basketball players (including the 1978 champion Washington Bullets). Among other visitors have been the Philadelphia Orchestra and the Boston Symphony and various educational and political groups, including a mayors' delegation and a governors' delegation. The Chinese have sent tennis, soccer, volleyball and basketball teams; acrobats, gymnasts and performing artists; educators, journalists and bureaucrats. Comedian Bob Hope took a troupe of entertainers to China in 1979, and made a three-hour TV special out of the trip later in the year.

Pingpong

No one expected, however, that the game of pingpong would be the vehicle for a breakthrough between the two countries.

"The ping heard round the world," as *Time* magazine put it, was first sounded on April 6, during the international championship table tennis competition in Nagoya, Japan, when the team from China invited members of the American team to visit the mainland before returning to the United States. No group of Americans had been allowed into China since the Communists took control in 1949. "We have . . . extended the invitation for the sake of promoting friendship between the peoples of China and the United States," the spokesman for the Chinese team said.

The invitation was accepted, and on April 10 the 15 Americans — nine players, four officials and two wives — walked across a bridge from Hong Kong into Chinese territory, where they were greeted by a delegation of smiling officials who escorted them to a train that took them to Canton. During the week of their visit, the Americans were kept on a full schedule of sightseeing, playing and entertainment.

They visited Peking, Shanghai, the Great Wall, a university and a rural commune. They participated in an exhibition pingpong match before a cheering audience of 18,000, attended a ballet staged by the wife of Party Chairman Mao Tse-tung, and were guests at a party April 14 at which Premier Chou En-lai engaged the visitors at length in good-humored chitchat. Chou impressed the visitors as a surprisingly genial host. In his formal greetings to them, he said: "You have opened a new page in the relations of the Chinese and American people. I am confident that this beginning again of our friendship will certainly meet with the majority support of our two people."

Equally significant with the invitation of the players, Peking permitted five American newsmen to enter China to report the trip. Chou said at the April 14 party that more American journalists would be granted visas to come to China, although "they cannot all come at one time."

On the day that Chou talked with the American players, April 14, the White House announced that a 20-year embargo on trade with China would be relaxed. The announcement stated:

● Visas for visitors from the People's Republic of China would be expedited.

● U.S. currency controls (imposed in 1950) would be relaxed so that China could use dollars to pay for exports.

● American oil companies would be allowed to provide fuel to ships or planes going to or from Chinese ports (except on Chinese-owned or chartered craft going to or from North Vietnam, North Korea or Cuba).

● U.S. vessels would be permitted to carry Chinese cargo between non-Chinese ports; U.S.-owned foreign flag carriers would be allowed to call at Chinese ports.

There followed on June 10 a further relaxation of trade restrictions when the White House announced a long list of goods that American businessmen could export to China. The items included farm, fish and forestry products; tobacco; many kinds of fertilizers and chemicals; coal; rubber and textiles; some metals; agricultural, industrial and office equipment; household appliances; some electrical appliances; automobiles; consumer goods; roadbuilding and construction equipment, and some relatively unsophisticated computers. The inclusion of construction equipment was regarded as significant because it was known that the Defense Department wanted to keep it off the list. The

U.S. Motivations for Rapprochement

Among the many factors that led to the establishment of friendlier relations in 1971-72 with the People's Republic of China, greater sympathy for the ideology and foreign ambitions of China was least among them. President Nixon had built much of his political career denouncing communism within the United States and abroad.

Like the once-intransigent Chinese, the Nixon administration and its advisers were motivated by some very pragmatic considerations in moving toward a re-evaluation of its position toward a former adversary.

Sino-Soviet-American Relations

A long-term relationship with Peking — drawing it into a constructive role in international affairs — appeared to be particularly necessary, not only for peace in Indochina but to give the Soviet leaders some pause for thought and reason for moderation in their own diplomacy. Nixon believed that China's continued isolation would be more dangerous to peace than their gradual involvement in world diplomacy.

One consequence of the deep Sino-Soviet ideological rift and the frequent military clashes along their common border was that both Peking and the Soviet Union viewed improved U.S. relations with either as collusion. Peking for its part had repeatedly attacked the collusion of U.S. "imperialism" and Soviet "revisionism" in arms control efforts, interpreted the U.S. position in the Sino-Soviet conflict as being pro-Soviet, and expressed fears of a pre-emptive Soviet nuclear attack.

Nuclear Threat

In addition to the benefits to be derived from a Sino-Soviet-American détente, another need for improved relations with China was that country's eventual nuclear capability. China detonated its first nuclear device in October 1964.

Supporting the overtures to Peking, Sen. Stuart Symington, D-Mo., said in 1969: "Now that all peoples are beginning to realize the true implications of a nuclear exchange, it would appear that a change in our China policy is long overdue." The reaction of other members of Congress to the growing Chinese nuclear capability was to suggest involving Peking in international disarmament talks. That did not happen, however.

Vietnam

There was little doubt in the United States that American involvement in Vietnam was another factor which had had a significant impact on U.S.-Communist Chinese relations. As long as the war continued, a major source of tension between the two countries would remain. Most importantly, because most of the Soviet military aid to North Vietnam traveled across China, only China could interdict the supplies.

Against this background, the Nixon administration's policy of withdrawing U.S. troops from Vietnam may have had a positive effect on Peking's willingness to negotiate with the United States and, finally, to stop the flow of Soviet military aid across China.

The Chinese also sent out signals suggesting they would back a new Geneva conference on Indochina and support the idea of a neutralized South Vietnam. So, as American troops continued to leave Vietnam at a rate of several thousand a week, it appeared that improved relations between the United States and China would permit the United States to make a face-saving exit from its Vietnam entanglement.

Asian Policy

The Nixon administration's intention of altering the U.S.' role as "global policeman" also required a change in U.S. relations with Peking. The first detailed expression of this policy was contained in the Guam Doctrine enunciated by President Nixon on the eve of a trip to Asia July 25, 1969. Henceforth, he said, the United States would seek to reduce its military presence on the Asian mainland, while providing Asian countries with the economic and military assistance they might need in assuming responsibility for their own defense.

The Chinese at first saw the Nixon Doctrine as contradictory in that while the United States proposed to reduce its commitments in the Pacific, it encouraged Japan and other countries to assume a larger military role. That in turn led to greater anxiety on the party of China. But, as the Chinese came to believe that the doctrine was not another American effort to encircle China, and that militarily strong and politically independent nations in Asia offered an important counterbalance to increased Soviet strength in the region, Peking came to support enthusiastically both a re-armed Japan and a strong Association of Southeast Asian Nations (ASEAN).

A major portion of the Nixon-Kissinger world view was a China that would participate actively with the United States in the maintenance of peace in East and Southeast Asia. A xenophobic and isolated Peking could not perform this role.

Trade

Despite reported interest by Peking in increasing trade with the United States, commerce with China had lain moribund under an embargo imposed by former President Harry S Truman in December 1950, after China attacked American forces in the Korean War. But President Nixon's progressive relaxation of cold war prohibitions against U.S. contact with China demonstrated his belief that the most populous nation on the earth had important political and economic roles to play in the world.

Nixon said as much in a speech July 6, 1971, three days before his assistant for national security affairs, Henry A. Kissinger, began secret meetings with Premier Chou En-lai in Peking which resulted in the invitation to the president to visit the Chinese capital. China was potentially "one of the five great economic superpowers," Nixon said, which would determine the course of great events in the remainder of the 20th century. An end to two decades of Chinese isolation, he said, would remove a threat to world peace but would mean "an immense escalation of their economic challenge."

Panda-Plomacy

Two giant pandas given to the United States by the People's Republic of China arrived at their new home in Washington's National Zoo on April 16, 1972. Zoos throughout the nation had competed for the animals, Ling-Ling and Hsing-Hsing *(above)*, but President Nixon decided on the Washington location because they were given by Chinese Premier Chou En-lai "in behalf of the American people."

The National Zoo prepared special air-conditioned quarters for the pandas. Attendance soared when the animals went on display.

Two musk oxen presented to China by the United States arrived in Peking April 9, 1972.

Pentagon's opposition to the sale of locomotives was also known, and they did not appear on the list.

Nixon Breakthrough

The dramatic thaw in relations took a new turn on July 15, 1971, when President Nixon announced he would visit Peking in early 1972 "to seek the normalization of relations between the two countries." Nixon said the meeting had been arranged during a secret visit to Peking in July by his national security adviser, Henry Kissinger. No American president had ever visited China.

The president described the event as "a major development in our efforts to build a lasting peace in the world." It was clearly a breakthrough portending a likely end to 21 years of American non-recognition of Mao Tse-tung's Communist government.

He stressed that his move would not be "at the expense of our old friends." This was interpreted primarily as reassurance for Nationalist China. But the Nationalist government was not assuaged. Premier C. K. Yen issued a statement of surprise and regret on July 16. Nixon assured Nationalist President Chiang Kai-shek, in a letter revealed July 20 in Taipei, that the United States would honor its mutual security treaty commitment to the government on Taiwan.

Kissinger Oct. 20 made a second trip to Peking to make "concrete" plans for President Nixon's China visit. Upon returning, he announced Oct. 27 that Nixon would visit China after the first of the year.

Chinese Response

During 1971, China's foreign policy continued to evolve away from its earlier, ideological approach. On May 1 the Peking *People's Daily* published an editorial defending the move and extolling the benefits that would accrue from "friendly exchanges between the peoples of various countries."

On Aug. 2 the Chinese Communist Party theoretical journal *Hongqi* published the fullest exposition of their policy to date. In an effort to explain why Peking, which had always treated the United States as the primary enemy of China, was moving to a rapprochement with the Western capitalists, the article stressed the critical situation in which China found itself internationally, and compared it to its situation during World War II. In the latter case, said the article, Party Chairman Mao Tse-tung had agreed to unite with any group (even anti-communists) in order to oppose the primary enemy — Japan. Today, the article declared, China must again distinguish between "the primary enemy and the secondary enemy." Thus, China would ally itself with the secondary enemy — the United States — in order to oppose the primary enemy — the Soviet Union.

As was the case during World War II, the Chinese Communists would form a "united front" with the enemies of its enemy, the Soviet Union.

On Feb. 14, 1972, three days before departing on his trip to the People's Republic of China, President Nixon ordered a further loosening of U.S. trade policy toward Peking.

The decision placed China under the same trade restrictions (labeled Group Y) as the Soviet Union and most of the Soviet bloc. China had previously been classified a Group Z country, with which no U.S. trade was allowed. Other Group Z countries included North Vietnam, North Korea and Cuba.

In addition, the president decided to modify remaining Foreign Assets Control Regulations pertaining to the People's Republic of China. He directed removal of the requirement that U.S.-controlled firms in countries (including Western Europe, Canada and Japan) which were members of COCOM — the international coordinating committee on strategic trade with communist countries — obtain a Treasury license in addition to a host country license for the export of strategic goods to the People's Republic of China. He also directed elimination of the requirement that U.S.-controlled firms abroad obtain prior Treasury licensing for the export of foreign technology to the People's Republic of China.

Nixon in China

Led by Premier Chou En-lai, Chinese officials gave Nixon a restrained welcome upon his arrival at Hongqiao Airport in Peking on Feb. 21, 1972. Later that day, however, the president met with Chairman Mao Tse-tung — an indication of the importance the Chinese leadership assigned Nixon's visit.

The hour-long Nixon-Mao meeting took place at Mao's residence somewhere in the old Forbidden City and was described afterwards only as "frank and serious." The president was accompanied by Kissinger. Mao was accompanied by Premier Chou and by his deputy director of protocol and an interpreter.

At a banquet that evening in the Great Hall of the People, Chou offered a toast to the Nixon party, including Mrs. Nixon, in which he said that the visit was a "positive move." President Nixon responded by noting that "more people are seeing and hearing what we say than on any other occasion in the whole history of the world." Nixon was referring to television coverage, beamed to the world via communications satellite. *(Text of the toasts, p. 323)*

The next day, Nixon and Chou met for four hours of policy discussions. Accompanying the president were Kissinger and John H. Holdridge and Winston Lord of the National Security Council. Secretary of State William P. Rogers and Foreign Minister Ji Pengfei held a separate conference. Nixon and Chou met again for talks each day of his visit.

Nixon spoke informally to reporters for the first time during his visit while on an excursion to the Great Wall of China. "As we look at this wall, we do not want walls of any kind between peoples," the president said. On the last day of his visit, in the Great Hall of the People, Nixon gave a banquet for Chou at which the president remarked that the two countries had "begun the long process of removing that wall between us." Chou noted that "whatever zigzags and reverses there will be in the development of history, the general trend of the world is definitely toward light and not darkness."

The Nixons then journeyed to Hangzhou and in the company of Chou En-lai, to Shanghai. A joint communiqué was released indicating that their talks had resulted in agreement on the need for increased Sino-U.S. contacts and for eventual withdrawal of U.S. troops from Taiwan. The 1,800-word communiqué, concluded after several nights of intensive negotiations, stated that progress toward "the normalization of relations" between the two sides was "in the interests of all countries." *(Text, p. 323)*

Henry Kissinger held a news conference in Shanghai on aspects of the communiqué. Asked what features of it indicated significant steps by China since its 1971 invitation to the U.S. table tennis team, Kissinger replied: "The formalization of exchanges encouraged by the two governments, the opening of trade encouraged by the two governments, the establishment of a diplomatic mechanism for continued contact, the joint statement of some general principles of international relations, the joint statement of some basic approaches to the view of the world with respect to, for instance, the section which includes the reference to hegemony — these, I believe, are matters that most of us would have considered unthinkable at the time of the invitation to the ping-pong team."

On their return, Feb. 28, President and Mrs. Nixon were greeted by crowds and a military band at Andrews Air Force base in Maryland. Vice President Spiro T. Agnew welcomed Nixon and remarked, "We feel easier tonight because of the trip you took." In a nationally televised address to the crowd, the president declared: "We did not bring back any written or unwritten agreements that will guarantee peace in our time." *(Excerpts of Nixon's homecoming address, p. 325)*

On the whole, Nixon's visit to China, and the promise it held out of closer relations with the People's Republic, were widely praised. Predictably, there were demurrals by the Nationalist Chinese *(text, p. 322)* and some members of Congress. *(Congressional reaction, p. 37)* Many congress-

men went to China for a first-hand look at the United States' new quasi-ally. *(Box, p. 38)*

Other 1972 Developments

Despite Nixon's assurances that no secret deals had been made in Peking, some of the closest allies of the United States feared that the Nixon visit might presage a U.S. withdrawal from Asia. Marshall Green, the assistant U.S. secretary of state, was sent on a tour of reassurance early in March. Green met with leaders in South Korea, Taiwan, the Philippines, South Vietnam, Laos, Cambodia and Thailand.

On March 13, 1972, the U.S. and Chinese ambassadors to France met in the Chinese Embassy in Paris for the first of a series of private discussions on matters of interest to the two countries. Arthur K. Watson represented the United States, and Huang Zhen represented the People's Republic of China. In announcing the talks three days earlier, White House press secretary Ronald L. Ziegler had said Paris was chosen as a "mutually convenient location." He said the problems to be discussed in the Paris meetings would be "far broader than anything ever taken up in Geneva and Warsaw," where previous Sino-U.S. ambassadorial contacts had taken place.

Returning from his May visit to the Soviet Union, President Nixon on June 1, 1972, told a joint session of Congress that his trips to Peking and Moscow were "part of a great national journey for peace" and were a move away from "perpetual confrontation" and toward "better understanding, mutual respect, point-by-point settlement of differences."

On June 19, 1972, Kissinger arrived in Peking and held four hours of talks with Premier Chou En-lai. Another four hours of discussions on the Indochina war took place June 20 between Kissinger and Chou, with Foreign Minister Ji Pengfei and other officials in attendance. After four days of meetings, an official joint statement was issued simultaneously in Washington and Peking June 24. It stated that the Kissinger-Chou meetings "consisted of concrete consultations to promote the normalization between the two countries."

On July 30, 1972, the Associated Press and Xinhua, the official Chinese press agency, agreed to an exchange of news and photographs. It was the first regular news contact with mainland China for a U.S. organization since December 1949, when the last Associated Press correspondent left the country. Late in 1972, a group of American newspaper editors under the auspices of the American Society of Newspaper Editors visited China.

1973 Developments

A major barrier to improved U.S.-Chinese relations was removed early in 1973 when Chinese authorities released a CIA agent shot down over China in 1952, as well as two U.S. airmen imprisoned after being shot down during missions in the Indochina war.

Downey Release. The White House announced on March 9 that the last three Americans held prisoner in China would be set free, one of them at the personal request of President Nixon to Premier Chou En-lai. Chou agreed to commute the sentence of John T. Downey, the CIA agent, and allow him to leave China. President Nixon had sent word to Chou that Downey's mother was critically ill in New Britain, Conn.

The White House also announced that two American pilots, Maj. Philip E. Smith of the Air Force and Lieut.

U.N. Membership for China . . .

At the beginning of the 92nd Congress in 1971 certain resolutions were introduced that reflected congressional interest in the admission of the People's Republic into the United Nations and the simultaneous expulsion of the Republic of China. Some members offered a "two-China" approach as an alternative to the expulsion of Taiwan.

For two decades, the United States steadfastly had opposed the admission of the People's Republic to the General Assembly and to the China seat in the Security Council.

Presidential Action

President Nixon on July 9, 1970, had directed the 50-member Commission on the Observance of the Twenty-fifth Anniversary of the United Nations to consult official and public opinion regarding U.S. participation in the United Nations.

The commission, headed by former U.S. Ambassador to the United Nations Henry Cabot Lodge and including prominent Americans from many professional fields, held public hearings in six cities before submitting its 100-page report.

On April 26, 1971, it urged that Communist China be admitted to the United Nations. The commission proposed that the United States:

● Adopt the position that all firmly established governments should be included in the U.N. system inasmuch as the benefits to the United States for having such governments within the United Nations and subject to the international obligations laid down by the charter far outweighed the problems raised by ideological differences between various states; and that no member of the organization living up to its obligations under the charter be expelled;

● "Under no circumstancs agree to the expulsion from the U.N. of the Republic of China on Taiwan but seek agreement as early as practicable whereby the People's Republic of China might accept the principles of the charter and be represented in the organization."

U.S. Acquiescence

The first indication that the United States would switch its stand opposing admission of Communist China to the United Nations came on June 4, 1971. The president at that time announced that "a significant change has taken place among the members of the United Nations on the issue of admission of mainland China," and the United States was "analyzing that situation."

Secretary of State William P. Rogers on Aug. 2 announced that the United States would oppose any efforts to "expel the Republic of China or otherwise deprive it of representation in the United Nations."

Avoiding a position on whether the Nationalist Chinese government on Taiwan should retain its seat on the U.N. Security Council, Rogers said the United States would abide by the views of the majority of U.N. members.

Chinese Response

Peking responded to the U.S. announcement by accusing Rogers of lying in order to push "the preposterous proposition of two Chinas." Rogers confirmed that he had no indication from either Peking or Taipei that they were willing to sit together in the United Nations. Premier Chou En-lai told James Reston, in an interview published in *The New York Times* August 10, that Peking would not join the United Nations unless Taiwan were excluded.

U.S. Resolutions

Just prior to the opening Sept. 21 of the U.N. General Assembly's 26th session in New York, the United States announced Sept. 16 its intention to vote to seat the People's Republic of China in the U.N. Security Council.

But the Nixon administration's efforts to prevent the ouster of Nationalist China from the United Nations encountered a setback Sept. 22 at a meeting of that organization's agenda committee.

The United States submitted two resolutions on the seating of a Chinese delegation in the United Nations. One text asked the General Assembly to agree that any move to oust Taiwan from its membership be considered an "important question" requiring the approval of two-thirds of the assembly's members. The other text recommended that Peking be admitted as a Security Council member but noted that Taiwan had a continued right of representation in the General Assembly.

The U.N. Assembly's General Committee voted Sept. 22 against a U.S. proposal to have the U.S. resolution and a previously submitted Albanian resolution on the seating of a Chinese delegation discussed simultaneously by the General Assembly. The motion was defeated by a vote of 12-9.

The committee voted 17-2 to put the Albanian resolution on the General Assembly's agenda as item 101. The U.S. resolutions, by a vote of 11-9, were to be placed on the agenda as item 105.

Comdr. Robert J. Flynn, would be freed. They were captured in 1965 and 1967 when they strayed over China during raids on North Vietnam.

Liaison Offices. Returning from a five-day visit to China on Feb. 22, 1973, Henry Kissinger announced that the two countries would establish liaison offices in each other's capitals. In a press briefing in Washington, Kissinger said the liaison offices would be established in the "nearest future" and would "cover the whole gamut of relationships."

Asked if the move was a prelude to establishing diplomatic relations between China and the United States, Kissinger said America "had no further steps in mind" and that "this is as far as we can go at this point."

A day earlier Sen. Edward M. Kennedy, D-Mass, had introduced in the U.S. Senate a resolution calling for "prompt establishment of full diplomatic relations" with China. He said the United States should end its diplomatic recognition of the Nationalist government on Taiwan and announce a unilateral guarantee for Taiwan's security.

. . . Took More than 20 Years

The Albanian resolution, submitted July 15, called on the General Assembly to admit Communist China, seat it in the Security Council, and expel Nationalist China from all U.N. bodies. A similar resolution had been supported by the assembly in 1970 by a vote of 51-49, but Peking's admission was blocked because the General Assembly had decided the question required a two-thirds majority.

The Albanian resolution was submitted well in advance of the assembly's Sept. 21 opening date, reportedly to emphasize Peking's insistence on the expulsion of Nationalist China as a condition for its own membership.

Nixon Support

In an unscheduled news conference at the White House Sept. 16 President Nixon declared that the United States would support Peking's seating in the Security Council because such a move "reflects the realities of the situation."

Nixon said "in the event that the People's Republic is admitted to the United Nations, the seat in the Security Council would go to the People's Republic and that, of course, would mean the removal of the Republic of China from the Security Council seat." The president added: "We will vote against the expulsion of the Republic of China [from the United Nations] and we will work as effectively as we can to accomplish that goal."

On Oct. 4 Secretary of State Rogers warned the General Assembly that the expulsion of Taiwan might endanger the membership of other nations and weaken the United Nations as a whole. The struggle over Taiwan's continued membership in the United Nations became the first test of strength between Peking and Washington since Nixon opened the dialogue between the two powers in mid-1971.

U.N. Vote on China

After a week of intense U.N. debate on the China issue during which the United States was accused of exerting undue pressure for dual representation, the U.N. General Assembly Oct. 25 voted to admit Peking and to expel the delegates of Taiwan. The vote was 76-35 with 17 abstentions. *(U.N. votes, pp. 365,366)*

The United States, despite supporting the seating of Communist China, thus lost in its effort to keep Taiwan in the United Naitons.

Prior to the vote, the U.S. resolution to declare the expulsion of Taiwan an important question requiring a

two-thirds majority was defeated 59-55 with 15 abstentions. The United States had predicted victory on that vote.

The U.S. resolution for dual representation of Peking and Taiwan never came to a vote because the Albanian resolution was considered first and adopted. On the eve of the debate, the Peking government stated that it would accept nothing less than its substitution for the Taiwan representatives.

U.S. efforts to retain Taiwan's seat were said to have been badly hurt by the White House's dispatch of Kissinger to Peking in the middle of the China debate and his presence there at the actual time of the vote Oct. 25. Kissinger in fact remained in Peking two days longer than scheduled, returning the day after the U.N. vote.

Congressional Reaction

Most members of Congress expressed anger at the United Nations for the expulsion of Nationalist China and many favored slashing U.S. contributions to the peacekeeping organization. Most of the reaction centered around the $3.2-billion fiscal 1972 foreign aid bill which was being debated in the Senate at the time of the U.N. action and which contained $141 million in outlays to various U.N. agencies. The bill was rejected Oct. 29 by a 21-47 roll-call vote. Foreign aid funds — including those for the United Nations — were restored by Congress near the end of its 1971 session.

Speaking for the administration, Secretary of State Rogers said the United States "will not support a reduction of funds for the United Nations in retaliation" for the vote. He emphasized that the United States would retain its ties with Nationalist China as before.

The White House had left all statements on the U.N. vote to Rogers in an apparent effort to keep the president's personal prestige separate from the voting setback and to avoid anything that might give offense in Peking and interfere with the president's 1972 China visit.

But, in what appeared to be a move to divert criticism from himself to the United Nations, Nixon, through press secretary Ronald L. Ziegler, denounced as "shocking" the "demonstration of undisguised glee shown by some delegates" after the Oct. 25 expulsion of Nationalist China. Ziegler said that Nixon supported the United Nations and wanted to see it succeed, but that action of some delegates "could lead to deterioration of support in Congress and the country" both for the United Nations and for the foreign aid program.

Envoys Appointed. On March 15, 1973, President Nixon announced at a news conference that he had selected Ambassador David K. E. Bruce to head the U.S. Liaison Office in Peking. Bruce, 75, was called from retirement after exercising diplomatic functions under four presidents. Nixon said he chose Bruce "because I thought it was very important to appoint a man of great stature to this position." The president said the liaison office would be opened about May 1, 1973, and would be staffed by 20 persons, including Alfred Jenkins of the State Department and John

H. Holdridge of the National Security Council.

Bruce arrived in Peking May 15, officially opening the U.S. Liaison Office. On May 29, 1973, the chief of the Chinese liaison mission, Huang Zhen, arrived in Washington to resume official contact with the United States after what he called a "20-year detour."

China's New Foreign Policy

For China, the 1971-74 period seemed to confirm the wisdom of their decision to side with the U.S. in opposing the Soviet Union. In December 1971 India, fortified by a new friendship treaty with Moscow, had invaded Pakistan, a Chinese ally. Then, in 1972, the Soviets had further increased their troop buildup along China's border. When the last American soldiers were withdrawn from Vietnam in 1973, China's southern flank was at last cleared of foreign troops, at least for the time being. Thus, in 1974, Peking promulgated the theoretical basis of its new foreign policy, the so-called "Theory of the Three Worlds."

On April 10, 1974, ranking Vice Premier Deng Xiaoping, speaking before the U.N. General Assembly, announced the new policy. *(Text, p. 326)* According to Deng, the world was no longer divided into two camps or blocs (communist and capitalist). On the contrary, the Soviet Union had betrayed its socialist heritage and, like the U.S., was a member of the first world, that of the superpowers. The second world was made up of all other industrialized nations, while the third world was comprised of all the remaining countries. In his speech, Deng offered Chinese leadership of this third world against exploitation and aggression by the other two.

The speech marked the formal end of the Chinese use of confrontation politics in international affairs, a view which had been predominant in Peking from 1958 to 1969.

Interregnum

After the flurry of activity surrounding the Nixon trip and its aftermath, the course of development of Chinese-U.S. relations slowed considerably in the next few years.

Even had he wished to pursue them, further initiatives toward China by the Nixon administration were hamstrung by the president's involvement in the Watergate scandal. And though his successor, Gerald R. Ford, indicated a willingness to perpetuate the Nixon policy on China, he did little more during his two-year presidency than to pay a visit to China that most observers agreed involved more show than substance. It would be left to his successor, Democrat Jimmy Carter, to take the next big step toward normalizing relations with the People's Republic.

Roughly the same period was a transitional one for the Chinese as well, as the last bitter years of the Cultural Revolution ended with the death or denunciation of its principals and the political resuscitation of it foes. *(Box, p. 199)*

Lin Piao was killed in 1971 and Liu Shao-ch'i was later reported to have died during this same period. In 1976 the two giants of the Chinese People's Republic since its formation — Mao Tse-tung and Chou En-lai — died, Chou in January of cancer and Mao in September of unknown causes. Mao was 82. Taking their place were two moderates: Deng Xiaoping, who had been in and out of the party hierarchy since the beginning of the People's Republic, and Hua Guofeng, a relative unknown who had played a prominent role in 1975 in the movement to modernize Chinese agriculture. *(Biographies, pp. 272, 274)*

Outwardly, little of dramatic significance seemed to be happening to change China's relations with the rest of the world, although its pragmatic foreign policy continued to evolve. In 1974 Peking announced its support for European unity; in 1975 it declared its support for a continued U.S. presence in the Pacific; in 1976 it said it would work with ASEAN nations *(p. 17)* in resisting Soviet expansion in Southeast Asia, while moving to moderate its stand on the eventual reunification of Taiwan with the mainland. Finally, in November 1977, the new leadership reaffirmed its commitment to a pragmatic, anti-Soviet foreign policy. The Sino-Soviet split was still unresolved as Peking as-

sumed an ever quieter role in the political affairs of third-world countries. At the same time, it went on expanding its trade relations with Western markets.

On its part, the United States officially ended the Vietnam War and continued quietly to negotiate with Peking on improving the diplomatic and commercial ties initiated by the Nixon-Mao breakthrough. In 1974 Congress repealed the 1955 Formosa resolution and in 1978 approved the sale of agricultural items to China through the Commodity Credit Corporation.

After the Carter administration took office in 1977, it began exploratory talks with the Chinese on the normalization issue during an August 1977 trip to Peking by Secretary of State Cyrus R. Vance. But there were reportedly no breakthroughs on the Taiwan issue during those talks.

Communist China Recognized

Then, on Dec. 15, 1978, came President Jimmy Carter's dramatic, unexpected bombshell. Beginning Jan. 1 of the new year, he announced in a joint communiqué with Peking, the People's Republic of China and the United States would formally recognize each other. They would exchange ambassadors and open embassies March 1. On Dec. 31, 1979, the United States would abrogate the mutual defense treaty with Taiwan.

"Normalization — and the expanded commercial and cultural relations that it will bring — will contribute to the well-being of our own nation, to our own national interest, and it will also enhance the stability of Asia," Carter said. "The normalization of relations between the United States and China has no other purpose than this — the advancement of peace." *(Text, p. 341)*

Breakthrough

The breakthrough was made possible by the willingness of both sides to make concessions on disputed issues that had been at the heart of U.S.-China relations for nearly 30 years. Each side claimed that the other had made the greater sacrifice.

For its part, the United States agreed to three conditions the Chinese long insisted had to be met:

● Ending recognition of the Republic of China on Taiwan.

● Termination of the U.S.-Taiwan mutual defense treaty.

● Withdrawal of the remaining U.S. troops on Taiwan.

The Chinese also made three major concessions. They:

● Tacitly agreed not to oppose continued American sales of arms to Taiwan.

● Agreed that the United States could terminate its defense treaty with Taiwan with one year's notice, rather than immediately.

● Agreed not to object to an American declaration of continued interest in the future of Taiwan.

Conservative critics argued that the Chinese concessions were merely rhetorical and that the United States essentially gave in to Peking's demands.

But the administration orchestrated a chorus of high-level officials who insisted that the United States had won essential points that would ensure Taiwan's independence for the foreseeable future.

The impetus for the breakthrough had been a trip to China in May by national security adviser Zbigniew Brzezinski, who impressed Chinese officials with his anti-

Soviet rhetoric. In July Leonard Woodcock, chief of the U.S. delegation in Peking, began serious negotiations with Chinese Foreign Minister Huang Hua. On Sept. 19 President Carter met with Chai Zemin, the new Chinese liaison officer in Washington, and laid out the American conditions for normalized relations. Negotiations then proceeded rapidly, with the two sides exchanging draft statements and proposals up until the day before the public announcement on recognition Dec. 15.

Reaction

Although the eventual normalization of relations between Washington and Peking had been taken for granted since President Nixon's trip to China in 1972, the sudden announcement caught most of the world by surprise. And among those most surprised were members of Congress, who thought Carter had promised to consult with them before changing the status of the Taiwan treaty.

On Capitol Hill, most conservatives were angered and most liberals were enthusiastic about Carter's announcement. But members of Congress of all political persuasions were upset that Carter acted so secretly, with little advance warning and no opportunity for congressional consultation.

A group of congressmen led by Sen. Barry Goldwater, R-Ariz., filed suit to have the abolition of the Taiwan defense treaty declared illegal because Carter had not consulted Congress. But the courts upheld the president. *(Details, p. 40)*

Taiwan

Most of the immediate attention after Carter's announcement was focused on whether the United States had obtained assurances for the future security of Taiwan, but even the harshest critics conceded that Carter had the legal authority to switch diplomatic recognition from Taiwan to mainland China.

Critics charged that Carter's action left Taiwan vulnerable to an invasion from mainland China, or at least a boycott or blockade. And even supporters of normalization said they were concerned about the future safety of Taiwan. Sen. John Glenn, D-Ohio, chairman of the Senate Foreign Relations East Asian subcommittee, said the U.S.-China agreement left a "nagging doubt" that China would leave Taiwan alone.

Administration officials did not alleviate fears for Taiwan's security when they flatly said they had never attempted to pressure the Chinese into making a commitment on Taiwan's future.

In his unilateral statement accompanying the joint communiqué, Carter said the United States "will continue to have an interest in the peaceful resolution of the Taiwan issue." His aides said that phrase indicated the importance the United States attached to the security of Taiwan. *(Text, p. 341)*

Referring to that phrase, Secretary of State Vance said: "We have expressed very clearly our deep concern that the welfare of the people of Taiwan be protected, and that the transition be a peaceful transition, that the Taiwan solution be a peaceful solution. This has not been contradicted by the People's Republic of China."

An additional factor, according to the administration, was the willingness of the Chinese to allow continued American arms sales to Taiwan. The United States already was committed to $625 million in heavy arms sales to Taiwan through 1983, including tanks, artillery and more than 100 F-5E fighters equipped to carry guided missiles.

Vance and other officials repeatedly said the strongest assurance for the safety of Taiwan was the "reality" of the military situation in east Asia. "It simply does not make sense for the People's Republic of China to do anything other than in a peaceful fashion," he said.

President Carter said China "does not have the capability" of launching a successful invasion of Taiwan, 100 miles off the mainland and "heavily fortified and heavily armed." One official said the Chinese would have to commit almost their entire armed forces to such an invasion, and that would mean withdrawing troops from the Russian front, which was China's greatest security concern.

However, officials said a Chinese naval blockade of Taiwan might be successful. Taiwan did not have an adequate capability to ward off the large mainland Chinese submarine fleet. Since Taiwan depended on imports for most of its food, oil and raw materials, a prolonged blockade could seriously damage the island's economy.

American businessmen with heavy investments in Taiwan apparently were not alarmed by the new status.

Administration officials said they expected China might be willing to adopt the same hands-off attitude toward Taiwan that it had toward Hong Kong.

U.S.-Soviet Relations. One of the most important questions concerned the long-term impact of U.S.-China relations on American relations with the Soviet Union. China and Russia had barely been on speaking terms since the early 1960s, and each side had massed several hundred thousand troops along the 5,000-mile border in a show of mutual mistrust. During that same time, the United States and the U.S.S.R. had pursued "détente" in achieving their most peaceful standoff since the Soviet invasion of Czechoslovakia in 1968.

In explaining his action, President Carter said: ". . . we have no desire whatsoever to use our relationships with China to the disadvantage of the Soviets or anyone else." Carter said he received a "very positive" message from Soviet President Leonid Brezhnev saying he accepted the need for the United States and China to normalize relations, but the Kremlin later disputed Carter's interpretation of the note, suggesting that the Soviets were seriously concerned about the new U.S. policy.

China, however, lost no time after the joint communiqué was issued in heaping further invective on the Soviets for their alleged plans for "hegemony," and the U.S.S.R. kept up its verbal attack on China, especially after China invaded Vietnam to do battle against Vietnamese forces close to its border.

Deng Visit

Chinese Vice Premier Deng Xiaoping took the next step in advancing U.S.-Chinese relations with a week-long goodwill tour of the United States Jan. 28 - Feb. 5, 1979. Deng proved a disarming spokesman for rapprochement in a whirlwind tour of Congress and in visits to Atlanta, Houston and Seattle.

Partly in an effort to allay the fears in Congress over the new agreement, the administration scheduled a full day of meetings between Deng and congressional leaders.

On Jan. 30 Deng dined with 85 senators, including the entire Foreign Relations Committee; had private talks with Senate Majority Leader Robert C. Byrd, D-W.Va., Minority Leader Howard H. Baker Jr., R-Tenn., and House Speaker Thomas P. O'Neill Jr., D-Mass.; and had tea with the House International Relations Committee, the leadership and 40 other House members. *(Box, p. 45)*

Another dozen members of Congress accompanied Deng, in relays, to Atlanta, Houston and Seattle after his departure from Washington Feb. 1.

At the conclusion of the visit to Washington, Deng and Carter signed agreements for science-and-technology and cultural exchanges. Negotiations were to continue on aviation, trade and other agreements, some of which would require congressional approval.

New Vietnam War. Even as the United States and China were celebrating the official beginning of new relations, the two nations were at odds over a new war in Vietnam. Vietnam invaded Cambodia in January and toppled the despotic regime backed by China. In retaliation, China invaded Vietnam Feb. 17, saying it wanted to "punish" its neighbor.

The Carter administration sharply criticized both invasions and urged the United Nations to do so.

Some critics argued that the war showed that the United States would have little influence over China, even with diplomatic recognition. With the withdrawal of Chinese troops from across the border in March, however, the issue died down for the time being.

Trade with China

With U.S. businessmen eager to get a toehold in a vast new market, support grew in Congress to end trade discrimination against the People's Republic of China by granting most-favored-nation (MFN) status to the Peking government.

The economics of MFN is relatively simple. It would invoke the principle of equal trade treatment for all countries by lowering U.S. tariffs on Chinese goods to a level equal to that of most other nations. Normalized trade relations would also make China eligible for low-interest credit provided by the U.S. Export-Import Bank.

Many observers thought Congress would approve early in 1980 the trade agreement with China signed by the two governments July 7, 1979, and submitted to Congress Oct. 23; they noted that on the merits current Chinese emigration seemed to meet the requirements of the Jackson-Vanik amendment to the 1974 Trade Act.

(Congress finally approved the treaty Jan. 24, 1980; *details, p. 69-72.*)

Mondale in Peking

During a 10-day trip to China that ended Aug. 31, 1979, Vice President Walter F. Mondale helped to confirm prospects for expanded U.S.-China trade. Mondale told his hosts that the U.S. would lend China $2 billion over five years through the Export-Import Bank, and more "if the pace of development warrants it." He promised quick congressional action on the Sino-American trade agreement. During his highly publicized visit, Mondale — the highest-ranking U.S. official to visit China since the agreements of December 1978 — performed a number of other diplomatic tasks:

● Met with Vice Premier Deng and Chairman Hua to affirm earlier agreements, and signed with them a cultural exchange pact and an agreement for the United States to help China develop hydroelectric power. During the "extremely productive and friendly" talks, as Mondale characterized them, the three leaders also discussed the situation in Indochina.

● Announced the acceptance by Chairman Hua of an invitation to visit the United States in 1980.

● Opened the first U.S. consulate in China in 30 years, in Canton. He also toured technological facilities in Xi'an.

● Delivered a highly conciliatory speech over national Chinese television in which he said: "any nation which seeks to weaken or isolate you in world affairs assumes a stance counter to American interests." He expressed U.S. approval of a "strong and modernizing" China. "Despite the sometimes profound differences between our two systems, we are committed to joining you to advance our many parallel and bilateral interests." *(Text, p. 345)*

Iran and Afghanistan

A dramatic case of parallel interests emerged several months later with the Soviet invasion of Afghanistan, as some 50-100 thousand Russian troops crossed the border to depose the Soviet-leaning but weak Marxist government headed by Hafizullah Amin (Amin was murdered) and replaced it with an overtly pro-Soviet group under Babrak Karmal on Dec. 27.

China — which shares a short western border with Afghanistan — joined with the United States, its European allies and most Middle Eastern nations in condemning the invasion and virtual occupation of Afghanistan by Russia.

Within a week, U.S. Defense Secretary Harold Brown was in Peking for eight days of talks with Chinese leaders. Although the trip had been planned before the Soviet invasion occurred, the situation in Afghanistan clearly had become the first order of business in the discussions. Brown renewed U.S. charges against the Soviet action and strongly suggested — for virtually the first time — the possibility of joint Sino-U.S. military action. He hinted at "wider cooperation on security matters" that "should remind others that if they threaten the shared interests of the United States and China, we can respond with complementary actions in the field of defense as well as diplomacy." Such actions were sure to include, at the very least, heavy outlays of U.S. and Chinese military aid to Pakistan.

At the time of Brown's trip, Chinese Vice Premier Deng Xiaoping had repeated his government's "firm demand" that Russia pull out of Afghanistan and promised that China would "work together with the Afghan people, and all countries and people who love peace and uphold justice, to frustrate Soviet acts of aggression and expansion."

Closer China-U.S. relations had already paid a dividend in Iran, next door to Afghanistan, when Iranian militants seized the U.S. Embassy in Tehran on Nov. 4. China tacitly supported U.S. efforts to condemn the action and its approval by the Ayatollah Ruhollah Khomeini, and joined the United States and ten other U.N. Security Council members in voting for a resolution stipulating that the council would consider economic sanctions against Iran if the hostages were not released. (On the subsequent vote actually to impose sanctions, however, the Chinese delegation did not participate.)

"Parallelism" in Future Relations

Even as the United States and China moved to cement their new, more peaceful relationship, the eruption of new and old trouble spots around the world made the rapprochement all the more significant for the future and strengthened it in specific, strategic areas as the two countries recognized the similarity of their attitudes to these new problems.

● **Afghanistan.** Both the United States and China reacted with outrage to the Soviet invasion. China called it "a threat to China's security"; the United States said it was a "blatant violation of accepted international rules of behavior," while cutting off grain and technology sales to the Soviet Union and threatening to boycott the 1980 Olympics if the games were held in Moscow.

But despite overwhelming censure by the U.N. General Assembly for its actions, the Soviet Union showed no inclination toward retreat from Afghanistan. Instead, it launched a propaganda campaign against Chinese and American threats to Afghanistan's autonomy, inviting speculation that Afghanistan might be only the first of the region's "dominoes" which Russia sought to topple in its search for access to a warm-water port. Under that theory, the two nations most directly threatened by further Soviet expansion were Pakistan and Iran, both bordering Afghanistan and the Indian Ocean.

● **Pakistan.** The invasion of Afghanistan made Pakistan — overnight — the most strategically important country in the world. Both China and the United States — even before normalization of relations between them — had supported Pakistan in its conflicts with India. The United States in 1979 had discontinued its intermittent military aid to Pakistan, ostensibly because that country seemed to be pursuing an independent nuclear development policy and had seemed in violation of President Carter's human rights criteria in qualifying for aid, but probably also in order to avoid further alienating India. With the Soviet overthrow of Afghanistan, however, and the concomitant danger to Pakistan, the Carter administration began immediately to make plans for restoring aid — perhaps as much as $1 billion worth — and appeared to be coordinating Pakistan's defense with stepped-up military aid efforts from China, which had supplanted the United States as Pakistan's primary source of weapons.

Despite these assurances of support, however, Pakistan at the same time faced renewed threats on its eastern flank from India, which in January 1980 restored Pakistan's *bête noir*, Indira Gandhi, to power. Mme. Gandhi immediately confirmed Pakistan's worst fears when India's U.N. delegation voted against condemning Russia for its Afghanistan invasion, although Mme. Gandhi criticized the Soviet action a short time later. The threats on both its borders seemed to guarantee a joint, continuing Sino-U.S. effort on Pakistan's behalf, but the stability of President Mohammed Zia ul-Haq's government was questionable.

● **Iran.** The future of Iran early in 1980 was unpredictable and dangerous, the fiercely Moslem nation still in the throes of revolution. The aftermath of the takeover of the U.S. Embassy in Tehran had proved that no one seemed to be in effective control of the Iranian government, as diplomats from all over futilely sought a rational avenue by which to negotiate release of the American hostages. But even the emotional campaign against alleged U.S. complicity in atrocities committed by the deposed Shah failed to unite the country, which under the aged Ayatollah Ruhollah Khomeini's rule often seemed on the verge of religious, political and economic anarchy. Although Islamic solidarity in Iran was believed to be a buffer against Soviet designs there, there seemed to be no outside power aligned with Iran that could deter an outright Soviet military move. The Soviets, seizing the moment, sought to curry favor with Iran by joining its impassioned attacks against the United States, perhaps seeking justification for intervention there against "American imperialism."

China, for its part, tried to maintain some leverage in Iran by refusing to join U.S.-sponsored moves against the embassy takeover in the United Nations, but China was thought to have little influence with Iranian leaders.

● **The Middle East.** The resurgence of Islamic and nationalistic fervor were major factors in both the Pakistani and Iranian situations and were sure to affect developments elsewhere in the Middle East and the Asian subcontinent. Saudi Arabia already had taken steps early in 1980 to defuse this kind of popular militancy by broadening representation in its government. In addition, anti-Israeli sentiment in the Eastern Mediterranean seemed in no way diminished by the initiatives of Israel and Egypt in 1978 and thereafter.

That remained a potential impediment to continuing Sino-U.S. accord. American support for Israel was unlikely to diminish appreciably, while China has traditionally assumed an anti-Zionist posture in seeking the friendship of the third world countries of the Middle East. It seemed probable that the two nations would attempt to smooth over such disagreements as they arose, at least for the time being.

● **Korea.** In Korea, where U.S. and Chinese troops had fought their only major war in the 1950s, the October 26 assassination of South Korean strongman Park Chung Hee introduced a new element of instability in the often-troubled region. When this was followed by a coup on December 12, the U.S. issued strong warnings to North Korea not to exploit the situation. In response, Chinese Premier and Party Chairman Hua Guofeng assured the West on Dec. 6, 1979 that Peking would use its not-inconsiderable influence in Pyongyang to reduce tension, and assured Japanese Prime Minister Masayoshi Ohira that there was "no possibility" of an invasion from the north. Hua also pledged to continue to press for a peaceful unification of the peninsula.

● **Thailand.** Another area of joint American-Chinese interest is Thailand, a long-time U.S. ally under the old SEATO treaty. As the Vietnamese invasion of Cambodia and Laos threatened to spill over into Thailand, both Peking and Washington professed their support for Bangkok. On Oct. 28 and again on Dec. 4 China declared that it would "stand on the side of Thailand" and also called for more "cooperation" between the two nations. On Nov. 16 U.S. Assistant Secretary of State for East Asian and Pacific Affairs Richard Holbrooke reiterated the U.S. position that American policy "will be based on strong support for Thailand." As Washington announced new arms sales to Bangkok, Peking declared its intentions to supply oil to Thailand at markedly reduced prices.

Thailand is also a member of ASEAN (Association of Southeast Asian Nations), a sort of Asian Common Market of five non-aligned nations. Both the United States and China have expressed their strong support for ASEAN as a hedge against Soviet expansion in the Southeast Asian region.

● **Japan.** As Soviet naval activity in Asia continued to increase, U.S. pressure on Japan to take over responsibility for its own defense was expected to grow during the 1980s. Originally, the Chinese had opposed any increase or improvement in Japan's military, and its 1950 friendship treaty with the Soviet Union had contained clauses condemning "Japanese militarism." By the late 1970s, however, Peking's position had changed significantly. It had abrogated the treaty with Moscow and signed a peace treaty with Tokyo, and backed U.S. calls for a stronger Japan with similar statements of its own.

The 1980s will almost certainly see new increases in Chinese trade with Japan, already America's number one trading partner.

On-going Diplomacy

Even without the impetus of mutual interests abroad to draw them closer together, China and the United States showed every sign of working together to build on their new relationship.

Continuing the policy of personal diplomacy established by his predecessors, President Carter planned a trip to China in 1980, preceded by a visit to America by Chinese Premier Hua Guofeng.

American politicians obviously felt the new China policy worked to their advantage. President Nixon — and many observers of his administration — called the China breakthrough the greatest achievement of his presidency.

Ex-President Nixon, in fact, returned in 1976 and 1979 to the scene of his triumph as an honored guest of Chinese leaders — to the discomfort of many diplomats and members of his own political party.

Clearly, the recognition by the United States of the People's Republic of China, and the promise it held for increasingly closer ties between the two disparate nations, was one of the major coups of modern diplomacy and an action that the people of both countries generally found hopeful and fruitful.

And as 1980 seemed to usher in a decade of renewed global tension, especially in the Persian Gulf area, the alignment promised to be one of immense strategic importance as well.

Historical Background

China's rapprochement with the United States and its Western allies in the 1970s was dramatic not only in terms of post-World War II events, but in light of China's relations with the Western world throughout its long history — during which the colonizing nations of Europe, and later the United States, imposed their will on a declining Chinese empire.

The West's first contacts with China began some 700 years ago. Much of the period since then has been marked by misunderstanding between the two cultures, contempt of one for the other, exploitation, outright hostility, and occasional resort to arms. Writing of China's bitterness and hatred toward Western nations in 1965, *New York Times* correspondent Harry Schwartz spoke of "a century of Chinese humiliation by the West." [1]

Early Contacts With the West

Marco Polo, the Venetian adventurer who lived in China for 17 years during the 13th century, was not the first Westerner to reach the Celestial Kingdom. Under Alexander the Great, the Greeks had penetrated to central Asia; traders from the Roman Empire had some commercial contact with the Chinese. During the reign of the Mongol emperor Kublai Khan, before Marco Polo arrived with his merchant uncles, Roman Catholic missionaries had journeyed from Europe to China and established small communities of Christian converts.

The influence on the West of the writings of Marco Polo was nevertheless wider than that of any occidental who preceded him. His book, *Description of the World,* or *Travels of Marco Polo,* became the principal European source of information on East Asia. A historian, Dun J. Li, has observed that the impact of this work on contemporary Europe was tremendous.

> That a more advanced society existed simultaneously with Europe was hard to believe, and most of the Europeans dismissed the book as mere fable. When the book finally won credence, it aroused great interest in China among the literate Europeans. Its readers included such men as Christopher Columbus. To the religiously devoted, there was a huge pagan world to conquer, and to the worldly merchants, there were enormous profits to be realized. [2]

Marco Polo's journal, Li wrote, paved the way "for the arrival of thousands of Europeans in the centuries to come."

Penetration by Traders and Missionaries

The greatest influx of Westerners into China did not come for several hundred years, not until the European people had begun the expansion "which culminated in political domination of the world." The Iberians were the first to arrive. A group of Portuguese traders sailed into Canton harbor in 1517. Though they met with no violence, the emperor, annoyed at their lack of respect, expelled the Portuguese. Others continued to come, trading and often looting along the coast. In an effort to restrict the intruders to a given area, Macao was "lent" to Portuguese merchants as a trading base in 1557.

As the Portuguese traders prospered, traders from other nations followed. The Dutch were the next to arrive; they operated from the Pescadores and Taiwan. By the beginning of the 18th century, England and France had joined in the commerce. The Chinese, hoping to put limits to the widening operations of the foreigners, in 1757 confined all foreign trade to the port of Canton. By 1784, when the first American ship, the *Empress of China,* sailed for the Orient, the British had established a pre-eminent position in the China trade.

The first extensive cultural contact between China and Europe began at the end of the 16th century, when Jesuit missionaries reached China by sea. The missionaries had a dual role:

> They not only diffused Western ideas in China, including elements of mathematics, astronomy, geography, hydraulics, the calendar, and the manufacture of cannon, but they also introduced Chinese . . . ideas into Europe. The Jesuits found it easier to influence China's science than her religion. Perceiving this, they used their scientific knowledge as a means of approach to Chinese scholars. [3]

One of the leading Jesuit missionaries was Matteo Ricci, who arrived in Macao in 1582 and in Peking in 1601. Father Ricci revealed an understanding of the Chinese and immersed himself in the study of China's language, literature and philosphy. He sought to detach himself and his mission from identification with the power of the European state and concentrated on cultivating scholars and high government officials. In return for the counsel of Father Ricci and his colleagues on matters of science and technology, the Chinese granted them permission to preach and proselytize. But despite the efforts of the Jesuits and of other missionaries who followed them to Peking, the number of Christian converts 100 years after Ricci's arrival in China was estimated at only between 100,000 and 250,000.

Cultural Gap

When Father Ricci was first in Peking, he observed the Chinese looked upon all foreigners "as illiterate and barbarous." They would not condescend "to learn anything from the books of outsiders because they believe that all true science and knowledge belongs to them alone." The Jesuits' superiority in technical subjects finally induced the Chinese to follow their lead, but in other aspects of society and intellectual life the Chinese held to their own views.

The emperor and his court officials, believing Peking to be the center of the world and all other nations inferior, had no understanding of the power of European nations. Scorning trade, they considered commercial contacts with foreigners as privileges they could grant or withhold. Accustomed to dealing with the small tributary states on their borders, they viewed pretentions to sovereignty by others as impertinence.

The first British emissary to China, arriving in 1793, sought an audience with the emperor to establish British representation in Peking, the opening of additional ports to trade, and reductions in Chinese tariffs. To the Chinese, the Briton was no more than a tribute bearer, but the emperor Chien-lung (Qianlong) granted him a hearing because he had come so far and was for the first time visiting "a superior country." However, the British requests were rejected as inconsistent with Chinese custom. No other state was allowed permanent representation in Peking.

Differences over trading rights and criminal jurisdiction exacerbated relations between the Chinese and Westerners. The Chinese considered permission to trade a favor which could be revoked; but trade was the principal interest of the Western voyagers, and they objected to limitations placed upon their activities by designation of where and with whom they could deal. In addition, bribes demanded by local officials doubled, even tripled, the official high tariff rates.

The Chinese insisted that the imperial government had jurisdiction over all criminal cases involving a Chinese national. The foreigners considered Chinese law and court procedures barbarous and were reluctant to accept Chinese jurisdiction. The Chinese held to the principle of joint responsibility for a crime: if one of a ship's crew had committed a crime and could not be found, the ship's captain should be brought to account. The Europeans maintained that only those directly involved were subject to trial and punishment.

Opium War of 1839-1842

Given the vast cultural differences between China and the West, a clash was probably inevitable. "The great tragedy," Harry Schwartz observed, "is that the clash occurred over an issue on which the West's position was morally indefensible by today's standards: the British demand that the Chinese government permit Western merchants to sell opium freely to Chinese." The conflict that became known as the Opium War of 1839-42 was "one that has cast a terrible shadow over China's relations with the West ever since." [4]

Opium originally was shipped to China in quantity by the Portuguese, but this trade was still relatively small in 1729, when the Chinese emperor prohibited the sale and use of opium in China. Despite the ban, the opium traffic grew rapidly as merchants, principally British, pressed the trade with the assistance of corrupt Chinese officials. Not only was the drug traffic a source of large profit; it also provided an alternative to silver in paying for Chinese tea, silk and porcelain.

By the late 1830s, opium addiction had spread from members of the nobility to artisans, merchants, women, and even members of the religious organizations. "If the opium traffic is not stopped," wrote a Chinese official, "the country will become poorer and poorer and its people

weaker and weaker." But even a direct appeal to the conscience of Queen Victoria proved unsuccessful. In 1838 Lin Tse-hsu (Lin Zexu) was named imperial commissioner at Canton and directed by the emperor to end the opium trade once and for all. He ordered that all opium held by foreigners be turned over to the government and burned.

When British traders refused to pledge that they would ship no more opium to China, Lin threatened to ban all commercial traffic. Meanwhile, a Chinese citizen had been killed in Kowloon by a group of English sailors. And when the British rejected Chinese demands for surrender of the sailors, Lin sent war junks toward the British naval force in Hong Kong. When the junks were fired upon, the war began. British naval superiority assured ultimate victory. When the British threatened a direct attack on Nanjing, the Chinese sued for peace.

The Treaty of Nanking (Nanjing) signed in 1842, resulted in the opening of China to Western traders. The treaty provided for (1) opening of five ports — Xiamen, Canton, Fuzhou, Ningbo and Shanghai — to British trade; (2) cession to Britain of the island of Hong Kong; (3) Chinese agreement to uniform and moderate tariffs on imports and exports, subject to change only by mutual consent; and (4) indemnity payments of $21 million. Under a supplementary treaty signed a year later, China granted the British extraterritorial jurisdiction in criminal cases and most-favored-nation status.

Opening of China

Other Western powers, through persuasion and threats of force, demanded and received the same or greater privileges. Because a most-favored-nation clause was incorporated in all later Chinese treaties with Western countries, a concession to one nation automatically became a concession to all. The Treaty of Wang-hsia, concluded with the United States in July 1844, extended the principle of extraterritoriality to civil as well as criminal cases. France was later granted the right to build Roman Catholic missions at treaty ports and freedom to proselytize without interference. Such concessions then were extended to all nations with missionaries in China.

The opening of China came at a time when the proselytizing zeal of American churches was at a high level. China became an irresistible magnet for missionary work. "China's vastness excited the missionary impulse; it appeared as the land of the future whose masses, when converted, offered promise of Christian and even English-speaking dominion over the world." The first American missionary arrived in China as early as 1811, but the main growth came later in the century. By 1925, there were 8,000 missionaries in China, most of them American. Their influence far outweighed their number and the number of their conversions. By the eve of World War II there were no more than 2.25 million Christians in China (1.5 million Roman Catholic and 750,000 Protestant). But the missionaries and their converts held favored positions in the Western-dominated parts of China and they provided major channels, through their schools, hospitals and other establishments, for the promulgation of Western ideas.

Of particular importance was the influence of the missionaries on the minds of Americans back home and indirectly on foreign policy. "Hardly a town in our land was without its society to collect funds and clothing for Chinese missions ... and to hear the missionaries' inspiring reports," Dean Acheson wrote. "Thus was nourished the love portion of the love-hate complex that was to infuse so much emotion into our later China policy."[5] The author of another account said: "It would be hard to over-emphasize the extent of the influence of the missionaries in shaping and directing the Far Eastern policies of the United States.... Beginning with President McKinley, they received ... special recognition from the executive branch.... For many years missionaries, businessmen and government officials collaborated in the movement to implant American social and economic institutions in China; and of the three the missionaries were by far the most powerful."[6]

Their view of China became the American view. They sympathized with the privations of the people in an industrially backward, strife-torn country and took the view that America was obligated to help them. "Congregations all over the United States listened to the returned missionary ... tell of the deserving qualities of the Chinese people and of the great reservoir of future Christians. The public impression was that America had saved China's integrity by the doctrine of the Open Door — a policy which called for equality of commercial rights in China among foreign interests. Missionary propaganda helped to create the image of China as protégé, an image which carried an accompanying sense of obligation toward the object of one's own beneficence."[7] Undetected by most Americans for many years was the undercurrent of resentment and sense of humiliation in China over its subservience to the foreign intruder.

Dun J. Li has pointed out that the Treaty of Nanking, "hopefully hailed by many westerners as the beginning of a new era in the relations between China and the Western world, created only a lull before another storm."[8] The Chinese, with more than 4,000 years of an inward-looking culture, were slow to understand the new reality of European power. Instead of adjusting to the future, they dreamed of the past, when the Celestial Emperor dealt peremptorily with the barbarians from the outer world. The policy of conciliation, evasion and negotiation followed by the Manchus for two decades after the Opium War amounted to merely a delaying action as the foreigners moved to enhance their power in China.

Century-Long Humiliation

The Opium War began more than 100 years of foreign humiliation of the Chinese government and people, a humiliation not fully ended until Mao Tse-tung and the Chinese Communists triumphed in 1949. Some of the Western nations regarded the Treaty of Nanking as too lenient. They wanted additional ports opened to trade and diplomatic representation at Peking. China's vulnerability was revealed during the Opium War, making a second conflict not unattractive to some Western states.

The second conflict was sparked by two incidents in 1856. One concerned the crew of a British-registered ship, the other the execution of a French Catholic missionary and some of his converts. British and French forces easily defeated the poorly trained Chinese. When the Europeans threatened to attack the city of Tianjin, the Manchu government again sued for peace. The treaties of Tientsin (Tianjin) granted new concessions to the West and enlarged older privileges. Britain and France were granted the right to maintain resident ministers at Peking and their nationals received unlimited travel privileges. New ports were opened to trade, and foreign ships were granted navigation rights on the Yangtze (Changjiang) River. Indemnities were paid, tariff rates lowered, and protection of missionaries guaranteed.

Utilizing the customary delaying tactics, the Chinese refused to ratify the new treaties. Britain and France then renewed the war, and the British commander ordered the burning of the Summer Palace in Peking, one of the architectural glories of the empire. The war came to a close with another treaty, signed in Peking in 1860, which gave still more privileges to the Europeans, including cession to the British of the Kowloon peninsula adjoining Hong Kong. The new privileges were extended to the other Western nations which had been accorded most-favored-nation status, including the United States and Russia.

Foreign powers later extended their dominion in Asia. Russia took over all of the mainland north of Korea and Manchuria. France colonized southern Indochina. Russia in 1868 completed a campaign to gain control of a large part of Xinjiang. Nepal, a tributary state, came under British control in 1881, and five years later Britain completed the conquest of Burma. At the close of the Sino-Japanese War in 1895, Japan exacted Taiwan from China and won paramount status in Korea. The Germans, French and British gained naval bases and ports on the Chinese mainland in 1898. Finally, following the Boxer uprising[9] and a lengthy siege of the European legation quarter in Peking in 1900, the Western powers imposed heavy indemnities and stationed foreign troops in the capital. "For over a decade after 1900, China was in fact a foreign-occupied country."[10]

The century which began with Chinese pride and arrogance, Robert S. Elegant relates, "ended with Chinese humiliation complete."

> Foreign envoys, once scorned, dictated terms in the Imperial City itself. Foreign missionaries, once barely tolerated, ranged everywhere to subvert the people from their proper duties to the emperor. In violation of Peking's express decrees, hundreds of thousands of Chinese emigrated to serve the imperialists abroad — and to create the overseas Chinese problem which vexes Southeast Asia today.[11]

China was saved from being carved up into colonies by disagreement among her conquerors, who jealously guarded their spheres of influence. The United States, which had no territorial possessions on the mainland, formalized the precarious status quo by proclaiming the Open Door policy in 1899. That policy guaranteed equality of commercial opportunity and enjoined further territorial seizures. Actually, the Open Door policy, which was supported by British power, was rooted in the most-favored-nation clauses of the Sino-Western treaties.

20th Century Sino-Western Relations

The Western powers were able to impose their will in China mainly because of the degenerate state of the Confucian dynasties which had ruled that country for 2,000 years. Chinese failure to recognize until too late that the West was a truly formidable adversary resulted from almost total Chinese ignorance of the world beyond the borders of the Celestial Empire. This lack of knowledge led to collapse of the empire itself, as the Chinese began to learn from the West and to use what they had learned to free themselves from foreign bondage.

Formation of the Republic

During the 19th century Chinese resentment of the privileged status of foreigners in their midst periodically flared into violence against Westerners. The most serious outbreak was the Boxer Rebellion, but as Chinese youth became more westernized, their resentment was directed at the Chinese authorities and the ineffectual imperial government. Young students, angered by the corruption, brutality and inefficiency which marked the declining years of the Manchu Dynasty, turned against the customs and religion of the older generation.

The youthful opposition joined in a revolutionary movement led by Sun Yat-sen and supported by overseas Chinese. The Empress Dowager and her successor died in 1908, leaving the succession to an infant emperor. A troop revolt which broke out in three cities in October 1911 led to the proclamation of a republic; the rebellion spread rapidly, and by the end of the year a national council had been set up. The council elected Sun Yat-sen president of the republic, and in February 1912 the boy emperor, P'u Yi, was forced to abdicate.

The new leaders had been united only by their opposition to the Manchu Dynasty, and China soon splintered into contending states headed by warlords and factions. Between 1913 and 1928, when the Kuomintang — or Nationalist Party — under the leadership of Chiang Kai-shek established a degree of control over the warring factions, the nation was split into the private domains of various warlords and was demoralized, disorganized and disunited. During this period, Robert S. Elegant noted, the only orderly government was "that imposed by foreigners in their various treaty ports."

> In westernized treaty ports and in inland hamlets, each new day added new weight to oppressive reality. The young Chinese tended to scorn other Chinese — and himself — for their degradation. The chief clubs of China's major cities either excluded Chinese or admitted a few as native curiosities. The Christian missionary enjoyed extraordinary privileges amounting to immunity from the law. . . . Foreign warships patrolled the coasts and rivers of China, enforcing payment of taxes for the foreigners' benefit.

"The most idealistic and talented youth of China," Elegant concluded, "grew to maturity in a miasma of hatred." [12]

Decline of Foreign Control

China entered World War I in August 1917 on the side of the Western allies, but, when the peace conferees at Paris decided to transfer German holdings in China's Shandong Peninsula to Japan, the representatives of China refused to sign the treaty. However, the Treaty of Versailles benefited China by depriving Austria and Germany of extraterritorial status and special concessions in China.

Further gains were made by the Chinese in the years following the war. At the Washington arms limitation conference of 1921-22, the Western powers and Japan agreed to respect the independence and territorial integrity of China, to refrain from seeking special privileges, and to give the Chinese an opportunity to achieve stable government. The powers agreed also to study the question of extraterritoriality with a view to its abolition. During the conference China and Japan also negotiated a treaty, ratified June 2, 1922, under which Japan surrendered the rights and concessions it obtained in Shandong.

The Bolshevik Revolution of November 1917 in Russia had opened the way for China to regain some of the ground lost to the Czars. Under an agreement concluded in 1924, for example, Russian extraterritorial privileges in China

were relinquished. Soon thereafter, pressure mounted in China for abolition of the concessions still enjoyed by foreigners in treaty ports. By 1930 more than half the foreigners in China had lost extraterritorial privileges, but the United States, Great Britain, France and Japan would not give ground. A Chinese attempt to resolve the question by simply decreeing that all remaining extraterritorial privileges would be withdrawn on a certain date was not successful, and some foreigners continued to enjoy such privileges until World War II.

Civil War and Communist Triumph

The Chinese Communist Party was formally organized in 1921 with no more than 50 registered members. It joined with the Kuomintang in support of Sun Yat-sen in 1924. Several Communists, including Mao Tse-tung, were elected alternate members of the Kuomintang's Central Executive Committee. This first period of cooperation ended in 1927, when the Kuomintang, under Chiang Kai-shek's leadership, purged the Communists.

The purge was followed by a lengthy struggle between Communists and Nationalists. The latter were ascendant in most of China, but in 1931 a Soviet republic was proclaimed in southern Jiangxi; under Mao's leadership the area became a microcosm of present-day China. Nationalist armies launched a number of campaigns against the republic, but, plagued by Japanese intrusions in Manchuria, these efforts were unsuccessful. Only in 1934, after a truce with Japan had been signed and an economic blockade of Jiangxi established, did Nationalist pressure damage the Communists. Rather than face annihilation, the Communist forces in 1934-35 staged the famed Long March.

Harried by government troops, by shortages of food and medicine and by the often harsh climate, Mao's wandering army overcame incredible hardships. It climbed major mountain ranges, crossed turbulent rivers on perilous and primitive bridges and inched its way across great swamps. A year after he had started, and 6,000 miles from his starting point, Mao called a halt. He had arrived at the other end of his country, in northern Shaanxi Province in northwestern China. Fewer than one-third of the 100,000 men who had begun the Long March completed it; most had fallen victim to battle, hunger, cold or disease. But in this poverty-stricken region of China, Mao created a new Communist area, set up his capital in Yanan and started over.

Confronted by further Japanese aggression in 1937, Communists and Nationalists again entered a period of cooperation. Before long, however, the struggle became a three-sided contest, with each Chinese faction attempting to enlarge its area of control at the expense of its rival while at the same time fighting the Japanese. After World War II ended in the Pacific with Japan's surrender, efforts to form a coalition Chinese government broke down and the civil war between Nationalists and Communists resumed.

By 1949, despite American military and economic aid to Chiang's forces, the Communist armies were clearly headed for victory. Early in that year, Chiang began to shift some of his forces as well as China's gold reserve to Taiwan, a large island separated from the mainland by the 100-mile-wide Taiwan Strait. The Nationalist withdrawal was accelerated as the Communists rapidly won most of the mainland. By Oct. 1, 1949, when the People's Republic of China was proclaimed in Peking, few areas were left in Nationalist hands.

The new Communist government was at once recognized by the Soviet Union and other communist states, and a treaty of friendship was signed between China and the U.S.S.R.

The Chinese Communist Party controlled all levels of government, the army, education and the media. Mao, as chairman of the party, ruled the country. Second in command was Chou En-lai, appointed premier and foreign minister. They remained the central figures in Chinese affairs until 1976, the year both died.

Footnotes

[1] Harry Schwartz, *China* (New York: Atheneum, 1965), p. 30.

[2] Dun J. Li, *The Ageless Chinese: A History* (New York: Charles Scribner's Sons, 1965), p. 376.

[3] Ssu-yu Teng and John K. Fairbank, *China's Response to the West* (Cambridge: Harvard University Press, 1965), p. 12.

[4] Schwartz, *China*, p. 33.

[5] Dean Acheson, *Present at the Creation* (New York: W. W. Norton & Co., 1965), p. 8.

[6] Richard Van Alstyne, *The Listener* (1961), quoted in Felix Greene, *A Curtain of Ignorance* (Garden City, N.Y.: Doubleday & Co., 1964), p. 4.

[7] Barbara W. Tuchman, *Stillwell and the American Experience in China* (New York: Macmillan Co., 1971), p. 32.

[8] Li, *The Ageless Chinese*, p. 394.

[9] Immanuel C. Y. Hsu, *China's Entrance into the Family of Nations: The Diplomatic Phase, 1858-1880* (Cambridge: Harvard University Press, 1960), pp. 10-11. Boxers were members of a secret sect which sprang up in 1898 among restive peasants. At first opposed by the Empress Dowager and later encouraged as a means of ridding China of foreigners, the Boxers killed scores of missionaries and their converts.

[10] Kenneth Scott Latourette, *China* (Englewood Cliffs, N.J.: Prentice-Hall, 1904), p. 121. Japan became one of the occupiers after its victory in the Russo-Japanese war of 1904-05. Railroad and other rights in South Manchuria granted by China to Russia in 1898 were transferred to Japan, laying the foundation for Japanese occupation of all of Manchuria in the 1930s.

[11] Robert S. Elegant, *The Center of the World: Communism and the Mind of China* (New York: Funk & Wagnall's, 1964), p. 69.

[12] Ibid., pp. 106-107.

Only in the case of Communist China has the Congress played a major role over a long period of time to confine narrowly the president's means of maneuver. In the late 1940s and early 1950s the Congress served as the forum for developing and expressing the version of why China went communist that was to permeate the public most deeply. Communist China's intervention in the war in Korea reinforced hostility to the regime.

Beginning in the early 1950s the Congress went on record each year, often more than once and usually with no dissenting voices, to oppose the seating of Communist China in the United Nations. The resolutions were symbols of the tangled and emotion-laden history of China policy. If they did not always explicitly endorse this resolving, the presidents expressed no dissent. By these resolutions, by amendments to various laws, and in other ways, the Congress constructed formidable walls for any president, if so inclined, to breach.

Holbert N. Carroll, "The Congress and National Security Policy," in David B. Truman (ed.) *The Congress and America's Future* (Englewood Cliffs, N.J.: Prentice-Hall, Inc., 1965, pp. 161-162.)

It is undisputed that the Constitution gave the President full constitutional authority to recognize the PRC and to derecognize the ROC. What the United States has evolved for Taiwan is a novel and somewhat indefinite relationship. . . . The subtleties involved in maintaining amorphous relationships are often the very stuff of diplomacy — a field in which the President, not Congress, has responsibility under our Constitution.

U.S. Court of Appeals, Nov. 30, 1979

Congress and China Policy, 1945-1980

The principal direction of congressional interest in Chinese and East Asian affairs has changed significantly since Mao Tse-tung's Communist forces routed Chiang Kai-shek's Nationalists and proclaimed the People's Republic of China in late 1949.

In the 1940s the most vocal congressional critics of U.S. Asian policy urged greater American support of the Nationalist government in the civil war against the Communists. By the mid-1960s, critics of U.S. China policy, although in a minority, suggested a softer stance toward China involving resumption of trade, diplomatic recognition of the People's Republic and Peking's admission into the United Nations. By the beginning of the 1980s, most legislators had fallen in line behind the initiatives for closer ties with China undertaken by Presidents Nixon and Carter.

Throughout the early post-World War II period, a majority prevailed on Capitol Hill which supported President Truman's hands-off policy in the Chinese civil war (1946-1949) and his defense of Taiwan after June 1950, then backed President Eisenhower's defense of Taiwan and the offshore islands, opposed recognition and U.N. membership for mainland China and, in an intimately related issue, supported and financed the U.S. military effort in Indochina under Presidents Kennedy, Johnson and Nixon.

Congressional support for the pro-Taiwan "China Lobby" point of view in the 1940s came mostly from Republicans; pressure for a "containment without isolation" policy toward China in the 1960s emanated for the most part from the Democrats, with the Senate Foreign Relations Committee as a base.

During this period, pro-Nationalist forces in the United States, aided by a well-organized lobbying coalition and an anti-communist political consensus fed by the Cold War with the Soviet Union and combat against the Communist Chinese in Korea, held sway in U.S. China policy deliberations.

Congress backed the emerging pro-Taiwan, anti-Peking policy of this period by passing the China Aid Act of 1948, the Mutual Defense Treaty of 1954 and the Formosa Resolution of 1955. In 1964 Congress sanctioned President Johnson's heavy commitment of U.S. forces to the Vietnam conflict by approving the Tonkin Gulf Resolution.

By the early 1970s, however, congressional conservatives on the China question found themselves in retreat. A Republican president famous for his anti-communism had eased trade and travel restrictions with China, reversed the traditional U.S. policy against U.N. membership for the People's Republic of China (PRC) and made an historic personal visit to Peking.

For the first time in two decades, Congress in 1971 failed to go on record against Peking's admission to the United Nations. Instead, most members of the House and Senate confined themselves to support of the administration's unsuccessful effort to save Taiwan's seat in the world organization.

By 1978, congressional sentiment had clearly shifted toward rapprochement with the PRC. Although President Carter's Dec. 15 announcement of normalization of relations generated a flurry of reaction on Capitol Hill, opposition was based less on disapproval of normalization than on Carter's failure to consult the legislative branch before terminating the Taiwan defense treaty, and on fears for the future security of Taiwan. Both these reservations, however, were dealt with in legislation passed during the first part of 1979 — and in a failed court suit brought by members of Congress — as Carter's diplomatic coup became a *fait accompli.*

Civil War 1946-1949

During the late 1940s, the Truman administration maintained a hands-off policy toward the Chinese civil war despite pressure from a vocal minority of senators and representatives for the increased involvement of the United States on behalf of Generalissimo Chiang Kai-shek and his Nationalist forces. The only significant concession to this minority was the China Aid Act, which cleared Congress in 1948.

On Feb. 18, 1948, President Truman sent a special message to Congress recommending a $570-million aid program for China. The administration program made no provision for military aid to the Nationalist government in its struggle against the Communists, who were then making rapid progress in Manchuria. The message said, however, that the proposed shipments of food, raw materials and fertilizers from the United States would permit the Nationalist government "to devote its [own] limited dollar resources to the most urgent of its other needs." On April 2, 1948, Congress passed the bill. The economic aid appropriation had been reduced to $338 million, but $125 million had been added for the Chinese government to use as it saw necessary, which presumably meant for military aid. The total amount was $463 million. On April 3, President Truman signed the bill into law. *(Text, p. 304)*

On Feb. 25, 1949, Sen. Pat McCarran, D-Nev., introduced a bill to provide a $1.5-billion loan to Nationalist China for military and economic purposes. Asked for comment by the Senate Foreign Relations Committee, Secretary of State Dean Acheson wrote April 14, 1949, that there was "no evidence" that such aid would "alter the pattern of current developments in China," to which the United States had given $2 billion since 1945 without stemming Communist forces. Sen. Styles Bridges, R-N.H., called for an investigation of China policy, accusing Acheson of what "might be called sabotage of the valiant" Nationalists. Sens. McCarran and William F. Knowland, R-Calif., supported Bridges. Sens. Tom Connally, D-Texas, and J. W. Fulbright, D-Ark., defended Acheson. No action was taken on McCarran's bill.

But on April 14, 1949, as the Nationalist position continued to deteriorate, Congress extended the 1948 China Aid Act by authorizing the president to use unobligated funds as he determined necessary for aid to those areas of China that remained free of Chinese Communist control. The funds were made available until Feb. 15, 1950.

In June 1949, when it was rumored that the State Department was studying the possibility of recognizing a Chinese Communist regime, 21 senators (16 Republicans and five Democrats) sent a letter to President Truman expressing bitter opposition to any such move and calling for increased aid to the Nationalists. Sen. Arthur H. Vandenberg, R-Mich., declared in a Senate speech that the U.S. policy toward China had been a "tragic failure." But Sen. Connally replied: "Would you send your own sons to fight in the Chinese civil war?"

China "White Paper"

On Aug. 5, 1949, the State Department released a "White Paper" on China, pointing out that the Nationalists were on the verge of collapse because of the military, economic and political shortcomings of the Chiang regime, and that no amount of additional aid would have prevented their defeat at the hands of Communist forces. The document set off a new burst of criticism from Republicans.

Among groups supporting Chiang and denouncing the White Paper were the China Emergency Committee, headed by Frederick C. McKee, and the American China Policy Committee, headed by Alfred Kohlberg.

Rep. Mike Mansfield, D-Mont., called Aug. 25 for an investigation of lobbying on behalf of the Nationalists. He suggested that money provided earlier "to help China, but siphoned off for private use, is being used to finance attacks on our Secretary of State and other officials charged with conducting our relations with China." Talk of a pro-Chiang "China Lobby" persisted for many years but the issue was never fully clarified. *(Box, pp. 30-31)*

The Senate Sept. 22 passed the Mutual Defense Assistance Act, adding to the funds requested by the president $75 million for use in the "general area" of China. The House accepted the item, for which Sen. Knowland was chiefly responsible, and it was retained in the final law.

Disunity Over Asia Policy

Early in 1950, bipartisan cooperation on questions of foreign policy was strained by the charges of Sen. Joseph McCarthy, R-Wis., that American policies in East Asia had been influenced by communist sympathizers in the State Department *(Box, p. 28);* by Republican demands that the president "fire Acheson"; by Truman's statements that Sen. Bridges and other minority senators were "trying to sabotage the foreign policy of the United States"; and by continuing complaints from GOP leaders that they were "never consulted" on East Asian policy.

A warning that congressional dissatisfaction with American policy in East Asia went deeper than the administration apparently had supposed was given early in the 1950 session of Congress when the House Jan. 19 defeated, 191 to 192, a bill to appropriate $60 million for additional economic aid to the Republic of Korea during the period Feb. 15 to June 30.

The president had requested $150 million. The appropriation of $60 million was later approved, 240 to 134, but only after an authorization for continued assistance to the Chinese Nationalists on Taiwan had been added to it.

Korean War

Less than five years after V-J Day, the United States in mid-1950 found itself locked in a full-scale war in a little-expected quarter — Korea. Political disunity receded after President Truman's June 27 action ordering American forces to South Korea and reversing previous policy by ordering the 7th Fleet to "prevent any attack on Formosa [Taiwan]." Subsequent American setbacks in the conflict brought all but unanimous support for the president's Korean policies and the legislation needed to implement them.

After Communist China's entry into the Korean War and its rejection of two U.N. appeals for a cease-fire in the conflict, the United States called on the General Assembly to label the Peking regime as an aggressor. Underscoring congressional support for this move, the House and Senate quickly passed resolutions to the same effect.

H Res 77, introduced by House Majority Leader John McCormack, D-Mass., called on the United Nations to "immediately act and declare the Chinese Communist authorities an aggressor in Korea." The House approved the resolution by voice vote on Jan. 19, 1951. The Senate Jan. 23, 1951, adopted a similar resolution (S Res 35), introduced by Sen. John L. McClellan, D-Ark., also by voice vote.

Following Senate action on S Res 35, McClellan called up two other resolutions. S Res 36 declared that Communist China should not be admitted to the United Nations. Sen. Brien McMahon, D-Conn., said that, although he agreed, the matter should be studied because the United States might want to change its position if a split developed between Moscow and Peking. Sen. Spessard Holland, D-Fla., said this would leave the administration in doubt as to the Senate's views. S Res 36 was adopted 91-0. (A similar resolution opposing China's U.N. membership passed every Congress until 1971. *Box, pp. 12-13)*

The third resolution (S Res 37), calling for "the complete interruption of economic relations" between U.N. members and Communist China, was referred by voice vote to the Senate Foreign Relations Committee on the motion of Majority Leader Ernest W. McFarland, D-Ariz. No further action was taken on S Res 37.

The House May 15, 1951, passed a resolution identical to S Res 36 after Secretary of Defense George C. Marshall had declared that the United States should use its veto in the Security Council, if necessary, to keep Communist China out of the United Nations. The secretary had also said that Taiwan "must never be allowed to come under control of a Communist government or a government under Soviet domination."

Also on May 15, both the House and Senate unanimously adopted a resolution (S Con Res 31) which urged the U.N. General Assembly to "take action leading to . . . an embargo on the shipment to Communist China of arms, ammunition, and all other materials which might add to the war-making potential of Communist China."

MacArthur

However, the unity that President Truman successfully had maintained in Congress was eroded with the president's removal of Gen. Douglas MacArthur April 11, 1951, from his Asian commands. Most Republicans and a few Democrats, dissatisfied with a situation that seemed to promise nothing better than a stalemate in Korea, bitterly attacked the president for his action. Some Republicans, such as Indiana Sen. William E. Jenner, talked openly of impeachment. Sen. McCarthy said it was the "greatest victory the Communists have ever won."

In the midst of the political storm, MacArthur returned to Washington. In an address before a joint session of Congress April 19 and in subsequent testimony before the joint Senate Foreign Relations-Armed Services committees, MacArthur recommended that China be blockaded, that restrictions on "air reconnaissance" of China's coastal areas and Manchuria be removed, and that the restrictions on the forces of the Republic of China on Taiwan also be removed, with "logistical support" of their operations against Communist China supplied by the United States. MacArthur said such actions would quickly bring Communist China to its knees.

1951 Hearings

The joint Senate committee hearings on Far Eastern policy, conducted in May and June of 1951, put on record a large number of secret documents, including the Wedemeyer report on Korea of September 1947 (part of a report on China by Lt. Gen. Albert C. Wedemeyer).

On June 1, over the protest of Secretary of State Acheson, the committees voted 15-9 to make public a State Department memorandum of Dec. 23, 1949, which said that Taiwan had "no special military significance" and that its loss to the Communists was expected.

Although the hearings were closed, transcripts of the testimony were made public after material directly relating to future war plans had been deleted. A Republican move to hold the hearings in the open was blocked in the Senate, 41 to 37, after all 70 senators who were not members of the Foreign Relations or Armed Services committees had been invited to attend by the two committees.

A skillful defense of administration policies during eight days of testimony and cross-examination apparently restored Secretary Acheson's prestige somewhat. In the House, a Republican amendment to the State Department's fiscal 1952 appropriation (HR 4740) which would have had the effect of removing the secretary from the federal payroll was defeated on July 26, 1951, by a standing vote of 171 to 81.

On Aug. 17 the joint committee voted 20-3 to file no formal report on the investigation. Richard B. Russell, D-Ga., said the group wished to avoid "renewal of bitter controversy" at a time when Korean truce negotiations were in progress. The hearings, he said, had "forced a definite policy in the Far East when we did not have one," had been partly responsible for a change in attitude toward the Nationalist Chinese on Taiwan and had led to an economic blockade of Communist China.

An Aug. 19 statement issued by the eight Republican members of the joint committee condemned the manner of Gen. MacArthur's dismissal, described the administration's East Asian policy as a "catastrophic failure," asserted that the constitutional authority of the Congress to declare war had been bypassed in Korea, and warned against any peace of "appeasement" with the Chinese Communists. Sen. Wayne Morse, then R-Ore., issued his own statement Sept. 5 praising the president for his actions.

Defense of Taiwan

As the eight years of fighting in Indochina between the French and the Vietminh ended, and as the Southeast Asia Treaty Organization (SEATO) became a reality, Communist China increased military operations against the offshore islands of Quemoy, Matsu and the Dachens. To underscore its support of the Taiwan regime, the United States Dec. 2, 1954, signed a mutual security pact with the Republic of China. Meanwhile, Sen. Knowland was calling for a blockade of the mainland to force the release of 13 Americans captured in Korea and sentenced Nov. 22, 1954, as spies by the Chinese Communists. Tensions were mounting as the Democratic-controlled 84th Congress convened Jan. 5, 1955, and President Eisenhower asked the Senate for prompt approval of the U.S.-Nationalist security pact. It was ratified on Feb. 9, 1955, and remained in effect until President Carter abrogated it as of Jan. 1, 1980.

"Formosa Resolution." On Jan. 18, 1955, Communist forces seized the offshore island of Yijiang, 210 miles north of Taiwan, and seemed prepared to invade the nearby Dachen Islands. The situation led the president to ask Congress, in a special message Jan. 24, for explicit authority to use American armed forces to protect Taiwan, the adjoining Pescadores Islands, and "related positions and territories." Despite some misgivings concerning aspects of the bill which they considered vague (such as the president's or Secretary Dulles' intent regarding Quemoy, Matsu and the offshore islands), the Democratic leaders in Congress hastened to comply with the president's request.

The Formosa Resolution (H J Res 159), authorizing him to "employ the armed forces of the United States as he deems necessary" in the defense of Taiwan, was reported by the House Foreign Affairs Committee the same day, unanimously and without amendment. The House passed it Jan. 25 on a 410-3 roll-call vote after hearing Speaker Sam Rayburn, D-Texas, state his belief that the resolution added nothing to the constitutional powers of the president and should not be taken as a precedent that would bind him in the future.

On Jan. 26 the Senate Foreign Relations and Armed Services committees, sitting jointly, voted 27-2 to report the resolution without change, after rejecting amendments to restrict the president's authority. In floor debate Jan. 26-28, Sens. Morse, D-Ore. and Ralph Flanders, R-Vt., warned of a "preventative war," while Sens. Estes Kefauver, D-Tenn., Hubert Humphrey, D-Minn., and Herbert Lehman, D-N.Y., attacked the resolution's ambiguity regarding the offshore islands. But the Senate Jan. 28 rejected three restrictive amendments by lopsided margins and passed H J Res 159 on an 85-3 roll call. Voting "nay" were Morse, William Langer, R-N.D., and Lehman. *(Text, p. 311)*

SEATO Treaty. Senate action on the Southeast Asia Collective Defense Treaty, submitted by the president Nov. 10, 1954, was postponed until the Formosa Resolution was approved. The Foreign Relations Committee cleared the treaty Jan. 21, 1955, and the Senate approved ratification Feb. 1, 1955, by an 82-1 roll-call vote.

China Treaty. On Feb. 8 the Senate Foreign Relations Committee voted 11-2 to approve the mutual security treaty signed with the Republic of China in December 1954. The committee, however, stated its understanding that its terms "apply only in the event of external armed attack, and that military operations by either party from the territories held by the Republic of China shall not be undertaken except by joint agreement." Two other "understand-

McCarthy and China Policy

A speech by Sen. Joseph R. McCarthy, R-Wis., Feb. 9, 1950, to the Ohio County Women's Republican Club in Wheeling, W.Va., led to one of the most bitterly controversial investigations in the history of Congress. A special subcommittee of the Senate Foreign Relations Committee was set up to investigate McCarthy's charges that communists were knowingly employed by the State Department and were directing its policies, especially in East Asia.

The subcommittee held 31 days of hearings between March 8 and June 28, 1950. During the course of the hearings, McCarthy charged 10 individuals by name with varying degrees of communist activity.

Among those named was Prof. Owen J. Lattimore of Johns Hopkins University. On the case of Lattimore, McCarthy said he would "stand or fall." In executive hearings, McCarthy March 20 said Lattimore was "the top of the ring of which [Alger] Hiss was a part." Asked if he was sure Lattimore was the biggest Russian spy, McCarthy said: "By far and away. I think he is the top Russian spy."

Lattimore spent three days on the stand, April 6 and May 2 and 3. He denied charges that he was a communist and challenged McCarthy to repeat his charges off the Senate floor "so he can be held accountable in a court of law."

Report. In the final report (S Rept 2108), filed July 20, 1950, the Democratic majority found "no evidence to support the charge that Owen Lattimore is the 'top Russian spy,' or for that matter, any sort of spy." Each of the other nine primary "cases" submitted by McCarthy was also found to be without substantiation or was rejected because the person involved had never been an employee of the government.

Aftermath. Although he soon lost interest in East Asia, McCarthy and his repeated accusations of communist influence throughout the government remained a key domestic issue. The main result of his accusations on U.S. Asian policy was a purge of the State Department's Asia section, and the creation of an atmosphere wherein scholars and officials favoring improved relations with Communist China were reluctant to speak out.

Taking over the chairmanship of the Senate Government Operations Committee and its Permanent Investigations Subcommittee in 1953, McCarthy investigated the State Department, Voice of America, Department of the Army and other agencies. An opinion-stifling "climate of fear" in many government agencies was said to be one of the results of his probes. The Army-McCarthy hearings, televised in the spring of 1954, were the climax of McCarthy's career, and led finally to his censure by the Senate Dec. 2, 1954. He died May 2, 1957.

ings" were expressed, to the effect that any extension of the treaty area would require the concurrence of a two-thirds majority in the Senate, and that nothing in the treaty "shall be construed as affecting or modifying the legal status or sovereignty" of Taiwan and the Pescadores.

Sen. Morse nevertheless proposed adding this last point to the text of the treaty. The Senate rejected the move, 11-57, as it did a second Morse amendment to strike out a reference to defense of "such other territories as may be determined by mutual agreement," 10-60. Ratification of the treaty was then approved Feb. 9, 1955, by a vote of 65-6. Opposed were Sens. Morse, Langer, Lehman, Dennis Chavez, D-N.M., Albert Gore, D-Tenn., and Kefauver. *(Text, p. 311)*

New Policy Proposals

In 1957 a handful of senators advocated revising U.S. China policy, with no substantial results. The most important recommendation was made by Sen. Theodore F. Green, D-R.I., chairman of the Senate Foreign Relations Committee. On Feb. 18 Green said the United States "should recognize Red China sooner or later. We don't like their form of government, but the country is a great country and organized, and I do not myself see why we should recognize these other Communist countries and withhold recognition of China unless we are going to apply that to other Communist countries." Secretary of State Dulles told a news conference Feb. 19 that it would be "premature, to say the least," to discuss recognizing Communist China, but he added that "none of us are talking here in terms of eternity."

On June 16, 1957, Sen. Fulbright, second-ranking majority member of the Senate Foreign Relations Committee, suggested during a television interview that recognition of Communist China by the United States was inevitable in course of time; the only question was "when and how you do it." Fulbright favored negotiations on recognition and on modification of the embargo in return for such concessions as a Peking pledge to stay out of Taiwan.

On July 18, 1957, after pressure was exerted by some members of Congress and the press, a crack in the American policy of trying to hold Communist China virtually in quarantine showed up for the first time when Secretary Dulles offered to validate the passports of a limited number of American newsmen for travel in China for a limited period. The Chinese Communists later refused to allow the newsmen into the country on grounds that the decision had not been reciprocal.

Taiwan — 1958

But the rising tide of congressional sentiment for a revision in U.S. policy toward China was quickly quelled in the fall of 1958 as Communist China resumed military operations against the Nationalist-held offshore islands. As President Eisenhower and Secretary Dulles alternated pledges of "no retreat" with pleas for a cease-fire, Senate Democrats voiced their concern. On Sept. 13 Sen. John F. Kennedy, D-Mass., commented that in Taiwan, "The weight of military, diplomatic, political, and historical judgment would dictate a contrary policy." Kennedy was joined by Sen. Ralph W. Yarborough, D-Texas, who asserted that Eisenhower was getting "bayonet-happy." Sen. Green expressed "profound concern" Sept. 12 over the president's policy of employing armed forces "in a way which might risk deeper military involvement." The president, Green said, "has a duty to request policy guidance from Congress."

On Oct. 4, 10 Democratic House members sent a telegram to President Eisenhower making a new demand for a special congressional session on the Far East. They said they had found "the great majority" of their constituents were "deeply disturbed with the administration's Quemoy policy," and they believed "we should disentangle ourselves from Chiang Kai-shek's aspirations on Quemoy, and should endeavor to bring the mantle of the U.N. over Formosa [Taiwan]. . . ."

Policy Studies

On Nov. 1, 1959, the Senate Foreign Relations Committee released a study prepared by a private research firm, Conlon Associates, Ltd., of San Francisco, Calif., on U.S. foreign policy in Asia. The study recommended that the United States gradually shift its policy, leading to recognition of Communist China, U.S. support for seating Peking in the United Nations, recognition of Taiwan as a new republic and its seating in the U.N. General Assembly. Committee Chairman Fulbright said the study was "very provocative. . . . [W]hile I do not believe that the U.S. should recognize Communist China at the present time . . . I do not believe it is wise to continue to ignore over 600 million people . . . in the naive belief that they will somehow go away."

On Jan. 3, 1960, Sen. Henry M. Jackson, D-Wash., chairman of a Senate Government Operations subcommittee, issued a report entitled "National Policy Machinery in Communist China," noting that "the Chinese Communist party has attained a degree of unity and stability at its higher levels which is unequaled by other major Communist parties." The report concluded that the Communist leadership in China had uplifted the country "from a prostrate colossus to a giant on the march, in ten short years."

Kennedy Administration

Despite some indications to the contrary, the Kennedy administration offered no immediate plans for basic changes in U.S.-China policy. On May 3, 1961, Senate Minority Leader Everett M. Dirksen, R-Ill., introduced a resolution restating congressional opposition to the seating of Communist China in the United Nations. An identical measure was introduced the same day in the House by Rep. Clement J. Zablocki, D-Wis., and 55 other members.

Dirksen submitted the resolution, which was also endorsed by Senate Majority Leader Mike Mansfield, following conferences initiated after Senate debate April 14 over the president's reaffirmation of longstanding U.S. policy on the question of Chinese representation in the United Nations. Asked if the resolution had been approved by Secretary of State Dean Rusk, Dirksen said "that is my definite understanding."

The resolution declared it "the sense of Congress that it supports the president in his affirmation that the United States shall continue to meet its commitments to the people and Government of the Republic of China and shall continue to support the Government as the representative of China in the United Nations [and] further, the United States shall continue to oppose the seating of the Chinese Communist regime in the United Nations so long as that regime persists in defying the principles of the United Nations Charter. Further, it is the sense of the Congress that the United States supports the President in not according diplomatic recognition to the Chinese Communist regime."

The Senate July 28 adopted S Con Res 34 by a 76-0 roll-call vote and sent it to the House. The Senate accepted two amendments offered by Sen. Thomas J. Dodd, D-Conn., which he said were designed to justify to the world the United States' "determination to keep Red China out of the United Nations." The amendments restated that Communist China should not be seated because it had "flagrantly violated basic human rights," had imposed a brutal regime on the Chinese people, had derived its authority from usurpation and tyranny and had become the "major source of the international illicit narcotics traffic."

On Aug. 31, 1961, the House unanimously passed the resolution. During debate, several members argued that the language of the resolution was too restrained. Only two members — Reps. Thomas L. Ashley, D-Ohio, and William Fitts Ryan, D-N.Y. — spoke against it. Both answered "present" on the roll call.

Indochina

The 1954 Geneva agreements on Indochina failed to resolve the political conflicts of the area, and by 1961 the Communist regime of North Vietnam was giving support to guerrilla operations against the U.S.-backed governments of Premier Boun Oum in Laos and President Ngo Dinh Diem in South Vietnam. In 1962 the scale of American aid increased rapidly as more than 10,000 U.S. military personnel undertook to train the expanded forces of President Diem and assist them in countering the highly effective guerrilla techniques of the Communist Viet Cong.

Vietnam Report

On Feb. 24, 1963, a special report was submitted to the Senate Foreign Relations Committee by a four-man panel headed by Senate Majority Leader Mike Mansfield. In an investigation of U.S. aid to Southeast Asia, the report concluded that "there is no interest of the United States in Vietnam which would justify, in present circumstances, the conversion of the war . . . primarily into an American war to be fought primarily with American lives." The report recommended that the United States conduct a thorough reassessment of its "over-all security requirement on the Southeast Asia mainland" aimed at consideration of a reduction in the U.S. aid programs, although "extreme caution" should be used, "for if the attempt is made to alter the programs via a congressional meat axe cut . . . it runs the risk of not merely removing the fat but of leaving a gap which will lay open the region to massive chaos and, hence, jeopardize the present Pacific structure of our national security."

On Sept. 12, 1963, Sen. Frank Church, D-Idaho, proposed a resolution calling for U.S. withdrawal from South Vietnam if "cruel repressions" of the Buddhists by the government continued. Church charged that the situation in Vietnam had "worsened" while the U.S. effort had increased.

Fulbright Criticism

On March 25, 1964, Sen. Fulbright, chairman of the Foreign Relations Committee, began to criticize the Johnson administration's East Asia policies. In a speech entitled "Old Myths and New Realities," a general criticism of American foreign policy, the senator called for a re-evaluation of U.S. East Asian policies and added that "whatever the outcome of a re-thinking of policy might be, we have been unwilling to take it because of the fear of many government officials, undoubtedly well-founded, that even the suggestion of new policies toward China or Vietnam would provoke a vehement outcry."

Fulbright asserted that the United States should "introduce an element of flexibility, or, more precisely, of the

The Rise and Fall of the American 'China Lobby' . . .

During the final stages of the Chinese civil war — which featured many reports of corruption among the Nationalists and the abandonment of U.S.-supplied arms to the Communists — there was considerable sympathy in the United States for the "plague-on-both-your-houses" view of Gen. George C. Marshall and a policy of "let the dust settle."

With the defeat of the Nationalists by the Communists in 1949, however, followed by the invasion by North Korea of South Korea in June 1950, U.S. policy in China became the subject of major political controversy that figured strongly in the 1952 presidential campaign, when conservative Republicans charged that the Democrats had "lost" China. The Truman administration, they said, had "substituted on our Pacific flank a murderous enemy for an ally and friend."

During this period an extensive propaganda war was waged between organizations opposing or supporting the Chinese Nationalists. Groups supporting the Chiang regime charged its opponents with being communist "dupes" and "fronts"; the latter helped to label the former as the "China Lobby," bought and paid for by the Nationalists.

Pro-Nationalist Groups

The pro-Chiang Kai-shek forces formed a loose and broad alliance of individuals having little in common except their opposition to the Chinese Communists. A number of the directors listed on the letterheads of the American China Policy Association and the Committee To Defend America by Aiding Anti-Communist China were people who had worked in China as religious or medical missionaries — as had Rep. Walter Judd, R-Minn. (1943-63) — or in other similar capacities.

Several of the listed directors were former communist leaders who broke with Stalinism: Jay Lovestone, of the Committee to Defend America, was once secretary general of the Communist Party, U.S.A., and later a top foreign policy adviser for the AFL-CIO; Freda Utley, of the American China Policy Association, had been a British communist; other listed directors had similar sympathies or affiliations in the past.

Among the early pro-Nationalist lobbies were:

● **American China Policy Association,** headed by Alfred Kohlberg, an import-export merchant, and William Loeb, publisher of the Manchester (N.H.) *Union-Leader,* and the **China Emergency Committee,** headed by Frederick C. McKee, a Pittsburgh industrialist. Serving as an adviser to both groups was Rep. Judd, a leading conservative spokesman on China policy throughout the history of debate.

● The **Committee to Defend America by Aiding Anti-Communist China** became active in the latter half of 1949 and issued a quantity of literature urging China aid. Chairman pro tem of the committee was Frederick C. McKee. On its board of directors were ex-Ambassador Arthur Bliss Lane; David Dubinsky, president of the International Ladies' Garment Workers' Union and second vice president of the American Federation of Labor; James A. Farley, chairman of the board of the Coca-Cola Export Corp., formerly chairman of the Democratic National Committee and Postmaster General.

● The **Committee on National Affairs** — another group headed by McKee — in 1949 sent congressmen reprints of an article, "An Aid Plan for Asia," by Harold E. Stassen, then president of the University of Pennsylvania and formerly Governor of Minnesota, calling for a billion-dollar-a-year "MacArthur Plan" for Asia to oppose the Chinese Communists. The Stassen article opposed backing any large central governments, and would have extended aid on a project basis.

● **Committee of One Million.** In 1953 the pro-Nationalists turned their attention to the problem of keeping Communist China out of the United Nations. Starting with a petition to the president signed by prominent members of both parties, a Committee of One Million Against the Admission of Communist China to the United Nations was created. (Just who the "one million" were was never documented.) In March 1954 the committee announced "the expansion of its activities to include opposition to trade with Red China."

After a period of dormancy in the 1960s, the committee in October 1970 announced "a nation-wide information program and petition drive." It said this was prompted partly by disclosure that "powerful, well-financed groups" were pressing for recognition of the Peking regime and its admission to the U.N. The committee sometimes distributed Nationalist China material to members of Congress, some of which was read on the floor of the House.

By the mid-1960s, all these groups were defunct except the Committee of One Million, which — now called the **Committee for a Free China** — was still lobbying for grass-roots support of Taiwan after normalization of U.S. relations with Peking in 1979.

In addition to those topical lobbies, a number of broader-based organizations campaigned in behalf of Taiwan. Among them were the executive council of the AFL-CIO; the American Legion; the American Security Council; the American Conservative Union; and Young Americans for Freedom.

Pro-Détente Groups

● The **Committee for a Democratic Far Eastern Policy,** which the pro-Chiang groups claimed was under communist influence, urged a hands-off policy towards China. In literature sent congressmen in 1949, the committee called for a congressional investigation of the "Chinese lobby" and the private wealth which Chinese officials and individuals "have stowed away in American banks and investments"; an immediate end to all American intervention in China; and no dealing with any remnant of the Kuomintang. In 1950 the committee circulated "Facts on the Korean Crisis" criticizing the "unprecedented haste" of the United States in persuading the United Nations to censure North Korea. That October the committee sent congressmen a resolution urging the United States to recognize the People's Republic; help seat it in the U.N.; recognize that Taiwan belonged to mainland China; cease giving military aid and advice to other nations for use in Asia; and withdraw from Korea.

... Pro-Taiwan Groups Were Influential in the 1950s

● The **Institute of Pacific Relations** came under heavy attack in 1950 during the hearings of Sen. Joseph R. McCarthy, R-Wis., into charges of communist influence in the State Department. *(Box, p. 28)*

William L. Holland, secretary of the IPR, in 1950 denied as "utterly false" the McCarthy communist-front charge. He described the Institute as "a reputable nonpartisan international research organization whose studies of Far Eastern and Pacific countries long have been valued and acclaimed by leading scholars and public figures." McCarthy's charges came in connection with his attacks on Owen Lattimore, who conducted research in Peking for the institute in the early 1930s and was editor of its magazine, *Pacific Affairs*, from 1934 to 1941.

● The **Committee for a New China Policy** was founded by Thomas B. Manton, Burma-born son of an American missionary, in April 1969. While director of international affairs for the United Church of Christ in 1970, Manton served as a part-time consultant to the U.S.-China committee of the Members of Congress for Peace Through Law.

● **Citizens to Change United States China Policy** was formed by Prof. Allen S. Whiting following a split-off from the Committee for a New China Policy (CNCP). Manton said Whiting and his backers walked out in disagreement primarily with the CNCP advocacy of an abrupt end to U.S. support of Nationalist China; Whiting favored gradualism.

Whiting said he had never been in CNCP but that a group split off from CNCP and asked him to head it.

Both the organization and Burton registered as lobbyists June 15, 1971. Policy objectives included ending all trade embargoes against mainland China; withdrawal of U.S. military from Taiwan; recognition of mainland China as the sole U.N. representative of China, and establishment of economic, social, cultural and diplomatic relations with Communist China "on the basis of the principles of equality, mutual respect, and nonintervention in each other's affairs."

● **National Committee on United States-China Relations Inc.**, was founded in June 1966 and described itself as an independent, non-partisan educational organization which received most of its financial support from the Ford Foundation and the Rockefeller Brothers Fund. Its chairman, Alexander Eckstein, testified at 1966 Senate hearings in support of closer U.S. relations with the China mainland, and the committee became a leading advocate of opening the door to the PRC.

Among its founders was Robert A. Scalapino, chairman of the political science department at the University of California, Berkeley, a consultant to the Rockefeller and Ford foundations, and a supporter of U.S. policy in the Vietnam War.

● **U.S.-China People's Friendship Association,** established after President Nixon's visit to Peking in 1972, is a non-profit organization that sponsors informational and educational programs, seminars and cultural exchanges emphasizing trade, cultural and commercial relations with the People's Republic of China.

Existing groups that have spoken out for a more moderate policy toward the PRC include Americans for Democratic Action, the Ripon Society and Members of Congress for Peace Through Law.

Changed Circumstances

The decline of the influence of the Nationalists' U.S. allies — who had held sway for nearly a quarter century — was signaled by President Nixon's overtures to the PRC in 1971-72. A number of factors accounted for the change in direction.

● The new moves toward closer relations with the People's Republic of China came, for the first time, from a Republican president with a reputation for opposing communism that dated back to the Alger Hiss case. This factor tended to subdue a renewal of the harsh domestic battles over alleged communist subversion which dominated earlier phases of China policy controversy.

● The Communist government had been in command of mainland China since December 1949. No longer was there debate over helping Chiang Kai-shek's Nationalists to regain the China mainland by force. Taiwan — and continued U.S. guarantees of its independence — had become the central issue.

● The leaders of the two big communist powers, China and the Soviet Union, had become adversaries. Some saw an opportunity to try to widen the wedge between them.

● Other nations — including many of the United States' allies — pragmatically decided to establish diplomatic relations with Communist China, vote to admit it to the United Nations and expand trade with it.

● Long before the Vietnam War ended, it became clear that North Vietnam was not a "puppet" state of Communist China. This defused the argument of the "domino theory" that communist forces in Indochina were part of a monolithic movement controlled by Peking.

● Death or political attrition removed many of the key figures in the China struggle — Chiang Kai-shek; Mao Tse-tung; Chou En-lai — and early U.S. debate over it — Secretary of State John Foster Dulles; Sen. Joseph McCarthy; William F. Knowland, the Senate GOP leader who told his party's national convention in 1956 he would oppose Red Chinese membership in the U.N. "as long as I have a voice and a vote" in the Senate; Gen. Douglas MacArthur, who commanded U.N. troops in Korea against the Chinese Communists; Alfred Kohlberg, whose letter-writing earned him a nickname he took to his grave, "the China lobby man"; Prof. Owen Lattimore, who called Knowland the "senator from Formosa" and was himself characterized by the Senate Judiciary Committee as "a conscious articulate instrument of the Soviet conspiracy."

● Years of discussion, much of it in small, information groups, had taken place in U.S. academic circles. During that period, the question of lowering the bars to the Peking government lost its stigma and became an openly debated possibility.

The pro-Nationalists would make a last-ditch effort to "save Taiwan" at the time of the recognition of the PRC by President Carter in 1978-79, but by then the "China lobby" clearly had been overtaken by events. *(See box, p. 46)* capacity to be flexible, into our relations with Communist China." He added that the foremost of the new realities about China "is that there are not really 'two Chinas' but only one, mainland China, and that is ruled by Communists and likely to remain so for the indefinite future." The Johnson administration disputed Fulbright's views.

Tonkin Gulf Resolution

The conflict in Vietnam went badly for the United States in the mid-1960s. The South Vietnamese government seemed unable to rally its people in the war against the Communists, while the U.S. commitment, both in men and money, was significantly increased. As congressional concern mounted, President Johnson May 18, 1964, requested $125 million in additional economic and military aid for South Vietnam. The request for $70 million in additional economic aid and $55 million in additional military aid for Vietnam was quickly approved May 20 by the House Foreign Affairs Committee.

On Aug. 2 and 4, U.S. destroyers patrolling the Gulf of Tonkin off the coast of North Vietnam reported torpedo attacks by Communist PT boats, and President Johnson ordered an air strike at their bases resulting in the destruction of 25 boats. On Aug. 5 the president asked Congress to enact a resolution to "give convincing evidence to the aggressive Communist nations, and to the world as a whole, that our policy in Southeast Asia will be carried forward, and that the peace and security of the area will be preserved."

Republicans as well as Democrats endorsed the president's actions. Only Sens. Morse, D-Ore., and Ernest Gruening, D-Alaska, objected that, in Morse's words, "continuation of the U.S. unilateral military action in Southeast Asia, which has now taken on the aspects of open aggressive fighting, endangers the peace of the world." On Aug. 7, 1964, the Senate voted 88-2 and the House 414-0 to pass a resolution declaring support for "the determination of the President as Commander-in-Chief, to take all necessary measures to repel any armed attack against the forces of the United States and to prevent further aggression." The resolution also affirmed U.S. intentions to aid any member or protocol state of the SEATO pact "requesting assistance in the defense of its freedom" (PL 88-408). *(Text, p. 314)*

Rising Costs

The escalating military situation in South Vietnam also meant a steep rise in costs. During 1965, the House May 5 and the Senate May 6, by nearly unanimous roll-call votes, passed and sent to the president a bill (H J Res 447) making fiscal 1965 supplemental appropriations of $700 million to meet mounting military requirements in Vietnam. The actions came less than 53 hours after President Johnson had appealed to Congress to "provide our forces with the best and most modern supplies and equipment" and to show "prompt support of our basic course: resistance to aggression, moderation in the use of power; and a constant search for peace." The president signed the bill May 7 (PL 89-18).

Vietnam Preoccupation

Beginning in 1966, the Vietnam conflict emerged as the dominant foreign policy issue in Congress. It overshadowed civil rights, the war on poverty and the other programs of Lyndon Johnson's Great Society. Its cost alone soared to more than $2 billion a month. By early 1968, more than

500,000 U.S. troops were committed to South Vietnam, and casualty figures had risen above the 100,000 mark.

As the war and the American commitment intensified, so did congressional debate. Possibly the key issue in the debate was the question of war aims. Both acrimonious and confused, the arguments centered on congressional and administrative perceptions of China and the Soviet Union. Thus, those who argued in favor of an American commitment to Vietnam usually cited the expansionist aims of a Communist China trying to establish a "sphere of influence" in Southeast Asia — much like that which the Soviet Union had established in Eastern Europe after World War II. Those who opposed U.S. activities in Vietnam took the opposite tack, citing the lack of evidence of direct Chinese involvement and stressing that the war in Vietnam was nothing more than a civil war between North and South. In both cases, however, one's view of the war in Vietnam, and all of Indochina for that matter, usually hinged on one's perception of China's role in that conflict. Thus, as opinions about Chinese belligerence began to soften during the late 1960s, there was increased pressure to withdraw from Vietnam. This perception changed slowly, however, and congressional critics of administration policy would remain in the minority until the 1970s.

Appropriations to carry out the administration's war policy were approved by large margins, since most dissenters found it awkward to vote against supplies or in favor of restrictions on the grounds that they did not wish to expose men already committed to battle to needless risks.

Congressional Debate

As congressional debate over Vietnam increased, the Senate Foreign Relations Committee on Jan. 7, 1966, released a report on Vietnam by Senate Majority Leader Mansfield. The new report, entitled "The Vietnam Conflict: The Substance and the Shadow," concluded that "the situation, as it now appears, offers only the very slim prospect of a just settlement by negotiations or the alternative prospect of a continuance of the conflict in the direction of a general war on the Asian mainland." Militarily, the report said that the large-scale introduction of U.S. forces "has blunted but not turned back the drive of the Viet Cong."

The Mansfield report and President Johnson's decision to end a 38-day pause in the bombing of North Vietnam touched off an even more heated congressional debate, especially in the Senate.

On Feb. 4, 1966, the Senate Foreign Relations Committee began hearings on an administration bill (S 2793) authorizing $415 million in supplemental fiscal 1966 foreign economic aid, of which $275 million was earmarked for emergency aid to South Vietnam. The hearings were televised nationally and were used by the committee as a springboard to conduct a public inquiry into the administration's "general policy" in Vietnam. Witnesses included David E. Bell, administrator of the Agency for International Development; retired Gen. James M. Gavin; George F. Kennan, former ambassador to the Soviet Union; retired Gen. Maxwell D. Taylor, special consultant to President Johnson; Secretary of State Dean Rusk; and Vice President Hubert H. Humphrey, who met informally with the committee after his return from South Vietnam.

On March 1, 1966, Congress moved nearer to action on supplemental appropriations for U.S. activities in Southeast Asia as it passed several authorizing bills. Passage of the measures came in contrasting atmospheres in the two chambers as senators continued lengthy, and at times acrimonious, debate of President Johnson's Vietnam policies while the House acted quickly and with only limited outright criticism of the increased U.S. commitment to the war. However, 78 House Democrats signed a statement which said that their vote for a defense supplemental appropriations authorization did not mean they supported an enlargement of the military effort.

China Hearings

On March 8, 1966, the Senate Foreign Relations Committee began hearings on U.S. policy toward Communist China, an outgrowth of the Vietnam hearings. By this time, some congressmen were concerned about China's reaction to the American build-up in Vietnam. Describing the hearings as "educational," Chairman Fulbright said: "At this stage, perhaps the most effective contribution the Committee can make is to provide a forum for recognized experts and scholars in the field of China."

The main theme to emerge from the next three weeks of testimony was that U.S. policy had not only tried to contain China, but also had attempted to isolate it, which had been both unwise and unsuccessful. Dr. John K. Fairbank of Harvard's East Asian Research Center typified the theme when he concluded: "Containment alone is a blind alley unless we add policies of constructive competition and international contact. . . . Peking's rulers shout aggressively out of manifold frustrations. . . . Isolation intensifies their ailment and makes it self-perpetuating, and we need to encourage international contact with China on many fronts."

The majority of witnesses proposed three basic changes in U.S. policy: official diplomatic recognition of Communist China, an expansion of trade relations, and admission of Communist China into the United Nations. These changes were opposed by a minority of witnesses, one of whom was former Rep. Walter H. Judd, R-Minn. Judd said that "our choice — with Red China just as it was with Japan and Hitler — is not between checking and not checking, it is whether to check early, while we can, and with allies — or try to check the aggression later, when it is stronger, closer and we have fewer and weaker friends and allies."

On May 19, 1966, the House Foreign Affairs Subcommittee on the Far East and Pacific released a report on its open hearings, held between Jan. 25 and March 10, on U.S. policy toward Asia. The report recommended that the United States, despite rebuffs, should continue to seek peaceful contacts with China while at the same time preventing her from any aggressive expansion. To do this, it continued, would require both increased assistance and cooperation from Western European allies and increased U.S. efforts to build up the strength of "the independent countries of the continent — from India and Pakistan to Japan and Korea."

Dissent on Vietnam

A major font of criticism of administration aims in the war was the Senate Foreign Relations Committee under Chairman Fulbright. By 1968, Secretary of State Dean Rusk repeatedly had refused to testify in public hearings conducted by the committee.

In 1967 the committee held three sets of hearings on subjects relating to the war:

● In January and February on the "responsibilities of the United States as a great power."

● In August on a resolution (S Res 151) asserting that

U.S. commitments to a foreign power required legislative approval. The committee Nov. 20 reported an amended resolution (S Res 187), but no floor action was taken.

● In October and November on two resolutions (S Con Res 44, S Res 180) urging that a solution to the war be sought through the United Nations. The committee Nov. 21 reported S Res 180, and the Senate Nov. 30 unanimously adopted the measure. No action was taken by the House.

House Action

Although there was less anti-war activity in the House than the Senate, 52 House members (48 Republicans and four Democrats) on Sept. 25, 1967, introduced resolutions (H Con Res 508, 509, 510) calling for a congressional review of U.S. war policy. Sponsors claimed that "a great uneasiness" among members and the public had emerged since the passage of the Gulf of Tonkin resolution of 1964. They also pointed out that 123 House members had not been members of Congress when the Tonkin Gulf resolution passed. The resolutions were referred to the Rules Committee, which took no action.

Three weeks later, a bipartisan group of 30 House members sent a letter to President Johnson asking him to halt the bombing of North Vietnam. Sixty-seven House Democrats had written Johnson June 23 asking him to renew efforts to have the U.N. Security Council consider the Vietnam conflict.

In 1968 there was not a single significant roll call taken on the Vietnam issue, although there were more hearings in the Senate. Instead, debate on the war shifted from Congress to the presidential campaign. The muting of congressional opposition was attributable in large measure to President Johnson's March 31 announcement that he had ordered an immediate bombing halt over most of North Vietnam and that he was withdrawing from the race for the presidency.

Nixon-Ford Administrations

Indochina

U.S. involvement in Indochina and the nation's global defense commitment provided the focus of congressional concern in foreign affairs during the 91st Congress (1969-70). U.S. activities in Asia, more than any other region, planted the seeds of congressional anxiety about the nature and repercussions of American commitments abroad.

In February 1970 President Nixon formally outlined what had become known as the "Nixon Doctrine," which had as its goal avoiding direct U.S. military involvement in remote corners of the globe. Nixon said the central thesis of his policy was "that the United States will participate in the defense and development of allies and friends, but that America cannot — and will not — conceive all the plans, design all the programs, execute all the decisions and undertake all the defense of the free nations of the world." *(See p. 189)*

But in 1969 and 1970, the apparent extension of the Vietnam conflict into neighboring Laos and Cambodia — at the same time the administration was attempting to "Vietnamize" the war in South Vietnam — gave rise to the fear that the United States was still bogged down in what Sen. Fulbright termed the "second Indochina war."

For the first nine months of 1969, Congress followed a "wait and see" course on the war. By the fall, with apparently no new policy shifts or initiatives forthcoming from the Nixon administration, resolutions were introduced in

Congress calling for a pullout from Vietnam by December 1970. In December, in an unusual secret floor session, the Senate voted 73-17 to prohibit a commitment of U.S. ground troops to Laos and Thailand. The prohibition, added to the defense appropriations bill, was retained in the House-Senate conference report. Although the amendment broke new ground on congressional limitations by restricting U.S. military activities in Southeast Asian countries, the bill was signed by President Nixon.

A number of senators in 1970 sponsored a succession of anti-war proposals. Chief among them were Majority Leader Mansfield and John Sherman Cooper, R-Ky., Frank Church, D-Idaho, George McGovern, D-S.D., Mark O. Hatfield, R-Ore., and Edward W. Brooke, R-Mass.

Cooper-Church

President Nixon's decision to send U.S. forces into Cambodia to clean out communist sanctuaries provoked a six-week Senate debate in May and June on a Cooper-Church amendment to bar use of U.S. funds for military operations in Cambodia. A weakened version of the amendment — barring use of ground forces but not aircraft — was passed in December, months after Nixon had removed the U.S. troops from Cambodia.

Other action on anti-war proposals in 1970 included repeal of the 1964 Tonkin Gulf resolution and defeat of two "end-the-war" amendments sponsored by Hatfield and McGovern.

In 1971 the Senate adopted amendments to three bills introduced by Mansfield calling for withdrawal of troops from Indochina by a certain deadline. Two of these survived House-Senate conferences with the withdrawal deadline deleted — the first time the House had gone on record urging an end to the war. The president, however, said the provision was not binding and that he would not follow it. A new Cooper-Church amendment, limiting use of U.S. military funds in Indochina to troop withdrawal, was defeated on the Senate floor in a series of close votes.

Congress in 1972 enacted no legislation restricting U.S. military involvement in Southeast Asia, although the Senate took its toughest stand on terminating U.S. involvement. But continued House support for the president's policies forestalled congressional action to set a date for withdrawal.

The Senate Aug. 2 posed its most serious challenge to the president's Vietnam policy by adopting on a 49-47 roll-call vote an amendment cutting off funds for U.S. participation in the war. The amendment barred use of funds for U.S. participation in the war four months after enactment. All U.S. ground, naval and air forces would have to be out of Indochina by that date if North Vietnam and its allies had released all American prisoners of war. House conferees refused to accept the amendment.

Peace Agreement

The longest war in United States history drew to a close on Jan. 23, 1973, when President Nixon announced an agreement "to end the war and bring peace with honor in Vietnam and Southeast Asia."

Formal signing of the agreement by representatives of the United States, South Vietnam, North Vietnam and the Viet Cong's provisional revolutionary government took place on Jan. 27. At 7 p.m. (EST) that day, an internationally supervised cease-fire went into effect.

Under the terms of the agreement, all U.S. prisoners of war in Indochina would be returned home within 60 days from the start of the cease-fire. During that same period, the 25,000 American troops remaining in South Vietnam would be withdrawn.

The agreement was initialed in Paris by Henry A. Kissinger, then Nixon's national security adviser, and chief negotiator Le Duc Tho of North Vietnam, ending three months of intensive negotiating. Anticipation that a settlement was finally nearing had been kindled Oct. 26, 1972, with Kissinger's statement that "peace is at hand." But hopes were dashed during the week of Dec. 16-22, 1972, when the United States announced a suspension of the Paris peace talks with Hanoi and a resumption of full-scale bombing of all of North Vietnam.

Implementation of the cease-fire agreement was not without setbacks and threats of disintegration. There were several impasses over the timetable for releasing prisoners of war and other issues; but in each case the stalemate was broken, and on March 29 U.S. military involvement in Vietnam came to an end. On that day, the remaining 67 American prisoners held by North Vietnam were freed in Hanoi, and the United States withdrew its remaining 2,500 troops from South Vietnam.

'Secret' Commitments

Two years later, on April 8, 1975, Sen. Henry M. Jackson, D-Wash., charged that the Nixon administration had worked out "secret agreements" with South Vietnam involving future military assistance for that nation.

Jackson said the Ford administration had intimated that Congress had reneged on "commitments" and "obligations" to the Saigon government. "The fact is," he continued, "that Congress is being accused of violating commitments and obligations it never heard of. . . . I call upon the president now to make public and to provide to Congress all documents embodying or reflecting these secret agreements. . . . We in the Congress cannot play our constitutional role in constructing a coherent foreign policy so long as information to which we are entitled is kept from us."

The White House responded in a statement issued April 9 that former President Nixon had assured South Vietnamese President Thieu in private correspondence that the United States would "react vigorously to major violations" of the Paris peace accords. The "confidential exchanges" between Thieu and Nixon did not differ in substance from what was stated publicly when the accords were signed in January 1973, the statement said, when the U.S. intentions to provide adequate economic and military assistance and to enforce the Paris agreements "were stated clearly and publicly by President Nixon."

Jackson later said that the White House statement was unsatisfactory because it was "only a partial disclosure" and Congress should have access to "all relevant papers."

Aid Controversy

Despite completion of the general withdrawal of U.S. combat troops from South Vietnam in 1973 after the signing of the Paris peace agreement, controversy surfaced again when an attempt was made in 1974 to increase U.S. military aid to South Vietnam and Laos. The effort was thwarted in Congress when members opposed to the war and in favor of shifting U.S. priorities joined with those angered by the Pentagon's failure to live within congressionally set Vietnam aid limits to defeat an amendment that would have raised the authorization ceiling for military aid for the two nations to $1.4 billion from the $1.126 billion set in 1973. In a related action, the House in 1974 voted to re-

Out of the Vietnam Quagmire

The war in Indochina ended in the spring of 1975 after more than three decades of bloody conflict, with North Vietnam the winner. The military victory finally extricated the United States from its long agony in Southeast Asia; 1975 was, as one headline writer put it, the year the light went out in the tunnel.

The end came in a final massive military drive by Hanoi forces and their allies which swept away the pro-Western governments in South Vietnam and Cambodia by the end of April and plunged the people of Indochina into further death, suffering and homelessness.

The communist victory ended for the United States one of the most traumatic and costly events in its history, comparable to the Revolution, the Civil War, the Great Depression and World War II.

The China Factor

Fear of Chinese expansion had been a principal reason behind the U.S. commitment in Indochina. Asian communism was believed to be a monolithic movement controlled by Peking through puppet governments in Southeast Asia — the "Domino Theory" of communist expansion. As John K. Fairbank noted, "We are in Vietnam because of the Chinese Communist revolution."

In 1965 both President Johnson and President-to-be Nixon expressed this belief. "The rulers in Hanoi are urged on by Peking," said Johnson. "The contest in Vietnam is part of a wider pattern of aggressive purpose." Said Nixon: "A United States defeat in Vietnam means a Chinese Communist victory."

But that rationale became increasingly insupportable as China refused directly to intervene in Vietnam and, indeed, became increasingly estranged from Hanoi, which turned to the Soviet Union as its patron. But by that time the war had taken on a life of its own for the United States, which began to rely on "peace with honor" and "upholding our commitments" to justify its continued presence in Vietnam. Four years after the final American withdrawal, China was itself engaged in open combat with Vietnam and sharing with the Western world the burdens of absorbing the flow of Vietnamese and Cambodian refugees cast adrift by the new government of Vietnam.

Congressional Role

The Vietnam misadventure had begun in 1950 when U.S. arms were shipped to the French fighting in Vietnam, and grew into an issue that divided the nation and became the symbol of Congress' frustration. Not until 1973, five months after a peace agreement was signed, was Congress successful in voting an end to funding of the war in Indochina.

In the end it was Congress — through its control of the purse strings — that forced the end of the U.S. presence in Indochina. It resisted President Ford's request in January 1975 for $522 million in emergency military aid for South Vietnam and Cambodia, despite administration protestations that the money was necessary for the two countries to defend themselves. Ford had warned that if approval of the aid were denied, Congress would be to blame if the two governments fell. A communist of-

fensive that was launched in early March began to overrun the armed forces of the two countries, and Ford a month later revised his request, asking for $722 million in military aid and $250 million in economic and humanitarian assistance for South Vietnam while tacitly conceding the downfall of Cambodia.

Ford and his advisers told Congress that the South Vietnamese still had the will and ability to defend themselves if given American funds. Secretary of State Kissinger viewed continued support as a moral commitment to Saigon in light of earlier promises, some of which had become known belatedly.

But Congress moved slowly on the requests, fearing a never-ending U.S. involvement. But debate was overtaken by military events, and the surrender of the Phnom Penh and Saigon governments came before any more funds were approved.

Even after the surrender, the scars of the earlier congressional experiences were deep, and Congress refused to give even belated approval to Ford's use of troops for the evacuation of the Americans and South Vietnamese or to authorize money to pay for it. Some members expressed concern that the legislation might provide a blanket authority that could be used in the future despite administration assurances otherwise. Ultimately, Congress agreed only to provide funds for the resettlement and assistance of more than 100,000 refugees who chose to live in the United States.

Toll on the Nation

The difficult issue of accounting for those American servicemen listed as missing in action, as well as the Vietnamese refugee problem, remained to be resolved. But Indochina soon dropped from the daily headlines and Americans began putting Vietnam out of their consciousness. Officially the "Vietnam Era" had ended by proclamation of the president on May 7, 1975.

But the healing process would take time. The costs of U.S. involvement in Indochina — those that could be measured — had been immense. The war caused more than 46,000 American combat deaths. More than 300,000 Americans were wounded. Vietnamese dead and wounded, from both sides, ran into the millions.

In dollars, the United States poured upwards of $140 billion into the war effort from 1965 on. But no exact figures existed for the total economic cost of Vietnam-related expenses since American aid first started flowing to help the French colonialists after World War II. Some estimates placed the figure at more than $350 billion; others at twice that amount.

But even more significant were the immeasurable costs to the United States' social fabric and national spirit. By the end of the war in 1975, America was a very different place than it was when the enormous infusion of U.S. troops began in the mid-1960s. Perhaps most damaging, and most difficult to measure for many years, was an apparent — or at least, a widely believed — disillusionment in government and American leadership by thousands of young Americans who in the next two to three decades would have to take control of the government themselves.

duce to $700 million the $1 billion that had been requested for military aid to South Vietnam as part of the fiscal 1975 Defense Department appropriations bill.

It was this remaining $300 million that President Ford in 1975 asked Congress to provide for South Vietnam. Congress rejected the request, thereby leaving itself open to blame for the defeat that was then taking place in Indochina. But the charge, which was not made, would have been hard to support because Congress had by then appropriated at least $140 billion for the war effort. *(Box, p. 217)*

China Issue Renewed

The Nixon administration's Vietnamization and troop withdrawal policy in Indochina, combined with its goal objective of a reduced U.S. military presence in Asia, prompted many members of Congress to call for a re-evaluation of U.S. policy toward China. There was stepped up activity in Congress concerning China in 1969 through 1971 in the form of policy declarations by leading members and House and Senate hearings on China policy.

In March 1969, Sen. Edward M. Kennedy, D-Mass., urged the United States to discard the "passions of the past," terminate restrictions on trade and travel to the China mainland, establish consular relations as a step toward full diplomatic recognition and reverse opposition to Peking's membership in the U.N. Kennedy said these steps should be taken without jeopardizing U.S. ties with Taiwan.

Kennedy was joined by Sens. Mark O. Hatfield, R-Ore., Jacob K. Javits, R-N.Y., Stuart Symington, D-Mo., and Rep. Paul Findley, R-Ill. On March 10 Senate Majority Leader Mansfield called for an end to special travel restrictions and said trade in non-strategic goods should be put on the same basis as U.S. trade with other communist nations.

On Sept. 25, by a 77-3 roll-call vote, the Senate passed a resolution (S Res 205) declaring the sense of the Senate that U.S. recognition of a foreign government did not "of itself imply that the United States approves of the form, ideology or policy of that foreign government." Secretary Dulles had argued against recognizing Peking because doing so would imply U.S. approval of the regime.

Although Alan Cranston, D-Calif., the author of the resolution, argued that it should not be construed primarily as laying the groundwork for recognition of Peking, Thomas J. Dodd, D-Conn., who voted against passage, said, "if the resolution is not intended to clear the way for the recognition of Communist China . . . then it is difficult to understand the motivation behind it. . . ."

A similar interpretation of the resolution was contained in a Nov. 21, 1969, letter to the president signed by a bipartisan group of 39 representatives and eight senators expressing "full support and agreement with your administration's policy of seeking ways to normalize relations with Peking." This endorsement, they wrote, was evidenced by passage of S Res 205.

But while members seeking changes in U.S. East Asia policy made most of these speeches, there was powerful opposition. In 1969 and 1970, Congress reaffirmed in routine resolutions its opposition to the seating of Communist China in the United Nations.

And during debate on a foreign aid bill (HR 15149) Dec. 9, 1969, the House adopted, 83-54, an amendment by H. R. Gross, R-Iowa, prohibiting U.S. assistance to countries that aided or traded with Peking. But the amendment subsequently was dropped from the final bill.

Finally, a group of powerful representatives attempted unsuccessfully in 1969-70 to give an additional $54.5 million in military assistance to Taiwan. Principal sponsors of the addition were Otto E. Passman, D-La., Robert L. F. Sikes, D-Fla., House Minority Leader Gerald R. Ford, R-Mich., and Armed Services Chairman L. Mendel Rivers, D-S.C. Argued Sikes: "Taiwan is a . . . needed brake on Red Chinese aggression."

And in reaction against early moves by the Nixon administration to relax tensions with the Peking regime, some Republicans criticized the president. In a Senate speech late in 1970, Sen. Barry Goldwater, R-Ariz., stated: "Nothing can be gained but a great deal can be lost by admission of Red China to the United Nations or its diplomatic recognition by the United States."

Hearings

In November 1969 and May 1970, the Senate Foreign Relations Subcommittee on U.S. Commitments Abroad held hearings in executive session on U.S. commitments to Nationalist China. The hearings, containing testimony by administration witnesses, published in July 1970, disclosed that U.S. policy toward Taiwan was in a period of transition as U.S. military assistance to Taiwan was being phased out (economic assistance had been ended in 1965).

In the fall of 1970 the House Foreign Affairs Subcommittee on Asian and Pacific Affairs held its first hearings on China policy since 1966. Most of the experts on China and the Soviet Union who testified before the subcommittee urged a normalization of relations with mainland China. Many of the same witnesses testified in June 1971 before the Senate Foreign Relations Committee again recommending improved relations with Peking.

1971-72 Breakthrough

By midsummer of 1971 the Nixon administration already had revealed two of its three major alterations in U.S. policy toward China: the end of the trade embargo (June 10) and the president's planned trip to Peking (July 15).

The third stage came Aug. 2, when Secretary of State William P. Rogers announced that the United States would support the seating of Communist China in the United Nations. The secretary said the United States would oppose any efforts to "expel the Republic of China or otherwise deprive it of representation" in the United Nations. He avoided the question of which China would serve on the Security Council, saying only that the United States would abide by the views of the majority of U.N. members on the question.

Involvement. White House congressional liaison chief Clark MacGregor said the State Department had briefed key members of Congress "well in advance" of Rogers' announcement. The secretary and other department officials had made 20 to 30 phone calls to House and Senate leaders, members of the Senate Foreign Relations and House Foreign Affairs committees and other members who had expressed particular interest in China policy, MacGregor said.

U.N. Commission. Eight members of Congress served on President Nixon's special commission on the United Nations which recommended April 26 that the People's Republic be admitted to the U.N.

The commission reported that it had found growing public support in the United States for the involvement of the Chinese Communists in the work of the United Nations as well as "a deep American commitment to the continued representation of the Republic of China on Taiwan."

The eight members of Congress serving on the commission were: Senate Foreign Relations Committee Chairman J. W. Fulbright, D-Ark., House Foreign Affairs Committee Chairman Thomas E. Morgan, D-Pa., Sen. George D. Aiken, R-Vt., Sen. John Sherman Cooper, R-Ky., Sen. John Sparkman, D-Ala., Sen. Robert Taft Jr., R-Ohio, Rep. Cornelius E. Gallagher, D-N.J. and Rep. Sherman P. Lloyd, R-Utah.

The 50-member commission, headed by Ambassador Henry Cabot Lodge and including prominent Americans from many professional fields, held public hearings in six cities before submitting its 100-page report.

Conservative Positions. On Sept. 28, 21 senators and 33 House members of both parties joined in issuing a statement declaring that if the Republic of China were expelled from the United Nations, "we would feel compelled to recommend a complete reassessment of U.S. financial and moral support of the U.N."

The statement was drafted by Sens. James L. Buckley, Cons-R-N.Y., and Bill Brock, R-Tenn. At a news conference the same day, Buckley said each member who signed the statement would have a different interpretation of the word "reassessment."

When the assembled members were asked why Congress had failed to go on record — for the first time in 20 years — as opposing Peking's admission into the United Nations, Sen. Strom Thurmond, R-S.C., stated that although he continued to support such a policy, "I'm not sure the majority of Congress would oppose the seating of Communist China in the United Nations this year." Thurmond added that he supported President Nixon's planned journey to Peking.

Walkout. But the news conference quickly broke up when two of Congress' staunchest conservatives, Reps. John G. Schmitz, R-Calif., and John R. Rarick, D-La., disassociated themselves from the statement and walked out.

Schmitz, a member of the John Birch Society, referred to the Peking regime as a "bandit government" run by a "bunch of butchers." He explained that he and Rarick could not accept any statement that would acquiesce in the admission of Communist China into the U.N.

Congressional Warning. On Oct. 11, Sen. Buckley visited the United Nations personally, met with U.S. Ambassador to the U.N. George Bush and then warned that, as the representative of 21 senators, he would "immediately introduce legislation calling for the dramatic reduction" of U.S. contributions to the U.N. if Taiwan were expelled. Buckley said his views reflected "the views of Congress."

On Oct. 13, President Nixon received a petition signed by 336 of the 430 members of the House (there were five vacancies) opposing "strongly and unalterably" the expulsion of Taiwan from the U.N. According to the White House, the president thanked the members who presented him with the petition — most of them among the more conservative members of the House — for their "support of the administration on this issue."

Reaction to U.N. Vote

The expulsion of Nationalist China from the United Nations Oct. 25, 1971, produced immediate response — mostly angry and accompanied by threats of retaliation — from members of Congress. Action, statements and floor speeches Oct. 26 included:

● A move by senators from both parties for a reduction in U.S. financial support of the United Nations, and specifically in the $141 million authorization for U.N. funds in the $3.2 billion foreign aid authorization bill on which debate began Oct. 26.

● A demand by Sen. Barry Goldwater, R-Ariz., that the United States withdraw from U.N. membership.

● Announcement by Sen. Buckley the night of the vote that he was drafting legislation calling for a major reduction in U.S. financial contributions to U.N. activities.

● A move to delete a provision in the foreign aid authorization bill repealing the Formosa Resolution of 1955. The resolution authorized the president to use armed force to protect Nationalist China against armed attack.

● A promise by Rep. John J. Rooney, D-N.Y., chairman of the State-Justice-Commerce Appropriations Subcommittee, to reduce U.N. funds in the bill when it came up again in 1972. They totaled $107.9 million in the fiscal 1972 bill, which was signed into law Aug. 10.

● A move to base U.N. contributions from each country on population. Under the proposal, made by Rep. Philip M. Crane, R-Ill., U.S. contributions to the U.N. would equal the same percentage as U.S. total population is to total population of all U.N. member nations, or 7.6 percent. If applied to total contributions, this would have cut the U.S. outlay from $318 million to about $80 million for 1972.

House Speaker Carl Albert, D-Okla., in answer to the proposals for retaliation against the U.N. and those countries which supported the ouster of Nationalist China, said, "I . . . feel it would be heaping one irresponsibility on another to diminish our support of the United Nations because of our displeasure with this vote." He was joined by Foreign Aid Appopriations Subcommittee Chairman Otto E. Passman, D-La.

Formosa Resolution Repeal. The Senate Foreign Relations Committee held hearings in June 1971 on five resolutions calling for changes in U.S. China policy.

The committee Sept. 21 reported S J Res 48 (S Rept 92-363), sponsored by Sens. Frank Church, D-Idaho, and Charles McC. Mathias, R-Md. The resolution, which would have the force of law, would withdraw authority granted to the president in 1955 to use armed force to protect Taiwan and the Pescadores from attack.

The committee attached S J Res 48 to the fiscal 1972 foreign aid authorization (HR 9910) when it reported the aid bill Oct. 20 (S Rept 92-404). Debate on the foreign aid bill began Oct. 26, the day after the U.N. General Assembly had voted to expel Nationalist China and seat the Peking government. The debate took place in an emotional atmosphere charged by the Taiwan expulsion, which contributed to general disillusionment with the foreign aid program. The Senate Oct. 29 by a 27-41 roll-call vote killed the foreign aid bill. (After repeated attempts, Congress Oct. 11, 1974, finally repealed the Formosa Resolution. But it left the 1954 mutual defense pact in force.)

Nixon China Trip

After his trip to Peking Feb. 21-28, 1972, President Nixon was met by a rising chorus of praise for establishing contacts with the Chinese government.

The praise was not unanimous, however. Nixon's argument that Taiwan was a part of China and that its future was a matter to be determined by the Chinese, evoked bitter criticism from some sources.

The statement was interpreted by some conservatives as meaning the abandonment of the Nationalist Chinese

Members of Congress Visit China

Members of Congress — never loath to check out U.S. foreign relations at first hand — have been traveling to China as guests of the People's Republic in ever-increasing numbers. Three members visited Peking in 1972; by 1978, the number had grown to 65. Visitors included:

1972

Senate Majority Leader Mike Mansfield, D-Mont., Senate Minority Leader Hugh Scott, R-Pa.; House Minority Leader Gerald R. Ford, R-Mich.

1973

Sens. Warren G. Magnuson, D-Wash., Robert P. Griffin, R-Mich., John Sparkman, D-Ala. and Gale W. McGee, D-Wyo.; Reps. John J. McFall, D-Calif., Jerry L. Pettis, R-Calif., Thomas E. Morgan, D-Pa. and W. S. Mailliard, R-Calif.

1974

Sens. Hiram L. Fong, R-Hawaii, and Henry Jackson, D-Wash.; Reps. William S. Broomfield, R-Mich., Peter H. B. Frelinghuysen, R-N.J., Barbara Jordan, D-Texas and Clement J. Zablocki, D-Wis.

1975

Sens. Sam Nunn, D-Ga., Charles Percy, R-Ill., Adlai E. Stevenson, D-Ill., James B. Pearson, R-Kan., Jacob K. Javits, R-N.Y. and Robert C. Byrd, D-W.Va.; Speaker of the House Carl Albert, D-Okla., House Minority Leader John J. Rhodes, R-Ariz.; Reps. Paul N. McCloskey Jr., R-Calif., Patricia Schroeder, D-Colo., Patsy Mink, D-Hawaii, John B. Anderson, R-Ill., Cardiss Collins, D-Ill., Edward J. Derwinski, R-Ill., Lindy Boggs, D-La., Gladys Noon Spellman, D-Md., Margaret W. Heckler, R-Mass., Millicent Fenwick, R-N.J., Helen Meyner, D-N.J., Bella Abzug, D-N.Y., Elizabeth Holtzman, D-N.Y. and John M. Slack, D-W.Va.

1976

Sens. Ted Stevens, R-Alaska, J. Bennett Johnston, D-La., Mike Mansfield, D-Mont., Carl T. Curtis, R-Neb., John Glenn, D-Ohio and Milton R. Young, R-N.D.; Reps. William R. Dickinson, R-Ala., Yvonne Brathwaite Burke, D-Calif., Bob Wilson, R-Calif., William J. Randall, D-Mo., Samuel S. Stratton, D-N.Y., Lester Wolff, D-N.Y. and G. William Whitehurst, R-Va.

1977

Sens. William V. Roth Jr., R-Del., John C. Culver, D-Iowa, Edward M. Kennedy, D-Mass., John A. Durkin, D-N.H. and Richard S. Schweiker, R-Pa.; Reps. Jack Edwards, R-Ala., George E. Danielson, D-Calif., Barbara A. Mikulski, D-Md., Silvio Conte, R-Mass. and Mark Andrews, R-N.D.

1978

Sens. Dale Bumpers, D-Ark., Alan Cranston, D-Calif., Gary Hart, D-Colo., Lawton Chiles, D-Fla., Richard Stone, D-Fla., Richard G. Lugar, R-Ind., Edmund S. Muskie, D-Maine, Charles McC. Mathias Jr., R-Md., Edward M. Kennedy, D-Mass., Donald W. Riegle Jr., D-Mich., Howard W. Cannon, D-Nev., Harrison A. Williams Jr., D-N.J., Henry Bellmon, R-Okla., Bob Packwood, R-Ore., James Abourezk, D-S.D., Lloyd Bentsen, D-Texas, Patrick J. Leahy, D-Vt. and Henry M. Jackson, D-Wash.

Reps. Tom Bevill, D-Ala., Jack Edwards, R-Ala., Bill Alexander, D-Ark., George Brown, D-Calif., J. Herbert Burke, R-Fla., Richard Kelly, R-Fla., William Lehman, D-Fla., Doug Barnard, D-Ga., Wyche Fowler, D-Ga., Daniel K. Akaka, D-Hawaii, Paul Findley, R-Ill., Edward Madigan, R-Ill., Robert H. Michel, R-Ill., George M. O'Brien, R-Ill., David Evans, D-Ind., John T. Myers, R-Ind., Berkeley Bedell, D-Iowa, Neal Smith, D-Iowa, Keith Sebelius, R-Kan., Larry Winn Jr., R-Kan., Tim Lee Carter, R-Ky., Gillis W. Long, D-La., Bill Frenzel, R-Minn., Tom Hagedorn, R-Minn., David R. Bowen, D-Miss., Harold Volkmer, D-Mo., Robert K. Garcia, D-N.Y., John J. LaFalce, D-N.Y., Charles B. Rangel, D-N.Y., Fred Richmond, D-N.Y., James H. Scheuer, D-N.Y., Lester L. Wolff, D-N.Y., L. H. Fountain, D-N.C., Stephen L. Neal, D-N.C., Mark Andrews, R-N.D., Thomas L. Ashley, D-Ohio, Tennyson Guyer, R-Ohio, Mary Rose Oaker, D-Ohio, Charles W. Whalen Jr., R-Ohio, James Weaver, D-Ore., Butler Derrick, D-S.C., James Mann, D-S.C., E. (Kika) de la Garza, D-Texas, Jack Hightower, D-Texas, J. Kenneth Robinson, R-Va., John M. Slack, D-W.Va. and Henry S. Reuss, D-Wis.

1979 (Partial)

Sens. Sam Nunn, D-Ga., Gary Hart, D-Colo., William S. Cohen, R-Maine, John Glenn, D-Ohio and Henry M. Jackson, D-Wash.; Reps. Dante B. Fascell, D-Fla., James C. Corman, D-Calif., Benjamin S. Rosenthal, D-N.Y., James H. Quillen, R-Tenn., John W. Wydler, R-N.Y., James J. Howard, D-N.J., David R. Obey, D-Wis., Robert A. Roe, D-N.J., Robert F. Drinan, D-Mass., Bill Archer, R-Texas, Cardiss Collins, D-Ill., Robert E. Bauman, R-Md., John L. Burton, D-Calif., Marty Russo, D-Ill., Allen E. Ertel, D-Pa. and Dan Mica, D-Fla.

government. Criticism came from such disparate candidates for president as Rep. John M. Ashbrook, R-Ohio, Nixon's conservative opponent for the Republican nomination, and Sen. Hubert H. Humphrey, D-Minn., the Senate's most articulate liberal in the years when U.S. policy on China was dominated in Congress by pro-Chiang forces, which included Nixon as a representative, as a senator and as a vice president.

"For over two decades," Ashbrook said, "it is we who have fostered and supported, both by words and deeds, the concept of an independent Republic of China on Taiwan. Now, in a single week, we have abandoned that position —

and in so doing we have set up the framework to abandon 15 million people to the tender mercies of a regime that during its tenure in office — its 23 years of enlightenment and progress — has managed to slay, at conservative estimate, 34 million of its own citizens."

Humphrey's concern was more for the native Taiwanese, as distinct from the Nationalist Chinese who came from the mainland.

"It is now clear," he said, "that the rug has been pulled out from under the Taiwanese, though the people of the island of Formosa [Taiwan] once aspired to determine their own destiny."

Humphrey also took issue with Nixon's statement (in his arrival speech) that no other nation's fate was being negotiated behind its back in the talks with Premier Chou En-lai and that no American commitment to another country was given up.

"It is apparent from the communiqué as I read it," Humphrey said, "that concessions were made by the president and by Dr. [Henry A.] Kissinger [Nixon's national security adviser], but not any, insofar as I have been able to interpret, were made by the Chinese."

Ashbrook's view was echoed by four House conservatives, Reps. Crane, Rarick, Schmitz and Robert L. F. Sikes, D-Fla.

Further criticism came from two other candidates for the presidency, Rep. Paul N. McCloskey Jr., R-Calif., and Sen. Henry M. Jackson, D-Wash. McCloskey welcomed the limited renewal of relations with China but said that, despite Nixon's trip, "we did not progress one inch toward settling the major problem of today, ending the Vietnam war." Jackson expressed disappointment that Nixon had not gained concessions on Vietnam from the Chinese government.

Sen. Buckley said that relaxation of the U.S. commitment to defend Taiwan would "vastly diminish" his regard for Nixon. But he said he still would support Nixon for reelection.

Sen. George McGovern, D-S.D., the eventual Democratic nominee for president, praised the Nixon trip, as did Sen. Edward M. Kennedy, D-Mass. Chairman J. W. Fulbright, D-Ark., of the Senate Foreign Relations Committee, a persistent critic of Nixon's Vietnam policy, indicated he was pleased with the results of the trip. So did Sen. Goldwater, the unsuccessful Republican presidential candidate in 1964. Goldwater said he was satisfied that "we have not given away one single thing to the Red Chinese" and that "we will uphold our treaty commitments to the Taiwan government."

During Nixon's visit, U.S. officials arranged for high-level visits to China by congressional leaders. Senate Majority Leader Mike Mansfield, D-Mont., and Minority Leader Hugh Scott, R-Pa., visited six Chinese cities from April 19 to May 3, and House Majority Leader Hale Boggs, D-La., and Minority Leader Gerald R. Ford, R-Mich., followed June 23-July 8.

Interim

Between President Nixon's initiatives in 1971-72 and President Carter's in 1978-79, Congress tended to support closer U.S. ties with China, the gradual withdrawal of American troops from Taiwan, and less military aid to the ROC. At the same time, Congress maintained its preoccupation with U.S.-Taiwan relations. In the 1978 foreign military assistance bill, for example, Congress approved a provision stating that "there should be prior consultation

between Congress and the executive branch on any proposed policy changes affecting . . . the Mutual Defense Treaty of 1954" with Taiwan. Such consultation became an issue after Carter's surprise announcement of recognition of China in 1978. (*See below*)

There were, however, several congressional attempts to move away from the narrow relationship the United States had with Taiwan. In 1974 Congress repealed the 1955 Formosa Resolution committing the United States to defend Taiwan against any perceived threat, while maintaining the Mutual Defense Treaty in force.

In 1978 Congress passed a bill allowing sales of agricultural items by the Commodity Credit Corporation to the People's Republic. The bill authorized the corporation to provide short-term credit for commercial sales of foodstuffs to China. The provision was designed to sidestep the Jackson-Vanik amendment to the 1974 Trade Act, which banned sales to socialist countries which failed to assure that they would permit free emigration by their citizens. (*Box, p. 71*)

Recognition of Communist China

In a joint communiqué issued Dec. 15, 1978, the United States and the People's Republic of China announced that they would formally recognize each other Jan. 1, 1979, and exchange ambassadors and establish embassies March 1. In addition, it was announced that Deng Xiaoping, the Chinese vice premier, would visit Washington Jan. 29.

The announcement meant that the United States would withdraw its recognition of the Republic of China (Taiwan) and terminate its mutual defense treaty with that nation at the end of 1979.

(Article X of the treaty stated either party could terminate the pact with one year's notice. The United States would also withdraw its remaining 753 non-combat troops from Taiwan.)

Consultation Flap

Congressional response to President Carter's announcement was unanimous on one point: Carter had brazenly ignored his promise to consult with Congress.

Just three months earlier Carter had signed a military aid bill that specified that the president should consult with Congress before taking any action on the mutual defense treaty with Taiwan.

The provision, passed by the Senate 94-0 July 25 as an amendment to the International Security Assistance Act of 1978 (PL 95-384) and incorporated in the final version with minor changes, said: "It is the sense of the Congress that there should be prior consultation between the Congress and the executive branch on any proposed policy changes affecting the continuation in force of the Mutual Defense Treaty of 1954."

Carter signed the bill on Sept. 26, just a week after his key meeting with Chinese officials that had speeded up the normalization process.

Predictably, members of Congress were angered when Carter unilaterally announced, without consulting them, that the treaty would be terminated at the end of 1979.

There were predictions that legislation to implement the new China policy would be stalled, or heavily amended, and that congressional wrath would spill over onto such crucial issues as the Strategic Arms Limitation Treaty.

In its report on Taiwan, the Senate Foreign Relations Committee criticized the lack of congressional consultation.

The committee noted that Carter's announcement "came as a surprise to Congress and the American people. There were no meaningful prior consultations with Congress" despite the consultation provision in the military aid bill.

"Executive branch agencies were caught off guard, resulting in last-minute efforts to draft executive orders and legislation to smooth the transition," the committee said.

Rep. Lester L. Wolff, D-N.Y., chairman of the House Subcommittee on Asian and Pacific Affairs, said: "The administration's failure to live up to its pledge of last summer creates needless potential domestic obstacles, and also raises serious concerns that we have returned to the era of secret agreements concluded primarily for the purpose of avoiding rigorous debate in Congress on the merits of the issues involved."

The provision did not legally obligate Carter to consult with the legislative branch, but it created an opening for a renewal of the debate about the role of Congress in foreign policy.

The amendment was the result of a series of compromises on several Taiwan-related resolutions introduced in the 95th Congress by conservatives. An aide to Sen. Edward M. Kennedy, D-Mass., said the amendment was passed only because consultation is a "motherhood" issue.

"This simply says, ideally, that the president should consult with Congress," said Jan Kalicki, foreign affairs aide to Kennedy. "Who can be against that?"

Senate Minority Leader Howard H. Baker Jr., R-Tenn., sent a telegram to Carter asking him to postpone the cancellation of the Taiwan defense treaty until Congress could consider that action. "Time must be given for Congress to deal with such an important foreign policy matter," Baker said.

But the president rejected that plea, saying it was important to go ahead and formally notify Taiwan that the treaty would be terminated at the end of 1979.

Congressional Approval Demanded

Acting to protect its prerogatives, the Senate on June 6, 1979, insisted that the president obtain Senate approval before ending mutual defense treaties with other countries. The vote was 59-35. Although proponents said the resolution was not aimed at the Taiwan treaty decision, the action was clearly an indirect slap at Carter's handling of the decision.

The issue of treaty terminations was forced on the Senate by Sen. Harry F. Byrd Jr., Ind-Va., who introduced S Res 15 on the first day of the session. Byrd's resolution stated it to be the sense of the Senate that Senate approval "is required to terminate any mutual defense treaty between the United States and another nation."

The Foreign Relations Committee held hearings on Byrd's resolution in April and subsequently drafted language thoroughly rejecting what Byrd had proposed. The committee added exceptions, which Byrd said created major loopholes under which the president could end treaties without Senate approval.

Committee Chairman Frank Church, D-Idaho, defended his panel's version of S Res 15 in Senate debate June 6, saying it "conveys a clear message to the president that the roles of the Senate and Congress in the treaty termination process must be respected." He said the committee sought to avoid a constitutional confrontation, "which would be in the interest of neither branch."

Byrd argued that the committee language gave the president "a blank check in the termination of future treaties" and did "precisely the opposite from the intent" of his original resolution.

Church made little effort to refute the arguments against the committee resolution. Apparently optimistic about the outcome, he said early in the debate that "the strength of the committee's position is such that I am prepared to have the Senate proceed to a vote."

But then the Senate voted 59-35 to substitute Byrd's original language for the committee-sponsored version. Byrd's resolution was supported by all but four Republicans, and by most moderate and southern Democrats.

Senate leaders agreed that the Senate should have had a voice in the decision to terminate the Taiwan treaty, but they were unable to agree on how to pose the issue to senators. Majority Leader Robert C. Byrd, D-W.Va., called for a majority vote endorsing Carter's action, while Sen. Barry Goldwater, R-Ariz., insisted that a two-thirds vote was necessary. So Byrd — foreseeing a potential simple majority approving the action, but not a two-thirds majority — shelved further action on the resolution.

Goldwater Suit

Carter's unilateral decision to end the Taiwan defense treaty generated a landmark court decision on a suit by Sen. Goldwater and other conservative lawmakers opposed to the president's new China policy. Goldwater sought to prevent Carter from abrogating the treaty on the grounds that the Senate should have been consulted.

Earlier on June 6, the same day the Senate voted on S Res 15, Federal District Judge Oliver Gasch dismissed the Goldwater suit. The judge said he agreed with Goldwater but threw out the case because the senator did not have legal standing to sue. Because Congress had not yet acted on the issue, there was no evidence that Congress, or individual members of Congress, had been legally injured by what Carter did, Gasch said.

Reversal No. 1

But Gasch reversed that decision Oct. 17 and ruled not only that Goldwater did have standing, but that he was correct in demanding a role for Congress in terminating the Taiwan treaty. Gasch said Carter had to get approval from two-thirds of the Senate or from a majority in each house of Congress in withdrawing from the pact.

The White House appealed that decision, and the case went before the eight-judge District of Columbia Court of Appeals on Nov. 13.

Oral arguments centered on whether the court should decide the issue by granting Goldwater and his colleagues legal standing to sue Carter on the issue, and the constitutional issue of how a treaty can be terminated.

Although the Constitution requires approval by two-thirds of the Senate before a treaty can take effect, it is silent on which branch of government can terminate treaties. The issue had never been decided by the courts.

Reversal No. 2

On Nov. 30, 1979, the appellate court overturned the Gasch decision and upheld President Carter's right to end the Taiwan treaty without approval by Congress.

The court said its decision was not a sweeping ruling that Congress never has a right in ending treaties. Four times in its opinion, the majority said it was ruling only on the Taiwan treaty, not on the overall issue of whether Congress ever has a role in ending treaties.

"History shows us that there are too many variables to lay down any hard and fast constitutional rules," the majority said.

Nevertheless, attorneys for both sides said the ruling might establish a precedent giving presidents the right to end any treaty without congressional approval. *(Text, p. 355)*

The Decision

The appellate court took three actions in the Goldwater case:

● By a vote of 7-0, the court ruled that the treaty issue was a legal matter that could be decided by the courts, rather than a political dispute between the legislative and executive branches. In effect, the court resisted the temptation to duck the dispute between Carter and Congress.

● By a vote of 5-2, the court ruled that Goldwater and his colleagues had the legal "standing" to sue the president, because members of Congress had suffered a legal "injury" when Carter deprived them of a role in deciding the treaty issue. The two judges in the minority — Chief Judge J. Skelly Wright and Judge Edward A. Tamm — said Congress had not done everything it could to overturn Carter's action.

● By a vote of 4-1, the court ruled that Carter did not have to seek the approval of Congress before ending the Taiwan treaty. The four in the majority were Patricia M. Wald, Carl M. McGowan, Spottswood W. Robinson III and Malcolm Richard Wilkey. One judge, George E. MacKinnon, said a majority vote of both houses of Congress is needed to terminate a treaty. Wright and Tamm did not participate in this ruling on the merits of the case.

Judge Harold H. Leventhal died Nov. 20, before the court made its decision.

Jody Powell, Carter's press secretary, said the president was "obviously very pleased" by the decision and would proceed with plans to terminate the treaty Jan. 1, 1980.

J. Terry Emerson, Goldwater's legal assistant, found several "encouraging signs" in the court decision.

The court's decision to grant Goldwater and his colleagues legal standing on the issue represented "an expansion of the rules" governing the right of members of Con-

---

"It would take an unprecedented feat of judicial construction to read into the Constitution" a requirement that Congress approve all terminations of treaties. Such a ruling "would unalterably affect the balance of power between the two branches."
—From the Appellate Court decision

---

gress to sue the executive branch, he said. The decision "went well beyond" previous court rulings on the subject. The most sweeping ruling until this case had been a 1974 decision by the same court that gave Sen. Edward M. Kennedy, D-Mass., the right to challenge in court a pocket veto by President Richard M. Nixon.

Emerson also praised the court's unanimous decision not to avoid the treaty termination issue because of its po-

litical overtones. Frequently, courts refuse to decide disputes between Congress and the executive branch because the conflicts involve political, rather than legal, issues. But none of the seven judges sought to avoid the Taiwan treaty issue for this reason.

The circumstances surrounding Carter's action in ending the Taiwan treaty "include a number of material and unique elements," the court said. These included the fact that Carter withdrew recognition from the Taiwan government — thereby reducing the "meaningful vitality" of the

---

"The appetite of the presidential office will be whetted by the court's decision." In the future, "a voracious president and Department of State" could use the decision "to develop other excuses to feed upon congressional prerogatives."
—From Judge George E. MacKinnon's dissent

---

treaty with that government — and that when the Senate approved the treaty in 1955 it did not reserve a role for itself in ending the treaty.

Judge MacKinnon harshly attacked the majority's insistence that it was ruling only on the Taiwan treaty.

The majority attempted to minimize the "harmful effect" of its ruling by saying it applied only to the Taiwan treaty, MacKinnon said. "History will not deal kindly with such an obviously expedient decision."

MacKinnon warned that "the appetite of the presidential office will be whetted by the court's decision today." In the future, he said, "a voracious president and Department of State" could use the decision "to develop other excuses to feed upon congressional prerogatives. . . ."

Congressional Role

The heart of the court's ruling was the 4-1 vote determining that Carter did not have to seek congressional approval before ending the defense treaty.

John M. Harmon, assistant U.S. attorney general, had argued the president had no constitutional obligation to seek congressional approval. Congress is free to pass resolutions objecting to the president's action, but had not done so, he said. "They ask this court to give them the political victory they have not been able to win in the Congress."

The majority noted that "the constitutional initiative in the treaty-making field [lies with] the president, not the Congress. It would take an unprecedented feat of judicial construction to read into the Constitution" a requirement that Congress approve all terminations of treaties. Such a ruling "would unalterably affect the balance of power between the two branches," they said.

The majority said "it is significant" that the treaty-making power is included in Article III of the Constitution, dealing with the presidency, rather than in Article I, dealing with Congress.

In dissent, MacKinnon said "the power to terminate treaties is one of the implied powers that the Constitution implicitly vested in the government," rather than in the presidency.

The majority ruled that treaties are not the same as other federal laws, which have to be amended or repealed by joint action of the president and Congress. Although they are equally supreme under the Constitution, treaties and laws "are not necessarily the same in their other characteristics, any more than the circumstances and terms of their creation are the same," they said.

MacKinnon challenged that ruling, saying that treaties and other laws are of "equal dignity." Since a treaty is the law of the land, "a treaty is to be terminated in the same manner as any other law — by a formal act of Congress approved by the president," he said.

MacKinnon relied heavily on past practice to contend that Congress should be involved in ending treaties.

The history of 52 past treaty terminations "convinces me that congressional participation in termination has been the overwhelming historical practice," he said.

MacKinnon mocked Carter's claim that 13 treaties have been ended by presidents without the involvement of Congress. Those cases involved such "relatively innocuous and noncontroversial" treaties as an 1865 agreement governing a lighthouse at the Strait of Gibraltar, he noted.

"In almost 200 years of American history these are the only instances that [Carter] has been able to dredge up in an effort to support his claim to absolute power," MacKinnon said. Of the 13 treaties Carter cited, "there were only two minor treaties in which the president could be said to have acted alone since 1788."

"It is almost farcical" for Carter to contend that "the president, acting alone, has the absolute power to terminate a major United States defense treaty," MacKinnon said.

"No prior president has ever claimed such power with respect to such important treaties; we should not allow the few prior instances where presidents, in relatively minor matters, may have acted alone to be magnified into a truly awesome power and a dangerous precedent."

Goldwater Legal Standing

In supporting Goldwater's contention that members had legal standing to sue Carter because they were legally "injured" by his action, MacKinnon and the four-member majority said the crucial issue was whether the members of Congress "have the effective power to block the termination of this treaty despite the president's action."

The four-member majority decided that "there is no conceivable senatorial action that could likely prevent termination of the treaty." At most, a resolution or bill passed by Congress would have "persuasive effect with the president," they said. Therefore, it is necessary for the court to intervene to protect Congress' rights, they said.

But Wright and Tamm rejected these arguments. They insisted the courts should not step into the dispute until Congress had taken all possible actions to overrule the president.

Until Congress "has taken all final action in its power to exercise its constitutional prerogative, any injury an individual legislator suffers" is caused by "his colleagues in Congress," not by the president, they said.

"Congress as a body has chosen not to confront the president directly on the treaty termination," Wright and Tamm said. Goldwater and his colleagues "have always had the legal, if not the political, power" to try to get Congress to pass legislation overturning Carter's action.

Byrd Resolution

The judges issued varying opinions about the legal impact of the Senate's June 6 vote in favor of a Senate role in ending mutual defense treaties. The Senate action was on a resolution sponsored by Harry F. Byrd Jr., Ind-Va.

The four-member majority merely noted that the Senate has not "purported to take any final or decisive action" on the treaty issue.

Judges Wright and Tamm noted that even some of the 59 senators who voted for the Byrd resolution disagreed about whether it would apply to the Taiwan treaty, or only to treaties in the future.

Supreme Court Action

On Dec. 13, 1979, the Supreme Court denied Goldwater's appeal, thus sustaining Carter's action.

Four members of the High Court — Chief Justice Warren E. Burger and Justices William H. Rehnquist, John Paul Stevens and Potter Stewart — voted to dismiss the Goldwater suit because the dispute between Goldwater and the president was a "political question." They did not address the constitutional issue of whether a president can terminate a treaty without congressional approval.

Justice Lewis F. Powell Jr. said Goldwater's complaint was "not ripe for judicial review," presumably because Congress as a body had not taken a position on the issue. Justice William J. Brennan Jr. was the only member of the court who rejected Goldwater's position that Carter acted unconstitutionally. Justice Thurgood Marshall concurred in the majority opinion but did not give a reason.

Only two justices, Byron R. White and Harry A. Blackmun, said Goldwater should have been given the opportunity to present his arguments before the court. Goldwater had asked the court to hold formal hearings on his appeal of the appeals court decision.

Implementing Normalization

Despite criticism, however, key pieces of the administration's new policy began to fall into place, nearly on schedule and over the objections of Capitol Hill friends of Taiwan. Even the harshest critics conceded that Carter had the legal authority to establish diplomatic relations with mainland China. And praise for Carter's action came from Senate liberals, who had long urged the United States to move rapidly toward normalization of relations.

Alan Cranston, D-Calif., Senate Democratic whip, said Carter's "courageous decision is a positive step toward world peace." Cranston in January 1978 had led a 10-member delegation to China that later called for prompt recognition of China.

The Senate on Feb. 26, 1979, confirmed Leonard Woodcock as ambassador to the People's Republic of China just three days before official U.S.-China diplomatic relations commenced. Woodcock could not make it to Peking in time for the March 1 ceremonies. His counterpart, Chai Zemin, presented his credentials to President Carter in a White House ceremony subdued by the strain between China and the United States over the Chinese invasion of Vietnam. *(See pp. 16, 43)*

In Peking, the two nations reached quick settlement on the issue of millions of dollars in bank accounts and other assets that had been frozen for nearly 30 years, the first step toward an important trade agreement.

And committees of the House and Senate reported bills providing for unofficial relations with Taiwan. Under that legislation, the United States would acknowledge the existence of Taiwan and "the people on Taiwan," but not the Republic of China government.

Woodcock Confirmation

Leonard Woodcock, the head of the United States Liaison Office in Peking since March 1977, became the first full-fledged American ambassador to mainland China since the 1949 Communist takeover.

Woodcock, the former president of the United Automobile Workers, was nominated for the post by President Carter Jan. 15, 1979, approved by the Senate Foreign Relations Committee Feb. 8 by a 14-1 vote after a brief hearing, and confirmed by the Senate 82-9 Feb. 26.

Sen. Jesse Helms, R-N.C., had threatened to filibuster Woodcock's nomination, but relented after just three hours of floor debate. Carter administration lobbyists had asked the Senate to confirm Woodcock before March 1 — the date the United States and China were scheduled to exchange ambassadors and open embassies.

Senate Debate

Although no one in the Senate challenged Woodcock's qualifications to be ambassador, a substantial number of Republicans argued for delaying his confirmation.

Some Republicans said he should not have been confirmed until after Congress had passed legislation supporting Taiwan; others maintained he should not have been confirmed while China was engaged in a war against Vietnam.

Peking's Feb. 17 invasion of Vietnam was the chief concern of much of the Senate during the debate. Helms said: "To confirm Mr. Woodcock at the present time, in light of the People's Republic of China's action in the Sino-Vietnamese war, would be, in the minds of many, a matter of the Senate putting an implicit stamp of approval on the Chinese invasion."

And Republicans Charles McC. Mathias of Maryland and S. I. Hayakawa of California said they voted against Woodcock solely because of the timing.

"I believe that were the U.S. Senate to approve this nomination now, it would send out another wrong signal to a very troubled region," Mathias said. "We should tell the Chinese clearly and forcefully that they cannot make war and expect our new relationship to prosper. The best way to get that message across at this point is to defer our consideration of the Woodcock nomination until a more propitious time."

"China seems to have assumed that we are an ally of theirs against Russia," Hayakawa said. "To take advantage of what they have regarded as implicit approval of everything they do, China has attacked Vietnam."

By "rushing headlong" into approval of an ambassador, the United States would be acting "as if these events had not taken place and as if China had not exposed itself as an aggressor nation, willing to use force against those of whom it disapproves across any of its borders," Hayakawa said.

In defense of the timing, Foreign Relations Committee Chairman Frank Church, D-Idaho, said the recognition of China and the appointment of an ambassador were unrelated to Chinese policies and actions.

"When the president . . . recognized the People's Republic of China . . . [he] did not create an alliance with China. Recognition of China did not officially approve of that government or its policies. All the president did was to say that . . . the time had finally come to set aside the illusion which had misguided American policy in Asia for 30 years; namely, that the government of China was situated on the island of Formosa [Taiwan]."

Recognition of Peking, Church said, "does not connote our approval of Peking any more than the fact that the many-year presence of an American ambassador in Moscow connotes our approval of the Soviet government."

Majority Leader Robert C. Byrd, D-W.Va., said delay of Woodcock's nomination "would give undue comfort to the Soviet Union. The Soviets know that normalization [by the United States] with the People's Republic is a reality, but I would imagine that they would not be at all unhappy to see an obstacle in the way of normalization."

Woodcock Role in Talks

Helms criticized Woodcock's role in the negotiations leading to the December 1978 agreement establishing diplomatic relations with mainland China. In testimony before the Foreign Relations Committee, Woodcock conceded that he had never tried during the talks with the Peking government to obtain a Chinese pledge not to use force to annex Taiwan to the mainland.

"I fully realize that policies Mr. Woodcock was following were dictated from the White House and from the State Department," Helms said. "But there was little evidence that Mr. Woodcock himself intervened" to obtain assurances for Taiwan."

Helms cited Woodcock's testimony that an American insistence on a Chinese promise not to invade Taiwan might have put a "roadblock" in the way of U.S.-China relations.

"There is not any question in this senator's mind about Ambassador Woodcock's unwillingness to broach that subject [of Taiwan] with the Communist regime in Peking," Helms said.

Senate Vote

The key vote on Woodcock came on a procedural motion allowing the Senate to consider the nomination. That vote was 56-29. All 29 votes against taking up the nomination were cast by Republicans.

On the final vote confirming Woodcock, only nine senators voted against the nomination. Aside from Mathias, a moderate, all the "no" votes were cast by conservative Republicans: Helms; Hayakawa; Ted Stevens, Alaska; James A. McClure, Idaho; Gordon J. Humphrey, N.H.; Harrison Schmitt, N.M.; John Tower, Texas; and Jake Garn, Utah.

Some of the Senate's most prominent conservatives, including Barry Goldwater, R-Ariz., and Paul Laxalt, R-Nev., voted for the nominee. Although Goldwater had earlier voted in effect against Woodcock on the procedural vote, he said the president "has a right to pick his ambassadors."

Funding of Taiwan Institute

Implementation of the new U.S. policy toward Taiwan, which was to have begun March 1, 1979, was delayed by an angered Sen. Ernest F. Hollings, D-S.C., until passage of the Taiwan Relations Act on April 10, 1979. As chairman of the Appropriations subcommittee that handled the State Department's budget, Hollings refused to allow the administration to transfer $2 million of State's fiscal 1979 budget.

The money had been budgeted for the American Embassy in Taipei, and the administration wanted to allocate it to the new American Institute in Taiwan, which was now to conduct American relations with Taiwan. State Department officials said the $2 million was necessary to open the institute's offices in Taipei and in Rosslyn, Va., a Washington suburb; without the money, there would be a "hiatus" in relations between the United States and Taiwan.

The institute was to be staffed by employees on leave from the U.S. government. Its offices in Taipei were not in the former American Embassy for "symbolic reasons," State Department China director Harvey Feldman said. Although the institute already had been incorporated under Washington, D.C., laws, legislation authorizing it to act on behalf of the United States needed congressional approval.

"We can't reprogram the money because there is no institute to transfer it to," Hollings said, adding that he would not allow the money to be reprogrammed until Congress passed the enabling legislation. President Carter called Hollings Feb. 27 to ask him to approve transfer of the money. "I told him I couldn't do it," Hollings said.

But Hollings also had other reasons for holding up the money. He said he was angered by the administration's treatment of Taiwan since the December announcement of the new China policy. "It appears to me that the State Department is moving swiftly to submerge Taiwan," he said. "They're going about it [dealing with Taiwan] in a high-handed fashion."

Hollings had a list of complaints that included:

● What he called State Department "pressure" on Taiwan to recall I-Cheng Loh, director of the Taiwan government's China Information Service in New York City, after Loh had written letters in January to several newspapers criticizing Carter's China policies. State Department officials said Loh engaged in "undiplomatic behavior" in addition to writing the letters, but they denied pressuring Taiwan to recall him.

● The lack of congressional oversight of the American Institute. "We won't hear anything more about Taiwan, if you leave it in the hands of the State Department," Hollings said. "They don't have that much interest in Taiwan." Hollings said he wanted legislation to create a commission, composed of both congressional and executive branch appointees, to oversee the institute.

● State Department "scheming" to turn the former Republic of China Embassy in Washington over to mainland China. Hollings said the embassy, called Twin Oaks, "rightfully belongs to Taiwan. I want to see to it that Taiwan gets its property back."

Funding of the institute proceeded with the signing of the Taiwan Relations Act on April 10.

In one setback for the administration, a Senate Appropriations subcommittee refused to expedite funding for the private corporation that was to conduct future American dealings, with Taiwan unofficially assuming the functions of the former U.S. Embassy there. Administration officials said there would be a brief "hiatus" in relations with Taiwan because the embassy in Taipei had been closed. *(Box, this page)*

The administration had wanted Woodcock confirmed and the American Institute funded and operating well before March 1.

Lobbying Efforts

Attempts by conservatives to delay or disrupt President Carter's policy were surprisingly restrained. Massive lobbying campaigns on behalf of Taiwan, promised by several conservative groups in December, did not materialize, partly because Taiwan officials themselves did not vocally press their own cause. *(Box, pp. 46-47)*

After some initial confusion and fumbling, the administration's lobbying efforts worked smoothly. As originally conceived, Carter's legislative proposal for continuing unofficial relations with Taiwan had been widely criticized on Capitol Hill as inadequate and poorly drafted.

But as the House and Senate committees began work on the bill, administration officials quickly accepted changes that gave additional assurances to Taiwan while giving members of Congress a chance to express themselves on the new policy. At the same time, Carter successfully sidetracked amendments that might have jeopardized the new relationship with Peking.

Deng as Salesman

An effective salesman for the administration's China policy was Chinese Vice Premier Deng Xiaoping during his visit to the United States Jan. 28-Feb. 5, 1979. In a one-day whirlwind tour of Capitol Hill, Deng told congressional leaders that China would let Taiwan alone if the Taiwan government agreed to give up its sovereignty. *(Box, p. 45)*

Some members of Congress said they were reassured by Deng's remarks. Tony P. Hall, D-Ohio, for example, attempted to get the House Foreign Affairs Committee to refer officially to Deng's statements in the Taiwan legislation. "His remarks were very reassuring," Hall said. "I don't think the vice premier of China would say anything to this committee in a frivolous manner."

But conservatives charged that Deng did not reassure Taiwan. "Quite frankly, I think the vice premier of China is a liar," said Edward J. Derwinski, R-Ill. "We've embraced a bunch of bums."

Although Chinese officials had repeatedly said the future of Taiwan was a domestic issue for China to solve, Deng willingly discussed the issue on Capitol Hill.

In response to questions Deng said mainland China did not intend to interfere in Taiwan, as long as Taiwan agreed formally to become part of the People's Republic of China.

"I'm sure you have already noted we no longer use the word 'liberation' of Taiwan," Deng told the senators. "We now say we want to solve the question of the return of Taiwan to the motherland and complete the great cause of reunification of the motherland. We say that, so long as Taiwan is returned to the motherland and that there is only one China, then we will fully respect the present realities on Taiwan."

Deng said Taiwan would be allowed to keep its current economic and social systems and its military defenses in-

Vice Premier Deng Welcomed on Capitol Hill

The Speaker of the House, the majority and minority leaders, 70 House members and two dozen Chinese officials were assembled in a Rayburn House Office Building hearing room Jan. 30 to welcome Deng Xiaoping, vice premier of the People's Republic of China.

Rep. Clement J. Zablocki, D-Wis., chairman of the House International Relations Committee, stepped to the microphone to speak the first words of greetings from the House side of Capitol Hill:

"Wo hen yukuai guoji guanxi weiyuanhui he wo geren huanying ni fuzongli," spoke the veteran legislator from South Milwaukee. "Women dajia dou xiwang bing qidao keyi baozhang zai yuandong de heping he wending." Obviously surprised, members of the assembled delegation smiled, then chuckled and broke into delighted applause as Zablocki grinned broadly.

Finally, for the benefit of his fellow legislators, Zablocki translated his words into English: "On behalf of the International Relations Committee and myself, it is a pleasure to welcome you, Mr. [Vice Premier]. All of us hope and pray that peace and stability in the Far East will be [preserved]."

Deng devoted six hours of his Washington visit to lobbying on Capitol Hill. Unlike most lobbyists, he did not have to seek out members of Congress for private backroom conversations.

Eighty-five members of the Senate showed up for a noon luncheon with Deng in the famous Caucus Room in the Russell Senate Office Building.

On the House side, members avidly sought invitations for a "tea and meeting" with Deng in the International Relations Committee room. Members of both houses stood in line to shake Deng's hand and even to get his autograph.

Rep. Paul Findley, R-Ill., upstaged his colleagues by presenting Deng with a coffee table-size book of photographs of Abraham Lincoln (the most famous resident of Springfield, in Findley's district). In return, Deng autographed a copy of *Time* magazine with his portrait on the cover. The next day, Deng received a second copy of the Lincoln book from the National Park Service while touring the Lincoln Memorial.

Deng was on Capitol Hill primarily to reassure anxious members of Congress about China's peaceful intentions toward Taiwan. The Carter administration had hoped that Deng would tell members what they wanted to hear: China would leave Taiwan alone.

The vice premier listened to welcoming speeches from four Senate leaders at lunch and from three House leaders at teatime. Each one made at least an indirect reference to American hopes for peace between China and Taiwan.

House Speaker Thomas P. O'Neill Jr., D-Mass., for example, told Deng: "We want you to know that we are vitally interested in the peaceful resolution of the Taiwan issue." In response, Deng acknowledged that "some of you may not be very clear about China's position. All of you are welcome to go to China for a look."

Deng's friendly attitude and apparently forthright responses to questions impressed most congressmen.

"He's a very good advocate of his country because he has a warm, friendly smile," said Sen. Henry M. Jackson, D-Wash., after the Senate luncheon. Speaking of Deng's week-long visit to the United States, Jackson predicted that "he'll be kissing a lot of babies here. . . ."

---

definitely. He refused to say, however, that China would never use force to take over Taiwan.

In a later interview, Deng said on the issue: "The question is, if we are to commit ourselves to not using armed force at all then that will be equivalent to tying our own hands, and the result then would be to have the Taiwan authorities refuse absolutely to negotiate with us for a peaceful reunification."

Several members of Congress said Deng's remarks reassured them that China was not about to try to conquer Taiwan. "These people obviously intend to preserve Taiwan's autonomy," said Sen. Paul Laxalt, R-Nev.

Sen. Henry M. Jackson, D-Wash., said he was not alarmed by Deng's refusal to renounce forever the use of force against Taiwan.

Complicating the new agreements was China's invasion of Vietnam on Feb. 17, 1979. The Chinese invasion seemed to toughen congressional determination to express American support for Taiwan. Clement J. Zablocki, D-Wis., chairman of the House Foreign Affairs Committee, said the invasion "simply reaffirms the need for us to take a strong, clear stand" in support of Taiwan.

One of the most vocal critics of Carter's China policy, Sen. Jesse Helms, R-N.C., used the Sino-Vietnamese conflict as an argument against confirming Woodcock as ambassador. The fighting ended, however, congressional tempers cooled, and Woodcock was confirmed. *(Box, p. 43)*

Trade with China

Treasury Secretary W. Michael Blumenthal opened negotiations with the Chinese on some of their mutual trade and economic issues in a visit to China the week of Feb. 25, 1979. Blumenthal was the highest American official to visit China since the United States recognized Peking in December 1978. He represented the United States at March 1 recognition ceremonies in Peking.

Blumenthal quickly completed a settlement of a 30-year-old dispute involving assets (such as bank accounts) frozen by the two nations since the Communist takeover of the mainland in 1949. China agreed to pay the United States $80.5 million in cash, over five years, to settle $196 million in American claims. In return, the United States would release Chinese assets that had been frozen here.

Administration officials said it would be difficult for the two nations to carry out normal trade and business relations until claims on those issues were resolved. Congress could have blocked the agreement but did not, and Chinese settlement payments to the United States began Oct. 1, 1979. The first of four installments was $20 million.

Trade Pact

The two countries also negotiated a basic three-year trade agreement, signed July 7, 1979, in Peking, that

Cautious Taiwan Effort Blamed for Failure . . .

The Taiwan government's most vocal supporters in the American political community said they failed to generate an effective lobbying campaign against President Carter's new China policy because Taiwan refused to confront the issue head on.

Although a loosely knit coalition of conservative groups was formed in December 1978 in opposition to Carter's decision to recognize the PRC and de-recognize the Republic of China on Taiwan, lobbying against the new China policy was conspicuously absent during debates in the Senate Foreign Relations Committee and House Foreign Affairs Committee over legislation defining the basis of future U.S.-Taiwan relations.

Pro-Taiwan forces in the United States also did not exploit the confirmation hearings of Leonard Woodcock as ambassador to China to enunciate their disapproval of what they viewed as the "abandonment" of Taiwan.

"There is a strategic focus lacking" among the pro-Taiwan groups, said Howard Phillips, national director of the Conservative Caucus.

The reason that focus was lacking in the committee debates boiled down to a fundamental disagreement between Taiwan and its friends in the American conservative community over the best strategy for preserving Taiwan's security and economic interests.

Taiwan chose a cautious course that accepted as a *fait accompli* President Carter's recognition of Peking. In seeking to minimize its losses, Taiwan did not want to antagonize the United States, on which, for better or worse, it must continue to rely for military support.

But American conservative groups thought Taiwan stood to gain more by fighting back and, in particular, by insisting on government-to-government relations with the United States and continuation of the 1954 mutual defense treaty. Although these groups did not oppose recognition of Peking, they opposed it if it meant derecognition of Taiwan.

Taiwan 'Capitulates'

If American groups had any intention of fighting Taiwan's battle, that country's agreement Feb. 13 to accept the administration-proposed American Institute in Taiwan (AIT) as the vehicle for continued relations, drew the final curtain on such plans.

"I think Taiwan chickened out and capitulated too early," said James Chieh Hsiung, a New York University professor of politics. "If Taiwan accepts the AIT, there's nothing we can do."

Washington-based pro-Taiwan groups insisted they would continue to fight on behalf of Taiwan and what they saw as U.S. security interests. But virtually all of them echoed Hsiung's pessimism concerning their ability to be of much help:

● "One of the difficulties in developing a confrontation with Congress on the Taiwan issue has been the unfortunate timidity, the willingness of the Taiwanese to cave in to State Department demands," said Gary Jarmin, legislative director of the 350,000-member American Conservative Union.

● "The Taiwanese blew it," said Anne Martin, executive director of the Committee for a Free China. "Since they gave in on the demand for government-to-government relations, I don't see how anyone could do anything for them."

● "You can't be more Catholic than the Pope," said Edwin J. Feulner Jr., executive director of the Heritage Foundation. "You can't tell them to go for a whole loaf if they're willing to go for half."

● "It is difficult for [Taiwan] supporters in the United States to launch a campaign if the people on behalf of whom you're working aren't taking a strong position," said William F. Rhatican, whose public relations firm organized a congressional tour to Taiwan in January 1979. The Taiwan issue, according to Rhatican, "had the potential to be a major confrontation, but it fizzled."

Only Rep. Robert E. Bauman, R-Md., chairman of the American Conservative Union (ACU), thought Taiwan had "made its views forcefully" at the time of Carter's recognition of Peking and saw "no wavering" since then.

Although conservatives generally viewed Taiwan's limited challenge to Carter as the underlying cause of their own weak response on behalf of Taiwan, three other factors hampered a forceful lobbying effort.

First, President Carter's Dec. 15 announcement caught pro-Taiwan forces off guard. With March 1 set as the date of establishing formal relations with Peking, and a new Congress just coming into town, Taiwan's friends had little time to mobilize a significant grass-roots effort.

Second, the U.S. business community failed to take a strong pro-Taiwan position, apparently finding the prospect of trade with mainland China irresistible.

Third, the foreign relations committees framed their debate in terms of providing greater assurances to Taiwan than Carter proposed, rather than insisting on full diplomatic relations.

Conservative Coalition

Most of the pro-Taiwan groups generally took a dim view of the Carter administration's foreign policy, arguing that the derecognition of Taiwan was the latest in a series of sellouts of longtime U.S. allies.

In a Dec. 30, 1978, fund-raising appeal for the Washington Legal Foundation — a group representing Sen. Barry Goldwater, R-Ariz., in a suit challenging Carter's termination of the 1954 mutual defense treaty with Taiwan *(see p. 40)* — Sen. Gordon J. Humphrey, R-N.H., lamented "the giveaway of the Panama Canal" and urged support for pro-Taiwan efforts. "[R]ight now I feel ashamed," Humphrey wrote. "First, we abandon the Vietnamese and the Cambodians. Then we tell the Koreans we're pulling out. And now we break our word to the people of Taiwan." Humphrey's appeal was largely consistent with that of other groups working on behalf of Taiwan, a coalition that read like a Who's Who of Washington conservative lobbies. These groups included:

● **The National Conservative Political Action Committee,** best known for pouring millions of dollars into the election campaigns of conservative congressional candidates.

● **The American Conservative Union,** the largest organization of conservatives in the country.

... to Defeat Carter's New Policy Toward China

● **The American Council for a Free Asia,** described by its national director, Gary Jarmin of ACU, as a "conservative anticommunist public interest lobby."

● The **Conservative Caucus,** which had been active in opposing abortion, busing, gun control and the Equal Rights Amendment, and decided to make Taiwan a major priority.

● The **Washington Legal Foundation,** which handled Goldwater's lawsuit, also represented congressmen suing the administration to stop the Panama Canal agreement in 1978.

● **The Heritage Foundation,** a conservative research organization founded and originally funded by Joseph Coors. Heritage Foundation public relations were handled by Hugh C. Newton, a registered foreign agent of the Taiwan government, and Herbert Berkowitz, a former employee of Newton's firm.

● **Young Americans for Freedom,** a student-oriented lobby.

● **The Committee for the Survival of a Free Congress,** a political and legislative action group headed by Paul Weyrich (a founder of the Heritage Foundation) which funds conservative candidates.

● **The Committee for A Free China,** the last organizational vestige of the "old China lobby," formed in 1953 as the Committee for One Million Against the Admission of Communist China to the United Nations, directed its efforts largely at generating grass-roots support for Taiwan. Its president in 1979 was former Rep. Walter H. Judd, R-Minn. (1943-63). Its treasurer, Charles A. Moser, was also treasurer of the Committee for Survival of a Free Congress.

● **Friends of Free China,** headed by Jack Buttram, a board member of the Committee for a Free China. The organization's national chairman was Barry Goldwater. Its national advisory board included Ronald Reagan. The "Friends" were the current owners of the Taiwan Embassy.

Grass-roots Lobbying

The lack of direct lobbying on the Taiwan bill surprised members of the foreign affairs committees and State Department officials. But the pro-Taiwan groups had not been totally inactive.

A four-part plan of action by the coalition was outlined by its organizer, John T. Dolan, executive director of NCPAC and a director of the Washington Legal Foundation: 1) grass-roots lobbying and mail campaigns, 2) support for the Washington Legal Foundation lawsuit, 3) lobbying on foreign aid and economic legislation and, 4) coordinating trips to Taiwan to encourage greater support for Taiwan.

A survey of 20 House and Senate offices in early 1979 showed the pro-Taiwan mail campaign was highly visible on Capitol Hill. Although mail was not nearly so heavy as that on the Panama Canal debate, one office reported receiving 10,000 letters or postcards while several said they received more than 3,000. Some, however, said they got as few as 15. Much of the mail was the product of organized writing campaigns, some of which originated from Taiwan.

The Committee for A Free China sent letters to more than 100,000 homes urging citizens to write Congress.

The American Council for a Free Asia, according to Jarmin, sent 300,000 letters urging people to sign a petition saying the Taiwanese should not be "enslaved or murdered by the Communists." NCPAC mailed 50,000 personalized letters through the Richard A. Viguerie direct mail company, enclosing postcards to be sent to senators saying, "Please do not let President Carter abandon the 17 million free people of Taiwan."

The Washington Legal Foundation sent out more than 500,000 of the Gordon Humphrey fund-raising letters, which included postcards almost identical to those sent out by NCPAC. An aide to Sen. William S. Cohen, R-Maine, reported that 3,000 of the 4,000 pieces of mail it received were foundation postcards.

Looking Ahead

If conservative groups failed in their efforts to "save" Taiwan, many nonetheless took credit for subsequent legislation supportive of the ROC and saw a silver lining in the future.

Many conservatives hoped to cash in on what they viewed as Carter's weakness in foreign policy in the 1980 presidential elections.

Phillips of the Conservative Caucus said, "In the 1980 presidential race any serious Republican candidate will be brought to heel on this. . . . We will discover how strongly the rank and file feel about Taiwan." Taiwan "will be a live issue in the 1980 campaign," Phillips said, touting the possibility that Ronald Reagan or Rep. Philip M. Crane, R-Ill., the former ACU chairman who was running for president, would re-establish relations with Taiwan.

Jarmin of ACU said his group hoped to "generate so much political pressure" on the Taiwan issue "that Carter won't be able to survive in 1980." And while he said defeating Carter was "not our sole objective," he added "to a large extent that is the objective of the American Council for a Free Asia."

Whatever life the Taiwan question may have had left as a campaign issue, however, was further vitiated by events in late 1979 and early 1980. The Iran hostage crisis and the Soviet incursion into Afghanistan served both to overshadow the Taiwan issue and in some respects seemed to justify the new U.S. China policy.

These crises guaranteed that the Middle East and containment of Soviet expansion — not China — would be the nexus of foreign policy debate in the 1980 elections and probably for years to come. At the same time, China's refusal to block U.S. retaliation against Iran, and its cooperation with America in denouncing the Soviet Afghan adventure and moving to block further Russian expansion in the area, were likely to be cited by the administration as benefits accruing from its China initiatives.

The Iran indignities and the Soviet threat aroused the American public and its politicians into a renewed spirit of opposition to foreign aggression. The focus of attention was on Pakistan and the Persian Gulf — not Taiwan and the Taiwan Strait — as the strategic area on which democratic and unaligned nations were to stand their ground.

Rabbit Meat

On Nov. 10, 1977, President Jimmy Carter vetoed a bill (HR 2521) requiring federal inspection of domestic rabbit meat and spot checks of imported rabbit meat. No override was attempted. A similar measure was vetoed by President Ford in 1976.

Among various reasons cited by the president for his veto, Carter noted that the bill required spot-check inspections of rabbit meat processing plants, including those in countries that exported meat to the United States. That requirement would "strain relations" with the People's Republic of China, the principal rabbit meat exporter to the United States, and could "severely restrict" or end the Chinese imports, he said. No health problems with rabbit meat from China had been found by FDA inspectors, he added.

Representatives of the $10-million-a-year rabbit industry and bill sponsor Rep. Keith G. Sebelius, R-Kan., had contended that rabbit eaters deserved the same protection as consumers of other meats. They added that the inspection fee under the voluntary program had driven rabbit prices up toward non-competitive levels, stemming the meat's growth potential as an American diet staple, and threatening the survival of the struggling domestic rabbit industry.

granted the Chinese "most-favored-nation" status, which would give that country the same trade and tariff privileges enjoyed by most nations deemed "friendly" by the United States.

But the Carter administration — despite reports of Chinese impatience — delayed sending the agreement to Congress. The White House was reportedly reluctant to submit the pact without sending Congress a similar agreement with the Soviet Union at about the same time. Both agreements faced the same obstacle: the Jackson-Vanik Amendment to the 1974 Trade Act which barred MFN and Export-Import Bank credits to communist countries that do not allow freedom of emigration.

On Oct. 23, President Carter finally sent the Sino-U.S. trade agreement to Congress. On the same day, Carter signed a proclamation waiving the requirements of the Jackson-Vanik amendment as applied to the China pact. In his letter of transmittal, Carter stated that China was moving to lift bans on emigration.

Congressional sentiment for approving the trade pact seemed strong during the final days of 1979, as committees acted to clear the agreement for early 1980 passage.

Approval became a certainty after Soviet troops unexpectedly occupied Afghanistan on Dec. 27. The Russian incursion influenced those advocating "evenhandedness" in dealing with China and Russia to withdraw their objections to granting MFN status to China alone.

On Jan. 24, 1980, two days after it convened, Congress approved the treaty, by votes of 294-88 in the House, 74-8 in the Senate. *(Details, pp. 69-72; Text, pp. 352-354)*

Future of Taiwan

The paramount issue throughout congressional debate on the China policy was the future of Taiwan: whether that island nation, with a capitalist economy and an autocratic political system dominated by mainland refugees, would be free from an eventual attack or boycott by China.

The Carter administration's answer to that question was yes, at least for the foreseeable future. But conservative backers of Taiwan said they were certain China would attempt as soon as possible to annex Taiwan, and the United States should not simply stand by and allow that to happen.

Sen. Helms said China still wanted to take over Taiwan. Citing its invasion of Vietnam, he said: "If China is willing to go to war over a border dispute, how much more willingly would they go to war over what they regard as [their own] province?"

In attempting to stave off a rigid commitment to defend Taiwan, the administration found many allies in Congress, including moderates, liberals and even some conservatives. They said the United States should support Taiwan through trade and arms sales and diplomatic pressure on the mainland. But few said they, or their constituents, were willing to go to war to save Taiwan from a communist takeover.

Taiwan Relations Act

A description of the American dilemma concerning Taiwan came from the Senate Foreign Relations Committee. In its March 1, 1979, report on the Taiwan relations legislation (HR 2479), the committee concluded that Taiwan "today is less important strategically to the United States than it was during the 1950s" when the mutual defense treaty was signed.

But the committee added that an attack on Taiwan "would pose grave problems" for the United States.

"The long United States-Taiwanese association would make it extremely difficult for the United States not to respond firmly to hostile activity directed against Taiwan," the committee said. Failure to help Taiwan "would seriously weaken the confidence of America's other allies in the reliability of United States protection."

Committee Chairman Frank Church, D-Idaho, repeatedly argued that Taiwan might be safer in the future because the United States could pressure Peking to leave Taiwan alone.

"Now we have the leverage that will come from the benefits that will flow from recognition of Peking," Church said. American relations with Peking, plus continued support of Taiwan, "will give a larger measure of security to the people on Taiwan than was previously the case."

Legislative Battle

During the early stages of floor debate on the bill the week of March 5, both houses narrowly rejected efforts to cripple Carter's policies toward Taiwan and mainland China. The votes reflected widespread dissatisfaction with the deal Carter made secretly with Peking in December 1978 without consulting Congress.

Overall, conservative critics of the Carter policy managed in both houses to insert modest amendments strengthening the American presence in and guarantees for Taiwan. But they were beaten in their efforts virtually to restore the full government-to-government relationship that existed before President Carter recognized the mainland.

As Senate conservatives persisted in pushing amendments to every section of the bill, Sen. Church suggested the bill was beginning to resemble the traditional congressional "Christmas tree." "We do not have to hang ornaments on every branch of this tree — ornaments that only detract from its pristine beauty," Church said, grinning.

Senate Action

The Senate completed action on its bill after four days of debate. Most controversial issues had been settled during the first two days, leaving secondary amendments and one sentimental issue for the final two days, March 12 and 13.

Conservatives managed to strengthen several technical provisions benefiting Taiwan, and all but six of them ended up voting for the bill.

In general, major amendments rejected during the floor debate would have strengthened American support for Taiwan security and raised the U.S.-Taiwan relationship to a more offical or semi-official status.

Taiwan Embassy. Brushing aside strenuous objections from the administration and a compromise proposal by Chairman Church, the Senate voted to ensure that the Taiwan government would be able to keep its embassy and chancery buildings in Washington. A similar provision had been placed in the House bill by the Foreign Affairs Committee. *(Box, p. 50)*

Senate Confirmation. The Senate rejected an attempt by Robert Dole, R-Kan., to require Senate confirmation of the director of the new American Institute in Taiwan to replace the embassy there. Dole's amendment also would have set a two-year term for the director.

Dole argued that the director should be subject to Senate confirmation because he would perform the same functions as an ambassador.

Joseph R. Biden Jr., D-Del., said the amendment would raise the status of the American presence in Taiwan, in violation of President Carter's agreement with Peking. Requiring Senate confirmation would make the institute director a government official and would disrupt "the delicate set of relationships this legislation is intended to promote," Biden said.

Dole's amendment was tabled on a 54-38 vote.

House Action

In two days of debate (March 8 and 13), House conservatives repeatedly tried and failed to add even a slice of official status to the institute that is to represent the United States in Taiwan. Unlike the Senate bill, the House version referred to a "designated entity" rather than naming the agency the American Institute in Taiwan.

Conservative members argued that the United States should continue at least some semblance of official ties with a nation that had been a close ally for 30 years. But backers of the administration's position said relations with Taiwan had to be entirely unofficial since the United States now recognized the mainland government as the sole government of China.

The closest the conservatives came in their efforts was a 172-181 vote March 8 rejecting an amendment to establish a governmental "liaison office" in Taipei. All other amendments on the issue were soundly defeated.

Taiwan Security. The House debated Taiwan security issues March 8, turning down several attempts to strengthen the American security commitment to the island.

In a March 13 discussion on the floor, Clement J. Zablocki, D-Wis., told the House the security provisions of the bill would not give the president additional power to conduct wars to protect Taiwan.

Paul Findley, R-Ill., said he was concerned the bill might produce the "same mischief" as the 1964 Gulf of Tonkin resolution, which President Johnson used as the legal basis for the Vietnam War.

Zablocki assured Findley that the bill did not directly authorize the president to take military action to protect Taiwan.

Under the War Powers Resolution (PL 93-148) the president must "in every possible instance" consult with Congress before sending troops into combat overseas, and then must obtain congressional approval for the action within 60 days.

Zablocki's interpretation of the bill was disputed by Robert E. Bauman, R-Md., a conservative who voted against HR 2479. Bauman argued that the "very broad draftsmanship" of the bill would add to the president's authority to take military action.

Bauman said the bill would give the president "a blank check" to transfer arms to Taiwan through the institute, "and that could be an act short of war, but certainly one that could have a great deal of consequences."

Quemoy and Matsu. Two tiny islands that figured prominently in the 1960 Kennedy-Nixon debates surfaced during House action. *(pp. 3, 58)*

Mickey Edwards, R-Okla., proposed an amendment expressing concern for the security of the two islands, which are located about 10 miles off the China coast, but are controlled by Taiwan.

Expressing U.S. concern for the islands through the legislation, Edwards said, "will help this nation, this great nation of ours, to do the right thing and keep its soul."

But administration supporters noted that not even the expiring U.S.-Taiwan mutual defense treaty covered Quemoy and Matsu. "We should not be expanding the U.S. security commitment beyond what was in the treaty," Zablocki said.

Edwards' amendment was rejected 146-256.

Conference Report

The House-Senate conference committee that wrote the final version of HR 2479 eliminated several provisions the administration said went too far in re-establishing formal ties with Taiwan.

● Both houses had included language expressing general concern for Taiwan's future security, but pledging no direct action other than the continued sale of defensive weapons. The final version incorporated Senate language promising arms to Taiwan for its self-defense.

● The House bill was titled the "U.S.-Taiwan Relations Act." Administration officials said that might be interpreted to mean the United States and Taiwan were continuing official relations. The committee changed the title to the "Taiwan Relations Act."

● The House bill did not specify the private agency that was to conduct future relations with the island. Instead, the House bill referred to a "designated entity." As a compromise, the conferees listed the American Institute in Taiwan "or such comparable successor" agency designated by the president.

● The administration had opposed a reference in the House bill to the performance of "consular" duties by employees of the new unofficial agency. The conferees referred to those duties "as if" they were consular functions.

● A House provision "strongly opposed" by the administration would have prohibited use of any federal funds for the institute without express authorization and appropriation by Congress. The administration said that would hamper the institute and make it impossible for government agencies to contract with the institute without prior approval of Congress. The provision was eliminated.

Saving the Taiwan Embassy

As finally passed by Congress over White House objections, the Taiwan relations bill prohibited the People's Republic of China from acquiring the former Washington embassy of Nationalist China, known as Twin Oaks.

Sen. Frank Church, D-Idaho, said senators had "sentimental reasons" for wanting to save Twin Oaks for Taiwan.

Under the committee-recommended bill, the Taiwan government would have been guaranteed its bank deposits, foreign exchange assets and other holdings earned in the United States after 1949 — when the Chiang Kai-shek government was forced to locate on Taiwan. But at the urging of the administration, the committee bill did not legislate the status of the embassy, which was acquired by the Nationalist Chinese government in 1945.

Administration spokesmen said the fate of the embassy should be left up to the courts. And the administration took the position that the embassy belonged to the mainland government, since it was now recognized by the United States as the legal government of China.

In an attempt to prevent Peking's acquisition of the property, the Republic of China on Dec. 22 sold the embassy and chancery for $10 to the Friends of Free China, a private, Washington-based group. The property was valued at more than $3 million. The group's chairman, Sen. Barry Goldwater, R-Ariz., took part in Senate debate on the issue, but then abstained from voting.

During committee hearings in February, State Department attorneys questioned the legality of the property transfer to the Friends of Free China.

Floor debate centered on the question of fairness versus legality. Proponents argued that Taiwan should be allowed to keep the embassy it occupied for 30 years, while opponents said the issue of property ownership legally should be resolved in the courts rather than by the Senate.

David L. Boren, D-Okla., argued that allowing Taiwan to keep its embassy would be "small compensation for a long and trusted ally. In light of the backhanded treatment received by our friend and ally on Taiwan, there is no justification for adding summary eviction to the list."

Referring to the general practice for dealing with diplomatic property, Boren said: "It may be normal diplomatic procedure to transfer control of such property when governments change, but there is very little normal about this whole issue."

Boren sponsored the embassy amendment, which stated that all property held by the Republic of China before Jan. 1, 1979, including the diplomatic property, would continue to belong to that government.

But Church said: "This is the first time in my experience in this body that the Senate has ever undertaken to determine the ownership of real property. I rather doubt that we have the authority to do that. I am positive we lack the competence to do it."

Congress, he said, should not "side with one side over the other for sentimental reasons."

And Church argued that legislation on the issue could prejudice the United States claims to 180 buildings on 51 tracts of land in mainland China that were seized in 1949.

Church and Javits offered a substitute amendment stating that the embassy ownership question should be resolved by the courts. That amendment was tabled on a 49-36 vote. Several moderate and liberal Democrats joined conservatives to kill the substitute.

The Boren amendment then was adopted by voice vote.

● Under the Senate bill, the United States was to have unofficial relations with "the people on Taiwan"; the House bill simply referred to Taiwan. The administration preferred the Senate version because it sounded less official. Conferees employed both phrases throughout the bill.

● The Senate bill would have established a joint commission of 12 members of Congress to oversee the American Institute. The conference version gave oversight authority to the "appropriate committees."

Passage of the Bill

The conference report on the bill was adopted by the House March 28, 1979, by a 339-50 vote and by the Senate on March 29 by a vote of 85-4.

The Taiwan Relations Act established unofficial relations between the United States and Taiwan and provided security assurances to the island. The final bill tied the United States closer to ensuring Taiwan's independence than the original legislation submitted by the Carter administration in January. Nevertheless, the White House found it acceptable, and President Carter signed it into law on April 10 (PL 96-8). *(Text, p. 343)*

Few, if any, members of Congress expressed great enthusiasm for the legislation, especially the provision for conducting relations with Taiwan through a private corporation.

Even the floor managers praised the bills only as the best legislation possible under the circumstances. Rep. Zablocki, chairman of the House Foreign Affairs Committee, referred to the proposed institute as a "Mickey Mouse operation."

The People's Republic of China on March 16 officially protested as "unacceptable" the Taiwan security provisions of the legislation. However, administration officials said Chinese unhappiness over the bill would not seriously disrupt U.S.-China relations.

The administration had wanted the legislation passed before the March 1 closing of the American Embassy in Taipei. Because that deadline was not met, the United States had no official or unofficial representation in Taiwan for more than a month.

The purpose of the legislation was to continue some form of relations with Taiwan even though the United States no longer recognized the Republic of China regime that governed the island. Under the legislation, the United States agreed to conduct its relations with Taiwan through a private corporation, the American Institute in Taiwan. Taiwan, in return, continued its ties with the United States through an unofficial Coordination Council for North American Affairs. *(Box, p. 44)*

The legislation assured that all trade, transportation and cultural links between the United States and Taiwan would remain in effect. *(pp. 52, 348)*

At the insistence of many members, the bill contained stronger language than President Carter wanted expressing American concern for the future security of Taiwan; it pledged continued arms sales to the Taiwan government and said the United States would take actions — not specified — in the event of an attack on Taiwan.

The changes made by Congress were "a vast improvement over the legislation initially proposed by the administration," said Frank Church, D-Idaho, chairman of the Senate Foreign Relations Committee, in explaining the final bill March 29. It "clarifies many uncertainties and ambiguities concerning trade, legal and economic issues."

Final Provisions

As cleared by Congress and signed by the president, the act:

● Stated it to be the policy of the United States "to preserve and promote extensive, close and friendly commercial, cultural and other relations between the people of the United States and the people on Taiwan."

● Declared that "peace and stability in the area are in the political, security and economic interests of the United States, and are matters of international concern."

● Declared that "the United States decision to establish diplomatic relations with the People's Republic of China rests upon the expectation that the future of Taiwan will be determined by peaceful means."

● Declared "any effort to determine the future of Taiwan by other than peaceful means, including by boycotts or embargoes, a threat to the peace and security of the Western Pacific area and of grave concern to the United States."

● Stated that the United States "will make available to Taiwan such defense articles and defense services in such quantity as may be necessary to enable Taiwan to maintain a sufficient self-defense capability." The nature and quantity of the defense services and arms were to be determined by the president and Congress "based solely upon their judgment of the needs of Taiwan."

● Declared that the United States will "maintain the capacity . . . to resist any resort to force or other forms of coercion that would jeopardize the security, or the social or economic system, of the people on Taiwan."

● Directed the president promptly to inform Congress of "any threat to the security of the social or economic system of the people on Taiwan and any danger to the interests of the United States arising therefrom." The president and Congress "shall determine, in accordance with constitutional processes, appropriate action by the United States in response to such danger."

● Authorized the United States to conduct its future relations with Taiwan through a private, non-profit, tax-exempt corporation, the American Institute in Taiwan, or "such comparable successor nongovernmental entity the president shall designate."

● Authorized U.S. government agencies, through the State Department, to contract with the institute for the purchase of services and supplies.

● Authorized the institute to enter into, perform and enforce agreements and other transactions with respect to Taiwan. Among other things, the institute was to channel the sale of arms by the United States to Taiwan.

● Directed the United States to deal with Taiwan through whatever unofficial agency was established by the Taiwan government in the United States.

● Authorized the institute to perform services to U.S. citizens such as those performed by consular offices.

● Directed the president to allow Taiwan in the future to maintain the same number of offices and personnel in the United States as it had before Jan. 1, 1979, the date the United States ended official relations with Taiwan.

● Mandated that all U.S. agreements and treaties with Taiwan would remain in effect unless otherwise terminated, except for the mutual defense treaty, which was to be terminated at the end of 1979.

● Recognized, for purposes of U.S. law, the validity of Taiwan domestic law, and of contracts entered into under Taiwan law.

● Stated that U.S. laws relating to foreign countries would apply to Taiwan.

● Stated that recognition of the People's Republic of China would not affect the ownership of property acquired by the Republic of China on Taiwan before Dec. 31, 1978. (This provision guaranteed continued ownership by the Taiwan government of its bank accounts and other assets in the United States, including its embassy and chancery property in Washington, D.C. The embassy had been claimed by Peking.)

● Authorized the secretary of state to treat Taiwan as a nation with a separate immigration quota. This would give both Taiwan and China annual quotas of 20,000.

● Exempted Taiwan, for three years, from restrictions on guarantees, insurance and loans by the Overseas Private Investment Corp. (OPIC). (OPIC guarantees were to be restricted in 1979 because per capita income on the island exceeded $1,000; under U.S. law OPIC could not issue guarantees in countries with incomes over that amount.)

● Provided that the House Foreign Affairs Committee and the Senate Foreign Relations Committee and "other appropriate committees" would monitor implementation of the legislation.

● Authorized the president to grant Taiwan representatives in the United States those diplomatic privileges and immunities "as may be necessary to the effective performance of their functions," provided that employees of the American Institute in Taiwan were granted comparable privileges.

● Authorized U.S. government employees to take temporary leaves of absence in order to work for the institute.

While at the institute they would not be considered employees of the U.S. government, but they would not lose seniority, pension or other benefits when they returned to government employment.

● Authorized funds appropriated to the secretary of state in fiscal 1980 to be used to carry out provisions of the legislation, including funding of the American Institute. Funds appropriated for the State Department were to finance the institute for the remainder of fiscal 1979.

● Defined "Taiwan" to include the islands of Taiwan and the Pescadores, "the people on those islands, corporations and other entities and associations created or organized under the laws applied on those islands, and the governing authorities on Taiwan recognized by the United States as the Republic of China prior to Jan. 1, 1979. . . ."

Continuing Taiwan Support

Despite congressional pledges in the Taiwan Relations Act and elsewhere to continue support for the Republic of China — and the failure of Sen. Goldwater's suit challenging the constitutionality of Carter's abrogation of the Taiwan defense treaty — Taiwan's friends on Capitol Hill kept up a barrage of charges that the Carter administration was betraying a longtime ally.

Goldwater and others cited several actions that, they said, added up to a deliberate policy of kicking Taiwan in the shins: the breaking off of diplomatic relations, the termination of the mutual defense treaty, the forced closing of five of Taiwan's 14 consulates in the United States, and the imposition of a one-year moratorium on arms sales to Taiwan.

Rumors circulated on Capitol Hill that the administration would continue in force a one-year moratorium, covering 1979, on arms sales to Taiwan. Then, Taiwan's representatives were turned away when they sought to meet with Commerce Department officials in Washington. Finally, in August Vice President Walter F. Mondale announced in Canton, China, that the United States was cancelling its 1946 aviation agreement with Taiwan in order to begin negotiations on an aviation agreement with China.

Goldwater took the Senate floor Sept. 25 to complain about Carter's attempts to "blackmail" Taiwan.

The proposed termination of the aviation agreement, he said, "is the latest slap in the face to Taiwan by the Carter administration. It is the latest demonstration by the State Department of its willingness to kowtow to the communist dictators who are suppressing human rights on the Chinese mainland."

The House Foreign Affairs Committee responded by holding hearings on recent treatment of Taiwan by the administration. At a hearing Oct. 23, representatives of American businesses in Taiwan echoed Goldwater's complaints. Deputy Secretary of State Warren M. Christopher responded to the complaints Nov. 8.

Aviation Agreement

Most of the controversy surrounded the administration's decision to end the aviation agreement, which determines schedules, fares and other details of air travel between the United States and Taiwan.

Robert P. Parker, president of the American Chamber of Commerce in Taiwan, said that ending the aviation agreement "is directly contrary to express representations made to American businessmen and to Congress" when Carter broke off relations with Taiwan.

Parker quoted statements by administration witnesses early in 1979 that the United States would maintain all treaties and agreements with Taiwan, other than the mutual defense treaty.

For example, State Department legal adviser Herbert J. Hansell told the Senate Foreign Relations Committee on Feb. 5: "Treaties and legal agreements and arrangements between the United States and Taiwan in force at the time of normalization [with China] will remain in force" except for the mutual defense treaty.

Similar assurances were made by Christopher, Assistant Secretary of State Richard Holbrooke and other officials.

Based on those assurances, Congress included a section in the Taiwan Relations Act approving "the continuation in force of all treaties and other international agreements" between the United States and Taiwan.

Parker charged that the decision to end the aviation agreement "contravenes the clear intent of Congress" that all agreements would continue in effect.

And Lester L. Wolff, D-N.Y., chairman of the House Asian and Pacific Affairs Subcommittee, told Christopher: "We were led to believe there would be a continuation of relations with the people on Taiwan. Now you're giving us a complete change of direction. I believe there was an intent to mislead the Congress in order to achieve passage of the Taiwan Relations Act."

In response, Christopher gave the following status of the 67 U.S.-Taiwan treaties and agreements: five, including the aviation agreement, "require current attention" and needed to be renegotiated; 29 agreements could remain in effect with no change; seven military agreements, including the mutual defense treaty, would be terminated at the end of 1979; two other agreements were rendered moot by the break-off of diplomatic relations; and 14 agreements were inactive or were no longer needed. *(See pp. 52, 348)*

Christopher said: "We do not have a policy to convert or terminate all of the treaties and agreements we maintain with Taiwan. Each agreement, as the circumstances require, will be considered on its own merits, on a case-by-case basis."

The aviation agreement "has become a hindrance to development of aviation relations with the PRC," Christopher said. Mainland China refused to negotiate an aviation agreement with the United States until Mondale announced that the U.S.-Taiwan agreement would be ended.

And Christopher argued that the U.S.-Taiwan agreement was outdated because "it purported to give us landing rights all through China," specifically in Nanjing and Shanghai on the mainland.

Christopher said the U.S.-Taiwan aviation agreement was being renegotiated, and would be converted into an agreement between the two unofficial agencies that represent the United States and Taiwan — the U.S. American Institute in Taiwan and Taiwan's Coordination Council for North American Affairs. A new agreement would allow for lower fares and more flights between the United States and Taiwan, he said.

Christopher's assurances satisfied some members of the House Foreign Affairs Committee, but not others.

Committee Chairman Clement J. Zablocki, D-Wis., said, "of course the aviation agreement has to be renegotiated. It's out of date." Zablocki said Wolff "is in error" about Congress being misled.

And Jonathan B. Bingham, D-N.Y., said: "I didn't feel misled at all" about the status of U.S.-Taiwan agreements.

"Surely we didn't intend that all agreements in force on a particular day would remain in effect in perpetuity."

But Republicans asked why the aviation agreement had to be ended.

"I don't understand why we can't amend the existing agreement, instead of bowing to pressure from the PRC in abrogating it," said Edward J. Derwinski, R-Ill. Mainland China "needs those flights into Peking more than we do."

And Benjamin A. Gilman, R-N.Y., complained that Congress was not told that some of the agreements with Taiwan would be ended. "Such terminations are contrary to the spirit of the law," he said.

Christopher promised to look into other complaints voiced by Taiwan's friends in Congress. Two such complaints were that the U.S. office in Taiwan was understaffed and that the United States withheld approval of permanent diplomatic license plates for Taiwan's representatives here.

But Christopher flatly rejected congressional complaints on the refusal of U.S. government officials to meet with Taiwan's representatives. Taiwan representatives were told in 1979 that they could not meet with officials of the U.S. Commerce Department in Washington.

"In neither country are the representatives of the unofficial agencies in contact with government officials," Christopher said.

Arms Sales to Taiwan

Upon ending diplomatic relations with Taiwan, Carter announced a one-year moratorium on new arms sales to the island. Deliveries of previous arms sales would be completed, he said.

The Taiwan Relations Act stated that the United States "will make available to Taiwan such defense articles and defense services in such quantity as may be necessary to enable Taiwan to maintain sufficient self-defense capability." But congressional conservatives charged that Carter planned to extend the freeze on arms sales through 1980.

In his testimony Nov. 8, 1979, Christopher said "there is no substance to the rumor." Starting next year "we shall continue to provide Taiwan access to selected defensive weapons."

Referring to other rumors that the United States might allow China to dictate what arms would be sold to Taiwan, Christopher said U.S. arms sales "will not be affected by a veto by any other party." And, he said, "we have not set an arbitrary limit on the dollar value" or "an arbitrary limit on the nature of weapons" to be sold to Taiwan.

Christopher refused to comment on specific weapons Washington would continue to sell Taiwan. But when Robert J. Lagomarsino, R-Calif., asked if Taiwan would be able to buy F-16 jet fighters, Christopher noted that Taiwan's previous requests for the F-16 had been rejected "on the grounds that it would violate the president's arms transfer policy." Under that policy, Carter pledged not to introduce more sophisticated weapons into any region. The F-16 was more advanced than any jet then in use by nations in South Asia.

Christopher denied reports that the administration had rejected Taiwan's request for the Harpoon anti-ship misssile. The request "is under consideration," he said.

In fact, arms sales did resume in 1980 with the State Department announcement, Jan. 3, that the United States would sell $280 million worth of weapons to Taiwan, thus ending the moratorium. Included in the deal were land- and sea-based air defense missiles and TOW anti-tank missiles. The U.S. again refused to sell Taiwan high-performance aircraft such as the F4, F16 or F18, but indicated its willingness to provide more F5Es. Congress had 30 days to review the decision, but was not considered likely to oppose it.

The Crisis in Afghanistan

The December 1979 Soviet invasion of Afghanistan raised concern in both Peking and Washington that the war there might spill over into Pakistan, a long-time ally of both China and the United States. On Jan. 4 President Carter contacted Congress about emergency legislation allowing the resumption of direct military aid to Islamabad — cut off earlier in 1979 — and received a positive response. At the same time, the U.S. sought to enlist the cooperation of China — which had supplanted the U.S. as Pakistan's primary source of arms — in an effort to demonstrate disapproval of Moscow's threat to the area, a request which was greeted warmly in Peking. The Soviet move also assured rapid passage of the China Trade Act as a further punishment against the Soviets in addition to other economic sanctions imposed on Russia by the United States. Congress promptly approved the treaty by lopsided margins on Jan. 24, 1980.

China wouldn't have gone Communist — if the Truman administration had had backbone.

Vice Presidential Candidate Richard Nixon, 1952

I can think of nothing more detrimental to freedom or peace than the recognition of Communist China.

Presidential Candidate Richard Nixon, 1960.

... We simply cannot afford to leave China forever outside the family of nations, there to nurture its fantasies, cherish its hates and threaten its neighbors.

Presidential Candidate Richard Nixon, 1967

Let me tell you what the world would be like if I had not taken the trip to Peking. One-fourth of all the people in the world live in the People's Republic of China. ... They are among the ablest people in the world. Their government is a Communist government. I do not agree with their philosophy. We will continue to have differences with their government. We will have disagreements with their philosophy. But if a billion people in the world, 10, 15, 20 years from now, were lined up in confrontation against the United States of America it would be a dangerous world.

I had to take the steps now to reduce that danger. We have done it so we have a better chance for a generation of peace for our young Americans.

President Richard Nixon, 1972

The China Issue in Presidential Campaigns: 1948-76

By 1976, China policy — once a major issue that inspired impassioned rhetoric — had moved from center stage to the wings as a subject for debate.

President Nixon's role in muting the China issue cannot be overestimated. Nixon — as senator and vice presidential candidate — had been a central figure in the anticommunist cold-war panic of the early post-war years, attacking the Democrats as "soft on communism" because of their policy toward China and the Soviet Union. "China wouldn't have gone communist," said vice presidential candidate Nixon in 1952, "if the Truman administration had had backbone."

President Nixon's sudden initiative toward rapprochement with Communist China in 1971-72 was so widely endorsed or at least tolerated that it not only deprived Democrat George McGovern, a foreign policy liberal, of a campaign issue in 1972 but provided the source for a Nixon boast of accomplishment during his first term.

The subject hardly came up during the next presidential contest, between Jimmy Carter and Gerald Ford, who had inherited Nixon's foreign policy and his chief China policy architect, Secretary of State Henry Kissinger.

Such a political consensus on the once-volatile issue could never have been predicted in the late 1940s.

1948

On Nov. 2, 1948, in the midst of some of the most severe fighting of the Chinese civil war, Harry S Truman surprised most political observers by winning a full term as president. Democrats not only won the White House over highly favored New York Gov. Thomas E. Dewey, R, but also regained control of the House and Senate.

Almost three months before the election — on Aug. 13 — Secretary of State George C. Marshall had advised the staff of the U.S. Embassy in Nanjing (the Nationalist regime's capital) that it was "not likely that the situation will make it possible for us at this juncture to formulate any rigid plans for our future policy in China."

Up to that point, support for much of the Truman administration's foreign policy had been bipartisan, due mostly to the efforts of Sen. Arthur H. Vandenberg Jr., R-Mich., chairman of the Senate Foreign Relations Committee and a converted isolationist.

Republicans Attack

But on Oct. 3 — one month before the presidential election — the House Foreign Affairs Subcommittee on World Communism, chaired by Rep. Frances P. Bolton, R-Ohio, issued a report calling China the "active theater" in the cold war. The report said the communists were using China as the testing ground for tactics they might employ in an attempt to take over the world. The subcommittee recommended that the United States give Chiang Kai-shek's Nationalist government a "guarantee of territorial and political integrity."

And in the Senate, Republicans H. Styles Bridges, N.H., Homer E. Capehart, Ind., William F. Knowland, Calif., William Langer, N.D., and Kenneth S. Wherry, Neb., urged the administration to provide more military and economic aid to Chiang Kai-shek.

During the campaign, Gov. Dewey, flanked by the brothers Dulles — John Foster (later to become secretary of state) and Allen W. (later director of the Central Intelligence Agency) — as foreign policy advisers, charged that the Truman administration had done far too little to protect China from communism.

The Republican platform for 1948 stated: "We will foster and cherish our historic policy of friendship with China and assert our deep interest in the maintenance of its integrity and friendship." The Democratic 1948 platform, in contrast, cited only the Truman administration's achievement in providing China with "vital aid."

Two days after the election, President Truman told Congress that "many difficulties" were involved in making aid to China effective and that U.S. officials constantly had to oversee how funds were expended.

1952

By 1952 the Chinese Communists had successfully routed the Nationalist forces, sent Chiang Kai-shek and his allies in flight to Taiwan, proclaimed the People's Republic and signed a 30-year treaty with the Soviet Union. The communist North Koreans had launched their Soviet-inspired attack on South Korea (June 25, 1950), and a successful U.S. military drive to the Yalu River in North Korea had brought masses of Chinese "volunteers" into the conflict (October 1950). The United Nations' "police action" had become a bloody and frustrating war, the conduct of which became a prime issue in the 1952 campaign.

Since Chiang's fall, the Truman administration had attempted to maintain a "hands off Taiwan" policy despite strong Republican objections. But the invasion of Korea prompted the president on June 27, 1950, to station the U.S. 7th Fleet in the Taiwan Strait both to protect the island from the communists and to prevent any further Nationalist attacks on the mainland.

McCarthyism

The four years between presidential elections also had seen the advent of McCarthyism, as Sen. Joseph R. McCarthy, R Wis., repeatedly charged that many State Department officials, especially those responsible for U.S. Far Eastern policy, were either communists, sympathizers or dupes. Although he subsequently lost interest in China, McCarthy and his accusations remained a key campaign issue.

Political rhetoric concerning the Far East was as bitter, emotional and often vicious in the months leading up to and during the 1952 election campaign as at any time during the postwar period. Republicans openly blamed the Democrats for the fall of Chiang and the invasion of South Korea. Many agreed with McCarthy that there had been communist influence on policy-making in the Far East and called for investigations.

As McCarthy and his allies increased their attacks, naming specific officials in the department, President Truman personally replied. On May 2, 1952, Truman condemned what he called "political gangsters" who "are motivated by such a lust for power that they are willing to wreck the lives and careers of innocent public servants" by creating "an atmosphere in which a charge is a conviction in the public mind despite the lack of evidence." He added: "I think they are worse than Communists, and I think they are partners with them."

As the election approached, the rhetoric sharpened. Campaigning for the GOP presidential nomination, Sen. Robert A. Taft of Ohio advocated arming the Nationalist Chinese for a full-scale attack on the mainland. On Jan. 12, 1952, he said the State Department's "pro-Communist policies . . . fully justified" Sen. McCarthy's demands that the department be investigated.

Another presidential contender, former Minnesota Gov. Harold E. Stassen, R, charged the "blinding, blundering, bewildering" Far East policy of the "spy-riddled" Truman administration was directly responsible for U.S. casualties in Korea.

GOP Convention

On July 7, 1952, Gen. Douglas MacArthur, whom Truman had dismissed as commander of U.S. and U.N. forces in the Far East because of the general's repeated public statements urging expansion of the conflict into Communist China, made the keynote speech of the Republican National Convention in Chicago.

MacArthur charged that the administration had "condemned" the people of China to "Communist tyranny" and contended that when the Chinese entered the Korean conflict, "our leaders lacked the courage to fight to a military decision, even though victory was readily within our grasp — a victory which . . . might well have saved continental Asia from Red domination."

John Foster Dulles wrote a strongly worded plank in the Republican 1952 platform charging that the administration had "squandered the unprecedented power and prestige" the United States had enjoyed since the end of World War II, had scuttled the Nationalist Chinese regime, had caused the Korean war through ambiguous policy statements and then "produced stalemates and ignominious bartering" after war broke out.

On July 11 the convention chose Dwight D. Eisenhower and Sen. Richard M. Nixon, Calif., as its presidential and vice presidential candidates. Nixon had won his Senate seat in 1950 in a hard-fought race against Rep. Helen Gahagan Douglas, a liberal Democrat. Nixon's charges that Douglas frequently voted with Rep. Vito Marcantonio, American Labor Party, N.Y., whose voting record often had been described as pro-communist, established Nixon's reputation, to some, as an unscrupulous campaigner.

Democrats

The Democrats, also meeting in Chicago, July 26 chose Illinois Gov. Adlai E. Stevenson and Sen. John Sparkman of Alabama as their candidates and adopted a platform pledging "a continued effort, by every honorable means, to bring about a fair and effective peace settlement in Korea in accordance with the principles of the United Nations' charter. . . . We reject the ridiculous notions that would have the United States face the aggressors alone. That would be the most expensive — and the most dangerous — method of seeking security."

It added: "Our military and economic assistance to the Nationalist Government of China on Formosa [Taiwan] has strengthened that vital outpost of the free world and will be continued."

Campaign

During the campaign, Eisenhower endorsed the Truman administration's decision to enter the Korean conflict but accused the president of allowing the nation to become militarily weak and of announcing "to all the world that it had written off most of the Far East as beyond our direct concern." Secretary of State Dean Acheson's 1950 definition of the U.S. "Asian defense perimeter" so as to exclude Korea had directly invited communist aggression, Eisenhower charged.

Stevenson defended the administration's conduct of the war, and on Oct. 18 President Truman charged in Providence, R.I., that Eisenhower "held out a false hope to the mothers of America in an effort to pick up a few votes" by calling for a withdrawal of U.S. troops from the front lines. Truman pointed out that 50 percent more South Koreans were fighting in the conflict than were Americans.

But on Oct. 24 Eisenhower found what many observers felt was a paydirt issue in a nation deeply disturbed by the war, its mounting casualties and the stalemate in truce negotiations. He told an audience in Detroit, Mich., that he would "forgo the diversion of politics" after the election and "concentrate on the job of ending the Korean War." The former general pledged: "I shall go to Korea" in an effort to end the conflict. Stevenson quickly denounced the proposed trip as a "slick idea that gets votes by playing upon our hopes for a quick end to the war." President Truman charged that Eisenhower was attempting a "superman" approach to the problem and that "anybody who poses and talks like a superman is a fraud."

On Nov. 4 Eisenhower and Nixon were elected by a wide majority. The Republicans also gained control of both houses of Congress by narrow margins.

1956

From 1952 through 1956, French power in Southeast Asia collapsed and the United States, although not signing the Geneva accord ending the seven-and-one-half-year war in Indochina, acquiesced to the partition of Vietnam while bolstering its campaign to thwart Communist China's designs on Taiwan and Southeast Asia.

1955 Taiwan Strait Crisis

On Jan. 18, Communist forces seized the offshore island of Yijiang, 210 miles north of Taiwan, and seemed prepared to invade the nearby Dachen Islands. The situation led President Eisenhower to ask Congress, in a special message Jan. 24, for explicit authority to use U.S. armed forces to protect Taiwan, the adjoining Pescadores Islands and "related positions and territories." It was essential to U.S. security that Taiwan "should remain in friendly hands," Eisenhower said.

What remained unclear was the administration's intent regarding Quemoy, Matsu and the other offshore islands. To many Democrats, these islands — unlike Taiwan — clearly belonged to mainland China, and the question of their disposition was an internal matter outside the scope of legitimate U.S. security interests. They feared that the Nationalists, in their efforts to regain the mainland, would use this "fatal ambiguity" over the offshore islands to maneuver the United States into a war with Communist China.

Congress Jan. 28 passed a resolution granting the president the authority he had requested. On Feb. 9, the Senate ratified a mutual defense treaty with Nationalist China (signed by Secretary of State Dulles on Dec. 2, 1954) whereby both countries agreed to meet an armed attack against U.S. or Nationalist territories, including Taiwan, the Pescadores islands and "such other territories as may be determined by mutual agreement."

The Nationalist government Feb. 5 requested U.S. protection of a withdrawal operation from the Dachen Islands. Fighting continued for some weeks in the Quemoy and Matsu area, then abated, although a formal cease-fire never was concluded.

Stevenson Statement

On an April 11 national radio program, Adlai Stevenson (who was to announce his candidacy for the 1956 Democratic presidential nomination seven months later) proposed that the United States should seek an international declaration "condemning the use of force in the Formosa Strait" and an agreement by free nations "to stand with us in the defense of Formosa [Taiwan] against any aggression, pending some final settlement of its status."

He stated: "The possibility of war just now seems to hinge upon Quemoy and Matsu, small islands that lie almost as close to the coast of China as Staten Island does to New York." He asked: "Are the offshore islands essential to the security of the United States? Are they, indeed, even essential to the defense of Formosa [Taiwan] — which all Americans have agreed upon since President Truman sent the 7th Fleet there five years ago?"

Stevenson concluded: "Should we be plunged into another great war, the maintenance of our allies and the respect and the good will of the uncommitted nations of Asia will be far more important to us than the possession of these offshore islands by Chiang Kai-shek ever could be."

Secretary Dulles replied the next day that Stevenson "suggests, as original ideas, the very approaches which the government has been and is actively exploring."

Chinese Offer. The State Department June 12, 1956, revealed it had rejected a Chinese proposal (made on May 12) that Secretary of State Dulles and Chinese Foreign Minister Chou En-lai meet to discuss Taiwan and other problems. The department said the proposed talks would be held on too short notice and pointed out that 13 Americans were still being held by the Communists.

Conventions. On Aug. 16-17, 1956, Adlai Stevenson and Sen. Estes E. Kefauver, Tenn., were nominated at the Democratic convention in Chicago.

The party's 1956 platform pledged "determined opposition to the admission of Communist China into the U.N.," and urged "a continuing effort to effect the release

of all Americans detained by Communist China." It charged that Secretary Dulles "brags of 'brink of war'" rather than making "our peaceful purpose clear beyond dispute. . . ."

On Aug. 22, President Eisenhower and Vice President Nixon were renominated at the Republican convention. In a convention speech, Senate Minority Leader William F. Knowland of California pledged to fight Chinese Communist membership in the United Nations "as long as I have a voice and a vote" in the Senate. (He was defeated two years later in the California gubernatorial election.)

The GOP platform pledged "to oppose the seating of China in the U.N." and denounced "any trade with the Communist world that would threaten the security of the United States and our allies."

Campaign

War in the Middle East and uprisings in Hungary and Poland dominated the news during the last weeks of the 1956 campaign, eclipsing domestic issues and changing the emphasis in international policy debates. China rarely was mentioned.

In a Sept. 5 news conference, President Eisenhower defended his Far East policy, stating that when he took office the French "were involved in a hopelessly losing war in Indochina" and could have lost "the whole peninsula." The Geneva settlement, the president said, "at least gave the free world a firm foothold and under stronger leadership." The Korean conflict was still going on, he said, "under conditions where it was impossible to win. We were suffering losses merely to hold the line we then had. It was settled and we still hold that line."

President Eisenhower was re-elected Nov. 6 with the largest popular vote in history and a plurality matched only three times in the last century, but the Democrats retained control of the House and Senate.

1960

In 1957 the administration restated its determination to keep Communist China out of the U.N. and its opposition to the establishment of diplomatic relations with Peking. But Secretary Dulles expressed some flexibility on the question of trade and, on Aug. 22, the State Department announced that restrictions on travel to China by some newsmen were being lifted. Three days later, the Chinese accused the United States of "insufferable arrogance" in agreeing to "send its correspondents to China just on the basis of its own unilateral decision" and "refusing reciprocal visas to Chinese correspondents."

Taiwan Again

While the United States was preoccupied with events in the Middle East, Communist China resumed military operations against the Nationalist-held offshore islands in August 1958, concentrating heavy artillery barrages against Quemoy. As in 1954-55, tensions mounted rapidly, buoyed by speculation that the Communists were preparing an invasion and that the United States was poised for massive intervention.

Through September and October, both sides mounted massive propaganda campaigns. Soviet Premier Khrushchev declared Moscow's solidarity with Peking, while President Eisenhower and Secretary Dulles alternated pledges of "no retreat" with pleas for a cease-fire. Dulles flew to Taiwan Oct. 20, reportedly to persuade Chiang Kai-shek to reduce the size of his forces deployed on the offshore islands, and the Communists soon scaled down the bombardment of Quemoy to an every-other-day affair of no military significance.

In the midst of the crisis, a number of Democrats in Congress expressed concern that the administration was overly anxious to get militarily involved in a situation that did not warrant such involvement.

One of them, Sen. John F. Kennedy, D-Mass, stated Sept. 13 that "the weight of military, diplomatic, political and historical judgment would dictate a contrary policy concerning Formosa [Taiwan]." His statement came one week after Vice President Nixon's observation that the United States "could make no greater mistake than by appearing to be a paper tiger" in the Far East, because "in dealing with dictatorships you do not maintain peace by appearing to be weak but only by maintaining strength militarily and diplomatically."

During the 1958 congressional election campaign, Nixon Oct. 13 rebutted a statement issued by the Democratic Advisory Council charging that the Republicans were leading "us to the brink of having to fight a nuclear war" and urging that the United States refer the dispute over Quemoy and Matsu to the United Nations. Nixon said the council had "the same defensive, defeatist, fuzzy-headed thinking which contributed to the loss of China and led to the Korean war."

Conventions

On July 13-14, 1960, the Democrats nominated Sen. Kennedy and Senate Majority Leader Lyndon B. Johnson, Texas, as their presidential and vice presidential candidates. The Democratic platform reaffirmed "our pledge of determined opposition to the present admission of Communist China" to the United Nations and "likewise to defending Formosa [Taiwan]." It added: "Although normal diplomatic relations between our governments are impossible under present conditions, we shall welcome any evidence that the Chinese Communist government is genuinely prepared to create a new relationship based on respect for international obligations, including the release of American prisoners."

The Republicans July 27 chose Richard Nixon as their candidate, with U.S. Ambassador to the United Nations Henry Cabot Lodge as his running mate. The GOP platform stated only that opposition to Communist China's entry into the United Nations and the establishment of diplomatic relations with Peking would continue.

Campaign

The only debate on China policy between Kennedy and Nixon during the campaign concerned the importance of defending Quemoy and Matsu.

In two televised debates on Oct. 7 and 13, the candidates expressed differing opinions. Kennedy criticized the ambiguity of the nation's commitment to defend the two offshore islands, saying it was "unwise to take the chance of being dragged into a war which may lead to a world war over two islands which are not strategically defensible," and that "our line should be drawn in the sea" between Taiwan and the mainland.

Nixon countered that "these two islands are in the area of freedom [and] we should not force our Nationalist allies to get off of them and give them to the Communists." The issue blossomed as Kennedy called Nixon "trigger-happy"

while Nixon said Kennedy was advocating a course of "surrender."

On Nov. 8, Kennedy defeated Nixon in the closest presidential election of the 20th century.

1964

The next four years witnessed the evolution of the Sino-Soviet split, the deterioration of the Chinese Communist economic program (the "Great Leap Forward"), the Chinese-Indian border dispute, the Cuban missile crisis and the assassination of President Kennedy.

Vietnam. But most important to U.S.-Chinese relations was America's growing involvement in Indochina. By the time of his death, President Kennedy's administration had supplied South Vietnam with 16,000 U.S. military advisers and large amounts of economic and military aid.

After Kennedy's death, the Johnson administration quickly moved to shore up what political stability there was in South Vietnam with increased military aid, including more troops.

Gulf of Tonkin. On Aug. 2 and 4, 1964, U.S. destroyers patrolling the Gulf of Tonkin off the coast of North Vietnam reported torpedo attacks by Communist PT boats, and President Johnson ordered a retaliatory air strike at their bases. Congress Aug. 7 overwhelmingly passed the Gulf of Tonkin Resolution authorizing the president "to take all necessary measures to repel any armed attack against the forces of the United States and to prevent further aggression."

Campaign

The Republicans July 15 had nominated Sen. Barry Goldwater (Ariz.) as their presidential candidate and adopted a platform stating: "We are opposed to the recognition of Red China. We oppose its admission into the United Nations. We steadfastly support free China." On Vietnam, the platform charged that the Democrats had "encouraged an increase of aggression in South Vietnam by appearing to set limits on America's willingness to act."

The Democrats Aug. 26 chose President Johnson as their candidate for president, with Sen. Hubert H. Humphrey of Minnesota as his running mate. The Democratic platform did not make the usual mention of Communist China, but said only: "We will support our friends in and around the rim of the Pacific and encourage a growing understanding of peoples, expansion of cultural exchanges and strengthening of ties."

U.S. policy in Vietnam became a double-edged campaign issue as Sen. Goldwater found in it evidence of the administration's "no-win" policy against communism while Johnson linked his actions in the Gulf of Tonkin to those of the United States in the Cuban missile crisis as examples of the successful application of force with restraint.

On Sept. 28, the president told a Manchester, N.H., audience that he was opposed to getting involved in "a war with 700 million Chinese." He also pledged that the United States was "not going north [in Vietnam] and drop bombs at this stage."

Johnson's overwhelming victory at the polls Nov. 3 supplied no answer to the increasingly pressing question in Vietnam — whether to step up the degree and scope of U.S. involvement in the war or encourage efforts to seek a negotiated settlement of the conflict.

1968

That question was answered in the next four years by Lyndon Johnson, who ordered the bombing of North Vietnam only three months after the 1964 election. From that point on, the U.S. commitment in the Vietnam struggle grew precipitously. It often overshadowed serious domestic problems, distorted the U.S. economy and loomed over U.S. foreign policy. Its costs soared to more than $2 billion a month; reflecting the expense of the war, the federal budget by fiscal 1969 was at a record $186 billion, with $80 billion of that for defense. The U.S. troop commitment by late 1968 was 535,000, and in the wake of the enemy's Tet offensive, U.S. casualties were running high. *(Details, pp. 29-36, boxes, pp. 35, 217)*

The burden of the conflict was brought home to the American people by regular television coverage, anti-war demonstrations, inflationary pressures and the 1968 tax surcharge, and by the presidential campaign bids of three Democrats strongly opposed to the war — Sens. Eugene J. McCarthy, Minn., Robert F. Kennedy, N.Y., and George McGovern, S.D.

The first indication of U.S. readiness to de-escalate the conflict came March 31, 1968, when President Johnson — in the same speech in which he announced he would not run for re-election — said he had ordered a limited bombing halt of North Vietnam. On Oct. 31, only days before the election, Johnson extended the bombing freeze to all of North Vietnam.

Conventions

The Republicans, meeting in Miami Aug. 5-8, chose Richard Nixon once again as their presidential candidate, with Maryland Gov. Spiro T. Agnew as his running mate.

The GOP platform's section on China stated: "We do not intend to conduct foreign policy in such manner as to make the United States a world policeman. However, we will not condone aggression, or so-called 'wars of national liberation,' or naively discount the continuing threats of Moscow and Peking. . . . Under existing conditions, we cannot favor recognition of Communist China or its admission to the United Nations."

The Vietnam plank was surprisingly dovish, calling for decreased U.S. involvement and for vigorous pursuit of negotiations. The section was widely interpreted as an eclectic effort, reflecting the thinking of New York Gov. Nelson A. Rockefeller and Nixon, with few concessions to the more conservative views of California Gov. Ronald Reagan. The plank was drafted primarily by Rep. Peter H. B. Frelinghuysen, N.J., a Rockefeller supporter, and it replaced a negatively worded plank in the original draft which warned that any negotiated settlement would be "unacceptable" unless it assured Vietnamese self-determination.

While violence erupted in the city streets and thousands of police and guards imposed security precautions unprecedented in the annals of American political conventions, the Democrats met in Chicago Aug. 26-29 and nominated Hubert H. Humphrey for president and Sen. Edmund S. Muskie, Maine, for vice president.

The Democratic platform did not mention the issue of recognizing Communist China or allowing it into the United Nations. Instead, the platform stated: "The immediate prospects that China will emerge from its self-imposed isolation are dim. But both Asians and Americans will have to coexist with the 750 million Chinese on the mainland. We shall continue to make it clear that we are prepared to cooperate with China whenever it is ready to become a responsible member of the international community. We would actively encourage economic, social and cultural exchange with Mainland China as a means of freeing that nation and her people from their narrow isolation."

Humphrey on July 12 had endorsed the removal of trade restrictions against Communist China and a "shift" in total U.S. foreign policy basis from one of "confrontation and containment" to one of "reconciliation and peaceful engagement."

The platform met the demands of the party's liberals word for word in almost every section except that which dealt with U.S. policy in Vietnam.

Unlike the GOP platform, which urged decreased U.S. involvement in Vietnam, Democrats called for a continued strong American war effort. While the Democrats agreed with Republicans that the South Vietnamese eventually should take over their nation's defense, they gave no indication that an expanded Vietnamese role could lead to U.S. troop reductions in the near future.

Campaign

The Vietnam war had dominated preconvention activity, especially among the Democrats. It loomed over the general election as the single most important issue. Both candidates knew that, but each had to play it differently. The burden of the issue was on Humphrey and the Democrats.

Nixon avoided most discussion of Vietnam policy because he said he did not want to jeopardize the peace negotiations under way in Paris.

But Humphrey, plagued by heckling by anti-war elements virtually everywhere he sought to speak, had to make a break and establish some measure of independence from the unpopular war program of the Johnson Administration. His significant step to win some of the anti-war Democrats to his side came in a Sept. 30 nationally televised address from Salt Lake City, Utah, when he said he would stop the bombing of North Vietnam "as an acceptable risk for peace."

President Johnson actually took that step one month later. Humphrey appeared satisfied. The combination of his own softened stand and the president's decision won him, at least for the moment, the support of many of the Democrats who had been most disaffected at Chicago.

But in a close election, Nixon weathered Humphrey's strong comeback and won by a half-million vote margin.

1972

By 1972, Nixon's establishment of contacts with the Chinese Communist government — publicized and symbolized by his trip to Peking in February 1972 — was a *fait accompli*, a reversal of the hard-line U.S. policy toward China of two decades, accomplished with surprising ease, suddenness and wide public support.

Paradoxically, the GOP four years earlier had reaffirmed its unyielding opposition to recognition of Communist China, while the Democratic Party's platform in 1968 had stressed coexistence and cooperation with the Peking regime and had spoken of "freeing that nation and her people from their narrow isolation."

By adopting, in effect, the Democratic Party's previous China position for his 1972 campaign, Nixon pre-empted the issue. In fact, he used his China trip as a campaign talking point, citing the diplomatic initiative as part of his search for a generation of world peace.

Nixon had cut his losses in Vietnam, too, at least in terms of public opinion. Even though he had widened the theatre of war in Indochina with the invasion of Laos and the bombing and invasion of Cambodia, he had met his commitment to an American public weary of the conflict to begin pulling U.S. troops out of South Vietnam.

As one-time Nixon aide Jeb Stuart Magruder opined: "At no time during the four years of his Presidency . . . was President Nixon ever considered to be at fault for that war . . . I don't think the public ever forgave the Democratic Party for that war."

Conventions

The Democratic platform adopted at the convention in Miami Beach in July 1972 commented only briefly on the China question, and the Democrats' discomfiture was evident. "The beginning of a new U.S.-China relationship is welcome and important," the platform stated. "However, so far, little of substance has changed, and the exaggerated secrecy and rhetoric of the Nixon administration have produced unnecessary complications in our relationship with our allies and friends in Asia and with the U.S.S.R.

"What is needed now is serious negotiation on trade, travel exchanges and progress on more basic issues. The U.S. should take the steps necessary to establish regular diplomatic relations with China."

The Republican platform, adopted at the national convention in Miami Beach a few weeks later, took credit for ending the isolation of China and for starting "constructive new relationships with the Soviet Union and the People's Republic of China."

"Before this administration," the GOP platform declared, "a presidential visit to Peking would have been unthinkable. Yet our President has gone there to open a candid airing of differences so that they will not lead some day to war. All over the world tensions have eased as . . . the strongest of the nations and the most populous of nations have started discoursing again. . . . While profound differences remain between the United States and China, at least a generation of hostility has been replaced by frank discussions. In February 1972 rules of international conduct were agreed upon which should make the Pacific region a more peaceful area now and in the future."

Campaign

The central and most passionately held concern of the 1972 Democratic presidential nominee, Sen. George McGovern of South Dakota, was peace. As a prominent "dove," he advocated improved relations with the communist world, China as well as the Soviet Union, Cuba and North Vietnam. But in 1972, Nixon — fortuitously or by political design — had co-opted much of McGovern's expected constituency through his spectacular China initiative and seemed to have persuaded many voters that "peace with honor" was right around the corner in Vietnam.

McGovern's campaign was plagued from the outset by a series of political gaffes, including his selection and later abandonment of Sen. Thomas F. Eagleton, D-Mo., as his running mate, and his roundly scored plan to give each U.S. resident an annual cash guarantee of $1,000. Nor did his criticism of Nixon's continuing bombing of Indochina catch hold with the voters. Nixon won the contest with one of the largest pluralities in U.S. election history.

1976

China remained muted as a campaign issue in the contest between Republican President Gerald Ford and Democrat Jimmy Carter.

After taking over the presidency from the departed Richard Nixon, who had resigned rather than face a likely impeachment trial stemming from the Watergate scandal, Ford largely continued the foreign policy of his predecessor and Secretary of State Henry Kissinger, who had stayed on in the Ford administration.

On Nov. 29, 1975, Ford began a five-day trip to mainland China; he had been there in 1972 as House minority leader. His reception, while cordial, differed from the elaborate welcome given Nixon in 1972. Mao's age and the illness of Premier Chou En-lai seemed to preclude any immediate significant advances in Sino-U.S. relations, but the trip at least symbolized Ford's desire to continue the Nixon initiatives.

For his part, Carter — when he spoke of China at all — generally endorsed the communications between the two countries that Nixon had begun. The brevity of his China utterances as a candidate made his subsequent moves toward recognizing China as president all the more unexpected and dramatic.

The final withdrawal of American forces in Vietnam, and the subsequent victory by the North Vietnamese, likewise removed the Indochina war as a major issue in the 1976 campaign.

Conventions

The Democratic platform adopted July 14, 1976, in New York City, was brief and unspecific on the subject of China. That plank, in its entirety, read: "The recent improvement in relations with China, which has received bipartisan support, is a welcome recognition that there are few areas in which our vital interests clash with those of China. Our relations with China should continue to develop on peaceful lines, including early movement toward normalizing diplomatic relations in the context of a peaceful resolution of the future of Taiwan."

The Republicans — who treated Nixon's China breakthrough as a feather in their cap in an otherwise downbeat and defensive post-Watergate campaign year — had more to say about China than did the Democrats. Ronald Reagan — President Ford's conservative challenger — did not make a serious issue of it at the convention.

The GOP platform, ratified Aug. 17, in Kansas City, Mo., stated:

A development of significance for the future of Asia and for the world came to fruition in 1972 as our communications were restored with the People's Republic of China. This event has allowed us to initiate dialogue with the leaders of a quarter of the earth's population, and trade channels with the People's Republic have been opened, leading to benefits for each side.

The People's Republic of China can and will play an increasingly important role in world affairs. We shall seek to engage the People's Republic of China in an expanded network of contacts and trade. Such a process cannot realistically proceed at a forced or incautious pace; the measured but steady growth of our relations best serves our interests. We do not ignore the profound differences in our respective philosophies, governmental institutions, policies and views on individual liberty, and we are hopeful that basic human rights will be extended to the Chinese people. What is truly fundamental is that we have established regular working channels with the People's Republic of China and that this process can form an important contribution to world peace.

Our friendly relations with one great power should not be considered as a challenge to any other nation, large or small. The United States government, while engaged in a normalization of relations with the People's Republic of China, will continue to support the freedom and independence of our friend and ally, the Republic of China, and its 16 million people. The United States will fulfill and keep its commitments, such as the mutual defense treaty, with the Republic of China.

Campaign

Candidate Carter gave little indication during the campaign that he planned any major innovations in China policy if he became president. On March 15, 1976, before his nomination, he told a Chicago group that "The United States has a great stake in a nationally independent, secure, and friendly China. The present turmoil in Chinese domestic politics could be exploited by the Soviets to promote a Sino-Soviet reconciliation which might be inimical to international stability and to American interests. I believe that we should explore more actively the possibility of widening American-Chinese trade relations and of further consolidating our political relationships."

In a June 23 statement, Carter advocated full diplomatic relations with the People's Republic of China but indicated that they were contingent upon guarantees by the PRC that it would leave Taiwan alone.

President Ford had even less to say on the subject — perhaps to forestall a confrontation with such conservative supporters of Ronald Reagan as Sen. Jesse Helms, R-N.C., a hard-line opponent of normalizing relations with Peking. In any case, China was not the subject of much presidential oratory in 1976, and when Ford was queried on his views by newsmen his responses were not of the kind that would ruffle many feathers: "Our interest is, I think, very pragmatic. Eight hundred million-plus individuals, a tremendous mass in a very strategic part of the world — it is an area where we have to continue the normalization process...."

In a debate between the two candidates on Oct. 6, both men advocated continued negotiations toward normalization of relations with Peking while asserting their support for Taiwan. Carter — attempting to turn Nixon's China initiatives to his own advantage — added that Ford had "frittered away" the promise held out by the Shanghai communiqué of 1972. *(Box, this page)*

China probably figured most prominently in Ford's campaign fortunes in an oblique way when ex-President Nixon accepted an invitation to pay another visit to Peking. The trip thrust Nixon back into the headlines — and served to remind voters of Ford's unpopular pardon of the disgraced president — just three days before the New Hampshire presidential primary.

Ford and Carter Debate China

The China issue was raised during the second nationally televised debate between President Ford and challenger Jimmy Carter on Oct. 6, 1976, in San Francisco.

Q. Mr. President, the policy of your administration is to normalize relations with mainland China. That means at some time establishing full diplomatic relations, and obviously doing something about the mutual defense treaty with Taiwan. If you are elected will you move to establish full diplomatic relations with Peking and will you abrogate the mutual defense treaty with Taiwan, and as a corollary would you provide mainland China with military equipment if the Chinese were to ask for it?

Ford: Our relationship with the People's Republic of China is based upon the Shanghai Communiqué of 1972 and that communiqué calls for the normalization of relations between the United States and the People's Republic. It doesn't set a time schedule, it doesn't make a determination as to how that relationship should be achieved in relationship to our current diplomatic recognition and obligations to the Taiwanese government. The Shanghai Communiqué does say that the differences between the People's Republic on the one hand and Taiwan on the other shall be settled by peaceful means. The net result is that this administration, and during my time as the President for the next four years, we will continue to move for normalization of relations in the traditional sense and we will insist that the disputes between Taiwan and the People's Republic be settled peacefully, as was agreed in the Shanghai Communiqué of 1972.

The Ford administration will not let down, will not eliminate or forget our obligations to the people of Taiwan. We feel that there must be a continued obligation to the people, the some 19- or 20-million people in Taiwan, and as we move during the next four years, those will be the policies of this administration.

Q: And, sir, the military equipment for the mainland Chinese?

Ford: There is no policy of this government to give to the People's Republic or to sell to the People's Republic of China military equipment. I do not believe that we, the United States, should sell, give or otherwise transfer military hardware to the People's Republic of China or any other Communist nation such as the Soviet Union and the like.

Q: Governor Carter?

Carter: ... I would certainly pursue the normalization of relationships with the People's Republic of China. We opened up a great opportunity in 1972, which pretty well has been frittered away under Mr. Ford, that ought to be a constant inclination towards friendship. But I would never let that friendship with the People's Republic of China stand in the way of the preservation of the independence and freedom of the people of Taiwan.

It is time to lift the embargoes [against China] pure and simple. It is an anachronism, a monument to bureaucratic rigidity and a symbol of a bankrupt China policy we have been pursuing for the last 20 years.

Prof. Alexander Eckstein,
testifying before the Joint
Economic Committee
Dec. 9, 1970

In trade, our interests are served by your expanding exports of natural resources and industrial products. And at the same time your interests are served by the purchases you can finance through those exports.

As you industrialize, you provide a higher standard of living for your people. And at the same time our interests are served — for this will increase the flow of trade, narrow the wealth gap between the developed and the developing world, and thus help alleviate a major source of global instability.

Vice President Walter Mondale,
address to the Chinese people in
Peking, Aug. 27, 1979

Trade With China

Perhaps the greatest support in the United States for closer relations with China has come from the business community, which is eager to open the huge China market to American goods. In statements accompanying the 1979 normalization initiatives, President Carter emphasized the importance of the trade issue, saying the normalization opens "a new vista for prosperous trade relationships with almost a billion people in the People's Republic of China."

The support of closer U.S.-China ties by the U.S. business community may — arguably — also have helped to soften the response of conservative politicians to recognition of the People's Republic and the termination of diplomatic relations with Taiwan. With business anticipating potentially big gains in a large, virtually untapped communist market, the customary alliance of American business interests and the political right was all but absent.

Background

Protectionist trade policy in the United States reached its peak in 1930 when Congress used its authority to set tariffs for the last time by enacting the Smoot-Hawley Tariff Act. The law, which raised tariffs to their highest levels in history, has often been cited as an important factor in prolonging the Great Depression. Tariffs on dutiable items amounted to 59 percent of value in 1932, when total U.S. imports were little more than $1 billion.

To reverse this flight to economic isolationism, and more specifically to assist economic recovery at home by expanding American exports, the Franklin D. Roosevelt administration proposed that Congress delegate some of its constitutional power to "regulate commerce with foreign nations" to the president by authorizing him to negotiate trade agreements with other nations. The administration asked to cut U.S. tariffs by as much as 50 percent in return for equivalent concessions from other nations. Prodded and persuaded by Secretary of State Cordell Hull, the Democratic-controlled 73rd Congress — over the nearly unanimous opposition of Republicans — made this grant of authority in the Trade Agreements Act of 1934. Subsequently, no serious effort was made to deprive the president of this power to modify tariffs.

By 1939, the U.S. had negotiated more than a score of reciprocal trade agreements; exports had risen to $3.1 billion, imports to $2.3 billion. But with the start of World War II, normal trade relations went out the window; military and other non-commercial criteria determined the flow of exports and imports. Six years later, a large part of Europe and East Asia lay in ruins while the United States, unscathed by war damage, had emerged as the world's foremost economic as well as military power. Such a dangerous imbalance of resources, it was clear, had to be corrected.

Trade liberalization entered a new phase after World War II when 23 Western nations agreed in 1947 on a complex set of rules and principles known as the General Agreement on Tariffs and Trade (GATT). One of the guiding principles of GATT was most-favored-nation (MFN) treatment, which required that each country extend equal trade treatment to the products of all other parties.

Trade With Communist Nations

Communist nations did not participate in the GATT negotiations, however, and Congress took action in 1951 to ensure they would not receive any of the benefits. The 1951 Reciprocal Trade Agreements Act directed the president to deny tariff-cutting benefits to any nation "dominated or controlled" by the "world communist movement." Poland and Yugoslavia were excluded from the definition.

The result was to establish a second column of duties applicable to communist countries; most of the rates were the original tariffs set in the 1930 Smoot-Hawley Act.

The difference between columns 1 and 2 varied greatly from item to item: in many cases duties were the same or only slightly higher. As a general rule tariff differentials tended to be lowest for raw materials and partially manufactured products and higher as products moved through successive stages of the manufacturing process. Beginning in the late 1960s, the gap between columns 1 and 2 tended to widen as column rates were cut following several rounds of GATT negotiations.

In the 1962 Trade Act, Congress directed the president to suspend trade benefits to "any country or area dominated or controlled by communism." The effect of the provision was to withdraw MFN from Poland and Yugoslavia. President John F. Kennedy withheld action on this provison, however, and it was repealed by Congress in 1963.

U.S. trade with mainland China meanwhile lay moribund under an embargo imposed by President Harry S Truman in December 1950, after China attacked American forces in the Korean War. But President Richard M. Nixon's progressive relaxation of cold war prohibitions against U.S. contact with China demonstrated his belief that the most populous nation on the earth had important political and economic roles to play in the world.

Nixon said as much in a speech July 6, 1971, three days before his assistant for national security affairs, Henry A. Kissinger, began secret meetings with Premier Chou En-lai in Peking which resulted in the invitation to the president to visit the Chinese capital. China was potentially "one of the five great economic superpowers," Nixon said, which would determine the course of great events in the remainder of the 20th century. An end to two decades of Chinese isolation, he said, would remove a threat to world peace but

China: Balance of Trade

(in millions of dollars)

	Total Trade				Communist Countries				Non-Communist Countries			
	Total	Exports	Imports	Balance	Total	Exports	Imports	Balance	Total	Exports	Imports	Balance
1950	1,210	620	590	30	350	210	140	70	860	410	450	−40
1951	1,900	780	1,120	−340	975	465	515	−50	920	315	605	−290
1952	1,890	875	1,015	−140	1,315	605	710	−105	575	270	305	−35
1953	2,295	1,040	1,255	−215	1,555	670	885	−215	740	370	370	0
1954	2,350	1,060	1,290	−230	1,735	765	970	−205	615	295	320	−25
1955	3,035	1,375	1,660	−285	2,250	950	1,300	−350	785	425	360	65
1956	3,120	1,635	1,485	150	2,055	1,045	1,010	35	1,065	590	475	115
1957	3,055	1,615	1,440	175	1,965	1,085	880	205	1,090	530	560	−30
1958	3,765	1,940	1,825	115	2,380	1,280	1,100	180	1,385	660	725	−65
1959	4,290	2,230	2,060	170	2,980	1,615	1,365	250	1,310	615	695	−80
1960	3,990	1,960	2,030	−70	2,620	1,335	1,285	50	1,370	625	745	−120
1961	3,015	1,525	1,490	35	1,685	965	715	250	1,335	560	775	−215
1962	2,670	1,520	1,150	370	1,410	915	490	425	1,265	605	660	−55
1963	2,775	1,575	1,200	375	1,250	820	430	390	1,525	755	770	−15
1964	3,220	1,750	1,470	280	1,100	710	390	320	2,120	1,040	1,080	−40
1965	3,880	2,035	1,845	190	1,165	650	515	135	2,715	1,385	1,330	55
1966	4,245	2,210	2,035	175	1,090	585	505	80	3,155	1,625	1,530	95
1967	3,915	1,960	1,955	5	830	485	345	140	3,085	1,475	1,610	−135
1968	3,785	1,960	1,825	135	840	500	340	160	2,945	1,460	1,485	−25
1969	3,895	2,060	1,835	225	785	490	295	195	3,110	1,570	1,540	30
1970	4,340	2,095	2,245	−150	860	480	380	100	3,480	1,615	1,865	−250
1971	4,810	2,500	2,310	190	1,085	585	500	85	3,725	1,915	1,810	105
1972	6,000	3,150	2,850	300	1,275	740	535	205	4,725	2,410	2,315	95
1973	10,300	5,075	5,225	−150	1,710	1,000	710	290	8,590	4,075	4,515	−440
1974	14,080	6,660	7,420	−760	2,435	1,430	1,010	420	11,645	5,230	6,415	−1,185
1975	14,575	7,180	7,395	−215	2,390	1,380	1,010	370	12,185	5,800	6,385	−585
1976	13,275	7,265	6,010	1,255	2,345	1,240	1,105	135	10,930	6,025	4,905	1,120
1977	15,055	7,955	7,100	855	2,520	1,370	1,150	225	12,530	6,580	5,950	630
1978	21,100	10,000	11,100	−1,100	3,200	1,600	1,600	0	17,900	8,400	9,500	−1,100

* Data are rounded to the nearest $5 million, with the exception of 1978 data which are preliminary and rounded to the nearest $100 million. Exports are f.o.b. (freight on board); imports are c.i.f. (cost, insurance and freight).

SOURCE: CIA National Foreign Assessment Center

would mean "an immense escalation of their economic challenge." *(Excerpts, p. 322)*

The president had begun in July 1969 to ease travel and trade restrictions with China. On June 10, 1971, he lifted restrictions on exports of a wide variety of non-strategic goods to China and on commercial imports from the mainland.

Nixon's Breakthrough

Nixon's historic trips to Moscow and Peking in 1972 substantially altered the U.S. trade picture.

From Peking the president returned with the hope of normalized relations. Liaison offices were established several months after the Nixon visit, followed by a resumption of trade.

From Moscow he brought back seven agreements, including a new trade pact. The U.S.-Soviet Trade Agreement marked the beginning of a long and heated debate in Congress over the U.S. policy of détente with the Soviet Union. When it was over, Congress had severely limited Export-Import Bank financing to the Soviet Union, and had made most-favored-nation status for communist countries conditional on their emigration policies. The Soviet Union subsequently abrogated the 1972 trade agreement.

1974 Trade Act Waiver

The 1974 Trade Act authorized the president to negotiate three-year bilateral trade agreements with communist countries, but — through the "Jackson-Vanik amendment" — established a procedure linking trade concessions to emigration. *(Jackson-Vanik amendment, box, p. 71)*

The act allowed the president to extend MFN if he found that emigration requirements were being met — that the country did not deny its citizens the opportunity to emigrate, or impose more than a nominal tax on emigration or emigration documents. Alternatively, the president could waive the emigration requirements if he found it would "substantially" promote freedom of emigration and if he had received "assurances" that the country's practices would "henceforth lead substantially" to freedom of emigration. The House and Senate were required to approve the agreement by adoption of a concurrent resolution.

As of late 1979, two countries — Hungary and Romania — had qualified. Congress passed a resolution (S Con Res 35) approving the U.S.-Romania Trade Agreement in mid-1975 by a vote of 88-2 in the Senate and 355-41 in the House. The resolution approving the agreement with Hungary (H Con Res 555) was adopted in May 1978 by a vote of 209-173 in the House and by voice vote in the Senate the following month.

U.S.-China Trade Increases

Trade between the United States and China remained relatively modest until 1978. Chinese exports to the United States grew steadily, reaching $203 million in 1977, but they remained a small fraction of China's total exports of $8 billion. Imports to the United States consisted largely of textiles and apparel, antiques and handicrafts, bristles and feathers, fireworks and non-ferrous metals.

U.S. exports to China fluctuated wildly, largely in response to Chinese demands for agricultural commodities such as wheat and soybeans. Large food shipments in 1974 boosted U.S. exports to $807 million, but better Chinese harvests in subsequent years caused a substantial decline. China in this period also bought 10 Boeing aircraft, eight ammonia plants and substantial amounts of equipment for the exploration and drilling of oil.

In 1978 trade between the two nations more than doubled, to more than $1 billion, primarily because of a resumption of U.S. food exports. Of total exports to China of $824 million, three-fourths ($614 million) were agricultural commodities, primarily wheat ($291 million), cotton ($157 million) and corn ($118 million). Agricultural exports alone were expected to have approached $1 billion in 1979.

Chinese exports to the United States also jumped substantially, rising from $203 million in 1977 to $324 million in 1978, with the pattern of exports remaining generally the same.

By 1979, the United States ranked third as a major supplier of goods to the PRC (behind Japan and West Germany) and third as a major market for PRC exports (behind Hong Kong and Japan). Trade for the first six months of 1979 already equaled trade for all of 1978.

During the first half of 1979, crude oil first exported that year became the leading Chinese export to the United States. And with vast oil deposits believed to be awaiting discovery, especially in the Bohai Gulf off north China, some observers thought oil would become the central factor in future U.S.-China trade. The United States was desperately seeking new foreign sources of oil — especially after the Iranian crisis of 1979 and concomitant oil price increases by the Arab bloc — while the Chinese were expected to need American help in developing their oil resources through more sophisticated exploration and drilling techniques and equipment.

Other leading imports from the PRC in 1979 included fireworks, antiques, white cotton shirting, shrimp, carpets, crude or processed bristles, bamboo baskets and bags, and feathers. Leading U.S. exports to China included yellow corn, cotton, wheat, soybeans and soybean oil, polyester fi-

bers, oil and gas drilling machines and parts, and chemicals.

China's Trade Potential

Further investment was certain, even without a new Sino-U.S. trade agreement, though the upper limits of Chinese investment in Western technology could only be roughly estimated: The National Council for U.S.-China Trade estimated that Peking would spend $40 billion on foreign capital investment between 1978 and 1985, while Commerce Department experts estimated spending in the $60 billion to $80 billion range.

A Commerce Department study cautioned against unrealistically high estimates of China's trade potential. The study predicted that in the 1978-1985 period Chinese imports would probably not exceed $136 billion, while exports would be unlikely to exceed $103 billion. The U.S. share of the Chinese import market in this period was estimated at $12 billion to $15 billion, or about 10 percent of total Chinese imports.

The study said total Chinese foreign trade, assuming an annual export growth of 10 percent and import growth of 15 percent, could approach $40 billion by 1985, with imports of about $22 billion and exports of about $16 billion. China's trade in 1978 totaled over $20 billion, about evenly divided between exports and imports.

Two-way trade between the United State and China was expected to continue upwards in the 1980s, with U.S. agricultural exports likely to make up more than half of total trade. A variety of possible new projects involving U.S. firms, in areas such as mining, energy, steel and hydroelectric facilities, was expected to boost trade substantially during the decade.

China in 1979 had an excellent credit rating and relatively little foreign debt. The chief impediment to trade was expected to be limited potential for export growth and the accumulation of foreign exchange to pay for China's imports. The Chinese were expected to rely on the development of their oil resources during the 1980s as a major source of foreign exchange, and to use compensation agreements — paying for a project with a share of the output — to pay back foreign debts.

Most-Favored-Nation Status

A 1978 study done for the congressional Joint Economic Committee by the Commerce Department's Bureau of East-West Trade predicted that U.S. imports from China would have been 30 percent higher in 1976 if China had been granted MFN.

The biggest predicted increases would have been in textile products such as household linens (tariffs would drop 43 percent with MFN), silk fabrics (50 percent tariff differential), and underwear and cotton fabrics. Substantial increases were also predicted for products such as basketwork (32 percent tariff differential), porcelain and chinaware and dried vegetables.

The study concluded that with Chinese imports to the United States at such a low level — less than one-tenth of 1 percent of total U.S. imports in 1976 — a 30 percent increase would have relatively little effect on the U.S. economy. A substantial portion of the increase would probably displace other foreign suppliers.

In the long run, the study suggested that high technology products not currently exported by China could be the greatest beneficiaries of MFN. Other Chinese exports of po-

Highlights of U.S.-China Trade

Millions of U.S. Dollars

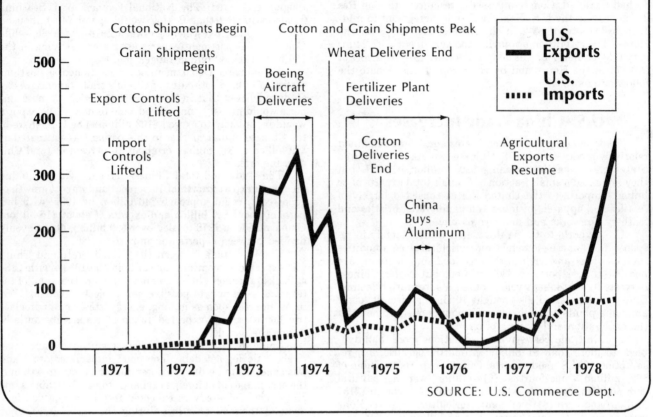

Cotton Shipments Begin

Grain Shipments Begin

Export Controls Lifted

Import Controls Lifted

Boeing Aircraft Deliveries

Cotton and Grain Shipments Peak

Wheat Deliveries End

Fertilizer Plant Deliveries

Cotton Deliveries End

China Buys Aluminum

Agricultural Exports Resume

U.S. Exports

U.S. Imports

1971 1972 1973 1974 1975 1976 1977 1978

SOURCE: U.S. Commerce Dept.

tential significance, such as oil and tin, had tariffs that were negligible under both MFN and non-MFN status.

An important contingency noted in the study — that quantitative restrictions on import-sensitive products such as textiles and footwear would negate the effect of tariff cuts granted by MFN — has substantially altered estimates of the impact of MFN on Chinese exports.

"From a psychological standpoint, MFN would certainly help," said Gary Teske, one of the authors of the study. "But from the point of view of an actual boost in import earnings, it would not be that great."

Most observers expected China's eligibility for Export-Import Bank financing to have a far larger impact than MFN tariff cuts.

Though the total amount of Export-Import Bank financing was expected to be relatively limited — the Commerce Department estimated total Export-Import Bank financing to China from 1978 to 1985 at $1 billion to $2 billion — the value of the financing was multiplied by its use in conjunction with commercial bank financing. In addition, the bank could facilitate commercial financing through the provision of loan guarantees.

(Vice President Walter Mondale, speaking on Chinese television Aug. 27, 1979, promised a minimum of $2 billion in ExImBank trade credits over a five-year period.)

1978 Breakthrough

Two factors added a dramatic new dimension to U.S.-China trade relations in 1978.

One was the Dec. 15 announcement that the two nations intended to normalize relations.

The second development was a significant new emphasis by the Chinese leadership, led by Vice Premier Deng Xiaoping, on international trade and foreign investment as a vital instrument in China's modernization plans.

The retreat from economic self-reliance was signaled by an explosion of new trade deals by Peking, which made commitments to buy roughly $8 billion in technology from Western Europe, Japan and the United States in 1978.

The Chinese purchases almost exclusively involved capital investment rather than consumer goods. The U.S. Steel Corp. agreed to build an iron ore processing plant worth about $1 billion; the Fluor Corp. signed a $10-million agreement heralding construction of a proposed $800-million complex to mine and process copper; and Pan American Airways, through its subsidiary Intercontinental Hotels, negotiated a $500-million agreement to build luxury hotel rooms. Other deals included purchase of three Boeing 747s with an option to buy two more, worth $250 million, and an agreement to sell and later bottle Coca-Cola.

China: Geographic Distribution of Trade, 1978

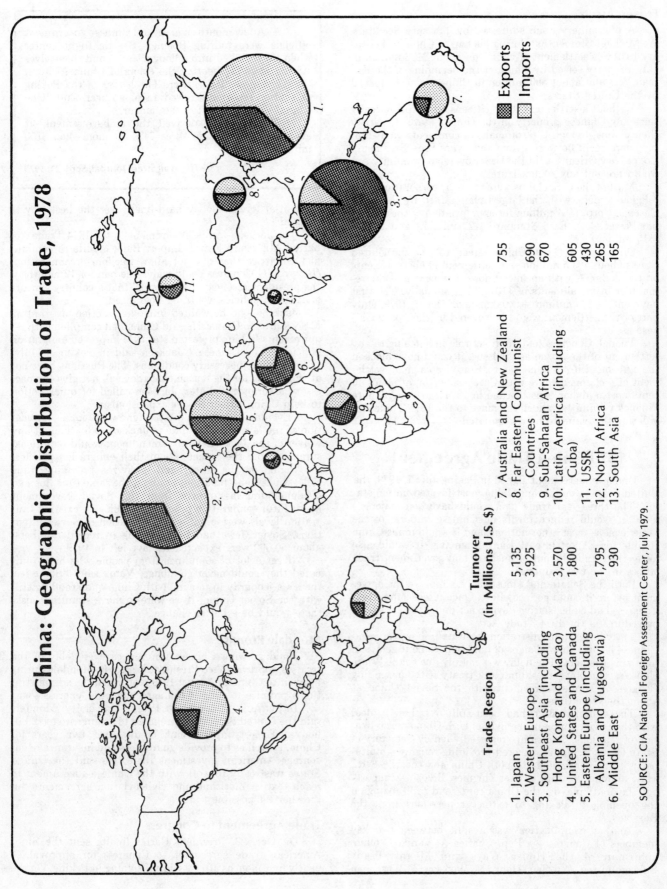

Exports **Imports**

Trade Region	Turnover (in Millions U.S. $)
1. Japan	5,135
2. Western Europe	3,925
3. Southeast Asia (including Hong Kong and Macao)	3,570
4. United States and Canada	1,800
5. Eastern Europe (including Albania and Yugoslavia)	1,795
6. Middle East	930
7. Australia and New Zealand	755
8. Far Eastern Communist Countries	690
9. Sub-Saharan Africa	670
10. Latin America (including Cuba)	605
11. USSR	430
12. North Africa	265
13. South Asia	165

SOURCE: CIA National Foreign Assessment Center, July 1979.

Frozen Assets

A preliminary issue addressed by Treasury Secretary W. Michael Blumenthal during his trip to China in February 1979 was settlement of claims on about $196 million in U.S. property seized by China at the beginning of the Korean War and about $80 million in Chinese assets blocked by the United States.

Without a settlement, U.S. citizens could theoretically seize any Chinese property in the United States to satisfy their claims, though U.S. officials, in comments on a shipping agreement between China and Lykes Bros. Steamship Co. of New Orleans, said the U.S. Sovereign Immunity Act would prevent any such seizures.

Most of the U.S. claims were made by corporations and religious orders, with the largest claims filed by the Boise Cascade Corp. ($54 million for expropriation of the Shanghai Power Co.), Esso Standard ($27 million) and Caltex ($15 million).

On March 2, 1979, China agreed to pay the United States about $80.5 million — a settlement of about 41 cents on the dollar — with an initial down payment and the remainder in installments of $10 million annually. The first payment — $20 million — was made on Oct. 1, 1979. Only part of the settlement would be covered by the frozen Chinese assets.

Though Congress had no direct role in agreeing to any settlement of the frozen assets issue, it could have blocked the agreement if it had chosen to. State Department settlement of a claims dispute with Czechoslovakia, at about 40 cents on the dollar, was blocked in 1974 when the Senate Finance Committee added language to the 1974 Trade Act ordering the claim to be renegotiated.

1979 China Trade Agreement

Under an agreement signed in Peking July 7, 1979, the United States would grant China most-favored-nation status. The three-year trade pact would have two major effects: It would reduce tariffs on Chinese imports to the same level as most other nations, and it would make China eligible for Export-Import Bank financing. It would also foster the establishment of business and government trade offices in the two countries.

Both the Senate and House had to approve the agreement before it could go into effect. Once it was submitted, Congress had 60 legislative days to act under the expedited procedures of the 1974 Trade Act.

The Carter administration hesitated, however, and Chinese leaders showed signs of impatience about delays in finalizing the pact. The delay was mainly due to the White House's reluctance to submit the treaty without sending Congress a similar agreement with the Soviet Union at about the same time.

The administration had been split over how to deal with the Soviet Union in the light of U.S.-China normalization of relations. One camp, reportedly led by Secretary of State Cyrus R. Vance, favored providing roughly simultaneous trade concessions to both China and the U.S.S.R., while national security adviser Zbigniew Brzezinski reportedly favored "playing the China card" and capitalizing on the opening to Peking to extract concessions from the Russians.

Another complication was a split between two key members of Congress — Rep. Charles A. Vanik, D-Ohio, chairman of the House Ways and Means Trade Subcommittee, and Sen. Henry M. Jackson, D-Wash., an

> "...A few months ago several Chinese government officials were touring Boeing's Seattle flight center when they walked into a hangar and found themselves staring at a 747 bearing the colors of China Airlines, the Taiwanese flag carrier. The leader of the Peking delegation reportedly raised a single finger, said, 'One China' — and departed the hangar.
>
> "Still, Boeing survived the embarrassment. It eventually sold China three 747s for more than $150 million."
>
> —*The Wall Street Journal*, Sept. 21, 1979

influential foreign policy hard-liner, over the best way to proceed.

The Jackson-Vanik amendment to the 1974 Trade Act barred MFN and Export-Import Bank credits to communist countries that did not allow freedom of emigration. *(Box, p. 71)* Congress could waive the ban for 12 months if the president received "assurances" that a country's future emigration policies would be liberalized.

Jackson said he wanted immediate action on granting MFN status to China. He said China had complied with requirements linking preferred status to improved emigration policies. "The Chinese," Jackson said in Peking in July, "have met the necessary conditions. The Russians have not at this point, for the reason that they will not give the necessary assurances." Later, Jackson called for quick action to help China "deter Soviet expansionism."

"Evenhandedness is inconsistent with equal application of the law," said an aide to Jackson, who thought any waiver of the Jackson-Vanik amendment would require assurances from the Soviets about their emigration policies.

Vanik, on the other hand, preferred providing trade concessions to both nations at about the same time. Instead of demanding assurances from the Soviet government about future emigration practices, Vanik said existing emigration levels were a sufficient indication of Soviet intentions. Soviet Jews had been leaving in record numbers; about 50,000 were expected to have left in 1979.

"I get a lot of soundings from people who have indicated they could never go along," Vanik said. "Some feel there's a jeopardy in moving with China and standing still with the Soviet Union. If we were to move simultaneously there would be a better chance."

Mondale Promise

Amid growing Chinese impatience over delay of the treaty's approval, Vice President Walter F. Mondale during his visit to China in August 1979 reaffirmed the administration's promise to submit the agreement to Congress soon.

In his Aug. 27 speech at Peking University, Mondale said the United States was prepared to arrange up to $2 billion in Export-Import Bank credits over five years for China, as well as to provide guarantees and insurance to encourage American investment there. He said the United States was ready to work with the Chinese government to reach textile, maritime and civil aviation agreements "in the shortest possible time."

Trade Agreement to Congress

On Oct. 23, President Carter finally sent the Sino-American trade agreement to Congress for approval — nearly four months after its July 7 signing in Peking. On the

Key Economic Sectors in China, 1972-78

	1972	1973	1974	1975	1976	1977	1978
Gross national product (billion 1978 US$)	294.0	332.0	344.0	368.0	368.0	398.0	440.0
Industrial production index (1957=100)	385.0	436.0	455.0	502.0	502.0	572.0	650.0
Electric power (billion kwh)	138.0	149.0	162.0	185.0	200.0	223.4	256.6
Coal (million metric tons)	376.5	398.1	410.6	479.6	488.0	550.0	618.0
Crude oil (million metric tons)	44.9	56.9	68.2	77.1	86.8	93.7	104.1
Crude steel (million metric tons)	23.0	25.0	21.0	24.0	20.5	23.7	31.8
Trucks (thousand units)	100.0	110.0	121.0	133.0	135.0	150.0	181.0
Tractors (thousand 15-hp units)	136.0	166.0	150.0	180.0	190.9	221.8	271.0
Chemical fertilizer (million metric tons)	19.8	24.8	24.9	28.8	24.3	38.0	48.0
Cement (million metric tons)	38.0	40.9	37.2	46.9	49.1	55.7	65.2
Paper (million metric tons)	5.6	6.0	6.5	6.9	7.0	7.1	—
Cotton cloth (billion linear meters)	—	—	—	9.6	8.9	10.2	11.0
Agricultural production index (1957=100)	126.0	142.0	146.0	148.0	148.0	146.0	159.1
Total grain (million metric tons)	240.0	266.0	275.0	284.0	285.0	282.8	304.8
Cotton (million metric tons)	2.1	2.6	2.5	2.4	2.3	2.0	2.2
Hogs (million head)	261.0	—	287.0	—	—	291.8	301.3
Modern transport index (1957=100)	314.0	339.0	356.0	392.0	397.0	446.0	—
Foreign trade (billion current US $)	6.0	10.3	14.1	14.6	13.3	15.1	21.2
Exports, f.o.b.	3.2	5.1	6.7	7.2	7.3	8.0	10.1
Imports, c.i.f.	2.8	5.2	7.4	7.4	6.0	7.1	11.1

Sources: CIA National Foreign Assessment Center, *China: Economic Indicators,* December 1978; and Communiqué of the State Statistical Bureau of the People's Republic of China on Fulfilment of China's 1978 National Economic Plan (June 27, 1979).

same day, Carter signed a proclamation waiving the requirements of the Jackson-Vanik amendment, which would bar granting most-favored-nation (MFN) status to China unless it guaranteed free emigration. *(Texts, p. 352)*

The Carter administration had withheld submission of the treaty while it tried to work out three essential problems: protectionist sentiment against import of Chinese textiles; opposition to granting MFN status to China without simultaneously awarding the Soviet Union the same privileges; and dispute over whether China's emigration policies qualified it for MFN status under the Jackson-Vanik amendment.

The administration was believed to have forestalled the opposition of U.S. textile interests by unilaterally imposing non-preferential textile import quotas on the Chinese on Oct. 30, 1979. But the other two related issues — Chinese emigration and MFN status for Russia — remained a problem.

Lobbying for the Trade Pact

The White House looked to American business for help in getting the Chinese trade agreement approved on Capitol Hill. Big businesses such as Coca-Cola, Bethlehem Steel and Pan American Airways were early entrants in the sweepstakes for trade with the mainland. Other businesses were favorably disposed to easing the way for trade there.

One group lobbying in Washington was the National Council for U.S.-China Trade, which represented banking, construction, transportation and other firms anxious to do business with 900 million Chinese.

Its president, Christopher H. Phillips, said lower tariffs on Chinese exports would boost China-U.S. commerce by about $540 million over the next three years and give the United States a wider variety of Chinese exports at prices comparable to those from other Asian nations. Among these

goods, he said, were light machine tools, hand tools, sporting equipment, toys and chemicals.

"In other words," Phillips said in November 1979, "at a time when inflation is moving at 13 percent a year, this will be one means of helping keep prices down — a welcome prospect for American consumers."

The National Foreign Trade Council also endorsed the pact. "In our opinion," said council official Cord Hansen-Sturm, vice president of the American Express Company, "this agreement will open up a substantial new market for exports of U.S. goods and services at a time when continued trade deficits have made export expansion a necessity."

Chinese Emigration

Although the emigration provisions of the 1974 Trade Act were aimed primarily at the Soviet Union, they were also applicable to China in the event an administration sought MFN status for the PRC.

Relatively little attention had been paid to Chinese emigration, although the Chinese in 1978-79 significantly relaxed their emigration policies after normalization of relations with the United States.

The State Department said applications from Chinese who had been allowed to enter Hong Kong to apply for U.S. visas had climbed from 500 in November 1978 to nearly 1,000 in December and an estimated 2,000 in both January and February 1979, after averaging only 25 to 30 a month a year earlier.

The report said emigrants had been granted exit visas after showing Chinese officials a U.S. government petition filed by relatives in the United States that said they met the requirement to apply for a U.S. visa. U.S. officials said petitions for about 18,000 Chinese who had not yet arrived in Hong Kong in early 1979 had been cleared by the U.S. Immigration Service.

U.S.-China Trade by Commodity, 1972-78

(in millions of U.S. dollars)

	1972	1973	1974	1975	1976	1977	1978	1979*
U.S. exports	63	740	819	304	135	171	864	395
Agricultural commodities:	61	628	668	80	0	64	573	—
Wheat	35	308	234	0	0	0	250	—
Corn	24	141	96	0	0	0	118	—
Soybeans	0	55	138	0	0	0	15	—
Cotton	0	101	186	80	0	18	157	—
Vegetable oils	2	19	8	0	0	28	26	—
Metals:	0	31	22	83	47	7	—	—
Steel scrap	0	24	12	13	4	Negl.	—	—
Aluminum	0	3	0	47	26	5	0	—
Iron and steel pipe	0	0	3	12	11	Negl.	—	—
Machinery and equipment:	2	69	107	121	57	56	93	—
Aircraft, including engines, parts and accessories	0	63	76	2	1	Negl.	Negl.	—
Other	0	12	22	22	23	48	—	—
U.S. imports	32	64	115	158	201	203	324	101
Foodstuffs and tobacco	4	7	16	16	24	26	—	—
Textiles and apparel	7	15	36	45	63	58	—	—
Silk and other fibers	4	6	5	4	8	8	—	—
Cotton and other fabrics	2	7	25	31	35	21	—	—
Clothing and footwear	1	2	6	10	20	29	—	—
Handicrafts:	8	15	20	22	42	49	—	—
Antiques, works of art	3	6	8	6	12	9	—	—
Bristles, downs and feathers	8	8	10	6	23	28	—	—
Chemicals, including fireworks	2	8	18	18	18	22	—	—
Nonferrous minerals and metals:	2	8	11	42	21	12	—	—
Tin	1	8	9	40	13	4	—	—
Other	1	3	4	11	10	8	—	—

* 1st quarter only.

Source: U.S. Commerce Department

Textiles

Discussions with the Chinese on the issue of textile imports began Jan. 22, 1979. U.S. trade negotiator Michael Smith said the United States would seek quantitative limits on about a dozen particularly sensitive textile products, and said China would be asked to conform to the requirements of the Multifiber Arrangement (MFA) limiting annual export growth to 6 percent.

"We cannot treat China any more favorably than other MFA participants," Smith said.

China, one of the largest suppliers of textiles and apparel products in the world, wanted to sell large quantities of both to the United States. But the Carter administration promised to protect the U.S. textile industry from just such an influx of foreign competition. The major concern was that large Chinese textile imports could lead directly to lower sales of U.S. textiles and then set off massive unemployment in the domestic industry.

Since the talks started, imports from China continued to contribute to the serious market disruption in the United States, textile industry and labor advisers to the U.S. negotiating team told *The Wall Street Journal* in April. The advisers said that the Chinese had adopted a "rigid position," which had "compelled the suspension of the talks" on April 20.

When talks resumed in May, President Carter's special trade negotiator, Robert Strauss, met with continued Chinese intransigence on the textile issue. After adjournment of this round of talks, the U.S. Commerce Department on May 31 announced that quotas on five categories of textile imports — including cotton blouses, shirts, trousers and gloves — would be imposed on China.

After protests from protectionist-minded congressmen like Sen. Ernest Hollings, D-S.C., who warned that China could "inundate" U.S. markets with cheap textiles at the expense of the domestic textile industry, the United States announced on Oct. 30 that further quotas would be imposed on Chinese textile imports. Hollings had threatened to block the 1979 Sino-U.S. trade agreement unless further limits were imposed.

Under the new quotas, China's ability to export textiles would be affected. China's leading export to the United States in 1978, for example, was white cotton shirts, on which duties would drop from 17 percent to 9.3 percent.

Jackson-Vanik Amendment

In 1973 the Nixon administration proposed a comprehensive new trade bill that included broader authority for the president to negotiate reductions in tariffs in the upcoming round of international negotiations.

As part of the U.S.-Soviet Trade Agreement, the bill included a proposal to extend most-favored-nation status to the Soviet Union. The Trade Act finally was cleared in December 1974, but only after a protracted debate over trade concessions for the Soviets.

Under the Jackson-Vanik Amendment, Congress insisted on linking most-favored-nation status for the Soviet Union with assurances that Russia would relax its restrictions against the emigration of Russian Jews. Senate leaders finally accepted a compromise, agreeing to waive denial of MFN for the USSR in return for administration assurances concerning Soviet emigration.

As part of the compromise, Secretary of State Henry A. Kissinger said in a letter to Sen. Henry M. Jackson, D-Wash., that he had received "clarifications" from Soviet leaders about their emigration practices, but he emphasized that the compromise did not represent a formal commitment by the Soviets.

Jackson said the agreement assumed that Soviet emigration would rise from the 1973 level of about 35,000, and that a benchmark of 60,000 annually would be considered a minimum standard of compliance.

Whatever assurances Kissinger had received from the Soviets, they were disavowed almost immediately after passage of the trade bill. In December the Soviets denied they had given any specific assurances about the linkage of emigration and trade or that emigration from the Soviet Union would increase; the following month Kissinger announced the Soviets would not put the 1972 trade agreement into effect.

Export-Import Bank Restrictions

While the debate over Soviet emigration policies captured public attention in late 1974, other restrictions on U.S.-Soviet trade were being simultaneously considered as part of the Export-Import Bank authorization bill.

With the U.S. economy stunned by the 1974 Middle East oil embargo and a severe inflation, debate focused on the propriety of subsidizing the export sector by providing financing to foreign borrowers at 6 percent interest.

Particularly controversial was the bank's role in supporting projects in the Soviet Union as part of the administration's policy of détente. In the year-and-a-half since the signing of the 1972 U.S.-Soviet Trade Agreement, the bank had provided $469 million in credits to finance over $1 billion in Soviet projects, with prospects for additional support in the event a major Soviet oil and gas exploration proposal was approved.

Running parallel to debate on the trade bill, debate on the Export-Import Bank bill was heated, with the Senate rejecting two conference reports before finally passing a compromise measure Dec. 19.

As cleared, the bill imposed several limits on the bank's lending to the Soviet Union, including a $300-million ceiling on total loans and guarantees, with congressional approval required for a higher ceiling, plus a total ban on financing for Soviet fossil fuel production and a $40-million limit on fossil fuel research. The bill also required a separate determination by the president that any loan over $50 million to a communist country was in the U.S. national interest.

The $300-million ceiling, proposed by Sen. Adlai E. Stevenson III, D-Ill., was also included in the Trade Act, though the cap on bank financing for the Soviets was originally conceived as an alternative to the trade bill's emigration provisions.

Jackson-Vanik: A Success?

Soviet Jewish emigration dropped sharply in the years after abrogation of the trade agreement, declining from a high of 35,000 in 1973 to 13,500 in 1975, 14,000 in 1976 and 16,700 in 1977.

Nonetheless, supporters of the Jackson-Vanik amendment generally maintained that the amendment has been a success.

"Jackson-Vanik served notice to the Soviets that although it could be in our national interest to develop trade, there was a foreign policy objective that transcended the pragmatic," said Marina Wallich, legislative director of the National Conference on Soviet Jewry. "It was a signal that we remained tough even in a period of détente."

Opponents contended the amendment had been counterproductive, that emigration declined and the U.S. economy suffered.

"I don't think it's been successful," said Stevenson. "It's curtailed emigration from the Soviet Union and has also heightened U.S.-Soviet tension."

"What we've lost has been tremendous," said Donald M. Kendall, head of Pepsico Inc. and former head of the U.S.-U.S.S.R. Trade and Economic Council. Kendall said the claim by the Soviets that the absence of credits had caused Moscow to transfer $2 billion worth of orders to other suppliers was the "minimal" loss incurred by U.S. business.

Soviet Emigration Trends

Emigration increases from the Soviet Union — almost 3,700 emigrants left in January 1979 — raised the possibility that total Soviet emigration that year could approach the 60,000 figure Jackson used in 1974 as a "benchmark" figure for free emigration.

Prospects for a waiver of the Jackson-Vanik amendment depended on several additional factors, however.

Staff members of the Commission on Security and Cooperation in Europe — an independent advisory agency established to monitor international compliance with the human rights provisions of the Helsinki Agreement — pointed out that although absolute numbers of Soviet emigrants had risen, procedural blocks such as long waiting periods still remained, and that the emigration of "refuseniks" — those turned down who reapply — had not improved much.

Moscow traditionally considered the emigration issue as interference in its internal affairs and still was presumed to be very sensitive about formal compliance.

Coke comes to China. The ideographs on the bottle can be literally translated as "Right for Your Mouth, Right for Your Happiness."

Further evidence of a relaxed attitude toward emigration on the part of the Chinese was vividly evident during Vice Premier Deng Xiaoping's trip to Washington in February 1979. When President Carter broached the subject of emigration, Deng replied: "I'll send you 10 million emigrants right away."

In his letter of transmittal accompanying submission of the 1979 China trade bill to Congress, President Carter said Peking had taken action to lift restraints on emigration.

No Equal Terms for Russia

Whatever objections remained over granting most-favored-nation status to the PRC without simultaneously bestowing the same benefits on the Soviet Union all but disappeared after the Soviet invasion of Afghanistan on Dec. 27, 1979.

Although the 96th Congress was in adjournment at the time of the Afghan incursion, it had become apparent before the legislature reconvened in January 1980 that it was likely to approve the China Trade Agreement — unilaterally bestowing MFN status on China but not the U.S.S.R.

— as a means of punishing the Soviets for their action. President Carter had already imposed various economic sanctions against the U.S.S.R. in halting scheduled U.S. grain, technological and other sales to Russia after the Afghanistan invasion.

Congressional Action

So — two days into its 1980 session — Congress without further ado overwhelmingly passed a joint resolution approving the trade agreement. There is no question that the speed of the vote and its lopsidedness — 294-88 in the House, 74-8 in the Senate — reflected Congress' eagerness for a vehicle by which to "get tough" with Russia.

But the China Trade Act had been expected to pass even without the impetus of the Soviet-Afghan crisis. Rep. Vanik, who favored joint MFN grants to China and Russia, had conceded that simultaneous action was impossible, on the grounds that the SALT II disarmament issue would have to be disposed of before Congress felt inclined to deal with improved trade status for Russia. After the Afghanistan invasion, ratification of SALT II and MFN status for the Soviet Union both became very remote possibilities as far as Congress and the president were concerned.

Terms of the Treaty

The principal provisions of the Sino-U.S. trade agreement were similar to the analogous understandings between the United States and Hungary and Romania approved earlier. As summarized by the Senate Finance Committee, the pact included the following provisions:

● The United States and the People's Republic of China would provide non-discriminatory (most-favored-nation) tariff treatments to imports from the other country.

● Safeguards arrangements were to be provided to remedy market disruption because of rapidly increasing imports, and to permit the taking of unilateral action following consultations.

● Arrangements for business and financial facilitation would be provided, including the establishment of business representation offices and provisions encouraging visits by economic, trade and industrial groups.

● The PRC would provide copyright, patent and trademark protection equivalent to the protection afforded the PRC by the United States. *(Text of agreement, p. 352)*

CHRONOLOGY OF EVENTS

CHART OF CHINESE, WORLD HISTORY FROM 2000 B.C.

Christian Calendar	Outside World	Key Facts	Dynasties	Religion and Thought	Art	Culture
2000 B.C.	Bronze Age First Dynasty, Babylon	Emergence from Stone Age	HSIA		Black pottery	Domesticated pig and dog Cultivated millet and wheat Potter's wheel Domesticated ox, goat, sheep, horse
1500	Dynasty XVIII, Egypt	Bronze Age		Religion animistic and orgiastic	White incised pottery	Script Practice of divination Silk culture
		Earliest writing			Bronze ritual vessels and weapons	Wheeled vehicles
		Urban development	SHANG	Recognition of spirit world	Carved ivory and stone Jades	Cowry shells
	MOSES					Brush and ink Composite bow
	Iron Age			Ancestor worship	Turquoise inlay	Books of bamboo slips
1000	*Rigveda*					Wet rice Fowl Water buffalo
	ZOROASTER	Raids cause shift of capital Feudalism	CHOU	*The Odes*		Use of rime
500	BUDDHA DARIUS	Iron Age First law code Canal and wall building		CONFUCIUS MO-TZÜ CHUANG-TZÜ LAO-TZÜ LORD SHANG	Bronze vessels Bronze mirrors Lacquer Jades Palace architecture	Advances in astronomy Traction plow Crossbow Round coins
	ALEXANDER CHANDRAGUPTA ASOKA	SHIH-HUANG-TI	CH'IN			Fighting on horseback Trousers, boots Iron sword
		Hsiung-nu raids Expansion under WU-TI	FORMER HAN	Civil examinations SSÜ-MA CH'IEN Canonical research Alchemy	Garden retreats Wall painting Sculpture	Mule, ass, camel introduced Soy bean Football
A.D.	JESUS	WANG MANG				
	KANISHKA			PAN KU PAN CHAO		Paper
	MARCUS AURELIUS		LATER HAN	Buddhist sutras translated	Glazed pottery	
	MANI		3 KINGDOMS	Taoism		Map of China Tea
		Buddhism firmly established	TSIN	Pilgrims to India	Calligraphy	Water mill
			WEI	TAO CH'IEN Chinese nuns	KU K'AI-CHIH	Sedan chair
500	ATTILA	South China colonized	SUNG CH'I		Greco-Indian influences in rock temples	Use of coal Kite
			CHI'I LIANG CHOU CH'EN			Firecracker
	MOHAMMED	Grand canal	SUI	Examination system Alien faiths HSÜAN-TSANG	Tomb figurines Painting	Law code Elephant chess Polo game
		Expansion up to 751	T'ANG	HAN YÜ Proscription of Buddhism	Porcelain	Block prints
	HARUN AL-RASHID	Block printing				
		Foot binding		Printing of all canonical works		Chairs
		WANG AN-SHIH	LIAO / 5 Dynasties	Classical renaissance Antiquarianism Judaism	Landscapes Private gardens	Paper money Ships for ocean travel Compass
1000			No. SUNG			
		JENGHIS KHAN	CHIN / So. SUNG	Drama CHU HSI Mathematics	Music	Cotton Gunpowder Sorghum
	Magna Carta The Polos			Islam Christianity	Cloisonne	Abacus Distillation of liquor Chaulmoogra oil
		Mongols expelled CHENG HO voyages	YUAN	Lamaism Encyclopaedias Gazetteers	Old and new styles in painting	Spectacles Syphilis
	COLUMBUS Magellan	Peking rebuilt Portuguese traders	MING	WANG SHOU-JEN Fiction	Colors on porcelain Under glaze blue and enamel	Maize and sweet potato
1500		Spaniards take P.I. Japanese raids		Jesuit influence Critical scholarship		Peanuts Tobacco and snuff
		The Manchus K'ANG-HSI era CH'IEN-LUNG era		Dictionaries Libraries		Imposition of queue Mexican dollar
		Mohammedan rebellions	CH'ING	Literary inquisition	European influences	Opium smoking Factories
		Tai-ping rebellion SUN YAT-SEN		Protestant Christianity Western education		Steamships Railroads Motor transport
1950	Two World Wars	Japanese invasions Communist control MAO TSE-TUNG	REPUBLIC	Mass education	Archeology	Aviation

Source: *A Short History of the Chinese People,* by L. Carrington Goodrich, Harper & Brothers, 1951.

Chronology of Events

Before 1945

Revolution of 1911 and Overthrow of Monarchy — May Fourth Movement — Nationalist-Communist Collaboration, 1923-27 — Chiang's Break with Communists, 1927 — Japanese Takeover of Manchuria, 1931-32 — Long March and Rise of Mao Tse-tung, 1934-35 — Japan's Attack on China, 1937 — Nationalist-Communist United Front, 1937-39 — Stilwell's Mission to China, 1942-44 — Cairo Conference and Declaration, 1943 — Hurley's Mission to China, 1944-45.

China's Republican Revolution. On Oct. 10, 1911, a mutiny of troops at Wuchang in the Yangtze (Changjiang) valley touched off revolution in China. Four months later, on Feb. 12, 1912, the last representative of the ancient Manchu (Manzu) dynasty, the infant Emperor Hsuan T'ung (Xuantong), abdicated. The act of abdication specified that Yuan Shih-k'ai (Yuan Shikai), long a supporter of the dynasty, was to organize a republican government at Peking (Beijing). To unify the country, Sun Yat-sen (Sun Zhongshan), father of the revolution and head of a provisional government at Nanjing, yielded the presidency to Yuan. Protracted civil strife, fed by rivalries among China's numerous warlords, prevailed over most of the country after Yuan Shih-k'ai died in 1916. In 1917 Sun Yat-sen established at Canton (Guangzhou) an independent republic to assume leadership of the struggle for national unification.

Founding of Parties. In 1912 the Kuomintang (Guomindang — Nationalist Party), a secret organization started before the revolution by Sun Yat-sen and other radical leaders, was turned into a political party, the first in China. On July 1, 1921, the Chinese Communist Party (CCP) was founded by 12 delegates, including Mao Tse-tung (Mao Zedong), who attended the first national congress of the party in Shanghai.

May 4 Movement. On May 4, 1919, the students of Peking University launched mass demonstrations which soon spread throughout China. The incidents were triggered by the announcement, made the same day, that the Versailles Conference had refused to return Japanese concessions in China, seized from Germany during World War I, to the Chinese. Many historians mark the demonstrations as the beginning of a new period when nationalism became the dominant force in Chinese politics.

May Fourth has also come to represent the culmination of a "literary and cultural renaissance" among China's intellectuals, 1917-21, during which they led China away from its traditional culture and toward an exposure to the new ideas invading China from the West. Centered at Peking University, the movement produced a new written language, tried to increase literacy and free the individual from the ideas of Confucianism that were written in the old style, and introduced new periodicals and books that espoused and debated all the social and philosophical ideas then current in the West: liberalism, socialism, social Darwinism and, after 1921, Marxist-Leninism.

Nationalist-Communist Collaboration. From 1923 until 1927, the Kuomintang accepted the aid and counsel of a Soviet mission invited to China to help the country "achieve unification and attain full national independence." The Nationalist Party was reorganized and Communists admitted, workers and peasants were mobilized in unions to give the party mass support and a Kuomintang military force was built under party control. In 1926 the "Northern Expedition" was launched against the northern warlords to extend the area of Nationalist control.

Chiang-Communist Break. Dissension among Nationalist leaders, growing since the death of Sun Yat-sen in 1925, came to a head early in 1927. At the end of March, military forces of Gen. Chiang Kai-shek (Jiang Jieshi), leader of the right wing, occupied Shanghai, massacred large numbers of workers, and dissolved trade unions. On April 18, 1927, Chiang set up a new government at Nanjing. Left-wingers in control of the established government, then in Wuhan, gave way to conservative pressures and made their peace with Chiang in June 1927. The Russians were then sent back to Moscow, and the Chinese Communists moved underground.

Unification of China. In June 1928 Peking fell to the armies of the Nationalists. On July 25, 1928, the United States became the first country to recognize the Nanjing government as the national government of the Republic of China. China's unification was completed, at least on the surface, when the Manchurian (Dongbei) provinces agreed to join the government at the end of 1928.

Communists in the South. After the Kuomintang-Communist split, dissident Communist army commanders,

Sources for the data in the chronology include Congressional Quarterly *Weekly Report* and *Almanac; China Quarterly; Current History; Facts on File; Foreign Broadcast Information Service; Survey of the China Mainland Press; China News Analysis; Foreign Affairs; Foreign Policy; Journal of Asian Studies; Issues and Studies; Far Eastern Economic Review; Asian Survey; Time; Newsweek; U.S. News & World Report; The New York Times; The Washington Post; The Times* of London; *The Toronto Globe and Mail; The Peking Review* (English language); *Hongqi* (Red Flag); *Renmin Ribao* (People's Daily); Xinhua (New China News Agency).

China Before the Revolution

17th-18th centuries: Russian migration eastwards, spearheaded by the cossacks, leads to military confrontations between Chinese and Russian troops in the 17th century. Treaties are signed at Nerchinsk (1689) and Kiakhta (1727) to define Sino-Russian boundaries and to establish limited commercial and diplomatic exchanges.

1784: First American ship, the "Empress of China," calls at Chinese port; Sino-American trade begins, mainly in U.S. food crops (maize, sweet potato, peanuts, tobacco) and Chinese arts, crafts and textiles.

1811: First American missionary arrives in China. Their ranks grow rapidly in the latter half of the century to about 8,000 in 1925.

1844: Treaty of Wang-hsia (Wangxia) signed by United States and China, granting America same rights imposed upon China by Britain after Opium War (1839-42) — extraterritoriality, most-favored-nation treatment and establishment of commercial centers, churches and hospitals in five ports.

1850: Beginning of two decades of substantial Chinese immigration into the United States.

1858-60: Through military occupations, ratified through so-called "unequal treaties" (including the June 18, 1858, Tianjin-Reed treaty), Russia takes all land north of the Amur River and east of the Ussuri River in Manchuria. This land was later called the Maritime Province, and has been a source of Chinese hostility towards Russia to the present day.

1861: U.S. Secretary of State Seward sends Anson Burlingame as first minister to Peking with instructions to cooperate with other foreign powers in assuring equal economic opportunity for all.

1864: Roughly 10,000 Chinese are recruited to work on the first transcontinental railroad across the U.S.

1868-70: Anson Burlingame conducts a worldwide tour to help revise treaties with foreigners in the hope of bringing "the shining banners of Western civilization" to China. Burlingame Treaty with China signed July 28, 1868.

1872-81: A total of 120 Chinese students travels to the United States.

1879: Congress, responding to increasingly violent agitation against Chinese immigration, passes bill limiting the number of Chinese permitted to arrive in U.S. to 15 per shipload. Although this bill is vetoed by President Hayes, both parties put immigration restrictions in their election platforms.

1882: Congress passes and President Arthur signs into law a bill to suspend Chinese immigration for ten years.

1892: Congress promulgates Geary Act, another exclusion law, which also required Chinese to register and carry identification.

Late 19th century: Although China manages to maintain most of its territories in the westernmost province of Xinjiang, Russian interest in East Asia increases through the late 19th century, particularly with the building of the Trans-Siberian Railway in the 1890s.

1899-1900: Secretary of State John Hay plays the leading role in having Western powers endorse the "Open Door Policy" which upholds the "equality of economic opportunity" for foreigners, and promises to protect the "territorial and administrative integrity" of China.

1900: America provides 2,100 men for an Allied force which suppresses the Boxer Rebellion and occupies the city of Peking. On July 3, 1900, Secretary Hay sends a circular note to the other nations participating in suppression of Boxer Rebellion to "preserve Chinese territorial and administrative integrity." In 1901 the United States is granted part of the indemnity paid by China because of the Boxer Rebellion. (Under arrangements provided through congressional action in 1908 and 1924, the U.S. returned all Boxer indemnity payments not already allocated, which were used for the education of Chinese students in the U.S. On Jan. 11, 1943, the U.S. yields all further claims to indemnity payments.)

1900-05: The Russian occupation of Manchuria, in the wake of the Boxer Rebellion of 1900, was a major cause of the Russo-Japanese War which led to the Russian defeat by Japan in 1905.

1902: U.S. exports to China reach $25 million, and investments total $19.7 million.

1905: Chinese students initiate boycotts of American goods, protesting U.S. immigration restrictions.

On Sept. 5 President Roosevelt uses his good offices to help Russia and Japan to negotiate an end to their war. The Treaty of Portsmouth wins Roosevelt the Nobel peace prize.

1908: On Sept. 5, in an exchange of notes between Secretary of State Elihu Root and Japanese ambassador to the U.S. Takahira, Japan agrees to American policy toward China. In the Root-Takahira Agreement, Japan agrees to maintain the status quo in the Pacific, to uphold the Open Door, and to support the "independence and integrity of China."

1909: In an effort to maintain the Open Door and to discourage any further penetration of Manchuria by Russia and Japan, the U.S. suggests that the railroads there be "neutralized" so that all powers could trade in the northeast. Despite this, in agreements signed on July 4, 1910, and June 25, 1912, Japan and Russia effectively close off Manchuria to trade with any other countries.

Sources: James R. Townsend (comp.), *The People's Republic of China: A Basic Handbook*, (New York: Council on International Affairs and China Council of the Asia Society, 1979); *United States Relations with China, with Special Reference to the Period 1944-49* (The China "White Paper") (Washington: U.S. State Dept., 1949).

including Mao Tse-tung, led thousands of soldiers into southern China. The Communist armies dominated extensive areas there from 1928 until Chiang Kai-shek, after repeated efforts, finally forced them out in October 1934.

Long March and Mao's Rise. In the famous Long March of 368 days, from October 1934 to October 1935, the escaping Communists made their way over 6,000 miles of often difficult terrain to establish a new center of power in the northwestern province of Shaanxi. Mao was successful in blaming the October 1934 defeat on the previous leadership, and in January 1935 this led to his election as chairman of the Politburo. This was the real beginning of Mao's control of the party.

Japan in Manchuria. On Sept. 19, 1931, Japanese troops stationed in South Manchuria to protect a sphere of interest that Japan had held there since 1905, bombarded the city of Mukden (Shenyang) and within three days subjected all of South Manchuria to Japanese control. Military occupation of the remainder of Manchuria was completed on Feb. 5, 1932. Meanwhile, on Jan. 7, 1932, U.S. Secretary of State Henry L. Stimson had proclaimed what became known as the Stimson doctrine of nonrecognition of territorial changes brought about by force.

Puppet State of Manchukuo. On Feb. 18, 1932, Manchuria was declared independent, and on March 1 it became the state of Manchukuo (Manzhouguo), controlled by the Japanese. On March 9, Henry P'u-yi, last of the Manchu emperors, was inaugurated as provisional dictator. On March 1, 1934, Manchukuo became a monarchy and P'u-yi was installed as Emperor K'ang Teh (Kangde).

Tangku Truce. On May 31, 1933, Japanese penetration into North China was halted by conclusion of the Tangku (Danggu) Truce, which established a demilitarized area stretching from the Great Wall to within 13 miles of Peking and from the coast 250 miles inland.

Chiang Kidnapped. On December 12, 1936, Chiang Kai-shek was kidnapped by troops of Marshal Chang Hsueh-liang (Zhang Xueliang), the former Manchurian warlord whose men, instead of fighting, were fraternizing with the Communists. Chiang was held captive at Xi'an until an understanding was reached to work for a Kuomintang-Communist alliance against the Japanese.

Japanese Attack. On July 7, 1937, a clash of Japanese and Chinese troops at the Marco Polo Bridge (Lukouqiao) outside of Peking led to the opening three weeks later of a full-scale Japanese offensive against China.

Kuomintang-Communist Alliance. On Sept. 22, 1937 the united front projected in December 1936 began to take form. On that day, the Central Committee of the Chinese Communist Party issued a manifesto proclaiming abandonment of efforts at insurrection and sovietization in favor of cooperation with the government against Japanese aggression. The following day, Chiang announced that the government would give up attempts at military suppression of communism in favor of seeking a political settlement.

Sinking of *U.S.S. Panay.* On Dec. 12, 1937, Japanese aviators bombed and sank the U. S. gunboat *Panay*, which was escorting U.S. tankers on the Yangtze River. Two Americans were killed and others injured. The crisis passed with Japan's statement of abject apologies.

Government Reforms. In March 1938 an Extraordinary National Congress of the Kuomintang, which included Communist Gen. Chou En-lai (Zhou Enlai) among the members of its presidium, established a People's Political Council to advise the government. On April 1, 1938, the National Congress adopted a Program of Armed Resistance and National Reconstruction containing a basic outline of principles to be followed by the wartime entente. The program called for governmental, economic and military reforms.

Kuomintang-Communist Friction. Late in 1938, relations between the Kuomintang and the Communists began to cool. In 1939 the government started to enforce a military blockade of Communist-held areas to prevent Communist infiltration of government-held areas. In January 1941, fighting broke out between government and Communist forces in the Yangtze valley. Similar clashes followed, but efforts to reach a political settlement continued.

Pearl Harbor. On Dec. 7, 1941, the Japanese attacked Pearl Harbor in Honolulu and on the following day the United States declared war against Japan.

Stilwell's Mission. On Feb. 2, 1942, Lt. Gen. Joseph W. Stilwell was ordered to Chongqing, the new Nationalist capital, as chief of staff to Generalissimo Chiang Kai-shek. On Feb. 7, 1942, the United States authorized a loan of $500 million to China.

Equal Rights for China. On Jan. 11, 1943, the United States and China signed a treaty, ratified May 20, 1943, by which the United Stated relinquished extraterritorial and related rights in China. On Dec. 17, 1943, President Franklin D. Roosevelt approved an act repealing discriminatory legislation affecting immigration of Chinese nationals into the United States and the naturalization of Chinese.

Recognition of China as a Great Power. On Oct. 30, 1943, upon U.S. insistence, a representative of China joined a conference of the the Big Three foreign ministers at Moscow to sign a Declaration of Four Nations on General Security. Acceptance of China as a signatory was interpreted as acknowledgement of China's status as a great power and of its right to participate with the other major powers in prosecuting the war, organizing the peace, and establishing machinery for postwar international cooperation.

Cairo Conference. The Cairo Declaration, issued Dec. 1, 1943, following a conference of President Roosevelt and British Prime Minister Winston Churchill with Chiang Kai-shek at Cairo, Nov. 22-26, voiced "their purpose that . . . all the territories Japan has stolen from the Chinese, such as Manchuria, Formosa [Taiwan], and the Pescadores [Penghu], shall be restored to the Republic of China." The declaration said also that the three powers were "determined that in due course Korea shall become free and independent."

Wallace's Mission. In late June 1944 Vice President Henry A. Wallace held long discussions with Chiang Kai-shek at Chongqing. Chiang told Wallace he desired a political agreement with the Communists.

Hurley's Mission. On Aug. 18, 1944, Major Gen. Patrick J. Hurley was named President Roosevelt's personal representative to China. Hurley arrived at Chongqing on Sept. 6; on Nov. 30, 1944, he was appointed U.S. ambassador to China. His first mission was to seek to improve relations between Chiang and Stilwell, but he found the two so near swords' points that he recommended that Stilwell be recalled. On Oct. 24 Lt. Gen. Albert C. Wedemeyer was designated to replace Stilwell. Hurley's second mission was to try to bring about a cessation of hostilities between the Nationalists and Communists. In December 1944 he reported that first steps toward that goal had been taken.

1945

Yalta Decisions on Asia — Hurley's China Activities — Death of Roosevelt and Succession of Truman — End of War in Europe — China's Rank as Great Power in United Nations — Atomic Bombs Dropped — Russia Enters War in East Asia — End of World War II — Sino-Soviet Alliance — Chiang-Mao Agreement — Nationalist-Communist Hostilities — Hurley's Resignation and Marshall's Appointment.

Yalta Conference. On Feb. 11 President Roosevelt, Prime Minister Churchill and Soviet Premier Joseph Stalin signed the Yalta Agreement on surrender terms, postwar treatment of the Axis nations, policies toward liberated countries, and plans for the United Nations. The three had met for a week at the Black Sea resort of Yalta.

Roosevelt had been urged by his military planners to seek a definite commitment for intervention of the Soviet Union in the Pacific war. The president also sought Stalin's agreement to give China an important place in the United Nations and allow Chinese repossession of lost territories.

The United States gained guarantees of Soviet entry into the Pacific war. In return, Outer Mongolia as well as strategic ports and railroads in Manchuria were conceded to the Soviet Union following the defeat of Japan "with the concurrence of Generalissimo Chiang Kai-shek," which Roosevelt agreed to obtain. For its part, the Soviet Union agreed "to conclude with the Nationalist government of China a pact of friendship and alliance."

It was further agreed that the Asian aspect of the agreement should remain secret because Russia had a neutrality treaty with Japan, and because information usually leaked from the Nationalists to Japan — an immediate announcement might sabotage negotiation of differences between Chinese Nationalists and Communists, which the U.S. ambassador to China, Major Gen. Hurley, felt were close to success. The Yalta terms were not officially disclosed to Chiang Kai-shek until June 15, 1945. *(See Aug. 14, 1945)*

Discussions in China. On Feb. 14 the Nationalist government announced that it had been negotiating with the Chinese Communists for two weeks with the assistance of Ambassador Hurley.

New Constitution for China. On March 1 Chiang Kai-shek announced that a national assembly would be convened Nov. 11, 1945, to draw up a constitution. Chiang invited the Communists to attend and to join the Nationalist government. On March 9 the Communists replied that the national assembly would be a "congress of slaves" and demanded that Chiang be removed from office.

U.S. Arms. On April 2 Ambassador Hurley announced that although the United States was sending arms and aid to China, none would go to the Communists. On April 28 Hurley noted that the United States, the Soviet Union and Great Britain agreed that China should be unified, and that "the Chinese must furnish their own leadership, make their own decisions and be responsible for their own policies."

Death of Roosevelt. On April 12 President Roosevelt died at Warm Springs, Ga., and Vice President Harry S Truman took the oath of office as president at the White House.

Hurley and Stalin. On April 15 Ambassador Hurley concluded a conference with Soviet Premier Joseph Stalin and Foreign Minister V. M. Molotov in Moscow and reported that Stalin "agreed unqualifiedly to America's policy in China as outlined to him during the conversation." On April 19 W. Averell Harriman, U.S. ambassador to the Soviet Union, who had participated in the conference, stated that he felt the Hurley report, while factually accurate, gave a "too optimistic impression of Marshal Stalin's reactions." Harriman warned that Stalin eventually "would make full use of and would support the Chinese Communists."

Harriman said he was certain that Stalin would not cooperate indefinitely with Chiang Kai-shek.

V-E Day. On May 8 the war ended in Europe. Both the United States and the Soviet Union shifted their attention to Asia.

China's Place in United Nations. On June 26, delegates to the organizing conference of the United Nations at San Francisco signed the U.N. Charter. The charter made the Republic of China, along with the United States, the Soviet Union, the United Kingdom and France, a permanent member of the Security Council and, as such, entitled to exercise the veto power.

Potsdam Conference. On July 17 President Truman, British Prime Minister Churchill and Soviet Premier Stalin met in Potsdam, Germany, to confer on the fate of the defeated Axis nations and the liberated areas. Concerning East Asia, Stalin asserted that the Chinese did not recognize the "pre-eminent interests of the Soviet Union" in the Manchurian port of Dairen (Dalian). President Truman indicated that the main interest of the United States was internationalization of that port, with the safeguarding of Soviet interests, as agreed at Yalta. Stalin replied that Dairen would be open to all nations and that he did not wish to "add in any respect to the Yalta agreement or to deceive the Chinese." It was reported later that President Truman was satisfied, but that Ambassador Harriman was convinced that the United States should obtain reaffirmation in writing of Stalin's oral assurances.

Atomic Bombs. On Aug. 6 a U.S. B-29 bomber, the *Enola Gay*, dropped the first atomic bomb on Hiroshima. On Aug. 9 another atomic bomb was dropped on Nagasaki.

Russia Enters War. On Aug. 8 the Soviet Union officially declared war on Japan. The next day, Soviet troops entered Manchuria.

Communists Move to Manchuria. On Aug. 11, units of the Chinese Communist army, about 100,000 strong, left their base in the northwest and began the move to Manchuria.

Japan Surrenders. On Aug. 14 Japan surrendered to the Allies.

Sino-Soviet Alliance. On Aug. 14 the Soviet Union and the Republic of China signed a Treaty of Friendship and Alliance, pledging mutual respect for their respective sovereignties and mutual non-interference in their respective internal affairs for a 30-year period. Chinese Premier T. V. Soong (Song Ziwen), brother of Mme. Chiang Kai-shek (Song Meiling) and Mme. Sun Yat-sen (Song Qingling), led the Chinese delegation to Moscow.

In separate agreements, the Soviet Union was granted ownership and management with China of the main Manchurian railways and joint use with China of Port Arthur (Lushun) as a naval base. Dairen was declared a free port. The Soviets agreed to respect Chinese sovereignty in Manchuria. China agreed to recognize the independence of Outer Mongolia if its people so voted in a plebiscite.

This treaty represented the acceptance and implementation of the Yalta accords by Russia and China.

Chiang's Appeal. On Aug. 15 Chiang Kai-shek sent a note to Mao Tse-tung in Yanan (the Communist headquarters) asking him to come to Chongqing, the Nationalist government's wartime capital, to confer on "many international and internal problems." On Aug. 26 Mao accepted the invitation. The next day the U.S. ambassador to China, Patrick J. Hurley, flew to Yanan to bring Mao to Chongqing. On Aug. 28 Mao and Hurley arrived in Chongqing.

Soviet Withdrawal. On Sept. 29, Soviet troops began withdrawing from Manchuria.

Communist-Nationalist Agreement. On Oct. 10, Nationalist and Communist representatives issued a joint communiqué in Chongqing, expressing vague agreement on democratization, local administration and reorganization of their troops. On Oct. 11 Mao Tse-tung returned to Yanan, following six weeks of negotiations that had preceded the agreement. Increased military activity by both sides rendered the agreement invalid within two weeks.

Outer Mongolia. On Oct. 22 the Soviet Union announced that an Outer Mongolian plebiscite showed an overwhelming vote for independence from China.

More Fighting. On Oct. 27 the Nationalist government reported that hostilities between Nationalist and Communist forces were continuing in 11 of China's 28 provinces despite the Oct. 10 agreement between Chiang and Mao. On Oct. 29 the government reported that Chinese Communist forces were massing near the area where U.S. ships were scheduled to land Nationalist troops in Manchuria. The report said the Communists had cut the rail lines between Peking and Hankou. The Communists rejected demands that they withdraw, and on Oct. 31, 100,000 Communist troops attacked Datong. On Nov. 2, as the Communist attacks continued, U.S. transports landed Nationalist troops at Huludao in Manchuria.

On Nov. 5 the radio in Yanan, the Communist headquarters and the *New China Daily News*, a Communist paper published in Chongqing, charged that U.S. troops sent to China to help disarm the Japanese were aiding the Nationalist forces against the Communists.

On Nov. 8 Lt. Gen. Albert C. Wedemeyer, Stilwell's replacement as chief of staff to Chiang, conceded that U.S. troops in Shanghai had been involved in skirmishes with the Communists. Fighting continued throughout the month with Nationalist forces making gains in Manchuria. There were also repeated reports of skirmishing of U.S. troops with Communist forces.

Sino-Soviet Agreement. On Nov. 27 the Nationalist government reported that the Soviet Union, which still had some troops in Manchuria, had agreed to aid the Nationalists in occupying Manchuria and had ordered the Chinese Communist forces to abandon Mukden and Changchun, large cities in eastern Manchuria.

Resignation of Hurley. On Nov. 27 U.S. Ambassador Patrick J. Hurley resigned to protest the U.S. decision to stop military aid to Chiang Kai-shek. At the same time, he charged that career officials had sabotaged his efforts to bring about a reconciliation between the Nationalists and the Communists. "A considerable section of our State Department is endeavoring to support communism generally as well as specifically in China."

Marshall Appointed. On Nov. 27 President Truman appointed Gen. George C. Marshall as the special representative of the president in China, with the personal rank of ambassador.

Troops in Manchuria. On Nov. 29 the Soviet Union announced it had agreed to a request from the Chinese government to defer withdrawing Soviet troops from Manchuria until Nationalist troops could take over.

Fighting in Shandong. On Nov. 30 it was reported that 200,000 Chinese Communist troops had invaded Shandong Province. On Nov. 28 the Chinese Communists in Yanan had charged that the United States "recklessly lines up with all the worst elements in China . . . to attack the Chinese people."

On Dec. 1 Lt. Gen. Albert C. Wedemeyer said the Chinese government was still receiving U.S. military aid through the lend-lease program.

Byrnes on China. On Dec. 4 Secretary of State James F. Byrnes said in a letter to Rep. Jack Z. Anderson, R-Calif., that "we favor the creation of a strong, united and democratic China" and "feel that collaboration" between the Soviet Union, China, the United States and Great Britain is "essential" to peace in East Asia.

Hurley's Testimony. On Dec. 5 Major Gen. Patrick J. Hurley told the Senate Foreign Relations Committee that five career diplomats had attempted to undermine U.S. policy in China. He identified them as George A. Atcheson Jr., John S. Service, John Davies, Fulton Freeman and Arthur Ringwalt.

Truman on China Fighting. On Dec. 15, in a major policy speech, President Truman called on the Chinese to stop fighting and urged the calling of a national conference of the major political elements in China to end the internal strife and unify the country. Truman also said each political element should be given a fair voice in the Chinese government. *(Text, p. 303)*

Marshall in China. On Dec. 22 Gen. George C. Marshall arrived in Chongqing and met with Nationalist Premier T. V. Soong and Communist Gen. Chou En-lai. On Dec. 27 Chou proposed a "nationwide and immediate unconditional truce."

Moscow Conference. On Dec. 27 U.S. Secretary of State Byrnes, Soviet Foreign Minister Molotov and British Foreign Minister Ernest Bevin announced they had reached a series of agreements after 11 days of discussion in Moscow. Concerning China, the three agreed "as to the need for a democratic and unified China under the National government, and for cessation of civil strife." Molotov said that withdrawal of Soviet forces from Manchuria "had been postponed until Feb. 1, [1946] at the request of the Chinese government." It was reported that Byrnes and Molotov had decided that both Soviet and American troops would be withdrawn from China "at the earliest practicable moment consistent with the discharge of their obligations and responsibilities."

Truce Proposal. On Dec. 31 the Nationalist government in effect accepted Chou En-lai's Dec. 27 truce proposal and suggested that Gen. Marshall act as mediator between the two sides.

1946

Marshall's Efforts to Mediate Between Nationalists and Communists — Civil War Truce — Soviet Removal of Machinery from Manchuria — Nationalist-Communist Clashes in Manchuria — Government Returns to Nanjing — Truce in Manchuria — More Fighting — New U.S. Ambassador — Sale of War Surplus to China — National Assembly Meets — End of Nationalist-Communist Negotiations — Adoption of Constitution — Chinese Inflation.

Marshall Mediation. On Jan. 7 Gen. Chang Ch'ün (Zhang Qun), Nationalist government representative, and Gen. Chou En-lai, Communist representative, met with Gen. Marshall in Chongqing.

Truce in Civil War. On Jan. 10 an agreement for cessation of hostilities in China's civil war was reached. Chiang Kai-shek and Mao Tse-tung both ordered their forces to cease hostilities and halt all troop movements. To enforce the truce, it was agreed to establish an executive headquarters in Peking manned by one representative each of the Nationalist government, the Communists and the United States. U.S. participation was to be solely for the purpose of assisting the Chinese members in implementation of the cease-fire.

Political Conference. On Jan. 10 the Political Consultative Conference (PCC) opened in Chongqing with a speech by Chiang Kai-shek pledging recognition of fundamental democratic rights. The delegates, representing almost every faction in the country, agreed on immediate organization of a coalition government. Resolutions were offered to convene a National Assembly on May 5 to adopt a constitution, to recognize the legality of all political parties and to pledge all parties to accept the national leadership of President Chiang Kai-shek.

On Jan. 31 the PCC adopted the resolutions. It was announced during the conference that both Communists and Nationalists would reduce their military forces.

Charges and Countercharges. On Feb. 15 the Chinese Communist Party in Yanan demanded joint control of Manchuria along with the Nationalist government. The statement noted that the Communists controlled an army of 300,000 in Manchuria.

Military Unification. On Feb. 25, amid reports of heavy fighting between Communists and Nationalists in Manchuria, a military accord was signed in Chongqing providing for gradual unification of the opposing armies.

Removal of Machinery. On Feb. 26, reports from Manchuria said the Soviet commander in Mukden conceded that "Japanese" machinery was being taken out of Manchuria. On March 1 the United States protested the removal as illegal, and anti-Soviet demonstrations erupted throughout China.

Kuomintang Meeting. On March 1-17 the Kuomintang's Central Executive Committee met in Chongqing to consider the resolutions adopted by the Political Consultative Conference on Jan. 31. Although the committee announced its approval of the resolutions, there were rumors that right-wing elements within the Kuomintang were attempting to "sabotage" the PCC program.

Troops in Manchuria. On March 14 the Nationalist government reported 300,000 Soviet troops, 200,000 Chinese Communist troops and 120,000 Nationalist troops were in Manchuria. On March 23 the Chinese foreign minister said the Soviet Union had given notice that the deadline for departure of Russian troops from Manchuria, originally Feb. 1, had been moved back to April 30 because of "technical difficulties."

Marshall Returns Home. On March 15 Gen George C. Marshall, returning from China, reported to the president. On March 16 Marshall said the situation in Manchuria was "extremely critical."

Reports from Manchuria. On March 30, Soviet troops unexpectedly began to withdraw from Manchuria. Nationalist and Communist forces continued to move in. Amid repeated reports of fighting between Nationalists and Communists in Manchuria, Gen. Chou En-lai, head of the Communist delegation at Chongqing, urged the United States to discontinue military aid to the Nationalist government until a new coalition government had been formed.

Battle for Changchun. On April 14, Soviet troops evacuated Changchun, capital of Manchuria, and fighting broke out immediately between Nationalists and Communists for control of the city.

Changchun Falls. On April 17, Communist forces occupied Changchun.

Marshall Back in China. On April 18 Gen. Marshall returned to Chongqing from Washington and proposed that field teams be sent to Manchuria to implement the Jan. 10 cease-fire agreements.

National Assembly Postponed. On April 24 President Chiang Kai-shek postponed indefinitely the National Assembly scheduled to meet May 5 to draw up a constitution. The Communists had refused to nominate delegates until Nationalist-Communist differences were settled.

Harbin Falls. On April 25, as Russian troops withdrew, Chinese Communist forces occupied the Manchurian city of Harbin. On April 28 the Chinese Communists occupied Qiqihar, a railroad center in Manchuria.

Russians Leave. On May 3 the last Russian troops left Manchuria.

Government Returns to Nanjing. On May 5 the Kuomintang government moved from Chongqing back to Nanjing. Forced out of Nanjing by the approach of Japanese forces in November 1937, the government had fled to Hankou and then, in October 1938, to Chongqing.

Changchun Recaptured. On May 23, Nationalist forces recaptured Changchun, capital of Manchuria.

Truce Announced. On June 7 a 15-day truce went into effect in Manchuria. Both sides announced that, during the truce, agreement would be sought on a permanent truce and on execution of the Feb. 25 agreement for military reunification.

Truce Extended. On June 21 President Chiang Kai-shek announced that the temporary truce in Manchuria had been extended to June 30 at the request of the Communists.

Truce Ended. On June 30 the temporary truce ended. On July 8 the Nationalist government announced that its troops had renewed the fighting in Manchuria. On July 16 the Communist representative in Nanjing, Gen. Chou En-lai, urged Gen. George C. Marshall to use his influence to renew the truce.

New U.S. Ambassador. On July 11 President Truman appointed Dr. J. Leighton Stuart, president of Yanjing University in Peking, as U.S. ambassador to China. Stuart succeeded Major Gen. Patrick J. Hurley, who had resigned in 1945.

U.S. Marines Ambushed. On July 28 a U.S. Marine convoy was ambushed by Communist troops near Peking. Three Americans were killed and 12 wounded. On Aug. 5 Washington announced it had no intention of withdrawing U.S. forces from China.

Truman's Letter to Chiang. On the same day, President Truman sent a note to President Chiang Kai-shek stating that the United States might have to redefine its position on China unless there was noticeable progress toward a peaceful settlement of differences with the Communists. Chiang issued a statement three days later blaming the Communists for a breakdown in negotiations and stating his demands for peace.

Sale of War Surplus to China. On Aug. 30 the United States signed an agreement for sale to the Nationalists of surplus supplies except combat material in China and the Pacific islands. The announcement caused the Chinese Communists to denounce the United States for attempting to mediate between the two Chinese factions while furnishing one of them with war materials.

Marshall Memorandum. On Oct. 1 Gen. George C. Marshall in a private memorandum informed President Chiang Kai-shek that he would recommend to President Truman that the United States discontinue its efforts at mediation unless "a basis for agreement is found ... without further delays." On the same day, Chou En-lai informed Marshall that if the Nationalist government did not halt its offensive against Kalgan, a Communist base in Chahar Province in Inner Mongolia, there would be "a total national split." On Oct. 2 the Nationalist government reported to Marshall that its "maximum concessions" would be to issue a cease-fire order if the Communists began to integrate their forces into the Nationalist army and appointed their delegates to the National Assembly.

Kalgan Falls. On Oct. 11 the Communist base of Kalgan in Chahar Province was seized by the Kuomintang.

Peace Talks Resumed. On Oct. 21 Communists and Nationalists resumed peace talks in Nanjing.

Sino-U.S. Treaty. On Nov. 4 a five-year Sino-American Treaty of Friendship, Commerce and Navigation was signed at Nanjing.

U.S. Elections. On Nov. 5 the Republican Party won a landslide victory in the off-year congressional elections, gaining a majority in both houses of the 80th Congress.

Nationalist Cease-Fire. On Nov. 8 Chiang Kai-shek ordered Kuomintang troops to cease hostilities at noon, Nov. 11, "except as may be necessary to defend their positions." Chiang again invited the Communists to par-

ticipate in the National Assembly scheduled to meet Nov. 15.

National Assembly Convenes. On Nov. 15 the National Assembly convened in Nanjing, with the Communists and a majority of third-party representatives boycotting the session. Chiang Kai-shek called the meeting the beginning of constitutional government for China.

Chou's Statement. On Nov. 16 Chou En-lai, Communist representative in Nanjing, charged that the Kuomintang's action in convening the assembly was contrary to the resolutions adopted Jan. 31 by the Political Consultative Conference. He said the Communist Party would not recognize the assembly and said the Kuomintang had "slammed" the door to negotiations. On the same day, Chou asked Gen. Marshall for transportation back to the Communist headquarters at Yanan.

Negotiations Cease. On Nov. 19 Chou En-lai returned to Yanan aboard a U.S. Army plane. With his departure, all negotiations between Communists and Nationalists, carried on intermittently since January, were terminated. By the end of November, fighting had resumed and the country was braced for full-scale war. On Dec. 4 the Communists notified Gen. Marshall they would not negotiate until the "illegal" assembly was dissolved and Nationalist troops were withdrawn to positions they held on Jan. 13.

Marshall's Warning. On Dec. 1 Gen. Marshall met with Chiang Kai-shek and warned that the Communist forces were too strong to defeat militarily. He said negotiations offered the only sensible way to avert the complete collapse of China's economy.

Truman Reaffirms U.S. Policy. On Dec. 18 President Truman reaffirmed U.S. belief in a "united and democratic China." He said he would continue the policy of avoiding involvement in Chinese civil strife while "helping the Chinese people to bring about peace and economic recovery in their country."

Constitution of China Adopted. On Dec. 25 the National Assembly in Nanjing adopted a constitution to go into effect on Dec. 25, 1947. The constitution contained no significant changes or reforms.

Chinese Hyperinflation. The Chinese economy, which had experienced serious but not critical inflation during the war, became hyperinflated in the 16 months following the war's end. By Dec. 31 the wholesale price index in Shanghai (1937 = 1) had hit 1,143,000 — i.e., it took more than 1 million yuan to buy what had cost 1 yuan in 1937.

1947

Marshall Reports in Washington — Mediation Effort Ended — Continuing Hostilities in China — U.S. Arms Aid — Wedemeyer's Fact-Finding Mission and Report — New U.S. Aid Program — Elections for National Assembly — New Chinese Constitution — Soviet Mediation Offer Rejected — Chinese Inflation.

Anti-U.S. Demonstrations. On Jan. 1 about 5,000 students in Shanghai demonstrated to protest the alleged rape of a Chinese girl by a U.S. Marine. On Jan. 3 the demonstrations spread to Nanjing where U.S. Ambassador J. Leighton Stuart told the crowd that the matter would be investigated. On Jan. 4 Nationalist Premier T. V. Soong ordered the demonstrations to cease.

Marshall Recalled. On Jan. 6 President Truman announced that Gen. George C. Marshall had been recalled to Washington. The U.S. effort at mediating the Chinese civil war had ended in failure.

Marshall to State Department. On Jan. 7 President Truman announced the nomination of Gen. Marshall as Secretary of State, replacing the ailing James F. Byrnes.

Marshall's Report. On Jan. 8 Gen. Marshall's report on China was made public. Marshall blamed the breakdown in Nationalist-Communist negotiations on the air of suspicion and the extremism in both camps. "The salvation of the situation," he said, "would be the assumption of leadership by the liberals in the government and in the minority parties, and successful action on their part under the leadership of the Generalissimo would lead to unity through good government."

U.S. Ends Mediation Effort. On Jan. 29 the United States announced termination of its efforts to mediate a settlement in China and immediate withdrawal of its troops. U.S. Ambassador J. Leighton Stuart made formal notification to President Chiang Kai-shek and to Wang Bingnan, the Communist representative in Nanjing. The last U.S. Marine convoy left China in June.

New Nationalist Offensive. On Feb. 2 the Nationalist government launched a new military offensive involving about 500,000 troops in southern Shandong Province. Communist forces either withdrew or deserted to the Nationalists.

AP Report. On Feb. 15 the Associated Press reported that President Chiang Kai-shek had said in an interview that the United States was responsible for prolonging the civil war because it was withholding arms shipments and credits from the Nationalist government. The AP said Chiang was convinced that the Communists had to be shattered militarily.

Taiwan Uprising. On Feb. 28 a major rebellion broke out on the island of Taiwan and was immediately suppressed by the Nationalist government. Over 3,000 Taiwanese were reportedly slain.

Soong Resigns. On March 1 Premier T. V. Soong resigned and President Chiang Kai-shek took his place (while remaining as president).

Hostilities. On March 1 it was reported that Communist forces had launched a new offensive against Changchun, capital of Manchuria, but on March 4 the Nationalist government's commander there stated that the Communists had been driven back. Reports from Yanan, the Communists' "capital," indicated the city was being evacuated as Nationalist forces approached.

Contacts Ended. On March 5 the last Communist representative, Wang Bingnan, left Nanjing. On March 10 the U.S. liaison detachment, which had monitored Communist activities since 1944, left Yanan. This ended all official contacts between the Nationalists and the Communists and marked the beginning of large-scale fighting.

Yanan Captured. On March 19, Nationalist forces occupied an already abandoned Yanan, the Communist "capital," and claimed to have routed over 100,000 Communist troops. U.S. Ambassador J. Leighton Stuart

called the claim a "gross exaggeration" and warned that such military actions only overextended the Nationalist supply lines and drained the national economy. Stuart noted that withdrawal "in the face of enemy pressure" was a Communist military tactic.

Taiwan. On March 22 the Central Executive Committee of the Kuomintang demanded the ouster of the governor of Taiwan, Ch'en Yi, and blamed him for the conditions that caused the Feb. 28 rebellion there. On March 31 the United Press reported that Ch'en had resigned.

Marines Killed. On April 5 five U.S. Marines were killed and 16 wounded during an attack by Communist troops on a Marine ammunition dump near Danggu.

Reorganization at Nanjing. On April 16 a government reorganization was announced at Nanjing. Gen. Chang Ch'ün (Zhang Qun) was appointed premier. Dr. Sun Fo (Sun Ke), a leftist and son of the founder of the Chinese Republic, Sun Yat-sen, was elected vice president. Although a number of representatives of third parties were installed in office, the Kuomintang's old guard remained in control of the government.

Anti-war Rioting. On May 16, students began rioting at the University of Nanjing. Until the end of June, the government was forced to contend with student demonstrations for an end to the civil war and for government action to improve the lagging economy.

New Taiwan Governor. On May 16 Dr. Wei Tao-ming (Wei Daoming) assumed office as the new governor of Taiwan and on the same day the island officially became a province of China.

Last Marines Leave China. On June 17 the last contingent of U.S. Marines in China began to leave.

U.S. Arms Aid to China. On June 20, as Communist forces in Manchuria closed in on Changchun, the provincial capital, Vice President Sun Fo appealed in Nanjing for more U.S. aid. On June 26 the U.S. lifted its embargo on the sale of arms to China. On June 27 the State Department announced it had sold $6.5 million worth of ammunition to the Nationalist government at one-tenth the procurement cost.

Marshall's Message. On July 6 Secretary of State George C. Marshall told President Chiang Kai-shek that the United States was "perturbed over the economic deterioration resulting from the spread of hostilities." Marshall's message warned that the United States could "only assist as conditions develop which give some beneficial results."

Wedemeyer Mission. On July 9 President Truman instructed Lt. Gen. Albert C. Wedemeyer, who had been Chiang Kai-shek's chief of staff from late 1945 till mid-1946, to proceed to China on a fact-finding mission "for the purpose of making an appraisal of the political, economic, psychological, and military situations. . . ."

On Aug. 24 Wedemeyer, just before leaving China after a month's stay, strongly criticized the Nationalist government for its corruption and inefficiency and the inadequacy of its military effort. Wedemeyer warned that the government could not defeat communism by force, but only with the enthusiastic support of the Chinese people gained through immediate political and economic reforms. The fate of the Nationalist government, he said, depended on the timeliness and effectiveness of reforms.

On Sept. 2 Premier Chang Ch'ün said the government would not change any of its domestic or foreign policies because of the Wedemeyer statements.

Chiang's Admission of Failure. On Sept. 9 the Fourth Plenary Session of the Kuomintang Central Executive Committee opened in Nanjing with an address by President Chiang Kai-shek admitting his "failure" to implement the principles of Sun Yat-sen, but blaming the party for China's unsolved problems and absolving himself of all responsibility. Chiang said the Kuomintang was doomed unless there was reform and admitted that the Communists had proven themselves abler and more devoted than the Nationalists.

Wedemeyer Report. On Sept. 19 Lt. Gen. Albert C. Wedemeyer submitted his report to President Truman, but it was not made public until the summer of 1949 because of the general's suggestion that Manchuria be placed by the United Nations under the guardianship of a five-power commission that would include the Soviet Union, or under a U.N. trusteeship. The president and Secretary of State Marshall both felt this recommendation would be highly offensive to the Chinese, for it would represent the government as incapable of governing its own territory. The report recommended a five-year program of economic and military aid to China. It stipulated that China accept U.S. advisers to assist "in utilizing U.S. aid in the manner for which it is intended." The report further stipulated that China must carry out economic, political and military reforms.

Elections Postponed. On Sept. 26 the Nationalist government's State Council in Nanjing postponed elections for the National Assembly from Oct. 21 to Nov. 21, 1947.

Communist Leaders Meet. On Oct. 5 the leaders of nine Communist nations, meeting in Poland, issued a manifesto stressing the need for stronger ties among various communist parties. This was the first international communist meeting since the abolition of the Communist International in 1941.

The manifesto declared that the entire world is divided into two blocs: (1) "the camp of imperialism and anti-democratic forces," and (2) "an anti-imperialist democratic camp." It was predicted that world history would be determined by the struggle between these two camps.

This notion of two competing blocs also characterized the views of U.S. leaders during the Cold War, although they labeled them "communist" and "free." This viewpoint would last until 1956 in the Soviet Union and longer in China and the United States.

Anarchy in Shanghai. On Oct. 15 the Nationalist government announced that Shanghai was in a state of anarchy and that the death penalty would be imposed for law violations, especially hoarding of food.

Communist Land Reform. On Oct. 18 the Chinese Communists announced they had embarked on a new land reform program, abolishing the ownership rights of "all landlords."

Aid Agreement Signed. On Oct. 27 a U.S. aid agreement was signed in Nanjing to provide the Chinese with food, supplies and other basic essentials of life.

Democratic League Outlawed. On Oct. 28 a Nationalist government decree outlawed the Democratic League, one of the minor parties, on the ground that it was subservient to the Communists.

New Aid Program. On Nov. 10 Secretary of State George C. Marshall, appearing before a joint session of the Senate Foreign Relations and House Foreign Affairs committees, announced the administration's intention to seek approval of a new China economic aid program. During hearings on the following days, Marshall tentatively estimated that the amount would be approximately $300 million over a 15-month period beginning April 1, 1948. The secretary added that the situation in China was "very decidedly one where we have found the greatest difficulty in trying to calculate a course where money could be appropriated with, as I put it, a 70 percent probability of effective use in the situation." On Nov. 15 Nationalist government leaders called the U.S. aid plan a "drop in the bucket" and urged the United States to give them $3 billion over a three-year period.

China Elections. On Nov. 21-23, a three-day popular election by secret ballot, the first in China's history, was held to choose representatives for the National Assembly. The government claimed that 20 million persons voted and that Kuomintang candidates won most of the seats.

New Constitution. On Dec. 25 the new Chinese constitution, adopted by the National Assembly a year earlier, went into effect.

Soviet Mediation Offer. On Dec. 30 President Chiang Kai-shek's private secretary informed the U.S. Embassy that the Soviet Union had offered to mediate between the Chinese factions, but that the Chinese government "neither desired nor believed possible any accommodation with the Chinese Communists at that time."

Chinese Hyperinflation. On Dec. 31 the wholesale price index at Shanghai (1937 = 1) hit 16,759,000. *(See Dec. 31, 1946)*

1948

Heavy Fighting in Manchuria — U.S., British Nationals Warned to Leave North China — Consideration of China Aid by Congress — Aid Agreement Signed — State Department Directives to U.S. Embassy at Nanjing — Communist Gains in Manchuria — Americans Urged to Leave Nanjing — Mme. Chiang Pleads for More Aid — Chinese Inflation.

Warning. On Feb. 15 the U.S. and British governments warned their nationals to leave northern China.

China Aid Program. On Feb. 18 President Truman submitted to Congress a $570 million program of economic aid for China. The sum of $510 million was to finance imports of essential civilian commodities and the remaining $60 million to finance selected industrial and transportation reconstruction projects.

Czech Coup. On Feb. 20-25, Czech Communists gained control of the government at Prague, assuring Soviet domination of Czechoslovakia.

Communists Take Luoyang. On March 12 the Communists captured the key northern city of Luoyang. The strategic initiative had gone to the Communist troops.

Action in National Assembly. On March 29 the Chinese National Assembly met in Nanjing and on April 19 re-elected Chiang Kai-shek as president, but Li Tsung-jen (Li Zongren), a longtime opponent of Chiang's, was named vice president over Chiang's objections. Many of the delegates from Manchuria and north China expressed discontent with the government's conduct of the war in their area.

China Aid Authorized. On April 2 Congress completed action on the foreign aid authorization bill. Economic aid authorized for China was reduced to $338 million, but $125 million was added to the bill for the Chinese government to use as it saw necessary, which presumably meant for military purposes. The total amount authorized thus was $463 million.

On April 3 President Truman signed the foreign aid bill. *(Text p. 304)*

Student Riots. On May 5 a student demonstration in Shanghai began an "anti-hunger and anti-civil war" movement that soon spread to other parts of the country.

Demonstrations Banned. On May 18 the Nationalist government prohibited all demonstrations and strikes. Although the order was largely ineffective, a nationwide strike set for June 2 was averted by resort to repressive measures.

New Chinese Premier. On May 24 President Chiang Kai-shek named Dr. Wong Wen-hao (Weng Wenhao) the new premier, succeeding Chang Ch'ün. Wong, considered a moderate, on May 31 chose an 18-man Cabinet that included six non-Kuomintang members. On June 11 he said it would take at least two years to defeat the Communists.

Berlin. On June 18 the Soviet Union instituted its blockade of Berlin.

Aid Agreement Signed. On July 3 the United States and China signed an aid agreement under which the Nationalist government was to receive $275 million for nonmilitary supplies and $125 million for use at its discretion.

Communists in United States. On July 31 the House Un-American Activities Committee opened hearings on Communist activity in the United States before and since World War II. The hearings led to the investigation of disloyalty charges against former State Department official Alger Hiss.

China Policy Directives. On Aug. 12 Secretary of State George C. Marshall advised the staff of the American Embassy in Nanjing (1) that the U.S. "must not directly or indirectly give any implication of support, encouragement or acceptability of coalition government in China with Communist participation," and (2) that the U.S. had "no intention of again offering its good offices as mediator in China."

On the following day, a second policy directive advised the embassy that it was "not likely that the situation will make it possible for us at this juncture to formulate any rigid plans for our future policy in China."

Jinan Falls. On Sept. 23 Jinan, an industrial and railroad center and capital of Shandong Province, fell to the Communists. Chiang Kai-shek on Oct. 10 called the loss "the greatest disaster."

House Report on China. On Oct. 3 the House Foreign Affairs Subcommittee on World Communism, chaired by Rep. Frances P. Bolton, R-Ohio (1940-69), issued a report calling China the "active theatre" in the cold war. The report said the Communists were using China as a testing ground for tactics they might use to take over the world. The subcommittee recommended that the United States give the Nationalist government a "guarantee of territorial and political integrity."

Changchun Falls. On Oct. 20 the capital of Manchuria, Changchun, fell to the Communist troops of Lin Piao (Lin Biao), who had been attacking the city since the year before. The loss of Changchun culminated a series of Nationalist defeats in Manchuria that had been characterized by poor leadership, poor morale, and numerous defections of Nationalist troops.

Two Blocs. On Nov. 1 Liu Shao-ch'i (Liu Shaoqi), second ranking leader of the Chinese Communist Party, articulated what would later be known as the "two bloc thesis." In an article entitled "Internationalism and Nationalism," Liu asserted: "The world today has been divided into two mutually antagonistic camps, on the one hand, the world imperialist camp, composed of the American imperialists and their accomplices — the reactionaries of all the world; on the other hand, the world anti-imperialist camp, composed of the Soviet Union and the New Democracies of Eastern Europe, and the national liberation movements in China, Southeast Asia, and Greece, plus the people's democratic forces of all countries of the world."

Mukden Falls. On Nov. 1 Mukden (Shenyang), regarded as the key to Manchuria, fell to the Communists. Thereafter, the smaller Manchurian cities and towns went down one after another. The Nationalist effort in Manchuria had cost the government 30 good divisions, half of which had been equipped by the United States. With this equipment in hand, the Communists were now free to transfer these troops to China proper.

Truman Re-elected. On Nov. 2 President Truman surprised almost all political observers by winning re-election. Democrats not only held on to the White House but also regained control of the House and the Senate. Truman's triumph at the polls dealt a serious blow to President Chiang Kai-shek, who felt that a Republican victory would result in more U.S. aid for China. On Nov. 4 President Truman told Congress that "many difficulties" were involved in making aid to China effective and that Americans had to oversee constantly how funds were expended. The United States, however, had approved Chinese purchases of arms worth $5 million on Nov. 1.

Americans in China Urged to Leave. On Nov. 5 the United States advised Americans in Nanjing to leave. On Nov. 17, U.S. consular officials warned Americans of the danger of remaining in any part of China except the far south and Taiwan. The U.S. Navy began to evacuate Americans from Shanghai.

Huai-hai Battle. On Nov. 7 the Communist forces launched a full-scale attack against the last large concentration of regular Nationalist units defending the central China plain. The battle lasted until Jan. 10, 1949, and was a complete defeat for the Kuomintang. Many of the Nationalists' best units were either destroyed, captured or defected to the Communists. The way was now clear for the Communists to invade southern China.

Supplies Not a Factor. On Nov. 16, responding to charges that the U.S. failure to aid the Nationalists had caused their recent defeats, Major General David Barr, chief of the U.S. Joint Military Advisory Group attached to the Nationalists, stated: "No battle has been lost since my arrival due to lack of ammunition or equipment. Their military debacles in my opinion can be attributed to the world's worst leadership and many other morale-destroying factors that lead to a complete loss of will to fight."

New Requests for Aid. On Nov. 18 President Chiang Kai-shek asked President Truman for an immediate increase in material aid. Truman's reply was non-committal. Experts in Washington were said to believe that it would cost $5 billion to "rescue" the Chinese Nationalists, and then only if it were certain the money would be spent wisely. On Nov. 24 President Truman and Secretary of State George C. Marshall conferred on China. Marshall said later that a large U.S. aid program might involve the United States directly in the civil war.

New Premier. On Nov. 26 Dr. Sun Fo, son of Sun Yat-sen, succeeded Dr. Wong Wen-hao as premier.

Mme. Chiang's Visit. On Dec. 1 Mme. Chiang Kai-shek arrived in Washington to plead personally for $3 billion in aid over a three-year period. The Democratic administration, since the election no longer under severe pressure from Congress, politely ignored her. The administration was reported to feel that, because China had received $2.5 billion in aid from the United States since the end of World War II, because Chiang had never really paid attention to the advice Secretary Marshall had given him in 1946, and, finally, because the Nationalist armies were not fighting with any degree of enthusiasm, only direct U.S. military involvement would stop the Chinese Communists. On Dec. 16 Acting Secretary of State Robert A. Lovett said that the United States definitely would not get involved in the Chinese civil war, nor, he said, would U.S. aid be increased if a coalition government were-formed.

Chinese Hyperinflation. On Dec. 31 the wholesale price index at Shanghai (1937=1) hit 21,568,000,000. *(See Dec. 31, 1946)*

1949

U.S. Declines Request to Mediate — Mao Calls on Nationalists to Surrender — Chiang Retires and Vice President Li Tsung-jen Becomes Acting President — Peking Falls — Government Moves to Canton — Red Terms for Peace Rejected — Nanjing Falls — Shanghai Falls — U.S. China Policy Review — U.S. Ambassador Leaves China — State Department's White Paper — People's Republic Proclaimed — Acheson Lists Conditions for Recognition — Canton and Chongqing Fall — Nationalist Government Moves to Taiwan.

Foreign Mediation Asked. On Jan. 8 the Chinese foreign minister requested the U.S., British, French and Soviet governments to mediate a restoration of peace with the Chinese Communists. The request was declined by the United States on Jan. 12. On Jan. 5 the Communists had announced over their radio that they would "fight to the finish" rather than negotiate with Chiang or any other "war criminal."

Mao's Demands. On Jan. 14 CCP Chairman Mao Tse-tung issued an "eight-point program" calling for surrender of the Nationalist government and punishment of "war criminals."

Chiang Retires. On Jan. 21 President Chiang Kai-shek announced his retirement and left Nanjing for Feng-hua, his native home. Vice President Li Tsung-jen became acting president. Despite his resignation, Chiang would continue to issue orders to those military units loyal to him personally.

Chinese Language Reform

Since the early part of the 20th century, the Chinese have been engaged in reforming their written language. During the 1920s, as a part of the New Culture movement, literate Chinese (then, as now, a small minority) abandoned the archaic "literary" Chinese, and began to rewrite the language into a more accessible form. The change was not unlike the replacement of Latin by the romance languages as the written language of Europe during the Middle Ages.

When the Chinese Communists came to power in 1949, they immediately began to study further reform of the written language. Their goal was to simplify the characters, reduce their complexity, and make them easier to learn, so that literacy could be increased. At the same time, an effort was made to standardize the language, both written and spoken. On Jan. 28, the State Council adopted proposals eliminating 1,055 characters which were declared as variant, and simplified most of the 4,000 characters in common use. The decision was also made to write from left to right.

The new proposals were instituted in the schools, the government, and the military, and are now in common use. Although literacy has increased, young Chinese are increasingly cut off from their cultural history and unable to read most of the Chinese classics, still only available in the traditional forms.

On Taiwan, where the literacy rate is much higher (97 percent), no such changes have been made.

Another aspect of the effort to simplify and reform the Chinese language is a series of proposals to alphabetize it. The first of these date to the 17th century, and were offered to the Chinese by Jesuit missionaries. In the 20th century, efforts to find suitable alphabetic equivalents for Chinese characters have centered on developing a standard base guide to teach pronunciation, not on eliminating the characters. The problem lies in the fact that although all Chinese tend to write the same, various regions of China have totally different pronunciations of the characters. The characters themselves offer no guide to "correct" pronunciation, since they represent only ideas, not sounds, as is the case in English. Thus reformers sought to teach all Chinese in all parts of China to pronounce characters in "correct" Mandarin phonetics. On Nov. 1, 1957, the State Council approved a proposal to use the roman alphabet for this purpose. The system was called *pinyin*. Despite determined efforts by the government, this system was not adopted widely, and all but disappeared during the Cultural Revolution. The recent government decision to use *pinyin* to romanize proper nouns in translations may indicate a new effort to revive the system in the schools, but does not solve the problem of Chinese opposition to a "foreign" writing system. *(See pinyin conversion tables, p. 361.)*

On Taiwan, the Chinese avoided this problem by inventing their own system, a syllabic alphabet, wherein each syllable of the language is represented by a separate symbol. Thus school children are taught to recognize the symbols as correct Mandarin Chinese before they learn any characters. The program is in use everywhere on Taiwan, and has been effective. Despite the varied origins of its inhabitants, all Chinese on Taiwan under age 25 speak standard Mandarin.

Peking Falls. On Jan. 23 Peking fell to the Communists.

Government Moved. On Feb. 5 the Nationalist government moved from Nanjing to Canton (Guangzhou), but acting President Li remained in Nanjing; although lacking the full support of Premier Sun Fo in Canton, Li continued to work for a peace agreement.

Negotiations for Peace. On Feb. 24, unofficial representatives of acting President Li met with Communist leaders Mao Tse-tung and Chou En-lai north of Peking. On March 3 Premier Sun Fo, joining the peace effort at Li's insistence, announced that the Nationalists would begin formal peace talks with the Communists soon after March 15. On March 5 the Communist radio called Sun a "war criminal."

U.S. Senate Action. On March 10, 50 senators — 25 Republicans and 25 Democrats — requested that the Senate Foreign Relations Committee take immediate action on a $1.5 billion aid-to-China bill introduced by Sen. Pat McCarran, D-Nev. (1933-1954).

Secretary of State Dean Acheson commented that there was "no evidence" that such aid would "alter the events in China" to which the U.S. had already given $2 billion since 1945.

Sun Fo Replaced. On March 12, following the resignation of Dr. Sun Fo as Nationalist premier, Gen. Ho Ying-ch'in (He Yingqin) was named to the office. A new Cabinet was formed, peace delegates chosen, and proposals made for discussions with the Chinese Communists.

Taiwan. On March 15 the Chinese Communists announced that they intended to "liberate" Taiwan because the United States wanted it as "a springboard for future aggression against China proper."

Nationalist Corruption. On March 16 the U.S. Chamber of Commerce in Shanghai sent a telegram to the State Department criticizing "the military, civil, and economic incompetence, or worse, of the Nationalist government." The message went on to say that the Chinese people did not believe in communism, but "they are battered, beaten, and helpless — accepting a fate they hate but feel cannot be worse than that which they have gone through the past four years.

Later in the month, the U.S. consul general in Tianjin sent a memorandum to Washington that took very much the same view and concluded that the U.S. policy of opposing communism, however warranted in other parts of the world, "should not oblige us to support a hopelessly corrupt government which has lost the support of its people."

Soviet-Korean Agreement. On March 17 the Soviet Union and North Korea signed a 10-year economic and cultural cooperation agreement providing for trade, technical assistance, and credit arrangements. It is believed that a secret military assistance pact was also signed at this time. Unlike pacts with other Russian satellites, however, there does not seem to have been a mutual defense treaty included in the agreements.

Communists Agree to Talk. On March 26 the Chinese Communists announced that they would participate in peace talks with the Nationalists. The broadcast said the Communists had already chosen their delegates and selected Peking as the site of the negotiations.

Chinese Hyperinflation. On March 31 the wholesale price index at Shanghai (1937 = 1) hit 2,432,000,000,000,000. This was the last compilation of the index, and marked the Chinese inflation as the worst of any nation in history. *(See Dec. 31, 1946)*

China Aid Extended. On April 14 Congress extended the 1948 China Aid Act by authorizing the president to use unobligated funds until Feb. 15, 1950, to aid those areas of China that remained free of Chinese Communist control.

Yangtze Crossed. On April 20, at midnight, Communist forces crossed the Yangtze (Changjiang) River and began a sweep into southern China. The government's cease-fire proposal was ignored.

Officials Flee. On April 23 the acting president, the premier, and other officials fled Nanjing for Canton.

Nanjing Falls. On April 24 Nanjing, already abandoned by Nationalist forces, was occupied by the Communists. On the following day, Communist troops invaded the U.S. Embassy and pulled U.S. Ambassador John Leighton Stuart out of bed for questioning.

Chennault's Plea. On May 3 Gen. Claire L. Chennault told the Senate Armed Services Committee that the United States must defend southern China. On May 4 Secretary of State Dean Acheson (who had become secretary after George C. Marshall resigned in January) said that U.S. policy toward China would not change.

Wuhan Falls. On May 17 Wuhan fell to the Communists.

Shanghai Falls. On May 25 Shanghai fell to the Communists.

New Premier. On June 3 Nationalist Premier Ho Ying-ch'in was succeeded by Yen Hsi-shan (Yan Xishan). It was reported that the government was preparing to move the capital from Canton to Chongqing.

Diplomatic Contacts. On June 6 Huang Hua, a representative of the Chinese Communists, contacted U.S. Ambassador to China John Leighton Stuart in Nanjing. One week later they met to discuss future American relations with the Communists. *(See June 28)*

Mao on Recognition. On June 15 Mao Tse-tung announced his willingness to discuss the establishment of diplomatic relations with any foreign government, on "the basis of the principles of equality, mutual benefit, and mutual respect for territorial integrity and sovereignty." *(See June 28, 1954)*

Reaction in U.S. Senate. On June 24, 21 senators (16 Republicans, five Democrats) in a letter to President Truman urged him not to recognize the Chinese Communist regime. Sen. Arthur H. Vandenberg, R-Mich., (1928-1951) said in the Senate that U.S. policy toward China had been a "tragic failure."

More Diplomatic Efforts. On June 28 Huang Hua again contacted U.S. Ambassador Stuart and invited him to come to Peking, where Communist Party Chairman Mao Tse-tung and Chou En-lai would "personally welcome" him. Stuart cabled Washington for instructions, but received no reply.

Mao on Communist Alliance. On July 1, in a paper called "On People's Democratic Dictatorship," Chinese Communist Party Chairman Mao Tse-tung enunciated his famous "lean to one side" policy. In an abrupt termination of the diplomatic feelers which had been extended to Washington, Mao announced that China must "either lean to the side of imperialism or to the side of socialism.... Neutrality is a hoax. No third path exists." Thus, concluded Mao, China will ally itself with "the Soviet Union, with every new democratic country, and with the proletariat and broad masses in all other countries." Soon afterward, the State Department cabled Stuart not to go to Peking. *(See Feb. 14, 1950)*

U.S. Policy Review. On July 27 Secretary of State Dean Acheson announced that U.S. East Asian policy was to be subjected to thorough review by a group of governmental and non-governmental specialists headed by Ambassador-at-Large Philip C. Jessup, who had successfully negotiated the agreement ending the Berlin blockade. Acheson told the panel to take it as their assumption that "the United States does not intend to permit further extension of Communist domination on the continent of Asia or in the Southeast Asian area." The committee was asked to examine possible plans, costs and necessary forces to implement such a policy, and to explore every possible approach. Acheson said that he wanted to be certain that "we are neglecting no opportunities that would be within our capabilities to achieve the purpose of halting the spread of totalitarian communism in Asia."

Stuart Leaves China. On Aug. 2 U.S. Ambassador John Leighton Stuart, who had remained in Nanjing since the Communists took over late in April, left for the United States.

White Paper on China. On Aug. 5 the State Department issued a 1,054-page report, *United States Relations with China, 1944-1949* (White Paper), on U.S. policy toward China. On the one hand, the administration sought to use the report to respond to Republican charges that Truman had "lost" China. Secretary Acheson, in a letter of transmittal to the president, blamed the Nationalist debacle on the inept leadership of the Kuomintang rather than any insufficiency of U.S. aid. Acheson said "the only alternative open to the United States was full-scale intervention in behalf of a government which had lost the confidence of its own troops and its own people." He asserted that intervention on the scale required to overcome the Communists would have been "resented by the mass of the Chinese people, would have diametrically reversed our historic policy, and would have been condemned by the American people.

On the other hand, the White Paper was an effort to put distance between the U.S. government and that of Chiang Kai-shek on Taiwan, thus holding open the possibility of diplomatic relations between Peking and Washington. This effort would continue until the Korean War. *(See Jan. 5, 1950)*

The White Paper was bitterly attacked by the Republicans, who termed it a "whitewash of a wishful, do-nothing policy which has succeeded only in placing Asia in danger of Soviet conquest." The report was not released publicly until the early 1970s. The White Paper has remained a subject of controversy.

Mansfield on China Lobby. On Aug. 25 Sen. Mike Mansfield, D-Mont., (1953-1977) called for an investigation of lobbying on behalf of Nationalist China. He suggested that U.S. funds appropriated as assistance to China were being used in the lobbying effort.

Paper Tiger. In August Mao Tse-tung met with U.S. newspaper correspondent Anna Louise Strong. In this interview, Mao characterized the U.S. atomic bomb as a "paper tiger." Mao noted that "it looks terrible, but in fact it isn't.... The outcome of a war," continued Mao, "is decided by the people, not by one or two new types of weapons."

People's Republic Proclaimed. On Sept. 21 the Chinese People's Political Consultative Conference met in Peking and proclaimed the People's Republic of China. The conference also adopted the Organic Law of the Central People's Government, ratified Mao Tse-tung's "new democratic" program as "the political foundation of the state," and on Sept. 27 renamed the capital Peking (meaning "northern capital") in place of Peiping (meaning "northern peace"). Three days later, Mao was elected chairman of the new government.

Soviet Atomic Explosion. On Sept. 23 President Truman announced that "We have evidence that within recent weeks an atomic explosion occurred in the U.S.S.R."

New Government Inaugurated. On Oct. 1 the People's Republic of China (PRC) was formally inaugurated. Chou En-lai was named premier and foreign minister. In his speech at the ceremony, Chou repeated Mao Tse-tung's three principles concerning recognition of the PRC. *(See June 15, 1949)*

Soviet Recognition. On Oct. 2 the Soviet Union recognized the Chinese government and terminated relations with the Nationalist government. In the following days, all other Soviet-bloc countries did likewise.

U.S. Position. On Oct. 3 a State Department official said the United States would not recognize the Chinese Communist government without first consulting Congress.

Conference on East Asian Policy. On Oct. 6 Secretary of State Acheson opened at the State Department a three-day conference on U.S. East Asian policy. The conference was attended by 24 leading scholars, academicians and businessmen. A majority agreed that the United States ought to recognize the Chinese government, establish trade relations with China, and withdraw recognition from the Nationalist government. Of those who did not concur, Harold E. Stassen was the most prominent.

Acheson News Conference. On Oct. 12 Secretary Acheson listed three conditions a new government must meet before receiving U.S. recognition: (1) It must exercise effective control in the country it purports to govern; (2) it must recognize its international obligations; and (3) it must govern with the consent of the people. The secretary doubted whether China adhered to the standards of international behavior required under the second condition.

Canton Falls. On Oct. 15 Canton was occupied by the Communists. The Nationalist capital was moved to Chongqing.

Angus Ward Affair. On Oct. 24, after holding the staff of the U.S. consulate general in Mukden under house arrest for nearly a year, local Chinese authorities jailed Consul General Angus Ward and four of his associates on charges of having assaulted a Chinese employee. The Chinese refused to allow Ward to communicate with Washington, and Peking ignored all protests. The Ward case became a cause célèbre in the U.S. President Truman declared the arrest an outrage, and the New York *World-*

Telegram, in a representative statement said, "We want Angus Ward out alive — or else." However, there was nothing the U.S. could do short of direct military intervention. The Chinese held Ward for another month, and then deported him. Ward returned to the U.S. something of a hero. *(See Jan. 14, 1950)*

Li Flees. On Nov. 20 Acting President Li Tsung-jen flew to Hong Kong. Shortly thereafter, he went on to New York for "medical treatment."

Chongqing Falls. On Nov. 30 Chongqing was occupied by Communist forces. The Nationalist government moved on to Chengdu, but now commanded few troops.

Nationalists to Taiwan. On Dec. 8, officials of the Nationalist government flew to Taiwan, where they set up headquarters the next day. On Dec. 10 Chiang Kai-shek arrived in Taiwan.

Chinese Buildup. On Dec. 11, following reports of a Chinese troop buildup on the mainland opposite Taiwan, *The New York Times* reported that "a communist conquest eventually — next spring or the following spring — is certain." The article also noted that Taiwan "alone . . . cannot fight China."

British Recognize Peking. On Dec. 16 British Foreign Minister Ernest Bevin informed Secretary of State Acheson of a Cabinet decision to recognize the Chinese Communist government early in January. The decision was believed to be influenced by the vulnerability of Hong Kong.

Mao to Moscow. On Dec. 16 Communist Party Chairman Mao Tse-tung arrived in Moscow for 10 weeks of negotiations with the Soviet Union. On Jan. 19, 1950, Chinese Premier and Foreign Minister Chou En-lai arrived to join Mao in the treaty talks. Discussions included the question of Soviet aid to China, the Soviet treaty with the Nationalist government, and the problems of trade. It is still not known if Korea was discussed by Mao and Stalin. *(See Feb. 14, 1950)*

Indian Recognition. On Dec. 30 the Indian government announced recognition of the PRC.

1950

State Department Writes Off Taiwan — Britain Recognizes Chinese Government — Acheson on Far East Policy — U.S. Personnel Recalled — Dispute Over China's Seat in U.N. — Soviet Boycott of Security Council — McCarthy's Charges on Communists in State Department — Soviet Treaty with China — Chiang Resumes Presidency — Start of Korean War — U.N. and U.S. Action — Seoul Captured — Russians Return to U.N. Security Council — U.S. Army Expansion — Wage-Price Control Authority — Seoul Recaptured — Truman and MacArthur at Wake Island — Chinese "Volunteers" in Korea — U.N. Troops Retreat — United Nations Asks Cease-Fire Negotiations — Truman Proclaims National Emergency — Communist Offensive Against Seoul.

State Department Advisory. On Jan. 3 United Press reporter Earnest Hoberecht revealed that the State Department had notified all its posts that the fall of Taiwan to the Communists was to be expected and the public should be told that the island meant little to U.S. security. This was in reference to a State Department memorandum dated Dec. 23, 1949, which stated that the island of Taiwan held "no special military significance."

No Aid for Taiwan. On Jan. 5 President Truman announced in Washington that the United States would "not provide military aid or advice to Chinese forces" on Taiwan. Secretary of State Dean Acheson explained that the Nationalists on Taiwan were able to obtain all the required military equipment for themselves. All they needed, Acheson said, was the "will to resist."

The announcement shocked both the Nationalists and Republicans. Sen. Robert A. Taft, R-Ohio, called it "inconsistent with what we have agreed to do in stopping the advance of communism in Europe," and Sen. William F. Knowland, R-Calif, said the decision "accelerated the spread of communism in Asia."

Britain Recognizes Peking. On Jan. 6 Great Britain recognized the Chinese Communist government.

Peking's Request. On Jan. 8 Chinese Premier and Foreign Minister Chou En-lai cabled U. N. General Secretary Trygve Lie to insist on Peking's right to U.N. admission. Chou demanded the immediate ouster of Dr. T. F. Hsiang, the Nationalist Chinese delegate, since he represented only "the Chinese Kuomintang remnant reactionary clique."

Peking Accepts British Recognition. On Jan. 9 the Chinese Communist government announced acceptance of British recognition and implied it would not take hostile action against Hong Kong. But due to British insistence on maintaining a consulate on Taiwan, ambassadors were not exchanged until 1972. *(See March 13, 1972)*

Soviet Walkout in United Nations. On Jan. 10 the U.S. representative to the United Nations Security Council announced that the U.S. would vote against a Soviet proposal to admit the People's Republic of China, but would not veto the resolution. Because the vote was delayed, the Soviet delegate, Yakov A. Malik, walked out of the U.N. Security Council. He returned two days later.

Acheson on Asian Policy. On Jan. 12 Secretary of State Dean Acheson delivered one of his most important speeches on East Asian policy before the National Press Club in Washington. Entitled "Crisis in China," Acheson first defended the administration's past actions in Asia and China, and then turned to the question of future U.S. military security in the region. He declared that America should be prepared to defend a line which ran from the Aleutian Islands to Japan, the Ryukyu Islands, south to the Philippines. The area delineated by Acheson thus excluded Taiwan and, most significantly in view of later events, Korea. As far as the U.S. was concerned, said the secretary, the military security of the countries beyond this defense perimeter "lay beyond the realm of any practical relationship." Should an attack on these areas occur, "the initial reliance must be on the people attacked to resist it and then upon the commitments of the entire civilized world under the charter of the United Nations."

Acheson added that the United States could not instill in the new nations of South Asia the "will to fight communism," but would be willing to grant them economic aid and advice if there were a "fighting chance" they could emerge without turning to communism.

Acheson was assailed, both at the time and in later years, for encouraging the communists to believe that if this were indeed American policy, they could attack either

Taiwan or Korea with impunity. Acheson replied that this was not his theory alone, but was also the view espoused by the Joint Chiefs of Staff and the State Department. *(Text p. 304)*

Second Soviet Walkout in United Nations. On Jan. 13 the Soviet resolution to admit the People's Republic of China to the United Nations was defeated 6-3 in the Security Council, with Norway and France abstaining. This would be the closest vote until 1970. Following the vote, U.S.S.R. delegate Yakov A. Malik walked out of the Security Council, only one day after his return from the first walkout. Malik said the Soviet Union would boycott the council until it ousted the Nationalist Chinese delegate and seated Peking.

American Personnel Recalled. On Jan. 14 the Chinese seized the U.S. consulate in Peking. The action culminated a series of anti-American incidents, including the arrest and beating of a U.S. vice consul in July 1949 and the jailing of the consul general in Mukden in October. *(See Oct. 24, 1949)* According to some scholars, this marked the end of whatever momentum there had been for U.S. recognition of the new Peking regime. Other scholars, who see no such momentum, argue that the U.S. used these incidents as a pretext not to recognize the PRC.

On the same day, the State Department recalled all official personnel from China.

Acheson Press Conference. On. Jan. 18 Secretary Acheson said that seizure of the Peking consulate made it obvious that Communist China did not want U.S. recognition.

Nationalist Air Attacks. On Jan. 18 the Nationalists announced that their planes had destroyed 2,000 Communist landing craft assembled for an attack on Nationalist-occupied Hainan Island, across the Gulf of Tonkin from Vietnam.

Tibet's Appeal. On Jan. 31 the Tibetan radio broadcast an appeal for aid against invasion by the Communist Chinese.

U.N. China Dispute. On Feb. 3 the Nationalist Chinese delegate in the United Nations told a Security Council committee that he would veto a resolution to recognize the right of the Communist regime to represent China in the organization. On Feb. 8 the committee decided that the General Assembly would have to solve the problem of Chinese representation.

McCarthy's First Charge. On Feb. 9 Sen. Joseph R. McCarthy, R-Wis., charged in Wheeling, W. Va., that 205 communists were working in the State Department. The department denied the charges.

Sino-Soviet Treaty. On Feb. 14 the Soviet Union and China signed a 30-year Treaty of Friendship, Alliance, and Mutual Assistance, and concluded two subsidiary agreements — one promising eventual return to China of Soviet-held properties in Manchuria and the other extending to China a $300-million loan for industrial equipment.

The two governments declared Russia's 1945 treaty with Nationalist China null and void, promised mutual assistance in case of "the resumption of aggression on the part of Japan or any other state that may collaborate in any way with Japan in acts of aggression," pledged both to work for peace under the United Nations, guaranteed the "independent status" of the Mongolian People's Republic, and made provisions for the restoration of Port Arthur (Lu-

shun), Dairen (Dalian), and the Chinese Changchun Railway to full Chinese control.

Foreign Ministers Vishinsky of the Soviet Union and Chou En-lai of China signed the pacts after nine weeks of negotiation in Moscow.

Acheson's Comment. On Feb. 15 Secretary Acheson commented that he felt the Sino-Soviet Treaty was detrimental to China since the Soviet Union would attempt to use it to convert China into a U.S.S.R. satellite.

McCarthy's Second Charge. On Feb. 20 Sen. Joseph R. McCarthy, R-Wis., leveled the charge that there were 57 communists in the State Department. He added that the loyalties of 81 employees were "questionable" and that some were being protected by superiors. Two days later the Senate voted unanimously for an investigation by the Foreign Relations Committee.

Chiang Reclaims Presidency. On March 1 Chiang Kai-shek announced he was reclaiming the presidency of China from Gen. Li Tsung-jen, who had been in New York for medical treatment since December 1949.

U.N. Representation Debate. On March 8 U.N. Secretary-General Trygve Lie implied in a memorandum to all the delegations that the PRC should be permitted to take the China seat at the U.N. Lie said U.N. policy should be to deal with whatever government exercises "effective authority" in a country and was "habitually obeyed by the bulk of its population." Secretary Acheson replied that the United States would not vote to seat the Communists while it recognized the Nationalists, but would also refrain from using the veto and accept the majority decision of the United Nations. Acheson's statement was severely criticized in Congress.

McCarthy Lists "Communists." On March 8 Sen. McCarthy accused Ambassador-at-Large Philip C. Jessup of having "an unusual affinity for Communist causes." McCarthy later added eight more names to his list of alleged security risks, including those of Prof. Owen J. Lattimore of Johns Hopkins University, and John Stewart Service, a veteran U.S. career diplomat who had served with the Dixie Mission in Yanan. Both had advised the State Department in formulation of East Asian policies.

Another McCarthy Charge. On March 23 Sen. McCarthy charged that Russia's "top espionage agent in America" was a consultant on Far Eastern affairs in the State Department and had access to secret files. Sen. Millard E. Tydings, D-Md., chairman of the Foreign Relations subcommittee studying McCarthy's charges, said the man in question had performed menial tasks for the department five years before and only for four months. McCarthy said this was "completely untrue." Three days later, it was disclosed that the man McCarthy had in mind was Prof. Owen Lattimore of Johns Hopkins University, who called the charges "moonshine" and "a hallucination."

Truman Denounces McCarthy. On March 30 President Truman denounced McCarthy, Sen. Styles Bridges, R-N.H., and Sen. Kenneth S. Wherry, R-Neb., as saboteurs of U.S. foreign policy and said they were the Kremlin's greatest asset in the Cold War.

Lattimore Defies McCarthy. On April 6 Prof. Owen Lattimore confronted McCarthy before the Senate Foreign Relations subcommittee. To McCarthy's charge that Lattimore was the architect of the country's policy of abandoning China to the communists, Lattimore replied: "I wish I had more influence. If I had, I think the Communists would not now control China." Lattimore called McCarthy a "base and contemptible liar" and said he was "either a fool or an enemy of his country."

Charge Filed in United Nations. On April 10 the Chinese Nationalist delegate filed a charge with the U.N. Secretariat that the Soviet Union was furnishing men and planes for the Chinese Communist air force and urged action on his request for U.N. observation of the Chinese civil war.

Famine Reported. On April 15 Peking reported that famine had affected 40 million persons in China since 1949 and that seven million were in "a most serious plight."

Russia Answers Nationalist Charge. On April 18 the Soviet Union called "slanderous" the Nationalist charge that Russians were serving in the Chinese air force.

Communists Seize Hainan. On April 19 the Communists launched an invasion of Hainan Island, a key Nationalist-held island off the coast of Guangdong Province. On April 22 a second amphibious assault force was landed.

McCarthy Attacks Gen. Marshall. On April 20, before the American Society of Newspaper Editors in Washington, Sen. McCarthy said Gen. George C. Marshall was "completely unfitted" to be the secretary of state during the China crisis while following advice from people like Lattimore.

Acheson Attacks McCarthy. On April 22 Secretary of State Acheson called the McCarthy attacks "mad" and "vicious."

Hainan Evacuated. On April 23 Chiang Kai-shek ordered evacuation of the 125,000 Nationalist troops on Hainan Island. The capital of Hainan was occupied by Communist troops the same day.

Hearings Continue. On May 2 Lattimore returned to the witness stand before the Foreign Relations subcommittee and denounced McCarthy. He said McCarthy "debased" Senate procedures, "has lied, distorted and vilified" and "has disgraced his party and the people of his state and nation."

Nationalists Appeal. On May 5 the Chinese Nationalists appealed for U.S. military aid "before it is too late." Chiang Kai-shek said the United States should give the Nationalists as much aid as the Russians were giving the Chinese Communists, in order to prevent a communist invasion of Taiwan or Southeast Asia.

Truman Discusses Famine. On May 9, in a speech in Wyoming, President Truman accused the Soviet Union of being "heartlessly indifferent" toward China's worst famine in a century. He said the United States would attempt to get relief to stricken areas in China through private American agencies. The president asserted that the Chinese Communists had "sent to the Soviet Union food which is desperately needed by the Chinese people."

McCarthy Speech. On May 15 Sen. McCarthy demanded in Atlantic City that President Truman fire Secretary of State Dean Acheson and Ambassador-at-Large Philip C. Jessup, whom he called "Pied Pipers of the Politburo."

Declaration of Conscience. On June 1, seven Republican senators, led by Sen. Margaret Chase Smith, R-Maine, issued a "Declaration of Conscience" denouncing McCar-

thy's tactics as "selfish political exploitation of fear, bigotry, ignorance and intolerance." In a Senate speech, Sen. Smith criticized "character assassinations," "trial by accusation," and "political smears," without mentioning McCarthy by name. The other signers were: Sens. Aiken, Vt.; Hendrickson, N.J.; Ives, N.Y.; Morse, then R-Ore.; Thye, Minn.; and Tobey, N.H.

U.N. Chinese Issue. On June 6 U.N. Secretary-General Trygve Lie disclosed that he had asked the Big Four Powers (United States, Soviet Union, Britain, and France) to end their deadlock over Chinese representation in the United Nations. It was generally understood that Lie wanted the Western powers to admit the PRC and let it occupy China's permanent seat in the Security Council.

Acheson Answers. The following day, Secretary Acheson told a news conference that the United States would not be "coerced" by Soviet walkouts into admitting Communist China to the United Nations. He said the United States did not favor transfer of Chinese representation to the Communists but would not use the veto to block the transfer if a majority of the Security Council so voted.

Bradley Testimony. On June 9 Gen. Omar N. Bradley, chairman of the Joint Chiefs of Staff, told a Senate Appropriations subcommittee that U.S. armed forces were not in shape to fight a major war and would not be for a year; however, they were being built up to the point where they could repel an enemy attack.

Korean War. Early in the morning of June 25 North Korea launched a surprise invasion of South Korea. About 75,000 North Korean troops poured across the 38th parallel, attacking at six main points along the border and making two amphibious landings on South Korea's east coast. North Korean radio immediately began broadcasting statements that the attack was "defensive" and that the South Koreans had attempted to invade the North.

United Nations Acts. That afternoon, the U.N. Security Council adopted a resolution calling for an immediate cease-fire in Korea and withdrawal of the northern invaders. The resolution also called on member nations "to render every assistance to the United Nations in the execution of this resolution." The latter section provided a basis for extension of U.S. air and sea support to South Korea. The resolution was adopted 9-0 with Yugoslavia abstaining. A probable Soviet veto was avoided because of the continued Russian boycott of the Security Council over the Chinese representation question. Two days later, Russia and North Korea asserted that the cease-fire resolution was invalid because neither the Soviet Union nor the PRC had attended the session at which it was adopted.

Truman Orders Military Action. On June 27 President Truman announced that he had ordered U.S. air and naval forces in the Far East to go to the aid of South Korea, had ordered the 7th Fleet to prevent any attack on Taiwan, and had ordered a speedup of military assistance to French forces in Indochina and a strengthening of U.S. forces in the Philippines. In fact, however, the 7th Fleet did not actually move into the Taiwan Strait until the next year.

Truman also said that any "determination of the future status of Formosa [Taiwan] must await the restoration of security in the Pacific." Despite its apparent ambiguity, this statement represented a significant upgrading in the status of Taiwan, which Truman had earlier abandoned.

U.N. Sanctions. Late that evening, the U.N. Security Council adopted a resolution urging U.N. members to give South Korea the assistance "necessary to repel the armed attack," thus in effect endorsing action already taken by President Truman.

China's Response. On June 28 Chinese Premier and Foreign Minister Chou En-lai characterized Truman's decision to use the 7th Fleet to protect Taiwan as "armed aggression against the territory of China." Chou went on to declare that "the fact that Taiwan is part of China will remain unchanged forever."

Land Reform in China. On June 28 the Chinese government passed the Agrarian Reform Law, by which land reform in China would be accomplished. Land reform, often violent, was completed by spring 1953.

Senate Hearings Suspended. On June 28 the Senate subcommittee investigating Sen. McCarthy's charges against the State Department voted to call off its hearings "for the time being." Subcommittee Chairman Millard E. Tydings said that all of McCarthy's accusations had been disproved.

Seoul Captured. On June 28 Seoul, capital of South Korea, fell to advancing North Korean troops.

Chiang Offers Troops. On June 29 Nationalist Chinese President Chiang Kai-shek offered 30,000 of his "best equipped troops" for use in Korea. The U.S., fearful of widening the war, refused the offer.

President Authorizes Use of U.S. Troops. On June 30 President Truman authorized Gen. Douglas MacArthur to send supporting ground forces from Japan to Korea. Truman also ordered the U.S. Navy to blockade the entire Korean coast and authorized the U.S. Air Force to bomb North Korea.

Troops Land. Hours after the president's announcement, 1,000 U.S. troops landed in South Korea from Japan under heavy air cover.

Marines Ordered. On July 3 U.S. Marine ground and air units were ordered to Korea.

U.N. Action. On July 7 the U.N. Security Council voted to appoint Gen. MacArthur as U.N. commander in Korea.

Truman Authorizes Draft. On July 7 President Truman authorized the armed forces to use the draft if necessary to build up their strength. Three days later, the U.S. Army put in a call for 20,000 draftees.

$10 Billion Request. On July 19 President Truman requested $10 billion from Congress for a huge rearmament program for the Korean War.

Chiang's Statement. On Aug. 1, following the visit of General MacArthur to Taiwan, Nationalist President Chiang Kai-shek announced that the talks had laid the foundation for the joint defense of Taiwan and "Sino-American military cooperation," and "final victory" against the Communists.

On Aug. 14 the U.S. government registered its protest, and told MacArthur that there would be no attack on the Chinese mainland: "The most vital national interest requires that no action of ours precipitate general war."

Soviets Return to United Nations. On Aug. 1 Soviet delegate Yakov A. Malik returned to the Security Council,

ending the six and one-half month Russian boycott without explanation or condition. The same day, the council voted to override an order by Malik, as president of the council for August, that the PRC take the Chinese seat in that body.

Aid to Viet Minh. On Aug. 12 the Vietnam government in Saigon announced that the Chinese Communists had initiated a large-scale program of military aid to Ho Chi Minh's Indochinese rebels.

North Korean Capital Moved. On Aug. 15 the North Korean government was moved from Pyongyang to Seoul, in South Korea. The North Korean army had pushed Gen. MacArthur's U.N. forces to a small perimeter around the southern seaport city of Pusan, where supplies and men streamed in from Japan, the United States, Britain, Australia, Canada, the Netherlands and Turkey.

Republican Charges. On Aug. 16 Sen. Kenneth S. Wherry, R-Neb., GOP floor leader, charged that "the blood of our boys in Korea is on [Secretary of State Dean] Acheson's shoulders and no one else." The following day, the president called Wherry's attack "a contemptible statement and beneath comment." The Republican members of the Senate Foreign Relations Committee had charged, earlier in the week, that "the major troubles of the world today" were caused by the "failure and refusal" of Presidents Roosevelt and Truman to recognize the true aims of the Russians. They accused the administration of "subtle betrayals of China" and of a Far Eastern policy which "consistently temporized with and capitulated to the ruthless demands" of the communists, and resulted in giving the Kremlin "a green light to grab whatever it could in China, Formosa, and Korea."

U.S. Should Unite Korea. On Aug. 17 Warren Austin, U.S. Ambassador to the United Nations, declared that the United Nations should not let Korea remain "half slave, half free." Although he did not recommend outright that U.N. forces should invade North Korea, it has been argued that his remarks were interpreted that way in Peking, and may have prompted Chinese intervention in the Korean War.

PRC Demands. On Aug. 24 the PRC demanded that the U.N. Security Council order U.S. "armed invading forces" to withdraw from Taiwan. The demands referred to the 7th Fleet. Chinese Premier and Foreign Minister Chou En-lai said that China was "determined to liberate" Taiwan and all other Nationalist territories from "the tentacles of the U.S. aggressors."

The U.S. responded by sending a letter to U.N. Secretary General Trygve Lie saying that U.S. did not want Taiwan for itself, and that the U.S. action was taken without prejudice to the future settlement of Taiwan's political status.

Tibet Invaded. On Aug. 25 Chinese Communist troops invaded Tibet. The fighting ended on March 6, 1951. *(See May 23, 1951)*

Chinese Forces. On Aug. 25 U.S. Army spokesmen said that two Chinese armies were massed on the Korean-Manchurian border and that 120 Russian tanks had been shipped from Manchuria to North Korea. Three days later, the Nationalist Chinese government asserted that four Chinese Communist armies had been in North Korea for a month.

MacArthur Statement on Taiwan. On Aug. 26 MacArthur urged that Taiwan be turned into a U.S. defense stronghold.

Truman Orders Withdrawal of Statement. On Aug. 28 President Truman directed that MacArthur's statement be withdrawn to "avoid confusion as to the U.S. position" on Taiwan. The president was criticized by Senate Republicans for "gagging" MacArthur.

Acheson News Conference. On Aug. 30 Secretary Acheson said the United States was doing everything possible to convince the PRC that there were no American designs on Taiwan or any other Chinese territory. Acheson said the Chinese would have no justification for entering the Korean War.

Malik Steps Down. On Aug. 31 Soviet delegate Yakov A. Malik's month as president of the U.N. Security Council ended. During August he had been successful in blocking debate on the Korean War.

Truman Announces Military Expansion. On Sept. 1 President Truman announced over nationwide radio and television that he planned to double the strength of U.S. armed forces "to close to three million" men.

Russia Uses Veto. On Sept. 6 the Soviet Union vetoed a U.N. Security Council resolution to condemn North Korea for "continued defiance of the U.N." The council then voted 8-1 against a Soviet resolution to demand that all "foreign troops" leave Korea.

Defense Production Act Approved. On Sept. 8 President Truman signed the Defense Production Act of 1950. The act gave the president authority to impose wage, price and rationing controls, to assign priorities on war materials, and to regulate consumer credit. Hoarding of food or other materials was made subject to heavy penalties.

Landing at Inchon. On Sept. 15 a large U.N. amphibious force landed at Inchon, 18 miles from South Korea's capital of Seoul and 150 miles north of the battlefront. At the same time, MacArthur's forces near Pusan, at the bottom of the peninsula, launched a major offensive. The North Koreans soon found themselves cut off from supplies and communications with the North and their military position disintegrating.

PRC Barred Again. On Sept. 19 the PRC was barred from taking China's seat in the U.N. General Assembly. An Indian motion to seat the Communists lost 33-16 with 10 abstentions. A Soviet motion to oust the Nationalist Chinese lost 38-10 with eight abstentions.

Seoul Recaptured. On Sept. 26 Seoul was recaptured, three months to the day after the first Communist forces had entered the city.

Chou's Public Warning. On Sept. 30 Chinese Foreign Minister Chou En-lai warned that his government would not stand aside if "the imperialists wantonly invaded the territory of North Korea."

Crossing the Parallel. On Oct. 1 South Korean troops crossed the 38th parallel into North Korea.

Chou Warns Again. On Oct. 2 Chinese Foreign Minister Chou En-lai formally notified Indian Ambassador to China K. M. Panikkar that if U.S. troops entered North Korea, China would intervene in the war.

U.N. Decision. On Oct. 7 the U.N. General Assembly adopted a resolution calling for "all appropriate steps" to "ensure conditions of stability throughout Korea." Gen. MacArthur was authorized by implication to do whatever he deemed necessary about invading North Korea. U.S. troops crossed the 38th parallel the same day.

China Intervenes. On Oct. 14 the first Chinese Communist units crossed into Korea in secrecy.

Truman and MacArthur Meet. On Oct. 15 President Truman and Gen. MacArthur met on Wake Island to discuss the Korean situation and U.S. policy throughout East Asia. Truman said later that he and MacArthur were in "complete unanimity" and that MacArthur was "one of America's great soldier-statesmen." It was later revealed that MacArthur had assured Truman that the risk of Chinese intervention in the Korean War was minimal and that the Chinese, even if they did intervene, could only transport, at most, 60,000 troops to the battlefield.

Pyongyang Falls. On Oct. 19 Pyongyang, capital of North Korea, fell to the United States and South Korean forces. One week later, on Oct. 26, South Korean troops reached the Manchurian border.

Chinese Accept Invitation. On Oct. 24 the Chinese accepted an invitation to attend a U.N. Security Council discussion of alleged U.S. aggression in Taiwan. *(See Nov. 28)*

China Attacks. On Oct. 26, Chinese Communist troops attacked the South Korean units which had reached the Yalu River. On Nov. 2, Chinese troops attacked U.S. forces on both the western and eastern fronts. The U.S. ordered a withdrawal.

China Breaks Off Attack. On Nov. 7 all Chinese Communist units broke off their attacks and withdrew.

GOP Demands New Investigations. On Nov. 9 Sen. Bourke B. Hickenlooper, R-Iowa, demanded a new Senate investigation of the McCarthy charges of communist infiltration of the State Department and another probe of the administration's enforcement of the Internal Security Act. In the following days, he was supported by other Republican senators. The demands for a new investigation were made in the wake of Republican gains in the off-year elections. Although the GOP was still in a slight minority in both houses of Congress, the Republican-Dixiecrat coalition often controlled legislative decisions.

Chinese Take Lhasa. On Nov. 9 the Chinese troops which had invaded Tibet in August entered the capital city of Lhasa.

PRC Message to United Nations. On Nov. 15 the Chinese Communists sent a message to the United Nations through the Soviet delegation asserting that the "sincere desire of the Chinese to assist the Koreans against U.S. aggression is absolutely natural, just, magnanimous, and lawful."

Acheson's Statement. On the same day, Secretary of State Acheson told reporters that the United States was ignorant of Chinese motives and that an effort should be made to determine whether a sincere but needless fear caused the Chinese to intervene in Korea. Acheson hinted that he would welcome direct talks with the Chinese Communists, but warned that deliberate precipitation of a war by China would be "a tragedy of the most colossal nature" and would be met by firm U.N. action.

U.N. Offensive Launched. On Nov. 24, promising to "bring the boys home by Christmas," MacArthur launched a U.N. offensive that began against little opposition.

Chinese Open Drive. On Nov. 26, 200,000 Chinese Communists troops opened an enormous counter-offensive that shattered the center of the U.N. line.

Communist China at United Nations. On Nov. 28 the PRC, carrying out its Oct. 24 acceptance of an invitation to attend a U.N. Security Council debate on alleged U.S. aggression, told the council that it should penalize the United States for "armed aggression" against China, Taiwan and Korea. The spokesman for a nine-man delegation said China would "liberate" Taiwan and aid the communists in Indochina, the Philippines and Japan. "The Chinese people have arisen," he concluded.

Acheson Speech. On Nov. 30 Secretary Acheson warned Peking that it faced its "hour of decision." He said no one "can guarantee that war will not come. . . . Whether reason will prevail is only partly for us to decide. We must hope and strive for the best while we prepare for the worst."

Truman Statement. On Dec. 1, speaking in response to Chinese use of "volunteers" in Korea, President Truman contended that the Chinese "are being forced into battle against our troops," and that U.N. forces "are in Korea to put down an aggression that threatens not only the whole fabric of the United Nations, but all human hopes of peace and justice."

Russian Vetoes. The same day, the Soviet Union vetoed a Security Council resolution requesting the Chinese to withdraw their troops from Korea on assurance that China's legitimate interests would be protected.

Pyongyang Regained. On Dec. 4 the Communists reoccupied the North Korean capital of Pyongyang after it had been abandoned by U.N. forces retreating to the 38th parallel. Americans trapped in the northeast began fighting their way to the sea.

Truman-Attlee Conference Ends. On Dec. 8 a five-day Washington conference of President Truman and British Prime Minister Clement R. Attlee ended with a joint statement that there would be "no appeasement" of China over Korea. Both leaders agreed to abide by U.N. decisions, although they disagreed on whether China should be admitted to the United Nations. According to his memoirs, Truman told Atlee that not only was Taiwan militarily significant, but more importantly, there was a "senatorial clamor" on behalf of Chiang Kai-shek. The administration, Truman indicated, was limited in its freedom of maneuver regarding East Asia because the U.S. could not act abroad without solid backing at home. If China were to be admitted to the U.N., concluded Truman, there would be "terrible divisions" among the American people and a "loss in public morale."

Following the Truman-Attlee talks, leading Republicans let up on criticism of administration East Asian policy and called for national unity to meet the crisis. Gov. Thomas E. Dewey, R-N.Y., chief spokesman of the GOP, said Dec. 8: "We can survive if we mobilize America's enormous potential strength and achieve a united front at home and with enough other free nations."

Trade Embargo on China. The same day, the U.S. Commerce Department announced a complete, although "informal," embargo on all U.S. exports to China. This embargo would last 21 years. *(See April 14, 1971)*

U.N. Asks for Cease-Fire. On Dec. 14 the U.N. General Assembly adopted a resolution asking China to negotiate with the U.N. for a cease-fire in Korea. A three-man U.N. committee was created to seek a truce.

Cease-Fire Plea Rejected. On Dec. 16 the head of the PRC delegation which had appeared before the U.N. Security Council Nov. 28 said the Communists would not stop fighting in Korea until all their demands were met.

President Proclaims National Emergency. On the same day, President Truman proclaimed "the existence of a national emergency" as a result of Korean setbacks. He warned the American people on a nationwide broadcast that "our homes, our nation, all the things we believe in, are in great danger." The president also announced creation of a new Office of Defense Mobilization.

PRC Delegation Departs. On Dec. 19 the PRC's visiting delegation at the U.N. departed for Peking.

Assets Frozen. On Dec. 29 President Truman declared that all assets of the People's Republic of China held in the U.S. were to be frozen. China retaliated by seizing all remaining U.S. property in China. The resultant claims question would not be settled until 1979.

Offensive Begins. On Dec. 31 the Chinese Communists and North Koreans began an offensive against Seoul with a heavy artillery barrage.

1951

Seoul Falls Again — U.N. Truce Appeal — U.N. General Assembly Labels China an Aggressor — Seoul Recaptured — MacArthur Hints U.N. Attack on China and Suggests Negotiations — State Department Reprimand — MacArthur Letter to Martin — Truman Dismisses MacArthur — MacArthur Hearings in Senate — Soviet Initiative on Korean Truce — Ridgway's Truce Proposals — Truce Talks Begin — Talks Shifted to Panmunjom — Provisional Agreement and Lull in Fighting — Provisional Agreement Lapses but Negotiations Continue.

Seoul Falls Again. On Jan. 4 Seoul fell to the Communists for the second time. U.N. forces abandoned the city in the face of impossible odds.

New U.N. Truce Appeal. On Jan. 13 the U.N. General Assembly's Political Committee appealed for acceptance of a new cease-fire and truce plan to stop the Korean War and establish peace in East Asia. On Jan. 17 Communist China rejected the appeal and said it would not talk peace until U.N. troops left Korea and U.S. forces gave up protecting Taiwan.

House and Senate Resolutions. On Jan. 19 the House adopted, by almost unanimous voice vote, a resolution asking that the U.N. immediately declare Communist China an aggressor in Korea. Four days later, the Senate adopted a similar resolution by a vote of 91-0.

U.N. Resolution on China. On Jan. 20 U.S. Ambassador to the U.N. Warren R. Austin, appearing before the U.N. Political Committee, introduced a resolution to declare China guilty of aggression in Korea and demand withdrawal of its forces from that country. The United States could not find a cosponsor for the resolution even though it had many supporters. India led an opposition Arab-Asian bloc of 12 nations which contended that the

United Nations should attempt to negotiate with China rather than risk spreading the war beyond Korea. The Indian delegate, Sir Benegal N. Rau, told the committee that the resolution would follow a "disastrous course" and would "isolate China even more than at present." He said that economic sanctions would harm the Chinese people far more than their leaders and added that the Communists might have acted in Korea because of "suspicious Chinese nationalism and not of aggressive communism."

Modified Chinese Position. On Jan. 22 India delivered at the United Nations a new communication from the Chinese which modified their earlier rejection of a cease-fire in Korea. The Communists offered to agree to a cease-fire as soon as a seven-nation Far Eastern peace conference went into session. The note added that "definite affirmation of the legitimate status of the People's Republic of China in the U.N. must be insured." In Washington, the State Department said the United States would be "stupid" to accept the new Chinese terms since they carried no guarantees on troop withdrawal or truce inspection. On Jan. 24 Indian Prime Minister Jawaharlal Nehru said he was "convinced" the Chinese Communists were "eager to have negotiations." The same day, Ambassador Austin said the Chinese must be shown "you can't shoot your way into the U.N." He insisted on condemnation of the Communists and "immediate" study of possible ways to punish them for aggression.

Senate Opposes Peking in U.N. On Jan. 23 the U.S. Senate voted 91-0 on a resolution (S Res 36) opposing Peking's admission to the United Nations. The House passed an identical resolution on May 15. Similar resolutions passed every Congress until 1971.

Last Warning. On Jan. 29 India told the U.N. Political Committee that the Communist Chinese had warned they would not talk peace if the U.N. branded them as aggressors.

PRC Labeled an Aggressor. The next day the U.S. resolution cleared the Political Committee by a vote of 44-7 with eight abstentions. On Feb. 1 the General Assembly itself adopted the resolution by the same vote. The resolution condemned China as an aggressor against Korea and the United Nations but left open a door for peace talks through a standing U.N. good offices committee.

Chinese Reaction. On Feb. 3 the Chinese Communists declared that adoption of the resolution "blocked the path to a peaceful settlement" and was ". . . an insult to the Chinese people."

Offensive Thwarted. On Feb. 18 the Chinese abandoned an attempt to break through the U.N. front in central Korea. U.N. forces launched a counteroffensive, which led eventually to the recapture of Seoul and drove most Communist forces back across the 38th parallel.

MacArthur Warning. On March 7 Gen. MacArthur warned that the Korean War "cannot fail" to become a "theoretical military stalemate" if the United Nations does not use more men and allow attacks on the enemy's Manchurian sanctuary. He said the Communists were building a new offensive for the spring and advised U.N. members to resolve "obscurities which now becloud U.N. objectives in Korea."

Seoul Recaptured. On March 14 Seoul was reoccupied by U.N. troops. It was the fourth time the capital had changed hands since the outbreak of hostilities. One week later, U.N. forces occupied Chunchon, a highway and rail center eight miles south of the 38th parallel. Its capture again raised the question of whether U.N. forces should cross the parallel.

MacArthur Statement. On March 24 Gen. Douglas MacArthur implied that the United Nations might soon decide to attack China proper. He also suggested that the enemy commander-in-chief meet him in the field for truce negotiations.

Reaction in Washington. The same day, the State Department said the political issues "which General MacArthur has stated are beyond his responsibility as a field commander, are being dealt with in the United Nations and by inter-governmental consultations." On March 26 the State Department received assurances from the Defense Department that MacArthur would be told to clear any future statements having political overtones. The following day, Defense Secretary George C. Marshall vetoed a full-scale invasion of North Korea by U.N. forces.

MacArthur's Warning. On April 2 Gen. MacArthur warned of an impending Communist offensive by more than 500,000 troops. On April 5, in a letter read to the House of Representatives by Minority Leader Joseph W. Martin Jr., R-Mass., MacArthur urged use of Chinese Nationalists to open a second front against the Communists on the mainland.

Ho Chi Minh's Orders. On April 7 Indochinese rebel leader Ho Chi Minh broadcast orders to his forces to abandon conventional tactics against the French and resume guerrilla raids. "We are to begin a new war of attrition," he said.

MacArthur Dismissed. On April 11 General of the Army Douglas MacArthur, 71, was dismissed by President Truman from all his commands in East Asia and replaced by Lt. Gen. Matthew B. Ridgway, 56, who had commanded the U.S. Eighth Army in Korea for three months. The White House charged that MacArthur had repeatedly violated orders not to make public statements demanding expansion of the war against Communist China. It was revealed later that the letter from MacArthur to House Minority Leader Martin had been the deciding factor in the president's decision.

GOP Reaction. On the day of the president's announcement, Republicans in Congress met, phoned MacArthur in Tokyo and got his consent to appear before a joint session of Congress, and then delivered a torrent of protest against the president. House Minority Leader Martin said some GOP conferees had talked of "impeachments." Sen. Joseph R. McCarthy, R-Wis., said the dismissal was "perhaps the greatest victory the Communists have ever won." Sen. William E. Jenner, R-Ind., said "Our only choice is to impeach President Truman," and Sen. William F. Knowland, R-Calif, warned of a Far Eastern "Munich." A few Republicans, including Sens. Henry Cabot Lodge, Mass., Leverett Saltonstall, Mass., and Wayne Morse, then-R-Ore., and most Democrats backed the president.

President's Rebuttal. On the night of April 11 the president addressed the nation by television and radio. He said he had to dismiss MacArthur because the general could not agree with the policy of continuing the "difficult and bitter task" of repelling the Communists in Korea without letting the "limited war" become "a general war." The president predicted the Communist forces would launch a spring offensive, but said he was "confident" it would fail.

MacArthur's Return. On April 19 Gen. MacArthur addressed a joint session of Congress following a hero's welcome back to the United States. MacArthur asserted that the Joint Chiefs of Staff had shared his military views on Korea. He said the Korean War must not be stalemated, and that Manchuria should be bombed and China blockaded. He also favored equipping the Nationalists on Taiwan for an invasion of the Chinese mainland. His conclusion — "Old soldiers never die, they just fade away" — brought thunderous applause from the Congress and galleries. The next day, the general, his wife and son were given the largest official welcome in New York City's history.

Aid to Nationalists Resumed. On April 21, following a decision made the month before, the U.S. Defense Department announced the appointment of a 100-man Military Assistance Advisory Group for Taiwan and, on this group's recommendation, the U.S. resumed direct military aid to the Nationalist government with a first allocation of $300 million.

New Communist Offensive Launched. On April 22 the Chinese and North Koreans launched their expected spring offensive and pushed U.N. forces south of the 38th parallel. U.N. commanders said their forces would retreat in good order and inflict heavy casualties on the massive Communist forces, while avoiding heavy U.N. casualties. A Communist air offensive in support of the ground attack never materialized, and U.S. planes continued to bomb supply lines and troop concentrations.

MacArthur Hearings Announced. On April 24, Democratic leaders announced that the Senate Foreign Relations Committee and the Senate Armed Services Committee would open joint hearings May 3 on Gen. MacArthur's dismissal and U.S. East Asian policy.

Offensive Thwarted. On May 1 the Chinese forces abandoned their attempt to recapture Seoul in the first phase of their spring offensive.

MacArthur's Testimony. On May 3 MacArthur told a joint session of the Senate Foreign Relations and Armed Services committees that the United States should serve an ultimatum on China to participate in truce talks or its "actions in Korea would be regarded as a declaration of war against the nations engaged there and those nations would take such steps as they felt necessary to bring the thing to a conclusion." MacArthur added that if Peking defied the ultimatum, the United States should use air power to block delivery of Russian supplies to China, institute a naval blockade of Chinese ports, and equip Nationalist Chinese forces for an attack on the mainland. He doubted that the Soviet Union would intervene. MacArthur said the Joint Chiefs of Staff had recommended to the Defense Department Jan. 12, 1951, that air operations over Manchuria be authorized, that the Chinese Nationalists be given "logistical" support, and that a naval blockade be instituted. He said he did not question "in the slightest" the right of President Truman to recall him, but the manner in which it was done "jeopardized" the national interest because it removed him too abruptly from the middle of vital and immediate operations. He said the reasons for the dismissal were "invalid," for "I have carried out every directive I have ever received."

Marshall's Testimony. On May 7 Gen. George C. Marshall told the two committees that the Chinese Communists could not be as easily defeated as MacArthur had indicated. On the question of the Chinese civil war, Marshall listed four reasons why the U.S. had not intervened directly: "In view of the general world situation, our own military weakness, the global reaction to this situation, and my own knowledge out of that brief contact with China we could not afford to commit this Government to such a procedure."

Communist Retreat. By May 10, Chinese and North Korean troops had retreated almost to the 38th parallel, where they regrouped for another attack.

Congress on Embargo. On May 15 both the House and Senate adopted a resolution (S Con Res 31) which urged the U.N. General Assembly to "take action leading to . . . an embargo on the shipment to Communist China of arms, ammunition, and all other materials which might add to the war-making potential of Communist China. *(See May 18)*

Bradley Testimony. On May 15 the chairman of the Joint Chiefs of Staff, Gen. Omar N. Bradley, began six days of testimony before the two Senate committees. He said that to expand the war beyond Korea would put the United States "in the wrong war, at the wrong time, and with the wrong enemy."

Another Offensive. On May 16 the Chinese and North Korean troops launched their second spring offensive with more "human sea" attacks, pushing U.N. forces farther south of the 38th parallel. But within a week, enormous casualties forced the Communists again to retreat across the 38th parallel. The U.S. estimate of Communist casualties for one day alone was 10,000.

Rusk's Statement. On May 18, sounding the theme that would characterize U.S. East Asian policy for the next two decades, Assistant Secretary of State for Far Eastern Affairs Dean Rusk stated that "The regime in Peiping (Beijing) . . . is not the government of China. . . . We recognize the national government of the Republic of China" even though its territory is small. "That government will continue to receive important aid and assistance from the United States." Rusk also noted that because the Communist government was under the control of the Soviet Union, "it is not Chinese," and cannot, therefore, be recognized by the United States.

U.N. Embargo on China. Also on that day, the United Nations unanimously adopted a resolution sponsored by the United States that asked "every state" in the world to refrain from sending arms or strategic materials to China.

The communist bloc nations refused to participate in the voting.

Agreement With Tibet. On May 23 a Tibetan delegation led by the pro-Chinese Panchen Lama concluded negotiations in Peking, and signed an agreement with the local government of Tibet. The Tibetans, however, led by the pro-Indian Dalai Lama, continued to resist Chinese domination.

Acheson's Testimony. On June 1 Secretary of State Dean Acheson testified before the committees that MacArthur's program for air and sea attacks on China might break up the world anti-communist alliance if carried out by the United States alone, and probably would not bring victory in the Korean War. Reviewing history, the secretary said the Soviet Union was in a position to take much more in Manchuria than the rights it was promised at the 1945 Yalta Conference.

Staging Area Overrun. On June 13, U.N. forces completed occupation of the "Iron Triangle," a Communist staging area in central North Korea.

Truce Plea. On June 23 Yakov A. Malik, Soviet delegate to the United Nations, said Russia would like to see negotiation of a cease-fire in Korea based on the 38th parallel. Secretary Acheson said the U.S. would be satisfied if the Communists withdrew behind the 38th parallel and gave satisfactory guarantees against a renewal of aggression. President Truman said he was hopeful but cautious.

Bid for Cease-Fire Parley. On June 30 Gen. Matthew B. Ridgway, commander of U.N. forces in Korea, broadcast the first specific proposal for a military cease-fire conference.

Communist Answer. On July 1 the Communists answered that the meeting should be held in the area of Kaesong on the 38th parallel. Two days later, Gen. Ridgway accepted the offer.

Truce Talks Begin. On July 10, military truce negotiations began in Kaesong between five-man delegations of the United Nations and North Korean-Chinese Communist commands. The chief negotiators were Vice Adm. Charles Turner Joy, 56, U.S. Navy commander in the Far East, and Lt. Gen. Nam Il, 38, chief of staff of the North Korean Army.

Agenda Agreement. On July 26 the negotiators agreed on an agenda, with this order of business: (1) a military demarcation line and the establishment of a demilitarized zone; (2) the composition, organization, and functions of an organization to supervise the implementation of the truce; (3) exchange of prisoners; and (4) recommendations to the governments of the countries concerned on both sides. The negotiations then centered on the first point. The Communists wanted the line on the 38th parallel, while the United Nations insisted on the existing battle lines, north of the parallel. A subcommittee was formed to work out a proposal.

New McCarthy Charge. On Aug. 9 Sen. Joseph R. McCarthy, R-Wis., named 26 past or present employees of the State Department, including Ambassador-at-Large Philip C. Jessup and Consul General John Carter Vincent, who, he said, were suspected of disloyalty.

Outcome of MacArthur Inquiry. On Aug. 17 the Senate Armed Services and Foreign Relations committees voted 20-3 not to make any formal report on the investigation of Gen. MacArthur's dismissal.

McCarthy Broadcast. On Aug. 24 Sen. McCarthy charged in a radio broadcast that President Truman had issued an executive order in 1948 forbidding government employees to "give Congress the truth about Communists who are in our government." McCarthy asserted also that Ambassador Jessup was once the editorial director of the official publication of a communist-front organization. The senator said that State Department aide John Stewart Service had been giving "top-secret military information" to Philip Jaffe, who "has been named under oath as a Communist spy."

U.S. Treaty with Philippines. On Aug. 30 the U.S. and the Philippines signed a mutual defense treaty in Washington.

Justice Douglas' Statement. On Aug. 31 Associate Supreme Court Justice William O. Douglas said on his return from East Asia that U.S. recognition of China would help undermine Peking's ties with Moscow and be "a real political victory" for the West. He said it would "require straightforward and courageous thinking by all Americans, but it is the only logical course."

World War II Peace Treaty Signed. On Sept. 8, 48 non-communist nations signed a peace treaty with Japan in San Francisco, officially ending World War II. No communist nation signed the treaty. In addition to ending the war, the treaty also deprived Japan of the right to have its own military forces, other than those used for maintaining order.

Mutual Security Treaty. On the same day, the U.S. and Japan also signed a mutual security treaty which gave the U.S., in effect, responsibility for the protection of Japan. The treaty gave the U.S. the right to deploy its land, sea and air forces in and about Japan and Okinawa. *(See Jan. 19, 1960)*

Marshall Resigns. On Sept. 12 Gen. George C. Marshall, 70, resigned as secretary of defense and was replaced by Deputy Defense Secretary Robert A. Lovett.

Atomic Tests. On Oct. 6 Soviet Premier Stalin was quoted as confirming that the Russians were testing atomic weapons.

Jessup Rejected. On Oct. 18 a Senate Foreign Relations subcommittee voted 3-2 against confirming Philip C. Jessup as a U.S. delegate to the United Nations. The next day, the Senate confirmed nine other appointments, but avoided voting on Jessup. On Oct. 22, two days after Congress adjourned, President Truman gave the ambassador-at-large a recess appointment, saying that charges against him were "utterly without foundation."

Korean Negotiations Resume. On Oct. 25, truce negotiations resumed in Panmunjom, an abandoned village six miles from Kaesong, after a 63-day lapse. On Nov. 1 a subcommittee reached agreement on an armistice line for the eastern half of the front. The Communists had abandoned their insistence on the 38th parallel, but the dispute continued as to where the line should be drawn in the west.

Provisional Agreement. On Nov. 27 the two sides reached a provisional agreement to establish a cease-fire line following the existing battlefront, to make the line permanent if a comprehensive armistice agreement was concluded within 30 days, and to let the provisional cease-fire agreement lapse if a general agreement were not reached by Dec. 27. On the following day, Nov. 28, fighting ceased on almost the entire front, although the provisional agreement obligated neither side to stop fighting until other truce questions were settled. Air action increased in the first part of December, but no major air or ground fighting occurred from mid-month to year's end.

Armistice Negotiations Continue. On Dec. 2, no final armistice agreement having been reached, the provisional agreement lapsed. However, truce negotiators continued efforts to resolve differences on arrangements for enforcing an armistice, exchanging prisoners, etc.

1952

French Stand on Indochina War — Washington Meeting on Indochina — Warning on Aggression in Southeast Asia — POW Riot in Korea — New Air Raids on North Korea — Eisenhower, Nixon Nominated — Stevenson, Sparkman Nominated — South Korea Elects Rhee — Release of POWs Wanting to Stay in South Korea — Eisenhower's Pledge to Go to Korea — Eisenhower Defeats Stevenson — Lie Resigns as U.N. Secretary General

Washington Conference on Indochina. On Jan. 11 a secret military conference involving the United States, Britain, and France was held in Washington to discuss the situation in Indochina and other threatened areas of Southeast Asia. The French representative said that France would need help if China entered the war in Indochina. Gen. Omar N. Bradley, chairman of the Joint Chiefs of Staff, represented the United States. The Associated Press reported four days later that the United States had sent 70 shiploads of military equipment to Indochina since July 1950.

Taft on China. On Jan. 12 Sen. Robert A. Taft, R-Ohio, advocated arming the Nationalist Chinese for a full-scale attack on the mainland, and also declared that the State Department's "pro-Communist policies . . . fully justified" Sen. McCarthy's demands that the department be investigated.

Korean Truce Stalemate. On Jan. 24 Gen. Matthew B. Ridgway, U.N. supreme commander in Korea, said the truce talks had reached "a complete state of paralysis."

Vincent Testimony. On Jan. 30 Foreign Service officer John Carter Vincent testified before the Senate Internal Security Subcommittee to deny Sen. McCarthy's charges that he was pro-communist. Vincent said he had accompanied former Vice President Henry A. Wallace to China in 1944 under orders from Secretary of State Cordell Hull.

Truman on McCarthy. On Jan. 31 President Truman assailed Sen. Joseph R. McCarthy, R-Wis., as "untruthful, pathological and a character assassin." McCarthy answered that the president was engaged in "name-calling."

Vincent Cleared. On Feb. 19 the State Department Loyalty and Security Board "completely cleared" John Carter Vincent of charges of pro-communism made against him by Sen. McCarthy.

Lattimore Testimony. On Feb. 26 Prof. Owen Lattimore of Johns Hopkins University testified before the Senate Internal Security Subcommittee. He denied that he was ever a communist, that the Institute of Pacific Relations, whose magazine he edited from 1934 to 1941, was communist, or that he influenced the State Department to abandon China to the communists.

McCarthy Sues Benton. On March 26 Sen. Joseph R. McCarthy sued Sen. William Benton, D-Conn., for libel, slander and conspiracy. McCarthy demanded $2 million and costs in U.S. District Court. Benton had filed accusations against McCarthy in connection with a resolution he introduced in 1951 for a Senate investigation of the Wisconsin Republican's fitness to hold his seat. McCarthy said Benton attacked him because he was "exposing Communists in the government."

Clark to East Asia. On April 28 President Truman announced that Gen. Mark W. Clark would succeed Gen.

Matthew B. Ridgway as U.N. supreme commander in Korea and commander of U.S. forces in the Far East. Ridgway was to succeed retiring Gen. Dwight D. Eisenhower as supreme allied commander, Europe.

Truman on Political Gangsters. On May 2 President Truman condemned "political gangsters" who "are motivated by such a lust for power that they are willing to wreck the lives and careers of innocent public servants" by creating "an atmosphere in which a charge is a conviction in the public mind despite the lack of evidence." Truman added, "I think they are worse than Communists, and I think they are partners with them."

Communist Prisoners Riot. On June 10, Communist prisoners on Koje Island fought with U.S. paratroopers for almost three hours, using spears, knives and clubs for weapons. The prisoners had captured an American general and held him hostage for three days in early May. The new uprising resulted in the deaths of 38 prisoners and one American. Some prisoners had been killed by their comrades because they wanted to surrender. On June 11 President Truman endorsed a proposal that five neutral countries investigate the uprising and U.N. measures to suppress it.

Power Plants Bombed. On June 23-26 more than 500 U.S. planes bombed five major hydroelectric power plants in the Yalu River area of North Korea in the biggest bombing raid of the war. The plants provided power for industries in Manchuria and large cities in North Korea, including Pyongyang. The Soviet news agency Tass reported on June 25 that "the American air pirates have started the massive bombing of peaceful towns which have no military objectives." Secretary of State Dean Acheson apologized to Prime Minister Winston Churchill on June 26 for failing to give Britain advance notice of the Yalu raids. Some British political leaders feared the raids might lead to world war.

Senate Committee's Report. On July 2 the Senate Judiciary Subcommittee on Internal Security issued a report charging that Prof. Owen Lattimore of Johns Hopkins University had been a "conscious, articulate instrument of the Soviet conspiracy" and had lied to the subcommittee five times. The subcommittee recommended that the Justice Department ask a grand jury to determine whether Lattimore should be indicted for perjury. Lattimore said the charges were "untrue" and "supported by no creditable evidence."

Republican Convention. On July 7 Gen. Douglas MacArthur, in a keynote address at the Republican National Convention in Chicago, asserted that the administration "gave over to Soviet control the industrial resources of Manchuria" and "condemned" the people of China to "Communist tyranny." MacArthur contended that when the Chinese entered the war, "our leaders lacked the courage to fight to a military decision, even though victory was then readily within our grasp — a victory which . . . might well have saved continental Asia from Red domination." He added that the administration had condemned U.S. forces to a "stalemated struggle" and Korea to "progressive obliteration." The armistice negotiations, in the general's opinion, only served to give the enemy time for military reinforcement.

Talks in Second Year. On July 10 the Korean truce negotiations entered their second year with the delegations engaged in secret talks over the prisoner exchange deadlock.

Eisenhower and Nixon Slate. On July 11 the Republicans nominated Gen. Dwight D. Eisenhower for president and Sen. Richard M. Nixon, Calif., for vice president.

John Foster Dulles wrote the strongly worded plank in the Republican platform charging that the administration had "squandered the unprecedented power and prestige" the U.S. had enjoyed since the end of World War II, had scuttled the Nationalist Chinese regime, had caused the Korean War through ambiguous policy statements and then "produced stalemates and ignominious bartering" after the war broke out.

Pyongyang Bombed. On July 11 Pyongyang, the North Korean capital, was heavily bombed in one of the biggest air raids of the war. Gen. J. Lawton Collins, U.S. Army chief of staff, warned of still heavier raids if the Communists insisted on "prolonging the war."

U.S. Report on Prisoners. On July 13 the United States said in a report to the United Nations Security Council that more than 100,000 prisoners in South Korea had said they would do anything rather than return to communist territory.

Stevenson and Sparkman Slate. On July 26 Gov. Adlai E. Stevenson, Ill., and Sen. John Sparkman, Ala., were nominated by the Democratic National Convention for president and vice president.

The Democratic platform stated: "Our military and economic assistance to the Nationalist Government of China on Formosa [Taiwan] has strengthened that vital outpost of the free world and will be continued."

Plant Bombed. On July 30, 63 B-29s bombed a North Korean aluminum plant 11 miles from the Manchurian border. On Aug. 5 the United States announced that the people of 78 North Korean towns and cities had been warned by radio and leaflets that their areas had been marked for destruction and should be evacuated.

Rhee Elected. On Aug. 5 South Korean President Syngman Rhee, 77, won a second four-year term in South Korea's first popular presidential election.

Stalemate. On Aug. 14 North Korean Premier Kim Il Sung conceded in a speech at Pyongyang that the Korean War had reached a stalemate. He said he would accept an armistice under which the "Americans are not the winners and the Koreans the losers."

Sino-Soviet Talks. On Aug. 19 Chinese Premier and Foreign Minister Chou En-lai arrived in Moscow for the first conference between Chinese and Soviet leaders since the Treaty of Alliance and Friendship was signed in February 1950. The talks were reported to cover the Korean conflict, its toll on the Chinese economy, and Sino-Soviet relations in general.

McCarthy Question. On Aug. 22 GOP nominee Dwight D. Eisenhower said he would support Sen. Joseph R. McCarthy, R-Wis., for re-election to the Senate if the senator won renomination in the Wisconsin primary. Both Eisenhower and Democratic nominee Adlai E. Stevenson had denounced McCarthy earlier in the week for attacking Gen. George C. Marshall.

Communist Protest. On Aug. 23 the Chinese and North Koreans, protesting air raids in North Korea, accused the United States of "blind and wanton bombings of

civilians. On Aug. 29 the U.S. Air Force announced that Pyongyang had undergone the heaviest air raid of the war.

McCarthy Renominated. On Sept. 9, in the first test of "McCarthyism" at the polls, Sen. Joseph R. McCarthy overwhelmingly won renomination in the Wisconsin Republican primary.

Prisoners Released. On Sept. 20 the United Nations announced that it had reclassified 11,000 Communist prisoners as South Korean civilians and released them. The Chinese asserted three days later that the action rendered the armistice talks "null and void." On Oct. 1, 52 rioting Communist prisoners were killed and 113 wounded by U.S. troops at a Cheju Island prison camp. North Korea immediately denounced the "bloody yet cowardly massacre" of the prisoners.

McCarthy-Eisenhower Agreement. On Oct. 3 Gen. Eisenhower said in Green Bay, Wis., that he and Sen. McCarthy agreed on the objective of cleansing the government of "the subversives and the disloyal," but that they differed on methods.

Eisenhower on Korea. On Oct. 8 Eisenhower criticized the Truman administration for allowing U.N. forces to accept the "trap" of negotiations in Korea in June 1951, at a time when they were "driving back" the enemy. Eisenhower said the lull allowed the Communists time to build up their positions. Earlier in the week, the general told an audience in Illinois that "if there must be war" in Asia, "let it be Asians against Asians, with our support on the side of freedom." He added that "the South Korean battle line today should be manned primarily by Koreans" and American troops should be used as reserves.

Truman Attacks Eisenhower. On Oct. 17 President Truman said in Lawrence, Mass., that the Soviet Union would have conquered Europe if the United States had failed to fight in Korea.

On the next day, the president charged that Eisenhower "held out false hopes to the mothers of America in an effort to pick up a few votes" by calling for the withdrawal of U.S. troops from the front lines and pointed out that 50 percent more South Koreans than Americans were fighting in Korea.

Korea in First Place. On Oct. 22 the Korean question was given first place on the U.N. General Assembly's agenda. On the following day, a representative of South Korea was admitted to the Korea debate.

Eisenhower Pledges Korean Trip. On Oct. 24 Gen. Eisenhower pledged to a Detroit audience that "I shall go to Korea" in an effort to end the war. Stevenson denounced the proposed trip as "a slick idea that gets votes by playing upon our hopes for a quick end to the war."

McCarthy Charge. On Oct. 27 Sen. McCarthy charged in a radio and television broadcast that Stevenson had helped the communist cause and had surrounded himself with leftist advisers, including Wilson W. Wyatt and Arthur Schlesinger Jr.

Eisenhower Wins. On Nov. 4 Gen. Eisenhower easily defeated Gov. Stevenson for the presidency. The GOP won control of both houses of Congress by narrow margins.

Lie Resigns. On Nov. 10 U.N. Secretary General Trgyve Lie of Norway resigned on the ground that Soviet hostility toward him prevented his working effectively for a Korean peace.

Formosa, Taipei and Taiwan

In 1590, when Portuguese explorers landed on a large island 100 miles off the coast of China, they named it "Ihla Formosa" or "Beautiful Island." Through Dutch, Spanish, Chinese, Japanese and U.S. occupation, the name Formosa was used despite the existence of an indigenous Chinese name — Taiwan. Following World War II, however, more and more colonial names gave way to the names used by the inhabitants themselves: the Belgian Congo became Zaire, for example, and Ceylon became Sri Lanka. During the 1960s, Western writers stopped using the colonial name Formosa and began referring to it by its Chinese name, Taiwan.

In 1945 the island was returned to the Chinese by the victorious allies, ending 50 years of Japanese occupation. Shortly thereafter, the island became a province. Chinese troops were sent to take possession, and a governor was appointed.

In 1949-50, as the Nationalist forces on the mainland crumbled under Communist attacks, the Kuomintang (KMT) leaders transferred key troops and, later, themselves to the island. In 1950 Chiang Kai-shek arrived, and the city of Taipei became the temporary capital of the Republic of China (Taichung remained the "provincial" capital). From that point on, Nationalist leaders insisted their stay on Taiwan was temporary and their return to the mainland imminent. In fact, they only controlled several islands off the coast of China, including the island of Taiwan, the Pescadores (Penghu), the Matsus (Mazu), and the Quemoys (Jinmen).

With the onset of the Korean War and the U.S. decision to defend the Republic of China against Communist attack, a legal fiction evolved that continued to plague Sino-American relations. In 1954 and 1955, the president and Congress went on record as defining the Republic of China in terms of the territories it actually controlled — the islands listed above. At the same time, however, the KMT itself defined the Republic of China (ROC) as the government of all of China, and its legislature was made up of proxy representatives from all of mainland China's provinces. The U.S. government tacitly accepted this latter definition by its official recognition of the ROC government and its non-recognition of the People's Republic of China in Peking.

During the three decades following the Communist victory, however, it became clear that despite the official rhetoric, two separate governments ruling two separate areas had evolved. Nonetheless, neither government would maintain relations with any third government which tried to promote the recognition of "two Chinas."

Thus the world was forced to choose between Taipei and Peking. During the 1970s, as more and more nations opted for Peking, nations were forced to take an official stand on the relation of Taiwan to China. Most used the Canadian or British "solutions" either "taking note of" or "acknowledging" Peking's position that Taiwan was part of China. Despite this, many governments continued to trade with the ROC, lend it money, sell it arms, and unofficially accept its "diplomats."

In 1979 President Carter's decision to recognize Peking confronted the United States with the same problems but — because of U.S. treaty links with the ROC and its longtime support for the government — on a much larger scale. As eventually worked out by the State Department and passed by Congress, the U.S. "acknowledged" that Taiwan was part of China and stopped all official reference to the ROC. In official U.S. parlance, the government of the ROC no longer existed.

Unfortunately for U.S. leaders, however, this did not answer the question of what to call the "non-nation" which the U.S. would continue to treat as a sovereign power. The solution was to refer to it simply as Taiwan, and to call the government there "authorities on Taiwan," or "people of Taiwan." This legal fiction remained confusing, however, because "Taiwan" still included all the other islands controlled by the ROC. In addition, as skeptical congressmen pointed out to beleaguered bureaucrats, the Taiwan "authorities" kept order, collected taxes and operated and commanded armed forces — in short, met all the requirements for nationhood. Its population and gross national product placed it among the world's richest states, yet it was not a state. It had no seat in the United Nations, nor would it be allowed to participate in future Olympics, at least as the ROC.

For their part, KMT leaders perpetuated their own fiction, insisting that there still was a Republic of China, located on the island of Taiwan, and that it was still the government of all of China. They still maintained two governments there: a "national" government and a "provincial" government. They steadfastly refused even to discuss the question of unity with the mainland as long as the Communists were in power.

Vishinsky on POWs. On the same day, Soviet Foreign Minister Andrei Y. Vishinsky told the General Assembly's Political and Security Committee that the Soviet Union would "never budge" from its opposition to voluntary repatriation of Korean prisoners of war. He rejected all pending compromise proposals.

Eisenhower Trip to Korea. On Dec. 2 U.S. President-elect Eisenhower departed on a three-day secret visit to Korea. After touring the battlefront and interviewing officials, Eisenhower announced at a press conference in Seoul on Dec. 5 that he had "no panaceas, no tricks" for settling the war. He said it was "difficult . . . to work out a plan that would bring positive and definite victory without possibly running a grave risk of enlarging the war."

Vincent Suspended. On Dec. 15 the State Department suspended John Carter Vincent as U.S. minister at Tangier and ordered him back to the United States. The suspension resulted from a report by the Civil Service Commission's Loyalty Review Board that there was "a reasonable doubt as to his loyalty."

Lattimore Indicted. On Dec. 16 Prof. Owen Lattimore was indicted by a federal grand jury in Washington on seven counts of perjury. Johns Hopkins put Lattimore on an indefinite leave of absence with full pay.

1953

U.S. Hydrogen Bomb — Chiang "Unleashed" — Death of Stalin — New Korean POW Proposals — POW Agree-

*ment — Syngman Rhee Frees Anti-Communist POWs —
Signing of Korean War Armistice — Korean War Casual-
ties — Soviet Hydrogen Bomb — U.S. Aid for France in
Indochina War — U.N. Excludes China — Clash Over
Plans for Korean Political Conference — Viet Minh Drive
to Borders of Thailand.*

Hydrogen Bomb. On Jan. 7, in his State of the Union
Message to Congress, President Truman confirmed the fact
that the U.S. had developed a hydrogen bomb. He added
that its use would be "unthinkable for rational men."

Taylor Replaces Van Fleet. On Jan. 23 Lt. Gen.
Maxwell D. Taylor, 51, was designated to replace retiring
Gen. James A. Van Fleet as commander of the U.S. 8th
Army in Korea.

Election in Vietnam. On Jan. 25, in the first local
elections ever held throughout Vietnam, candidates supporting the pro-French Vietnam government were successful in all localities except Hanoi. Despite threats of terrorism from the rebels, 80 percent of those registered voted.

Chiang "Unleashed." On Feb. 2 President Eisenhower announced in his State of the Union Message that he
was "issuing instructions that the Seventh Fleet no longer
be employed to shield Communist China" from an attack
by Nationalist forces on Taiwan. The president said the
order did not imply aggressive intent against Communist
China on the part of the United States, "but we certainly
have no obligation to protect a nation fighting us in Korea."

China and Truce Talks. On Feb. 4 Chinese Premier
Chou En-lai requested the United States to return to the
Korean truce talks. China, he said, was "ready for an
immediate cease-fire on the basis of the agreement already
reached in Panmunjom." The United States answered it
would return when the Communists conceded on their
demands for forced repatriation of prisoners of war.

First Five-Year Plan. On Feb. 4 the Chinese government declared the post-civil war recovery period over and
launched the first five-year plan, a systematic attempt to
develop China based on the Soviet model and using Russian aid and advisors.

Blockade Proposal. On Feb. 6 Rep. Dewey Short, R-
Mo., House Armed Services Committee chairman, reported
that the president and his advisers were studying proposals
for a naval blockade of China. Secretary of State John
Foster Dulles and Gen. Omar N. Bradley, chairman of the
Joint Chiefs of Staff, told the Senate Foreign Relations
Committee on Feb. 10 that the Joint Chiefs still believed
that a blockade by the United States alone might split the
allies and bring on war with the Soviet Union; and that the
flow of U.S. arms to the Nationalists on Taiwan was
"stepping up."

Chiang's Statement. On Feb. 12 Chiang Kai-shek
said the Nationalists could attack China whenever they
chose without U.N. sanction or fear of Soviet intervention.
Chiang conceded that his forces were not "adequately
equipped" for a full-scale invasion, but he felt they could
"not afford to wait until we are fully prepared."

Eisenhower Press Conference. On Feb. 17 President
Eisenhower said at his first news conference that he was not
then considering blockading or embargoing mainland
China. Secretary of State John Foster Dulles told a news
conference the following day that the administration was
seeking ways to isolate China from vital trade with non-

communist nations. He said that an embargo and blockade
were only two of a "whole series of measures of varying
kinds which could be adopted."

Vincent Cleared. On March 4 Secretary of State
Dulles announced that he had cleared career diplomat John
Carter Vincent of disloyalty charges. At the same time,
Dulles said Vincent's performance of his duties fell short of
necessary standards, and he was therefore accepting his
application for retirement.

Stalin Dies. On March 5 Soviet Premier Joseph V.
Stalin died of a brain hemorrhage. He was 73. The new,
collective leadership was much more conciliatory towards
the West, and took steps to ease tensions with the U.S.
Some analysts maintain that the first of these steps was towards a settlement of the Korean War. *(See April 26)*

Agreement on Sick and Wounded. On April 11 a final
agreement was reached on exchange of sick and wounded
prisoners in Korea, starting April 20. The Communists
asked for a resumption of talks on the entire prisoner issue
and assured the United Nations that it was the only
remaining obstacle to a cessation of hostilities.

Main Truce Talks Resume. On April 26 the Korean
truce talks were resumed at Panmunjom. The Communists
immediately rejected U.N. proposals for prisoners refusing
repatriation, but when the U.N. delegation threatened to
recess the talks again, the Communists modified their
stand.

POW Agreement Signed. On June 8, after more than
a month of proposals and rejections, U.N. and Communist
delegates to the truce talks in Panmunjom signed an
agreement on prisoners of war — an issue that had deadlocked negotiations for a year. The agreement called for
establishment of a supervising commission composed of
representatives of Czechoslovakia, India, Poland, Sweden
and Switzerland. The United Nations agreed that all prisoners should be repatriated provided they were willing to go
home; each side would be given 90 days to attempt to
change the minds of those unwilling to return. The supervising commission would have charge of those who were
unwilling, and they would be released after the 90-day
"convincer" period ended.

Rhee Agrees to Armistice. On July 11 the United
States announced that South Korean President Syngman
Rhee had agreed to an armistice on terms acceptable to the
United Nations. On the following day, Rhee and U.S.
Assistant Secretary of State for Far Eastern Affairs Walter
S. Robertson issued a joint statement implying that Rhee
had accepted President Eisenhower's views on a truce and a
U.S.-South Korean defense pact. Robertson had been in
Seoul for two weeks in an effort to persuade the South
Korean president to accept the truce. Truce negotiations
had been broken off on June 20 by the Communists after
Rhee had released 25,000 anti-communist prisoners of war.
Secret negotiations were resumed on July 10, but the
Communists refused to sign the agreement, asserting that
there was only "vague" assurance that the United Nations
could control South Korea.

New Offensive. On July 13 Chinese forces launched
their largest offensive since May 1951, in the central-front
area of Korea. U.N. forces retreated about four miles but by
July 16 were able to halt the offensive with heavy artillery
fire and bombing attacks. U.N. forces then counterattacked
and regained most of the lost ground.

It was later revealed that during the renewed fighting, President Eisenhower informed Peking, via India, that he "would no longer regard this war as being limited." Eisenhower's threat to use nuclear weapons was confirmed by Secretary of State John Foster Dulles. *(See Jan. 11, 1956)*

Armistice Signed. On July 27 an armistice was finally signed. The truce talks had been the longest in history, lasting two years and 17 days and including 575 separate meetings. The agreement provided for a prisoner exchange, freezing of the military fronts as a demarcation line, and establishment of a demilitarized zone four kilometers wide between the opposing forces. The size of forces on both sides also was frozen, but each side was permitted to rotate limited numbers of troops and equipment. A Military Armistice Commission of five U.N. and five Communist members was to supervise execution of the agreement. A political conference was to be held, after completion of the prisoner exchange, to discuss the future status of Korea and related problems.

Eisenhower's Warning. On Aug. 4 President Eisenhower told the Governors' Conference in Seattle that Burma, India and Indonesia would be in peril if the communists overran Indochina. He said that U.S. economic and military aid to anti-communist forces there offered the "cheapest way" to avoid a serious threat to U.S. security.

Prisoner Exchange Begins. On Aug. 5 the first U.N. and Communist prisoners of war in Korea were exchanged at Panmunjom.

Korean War Casualties. On Aug. 7 the U.N. Command estimated that U.N. military casualties totaled 455,000, of whom 300,000 were South Koreans. Estimates of Communist casualties ranged from 1,500,000 to 2,000,000. The Defense Department on Aug. 19 announced a total of 142,277 American casualties in Korea: 25,604 dead, 103,492 wounded, 8,529 missing, 2,219 captured, and 2,433 previously listed as captured or missing but later returned to duty.

Treaty with Korea. On Aug. 8 the U.S. signed a mutual defense treaty with South Korea in Seoul. The agreement provided for consultation if either nation were threatened by attack, and joint action "to meet a common danger." The U.S. was also permitted to maintain "air, land and sea forces" in Korea.

Hydrogen Bomb. On Aug. 8 Soviet Premier Georgi M. Malenkov said the Soviet Union had the hydrogen bomb. On Aug. 20 Malenkov announced that the Soviet Union had tested a hydrogen bomb. The test was later confirmed by the U.S. Atomic Energy Commission.

Dulles Warns China. On Sept. 2 Secretary of State Dulles warned China — "in hope of preventing another aggressor miscalculation" — that a renewal of the Korean conflict or a transfer of Communist forces into Indochina might mean war against the mainland itself. The secretary said the United States had learned one lesson from the Korean conflict: "If events are likely which will in fact lead us to fight, let us make clear our intention in advance; then we shall probably not have to fight."

Prisoner Exchange Completed. On Sept. 6 the exchange of prisoners of war was completed. The Communists released 12,760 prisoners (3,597 Americans), and the United Nations released 75,799 (5,640 Chinese). On Sept. 9 the United Nations demanded in the Military Armistice Commission that the Communists account for 3,404 other men, including 944 Americans. On Sept. 10 the United Nations began to move into the neutral truce zone 14,710 Chinese and 7,918 North Koreans who had refused repatriation. A 5,000-man Indian army guard force was being assembled to police the neutral camps.

Aid to French in Indochina. On Sept. 10 the National Security Council recommended that U.S. aid to France for the war in Indochina be increased by $385 million. Congress had already provided $400 million.

China and United Nations. On Sept. 15 the U.N. General Assembly adopted, 44-10, a U.S. resolution to keep the question of a seat for China off the assembly's 1953 agenda.

Indochina. On Nov. 20 French forces in Indochina seized Dienbienphu in western North Vietnam. The fortress had been a stronghold for the Viet Minh rebels.

U.N. Atrocity Resolution. On Dec. 3 the U.N. General Assembly adopted a U.S.-sponsored resolution charging that North Korea, China, and the Soviet Union were guilty of atrocities against prisoners of war.

Dean's Prediction. On Dec. 21 U.S. truce-talk negotiator Arthur H. Dean predicted that there would not be a renewal of fighting in Korea even if the political conference were not held. Dean had returned to Washington after walking out of preliminary discussions in Panmunjom.

Viet Minh Offensive. On Dec. 22 the Viet Minh launched a five-day offensive which severed Indochina at its narrowest point, driving across both Vietnam and Laos. The offensive ended when the Communist forces reached the Mekong River, the border of Thailand.

1954

Doctrine of Massive Retaliation — Eisenhower on Indochina War — Dulles on Troops for Indochina — Geneva Conference (Part I, Korea) — Fall of Dienbienphu — Geneva Conference (Part II, Indochina) — Ngo Dinh Diem to South Vietnam — Indochina Settlement — SEATO Treaty — Mutual Defense Treaty with Nationalist China — Senate Censure of McCarthy.

Massive Retaliation. On Jan. 12 Secretary of State John Foster Dulles, addressing the Council on Foreign Relations in New York City, outlined the doctrine of massive retaliation. The threat of "a great capacity to retaliate, instantly, by means and at places of our choosing" was held out as "a maximum deterrent at a bearable cost" against "a potential aggressor . . . glutted with manpower."

Unrepatriated POWs Returned. On Jan. 21 the Indian forces in Korea, acting for the supervisory commission on prisoners of war, moved back from the neutral truce zone all prisoners who had refused to be repatriated. The U.N. forces received 14,209 Chinese and 7,582 North Korean prisoners. On Jan. 28, 347 pro-Communists were handed over to the Chinese and North Koreans; the number included 21 Americans.

Viet Minh Invasion. On Jan. 30 the Viet Minh rebels launched an invasion of northern Laos. By Feb. 11, three Viet Minh forces had reached the outer defenses of Luang Prabang, the Laotian royal capital. French forces at Dienbienphu in Vietnam began attacking Communist troops who had surrounded that stronghold.

Eisenhower's Statement. On Feb. 10 President Eisenhower said it would be a "great tragedy" for the U.S. to get involved in the war in Indochina and that everything he did was calculated to prevent involvement. The French privately protested later that the president's statement had lowered both French and Indochinese morale and might encourage China to intervene.

Plans for Geneva. On Feb. 18 the Big Four foreign ministers, conferring in Berlin, agreed on proposals for a Far Eastern peace parley. The plan provided for a meeting in Geneva on April 26 to be attended by South Korea, the U.S., Britain, France, and 13 other nations represented in the U.N. Korean command and by China, North Korea, and the Soviet Union "for the purpose of reaching a peaceful settlement of the Korean question." The ministers agreed that the problem of Indochina also would be discussed. They said the conference should not be deemed "to imply diplomatic recognition in any case where it has not already been accorded."

U.S. Defense Agreement with Japan. On March 8, after eight months of negotiation, the U.S. and Japan signed a mutual defense treaty in Tokyo. The U.S. promised military and economic aid in return for a Japanese pledge to rebuild its armed forces under American guidance and to make "full contribution" to the strength of the anti-communist world.

Peking charged that the agreement was an attempt to revive Japanese militarism.

France to Negotiate. On March 9 the French National Assembly agreed to negotiate an Indochina peace settlement at the Geneva conference.

Dienbienphu Offensive. On March 13 the Viet Minh launched an attack on the French stronghold of Dienbienphu. The rebels had completely surrounded the fortress and damaged the airfield, the only means of supply for the French forces.

U.S. Aid in Indochina. On March 16 it was announced to the French National Assembly that the U.S. was paying 78 percent of the cost of the Indochina war. U.S. aid in 1954 would amount to $1.4 billion, while the French would provide only $394 million. On March 23 Secretary of State Dulles said in Washington that the U.S. would give France all the supplies and equipment necessary to defeat the Viet Minh rebels. The secretary predicted the French would win in Indochina even if the Chinese continued to support the rebels.

Dulles on Southeast Asia. On March 29 Secretary of State John Foster Dulles said in a New York speech that a Viet Minh victory in Indochina would lead to communist domination of all Southeast Asia. He said also that the U.S. would stand firm against recognition of China and against its admission to the U.N.

Dienbienphu Attacked. On March 30, Viet Minh forces staged a massive attack on Dienbienphu. After three days of heavy fighting, they had advanced to within a mile of the stronghold's center but then withdrew to regroup.

Dulles on S.E. Asia Defense. On April 5 Secretary Dulles proposed that the U.S. and its allies join in warning China against further aggression in Indochina or elsewhere in Southeast Asia. On April 10 the Secretary flew to London and later to Paris to confer on the prospects of establishing "a united front to resist communist aggression in Southeast Asia." He returned April 15 with French and British pledges to examine the possibility of "collective defense" for Southeast Asia and the Western Pacific.

Geneva Conference — Part I. On April 26, at the opening of the first part of the Geneva Conference, which was restricted to Korean questions, Chinese Premier and Foreign Minister Chou En-lai demanded that the U.S. and other Western powers be excluded from East Asian affairs. Secretary of State John Foster Dulles answered that the "authority of the U.N." was "at stake," and if "this conference is disloyal to the U.N. and its decisions on how to make peace and unify Korea, then each of us will bear a share of responsibility for destroying what protects us all." Chou replied that "the countries of Asia should consult among themselves, . . . seeking common measure to safeguard peace and security in Asia." Chou demanded removal of all foreign military personnel and bases from Asia. The following day, the Soviet Union announced its support of Chou's stand and condemned the U.S. for refusing to recognize Communist China.

French Pledge to Vietnam. On April 28 France pledged "total independence" to Vietnam, which promised to "maintain and consolidate" its friendship with France.

Sino-Indian Agreement. On April 29 China and India signed an agreement regulating trade and travel between India and "the Tibet region of China." The agreement made no reference to the Sino-Indian border dispute, which remained unresolved.

Indochinese Invited to Geneva. On May 3 Cambodia, Laos and the Viet Minh rebels were invited to the Geneva Conference as preparations began to arrange a truce or peace in Indochina.

Dienbienphu Totters. On May 4, Viet Minh forces, by means of "human sea" attacks, pushed to within 500 yards of the French command post in Dienbienphu.

Dienbienphu Falls. On May 7 the French fortress at Dienbienphu was overrun — the first time in the Indochinese war that a French stronghold had been conquered by direct assault. The final attack climaxed eight weeks of siege. The Communists on May 10 claimed to have taken 10,000 prisoners, including Brig. Gen. Christian de Castries, commander of the fortress. They said an additional 6,000 were killed or wounded.

Dulles Broadcast. On May 7 Secretary of State Dulles said over radio and television that the U.S. might have to make "serious commitments" to defend Southeast Asia, although the president would not order military action in Indochina without the support of Congress.

Geneva Conference — Part II. On May 8 the Geneva Conference turned its attention to Indochina. Nine states — the U.S., France, Britain, Russia, China, Cambodia, Laos, North Vietnam, and South Vietnam — participated in the second part of the conference. Discussions were promptly deadlocked by the Communists' refusal to accept independence for Laos and Cambodia.

New French Government. On June 13 Pierre Mendes-France replaced French Premier Joseph Laniel, whose government had lost a vote of confidence in the National Assembly on June 12.

Korean Talks Ended. On June 15 the Korean phase of the Geneva talks was terminated by the U.N. allies, who pointed out that the Communists had rejected "every effort to obtain agreement." The South Korean foreign minister said the failure of the talks left his government "free to take action."

Diem Becomes Premier. On June 15 Ngo Dinh Diem became premier of South Vietnam. He had lived in France for three years, protesting colonialism in Indochina.

Chinese Offer at Geneva. On June 16 Chinese Foreign Minister Chou En-lai offered a new compromise proposal on Indochina at the Geneva Conference, breaking what had seemed an insurmountable deadlock. The Chinese dropped their demand that rebel forces in Laos and Cambodia be recognized as "governments," said those forces would be withdrawn under a cease-fire, and asked that the Viet Minh rebel command represent the Communists in truce talks in Vietnam.

French-Chinese Meeting. On June 23 French Premier Mendes-France and Chinese Premier Chou En-lai met in Bern, Switzerland. The two agreed that a unified Vietnamese government should be established but that the military would remain divided; that a general election should be held after a period of truce; and that Laos and Cambodia should remain sovereign but be neutralized.

Sino-Indian Agreement. On June 28 Indian Prime Minister Jawaharlal Nehru and Chinese Premier Chou En-lai, meeting in New Delhi, issued a joint communiqué, in which India promised neutrality in the Cold War, and the Chinese promised not to commit aggression against India. The communiqué included China's first use of the "Five Principles of Peaceful Coexistence," which have guided China's foreign policy with the Third World ever since.

The Five Principles are: (1) mutual respect for each other's territorial integrity and sovereignty; (2) non-aggression; (3) non-interference in each other's internal affairs; (4) equality and mutual benefit; and (5) peaceful coexistence. The principles represented an elaboration of those first offered by Mao Tse-tung in 1949. *(See June 15, 1949)*

French Withdrawal. On June 29 French forces in Indochina withdrew from the southern section of the Red River delta to lines around Hanoi and Haiphong.

China-U.N. Dispute. On July 1 U.S. Senate Majority Leader William F. Knowland, R-Calif., announced that if China were admitted to the U.N., he would resign as majority leader to "devote my full efforts" to terminating U.S. membership. Senate Minority Leader Lyndon B. Johnson, D-Texas, said on the Senate floor, July 2, that "the American people will refuse to support" the U.N. if China is admitted. President Eisenhower said he was "completely and unalterably opposed under the present situation to the admission of Red China," but he implied opposition to U.S. withdrawal.

Hanoi and Haiphong Attacked. On July 12, Viet Minh forces intensified their attacks on French defenses at Hanoi and Haiphong.

Dulles Confers on Truce. On July 12 Secretary of State Dulles gave some support to Indochinese truce terms advocated by French Premier Mendes-France. Dulles had flown to Paris to meet with the French premier and British Foreign Secretary Anthony Eden on a collective defense alliance in Southeast Asia.

Indochina Settlement. On July 21, separate armistice agreements signed in Geneva with Cambodia, Laos and Vietnam ended the seven and one-half year war in Indochina. The U.S. refused to sign the agreements but promised that it would use no threat or force to upset them. South Vietnam also refused to sign. Under the provisions of the agreements, Vietnam was divided into two parts along the 17th parallel, the northern section controlled by the Viet Minh and the southern by the pro-French government in Saigon. Rebel forces in southern Vietnam were to be withdrawn to the north within 10 months and the French were given the same amount of time to evacuate the Hanoi area. Neither foreign troops nor arms and munitions of any kind were to be introduced into Vietnam. Cambodia and Laos were to be demilitarized (with the exception of two French outposts) and the territorial and political integrity of both was to be recognized by the Communists (rebel forces were permitted to remain in two Laotian provinces on the North Vietnamese border). Civilians were to be allowed to move from North to South Vietnam or vice versa and war prisoners were to be exchanged within 30 days. An International Control Commission was established, composed of India, Poland and Canada to supervise the agreements.

Final Geneva Declaration. On the day the armistice agreements were signed, the Geneva Conference ended with a "final declaration" which obligated the signatories (again not including the U.S. or South Vietnam) to observe certain additional stipulations:

1. Laos and Cambodia were not to request foreign military aid except for self-defense.

2. The military demarcation line in Vietnam (the 17th parallel) was not to be "interpreted as constituting a political or territorial boundary."

3. General elections were to be held in Vietnam in July 1956 "under the supervision of an international commission composed of representatives of the member states of the International Supervisory [Control] Commission." Consultations on the elections were to be held "from April 20, 1955, onwards."

4. The signatories were to "respect the sovereignty, the independence, the unity, and the territorial integrity" of Cambodia, Laos and Vietnam and "refrain from any interference in their internal affairs."

Eisenhower's Reaction. On July 21 President Eisenhower told a news conference that the Geneva agreement contained "features we do not like, but a great deal depends on how they work in practice." He said he could not offer a better proposal and would therefore not criticize the conference. The president added that the U.S. was "actively pursuing discussions [aimed at] rapid organization of a collective defense in Southeast Asia . . . to prevent further direct or indirect communist aggression in that general area."

Casualties in Indochina. Total pro-French casualties in the Indochinese war were estimated at 253,000 with 92,000 dead or missing. More than 200,000 Viet Minh soldiers died, according to unofficial estimates.

Chinese Air Attacks. On July 23, Chinese fighter planes shot down a British airliner in the South China Sea, 30 miles south of Hainan Island. On July 26 three American planes searching for survivors were fired on by two Chinese aircraft. The American pilots shot down both. Peking expressed regret for the first incident, explaining that the British aircraft was mistaken for a Chinese Nationalist warplane, but it said the U.S. planes had "committed an act of aggression." Secretary of State Dulles called the incident a "belligerent interference with a humanitarian rescue operation being conducted over the high seas."

Chou's Statement. On Aug. 11 Chinese Premier and Foreign Minister Chou En-lai urged the "liberation" of Taiwan and warned that "foreign aggressors" who intervened would face "grave consequences."

On Aug. 17 President Eisenhower commented that the Communists would have to contend with the 7th Fleet before reaching Taiwan.

First Taiwan Strait Crisis. On Sept. 3 Communist artillery began shelling the Nationalist-held island of Quemoy (Jinmen), and the Nationalists returned fire. *(Map, p. 105)* On Sept. 4 Secretary Dulles ordered the 7th Fleet to recommence patrolling the Taiwan Strait. On Sept. 7 Taiwan began large-scale air strikes against the mainland.

Creation of SEATO. On Sept. 8, eight nations signed in Manila a U.S.-sponsored Southeast Asian collective defense treaty. Sometimes referred to as the Manila Pact, the signatories were Australia, Britain, France, New Zealand, Pakistan, the Philippines, Thailand, and the U.S. The agreement, which established the Southeast Asia Treaty Organization, pledged each of the member states in the event of armed aggression against any one of them to consult on joint measures to meet the threat raised by "any fact or situation [other than armed attack] which might endanger the peace of the area." The area covered by the treaty was defined as the "general area of Southeast Asia, including the "entire territories" of the Asian parties to the treaty, and the "general area of the Southwest Pacific" below a line running to the south of Taiwan.

An official "understanding," filed with the treaty, made it clear that the American commitment applied only to "Communist aggression," but that the U.S. would consult with SEATO members in the event of "other aggression or armed attack." The word "Communist" did not appear in the treaty.

The U.S. Senate ratified the treaty by an 82-1 roll-call vote on Feb. 1, 1955

Dulles on SEATO. On Sept. 8 Secretary of State Dulles called the SEATO treaty an "Asiatic Monroe Doctrine." He said in Manila that it "promoted unity rather than disunity" and was "a major step in building security" for Southeast Asia.

Dulles Assures Taiwan. On Sept. 12 Secretary Dulles told newsmen in Denver that he believed the Chinese would not invade Taiwan. He said that invasion would be impossible against "such opposition as we would interpose" and that, in his opinion, Quemoy also was secure.

According to a statement made later by Dulles, China backed down after the U.S. had threatened to use nuclear weapons against China. *(See Jan. 11, 1956)*

China Question in U.N. On Sept. 21 the General Assembly bypassed a Soviet resolution urging admission of China to the U.N. and adopted, by a 43-11 vote, a U.S. resolution putting off debate on the question to September 1955.

Viet Minh in Hanoi. On Oct. 9, Viet Minh forces occupied Hanoi and were greeted by flag- and banner-waving residents.

Soviet Credits to China. On Oct. 11 the Soviet Union and China issued a joint communiqué in Peking announcing that the Soviet Union had agreed to grant China a second credit, of $130 million. The Soviets also agreed to the implementation of the remaining provisions of the 1950 Sino-Soviet Treaty, which the Korean War had delayed.

Eisenhower Note to Diem. On Oct. 23 President Eisenhower sent a note to South Vietnamese Premier Ngo Dinh Diem urging "needed reforms" in return for U.S. aid. The president said the aid would help South Vietnam to develop and maintain "a strong viable state capable of resisting attempted subversion or aggression through military means."

Nehru on China. On Oct. 31 Indian Prime Minister Jawaharlal Nehru reported on his return from China that Mao Tse-tung had assured him that China wished to avoid war because it would interfere with the country's economic development. Nehru said that Mao thought the Geneva Conference "had eased the world situation greatly," but he felt that Korea, Taiwan and Indochina were still major threats to world peace.

U.S. Midterm Elections. On Nov. 2 the Democrats gained slender majorities in both chambers of Congress. President Eisenhower announced his intention to cooperate fully with Democratic leaders.

Chinese Sentence Americans. On Nov. 22 a Chinese military tribunal sentenced 11 U.S. airmen and two civilian U.S. Army employees to long prison terms as spies. They had been captured in two groups when their planes were shot down during the Korean War. The State Department sent the "strongest possible protest." *(See Dec. 12, 1971)*

Knowland Reaction. On Nov. 27 Senate Majority Leader William F. Knowland, R-Calif., urged that the U.S. establish a naval blockade of mainland China "until these Americans are released."

Dulles on Blockade. On Nov. 29 Secretary of State Dulles told a Chicago audience that a U.S. blockade of China would be an act of war and that imprisonment of the 13 Americans was "a challenge to us . . . to find ways, consistent with peace, to sustain international rights and justice." Dulles added that the U.S. was obligated to settle disputes within the framework of the U.N. "in such a manner that international peace is not endangered." On Dec. 1 he said a blockade was "certainly a possibility" if all peaceful efforts to obtain the release of the Americans failed.

Mutual Defense Treaty. On Dec. 2 Secretary of State Dulles signed a mutual defense treaty with the Republic of China. The Senate ratified the treaty on Feb. 9, 1955, and President Eisenhower signed the resolution of ratification on Feb. 11. The treaty required the U.S. and the ROC to:

(1) Maintain and develop "jointly by self-help and mutual aid" their individual and collective capacity to resist armed attack and Communist subversion directed against them "from without."

(2) Cooperate in economic development.

(3) Consult on implementation of the treaty.

(4) Act to meet an armed attack "in the West Pacific area directed against the territories" of either the U.S. or the Republic of China, including Taiwan, the Pescadores Islands, and "such other territories as may be determined by mutual agreement." *(Text, p. 311)*

The treaty did not cover Nationalist-held islands along the coast of China. *(See Jan. 24, 1955)*

In an exchange of notes signed Dec. 10, the government of the Republic of China issued a formal understanding to the U.S. that its forces would not attack the mainland without prior consultation with the U.S. *(See Jan. 14, 1955)*

1955

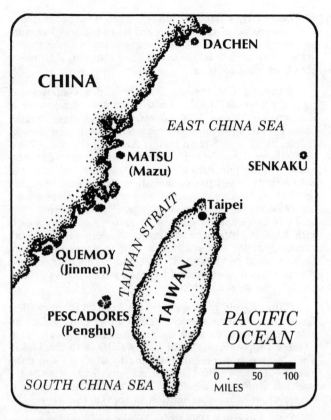

Hammarskjold in Peking — China Threatens Taiwan — Congress Authorizes Use of U.S. Armed Forces to Defend Taiwan — Differences Over Offshore Islands of Quemoy and Matsu — Chou En-lai at Bandung Conference — Progress Toward Release of Americans in China — Premier Diem of South Vietnam Becomes President.

Raids on Dachen Islands. On Jan. 10 the Nationalist Chinese Defense Ministry announced that the Communist Chinese had launched the largest air attacks of the civil war against the Nationalist-held Dachen Islands, 200 miles north of Taiwan. *(Map, this page)*

Hammarskjold Trip. On Jan. 13 U.N. Secretary General Dag Hammarskjold returned to New York from Peking and reported that his visit had been important as "a first stage" in obtaining release of the 13 Americans. Hammarskjold told reporters: "I feel my talks with Mr. Chou En-lai were definitely useful for this purpose. We hope to be able to continue our contact. The door that is opened can be kept open, given restraint on both sides." On Jan. 14 Hammarskjold told a news conference he had made "no deals of any kind" with the Chinese, but that he did feel it would be "useful" if they were allowed to enter the U.N.

Nationalist Pledge. On Jan. 14 it was reported that Chinese Nationalist Foreign Minister George K. C. Yeh had pledged, in a private letter to the U.S., that under the U.S.-Nationalist Chinese mutual defense treaty, his country would not invade the Chinese mainland without prior U.S. approval. On Jan. 16 U.N. Secretary General Dag Hammarskjold said he planned to send a message to Peking informing the Chinese Communist leaders of the Nationalist pledge.

Communists Seize Yijiang. On Jan. 18 Chinese Communist forces invaded Yijiang Island, eight miles north of the Dachen Islands and 210 miles north of Taiwan. The small Nationalist force defending the island quickly surrendered. The following day, over 200 Communist aircraft bombed the Dachens and the Nationalist Air Force retaliated by bombing shipping along the China coast. On Jan. 19 President Eisenhower told a news conference he hoped the U.N. would "exercise its good offices" to obtain a cease-fire in the Taiwan Strait.

Chou Threatens Taiwan. On Jan. 24 Chinese Premier and Foreign Minister Chou En-lai reiterated his country's intention to invade Taiwan and rejected the possibility of a cease-fire. Chou said the U.S. was "using war threats and brandishing atomic weapons to force the Chinese people into tolerating" the "occupation" of Taiwan. He demanded that American forces depart from the area.

Eisenhower's Message. On Jan. 24 President Eisenhower sent a special message to Congress requesting emergency authorization to use American armed forces to protect Taiwan and the Pescadores Islands. The resolution went beyond the mutual defense treaty by implicitly pledging the U.S. to help Taiwan defend the offshore islands of Quemoy and Matsu "for the specific purpose of securing and protecting Taiwan and the Pescadores against armed attack."

Formosa Resolution. On Jan. 25 the House adopted the administration resolution (H J Res 159) by a 410-3 roll-call vote and sent it to the Senate without amendment. On

Senate Censures McCarthy. On Dec. 2 the Senate by a 67-22 roll-call vote condemned Sen. Joseph R. McCarthy, R- Wis., for failing to cooperate with a Senate subcommittee that had inquired into his financial affairs in 1951-52, and for leveling abusive charges against the bipartisan Select Committee which had recommended that he be censured.

McCarthy Displeased. On Dec. 7 Sen. McCarthy assailed President Eisenhower because he "on one hand congratulates the Senators who hold up the work of our Committee, and on the other hand urges that we be patient with the [Chinese] Communist hoodlums who at this very moment are torturing and brainwashing American uniformed men in Communist dungeons."

U.N. Resolution. On Dec. 7, the 16 Korean War allies offered a resolution in the General Assembly accusing China of violating the Korean armistice by jailing 13 Americans as spies *(see Nov. 22, 1954)* and detaining other captured U.N. personnel who wanted to be repatriated. On Dec. 10 the General Assembly adopted the resolution and instructed Secretary General Dag Hammarskjold to seek immediate release of the prisoners. On Dec. 13 Peking radio said the U.N. had no right to interfere with the conviction and punishment of the Americans.

Warning on Taiwan. On Dec. 8 Chou En-lai, Chinese premier and foreign minister, speaking in response to the American signing of a mutual defense treaty with Taiwan, warned the U.S. that it would face "grave consequences" if it did not withdraw "all its armed forces" from Taiwan. Chou said that China was determined to "liberate Taiwan" and that the island "is entirely within the purview of China's sovereignty and a purely internal affair of China."

On Dec. 15 the Soviet Union announced "full support" of the Chinese demands.

Jan. 28 the Senate adopted the resolution by an 85-3 roll-call vote without amendment. The negative votes were cast by Sens. Wayne Morse, D-Ore., William Langer, R-N.D., and Herbert H. Lehman, D-N.Y. *(Text, p. 311)*

President Signs Resolution. On Jan. 29 President Eisenhower signed H J Res 159 into law (PL 84-4). He said "We are ready to support a United Nations effort to end the present hostilities in the area, but we are also united in our determination to defend an area vital to the security of the United States and the free world." *(See Oct. 11, 1974)*

Dachen Withdrawal. On Feb. 5 the United States announced that the Nationalist government had decided to withdraw from the Dachen Islands, and had requested U.S. assistance. The 7th Fleet covered the withdrawal.

New Soviet Leadership. On Feb. 8 the U.S.S.R. Supreme Soviet announced the removal of Georgi M. Malenkov from the premiership. The first secretary of the Communist Party's Central Committee, Nikita S. Khrushchev, emerged as the strongest figure in the Communist Party.

Defense Treaty Ratified. On Feb. 9 the Senate ratified the mutual defense treaty with Nationalist China. *(Text, p. 311)*

Dulles' Policy Review. On Feb. 16 Secretary of State John Foster Dulles, speaking before the Foreign Policy Association in New York, presented what the State Department billed as a "review of [the basic U.S. East Asian and Southeast Asian] positions as of 1955."

In the speech, Dulles outlined the steps which had been taken to cut off and isolate mainland China, including the mutual security treaties with South Korea, Japan and Nationalist China, as well as the SEATO pact. Because of this, said Dulles, "free men throughout the world can face the future with better hope and new confidence," *(Text, p. 311)*

Nationalist Military Action. On Feb. 22 the Nationalist government on Taiwan claimed its largest military victory since leaving the mainland in 1949. The Nationalists said their ships and warplanes had launched successful strikes against Chinese Communist convoys en route to the Communist-held Daishan islands.

SEATO Meeting. On Feb. 23, the foreign ministers of the eight SEATO nations met in Thailand to formulate its defense plans. It was the first meeting of the council. The treaty had gone into effect on Feb. 19.

Dulles Warning to China. On March 8 Secretary of State John Foster Dulles, in a nationwide broadcast, warned China not to underestimate U.S. determination to meet aggression in East Asia. Dulles said that American naval and air forces were "equipped with new and powerful weapons of precision, which can utterly destroy military targets without endangering unrelated civilian centers."

Chinese Free to Leave U.S. On April 2 the State Department announced that 76 Chinese students with technical training who had been refused exit permits after the start of the Korean War, because they might have helped the Communists in Korea, were now "free to depart" from the U.S. The department denied there was any deal for release of Americans held in China, though "We would like Americans of all categories in China to be released for whatever reason appeals to the Red Chinese authorities."

Dean Urges Recognition. On April 8 Arthur H. Dean, U.S. negotiator in the Korean armistice talks at Panmunjom and a former law partner of Secretary of State Dulles, urged in an article in *Foreign Affairs* that the U.S. recognize Communist China.

Bandung Conference. On April 18 a conference of representatives of 29 Asian and African nations convened in Bandung, Indonesia. The following day, Chinese Premier Chou En-lai, addressing the conference, indicated a major change in Chinese foreign policy. Avoiding use of the "two-bloc" thesis, Chou began a courtship of the sitting governments of Asia and Africa. Because they were all countries only recently freed from colonialism, Chou said that they should "seek common ground, and not create divergence."

Now called the "Bandung phase" of Chinese foreign policy, Chou's speech marked increased Chinese contacts with Asia and Africa, a cooling of tensions along China's various borders, and a Chinese shift to an assertion that Taiwan could be "liberated" peacefully. This milder phase of Chinese policy would end with the second Taiwan Strait Crisis. *(See Aug. 23, 1958)*

China Ready to Negotiate. On April 23 Premier Chou En-lai, in another statement at Bandung, said: "The Chinese people are friendly to the American people. The Chinese people do not want to have war with the U.S.A. The Chinese government is willing to sit down and enter into negotiations with the U.S. government to discuss the question of relaxing tension in the Far East and especially the question of relaxing tension in the Taiwan area."

U.S. Reaction. The State Department said the same day that the U.S. would agree to negotiations if the Chinese Communists would allow Nationalist China's participation in the discussions as an equal, would release Americans imprisoned in China, and would accept the "outstanding invitation" of the U.N. Security Council "to participate in discussions to end hostilities in the Formosa [Taiwan] region."

On April 26 Secretary of State Dulles said at a news conference: The "first thing is to find out whether there is a possibility of a cease-fire in the area [of Taiwan]. That is a matter which can be discussed, perhaps bilaterally, or at the U.N., or possibly under other circumstances. But I regard a cease-fire as the indispensable prerequisite to anything further. When you get into further matters, then the interests of the Chinese Nationalists would naturally come to play a very large part."

Conference Adjourns. On April 27 the Bandung Conference adjourned.

Nehru's Announcement. On April 30 Indian Prime Minister Jawaharlal Nehru announced that Indian U.N. delegate V. K. Krishna Menon had been invited to Peking by Chinese Premier Chou En-lai to discuss the Taiwan crisis. Nehru said the Indian government would attempt to avert "the grim alternative that faces us if there are to be no negotiations."

Air Skirmish Near Korea. On May 11 the U.S. lodged a protest with the Korean Armistice Commission against a Chinese Communist attack on U.S. fighter planes "over international waters" near North Korea. The U.S. reported it had shot down two or three Communist planes in the skirmish. The Chinese claimed they had shot down one U.S. plane and damaged two more. The Communists said the U.S. aircraft had violated China's "territorial air" by passing over two Chinese islands off the Manchurian coast.

Four Fliers Released. On May 30 Indian U.N. delegate V. K. Krishna Menon announced in New Delhi that the Chinese would release four American airmen who had been imprisoned in China for more than two years. Menon said the Chinese still held 11 U.S. fliers who had been convicted of espionage and sabotage. The Indian diplomat had conferred with Chinese Premier Chou En-lai for 11 days in Peking. On June 1 he flew to Washington for discussions on "lowering tensions" between the U.S. and China.

On May 31 U.N. Secretary General Dag Hammarskjold asked the Chinese government to release all other Americans imprisoned in China. On June 1 the four released fliers said that Hammarskjold's January visit to Peking "had very much to do with our release."

Lattimore Case Dropped. On June 28 Attorney General Herbert Brownell Jr. announced that the government was dropping its perjury case against Johns Hopkins Prof. Owen Lattimore because "there is no reasonable likelihood of a successful prosecution. . . ."

Aid to North Vietnam. On July 8 Peking radio announced a $338 million economic aid program for North Vietnam. North Vietnamese President Ho Chi Minh had visited Peking to ask for aid and had joined Chinese Premier Chou En-lai in accusing the U.S. of seeking to prevent "peaceful unification" of Vietnam through elections.

Prisoners Return. On July 10 three of the 23 Americans who had been captured during the Korean War and elected to stay in China left for Hong Kong.

Chou on Trade and Taiwan. On July 30 Chinese Premier Chou En-lai told the National People's Congress in Peking that the "number of American civilians in China is small and their question can be easily settled." Chou expressed concern over "the extremely unjust policy of blockade and embargo which obstructs trade between countries" and stated that it should be possible "to remove such barriers so that peaceful trade between all countries will not be hindered."

Chou observed that after "the Korean armistice and the restoration of peace in Indo-China, the situation in the Taiwan area has become the most tense in the Far East." He continued: "Provided that the U.S. does not interfere with China's internal problems, the possibility of peaceful liberation of Taiwan will continue to increase. If possible, the Chinese government is willing to enter into negotiations with the responsible local authorities of Taiwan to map out concrete steps for Taiwan's peaceful liberation. It should be made clear that there should be negotiations between the central government and local authorities. The Chinese people are firmly opposed to any ideas or plots of the so-called 'two Chinas.'"

Ambassadorial Talks. On Aug. 1 the Chinese ambassador to Poland, Wang Bingnan, began talks with the U.S. ambassador to Czechoslovakia, U. Alexis Johnson, in Geneva. This first meeting represented an upgrading of the talks, which first began in 1954, from the consular to the ambassadorial level. *(Box, p. 149)* The same day, China announced the release of 11 U.S. fliers who had been imprisoned as spies in China.

Dulles on Chou's Speech. On Aug. 2 Secretary of State Dulles told a news conference that Chou En-lai's speech "indicated his going further in renunciation of force than anything he had said before." Dulles went on to say: "What we hope to arrive at by progressive steps is a situation where the Chinese Communists will have renounced the use of force to achieve their ambitions. If they want to use force . . . that will almost surely start up a war, the limits of which could not be defined in advance."

On Aug. 16 the secretary expressed disappointment that the Chinese-U.S. talks in Geneva still had not resulted in release of 41 U.S. civilians held in China. He had hoped, in light of Chou's speech, that the matter would be "promptly settled."

Civilians Released. On Sept. 6 Wang Bingnan, China's ambassador to Poland, announced to U. Alexis Johnson, U.S. ambassador to Czechoslovakia, that the Chinese government would release 12 of the 41 American citizens held in China. The State Department called the action "encouraging" but reaffirmed demands that all of the civilians be released.

Repatriation. On Sept. 10 the Geneva ambassadorial talks resulted in the issuance of "agreed parallel unilateral statements" by China and the U.S., which were to resolve the problem of the repatriation of the remaining civilians held by both nations. Wang said that some would be released "soon" and some "expeditiously." Meanwhile, the U.S. also began repatriating some of the 129 Chinese students and scientists who were being detained in the U.S. The agreements foundered on the Chinese refusal to return any actual "prisoners," but only "civilians." *(See Jan. 6, 1956)*

U.N. Turns Down China. On Sept. 20 the U.N. General Assembly adopted a U.S. resolution to defer consideration of representation for Communist China for another year. The vote was 42-12 with 6 abstentions.

Diem Becomes President. On Oct. 23 a national referendum in South Vietnam deposed Emperor Bao Dai, who was living in France, and elevated Premier Ngo Dinh Diem to chief of state. Diem received 98.2 percent of the votes. On Oct. 26 he declared South Vietnam a republic and proclaimed himself president. He said the country would have a new constitution and an elected National Assembly "before the end of the year."

Dulles on Prisoners. On Dec. 6, following the Chinese release of 10 more U.S. prisoners, Secretary of State Dulles said he was still disappointed with the progress of the releases, and noted the Chinese still held 19 Americans and were examining their cases "one be one." After the release of six more civilians, Peking retained only the 13 Americans imprisoned as spies in 1954. *(See Nov. 11, 1954)*

1956

Stir Over Dulles Views on Brinkmanship — Exchanges with Peking on Taiwan Question — Soviet Leaders Assail the Stalin Cult of Personality — Khrushchev's Denunciation of Stalin — Washington Turns Down Peking Bid for Dulles-Chou Talks — Chou En-lai Bid — Chinese Troops in Burma — State Department Bars Acceptance of Chinese Communist Offer of Visas to Newsmen — Republican and Democratic Party Platforms Oppose Admission of China to U.N. — General Assembly Defers Question of Chinese Representation.

Peking on U.S. Civilians in China. On Jan. 6 a spokesman for the Chinese Foreign Ministry said that Chinese-held American civilians who "offended against the law in China must be dealt with in accordance with Chinese legal procedures, and no time limit can be set for their release."

Dulles Brinkmanship. On Jan. 11 *Life* magazine published an article, entitled "How Dulles Averted War," in which Secretary of State John Foster Dulles was quoted as saying it was "a pretty fair inference" that the Eisenhower administration's "policy of deterrence" had "brought the Korean War to an end ... kept the Chinese from sending their Red armies into Indochina" and "stopped them in Formosa [Taiwan]." The article by James Shepley, chief Washington correspondent for Time-Life, said that Eisenhower had decided that if truce negotiations failed in Korea, the U.S. would "fight to win," attacking bases in Manchuria and resorting to "tactical use of atomic arms." This decision, the article continued, was relayed to Indian Prime Minister Nehru through Dulles in May 1953, in the belief that Nehru would inform the Chinese Communist leaders. "Within two weeks," Shepley wrote, the Communist negotiators in Korea "began to negotiate seriously."

In the Indochina war, Secretary Dulles and Admiral Arthur W. Radford, chairman of the Joint Chiefs of Staff, were said to have been given the president's approval to employ U.S. air power to destroy Communist staging areas in China if the Chinese Communists "intervened openly." Shepley added that "Dulles had seen to it that [China and the Soviet Union] knew that the U.S. was prepared to act decisively to prevent the fall of all of Southeast Asia."

The article said, in addition, that a war over Taiwan was avoided by the congressional resolution of Jan. 28, 1955, authorizing the president to use what force he deemed necessary if the Chinese attacked Taiwan or the Pescadores. According to Dulles, "We walked to the brink and looked it in the face. We took strong action." Shepley reported that Dulles was the author of the Formosa Resolution and that he had sent a second warning to Communist leaders, via Burmese Prime Minister U Nu, that the U.S. "meant business."

Reaction to Dulles Claims. The *Life* article brought immediate criticism from the Democrats. Sen. Hubert H. Humphrey, D-Minn., told the Senate Jan. 13 that "Mr. Dulles' 'art' ... comes precariously close to rejecting the traditional American conviction that we must not strike the first blow [nor] bear the awful responsibility for beginning atomic war." He said the secretary's policy of "massive retaliation" would cause "untold trouble with our allies."

On Jan. 14 Adlai Stevenson said in Chicago that he was "shocked that the Secretary of State is willing to play Russian roulette with the life of our nation.... The art of diplomacy, especially in this atomic age, must lead to peace, not war or the brink of war."

On the same day, Vice President Richard M. Nixon told an audience in Springfield, Ill., that "the test of a foreign policy is its ability to keep the peace without surrendering any territory or principle," and that this "great fact about the Eisenhower-Dulles foreign policy will stand out long after the tempest in a teapot over the expression ["brink of war"] is forgotten." Both Nixon and Harold E. Stassen, presidential special assistant on disarmament, criticized Stevenson for describing Dulles' strategy as "Russian roulette."

On Jan. 17 Secretary Dulles told a news conference that "the surest way to avoid war is to let it be known in advance that we are prepared to defend" our interests. He added that the U.S. was "brought to the verge of war" because of communist threats against Korea, Indochina, and Taiwan.

On Jan. 19 President Eisenhower told a news conference that he had "complete faith" in Dulles as "devoted to peace" and "to my mind the best Secretary of State I have ever known."

The next day, Sen. Mike Mansfield, D-Mont., said Dulles should have warned the Senate Foreign Relations Committee when the U.S. was on the "brink" of wars. He charged: "For three years we have lived on borrowed time in foreign relations.... Nothing has been settled in Korea.... [Quemoy and Matsu] may yet lead us into a military involvement with Communist China if not to World War III itself. In Indochina ... the danger of catastrophe is not yet passed."

Dulles answered that "constructive discussion of foreign policy" was "entirely proper and appropriate" up to a certain "danger point" where it might cause "doubt" over U.S. "determination" to fulfill its "commitments."

Peking on Dulles. On Jan. 18 the Chinese Foreign Ministry in Peking released a report on the Geneva ambassadorial discussions because "the U.S. has recently stepped up military activities in the Taiwan area to aggravate the tension, and U.S. Secretary of State Dulles even renewed the clamors for an atomic war against China." The Communist statement said Dulles had "openly cried out recently that in order to hold on to China's territory and infringe China's sovereignty, he would not scruple to start an atomic war."

Washington-Peking Exchanges. On Jan. 21 the State Department released its own report on the Geneva ambassadorial talks because it was "necessary that the record be set straight." Both Washington's and Peking's reports said the U.S. had proposed a joint statement committing the two countries to a mutual renunciation of the use of force. The Communists said they would agree as long as the renunciation did not apply to the "internal affair" of Taiwan. The U.S. said the Chinese were attempting to exempt those areas they planned to seize by force, and that until there was agreement on a declaration renouncing the use of force "generally, and particularly in the Taiwan area," progress toward a Sino-American settlement would be obstructed.

Peking answered: "Taiwan is China's territory. There can be no question of defense so far as the U.S. is concerned. The U.S. has already used force and the threat of force against China in the Taiwan area.... Yet the U.S. has demanded the right of defense in the Taiwan area. Is this not precisely a demand that China accept continued U.S. occupation of Taiwan and that the tension in the Taiwan area be maintained forever?"

The State Department replied that "the Communists so far seem willing to renounce force only if they are first conceded the goals for which they would use force."

Peking further charged that "the great majority" of "tens of thousands of Chinese in the U.S." had "not been able or not dared to apply for returning to China" because of "obstructions and threats ... in violation of the agreement." The Chinese called U.S. charges concerning the detention of Americans in China "groundless."

The State Department answered that, four months after Peking had promised their release, "thirteen Americans are still held in Communist prisons." The Department demanded their immediate release "not only for humanitarian reasons but because respect for international undertakings lies at the foundation of a stable international order."

On Jan. 24 Secretary of State Dulles told a news conference: "Negotiations with the Chinese Communists are usually slow and prolonged," but "we are planning to go ahead . . . and we continue to be patient and persistent in our effort to obtain a greater assurance of peace and renunciation of force in that area." *(Box, p. 149)*

Controls on China Trade. On Feb. 1 President Eisenhower and British Prime Minister Anthony Eden, who was visiting Washington, announced they had "agreed that trade controls [against China] should continue and should be reviewed . . . periodically as to their scope, in the light of changing conditions, so that they may best serve the interests of the free world."

Policy Changes in Moscow. On Feb. 14 Soviet Communist Party First Secretary Nikita S. Khrushchev, in a seven-hour speech opening the 20th Soviet Party Congress, said war with "capitalist imperialism" was no longer inevitable, implicitly because of Soviet possession of nuclear weapons. Noting that peaceful coexistence was gaining "increasingly wider international recognition," Khrushchev said: "Indeed, there are only two ways: either peaceful coexistence or the most devastating war in history." Thus, stated Khrushchev, other communist parties should try to find a "peaceful" road to power.

On Feb. 24, in a secret speech to the congress, Khrushchev delivered a violent and detailed denunciation of the late Premier Joseph Stalin, his policies and his actions.

The two speeches sent shock waves through the world's communist parties. For the Chinese, it meant that they would be less able to rely on the Soviet Union in foreign affairs and that, in particular, they had lost the protection of the Soviet nuclear "umbrella." Khrushchev's attack on Stalin's "cult of personality" raised problems for Chinese Chairman Mao Tse-tung, who had also created such a "cult."

The Chinese Communists date the origins of the Sino-Soviet split from these speeches.

Sino-Cambodian Agreement. On Feb. 18, Chinese and Cambodian leaders signed a joint communiqué in Peking. The communiqué embodied the "five principles of coexistence," as well as provisions for economic aid to Cambodia.

The "Hundred Flowers" Movement. On May 2 Mao Tse-tung, in a speech to the Supreme State Conference, developed various themes with liberal overtones, and illustrated them with a quotation from the Chinese classics: "Let a hundred flowers bloom, let a hundred schools contend." Although a complete text of this speech has never become available, the theme was picked up several days later by Lu Dingyi, head of information and propaganda in the Chinese Communist Party, in a speech at a conference of writers. The essence of Lu's comments was that the regime did not fear criticism, and even welcomed it, arguing that there was no need for artists and authors to deal only with subjects directly related to communist ideology.

These two speeches provoked a slow but steadily increasing amount of criticism of the Communist regime, and of all aspects of life in China, and seemed to point to a liberalization of the regime. *(See Feb. 27, 1957)*

Chinese Offer Talks. On May 12 Peking proposed that Chinese Foreign Minister Chou En-lai meet with Secretary of State Dulles to discuss Taiwan and other problems. *(See June 12)*

British to Expand China Trade. On May 16 Britain informed the U.S. that it planned to expand trade with China by "excepting" a number of items currently on the list of strategic goods not to be exported to mainland China. British officials said they would move "cautiously" to avoid selling any important strategic goods to the Communists.

Egypt Recognizes China. On May 16 Egypt extended recognition to the PRC. On May 22 Secretary of State Dulles said it was "an action that we regret." On May 24 Egyptian Premier Gamal Abdel Nasser accepted an invitation to visit China and reciprocated by inviting Chinese Premier Chou En-lai to visit Egypt.

Dulles Rejects Chinese Offer. On June 12 the State Department announced rejection of a Chinese proposal for discussions between Secretary of State Dulles and Chinese Premier and Foreign Minister Chou En-lai. The proposal, made May 12, was disclosed in Geneva on June 12 by the Chinese ambassador to Poland, Wang Bingnan. The U.S. said the proposed talks would be held on too short notice. It also pointed out that 13 Americans were still imprisoned in China.

Dulles for Renouncing Force. On June 21 Secretary of State Dulles told an audience in San Francisco: "While the Soviet successors to Stalin at least profess to have renounced the use of force in international affairs, the Chinese Communists still refuse this."

China for Greater Leniency. On June 25 the Chinese Communist Party Central Committee adopted a policy of "domestic peaceful coexistence," conceding that "counter-revolutionaries" had been handled too harshly and should be treated with "greater leniency."

Chou's Speech. On June 28 Chinese Premier Chou En-lai told the National People's Congress that "traditional friendships," between the American and Chinese people eventually will lead to U.S. diplomatic recognition of the Communist government. Chou said the Chinese government was "willing to discuss" with Taiwan authorities "specific steps for the peaceful liberation of Taiwan." On June 29 the Nationalist government answered: "What needs liberating now is . . . the mainland under the bloody Communist reign."

Burma Hostilities. On July 31 the Burmese government charged that several thousand Chinese Communist troops had occupied a large area in northeastern Burma. Burmese officials said there had been sporadic fighting between Chinese and Burmese troops, but that the threat was not regarded as very serious and negotiations already had begun with the Chinese Communists for removal of their forces.

Chou's Interview. On Aug. 5 Chinese Premier Chou En-lai told an Australian newsman that U.S. refusal to recognize the Peking government was ostrichlike. He rejected U.S. participation in any discussions on Taiwan, asserting that the island was a Chinese province. Chou said also that China soon could "enlarge the democratic base of our system of government" with more meetings of the National People's Congress, increased self-criticism, and extension of voting privileges.

Travel to China. On Aug. 6 the Chinese government offered visas to 15 U.S. newsmen who had requested them. The following day, the State Department announced it would continue to bar travel to China as long as Americans were held there as "political hostages."

Burma. On Aug. 7 Burmese Premier U Ba Swe said his country would not negotiate with the Chinese Communists until their troops were withdrawn from Burma's border provinces. On Aug. 14, Burmese military authorities said that 4,500 Chinese Communist troops had entrenched themselves in Burma as the first unit of a "planned invasion."

Stevenson and Kefauver Nominated. On Aug. 16 Adlai E. Stevenson was again nominated for president at the Democratic National Convention in Chicago. The next day, the party nominated Sen. Estes E. Kefauver, Tenn., for vice president. The party's platform stated: "We pledge determined opposition to the admission of the Communist Chinese into the U.N., . . . urge a continuing effort to effect the release of all Americans detained by Communist China."

Plane Downed. On Aug. 22, Chinese Communist fighter planes shot down a U.S. patrol aircraft with 16 men aboard, 32 miles from the Chinese mainland. The Communists said their pilots had mistaken the plane for a Chinese Nationalist aircraft.

Eisenhower and Nixon Nominated. On Aug. 22 President Dwight D. Eisenhower and Vice President Richard M. Nixon were renominated at the Republican National Convention in San Francisco. Senate Minority Leader William F. Knowland, R-Calif, said in a speech at the convention that he would fight Communist Chinese membership in the U.N. "as long as I have a voice and a vote" in the Senate. The Republican platform carried a pledge to "oppose the seating of China in the U.N." and denounced "any trade with the Communist world that would threaten the security of the U.S. and our allies."

Eisenhower and Nixon Elected. On Nov. 6 President Eisenhower and Vice President Nixon were re-elected in a landslide victory. The Democrats retained control of both chambers of Congress.

U.N. Bars China. On Nov. 12 the U.N. General Assembly voted 37-24 (eight abstentions) to postpone consideration of U.N. membership for Communist China for another year.

New Delhi Talks. On Nov. 28 Chinese Premier Chou En-lai arrived in New Delhi, the second stop of a seven-country tour of Asia. Chou told the Indian Parliament the next day that only through "solidarity" could the newly independent Asian and African countries frustrate attempts to destroy them again, one by one. On Dec. 1 he hinted that Americans imprisoned in China might be released on good behavior. He suggested later that the U.S. would have to make the next move if it wanted release of the prisoners and a general settlement in East Asia.

Nehru Comment. On Dec. 12 Indian Prime Minister Jawaharlal Nehru told American reporters that Chou's "attitude seemed to be one of desiring to have much better relations" with the U.S.

Nehru Visit to U.S. On Dec. 16 Prime Minister Nehru arrived in the U.S. for talks with President Eisenhower. On Dec. 19 Nehru said at a news conference that U.S. foreign policy was "a flexible policy adapting itself to circumstances" and "not as rigid as I thought." The Indian prime minister added: "I would say that they [the Chinese Communists] have certain complaints . . . in the sense of steps taken or not taken." They asserted, for example, that they "have gone several steps forward, but there has been no favorable reaction" from the U.S. Nehru pointed out that "legally and constitutionally speaking, there is only one China," and each side "claims to be the real article."

Chou in Burma. On Dec. 20 Chinese Premier Chou En-lai and Burmese Premier U Ba Swe issued a joint statement saying that they had not resolved the border dispute between their countries, but that it was "nearer to a solution." An interview with Chou filmed by Edward R. Murrow during his visit to Burma was shown on CBS's *See it Now* Dec. 30. The Chinese premier reiterated Chinese demands for control of Taiwan and the Chinese seat in the U.N.

1957

Sino-Soviet Joint Policy Statement — State Department Refusal to Let U.S. Newsmen Go to China — American Policy on Trade with Mainland China — Sen. Green Advocates Recognition of Communist China — Mao's "Hundred Flowers" Speech — New Statement of U.S. Policies Toward China — Dulles on China and the Bomb — Anti-Rightist Drive in China — Young Americans Visit China and Lose Passports — State Department Lifts China Travel Ban for 24 Newsmen — Peking Refuses to Admit U.S. Newsmen.

South Korean Demand. On Jan. 7 the South Korean ambassador to the U.S., You Chan Yung, urged the U.N. to demand that all Chinese forces abandon North Korea. He said there had been sharp increases in Communist ground and naval forces in North Korea since the armistice.

Unification of Korea. On Jan. 8 the Political Committee of the U.N. General Assembly adopted a U.S. resolution, 57-8, calling for unification of Korea through U.N.-sponsored free elections.

Sino-Soviet Policy Statement. On Jan. 18 a joint policy statement signed by Soviet Premier Nikolai A. Bulganin and Chinese Premier Chou En-lai, who was visiting Moscow, said the two nations were "ready to continue rendering support" to the "peoples of the Near and Middle East to prevent aggression and interference in the internal affairs of the countries of this area." The statement charged that the "so-called Eisenhower Doctrine" was a "colonialist" policy designed to "suppress the movement for national independence and enslave the peoples of these countries." (The term "Eisenhower Doctrine" stemmed from the president's request of Congress, Jan. 5, for authority, granted in modified form by a joint resolution approved March 9, 1957, to use military force and economic aid to combat threats of direct or indirect communist aggression in the Middle East.)

The joint statement noted that Russia and China held "complete unanimity of views" on the international situation; that "American imperialism is trying" to "take the place of the colonialist powers" in the Middle East; that both Russia and China favored the reunification of Germany, Korea and Vietnam; and that the "great alliance of the Soviet Union and China" was "an important mainstay of peace all over the world."

Chou had arrived in Moscow on Jan. 7. Going on to Warsaw, he declared there, on Jan. 11, that the Soviet Union was the primary leader of the communist countries and that "strengthening the solidarity of the Socialist camp" was of "utmost importance," because "imperialism has never stopped its diversionist activities" in the communist countries. Chou later promised that the "Polish nation may always count on the support of the Chinese nation," adding that while "abnormal relations" could arise between communist nations, their policies should avoid "fundamental conflicts."

On Jan. 17, before returning to Moscow, Chou visited Hungary and signed a joint declaration with Hungarian leaders in which he supported Soviet suppression of the recent Hungarian revolt and advised the Hungarian people to "stand solidly with the Soviet Union, leader of the Socialist camp."

Ban on China Travel. On Feb. 6 Secretary of State John Foster Dulles told a news conference that the State Department had banned travel to Communist China for reporters because China was "trying to get reporters — preferably those it picked — to come," and had "tried to use the illegal detention of Americans" in China to force the State Department's approval of the trips. The secretary said the U.S. could not allow other governments to "throw into jail American citizens, so they can put a price on their release." He added: "The issuance of passports to a regime which is not recognized is something which is never done."

Green on Recognizing China. On Feb. 18 Sen. Theodore F. Green, D-R.I., chairman of the Senate Foreign Relations Committee, said the U.S. "should recognize Red China sooner or later." He explained: "We don't like their form of government, but the country is a great country and organized, and I do not myself see why we should recognize these other Communist countries and withhold recognition of China unless we are going to apply that to other Communist countries."

Green later said his remarks should not be construed as endorsing immediate recognition of Communist China. "This is not the case," he added. "Red China has not purged itself of its aggression of the United Nations in Korea, and it still holds American citizens prisoner against their will. In time — sooner or later, as I said — the President — whose responsibility it is — must determine if we are to continue forever to live without official contact with 300 million Chinese [actual population about 600 million]."

On Feb. 19 Secretary of State Dulles told a news conference it would be "premature, to say the least," to discuss recognizing China, but he added that "none of us are talking here in terms of eternity."

Mao Ideological Speech. On Feb. 27 Communist Party Chairman Mao Tse-tung delivered a four-hour speech to a closed session of the Supreme State Conference in Peking entitled "On the Correct Handling of Contradictions among the People." Mao issued an unprecedented call for criticism of his regime: "As a scientific truth, Marxism fears no criticism." Thus, stated Mao, counterrevolutionary ideas should be greeted not with "coercive measures," but with "discussion, criticism, and reasoning."

The slogan for the new movement, said Mao, was "Let a Hundred Flowers Bloom and Let a Hundred Schools of Thought Contend." *(see May 2, 1956)* The speech also contained criticisms of Soviet leaders and their policies which were deleted from the official text.

Published in June, the speech soon prompted a large increase in criticism of Chinese life and politics.

Newsmen's Travel. On March 5 Secretary Dulles told a news conference that newsmen's travel to China "would be bearable by us" but could have "dangerous consequences in other areas." The secretary said the U.S. would attempt "to satisfy better the demand for news coverage without seeming to drop the barriers down generally."

Chou's Charges. On March 5 Chinese Premier Chou En-lai said in a statement to the Political Consultative Conference in Peking that the U.S. did not want "to negotiate seriously on the question of tension in the Taiwan area." He charged that the U.S. was "planning to install guided missiles" on Taiwan to convert the island into an American "dependency, like Hawaii," and was plotting to "overthrow the [present] Taiwan authorities." Chou again pledged to "liberate" Taiwan peacefully.

Dulles' View of Asian Communism. On March 11 Secretary of State Dulles told a meeting of the SEATO Council of Ministers in Canberra, Australia, that communism was "a passing and not permanent phase" in Asia and that U.S. recognition or U.N. membership for Communist China "would serve no national purpose" and would "encourage influences hostile to us and to our allies."

Celler Resolution. On March 18 Rep. Emanuel Celler, D-N.Y., chairman of the House Judiciary Committee, introduced a resolution (H Con Res 153) designed to permit U.S. newsmen to travel anywhere in the world, including Communist China.

Newsman Testifies. On March 29 William Worthy, reporter for the Baltimore *Afro-American,* who defied the State Department ban on travel to China, protested before the Senate Judiciary Constitutional Rights Subcommittee the department's delay in processing his application for passport renewal. Also opposing the travel ban were representatives of the American Society of Newspaper Editors, the *Saturday Review,* the American Newspaper Guild, the American Civil Liberties Union, *The Washington Post,* and United Press International.

Communist China Trade. On April 4 Secretary of Commerce Sinclair Weeks said the U.S. ban on all trade with Communist China would remain intact, but he found "some merit" in the desires of other free world countries for relaxation of the ban, observed by them, on exports of strategic goods to communist countries. Weeks said he favored a policy of easing some restrictions against China for tighter restrictions against trade with the Soviet bloc.

Trade Controls. On April 20 the State Department notified 14 allied nations participating in the system of controls on trade with China and the European Soviet bloc that the United States would consider "certain modifications" of the general controls but would "continue its unilateral embargo on all trade with Communist China." A department spokesman said the U.S. had been "repeatedly pressed by its allies" to relax controls and would consider the following modifications:

● Certain items for peaceful use embargoed for shipment to China would be "removed from controls" and given the same status as similar items traded with the European Soviet bloc.

● Other items embargoed for China would remain embargoed and added to the European Soviet bloc list, but with a "lesser degree of control."

● Tightening the "exceptions" procedure used for trade when an embargo was deemed "unfair."

Travel Ban Problem. On April 23 Secretary of State Dulles told a news conference that the State Department was willing to allow a "pool" of American newsmen to visit China provided existing bans on travel by other Americans to the Chinese mainland could be maintained. But he said the department and leading news executives with whom the problem had been discussed were bankrupt of ideas on how this could be done successfully.

McCarthy Dead. On May 2 Sen. Joseph R. McCarthy, R-Wis., 48, died in Bethesda Naval Hospital of acute hepatitic failure.

Missiles in Taiwan. On May 7 the U.S. and the Nationalist Chinese signed an agreement for the emplacement on Taiwan of Matador missiles, with a range of about 600 miles and capable of carrying nuclear warheads.

Dulles on Reporting China. On May 14 Secretary of State Dulles pointed out that American newspapers could send anyone to China so long as he did not travel on a U.S. passport not validated for travel to that country. Dulles added that there were "ample ways" to obtain news from China "without sending American correspondents . . . into areas where that would involve a conflict with [U.S.] foreign policy." The secretary concluded that if China released U.S. prisoners "we would certainly take a new look at the situation."

Taiwan Riot. On May 24 an anti-American riot erupted in Taipei (Taibei), Taiwan, after a U.S. military court had acquitted an American soldier charged with the murder of a Chinese he said he had caught peeping through a window at his wife while she was taking a bath. The soldier said he shot the victim in self-defense after the Chinese man approached him with a club. About 3,000 rioters raided the American Embassy and the U.S. Information Service in Taipei, injuring 13 Americans. On May 25 the city was placed under martial law and occupied by 33,000 Nationalist troops. At least two Chinese were killed during the rioting.

British Trade With China. On May 20 the British government announced it would apply the same restrictions on trade with Communist China as those applied on trade with the Soviet bloc. The same day, the State Department, "most disappointed" by the British move, said the U.S. contemplated no change in its total embargo on trade with China. Senate Democratic Leader Lyndon B. Johnson, Texas, said June 1 that the U.S. would have to re-evaluate the China trade situation.

On June 5 President Eisenhower observed at his news conference: "I don't see as much advantage in maintaining the differential [between restrictions on Soviet and Chinese trade] as some people do, although I have never advocated its complete elimination."

On June 2 Sen. Allen J. Ellender, D-La., said the U.S. should consider lifting its total embargo.

On June 11 Secretary Dulles told a news conference that the president supported continuation of a "differential" on trade with China and East Europe.

On June 16 Sen. Warren Magnuson, D-Wash., chairman of the Senate Interstate and Foreign Commerce Committee, said the possibility of starting American passenger and mail flights to China would be explored at upcoming hearings on U.S. trade policies. "We have got to be realistic," Magnuson said. "We can't keep 400 million [actual population over 600 million] people behind an economic bamboo curtain just because we don't like their government." Senate Republican Leader William F. Knowland, Calif., said he doubted if the hearings would alter administration opposition to trade exchanges and said: "I don't believe that sentiment has changed in the Senate."

Russia Denounced at Peking. On June 20 the Xinhua news agency reported that the vice chairman of the Chinese Communist National Defense Committee, Gen. Lung Yun (Long Yun — a former KMT warlord), had denounced the Soviet Union for removing "huge quantities of industrial equipment" from China after World War II, and for allowing China "to pay all expenses of the Korean War." Lung pointed out that the United States had "given up her claims for loans she granted to her allies during the first and second world wars, yet the Soviet Union insists that China must pay interest on Soviet loans." He added that "China could not possibly reimburse the Soviet loans within 10 years or more." On June 23 it was reported that the Kuomintang Revolutionary Committee, an organization of former Chinese Nationalists who had defected to the Communists, had denounced Lung and two other generals for "rightist deviation."

Trade Controls Relaxed. On June 21 the Italian government announced relaxation of its restrictions on trade with China. The Danish and French governments had announced revision of their embargo lists earlier in the week.

Korean Military Buildup. On June 21 the U.N. Korean Command announced in Panmunjom that it would no longer abide by the armistice terms covering amounts of military equipment to be allowed in South and North Korea. The U.N. Command explained that continued Communist violation of the terms had resulted in a "vastly superior" Communist force in North Korea.

Refusal for Mrs. Roosevelt. On June 25 Mrs. Franklin D. Roosevelt said the State Department had denied her permission to travel to China and interview Chinese leaders.

Wilting of the Hundred Flowers. On June 26 Chinese Premier Chou En-lai, obviously upset over the outpouring of criticism which had followed the recent publication of Mao's "Hundred Flowers" speech *(see Feb. 27, 1957)*, warned that those who continued to criticize the government would be classified as "enemies of the people," and hoped that they would "repent and accept opportunities of remolding themselves." Speaking to the National People's Congress in Peking, the premier stated that the Communist Party would "allow no wavering on the basic state system of our country."

Henceforth, critics of the regime would be labeled as "rightists," and a systematic purge of these "rightists" was begun which would last until the end of the year. By that time, all non-party officials (including three Cabinet ministers) had been purged from the government, and critics of the regime had been forced to recant and "confess their errors."

The Minister of Security Luo Reiqing later claimed that 100,000 had been purged between June 1955 and October 1957.

Dulles' Policy Pronouncement. On June 28 Secretary of State John Foster Dulles, addressing a convention in San Francisco, made what the State Department called a major policy pronouncement on China. Affirming that the U.S.

would continue to oppose Chinese membership in the U.N. and to withhold diplomatic recognition of the Peking regime, Dulles declared that China failed "to pass even those tests which . . . the Soviet regime seemed to pass."

Dulles pointed out that "diplomatic recognition gives the recognized regime valuable rights and privileges, and, in the world of today, recognition by the United States gives the recipient much added prestige and influence at home and abroad."

"Normal peacetime trade with China, from which the American and Chinese peoples would benefit, could be in the common interest," he conceded. "But it seems that that kind of trade is not to be had in any appreciable volume. Trade with Communist China is wholly controlled by an official apparatus and its limited amounts of foreign exchange are used to develop as rapidly as possible a formidable military establishment and a heavy industry to support it. The primary desire of that regime is machine tools, electronic equipment, and, in general, what will help it produce tanks, trucks, planes, ammunition, and other military items."

Dulles went on to predict the "passing of Communism" in China, and declared that "we owe it to ourselves, our allies, and the Chinese people to do all that we can do to contribute to that passing." Thus, Dulles opposed all cultural and commercial relations because they do not contribute to the "passing," any more then diplomatic recognition or admission to the U.N. would do.

Finally, the secretary said that although there were "basic power rivalries between Russia and China in Asia" the Soviet and Chinese Communist parties were bound together by close ideological ties. At the same time, "if the ambitions of the Chinese Communists are inflated by successes, they might eventually clash with Soviet Russia."

Trade With China. On July 3 Sen. Charles E. Potter, R-Mich., said that "the stakes are too high, the dangers too great" for the U.S. to assume the "calculated risk of trade with Red China." Potter asserted that "Anyone who believes we can trade with Communist China to any appreciable degree in any types of goods without augmenting her war machine is simply deluding himself." On July 9 Secretary of Commerce Sinclair Weeks said the administration would "not gamble with national security" by a premature removal of this country's total embargo on trade with China. Weeks said China "continues to constitute a serious threat to the security of the Far East."

Moscow Reaction. On July 16 the Soviet Communist Party newspaper *Pravda* said that Mao Tse-tung's speech on "contradictions" was "an outstanding event in China's political life" and "furnishes the Chinese people with a new clear-cut orientation in the new situation." The newspaper added that the speech "has multiplied the strength of the millions of supporters of socialism in China who have turned to a decisive offensive against . . . right-wing bourgeois elements." *(See Feb. 27)*

Trip To China. On Aug. 14, 41 young Americans left Moscow on a trip to Peking despite warnings from the State Department that the U.S. and China were in a "quasi state of war" and that the trip "would be subversive of [U.S.] foreign policy." The youths attempted to avoid violating American passport laws by obtaining visas from the Chinese Communist government. The 41 were members of a U.S. delegation to Russia's Sixth World Festival of Youth and Students in Moscow. Before leaving on their three-week tour of China, 35 of the youths issued a statement

saying they were making the trip to confirm "the right of [U.S.] citizens to travel." On Aug. 21 President Eisenhower said the youths were "doing the country a disservice."

Travel Authorization. On Aug. 22 Secretary of State Dulles authorized 24 news organizations (newspapers, news services, periodicals, and radio-TV networks) to send correspondents to China for a seven-month trial period. The State Department said it was modifying its eight-year travel ban because "new factors have come into the picture, making it desirable that additional information be made available to the American people respecting current conditions within China.

The newsmen's entry hinged on issuance of visas by the Chinese government; the State Department said the U.S. would not accord reciprocal visas to newsmen from China. It warned that those entering China faced "abnormal personal risks." A department spokesman said renewal of the passport validation, after the seven-month trial period, would depend on whether the newsmen were allowed to report freely.

Sen. J. William Fulbright, D Ark., had introduced a resolution (S Res 190) Aug. 20, calling on the State Department either to "encourage and facilitate" entry of newsmen into China or refrain from taking reprisals against those entering on their own responsibility.

Chinese Reaction. On Aug. 25 the Peking *People's Daily* called the State Department's plan "completely unacceptable to the Chinese people." It denounced the U.S. for "insufferable arrogance" in agreeing to "send its correspondents to China just on the basis of its own unilateral decision" and "refusing reciprocal visas to Chinese correspondents." The paper asserted that the U.S. State Department "wants to collect intelligence in China through its correspondents [and] carry out subversive activities." "The principle of equality and reciprocity," it added, "requires that newsmen of both sides be allowed to stay in each other's country."

Soviets Test ICBM. On Aug. 26 the Soviet Union conducted its first successful test of an ICBM, which could reach either the U.S. or Western Europe. The first U.S. tests had failed. *(See Oct. 4, 1957)*

Journalists Purged. On Aug. 26 the Xinhua news agency said that 90 journalists had been "ferreted out from press and radio operations all over China" in "a struggle against rightists in the journalistic field." In the following weeks, the Chinese government announced the arrest and execution of a number of counterrevolutionaries and admitted there had been student and peasant uprisings against the government.

Dulles on Newsmen. On Aug. 27 Secretary of State Dulles told a news conference that if any Chinese newsman applied for entry into the U.S., his application would be studied "on its merits." Dulles commented: "So far as I know, we have never laid down any absolute rule that no Chinese Communist could come to this country," but there had been "no application for anyone" from China. The secretary explained that when travel of American newsmen to China was authorized, no reciprocal offer to admit Chinese newsmen was made because "We wanted to obviate any claim by the Chinese Communists that they would be entitled as a right to send a corresponding number" of reporters to the U.S. "That we could not do under the law," he said, which "hedges about very strictly the possibility of Communists coming to this country." Dulles said there must "be a finding made by the Attorney General to permit any Communist to come. Whether or not he could make these findings I do not know."

On Sept. 1 Sen. William F. Knowland, R-Calif., said in a television interview that the State Department could issue "temporary news certificates" to Chinese reporters and still maintain the ban on Chinese Communist visitors. On Sept. 6 Sens. Bourke Hickenlooper, R-Iowa, and Mike Mansfield, D-Mont., of the Senate Foreign Relations Committee endorsed Knowland's suggestion.

On Sept. 10 Under Secretary of State Christian A. Herter said the U.S. had opened the way for an exchange of newsmen with China and the matter "is now up to the Chinese government." Herter added that if China were interested in reciprocal exchange of newsmen, its reporters should apply for admission to the U.S.

On Sept. 24 Dulles said he was expressing his own opinion in relation to the specific problem of newsmen's entry into China when he said Constitution-guaranteed freedom of the press "relates to publication and not the gathering of news." Dulles, in a letter to Executive Editor J. R. Wiggins of *The Washington Post* made public Oct. 3 said it was his "firm belief that insofar as the gathering of news can be carried out without prejudice to the national interest, that activity should be facilitated and it is our policy to do that."

Soviets Launch Sputnik. On Oct. 4 the Soviet Union launched the first "artificial earth satellite," dubbed "Sputnik." On Nov. 3 the Soviets launched a second satellite, this time carrying a dog. These successes, combined with the earlier successful test firings of an ICBM, seemed to give the Soviets a lead over the U.S. both in space exploration and nuclear capability. On Nov. 5 Secretary of State John Foster Dulles conceded that this was the case, but said that the U.S. would catch up soon.

Visitors to China Return. On Oct. 5, 14 of the 41 American youths who had visited China returned to Moscow and were informed by a U.S. consular official that their passports were valid only for return to the U.S. The State Department had said on Sept. 18 that it would revoke the passports of all 41 youths. The students reported that Chinese Premier Chou En-lai had told them on Sept. 6 that China's "door is always open" but "it should be on an equal and mutual basis." On the following day, Chou told 10 of the American visitors that the State Department "put an end to the matter by refusing reciprocal rights of coverage to Chinese reporters."

Sino-Soviet Nuclear Agreement. On Oct. 15 the Soviet Union and China signed a secret agreement which stated that the Russians would help the Chinese develop a nuclear capability. *(See June 20, 1959)*

Kennedy on China. In October *Foreign Affairs* magazine published an article by Sen. John F. Kennedy, D-Mass., that called for a new American foreign policy towards China. Entitled "A Democrat Looks at Foreign Policy," the article criticized current U.S. policy as "exaggeratedly military" and "probably too rigid." Kennedy went on to say that "there have been — and still are — compelling reasons for the nonrecognition of China but we must be very careful not to straight-jacket our policy as a result of ignorance and fail to detect a change in the objective situation when it comes."

Mao in Moscow. On Nov. 6 Mao Tse-tung, in Moscow to attend a conference of the twelve communist parties,

said that China would maintain strong ties with the Soviet Union, although it had the right to travel "separate roads to socialism."

On Nov. 19 Mao, speaking to a group of Chinese students in the Soviet Union, declared that "The East wind is prevailing over the West wind."

Geneva Talks Suspended. On Dec. 12 the U.S. suspended the on-again off-again ambassadorial talks between the U.S. and China at Geneva. The talks would not reopen for nine months. *(See Sept. 15, 1958)*

U.S. Trade. On Dec. 16 Assistant Secretary of Commerce for International Affairs Harry Kearns said the World Trade Advisory Committee of the Commerce Department was critical of U.S. policy on trade with Communist China; committee members called the rigid trade ban "unrealistic."

Drive Terminated. On Dec. 29 the Chinese Communist Party announced that the movement against "rightists" in China had been terminated.

1958

Sino-Soviet Trade Pact — ADA Asks Negotiations for Recognition of China — China's First Atomic Reactor — State Department Rejects Concept of Two Chinas — China Threatens Taiwan and Offshore Islands — Pentagon Strengthens U.S. Forces in Taiwan Strait — U.S. Reaffirms Determination to Defend Taiwan — Resumption of U.S.-Chinese Ambassadorial Talks Proposed — Five-Year Sino-Korean Trade Pact — Foreign Policy in U.S. Midterm Campaign — Chiang Renounces Use of Force to Return to Mainland — Partial Truce on Offshore Island Bombing — Mao Tse-tung Resigns as Chairman of People's Republic.

China Visit. On Jan. 7 the mothers of three Americans held prisoner in China were allowed to visit their sons.

Chou's Warning. On Jan. 10 Chinese Premier Chou En-lai charged in an interview that the U.S., Britain and Japan were attempting to create a permanent Nationalist government on Taiwan in order to "manufacture two Chinas." Chou said that as the U.S. "exerts pressure on us, the more we will resist." "If the [U.S.] insists on waging war, we will fight."

The interview followed repeated reports from the China mainland that the government continued to arrest governmental and religious leaders as "counter-revolutionaries." On Jan. 17 the vice chairman of the Nationality Affairs Committee said in Peking that "mounting regional nationalism" among minorities had "become a danger that must be taken seriously."

Dulles on China. On Jan. 16 Secretary of State Dulles told the National Press Club that he did not think there was "any occasion at the present time to meet Communist China at the summit," but the U.S. would negotiate with that government or even recognize its regime "any time it will serve the interest of the United States."

The "Great Leap Forward." On Jan. 28 Chinese Communist Party Chairman Mao Tse-tung, in a speech to the Supreme State Conference, said China could and should catch up with Britain within 15 years. *(See May 5, 1958)*

Korea. On Feb. 7 Premier Chou En-lai renewed a proposal that both the U.N. and Chinese forces withdraw from Korea "within a set period of time."

New Chinese Foreign Minister. On Feb. 11 Chou En-lai resigned as China's foreign minister and was replaced by Marshal Chen Yi. Chou remained in the government as premier.

Chinese Withdrawal. On Feb. 19 the Chinese and North Korean governments announced that all Chinese forces would be withdrawn from Korea by the end of 1958. The joint statement said the "Chinese government is taking the initiative in withdrawing its volunteer forces in support of North Korea's demand for withdrawal of all foreign troops in Korea."

The State Department announced the same day that the U.S. would not remove its troops from South Korea but hoped that China "would go further" and "agree to genuinely free elections" to unite the country. On Feb. 22 the South Korean National Assembly voted unanimously for a resolution demanding that the U.N. Command discard the 1953 truce agreement with North Korea and China.

Soviets Warn SEATO. On March 8 the Soviet Union warned SEATO member nations not to accept U.S. missiles and atomic weapons because they would then bear "serious responsibility" for increased tension in Southeast Asia. On March 11 Secretary of State Dulles told the SEATO Ministerial Council in Manila that communist pressure "should alert us to the possibility that there may be new aggressive Communist plans for this area, plans which Communist rulers fear SEATO might block."

Soviets Stop Testing. On March 31 Soviet Premier Khrushchev announced that the Soviet Union would unilaterally cease nuclear testing in order to prevent further proliferation of nuclear arms.

Wheat to China. On March 31 it was disclosed that China and four companies — three Canadian and one American — had signed an agreement for shipment of Canadian wheat to China.

U.N. on Korean Elections. On April 9 the U.N. Command asked China and North Korea to clarify their proposals for unification of Korea through free elections. The command queried the Communists as to whether they would approve of U.N. supervision of the elections, and whether they would accept a unified Korean National Assembly based on proportional representation. South Korea's population is almost three times that of North Korea.

Production in China. On April 10 Peking radio reported that light industrial production had almost doubled during China's first five-year plan (1953-1957). During the same period, the broadcast said, there had been a 39 percent increase in the wages of light industrial workers.

Sino-Soviet Trade Pact. On April 22 China and the Soviet Union signed a trade agreement providing for the increased exchange of Chinese food products and Soviet industrial machinery.

The "Great Leap Forward." On May 5 the second session of the 8th Congress of the Chinese Communist Party opened in Peking. The congress officially implemented Mao Tse-tung's earlier call for a "Great Leap Forward." *(See Jan. 28, 1958)* In what was obviously a decision to abandon the Soviet model of development, the congress proposed its own "great revolutionary leap toward the building of socialism." Capital-poor China thus stopped the emphasis on heavy industry which had been

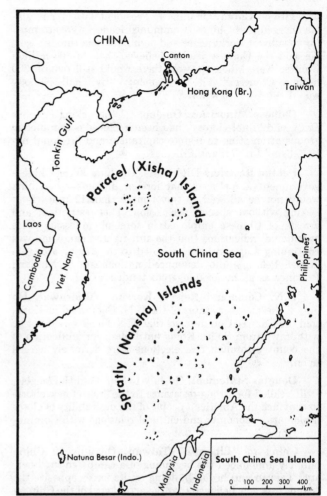

the basis of the first five-year plan (1953-1957) and switched to the use of China's vast population in mass labor projects. No mention was made of the second five-year plan, which appears to have been abandoned.

The most famous (and ill-fated) example of the change was the effort to match England in steel production within 15 years by the use of "backyard furnaces," which all families were ordered to build. The steel which was produced was useless, and the time lost to farm production probably contributed to the disastrous harvests of 1960 and 1961. *(See Jan. 20, 1961)*

ADA Resolution. On May 18 Americans for Democratic Action, meeting in annual convention, called for an immediate start on negotiations looking toward recognition of China. An earlier resolution, which would have recommended immediate recognition, was defeated after a floor fight. The final resolution said: "ADA urges immediate initiation of negotiations toward diplomatic recognition of the Peking regime, not as a gesture of moral approval — which the Chinese Communists obviously do not merit — but as a means of establishing the normal channels of international communication between the two nations."

De Gaulle Becomes Premier. On June 1 Gen. Charles de Gaulle became the 26th postwar premier of the French Fourth Republic.

China's Atomic Reactor. On June 13 China's first experimental atomic reactor, built with Russian help, began operating.

Tito on China. On June 15 President Tito of Yugoslavia charged that Chinese Communist leaders were attempting to subvert world peace and dominate Asia through war. He said the Chinese leaders believed that "if 300 million Chinese were killed [in war] there would still remain 300 million Chinese." Tito's comment: "By God! Nobody would survive a new war."

Chinese Minorities. On June 27 the Peking *People's Daily* said "final victory" had been achieved over minority groups attempting to restore capitalism and "regional nationalism" in Xinjiang Province.

Peking Restricts Diplomats. On June 30 the Chinese government announced that foreign diplomats in China would not be allowed to travel more than 12 miles from Peking without special permission. This restriction, and arrests of Chinese employed in foreign embassies, were considered indications that the anti-rightist campaign was continuing and had been extended to the Peking area. On July 5 Peking radio denounced nationalism in Xinjiang Province as a "major dangerous tendency."

U.N. Command Rejects Korean Withdrawal. On July 2 the member states of the U.N. Command in Korea told the Chinese Communists that U.N. forces would not be withdrawn from South Korea until plans for unification of the country through free elections were definitely agreed upon.

Douglas Statement. On July 15 Sen. Paul H. Douglas, D-Ill., called for strong resistance to the "rise of new efforts to convince the American people of the desirability of closer diplomatic, economic and cultural relations with Communist China."

China to "Liberate" Taiwan. On July 22 China publicly announced the beginning of a campaign to "liberate" Taiwan and began building up its forces opposite the island. It is now believed that the actual goal of the Chinese was only the seizure of the offshore islands. *(See Aug. 28, 1958)*

Khrushchev to Peking. On July 31 Soviet leader Nikita Khrushchev arrived in Peking for a four-day visit. Although no details were released at the time, it is now believed that during his talks with Chinese Party Chairman Mao Tse-tung, Khrushchev refused to provide wholehearted support for the Chinese during their planned actions against the Nationalist-held islands in the Taiwan Strait, thus widening the Sino-Soviet split.

Nationalist Alert. On Aug. 6 the Chinese Nationalist government ordered a state of emergency on Matsu (Mazu) and the Pescadores Islands because of increasing Communist activity in the Taiwan Strait area. On Aug. 8 the State Department announced that Communist China was attempting to "increase tension and raise the specter of war" in the Taiwan Strait area by increasing the size of its air force on the mainland nearest Taiwan.

U.S. Policy Statement. On Aug. 9 the State Department issued a memorandum, which had been circulated to all its embassies, reaffirming the policy of not recognizing China. The memorandum said that "one day [Communist rule in China] will pass" and by "withholding diplomatic recognition from Peiping, [the U.S.] seeks to hasten that passing." The "two Chinas" theory was rejected on the ground that the Nationalist government on Taiwan "would not accept any diminution of its sovereignty over China." The memorandum noted also that the Chinese Communists had rejected any solution that included diplomatic recognition of both the Nationalist and the Communist governments. It added that the U.S. would "readjust its present policies" if "the situation in the Far East were so to change in its basic elements as to call for a radically different evaluation of the threat Chinese Communist policies pose to [the U.S.]."

Second Taiwan Strait Crisis. On Aug. 23, four years to the day after the first Taiwan Strait crisis, the Chinese Communists began intensive shelling of Quemoy (Jinmen) and the Tan (Dan) Islands, just to the south of Quemoy. On the same day, Secretary of State Dulles asserted in a letter to Acting Chairman of the House Foreign Affairs Committee Thomas E. Morgan, D-Pa., that an invasion of the offshore islands would be a "threat to peace in the area." He said that if the Communists did attack the islands, "President Eisenhower will decide as to the . . . value of certain coastal positions to" Taiwan.

On Aug. 27 President Eisenhower declared that the U.S. would not "desert our responsibilities or the statements we have already made" concerning Taiwan and the offshore islands. Adding that "the Nationalist Chinese have now deployed about a third of their forces to . . . these islands," the president noted that "that makes a closer interlocking between the defense systems of the islands with Formosa [Taiwan] than . . . before." In fact, the U.S. had already ordered six aircraft carriers to the region, and later provided eight-inch howitzers capable of firing atomic shells to the garrison on Quemoy.

Chinese Demands. On Aug. 28 the Chinese "Fujian Front Command" broadcast a demand that the Nationalists evacuate the offshore islands. Nothing was said about Taiwan, giving the U.S. no reason to invoke the 1955 Formosa Resolution.

On the next day, the State Department warned that a Communist attempt "to change the situation" in the Taiwan Strait by force "could [not] be a limited operation." The Defense Department announced that U.S. forces in the area were being reinforced.

Communes Organized. On Aug. 29 an enlarged meeting of the Politburo of the Chinese Communist Party passed the so-called "Beidaihe Resolution," which formalized the Great Leap Forward in Agriculture. *(See May 5)* Noting that the collectivization of agriculture (completed in 1957) had not produced rapid enough results, the resolution laid down the guidelines for the creation of communes throughout China. Because of China's heavy dependence on agriculture, the results were even more disastrous than in industry. Although the 1958 harvest was excellent, that of 1959 was poor, and those of 1960 and 1961 disastrous. The communes were drastically reorganized in 1962.

Soviet Support. On Aug. 31 the Soviet Union announced it would send "moral and material aid" to the Chinese in their efforts to overthrow the "aggressors" in the Taiwan area.

China Proclaims 12-Mile Limit. On Sept. 4 Communist China laid formal claim to all waters within 12 miles of its coasts, and thus claimed the Nationalist-held islands of Quemoy (Jinmen), Matsu (Mazu), and other islands within the proclaimed limit of its territorial waters. Peking forbade foreign vessels and aircraft to enter the area without permission, thus trying to block U.S. convoys that were supplying the islands. The U.S. immediately said it would recognize only the traditional three-mile limit.

U.S. Ready to Use Force. On Sept. 4 Secretary of State John Foster Dulles, in a statement cleared by President Eisenhower, warned China that the president "would not hesitate" to use armed force "in insuring the defense of" Taiwan if he deemed such action necessary. The statement, issued following a conference at the Newport, R.I., summer White House, said the president "has not yet made any finding" on the need for armed action, but if he should, "action both timely and effective" would follow.

The statement stressed U.S. obligations to employ U.S. armed forces to defend not only Taiwan but also "related positions . . . now in friendly hands." The Dulles statement pointed out that securing of the offshore islands of Quemoy and Matsu "has increasingly become related to the defense of Taiwan." Dulles said any "naked use of force" by the Chinese Communists "would pose an issue far transcending the offshore islands and even the security of Taiwan." It would "forecast a widespread use of force in the Far East which would endanger vital free world positions and the security of the United States."

Ambassadors to Discuss Taiwan. On Sept. 6 Chinese Premier Chou En-lai proposed resumption of the Sino-U.S. ambassadorial talks for discussion of the Taiwan question. The U.S. replied the same day that Jacob Beam, U.S. ambassador to Poland, "stands ready to meet promptly" with the Chinese ambassador to Poland, Wang Bingnan, who had conducted the talks for China since their inception at Geneva. The statement said the U.S. would "adhere to the negotiating position . . . that we will not . . . be a party to any arrangement which would prejudice the rights of our ally, the Republic of China."

Khrushchev Letter. On Sept. 8 President Eisenhower received a letter from Soviet Premier Nikita Khrushchev warning that an attack on China would be "an attack on the Soviet Union." *(See Sept. 13)*

Dulles on Warsaw Talks. On Sept. 9 Secretary of State Dulles told a news conference that a meaningful renunciation of force by China would ease the Taiwan Strait crisis, and he said there might be "further consequences." Dulles hinted that the U.S. was ready to offer concessions under such circumstances at the proposed ambassadorial talks in Warsaw. The secretary said the U.S. would seek agreement along detailed, specific lines but could not itself negotiate the future of Quemoy and Matsu, because those islands belonged to Nationalist China.

Letter to Khrushchev. On Sept. 13 President Eisenhower, replying to a letter received from Soviet Premier Khrushchev on Sept. 8, suggested that he carry out his asserted desire for peace by urging China to discontinue military operations in the Taiwan Strait area.

Successful Convoy. On Sept. 14 the Nationalist Chinese accomplished their first successful convoy to the beleagured island of Quemoy, marking a shift in military advantage away from Peking.

British Policy on Taiwan. On Sept. 15 British Labor Party Leader Hugh Gaitskell demanded in a letter to Prime Minister Harold Macmillan that he "make it plain that, even if the U.S.A. becomes involved in a war to defend Quemoy, Britain would not join in." Macmillan replied that Britain "strongly supported" the U.S. "in opposing any attempt to settle the dispute by . . . force." Macmillan noted that "Our American allies have neither sought nor received promises of military support from us in the Formosan [Taiwan] area."

Anti-Communist China Lobby. On Sept. 15 Marvin Liebman, secretary of the Committee of One Million Against the Admission of Communist China to the United Nations, said the organization was "redoubling and tripling our efforts to stem this tide of pro-appeasement sentiment" concerning China. Liebman said the Communist shelling of Matsu and Quemoy helped the committee's campaign because "it shows up the Chinese Reds for what we always said they were; proves they are prepared and willing to shoot their way into the United Nations;" and brings the whole issue out into the open for debate.

The Committee of One Million listed 23 senators as members, including Paul H. Douglas, D-Ill., William F. Knowland, R-Calif., Mike Mansfield, D-Mont., Everett M. Dirksen, R-Ill., Jacob K. Javits, R-N.Y., and A. S. Mike Monroney, D-Okla. It also listed 83 representatives; four Governors; Robert S. Allen, columnist; H. V. Kaltenborn, radio commentator; Gen. George C. Marshall; Henry R. Luce of *Time* and *Life;* Warren R. Austin, first U.S. Ambassador to the U.N.; and Adm. Arthur W. Radford, former chairman of the Joint Chiefs of Staff.

Warsaw Talks. On Sept. 15 the U.S. and Chinese Communist ambassadors to Poland (Jacob D. Beam and Wang Bingnan) opened talks on the Taiwan Strait crisis.

Dulles at U.N. On Sept. 18 Secretary of State Dulles told the U.N. General Assembly that debate on the Taiwan and Quemoy-Matsu dispute should be postponed until the outcome of negotiations in Warsaw between the U.S. and China. He expressed hope that the negotiations there would bring a cease-fire but reserved the right to bring the problem to the U.N. if it became necessary.

Aid to Taiwan. On Sept. 18 Defense Department spokesmen said the U.S. had sent $90 million in military supplies to Taiwan in the three weeks since the Quemoy crisis began. The Pentagon announced also that American pilots were authorized to follow a "hot pursuit" policy against any Chinese Communist plane which might attack them, including following the plane over communist-held territory.

Nationalist View. On Sept. 19 Nationalist Chinese Premier Ch'en Ch'eng told the Nationalist Parliament that the Nationalist government would "not accept any resolution reached in Warsaw that might prejudice the rights of [Nationalist] China." He added: "Nobody has the right to make us demilitarize these islands. Communist occupation of Quemoy and Matsu would pose a serious threat to the security of all the Far East area."

Khrushchev Letter Rejected. On Sept. 20 the White House rejected a letter from Soviet Premier Khrushchev because it was "replete with false accusations." The letter said that neither Russia nor China was frightened by what they considered "atomic blackmail," and that there should be no doubt of Russia's intention to support its Chinese allies. On Sept. 21 the official Soviet news agency Tass said the rejection indicated that President Eisenhower was unwilling to "listen to the voice of reason."

Quemoy Casualties. On Sept. 21 the Nationalist government announced that the Chinese Communist bombardment of Quemoy from Aug. 23 to Sept. 21 had resulted in 3,000 civilian and 1,000 military casualties.

U.N. Action. On Sept. 23 the U.N. General Assembly approved, by a 44-28 vote with nine abstentions, a U.S. proposal to postpone for another year any consideration of

China's admission to the U.N. U.S. representative to the U.N. Henry Cabot Lodge on Sept. 22 told the assembly that the Chinese were "rapidly shooting themselves and shooting the world" out of a peaceful Taiwan settlement. He said their bombardment of the offshore islands was "a further disqualification" for U.N. membership.

Sino-Korean Pact. On Sept. 27 China and North Korea signed a five-year trade agreement.

Chiang's Statement. On Sept. 29 Chiang Kai-shek told a news conference that the offshore islands had become a "shield" for the protection of Taiwan rather than a springboard for invasion of the mainland, and for that reason the Nationalist government was determined to defend them. He added that "talks with the Communists under any circumstances are futile, and the Warsaw talks are no exception."

Morse's Statement. On Oct. 1 Sen. Wayne Morse, D-Ore., said that before the Senate ratified a defense treaty with Chiang Kai-shek in 1955, Secretary Dulles was "forced into an understanding" with the late Sen. Walter F. George, D-Ga., then chairman of the Foreign Relations Committee, that the Senate would be asked to ratify any U.S. move to defend Quemoy and Matsu.

Passports. On Oct. 2 a Federal judge upheld the State Department's refusal in 1957 to renew the passport of William Worthy Jr., a newspaperman who violated the ban on travel to China.

Warsaw Meeting. On Oct. 4 the discussions between the U.S. and China in Warsaw were reported to have made no progress toward a solution of the Taiwan crisis.

Congressional Telegram. On Oct. 4 a demand for a special session of Congress on the East Asian situation was made by 10 Democratic congressmen in a telegram to the president. They said they had found "the great majority" of their constituents "deeply disturbed with the Administration's Quemoy policy," and they believed "we should disentangle ourselves from Chiang Kai-shek's aspirations on Quemoy, and should endeavor to bring the mantle of the U.N. over Formosa [Taiwan]."

Cease-Fire. On Oct. 6 China's Defense Minister Peng Dehuai announced over the radio a one-week cease-fire in the Taiwan Strait area. He said the Nationalists would be "fully free to ship in supplies [to Quemoy] on condition that there would be no American escort." Peng reiterated the Chinese Communist position that the warfare was "an internal Chinese matter" and "not a matter between China and the U.S.," so "the question of a cease-fire does not arise" between the two countries. He added that "of all choices, peace is best. . . . We propose that talks be held to effect a peaceful settlement." On the same day, the Nationalist government rejected the proposal for talks, because the Communists "never will keep their word."

U.S. Halts Convoys. On Oct. 8 the State Department announced a halt in convoying of Nationalist Chinese supply vessels to Quemoy as a result of Communist China's Oct. 6 announcement of a one-week cease-fire in the Taiwan Strait area. The department said the halt in convoys followed "full consultation" with the Chinese Nationalists, but that the escort system would be resumed if the Communists resumed their attacks.

Cease-Fire Extended. On Oct. 13 China extended its Oct. 6 order for a one-week cease-fire in the Taiwan Strait area for two additional weeks "to see what the opposite side is going to do and enable our compatriots on Quemoy, both military and civilian, to get sufficient supplies, including food and military equipment." The statement said the bombardment would "start at once" if the U.S. resumed "escort operations in the Quemoy water area." It added that the dispute was "China's internal affair, and no foreigner has any right to meddle with it."

No Plan to Coerce Chiang. On Oct. 14 Secretary of State John Foster Dulles told a news conference there would be no effort to coerce Nationalist President Chiang Kai-shek into reducing his Quemoy Island garrison. Dulles said the Communists were interested only in "driving a wedge" between the U.S. and the Nationalists, that he saw no indications that "a deal could be made with the Communists which was confined to the Quemoy or Matsu situation," and that he did not "want to give the impression that we . . . plan to press the Republic of China to do something against its own better judgment."

Thus, unlike its actions during the first Taiwan Strait crisis, the U.S. did not try to force the Nationalists to evacuate the islands. On the contrary, the second crisis was followed by a massive buildup of the islands, using U.S. aid, in exchange for Chiang Kai-shek's pledge of Oct. 23.

Foreign Policy in Politics. On Oct. 14, at a news conference, Secretary Dulles decried the continuing injection of foreign policy into the current election campaign and said he hoped both parties would "calm down" on foreign policy, though there were "some basic problems which can be discussed in terms of underlying principles." On the same day Vice President Richard M. Nixon replied to an Oct. 11 statement by the Democratic Advisory Council, which criticized "six years of leaderless vacillation" and urged presentation of the Taiwan question to the U.N. Nixon said the statement was an example of "the same defensive, defeatist, fuzzy-headed thinking which contributed to the loss of China and led to the Korean War."

Bombardment Resumed. On Oct. 20 China, ending its cease-fire a week ahead of schedule, resumed bombardment of the offshore islands. It said the U.S. had broken the truce by escorting Nationalist supply ships to Quemoy the previous day. A U.S. Navy spokesman denied the charge.

Chiang Renounces Force. On Oct. 23, after three days of talks at Taipei, Chinese Nationalist President Chiang Kai-shek and Secretary of State Dulles said in a joint communiqué that return to the mainland was still Chiang's sacred mission, but that the principal means of accomplishing that mission was through implementation of Sun Yat-sen's Three People's Principles (nationalism, democracy and social well-being) "and not the use of force." The U.S. and the Nationalists both "recognized that under present conditions the defense of the Quemoys together with the Matsus is closely related to the defense of Taiwan and [the Pescadores] islands."

Elaborating on the talks at an Oct. 23 news conference, Assistant Secretary of the State Walter S. Robertson said the Nationalists had asked for convoy escorts; he added that "we have reassured them" that "when it is considered by military authorities to be necessary, they will be resumed."

Dulles Statement. On Oct. 24, after reporting to President Eisenhower on his trip to Taiwan, Secretary Dulles said that the Nationalist government was "dedicated to the peaceful achievement of its high mission." He added that "Apparently the Communists desire to throw roadblocks in the way of stabilized tranquility," but that he was "confident that the Chinese Communists will not gain their ends either through their military efforts or their propaganda guile."

Withdrawal From Korea. On Oct. 25 the Chinese announced completion of their troop withdrawal from North Korea.

Every-Other-Day Truce. On Oct. 25 China announced there would be no bombardment of Quemoy airfield, wharf, or beach landing areas on "even dates" of the month (so the offshore islands could get supplies), but that "exception will be taken if there should be escorts." The Communists said they would "not necessarily conduct shelling on odd dates," but they warned the Nationalists to supply the island on even dates "to avoid possible losses."

Dulles on Truce and Talks. On Oct. 28 Secretary Dulles told a news conference that the Chinese Communist announcement of a partial truce showed that "the killing is done for political purposes and promiscuously," and that the Communists "are trying to save themselves from a loss of face and a defeat in the effort which they had initiated but had been unable to conclude successfully." Dulles said the most important achievement of his talks with Chiang Kai-shek was "a fresh formulation of the mission of the government of Free China" with "the emphasis on winning through peaceful processes."

Election. On Nov. 4 the Democrats made important gains in congressional and gubernatorial elections as a record number of Americans went to the polls for the midterm voting. The Democrats gained 13 Senate seats, 47 House seats, and five governorships.

Eisenhower on China. On Nov. 5 President Eisenhower said at a news conference, regarding China policy: "As far as I am concerned, our position has not changed as long as Red China continues to do some of the things which we cannot possibly stomach, one of them being that after two years ago promising to give back all our prisoners, and people that we think are illegally held, they still will do nothing about it. And there are a good many other accusations of the same kind."

Dulles Speech. On Nov. 13 Secretary of State Dulles told a meeting of the Seattle, Wash., Chamber of Commerce that China's leaders were creating a vast slave state to increase the power of international communism; because they recognized that their activities were "bound to induce hatred on the part of the Chinese people," they were trying to divert hatred away from themselves by directing it against foreigners.

Mao Resigns. On Dec. 17 the Chinese Communist Party Central Committee announced that Mao Tse-tung (Mao Zedong), 65, would retire as chief of state of the Chinese People's Republic when his current term expired in January 1959. The announcement said Mao was resigning to devote full time to his job as Communist Party chairman. Chinese Foreign Minister Chen Yi said Mao was retiring "to conserve himself [for] still more important tasks." He denied that difficulties with the commune system — which was intended to enable China to make a "great leap forward" in agricultural and industrial production — or the failure to gain control of the offshore islands had anything to do with Mao's decision. Mao was suc-

ceeded as chief of state by Liu Shao-ch'i (Liu Shaoqi), whom Mao would purge during the power struggles of the late 1960s.

Commune Slowdown. On Dec. 18 the Chinese Communist Party Central Committee announced a decision, made Dec. 10, to put off introduction of large-scale communes in big cities pending solution of special problems encountered in urban centers. Meanwhile, the rural communes, where friction between peasants and party workers had arisen, were to be "tidied up, checked over and consolidated."

1959

Sino-Soviet Aid Pact — Anti-Chinese Revolt in Tibet — Nehru Charges China — Dalai Lama Escapes to India — Liu Shao-ch'i New Chief of State of PRC — Unrest in China's Communes — Dulles Dies — China's Economic Progress — Laos Asks for U.N. Emergency Force to Stop North Vietnamese Aid to Laotian Rebels — Development of Chinese Border Dispute with India — Khrushchev in Washington — Lin Piao Named China's Defense Minister — Khrushchev in Peking — Marshall Dies — Indian-Chinese Border Clash — Failure of Nehru and Chou to Find Basis of Negotiation.

Chou in Moscow. On Jan. 28 Chinese Premier Chou En-lai told the 21st Soviet Communist Party Congress in Moscow that the Soviet Union and China shared "a common destiny" and a friendship that was "eternal and inviolable."

Sino-Soviet Aid Pact. On Feb. 7 Soviet Premier Nikita S. Khrushchev and Chinese Premier Chou En-lai signed a technical aid agreement in Moscow to provide China with $1.25 billion worth of equipment and assistance by 1967 for construction of 78 heavy industrial installations.

Sino-Soviet Unity. On Feb. 14 a joint Soviet-Chinese statement, issued in Moscow by the Chinese-Soviet Friendship Association, asserted that the "unbreakable unity" of China and Russia could not be broken by "American imperialists and . . . revisionists of Yugoslavia," who were both "spreading infamous insinuations about the 'big leap' in our countries and the development of the people's communes."

Sino-Soviet Trade Pact. On Feb. 26 it was disclosed that the Soviet Union and China had signed a $1.75-billion trade agreement in Moscow. Russia was slated to export industrial equipment to China, while the nature of the Chinese goods sent to Russia was not mentioned.

Tibetan Revolt. On March 10, demonstrations against the Chinese began in Tibet. On March 17, Chinese troops fired on crowds in Lhasa demonstrating in support of Tibet's spiritual and temporal leader, the Dalai Lama, who fled Lhasa the same day. On March 19 heavy fighting broke out in Lhasa.

Tibet. On March 25 the Tibetan Cabinet declared independence from China and demanded that the Chinese withdraw from Tibet. On the same day, Chinese troops occupied Lhasa after heavy fighting. They apparently were not able to re-establish control over the rebels in southern Tibet.

On March 28 Chinese Premier Chou En-lai ordered the Tibetan government dissolved and replaced by a regime headed by the Panchen Lama, 21, who said the following day he would serve until the return of the Dalai Lama to Lhasa. Chou charged that Tibetan officials had "colluded with imperialism, assembled rebellious bandits, carried out rebellion," and "put the Dalai Lama under duress." The State Department on March 28 accused China of "barbarous intervention" and of attempting to "destroy the historical autonomy of the Tibetan people."

Nehru's Statement. On March 30 Indian Prime Minister Nehru charged that the Chinese had broken pledges to allow Tibet "full autonomy." He said India sympathized with the Tibetan rebels and would admit refugees from Tibet on an individual basis.

Dalai Lama Escapes. On March 31 the Dalai Lama reached India after a 300-mile journey over the southern mountains of Tibet. On the same day, the Peking *People's Daily* said the Chinese army had "swiftly put down the rebellion in the Lhasa area" and was "mopping up the rebels in some other places in Tibet."

Dulles Resigns. On April 15 Secretary of State John Foster Dulles resigned. Doctors had found that cancer had spread to his neck. President Eisenhower, in an emotional press conference, commented: "I personally believe he has filled his office with greater distinction than any man our country has known." On April 18 Eisenhower announced that Christian A. Herter would replace Dulles as secretary of state. He was sworn in on April 21. ·

Liu Elected. On April 27 the National People's Congress in Peking elected Liu Shao-ch'i (Liu Shaoqi) as the new chief of state of the PRC. Mao's resignation from the post was announced Dec. 17, 1958. Liu was known as a leading communist theoretician and organizer.

Commune Unrest. On May 16, sources in Hong Kong reported that the Chinese government had eased control of agricultural production in southern communes due to spreading dissatisfaction among peasants.

Dulles Dies. On May 24 former Secretary of State John Foster Dulles died of cancer at age 71.

Peasant Uprising. On May 25 the Nationalist Chinese reported that 10,000 peasants had revolted near Nanjing on May 17 and killed 80 communist officials. At least 200 rioters were said to have been killed before troops suppressed the uprising.

Nationalist China and Olympics. On May 28 the International Olympic Committee voted "almost unanimously" to withdraw recognition from Nationalist China because "it no longer represents sports in the entire country of China." The president of the IOC, Avery Brundage, an American, said that if China applied for membership, it would be recognized as the "representative of China." On June 2 the State Department charged that the action was "a clear act of political discrimination" against the Nationalist Chinese "to obtain the later admission of the Chinese Communists." On June 3 the House of Representatives voted unanimously to withhold U.S. financial support of the 1960 Winter Olympics at Squaw Valley, Calif., if the IOC refused to allow entry of athletes from any "free nation."

Chinese Athletes. On June 12 the State Department announced it would give visas to any bona fide athletes sent from Communist China to the Winter Olympics in Squaw Valley, Calif.

Food in China. On June 20 *The New York Times* reported that China's 1959 food production had fallen below 1958 levels as a result of floods and drought.

Soviets Withdraw Nuclear Help. On June 20 the Soviet Union secretly told China that it was abrogating its Oct. 15, 1957, secret agreement promising to help the Chinese develop a nuclear arsenal.

Americans Slain in Vietnam. On July 8 two Americans were killed and one wounded during a Viet Minh attack on a compound 20 miles northeast of Saigon. The Americans were members of the U.S. Military Assistance Advisory Group in South Vietnam.

Peng Dehuai Purged. On Aug. 2-16 at the 8th Plenary Session of the Chinese Communist Party Central Committee, at Lushan, Marshall Peng Dehuai, the minister of defense, was purged. He was later replaced by Marshall Lin Piao (Lin Biao), one of the most devoted followers of Mao Tse-tung.

Reportedly, Peng was critical of the Great Leap Forward, and upset over the effect which the growing Sino-Soviet split would have on the Chinese army's ability to procure arms, especially in light of the crisis in Tibet and the growing tension with India.

China's Economic Progress. On Aug. 16 the National Planning Association reported that China distributed $647 million in foreign aid to Asian and Middle Eastern nations from 1952 to 1957 and received $430 million in aid from the Soviet Union during the same period. A report by A. Doak Barnett for the Rockefeller Foundation said that Soviet technical aid had been "indispensable" to China, but that the "Chinese Communists have had to pay their own way in relations with the Russians."

The Barnett report called China's economic progress "very impressive" and its growth since 1958 "revolutionary and . . . startling" but said it was "impossible to evaluate [the situation] at this time with any sense of confidence." Barnett said that China's establishment of a commune system and its decentralization of industry constituted the "most radical political, economic and social reorganization ever attempted in so short a time by a large nation." The report predicted that if the communes succeeded, "great opportunities for accelerated development may be opened up for the Peking regime." If they failed, there would be "a very adverse effect upon every aspect of the Chinese Communists' program."

Indian Border Violations. On Sept. 3 it was reported in New Delhi that Chinese forces had violated India's northern border, and that Indian troops had been dispatched to two Himalayan mountain passes to guard roads from Tibet to Sikkim and India.

Charges Against India. On Sept. 4 Indian Prime Minister Nehru announced that the Chinese had accused India of "aggression" and demanded that India evacuate "one or two areas which they claim to be Chinese territory." Nehru said the general line defining the Tibetan-Indian frontier "has to be accepted," although he would be willing to make some minor revisions. He called the dispute "rather absurd" and said it was "not a question of two or three miles of territory, but [of] national prestige and self-respect."

Laos Appeals to U.N. On Sept. 4 Laos appealed to the U.N. for "dispatch of an emergency force" to counter aggression by North Vietnamese-supported rebels. Laotian

Foreign Minister Khampan Panya sent a note to U.N. Secretary General Dag Hammarskjold asserting that "foreign troops have been crossing the frontier [from North Vietnam] and engaging in actions against garrison units . . . stationed along the northeastern frontier of Laos." It charged that "these attacks would not have taken place if the attackers had not come from outside the country and would not have continued" without reinforcement and supplies . . . from outside." On Sept. 5 the U.S. warned the Soviet Union and China it would help to counter any "new danger to peace" caused by "further augmentation of the invading force or continued military support thereof by Communists in North Vietnam."

U.N. Action. On Sept. 8 the U.N. Security Council voted 10-1 (Russia opposed), to establish a subcommittee to examine the Laotian complaint.

Soviets Ask Conference. On Sept. 14 the Soviet Union asked that an international conference be "called without delay by the countries that attended the 1954 Geneva Conference" to discuss the hostilities in Laos. The Soviets said the dispute had to be settled "within the framework of the Geneva agreements, which provide the foundations for peace and security in Indochina."

U.S. Rejects. On Sept. 15 the State Department called the Soviet request "unnecessary and disruptive" and said solution of the Laos problem was "not to be found in international conferences but in cessation of intervention and subversion" by "Lao Communists and their supporters."

Khrushchev Arrives. On Sept. 15 Soviet Premier Nikita Khrushchev arrived in Washington for a two-week visit in the U.S. The talks, held at Camp David, were extremely cordial and resulted in an extraordinary, if short-lived, easing of Soviet-American tensions.

U.N. China Action. On Sept. 22 the U.N. General Assembly adopted, 44-29 with nine abstentions, a U.S. resolution to delay consideration of a U.N. seat for Communist China for another year.

Khrushchev Leaves. On Sept. 27 Soviet Premier Khrushchev left the U.S. for Moscow. Two days later, he flew to Peking to attend China's 10th anniversary celebrations.

Khrushchev Statements. On Sept. 30 Khrushchev told members of a banquet held in his honor in Peking: "We [Soviet-bloc nations] . . . must do everything possible to preclude war as a means for settling outstanding questions"; although communist countries had "created a mighty potential," "this certainly does not mean that . . . we should test the stability of the capitalist system by force"; "even such a noble and progressive system as socialism cannot be imposed by force of arms against the will of the people," because they "would never understand and would never support [it]."

China's Anniversary Celebration. On Oct. 1 China celebrated its 10th anniversary with an enormous parade in Peking, reviewed by Mao, Khrushchev, and other leaders of both countries.

Chinese Defense Minister Marshal Lin Piao told the huge crowd in Peking's Tiananmen Square that China would "never invade anyone nor . . . allow anyone to invade us." But he reiterated China's determination to "liberate" Taiwan "in one way or another" and warned all foreign powers not to intrude.

Indian-Chinese Notes. On Oct. 3 Indian Prime Minister Nehru sent a note to Chinese Premier Chou En-lai stating that "No discussions can be fruitful unless the posts on the Indian side of the traditional frontier now held by Chinese forces are first evacuated by them and further threats . . . cease." Chou, replying Oct. 7, said in a note to Nehru that the border dispute between the two countries was "merely an episode in our age-old friendship." On the following day, Nehru told newsmen that he was somewhat optimistic about the Chinese note and that India would not "start military operations . . . at this stage, when we are dealing with this matter on a political level." He added that another Chinese attack would be "fully resisted."

Chen's Article. On Oct. 4 Chinese Foreign Minister Chen Yi wrote in the Peking *People's Daily* that during the past decade U.S. "imperialists have carried out a series of aggressive acts and war threats against new China, fully revealing that they are the enemy of the Chinese people." He added: "We firmly demand that American troops pull out of the Taiwan area. Taiwan is Chinese territory and the Chinese people are determined to liberate it." This article, as well as the Oct. 1 speech by Lin Piao, are now interpreted as reactions to Khrushchev's private statements to Chinese leaders that the Soviet Union would not support them in an attack on Taiwan. Supposedly, Khrushchev also told the Chinese that the Soviet Union would remain neutral in the Sino-Indian border dispute, a statement that further infuriated Peking.

Herter on Sino-Soviet Relations. On Oct. 6 Secretary of State Herter said at a news conference: "There is no question in our minds that the [Soviet Union's] demand for recognition as the leader of the Communist world places upon the Russians a degree of responsibility for the actions of other members of the bloc that is very real." Herter admitted that Russia followed "a rather different line" from China. However, Premier Khrushchev had "talked quite eloquently" about peaceful coexistence during his trip to China. Chairman Mao Tse-tung "never made any statement" on the subject "either on Mr. Khrushchev's arrival or . . . departure." The secretary said it was "very difficult" to determine how "deep the differences" were between the two communist powers, but from "outward appearances" they "are working very closely together."

China as Threat to Peace. On Oct. 16 Assistant Secretary of State for Public Affairs Andrew H. Berding told the National Association of Broadcasters that since the "improvement in the international atmosphere" brought about by the talks between President Eisenhower and Soviet Premier Khrushchev, China stood as the world's chief threat to peace. Berding lauded Khrushchev for advising the Chinese not to spread "socialism by force of arms," and he added: "We believe that if the Soviet Union is sincere in wanting to safeguard the peace, it has the leverage . . . to insure a measure of responsibility on the part of the Chinese Communists."

Border Clash. On Oct. 20-21, following a series of minor incidents, the most serious fighting to date broke out between Chinese and Indian troops at the Kongka Pass, a remote section of Kashmir. Nine Indians were killed, and ten were taken prisoner. On Nov. 1 Prime Minister Nehru said that India was making "adequate military preparations" against the threat.

Travel Ban Upheld. On Dec. 7 the U.S. Supreme Court refused to review three lower court decisions sustaining a State Department ban on travel to China. Appeals had been filed by Rep. Charles O. Porter, D-Ore., reporter William Worthy Jr. of the Baltimore *Afro-American*, and Waldo Frank, lecturer and author. The State Department had refused to validate the passports of Porter and Frank for travel in China and had denied Worthy a new passport unless he agreed to respect the ban. In each case the applicants appealed on the ground that the secretary of state had no authority to restrict the travel of a citizen.

Rockefeller Report on Foreign Policy. On Dec. 7 a broad survey of U.S. foreign policy needs for the future was made public by the Rockefeller Brothers Fund. The report was prepared by a 14-man panel headed by two former assistant secretaries of state, Adolph A. Berle Jr. and Dean Rusk, president of the Rockefeller Foundation.

The members of the panel asserted that no responsible communist state should be barred from membership in the international community of nations. While not proposing U.S. recognition or U.N. membership for Communist China, they called for reassessment of China's position in the modern world and cautioned against permitting "emotion or differences of ideology" to stand in the way of improved relations with the Chinese people. However, the report pointed out that "Communist China is in a posture which, in the past historical experience, has almost invariably led to aggression" and it "looks upon the United States as its supreme enemy."

A rift in the alliance between the Soviet Union and China was not to be expected in the near future, the report observed, but the coming decade might see a strain in the relations between the two powers. The panel warned against a policy that might drive China closer to Russia but said that actions specifically designed to split the two powers probably would fail.

Eisenhower in India. On Dec. 9 President Eisenhower arrived in New Delhi for a four-day state visit.

1960

Senate Report Calls China a Giant on the March — Bishop Walsh Imprisoned in China — Chou En-lai Visits India — South Korean President Rhee Resigns — U-2 Incident — Growing Sino-Soviet Split — Eisenhower in Taiwan — Communists on Coexistence and War — U.S. Party Platforms on China Questions — Cuba Recognizes China — Kennedy-Nixon Debates on Quemoy and Matsu — Kennedy Elected — Manifesto Unites 81 Communist Parties in Fight Against Capitalism.

Report on China. On Jan. 3 Sen. Henry M. Jackson, D-Wash., chairman of a Senate Government Operations subcommittee, issued a report, "National Policy Machinery in Communist China," noting that "the Chinese Communist Party has attained a degree of unity and stability at its higher levels which is unequalled by other major Communist parties." The report said the Chinese Communist leaders had lifted the country "from a prostrate colossus into a giant on the march, in 10 short years."

Brucker on Taiwan Defense. On Jan. 10 Secretary of the Army Wilber M. Brucker, visiting U.S. bases on Taiwan, said the defense agreement between the U.S. and Nationalist China "included not just Taiwan but any part of the Republic of China where aggression would occur by the Communist Chinese."

U.S. Pact with Japan. On Jan. 19 the U.S. and Japan signed a mutual cooperation and security treaty in Washington. The new agreement, which superceded the 1951 treaty, returned full sovereignty to Japan in defense matters, and made the two countries equal partners in maintaining "international peace and security in the Far East." The signing was marked by wide-scale rioting in Japan. *(See June 16)*

Burma-China Agreement. On Jan. 28 Burmese Premier Ne Win and Chinese Premier Chou En-lai signed a border agreement, a 10-year non-aggression pact, and a treaty of friendship.

Newsman Jailed. On Feb. 6 Bill Yim, a United Press International newsman accused of "spy activities" in China, was reported to have been sentenced to one year in jail. Yim had been arrested while visiting Canton in 1959.

China and Disarmament. On March 16 President Eisenhower told a news conference: "If disarmament comes into the realm of practical negotiation and enforcement, you will ... unquestionably have to take into account the armaments of Red China." But he added, "there has to be a very great deal of progress, before we are into the stage of worrying too much about Red China."

Bishop Imprisoned. On March 18 a court in Shanghai sentenced an American Roman Catholic missionary, Bishop James Edward Walsh, 69, to 20 years imprisonment. Walsh, who had been under house arrest since October 1958, was charged with espionage and counterrevolutionary activities. On March 22 the U.S. called the imprisonment of Bishop Walsh "inexcusable" and said it was "one more step in the ... persecution of religion in Communist China."

Sino-Soviet Trade. On March 29 the Soviet Union and China signed an agreement to increase their 1960 trade by 10 percent over that of 1959.

Sino-Soviet Split. On April 16 the Chinese Communist Party theoretical journal *Hongqi* published the first public indication of the Sino-Soviet split. Entitled "Long Live Leninism," the article sought to demonstrate the theoretical legitimacy of Chinese Communism and Mao Tse-tung, and the deviation and heresy of the Soviet Union.

It was argued that Mao, not Khrushchev, was the heir to the communist tradition, and the logical successor to Marx, Lenin and Stalin. The result would be that Peking, and not Moscow, should be the leader of the communist world. The Soviets had forfeited their right to this title.

Without naming Soviet Premier Khrushchev, the article said he was a "distorter" of Lenin's teachings and labeled him a "revisionist," a reference to his attempts to work in harmony with the West. The Chinese argued that Khrushchev was bound to fail in his efforts, and restated their notion that "wars of one kind or another will always occur." (Khrushchev had earlier disputed the Leninist idea that war with the capitalist world is inevitable.) The article concluded that there was no "peaceful road to socialism," and stated that a nuclear war would be followed by "a civilization thousands of times higher than the capitalist system."

Soviet Reply to China. On April 22 a member of the Soviet Communist Party Presidium, Otto V. Kuusinen, answered the Chinese charge of April 16 in a speech given in Moscow. The essence of his reply was that the Chinese were "dogmatists" (adhering too rigidly to earlier communist writings) while Khrushchev's tactics represented an application of creative Leninism. This ideological debate would soon become a continuing disagreement on virtually all the fundamental issues facing the two nations.

Indian-Chinese Talks. On April 25 Indian Prime Minister Nehru and Chinese Premier Chou En-lai issued a joint statement after a week of talks in New Delhi on the border dispute between the two countries. Nehru and Chou admitted that the talks "did not result in resolving differences that had arisen," but they agreed "to avoid friction and clashes in the border areas" while their respective diplomats discussed their differences during the coming summer.

Rhee Resigns. On April 26 South Korean President Syngman Rhee, 85, resigned at the climax of a government crisis marked by extensive student rioting. The crisis was precipitated by charges that the March 15 election won by Rhee and his handpicked vice presidential candidate, Lee Ki Poong, had been rigged. The State Department said, April 19, that it had notified the South Korean government of "growing and profound" U.S. concern over unrest in that country and had urged restoration of public confidence by actions aimed to protect democratic rights and prevent political discrimination. Shortly before resigning, Rhee ordered new elections. South Korea's foreign minister, Huh Chung, was named Acting President on April 27. He pledged reforms, including elimination of "waste" of aid. The suicides of Lee Ki Poong, his wife and two sons were announced April 28.

Eisenhower's Reaction. On April 27 President Eisenhower told a news conference that the U.S. in no way had interfered in the South Korean crisis. The president said Rhee was a "tremendous patriot" who had "made some mistakes as he grew older."

China-Nepal Agreement. On April 29 Chinese Premier Chou En-lai left Nepal after signing a treaty with Nepalese Premier B. P. Koirala. A joint statement issued after Chou's departure announced ratification of the treaty, which settled Nepalese-Tibetan border disputes. Chou had told a joint session of the Nepalese Parliament on April 28 in Katmandu that the agreement was a step toward "peaceful coexistence between countries of different social systems."

U-2 Incident and Paris Summit. On May 5 the Soviet Union announced that on May 1 a U.S. high-altitude reconnaissance U-2 aircraft had been shot down near Sverdlovsk in the heart of the U.S.S.R. The incident, disclosed by Soviet Premier Nikita S. Khrushchev, produced almost hourly reverberations during the ensuing week. The most sensational was the belated but unequivocal acknowledgment by the U.S. of efforts to penetrate Soviet secrecy by such techniques as overflights.

Khrushchev told the Supreme Soviet May 5 that the flight was an "aggressive provocation aimed at wrecking the summit conference" scheduled to open in Paris on May 16. The Big Four conference did, in fact, collapse almost as soon as it opened. Khrushchev refused to proceed to a discussion of outstanding issues unless President Eisenhower bowed to an ultimatum that he apologize for the U-2 flight and agree to punish "those who are directly guilty." The president refused, and two days later both men left Paris and headed for home. Meanwhile, Khrushchev had canceled Eisenhower's scheduled state visit to Russia, which was to begin June 10. Observers believed Khru-

shchev destroyed the Paris summit due to Chinese opposition to peaceful negotiations with the West. *(See April 16)*

"Liberal Project" Study. On May 23 the "Liberal Project," a group of House members and scientists, scholars and political scientists formed April 15 to expound a liberal point of view, released its first study. "A Reexamination of U.S. Foreign Policy," written by James P. Warburg. On East Asian foreign policy, the study said: "We cannot see how our Government can hope to ease tensions, to arrive at fair settlements of disputes or, above all, to achieve disarmament without establishing direct channels of communication with Peking." It recommended that the U.S. withdraw its opposition to Communist China's admission to the U.N., "provided that the Peking regime will reaffirm the renunciation of force which it signed at the Bandung Conference of 1955, . . . undertake the obligations imposed by the Charter of the United Nations, and agree to cooperate in working toward universal total disarmament adequately enforced under world law."

The study also said: The U.S. should recognize Communist China's "unquestionably valid" claim to the off-shore islands in return for free evacuation of Chinese Nationalist troops and citizens; the U.S. has "more than fulfilled its obligations to the Nationalist regime" and should ask political amnesty for or offer asylum to Nationalist leaders who wish it; and the U.S. should seek an agreement with Russia and China whereby all three would withdraw from Korea and Vietnam.

Reaction. On May 24 the Committee of One Million Against the Admission of Communist China to the United Nations said the Liberal Project's objectives, particularly the recognition of Communist China, were "contemptible." The committee voiced confidence that "the other 427 members of the House . . . have learned full well the bitter lessons of appeasement and will continue to maintain and expand the only foreign policy possible to counter Communist aggression — strength and adherence to the principles of freedom and the preservation of our national security and honor."

Chinese Charge Overflights. On May 27 China charged that American U-2 jets had made at least three flights over the Chinese mainland.

Sino-Mongolian Treaty. On May 31 China and Mongolia signed a Treaty of Friendship and Mutual Assistance in Ulan Bator. Mongolia, which shares a 2,500-mile border with China and a 1,700-mile border with the Soviet Union, tended to lean toward Russia in the Sino-Soviet dispute.

Ike's Visit Cancelled. On June 16 it was announced in Washington that President Eisenhower had cancelled his upcoming trip to Japan, scheduled for June 19. The decision followed three weeks of rioting by leftist students in Japan protesting the recent signing of a security treaty with the U.S. *(See Jan. 19, 1960)*

Anti-Peking Campaign in U.S. On June 16 the Committee of One Million Against the Admission of Communist China to the United Nations called on the public to support its campaign to have planks included in the Democratic and Republican platforms expressing opposition to any concessions to the Peking government. The committee asked citizens to write to their senators and representatives, urging support of an anti-Communist China plank drafted by the committee. The president of the committee, former Gov. Charles Edison of New Jersey, said the plank had already been endorsed by 212 members of Congress — 100 Republicans and 112 Democrats.

Communist Shelling. On June 17, while President Eisenhower was enroute by sea from Manila to Taiwan on the second leg of an East Asian trip, Chinese Communist batteries fired a record 86,000 artillery shells at Nationalist-held Quemoy Island in what Peking radio called a "gesture of contempt and scorn" for the president and the United States.

Taiwan Visit. On June 18 President Eisenhower arrived in Taiwan and told a rally: "The United States does not recognize the claim of the warlike and tyrannical Communist regime in Peking to speak for all the Chinese people. In the United Nations we support the Republic of China, a founding member, as the only rightful representative of China in that organization."

Communists on Coexistence and War. On June 22, leaders of 12 communist nations, including China and the Soviet Union, met in Bucharest, Romania, and reaffirmed support of Soviet ideas on peaceful coexistence. In statements clearly aimed at the Chinese, Soviet Premier Khrushchev had told the Romanian Communist Party Congress a day earlier that "under present conditions, war is not inevitable," and that "he who does not understand this does not believe in the . . . great attractive force of socialism, which has manifestly demonstrated its superiority over capitalism. . . . [I]n our day only madmen and maniacs" advocate a new war. The Soviet premier had said at an earlier press conference that "Coexistence is the only . . . path to take; any other way means death and destruction for all of us."

Chinese on Peace. On June 29 the Peking *People's Daily* said: "Only when the imperialist . . . and capitalist systems . . . are really abolished can there really be lasting world peace."

Eisenhower on Sino-Soviet Split. On July 6 President Eisenhower discussed the Sino-Soviet split at a news conference: "As [both communist powers] have gotten more productive, they have a much bigger collection of productive mechanisms. In other words, they have accumulated wealth, and they've also got a great arsenal of powerful weapons; I think . . . there comes a time when their views as to the methods they will use to dominate the world . . . might be changed. And I think there is a change going on there that probably the Red Chinese have not yet decided upon. As of this moment, they seem to be much more belligerent and much more . . . quarrelsome than are their associates."

Kennedy Nominated. On July 13 the Democratic National Convention in Los Angeles nominated Sen. John Fitzgerald Kennedy, 43, of Massachusetts for president. The following day, Kennedy picked Sen. Lyndon B. Johnson, 51, of Texas as his running-mate.

The Democratic platform, in its section on China, said: "We deeply regret that the policies and actions of the government of Communist China have interrupted the generations of friendship between the Chinese and American peoples. We reaffirm our pledge of determined opposition to the present admission of Communist China [to the U.N.]."

Soviet Advisers to Leave China. On July 16 the Soviet Union informed China that it had decided to recall its 1,390 experts in China, terminate most of their agreements and contracts, and to discontinue supplies of much equipment and materials.

Nixon Nominated. On July 27 the Republican National Convention in Chicago nominated Vice President Richard Milhous Nixon, 47, for president. The following day, Nixon picked U.S. Ambassador to the U.N. Henry Cabot Lodge, 58, as his running-mate.

The Republican platform, in its section on China, said: "Recognition of Communist China and its admission to the United Nations have been firmly opposed by the Republican administration. We will continue in this opposition."

Chou's "Peace Pact" Offer. On Aug. 1 Chinese Premier Chou En-lai, attending a reception at the Swiss embassy in Peking, proposed a "peace pact" between China, the U.S., and other Pacific powers to establish a "non-nuclear zone in Asia and the Western Pacific." Chou added that China had not "given up its policy of seeking peaceful relations with countries with different social systems." On the same day, State Department spokesman Lincoln White said Chou's proposal was a "propaganda gesture" and added that the offer had never been discussed at the Chinese-American meetings in Warsaw.

Laotian Coup. On Aug. 15 an army rebellion overthrew the government of Premier Tiao Somsanith and a Cabinet dedicated to neutralism was formed under Prince Souvanna Phouma.

Cuba-China Ties. On Sept. 2 Cuban Premier Fidel Castro announced in Havana that Cuba would become the first Latin American country to recognize Communist China. He said his country would break diplomatic relations with Nationalist China.

Kennedy-Nixon Debate. On Oct. 7 Sen. John F. Kennedy and Vice President Richard M. Nixon held their second radio and television debate of the presidential campaign. The nominees disagreed about defense of Quemoy and Matsu.

Sen. Kennedy said: "These islands are a few miles, five or six miles off the coast of Red China within a general harbor area, and more than 100 miles from Formosa [Taiwan]. We have never said flatly that we will defend Quemoy [Jinmen] and Matsu [Mazu] if it is attacked. . . . I think it is unwise to take the chance of being dragged into a war which may lead to a world war over two islands which are not strategically defensible, which are not . . . essential to the defense of Formosa [Taiwan]."

Vice President Nixon answered: "I think as far as Quemoy and Matsu are concerned that the question is not these two little pieces of real estate. They are unimportant. . . . It is the principle involved. These two islands are in the area of freedom. . . . We should not force our Nationalist allies to get off them and give them to the Communists. If we do that, we start a chain reaction, because the Communists aren't after Quemoy and Matsu. They are after Formosa [Taiwan]."

U.N. Vote on China. On Oct. 8 the U.N. General Assembly voted 42-34 (22 abstentions) in favor of a U.S.-backed resolution to take no action at the current session on admission of Communist China. The resolution carried by the smallest margin in 10 years.

Sen. Wayne Morse, D-Ore., a member of the U.S. delegation, told newsmen the next day that the vote showed that Communist China's admission was "inevitable."

Morse said that in 1961 the U.S. must "be willing to have the U.N. negotiate conditions" for such admission. Senate Foreign Relations Chairman J. W. Fulbright, D-Ark., told an Oct. 10 news conference he agreed that admission of Communist China was inevitable.

More Debate. On Oct. 13 one of the chief questions at issue in the third Nixon-Kennedy debate was again Quemoy and Matsu. Nixon said that if a Chinese Communist attack on the offshore islands was "a prelude to an attack on Formosa, which would be the indication today, . . . there isn't any question but that the United States would then again, as in the case of Berlin, honor our treaty obligations and stand by our ally." Nixon asserted that surrender of the islands would not lead to peace. On the contrary: "It is something that would lead, in my opinion, to war. . . . Now what do the Chinese Communists want? They don't want just Quemoy and Matsu. They don't want just Formosa. They want the world. . . ."

Sen. Kennedy said in reply: "Mr. Nixon suggests that the United States should go to war if these two islands are attacked. I suggest that if Formosa is attacked, or the Pescadores [Penghu], or if there is any military action in any area which indicates an attack on Formosa and the Pescadores, then, of course, the United States is at war to defend its [security] treaty [with Nationalist China]. . . ."

Election. On Nov. 8 Democratic presidential nominee John F. Kennedy defeated Vice President Richard M. Nixon, the Republican nominee, in the closest presidential election of the 20th century. The Democrats maintained their heavy majorities in the Congress and among the nation's governors.

Communist Manifesto. On Dec. 6, representatives of 81 communist parties, attending the 2nd World Conference of Communist Parties in Moscow, issued a manifesto claiming unity in the fight against capitalism. Soviet Premier Khrushchev and Chinese chief of state Liu Shao-ch'i had exchanged strong criticisms for at least 10 days before a compromise was reached. The manifesto's wording was more aggressive than that of previous Soviet statements, due to Russian concessions to Chinese demands. China's views had the support of representatives of communist movements in Latin America, Albania, and some sections of Asia. The Soviet position was supported by the majority of the participants, most of them from the East European nations.

After declaring that "U.S. imperialism is the main force of aggression and war. . .," the manifesto said: "The aggressive nature of imperialism has not changed. But real forces have appeared that are capable of foiling its plans of aggression. War is not fatally inevitable. Had the imperialists been able to do what they wanted, they would have already plunged mankind into the abyss of the calamities and horrors of a new cold war. But the time is past when the imperialists could decide at will whether there should or should not be war. . . .

"Peaceful coexistence with countries of different systems or destructive war — this is the alternative today. There is no other choice. Communists emphatically reject the U.S. doctrine of cold war and brinkmanship, for it is a policy leading to thermonuclear catastrophe. . . ."

Laos. On Dec. 9 the neutralist government of Laos under Prince Souvanna Phouma collapsed under pressure from U.S.-supplied rightist forces attacking Vientiane, the Laotian capital.

Rusk Named. On Dec. 12 President-elect Kennedy announced that Dean Rusk, president of the Rockefeller Foundation, would be his secretary of state. The next day, Kennedy announced he would nominate Robert S. McNamara as secretary of defense.

Sino-Cambodian Treaty. On Dec. 19 Prince Sihanouk of Cambodia signed a treaty of friendship and non-aggression with China in Peking. Several economic agreements were also signed.

Chinese Agriculture. On Dec. 29 Peking radio said that over one-half of China's farmland had been crippled during 1960 by the worst "natural calamities" in a century. The report said millions of acres had been "seriously affected" by droughts, plant diseases, and typhoons.

1961

Burma-China Treaty — Kennedy Inaugurated — Kennedy on Reported Sino-Soviet Split — Warsaw Talks Resume — Kennedy on Laotian Neutrality — Johnson's Trip to Asia — Geneva Conference on Laos Opens — Kennedy-Khrushchev Meeting — Restatement of U.S. Opposition to Admitting China to U.N. — Chinese Praise for Soviet Resumption of Nuclear Testing — Hammarskjold Killed — Communist Countries Meet in Moscow — China, Albania Affirm Ties — Stalinists Purged in USSR — U.N. Debates China Representation, Rejects Admission

Burma Treaty with China. On Jan. 4 Burmese and Chinese Premiers U Nu and Chou En-Lai, meeting in Rangoon, completed action on a border agreement between the two countries. The two also negotiated an agreement for an $85 million six-year loan for a Chinese technical assistance program.

U.S. Nominees Approved. On Jan. 18 the Senate Foreign Relations Committee approved the nominations of Dean Rusk as secretary of state and Adlai E. Stevenson as U.S. ambassador to the U.N. On Jan. 19 the committee approved Chester Bowles as under secretary of state.

All three were questioned closely on their attitude toward Communist China. Rusk said Jan. 12 he saw "no promise at the present time that normal relations could be established with the regime in Peking," primarily because the Chinese Communists set as a prerequisite "the abandonment of the government and people of Formosa [Taiwan]." On Jan. 18 Stevenson testified that the U.S. "would have to face the possibility" of Communist China's admission to the U.N. He said he had never advocated such a step but it might be "impossible to prevent." Bowles testified Jan. 19 that U.S. recognition of Communist China was "completely unnegotiable" for "the time being" in the light of that government's demands. He said, "We are going to defend Formosa — whatever the risk, whatever the costs."

Kennedy Inaugurated. On Jan. 20 John Fitzgerald Kennedy, 43, was sworn in as 35th president of the United States.

Great Leap Reversed. On Jan. 20 the Central Committee of the Chinese Communist Party announced that in the light of the recent crop failures, industrial production would be curtailed and new efforts made to expand lagging farm production. The announcement marked the effective end of the Great Leap Forward in industry. *(See May 5, 1958.)*

Interview with Chou. On Jan. 31 *Look* magazine published an interview by Edgar Snow with Chinese Premier Chou En-lai. Chou told the American journalist that although the Soviet Union and China had differences, they agreed on the desirability of disarmament and peaceful coexistence. He said a settlement with the U.S. would be possible only after it had accepted Peking's position that Taiwan was a Chinese internal problem. U.S. forces would have to be withdrawn from the island.

British View. On Feb. 8 Lord Home, British foreign secretary, told the House of Lords that "the facts of international life require that Communist China be seated in the United Nations." On Feb. 9 the State Department said the U.S. did not share the British view.

Food for China. On Feb. 23 the White House announced that President Kennedy had rejected a proposal by Rep. James J. Lane, D-Mass., that the U.S. send food to China in exchange for release of Americans held prisoner there. It was reported two days later that Chinese Foreign Minister Chen Yi had said that China would not "stoop to beg for food from the United States."

Relations With Russia. On March 1 President Kennedy was asked during a news conference if the reported Sino-Soviet split might result in better relations between the U.S. and the U.S.S.R. The president expressed hope that it would and added that "We are attempting, and will be attempting in the coming months to determine whether any effective agreements can be accomplished with the Soviet Union which will permit a relaxation of world tension."

Warsaw Talks Resumed. On March 7, U.S.-Chinese Warsaw talks resumed with U.S. Ambassador to Poland Jacob D. Beam proposing that he and Chinese Ambassador Wang Bingnan discuss an exchange of newsmen between their two countries, the release of imprisoned Americans in China, and a general settlement of U.S.-Chinese disputes. Wang immediately rejected all three proposals, saying that nothing could be negotiated until the U.S. withdrew its forces from Taiwan.

Kennedy on Laos. On March 23 President Kennedy told a news conference that local communist forces in Laos had "increasing direction and support from outside" aimed at destroying Laotian neutrality, and if that neutrality was lost the security of all Southeast Asia would be endangered. The president said the U.S. "strongly and unreservedly" supported the goal of a "truly neutral" Laos.

Soviet-Chinese Agreement. On April 7 the Soviet Union and China signed a trade and economic aid agreement, the total value of which was reported to be smaller than in either 1959 or 1960. Although China was believed to be in a state of near-famine, the agreement contained no provisions for food shipments except for a loan of 500,000 tons of sugar. The Soviet Union conceded a five-year postponement of payments due from China under previous trade agreements.

Cuban Invasion. On April 17, anti-Castro Cuban rebels launched an attack on Cuba, landing at Cochinos Bay (Bay of Pigs), south of Havana. The force of 1,200 to 1,500 Cuban refugees, reportedly trained and supplied by the U.S. Central Intelligence Agency, encountered unexpectedly strong resistance and was overwhelmed in little more than 48 hours. The U.S. government became the target of strong criticism at home and abroad. On April 24 a White House statement asserted that the president "bears sole responsibility for the events of the past few days" and "is strongly opposed to anyone within or without the administration attempting to shift the responsibility."

Canadian-Chinese Agreement. On May 2 Canada announced it had agreed to sell $362 million worth of wheat, barley and flour (six million tons) to China. Peking radio reported 10 days later that "natural calamities" had caused massive crop losses.

Johnson's Trip to Asia. On May 9 Vice President Lyndon Johnson left Washington carrying personal letters from President Kennedy to Asian leaders assuring them of continuing and increased U.S. support. Johnson's first stop was in Saigon, capital of South Vietnam, where he met May 12 with President Ngo Dinh Diem to discuss the critical problem of infiltration by guerrilla forces from Communist North Vietnam.

Johnson next visited Manila for talks with President Carlos P. Garcia of the Philippines; a joint communiqué announced their "complete agreement on the seriousness of the situation in Southeast Asia." From Manila, Johnson flew to Taipei, May 14, where he assured Chinese Nationalist President Chiang Kai-shek of America's continuing support. After a stopover in Hong Kong, Johnson moved on to Bangkok May 16 for talks with Thailand's premier, Field Marshal Sarit Thanarat, about the precarious situation in adjoining Laos.

Second Geneva Conference. On May 12 the 14-nation conference on Laos opened in Geneva following a cease-fire between communist-backed and U.S.-supported forces in Laos. The conference promptly became deadlocked over a procedural question. The Soviets insisted that representatives of the communist-led Pathet Lao rebels be seated along with spokesmen for the pro-Western Laotian government and for neutralist Prince Souvanna Phouma. Secretary of State Dean Rusk opposed the move as tantamount to recognition of the rebels as a component of the future Laotian government — a step the U.S. felt would sabotage the objective of creating a truly neutral regime in Laos. With tension high — in part because of the presence of Communist China at the conference table — the principals finally agreed May 15 to seat all three Laotian groups as "spokesmen" for forces operating in Laos.

The conference formally opened on May 16. On May 17, both the U.S. and the Soviet Union proposed that all foreign troops be withdrawn from Laos. But the Soviets proposed also that the three-member International Control Commission — composed of India, Canada and Poland — adhere to the rule of unanimity in carrying out its truce-inspection duties, and also that it act only on the instruction of the co-chairmen of the conference, Britain and the Soviet Union. U.S. delegates said such a plan would give the Soviets a "double-barreled veto." By May 20 Secretary of State Rusk and other delegation leaders had returned home, leaving deputies in charge of the negotiations, which lasted until July 23, 1962. *(See June 11, 1962.)*

Kennedy on China. On June 2 President Kennedy, en route to Vienna to meet with Soviet Premier Nikita Khrushchev, was asked during a news conference in Paris how China could normalize its relations with the West and be admitted to the United Nations.

The president replied: "We desire peace and we desire to live in amity with the Chinese people. But I will say that since long before I assumed office, and in the first days of our new administration before really any actions were taken, the attacks upon our government and the United States were constant, immediate, and in many cases malevolent."

Kennedy-Khrushchev Meeting. On June 3 President Kennedy and Soviet Premier Khrushchev met in Vienna for two days of discussions. The president said: "The one area which afforded some . . . prospect of accord was Laos. Both sides endorsed the concept of a neutral and independent Laos. . . . And, of critical importance to the current conference on Laos in Geneva, both sides recognized the importance of an effective cease-fire."

Geneva Conference. On June 12 Chinese Foreign Minister Chen Yi told the 14-nation conference on Laos, meeting in Geneva, that Laos was "a victim of the United States policy of intervention" and warned that China "will never be a party to . . . enforcing an international condominium over Laos in the name of international control over its neutrality." The delegation from Thailand walked out during Chen Yi's speech.

Khrushchev Letter on China. On July 2 the London *Sunday Times* reported that Soviet Premier Khrushchev had sent a letter to the leaders of all communist parties denouncing the Chinese for what he felt was an overly aggressive policy. Peking's Taiwan policy was said to have come in for special criticism because it risked all-out war. On the same day it was learned that no Soviet officials had attended the celebration in Peking of the 40th anniversary of the founding of the Chinese Communist Party.

Sino-Korean Treaty. On July 11 China and North Korea signed in Peking a Treaty of Friendship, Cooperation and Mutual Assistance. The treaty represented a Chinese diplomatic coup, tying Korea more closely to China and drawing Pyongyang away from the Soviet Union.

China Resolution in Senate. On July 28 the U.S. Senate adopted, by a 76-0 roll-call vote, and sent to the House a resolution restating congressional opposition to the admission of Communist China to the United Nations and to U.S. recognition of the Peking government; the resolution also reaffirmed congressional support for continued recognition of the Nationalist Chinese government "as the representative of China in the U.N." The resolution was adopted by the House in a 395-0 roll-call vote on Aug. 31.

White House Communiqué. On Aug. 2, in a joint communiqué issued after two days of discussions between President Kennedy and Nationalist Chinese Vice President Ch'en Ch'eng (Chen Cheng), Kennedy pledged U.S. support for "continued representation of the Republic of China in the United Nations" and "reaffirmed the U.S. determination to continue to oppose admission of the Chinese Communist regime."

Berlin Wall. On Aug. 13, East German troops, police and factory workers sealed the border between East and West Berlin for reasons of "protection and control." Secretary of State Dean Rusk immediately charged that "Limitation on travel within Berlin is a violation of the four-power status of Berlin and . . . of the right of free circulation throughout the city. Restrictions on travel between East Germany and Berlin are in direct contravention of the four-power [Paris] agreement" of June 20, 1949. On Aug. 20, American troops began arriving in West Berlin to reinforce the U.S. garrison there.

Atomic Tests Resumed. On Aug. 31 the Soviet Union announced it would break the unofficial moratorium on atomic testing "reluctantly and with regret" because the U.S. "is standing at the threshold of carrying out underground nuclear explosions and only waits for the first suitable pretext to start them."

Chinese Reaction. On Aug. 31 the Chinese praised the Soviet Union for deciding to resume testing "in the interest of the defense of world peace." China called the decision "a cooling dose for hotheaded war plotters but a powerful inspiration to all peoples striving for world peace."

Kennedy Orders Atomic Tests. On Sept. 5 President Kennedy ordered resumption of U.S. underground nuclear testing because "We have no other choice."

Khrushchev on Big Bomb. On Sept. 8 *The New York Times* published a lengthy statement by Soviet Premier Khrushchev, given to C. L. Sulzberger to clarify statements in an earlier interview. Khrushchev said that "We already have" a bomb "equal in capacity to 100 million tons of TNT" and would "test the explosive device for it." He also said that the Soviet Union had given neither nuclear weapons nor long-range missiles to Communist China or any other nation. He denied that any weapons of that type were stationed outside the borders of the Soviet Union unless "possibly in East Germany."

Hammarskjold Killed. On Sept. 18 U.N. Secretary General Dag Hammarskjold was killed in a plane crash near Ndola, Northern Rhodesia, where he was to meet President Moise Tshombe of Katanga Province to arrange a cease-fire between Katangan and U.N. Congo forces.

China Debate. On Sept. 21 the U.N. General Assembly's Steering Committee voted to recommend debate on the question of Chinese representation. In a change of policy, the U.S. supported the proposed debate instead of seeking to have it postponed a year.

U.S. Involvement. On Oct. 11 State Department spokesman Lincoln White denied reports that the U.S. was considering sending troops to South Vietnam. White said: "There has been no such decision. Furthermore . . . Vietnam assures us . . . that with U.S. material assistance and training services, it can handle the present Communist aggressive attacks." He admitted he had doubts about South Vietnamese optimism. The U.S. was reported to have 685 men in a U.S. Military Advisory Group in South Vietnam.

Chou Warns of U.S. Imperialism. On Oct. 12 Chinese Premier Chou En-lai warned that his country "cannot be indifferent to the increasingly grave situation caused by United States imperialism in South Vietnam." Chou made the statement at a reception for North Vietnamese Premier Pham Van Dong in Peking.

Communist Party Congress. On Oct. 17 the 22nd Congress of the Soviet Communist Party convened in Moscow. Delegations from 83 countries were present. Representatives from Albania and Yugoslavia were notably absent. At the opening session, Soviet Premier Khrushchev denounced Albania for continuing to pursue the "cult of the individual," which in Soviet terms connoted Stalinism.

On Oct. 19 Chinese Premier Chou En-lai took issue with Khrushchev: "If there are quarrels in the Socialist camp we consider that they should be settled through bilateral contacts and that a public denunciation does not contribute to the cohesion of the Socialist camp.

On Oct. 20, foreign communist delegations began to voice support of Khrushchev's position, but on Oct. 21 the Chinese position was supported by President Ho Chi Minh of North Vietnam, Premier Kim Il Sung of North Korea, and a representative of the Japanese Communist Party.

The 22nd Congress adopted the "Third Program of the Soviet Communist Party," which called for bringing the Soviet Union to the threshold of communist abundance and perfection by 1980. At a time when hundreds of millions were hungry in China and the Great Leap Forward was in tatters, this represented the Soviet reply to Peking's 1958 claim that it would be the first to achieve communism. The Soviets already had begun to cut their aid to China, and this new message was clear evidence that they now expected the Chinese to get along on their own as long as they persisted in attacking the Soviet Union.

Biggest Bomb Exploded. On Oct. 30 the Soviet Union detonated the largest nuclear weapon in history — exceeding 50 megatons. The White House announced that "the explosion took place in the atmosphere" and would produce "more radioactive fallout than any previous explosion." On Nov. 2 President Kennedy said the U.S. would consider atmospheric nuclear testing if "it becomes necessary."

New Secretary General. On Nov. 3 U Thant, Burma's ambassador to the U.N., was appointed secretary general to replace the late Dag Hammarskjold.

Kennedy on Split. On Nov. 8 President Kennedy told a news conference: "None of us can talk with precision about the details of relationships between Russia and China. It is a matter of surmise and on this experts may differ. Therefore, I don't feel that it is probably useful now for us to attempt to assess it."

China and Albania. On Nov. 8 the Chinese Communist Party Central Committee asserted, in a message to the Albanian Communist Party on its 20th anniversary, that the Chinese-Albanian alliance "can be shaken by no force on earth." Two days later, it was reported in the U.S. press that Enver Hoxha, first secretary of the Albanian Communist Party, had said on the party's 20th anniversary: "It is not our party but the present Soviet leadership headed by Khrushchev who have slipped from Marxist-Leninist positions by demanding that other Communist parties submit to the Russian views and obey them." He said the Soviet Union was "afraid of imperialism" and had "delayed . . . from year to year" a showdown on the Berlin problem.

Purge of Stalinists. On Nov. 11 it was reported from Moscow that ex-Foreign Minister Vyacheslav M. Molotov and ex-Premier Georgi M. Malenkov had been expelled from the Soviet Communist Party because of their associations with Stalin and their 1957 "anti-party" conspiracy against Soviet Premier Khrushchev. On the same day, it was announced that Stalingrad had been renamed Volgograd, and that smaller cities, streets, squares and highways throughout the Soviet Union and Eastern European countries bearing Stalin's name had been renamed.

Wall Reinforced. On Nov. 19, East German workers began building a permanent wall between East and West Berlin. The following day, the deputy mayor of West Berlin, Franz Amrehn, inspected the new wall and commented: "That is a wall for 1,000 years."

China Debate in U.N. On Dec. 1, debate on China's membership in the U.N. began with a warning by U.S. Ambassador Adlai Stevenson that "the whole future of the United Nations may be at stake." Stevenson denounced the Chinese for aggression in Tibet, Korea and Vietnam. Later in the day, the Soviet delegation walked out during a speech by the Nationalist Chinese representative, who called China's leaders "even more bellicose than their Russian comrades, if that is possible." The Soviet ambassador to the U.N., Valerian A. Zorin, had called the Nationalist government on Taiwan "a rotten political corpse" kept "alive by sops from the master's table." It was the first time since 1950 that a resolution for China's admission to the U.N. had been debated in the General Assembly. The question previously had not gone beyond the assembly's Steering Committee.

U.N. Action on China. On Dec. 15 the U.N. General Assembly rejected a Soviet resolution for admission of China to the United Nations and expulsion of Nationalist China. The vote was 48 to 37 with 19 abstentions. A second resolution — to admit China without expelling Nationalist China was rejected the same day by a 45-30 vote with 29 abstentions. A third resolution, sponsored by the U.S. and providing that any new General Assembly resolution dealing with Chinese representation would require a two-thirds majority vote for adoption, was approved 61-34 with seven abstentions.

Canadian Wheat. On Dec. 21 the Canadian minister of agriculture announced that Canada had signed a new agreement with China for sale of $71 million worth of wheat and barley.

1962

Problem of Laos — More Aid for Vietnam — China Warns U.S. — Chinese-Cuban Trade Agreement — Communist Offensive in Laos — U.S. Troops Ordered to Thailand — Refugees From China — Agreement for Coalition Government in Laos — Geneva Conference on Laos — Drop in China's Trade with Soviets — Indian-Chinese Border War — Cuban Missile Crisis — Aid for India — Sino-Soviet Polemics Over Cuba and India — Kennedy on U.S. Actions in Vietnam.

Kennedy on Laos. On Jan. 15 President Kennedy was asked during a press conference if the U.S. were taking a chance in supporting a coalition type of government in Laos. The president replied: ". . .There is no easy, sure answer for Laos, but it is my judgment that it is in the best interests for our country to work for a neutral and independent Laos and we are attempting to do that. I can assure you that I recognize the risks that are involved. But I also think that we should consider the risks if we fail, particularly of the possibility of escalation of military struggle in a place of danger."

Laotian Agreement. On Jan. 19 the three princes representing the rightist, neutralist and leftist factions in Laos announced that they had reached an agreement on formation of a coalition government. The announcement was made by Prince Souvanna Phouma, whose government had collapsed on Dec. 9, 1960, and been replaced by the rightist faction. Souvanna was to become the new premier under the coalition agreement. But on Jan. 25 it was reported that Communist Pathet Lao forces had staged a large attack northwest of Luang Prabang, the royal capital of Laos.

Kennedy's Reaction. On Jan. 31 President Kennedy told a news conference that "if the fighting and hostilities

Third Taiwan Strait Crisis

Following the disastrous harvests in mainland China in 1960 and 1961 and the complete failure of the Great Leap Forward *(see May 5, 1958)*, the Nationalist government on Taiwan began to prepare for its long-awaited invasion of the Chinese mainland. In early 1962 Chiang Kai-shek announced that "we can no longer vacillate or hesitate to perform our duty to deliver our people . . . from catastrophe." The Nationalists began to prepare for the invasion with a troop buildup on the offshore islands, and launched a campaign in the U.S. to induce Washington to support their plans.

According to Roger Hilsman, then director of the Bureau of Intelligence and Research in the State Department, the Nationalist initiative posed real problems for the Kennedy administration: "The dilemma was clear. If the United States encouraged Chiang, and it turned out that the Communist regime was not ready to topple, it would be the Bay of Pigs all over again, only much, much worse. . . . On the other hand, if the Communist regime was really ready to topple and the United States failed to support the Nationalists, the Democrats would stand accused of being the only party in history that lost China twice."*

After much discussion, the administration decided to refuse Chiang's offer politely, and took pains to inform Peking of their decision on June 26, 1962.

---

* Roger Hilsman, *To Move a Nation* (Garden City, New York: Doubleday and Co., 1967), pp. 311-312.

began" in Laos, "the hope of a settlement would substantially diminish." The president cited "the great dangers to both sides in a resumption of hostilities" and added: "We are making every effort to attempt to get an accord before the cease-fire, which appears to be strained somewhat after many months — to try to get an accord before we have a breakdown of the cease-fire."

Laos Discussions Broken Off. On Feb. 2 Prince Boun Oum, rightist premier of the Laotian government, announced that he was breaking off negotiations with the princes representing the neutralist and leftist positions. He said he would boycott the meetings until Communist Pathet Lao troops ceased their attacks.

U.S. in Vietnam Action. On Feb. 4, South Vietnamese troops attacked a Viet Cong-held village in South Vietnam's southern tip and captured three guerrillas. The troops were lifted into the area aboard 15 U.S. Air Force helicopters, manned by U.S. crews.

Kennedy on Vietnam. On Feb. 7 President Kennedy was asked at a news conference how deeply the U.S. was involved in Vietnam. The president replied: "The United States . . . has been assisting Vietnam economically to maintain its independence, viability and also sent training groups out there, which have been expanded in recent weeks, as the attacks on the government and the people of South Vietnam have increased. We are out there on training and transportation, and we are assisting in every way we possibly can the people of South Vietnam, who with the greatest courage and under danger, are attempting to maintain their freedom."

China and Disarmament. On Feb. 14, at a news conference, President Kennedy said the PRC would have to be included in any disarmament agreement among the world powers before the U.S. "would be able to have any confidence in" such an agreement. "I quite recognize the hazards and the difficulties of attempting to bring them in. But if we are making progress . . . it is a question which waits for us before the end of the road is reached."

Glenn's Flight. On Feb. 20 U.S. Marine Lt. Col. John H. Glenn, 40, orbited the earth three times in a Mercury space capsule and was safely recovered in the Atlantic Ocean.

Peking Warns U.S. On Feb. 24 the Chinese Foreign Ministry charged that U.S. action in South Vietnam was "a direct threat" to North Vietnam and therefore "seriously affects the security of China and the peace of Asia." It charged that a recently established military command in South Vietnam was "by no means merely one for military assistance, but an operational command of the United States imperialists for direct participation. . . . The United States is already in an undeclared war in South Vietnam." Peking urged Britain and the Soviet Union, co-chairmen of the 1954 Geneva Conference, to take "appropriate measures" regarding U.S. intervention in the area. The Soviet Union echoed Chinese sentiments, but the British replied that "The tension in South Vietnam arises directly from the North Vietnamese [effort] . . . to overthrow the established government by force."

The U.S. Defense Department had said on Feb. 9 that "this is a war we can't afford to lose" and that "we're drawing a line" against communist aggression in South Vietnam. *The New York Times* had reported the day before that the U.S. had 5,000 personnel in South Vietnam, mostly on an "adviser" basis. The article pointed out that the 1954 Geneva agreements sought to limit South Vietnam to no more than 685 foreign military advisers and specified amounts of military equipment.

U.S. A-Tests. On March 2 President Kennedy announced that the United States would resume testing nuclear weapons in the atmosphere.

Burmese Coup. On March 2 Burmese Prime Minister U Nu was deposed in a coup led by Defense Minister Gen. Ne Win, who was named prime minister three days later.

Imperialists and Imperialism. On March 7 it was reported from Hong Kong that *Hongqi*, the Chinese Communist Party theoretical journal, had printed an article saying that "unconditional peaceful coexistence" meant "constant concessions toward imperialism," and that it was harmful "not to oppose . . . the policies of war and aggression of the United States and other imperialists." An article in the Peking *People's Daily* declared that the anti-Chinese world movement was perpetrated by "imperialists" and "revisionists."

Training of Vietnamese Pilots. On March 9 the State Department said that American pilots had participated in bombing missions against Communist guerrillas in South Vietnam. The statement said the action was necessary to train the South Vietnamese pilots who accompanied the Americans.

Rusk on Split. On April 5 Secretary of State Dean Rusk testified before the Senate Foreign Relations Committee that there was "considerable evidence of deep differences" between the Soviet Union and China. The secretary said the dispute concerned a "doctrinal debate" between the "hard-line" Chinese and the "peaceful coexistence" theory of the Russians, and that both vied for control of foreign communist parties and influence in underdeveloped nations.

Trade Agreement. On April 20 China and the Soviet Union signed a trade agreement for an undisclosed amount of goods. *The New York Times* three weeks earlier had carried a report from Polish sources that China currently ranked as the Soviet Union's fourth largest trading partner. It had ranked second in 1960, when Sino-Soviet trade totaled 1.5 billion rubles ($1.38 billion).

Indian Warnings to China. On April 23 India notified China that a 1954 trade agreement due to expire June 3 would not be renewed until Chinese forces had withdrawn from traditionally Indian territory. The Indian Minister for External Affairs, Mrs. Lakshi Menon, had told the Indian Parliament on April 19 that the Chinese had been warned of "grave consequences" if they "persist in their systematic and deliberate encroachments into Indian territory."

Chinese-Cuban Agreement. On April 26 China and Cuba signed a one-year trade agreement providing for Chinese shipments to Cuba of 134,000 tons of food, machinery, and medicine in exchange for 1,120,000 tons of sugar, nickel, copper, tobacco and canned fruits.

China Tallies U.S. "Intrusions." On April 27 Peking said: "During the past 15 months of the Kennedy administration the record of United States intrusions into China's territorial waters and airspace is 52 warships on 40 occasions and 64 sorties by United States aircraft. The criminal violation of China's sovereignty by United States imperialism has further laid bare the piratical nature of the Kennedy administration." It was "more obsessed and malignant" than the Eisenhower administration in "pursuing an aggressive policy which is stubbornly hostile to the Chinese people."

Pathet Lao Attacks. On May 3 the Communist Pathet Lao launched an offensive in northwestern Laos, utilizing about four battalions with support from two battalions of North Vietnamese troops. On May 6 the Pathet Lao captured Nam Tha, the northwestern provincial capital.

Troops to Thailand. On May 15 President Kennedy ordered an immediate buildup of U.S. troops in Thailand to a total of 5,000 and said the move was "considered desirable because of recent attacks in Laos by Communist forces, and the subsequent movements of Communist military units toward the border of Thailand." Kennedy emphasized that "this is a defensive act."

Prior to the president's order, 1,000 troops were in Thailand — retained there after recent maneuvers by SEATO forces. On May 16, U.S. jet bombers landed in Bangkok to spearhead ground and air forces, and on May 17 a task force of 1,800 Marines arrived. On May 10 a carrier task force of the U.S. Seventh Fleet had been ordered into the Gulf of Siam, off Thailand and Cambodia.

Kennedy on Food for China. On May 23 President Kennedy, questioned on the prospects of a Food for Peace program for mainland China, commented: "There has been no indication of any expression of interest or desire by the Chinese Communists to receive any food from us as I have said from the beginning, and we would certainly have to have some idea as to whether the food was needed and

under what conditions it might be distributed. Up to the present, we have no such indications."

Refugees From China. On May 23 President Kennedy announced that the U.S. would admit, under special provisions of the McCarran-Walter Act, "several thousand" Chinese refugees in the Hong Kong area who had been previously cleared by consular officials but could not enter the U.S. because the immigration quota for Chinese nationals was limited to 100 a year. The refugees were to be allowed to enter under the same McCarran-Walter provision as that utilized for admission of Hungarian refugees in 1956 and more recently of Cuban refugees. Preference would be given to those with technical skills in greatest demand or with family ties in the U.S. The president said that admission of some refugees to the U.S. and the continued availability of U.S. food for about half a million Hong Kong refugees would not eliminate "the basic problem which is that of a tremendous country, 650 million people, where food supplies are inadequate."

New Laotian Offensive. On May 26 the Communist-led Pathet Lao rebels launched another offensive in southern and northwestern Laos, in what was described by U.S. military advisers as a "concentrated assault" led by North Vietnamese units. It was reported that loyal government forces in the northwest had been forced for the second time to flee into Thailand. In Washington the same day, Kennedy administration spokesmen confirmed reports that American officials had reproached Laotian government leaders for refusing to negotiate with the Pathet Lao and the neutralist faction on formation of a coalition government.

Sino-Indian Dispute. On May 31 India protested to China that proposed negotiations between China and Pakistan over the Kashmir border formed a part of China's "aggressive designs" against Indian territory. India asserted that Pakistan had no right to negotiate a Kashmir border agreement because Kashmir belonged to India. The Chinese replied that India was pursuing a policy of "out-and-out great power chauvinism." On June 2 India announced it would not renew its trade agreement with Tibet because of China's refusal to discuss Indian-Tibetan border problems.

Laotian Agreement. On June 11 Laos neutralist Prince Souvanna Phouma announced that Prince Boun Oum, the current premier, and Prince Souphanouvong of the Pathet Lao pro-communist guerrillas had joined him in signing an agreement establishing a coalition Cabinet to rule the nation. Of the 19 Cabinet appointees, 11 were neutralists, four rightists, and four Pathet Lao.

Soviet Premier Khrushchev June 12 cabled President Kennedy that the agreement was "good news" for Laos. He said it strengthened the conviction that other international problems could be resolved by "cooperation with mutual account of the interests of all sides." In a June 13 note to Khrushchev, President Kennedy said he shared the view that the agreement was "encouraging." He said "continued progress in the settlement of the Laotian problem" could be helpful in leading toward resolution of other international problems.

3rd Taiwan Strait Crisis. On June 20, following a Nationalist build up on the offshore islands, the Chinese Communists were reported massing troops and military equipment, including aircraft, on the mainland opposite Quemoy and Matsu Islands. *(Map, p. 105)* On the same day, White House press secretary Pierre Salinger admitted the Chinese buildup was causing some concern.

On June 23 Peking admitted its military buildup and alerted the country for an invasion from Taiwan. On June 24 Under Secretary of State George W. Ball warned China that it would suffer "extremely costly" consequences if it attacked any of the offshore islands. On June 25 Chinese Foreign Minister Chen Yi said China was "watching vigilantly" for a "large-scale military adventure involving the invasion of the coastal areas of the mainland" by U.S. and Nationalist forces. Radio reports from the mainland indicated that the Communists had mobilized the peasants and city workers "to go into action" at any time. *(Box, p. 129)*

New Laotian Government. On June 22 the new coalition government of Laos was formally installed. The new premier, Prince Souvanna Phouma, declared that the coalition was "resolved to follow the way of peace and neutrality in conformity with the interests . . . of the Laotian people." He added that it was pledged "not to permit the establishment of any foreign military bases on Laotian territory and not to permit any country to use Laotian territory for military means."

U.S. Assures Peking. On June 26 the U.S. ambassador to Warsaw was secretly instructed to inform his Chinese counterpart that there would be no U.S. support for "any Nationalist attempt to invade the mainland."

U.S. Warning to Peking. On June 27 President Kennedy told newsmen that the U.S. would "take the action necessary to assure the defense of Taiwan and the Pescadores" provided for in the 1955 congressional "Formosa resolution" if China were to take "aggressive action against" Quemoy and Matsu. Kennedy said that "any threat to the offshore islands must be judged in relation to its wider meaning for the safety of Formosa [Taiwan] and the peace of the area."

Troop Withdrawal in Thailand. On July 1 the Defense Department announced that President Kennedy had ordered withdrawal of 1,000 Marines from Thailand. On July 3 Prince Souphanouvong, leader of the pro-Communist Pathet Lao in Laos, demanded that the remainder of U.S. troops leave Thailand.

Soviet Warning to U.S. On July 2 Soviet Premier Nikita Khrushchev warned during a television broadcast from Moscow that "anyone who dares to attack" China "will meet a crushing rebuff from the great Chinese people, the peoples of the Soviet Union and the whole Socialist camp." He said this was "not the first time the imperialists are trying to test the power of . . . Soviet-Chinese friendship." On the same day, Secretary of State Dean Rusk called Khrushchev's statements "nonsense." He said the U.S., instead of being "aggressive," had urged the "abandonment of force in settling matters in the Formosan [Taiwan] Strait."

Laos Conference Ends. On July 23 the 14-nation Geneva Conference on Laos, which had begun May 16, 1961, ended with the signing of an agreement to guarantee that country's neutrality and independence. The final ceremonies in Geneva were attended by Secretary of State Dean Rusk, Soviet Foreign Minister Gromyko, British Foreign Secretary Lord Home, Chinese Foreign Minister Chen Yi, and representatives from Thailand, Burma, Cambodia, India, South Vietnam, North Vietnam, Canada, Poland, France and Laos.

U-2 in North Pacific. On Sept. 2 the Soviet Union charged that a U.S. reconnaissance aircraft had flown over the Soviet island of Sakhalin in the northern Pacific. The U.S. admitted that the violation might have occurred but said it was unintentional.

Chinese-Laotian Relations. On Sept. 7 it was announced that Laos and China had established diplomatic relations. Nationalist China severed relations with Laos the same day.

U-2 Over China. On Sept. 9 China shot down a "U.S.-made U-2 high-altitude reconnaissance plane" flown by the Nationalists.

Sino-Soviet Trade Drops. On Sept. 20, *The New York Times* reported that Soviet-Chinese trade in 1961 fell almost 50 percent below the 1960 level to the lowest since 1951. "While Soviet exports to China last year declined from more than $800 million to $360 million, Chinese exports to the Soviet Union declined by only a little more than a third from $840 million to $540 million. . . . These figures seem to indicate that Moscow has been putting pressure on the Chinese to repay their debts to the Soviet Union."

Soviet Consulates Closed. On Sept. 26 *The New York Times* reported that the Soviet Union had closed its last two consulates in China, at Shanghai and Harbin.

Chou on China's Struggle. On Sept. 30, on the eve of the China's National Day, Premier Chou En-lai said at a reception in Peking that "Socialist construction work of the Chinese people has not been plain sailing." He pointed out that "serious natural disasters for three consecutive years, from 1959 to 1961, and shortcomings and mistakes in work have indeed caused difficulties," but he insisted that "a preliminary foundation has been laid for an independent, comprehensive and modern national economy."

Chinese National Day. On Oct. 1 China celebrated its 13th National Day with an enormous parade in Peking, attended by Communist Party Chairman Mao Tse-tung and other leaders. Foreign officials, including Soviet leaders, were noticeably absent. Chinese Foreign Minister Chen Yi told the crowd that "We are still confronted with many difficulties . . . yet the most difficult period has already passed."

U.S. Out of Laos. On Oct. 5 the U.S. withdrew its remaining military advisers from Laos, one day before the deadline.

Troops to Leave. On Oct. 9 the State Department announced that the 3,000 U.S. troops remaining in Thailand would be withdrawn.

Wheat to China. On Oct. 10 Australia announced it had agreed to sell 670,000 tons of wheat to China.

Chinese-Indian Fighting. On Oct. 10 serious fighting broke out between Chinese and Indian troops near the Indian outpost of Dhola on the northeastern frontier. At least six Indians and 22 Chinese were killed in a battle that lasted 12 hours.

French Sales to China. On Oct. 13 France announced it was selling surplus cereals to China.

Sino-Indian War. On Oct. 20 the mounting tension between China and India erupted into war as the Chinese opened an offensive that drove Indian forces back in the northeast and also in the Ladakh section of Kashmir. The Chinese offensive followed six months of Indian buildups on the disputed borders, and was probably triggered by the prospect of additional buildups promised by Nehru on Oct. 12. During the fighting, which lasted until Oct. 27, the Indian troops did poorly. Inadequately supplied and not reinforced, entire units were decimated.

U.S. Reaction. On Oct. 21 the State Department said the U.S. was "shocked at the violent and aggressive action of the Chinese Communists against India." It added that "our sympathy is with India as it seeks to meet this unprincipled challenge to its national authority." A State Department official said that any Indian request for aid would be "considered sympathetically." Surprisingly, the U.S. statement was not followed by any support from the various Third World nations of which India had been considered the leader. Nehru's reckless handling of the Sino-Indian dispute, in addition to his appeal for U.S. assistance, is generally considered to have marked the end not only of India's undisputed leadership of the Third World but of Nehru's dominance of Indian politics.

Cuban Missile Crisis. On Oct. 22 President Kennedy announced in a nationwide television and radio address that the U.S. had learned that the Soviet Union was establishing medium-range missile bases in Cuba. "To halt this offensive buildup," the president said, "a strict quarantine of all offensive military equipment under shipment to Cuba is being initiated." Kennedy warned that the U.S. would "regard any nuclear missile launched from Cuba against any nation in the Western Hemisphere as an attack by the Soviet Union on the United States requiring a full retaliatory response upon the Soviet Union."

On Oct. 23 the Soviet Union rejected Kennedy's warning and declared that aggressive action by the United States toward Cuba or its sea lanes to the Soviet Union might bring thermonuclear war. On the same day, the Organization of American States adopted a U.S.-sponsored resolution by a vote of 19-0 authorizing the use of force in blockading Soviet weapons en route to Cuba.

On the same day, Cuban Premier Fidel Castro called the blockade "a violation against the sovereign rights of our country and all the peoples" and a prelude to "direct military intervention" in Cuba. On Oct. 24 China called the blockade "flagrant piracy" and urged that all communist nations unify against "this most serious menace."

On Oct. 24 the blockade, established by a proclamation signed by President Kennedy Oct. 23, went into effect. The proclamation blamed China as well as the Soviet Union for the Cuban crisis. It said that world peace and the security of the Western Hemisphere were "endangered by reason of the establishment by the Sino-Soviet powers of an offensive military capability in Cuba." *(See Oct. 28)*

Chinese Proposal. On Oct. 24 China proposed that Indian Prime Minister Nehru and Chinese Premier Chou En-lai meet to settle the border dispute between their countries. The Chinese proposal called for a cease-fire and withdrawal of the forces of both sides a distance of 12 miles from the "line of actual control," India called the offer "a deceptive device that can fool nobody." It demanded withdrawal of Chinese troops from Indian-claimed territory prior to any conference.

On Oct. 26 the Soviet Union termed China's proposal "a display of sincere concern over relations with India and a desire to end the conflict." The statement said the "imperialists dream of inciting these two great powers to quarreling

and also to disrupt the friendship of the Soviet Union with fraternal China and with friendly India."

Indian Plea for Aid. On Oct. 26 India declared a state of emergency and appealed to the U.S., Britain, France and Canada for military aid. All four countries immediately responded affirmatively.

Chinese Charge. On Oct. 26 the Peking *People's Daily* said Nehru was attempting to establish an Indian sphere of influence in Asia that "would far surpass that of the colonialist system formerly set up in Asia by the British Empire."

Missile Crisis Ends. On Oct. 28 Soviet Premier Khrushchev announced that he had ordered the dismantling of Cuban missile bases and withdrawal of Soviet missiles from Cuba. President Kennedy called the action, amounting to compliance with his demands, a "statesmanlike decision" and an "important and constructive contribution to peace."

Aid for India. On Oct. 29 Indian Prime Minister Nehru made a direct appeal to the U.S. for arms and military equipment to use in the struggle with China. On the same day, U.S. Ambassador to India John Kenneth Galbraith informed Nehru that the U.S. would airlift infantry weapons to India as quickly as possible and said that heavier weapons would follow if needed. On the same day, British Prime Minister Harold Macmillan told the House of Commons that Britain would be willing to supply India with any military aid needed to combat China's "brutal and ruthless pressure."

China and the U.N. On Oct. 30 the U.N. General Assembly voted 56 to 42 with 12 abstentions to reject a Soviet resolution for Communist China's admission to and Nationalist China's removal from the United Nations. U.S. ambassador to the U.N. Adlai E. Stevenson had asserted Oct. 22 that China's "naked aggression" against India was proof of its "scorn" for the U.N. Charter. India, however, argued that China should be admitted to the U.N., where it would be open to the "views and discipline" of the organization.

Chinese on Cuba. On Oct. 31 the Peking *People's Daily* charged indirectly that Soviet Premier Khrushchev had surrendered to the "U.S. imperialist attempt to browbeat the people of the world into retreat at the expense of Cuba."

Indian Communists. On Nov. 1 the Indian Communist Party's National Council adopted a resolution appealing to "all sections of the Indian people to unite in defense of the motherland against Chinese aggression" and supporting Prime Minister Nehru's "stirring appeal for national unity in defense of the country."

U.S. Arms. On Nov. 3 the first planeload of U.S. small arms arrived in India. Within three days, one U.S. plane was landing every three hours.

Midterm Elections. On Nov. 6 the Democratic Party retained heavy majorities in both chambers of the U.S. Congress and among the nation's governors. Most observers believed that the Democratic victory resulted in part from President Kennedy's handling of the Cuban missile crisis.

Airlift to India Ends. On Nov. 10 the State Department announced that the arms airlift to India had been completed. Chinese troops were reported to have seized

3,000 square miles of the Ladakh territory since fighting broke out in Oct. 20 — adding it to 12,000 square miles taken since 1957.

Sino-Japanese Trade. On Nov. 11 China and Japan signed an unofficial memorandum trade agreement by which the two countries resumed regular trade relations. This informal agreement remained in effect until Tokyo and Peking opened full diplomatic relations in 1975. *(See Dec. 1, 1962)*

More Fighting in India. On Nov. 14, Nehru's birthday, Indian troops opened an offensive against the Chinese. This was quickly defeated, and a Chinese counteroffensive launched. Once again, the poorly led and poorly supplied Indian troops disintegrated. The Chinese had cleared all the disputed territory of Indian troops by Nov. 20.

Chinese Assail Revisionists. On Nov. 16 the Peking *People's Daily* and other leading Chinese newspapers launched a campaign against "modern revisionists [i.e. Khrushchev]," who, they said, had bowed to U.S. pressure in Cuba and thereby betrayed Marxist principles. The newspaper said it was "nonsense" that "peace had been saved" by the withdrawal of Soviet missiles from Cuba.

Soviet Reply. On Nov. 18 *Pravda* condemned Khrushchev's critics within the Communist bloc for "pushing mankind toward thermonuclear war." It said the Albanian (and by implication Chinese) leaders had undertaken "an especially shameful ... and provocative campaign in connection with the crisis in the Caribbean." However, "neither bourgeois propagandists nor other falsifiers" with their "unlimited slander" could detract from Khrushchev's contribution to peace.

India Asks More Aid. On Nov. 19 Indian Prime Minister Nehru, in a letter to President Kennedy, detailed the state of India's defenses and appealed for a "massive" U.S. military aid program, including a request for the transfer of 15 fighter squadrons. One U.S. aircraft carrier began to move, but the rest of the request was denied.

Cuban Blockade Ended. On Nov. 20 President Kennedy announced that the Soviet Union had agreed to withdraw its Il-28 jet bombers from Cuban bases, and that consequently he had instructed the Secretary of Defense to "lift our naval quarantine" of Cuba.

Chinese Cease-Fire. On Nov. 21 the Chinese government announced a unilateral cease-fire and withdrawal to begin at midnight of the same day. The announcement said: "Chinese frontier guards will withdraw to positions 20 kilometers [12.5 miles] behind the lines of actual control which existed between China and India on Nov. 7, 1959." The statement concluded that China was willing to negotiate "provided that the Indian government agrees to take corresponding measures." *(See Oct. 24.)*

What had been taken to be a Chinese invasion was thus, in fact, only a punitive expedition.

China-Japan Trade Agreement. On Dec. 1 Japan signed an unofficial five-year trade agreement with China providing for an exchange of $50 million worth of goods during 1963.

Nehru Rejects China Offer. On Dec. 1 Indian Prime Minister Nehru formally rejected China's proposal for negotiating a settlement of the border dispute between the two countries. On the same day, China began to withdraw its troops "in accordance" with its own cease-fire proposal.

China-Laos Agreement. On Dec. 4 China announced that it had made a long-term loan to Laos for industrial construction and would build a road from China to Laos.

Vietnam Situation. On Dec. 12 President Kennedy, asked at a press conference for an assessment of the situation in Vietnam, replied: The U.S. is "putting in a major effort in Vietnam.... We have about 10 or 11 times as many men there as we had a year ago. We have had a number of casualties. We put in an awful lot of equipment.... In some phases, the military program has been quite successful. There is great difficulty, however, in fighting a guerrilla war. You need 10 to one, or 11 to one, especially in terrain as difficult as South Vietnam. So we don't see the end of the tunnel, but I must say I don't think it is darker than it was a year ago, and in some ways lighter."

Khrushchev Objects to China's Criticism. On Dec. 12 Soviet Premier Nikita S. Khrushchev denounced the Chinese for criticizing Soviet Cuban policies. It was believed to be the first time a high-ranking Soviet official had publicly assailed the Chinese position on Cuba. Addressing the Supreme Soviet in Moscow, Khrushchev said: "In what way have we retreated, one may ask. Socialist Cuba exists. Cuba remains a beacon of Marxist-Leninist ideas in the Western Hemisphere. The impact of her revolutionary example will grow. The ... United States has given a pledge not to invade Cuba. The threat of thermonuclear war has been averted. Is this a retreat?" Khrushchev warned that the world was living above a "mined cellar full of nuclear weapons" and that those who brand imperialism as a "paper tiger" (as had the Chinese) should remember that "the paper tiger has nuclear teeth."

Colombo Peace Effort. On Dec. 12 a conference of six neutral nations — Ceylon, Burma, Cambodia, Ghana, Indonesia and the United Arab Republic — which had met in Colombo, Ceylon, to try to settle the Indian-Chinese border dispute, announced agreement on proposals to bring the two nations together for "negotiations to consolidate the cease-fire and settle the boundary dispute between them." Although both China and India announced their acceptance of the proposals, they were never implemented.

Tito in Russia. On Dec. 13 Yugoslav President Tito, in the Soviet Union on a "holiday," told the Supreme Soviet in Moscow that during the Cuban crisis Soviet Premier Khrushchev had acted "bravely at the most critical moment, taking into account the interests of all humanity and showing the farsightedness of real statesmen." Referring to Chinese criticism of Soviet Cuban policy, Tito stated: "Unfortunately there are strange views about this policy ... which are dangerous, as they might lead certain circles to a false assessment of the motive for this wise and peace-loving action. I think that it is shortsightedness to consider these actions as a sign of weakness."

China Accuses Soviet Leaders. On Dec. 15 an article in the *People's Daily*, reportedly written by Mao Tse-tung, said the Soviet Union had been "scared out of its wits" during the Cuban missile crisis. Soviet leaders were denounced for neutralism in the Chinese-Indian border dispute and for recent friendly relations with the "Tito clique" in Yugoslavia.

The article further accused the Soviet Union of following a policy of "moderation" and making "sensible compromises" with the "saber-rattling enemy" while refusing "to be conciliatory toward fraternal parties and fraternal countries." It declared that "No matter how the imperialists, the reactionaries and the modern revisionists may abuse and oppose us, our stand in upholding Marxism-Leninism and truth is absolutely unshakable."

Sino-Mongolian Boundary Treaty. On Dec. 16 China and Mongolia signed an agreement delineating their 2,500-mile border. The agreement was extremely favorable to Mongolia, and represented a Chinese effort to woo Ulan Bator away from Moscow. On Dec. 25, after signing a border agreement with China, the Premier of Outer Mongolia, Yumzhagiin Tsedenbal, said at a banquet in Peking that international disagreements should be solved "exclusively by peaceful means and negotiations." He urged the "continuous consolidation of the unity and solidarity of the Socialist camp, the guarantee for safeguarding world peace and preventing world thermonuclear war," a forceful affirmation of Outer Mongolia's support for Moscow's position in the Sino-Soviet dispute.

Pakistan-China Agreement. On Dec. 26 China and Pakistan announced "complete agreement in principle in regard to the alignment of the common border of the China-Xinjiang contiguous area, the defense of which is the responsibility of Pakistan." The treaty constituted Chinese recognition of Pakistan's control over the Kashmir, which was still being disputed between Pakistan and India. *(See March 2, 1963.)*

Wheat Agreement. On Dec. 28 Australia announced it would sell 50 million more bushels of wheat to China. The following day, *The Washington Post* reported: "The sale would bring total Australian wheat sales to Communist China since December 1960 to about 190 million bushels — 45 million bushels for cash and the balance on terms."

Nationalist Guerrilla Action. On Dec. 31 Peking radio announced that nine groups of Nationalist Chinese guerrillas had raided the Chinese mainland since October, but that all of them had been exterminated. The broadcast asserted that the guerrillas had operated "under the direct planning and organization of U.S. espionage organizations." On the same day, Nationalist China admitted there had been guerrilla raids supported by U.S. arms, but insisted that American personnel had not been involved.

Chinese Views. On Dec. 31 the Peking *People's Daily* published a long article in answer to Soviet Premier Khrushchev's Dec. 12 speech to the Supreme Soviet. The article said that peaceful coexistence between socialist and capitalist countries was "inconceivable without struggle," that thermonuclear war "would result in the extinction of imperialism and definitely not in the extinction of mankind," and that disarmament would be possible only when "socialist nations" had "great nuclear superiority."

1963

Sino-Soviet Feud — Chinese Trade with West — Fighting in Laos — Lodge Appointed Ambassador to South Vietnam — Buddhist Demonstrations — Nuclear Test-Ban Treaty and China's Reaction — Kennedy on China Threat — Chinese Denunciation of Khrushchev — China and Soviet Nuclear Aid — Chou on A-Bomb — Kennedy: "It's Their War" — Peking's Charges of Soviet Subversion in Xinjiang — Moscow's Charges of Chinese Border Violations — McNamara-Taylor on Duration of Vietnam War — Overthrow and Death of Diem — Assassination of President Kennedy — Hilsman Speech on U.S. China Policy.

Vietnam Casualties. On Jan. 2 five U.S. helicopters transporting South Vietnamese troops in the Mekong River delta area were shot down by Viet Cong gunfire. Fourteen of the 15 helicopters involved in the mission were hit by ground fire. Three American military advisers were killed and 10 wounded, bringing the total of U.S. deaths in Vietnam to 49.

Communist Feud: Soviet Round. On Jan. 15, Chinese and Soviet differences surfaced at the Sixth Congress of the East German Communist Party in East Berlin. The congress was attended by 70 delegations from national communist parties, most of whom sided with Soviet Premier Khrushchev. Walter Ulbricht, First Secretary of the East German Communist Party, denounced China for "unleashing" the "highly unnecessary" India-China border war without consulting or informing the other communist countries.

Communist Feud: Chinese Round. On Jan. 18 the head of the Chinese delegation in East Berlin, Wu Xiuquan, presented Communist China's reply to Khrushchev. According to Jack Altman of Reuters, the only Western newsman allowed to cover the congress, Wu was humiliated by other delegates who periodically silenced him by whistling, shouting, and stamping their feet. Despite the commotion, Wu made the following points:

"More and more people in the world have come to realize that U.S. imperialism is ... the most ferocious enemy of world peace."

"The Chinese Communist Party and the Chinese government have always stood for peaceful coexistence."

"China has consistently sought a fair and reasonable solution of the Indian border dispute through peaceful negotiation.... Confronted with the massive attacks of the Indian forces, China ... on her own initiative ceased fire and withdrew her troops."

Wu concluded that there should be an immediate world communist meeting. There was "danger of a split" if it did not occur.

Vietnam Report. On Feb. 24 a report on U.S. aid to Southeast Asia, requested by President Kennedy in 1962, was submitted to the Senate Foreign Relations Committee by a four-man panel headed by Senate Majority Leader Mike Mansfield, Mont. The report concluded that "there is no interest of the United States in Vietnam which would justify, in present circumstances, the conversion of the war ... primarily into an American war to be fought primarily with American lives."

New Chinese Attack on Soviets. On Feb. 27 China gave a new twist to its attacks on the Soviet bloc. The *People's Daily* accused the Soviet Union of "disregarding international practice" by "perfidiously and unilaterally" tearing up "hundreds of agreements and contracts they had concluded with a fraternal country [China]."

Russian Pledge. On Feb. 27 Soviet Premier Khrushchev said the Soviet Union desired to live in "peace and friendship with all peoples," but, he added, "if an attack is made on Cuba or on the People's Republic of China, which is being threatened from Taiwan," or on North Korea, North Vietnam, East Germany, "or indeed any Socialist country, the Soviet Union will come to the assistance of its friends and strike a devastating blow at the aggressors."

Chinese-Pakistani Agreement. On March 2 the foreign ministers of Pakistan and China signed an agreement defining the 300-mile boundary between China's Xinjiang Province and the section of Kashmir controlled by Pakistan but claimed by India. India immediately protested the agreement.

Chinese Trade With West. On March 14 the West German Chamber of Commerce announced that a Chinese trade delegation was negotiating with two West German steel and engineering concerns. The statement said China had been seeking contracts with the West since the Soviet Union had withdrawn its technicians from China.

On March 21 a Chinese trade delegation arrived in London for a three-week visit at the invitation of the British government. On the same day, the London *Times* reported: "Chinese trade with the Soviet Union and eastern Europe has fallen sharply in the last three years, partly owing to political differences and partly to bad harvests in China, which have seriously affected Chinese industrial plans. This will mean a switch of Chinese trade to Japan and western Europe."

Soviet Invitation. On March 30 the Soviet Communist Party's Central Committee sent a letter to the Central Committee of the Chinese Communist Party turning down China's March 10 invitation to Khrushchev but proposing a high-level meeting between the two countries in Moscow around May 15. The letter reviewed the Soviet position in the current ideological dispute. *(See May 9.)*

Laotian Fighting. On March 30 sporadic fighting broke out in Laos between Communist Pathet Lao forces and those of neutralist Gen. Kong Le, a supporter of the coalition government headed by Premier Souvanna Phouma.

Foreign Minister of Laos Slain. On April 1 the foreign minister of Laos, Quinim Pholsena, was assassinated by one of his own guards, who said later that the foreign minister, who had close connections with the Pathet Lao, had wanted "to overthrow the coalition government."

Prisoner Exchange. On April 2 the Chinese Foreign Ministry announced that all 3,213 Indian soldiers captured during the Chinese-Indian border conflict would be released beginning April 11. The Indian government reciprocated on April 14, returning 800 Chinese troops.

Chinese Visit Indonesia. On April 11 Chinese chief of state Liu Shao-ch'i and Foreign Minister Chen Yi left Peking for a goodwill tour of Southeast Asia. It was Liu's first visit to non-communist nations. On April 12 they arrived in Indonesia and were greeted by President Sukarno as "comrades in arms." Sukarno pledged Indonesian support of China's "just struggle to liberate Taiwan" and to attain its "legitimate rights" in the United Nations.

Liu in Burma. On April 20 Chinese chief of state Liu Shao-ch'i arrived in Burma and in a joint statement with Burmese leaders called for the termination of "outside interference" in Laos.

Sino-Soviet Trade Agreement. On April 20 the Soviet Union and China signed a trade agreement for 1963. The values and quantities involved were not disclosed.

Cease-Fire in Laos. On April 21 Laotian Premier Souvanna Phouma announced that a cease-fire had been arranged between the neutralist and Communist Pathet Lao forces. In the last days of fighting, the Pathet Lao troops had successfully dislodged the neutralists from most of their outposts in the Plaine des Jarres.

Soviet Action. On April 26 the Soviet Union, after a three-hour meeting between Soviet Premier Khrushchev and Under Secretary of State Averell Harriman, announced that it joined the U.S. in support of the 1962 Geneva accords for a neutral and independent Laos.

Liu in Cambodia. On April 27 chief of state Liu Shao-ch'i met with Cambodian leaders and in a joint statement pledged China's support for Cambodia's "fight against foreign imperialism." The statement referred to Cambodia's border disputes with Thailand and South Vietnam.

Buddhist Demonstrations. On May 8, anniversary of the Viet Minh victory over the French in 1954 at Dienbienphu, 9,000 Buddhists demonstrated in the South Vietnamese city of Hue. Troops and police dispersed the demonstrators, and in the process nine people were killed. The demonstrations were to protest an order by South Vietnamese President Ngo Dinh Diem (a Roman Catholic) forbidding Buddhists to display religious signs or parade on the birthday of Buddha (May 8).

Chinese Accept Bid to Moscow. On May 9 Chinese Premier Chou En-lai informed the Soviet ambassador that the Central Committee of the Chinese Communist Party had accepted the March 30 invitation of the Central Committee of the Soviet Communist Party to send a delegation to Moscow to discuss the ideological dispute. The Chinese delegation was to be headed by Deng Xiaoping, general secretary of the party, and Peng Zhen, a member of the Politburo. On May 10 the Peking *People's Daily* attacked the policies of Yugoslavia and the Soviet Union, which it described as "peaceable coexistence and active cooperation" with the West.

Liu in North Vietnam. On May 16 chief of state Liu and North Vietnamese President Ho Chi Minh issued a joint statement denouncing "revisionism, in other words rightist opportunism" as "the principal danger inside the international Communist movement." The statement urged bolstering of the "national defense might of the countries in the socialist camp, including development of a nuclear superiority in the socialist countries," and reaffirmed "the necessity of calling a meeting of representatives of Communist and workers' parties of the whole world to eliminate differences and strengthen unity."

Appeal to Stop Fighting in Laos. On May 23 the International Control Commission on Laos asked the Soviet Union and Great Britain, co-chairmen of the 1962 Geneva conference, to urge the Pathet Lao and neutralist factions in Laos to cease their fighting, which had broken out again on May 14 in the Plaine des Jarres. On May 29 the U.S.S.R. and Britain responded with an appeal to the two factions to end the hostilities and effect "peace, concord, and strict neutrality."

Aid to India. On May 24 an Indian delegation in Washington announced, after a meeting with President Kennedy, that the U.S. had pledged long-term military aid to India for defense against possible renewed attacks by China.

Australian Wheat. On May 31 Australia announced it had sold 46 million bushels of wheat to China, bringing the total of Australian wheat purchased by China since 1960 to 263 million bushels valued at $330 million.

North Korean Visit. On June 6 the North Korean head of state, Choi Yong Kon, arrived in China for a state visit. A joint statement issued later with Chinese chief of state Liu Shao-ch'i asserted that "both sides were completely identical in their stands and views." The statement denounced "modern revisionism" and "United States imperialism."

Kennedy on Ending the Cold War. On June 10, President Kennedy told a commencement audience at American University that it was time for a re-examination of American ideas about the Soviet Union and the Cold War. For the first time since World War II, an American president had raised the possibility of friendship with the Soviets. Clearly a response to earlier Soviet initiatives, Kennedy said that "No government or social system is so evil that its people must be considered as lacking in virtue. As Americans, we find Communism profoundly repugnant. . . . But we can still hail the Russian people for their many achievements." Stressing the good relations which the two nations had enjoyed earlier in the century, the president insisted that the two countries must stop "devoting massive sums of money to weapons that could be better devoted to combat ignorance, poverty and disease."

Kennedy stated that to further the progress towards peace, the U.S. would henceforth stop all atmospheric testing of nuclear weapons, and he asked Moscow to observe the same ban. The Soviets printed the speech in full the next day, a move which usually indicated their agreement.

Chinese Letter to Moscow. On June 14 the Chinese Communist Party's Central Committee, replying to the Soviet letter of March 30, proposed 25 points for discussion at a July 5 meeting in Moscow to discuss Sino-Soviet differences. The letter criticized the Soviet Union for seeking "peaceful coexistence" while ignoring "the revolutionary struggles of the people." It said: "To make no distinction between enemies, friends and ourselves and to entrust the fate of the people and of mankind to collaboration with United States imperialism is to lead the people astray. The events of the last few years have exploded this illusion."

The Chinese asserted that "Certain persons [i.e. Khrushchev] now go so far as to deny the great international significance of anti-imperialist, revolutionary struggles of Asian, African and Latin American peoples . . . and to hold down those struggles." It concluded that "if the imperialists are forced to accept an agreement to ban nuclear weapons, it decidedly will not be because of their love of humanity but because of the pressure of the people of all countries and for the sake of their own vital interests."

Reaction in Moscow. On June 18 the Central Committee of the Soviet Communist Party condemned the Chinese letter and ordered the Soviet press not to print it. Leonid F. Ilyichev, secretary of the Central Committee, reiterated Soviet Premier Khrushchev's policy of peaceful coexistence, but added: "There has never been and can never be any peaceful coexistence of ideologies. As long as antagonistic classes exist, an irreconcilable class struggle has been, is, and will be going on."

On June 21 Khrushchev told the Central Committee that "the leaders of the Communist Party of China had exacerbated in the extreme their differences with the Communist Party of the Soviet Union and the entire Communist movement." He said that "Those who reject the principle of peaceful coexistence of states with different social systems, the principle of peaceful competition, show they do not have faith in the revolutionary strength of the working class, in the mighty power of the ideas of Marxism-Leninism."

Lodge Appointed. On June 27 President Kennedy announced appointment of Henry Cabot Lodge Jr. as ambassador to South Vietnam. Lodge was to replace Frederick E. Nolting Jr.

Sino-Soviet Talks Begin. On July 5 the Moscow talks between representatives of China and the Soviet Union began. The Soviet delegation was headed by Mikhail A. Suslov, secretary of the Central Committee, and the Chinese delegation by Deng Xiaoping, who held the same post in the Chinese party.

Test-Ban Talks. On July 15, talks between the U.S., Great Britain and the Soviet Union on a treaty to limit nuclear tests opened in Moscow.

Chinese on Test Ban. On July 19 an editorial in the Peking *People's Daily* called the nuclear test-ban talks in Moscow a "capitulation in the face of imperialist nuclear blackmail." The editorial noted that Mao Tse-tung had said in 1957 "that mankind will definitely not be destroyed even if the imperialists insist on a nuclear war" and that World War III would "hasten the complete destruction of the world capitalist system."

Sino-Soviet Talks End. On July 21 Moscow and Peking announced in a joint statement that their talks in Moscow had been recessed the day before and were scheduled to continue "at some later time." The statement said the two delegations had failed to reach any agreement except to recess.

Test-Ban Treaty. On July 25, representatives of the Soviet Union, Great Britain and the U.S. initialed a treaty prohibiting nuclear tests in the atmosphere, in outer space, and underwater. On the following day, President Kennedy described the action as a "victory for mankind" and "a shaft of light into the dark threat of thermonuclear war."

Border Dispute. On July 26 the Indian Foreign Ministry announced that Chinese troops had re-entered areas on the Chinese-Indian border abandoned after the 1962 invasion. The announcement followed a long exchange of charges between the two countries concerning border violations. On July 28 Peking radio denied the Indian charges. Indian Prime Minister Nehru told a mass meeting two days later that "the Chinese intentions in their present military buildup in Tibet are obviously not good."

Harriman on Test-Ban Treaty. On July 27 Under Secretary of State W. Averell Harriman, who represented the U.S. at the test-ban treaty negotiations, returned from Moscow, reported to the president, and then told reporters that it was "fairly plain" that Soviet Premier Khrushchev had desired the treaty because he "wanted to show . . . the Chinese that his policy of coexistence could produce some results." Harriman said he also thought that "the Soviet people want to have relief from tensions."

Chinese Reaction to Test Ban. On July 31 a statement by the Chinese government termed the treaty "a big fraud to fool the people of the world." The statement went on to say that "The people of the world demand a genuine peace; this treaty provides them with a fake peace." The Chinese government concluded with a demand for a conference of world leaders "to discuss the question of complete prohibition and thorough destruction of nuclear weapons," and said that it would not sign any agreement which resulted from negotiations in which it had not been allowed to participate.

Kennedy on the China Threat. On Aug. 1 President Kennedy was asked at a news conference to appraise the power and the threat of China. He said that China, with its 700 million people, with a "Stalinist internal regime," with its determination for war "as a means of bringing about its ultimate success," and with its future potential as a nuclear power, might present in the next decade a "potentially more dangerous situation than any we faced since the end of the second war."

Canadian Wheat. On Aug. 2 Canada announced it had agreed on another sale of wheat to China. The new agreement provided for shipment of from three million to five million long tons of wheat over a three-year period.

Soviets Condemn China. On Aug. 3 the Soviet Union countered China's July 31 attack on the nuclear test-ban treaty with a statement denouncing the Chinese for "trying to cover up their refusal to sign a nuclear test-ban treaty." It said: "Trying to discredit . . . the assured success in the struggle for diminishing the war danger, to vilify the peace-loving foreign policy of the Soviet Union, the leaders of China have shown . . . that their policy leads to the aggravation of international tensions, to the further stepping up of the nuclear arms race, to the still further expansion of its scope and scale. This position is tantamount to actual connivance with those who advocate world thermonuclear war."

Nuclear Treaty Signed. On Aug. 5, the treaty to ban nuclear tests in the atmosphere, outer space, and underwater was signed in Moscow by U.S. Secretary of State Dean Rusk, Soviet Minister of Foreign Affairs Andrei A. Gromyko, and British Foreign Secretary Lord Home. President Kennedy Aug. 8 submitted the treaty to the Senate for approval. In an accompanying message the president said the treaty would "assure the security of the United States better than continued unlimited testing on both sides." The Senate ratified the treaty Sept. 24, 1963.

France and China had refused to sign the treaty.

Chou's Message to Hiroshima. On Aug. 6 Chinese Premier Chou En-lai said in a message to the World Conference Against Nuclear Weapons, meeting in Hiroshima, Japan, that "the danger of nuclear war, instead of being reduced, has increased." Chou declared: "Only by completely, thoroughly, totally, and resolutely prohibiting and destroying nuclear weapons and by taking effective measures agreed upon by all can the threat of nuclear war be removed."

Japanese Plant for China. On Aug. 20 the Japanese government approved a contract for the construction in China of a $20 million synthetic textile plant by a private Japanese company.

"Hot Line" Established. On Sept. 1 the U.S. and the U.S.S.R. opened the "hot line," a direct telephone link between Washington and Moscow.

Kennedy on Vietnam War. On Sept. 2 President Kennedy, discussing the Vietnam war in a television interview, said: "In the final analysis, it's their war. They are the ones who have to win it or lose it. We can help them, give them equipment, send our men out there as advisers, but they have to win it, the people of Vietnam against the Communists." Kennedy, emphasizing that victory depended on popular support, said that in his opinion the Diem government had "gotten out of touch with the people." He thought it might regain popular support by

"changes in policy and perhaps . . . personnel." Most sources interpreted the president's remarks as an invitation to Diem to oust his brother, Ngo Dinh Nhu, and Mme. Nhu, from positions of power.

Trouble in Xinjiang. On Sept. 6, Moscow dispatches said that China's charges of subversion in Xinjiang confirmed reports that around 50,000 Kazakh nomads had fled from that province of China into the Soviet Union because of hunger and religious persecution. Hong Kong dispatches said travelers arriving from Xinjiang had reported that Kazakh tribesmen staged an uprising there and appealed to the Soviet Union for arms to fight their Chinese overlords.

The New York Times on Sept. 7 called the incident in Xinjiang "clearly the most delicate matter yet raised in the [Sino-Soviet] dispute." It explained: "Xinjiang is one of China's colonial possessions and its predominantly Moslem peoples . . . are no more Chinese than the people of Tibet. Anti-Chinese feeling and revolutionary activity in Xinjiang have ancient historical roots. Under both the czars and the commissars, Russia has often intervened in this area during the past century. . . . There is substantial evidence indicating that Stalin's long-term goal was to absorb Sinkiang into the Soviet Union."

China on Sino-Soviet Split. On Sept. 6 the Peking *People's Daily* and the Communist Party theoretical journal *Hongqi* published the first installment of what would eventually be a nine-part Chinese "white paper" on the origins and development of the Sino-Soviet split. These articles placed the blame for the split on the Soviets, and traced the origin of the problem to Khrushchev's "secret speech" at the 20th Soviet Party Congress *(see Feb. 14, 1956).* Since that time, the article continued, the Soviet leaders tried to force other communist parties to follow Moscow's lead in attacking Stalin. The Chinese resisted this trend and thus were criticized and pressured by the Soviet Union. The article concluded that the result has been to produce a serious, but not yet irreparable split in the Socialist camp. The series ran until July 13, 1964.

Liu's Statement. On Sept. 15 Chinese chief of state Liu Shao-ch'i arrived in North Korea for a state visit. He criticized the belief of Soviet leaders that "the philosophy of survival has replaced the revolutionary theories of Marxism-Leninism" and added that "what really counts is the people . . . the decisive factor in war is man, not one or two weapons of a new type."

Russia Charges Border Violations. On Sept. 21 the Soviet government, in an article in *Izvestia*, defended the nuclear test-ban treaty and denounced the Chinese position as "a complete apostasy from the common, collectively formulated line of the Communist movement." In addition, the article charged that the Chinese had "systematically" violated the Sino-Soviet border since 1960. It said that 5,000 violations were reported in 1962 and that "there have even been attempts in the most flagrant manner to appropriate individual sections of Soviet territory." A "decisive rebuff" was threatened if China continued its "hostile activities."

North Korean Statement. On Sept. 27 Chinese chief of state Liu Shao-ch'i and North Korean President Choi Yong Kon issued a joint statement at the completion of Liu's two-week visit to North Korea. The statement affirmed a "complete identity of views" on all policy matters and noted the common opposition of the two countries to the policies of the Soviet Union.

French-Chinese Relations. On Sept. 28 a French economic mission arrived in Peking. Visits by various French officials followed, and the French press reported that China's leaders were openly encouraging France to recognize the Peking regime.

Vietnam Prediction. On Oct. 2 Secretary of Defense Robert S. McNamara and Chairman of the Joint Chiefs of Staff Maxwell D. Taylor reported to President Kennedy on their return from an eight-day visit to South Vietnam. Later that day, a White House statement said that "Secretary McNamara and Gen. Taylor reported their judgment that the major part of the U.S. military task [in Vietnam] can be completed by the end of 1965, although there may be a continuing requirement for a limited number of . . . training personnel."

Kennedy on Diem Regime. On Oct. 9 President Kennedy told his news conference that he saw no improvement in the Diem regime since his Sept. 2 remarks on television suggesting that "changes in policy and personnel" were necessary. "I think we are still dealing with the same problems we were dealing with a month ago," he said.

Chou on Pact with Soviets. On Oct. 11 Chinese Premier Chou En-lai told a reporter for Reuters that the Soviet-Chinese treaty of friendship and alliance was still in effect despite the ideological differences between the two countries. "If any act of aggression occurs against any socialist country," he said, "this would be an act of aggression against the whole socialist camp. It would be impossible not to give support. If a country refused to give support, it would not be a socialist country." Chou had declared earlier that a diplomatic break between the Soviet Union and China was impossible.

Soviets Denounce Chinese Leaders. On Oct. 24 the Soviet Communist Party's ideological journal *Kommunist* carried an editorial denouncing the leaders of China, who, it said, "want to destroy the international Communist movement and create under their aegis a new movement." It added that "the Communist movement now finds itself threatened by an attempt to replace Leninism with Maoism."

China's Nuclear Program. On Oct. 28 it was reported that Chinese Foreign Minister Chen Yi had told a group of Japanese newsmen in Peking that it would be several years before China began testing nuclear weapons and many years before China could be considered a nuclear power. It was the first public statement by a Peking official concerning China's nuclear program. The foreign minister attributed the lag in China's nuclear program to industrial and technological inadequacies, withdrawal of Soviet technicians from China, and the U.S. economic blockade of the country.

Vietnam Coup. On Nov. 1, in mid-afternoon, military forces headed by Gen. Duong Van Minh moved into Saigon to oust the government of President Ngo Dinh Diem. At the end of an 18-hour battle, Gen. Minh proclaimed the downfall of the regime, establishment of a military caretaker government, suspension of the Constitution, and initiation of a more vigorous campaign against the Viet Cong guerrillas.

President Diem and his brother Ngo Dinh Nhu reportedly fled to a Catholic church outside Saigon where they surrendered to the rebel forces. The victorious military commanders asserted that Diem and Nhu committed "ac-cidental suicide," while other reports said the two brothers were murdered by their captors.

The military junta Nov. 5 announced that Nguyen Ngoc Tho, 55, vice president during the Diem regime, would act as provisional premier pending democratic elections "when the situation permits." A statement by the victorious generals Nov. 2 said: "The armed forces are not aiming at setting up a military dictatorship, because they are well aware that the best weapon to fight communism is democracy and liberty."

U-2 Shot Down. On Nov. 1 Peking radio announced that a high-altitude reconnaissance U-2 plane "of the Chiang Kai-shek bandit gang" was "shot down by the air force" near Shanghai while flying "on a harassing mission." On Nov. 2 the Nationalist Chinese government admitted the loss of a U-2.

Russians on Rift with China. On Nov. 6 Nikolai V. Podgorny, a secretary of the Central Committee of the Soviet Communist Party and a member of the Presidium, said during a speech: "We sincerely want to normalize the relationship with the Chinese People's Republic, the great, industrious and talented Chinese people with whom we are bound in great friendship. There are no objective reasons which could prevent a return to the good relations which existed in the not too distant past between the U.S.S.R. and the C.P.R."

On the same day, Soviet Premier Khrushchev told a group of visiting American businessmen that the dispute with China "causes us deep concern . . . [and] merely causes joy on your part. . . . So let us take the whole matter off the agenda, because it is one that concerns only ourselves and China. We will find a method to discuss this with China, and I do not think that your nose would be quite in place in such a discussion." He added: "You are rejoicing that we are arguing with the Chinese, but the more pleased you feel now, the worse you will feel later on."

New Vietnam Regime. On Nov. 7 the U.S. extended diplomatic recognition to the new provisional government in South Vietnam. Secretary of State Rusk voiced hope that the new regime would "be able to rally the country" against the communists.

Kennedy on China Trade. On Nov. 14 President Kennedy, asked at a press conference what would be the conditions for a resumption of trade with China, said: "We are not planning on trade with Red China in view of the policy that Red China pursues. If the Red Chinese indicate a desire to live at peace with the United States, with other countries surrounding it, then quite obviously the United States would reappraise its policies. We are not wedded to a policy of hostility to Red China. It seems to me Red China's policies are what create the tension between not only the United States and Red China but between Red China and India, between Red China and her immediate neighbors to the south, and even between Red China and other Communist countries."

Cambodia Rejects U.S. Aid. On Nov. 19 Cambodian chief of state Prince Norodom Sihanouk ordered termination of all U.S. military and economic aid to his country. He charged that U.S. military advisers and the CIA had been aiding opponents of his government. The State Department immediately denied that charge. From 1955 through June 30, 1963, the U.S. had given Cambodia about $360 million in economic aid and $86 million in military assistance. Current aid totaled about $30 million a year.

Kennedy Assassinated. On Nov. 22 President John Fitzgerald Kennedy was assassinated in Dallas, Texas, and Vice President Lyndon Baines Johnson was sworn in as his successor. China's press and radio announced the assassination without comment. On Nov. 24 President Johnson said he would follow Kennedy's policies in South Vietnam.

On Nov. 27 Chinese newspapers described Johnson as "a firm supporter of all Kennedy's reactionary policies."

Chilean Copper to China. On Nov. 27 the Chilean government announced it had signed an agreement to sell China 10,000 tons of copper.

Chinese Rice to Indonesia. On Dec. 1 the Indonesian government announced it had signed an agreement to buy from China 40,000 tons of rice to help alleviate food shortages in Indonesia caused by flood and rodent damage.

China and Pakistan. On Dec. 2 the Chinese minister of trade pledged, during a visit to Pakistan, that China would support Pakistan in case of "fresh aggression" by India.

World Communists Support Russia. On Dec. 4, representatives of 80 countries attending a communist-dominated World Peace Council, held in Warsaw, repeatedly rejected pro-Chinese and anti-Soviet resolutions. On Dec. 5 Reuters reported: "The final session was several times postponed while delegates tried to work out a compromise to prevent a split in the movement.... In their bid for leadership of the smaller countries of Asia, Africa and Latin America, the Chinese Communists have called for 'active support' of armed 'revolutionary struggles' particularly in South Vietnam, Laos, Angola, Portuguese Guinea, Venezuela and Guatemala. Asian sources said committee balloting had yielded 27 votes in favor of the broad lines of Soviet policy and five in support of Peking. Voting with the Chinese throughout the meeting were Albania, North Korea, North Vietnam, Indonesia, and the delegate of one of the Japanese peace organizations."

Canadian Wheat Trade. On Dec. 4 the Canadian government announced that China had ordered 18,700,000 bushels of wheat from Canada for $35 million.

Chinese Editorial. On Dec. 4 the Peking *People's Daily* charged that withdrawal from China of Soviet experts and economic aid was responsible for disarrangement of their original economic plan because it happened when China was having "enormous difficulties."

Soviet Editorial. On Dec. 6 the Soviet Communist Party newspaper *Pravda* commented that "the open polemics have gone too far and in many instances overstepped the standards of relations between Communist parties." *Pravda* urged that the dispute be limited to "the normal course of interparty relations."

Sixth Article. On Dec. 11 the Peking *People's Daily* and the Chinese Communist Party's theoretical journal *Hongqi* published their sixth article on the Sino-Soviet split. The article, "Peaceful Coexistence — Two Diametrically Opposed Policies," included a lengthy analysis of "Lenin's and Stalin's policy of peaceful coexistence, which all Marxist-Leninists, including the Chinese Communists, stand for," compared to "the anti-Leninist policy of peaceful coexistence, the so-called general line of peaceful coexistence advocated by Khrushchev and others."

Hilsman's Speech on China. On Dec. 13 Assistant Secretary of State for Far Eastern Affairs Roger Hilsman Jr., addressing the Commonwealth Club of San Francisco, said that the U.S. was "determined to keep the door open to the possibility of change [in China], and not to slam it shut against any developments which might advance our national good, serve the free world, and benefit the people of China."

Hilsman declared that "We have no reason to believe that there is a present likelihood that the Communist regime will be overthrown," but he said there was "some evidence of evolutionary forces at work in mainland China" among the intellectuals and the "more sophisticated second echelon of leadership" which would one day come into power. Hilsman added that U.S. defense of Taiwan was a matter of "basic principle" and there could be no "basic improvement" in U.S.-Chinese relations until China accepted that fact.

Representing, as it did, the first public admission that the U.S. policy of "isolation" had failed to bring down the Peking leadership the speech is often considered an indication that President Kennedy had been contemplating a new U.S. policy toward China. Due to Kennedy's death and the subsequent military buildup in Vietnam, however, this potential new opening was firmly closed, just as the earlier 1949-1950 effort had been blocked by the Korean War. *(See March 16, 1966)*

Chou in Cairo. On Dec. 14 Chinese Premier Chou En-lai, starting a two-month tour of Africa with Foreign Minister Chen Yi, arrived in the United Arab Republic for a six-day visit. He met with U.A.R. President Gamal Abdel Nasser and told a news conference Dec. 20 that he knew nothing of Chinese development of atomic weapons.

On Dec. 21 Chou and Nasser issued a joint statement denouncing "the imperialist policy adopted in the Middle East" and warned against "the threat of such a policy to world peace and security." Nasser supported the Chinese Communist claims to Taiwan, and Chou supported the U.A.R. on the Arab refugee problem.

Soviet Action in U.N. On Dec. 17 the Soviet Union voted against a proposal before the U.N. General Assembly to revise the U.N. charter to enlarge the Security Council and the Economic and Social Council to give greater representation to Asian and African nations. The Soviet delegates said they voted against the resolution because they felt there should be no expansion until Peking became China's representative in the U.N..

On Dec. 18 the Peking *People's Daily* said the Soviet Union had misrepresented China by voting against the resolution. The newspaper stated that "the Chinese government has consistently and actively supported the Asian and African nations' efforts to obtain an increase in the number of their seats in the principal U.N. bodies."

McNamara Mission. On Dec. 21 Secretary of Defense Robert S. McNamara reported to President Johnson on his return from a two-day fact-finding mission to South Vietnam. Following their meeting, it was announced that the previous plan *(see Oct. 2, 1963)* to withdraw most U.S. military personnel from Vietnam by the end of 1965 had been abandoned. McNamara reportedly told the president that the Viet Cong had made progress in the wake of the chaos created by overthrow of the Diem regime.

Chou in Algeria. On Dec. 21 Chinese Premier Chou En-lai and Foreign Minister Chen Yi conferred with Algerian President Ahmed Ben Bella. In a speech to National Liberation Front Groups, Dec. 24, Chou asserted that the current international situation was "excellent for revolutionary struggle and the pursuit of national liberation." Declaring that Algeria could be called "the Cuba of Africa," he predicted that there would be more such revolutions in Africa and Latin America. Chou called for "a second Asian African conference," similar to the 1955 conference at Bandung, Indonesia.

Chou in Morocco. On Dec. 27 Chinese Premier Chou En-lai and Foreign Minister Chen Yi arrived in Rabat, Morocco, where they met with King Hassan and other officials. The Moroccans had been disturbed by China's support of Algeria in that country's border dispute with Morocco.

Chou in Albania. On Dec. 31 Chou arrived in Tirana, Albania. He and Albanian Premier Mehmet Shehu asserted in a joint statement that it was "now the sacred duty of Communists of all countries to combat modern revisionism and modern dogmatism, and to safeguard the purity of Marxism-Leninism." Shehu praised China for aiding Albania to overcome the effects of the Soviet bloc's economic blockade of his country.

1964

African Tour of Chou and Chen — France Recognizes China — McNamara on Withdrawing Troops From Vietnam — De Gaulle Urges Neutralization of Southeast Asia — Washington and Hanoi Reject Neutralization — Rusk on Far East Policy — White House Pledge to Vietnam — Fulbright on Far East Policy — Khrushchev's Opinion of China's Leaders — U.S. Troops to Stay in Vietnam — China's Foreign Minister on Relations With U.S. — Lodge Resigns as Ambassador to South Vietnam — Goldwater Nominated — Gulf of Tonkin Crisis — Congressional Resolution Supporting Johnson's Southeast Asian Policies — LBJ Nominated — Charges Against Chinese in Africa — China's First Nuclear Explosion — LBJ Wins — Chou in Moscow — Hints of Wider Vietnam War — Huong Declares State of Siege in Saigon — Tito on Sino-Soviet Split — Chou Denounces U.S. Action in Southeast Asia.

China's Chief Task for New Year. On Jan. 1 the Peking *People's Daily* said that an increase in agricultural output would be China's "most important task" in 1964. The editorial said that "all efforts will be devoted" to the increase, even if workers from other occupations have to be transferred to agricultural production.

Message to Vietnam. On Jan. 1 President Johnson, in a message to Maj. Gen. Duong Van Minh, chairman of the ruling South Vietnamese military junta, said the U.S. would "continue to furnish you and your people with the fullest measure of support in this bitter fight" and "maintain in Vietnam American personnel and material as needed to assist you in achieving victory." The message added that "As long as the Communist regime in North Vietnam persists in its aggressive policy, neutralization of South Vietnam would be another name for a Communist takeover."

Goldwater Announces. On Jan. 3 Sen. Barry Goldwater, R-Ariz., announced he would seek the 1964 Republican presidential nomination. He previously had summarized his prime foreign policy objective as "total victory" in the face of "the all-embracing determination of communism to capture the world and destroy the United States." Believing that negotiations with the communists were dangerous, Goldwater favored severance of diplomatic relations with the Soviet Union and liberation of Cuba and Eastern European satellites. He was one of eight Republican senators who voted against ratification of the 1963 limited nuclear test ban treaty. He thought the U.S. should withdraw from the United Nations if China were admitted.

Chou and Chen in Africa. On Jan. 9 Chinese Premier Chou En-lai and Foreign Minister Chen Yi arrived in Tunisia. On the following day, Chou and Tunisian President Habib Bourguiba announced that their countries would establish diplomatic relations and "build up economic and human exchange."

On Jan. 12 Chou and Chen Yi arrived in Ghana. On Jan. 16 the Chinese premier joined President Kwame Nkrumah in proposing an Asian, African, Latin American "anti-imperialist" conference and a conference of the world's leaders "if it could be convened for the purpose of prohibiting the development and use of all nuclear weapons and the complete destruction of existing nuclear weapons."

On Jan. 16 the Chinese leaders arrived in Mali, where, on Jan. 21, Chou and President Modibo Keita announced Mali's "determination to move forward on the road to socialism," with increased aid from China. On Jan. 20 a *New York Herald Tribune* dispatch pointed out that the Soviet Union had "spent more than $50,000,000 on economic aid to Mali," while the Chinese Communists to date had "sent 300 to 400 technicians to teach improved methods on rice paddies, and sugar and tea plantations."

On Jan. 21 Chou and Chen arrived in Guinea. Five days later, Chou and President Sekou Toure said they wished "to further develop the relations of friendship and cooperation, in particular in the economic field." Asian and African countries, they added, "must first of all depend on their own efforts and rely on their own people," but "self-reliance does not exclude foreign aid, which is only an auxiliary means" to which "no political conditions or privileges whatsoever should be attached."

Castro on Russia's Side. On Jan. 23 Cuban Premier Fidel Castro, winding up a nine-day visit to the Soviet Union, declared his support for the U.S.S.R. in its ideological dispute with China.

Laos. On Jan. 23 Communist Pathet Lao forces in central Laos launched a new military offensive against rightist and neutralist government forces.

France Recognizes China. On Jan. 27 France established diplomatic relations with China. In the statement issued at the time, no reference was made to Taiwan.

The State Department called the French action "an unfortunate step, particularly at a time when the Chinese Communists are actively promoting aggression and subversion in Southeast Asia and elsewhere." The statement said the U.S. would "stand firmly by its commitments" to Nationalist China, South Vietnam, and other countries endangered by Communist China. On Feb. 10, Taiwan broke relations with France.

McNamara on Southeast Asia. On Jan. 27 Secretary of Defense Robert S. McNamara told the House Armed Services Committee that the administration was hopeful of withdrawing a majority of the 15,000 American troops in South Vietnam before the end of 1965. The secretary said he did not feel the United States should assume the primary responsibility for the war in South Vietnam."

On the dispute between China and Russia, McNamara said it was "now quite evident that we are witnessing more than a disagreement on ideological matters and on strategy in opposing the free world," and that "what is involved is a direct clash of national interests." Because this clash led to a major cutback of Soviet military aid, the Chinese probably would not undertake any major military campaigns in 1964 but "will certainly continue to support subversion and insurrection in Southeast Asia and will attempt to gain control of revolutionary movements elsewhere in the world."

South Vietnamese Coup. On Jan. 30 Maj. Gen. Nguyen Khanh, commander of the Vietnamese Army's First Corps, led a bloodless rebellion against the military junta which had been in control of the government since the Diem regime was ousted in November 1963. Maj. Gen. Duong Van Minh, leader of the junta, was placed under house arrest in Saigon.

Chou in Ethiopia. On Jan. 30 Chinese Premier Chou En-lai and Foreign Minister Chen Yi arrived in Ethiopia. On Feb. 1 Chou and Emperor Haile Selassie announced their intention to expand economic and cultural relations between the two countries.

De Gaulle on Southeast Asia Neutralization. On Jan. 31 French President Charles de Gaulle said at a news conference in Paris that French recognition of China was justified because France could no longer ignore "the fact that for 15 years almost the whole of China is gathered under a government which imposes its laws, and that externally China has shown herself to be a sovereign and independent power." Going on to propose neutralization for Southeast Asia, de Gaulle said: "There is in Asia no political reality ... that does not concern or affect China. There is ... neither a war nor a peace imaginable on this continent without China's being implicated in it. Thus it would be ... impossible to envisage, without China, a possible neutrality agreement relating to the Southeast Asian states — a neutrality, which by definition, must be accepted by all, guaranteed on the international level, and which would exclude both armed agitations ... and the various forms of external intervention; a neutrality that ... seems ... to be the only situation compatible with the peaceful coexistence and progress of the peoples concerned."

Johnson Rejects Neutralization. On Feb. 1 President Johnson, commenting on the possibility of neutralizing Southeast Asia, said: "I do not agree with Gen. de Gaulle's proposals. I do not think that it would be in the interest of freedom to share his view.... I think that the present course we are conducting is the only answer ... and I think that the operations should be stepped up there."

Chou in Somalia. On Feb. 1 Chinese Premier Chou En-lai and Foreign Minister Chen Yi arrived in Somalia. Chou told French newsmen that U.S. "aggression and intervention" had prevented reunification of Vietnam under the 1954 Geneva agreements. He added that all peaceful countries "should join efforts" to force the U.S. to withdraw from South Vietnam.

Seventh Article on Split. On Feb. 3 the Peking *People's Daily* and the Chinese Communist Party's theoretical journal *Hongqi* published the seventh article in a series on the Sino-Soviet split. Entitled "The Leaders of the Communist Party of the Soviet Union Are the Greatest Splitters of Our Time," the article asserted that "The Soviet Communist Party leaders have completely reversed enemies and comrades ... [and] are bent on seeking

Soviet-United States cooperation for the domination of the world.... By embarking on the path of revisionism and splittism, the Soviet Communist Party leaders automatically forfeited the position of 'head' of the international Communist movement."

Chou and Chen Return to China. On Feb. 5 Chinese Premier Chou En-lai and Foreign Minister Chen Yi returned to Peking. Their trip through 10 African countries and Albania had lasted 55 days.

Khrushchev on Communist Unity. On Feb. 14 Soviet Premier Khrushchev told a plenary meeting of the Soviet Communist Party's Central Committee that the U.S.S.R. was attempting to restore "the monolithic unity of the world socialist system." He said: "We have fought and will continue to fight against revisionists, dogmatists, the newly-baked Trotskyites who, while making high-sounding revolutionary phrases about the struggle against imperialism, undermine in fact the unity of the world Communist movement by splitting their activities."

Chou's New Trip. On Feb. 14 Chinese Premier Chou En-lai and Foreign Minister Chen Yi arrived in Burma. On Feb. 18 Chou and General Ne Win, head of Burma's military junta, said in a joint statement that the emerging nations of Africa and Asia should concentrate on building "their independent national economy ... [depending] on the efforts of their peoples and their own material resources." The statement warned the emerging nations to "beware of attempts by colonialists and neo-colonialists to dominate newly independent countries by taking advantage of the financial and economic difficulties with which they are faced."

On Feb. 18 Chou and Chen Yi proceeded to Pakistan, where, after talks with President Mohammed Ayub Khan, Chou reaffirmed support of Pakistan's position on Kashmir.

Argentine Wheat for China. On Feb. 19 Argentina signed an agreement to sell China 400,000 tons of wheat.

China and the Congo. On Feb. 22 the Republic of the Congo (Brazzaville) recognized China.

Rusk on Far East Policy. On Feb. 25 Secretary of State Dean Rusk, addressing a world affairs conference in Washington sponsored by the AFL-CIO International Union of Electrical, Radio and Machine Workers, said: "We have special and very grave concerns about Communist China. And here let me clear away a myth. We do not ignore the Chinese Communist regime.... We talk with it regularly through our respective ambassadors to Warsaw. There have been 119 of these talks. And what the Peiping regime itself says to us is among the reasons why we continue to have very grave concerns about it.

"Peiping continues to insist upon the surrender of Formosa [Taiwan] as the *sine qua non* of any improvement whatever in the relations with the United States. We are loyal to our commitments to the government of the Republic of China; and we will not abandon the 12 million people of Free China on Taiwan to Communist tyranny.

"Peiping incites and aggressively supports the aggression in Southeast Asia in violation of the Geneva Agreements of 1954 and the Geneva Accords of 1962.

"Peiping attacked India and occupies a position from which it continues to threaten the subcontinent of South Asia.

"Peiping is attempting to extend its tactics of terror and subversion into Africa and Latin America.

"In other words, Peiping flouts the first condition for peace: leave your neighbors alone.

"And we in the United States have not forgotten Peiping's aggressive intervention in Korea — an act for which it stands condemned by the United Nations.

"The American people cherished their close and cordial ties with the people of the Chinese mainland. They look forward to the time when it will be possible to renew this historic friendship."

Chou in Ceylon. On Feb. 26 Chinese Premier Chou En-lai and Foreign Minister Chen Yi were greeted cooly in Ceylon. On Feb. 29 Chou and Mrs. Sirimavo Bandaranaike, Ceylon's prime minister, jointly urged an Asian-African conference, establishment of nuclear free zones in "various parts of the world," and reaffirmation of the Ceylonese view "that Taiwan is an integral part of China."

Romania and China. On March 2 a delegation from Romania began talks with Chinese chief of state Liu Shao-ch'i in Peking on "the question of unity of the Socialist camp." On March 11 a joint statement said only that the talks had been held "in a friendly atmosphere."

Canadian Barley to China. On March 3 the Canadian government announced the sale of 16.3 million bushels of barley to China.

Viet Cong and Paper Tiger. On March 4 the Peking *People's Daily* ran an article asserting that the "U.S. paper tiger had been punctured and exposed" by the Viet Cong in South Vietnam. The article added that the Vietnam experience had proved that "the people of any country ... subjected to U.S. aggression can win victory if only they are not overawed by its apparent strength and ... know how to struggle."

McNamara Mission. On March 8 Secretary of Defense Robert S. McNamara arrived in Saigon for the fourth time during the Vietnam War. Before leaving Washington, he had told newsmen that there was "evidence that in the last six months the North Vietnamese support of the Viet Cong had increased," and that weapons recently captured from the enemy "were obviously of Chinese Communist manufacture."

Gruening and Morse on Vietnam. On March 10 Sen. Ernest Gruening, D-Alaska, in a Senate speech called the war in Vietnam "a bloody and wanton stalemate." He said: "The time has come to cease the useless and senseless losses of American lives in an area not essential to the security of the U.S. This is a fight which is not our fight, which we should not have gotten into in the first place." Sen. Wayne Morse, D-Ore., added: "Southeast Asia may very well be essential to the defense of some of our allies, but who are they? They ran out on us. We should never have gone in. We should never have stayed in. We should get out."

Chinese Arms for Cambodia. On March 15 a planeload of arms arrived in Cambodia from China. At the airport, Prince Sihanouk told the Chinese ambassador: "Since our liberation from conditional American aid, our two armies have been able fraternally to extend hands. This is not conceived, as Thailand maintains, to menace the peace and encourage Cambodia to become aggressive. Our only worry is to have sufficient military force to dissuade instigators of imperialistic war who menace the Cambodian peace."

White House Statement on Vietnam. On March 17 the White House, in a rare public statement following a meeting of the National Security Council, pledged the U.S. "to furnish assistance and support to South Vietnam for as long as it is required to bring Communist aggression and terrorism under control." The NSC meeting followed a five-day inspection trip to Vietnam by Defense Secretary MacNamara, Chairman of the Joint Chiefs of Staff Gen. Maxwell D. Taylor, and other high ranking officials.

China Supports Palestine Arabs. On March 17 the Peking *People's Daily* declared that China supported "the restoration of the lawful rights of the Arab people of Palestine," and that "Israel, created and nurtured by the United States, has all along been used as an instrument of aggression against the Arab countries."

U.S.-Indonesian Relations. On March 24 Secretary of State Dean Rusk warned Indonesian President Sukarno that the U.S. would cut off aid shipments to Indonesia if that country did not settle its "confrontation" with Malaysia.

Fulbright on Far East Policy. On March 25 Sen. J. William Fulbright, D-Ark., chairman of the Senate Foreign Relations Committee, spoke in the Senate on "Old Myths and New Realities," strongly criticizing American foreign policy.

He asserted that "We are committed, with respect to China and other areas of Asia, to inflexible policies of long standing from which we hesitate to depart because of the attribution to these policies of an aura of mystical sanctity. ... Whatever the outcome of a re-thinking of policy might be, we have been unwilling to take it because of the fear of many government officials, undoubtedly well-founded, that even the suggestion of new policies toward China or Vietnam would provoke a vehement outcry." Nevertheless, the Senator asked for a re-evaluation of U.S. East Asian policy. For himself, he said:

"I do not think that the United States can or should recognize Communist China or acquiesce in its admission to the United Nations under present circumstances. It would be unwise to do so because there is nothing to be gained by it so long as the Peking regime maintains its attitude of implacable hostility towards the United States. I do not believe, however, that this state of affairs is necessarily permanent. ... It is not impossible that in time our relations with China will change again, if not to friendship, then perhaps to 'competitive coexistence.' It would therefore be an extremely useful thing if we could introduce an element of flexibility, or, more precisely, of the capacity to be flexible, into our relations with Communist China."

Fulbright said the foremost of the new realities about China "is that there are not really 'two Chinas' but only one, mainland China, and that is ruled by Communists and likely to remain so for the indefinite future." He expressed hope that "a new generation of leaders" both in Communist China and Nationalist China "may put a quiet end to the Chinese civil war."

Khrushchev on the Chinese. On April 1 Soviet Premier Khrushchev said in a speech delivered on a visit to Budapest: "There are people ... who call themselves Marxists-Leninists, and at the same time say there is no need to strive for a better life. According to them, only one thing is important — revolution. What kind of Marxism is this?"

Khrushchev on April 3 called China's leaders a "great danger." Two days later, while touring Hungary, he said they were "crazy" to try to develop China economically without outside aid; "only an idiot could pretend that it is easier to build socialism alone than by using the possibilities and support of the fraternal community of peoples who had previously taken the road."

China as Threat to Unity. On April 3 the Soviet government published a report by Mikhail Suslov, the Communist Party's chief theoretician, charging that "the policy and activities of the Chinese leaders represent today the main danger to the unity of the world Communist movement." The report denounced Mao Tse-tung as the source of China's "subversive policies."

Laos and China. On April 4 Prince Souvanna Phouma, premier of Laos, visited Peking and appealed for assistance in bringing peace to his country. Chinese Premier Chou En-lai replied by blaming Laotian difficulties on the U.S. and demanding that U.S. forces be withdrawn from South Vietnam.

Australian Wheat to China. On April 5 Australia announced the sale to China of 21 million bushels of wheat for about $35.8 million. This transaction brought the three-year total of Australian wheat sold to China to 300 million bushels valued at $448 million.

USIA Report on China. On April 8 the U.S. Information Agency in a report entitled "Asian Communist Bloc Propaganda Offensive" asserted: "Peking sustained a massive propaganda effort in 1963 to increase Chinese influence abroad and to gain friends both inside and outside the Communist bloc in its ideological confrontation with Moscow. . . . Freed from Moscow's restraining hand and flushed by what it held to be the promise of an economic take-off on the mainland, Peking moved confidently to break out of isolation and to establish its own image internationally. These goals, together with the worsening of Sino-Soviet relations, the persistence of United States pressure of containment in the Far East, and opportunities for exploiting political, social and economic turmoil in the underdeveloped world, provided the major stimuli for the continuous growth of Peking's propaganda mechanisms."

The report said that Peking, "determined to reduce its dependence on the Soviet bloc . . . made a prodigious effort in 1963 to seek out technical assistance, capital goods and raw materials from the West and new markets for Chinese exports." China concluded trade agreements with Japan, Britain, the Netherlands, Finland, Italy, Afghanistan, Cambodia, Ceylon, Guinea, Iraq, Argentina, Canada, Australia and Mexico.

Poles Assail China. On April 13, Polish officials arrived in Moscow for talks with Soviet leaders. A joint statement issued later accused the Communist Party of China of organizing "a brazen and slanderous campaign against the CPSU [Communist Party of the Soviet Union] and its Leninist leadership." The statement nevertheless advocated admission of China to the U.N., "ending of the occupation of Taiwan by American troops, and the reunification of this age-old Chinese territory with China."

Laotian Coup. On April 19 the Laotian coalition government under Prince Souvanna Phouma was ousted by a rightist military junta. The coup followed the failure of another attempt to unite the three Laotian factions: Pathet Lao, neutralists and rightists. On the same day, the U.S., Great Britain and France denounced the coup as a violation of the 1962 Geneva agreements. The military junta announced April 23 that Prince Souvanna Phouma had been reinstated as premier and would form a new coalition government. On May 2 Souvanna Phouma announced formation of a coalition of neutralists and rightists under his leadership.

Nuclear Materials Production. On April 20 President Johnson and Soviet Premier Khrushchev simultaneously announced that both countries would cut down production of nuclear materials. On the following day, Britain joined in the agreement. France refused to join.

Troops to Stay in Vietnam. On April 24 Defense Secretary Robert S. McNamara said at a news conference that the administration had been forced to give up plans for withdrawing American military personnel from Vietnam by the end of 1965.

Chen Yi on Relations With United States. On May 3 Chinese Foreign Minister Chen Yi, in answer to questions asked by Western newsmen, said the initiative for better relations between the U.S. and China would have to come from the State Department and that China could only wait patiently. He said the State Department's policy toward Communist China had remained much the same despite eight years of negotiations (in Warsaw), and that the policy was exemplified by American refusal to recognize China and to withdraw its forces from Taiwan. The foreign minister asserted that the American people were not at fault, only the U.S. government since the time of President Truman.

Soviet Charges Against China. On May 4 the Soviet government newspaper *Izvestia* published a statement accusing China of attempting to use racism as a weapon against the Soviet Union in Asia and Africa, and of constructing "a Chinese wall between white, yellow and black nations." There followed an angry exchange of statements, one of which revealed that the Chinese Communist Party had rejected a Soviet proposal for a world conference of communist parties to solve the Sino-Soviet dispute. On May 10 the Soviet Union, through *Pravda*, charged that Chinese leaders, especially Mao Tse-tung, wished to usurp the leadership of the international communist movement.

McNamara's Fifth Mission. On May 12 Secretary of Defense Robert S. McNamara, in Saigon, announced that the U.S. would send more fighter planes to Vietnam. He warned that "It's going to be a long war."

Crisis Over Laos. On May 13 Chinese Foreign Minister Chen Yi sent letters to Foreign Ministers R. A. Butler of Britain and Andrei Gromyko of the Soviet Union (the two countries that were co-chairmen of the 1962 Geneva Conference on Laos) charging that the U.S. had promoted the rightist military coup of April 19 in Laos to "endeavor to completely undermine the Laotian government of National Union, rekindle the flames of civil war in Laos and to create the division of Laos." Chen Yi said that "Laos is now faced with the dangers of all-out civil war as a result of provocations of United States imperialists and the Laotian right wing." *(See April 19)* The Chinese foreign minister proposed a new Geneva Conference on the entire Indochina question.

Chinese-Soviet Trade. On May 13 China signed a trade agreement with the Soviet Union. Russia was to send China aircraft, tractors, trucks, tools, oil and chemicals; China was to send Russia metals, ores, frozen and canned pork, egg products, fruit, wool and silk. The value of the trade agreement was not disclosed.

China and Sudan. On May 16 the president of Sudan, Ibrahim Abboud, arrived in Peking for a state visit and was met by Mao Tse-tung in one of his rare public appearances. During his visit, the Sudanese president signed an agreement with China for export of Sudanese cotton in return for machinery and electrical equipment.

Aid to South Vietnam. On May 18 President Johnson asked Congress for $125 million in additional economic and military aid for South Vietnam. The request for $70 million more in economic aid and $55 million more in military aid was approved May 20 by the House Foreign Affairs Committee. A total of about $500 million for Vietnam had already been requested in the budget for the fiscal year beginning July 1.

Chinese Aid to Kenya. On May 20 Kenya announced that China had agreed to grant that country $3 million immediately and to give it later a five-year, interest-free loan of $16 million.

Nehru Dies. On May 27 Jawaharlal Nehru, prime minister of India during the 17 years since the country became independent, died in New Delhi. Home Minister G. L. Nanda was sworn in as acting prime minister.

China and Yemen. On June 1 the president of Yemen, Abdullah al-Sallal, arrived in China for a state visit. The next day, Liu Shao-ch'i, China's chief of state, pledged his country's support for the people of "Aden, South Yemen and Oman in their just struggles against colonialism." All three countries were under British protection.

New Indian Leader. On June 2 Lal Bahadur Shastri was appointed prime minister of India.

Talks on Laos. On June 3 in Vientiane, Laos, talks began among six of the fourteen countries that signed the 1962 Geneva accords providing for Laotian neutrality. India, Great Britain, the U.S., Canada, South Vietnam and Thailand discussed recent violations of the accords by the Communist Pathet Lao forces. The U.S. continued to oppose a French proposal which Russia and China supported. The U.S. was reportedly interested, however, in a Polish plan, which also had Soviet support, for a six-nation meeting without the U.S. or China. The Polish proposal would include Britain and the Soviet Union, as co-chairmen of the 1962 Geneva Conference; India, Canada and Poland, as the members of the International Control Commission for Laos; and Laos itself, represented by the three factions in its coalition government.

South Korean Riots. On June 3, full-scale riots broke out in Seoul against the government of South Korean President Park Chung Hee. The rioters, mostly students, charged that there was corruption in the government and that Park misused his power. On the same day, Seoul was placed under martial law.

China and Tanganyika. On June 11 a delegation from Tanganyika arrived in China. On June 16 Vice President Rahidi Kawawa, head of the delegation, signed a treaty for cooperation with China. It was learned later that China had given Tanganyika a small grant and an interest-free loan of $28 million.

China and Japan. On June 20 Chinese Foreign Minister Chen Yi told a Japanese journalist during a radio and television interview: "The present state of Sino-Japanese relations still falls far short of the two people's strong desire for restoring diplomatic relations. . . . The Chinese government has always held that in relations between China and Japan, politics and economics are inseparable." On June 27 Japan and China agreed to exchange trade representatives. The U.S. and Nationalist China both strongly objected.

Lodge Resigns. On June 23 President Johnson accepted the resignation of Henry Cabot Lodge as ambassador to South Vietnam and named Gen. Maxwell D. Taylor, chairman of the Joint Chiefs of Staff, to replace him.

Chinese Warning on Vietnam. On July 6 Chinese Foreign Minister Chen Yi said that any attack against North Vietnam would threaten Chinese security and that "the Chinese people naturally cannot be expected to look on with folded arms" if such an attack occurred.

Thant on Vietnam. On July 8 U.N. Secretary General U Thant urged that the 1954 Geneva Conference reconvene to negotiate an end to the war in Vietnam. Thant said that "military methods will not bring about peace in South Vietnam" and that the "only sensible alternative is the political and diplomatic method of negotiation."

Romania and China. On July 8 it was announced that Romania and China had agreed to expand their trade and to step up cooperation in scientific and technical fields.

China to Defend Vietnam. On July 9 the Peking *People's Daily* announced that China would "defend" North Vietnam. The editorial added: "The Chinese people have always maintained that it is an unshrinkable proletarian internationalist duty of all Socialist countries to safeguard the peace and the security of the entire Socialist camp, to protect all its members from any imperialist invasion and to defend the Socialist camp."

Ninth Article. On July 13 the Peking *People's Daily* and the Chinese Communist Party's theoretical journal *Hongqi* published the ninth and most vituperative article in a series on the Sino-Soviet split. Entitled "On Khrushchev's Phony Communism and its Historical Lessons for the World," the article asserted that the Soviet premier headed a "privileged stratum" in his country that was attempting to restore capitalism while "the broad masses" were "seething with discontent in the face of oppression and exploitation practiced by the privileged stratum." The article charged that Soviet leaders "appropriated the fruits of the Soviet people's labor" and made annual incomes "a dozen or even a hundred times those of the average Soviet worker and peasant." The Soviet leadership "carried out one purge after another, planting their protegés in all leading posts," until, under Khrushchev, the growth of a "new bourgeoisie" confronted the Soviet Union with "the unprecedented danger of capitalist restoration." *(See Sept. 6, 1963)*

More Americans to Vietnam. On July 14 the Defense Department announced that 600 more "military advisers" were being sent to South Vietnam. On July 27 the U.S. announced that 5,000 more men would be sent to Vietnam, bringing the total of U.S. military personnel there to 21,000.

Goldwater Nominated. On July 15 the Republican Party nominated Sen. Barry Morris Goldwater of Arizona for president and Rep. William E. Miller of New York for vice president. On China, the party's platform said: "We are opposed to the recognition of Red China. We oppose its admission into the United Nations. We steadfastly support free China."

Khanh Urges Invasion of North Vietnam. On July 19 South Vietnamese Premier Nguyen Khanh, during a speech to 100,000 people in Saigon, demanded an invasion of North Vietnam. Asserting that the Vietnamese people had "called for the war to be carried to the north," Khanh said that "the government cannot remain indifferent before the firm determination of all the people who are considering the push northward as an appropriate means to fulfill our national history."

On July 23 the new U.S. ambassador to South Vietnam, Maxwell D. Taylor, conferred with Premier Khanh and reportedly voiced displeasure over Khanh's pronouncements on carrying the war to the north.

Chinese Loan to Pakistan. On July 31 Pakistan announced it was to receive an interest-free $60-million loan from China for purchase of heavy machinery, sugar mills and cement plants, and would repay the loan over a 30- to 40-year period with agricultural and manufactured goods. It was the first such agreement between the two countries, and was concluded at a time when Pakistan's relations with the U.S. had been rapidly deteriorating because the U.S. had supplied India with arms.

Gulf of Tonkin Crisis. On Aug. 2 the U.S. destroyer *Maddox* was attacked by three North Vietnamese PT boats in international waters about 30 miles off the coast of North Vietnam. The Defense Department said the 7th Fleet vessel was on a routine patrol in the Gulf of Tonkin when the PT boats attacked with torpedoes and gunfire. Joined by four U.S. aircraft from a carrier, the *Maddox* returned the gunfire and drove off the attacking boats. Informed of the attack, President Johnson held White House briefings with top U.S. military and diplomatic officials.

On Aug. 3 the president announced the following instructions to the Pacific naval command: (1) Continue the patrols in the Gulf of Tonkin; (2) double the destroyer force off North Vietnam; (3) provide a "combat air patrol" over the destroyers; (4) attack any force which attacks U.S. naval patrols and attack "with the objective of not only driving off the force but of destroying it."

The State Department said it was sending a strong protest to North Vietnam over "the unprovoked attack on an American ship in international waters." The protest warned the Hanoi government that it should be "under no misapprehension as to the grave consequences which would inevitably result from any futher unprovoked offensive military action against United States forces."

On Aug. 4 the Defense Department announced that a second "deliberate attack" had been made by an undetermined number of North Vietnamese PT boats on two U.S. destroyers. The *Maddox* and the *C. Turner Joy* were fired on "while on routine patrol in the Tonkin Gulf international waters about 65 miles from the nearest land." The destroyers and their covering aircraft followed the president's orders of the previous day, returning the attack and apparently sinking at least two of the PT boats.

On Aug. 5 Secretary of Defense Robert S. McNamara told a news conference that 64 air sorties, launched from two 7th Fleet carriers, were made against North Vietnamese PT boat bases and the supporting oil storage depots in four areas. The secretary said the strikes resulted in destruction of approximately 25 North Vietnamese vessels, while two American planes were lost and two others damaged.

Tonkin Gulf Resolution. On Aug. 7 Congress voted overwhelming approval of a resolution supporting President Johnson's actions in Southeast Asia (H J Res 1145). The House approved the resolution by a 416-0 vote. The Senate adopted it the same day by a vote of 88-2. Sens. Wayne Morse, D-Ore., and Ernest Gruening, D-Alaska, dissented.

The resolution recorded that "Congress approves and supports the determination of the president, as commander-in-chief, to take all necessary measures to repel any armed attack against the forces of the United States and to prevent further aggression." It stated also that the United States was "prepared, as the president determines, to take all necessary steps, including the use of armed force, to assist any . . . [state protected by SEATO, including South Vietnam] requesting assistance in defense of its freedom." *(Text, p. 314)*

Emergency Declared at Saigon. On Aug. 7 South Vietnamese Premier Nguyen Khanh declared a state of emergency with tightened government controls over travel, food distribution and curfews. Khanh asserted that Chinese troops were massing along China's southern frontier and that "the coming weeks will decide the destiny of our entire people."

U.N. Action. On Aug. 7 the U.N. Security Council extended an invitation to North Vietnam to testify on the armed clashes in the Gulf of Tonkin. On Aug. 8 the crisis atmosphere began to ease as the Security Council adjourned the Southeast Asia debate pending a response to its invitation to North Vietnam.

Response of Hanoi and Peking. On Aug. 9 North Vietnam rejected the Security Council's invitation, declaring that the council "has no right to examine U.S. war acts" in Vietnam.

On Aug. 10 Assistant Defense Secretary Arthur Sylvester confirmed reports that China had been moving Russian-built MiG-15s and MiG-17s into North Vietnam. Sylvester said that "This has been expected for some time because of known preparations such as lengthening of runways of airfields in the Hanoi area."

Tshombe's Statement. On Aug. 20 the new premier of the Congo, Moise Tshombe, sent a note to U.N. Secretary General U Thant asserting that China was attempting to exploit the strife in the Congo "to maintain a permanent center of subversion on Congolese soil." Tshombe appealed to the U.N. for aid in checking the Communist infiltration.

Johnson-Humphrey Ticket. On Aug. 26 President Lyndon B. Johnson was chosen Democratic nominee for president. On the same day, he recommended Sen. Hubert H. Humphrey, Minn., as his running-mate and Humphrey was duly nominated for vice president. The Democratic platform did not make the usual mention of Communist China but said only: "We will support our friends in and around the rim of the Pacific, and encourage a growing understanding among peoples, expansion of cultural exchanges, and strengthening of ties."

Government Crisis in Vietnam. On Aug. 28 South Vietnam's Finance Minister Nguyen Xuan Oanh was named acting premier after a week of anti-government demonstrations which forced Premier Nguyen Khanh to step down temporarily as head of the wartime military government.

China and Africa. On Sept. 8 the prime minister of Malawi, Hastings Kamazu Banda, charged that Chinese

Embassy officials in Tanganyika had offered his political opponents either a $50-million economic aid program or the assassination of Banda in exchange for diplomatic recognition of China.

On Sept. 10 Prime Minister Jomo Kenyatta of Kenya was urged by his political opponents to expel Chinese diplomats from the embassy in Nairobi because they had issued a statement criticizing Premier Tshombe of the Congo.

Attempted Coup in Saigon. On Sept. 13 a group of South Vietnamese army officers failed in an attempt to oust Premier Nguyen Khanh. Khanh owed the survival of his regime mainly to the loyalty of Air Commodore Nguyen Cao Ky, who had his planes circle over military units of the rebels until they withdrew.

Opium Traffic. On Sept. 13 *Pravda* charged that China was engaged in illegal opium traffic grossing nearly $500 million a year. The article asserted that the profits were used to pay for anti-Soviet propaganda.

Revisionism in China. On Sept. 13 the Chinese Communist Party theoretical journal *Hongqi* published an article denouncing all those who had deviated from Mao Tse-tung's teachings. On Sept. 14 *The New York Times* suggested that a purge of intellectuals similar to the anti-rightist purge of 1958 might be developing. "Analysts believe," the *Times* said, "that such old-guard leaders as Mao Tse-tung, the party chairman, are afraid that Chinese Communist society is harboring trends similar to those that led the Soviet party to emphasize living standards and to compromise its international revolutionary goals."

Cambodia's No. 1 Friend. On Sept. 26 Cambodian chief of state Prince Norodom Sihanouk arrived in Peking on a state visit. In a joint statement Oct. 5 China pledged "all out support" of Cambodia in case of "foreign armed aggression." In a Peking speech, Sihanouk thanked China for "new and most important unconditional economic and military aid" and said that China was Cambodia's "number one friend."

China and Africa. On Sept. 28 Alphonse Massemba-Debat, president of the former French Congo Republic, visited Peking. A joint statement Oct. 3 with Chinese chief of state Liu Shao-ch'i said that China supported the Republic against "imperialist threats, interference and subversion" emanating from the former Belgian Congo. A day earlier, Massemba-Debat had signed a treaty of friendship and an economic agreement with China.

On Sept. 29 the president of Mali, Modibo Keita, arrived in Peking on a state visit. China and Mali already had close economic and cultural ties.

On Sept. 29 China and the Central African Republic established diplomatic relations.

On Oct. 31 China and Zambia established diplomatic relations.

Resistance to Expanding War. On Sept. 28 President Johnson said in a speech at Manchester, N.H., that he was opposed to involving the U.S. in "a war with 700 million Chinese." The president said also that the U.S. was "not going north [in Vietnam] and drop bombs at this stage."

China and Czechoslovakia. On Sept. 29 China announced it had signed an agreement with Czechoslovakia for scientific and technical cooperation.

Chen Yi's Press Conference. On Sept. 29 Chinese Foreign Minister Chen Yi held a press conference in Peking.

Expressing Chinese concern over what it felt was a U.S. encirclement of China, Chen reacted: "If the U.S. imperialists are determined to launch a war of aggression against us, they are welcome to come sooner, to come as early as tomorrow.... For 16 years we have been waiting for the U.S. imperialists to come in and attack us. My hair has turned gray in waiting."

Cairo Conference. On Oct. 5, leaders of 47 nonaligned nations met in Cairo for their second conference (the first was in Belgrade in 1961). On Oct. 7 Indian Prime Minister Lal Bahadur Shastri proposed that the conferees "consider sending a special mission to persuade China to desist from developing nuclear weapons." Shastri also urged the conference to oppose "any changes brought about by use of force as well as by quiet penetration of borders or subversion." On Oct. 10 China called the proposal "provocative" and said: "The Indian government has vainly attempted to use the aid provided by the Khrushchev clique as a fig leaf on its signboard of nonalignment. But whether coming from the United States or the Soviet Union, arms obtained by expansionist India constitute the same threat to her neighbors."

China on Khrushchev. On Oct. 11 China issued a statement again personally attacking Soviet Premier Khrushchev. It said: "A comparison between Khrushchev's statements yesterday and today exposes this big conspirator, careerist and double-faced hypocrite in all his ugliness. Yesterday, using the most obsequious language, he fervently extolled Stalin.... Today, in the language of Trotskyites, he maliciously vilifies Stalin.... Khrushchev is the biggest revisionist of the present time and the biggest leader by negative example in the history of the ... international Communist movement."

Three Russians in Orbit. On Oct. 12 the Soviet Union orbited a three-man space capsule, the first to contain more than one man. The flight lasted 16 orbits and 24 hours.

Khrushchev Ousted. On October 14 Nikita S. Khrushchev was forced to resign as premier and first secretary of the Soviet Communist Party. He was replaced as party secretary by Leonid Brezhnev, 57, and as premier by Aleksei Kosygin, 60. On Oct. 16, China's leaders extended "warm greetings" to the new Soviet leaders and voiced "our sincere wish" that they "will achieve new successes ... in all fields and in the struggle for the defense of the world peace." The message also expressed hope that the "fraternal, unbreakable friendship" between China and the Soviet Union will "continuously develop."

Chinese Nuclear Test. On Oct. 16 China successfully tested its first nuclear device. The official statement announcing the test said China "will never ... under any circumstances be the first to use nuclear weapons." The statement again called for a "summit conference" of all nations to discuss "complete prohibition and thorough destruction of nuclear weapons."

New South Vietnam Government. On Oct. 24 the High National Council of South Vietnam, charged with preparations for a return to civilian government, chose a civilian, Phan Khac Suu, as chief of state. Suu, who under the new constitution was limited (for the most part) to performing ceremonial functions, appointed as premier and administrative head of the government former Saigon Mayor Tran Van Huong.

Premier Nguyen Khanh, responding to demands for a civilian government made by Buddhists and student groups during riots in August, had appointed the 17-man National Council nearly two months earlier to draw up a new constitution. Khanh had promised at that time to step down as head of the military regime by Oct. 27.

New Soviet Goals. On Oct 26 the Soviet government newspaper *Izvestia* published an article entitled, "A Commonwealth of Equals," in which the new administration outlined its goals for unity of the communist movement with equality and autonomy for each party. On Oct. 30 it was reported in the American and Western European press that a document listing 29 reasons why Khrushchev had been removed as Soviet Premier had been circulated among party officials. One of the main reasons cited was Khrushchev's handling of the Sino-Soviet rift. He was accused of allowing the situation to deteriorate to the point where the leaders of both sides were waging a conflict of personal polemics.

China's Support of Cambodia. On Oct. 27, after repeated charges by the Cambodian government that South Vietnamese and American planes had strafed and bombed Cambodian villages, the government sought China's support against "the criminal aggression of the American-South Vietnamese forces of oppression."

On Oct. 31 Peking replied that it "cannot ignore . . . grave crimes . . . against the Cambodian people." On Nov. 9 Chinese head of state Liu Shao-ch'i and Premier Chou En-lai wired the Cambodian government leaders that "650 million Chinese" supported Cambodia's "just struggle in defense of independence, neutrality and territorial integrity." China was "indignant at the grave crimes recently committed by the armed forces of the United States and its puppets."

De Gaulle on Nuclear Negotiations. On Oct. 30 French President Charles de Gaulle said in a message to Chinese Premier Chou En-lai that his country would be willing "at any moment" to enter into "any serious negotiations" with the five nuclear powers. France was the only other nuclear power aside from China that had refused to sign the 1963 nuclear test-ban treaty.

Soviet Pledge to India. On Nov. 1 the Indian Minister of Information, Mrs. Indira Gandhi, told a news conference in New Delhi following her return from Moscow that the new leadership in the Soviet Union had pledged to continue the policy of giving India both economic and military aid. Mrs. Gandhi said that, in her opinion, the Soviet policy toward China would remain the same because "great differences make it very difficult for them to come to terms," although the new Soviet leaders might attempt to "smooth the edges" in their dispute.

Chinese-British Trade. On Nov. 2 the British Trade Fair, largest Western trade fair to be held in China, opened in Peking. The president of China's Council for the Promotion of International Trade, Nan Hanchen, urged at the opening ceremony that all obstacles to expansion of Chinese-British trade be eliminated. He said that "United States imperialism is always creating artificial barriers in an attempt to hinder the development of trade" between Britain and China.

U.S. Election. On Nov. 3 President Johnson led the Democratic Party to its biggest national victory since 1936. Johnson amassed the largest vote of any presidential candidate in history and helped the Democrats score major gains in the House of Representatives and increase their already large majority in the Senate.

Chou in Moscow. On Nov. 5 Chinese Premier Chou En-lai arrived in Moscow, along with delegates from every communist state except Albania, to celebrate the 47th anniversary of the Bolshevik revolution. On Nov. 6, eve of the anniversary, the Soviet party's first secretary, Leonid Brezhnev, told the delegates that the new Soviet government would press for improved relations between the communist and capitalist worlds "to prevent a world thermonuclear war." He also urged greater unity within the communist world, more East-West trade, and "ever more democracy for the Soviet people."

Constantly mentioning the equality of all the communist nations and parties, Brezhnev declared that "a world war is not inevitable in contemporary conditions." He advocated "reuniting" Taiwan "with its homeland," the Chinese mainland, and withdrawing U.S. troops from South Korea and South Vietnam in order that "a peaceful reunification . . . on democratic principles" might be effected in those countries.

On Nov. 7 the Peking *People's Daily* published an editorial advocating unity between China and the Soviet Union so that they may fight "the common enemy . . . the nefarious United States imperialists and their lackeys." It also expressed optimism that "the difficulties which have temporarily appeared between China and the Soviet Union and between the two parties . . . can be gradually resolved."

On Nov. 13, after a series of long talks with the new Soviet leaders, Chinese Premier Chou En-lai returned to Peking. A Soviet statement that day said only that the talks had been held in a "frank, comradely atmosphere."

Southeast Asia Politics. On Nov. 5 the new government of South Vietnam began to disintegrate as Dr. Nguyen Xuan Chu, chairman of the High National Council, resigned in protest against the Cabinet appointments of Premier Tran Van Huong. Chu said the political factions were not adequately represented and that "such a government cannot win the confidence of the population."

China and Africa. On Nov. 12 the African state of Dahomey announced it would establish diplomatic relations with China. On Dec. 6 the prime minister of Malawi, H. Kamazu Banda, announced that his country also would recognize China.

U-2 Flight. On Nov. 16 China announced it had shot down a pilotless U-2 high-altitude reconnaissance plane over south-central China. On Nov. 18, American military sources in Saigon said the U.S. was launching pilotless reconnaissance aircraft (drones) from mother planes in South Vietnam on missions over North Vietnam. They could not report with certainty that any of the drones had been guided over Chinese territory.

Chinese Rejection. On Nov. 22 the Peking *People's Daily* announced that China had rejected U.N. Secretary General U Thant's proposal that the five nuclear powers hold disarmament talks and that China participate in the 17-nation Geneva disarmament conference.

China's Support of Congo Rebels. On Nov. 24, Belgian paratroopers were dropped from U.S. planes in Stanleyville in the Congo to rescue white hostages held prisoner by Congolese rebels. Later in the day, the Congolese government's army, led by white mercenaries, arrived in the city and drove the rebels out. On Nov. 28 Chinese Communist Party Chairman Mao Tse-tung personally announced China's full support of the Congolese rebels and called on all the peoples of the world to "unite and defeat the U.S. aggressors." On the next day, 700,000 people demonstrated in Peking against U.S. policy in the Congo.

State of Siege in Saigon. On Nov. 26 South Vietnamese Premier Huong, after five days of anti-government demonstrations and mob violence inspired by political factions excluded from the civilian Cabinet, imposed a state of siege in Saigon. Buddhist leaders demanded that the rioters be released and Huong ousted. Huong attributed the disorders to "dissatisfied politicians" and the Viet Cong.

On Dec. 12 the Peking *People's Daily* warned that "should U.S. imperialism dare to invade the liberated areas of Laos, Cambodia, or the Democratic Republic of [North] Vietnam, it will be severely punished." On Dec. 24 that warning was repeated with the added admonition that if the U.S. bombed the Ho Chi Minh trail, "the flames of war will spread to the whole of Indochina."

China on the U.N. On Dec. 4 the Peking *People's Daily* announced that China would not accept membership in any U.N. organizations until Nationalist China was ousted from every U.N. organization.

Tito on Sino-Soviet Split. On Dec. 7 President Tito of Yugoslavia, addressing the League of Communists of Yugoslavia, acknowledged that there was no real unity in the international communist movement. He said the Sino-Soviet dispute was rooted in the "conflicting foreign policies of two great powers." The ideological differences between the two countries, he added, were only a "smoke screen" to hide the real reasons for the split.

Increased Aid to Vietnam. On Dec. 11 the South Vietnamese government announced that the U.S. would send increased economic and military aid to South Vietnam.

Chinese Agriculture. On Dec. 12 it was reported that China had reaped its greatest harvest since 1957, due mainly to good weather and more scientific farming methods. It was reported also that China had imported more grain during 1964 than in any previous year.

Dissidence in Saigon. On Dec. 19 a group of South Vietnamese military officers overthrew the High National Council, arrested seven of its nine active members, and jailed the leading political opponents of Premier Tran Van Huong. The officers announced that the action had been taken "because we trust the prime minister and the chief of state and we do not [trust] the High National Council."

Nuclear Submarine on China Station. On Dec. 26 the Defense Department announced that a U.S. submarine carrying nuclear missiles was on station off the coast of China. On Dec. 29 China called the action a "naked provocation by United States imperialism against the Chinese people" and an "utterly shameless act of nuclear blackmail."

Chinese Aid to Cambodia. On Dec. 27 Cambodia announced that China had agreed to give it more military aid, including heavy artillery.

1965

Communist Front in Thailand — Bombing of North Vietnam — McNamara on the Stakes in Vietnam — Proposals for Vietnam Negotiations — Marines Land in Vietnam — Explosion Outside U.S. Embassy in Saigon — Johnson's Johns Hopkins Speech — Five-Day Bombing Pause — Washington Teach-in— Chou on Risk of World War — Commitment of U.S. Troops to Combat — First B-52 Raids — Ky Government Installed — Lodge Replaces Taylor at Saigon Embassy — Ho Chi Minh's Four Points for Peace — Lin Piao's Call for People's War Against Imperialists — Communist China's Conditions for Entering U.N. — Trouble in Indonesia — Anti-War Demonstrations in U.S. — Chinese-Soviet Exchange — Christmas Cease-Fire in Vietnam — Year-End Peace Offensive

Indonesia Leaves U.N. On Jan. 1 the Indonesian delegation to the U.N. announced it had received orders to withdraw from the organization. Indonesian President Sukarno had warned Dec. 31, 1964, that Indonesia would leave the U.N. if Malaysia took the Security Council seat to which it had been elected Dec. 29. It was the first time any member had quit the organization.

On Jan. 6 the Peking *People's Daily* announced China's support of the Indonesian action and added that Malaysia's election to the Security Council proved that the U.N. was "an American imperialist instrument of aggression, an infamous organ in the service of old and new colonialism, and a vile place for a few powers to share the spoils." U.S. officials asserted that Indonesia's move gave indication of an emerging "Peking-Jakarta axis" in Southeast Asia. Indonesia's departure took formal effect Jan. 21, when Ambassador L. N. Palar handed U.N. Secretary General U Thant a letter of resignation.

Soviets for Outlawing Nuclear Weapons. On Jan. 3 the Soviet news agency Tass reported that the Soviet Union had informed China of its support for the latter's proposal of a world conference on the outlawing and destruction of all nuclear weapons. The Soviet note, Tass reported, said that Russia favored a "radical" disarmament agreement, but would also favor any agreement to "limit" or "slow down" production of nuclear weapons.

China and Cuba Trade. On Jan. 5 China and Cuba announced a five-year trade agreement under which Cuban sugar, nickel and copper were to be traded for Chinese rice, cotton fabrics, laminated steel, industrial machinery and other products.

Sato in Washington. On Jan. 12 Japanese Premier Eisaku Sato conferred with President Johnson. In a joint statement issued the next day, the president reiterated U.S. support of Taiwan and warned that "China's militant policies and expansionist pressures against its neighbors endanger the peace of Asia." Sato said it was his country's policy to maintain friendly relations with the Nationalist government on Taiwan, but "at the same time to continue to promote private contact" with China, especially on matters concerning trade.

U.S. Planes in Laos. On Jan. 13 the U.S. acknowledged that two U.S. Air Force bombers had been shot down over Laos. The disclosure was the first public admission that U.S. forces were engaged in attacks on Communist supply lines beyond the borders of South Vietnam.

U.S. to End Aid to Taiwan. On Jan. 14, in his foreign aid message to Congress, President Johnson announced that aid to Nationalist China was a "striking example" of the success of the program, and that Taiwan "no longer needs assistance." *(See June 30)*

China and India. On Jan. 18 China, in a note to India, charged that Indian troops and reconnaissance planes had violated Chinese territory. It was the second such charge made by the Chinese. The Indian government had rejected the first as a "fantastic fabrication." During the first weeks of 1965, the Indian government had arrested more than 800 communists on charges that they were Chinese agents preparing "subversive and revolutionary action."

Communist Front in Thailand. On Jan. 22 the Peking radio announced that a "Patriotic Front," similar to the National Liberation Front in South Vietnam, had been established in Thailand. Thai Premier Thanom Kittikachorn had warned the previous week that Chinese Communist agents were infiltrating Thailand from Laos.

Canadian Wheat to China. On Jan. 25 Canada announced the sale of 27 million bushels of wheat to China.

Vietnam Coup. On Jan. 27, following a series of Buddhist demonstrations, South Vietnamese military commanders ousted Premier Tran Van Huong. Deputy Premier Nguyen Xuan Oanh was named acting premier.

China and Indonesia. On Jan. 28 Chinese Premier Chou En-lai and Indonesian Foreign Minister Subandrio issued a joint statement declaring that China will "absolutely not sit idly by" if the U.S. or Britain "impose[s] war on the Indonesian people." Indonesia denounced the U.S. "war of aggression in Indochina" and the futility of "peaceful coexistence" with the Western countries.

Burundi Breaks With China. On Jan. 30 Premier Joseph Bamina of Burundi broke off diplomatic relations with China and ordered the Chinese ambassador and his staff to leave the country within 48 hours. It had been reported that Chinese were training Congolese rebels in Burundi.

China and Niger. On Feb. 2 the president of Niger, Hamani Diori, charged that China had plotted and financed an unsuccessful revolt against his government in the fall of 1964. He denounced Chinese influence in Africa.

De Gaulle's Proposal for Revising United Nations. On Feb. 4 President Charles de Gaulle of France proposed at a news conference that a five-power conference, including China, be convoked to revise the U.N. Charter.

Kosygin Abroad. On Feb. 5 Soviet Premier Aleksei Kosygin received a cool reception in Peking, where he stopped on his way to Hanoi. At a dinner the next night, North Vietnamese Premier Pham Van Dong urged that Soviet and other communist leaders forget their differences and work together in the fight against U.S. imperialism.

On the following day, Kosygin told a mass rally in Hanoi that his country would supply North Vietnam with "all necessary assistance if aggressors dare to encroach upon [its] independence and sovereignty," and he "severely warns the United States against its schemes to provoke acts of war against North Vietnam."

North Vietnam Bombed. On Feb. 7, responding to major attacks by Viet Cong guerrillas against U.S. installations in South Vietnam, American and South Vietnamese aircraft engaged in "joint retaliatory attacks" on North Vietnamese training and staging areas. The attacks continued Feb. 8 and 11. Announcement of the first U.S. attack was made Feb. 7 by President Johnson, who said it had been launched "in response to provocation ordered and directed by the Hanoi regime."

Viet Cong troops had carried out a major raid Feb. 6 against a U.S. airfield and billeting area at Pleiku, South

Warsaw and Geneva Talks

From 1954 to 1972, despite the obvious hostility between the U.S. and China, the two countries did maintain one tenuous link — "a frail little thread," said Kenneth T. Young — which allowed officials of the two governments to talk face-to-face. Begun in 1954 at the consular level and raised to the ambassadorial level in 1955, meetings were held between the U.S. and Chinese ambassadors to, first, Switzerland, and, after 1958, Poland. This was the only contact point between Peking and Washington for 17 years.

Because the actual proceedings of the talks are still classified, little is known of the details of the discussions which were held. Nonetheless, Young, a State Department official who participated in some of the negotiations, has written an extensive memoir of the meetings.

In all, 139 meetings were held, which produced 19 formal proposals. There was only one agreement, in 1955, which was soon broken. But this is no accurate measure of the importance of the meetings, which were designed to avoid problems, not necessarily to solve them. In 1958 and 1962, during the second and third Taiwan Strait Crises *(pp. 3, 129)*, the participants were able to use the talks to explain their positions and avoid misunderstandings about the limited nature of their commitments. In both cases, the talks made an important if not crucial contribution to the easing of tensions. From 1965 to 1967, President Johnson was able to use the talks to explain the American military escalation in South Vietnam to Peking, thus avoiding the type of misunderstanding which had resulted in the Chinese intervention in the Korean War. According to some analysts, these U.S. assurances were enough to force the ouster of the so-called "interventionist clique" in Peking who were demanding just such a Chinese intervention in Vietnam. Later the Chinese were able to resist Soviet demands for all-out aid to Vietnam, secure in their belief that there were limits to the U.S. escalation.

At other times, the talks were used to discuss such issues as the Laos crisis of 1962, nuclear disarmament and the test ban treaty, return of prisoners, and the exchange of newsmen. Although little in the way of concrete results came from these talks, they were used by both sides to explain their actions to one another in an atmosphere of calm and secrecy far removed from the hostility and belligerence of their public announcements.

The talks were discontinued in 1972, probably as a result of Henry Kissinger's frequent trips to Peking, and were supplanted altogether with the establishment of the liaison offices on May 1, 1973.

Source: Kenneth T. Young, *Negotiating with the Chinese Communists: The United States Experience, 1953-1967* (New York: McGraw-Hill Book Company, 1968).

Vietnam, killing eight Americans and wounding more than 100. They also had made two smaller attacks in two other areas. The raids followed by only a few hours the arrival of Soviet Premier Kosygin in Hanoi.

More Action in Vietnam. On Feb. 9, Viet Cong forces blew up a U.S. Army barracks on Quinhon, approximately

275 miles northeast of Saigon. Two Americans were killed, 23 were listed as missing, and 18 were wounded. On Feb. 11 the Defense Department announced that U.S. and South Vietnamese aircraft had bombed two more staging areas in North Vietnam in retaliation for the latest attack.

Reaction to Bombing of North Vietnam. The action in Vietnam received general support from members of Congress. Senate Majority Leader Mike Mansfield, D-Mont., said: "In view of the circumstances, I think the president did the only thing he could do. He had little choice in the matter."

Sen. Wayne Morse, D-Ore., a critic of U.S. policy in Vietnam, said: "The United States is carrying out the war escalation plans that both the Pentagon Building and the State Department have been manipulating for the past several months. The violations of international treaties by Communist nations and groups in Asia are inexcusable, but they do not justify the United States committing the same wrongs the Communists have been committing."

Sino-Soviet Exchange. On Feb. 14 China and the Soviet Union exchanged messages on the 15th anniversary of the signing of their treaty of mutual assistance and friendship. The Chinese note was far more militant, especially against the U.S., than the Soviet message, which did not mention the U.S. as an enemy or Vietnam as a problem.

On the following day Chinese Foreign Minister Chen Yi said during a reception at the Soviet Embassy in Peking that "peaceful coexistence with United States imperialism, which is pushing ahead its policies of war and aggression, is out of the question." He added that "only in concrete action against United States imperialism and its followers can the Chinese-Soviet alliance be tested and tempered and Chinese-Soviet unity be consolidated and developed."

Chinese Threat to Enter War. On Feb. 15 the Peking *People's Daily* published an editorial warning that if the U.S. sent troops beyond the 17th parallel (the boundary separating North and South Vietnam), China would enter the Vietnamese conflict and also reopen the Korean War. "If the United States expands the war in Vietnam," the editorial warned, "the front will extend from Vietnam to Korea."

Another Coup in Saigon. On Feb. 16 a new civilian government was formed in Saigon, headed by Dr. Phan Huy Quat. Lt. Gen. Nguyen Khanh was ousted as commander-in-chief of the armed forces and chairman of the Armed Forces Council. Phan, a former foreign minister, replaced acting Premier Nguyen Xuan Oanh, who had been appointed by Khanh's Armed Forces Council after it had overthrown Premier Tran Van Huong on Jan. 27.

McNamara on Stakes in Vietnam. On Feb. 18 Secretary of Defense Robert S. McNamara told the House Armed Services Committee that "the stakes in South Vietnam are far greater than the loss of one small country to communism.... The choice is not simply whether to continue our efforts to keep South Vietnam free and independent, but, rather, whether to continue our struggle to halt Communist expansion in Asia."

China and Tanzania. On Feb. 20 China and Tanzania signed a treaty of friendship and, in a joint statement, condemned the "imperialists."

U.S. Bombing in South Vietnam. On Feb. 24 a U.S. Embassy spokesman in Saigon announced that American jet aircraft manned solely by American crews had taken part in bombing raids against the Viet Cong in South Vietnam since Feb. 17. The statement said the American attacks, staged "at the request of the government of Vietnam," were considered "appropriate, fitting and measured" in response to increased infiltration and provocations by the Viet Cong. All previous airstrikes in South Vietnam had been made by South Vietnamese pilots, sometimes "assisted" by U.S. copilots.

White Paper on North Vietnam Aggression. On Feb. 27 the State Department issued a 14,000-word white paper documenting North Vietnamese aggression against South Vietnam. The report, entitled "Aggression from the North," concluded that stepped-up communist involvement in South Vietnam could no longer be met by military efforts in the South alone.

The white paper did not predict new air strikes against North Vietnam, but it invited the North Vietnamese to choose between peace and an "increasingly destructive" conflict. U.S. officials said the purpose of the paper was to counter pressures at home and abroad for a negotiated settlement. Opponents of U.S. policy in Vietnam had contended that the conflict was a civil war and the U.S. had no justification for involvement. The white paper represented a departure from the former insistence that, despite North Vietnamese participation, the war would have to be won in the South.

To document North Vietnamese aggression, the white paper included case histories of North Vietnamese infiltrators who defected or were captured in the South, photographs of North Vietnamese and Chinese arms caches captured in or on the way to South Vietnam, captured documents describing infiltration activities, and lengthy appendices detailing arms shipments and troop movements.

Communist Parties Meet in Moscow. On March 1 delegations from 19 communist parties met in a suburb of Moscow to lay plans for a unity conference of the world's 81 communist parties. The parties of Albania, China, Indonesia, Japan, North Korea, North Vietnam and Romania had turned down invitations to attend. The meeting, held in secret, ended March 5. A public statement issued March 10 supported the plan for a global conference to re-establish unity in the world communist movement but only after several years of preparation, which would include bilateral party talks and a preliminary meeting of the 81 parties. The statement called meanwhile for "an end to the public polemics, which have a character which is unfriendly and offensive for fraternal parties."

Air Strikes on North Vietnam. On March 2 the U.S. joined South Vietnam in the heaviest air strikes so far against North Vietnam. At least 100 U.S. and 60 South Vietnamese planes took part. For the first time since selective air attacks on North Vietnamese targets began in August 1964, the strikes were not described as in direct retaliation for specific North Vietnamese or Viet Cong attacks. On March 3 more than 30 U.S. Air Force jets reportedly bombed the Ho Chi Minh trail in eastern Laos.

Moscow Students Mob U.S. Embassy. On March 4, 2,000 Russian, Asian (many Chinese), African and Latin American students broke through police barricades in Moscow to storm the U.S. Embassy in protest against American air strikes on North Vietnam. The students broke windows and spattered the building with ink; 600 policemen were forced to call in 500 army troops to quell the rioters. Several soldiers, policemen and demonstrators were seriously injured.

Marines Land in Vietnam. On March 8, 3,500 Marines landed in South Vietnam to defend the U.S. base at Danang.

U.S. Wary of Vietnam Negotiations. On March 9 the State Department announced it had rejected U.N. Secretary General U Thant's proposals for negotiations on the Vietnam question. It said the U.S. did not "see any indication that whatever the procedure, the Hanoi regime is prepared to stop trying to take over South Vietnam by violence."

Nixon on Vietnam and China. On March 15 Richard Nixon declared that the Vietnam War was not one between the North and South, nor between the U.S. and North Vietnam, but was in fact a war between the U.S. and China. "A United States defeat in Vietnam," said Nixon, "means a [Chinese] Communist victory."

Indonesia and the U.S. On March 19 the Indonesian government seized properties of three American oil companies. It had already taken over two American tire and rubber plants. The U.S. Information Agency had announced March 4 that it was "most reluctantly" closing its five libraries and reading rooms in Indonesia because of government harassment.

Chinese Restraint on Vietnam. On March 20 Chinese Premier Chou En-lai said in an interview in the Manila *Times* that his country was "against world war and would never provoke it," and that China had "shown restraint" in Vietnam, although "our restraint has limits." He added that China was not afraid of the U.S. since the latter's forces were scattered all around the globe.

China Ready to Intervene. On March 21 Chinese Foreign Minister Chen Yi said in an interview with an Italian journalist that China would actively fight in Vietnam if U.S. troops invaded North Vietnam or if the North Vietnamese government requested them to enter the war.

Nausea Gas. On March 21 a U.S. military spokesman in Vietnam said that U.S.-supplied nausea gas was being used against communist guerrillas. The announcement aroused strong criticism in the press of allied countries as well as in neutralist and communist countries.

Chen Yi's Trip. On March 22 Chinese Foreign Minister Chen Yi arrived in Afghanistan to sign an agreement for a long-term $27.5 million no-interest loan to that country. On March 24 he went on to Pakistan to sign a border agreement formalizing the boundary between China and that part of Kashmir controlled by Pakistan. On March 29 the foreign minister, now in Nepal, pledged China's aid for Nepal's new five-year plan.

Chinese Ready to Give Aid. On March 25 the Peking *People's Daily* said that China, in response to the March 24 declaration of the National Liberation Front, would "join the people of the whole world in sending all necessary material aid, including arms and other war materials, to the heroic South Vietnamese people who are battling fearlessly." The article added that China was "ready to send" its "own men whenever the South Vietnamese people want them, to fight together with the South Vietnamese people to annihilate the United States aggressors." It concluded: "The South Vietnamese people will not lay down their arms

until the last American soldier leaves their land. . . . All negotiations with the United States imperialists at this moment are utterly useless if they still refuse to withdraw from South Vietnam."

Moscow-Hanoi Agreement. On March 26 the Soviet Communist Party's Central Committee ratified a military aid agreement between the Soviet Union and North Vietnam aimed at "repelling aggression on the part of United States imperialism."

Neutrals Ask Vietnam Settlement. On April 1 leaders of 17 neutral nations appealed for a "peaceful solution through negotiations" of the war in Vietnam "without any preconditions." Copies of the appeal were sent to North and South Vietnam, the U.S., China, Britain, the Soviet Union, France, the National Liberation Front, Poland and Canada (the last two because they were members of the International Control Commission on Vietnam).

The statement said a peaceful solution of the Vietnam conflict was impeded by "foreign intervention in various forms, including military intervention, which impedes the implementation of the Geneva agreements on Vietnam." It added that "a political solution to the problem of Vietnam" should be found "in accordance with the legitimate aspirations of the Vietnamese people and in the spirit of the Geneva agreements."

Vietnam Buildup. On April 2 the Johnson administration announced it would send more economic aid and more troops to South Vietnam. A decision was also made at a meeting of the National Security Council to increase the number and intensity of air strikes over North Vietnam and to extend them farther to the north. The number of American troops currently in South Vietnam was 27,500.

Chou's Reply to U Thant. On April 6 Chinese Premier Chou En-lai replied through an intermediary to U.N. Secretary General U Thant's appeal for negotiations to end the Vietnam conflict. Chou said that any negotiations would have to be undertaken directly with the Viet Cong rather than with China or North Vietnam.

Mao's Advice to Arabs. On April 6, in one of his infrequent public appearances, Chinese Party Chairman Mao Tse-tung told an Arab delegation visiting Peking: "Asia is the biggest continent in the world. The West wants to continue to exploit it because the West likes neither us nor you. We must all understand this fact. The Arab battle against the West is actually a battle against Israel, so you Arabs must boycott Europe and America." Mao added that China was winning "in all the battles we are fighting, especially in Vietnam."

Johnson's Speech at Johns Hopkins. On April 7 President Johnson, in a speech at Johns Hopkins University in Baltimore, Md., said the U.S. was willing to begin "unconditional discussions" to end the war in Vietnam. The president also proposed a joint development plan for Southeast Asia under United Nations auspices and said the U.S. would contribute $1 billion. The speech was considered in part a response to the April 1 plea by 17 neutral countries for immediate negotiations "without any preconditions" to achieve a solution of the Vietnam problem.

While saying the U.S. was willing to begin negotiations without prior conditions, Johnson made it clear that any settlement must guarantee "an independent South Vietnam." He said: "We will not be defeated. We will not grow tired. We will not withdraw, either openly or under the cloak of a meaningless agreement."

The president expressed hope that "all other industrialized nations, including the Soviet Union," would join in a regional program for development of Southeast Asia, and that U.N. Secretary General U Thant would initiate such a plan "as soon as possible." He announced that he would appoint Eugene R. Black, former president of the International Bank for Reconstruction and Development, to head a special team of Americans "to inaugurate our participation in these programs."

Concerning China, the president said: "Over this war and all Asia is another reality: the deepening shadow of Communist China. The rulers in Hanoi are urged on by Peking. This is a regime which has destroyed freedom in Tibet, which has attacked India and has been condemned by the United Nations for aggression in Korea. It is a nation which is helping the forces of violence in almost every continent. The contest in Vietnam is part of a wider pattern of aggressive purposes."

Reaction to Johnson's Speech. Peking radio charged April 9 that the president's speech was "full of lies and deceptions." It said that "while the United States trumpets peace by word of mouth, it is actually pushing on with preparations for expansion of the war." Peking viewed the proposals as "an old device presented in new form for the sole purpose of luring the South Vietnamese people to lay down their arms." The Soviet Communist Party newspaper *Pravda* called the speech "noisy propaganda" that "cannot change the fact that the United States aggression in Vietnam is going on and that the situation there is getting worse, endangering peace in Southeast Asia and elsewhere in the world." North Vietnam's party newspaper *Nhan Dan* said Johnson's offer "smells of poison gas" and called his economic aid proposal "bait" held out by "stupid pirates."

Soviet Supplies for Vietnam. On April 7 it was reported that China and the Soviet Union had reached agreement on shipment of military equipment from Russia through China to North Vietnam. The report followed repeated stories that China had refused to allow the U.S.S.R. to send supplies to North Vietnam by rail, forcing the Russians to make shipments by sea (a distance of nearly 12,000 miles) and risk interception by the U.S. 7th Fleet.

U.S. Reply to Neutrals. On April 8 the Johnson administration, replying to the 17 neutral nations which had appealed for negotiations on Vietnam, said the U.S. was "ready and eager to withdraw its forces from South Vietnam . . . when conditions have been created in which the people . . . can determine their own future free from external interference." Belief was expressed that "peace can be achieved in Southeast Asia the moment that aggression from North Vietnam is eliminated."

Chinese-U.S. Air Clash. On April 9 China asserted that MiG jet fighters of its air force had been involved in a dogfight with 16 U.S. jets over the Chinese island of Hainan in the South China Sea. Peking said one U.S. jet had been shot down by a missile fired from another U.S. plane. According to the U.S. version, the encounter had taken place 35 miles from Hainan Island, and four U.S. fighter-bombers had shot down one Chinese plane and lost one of their own. The U.S. insisted that the American aircraft had not violated Chinese air space.

Communist Peace Position. On April 14 Soviet Premier Aleksei Kosygin and North Vietnamese Premier Pham Van Dong issued a joint statement which contained a four-point program for ending the war in Vietnam. The statement called for the removal of foreign bases and foreign troops from Vietnam, and the eventual reunification of the country through free elections.

The insistence on the removal of foreign — i.e., the United States — troops prior to negotiations, along with the call for implementation of the 1954 Geneva accords, would continue to characterize the communist position on the cessation of the war.

On April 20 the Standing Committee of the National People's Congress of China announced their endorsement of the proposals.

Air Strikes and Missile Bases. On April 15, in the biggest air action of the Vietnam war, 230 American and South Vietnamese planes struck a suspected Viet Cong outpost 72 miles west of Saigon. U.S. and South Vietnamese planes continued daily air strikes in North Vietnam. It was reported in Washington that U.S. reconnaissance planes had spotted preparations in North Vietnam to construct defensive missile sites, presumably for Soviet SAM missiles which could hit aircraft flying as high as 100,000 feet. On April 16 the State Department confirmed the reports.

Johnson Refuses to Halt Bombing. On April 17 President Johnson rejected appeals that he discontinue air strikes over North Vietnam in the hope that such action would help bring about peace negotiations. The president reiterated his offer of "unconditional negotiations" and criticized the communists for rejecting the April 7 proposal. "It has been a week of disappointment," he said, "because we tried to open a window to peace, only to be met with tired names and slogans — and a refusal to talk."

On the same day, Chairman J. William Fulbright, D-Ark., of the Senate Foreign Relations Committee commented: "There might be some value in stopping the bombings temporarily. I don't know if it would work, but it seems worth trying."

On April 17, 15,000 demonstrators at a rally and march in Washington protested the bombing of North Vietnam.

Volunteers for Vietnam. On April 18, following a meeting of Soviet and North Vietnamese officials in Moscow, the Soviet Union said that if the war in Vietnam intensified, it would allow Russian volunteers to join the fighting forces of North Vietnam whenever Hanoi asked for them. Two days later, a similar offer was made by China.

Johnson Repeats Peace Talk Offer. On April 27 President Johnson, at a news conference, reaffirmed his offer to engage in unconditional peace talks with "any government, anywhere, any time." He said the U.S. had not changed its "essential position" on Vietnam — to obtain a "peaceful settlement," to "resist aggression," and to "avoid a wider war." Responding to a question on possible use of nuclear weapons in Vietnam, the president said he had "never had a suggestion from a single official of this government . . . concerning the use of such weapons in this area."

Sino-Soviet Trade. On April 29 the Soviet Union and China signed a trade agreement providing for shipment to China of machine tools, automobiles, airplanes, tractors, and other equipment in exchange for shipment to the U.S.S.R. of fruit, eggs, livestock, chemicals and shoes.

French-Soviet Statement. On April 29 Soviet Foreign Minister Andrei Gromyko and French Foreign Minister

Maurice Couve de Murville wound up three days of talks in Paris. A joint statement urged that the 1954 and 1962 Geneva agreements be implemented to reaffirm the independence of Vietnam, Cambodia and Laos. The statement said the "situation in the Indo-Chinese Peninsula, and in particular Vietnam . . . creates dangers for peace." On April 28 the Soviet government newspaper *Izvestia* had denounced President Johnson and Secretary of Defense McNamara for having "refused to rule out the use of nuclear weapons" in Southeast Asia. *(See April 27)*

China on Dominican Intervention. On April 30 the Chinese Xinhua news agency, commenting on American intervention April 28 in the Dominican Republic, said: "The new intervention on the part of the United States, which came at a moment when United States imperialism was wildly extending its aggression in Vietnam, threw further light on its hideous feature as the international gendarme."

On May 12 Chinese Communist Party Chairman Mao Tse-tung declared: "U.S. military intervention in the Dominican Republic has aroused a new wave against U.S. imperialism among the people of Latin America and the world. . . . In the eyes of the U.S. imperialist aggressor, the United Nations, the Organization of American States and whatnot are just tools in their hands."

On the following day, an enormous demonstration was held in Peking protesting the American intervention in the Dominican crisis.

Cambodia Breaks With U.S. On May 3 Cambodia severed diplomatic relations with the United States. Prince Norodom Sihanouk, head of state, said the action was taken because of an attack on two Cambodian villages April 28 by South Vietnamese airplanes, and because of a *Newsweek* article criticizing Sihanouk's mother. Sihanouk added that "Diplomatic relations may be restored . . . if the United States conducts itself correctly towards Cambodia."

Appropriation for Vietnam. The House May 5 and the Senate May 6, by roll-call votes of 408-7 and 88-3, respectively, passed and sent to the president a bill (H J Res 447) making fiscal 1965 supplemental appropriations of $700 million to meet mounting military requirements in Vietnam. House and Senate action was completed only two days after President Johnson appealed to Congress in a special message to "provide our forces with the best and most modern supplies and equipment" and to show "prompt support of our basic course: resistance to aggression, moderation in the use of power, and a constant search for peace." The president signed the bill May 7 (PL 89-18).

Soviet-Chinese Thrusts. On May 7 at a Moscow rally celebrating the anniversary of V-E Day, Soviet Premier Aleksei N. Kosygin, referring to the Chinese Communists, said that "Some people contend that only a new world war can bring about the unity and solidarity of the . . . international Communist movement." He added: "We decisively reject such a position. . . . We have no more important task than to prevent a new world conflagration."

On May 9 the Peking *People's Daily* accused the Soviet leaders of "colluding with the United States aggressors and plotting to sell out the basic interests of the people of Vietnam and of all other countries, including the Soviet Union."

Bombing Pause. U.S. bombing raids on North Vietnam were suspended from May 13 until May 18. According to news reports, the raids were stopped to give North

Vietnam a face-saving opportunity to accept the president's offer of talks. The administration made no official statement, but Robert J. McCloskey, State Department press officer, voiced disappointment that North Vietnam made no move toward negotiations during the bombing suspension. On May 18 North Vietnam charged that the suspension was "an effort to camouflage American intensification of the war and deceive world opinion."

Second Bomb Test. On May 14 China announced it had exploded its second atomic bomb. The announcement indicated that the bomb had been dropped from the air. China's first successful nuclear test took place Oct. 16, 1964.

Rejection of Cease-Fire. On May 14 China labeled "preposterous" a proposal by India on April 24 for a Vietnam cease-fire to be enforced by Asian and African police detachments. The next day North Vietnam called the proposal "an offense" against the North Vietnamese people and charged that India had expressed "erroneous viewpoints that only benefit the United States imperialists."

Teach-Ins. On May 15 a "teach-in" protesting the war in Vietnam was held in Washington and broadcast by radio and television to college and university campuses throughout the nation. The U.S. policy was condemned and defended by government officials, professors, historians and writers. The teach-in was one of many of a similar kind held in past months.

Funds for Asian Development. On June 1 President Johnson told a news conference that he was asking Congress for a special appropriation of $89 million to start the economic development program for Southeast Asia that he proposed April 7. "This is the only way that I know in which we can really win not only the military battle against aggression but the wider war for the freedom and for progress of all men," the president said.

China and the Viet Cong. On June 1 the Peking *People's Daily* warned that U.S. air strikes in Vietnam "threatened China's security in an increasingly serious manner" and that China and North Vietnam were "all the more entitled" to assist the Viet Cong. The article also charged that the U.S. had "made a farce of the boundaries between Laos, Vietnam and Thailand" by "turning this entire nation into one battleground where it moves as it wishes."

Australians in Vietnam. On June 2 the first contingent of Australian troops arrived in South Vietnam.

Chou's Trip to Africa. On June 4 Chinese Premier Chou En-lai arrived in Tanzania after a brief stopover in Pakistan. At a reception the same day, Tanzanian President Julius K. Nyerere expressed gratitude for China's aid but cautioned that "From no quarter shall we accept direction or neo-colonialism, and at no time shall we lower our guard against the subversion of our government and people."

On June 8 Chou and Nyerere urged in a joint statement that an international conference be convoked to discuss elimination of all nuclear weapons. Prior to Chou's visit, China had increased its economic and military aid to Tanzania. It was reported that 300 Chinese technicians were in the country and that Chinese were operating a military training camp for the Tanzanian armed forces on Zanzibar.

Before returning to Peking, Chou briefly visited the United Arab Republic and Ethiopia. The African trip was only partly successful because Chou did not receive hoped-for invitations to visit Kenya, Uganda and Zambia.

Combat Role of U.S. Troops. On June 8 Robert J. McCloskey, State Department press officer, said that U.S. military commanders in Vietnam had recently been given authority to commit U.S. ground troops to combat if their assistance was requested by the South Vietnamese army.

Vietnam Protest Rally. On June 8, 17,000 people gathered in New York's Madison Square Garden to protest the war in Vietnam. Sen. Wayne Morse, D-Ore., told the crowd that President Johnson's "consensus" was "not the consensus of our people, nor even the community of nations; it is a consensus among the State Department, Defense Department, Central Intelligence Agency and the White House staff."

Threat to Send Volunteers to Viet Cong. On June 9 China's Xinhua news agency reported that South Vietnam's National Liberation Front had asserted that President Johnson's "declaration to put Vietnam and its adjacent waters in the combat zone of the United States armed forces and to order the expeditionary forces to take a direct part in the fight ... blatantly violates the 1954 Geneva agreement on Vietnam." The news agency said the NLF, because of Johnson's action, was "entitled to call for volunteers from the armies of North Vietnam and other friendly countries to join in the fight against the United States aggression."

South Vietnam's Premier Resigns. On June 12 South Vietnamese Premier Phan Huy Quat resigned and announced that his civilian regime would remain in office until another government had been formed.

More Troops to South Vietnam. On June 16 Secretary of Defense Robert S. McNamara announced that U.S. military strength in Vietnam would be increased to between 70,000 and 75,000 men, including 21,000 ground combat troops. The total current strength in Vietnam was 54,000 men.

First B-52 Raids. On June 17, 27 long-range heavy jet B-52 bombers of the U.S. Strategic Air Command were employed for the first time to bomb a Viet Cong-controlled area 30 miles from Saigon. The bombers made a round-trip flight of over 4,000 miles from Guam to South Vietnam and back again.

New Saigon Government. On June 21 South Vietnamese Air Vice Marshal Nguyen Cao Ky, 34, became premier following Dr. Phan Huy Quat's resignation June 12. The new government was the tenth in 19 months. Premier Ky on June 24 announced severance of diplomatic relations with France. The move had been opposed by U.S. officials in Saigon, but South Vietnamese Foreign Minister Tran Van Do asserted that Paris "has always directly or indirectly helped our enemies."

Military "Firsts" in Vietnam. On June 22, U.S. Air Force planes bombed North Vietnam sites north of Hanoi for the first time. On June 28, U.S. paratroopers and Australian and South Vietnamese troops launched a joint probing operation in Zone D, a Viet Cong stronghold northeast of Saigon, but failed to make substantial contact with the enemy. It was the first time American soldiers had taken the offensive. The U.S., since bombing of North Vietnam began Feb. 7, had limited air raids to targets in the southern part of North Vietnam and had limited ground operations to support of the South Vietnamese against Viet Cong assault.

Japan and South Korea. On June 22 Japan and South Korea opened full diplomatic relations, ending a 55-year rupture.

President's U.N. Address. On June 25 President Johnson, in a speech in San Francisco at the 20th anniversary celebration of the signing of the United Nations charter in that city, appealed to the U.N. to help get North Vietnam to the conference table for peace negotiations. He said: "I now call upon this gathering of the nations of the world to use all their influence, individually and collectively, to bring to the tables those who seemed determined to make war. We will support your efforts, as we will support effective action by any agent or agency of these United Nations."

France Urges China's Entry to U.N. On June 26 French ambassador to the U.N. Roger Seydoux urged admission of Communist China to the world organization, saying that "So long as the United Nations does not accurately reflect the world as it exists, its effectiveness will be impaired and even its role may be called into question."

U.S. Ends Aid to Taiwan. On June 30 the U.S. Agency for International Development announced that U.S. non-military aid to Nationalist China had been ended after ten years. The announcement stated that during the period, Taiwan had received $1.5 billion in economic aid from the U.S. Military aid to the island nation would continue.

Lodge Again. On July 8 Henry Cabot Lodge, former U.S. ambassador to South Vietnam, was named to the post a second time, replacing Gen. Maxwell D. Taylor, whose resignation was announced the same day.

Stevenson Death. On July 14 Adlai Ewing Stevenson, U.S. ambassador to the United Nations since 1961 and the Democratic presidential candidate in 1952 and 1956, died suddenly in London. On July 20 Supreme Court Justice Arthur J. Goldberg was appointed by President Johnson to take Stevenson's place at the U.N.

Aid to North Vietnam. On July 17 the Chinese Xinhua news agency reported that China and North Vietnam had concluded an agreement under which China would send "equipment, whole sets of installations, and supplies in the national defense and economic fields" to North Vietnam. During the previous week, similar agreements had been made by North Vietnam with the Soviet Union and North Korea.

McNamara's Views on Vietnam. On July 21 Secretary of Defense Robert S. McNamara, completing a five-day visit in South Vietnam, said at a news conference in Saigon: "The overall situation continues to be serious. As a matter of fact, in many aspects there has been a deterioration since I was last here 15 months ago. The size of the Viet Cong forces has increased; their rate of operations and the intensity of their attacks has been expanded; their destruction of the lines of communications, both rail and sea and road, is much more extensive; and they have intensified their campaign of terror against the civilian population." But he added: "the picture is not all black by any means. The Vietnamese people continue to be willing to fight and

... die in their own defense. The Viet Cong ... are suffering increasingly heavy losses, and the U.S. combat forces are adding substantially to the military power of the government." McNamara pledged that the U.S. would do whatever was necessary "to support the people of Vietnam in their fight to win their independence."

The day before, North Vietnamese President Ho Chi Minh had declared that his country would fight another 20 years if necessary. He urged the U.S. to abandon South Vietnam.

U.S. Bombing of Missile Sites. On July 24 the war in Vietnam took on a new dimension with the downing of a U.S. military plane and the damaging of three others by Soviet surface-to-air (SAM) missiles. U.S. Air Force fighter-bombers retaliated July 26 by attacking two of the missile sites 40 miles west of Hanoi. One site was destroyed and another badly damaged. Five U.S. planes were lost in the raids.

Troop Increase. On July 28 President Johnson announced at a news conference that U.S. troop strength in Vietnam would be increased from the current 75,000 to 125,000, and that monthly draft calls would be raised from 17,000 to 35,000.

Chinese Criticism. On July 31 the Peking *People's Daily* reiterated charges that the "Khrushchev revisionists" in the Soviet Union were attempting to "work hand-in-glove with the United States imperialism in order to push the scheme for 'peace talks' in Vietnam."

More U.S. Money for Vietnam. On Aug. 4 President Johnson asked Congress to appropriate an additional $1.7 billion to finance the war in Vietnam.

War in Kashmir. On Aug. 5 fighting broke out between India and Pakistan in the disputed state of Kashmir.

Chinese Volunteers. On Aug. 7 China, noting that it had "repeatedly pledged to the Vietnamese people our all-out support and assistance, up to and including the sending ... of our men to fight shoulder to shoulder with them," warned "once more that we Chinese people mean what we say." The statement commented that while President Johnson was "announcing the sending of large reinforcements to South Vietnam, he hypocritically talked about America's willingness to begin unconditional discussions with any government, at any place, at any time."

Anti-U.S. Mobs in Indonesia. On Aug. 7, 7,000 Indonesian youths and students mobbed the U.S. consulate in Surabaya while Indonesian police looked on. The U.S. consulate in Medan, Indonesia, had received the same treatment on July 30.

Rivers on China's Bomb. On Aug. 11 Rep. L. Mendel Rivers, D-S.C., chairman of the House Armed Services Committee, speaking in Hartford, Conn., said the U.S. must be prepared to use atomic weapons on China before China used them on the United States. "Even if we win the war in South Vietnam," he said, "I cannot help but think that we are merely postponing the final victory of Red China — unless the nation is prepared to risk the possible consequences of destroying her nuclear capability. And unless we make that decision, it is possible that all our fighting in South Vietnam will have been in vain."

Ho's Terms. On Aug. 12 North Vietnamese President Ho Chi Minh, in an interview appearing in the Paris newspaper *Le Monde,* said his country would agree to negotiations on the Vietnam War when the U.S. accepted North Vietnam's four-point proposal.

The four points were: (1) Total U.S. withdrawal from all of Vietnam; (2) following "peaceful reunification" of the country, its "two zones must refrain from joining any military alliance with any foreign countries" and "there must be no foreign military bases, troops, or military personnel in their respective territories"; (3) South Vietnam's "internal affairs ... must be settled by the people themselves in accordance with the program" of the National Liberation Front, the Viet Cong's political arm; (4) the Vietnamese people must be responsible for peaceful reunification of the country "without any foreign interference."

Independent U.S. Fighting. On Aug. 18 U.S. forces staged their first ground action in support of South Vietnamese troops.

Vietnam Funds. On Aug. 25 the Senate, by an 89-0 roll-call vote, passed and sent to conference a bill (HR 9221) that included a stopgap $1.7-billion appropriation for military operations in Vietnam.

Coupled with a $700-million fiscal 1965 supplemental appropriation, HR 9221 brought additional calendar 1965 outlays earmarked for Vietnam to a total $2.4 billion.

China and Nepal. On Aug. 29 China signed an agreement to grant Nepal $28 million to build a 140-mile east-west highway.

Negotiations and Bombing. On Aug. 29 President Johnson denied news reports that North Vietnam had signified willingness to start peace negotiations if the U.S. stopped bombing North Vietnam: "We hear a lot of reports. There is nothing official about them. I expect some newspaperman was speculating."

News reports suggested also that the administration had made offers to North Vietnam, through undisclosed third parties, to exchange demonstrations of willingness to slow down the war. Secretary of State Dean Rusk, at an Aug. 27 news conference, said such an assertion was too precisely worded, but he acknowledged that there had been "many" third party contacts with Hanoi. Rusk emphasized that the U.S. was "prepared to consider" ending its bombing attacks on North Vietnam if such an action would be a "step toward peace."

Lin Piao's Article. On Sept. 2, 20th anniversary of Japan's surrender to the Allies, Chinese Defense Minister Lin Piao issued a major policy statement which was published in newspapers all over China. It called for a "people's war" utilizing the same techniques as those used by Mao Tse-tung in the Chinese civil war of the late 1940s.

"It must be emphasized," Lin said, "that Comrade Mao Tse-tung's theory of the establishment of rural revolutionary base areas and the encirclement of cities from the countryside is of outstanding and universal practical importance for the present revolutionary struggles of all the oppressed nations and people, and particularly [those] ... in Asia, Africa and Latin America, against imperialism and its lackeys. . . . The countryside, and the countryside alone, can provide the revolutionary bases from which the revolutionaries can go forward to final victory. . . . [I]f North America and Western Europe can be called 'the cities of the world,' then Asia, Africa and Latin America constitute 'the rural areas of the world.' "

Lin contended that nuclear weapons could not save U.S. imperialism, which "has been condemned by the people of the whole world for its towering crime of dropping two atomic bombs on Japan. If it uses nuclear weapons again, it will become isolated in the extreme."

In Lin's view, U.S. troops "cannot possibly be endowed with the courage and the spirit of sacrifice possessed by the revolutionary people," whose "spiritual atom bomb... is a far more powerful and useful weapon than the physical atom bomb. The struggles waged by the different peoples against U.S. imperialism reinforce each other and merge into a worldwide tide of opposition to U.S. imperialism," which, "like a mad bull dashing from place to place, will finally be burned to ashes in the blazing fire of the people's wars it has provoked by its own actions."

It was Lin's opinion that the U.S. had made Vietnam a "testing ground for the suppression of the people's war." The Vietnam conflict was "now the focus of the struggle of the people of the world against U.S. aggression." Lin insisted that China's determination to support the communists in Vietnam was "unshakable."

Pakistan-India-China. On Sept. 7 China denounced Indian "aggression" in Pakistan and pledged full support of Pakistan in the struggle on the subcontinent. The Soviet Union on Sept. 7 offered its good offices in the search for a settlement of the dispute. Open warfare between India and Pakistan, which started in Kashmir in August, was intensified in September when the fighting reached into India and Pakistan proper. Violent air and ground action ensued.

U.S. Jet Downed. On Sept. 20 China said its planes had shot down an American jet fighter over Hainan Island and that the pilot had been captured.

Thant Urges China's Admission to U.N. On Sept. 21 U.N. Secretary General U Thant urged that China be admitted to the U.N. "Both the Vietnam situation and the disarmament impasse," Thant said, "point once again to the imperative need for the United Nations to achieve universality of membership as soon as possible."

Cease-Fire in Kashmir. On Sept. 22 Pakistan joined India in accepting a U.N. Security Council demand for a cease-fire in the war over Kashmir and withdrawal of all Indian and Pakistani troops to the positions they occupied on Aug. 5. A U.N. Observer Mission was established Sept. 23 to supervise the cease-fire. Both countries also announced acceptance of Soviet Premier Aleksei N. Kosygin's offer to mediate the dispute.

Goldberg Opposes China in U.N. On Sept. 23 U.S. Ambassador to the United Nations Arthur J. Goldberg appealed to the U.N. to keep China out of the organization. In his first major policy speech to the General Assembly, Goldberg described the "incredible manifesto" of Chinese Defense Minister Lin Piao on Sept. 2 as "the antithesis of everything this organization stands for." He said the U.N. had a "common responsibility to demonstrate to those who use violence that violence does not pay." He asked for U.N. aid in beginning "serious discussions" for a resolution of the Vietnam conflict.

Soviet Foreign Minister Andrei A. Gromyko, in a policy speech to the General Assembly the next day, condemned U.S. "aggression" in Vietnam and stressed Soviet support of "national liberation wars" in any part of the world. He also submitted a draft treaty which provided that any nation possessing nuclear weapons must not transfer them "in any form" to any nation that did not. Finally, Gromyko asked that China be given a seat in the U.N.

The General Assembly agreed without dissent Sept. 25 to debate the question of seating China.

Attempted Coup in Indonesia. On Sept. 30 the Indonesian armed forces crushed an uprising against the regime of President Sukarno. On Oct. 2 he announced appointment of Gen. Suharto as temporary head of the army in place of Gen. Abdul Haris Nasution, who had been injured when the insurgents attempted to kidnap him.

After a few days, it became apparent that the coup had been led by Lt. Col. Untung, a battalion commander in Sukarno's bodyguard, who was backed by the Indonesian Communist Party. Following the attempted coup, the government moved to destroy the PKI (Indonesian Communist Party), the largest non-ruling communist party in Asia, and a faithful ally of the Chinese Communist Party. Incidents against the large Chinese population in Indonesia became numerous. *(See Feb. 3, 1966)*

Vietnam Demonstrations. On Oct. 15-17, student-organized demonstrations against American military involvement in Vietnam flared up across the U.S. in marches and rallies in 40 cities. The biggest demonstrations were in New York City and Berkeley, Calif. Similar protests took place in London, Dublin, Brussels, Copenhagen, Stockholm, Rome and Tokyo. Protests against the military draft formed a major part of the weekend demonstrations.

Pro-Administration Demonstration. On Oct. 30 about 25,000 persons paraded down New York's Fifth Avenue to demonstrate support for the administration's policy on Vietnam.

Cultural Revolution Begins. On Nov. 10 Yao Wenyuan, editor of a Shanghai newspaper, wrote a signed article violently attacking a well-known and highly esteemed university professor and sometime playwright and, since 1949, one of the deputy mayors of Peking. It soon became clear that the article was a signal for a wide-ranging campaign against all forms of culture. It is now taken to mark the beginning of the Great Proletarian Cultural Revolution.

Chinese Fliers Defect. On Nov. 11 three Chinese pilots defected to Nationalist China in a Russian-made bomber. The plane crashed while landing, and one of the three defectors died.

China's U.N. Seat. On Nov. 17 the U.N. General Assembly defeated a resolution to award China's seat in the United Nations to Communist China and expel the representatives of Nationalist China. The vote was 47-47, with 20 abstentions. Prior to rejecting the change in representation, the assembly decided by a vote of 56-49, with 11 abstentions, that the matter was an "important question" requiring a two-thirds majority for adoption. With 94 members present and voting, 63 affirmative votes were needed.

Although the resolution fell far short of adoption, Peking's supporters claimed a political victory in having denied Nationalist China a plurality for the first time since the question was initially voted on in 1950. In each of the previous votes, the U.S.-backed Nationalists had attained wide margins. In 1963, when the question had last come to a vote, the Nationalists won by 57-41, with 12 abstentions.

McNamara to Vietnam. On Nov. 28 Secretary of Defense Robert S. McNamara, on a 30-hour inspection tour of Vietnam, announced that American air attacks on North Vietnam and Viet Cong supply routes would be stepped up to offset Communist military infiltration in the South.

China and Disarmament. On Nov. 29 the U.N. General Assembly approved a resolution urging convocation of a world disarmament conference, "not later than 1967," that would include China. The vote was 112-0 with France abstaining and Nationalist China absent.

On Dec. 1 China declared that "China will never enter into relations with the United Nations and any conference connected with it before the restoration of her legitimate rights in the United Nations and expulsion of the Chiang Kai-shek clique from the organization."

India-China Border Trouble. On Nov. 30 Indian Defense Minister Y. B. Chavan told the Indian Parliament that communist intrusions across the disputed Chinese-Indian border had been getting steadily bigger. "Where we used to see 10 or 12 Chinese coming across, we now see 50 or 60." On Nov. 28 the two countries had exchanged protest notes, each charging the other with border violations amounting to "aggression."

Church Council on Vietnam. On Dec. 3 the National Council of Churches called on the U.S. government to halt the bombing of North Vietnam long enough to establish a more favorable atmosphere for peace negotiations. The council's appeal was the first policy statement on the Vietnam War by a major U.S. religious body.

Chinese Aid to North Vietnam. On Dec. 5 China and North Vietnam signed an agreement providing for more loans to North Vietnam. The amount was not disclosed.

Anti-Chinese Attacks in Indonesia. On Dec. 10, 2,000 Indonesian demonstrators attacked China's consulate in Medan, North Sumatra. Three persons were killed when police fought to keep the demonstrators from entering the building. Homes and business establishments of Chinese residents also were attacked. On Dec. 18 President Sukarno appealed to Indonesians to stop attacking Chinese in Indonesia because, he said, "we are struggling against imperialism and we cannot do it alone."

Thailand Buildup. On Dec. 12 a dispatch to *The New York Times* from Bangkok reported that the U.S. had begun construction of a huge military base on the Gulf of Siam in Thailand. The dispatch reported also that pro-communist activity in northern Thailand had increased in the past six months. Communists were said to be using the same tactics in Thailand that the Viet Cong had used in South Vietnam before the large-scale American buildup there.

Air Strike Near Haiphong. On Dec. 15, U.S. planes made their first strike on a major industrial center in North Vietnam, destroying a thermal power plant 14 miles north of Haiphong, North Vietnam's major port.

U.N. Resolution on Tibet. On Dec. 18 the U.N. General Assembly adopted a resolution urging "cessation of all practices which deprive the Tibetan people of the human rights and fundamental freedom that they have enjoyed." The vote was 43-26, with 22 abstentions. All communist nations voted against the resolution.

China Ready to Fight U.S. On Dec. 20 Chinese Premier Chou En-lai, at a reception in celebration of the fifth anniversary of the founding of the National Liberation Front in South Vietnam, accused the U.S. of "making preparations" to extend the war in Vietnam to all of Southeast Asia and into China. Chou warned that if the U.S. decided on "going along the road of war expansion and

having another trial of strength with the Chinese people," China would "take up the challenge and fight to the end."

Soviet-North Vietnamese Agreement. On Dec. 21 the Soviet Union and North Vietnam signed an agreement providing for shipment of "supplementary technical assistance" and "additional free economic assistance" to North Vietnam.

Cambodian Sanctuary. On Dec. 21 the State Department confirmed reports that U.S. forces in South Vietnam had been authorized to pursue Viet Cong or North Vietnamese forces into Cambodia "in the exercise of the inherent right of self-defense to protect their forces." It was disclosed also that U.S. military commanders had been authorized to call in air strikes on North Vietnamese and Viet Cong forces hiding in Cambodia.

Christmas Cease-Fire. On Dec. 22 the U.S. military command ordered a 30-hour Christmas cease-fire, to apply generally unless firing became necessary in self-defense. Similar orders were issued by South Vietnam's military leaders, who referred to Pope Paul's appeal for a Christmas truce. Pressure immediately mounted to stretch the cease-fire into a lasting truce.

On Dec. 26, almost immediately after termination of the truce, allied ground forces resumed military action in the face of heavy Viet Cong attacks, but bombing raids on North Vietnam remained suspended.

On Dec. 28 a National Liberation Front broadcast proposed a four-day cease-fire between communist forces and South Vietnamese troops during the lunar New Year, Jan. 20-23. The offer was not extended to U.S. troops, but American officials said the U.S. would observe such a truce if it were agreed to by South Vietnam.

Peace Offensive. On Dec. 29, despite administration silence on continuation of the bombing pause begun Christmas Eve, it was apparent that a significant diplomatic operation was underway. Administration officials confirmed Dec. 30 that the president had been sending top aides to various world capitals in an all-out effort to bring peace in Vietnam.

But no positive response to these efforts was discerned in Hanoi's public statements, nor was there any indication that North Vietnam was reducing its war effort as a prelude to peace talks. On the contrary, Hanoi was getting ready to reject the president's peace offensive (on Jan. 4, 1966) as a "deceptive peace campaign and a trick."

1966

China-Cuba Trade — Tashkent Agreement — Vietnam Bombing Resumed — China Hearings — Honolulu Declaration — McNamara on Chinese A-Bomb — Suharto Takes Over Indonesia — Sino-Soviet Dispute Over Vietnam — U.S. Anti-War Protests — Cambodian Bombing — China-Albania Accord — ASPAC Formed — Red Guards Established — Lin Piao Leads Red Guard — Manila Conference — Two-China Policy Urged — China Atomic Test — Congress Backs Vietnam Policy — Non-Proliferation Treaty — Sino-Soviet Border Tension — Chinese Purge Expanded — China U.N. Bid Turned Down — U Thant's Peace Efforts — Mme. Mao Speaks Out — U.N. Space Treaty — Liu "Confesses" — Chinese Warning on Hong Kong

China-Cuba Trade. On Jan. 2 Cuban Premier Fidel Castro announced that China was reducing its trade with

China vs. the Soviet Union: A Schism . . .

Since the Communist victory in 1949, China's relations with the Soviet Union have proved to be one of the single most important factors in its foreign policy. Yet despite a brief period of relative harmony from 1950 to 1956, these relations have almost always been bellicose.

A Centuries-Old Conflict

The problems date at least to the 17th century, when Russia and China ended a series of border wars with a series of treaties. An uneasy peace followed until the 19th century when, faced with a weak and ineffective government in China, Russia, like all the other major powers, seized land along China's borders and forced the Chinese emperor to sign treaties legalizing the transfers. The Chinese Communists have said that they do not recognize these agreements, which they term "unequal treaties" and insist must be renegotiated. The Russians have refused. Thus most of China's border with the Soviet Union remains undefined.

In the 20th century, Soviet aid to the Chinese Communists prior to their victory often came with strings attached, and the Chinese felt betrayed by Moscow's interference in 1927 and 1945.

In 1950, when Chinese Communist Party Chairman Mao Tse-tung went to Moscow and signed a treaty of friendship and alliance with the Soviet Union, Western observers saw it as the logical union of the two communist giants. In fact, their similarities in ideology obscured fundamental differences between the two nations, and did nothing to halt Soviet efforts to interfere in internal Chinese politics: in Xinjiang, 1950-1953; in Manchuria, 1950-1954; and even in Peking, 1957-1959.

Khrushchev Muddies the Waters

In 1956 Nikita Khrushchev's speeches to the 20th Congress of the Soviet Communist Party mark what is now seen as the beginning of the Sino-Soviet split, although it was not apparent as such at the time. Khrushchev's attack on Stalin, while necessary to establish his own independent political position within Russia, posed problems for all the other communist states. First, because Moscow was still seen as the leader of the communist world, the speech seemed to represent a Soviet attack on one-man, police-state, totalitarian rule in other communist countries. In China, Mao Tse-tung and other Chinese leaders saw it as an attack on Mao himself. In both Peking and Eastern Europe, the leaders responded by loosening censorship, encouraging criticism, and liberalizing their rule. In China, however, the intensity of the resulting criticism caught the regime unawares, and the lid was quickly slammed down.

At the same time, the attack on Stalin also seemed to represent an attack on the way Stalin had administered the communist bloc as a whole, particularly his support for satellite states in their own confrontations with the anti-communist world.

These fears were soon confirmed in Khrushchev's second speech to the congress, when he called for an end to confrontation with the West and the beginning of an effort to achieve "peaceful coexistence."

To the Chinese leadership of that day, such notions were unthinkable. Since 1950 the avowed intention of the U.S. had been to surround China, cut it off from the world, and try to oust the communist regime and replace it with the government of Chiang Kai-shek on Taiwan. There were U.S. troops all around China: on Taiwan, in Japan, in the Philippines and in South Korea. There were U.S. advisers in South Vietnam, and British troops in Burma and Malaysia. China's only opening to the outside world was via the Soviet Union and, at least in the eyes of the Chinese leaders, Moscow's atomic weapons were China's only protection against the imperialistic West.

Faced with Khrushchev's actions, and with the failure of their attempts at liberalization, the Chinese announced their decision that Moscow was wrong, that peaceful coexistence with the capitalist-imperialist West was impossible, and that Khrushchev had violated the basic tenets of Leninist orthodoxy.

The True Believers

In 1958, with the decision to launch the Great Leap Forward, the Chinese tried to solve all their problems at once. First, they began to claim that Peking, not Moscow, was the center of true communist ideology. Second, they claimed that, faced with U.S. encirclement and Soviet abandonment, they would modernize on their own. Announcing that Mao had discovered a shortcut to communism, the Chinese espoused the principle of "self reliance." Mao explained that no longer would the Chinese "lean to one side" (toward Moscow), but would "walk on two legs."

Not surprisingly, Moscow reacted harshly to the Chinese initiatives. They heaped scorn on the Great Leap Forward (which soon stumbled), and chastized the Chinese upstarts who dared claim that they understood Lenin better than the Russians themselves. At the outset, this war of words was limited to ideological issues only, and no names were ever mentioned. The Soviets criticized Albania, not China, as "adventurist" and "infantile" for its insistence on direct confrontation with the West. For its part, the Chinese attacked Yugoslavia, not Moscow, calling it "revisionist" for its efforts to seek "coexistence" with the West. Thus, both sides had tacitly agreed that the dispute was ideological — between the two communist parties — and not a political dispute between the two states. In the United States, analysts saw only the war of words, and refused to believe that much deeper issues were involved. For most, the fundamental unity of the two nations remained unchanged.

In July 1960, the Soviets began to withdraw their technicians from China, and all agreements for scientific and technical cooperation (343 contracts and 257 projects) were suspended. The ideological quarrel had moved into the realm of state relations.

The war of words reached a crescendo in 1962-1963, with the Soviet refusal to help China in its war with India, and Khrushchev's decision to withdraw the missiles which the Russians had placed in Cuba. The Chinese press attacked both these moves as "retreats" and said that they had made no contribution to peace. At this point, the

. . . Develops In the Communist Movement

two sides stopped using veiled and obscure references, and began criticizing each other by name.

The accusations and counteraccusations continued to escalate until 1966 when, following the U.S. buildup in South Vietnam and the Soviet decision to increase aid to Hanoi, new problems arose. Moscow demanded that Peking cooperate in helping Vietnam, calling for "united action" between the two countries. Specifically, the Soviets wanted their arms shipments to Vietnam to pass through China unhindered. The Chinese saw this as an infringement on their sovereignty, more Soviet interference in internal Chinese affairs and, most importantly, a Soviet effort to push the Chinese into direct confrontation with the United States. China demurred.

Border Clashes

In response, the Russians tried to pressure the Chinese into agreement by building up troops along their 7,000-mile border.

During 1967, when the Chinese Cultural Revolution moved into its most radical phase, units of Red Guards began seizing the trains and distributing the arms amongst themselves. Tensions along the northern border continued to increase until 1969, when fighting flared all along the border.

Meanwhile, in 1968, Moscow had given the order to send troops into Czechoslovakia, ending that country's brief effort to draw away from the communist bloc and move closer to the West. For the Chinese, the invasion was an ominous portent of what might happen to them. Despite their claims, the Chinese had to be aware that their army had no hope of stopping the Russians if they decided upon a similar move in the east.

Thus, although very little is known about what goes on within the leadership in Peking, it seems that the combination of the invasion of Czechoslovakia and the 1969 border clashes forced the Chinese to undertake a complete overhaul of their foreign policy. On the one hand, they dropped the previous notion of a world dominated by the struggle between the imperialists and the communists, and adopted the "Theory of the Three Worlds," which explained that communists, too, could be imperialists, and China's true friends were not necessarily communists, but included all nations oppressed by either of the two superpowers: the Soviet Union and the United States.

At this point, the Chinese began to work with any country they could perceive as an ally — real or potential — against the Soviet Union. At the same time, they resurrected the traditional Chinese notion, first developed in the wars with the nomads along the northern border 2,000 years earlier, to "ally with the enemy far away (the U.S.) in order to fight the enemy who is at the gate (the Soviet Union)."

Freed from the radical excesses of the Cultural Revolution and the leadership of the "gang of four," China, for the time being at least, adopted what seemed to be a much more pragmatic approach to world politics. The realities of their enormous border with the Soviet Union have proved to be more important than ideology.

A Concurrence of Interests

The announcement of the Nixon Doctrine in 1969 *(p. 189),* and the subsequent American gestures toward China, came at a time when the Chinese themselves were looking toward a new foreign policy, and seeking new allies. Thus, unlike earlier initiatives, this one was embraced enthusiastically by the Chinese, and President Nixon made his historic trip to Peking.

The Chinese were reinforced in their decision when, in addition to the border confrontations, China and the U.S.S.R. fought "proxy wars" in 1971 and again in 1978. The first, which broke out in December, 1971, saw Pakistan, a Chinese ally, at war with India, supported by Moscow. In 1978, Vietnam, supported by the Russians, invaded Cambodia in order to force out the Pol Pot regime, which was backed by Peking. Direct confrontation between the two Asian giants threatened again when, in early 1979, the Chinese retaliated with their "punitive" invasion of Vietnam. And the Soviet invasion in late 1979 of Afghanistan — which borders China — drew China and the United States even closer together against the Russian threat to the balance of power.

Nonetheless, the extent to which good relations between China and America depend on the Sino-Soviet split may limit the durability of the new relationship. Some observers felt that unless the U.S. could find other common ground with China and work to build an affirmative relationship that does not depend on Chinese fear of Moscow, any warming in Sino-Soviet relationships could spell the end of Peking's opening to Washington and a return to the Sino-American hostility of an earlier era. Other, more optimistic observers felt that a lessening of Sino-Soviet hostility could only be beneficial to the West by reducing tension worldwide.

New Sino-Soviet Accord?

Reports of a possible thaw in relations between China and the Soviet Union had, in fact, begun to surface in the summer of 1979.

In September, a delegation from Peking led by Deputy Foreign Minister Wang Youping arrived in Moscow for talks with Soviet officials led by Soviet Deputy Foreign Minister Leonid F. Ilyichev.

Wang released a statement noting that "differences of principle between China and the Soviet Union should not hamper the maintenance and development of their normal state relations," and expressed hope that the talks would generate "genuine improvements" between the two countries.

The talks — proposed by China at the same time it announced it would not renew its 30-year alliance pact with the U.S.S.R. — got off to a rocky start, however, with accusations in the press of both nations. Xinhua, the Chinese news agency, charged the Soviets with creating "suspicions over the motive of the Chinese side," while Tass, the Soviet news agency, accused China of duplicity in negotiations with North Vietnam.

This round of talks ended Nov. 30, 1979, with little indication of progress, and the Soviets' Afghanistan invasion began a month later.

Cuba from an exchange of $250 million in 1965 to $170 million in 1966.

Tashkent Agreement. On Jan. 10 Indian Prime Minister Shastri and Pakistani President Yahya Khan signed an agreement in Tashkent, Russia, under which both countries agreed to withdraw from the positions they had occupied during the border conflict. The Soviet Union had acted as mediator in the discussions.

Russo-Mongolian Treaty. On Jan. 15 the Soviet Union and the People's Republic of Mongolia signed a Treaty of Friendship, Cooperation and Mutual Assistance in Ulan Bator. The pact seemed to be aimed at China, with which Mongolia has a 2500-mile border.

Indira Gandhi. On Jan. 19 Indira Gandhi, 48, was named India's new prime minister. The daughter of the late Prime Minister Jawaharlal Nehru, she succeeded Lal Bahadur Shastri, who died Jan. 11 in Tashkent.

Bombing Resumption. On Jan. 31 President Johnson announced in a nationally televised address that U.S. aircraft had resumed bombing of North Vietnam, ending the pause that began Dec. 24. The strikes, Johnson said, were directed against military targets, such as lines of supply which support the movement of men and arms from North Vietnam to South Vietnam.

U.S. Resolution at U.N. On Jan. 31 U.S. Ambassador Arthur J. Goldberg submitted to the U.N. Security Council a draft resolution asking the council: (1) to call for immediate discussions among the "appropriate interested governments," without preconditions, on arranging a conference "looking toward" application of the 1954 and 1962 Geneva agreements and the establishment of a durable peace in Southeast Asia; (2) to recommend that the first order of business of such a conference be the arrangement of an effectively supervised cease-fire; and (3) to offer U.N. mediation to help achieve the purposes of the resolution. The council on Feb. 2 voted 9-2 (U.S.S.R. and Bulgaria), with four abstentions (France, Mali, Nigeria, Uganda) to take up the resolution.

Goldberg asserted in an interview on Feb. 5 that there was a broad consensus in the Security Council that a reconvened Geneva conference was the proper place to deal with the Vietnam War.

Chinese Charges. On Feb. 2 the Peking *People's Daily* charged that the Soviet Union was supporting U.S. efforts to achieve the "military encirclement of China." The article claimed that Soviet policy "on Vietnam, India-Pakistan and Japan questions completely conforms with the requirements of United States imperialism, especially with the latter's policy of encircling China." The *People's Daily* had earlier published a map showing the positions of U.S. air bases, troop concentrations, ships and naval bases throughout Asia. The map was entitled: "The Military Encirclement of China by American Imperialism."

Chinese Embassy Sacked. On Feb. 3 a series of anti-Chinese incidents in Indonesia, dating from the abortive coup of 1965 *(see Sept. 30, 1965),* culminated in the burning of the Chinese Embassy in Jakarta, and the rough handling of several employees.

Senate Hearings Begin. On Feb. 4 the Senate Foreign Relations Committee opened hearings on an administration bill (S 2793) authorizing $415 million in supplemental fiscal 1966 foreign economic aid, of which $275 million was earmarked for South Vietnam. The hearings, televised

nationally, were used by the committee as a springboard for a public inquiry into the administration's "general policy" in Vietnam.

Attempts to Limit the Cultural Revolution. On Feb. 5 Peng Zhen, mayor of Peking and often referred to as a possible successor to Party Chairman Mao Tse-tung, called a meeting of the "Committee of Five," which was directing the Cultural Revolution. In an effort to limit the impact of the purge, Peng issued the "February Outline Report," which was then distributed secretly among ranking party leaders.

Peng was later accused of trying to organize a coup against Mao during this period.

China and Cuba. On Feb. 6 it became clear that the split between China and Cuba had widened. The Cuban Communist Party newspaper *Granma* published an article by Cuban Premier Fidel Castro in which he accused China of "blackmail" and the "betrayal" of the Cuban revolution. He asserted that China had attempted to intervene in Cuba's internal affairs, and that Cuban action to stop a Chinese propaganda campaign on the island was the "true motive for the Chinese conduct."

Honolulu Declaration. On Feb. 8 the United States and South Vietnam issued a Declaration of Honolulu and a joint communiqué following a three-day meeting between President Johnson and leaders of the Saigon government. The declaration confirmed U.S. commitments to South Vietnam and stressed not only expansion of military efforts but also political and social reforms in South Vietnam. The president announced that he had asked Vice President Hubert H. Humphrey to fly to Saigon with the Vietnamese leaders and from there commence a tour of other Southeast Asia nations.

U.S. Ready to Admit Chinese Journalists. On Feb. 14 the State Department announced that the U.S. was prepared to allow Chinese journalists to visit the United States. A spokesman said the offer, advanced during one of the regular meetings of U.S. and Chinese diplomats in Warsaw, was not dependent on reciprocal admission of American newsmen by China. The spokesman added that China "has neither taken up the offer nor rejected it."

Johnson Reply to Critics. On Feb. 23 President Johnson, in a speech at Freedom House in New York, said that the "strength of America can never be sapped by discussion," but he also warned that "no foe . . . should mistake . . . our debate for weakness." Reciting his replies to the "questions that are still being asked," Johnson said, "there is not and there will not be a mindless escalation [of the Vietnam War]." There was no risk of confrontation with China, he insisted, as long as "there is any reason left behind the wild words from" Peking.

No Progress at U.N. On Feb. 26, after three weeks of deliberation, it was reported that the U.N. Security Council had been unable to make progress toward agreement on the U.S. resolution to promote a negotiated settlement of the Vietnamese conflict. *(See Jan. 31, 1966)*

Ghana Ousts Communists. On March 1 the new regime in Ghana ordered all Soviet, Chinese and East German personnel and their families to leave the country. About 130 Russians and 150 Chinese departed during the first week of March.

McNamara on China's Bomb. On March 7 Secretary of Defense Robert S. McNamara told the Joint Congressional Committee on Atomic Energy that he was disturbed about the future nuclear capability of China, especially because of the "aggressive statements of her leaders." McNamara said that within two or three years China would have a nuclear "warhead delivery capability" within a 700-mile radius. China then would be able to support the aggressive statements of its leaders "with instruments of war of the most terrible kind."

China Hearings. On March 8 the Senate Foreign Relations Committee began a series of hearings on "U.S. Policy with Respect to Mainland China." Dubbed the "Second Great China Debate," the atmosphere was markedly different from the first, in the 1950s, which had seen the acrimonious presence of Sen. Joseph R. McCarthy.

The hearings were triggered by the expansion of the war in Vietnam and fear that the Chinese might intervene, as they had in Korea. The witnesses, including virtually all of the most prestigious China scholars in the U.S., although divided on the Vietnam War itself, were almost unanimous in arguing that although the U.S. should probably continue to try to "contain" China, the policy of "isolation" should be admitted to have failed, and be dropped. In turn, it was argued that the U.S. should step up cultural, educational, and technical contacts with the PRC.

On March 10 Dr. John K. Fairbank, director of the East Asian Research Center at Harvard University, testified that use of American military power in Asia should be tempered by constructive "nation-building." He thought that the alternatives to war with Peking were (1) to be more constructive socially and politically in Vietnam, so that "the non-Communist model of nation-building there can compete more effectively with the Chinese Communist model," and (2) to "dampen Peiping's [Beijing] militancy by getting China into greater contact with the outside world." In addition to proposing admission of China to international organizations, Fairbank pointed out that "the Chinese people positively need certain kinds of aid through exchanges of technology or of goods, like all developing countries."

He concluded: "Containment alone is a blind alley unless we add policies of constructive competition and international contact.... Peiping's rulers shout aggressively out of manifold frustrations.... Isolation intensifies their ailment and makes it self-perpetuating, and we need to encourage international contact with China on many fronts."

On March 21 Donald S. Zagoria, professor of government at Columbia University, testified: "Our only hope to achieve a stable and tolerable relationship with Communist China is to do all we can to promote not a change of the system — which can be done only by war — but a change within the system. The kind of evolution which is already transforming Russia and the East European Communist countries will have to come.... We can help to hasten its growth."

On March 28 Dr. George E. Taylor, professor of Far Eastern History at the University of Washington, disagreed that increased Sino-American contacts would lessen the chances of war or have any impact on internal Chinese policy, "unless there were a radical change in the attitude of the Communist regime."

The hearings ended March 30.

French to Leave NATO. On March 9 France formally announced that it planned to withdraw from the North Atlantic Treaty Organization. No date was specified.

Travel to Communist Countries. On March 9 it was disclosed that President Johnson had decided to ease travel restrictions for scholars wanting to visit Albania, China, North Vietnam, North Korea or Cuba.

Kenya Expels Communists. On March 10 the government of Kenya announced that it had ordered Chinese, Russian and Czech diplomats and journalists to leave the country. No reason for the action was given.

Sukarno Yields. On March 12, following weeks of demonstrations in Jakarta, President Sukarno relinquished all governmental power. Lt. Gen. Suharto, army commander, assumed leadership of the country. Sukarno, Foreign Minister Subandrio and other Cabinet ministers were placed under house arrest. Suharto immediately banned the PKI, the Indonesian Communist Party. Suharto said the new regime had no "intention of turning our revolution to the right as charged by some people, nor will we return it to the extreme left, because it is already leftist."

Humphrey on China Policy. On March 13 Vice President Hubert H. Humphrey, during a broadcast interview, said that U.S. policy toward China should be one of "containment without necessarily isolation." Humphrey added that the "program of responsible containment, the building of collective security in the West, but at the same time a probing and trying to find ways of communication, has been relatively successful, and I think it is in our interest and in the interest of humanity that the same kind of approach be exercised in Asia." He asserted that departure of the "Mao generation" from "positions of leadership" was necessary before there could be improved relations between China and the West. "In the meantime, we ought to maintain ... a spirit of friendship toward the Chinese people, but recognizing what the regime is, and making that regime understand they cannot achieve their purpose by military power."

Rusk on China. On March 16 Secretary of State Dean Rusk testified before the House Foreign Affairs Subcommittee on the Far East and the Pacific. After reviewing U.S.-China relations to date, Rusk summed up the elements of future U.S. policy, and listed ten elements in that policy:

These were: (1) firmness in assisting allied nations which sought U.S. help against Chinese aggression; (2) continued assistance to the nation-building process in Asia; (3) honoring of commitments for the defense of the Republic of China on Taiwan; (4) continued efforts to prevent the expulsion of the Republic of China from the United Nations, and opposition to Communist China's U.N. membership; (5) reassurance to Peking that the U.S. did not intend to attack the mainland; (6) avoidance of the assumption that hostility between the U.S. and China was "unending and inevitable"; (7) enlargement of possibilities for unofficial contacts between China and the United States, including permission for American universities to invite Chinese scientists to visit them; (8) continued direct diplomatic contacts with the Chinese ambassador in Warsaw; (9) willingness to discuss with Peking and other countries the critical problems of disarmament and non-proliferation; and (10) exploration and analysis of all available information on China in order to keep U.S. policies up to date.

The only change indicated in this statement was that the U.S. finally agreed to the 1956 Chinese proposal for cultural contacts. The Chinese had long since dropped the offer. *(Text, p. 315)*

There was no reference to the Vietnam War as an issue in Sino-American relations. *(See April 1, 1966)*

U.S. Reassures China. On March 20 the U.S. assured China that despite its buildup in Vietnam, the U.S. had no intention of invading China. The assurance was passed to the Chinese during the monthly meeting of U.S. and Chinese representatives at Warsaw.

European Steel Plant for China. On March 20 Secretary of State Dean Rusk, during a television interview, protested a plan by West German and other European companies to construct a $150-million steel plant in China. Rusk voiced hope that "our friends in Europe would keep this matter under review, and before they get into a situation where they are producing two million tons more of steel for Peiping, that they would give some thought to the problems of peace."

Soviet Letter Attacking Chinese Communists. On March 22 a letter reportedly written by the Soviet Communist Party's Central Committee to the East European parties was published by a West German newspaper (*Die Welt* of Hamburg). An English translation appeared two days later in *The New York Times*. The letter said there was "every reason to assert that it is one of the goals of the policy of the Chinese leadership in the Vietnam question to originate a military conflict between the U.S.S.R. and the United States . . . so that they may, as they say themselves, 'sit on the mountain and watch the fight of the tigers.'

"The Soviet Union delivers large amounts of weapons to the DRV, including rocket installations, anti-aircraft artillery, airplanes, tanks, coastal guns, warships and other items. In 1965 alone, weapons and other material worth about 500 million rubles [$550 million] were placed at the disposal of the DRV. The DRV is receiving support in the training of pilots, rocket personnel, tank drivers, artillerymen and so on. Our military aid is being rendered to the extent the Vietnamese leadership thinks necessary."

The Soviet leaders had proposed "more than once" to the Chinese leaders "that joint actions to support Vietnam be organized." But the Chinese leadership opposed such action. "By stating openly that they do not desire joint action with the U.S.S.R. and other Socialist countries, by emphasizing their differences of views with the Soviet Union, and by hindering its aid to the DRV, the Chinese leaders basically encourage the United States aggressors in their war acts against Vietnam." Moscow also accused Peking of needing a prolonged Vietnam War to "maintain international tensions and to represent China as a besieged fortress."

Going on to accuse the Chinese leadership of propagating "ever more obstinately the thesis of potential military clashes between China and the Soviet Union," the Russians referred to a recent increase in border conflicts and said they were provoked by the Chinese. "The Chinese government refuses to resume the negotiations suspended in May 1964 on a precise delimitation of the border. It obviously prefers to leave this problem unsettled. At the same time, allegations are being spread to the effect that the Soviet Union unlawfully holds Chinese territory in the Far East." On the contrary, the Russians emphasized, the area in question had always belonged to the U.S.S.R.

Finally, the Soviet Communists accused the Chinese of attempting to split the international communist movement and lead the world toward war. The letter said that Lin Piao's article on the "struggle of the world village against the world city" was "tantamount to the rejection of the leading role of the working class and constitutes a complete revision of the Marxist-Leninist doctrine of the world-historical mission of the working class."

The letter concluded that the Chinese Communists were seeking to dominate the entire communist movement and added that while the Chinese criticized others because they were not sufficiently militant, they themselves "show extraordinary caution in their own political deeds, as well as extreme patience toward imperialist powers and their policy, including the policy that is aimed against China itself."

Chinese Refuse Bid to Moscow. On March 23 China refused the Soviet Union's invitation to attend the 23rd Congress of the Soviet Communist Party. The Chinese statement, referring to the Soviet Party's anti-Chinese letter, said that "Since you have gone so far, the Chinese Communist Party . . . cannot send its delegation to attend this congress of yours."

Vietnam Protests in U.S. On March 26, anti-war demonstrations took place in numerous American cities. The largest was in New York; other demonstrations were staged in San Francisco, Chicago, Washington, Detroit and Cambridge, Mass. The rallies and parades were organized by the National Coordinating Committee to End the War in Vietnam, with headquarters in Madison, Wis.

Goldberg on China Policy. On March 28 Ambassador to the U.N. Arthur J. Goldberg said that U.N. members were currently less favorably disposed to seating Communist China than in 1965. He said the reason was due mainly to China itself and its self-imposed isolation. Goldberg said the U.S. was willing to terminate this isolation in limited ways, such as preliminary talks to determine whether a world disarmament conference should be held, a non-proliferation of nuclear weapons agreement, and exchanges of technical personnel.

Soviet Congress. On March 29 the 23rd Soviet Communist Party Congress convened in Moscow. In the opening speech, Communist Party First Secretary Leonid I. Brezhnev stressed unity and called relations with China and Albania "unsatisfactory." He said the Soviet Communist Party condemned "with deep indignation the anti-Communist terror in Indonesia."

China's Response to "Flexibility." On April 1 the *Peking Review* carried an article by "Observer" (indicating high-level approval) which rejected the recent U.S. efforts to improve relations with China. Entitled "Old Tune, New Plot," the article stated that the U.S. was still hostile toward China and "will not depart a whit from its fundamental China policy." It criticized the easing of travel restrictions to China as a ruse, designed only to fool people. *(See April 10)*

Chou's Response to "Flexibility." On April 10 Chinese Premier Chou En-lai, in an effort to relieve U.S.-China tension, stated that "China will not take the initiative to provoke war with the United States." At the same time, however, he stressed the key role which the Vietnam War had come to play in Sino-American relations: "The Chinese government and people will definitely support" any government which "meets with aggression by the imperialists."

B-52 Raids in North. On April 12, B-52 heavy jet bombers staged bombing raids over North Vietnam for the first time.

Offer to Chinese Scholars. On April 14 the State Department disclosed that several American universities had been notified that scientists and scholars from China would be permitted to visit the United States. The offer was rejected by China two days later.

China and the U.N. On April 19 Arthur J. Goldberg, U.S. ambassador to the U.N., speaking at the National Press Club in Washington, outlined the minimum conditions under which the U.S. would agree to China's admission to the United Nations. Peking would have to abandon its demand for expulsion of Taiwan; withdraw its demand that the U.N. rescind its condemnation of China for aggression in Korea and brand the U.S. as the aggressor; withdraw its demand that the U.N. be reorganized and that unnamed "lackeys" of the United States be expelled; and promise to observe the provisions of the U.N. Charter. While indicating that the administration was reconsidering its past position on China's admission, Goldberg said: "This is a highly intricate question, and no change in our policy has been made. Our tactics, of course, are under review." He said also that "along many avenues, even in the face of numerous rebuffs," the U.S. was trying to get China to "come into the mainstream of the international community."

Fulbright Speech. On April 21 Sen. J. William Fulbright, D-Ark., chairman of the Senate Foreign Relations Committee, said in a lecture April 21 at Johns Hopkins University School of Advanced International Studies that the U.S. was "gradually but unmistakably . . . succumbing to the arrogance of power" and that those protesting the Vietnam War "deserve our sympathy and respect." Fulbright also said the Senate "should undertake to revive and strengthen the deliberation function" in foreign policy-making which it had let atrophy during the past 25 years.

Cambodian Border Fighting. On May 3 the U.S. Military Command in Saigon acknowledged for the first time that American ground forces had fired on targets in Cambodia, delivering "a heavy volume of artillery" fire into a Viet Cong position on the Cambodian side of the Cai Bac River which forms the border.

Transit of Soviet Aid to Vietnam. On May 4 Peking radio broadcast a Chinese Foreign Ministry statement that "China has never hampered the transit of Soviet aid materials to North Vietnam." Peking insisted that "All military aid materials Vietnam asked for and the Soviet Union delivered to China have been transported to Vietnam by China with priority, at high speed and free of charge."

Mao's Orders to Army. On May 7 Party Chairman Mao Tse-tung ordered that the Chinese army and the Chinese people be brought into closer contact, with the army carrying out some civilian tasks and the general populace learning from the army, China's "great school."

Mao also called for the elimination of all individual interests and occupational differences, leading to the creation of a completely selfless and interchangeable man. Mao's order was made public on Aug. 2.

Mao and the Albanians. On May 10 the Xinhua news agency reported that Chinese Communist Party Chairman Mao Tse-tung had met with Albanian leaders in Peking a few days earlier. A picture of Mao and the Albanians was published. During their visit, the Albanians were reported to have joined the Chinese in warning the North Vietnamese "against remaining friendly with the Russians." They were said to have insisted that there could be "no neutrality in the dispute and that the struggle against Soviet revisionism must be carried through to the end."

Johnson on Use of U.S. Power. On May 11 President Johnson, in remarks at the dedication of the new building of the Woodrow Wilson School of Public and International Affairs, Princeton University, asserted that "the issue for this generation . . . has to do with the obligations of power." Apparently replying to statements by Sen. J. William Fulbright, D-Ark., the president said that: "The exercise of power in this century has meant for the United States not arrogance but agony. We have used our power not willingly and recklessly but reluctantly and with restraint."

Demonstration in Washington. On May 15 some 10,000 people demonstrated in Washington against the war in Vietnam and pledged themselves to fight politically for candidates in the coming elections who would support a showdown of the Vietnam conflict, looking toward a cease-fire.

Cultural Revolution Heats Up. On May 16, following a series of high-level Communist Party meetings in Peking, the "May 16 Circular" was issued, to be distributed secretly among the upper echelons of the party. Made public a year later, the circular rejected Peng Zhen's efforts to limit the Cultural Revolution to academic and intellectual circles, and called for a drastic expansion of the purge. One of the first victims of the new effort was Peng himself, the first major political figure to fall.

The circular was vague concerning who else should be purged, stating only that "some of them we have already seen through, others we have not," a slogan later used to purge those who, for whatever reason, opposed the purge.

Lu Dingyi, minister of culture and official spokesman for the government since 1949, was purged along with Peng, as well as several of Lu's assistants.

Intrusion Into China. On May 17 the Xinhua news agency asserted it could prove that five U.S. planes shot down a Chinese training plane over Chinese territory.

UAW on China. On May 21 the annual convention of the United Auto Workers (AFL-CIO), in a break with AFL-CIO policy, called for diplomatic recognition of China.

Program of the Cultural Revolution. On June 1 the Peking *People's Daily* published the first article in a five-part series which seems to have been designed to introduce the Cultural Revolution to the general public. Entitled "Sweep Away All Monsters," the article announced that a huge revolutionary, cultural, and proletarian wave was gathering force in China, and had been "sweeping away a horde of monsters that have entrenched themselves in ideological and cultural positions." This wave, concluded the article, will rout the "specialists," the "scholars," and various "authorities."

The article marks the beginning of what was later identified as a "red" versus "expert" dispute, in which it was more important to be "red" (a good revolutionary and fervent supporter of Mao Tse-tung) than it was to be "expert" (a non-fervent bureaucrat, technician, or cadre).

On June 8 the last important editorial in the series appeared. Entitled "We Are the Critics of the Old World," it was a call for all of the people of China to rise up and destroy the traditional Chinese culture. The origin of the Red Guards, and of their excesses, can be traced to this article.

Asian Council. On June 16 nine non-communist nations established the Asian and Pacific Council (ASPAC) at a meeting in Seoul, South Korea. The members included South Korea, Nationalist China, Japan, South Vietnam, Malaysia, Thailand, the Philippines, Australia and New Zealand. Laos was represented by an observer. In a joint statement the nine nations voiced their determination "to preserve their integrity and sovereignty in the face of external threats." They also supported "the inherent right of the Vietnamese people to self-defense and to choose their own way of life and their own form of government free from external aggression and subversion."

Mansfield Urges Meeting With China. On June 16 Senate Majority Leader Mike Mansfield, D-Mont., in a speech at Yeshiva University in New York City, said that what was needed in the face of the current danger in South Vietnam was an "initiative for a direct contact between the Peking government and our own Government on the problem of peace in Vietnam and Southeast Asia." He favored a meeting on the foreign-minister level. Mansfield called it "unrealistic to describe the situation in South Vietnam in a clear-cut ideological context" or to view the conflict "as wholly one of an aggression of the North against the South."

Reassurance to Taiwan. On July 3 Secretary of State Dean Rusk, upon arrival at the airport in Taiwan, pledged that "we are constant in our relations and in our alliance to the Republic of China, that we oppose the seating of the Peiping regime in the United Nations, and I have no doubt that that will be the basis of our relationship in weeks, and months, and years to come." Rusk's statement quelled fears in the Chiang Kai-shek government that the United States was considering a more flexible or "soft-line" policy toward China.

Chinese Charge Against Soviets. On July 10 Chinese Foreign Minister Chen Yi charged at a Peking rally that the Soviet Union was "making military deployments along the Chinese border in coordination with United States imperialist encirclement of China." He said:

"Fabrications are made and lies and slander spread everywhere, accusing China of obstructing transit of aid material to Vietnam in an attempt to undermine the unity between the peoples of China and Vietnam and to sabotage the Vietnamese people's war of resistance against United States aggression and for national salvation.... The facts are very clear. The Soviet revisionist ruling clique is redoubling its efforts to take united action with United States imperialism in a big way to sabotage the revolutionary struggle of all peoples of the world."

Doors Closed. On July 11 the Chinese government suspended most visas and closed China's doors to foreign travelers, with the exception of visitors whose business was considered essential to the Chinese state. The action was generally interpreted as a move to keep the "Cultural Revolution" under as close wraps as possible.

President on China and a Pacific Era. On July 12 President Johnson asserted in a nationally televised speech to the American Alumni Council at White Sulphur Springs, W.Va., that eventual reconciliation with China was necessary and possible, and that the U.S. would persist in efforts to reduce tensions between the two countries. "A peaceful mainland China is central to a peaceful Asia," the president said. "A hostile China must be discouraged from aggression. A misguided China must be encouraged toward

understanding of the outside world and toward policies of peaceful cooperation."

Travel to China. On July 16 the State Department relaxed restrictions on tourist travel to China. The only condition imposed by the new regulations was that the traveler's business or professional stature be such that his trip would benefit the United States. China, meanwhile, refused to grant visas to Americans.

Two-China Policy. On July 20 Sen. Edward M. Kennedy, D-Mass., said in the Senate that both Communist China and Nationalist China should be seated in the United Nations. Later in the day, President Johnson told a news conference that although the administration would "do everything we can to increase our exchanges" with Communist China, it was not ready to adopt a "two-China" policy.

Liu Warns U.S. On July 22 Chinese chief of state Liu Shao-ch'i urged the United States to avoid further escalation of the Vietnam conflict. "If you think you can unscrupulously escalate the war of aggression, without meeting due punishment," Liu's statement said, "then you will find it too late to repent." The theme was repeated the same day at a huge anti-American rally in Peking.

Big Splash. On July 25 the Xinhua news agency reported that Communist Party Chairman Mao Tse-tung, 72, had demonstrated his "wonderful health," after recovering from a long illness, by swimming for nine miles in the Yangtze River in view of thousands of spectators, many of them foreigners.

Schools Close in China. On July 26 all universities and secondary schools in China were closed so that students might participate in the Cultural Revolution. It was announced that the schools would be closed for six months, but they were not reopened for several years. *(See Nov. 24, 1966)*

DMZ Bombed. On July 30 U.S. aircraft bombed the demilitarized zone between North and South Vietnam for the first time. U.S. officials claimed that the zone had been used by North Vietnamese and Viet Cong as a sanctuary and infiltration route.

Mao's Wall Poster. On Aug. 5 a wall poster, supposedly written by Chinese Party Chairman Mao Tse-tung, appeared in Peking. It encouraged the Red Guards to "Bombard the Headquarters" of the Chinese Communist Party.

Official Approval for Cultural Revolution. On Aug. 8 the Central Committee of the Chinese Communist Party released its decision on the Cultural Revolution. Known as the "16 Points," the statement said that certain persons "taking the capitalist road" held leading positions within the party, and must be removed. This would be done by the masses, who would "revolutionize" themselves. The party also ordered the formation of "cultural revolutionary groups and committees" to attack the "anti-party, anti-socialist rightists." Announcing that "disorders were not to be feared," the "16 Points" thus set up mass organizations outside the party which were to be used to attack the party, opening the way for the chaos and anarchy which followed.

All of this activity would take place under the banner of the infallibility of Mao Tse-tung and his writings.

In this directive and others, the participation of the peasants in the Cultural Revolution was forbidden. In an obvious effort to maintain the agricultural output on which China depended, Red Guard activities were also limited to urban areas.

Birth of Red Guards. On Aug. 18 the first of many mass rallies was held in Peking to celebrate the Cultural Revolution, now in full swing. Over one million people gathered in Tiananmen Square to hear speeches by Chinese leaders, particularly those of Minister of Defense Lin Piao, who would lead the movement. During the rally, Mao Tse-tung gave official recognition to the "Red Guards," who were to be the soldiers leading the purge.

Two days after the rally, the city of Peking experienced near anarchy as Red Guards ran through the streets attacking people and property. This chaos soon spread to the other cities of China.

Fulbright on Purpose of U.S. in Asia. On Aug. 23 Sen. J. William Fulbright, D-Ark., chairman of the Senate Foreign Relations Committee, asserted during a committee session that the "real purpose" of the U.S. was to stay in Asia indefinitely to counterbalance the influence of China. The senator added that the massive construction of military bases in Thailand afforded proof of his point. "It is almost incredible to think that we are doing this as a temporary operation." he said.

Anti-Russian Rally. On Aug. 29, thousands of Red Guards marched past the Soviet Union's embassy in Peking in an all-day demonstration against "revisionism." Although the parade was well-disciplined, Chinese soldiers and police guarded the building against possible attack.

Red Guards Cautioned. On Aug. 31 the militant Red Guards held another rally in Peking and were reviewed by Mao, Lin and other leaders. A directive issued the same day stated that the Red Guards had been overly zealous in their anti-bourgeois campaign.

Chinese Bellicosity. On Sept. 2 the Xinhua news agency reported that China had assured North Vietnam that "every preparation" had been made to deal "joint blows at the U.S. aggressors until final victory is achieved."

Lin Piao to Lead Red Guards. On Sept. 4 Peking radio announced that Defense Minister Lin Piao, heir-apparent to Mao Tse-tung, had been designated by the Red Guards as their leader. It was reported also that Premier Chou En-lai had been named an adviser to the group.

Chinese Report and Warning. On Sept. 5 the Xinhua news agency reported that U.S. airplanes on Aug. 29 had sunk one Chinese ship in the Gulf of Tonkin and damaged another, killing nine Chinese seamen and injuring seven others. U.S. officials said the report would be investigated. According to the news agency, the Chinese Ministry of National Defense had said the attack was one of many.

Hanoi and Moscow. On Sept. 9 a Moscow dispatch to *The New York Times* reported that North Vietnam had "moved reluctantly into the Soviet political sphere of influence ... after Communist China allowed its once-predominant influence in Hanoi to be dissipated." The Chinese purge, the report said, "is believed to have disillusioned the North Vietnamese with their Chinese alliance and, consequently, raised their dependence on Moscow."

Peking Rally. On Sept. 15 more than one million Red Guards and soldiers crowded into Tiananmen Square (renamed the East-is-Red Square) in Peking to hear Premier Chou En-lai urge them to halt temporarily their anti-

bourgeois campaign and join the peasants in the countryside in harvesting the crops. Lin Piao, defense minister and Mao's heir-apparent, urged the crowd to "uphold Chairman Mao's teachings, strengthen the power of the revolution by uniting with the workers, peasants and soldiers, and firmly concentrate on production."

On the same day, the Peking *People's Daily* said in an editorial that the Cultural Revolution may be "suspended temporarily during the busiest period of the autumn harvest." It added: "It is not necessary for Red Guards and revolutionary teachers and students from colleges and middle schools to go to factories and rural areas to exchange revolutionary experiences and interfere with arrangements there."

Philippines and Viet Nam. On Sept. 15 substantial increases in U.S. economic aid to the Philippines were announced. On the following day, the first contingent of Philippine troops arrived in South Vietnam. On Sept. 16 Philippine President Ferdinand E. Marcos, addressing the National Press Club in Washington, said he supported the U.S. effort in Vietnam but was "concerned about the apparent failure of economic development measures in Vietnam to date."

Chinese Charge Plane Attack. On Sept. 16 China charged that two U.S. warplanes had attacked across the Chinese border, wounding three peasants. The Chinese asserted that the U.S. planes had been scared away by Chinese Air Force fighters. On the same day, Secretary of State Dean Rusk said the United States would investigate the charges. *(See Sept. 5, 1966.)*

U.S. to Oppose China at U.N. On Sept. 16 Secretary of State Dean Rusk told a news conference that the United States would again oppose admission of Communist China to the United Nations. He added, however, that the administration's current policy goals centered around the possibility of visitor exchanges with China to help "break through the walls of isolation that Peking has built around itself."

North Korea and China. On Sept. 18 the Soviet newspaper *Pravda* published an article from the North Korean Communist Party newspaper *Rodong Shinmoon* criticizing recent political events in China and implying that the North Korean party had defected from the Chinese camp.

Pravda Report on Red Guards. On Sept. 23 the Soviet Communist Party newspaper *Pravda* published a report from Peking that Red Guards were beating and murdering officials of the Chinese Communist Party. A Sept. 25 *Pravda* dispatch said the Red Guards had ordered "the destruction of all books which did not conform to the spirit of Chairman Mao's ideas."

Chinese Arms to Arabs. On Sept. 25 China was reported to be shipping small amounts of weapons to the Palestine Liberation Organization of the Arab countries.

Poles Denounce China. On Sept. 29 the Polish Communist Party, which had resisted Soviet attempts to exclude China from the international communist movement, for the first time strongly denounced China for disrupting the unity of the communist nations.

Chinese Rally. On Oct. 1, 17th anniversary of the founding of the Chinese People's Republic, more than 50 Soviet-bloc diplomats, their wives and families, left the reviewing stand during the mammoth ceremonies in Peking. They were protesting a charge by Defense Minister Lin Piao that the Soviet Union was plotting with the United States in Vietnam.

"We must turn the whole country into a great school of Mao Tse-tung's thought," Lin declared, adding that China was ready to wage "the struggle against U.S. imperialism and its lackeys and the struggle against modern revisionism, with the leadership of the Communist Party of the Soviet Union as its center, to the end."

In the parade, about 5,000 goose-stepping soldiers were followed by thousands of Red Guards, taking more than four hours to pass the reviewing stand where Mao, Lin and other officials were standing. Although the Red Guards made constant requests, Mao refused to speak.

At a banquet the night before, it was noted that chief of state Liu Shao-ch'i was absent, but he attended the National Day ceremonies.

Soviet Aid to North Vietnam. On Oct. 3 the Soviet news agency Tass reported that the Soviet Union and North Vietnam had concluded agreements for economic assistance and military aid. No figures were released.

Analysis of China's Position. On Oct. 4 U. Alexis Johnson, the new ambassador to Japan and former deputy under secretary of state, told the 18th annual Far East Conference in Washington that China's loss of prestige in the economic and political fields might force it to move toward a "live-and-let-live" policy toward the rest of the world. Noting that the non-communist nations of Asia were making rapid economic progress, Johnson said that China had made no progress in gross national product per capita since 1956. He added that the spread of Chinese-style communism had suffered a disastrous defeat in Indonesia and would again in Vietnam. The latter event, he said, might be a turning point for China, forcing the people to give up violence and attempt to live peaceably with their neighbors.

Chinese Students to Leave Russia. On Oct. 7 the Soviet Union announced it had ordered all 65 Chinese students in the U.S.S.R. to leave the country by the end of October. Peking on Sept. 20 had told Russian students in China to return home because their teachers were preoccupied with the Cultural Revolution.

Kosygin Accuses China. On Oct. 13 Soviet Premier Aleksei N. Kosygin, in a speech in Sverdlovsk, accused China of preventing a North Vietnamese victory in the Vietnam War by blocking efforts of socialist countries to assist North Vietnam. He said: "If American imperialism had met such general resistance from all the countries of socialism, with a unity of policy, there would be no doubt but that its outrages in Vietnam would have been brought to a halt in a short time." Kosygin went on to say: "The policies of China have become a serious obstacle in the struggle for this sacred cause. . . . They are causing great concern to all Communist and progressive people, to whom the defense of the Vietnamese people's freedom and independence is dear, because these policies are resulting in ever greater damage to the interests of the Vietnamese and the interests of world socialism."

On the same day, the Italian Communist Party condemned China for the first time, objecting mainly to the "Cultural Revolution."

LBJ Trip. On Oct. 17 President Johnson flew from Washington to Honolulu on the first leg of a trip to be climaxed by a conference at Manila with the leaders of six other nations. Upon arrival in the Hawaiian capital, the president said he was "convinced that we have reached a turning point in Asia's history, in Asia's relations with the United States, and in Asia's relations with the rest of the world." He added: "All hatred among nations must end in reconciliation, and we look to the day when the policies of mainland China will permit such a reconciliation."

Two-China Policy Urged. On Oct. 20 the United Nations Association, an independent, non-partisan organization devoted to support of the United Nations, published a study of the problem of China, the United Nations and United States policy. The study, prepared by a panel of 27 prominent persons, urged that the United States adopt a "two-China policy," permitting representation of both Communist China and Nationalist China in the United Nations.

The panel warned that if the United States continued to oppose the entry of China, the General Assembly might vote Nationalist China out of the organization and assign China's seat to the Communist regime. To save Nationalist China's membership, the study said, the United States should promptly adopt a "two-China policy." Communist China might initially reject an offer of U.N. membership if Nationalist China were to remain in the organization, but the panel felt that the offer "could strengthen the position of moderate voices in Peking and thereby have some influence in the changes" of leadership expected to occur in the Chinese hierarchy.

Nationalist Reaction to Two-China Plan. On Oct. 21 the Nationalist Chinese representative to the United Nations, Liu Chieh (Liu Jie), said the proposal that the United States move toward a "two-China policy," offered by a panel of prominent citizens Oct. 20, was "ill-timed" and "unrealistic." Liu added that the proposal would "encourage the extremists in the Chinese Communist Party to believe that their policy has proved effective and that Peking is to be accepted into the United Nations because of that policy."

China Tests Atomic Missile. On Oct. 27 the Xinhua news agency announced that China on Oct. 26 had "successfully conducted over its own territory a guided missile-nuclear weapons test." The agency said the test demonstrated that "China's defense capabilities are advancing at even greater speed."

Support of Asia Policy in Congress. On Oct. 28 a Congressional Quarterly survey of members of Congress showed that 313 senators and representatives, 58.5 percent of the membership, favored the basic course the United States was taking in Vietnam. But 141 members, or 26.4 percent of the Senate and House, favored more decisive military action: 81 members, or 15.1 percent of the total, favored increased stress on peace talks.

U.S. Elections and the War. On Nov. 8, Republican candidates in the midterm elections won three additional U.S. Senate seats and 47 additional House seats. The election results indicated continuing broad support in Congress for President Johnson's Vietnam policies. The voters, rather than electing opponents of the war, chose new representatives who seemed more in favor of stepped-up military efforts in Vietnam than were their predecessors.

Red Guard Logistics. On Nov. 8 Stanley Karnow of *The Washington Post* reported that the Red Guards were "causing havoc in China's inadequate transportation system." The Chinese leadership had therefore instructed the youth group to emulate the Long March of 1934-35 and travel by foot rather than rail. A Nov. 8 dispatch by the Xinhua news agency reported that "thousands upon thousands" of the youths were marching throughout the country, spreading the thoughts of Chairman Mao. "In a recent statement," Karnow reported, "Chinese Premier Chou En-lai calculated that 30 percent of China's road and rail facilities have lately been devoted to moving the youths in and out of Peking for assorted rallies and other demonstrations. A clue to the magnitude of the movement is suggested by the official claim that a total of six million youngsters attended the five main rallies held in the Chinese capital between Aug. 18 and Nov. 3." After that, there were two more such rallies.

Soviet Troop Movements. On Nov. 10 *The Washington Post* reported that communist sources in the United Nations had indicated that several divisions of Soviet troops had been switched from Eastern Europe to the Sino-Soviet border. As a result, the number of Soviet troops deployed in Asia was believed to exceed the number stationed in Eastern Europe.

China's Prestige. On Nov. 13 Max Frankel pointed out in an article in *The New York Times* on China's prestige: "In just a year the upheavals inside China have changed its reputation from that of a formidable challenger of the United States throughout Asia and of the Soviet Union inside the Communist world to that of a hobbled giant riddled by dissent and thus incapable of sustained growth and self-assertion."

In a separate article, Frankel maintained that the split in the Chinese hierarchy was not yet resolved and that "the Chinese drama is far from over." He said: "The conflict runs so deep that it appears it cannot be resolved without further major changes of personalities and policies, a convulsion that is bound once again, as in the period of the Great Leap Forward eight years ago, to sacrifice economic progress to political controversy." The war in Vietnam, Peking's relations with Moscow and general problems of national defense, Frankel noted, were among the issues being vehemently debated in China. "But the overriding pressures and preoccupations are domestic, related above all to the problem of governing China and, if anything, divert attention and energy from foreign affairs."

Nuclear Non-Proliferation Treaty. On Nov. 15 an article in the Peking *People's Daily* declared that China would never agree to a treaty banning the spread of nuclear weapons. The article said the proposed treaty had been "cooked up" by the United States and the Soviet Union in the United Nations and was "all part and parcel of the big collusion between the United States and the Soviet Union on a global scale." The treaty plan, the article said, meant that "nuclear weapons should be regarded as a thing to be monopolized by the two nuclear overlords, the United States and the Soviet Union, and that they and they alone should be allowed to possess such weapons, and not anyone else."

Sino-Soviet Border Tension. On Nov. 21 *The New York Times* reported from Washington that Soviet diplomats had openly discussed with American officials the growing concern of Moscow over a nuclear-armed China. According to the *Times*, a U.S. official described recent talks between Secretary of State Dean Rusk and Soviet

Foreign Minister Andrei A. Gromyko as the "most direct, honest, objective and non-ideological in several years." The official added, "Mr. Gromyko made clear that the break with China is quite fundamental and that Russia is now more interested than ever in settling other outstanding issues."

The Soviet foreign minister "was said to feel that none of the border disputes [with China] were worth a war, but that in a period of continuing ill-will between the two countries, there was always the danger that neither would be willing to back off from a small border clash and that such clashes could escalate and lead to a nuclear explosion." Reports of a large Soviet military buildup on the Sino-Soviet border continued.

Chinese Purge Expanded. On Nov. 23, twenty-page wall posters attacking Chinese chief of state Liu Shao-ch'i, Communist Party General Secretary Deng Xiaoping, and others, appeared in the streets of Peking. These were the first explicit attacks on the two leaders, whose names had not appeared in earlier criticisms.

Extended Vacation for Red Guards. On Nov. 24 the Soviet news agency Tass reported that Chinese Premier Chou En-lai had informed students that "studies at educational establishments will not begin until at least the summer vacations next year." The schools had originally been scheduled to reopen in December 1966. The dispatch said the Red Guards had welcomed Chou's announcement by plastering the city with posters reading: "There are another ten months ahead of us for carrying on the Cultural Revolution." *(See July 26, 1966)*

U.N. Vote on China. On Nov. 29 the U.N. General Assembly defeated 46-57 an Albanian-sponsored resolution to assign China's seat in the U.N. to the Communists and expel the Nationalists; 17 members abstained. The vote was interpreted as an appreciable gain for U.S. policy, because the 1965 contest over Chinese representation had ended in a 47-47 tie vote with 20 abstentions. Many African and Asian delegations, reacting to what they called Communist China's "aggressive" or "subversive" policies, abandoned their previous pro-Peking stand.

The assembly also rejected, 34-62 with 25 abstentions, the Italian resolution for a study of the question of Chinese representation. Many observers thought such a study might lead to a recommendation that both Chinese governments be seated in the U.N.

Chinese Primary Schools to Reopen. On Dec. 2, reports from Peking indicated that the Chinese Communist Party's Central Committee had ordered the country's primary schools to reopen. They had been closed for seven months. Primary schools include children from the ages of six to 12. It was reported that secondary schools, colleges and universities would remain closed.

Red Guards Ordered Home. On Dec. 3 the Chinese Communist Party's Central Committee ordered Red Guards remaining in Peking and other cities to return home. The order said the army would be responsible for seeing that the Guards left the cities by the appointed times.

Red Guard Violence. On Dec. 3 the Soviet news agency Tass reported that hundreds of people had been injured and several killed in China during recent fights between Red Guards and workers. The news agency said the most recent such disorders had taken place in Shanghai, where workers had rioted against the militant youth group after the Guard had tortured a local party official.

Macao Riot. On Dec. 3 a mob of pro-Communist Chinese stormed through the Portuguese enclave of Macao on the South China coast, beating officials and police and sacking the city hall.

Thant's Peace Efforts. On Dec. 4 U.N. Secretary General U Thant said in an interview in *Newsweek* that the United States thwarted his efforts to bring about peace talks between Washington and Hanoi three times between late 1964 and early 1965. Thant told columnist Emmet John Hughes that U.S. officials remained silent about the first peace probe, rejected the second because they thought Hanoi was insincere, and rejected the third on the ground that such talks would weaken the South Vietnamese government.

Mme. Mao's Ascent. On Dec. 4 Peking radio reported that Mao Tse-tung's wife, Jiang Qing, had demanded that all those opposing her husband be "wiped out once and for all." The broadcast said Jiang had been appointed as a consultant to the General Political Department of the Chinese army. She was reported to have strongly criticized the Peking branch of the Communist Party for being "as rotten as ever." The Peking branch had been one of the first targets of the Cultural Revolution in June when its secretary, Mayor Peng Zhen, was relieved of his post.

Jiang Qing was quoted as saying: "The old Peking municipal party committee was collaborating with reactionary powerholders.... The new Peking municipal committee is also resisting revolution. It is the same old stuff as the old committee. They are reactionary, two-faced; they insult Chairman Mao. They must be wiped out once and for all. For if we do not wipe them out, how can we carry on the revolution?"

Kosygin on U.S. and Vietnam. On Dec. 6 Soviet Premier Aleksei N. Kosygin, visiting France, told reporters in Lyons that he saw a "community of interests" between the United States and the Soviet Union, but he added: "The United States is bombing defenseless people in Vietnam. We don't see any indication of the way the United States is going to end the war. If it were ended, relations would improve.... We want a better understanding with the United States."

Panel on China Policy. On Dec. 7 the State Department announced appointment of a 10-member civilian panel to help "stimulate ideas" on U.S. policy toward China. The panel included several China scholars who had criticized U.S. policy during the Senate Foreign Relations Committee hearings on China in March 1966.

Space Treaty. On Dec. 8 President Johnson announced at a news conference in Texas that the United States and the Soviet Union had agreed on terms of a U.N.-sponsored treaty to bar the orbiting or installation of weapons of mass destruction in space. The president said the treaty was "the most important arms control development since the limited test-ban treaty of 1963." The treaty came into force Oct. 10, 1967, upon ratification by the United States, the Soviet Union, Great Britain, and eight other countries.

Opinions of Chen Yi. On Dec. 10 the Associated Press carried an interview with Chinese Foreign Minister Chen Yi by a Brazilian lawyer who had defended nine Chinese Communists accused of spying in Brazil. In the interview,

Peiping, Peking & Beijing

As if to further confuse students of China attempting to keep up with the shifting dicta concerning its language, the country's capital city is now called Beijing under the new *pinyin* system of transliteration. Before that, it was Peking (the spelling retained in this book), and before that, Peiping (Beiping).

Writing in *The New Yorker* April 23, 1966, Hans Koningsberger described the earlier change:

By then (1949) Peking (the name means 'Northern Capital') had been rechristened Peiping (which means 'Northern Peace') by Chiang Kaishek, and the capital had been moved to Nanjing. In 1949, when the Communists took the town, they made it the capital once more and gave it back the name Peking. The United States State Department (off and on) and most American mapmakers have gone on talking about the nonexistent town of Peiping and putting it in atlases — an interesting example of a nominalistic, well-nigh old-Chinese view of reality. It is reminiscent of that Ming emperor who, instead of bothering to build dikes, changed the name of a turbulent river from the Wild One to the Peaceful One. It didn't help.

Chen Yi was quoted as saying: "The Soviets have 13 divisions on the Chinese frontier, moved there from Eastern Europe. We do not fear a Soviet-American attack. The Chinese people are prepared for the war and confident of final victory.... The Soviet Union plots world domination with the United States. Politically, the Soviets and North Americans are already united."

The Chinese foreign minister said that Vietnam was a good example of the U.S. military failure "since 300,000 super-equipped men with the support of powerful land, sea and air forces have failed to defeat the guerrillas of a poor country." He accused the Soviets of wanting "to sell peace negotiations because they know that the Vietnamese and Chinese are united side by side against the imperialists, who will join forces to halt the march of nations toward communism."

Chen was pessimistic about U.S.-Chinese relations. "In the last ten years," he said, "we have had ambassadorial-level meetings with the United States which could have brought forth a Chinese-North American agreement. But invariably the representatives of Washington rejected the precepts of peaceful coexistence and refuse to withdraw their forces from Taiwan and the Strait of Taiwan.... We must first resolve the most important problem, Taiwan. And then, at the opportune moment, we will claim Macao and Hong Kong, today referred to by the Red Guards as the vacationland of the imperialists."

Soviet Defense Spending Raised. On Dec. 15 the Soviet Union announced it would increase its defense spending in 1967 by 8.2 percent due to "aggressive" U.S. policies, especially in Vietnam. On the same day, United Press International reported that U.S. officials had indicated "that Russia's increased military budget undoubtedly reflected concern over the situation" along the Sino-Soviet border. Both China and the Soviet Union, the report said, had heavily reinforced the border area "where China still claims 600,000 square miles of Soviet territory."

Javits Quits Committee. On Dec. 17 Sen. Jacob K. Javits, R-N.Y., announced he had withdrawn from the Committee of One Million Against the Admission of Communist China into the United Nations. In a letter to the committee's secretary, Marvin Liebman, Sen. Javits said: "I deeply believe that I must now, in any case, withdraw from membership in the interest of my duty as United States Senator to retain freedom of action regarding Communist China." On the same day, Liebman sent memorandums to all congressional members of the committee stating that the committee would no longer use their names on letterheads and other publications. *(Box, pp. 30-31)*

Chinese Advice. On Dec. 20 the Peking *People's Daily* published an editorial urging North Vietnam and the National Liberation Front (Viet Cong) to fight the war in Vietnam to the end and avoid all negotiations with the United States. The editorial said: "To realize the complete liberation and unification of their fatherland and defend the fruits of their victory, it is necessary for the Vietnamese people to carry through to the end the struggle against U.S. aggression and for national salvation and, without a single exception, to drive all of the U.S. aggressors out of their national soil."

Liu's "Confession." On Dec. 26 Chinese chief of state Liu Shao-ch'i "confessed" to taking an erroneous course. Red Guard newspapers and posters published the text of the confession, which was described as insincere and superficial. Liu, one of the leaders of the faction opposing Chairman Mao Tse-tung, had been the target of repeated Red Guard demands that he be dismissed. Official party publications were silent about Liu's statement.

Chinese Warning on Hong Kong. On Dec. 29 the Xinhua news agency reported that China had warned Great Britain it was "courting disaster" by allowing U.S. Navy ships to visit Hong Kong. The dispatch said Britain was "toeing the U.S. line and turning Hong Kong into a U.S. military base."

Student Letter to Johnson. On Dec. 29 presidents of student organizations and campus editors from 100 colleges and universities sent a letter to President Johnson voicing concern and doubt over U.S. involvement in the Vietnam War. "Unless this conflict can be eased, the United States will find some of her most loyal and courageous young people choosing to go to jail rather than to bear their country's arms," the letter said. "There are many who are deeply troubled for every one who has been outspoken in dissent.... There is increasing confusion about both our basic purpose and our tactics, and there is increasing fear that the course now being pursued may lead us irrevocably into a major land war in Asia — a war which many feel could not be won without recourse to nuclear weapons, if then."

1967

Thant Dismisses Importance of Vietnam to West's Security — Waning of China's Influence in Asia — Turning Point in Cultural Revolution — Anti-Maoist Gains — Reported Order to Use Army Against Mao's Opponents — Maoists and Army Dissidents — Red Guards Harass Russians — Party Criticism of Red Guards — Red Guard Self-Rectification — Reopening of Schools in China — Kennedy Plan for Peace in Vietnam — Bunker to Replace Lodge — Canton Under Army Rule — Guam Conference — Johnson-

Ho Exchange of Letters — Attacks on Liu Shao-ch'i — Mao Controls Politburo — New Peking Government — May Day in Peking — Clashes Among Maoists in Provinces — Friction Between Red Guard Groups — Trouble in Hong Kong — Harassment of British in Shanghai — Reports of Anarchy in China — China's Middle East Policy — Demoralization in Schools — Explosion of Hydrogen Bomb — Campaign to Unify Maoist Factions.

Cultural Revolution in Factories. On Jan. 1 an editorial in the Peking *People's Daily* ordered that the Cultural Revolution, which had been limited to students and intellectuals, be extended into China's factories. The editorial attacked those (like Chou En-lai) who believed that "revolution" and "production" were incompatible: "If the Great Proletarian Cultural Revolution develops in offices, schools and cultural circles only, it will stop halfway." Now, Red Guards were encouraged to go into the factories to mingle with the great masses of workers and peasants.

Not surprisingly, the workers resisted this directive, and fighting broke out all over China.

Pope Paul and Chinese Communists. On Jan. 6 Pope Paul VI said he would like to renew old contacts on the Chinese mainland and "discuss peace" with Chinese leaders.

Violence in Nanjing. On Jan. 7 reports from Peking said that bloody battles between Red Guards and masses of workers had placed Nanjing "in the grip of terror." The Czechoslovak news agency Ceteka reported that 60,000 prisoners had been taken by both sides, and that many of them had been tortured. "Their fingers, noses and ears were chopped off. Their tongues were cut out," the dispatch said. Japanese news sources reported that 54 people had been killed, 900 wounded and 6,000 arrested. The reports said the trouble had begun when an estimated 100,000 workers in Nanjing, led by the local party secretary, attacked the city's Red Guard headquarters. A huge battle ensued, lasting at least three days.

Peking's Ambassadors Called Home. On Jan. 9, reports from foreign capitals throughout the world indicated that most of China's ambassadors to other countries were being ordered home.

U Thant Differs on Vietnam. On Jan. 10 U.N. Secretary General U Thant told a news conference that he did not agree with the U.S. argument that Vietnam was vital to the interests and security of the West, nor did he believe in the so-called domino theory that if Vietnam fell to the communists, other countries would follow.

China Limits Red Guards. On Jan. 10 Peking radio and press reported that strikes were continuing in Shanghai and Fuzhou. Japanese correspondents in Peking reported that Chinese Premier Chou En-lai, who had opposed extending the Cultural Revolution to industry and the labor unions for fear of upsetting the economy, was attempting to moderate the campaign while remaining in the pro-Mao faction. Wall posters in Peking quoted Chou as saying: "We must thoroughly smash the bourgeois reactionary line represented by Liu [chief of state Liu Shao-ch'i] and Deng [General Secretary Deng Xiaoping], but it should be distinguished from excessive individual attacks against them."

No Nationalist Invasion. On Jan. 10 the State Department made it clear that Chiang Kai-shek's Nationalist forces could not make any military moves against China without U.S. approval. This put the damper on reports that

Great Proletarian Cultural Revolution

For some scholars, the Cultural Revolution was the result of Chinese Communist Party Chairman Mao Tse-tung's dissatisfaction with the lack of revolutionary ardor within both the party and the state organizations. Thus, says Merle Goldman, "Mao embarked on a final effort to revitalize the party by recapturing the ideological values that had prevailed" prior to the Communist victory in 1949: "idealism, self-sacrifice and willingness to work without concern for material incentives." To do this, says Goldman, Mao intended to utilize the masses of China, tap their revolutionary potential and turn them against the Communist Party, removing those who had lost touch with the Chinese revolution and the Chinese people. Mao — approaching his own death — would leave this legacy: "new Communist men who were selfless, disciplined, industrious and willing to die for the revolution."*

Other analysts have offered a more prosaic explanation, comparing the Cultural Revolution to other purges and power struggles which occur periodically in totalitarian states. With the failure of the Great Leap Forward in 1959, and the disastrous harvests that followed the formation of the communes, Mao had been forced out as chief of state and replaced by Liu Shao-ch'i. Faced with the real possibility of becoming only a figurehead, Mao struck back in 1966 and 1967 to consolidate his power, purging not only Liu himself, but all of his supporters, including Deng Xiaoping and Peng Zhen. Mao's ally in the purges was the army, led by the minister of defense, Lin Piao. But the victory proved costly for Mao, who found that he had destroyed one rival group, only to be faced with another: by 1969, China was under effective military control, and Lin was more powerful than Liu Shao-ch'i had ever been. In 1971 Mao turned on Lin, who was allegedly killed while trying to flee to the Soviet Union.

Political Chaos

Whether a power struggle or an effort to create the new communist man, the impact of the Cultural Revolution on China's foreign relations was disastrous. During the period of upheaval, as China turned ever more inward, 44 of China's 45 ambassadors were recalled, and several embassies closed altogether. As increasingly bizarre and bellicose statements emanated from Peking, several countries demanded the recall of certain Chinese emissaries, and some broke relations altogether. North Vietnam moved from the Chinese to the Soviet orbit, and North Korea developed a careful neutrality. The Soviet Union began its massive buildup on China's northern border, concurrent with the U.S. buildup in the south.

By 1971 China had returned to "normal," and once again became extremely active in foreign relations. But some of the damage could not be undone easily. A united Vietnam became a Soviet satellite, and the Russians maintained their troops on the border. Until China solved these problems, the legacy of the Cultural Revolution would remain a problem for Chinese foreign relations.

The 'Gang of Four'

During the Cultural Revolution, power *seemed* to be in the hands of the "gang of four," a sobriquet applied to Jiang Qing (Mme. Mao), Yao Wenyuan, Zhang Chunqiao and Wang Hongwen *(biographies, p. 285),* a group of radicals who had come to power during the Cultural Revolution and continued to hold that power by invoking the name of Mao, who no longer appeared in public. (In fact, many visitors to China reported that by this time Mao was only occasionally coherent, and may have been suffering from advanced senility.) But the "gang" were never able fully to consolidate their power, and were resisted at every turn by the chief of the moderates, Chou En-lai. Chou's death in January 1976 seemed to offer them new opportunities, but Mao's death, in September, removed their most important prop. On Oct. 6, in an apparent coup, Premier Hua Guofeng arrested all four, and apparently ended the Cultural Revolution once and for all.

A New Moderation

The removal of the "gang" opened the way for a new wave of moderation in Chinese politics, both internal and external.

First, hundreds and perhaps thousands of moderates, some of whom had been purged more than 15 years earlier, were returned to power. Following the lead of Deng Xiaoping, Chou En-lai's long-time supporter, these men began to work for the rejuvenation and modernization of China's economy, wracked by the years of inner turmoil.

Second, these same leaders, some of whom had been in prison for more than a decade, began to allow somewhat freer criticism of the regime. Reports of dissent in China, brought back by visitors, were difficult to evaluate and could be only ephemeral. But whatever the future of "democracy" in China, there could be no doubt that the end of the Cultural Revolution and the "gang of four" meant new freedom of expression in the arts, and was symbolic of the end of the radical oppression of the earlier period.

Third, and concurrent with Western overtures, China was again looking outward. The modernization effort meant that China would have to import technology, some of it very advanced, which could come only from the industrialized nations. Thus, since 1970, China had responded favorably to initiatives from Europe, the United States and Japan. The flow of goods, loans and people had increased rapidly, and was expected to continue, although not, perhaps, as fast as some had claimed. In its effort to rally all the nations of the world to oppose the Soviet Union and its satellites, China had given up its insistence on revolutionary purity, dominant during the Cultural Revolution, and had opted for the path of pragmatic politics.

---

* Merle Goldman, "The Aftermath of China's Cultural Revolution," *Current History* 61, no. 9 (September 1979): 165-170.

Chiang hoped to take advantage of the political crisis on the mainland and invade with his 600,000-man army.

Another Purged. On Jan. 11 David Oancia of the Toronto *Globe and Mail* reported that Bo Yibo, one of Communist China's leading economists, had been jailed by the Red Guards. The report said Bo had been arrested in Canton, brought to Peking, and was being "held under what are reported to be extremely rugged conditions along with the former mayor of Peking, Peng Zhen; the former army chief, Luo Reiqing; the propaganda director, Lu Dingyi; a Central Committee member, Yang Shangkun; and former Defense Minister Peng Dehuai, who was replaced by Lin Piao in 1959."

Mme. Mao's Role. On Jan. 11 Jiang Qing, Mao Tse-tung's wife and one of the most vocal of the radical leaders, was added to the army's "Cultural Revolution Group."

Waning of China's Influence. On Jan. 12 a *New York Times* dispatch from the United Nations suggested that the new political crisis in China was significantly "changing the balance of power in Asia." The dispatch said that "From Moscow and Kabul, eastward to Seoul and Tokyo, governments are contemplating the possibility that internal conflict will inhibit China's ability to initiate military or political action and will reduce the influence of Chinese communism on Communist parties in neighboring countries."

Turning Point in Cultural Revolution. On Jan. 15 Peking radio, announcing that the Cultural Revolution had reached "a new turning point," urged all supporters of Chairman Mao Tse-tung to "take political and economic authority into your own hands." The night before, Chinese Premier Chou En-lai had told a banquet audience in Peking that Mao had ordered "an all-out general offensive" against his opponents.

U.S.-China Deal. On Jan. 15 René Dabernat, foreign editor of *Paris-Match*, said in an interview in *U.S. News & World Report* that China had informed the United States through Paris, in the spring of 1966, that it would not become involved in the Vietnam War if the United States refrained from invading China or North Vietnam and from bombing the latter's Red River dikes. Dabernat said that subsequent public statements by President Johnson and other U.S. officials demonstrated that they had "agreed to these conditions." The State Department replied with a "no comment," but other officials acknowledged that the United States had received a number of messages from China through a number of different third parties. *(See March 20, 1966)*

Peasants Told to Stay Home. On Jan. 21 Peking radio and the Peking *People's Daily* carried orders to Chinese peasants to remain in their villages and stay away from the cities. The order was believed to be aimed specifically at Shanghai, where reports continued to emphasize clashes between workers and peasants. The Peking broadcast charged that opponents of Mao were sending the peasants into the cities to demand higher wages — a tactic denounced by Maoists as "economism." More than three million peasants were reported to have entered Shanghai.

Order to Seize Power. On Jan. 22 the Peking *People's Daily* published an editorial calling for the Red Guards to "seize power." The article said that "everything boils down to the matter of their holding in their own hands the seals of authority! ... Band together and rise up. Seize power!

Seize power!" The new order was followed by "power seizures" in a number of localities. *(See Feb. 5)*

Anarchy and Revolution. On Jan. 25 the Xinhua news agency reported: "Everywhere on both banks of the Yellow River, north and south of the Yangtze, all of China is [in] a frenzy.... Only one word can describe the circumstances. That word is 'anarchy.' Without anarchy there can be no revolution!"

U.S-Chinese Meeting. On Jan. 25 the U.S. and Chinese ambassadors to Poland met in Warsaw for a secret three and one-half hour talk. Neither the U.S. ambassador, John A. Gronouski, nor the Chinese ambassador, Wang Guoquan, would discuss the content of the talk. The next meeting was scheduled for June 7, 1967.

Chinese-Russian Clash in Moscow. On Jan. 26 the Chinese Embassy in Moscow protested to the Kremlin that Chinese students had been attacked "without provocation" by Russian soldiers when they sought to place a wreath at the Lenin Mausoleum in Red Square. The Soviet government answered that the protest was made up of "unpardonable lies." It accused the Chinese students of provoking the "wild scene." On the same day, huge crowds gathered outside the Soviet Embassy in Peking, shouting such slogans as "Down with the Soviet pigs!"

Chinese Demonstrations in Paris. On Jan. 27, Chinese students demonstrating outside the Soviet Embassy in Paris were arrested by French police after they began splashing red paint on the building.

On Jan. 29, Chinese students again clashed with French police outside the embassy.

Anti-Soviet Demonstrations in Peking. On Jan. 28, Chinese soldiers took part in an enormous demonstration outside the Soviet Embassy in Peking. The troops wielded rifles and fixed bayonets in the third demonstration in as many days. The embassy's walls were plastered with posters reading "Shoot Brezhnev" and "Fry Kosygin." On Jan. 29, hundreds of thousands again marched in front of the Soviet Embassy in Peking. Meanwhile, the Soviet government said in a note of protest to the Chinese Embassy in Moscow: "The Soviet side reserves the right to take the necessary measures if the Chinese authorities fail to provide normal conditions for the activity of the Soviet representation." The attacks ceased shortly afterward.

The Army Intervenes. On Jan. 28 the Military Affairs Committee of the Chinese Communist Party announced that the army would no longer remain neutral in the power struggles in China, and that it had been ordered to "support the left." The order followed repeated reports that the Red Guards, in their efforts to purge certain regional and provincial leaders, had been encountering armed opposition, probably organized by those who were to be purged. Although Lin Piao, minister of defense and leader of the Cultural Revolution, was silent on the new orders, they surely came with his approval.

The army began to intervene in the various local struggles almost immediately, as China appeared to be heading for a new round of chaos. Since each contending local group would claim support for the policies of Chairman Mao Tse-tung, the army commanders could only stop the fighting to maintain order. The eventual result was a virtual army takeover of China, with Lin Piao as China's most powerful leader. This was not completed until the spring of 1968. *(See May 31, 1968)*

Kennan on U.S.-Soviet Relations. On Jan. 30 former U.S. ambassador to the Soviet Union George F. Kennan told the Senate Foreign Relations Committee that the irreparable disunity of the communist world presented the United States with a perfect opportunity to take "greatly exciting" steps to improve U.S.-Soviet relations.

"Great Alliance." On Jan. 30 the Peking *People's Daily* called on supporters of Party Chairman Mao Tse-tung to form a "great alliance" after first settling "petty bourgeois" differences among themselves. "Only when such an alliance is forged is it possible to engage successfully in a struggle to seize power.... Any hasty attempt to seize power without this alliance is either empty talk or an ill-considered action that is bound to be unsuccessful."

Demonstrations. On Jan. 31, Chinese demonstrated outside the French Embassy in Peking, protesting the treatment of Chinese students who had been demonstrating against the Soviet Embassy in Paris. There were reports that Chinese in Hanoi demonstrated in front of the Soviet Embassy there. Large and noisy demonstrations continued in front of the Soviet and Yugoslav embassies in Peking.

Peking Harasses French Diplomat. On Feb. 1 the commercial counselor of the French Embassy in Peking and his wife were forced by a mob of demonstrators to stand outside the embassy in below-freezing weather for seven hours. During that time, loudspeakers accused the Frenchman of injuring several Chinese while backing his car. Reuters described the incident as a response to the recent arrest of Chinese students in Paris.

Russia Warns China. On Feb. 4 in an official note to Peking, Moscow demanded that China stop vilifying the Soviet Union and humiliating Soviet citizens in Peking. The note denounced the "anti-Soviet hysteria" in China and warned that "the restraint and patience of the Soviet people is not boundless." Retaliatory measures were threatened if such actions continued.

The Soviet note coincided with an emergency evacuation of most of the Soviet diplomatic staff and their dependents from China. By Feb. 7, it was reported that the remaining diplomats were virtual prisoners within their compound, due to China's refusal to guarantee their safety outside the area.

The Shanghai Commune. On Feb. 5 the leaders of several Red Guard organizations "seized power" in Shanghai municipality and declared the "Shanghai Commune," modeled after the Paris Commune of 1871. The new organization proved unable to administer the city, and disappeared later in the month. *(Box, p. 177)*

Abrogation of Consular Agreement. On Feb. 11 Peking radio reported termination of the consular agreement between Russia and China. Travel without visas to and from the two countries would no longer be permitted. According to *The New York Times'* dispatch, Russian diplomats feared further Chinese measures to block Soviet aid to North Vietnam. The agreement had guaranteed Russian specialists freedom of transit through China en route to North Vietnam.

Criticism of Red Guards. On Feb. 23 an editorial in the Chinese Communist Party theoretical journal *Hongqi* demanded that Red Guards halt attacks on government and party officials. The editorial criticized "the shortcomings and mistakes" of the Red Guards, saying that "they lack experience in struggle, are not yet mature politically, and at crucial turning points in the course of the revolution they frequently cannot see the direction clearly." *Hongqi* rejected the idea that "all those in authority are no good and unreliable and should therefore, without exception, all be overthrown." It called "those cadres who follow the proletarian revolutionary line represented by Chairman Mao the treasure of the party and the people."

Revolution in Education. In a Feb. 27 speech to the School of Military Warfare, Mao Tse-tung told the audience that "A little reading of books is all right, but a lot of it harms people — it really harms them."

A few days later Chen Boda expanded on Mao's remarks, stating that middle schools and primary school terms are too long: "This is intolerable.... Once people graduate, if they have no work to do there is a new problem." Chen's answer was to drastically shorten the amount of formal education given China's youth.

Back to School. On March 1 the *Far Eastern Economic Review* reported that secondary schools in China, closed since June 1966 to allow the pupils to participate in Red Guard activities, had reopened. Elementary schools had been ordered to reopen Feb. 9.

Senate Support for Johnson. On March 1 the U.S. Senate added to a war appropriations bill an amendment voicing support of efforts by President Johnson and "other men of good will" to prevent expansion of the Vietnam War and to reach a negotiated peace. Senate Majority Leader Mike Mansfield, D-Mont., author of the amendment, included a pledge of congressional support of the 1954 Geneva accords and urged convening of a similar conference as soon as possible to bring the Vietnam conflict to "an honorable conclusion in accordance with the principles of those accords." The Mansfield amendment was the first Senate policy statement on the Vietnam War since the Gulf of Tonkin resolution of 1964, which backed "all necessary steps" in defense of Southeast Asia.

Army Takes Over Education. On March 7 Chinese Communist Party Chairman Mao Tse-tung issued a secret directive to the Chinese army, ordering it to take over most of the political and military education in China, apart from the universities.

Canton Under Army Rule. On March 15 Reuters reported that the army had taken over and was ruling Canton and the remainder of the province of Guangdong. Large crowds welcomed the troops with celebrations, demonstrations and marching of Red Guards. *(See July 21)*

Reischauer Against China Trade Embargo. On April 6 Harvard Prof. Edwin O. Reischauer, former U.S. ambassador to Japan, suggested to the Joint Economic Committee of Congress that the United States lift its total embargo on trade with mainland China. Reischauer said the policy "has had no effect at all on China's economy, but has put a strain on U.S. relations with its allies, particularly Japan." He asserted that, in fact, "a rich and strong China might serve American interest and the cause of world peace better than an unstable and sick one."

Hong Kong Governor Assailed. On April 12 two Chinese Communist newspapers published in Hong Kong sharply denounced by name for the first time the British governor of the colony, Sir David Trench. The attack was part of a continuing protest against allowing American naval vessels to call at Hong Kong and American soldiers to go there for rest and recuperation.

Peace Demonstration. On April 15 the largest peace rally since the United States became involved in the Vietnam War was staged in New York City. An estimated 125,000 demonstrators marched from Central Park to the United Nations and listened to speeches by the Rev. Martin Luther King Jr. and Dr. Benjamin Spock. A parallel march, also sponsored by the Spring Mobilization Committee to End the War in Vietnam, took place in San Francisco the same day.

Drugs for China. On April 20 the U.S. Department of Commerce announced its willingness to license exports of drugs to combat reported epidemics of meningitis, cholera and contagious hepatitis in China. Nine days later, China rejected the offer, calling it a "dirty trick." The Peking *People's Daily* asserted that the United States was trying to "present heinous U.S. imperialism as a god of mercy to deceive the people of the world."

Indonesia Expels Chinese Diplomats. On April 24 the Indonesian government ordered the Chinese charge d'affaires and the consul general to leave the country within five days. On the same day, China gave similar instructions to the Indonesian charge d'affaires and information chief in China. The expulsions followed several days of violent anti-Chinese demonstrations in Indonesia.

U.S. Planes Over China. On April 25 Peking radio broadcast that two American F-4B Phantom aircraft had been shot down over Guangxi Province in southwestern China. American military spokesmen in Saigon, while denying that any U.S. planes had flown over China, reported four planes missing.

May Day in Peking. On May 1, for the first time in eight years, Chairman Mao Tse-tung joined the May Day parade through Peking. Mao stood in a jeep with Defense Minister Lin Piao at his side. Anthony Grey, Peking correspondent of Reuters, interpreted the appearance as a move to emphasize Mao's "immense personal stature at a time when the Cultural Revolution was officially reported to be moving into a decisive phase." Tillman Durdin of *The New York Times* noted, however, that several of the leaders under Red Guard attack — Zhu De, Chen Yun and Chen Yi — occupied places of honor at the celebrations. He concluded that "the failure to complete the ousting [of some leaders] . . . suggests that the ruling Maoist faction feels it does not yet have the support to carry through such a move."

Britain Cuts Back in Asia. On May 1 British Minister of Defense Denis Healey announced a sharp cutback of British forces in the Far East. Healey said that by April 1968, 20,000 troops would have been withdrawn from the Singapore-Malaysia area.

Dropping of Bombs Over China Charged. On May 2 the Peking *People's Daily* reported that the United States had dropped four bombs on the town of Ningming in Guangxi Province, 20 miles north of the Vietnamese border. A U.S. military spokesman in Saigon stated that U.S. pilots had bombed rail lines between Hanoi and the Chinese border but denied that any bombs had been dropped on Chinese territory. On May 3 the Defense Department asserted in Washington that "reports failed to show any evidence that these propaganda allegations are true."

Visitor from Taiwan. On May 10 President Johnson assured C. K. Yen (Yan Jiagan), visiting vice president of the Republic of (Nationalist) China, that the United States would continue to defend Taiwan militarily and to support Nationalist China's rights in the United Nations.

Labor Riot in Hong Kong. On May 11, riots flared at an artificial flower factory in Hong Kong as striking workers, shouting Maoist slogans, battled with police. Twenty persons were injured in the most recent outbreak of labor trouble in the British colony.

Hong Kong Friction Grows. On May 12, thousands of workers rioted in the Hong Kong industrial area of Kowloon (Jiulong). Cars were burned, and police were struck with stones and bottles as they threw tear gas into the crowds and arrested 200 rioters. Stanley Karnow, in a dispatch to *The Washington Post*, said that "strong Communist trade unions, exalted by Mao Tse-tung's Cultural Revolution, have turned labor disputes into an angry political campaign against the British colonial government." Other observers in Hong Kong questioned China's intentions, for, as Karnow remarked, "Peking recognized that Hong Kong would be worthless as a piece of Communist real estate." Accordingly, "Mao may loudly voice support for the colony's revolutionaries while quietly advising them to calm down."

More Rioting in Peking. On May 13, hundreds of Red Guards broke into the Chinese foreign ministry in Peking, beat up employees and ransacked confidential files. This was the first of a series of such incidents at the foreign ministry, and followed the refusal of Chinese Foreign Minister Chen Yi to accede to various Red Guard demands. *(See Aug. 22)*

China Protests to Britain. On May 15 the Xinhua news agency published a statement of protest issued at the Chinese Foreign Ministry and communicated to the British charge d'affaires in Peking. The statement demanded that the British government in Hong Kong "accept the just demands put forward by Chinese workers, immediately stop all fascist measures, set free all arrested persons, punish the culprits responsible for sanguinary atrocities, and guarantee against similar incidents." Anthony Lewis, the *New York Times* bureau chief in London, reported that the Chinese statement on Hong Kong "was taken very seriously here. . . . What was most disturbing . . . was its close parallel to the Chinese position in the Macao riots last December."

Chou's Interview. On May 15 Simon Malley reported in a dispatch to the *Chicago Daily News* that Premier Chou En-lai had told Malley in a 2-1/2 hour interview in March that war between China and the United States was inevitable. "Sooner or later the United States will find itself in a situation where the realization of its imperialist objectives will require the violation of our sovereignty and territorial integrity. And that day a military showdown will have become inevitable." On May 16 the Xinhua news agency denied that Chou had granted the interview. The agency called Malley's dispatch "an out and out fabrication put out with ulterior motives."

British Diplomat Abused. On May 16 Reuters reported that Chinese demonstrators had ransacked the Shanghai residence of British diplomat Peter Hewitt. On the same day, tens of thousands of Chinese in Peking protested alleged "fascist outrages" by the British in Hong Kong.

Army Strength in Peking. On May 22 David Oancia of the Toronto *Globe & Mail* reported an increase of armed strength in Peking. New orders issued by the Peking Revolutionary Committee were described as "little more than a step away from a declaration of martial law."

War in the Middle East. On June 5 serious fighting broke out between Israeli and Arab troops in the Sinai peninsula and Jerusalem. During the subsequent war, which lasted six days, Israeli troops captured all of the Sinai, the Gaza strip, and Jerusalem. On June 11 Israel and Syria signed a ceasefire, leaving Israel in possession of the large new territories captured by its armies.

China Faces Anarchy. On June 6 the Chinese Communist Party's Central Committee, the State Council, the Military Affairs Committee, and the Cultural Revolution Group issued a joint order aimed at curbing China's slide into complete anarchy. Dubbed the "Seven Point Circular," the order said that state organizations alone had the power to carry out arrests and searches and to pass judgements; that property was to be protected everywhere by the masses; and that physical violence was forbidden. The armed forces were to be responsible for ensuring that these measures were applied.

The immediate result of the order was further violence, as the army moved to consolidate its authority in the provinces. *(See July 19 and July 21)*

China's Middle East Policy. On June 11 an editorial in the *People's Daily* called the Soviet Union "a false and treacherous friend of the Arabs," while referring to the Chinese as "loyal, reliable comrades in arms." The *Economist* of London had suggested, June 10, that China had "high and not unfounded hopes of coming out of this [Middle East] crisis one up on the Russians." Harald Munthe-Kaas, a Scandinavian correspondent in Peking, wrote in the *Far Eastern Economic Review* that the crisis was "a gift for China in the Middle East." The *People's Daily* editorial urged the Arabs to carry on the struggle against the "paper tigers," U.S. imperialism, British imperialism, Soviet revisionism, and Israeli aggression.

On June 11 the Egyptian newspaper *Al Ahram* disclosed that the Chinese government had offered 150,000 tons of wheat and a $10-million interest-free loan to Egypt in appreciation of its "heroic stand against the vicious imperialist conspiracy." The *Economist* noted that "at this time and in this quantity the shipments to Egypt mean a sacrifice of some dimension."

Two Indian Diplomats Expelled. On June 14 two Indian diplomats, Krishnan Raghunath and P. Vijai, were expelled from China on espionage charges. The two officials were accused of photographing a military area in the western hills of Peking, a charge which the Indian government called "a fabrication." The Indian charge d'affaires in Peking delivered a strong protest to the Chinese Foreign Ministry against "inhuman treatment" accorded the two men at the airport on their departure. The next day, two Chinese diplomats were ordered to leave India.

China's Schools Chaotic. On June 15 Stanley Karnow, in a dispatch to *The Washington Post,* described the "hopeless breakdown of China's education system" from primary schools through universities. Karnow reported that since the recent resumption of regular classes, buildings had been damaged, teachers and students had been demoralized, and a properly Maoist curriculum had not been devised. He concluded that "in reality, studies are at a standstill and are likely to remain paralyzed for the foreseeable future."

Harald Munthe-Kaas, Scandinavian news agency correspondent in Peking, summarized in the *Far Eastern Economic Review* of June 15 the latest plans for trying to improve the situation. The Central Committee of the Chinese Communist Party called for emphasis on class criteria and political attitudes in selection of students and teachers, for institution of a half-work, half-study curriculum, for teaching through the medium of free discussions, and for abolition of examinations. Munthe-Kaas commented that "in short, schools are to be run on the lines of the Anti-Japanese Military and Political College of Yenan [Yanan] days."

No Reading of Wall Posters by Foreigners. On June 16 Reuters reported that the Chinese Foreign Ministry had announced that foreign journalists and diplomats gaining information from wall posters or Red Guard newspapers would be accused of spying. The announcement followed by two days the expulsion from China of two Indian diplomats charged with espionage.

Chinese Embassy in India Mobbed. On June 16, eight Chinese Embassy officials in New Delhi were assaulted and injured by a crowd of Indian students. The students forcibly entered the embassy, ransacked Maoist exhibits, and broke windows. The action apparently was in retaliation for massive protests outside the Indian Embassy in Peking and harsh treatment of the two Indian diplomats expelled from China June 14.

China Explodes Hydrogen Bomb. On June 17, two years and eight months after China's first detonation of a nuclear device, the Xinhua news agency announced detonation of the country's first hydrogen bomb, at the Lop Nor test site in Xinjiang province. The official statement called the accomplishment a "decisive victory of the great Cultural Revolution in our country" and a "fresh great victory of Mao Tse-tung's thought." The announcement stated that "as in the past, the Chinese people and government will continue to make common efforts and carry on an unswerving struggle together with all the other peace-loving people and countries of the world for the noble aim of completely prohibiting and thoroughly destroying nuclear weapons."

Foreign analysts commented that the detonation was timed for its best propaganda effect, to dramatize the power of China. Soviet Premier Aleksei N. Kosygin, whom the Chinese called "a paper tiger," was at the United Nations attending General Assembly sessions on the Middle East crisis. *The Washington Post* reported that American weapons experts were "frank to express admiration for the rapid pace of China's nuclear program." The Chinese pointed out that it took the United States seven years and the Soviet Union four years to accomplish the same feat. George Wilson, Pentagon correspondent of *The Washington Post*, predicted that the latest demonstration of China's growing nuclear capacity would increase pressure in the United States to install an anti-ballistic missile system. American officials were reported to be concerned about China's simultaneous development of missiles for carrying the bombs.

Indian Prime Minister Indira Gandhi said the event was "a matter of anxiety." The Japanese Foreign Ministry expressed "deep regret" and called the test a "reckless act." France's high commissioner for atomic energy, on the other hand, asserted that "this bomb has a much greater impact from the propaganda viewpoint than from the military viewpoint, at least in the near future."

Indian Embassy Besieged. On June 17 Reuters reported that the Indian Embassy in Peking was under siege. Communications between the embassy and its government had been cut off, and the staff and families were being held at the embassy compound, surrounded by Chinese demonstrators.

Hanoi-Peking Relations. On June 24 Stanley Karnow, in a dispatch to *The Washington Post* from Hong Kong, reported a cooling off in Hanoi-Peking relations. "This development has been gradual rather than dramatic," Karnow wrote. He pointed to Hanoi's increasing anxieties about the Cultural Revolution and to an upsurge in Hanoi's friendliness toward the Soviet Union.

Peking Denounces Glassboro Talks. On June 25 the Xinhua news agency denounced the meetings of Soviet Premier Kosygin and President Johnson at Glassboro, N.J., on June 23 and 25. The Chinese contended that the purpose of the summit talks was to establish "a global American-Soviet deal intended to enhance the anti-China, anti-Communist, anti-people and counter-revolutionary Washington-Moscow alliance." The news agency concluded that the meetings were "first and foremost directed against the Chinese."

Chinese Problems with Burma. On June 26 and 27, several Chinese teachers in Rangoon, in an effort to bring the Cultural Revolution to the Chinese in Burma, provoked anti-Chinese rioting and an attack on the Chinese embassy. The Chinese claimed that more than 50 of their compatriots had been killed. Shortly thereafter, all Chinese technicians were withdrawn, and the Chinese press began to refer to Burmese leader Ne Win as a "fascist reactionary" and a "new Chiang Kai-shek."

Kenya Expels Chinese Ambassador. On June 29 Kenya ordered expulsion of the Chinese ambassador and recalled its ambassador from China. The break between the two countries followed a dispute over Chinese interference in Kenya's domestic affairs.

China-East Germany Dispute. On June 30 a demonstration was staged by the Chinese Embassy staff in East Berlin to protest the death of three Chinese diplomats in an automobile accident in East Germany. David Binder of *The New York Times* noted that relations between the two governments had been "steadily deteriorating since the sharpening of the Cultural Revolution in China."

Anti-Chinese Demonstrations. On July 1, violent anti-Chinese incidents, a side-effect of the Cultural Revolution raging in China, occurred in Katmandu, Nepal, but good relations were restored almost immediately.

China Criticizes Soviets. On July 4 the Xinhua news agency said that "Soviet aid to African countries is zero."

Provincial Rebellion. On July 19 two high-level officials sent by Peking to settle the fighting in Wuhan were arrested by local officials and beaten. When Peking threatened military invasion, the local military commander yielded, and the two officials returned to Peking on July 22.

There had been serious fighting in Wuhan since February; one report said that 10,000 people had been arrested by April, and another that 300 people had been killed. Then, on June 14, when one of the factions had closed the strategic railroad bridge over the Yangtze (Changjiang) River, Peking sent Premier Chou En-lai and two other officials to sort out the problem. Chou remained in Wuhan

briefly and then returned to the capital. After his departure, the other two officials were arrested at a meeting they had called to end the fighting.

The incident marked a new plateau in the violence which was wracking China, and the only case thus far of open rebellion against the central government.

More Rioting in China. On July 21 the most serious fighting to date broke out in Canton between various factions of the Red Guards. Violence continued to escalate until August 12, when the factions fought a full-scale battle in the streets of the city. Although this was the most serious incident, similar ones were occurring throughout China.

China's Nuclear Progress. On Aug. 2 the Joint Congressional Committee on Atomic Energy reported that China had made "rapid progress" in its development of a thermonuclear warhead and that it would be able to launch a limited missile attack on the U.S. by the 1970s.

Chinese Reaction to ASEAN. On Aug. 6 the Peking *People's Daily* sharply attacked the formation of the Association of Southeast Asian Nations (ASEAN) as "another instrument for U.S. imperialists and Soviet modern revisionists in their pursuit of neocolonialism in Asia." The article also charged that the new organization was an "out-and-out counter-revolutionary alliance against China, communism, and the people."

ASEAN Established. On Aug. 8 the foreign ministers of Thailand, Indonesia, Singapore, the Philippines and Malaysia signed a seven-point declaration in Bangkok to establish the Association of Southeast Asian Nations (ASEAN). The major purpose of the organization was to "accelerate the economic growth, social progress, and cultural development in the region through joint endeavor."

ASEAN supplanted the six-year-old Association of Southeast Asia, which was later dissolved on June 30, 1977.

"Revcoms" Spread. On Aug. 8 Agence France-Presse reported that the formation of revolutionary committees (revcoms), ordered in January, had proceeded apace. Based on the leadership lists published by China on Army Day, it was concluded that revcoms had been formed in seven provinces and municipalities, and that seven more were in the process of formation. The 13 remaining provinces were still under military control. *(See Jan. 1, 1968)*

The revcoms were intended to hold sway in place of the party, which ostensibly had been destroyed by the Cultural Revolution.

Rioting in Peking. On Aug. 22, Red Guards invaded the British compound in Peking, set buildings afire, and attacked Donald C. Hopson, charge d'affaires. The attack followed Britain's refusal to accede to a Chinese demand that Hong Kong lift the suspension of three pro-communist newspapers there.

On Aug. 29 British police clashed with Chinese students behind the Chinese diplomatic mission in London.

Following these incidents, Britain downgraded its relations with China until 1972. *(See March 13, 1972)*

Red Guards Ordered to School. On Aug. 23 the Peking *People's Daily* published a government statement ordering the Red Guards to return to school and said that those who refuse "should be corrected immediately."

Cultural Revolution Moderated. On Sept. 1 the Peking Municipal Committee published an important resolution which emphasized that "politics" rather than armed struggle should be the chief means of attacking "capitalist roaders." While praising the contributions of the Red Guard, the committee ordered a cessation of "struggles by force" and demanded that future work be done "in a planned and organized manner." *(See Sept. 5, 1967)*

China Leaves Red Cross. On Sept. 3 the Chinese government announced its decision to withdraw from the International Executive Committee of the Red Cross. Peking announced that U.S. domination of the organization had triggered the decision.

Thieu Elected President. On Sept. 3 Nguyen Van Thieu was elected president of South Vietnam. He was unopposed.

Chinese Aid to Africa. On Sept. 5 China signed an agreement with Tanzania and Gambia to build, at high cost, a 1,600-kilometer railway line from Dar es Salaam to Lusaka. Work began Oct. 26, 1970, and the line was completed in 1976.

Army Orders Expanded. On Sept. 5 a combined order of the Chinese Communist Party Central Committee, the Military Affairs Committee, the State Council and the Cultural Revolution Group expressly forbade the "seizure of arms, equipment, and other military supplies" by the Red Guards, and gave the army the right to return fire if attacked by Red Guards.

On the same day, Jiang Qing, wife of Party Chairman Mao Tse-tung and one of the most vocal supporters of the Cultural Revolution, announced her opposition to the armed struggle and factionalism which were plaguing China, and severely criticized Red Guard attacks on the army to obtain guns. She pointed out that military goods slated for Vietnam had been seized, and declared that attacks on foreign embassies must cease.

Sino-Indian Fighting. On Sept. 7 fighting broke out between India and China on the Sikkim-Tibetan border and continued intermittently for a week. Both sides filed official protests. The fighting was the most serious since the border war of 1962.

Correspondents Leave China. On Sept. 10 China ordered three Japanese correspondents recalled because they had sent "anti-Chinese" dispatches.

Earlier, on July 30, David Oancia of the Toronto *Globe and Mail* had left China after being physically attacked. On Aug. 11 the Scandinavian news agencies had ordered the withdrawal of all of their correspondents in China following similar incidents.

Disorder in China Reduced. On Sept. 13 the highest levels of the state, the army, and the Communist Party issued directives urging the Chinese people to return home and give priority to the autumn harvest. Shortly thereafter, the Chinese press redoubled its attacks on the most extreme cases of violence. The mission of the army was enlarged, and late in September Mao made a brief tour of the provinces, further easing the tensions. The hiatus lasted only until January 1968.

ABM Proposed. On Sept. 18 U.S. Defense Secretary Robert McNamara announced that the U.S. would deploy a network of missiles capable of defending against the sort of limited attack that China was believed capable of mounting within a decade. McNamara said that although "it would be insane and suicidal" for China to launch a missile attack against the U.S., "one can conceive conditions under

which China might miscalculate," and the U.S. wanted to reduce the dangers of such a decision. *(See July 11, 1968)*

Mao Tours China. On Sept. 25 the Xinhua news agency reported that Chinese Communist Party Chairman Mao Tse-tung had returned to Peking after having "toured and inspected" various areas throughout China. Western observers commented that Mao had made the trip in an effort to pacify China's various feuding organizations and to urge unity.

This was only the second such extended trip by Mao reported since 1949. The first had been made in 1958, following the failure of the Great Leap Forward.

Nixon on China. In October *Foreign Affairs* magazine published an article by Richard M. Nixon outlining his proposals for dealing with China. Entitled "Asia after Viet Nam," the article proposed little that was new, but it represented a moderation of Nixon's earlier views. Declaring that American policy "must come urgently to grips with the reality of China," Nixon said that this did not mean "rushing off to grant recognition to Peking, to admit it to the United Nations and to ply it with offers of trade." The U.S. must recognize the threat posed by China, and work to meet it, but not by direct intervention.

In a foreshadowing of his later proposals, Nixon called for the non-communist nations of Asia to play a greater role in their own defense, and for the formation of new Asian organizations to replace SEATO, which he called an "anachronistic relic." As for the U.S., Nixon said that it should try "to persuade China that it *must* change; that it cannot satisfy its imperial ambitions." Once this has been accomplished, concluded Nixon, we can "pull China back into the family of nations."

China's Diplomatic Problems. On Oct. 1, as China celebrated its National Day, only five foreign governments sent representatives. At this point in the Cultural Revolution, China had managed to pick quarrels with 32 countries; many of them had broken off or downgraded relations with China.

During the parades which marked the celebrations, the Red Guards participated, but marched well to the rear. Minister of Defense Lin Piao gave the only speech at the rally in Peking, in which he called for an all-out effort to crown the great victories of the Cultural Revolution with final success. He said that the crucial tasks ahead were to promote production, purify class ranks, consolidate and rebuild the party, and simplify administration. His stress was on a return to order under the leadership of the proletariat and the army.

Chinese Computer. On Oct. 5 the Xinhua news agency reported that a transistorized general-purpose digital computer had been trial-tested by the Computer Technology Institute of the Chinese Academy of Sciences during the Cultural Revolution. It was said to be capable of assisting in the solution of problems arising in nuclear research, rocketry and space flight. Every time it was turned on, said the report, the computer sang the song "The East is Red," drew a picture of Chairman Mao and, in an imitation of his handwriting, wrote the slogan "Serve the People."

Production Down. On Oct. 10 Chinese Premier Chou En-lai admitted that the Cultural Revolution had adversely affected China's production. Addressing a crowd of 100,000 at a rally in Wuhan, Chou said that "production is affected to a certain extent, but this is only a temporary thing. As

The Shanghai Commune

For the most part, the efforts of the Cultural Revolution and its shock troops, the Red Guards, were limited to an attack on the Communist Party, while the government was declared immune from attack. This was not so simple in practice, because leading party figures also held governmental office. Thus — particularly at the local level — attacks on the party spilled over into attacks on the government.

This conflict reached its peak on Jan. 4, 1967, when groups of Red Guards and "revolutionary rebels" seized power in Shanghai, the original base of the Cultural Revolution. Following the power seizure, the leaders declared the formation of a Shanghai Commune, explicitly modeled after the Paris Commune of 1871. The new system of rule by committee did not work, however; authority disappeared, essential services went unprovided, and widespread work stoppages began throughout the city.

This provoked alarm in Peking, which announced that this time Shanghai should *not* be taken as an example for the rest of the country. On the contrary, the army was sent in to restore order.

The Jan. 23 order to the army marked the beginning of the end of the most radical phase of the Cultural Revolution, although full military occupation of other troubled areas would not come until later in the year.

soon as disorder is turned into order, production can quickly pick up and rise."

Rusk on China. On Oct. 12 U.S. Secretary of State Dean Rusk defended the U.S. actions in Vietnam as a way of blocking Chinese expansion in Southeast Asia, but noted that the administration was "not picking out Peking as some sort of special enemy." On the contrary, said Rusk, "Peking has nominated itself by proclaiming a militant doctrine of the world revolution, and doing something about it."

Dissenting Views. On Oct. 16 the Shanghai *Wenhuibao* (newspaper) published an article calling for experienced managers to be put back in charge of production. The article charged that although the Cultural Revolution had seen "proletarian revolutionaries" put into positions of power, "they lack experience." Citing examples of the problems caused by the new leadership, the article concluded: "It is absolutely necessary" to put experienced cadres "back in management posts."

The article represented one of the few dissenting voices claiming that "expert" is better than "red." *(See June 1, 1966)*

Humphrey on China. On Oct. 23 Vice President Hubert H. Humphrey said that the non-communist Southeast Asian leaders believed that if the U.S. failed in Vietnam, "they would be under unbearable pressure from a nuclear-armed Communist China."

Humphrey went on to moderate his position somewhat, saying: "We do not seek to make mainland China our enemy. We do not seek to encircle or crush her. What we seek is to help the independent nations of Asia strengthen themselves against subversion and aggression so that a new generation of mainland Chinese leaders may, in time, see the futility" of their hostile acts.

More Purges Reported. On Nov. 11 it was reported in Taiwan that 11 of the 17 members of the Chinese Cultural Revolution Group, the ad hoc body leading the Cultural Revolution, had been purged since January. Analysts made reference to the radical phase of the French Revolution, when the revolution began killing its own leaders.

Fighting in Hong Kong to End. On Nov. 30 the Xinhua news agency announced that Britain had agreed to six conditions to end the seven months of violence along the China-Hong Kong border.

Intellectuals Dissent. On Dec. 19, 14 prominent U.S. scholars of Asian affairs issued a statement saying that although it was necessary for the U.S. to "deter, restrain, and counterbalance" China's power in Asia to prevent a major war in the region, "we must establish an elaborate structure of inducements to moderation," including an entire series of exchanges at all levels and in many areas, in addition to a de-escalation of the Vietnam War.

1968

Cultural Revolution Restructured — Pueblo Seized — Chinese Army in Power — Tet Offensive — McCarthy Primary Victory — Kennedy Candidacy — Travel Ban Eased — Vietnam Bombing Halt — Johnson Withdraws — Chinese Killings — More 'Revolutionary Committees' — Chinese Internal Fighting Stops — Nuclear Non-Proliferation Treaty Signed — Internecine Chinese Fighting Renewed — Humphrey Endorses Ties — Red Guards Dissolved — Soviets Invade Czechoslovakia — Nixon Nominated — Humphrey Nominated — Agricultural Production Drive — "Limited Sovereignty" Doctrine — Liu Shao-ch'i Purged — Resumption of China-U.S. Talks — Vietnam Bombing Halt — Nixon Elected — Warsaw Talks to Resume

Peking Declares Goals. On Jan. 1 the Peking *People's Daily* published an editorial which summed up the accomplishments of the Cultural Revolution in 1967 and set the goals for 1968. According to the article, the Cultural Revolution had won a "decisive victory in 1967," and 1968 would begin the rebuilding process. Specifically, the Communist Party, in chaos after the events of 1967, was to be rebuilt. At the same time, the revolutionary committees, of which there were only a few, would be organized at all levels of Chinese society.

In this effort, concluded the article, the Chinese army would be the "main pillar" supporting the new structure, and the "steel wall defending the socialist motherland." In 1967, said the article, the contributions of the army had been "tremendous," and it would "undertake still more tasks of still greater importance" in 1968.

Revcoms Expand. On Jan. 1 it was reported that only six provincial revolutionary committees existed out of the 29 planned. These committees — "revcoms" — were established to take the place of the local party and government organizations which had been destroyed by the Cultural Revolution. The army had been ordered to begin organizing the committees in January 1967 but had encountered armed resistance. In those areas with committees, the army made up the majority of the membership. In areas without committees the army ruled by fiat. *(See May 31, 1968)*

Pueblo Seized. On Jan. 23, North Korean troops boarded the U.S. Navy intelligence ship *Pueblo* off Wonsan and took the ship and her 83-man crew into the North Korean port.

The U.S. Defense Department claimed that the *Pueblo* had been cruising in international waters. The North Koreans claimed that the ship had been spying in the territorial waters of North Korea.

U.S. reaction to the seizure was loud and indignant. Sen. Wallace Bennett, R-Utah, urged the U.S. to send "an armada steaming into Wonsan harbor, throw a tow rope around the *Pueblo* and get her out of there." Sen. Frank Church, D-Idaho, called the seizure "an act of war," adding: "The ship must be returned at once, with all Americans aboard. Our national honor is at stake." But President Johnson was cautious. He moved first to ask Moscow to put pressure on the North Koreans for the release of both the ship and her crew, but was ignored.

The U.S. also raised the issue in Warsaw, in the ongoing talks with the Chinese. No results ensued. Although the U.S. made some threatening moves, such as calling up the reserves and ordering a naval group into the area, President Johnson continued to espouse a soft line: "We will not shoot from the hip." *(See Dec. 22, 1968)*

Chinese Army in Power. From Jan. 24 to May 31, the Chinese Army set up "revolutionary committees" (revcoms) in all of the provinces of China, thus restoring order while claiming to be furthering the Cultural Revolution. The need for new organizations of provincial power followed the destruction of the old organs by the activities of the Red Guards during the preceding two years.

Due to the ad hoc nature of these new bodies, the political situation remained extremely confused, and fighting again broke out in several areas of China in April.

Tet Offensive. On Jan. 30 the Communist forces in Vietnam launched the Tet offensive, which soon became one of the major battles of the war, and included attacks on almost all the capitals of South Vietnam's 44 provinces. The offensive served to repudiate U.S. claims that the end of the war was near. Thus, despite the military defeat, the Communists won a psychological victory that contributed to President Johnson's decision not to run for re-election.

More Fighting in China. On Jan. 30 the Toronto *Globe and Mail* reported from Peking that public executions were continuing as the army moved to take power in China. Other reports from China indicated that factional strife and fighting had broken out in nine different provinces in January.

Chinese Attack on Soviets. On Feb. 5 the Peking *People's Daily* published an article by "Commentator" — indicating high-level approval — condemning Soviet Premier Aleksei Kosygin's recent visit to India, charging that he had "completely taken over Khrushchev's policy of supporting India against China, and has gone even further."

McCarthy's "Moral Victory." On March 12 Sen. Eugene J. McCarthy, D-Minn., received 42.2 percent of the vote in the New Hampshire presidential primary, while incumbent President Johnson received 49.2 percent. Despite his defeat, most observers saw the votes received by McCarthy as a repudiation of the U.S. policies on Vietnam, due to the essentially conservative nature of the New Hampshire electorate.

Kennedy to Run. On March 16 Sen. Robert F. Kennedy, D-N.Y., announced that he would run for the presidency, reversing his previous denials. It was thought that Kennedy's decision was prompted by McCarthy's showing in the New Hampshire primary. *(See March 12)*

Travel Ban Eased. On March 28 the U.S. State Department announced that American citizens who traveled to communist countries declared "off limits" for U.S. travelers would no longer be punished, and that their passports would no longer be revoked.

Johnson to Halt Bombing. On March 31, in a televised address to the nation, President Johnson announced a partial halt to the bombing of North Vietnam, in the hope that it would bring new peace talks.

At the end of his statement, President Johnson, who had been faced with criticism of his Vietnam policy both within and outside of the Democratic Party, announced that he would not run for another term as president, stating "I should not permit the Presidency to become involved in the partisan divisions that are developing in this political year."

Executions in Canton. On April 3 Moscow radio reported that authorities in Canton, long the scene of the bloodiest fighting during the Cultural Revolution, had carried out more than 900 executions in 1968.

Peking on Johnson. On April 5 the Chinese finally commented on President Johnson's speech of March 31. The Xinhua news agency referred to the American proposals as a "new fraud of inducing peace talks by suspending bombing . . . to win a respite on the battlefields of Vietnam to expand the war further." The Chinese made no comment on the Vietnamese agreement to hold peace talks, a decision with which they disagreed. The Chinese attitude remained that the idea of peace talks was a fraud and that a prolonged war was the only way to defeat the U.S. *(See Sept. 2, 1968)*

U.S. Troop Limits. On April 11 U.S. Defense Secretary Clark M. Clifford announced that American troop strength in Vietnam would not exceed 550,000 men. Clifford also disclosed that the U.S. had made "the policy decision . . . to turn over gradually the major effort to the South Vietnamese" in conducting the war.

Army Takes Over Court. On April 21 *The Washington Post* reported that the Chinese army had taken over the Supreme People's Court, China's highest judicial body. A five-man military committee was named to administer the court and carry out whatever purges were "necessary."

Humphrey on China. On April 22 Vice President Hubert H. Humphrey called for a total reappraisal of U.S. foreign policy, and stressed the need to replace "iron curtains" with "open doors." Humphrey went on to say that he looked forward "to the day when the great Chinese people, no longer victimized from within, take their place in the modern world." Humphrey said that he felt that the U.S. could hasten this process by "the building of peaceful bridges to the people of mainland China."

Moscow Castigates Peking. On April 24 the Soviet Communist theoretical journal *Kommunist* published the first of three long articles attacking Chinese Party Chairman Mao Tse-tung and the Cultural Revolution. The first article claimed that "Mao Tse-tung's group . . . in line with its great power adventurist ambitions, had deliberately broken with Marxist-Leninism." In the second article, which dealt mainly with foreign policy, the Soviets accused

Mao and his group of trying to prolong the Vietnam War with the "secret aim" of trying to set the U.S. and the Soviet Union on a nuclear collision course. In the third article, Moscow said that the Cultural Revolution had caused severe damage to China's industry, had virtually destroyed the Communist Party, and had led to the establishment of a "military-bureaucratic dictatorship," the extreme idolization of Mao, and the "fanning of great power nationalist passions."

Rockefeller for Closer Ties. On May 1 Gov. Nelson A. Rockefeller of New York, opening his campaign for the GOP presidential nomination, called for more "contact and communication" with China.

U.S. Invites Reporters. On May 2 Leonard Marks, director of the U.S. Information Agency, invited China to send journalists to cover the 1968 American presidential elections. Speaking at a convention of the American Women in Radio and TV, Marks stated: "We stand ready to discuss such exchanges on a broad, general basis or on specific points."

Liu Charged. On May 17 President Liu Shao-ch'i was accused by the official Chinese news agency Xinhua of being an agent of the Kuomintang — Chiang Kai-shek's Nationalist Party. *(See Oct. 11, 1968)*

Officials Call for New Policy. On May 21 in separate speeches, two U.S. under secretaries of state, Nicholas deB. Katzenbach and Eugene V. Rostow, urged China to reconsider its policy of isolation and accept U.S. offers of new contacts and exchanges. Rostow said that the U.S. "had made known our willingness to welcome Chinese scientists, scholars and journalists to the United States and have encouraged our own academics to establish contact with their counterparts on the mainland."

In his speech, Katzenbach hinted that the U.S. was ready to reconsider its policy of not trading with China.

More Revcoms Formed. On May 31 the province of Sichuan announced that it had formed its revolutionary committee, to replace the older leadership organization destroyed by the Cultural Revolution. The formation of this committee meant that all of China proper had been brought back under control, and that order had been established in most areas. *(See Jan. 1, 1968)*

In most cases the committees were dominated by the military; that seemed to make Defense Minister Lin Piao the most powerful man in China. The last two revolutionary committees were formed in September. *(See Sept. 6, 1968)*

Robert Kennedy Assassinated. On June 5, shortly after midnight, Robert Kennedy was shot by an assassin at a hotel party celebrating his victory in the California presidential primary.

Fighting to Stop. On June 13 Peking ordered the officials of Guangxi Province in southwestern China to halt factional fighting and normalize the shipment to Vietnam of Chinese and Soviet military and economic aid. Guangxi had long been one of the areas hardest hit by the Cultural Revolution, and the fighting had disrupted the rail lines to Vietnam almost completely.

The order, signed by the Communist Party Central Committee, the State Council, the Military Advisory Committee and the Cultural Revolution Group, said that "certain mass organizations" had "carried out armed attacks against trains and had damaged railways."

'Mangoes Make History'

"On July 27, 1968, a group of workers from various Peking factories took over Tsinghua [Jinghua] University, one of the most famous institutions of higher learning in China. Entering the 'students' dormitories and the homes of teachers and staff,' they immediately launched a propaganda campaign employing 'broadcasts, big-character posters and forums. . . .'

"A few days later . . . a curious thing happened. Mao had a basket of mangoes sent to Tsinghua to this very Worker Team. . . . 'People immediately gathered around Chairman Mao's gift, jubilantly cheering and singing . . . with tears in their eyes.' During the evening of this memorable day, the Tsinghua team had 'all kinds of celebration.' But this was not enough, so they telephoned 'the joyous and inspiring news' to all the factories from which they had come. Finally, despite rain, they marched to Party Headquarters to 'express their loyalty to the great leader.'

". . . It seems that the mangoes were distributed among the factories represented in the Worker Team. A breathless story in the country's leading newspaper tells us what happened next in one of these factories — a Peking printing plant. A rally was held in honor of the mango; but when the rally was over at 11 p.m., the workers began to think that it was unbearable that the mango should be allowed to decay and perish. Some way must be found, it was decided, to preserve it so that it could be handed down to 'future generations' in order that they will 'remain eternally loyal to Chairman Mao.' A frantic search was immediately begun for a suitable chemical to treat the mango before it commenced to spoil in the summer heat. It was not an easy search. Not even the Peking Agricultural Display Center could help. Fortunately, the Peking Museum of Natural Sciences came up with a formula. At once, the printing plant's carpenters went to work, 'going without their dinner in order to make in time a large glass box to put the mango in.' The workers proudly said: 'Preserving the mango is a matter of great importance. We must preserve it well and stamp Chairman Mao's proletarian revolutionary line in our minds forever.'

"In this manner the mango was preserved at the printing plant. All over the country, pictures of the preserved mango, surrounded by jubilant workers, appeared. . . . These events inspired others to try extraordinary things. For instance, a peasant woman on a farm near Peking decided to transplant mangoes to the harsh climate of North China so as to 'have the poor and lower-middle peasants think of our beloved Chairman Mao every time they see the mangoes, and let Chairman Mao's mangoes remain in the hearts of the poor and lower-middle peasants . . . for thousands and generations to come.' Indeed, the mango story shows graphically the high pitch of excitement in which the population of China was kept during the Cultural Revolution. Because the Chinese have been well-known in the past for a subtle sense of humor, one cannot but wonder if some of this has not been received with tongue in cheek."

Source: Klaus Mehnert, *Peking and the New Left: At Home and Abroad,* University of California Center for Chinese Studies, Berkeley, 1969, pp. 43-44.

On July 3, citing non-compliance with the first order, Peking again told the Guangxi officials to stop the fighting and to restore communications within the province.

Chinese Criticize Treaty. On June 13 the Peking *People's Daily* criticized the non-proliferation treaty which had been adopted the day before by the United Nations. The article claimed that the treaty would serve only to "bind hand and foot" the non-nuclear states and turn them into "protectorates" of the U.S. and the Soviet Union.

Call for Lifting Embargo. On June 21 Vice President Hubert H. Humphrey, in an interview with editors of *The New York Times,* said that the U.S. should lift its embargo on trade with China except for strategic materials.

Non-proliferation Treaty Signed. On July 1, 62 nations, including the U.S., the Soviet Union, and Great Britain, signed a Treaty on the Non-proliferation of Nuclear Weapons in identical ceremonies in the various capitals. The signing followed ratification of the treaty by the United Nations in June.

It was reported that on June 27 Peking had refused U.N. Secretary General U Thant's invitation to China to attend, as an observer, the upcoming Aug. 29-Sept. 28 Geneva meeting of the signatories. Peking based its decision on the U.N.'s refusal to recognize the People's Republic of China as the government of China.

Contract Voided. On July 3 the Peking Municipal Intermediate People's Court declared that a contract signed between a British company, Vickers-Zimmer, Ltd., and the China National Technical Import Company was to be annulled. Vickers-Zimmer had signed a contract in November 1964 to build a synthetic fiber plant in Lanzhou. The plant was well behind schedule, and construction on the site had been delayed by the Cultural Revolution.

ABM Approved. On July 11 Congress passed a military construction bill which contained funds for building the Sentinel anti-ballistic missile system. During the debate, the major argument offered in favor of the system was its use as protection against China's growing nuclear arsenal. On Sept. 18 Congress approved the remaining funds for the system.

Humphrey Policy Shift. On July 12 Vice President Hubert H. Humphrey endorsed the removal of trade restrictions against China and a "shift" in total U.S. foreign policy from one of "confrontation and containment" to one of "reconciliation and peaceful engagement."

More Fighting in China. On July 17 *The Washington Post* said that beginning in May, observers in Hong Kong were receiving reports of almost daily fighting in Canton.

Another report said that there had been more than 3,000 arrests in Canton, and many executions. In addition, it was reported that over 2,000 buildings had been destroyed and 40,000 made homeless by the fighting.

Green Light to Army. On Aug. 1, China's Army Day, the Peking *People's Daily* published a joint editorial which ordered the masses to "at all times have faith in and rely on the People's Liberation Army and back up and support it." Western observers who had been following the growing power of the army in China since January 1967 characterized the editorial as a "green light" for further army intervention in China's politics.

Factionalism Criticized. On Aug. 5 the Peking *People's Daily* published an editorial decrying factionalism and the development of "many centers" in China, and called for national unity. The article said that the "proletarian headquarters" headed by Mao Tse-tung and Lin Piao "is the one and only leading center" of leadership for the army, the Communist Party and the people. The article concluded by urging "boundless unity" with Mao and Lin.

Worker Propaganda Teams. On Aug. 7 the Peking *People's Daily* revealed the formation of "Mao Tse-tung Thought Propaganda Teams" designed to help "strengthen the sense of organization and revolutionary discipline" in China. Officially comprised of workers, peasants and soldiers — actually, mostly workers — the teams were first sent to China's universities to counter "erroneous tendencies."

Nixon Nominated. On Aug. 8 Richard M. Nixon easily won the Republican nomination for the presidency on the first ballot.

In his acceptance speech, Nixon said that he would "extend the hand of friendship to all peoples" and specifically to the peoples of Russia and China.

The Republican platform took a somewhat stronger tone, stating that the U.S. will not "condone aggression, or so-called 'wars of national liberation,' or naively discount the continuing threats of Moscow and Peking." Specifically, the platform also pledged to continue to oppose admission of China to the U.N.

Red Guards Dissolved. On Aug. 14 *The Washington Post* reported that Peking had begun to dissolve some Red Guard organizations earlier in the summer. The report also made reference to the fact that Party Chairman Mao Tse-tung was disillusioned with the Red Guards, who had been the motivating force for the Cultural Revolution.

On Aug. 16 Canton radio reported that large numbers of "illegal" student and worker organizations had been disbanded. August saw similar reports from various parts of China. *(See Aug. 30, 1968)*

Britons Freed. On Aug. 14 Sir Donald Hopson, charge d'affaires of the British Embassy in Peking, was finally allowed to leave China. Hopson had been a virtual prisoner in the compound since August 1967. *(See Aug. 22, 1967)* In mid-September, the remaining British employees were also allowed to leave.

Soviets Invade Czechoslovakia. On Aug. 21, Soviet, Polish, Hungarian, Bulgarian and East German troops invaded Czechoslovakia. Following a Prague radio announcement not to resist, there was little fighting. The invasion put an end to the "Prague spring," a period during which Czech Communist Party First Secretary Alexander Dubcek had been liberalizing life in Czechoslovakia and leading the country away from its ties to the Soviet Union.

Russia's decision to intervene forcefully in another communist state raised fears in Peking, and is often credited as one of the major factors which led Chinese leaders to respond favorably to U.S. initiatives for rapprochement.

Chinese Reaction. On Aug. 23 the Peking *People's Daily* published the first public Chinese reaction to the Warsaw Pact's invasion of Czechoslovakia. In a large-character front page article by "Commentator" — indicating high level approval — the Soviets were accused of wanting to "found a colonial empire."

The same day, Chinese Premier Chou En-lai stated that the invasion was "the most barefaced and most typical specimen of fascist power politics played by the Soviet revisionist clique of renegades and scabs. It marks the total bankruptcy of Soviet modern revisionism."

Democrats Nominate Humphrey. On Aug. 28, against a background of continued battles between police and young anti-war demonstrators that had raged for several days, the Democratic National Convention nominated Hubert H. Humphrey on the first ballot.

The Democratic platform, adopted on the same day, made little reference to China, stating that prospects for change were "dim." Nonetheless, the platform went on to call for "economic, social and cultural exchange as a means of freeing that nation and her people from their narrow isolation."

China's Schools Taken Over. On Aug. 28 the Xinhua news agency reported that worker propaganda teams had taken over 49 colleges and universities in Peking, 26 in Shanghai, six in Tianjin, and 38 in Nanjing. The report also said that hundreds of other teams were in training for similar work.

Red Guards Criticized. On Aug. 30 the *Peking Review* published an article accusing certain Red Guards of undermining national unity. Written by Yao Wenyuan, one of the most important leaders of the Cultural Revolution, the article said that some Red Guards had "incited the masses to struggle against each other, and set themselves to sabotage the great cultural revolution . . . and obstruct the work of purifying the class ranks and of party" reform and rebuilding.

Worker Propaganda Teams. On Aug. 30 the Communist Party theoretical journal *Hongqi* published an article by Yao Wenyuan, one of the most vocal supporters of the Cultural Revolution, further elaborating on the role of the worker propaganda teams which had been established earlier in the month. Entitled "The Working Class Must Exercise Leadership in Everything," the article said that the teams should "systematically and in a planned way go to" all of China's schools and other places where the "struggle-criticism-transformation [purge] has not been carried out well."

On the same day, Party Chairman Mao Tse-tung said the teams should stay permanently in the schools to direct the struggle-criticism-transformation process.

Chou Criticizes Talks. On Sept. 2 Chinese Premier Chou En-lai, speaking at a Peking celebration of Vietnam's National Day, spent most of his time condemning the Soviet invasion of Czechoslovakia, which Vietnam had supported. Chou blamed the "peace talk schemes" on the joint machinations of the Soviet Union and America, and reiterated China's contention that only by fighting a "protracted war" could the Vietnamese win.

Last Revcoms Formed. On Sept. 6 it was announced that the last of the revolutionary committees — local organizations set up to replace the previous local party organizations — had been established. Begun in January 1967, the revcoms were officially comprised of a "three-in-one alliance" of military leaders, party officials and leaders of activist mass organizations (Red Guards). As the revcoms emerged, however, it became clear that they were dominated by the military and that China had just undergone a military takeover at the local and provincial level.

Xiafang. On Sept. 13 a radio broadcast from Henan Province said that the province had sent 630,000 students to the "front line of agricultural production" by Sept. 10.

On Sept. 27 *The Times* of London reported that 20,000 students from Peking and 120,000 from Liaoning Province had been sent to areas "where conditions are the most arduous."

In what was commonly called the *Xiafang* or "down-to-the-countryside-movement," hundreds of thousands of students from all of China's cities would be sent to rural areas to "learn from the masses." *(See Dec. 23, 1968)*

China Air Space Violated. On Sept. 16 China charged that the Soviets had violated its northeastern borders 29 times between Aug. 9-29, 119 times during the past year. *Izvestia* denied the charges Nov. 9.

China and South Yemen. On Sept. 17 China signed economic and technical agreements with the People's Democratic Republic of South Yemen in Peking.

Peking Lauds Albania. On Sept. 20 the Peking *People's Daily* published an editorial welcoming Albania's decision, announced on Sept. 12, to withdraw from the Warsaw Pact. The article said that the Warsaw Pact had "long become an instrument for aggression in the hands of the Soviet revisionist renegade clique."

Thant Urges U.N. China Membership. U.N. Secretary General U Thant, in his annual report released Sept. 26, called Chinese membership in the U.N. "desirable and, indeed, necessary . . . to achieve universality of membership."

Doctrine of "Limited Sovereignty." On Sept. 26 the Soviet party organ *Pravda* advanced a new, ideological argument to justify the invasion of Czechoslovakia by the Warsaw Pact nations. The article said, in effect, that the world socialist community had a right to intervene when socialism came under attack in a fraternal socialist country, and denied that this had in any way violated Czechoslovakia's "real sovereignty."

Since "anti-socialist forces" had attacked the very basis of socialism in Czechoslovakia, the article asserted, the country's "real sovereignty" required that its allies defend it from the threat to the "very foundation of the country's independence and sovereignty."

Thus, continued the article, although there are different types of socialism, "each communist party is responsible not only to its own people, but also to all the socialist countries, to the entire socialist movement." The article concluded that "The sovereignty of each socialist country cannot be opposed to the interests of the world of socialism."

Soon labeled the doctrine of "limited sovereignty," the article — later elaborated on by Soviet party leader Leonid Brezhnev and Foreign Minister Andrei Gromyko — seems to have caused apprehension in Peking, which could foresee its application to their own case, with subsequent Soviet invasion.

China's Power Decentralized. On Oct. 1 *The Washington Post* published an article by Stanley Karnow which said that the Cultural Revolution had shattered the party bureaucracy, the only national political machinery in China. The 29 revolutionary committees which had been established since then apparently possessed more power than the six regional party bureaus which they replaced, which meant that political power in China was much more decentralized. Karnow also noted that the revcom chairmen seemed much more responsive to local conditions than to orders from Peking.

Red Guards Downgraded. On Oct. 5 Chairman Mao Tse-tung and Defense Minister Lin Piao received 10,000 workers from all parts of China, a move designed to underline the new leading role of the proletariat at the expense of the Red Guards.

Reports from Sichuan and Xinjiang indicated that Red Guard units there were already disbanded.

Mao's Directive. On Oct. 4 Chinese Communist Party Chairman Mao Tse-tung issued a new directive ordering youth to the countryside: "Sending the masses to do manual work gives them an excellent opportunity to study once again; this should be done by all cadres except those who are too old, weak, ill or disabled."

Red Guards Warned. On Oct. 7 the Chinese Communist Party Central Committee issued a directive warning the Red Guards and others against interfering with foreigners in China. The order said that all foreigners in China were there with the "knowledge and will" of Peking and were "under the protection of the authorities" of China. The order also threatened to "punish" any who continued to harass or interfere with the activities of foreigners.

Communist Party to Be Rebuilt. On Oct. 10 the Peking *People's Daily* published a joint editorial stressing the need to rebuild the Chinese Communist Party, which had been destroyed during the Cultural Revolution: "We must give a very important position to the work of consolidating and building the party."

Liu Shao-ch'i Purged. On Oct. 11, the 12th Plenum of the Eighth Central Committee of the Chinese Communist Party met in Peking. The meeting declared that the struggle against the "revisionists in the Party" had been victorious, and announced that Chinese chief of state Liu Shao-ch'i, the foremost "revisionist," had been removed from all his posts in the state and party, and expelled from the party forever. Shortly afterward, the drive to expel Liu's supporters in the provinces touched off new waves of violence in China.

Complete Bombing Halt. On Oct. 31 President Johnson announced that he was ordering a complete halt to all American air, naval, and artillery bombardment of North Vietnam as of Nov. 1. *(See Dec. 26, 1971, April 6, 1972 and p. 35)*

Nixon Elected President. On Nov. 5 Richard M. Nixon defeated Vice President Hubert H. Humphrey for the presidency. The Republicans made gains in both the Congress and statehouses.

Warsaw Talks Postponed. On Nov. 18 the U.S. State Department announced that the 135th ambassadorial meeting between China and the U.S. which was to have been held in mid-November — already postponed from May — would presumably not take place because the Chinese had failed to name a date.

China on Warsaw Talks. On Nov. 26 the Chinese Foreign Ministry denied that China had caused a postponement of the Warsaw talks *(see above)*, and put the blame on American unwillingness to hold further talks before the new administration took office.

The statement went on to say that Peking was willing to resume in February after Nixon's inauguration, and prescribed conditions for the talks which amounted to a return to their negotiating platform before the Cultural Revolution — that the U.S. should withdraw from Taiwan and should agree "on the principles of peaceful coexistence."

Washington Accepts. On Nov. 29, officials in Washington said that the U.S. had decided to accept the Chinese proposal to reopen the Warsaw talks.

Members of the Johnson administration had cleared the decision with a representative of President-elect Nixon in accordance with the agreement to coordinate foreign policy during the transition period prior to Nixon's inauguration. *(See Feb. 18, 1969)*

Report of Chinese Troops. On Dec. 8 the London *Observer* reported that during Chinese Chief of Staff Huang Yongsheng's late-November trip to Albania, the two countries had agreed to allow Chinese troops to be stationed there. The report was never confirmed officially.

Goldberg's Proposals. On Dec. 10 ex-ambassador to the United Nations Arthur Goldberg said he favored seating both China and Taiwan in the U.N. In a televised interview Goldberg also said that the U.S. should drop its refusal to admit Peking, because such a change would "revolutionize the attitude of the world community to the United States, and I think . . . would have profound effects in helping liberalize developments on Mainland China."

Intellectuals Criticized. On Dec. 12 the Chinese news agency Xinhua published an article criticizing China's intellectuals and applauding the move to send them "down to the countryside." The article noted that "a special characteristic of intellectuals is that they are cocky. We don't want these intellectuals who smell good, we want those who stink. Only when they know they stink will they feel the need to transform themselves."

Moscow's Reaction. On Dec. 14 Moscow criticized the proposed meeting between U.S. and Chinese representatives at Warsaw. The Soviet news agency Tass said that those people within China "who believe in the anti-imperialist demagogy" of Mao "should react to the offer of peaceful coexistence with the U.S. as to an 'alliance of the great helmsman [Mao Tse-tung] with the devil himself.'"

North Vietnam Stresses Independence. In a Dec. 21 address, North Vietnamese Defense Minister Vo Nguyen Giap reiterated his country's commitment to political independence. The speech was interpreted as a warning to China not to interfere in internal North Vietnamese affairs.

Chinese Troops on Border. On Dec. 22 Indian Defense Minister Swaran Singh told the Parliament in New Delhi that China had between 13 and 16 divisions on the Indian border with China.

Pueblo Crew Returned. On Dec. 22 the 82 surviving crew members of the *Pueblo*, seized by North Korea earlier in the year, were released, although the ship itself was not. The release followed the American signing of an agreement acknowledging that the *Pueblo* had intruded into North Korean waters, and apologizing for the intrusion. But Maj. Gen. Gilbert H. Woodward, U.S. chief negotiator at the talks, was allowed to read a U.S. statement disavowing the agreement — and the confession — prior to the signature.

When asked about the move, Secretary of State Dean Rusk called it a "strange procedure." *(See Jan. 23, 1968)*

Mao Approves *Xiafang*. On Dec. 23 Chinese Communist Party Chairman Mao Tse-tung declared: "The young rebels must go to the villages and accept re-education by the poor and lower middle peasants. This is a necessity."

'Détente'

"The term 'détente' is frequently used to describe the state of United States-Soviet relations since the Cuban missile crisis of 1962. Harold Nicholson, the noted British diplomat, defined 'détente' as simply a 'relaxation of tension.' The existence of a détente between two powers does not mean that fundamental problems in their relations have been solved. It does not mean that formal, or even informal, agreements have been reached between them. It in no way implies that the relaxed atmosphere is stable or permanent.

"Of course, problems may be solved, agreements reached, and a stable relationship achieved during a period of détente. But if and when these things occur, it is due not to the détente itself, but to the attitudes and skills of those who direct the foreign policies of the nations in question. A détente is a starting-point for conciliation and accommodation, not the product of these processes."

Source: Stephen S. Anderson, "United States-Soviet Relations: The Path to Accommodation," *Current History* 55, no. 327 (November 1968): 281.

Mao's announcement approving the *Xiafang* ("down to the countryside") movement accelerated the process, begun in September.

Although the avowed purpose of the action was to allow China's youth to "learn from the masses," a more pragmatic analysis has argued that removal of the Red Guards from the cities was a prime prerequisite for the restoration of order by the military. In fact, the fighting which had plagued China since 1966 did end at about this time.

It has been estimated that some 15 million Chinese youth were affected by the campaign.

China A-Test. On Dec. 27 China test-exploded its eighth nuclear bomb — a three-megaton device. The Chinese news agency Xinhua called it "another great victory for the invincible thought of Mao Tse-tung."

1969

Peace Talks Begin — Nixon Inaugurated — Nixon Announces New China Policy — China-U.S.S.R. Clash — Non-proliferation Treaty Ratified — Travel Eased — Ninth Chinese Party Congress — Russia, U.S. Denounced by Lin Piao — Diplomatic Openings by China — Grievances Against Soviet Union Aired — Asian Alliance Sought — Pullout of U.S. Troops from Vietnam — More Sino-Soviet Conflict — Nixon Doctrine — Ho Chi Minh Dies — Sino-Soviet Border Talks — U.S. Ends Taiwan Patrol — SALT Talks Begin — Okinawa Returned to Japan — China Releases American Prisoners — Congress Limits Combat Troops

Peking Stresses Unity. On Jan. 1 the Peking *People's Daily* published an editorial quoting Chinese Party Chairman Mao Tse-tung's calls for unity: "When people have divergent views and no unified thinking, it is impossible to establish centralism." *(See May 5, 1969)*

China Rebuilds. On Jan. 18, reports began to appear from localities throughout China concerning the re-estab-

lishment of law enforcement and public order authorities. These had been destroyed during the Cultural Revolution, and later were taken over by the army.

Peace Talks Begin. On Jan. 18, expanded peace talks aimed at ending the war in Vietnam opened in Paris, with representation by the U.S., North Vietnam, South Vietnam, and the National Liberation Front (Viet Cong). The talks would continue for four years. *(See Jan. 27, 1973)*

Nixon Inaugurated. On Jan. 20 Richard M. Nixon was inaugurated as the 37th president of the U.S. In his inaugural address, Nixon suggested that he would move to make fundamental changes in U.S. foreign policy: "After a period of confrontation, we are entering an era of negotiation." *(Text, p. 319)*

Peking on Nixon. On Jan. 23 the Peking *People's Daily* published an editorial commenting on the election of President Nixon; it marked an end to the more muted criticism of the U.S. during the latter part of the Johnson administration: "Like Eisenhower, Kennedy and Johnson before him, Nixon is an agent of the American monopoly groups which have now chosen him as their front man. It goes without saying that Nixon will pick up the line ... pursuing the reactionary policies of oppressing and exploiting the American people at home and carrying out aggression and expansion abroad."

Other, equally harsh editorials followed.

Nixon on China Prospects. On Jan. 27, in his first presidential news conference, when asked about the future of Sino-American relations, Richard Nixon stated that: "Until some changes occur on their side ... I see no immediate prospect of any change in our policy" toward China.

Nixon Orders New China Policy. On Feb. 1 newly elected President Richard Nixon, in a secret memorandum to Henry Kissinger, adviser for national security affairs, ordered a re-examination of U.S. policy toward China. The memo also stated: "We should give every encouragement to the attitude that this Administration is exploring possibilities of rapprochement with the Chinese," and that this should be done in absolute secrecy.

U.S. Reaction to Chinese Probe. On Feb. 18 Secretary of State William Rogers said that the U.S. was willing to accede to the Chinese desire for a reopening of the Warsaw talks.

This was the second positive response by the U.S. to the Chinese initiative. *(See Nov. 29, 1968)*

Warsaw Talks Canceled. On Feb. 18 China abruptly canceled the Warsaw talks with the U.S., which the Chinese had requested and which were to open on Feb. 20. The reason given was the defection of a Chinese diplomat to the U.S., but the actual cause may have been basic foreign policy differences within the Chinese leadership.

China to Retrench. On Feb. 21 the Peking *People's Daily* published an editorial which revived slogans from the period of retrenchment immediately following the Great Leap Forward of 1958. Thus, despite press references to a "new flying leap," the specific proposals in this article seemed to indicate that there would be no return to the radical policies of the past. *(See Nov. 2, 1969)*

Nixon and DeGaulle. On March 1 President Nixon met with French President Charles de Gaulle in Versailles. Nixon took the opportunity to ask de Gaulle to tell the

Chinese that the U.S. was interested in expanding communications with Peking.

Sino-Soviet Fighting. On March 2, following a series of minor incidents, serious fighting flared on the Sino-Soviet border as Chinese forces ambushed a Russian company making a routine patrol of Zhenbao (Damansky) Island in the Ussuri River; the island was in disputed territory. Thirty-eight were killed and 14 wounded. On March 15 the Soviets retaliated with artillery and tanks, causing heavy Chinese casualties.

In all, there would be more than 400 skirmishes along the border in 1969.

In 1978 former presidential adviser Robert Haldeman claimed that following the clashes, the Soviet Union sought to have the Nixon administration join Moscow in a joint nuclear attack on China. Haldeman's assertions have been denied by the Soviet Union, former Secretary of State William Rogers and former Secretary of State Henry Kissinger. *(See July 10, 1970)*

Nixon on China Prospects. On March 3 President Nixon, responding to questions at a news conference, said that although relations with China might improve in the long run, "we should not hold out any great optimism for any breakthroughs . . . at this time."

Demonstrations in China. From March 3 to March 7, 260 million people participated in anti-Soviet demonstrations throughout China. In Peking the demonstrations were directed against the Soviet Embassy, which was put under siege.

Chinese Criticize Soviets. On March 4 the Peking *People's Daily* printed an editorial which signaled an escalation of the Sino-Soviet battle of words. Entitled "Down with the New Tsars," the article claimed Chinese sovereignty over the disputed Zhenbao (Damansky) Island, even under the terms of the "unequal treaty imposed on the Chinese people in 1860 by Tsarist Russian imperialism," and accused the Russians of premeditation: "The armed provocation by the Soviet Revisionist clique against our country is a frenzied action it has taken out of the need of its domestic and foreign policies at a time when it is beset with internal difficulties and landed in an impasse."

China Accuses Taiwan. On March 6 the Peking *People's Daily* accused the Soviet government of carrying on negotiations with the Nationalist government on Taiwan. The article referred to the visit of the Soviet "journalist" Victor Louis (Vitali Yevgenevitch) to Taiwan in October 1968. During his visit, he was supposed to have talked with Minister of Defense and heir-apparent Chiang Ching-kuo.

On April 1 the *Christian Science Monitor* reported that the Victor Louis visit was followed by a trip by Ku Yu-hsiu, former deputy minister of education in the Nationalist government, to Moscow.

Non-proliferation Treaty Ratified. On March 13, after an eight-month delay caused by the Soviet invasion of Czechoslovakia in August 1968, the Senate ratified the treaty banning the spread of nuclear weapons.

On Nov. 24 President Nixon signed the instrument of ratification.

China Blocks Aid. On March 14 it was reported in Moscow that China had halted all Soviet shipments across its territory to North Vietnam. Soviet trade ministry officials said the blockade had come into effect after March 2,

the date of the outbreak of fighting on the Sino-Soviet border. Without passage across China, the only way Soviet shipments could reach Hanoi was by sea — around the Cape of Good Hope.

Le Monde, quoting communist diplomats at the United Nations, confirmed the reports.

Nixon on ABM. On March 14 President Nixon called for a substantial modification of the Sentinel anti-ballistic missile system, claiming that it would be a "safeguard against any attack by the Chinese Communists that we can foresee over the next ten years."

On May 18 Nixon said that American diplomacy in the Pacific area would not be credible "unless we could protect our country against a Chinese attack aimed at other cities. The ABM will do that and the ABM Safeguard System has been adopted for that reason."

Travel Ban Extended. On March 15 the U.S. State Department announced that the annual extension of the travel ban to China, North Vietnam, North Korea, and Cuba would only be extended for six months, instead of one year, prompting speculation that it would soon be ended altogether. *(See Sept. 15, 1969)*

China to Use A-bombs. On March 21 the Hong Kong newspaper *The Star* quoted Chinese Party Chairman Mao Tse-tung as saying that China was prepared to use nuclear weapons in the event of a Soviet nuclear attack.

More Discussion of China. On March 21-22 the National Committee on United States-China Relations sponsored a conference in New York which drew an audience of some 2,500 persons for a frank review of American policy toward China. Among the speakers, some condemned what they called "irresponsible and uninformed denunciation" of earlier U.S. actions, and restated old arguments for the containment and isolation of Peking. The majority, however, insisted on the need for a reconsideration of U.S. objectives.

Theodore Sorenson, Arthur Goldberg, Sen. Jacob Javits, R-N.Y., and Sen. Edward Kennedy, D-Mass., agreed that the passions of the past should be discarded and U.S. attitudes toward China readjusted in terms of East Asian realities. Espousing ideas that only a few years earlier might have been politically suicidal, Kennedy made a series of specific recommendations including an end to the trade embargo, reopening of American consular offices on the mainland, supporting Peking's recognition in the United Nations, and extending diplomatic recognition to the PRC. Kennedy also said the U.S. should withdraw its token military presence from Taiwan.

Moscow Attacks Mao. On March 23, in one of the harshest Soviet criticisms ever directed at China, the Soviet defense ministry newspaper *Red Star* portrayed Chinese Party Chairman Mao Tse-tung as a killer and obliquely compared him with Adolf Hitler. Mao was described as "simply a traitor to the sacred cause of communism." In an indirect reference to Chinese claims to Soviet territory in East Asia, the article said: "Once upon a time a certain Adolf Hitler marked Moscow and the Urals as his own territory on his maps. He marked them — and rotted away."

Chinese Communist Congress. On April 1 the Ninth Congress of the Chinese Communist Party opened in Peking. Wracked by the internal power struggle, the congress had been delayed eight years. The congress represented the culmination and, to some extent, the termination, of the Cultural Revolution, hailed as a "great victory." The party was reaffirmed as "the core of leadership of the Chinese people," but the party was now organized around the thought and will of one man, Chairman Mao Tse-tung. The congress saw the end of the diversity of membership which had given it much of its strength, as membership now depended almost solely on loyalty to Mao and, to a lesser extent, his designated heir, Minister of Defense Lin Piao. The congress formalized the changes in leadership which had occurred during the purges of the past three years, and membership of the top power organs was limited to the leaders of the Cultural Revolution. The sole exception was the moderate Chou En-lai, who had not only managed to hold on to power, but during the recent upheavals had become responsible for the day-to-day running of the country. But the Army's membership on the Central Committee and the ruling Politburo increased dramatically.

The congress also announced changes in the goals of the party. In 1956 it had declared that its chief mission was to "satisfy to the maximum extent the material and cultural needs of the people." In 1969 the party announced that its goal was to bring about "the complete overthrow of the bourgeoisie," and to practice the "theory of permanent revolution."

Lin's Report to 9th Congress. On April 1 Defense Minister Lin Piao restated Chou En-lai's declaration of the year before denouncing Soviet-U.S. détente as the vain attempts of "American imperialism" and Soviet "social-imperialism," which "collude and at the same time contend with each other," and which "act in coordination and work hand in glove in opposing China, opposing Communism, and opposing the people." Reacting to the recent Sino-Soviet border incidents, Lin aimed his harshest attacks at the "Soviet revisionist clique" whose turn it now was to be called a "paper tiger."

Lin also called for a new series of mass mobilization campaigns based on the Great Leap Forward of the late 1950s. Despite the seeming victory of the left in the Cultural Revolution, this suggestion met with much opposition, and probably triggered Lin's eventual downfall.

U.S. Spy Plane Downed. On April 15, North Korean MiGs shot down an EC-121 U.S. reconnaissance plane over the Sea of Japan. The U.S. claimed that the propellor-driven plane had been operating over international waters at the time of the incident. No survivors were reported among the 31-man crew.

On April 18 President Nixon announced that the flights would continue, and that they would be escorted.

Two Chinas. On April 21 Secretary of State William Rogers, in an important policy statement, announced the inauguration of the new policy toward China. The U.S., Rogers said, accepts the existence of a Communist China on the mainland and a Nationalist China on Taiwan as "facts of life" that cannot be ignored. He spoke of U.S. treaty relations with the latter, a political entity but not representative of all China, and expressed the hope that the problems to which these relations gave rise could be peacefully settled.

Rogers said Peking was currently in deep trouble and displaying a hostile attitude to America. Rogers said he believed this attitude would change but, in the meantime, "we shall take the initiative to reestablish more normal relations with Communist China and shall remain respon-

sive to any indications of less hostile attitudes from their side."

Chinese Publications Banned. On April 21 the U.S. Supreme Court rejected a challenge to federal regulations that prohibited the receipt of publications from China, North Vietnam, and North Korea without government permission. The 7-2 decision did not indicate the reason for dismissal.

Sino-Soviet Skirmish. On May 3, Chinese and Russian troops clashed in the Bakhty region of Kazakhstan.

Peking Stresses Unity. On May 5 the Peking *People's Daily* published an editorial calling on the Chinese people to restore unity. Entitled "The Proletariat Must Unite the Overwhelming Majority of the People Around Itself," the article said that "with the exception of ... a very few absolutely unrepentant diehards," all the other people of China should unite. This theme was quickly picked up by other periodicals and repeated throughout China.

China Emerges from Isolation. On May 16 the Chinese government named Geng Biao ambassador to Albania; he was the first ambassador to be named since the beginning of the Cultural Revolution in 1966, when all of China's ambassadors had been recalled.

The appointment marked the end of China's self-imposed diplomatic isolation as 16 more ambassadors were named during June and July. But the full complement of Chinese ambassadors did not return to their posts until the end of 1970.

Chinese Policy Statement. On May 24 the Chinese government issued an unprecedented public policy statement on the Sino-Soviet border dispute. The statement followed repeated failures to negotiate the problem, as well as a recent Soviet threat to use nuclear weapons if serious fighting were to break out on the border. Stating that the Chinese position had always been that "the status quo of the boundary should be maintained and conflicts averted," the Chinese traced the history of the dispute and articulated their specific boundary claims. By opening the dispute to world public opinion, the statement amounted to a serious escalation of the Sino-Soviet split.

American Feeler. On May 24 President Nixon had Secretary of State William Rogers, then in Pakistan, ask Pakistani chief of state Yahya Khan to feel out the Chinese about expanded talks with Washington. *(See Aug. 1)*

Sino-Romanian Trade Agreement. On June 3 Romania and China signed a trade agreement in Peking. In speeches celebrating the pact, Chinese leaders referred to Romania as the only member of the Soviet bloc that had sent greetings to the Ninth Congress of the Chinese Communist Party, and the only one that had not criticized China during the Moscow Conference of Communist Parties earlier in the month.

Asian Collective Security System. On June 7, speaking at the Moscow summit conference of the world's communist parties, Soviet party leader Leonid Brezhnev called for the formation of an "Asian collective security system," clearly aimed at limiting Chinese activity in Southeast and South Asia.

On June 10 Soviet Foreign Minister Andrei Gromyko offered more details of the plan, which sought to fill the power vacuum created by the British withdrawal from their East Asian, Indian Ocean, and Persian Gulf bases, as well as the contemplated U.S. withdrawal from Vietnam. The move was seen by Western analysts as an effort to stop China from moving to fill that vacuum.

Nixon Begins Vietnam Withdrawal. On June 8 President Nixon announced that he was ordering the withdrawal of 25,000 American troops from Vietnam. Nixon also announced that further reductions would occur "as decisions are made." At the time of the announcement, the U.S. had 540,000 troops in Vietnam.

Later in the year Nixon announced two additional troop cuts, reducing the American commitment to Vietnam by about 23 percent.

Sino-Soviet Fighting. On June 10, Chinese and Russian troops fought at Dazheng north of Yumin in the Barluk mountains (northwestern Xinjiang).

Cambodia-U.S. Relations. On June 11 the U.S. and Cambodia re-established relations, which had been broken in May 1965. This followed an increase in Chinese-inspired guerrilla activity, and Cambodia's recall of its diplomats in Peking.

Sino-Soviet Fighting. On July 8, Chinese and Russian troops clashed on Pacha (Goldinsky) Island in the Amur (Heilong) River.

Moscow on Border Clashes. On July 10 Soviet Foreign Minister Andrei Gromyko told the Supreme Soviet in Moscow that "even our worst enemies have never resorted to such unseemly methods" as China was now using against the Soviet Union.

Chinese Reaction. On July 13 Chinese Premier Chou En-lai strongly denounced the "Asian collective security system" proposed by Moscow as an anti-Chinese military alliance and a concealed attempt at aggression against Asian countries. (See June 7, 1969)

Travel and Trade with China. On July 21 the State Department announced a slight easing of travel and trade restrictions. Beginning July 23, U.S. citizens traveling abroad could bring back $100-worth of goods from communist countries, and some categories of citizens were allowed to visit China. This was done "to relax tension and facilitate the development of peaceful contacts."

Nixon Doctrine. On July 25, on the eve of a trip to Asia, President Nixon gave reporters on Guam a background briefing which signaled a complete reversal of U.S. East Asian foreign policy, and is now called the Nixon Doctrine. Stating that the U.S. could no longer act as the "global policeman," Nixon said that the U.S. would reduce its military presence on the Asian mainland and would provide Asian nations with the means to defend themselves.

The use of American troops to contain what was thought to be a hostile and aggressive China had been a cornerstone of U.S. foreign policy since the Korean War. Now it would be abandoned, said Nixon, and the U.S. would use money and arms in place of men and treaties.

This doctrine, generally attributed to the president's national security adviser, Henry Kissinger, would be formally announced in 1971 (see Feb. 25, 1971), would force all of the nations on the periphery of China to reappraise their positions, and open the way for the normalization of relations with China by the implementation of a fundamental Chinese demand which dated from 1950 — the removal of U.S. troops which "encircled" China.

More U.S. Feelers. On Aug. 1 President Nixon, visiting Pakistan, asked Pakistani chief of state Yahya Khan to explore with Chinese leaders the possibilities for expanded talks between the two countries. (See Oct. 25, 1970)

On Aug. 2, while visiting Romania, Nixon made similar proposals to Nicolae Ceausescu.

Rogers on China Talks. On Aug. 8 Secretary of State William Rogers, during an Asian tour, expressed the U.S.' desire to renew diplomatic talks with China at Warsaw.

ANZUS Voices Support. On Aug. 8 Australia and New Zealand announced their support for the U.S. policy of conciliation toward China, which had been enunciated in Canberra by Secretary of State Rogers at a one-day meeting of the ANZUS Treaty Council. In his speech, Rogers had said that the U.S. would "soon be making another approach to see if a dialogue with Peking can be resumed." Rogers went on to point out that "We intend to disregard Peking's denunciations of United States efforts to negotiate with the Soviet Union and we intend to disregard Soviet nervousness at steps we take to re-establish contacts between us and the Chinese Communists."

In the joint communiqué issued at the end of the meeting, Australia and New Zealand "agreed that efforts should be continued to resume a dialogue with the Peking regime."

Sino-Soviet Agreement. On Aug. 8 China and the Soviet Union signed a protocol "recording agreement by the two sides to carry out certain measures during the 1969 navigational season to improve the shipping" on various rivers along the border.

Sino-Soviet Fighting. On Aug. 13, Chinese and Soviet troops clashed again in the Yumin area, this time at Tiehlieketi.

Chinese Protest to Moscow. On Aug. 19 Peking accused the Soviets of 429 border incidents during June and July. In a note delivered to the Soviet Embassy in Peking, China charged that the Soviets "must be held fully responsible for all the grave consequences."

Rogers on Border Fighting. On Aug. 20 U.S. Secretary of State William Rogers declared that "our best judgment is that border clashes and incidents will continue.... We are convinced that the hostility between them is deep." Rogers also noted that it was doubtful whether the incidents would result in all-out war between Russia and China.

Soviet Pre-emptive Strike. On Aug. 28 the State Department acknowledged that it had heard reports that the Soviet Union had sounded out other communist countries in Eastern and Western Europe concerning a possible pre-emptive strike against China's nuclear installations.

Czech Protest. On Aug. 28, as China continued to publish criticism of the Soviet invasion of Czechoslovakia, the Czech Foreign Ministry filed an official protest with the Chinese government which accused the Chinese of misinforming its own and the international public about "the activities and intentions of counter-revolutionary forces in Czechoslovakia" and using the opportunity for "disruptive activities against the unity of the Socialist countries."

Ho Chi Minh Dies. On Sept. 3 North Vietnamese President Ho Chi Minh died. In his will, which was soon made public, Ho expressed sorrow about divisions in the world communist movement.

U.S. on Sino-Soviet Split. On Sept. 5 U.S. Under Secretary of State Elliott L. Richardson, addressing a convention of the American Political Science Association in New York, expressed concern lest any increase in Sino-Soviet tension escalate "into a massive breach of international peace and security." Richardson stated that the administration would not seek to exploit the rift, but would try to "pursue a long-term course of progressively developing better relations" with both countries. Richardson went on to say that "Soviet apprehensions" would not prevent the U.S. from "attempting to bring China out of its angry, alienated shell."

Kosygin to Peking. On Sept. 11 Soviet Premier Aleksei Kosygin arrived in Peking for talks with Chinese leaders. Most of the discussion centered on the Sino-Soviet border problems. The Soviets later revealed that Kosygin had called for more talks. *(See Oct. 20)*

In 1974 the Chinese claimed that Kosygin and Chinese Premier Chou En-lai had reached agreement on a border cease-fire and a mutual pullback from "disputed areas." Moscow has always denied that such an agreement was reached, and it has never been put into effect.

Western analysts feel that the Kosygin visit was a failure, given his refusal to help ease the problem, and that this failure helped push the Chinese toward the more pragmatic, anti-Soviet foreign policy they would adopt in 1970.

Travel Ban Extended. On Sept. 15 the State Department again extended the ban on travel by U.S. citizens to China, North Vietnam, North Korea and Cuba, but again for only six months. *(See March 15, 1969)*

Soviets Might Attack China. On Sept. 16 Victor Louis (Vitali Yevgenevitch), Moscow "correspondent" for the *London Evening News,* indicated that the Soviets might launch a surprise attack on China. "Events of the past year indicate that the Soviet Union is adhering to the doctrine that Socialist countries have the right to interfere in each other's affairs in their own interest. . . . Whether or not the Soviet Union will dare to attack Lop Nor, China's nuclear center, is a question of strategy."

Chinese Oil. On Sept. 18 the Xinhua news agency reported that China was now "entirely self-sufficient in the supply of oil for the country's national economy, for national defense construction, and for the development of science and technology, as regards quantity, variety, and quality." No figures were given, but this was the first time such a claim had been made. Previous reports had stated that China was self-sufficient "in the main."

China's Nuclear Test. On Sept. 23 China conducted its first underground nuclear test. The U.S. Atomic Energy Commission estimated that the test had taken place in the Lop Nor testing area, and that the device had been in the 20-200 kiloton range.

Senate on Recognition. On Sept. 25 the U.S. Senate passed a resolution declaring that "when the United States recognizes a foreign government and exchanges diplomatic representatives with it, this does not of itself imply that the United States approves of the form, ideology, or policy of that foreign government."

In debate on the resolution, which was non-binding, Sen. Alan Cranston, D-Calif., said that the policy of withholding recognition in order to influence political events within a country was "doomed to failure." The resolution represented a reversal of the concept of "democratic legitimacy" which had been associated with the extension of diplomatic recognition since the Wilson administration. Apart from the U.S., few countries have ever applied this concept.

Peking and Moscow to Talk. On Oct. 7 the Xinhua news agency announced that China and the Soviet Union had agreed to hold their first formal negotiations since 1964 on ending their border dispute. The report credited Chinese Premier Chou En-lai with originating the proposal.

New Economic Policy. On Oct. 13 the Chinese Communist theoretical journal *Hongqi* announced the inauguration of a new economic policy for China, the first such comprehensive policy since the beginning of the Cultural Revolution. The new plan stressed heavy industry, but in conjunction with agriculture and light industry. It called for the dispersal of Chinese industry as a precaution against war. The article also condemned former chief of state Liu Shao-ch'i and stressed that no material incentives of any kind would be used.

Vietnam Moratorium. On Oct. 15 an estimated one million persons in the U.S. participated in a nationwide protest against the Vietnam War. Labeled a "moratorium," the demonstrations were a protest against "business as usual" during the war.

China-U.S.S.R. Negotiations. On Oct. 20 Chinese Deputy Foreign Minister Qiao Guanhua and Soviet Deputy Foreign Minister Aleksei Kuznetsov opened negotiations in Peking on the Sino-Soviet border problems. The opening of the talks during the onset of winter marked the end of the long series of border clashes which had occurred during the spring and summer.

The onset of the talks was accompanied by a decrease in the accusations which the two sides had been hurling at one another since the early 1960s. The Chinese resumed their harsh criticisms of the Russians in 1971, but the Soviet response remained muted. *(See Aug. 28, 1971)*

Brezhnev on Border Talks. On Oct. 27 Soviet party leader Leonid Brezhnev expressed the hope that the Sino-Soviet border talks, just under way, might ease tensions between the two communist giants. In his speech, Brezhnev — in a conciliatory gesture — referred to Chinese Premier Chou En-lai as "comrade."

A New "Great Leap Forward." On Nov. 2 Changsha radio declared that a "flying leap" in production would soon emerge. This was soon followed by similar claims from other provincial news sources throughout China and suggested a return to the policies of the Great Leap Forward of 1958. *(See Feb. 21, 1969)*

Sino-Soviet Boundary Talks. On Nov. 6 the English language edition of the Hong Kong communist newspaper *Dagongbao* quoted its Canton correspondent as saying that "negotiations on the boundary question [between China and the Soviet Union] have not been proceeding as smoothly as some in the outside world have made them out to be."

U.S. Ends Patrol of Taiwan Strait. On Nov. 7 the U.S. quietly ended the 19-year presence of the 7th Fleet in the Taiwan Strait, which separates Taiwan from mainland China. Placed there to protect the government on Taiwan from a Chinese invasion, the patrol had become a symbol of U.S. commitment to Chiang Kai-shek. The decision to end the patrols may have prompted the Chinese to reopen the Warsaw talks in January 1970.

SALT Talks Begin. On Nov. 11 the U.S. and the U.S.S.R. formally opened preliminary talks in Helsinki, Finland, to limit the strategic arms race. Both sides pledged to avoid any agreement that would place the other side at a military disadvantage.

Second Moratorium. On Nov. 13, antiwar demonstrators began the second Vietnam Moratorium protest with ceremonies in Washington, D.C.

On Nov. 15 at least 250,000 war protesters marched and demonstrated peacefully in Washington. Some 100,000 protesters demonstrated in San Francisco in the largest peace demonstration ever held on the West Coast.

Okinawa to Revert to Japan. On Nov. 21 Japanese Prime Minister Eisaku Sato ended a three-day visit to the U.S. by issuing a joint communiqué with President Nixon. The communiqué stated agreement between the U.S. and Japan that the island of Okinawa, captured by the U.S. in World War II, would revert to Japan by the end of 1972. The U.S. would maintain its extensive military facilities on the island, but all nuclear weapons would be removed. *(See June 17, 1971)*

Peking Attacks Sato. On Nov. 28 the Peking *People's Daily* editorially attacked Japanese Prime Minister Eisaku Sato for saying, during a recent trip to the U.S., that Taiwan was "a most important factor for the security of Japan" and that Korea was "essential to Japan's own security." The article claimed that this was very similar to Japanese claims prior to the 1937 invasion of China by Japan, and concluded that Japan was seeking "to obstruct by force of arms the Chinese people's liberation of Taiwan."

China Prepares Defenses. On Dec. 1 *The Times* of London reported extensive digging of what were said to be air-raid shelters in the streets of Peking and other major cities. Earlier, a Tokyo newspaper had claimed that a directive of Chairman Mao Tse-tung in late October had ordered tunnels to be built in towns along the Sino-Soviet border and near military bases.

China Releases Prisoners. On Dec. 7 China released Simeon Baldwin and Bessie Hope Donald, two Americans whose private vessel had been seized by Chinese patrol boats while traveling from Hong Kong to Macao in February.

U.S. Asks Import Limits. On Dec. 8 the U.S. opened talks with South Korea in Geneva in an effort to persuade Seoul to limit voluntarily low-cost woolen and man-made fiber textile shipments to the U.S. market.

On Dec. 10, similar talks opened with Nationalist China. Conferences with Hong Kong were scheduled later.

Okinawa Missiles to Be Removed. On Dec. 15 the U.S. announced that all nuclear missiles on Okinawa would be removed to help cut defense costs. According to the U.S. agreement with Japan, the missiles were not slated for removal until 1972. It was reported that the missiles had been aimed at China.

Trade Restrictions Eased. On Dec. 19 the U.S. announced that, effective Dec. 22, subsidiaries and affiliates of U.S. firms abroad would be permitted to buy and sell non-strategic goods with China, ending a ban imposed in 1950. *(See Dec. 8, 1950)*

Congress Limits President. On Dec. 30 President Nixon signed a $70-billion defense appropriation bill which included a ban on the use of U.S. combat troops in Thailand and Laos.

1970

Warsaw Talks Resume — Planes to Taiwan — Travel Bans Ended —Coup in Cambodia — Chou En-lai in Korea — China Attacks Brezhnev Doctrine — Chiang Ching-kuo Escapes Assassination —First China Satellite — U.S. Invades Cambodia — Warsaw Talks Suspended — Cambodia Invasion Ends — ROC Raids on Mainland — China Backs Palestinians — Canada Recognizes PRC — U.S. China Policy Softened — China Asks Nuclear Ban — Italy Recognizes PRC — Yahya Khan Mediates with Chinese — Sino-Soviet Trade Pact — Nixon Threatens Hanoi

Agnew on China. On Jan. 3, speaking to newsmen while en route from South Vietnam to Taiwan, Vice President Spiro Agnew said that the U.S. would seek a "meaningful dialogue" with mainland China.

While on Taiwan, Agnew was reported to have informed Nationalist Chinese leader Chiang Kai-shek of the U.S.' intention to move closer to mainland China.

Moscow on Sino-Soviet Split. On Jan. 6 the Soviet Communist Party newspaper *Pravda* charged that China was slandering the Soviet Union and preparing for war. The paper also said Western "imperialists" welcomed the differences between the two countries and were "despondent at the very thought" of leadership changes in China that might lead to mending the rift.

Warsaw Talks to Resume. On Jan. 8 Peking and Washington announced that the Warsaw talks, suspended since Jan. 8, 1968, would resume on Jan. 20. Robert J. McCloskey, a State Department spokesman, made the announcement, stating that the talks would be held "at the embassy of the People's Republic of China." Never before had any U.S. spokesman referred to the Peking regime by its official name.

Jets to Taiwan. On Jan. 9 the White House confirmed that the U.S. had agreed to give the government of Nationalist China a squadron of F-104 Starfighter jets from "excess" Air Force stocks.

Talks with China Resume. On Jan. 20 the U.S. and China met in the Chinese Embassy in Warsaw, resuming the ambassadorial talks which had lapsed since 1968. The delegates agreed to resume meeting on the 20th of each month.

Planes to Taiwan Rejected. On Jan. 28 Congress passed the fiscal 1970 foreign aid bill after seven months' delay. One of the major reasons for the delay was dispute over $54.5 million added by the House, but not requested by the administration, for the sale of a squadron of Phantom F-4D fighter jets to Taiwan. The final bill did not include the money.

During the dispute, the administration, which was trying to improve relations with China while maintaining its commitments to Taiwan, had remained neutral.

Jets to Taiwan. On Jan. 31 the Pentagon announced that the U.S. was supplying 34 F-100 Super Sabre fighter bombers to Taiwan.

Peking Supports Arabs. On Feb. 1 Chinese Premier Chou En-lai sent a message to Egyptian President Gamal Abdel Nasser supporting his stand against Israel: "The Chinese people will forever remain the most reliable friend of the U.A.R., Palestine, and other Arab countries." Chou also criticized President Nixon for his January promise to supply more U.S. military aid to Israel.

This was the first official Chinese statement on the Middle East since 1967.

Moscow Responds to Predictions. On Feb. 15 the Soviet newspaper *Pravda* published a long article criticizing Western press predictions of a Soviet attack on China.

On the previous day, the Soviet news agency Tass had issued an official statement describing such predictions as "insinuations" and stating that they were "without any foundation whatsoever" and were "designed to increase tension in the relations between the Soviet Union" and China. The article also accused the Chinese of using these articles as propaganda within China, which had launched a campaign to "prepare for war."

Nixon on China. On Feb. 18 President Nixon addressed Congress on a wide range of foreign policy issues. On the question of China, Nixon explained that the U.S. had "taken specific steps that did not require Chinese agreement but which underlined our willingness to have a more normal and constructive relationship." In this effort, said Nixon, "we have avoided dramatic gestures which might invite dramatic rebuffs." Nixon denied that the U.S. was seeking to exploit the Sino-Soviet split.

Warsaw Talks. On Feb. 20 the Chinese and American ambassadors to Poland met for their monthly talks. As it turned out, this was to be the last China-U.S. meeting held in Warsaw. *(See March 10, 1972)*

It was later revealed that the U.S. had used the meeting to convey to the Chinese a secret proposal from President Nixon that a high administration official go to China for further negotiations.

Travel Restrictions Eased. On March 16 the State Department announced further easing of restrictions on travel to China.

Coup in Cambodia. On March 18 Prince Norodom Sihanouk, leader of Cambodia for 29 years, was ousted from power by General Lon Nol. Sihanouk was in Peking at the time seeking Chinese support for his request to have North Vietnamese troops withdrawn from Cambodia. Lon Nol immediately announced the end of Cambodian neutrality in the Indochina War and adopted a position of defiant anticommunism. The war soon engulfed the country.

On March 19 Sihanouk announced that a Cambodian government in exile and a National United Front of Kampuchea had been formed in Peking. Sihanouk headed both organizations. *(See May 2)*

Arms to Taiwan. On March 29 it was revealed in Washington that the U.S. had supplied Taiwan with $157 million worth of fighter and cargo aircraft, destroyers, antiaircraft missiles, tanks, and rifles during the previous year. With the exception of the four destroyers, for which the Nationalists had paid $1 million, the arms had been supplied without charge from "surplus" stocks.

Chou En-lai to Korea. On April 5 Chinese Premier Chou En-lai arrived in Pyongyang for a three-day visit, in an effort to restore the good relations which China had had with North Korea prior to the Cultural Revolution.

The Nixon Doctrine and the Cold War

On Jan. 20, 1969, after almost 25 years of open hostility between what had been known as the "free" and "communist" worlds, Richard M. Nixon in his presidential inaugural address announced the end of the "cold war" and the beginning of "détente." *(Box, p. 189)* Building on initiatives taken during the Kennedy and Johnson administrations, Nixon announced: "After a period of confrontation, we are entering a period of negotiation." *(Excerpts, p. 319)*

The pacific sentiments expressed by Nixon were by no means an instant solution to the cold war, but they did mark a turning point in U.S. policy.

Beginning almost immediately after the end of World War II, the United States and the Soviet Union — uneasy allies during the war — found they could not work together peacefully once their common enemy, Germany, had been destroyed. The postwar era came to be marked by increasing tension and hostility, and sometimes open warfare between allies of the two nations. The world had replaced the Axis and Allied blocs of the war with the democratic and communist blocs of the cold war. Richard Nixon, who had built his early political reputation on implacable opposition to communism, unexpectedly became the architect of a policy designed to reduce tension. Nixon proposed an "open world" in which all could participate in negotiating differences. "We cannot expect to make everyone our friend, but we can try to make no one our enemy."

On July 25 Nixon elaborated on these remarks in an off-the-record briefing to reporters on Guam. A more formal statement of what would become known as the "Nixon doctrine" came in a televised address on Feb. 25, 1971. In this speech, Nixon enumerated the three fundamental aspects of the doctrine:

● The United States would keep all its treaty commitments.

● The United States would provide a "shield" if a nuclear power threatened a nation allied with the United States or one whose survival the United States considers vital to its security.

● In cases involving other forms of aggression, the United States would furnish military and economic assistance, but no troops. *(Text, p. 321)*

Thus the United States would move to reduce world tension, especially in Asia, where the Vietnam war made progress toward better U.S. relations with the U.S.S.R. and China all but impossible. The new policy would not be one of open hostility to the two communist powers, but an effort to work with them to ensure peace and security.

In these statements, Nixon admitted that the United States had failed in its self-appointed role as "world policeman," and demanded that the nations of the world do more to insure their own security.

At the same time, the administration moved to improve its relations with Soviet leaders, and to establish relations with China's. Both efforts were successful. Although Nixon would be swept out of office by the Watergate scandal, the new role which he created for America in the world would continue to dominate contemporary U.S. foreign policy.

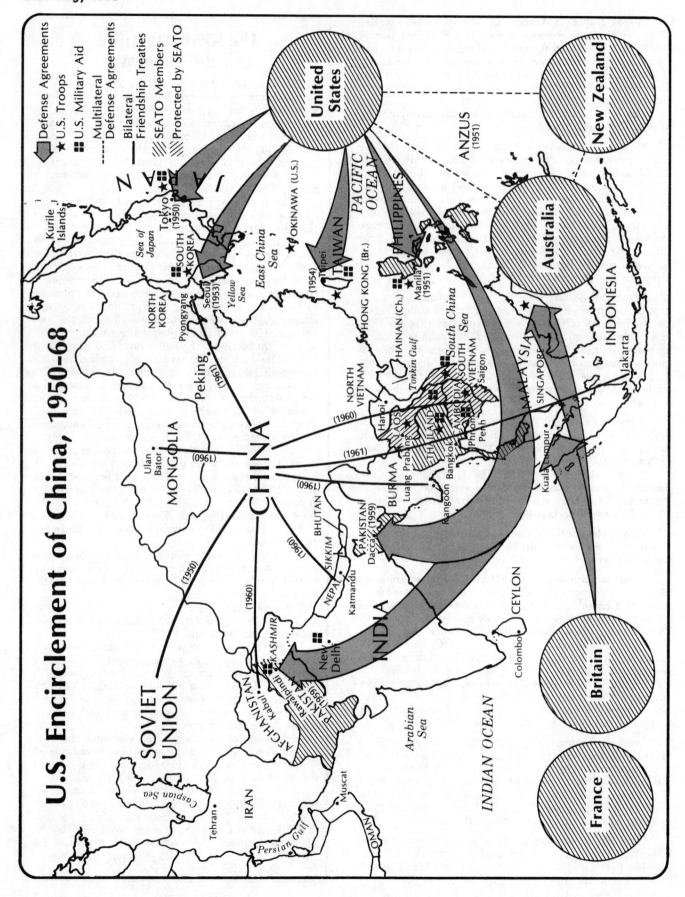

U.S. Encirclement of China, 1950-68

Legend:
- Defense Agreements
- ★ U.S. Troops
- ■ U.S. Military Aid
- ---- Multilateral Defense Agreements
- Bilateral Defense Agreements
- —— Friendship Treaties
- SEATO Members
- Protected by SEATO

United States

New Zealand

ANZUS (1951)

Australia

Britain

France

PACIFIC OCEAN

Kurile Islands

Sea of Japan

Tokyo (1950)

SOUTH KOREA

Seoul (1953)

Pyongyang

NORTH KOREA

Yellow Sea

East China Sea

OKINAWA (U.S.)

TAIWAN

Taipei (1954)

HONG KONG (Br.)

HAINAN (Ch.)

PHILIPPINES

Manila (1951)

South China Sea

Peking (1961)

Ulan Bator

MONGOLIA (1960)

CHINA (1961)

(1960)

NORTH VIETNAM

Hanoi

Tonkin Gulf

SOUTH VIETNAM

Saigon

LAOS

Luang Prabang

CAMBODIA

Phnom Penh

THAILAND

Bangkok

BURMA

Rangoon

MALAYSIA

SINGAPORE

Kuala Lumpur

INDONESIA

Jakarta

BHUTAN

SIKKIM

NEPAL

Katmandu

PAKISTAN Dacca (1959)

INDIA

New Delhi

KASHMIR

Rawalpindi

PAKISTAN (1959)

AFGHANISTAN

Kabul

SOVIET UNION (1950)

(1960)

CEYLON

Colombo

Arabian Sea

INDIAN OCEAN

IRAN

Tehran

Caspian Sea

Persian Gulf

Muscat

OMAN

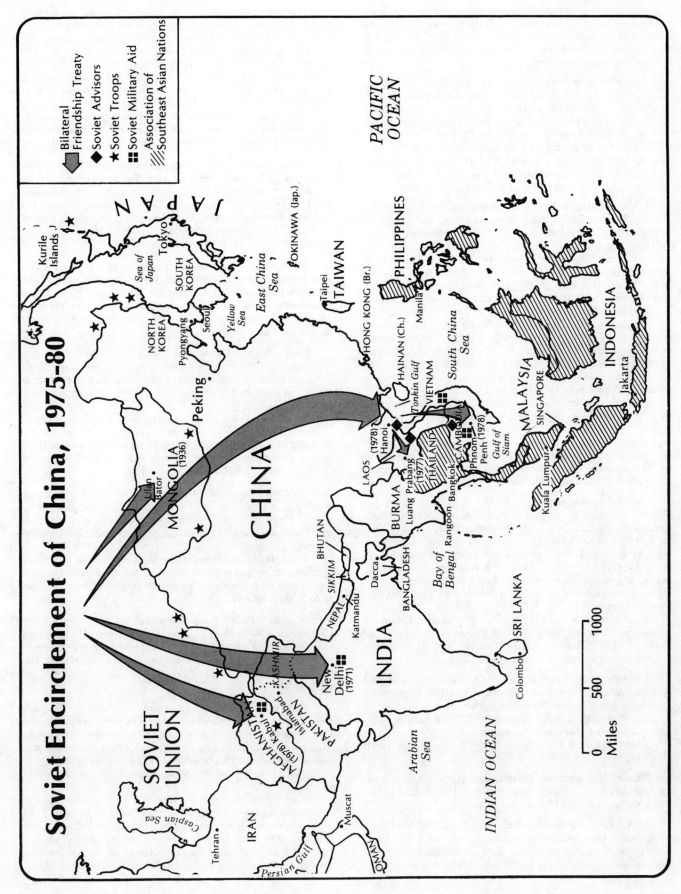

Soviet Encirclement of China, 1975-80

Legend:
- Bilateral Friendship Treaty
- ◆ Soviet Advisors
- ★ Soviet Troops
- ▦ Soviet Military Aid
- ///// Association of Southeast Asian Nations

SOVIET UNION

MONGOLIA (1936)

Ulan Bator

Peking

CHINA

JAPAN

Kurile Islands (J.)

Tokyo

Sea of Japan

NORTH KOREA

Pyongyang

SOUTH KOREA

Seoul

Yellow Sea

East China Sea

OKINAWA (Jap.)

TAIWAN

Taipei

HONG KONG (Br.)

PACIFIC OCEAN

PHILIPPINES

Manila

HAINAN (Ch.)

Tonkin Gulf

VIETNAM

South China Sea

LAOS (1978)

Hanoi

Luang Prabang

BURMA

THAILAND (1977)

Bangkok

Rangoon

CAMBODIA

Phnom Penh (1978)

Gulf of Siam

MALAYSIA

SINGAPORE

Kuala Lumpur

INDONESIA

Jakarta

BHUTAN

SIKKIM

NEPAL

Katmandu

Dacca

BANGLADESH

Bay of Bengal

INDIA

New Delhi (1971)

KASHMIR

Islamabad

PAKISTAN

AFGHANISTAN (1978)

Kabul

SRI LANKA

Colombo

INDIAN OCEAN

IRAN

Tehran

Caspian Sea

Arabian Sea

Persian Gulf

Muscat

OMAN

1000

500

0

Miles

On April 7 the two governments released a joint communiqué which condemned Japanese militarism and warned of its dangers. The communiqué concluded: "It is imperative for the Chinese and Korean peoples to unite against the common enemy."

More Sino-Soviet Criticisms. On April 21 Soviet party leader Leonid Brezhnev condemned the anti-Soviet campaign in China: "With their attacks on Lenin's country . . . the initiators of this campaign have exposed themselves . . . as apostates from the revolutionary Leninist cause."

On the same day, the Peking *People's Daily,* in a heavily footnoted joint editorial, declared that the activities of Brezhnev were "an outrageous insult to Lenin" and went on to call for the overthrow of the Soviet government.

Chinese Attack Brezhnev Doctrine. On April 22 the Peking *People's Daily,* the *Liberation Daily,* and the Communist Party theoretical journal *Hongqi* published a joint editorial criticizing the Russian invasion of Czechoslovakia and attacking Soviet party leader Brezhnev's defense of the invasion, commonly known as the Brezhnev Doctrine. *(See Sept. 26, 1968)* Although delighted with the damage which the invasion had done to the Soviet position in Eastern Europe, the Chinese were fearful that the doctrine could be used to justify a similar attack on China. Thus the editorial strongly criticized the Soviet notion of the "limited sovereignty" supposedly enjoyed by all communist countries except the Soviet Union, which, according to Brezhnev, had a "supreme sovereignty" that was more important than others and legitimatized the Soviet invasion.

Peking said Brezhnev's support of a "socialist community" was nothing more than a "synonym for a colonial empire" with Russia at the center.

The editorial concluded by stating that the Brezhnev doctrine was "hegemonism" (i.e., rule by force, instead of by right or law), introducing yet another element of dialectic into the Sino-Soviet dispute.

Assassination Attempt. On April 24, during his 10-day visit to the U.S., Nationalist Chinese Vice Premier Chiang Ching-kuo (son and heir-apparent to Chiang Kai-shek) escaped without injury an assassination attempt in New York City. The police took into custody Peter Huang, a member of the World United Formosans for Independence, a group of Taiwanese in the U.S. who demanded a Taiwan independent of both the Nationalist and Communist governments.

During his trip to the U.S., Chiang met with President Nixon, Secretary of State William Rogers and Secretary of Defense Melvin Laird, urging them to halt U.S. moves toward reconciliation with mainland China.

China's First Satellite. On April 24 China launched its first satellite from an unknown location in western China. Weighing only 381 pounds, the capsule alternated broadcasts of the popular Chinese song "The East is Red" with its normal telemetric broadcasts.

China became the fifth nation to launch an earth satellite.

Trade Restrictions Eased. On April 29 the U.S. authorized the selective licensing of goods for export to the People's Republic of China.

U.S. Invades Cambodia. On April 30 President Nixon, in a televised address, announced that U.S. troops were to conduct an "incursion" into Cambodia designed to disrupt sanctuaries which the North Vietnamese enjoyed in

that country. In addition, U.S. troops were to destroy supply caches and interdict supply routes. Despite the fact that the U.S. was withdrawing its troops, said Nixon, this was no indication of American weakness. "If, when the chips are down, the world's most powerful nation . . . acts like a pitiful, helpless giant, the forces of totalitarianism and anarchy will threaten free nations and free institutions throughout the world." *(See June 30, 1970)*

The Cambodian invasion sparked a public outcry in the United States, with demonstrations on most of the nation's campuses. *(See May 4, 1970)*

Sihanouk on Cambodian Invasion. On May 2 Prince Norodom Sihanouk, deposed Cambodian leader then in exile in China, issued a statement in Peking condemning the U.S. invasion of Cambodia. Calling himself the Head of State of Cambodia and Chairman of the National United Front of Kampuchea, Sihanouk called for the Cambodian people to unite in resisting the invasion.

Kent State Shooting. On May 4, hundreds of campuses across the U.S. continued demonstrations against the American invasion of Cambodia. At Ohio's Kent State University, National Guardsmen, attempting to clear an area of rock-throwing students, opened fire. Four students were killed and 11 wounded.

Executions in China. On May 5 *The Times* of London reported that "during the past two months" more than 1,000 people had been executed in China, and that several thousand more had been sent to labor reform camps run by the Chinese army.

The New York Times attributed the increase in crime to the campaign to shift people from the cities to the countryside. People who were designated to move lost their urban food ration privilege and, if they decided to stay in the city, were forced to steal to live.

China on Cambodian Invasion. On May 8 the *Peking Review* published China's first comment on the U.S. invasion of Cambodia, calling it not only an attack on Cambodia "but also frantic provocations against the Chinese people."

The relative mildness of the Chinese attack, as well as the long delay prior to its publication, indicated Chinese desire not to jeopardize the recent improvement in Sino-American relations.

Warsaw Talks Suspended Again. On May 18 the Chinese cancelled the 137th meeting between Chinese and U.S. ambassadors at Warsaw, which had been scheduled to open the next day. The Chinese refused to attend the meeting as a protest against the U.S. invasion of Cambodia.

Mao on Cambodian Invasion. On May 20 Chinese Communist Party Chairman Mao Tse-tung criticized the U.S. invasion of Cambodia, but the criticism was muted. Mao concluded by noting that: "The danger of a new world war still exists, and the people of all countries must get prepared. But revolution is the main trend in the world today."

The announcement of whether China sees war or revolution as the main trend is considered to be one of the most accurate barometers of the thinking in Peking. Thus the fact that Mao himself chose to announce that revolution, and not war, was the main trend further underlined Peking's commitment to rapprochement with the U.S.

Chou's View. On June 5 Chinese Premier Chou En-lai said he looked forward to a continuation of talks with the U.S. at Warsaw. *(See June 20)*

New Economic Policies. On June 6 *The New York Times* noted a shift in Chinese economic policies aimed at strengthening agriculture and small rural manufacturing. *The Washington Post* published a similar analysis on June 9.

On June 8 the Chinese Communist theoretical journal *Hongqi* said the new policy was called "walk on two legs," which had been the phrase used to describe the economic policies of the Great Leap Forward. *(See May 5, 1958)*

Later analysis attributed these new initiatives to Defense Minister Lin Piao as he tried to recreate the mass mobilization campaigns of the 1950s.

Warsaw Talks Suspended. On June 20 Peking radio announced that Chinese liaison officers in Warsaw had informed the U.S. that "in view of the fact that both sides clearly understand the current situation, the Chinese Government feels that to discuss at present the meeting date of the Chinese-U.S. ambassadorial talks is not suitable."

On the same day, the U.S. State Department issued a formal statement of regret and announced that it hoped for an early resumption of the talks.

Japan Renews Treaty. On June 22 the Japanese government formally announced plans to allow the automatic extension of its security treaty with the U.S. when it expired at midnight.

On June 23 the Peking *People's Daily* charged that the treaty extension was an effort by the U.S. to help "Japanese militarism to maintain its tottering neocolonialist system in Asia" by "using Asians to fight Asians."

Cambodian Invasion Ends. On June 30 the last U.S. troops withdrew from Cambodia.

On July 4 China said that the U.S. had suffered a "big defeat" in Cambodia and that the withdrawal was only "a smokescreen."

Sino-French Relations. On July 7 André Bettencourt, French minister in charge of planning and territorial development, arrived in Peking. This was the first governmental delegation to China since relations had been established in 1964.

On July 14 Chinese Premier Chou En-lai, speaking at a banquet, explained why China was dealing with countries that had "different social systems." According to Chou, French President Pompidou had said he would follow the foreign policy of former President de Gaulle, who had supported the independent neutrality of Cambodian Prince Sihanouk and had pressed the U.S. to withdraw from Vietnam.

U.S. and U.N. On July 9 President Nixon directed the 50-member Commission on the Observance of the Twenty-Fifth Anniversary of the United Nations to consult official and public opinion concerning U.S. participation in the United Nations. Headed by former U.S. Ambassador to the U.N. Henry Cabot Lodge, the commission held public hearings in six U.S. cities. *(See April 26, 1971)*

Xiafang to Be Continued. On July 9 the Peking *People's Daily* published another editorial on *Xiafang*, the "down to the countryside" movement. The article stressed that it was "not simply a temporary measure for the relocation of the labor force but an important means of training and bringing up revolutionary successors."

Soviets Propose Joint Action. On July 10 the Soviet SALT negotiators reportedly proposed that the U.S. and the Soviet Union agree to "joint retaliatory action" in response to any "provocative" acts or direct attacks by China. The proposal was not revealed publicly until 1973, and was denied by the Soviets at that time.

Bishop Walsh Released. On July 10 the Rev. James Edward Walsh, former Roman Catholic bishop of Shanghai sentenced in 1958 to 20 years imprisonment for "espionage and sabotage under the cloak of religion," was released by the Chinese. *(See March 18, 1960)*

Peking Accuses Tokyo. On July 11 the Peking *People's Daily* accused "Japanese militarism" of trying to annex Taiwan, dominate Korea, and revive the Greater East Asian Co-prosperity Sphere of World War II.

Classes Resume. On July 21 the Xinhua news agency announced the resumption of classes at Jinghua University in Peking, widely regarded as the birthplace of the Red Guards in 1966. This was the first known instance of a university's return to normal activity since the schools had stopped admitting new students four years before. The statement also said that admission would place emphasis on those with worker and peasant backgrounds. *(See Sept. 22, 1970)*

Hearings on Taiwan. On July 21 a special Senate Foreign Relations Subcommittee on U.S. Security Agreements and Commitments Abroad released a 200-page, heavily censored transcript of its hearings on Taiwan during 1969 and 1970. The hearings disclosed that the Nationalist Chinese were conducting significantly more small-scale military raids against the mainland than Peking was conducting against Taiwan. In addition, questions had been raised about a joint U.S.-ROC military exercise, known as "Forward Thrust," which had been conducted annually on Taiwan for 10 years and which closely resembled a planned effort to invade mainland China. In both cases, senators questioned whether such activities were consistent with the administration policy of trying to improve relations with Peking.

China and Romania. On July 23 a Romanian military delegation, headed by Minister of the Armed Forces Ion Ionita, arrived in China for a two-week visit. During the trip, they met with both Chairman Mao Tse-tung and Premier Chou En-lai. The Chinese emphasized the independence of Romania and its refusal to accept orders from "those assuming the posture of an overlord."

Rebuilding the Party. On July 24 the Peking *People's Daily* published another editorial that presented guidelines for the rebuilding of the Chinese Communist Party after the Cultural Revolution. Entitled "Conscientiously Study Chairman Mao's Thesis on the Party," the article quoted extensively from Mao's writings and emphasized the need for outstanding people in the party, party supremacy over the army, and the struggle against "erroneous" trends.

Chou Proposes United Front. On July 27 Chinese Premier Chou En-lai was interviewed by French journalists in Peking. During the talk, Chou criticized both "superpowers" for their exploitation and oppression of smaller states and proposed the formation of a "united front" to oppose them. Although Chou made no obvious distinction between the U.S. and the Soviet Union, it soon became clear that the united front would be aimed at Moscow.

U.S. Trade with China. On July 28 the U.S. Commerce Department approved the sale by an Italian company of 80 dump trucks with General Motors engines and parts to China.

China and South Yemen. On Aug. 1 the Premier of South Yemen arrived in Peking. During his stay, economic and technical agreements were signed. He left on Aug. 13.

Sino-Soviet Border Talks. On Aug. 15 Leonid Ilyichev arrived in Peking to succeed Aleksei Kuznetsov, the former Soviet envoy to the border talks, who had fallen ill. Sino-Soviet polemics remained muted.

Barefoot Doctors. On Aug. 20 the Peking *People's Daily* reported that rural medical technicians trained in the use of herbs for curing purposes were also performing major surgery. The report said that the technicians, also known as "barefoot doctors," had performed such operations as caesarian sections, appendectomies, and ovariocystectomies. The barefoot doctors, who were believed to be fanning out over all of rural China, were hailed as a "new development in the medical revolution."

Trade with China. On Aug. 26, restrictions prohibiting U.S. oil companies abroad from permitting foreign ships to use refueling facilities to and from China were lifted.

Peking Again Accuses Tokyo. On Sept. 3 the Peking *People's Daily* published a joint editorial commemorating the 25th anniversary of Japan's defeat in World War II. The article listed nine points purporting to demonstrate the revival of "Japanese militarism," which was referred to as an "indisputable reality." According to the article, the militarism had been revived by the U.S. and "encouraged and abetted by socialist imperialism [the Soviet Union]."

Travel Restrictions Retained. On Sept. 15 the U.S. State Department announced that it would continue to restrict travel to Cuba, mainland China, North Vietnam and North Korea.

Hearings on China. On Sept. 15 the House Foreign Affairs Subcommittee on Asian and Pacific Affairs opened hearings on U.S. policy toward China and invited expert testimony. The hearings lasted until Oct. 6.

Chinese Back Palestinians. On Sept. 21 the Chinese government strongly protested the Jordanian attack on the El al-Fatah commandos, to whom the Chinese had been supplying light arms. On Sept. 19 and 24, the Peking *People's Daily* published editorials condemning Jordan.

Admission Requirements. On Sept. 22 the Communist Party theoretical journal *Hongqi* published additional information concerning college admission policies. Following the lead of the radicals, the article said students would be selected on the basis of their political activity and class background. "Before the Cultural Revolution the sons of workers and peasants were left out of the universities. Now students should be selected from among the young activists."

New Peace Proposals. On Oct. 8 David Bruce, chief U.S. negotiator at the Paris peace talks, presented new U.S. proposals for settling the war in Vietnam which involved significant U.S. concessions. These involved a "cease-fire in place," which meant that the North Vietnamese would be allowed to hold those parts of South Vietnam which they already occupied, and an eventual total withdrawal of all U.S. troops from Vietnam.

These proposals were rejected by North Vietnam.

Soviet Ambassador Returns. On Oct. 10 Vasily S. Tolstikov, the new Soviet ambassador to China, arrived in Peking. His predecessor had been recalled in April 1967. *(See Nov. 22, 1970)*

Canada Recognizes PRC. On Oct. 13 the governments of Canada and China issued a joint communiqué announcing their intention to open full diplomatic relations. The statement said that "the Chinese government reaffirms that Taiwan is an inalienable part of the territory of the P.R.C. The Canadian Government takes note of this position of the Chinese government."

This sentence was the result of 18 months of negotiations between the two countries, and the handling of the Taiwan problem in this way became a model for many other countries.

Nixon Message to Peking. On Oct. 25 President Nixon met with Yahya Khan, Pakistan's head of state, after a White House dinner. Nixon asked Khan, who would soon be visiting China, to convey to the Chinese an American proposal that the U.S. and China conduct "high-level" talks in Peking. *(See Nov. 10)*

U.S. Policy on China. On Oct. 25 White House press secretary Ronald L. Ziegler indicated the first softening of the U.S. position on the admission of the People's Republic of China to the United Nations. Ziegler said: "The U.S. opposes the admission of the Peking regime into the U.N. at the expense of the expulsion of the Republic of China."

Ziegler thus gave the first hint of U.S. support of a "two-China" policy, which would continue to be the U.S. position until 1971. *(See Aug. 2, 1971)*

China Calls for Nuclear Ban. On Nov. 1 the Chinese government called on the world's nations to conclude a ban on nuclear weapons as a first step toward the "complete prohibition and thorough destruction" of such weapons. The announcement, a repetition of proposals made in previous years, was contained in a communiqué issued by the Xinhua news agency.

Italy Recognizes PRC. On Nov. 6 Italy established diplomatic relations with the People's Republic of China. In their joint communiqué, the two nations dealt with the Taiwan problem using the Canadian example. *(See Oct. 13)*

Yahya Khan to Peking. On Nov. 10 General Yahya Khan, Pakistani chief of state, visited Peking. The joint communiqué issued on this occasion stressed the "deep, all-around development" of the friendship between the two countries.

During his visit, Yahya Khan passed to Chinese Premier Chou En-lai the American proposal, conveyed earlier to the Pakistani chief of state *(see Oct. 25.)*, that the U.S. would like to dispatch a "high-level" official to Peking for talks with Chinese leaders. The following day, after conferring with Mao Tse-tung, Chou told Yahya Khan: "We welcome the proposal from Washington for face-to-face discussions. We would be glad to receive a high-level person for this purpose, to discuss the withdrawal of American forces from Taiwan."

After Khan returned to Islamabad, this message was cabled to the Pakistani embassy in Washington, and then passed to the White House. After discussion there, it was decided to accept the "invitation" but to ignore the Chinese' stated purpose for the talks.

Prior to national security adviser Henry Kissinger's visit to Peking in 1971, approximately a dozen messages were exchanged between Washington and Peking via the Pakistani embassies in the two countries.

U.S. Hints Change. On Nov. 12, during the first day of the annual debate within the United Nations over the admission of Peking, U.S. Deputy Permanent Representative Christopher H. Phillips appealed to the U.N. not to expel Nationalist China. Phillips did not use the hostile language which had been directed at Peking in earlier years, and he reviewed recent U.S. efforts to expand contacts with China. In addition, Phillips said that the U.S. was "as interested as anyone" in seeing China "play a constructive role among the family of nations." The moderate language and general focus of the speech led many observers to believe that the U.S. was moving toward a two-China policy. *(See Dec. 10)*

Chinese Ambassador Returns. On Nov. 22 Li Xinquan arrived in Moscow to take up his duties as Chinese ambassador to the Soviet Union. The last Chinese ambassador left Moscow in 1966 during the Cultural Revolution. Li's appointment was one of 16 made during 1970 as China reopened full relations with almost all of the countries with which it had had relations prior to the Cultural Revolution. *(See Oct. 10, 1970)*

Sino-Soviet Trade Pact. On Nov. 22 the Soviet Union and China signed a trade agreement, the first since 1967. The agreement did not seem to be accompanied by any other lessening of tension between the two countries.

Nixon Warns Hanoi. On Dec. 10 President Nixon at a news conference said he would order the bombing of military targets in North Vietnam if the North Vietnamese increased the level of fighting in South Vietnam as U.S. troops were withdrawn. Referring to his interpretation of an understanding supposedly reached with North Vietnam under President Johnson's administration, Nixon said that he would order the bombing of military complexes in North Vietnam if U.S. reconnaissance planes over North Vietnam were fired upon.

Nixon also announced that there had been no change in U.S. policy concerning the admission of China to the United Nations but went on to say, "We are going to continue the initiative" of relaxing trade and travel curbs and trying to open channels of communication with China. "Looking toward the future we must have some communication and eventually relations with Communist China."

No Subs to Taiwan. On Dec. 31 Congress cleared for the president's signature a bill (PL 91-682) authorizing the loan of surplus U.S. Navy ships and submarines to foreign countries. The Senate amendment to the House-passed bill deleted the authorization for a loan of three submarines to the Republic of China which had not been requested by the administration. Opponents of the loan cited U.S. efforts to improve relations with Peking, and the destabilizing and potentially provocative effect such a loan might have on the Pacific area.

1971

Tonkin Gulf Resolution Repealed — Scientific Exchange with China — South Vietnam Invades Laos — Nixon Doctrine Expanded — Chou En-lai in Hanoi — East Pakistan Revolts — Pingpong Breakthrough — China Backs Pakistan — China Trade Embargo Eased — North Vietnam-U.S. Peace Talks — Bangladesh Nation Declared — Nixon China Visit Hinted — Australia, New Zealand Overtures to Peking — Austria Recognizes PRC — Pentagon Papers Appear — Okinawa Treaty Signed — Kissinger to China — Nixon Announces Visit to China — Okinawa A-Bombs Disposal — U.S. Suspends China Spy-Plane Flights — Turkey-China Accord — U.S. Announces Two-China Policy — Burma-China Talks — India-Soviet Pact — Iran-China Agreement — Lin Piao Dies — Kissinger in China — PRC Admitted to U.N. — Belgium Recognizes PRC — China-Italy Trade Pact — India Invades Pakistan — U.S. Bombing of North Vietnam Renewed

Gulf of Tonkin Resolution Repealed. On Jan. 2 the House voted to repeal the 1964 Gulf of Tonkin Resolution (PL 88-408). Because the Senate had already voted for repeal on July 10, 1970, the repeal became effective with the House action. Presidential signature was not required.

President Johnson had used the resolution as an authorization for his buildup of U.S. troops in Vietnam. *(Text p. 314)*

Sato on China Relations. On Jan. 22 Japanese Prime Minister Eisaku Sato reiterated his desire to improve relations with the People's Republic of China.

Chinese Students in Moscow. On Jan. 25 a group of about 60 Chinese students clashed with Soviet police in front of Lenin's tomb.

U.S. Scientific Exchange with China. On Jan. 26 the U.S. State Department revealed that the U.S. had been exchanging scientific information with China prior to 1949 and had continued to do so.

South Vietnam Invades Laos. On Feb. 8 the troops of South Vietnam, supported by U.S. air power, invaded Laos. The goal of the incursion was to cut the Ho Chi Minh trail, by which North Vietnam supplied its troops in the south. The performance of the South Vietnamese troops was inconsistent, despite U.S. claims about the success of the Vietnamization program. After 45 days the troops were withdrawn, claiming a military victory. In fact, the poor performance of the units marked another psychological victory for the North Vietnamese. The U.S. followed the attack with another secret peace effort. *(See April 26)*

China registered its disapproval of the move by terminating, for six weeks, the secret exchange of letters between Peking and Washington, via Pakistan, which had begun in December 1970.

Chinese Response to Invasion. On Feb. 8 China reacted strongly to the U.S.-assisted invasion of Laos by South Vietnamese troops. The Chinese foreign ministry called the attack "rabid acts" and a "grave provocation."

On Feb. 12 the Chinese government termed the invasion a "grave menace to China."

On Feb. 20 the *People's Daily* published an editorial entitled, "Nixon, Don't Lose Your Head," which constituted a warning to the U.S. to curtail its support of South Vietnam.

The relative mildness of the Chinese response has been attributed to Chinese desire not to destroy the nascent opening to the U.S.

Seabed Treaty. On Feb. 11, 63 nations signed a treaty prohibiting the installation of nuclear weapons on the ocean floor. France and China did not sign the treaty. *(See March 1, 1971)*

U.S. Assurances to China. On Feb. 17 President Nixon at a White House press conference emphasized that the U.S. operations in Laos presented "no threat" to China and "should not be interpreted by Communist China as being a threat against them."

Nixon Doctrine. On Feb. 25 President Nixon presented his second annual State of the World Report to the U.S. Congress. In what amounted to a formal enunciation of the Nixon Doctrine *(see July 25, 1969)*, Nixon stressed his desire for improvements in U.S. relations with China, and said: "The United States is prepared to see the People's Republic of China play a constructive role in the family of nations."

This was the first time Nixon used the formal name adopted by the government of mainland China in 1949. *(Text, p. 321)*

Chinese Score Treaty. On March 1 China strongly criticized the recently signed seabed treaty *(see Feb. 11)* as "a move by the two superpowers to share and dominate the seas" in order "to continue, with even fewer scruples, their gunboat diplomacy and go in for nuclear threats and blackmail against the people."

Chou to Hanoi. On March 5 Chinese Communist Party Chairman Mao Tse-tung sent Chinese Premier Chou En-lai to Hanoi to tell the Vietnamese that, despite the invasion of Laos by the U.S. and South Vietnam, China would not intervene because Peking was convinced the U.S. was withdrawing from Indochina.

Travel Ban Ended. On March 15, the date usually reserved for the annual announcement of the extension of travel bans, the U.S. State Department announced that all restrictions on the use of U.S. passports for travel to China had been ended.

At the same time, it was announced that the U.S. was working through diplomatic channels to reopen the Warsaw talks between Washington and Peking.

Sino-Soviet Polemics Resume. On March 17, on the eve of the 24th Soviet Party Congress, China and the Soviet Union resumed their battle of words after a nine-month pause. The Xinhua news agency accused the Soviets of the "most savage and brutal means to deal with revolutionary people."

On the same day, Moscow warned Peking against playing a "dangerous game" by trying to improve relations with the U.S. On March 21 the Soviet news agency Tass denounced the Chinese for their "rude attacks and slander" and said that their doctrines were "a distortion of Marxist-Leninist teaching."

East Pakistan Revolts. On March 25 serious fighting broke out in East Pakistan following its declaration of independence. The leader of Pakistan, Yahya Khan, vowed to crush the revolt.

Brezhnev Attacks Chinese. On March 30, speaking before the 24th Soviet Party Congress in Moscow, Soviet party leader Leonid Brezhnev said that the Soviets resolutely opposed Chinese attempts to distort Marxist-Leninism and split the world communist movement.

Hijacked Plane Returned. On March 30 a Philippine Air Line passenger plane en route from Manila to the southern city of Davao was hijacked by six armed students and forced to fly to Canton. The plane, its crew and all the passengers were released by the Chinese and flew back to Manila on the next day. The students, described as Maoists, were detained in China. The captain of the aircraft said that Chinese authorities had told him that they disapproved of air hijacking.

Pingpong Diplomacy. On April 6, during the international table tennis championships at Nagoya, Japan, China invited the U.S. team to visit China prior to their return to the United States. *Time* magazine called it "The ping heard round the world."

State Department Warning. On April 9 a U.S. State Department spokesman reported that U.S. oil companies risked the seizure of their ships if they persisted in exploring for oil deposits near the Senkaku Islands in the East China Sea. The disputed islands had been claimed by Japan, China and Taiwan. *(Map, p. 105)*

Pingpong Team to China. On April 10, 15 Americans (including nine table tennis players, four officials, and two wives) crossed the border from Hong Kong to China, beginning their historic visit.

On April 11 seven newsmen, including three Americans, arrived in China; two other American journalists joined them on April 14. They had been granted visas to cover the visit of the U.S. table tennis team. This was the first sizable group of Americans to visit China since the 1950s. From that point on, American journalists were able in Ottawa to obtain visas to visit China.

China Backs Pakistan. On April 13 Chinese Premier Chou En-lai sent a letter to Pakistani chief of state Yahya Khan announcing China's strong support for Pakistan's efforts to put down the autonomy movement in East Pakistan. Chou also pledged Chinese support "should Indian expansionism dare to launch aggression against Pakistan." *(See Dec. 3, 1971)*

Some analysts have argued that China's decision not to support the secession movement represented Chinese abandonment of its revolutionary principles.

U.S. Eases Chinese Embargo. On April 14 the U.S. announced that the 21-year embargo on trade with China would be relaxed. In addition, it was stated that visas for visitors to China would be expedited, and that U.S. currency controls, also dating from 1950, would be relaxed. U.S. vessels would be allowed to carry Chinese cargo between non-Chinese ports, and a list of goods which could be traded would be released soon. *(See June 10, 1971)*

Chou En-lai on Sino-American Relations. On April 14 Chinese Premier Chou En-lai addressed the visiting U.S. pingpong team in Peking, stating that "a new page has been turned. A new chapter has been opened in the relations between our two peoples. Your visit to China has opened the door to friendly contacts between the peoples of the two countries."

Chou also said U.S. newsmen would be allowed to enter China "but they cannot all come at one time, they will have to come in batches." Chou then told John Roderick of the Associated Press, "Mr. Roderick, you have opened the door."

Nixon "Hopes" to Visit China. On April 16 President Nixon, meeting with the American Society of Newspaper Editors, said that he hoped that he could visit China someday.

United Asks for Routes. On April 19 United Airlines applied to the Civil Aeronautics Board for permission to extend its routing system to including Peking, Shanghai and Canton.

Rogers on China Relations. On April 23 Secretary of State William Rogers said at a press conference: "I think it was the [Premier] of the People's Republic of China who said that it was a new page in our relations. We would hope that it becomes a new chapter, that there will be several pages to follow."

Kissinger Peace Efforts. On April 26 national security adviser Henry Kissinger held a second secret meeting with chief North Vietnamese negotiator Le Duc Tho. Talks continued until Sept. 13, when negotiations were again broken off.

Commission Report on China. On April 26 the special presidential commission *(see July 9, 1970)* headed by Henry Cabot Lodge, former U.S. ambassador to the United Nations, released a 100-page report on the role of the U.S. in the U.N. The report came out in support of President Nixon's two-China policy, and said that although the People's Republic of China possibly should be admitted to the U.N., "under no circumstances" should the Republic of China be expelled.

Romania an Intermediary. On April 27 U.S. administration officials disclosed that Romania was acting as an intermediary between the U.S. and China. It was said that Vice Premier Gogu Radulescu had transmitted U.S. hopes for improved relations during meetings with Chinese Premier Chou En-lai in Peking in November 1970 and again on March 22, 1971.

Pakistan Claims Victory. On April 28 Pakistan anounced that all "anti-state elements" in East Pakistan had been crushed.

Earlier, on April 18, the insurgents had declared themselves the independent nation of Bangladesh.

Nixon on China. On April 29 President Nixon, responding to a question about U.S.-China relations at a press conference, sounded a note of caution: "What we have done has broken the ice. Now we have to test the water to see how deep it is."

Later, Nixon said: "I hope and, as a matter of fact, I expect to visit mainland China sometime in some capacity."

Flap Over Two-China Policy. On April 28 Charles W. Bray, a State Department spokesman, said it might be possible to resolve the status of Taiwan by direct negotiations between Peking and Taipei.

On April 29 President Nixon said direct talks were "completely unrealistic."

On April 30 Nationalist Chinese Foreign Minister Chow Shu-kai said his government was "surprised and amazed" that Bray had even raised the issue.

On May 4 the Peking *People's Daily* accused the U.S. of "brazen interference" in China's internal affairs.

Rogers on Nixon Visit. On April 28 Secretary of State William Rogers declared in an interview taped for British television that a visit to China by President Nixon "might well be possible" if relations between the two countries continue to improve. Rogers went on the describe himself as "very much in favor" of an exchange of journalists, students and professional people with China in the near future.

Mao Says Nixon Welcome. On April 30 *Life* magazine published a long interview with Chinese Party Chairman Mao Tse-tung by Edgar Snow. During the interview, which had been held Dec. 18, 1970, Mao told Snow that Nixon was welcome to come to China, either as president or as a tourist.

Taiwan to Cancel Visas. On May 1 the Nationalist Chinese government announced that visas issued for visiting Taiwan would be rendered invalid by travel to mainland China. This policy was relaxed in 1979.

Peking on Okinawa. On May 1 the Chinese government, alarmed by what it saw as the rebirth of a strong Japan, issued a statement condemning the reversion of Okinawa to Japan. The report was especially critical of the inclusion of Senkaku Island, which both Chinese governments claimed as Chinese territory.

China's Moderate Foreign Policy. On May 1 the Peking *People's Daily* published an editorial defending the more moderate foreign policy adopted by China after the end of the Cultural Revolution in 1969: "We have always maintained that friendly exchanges between the people of various countries and the Chinese people and the friendship visits to China of friends from other lands are a support and encouragement to the Chinese people and provide us with good opportunities to learn from other peoples."

Trade with China. On May 7 U.S. Treasury Secretary John B. Connally announced a general license for the use of dollars in transactions with China. In the past, the use of dollars in such deals had been banned.

Australian Trade Bans Eased. On May 13 Australian Prime Minister William McMahon announced a relaxation of restrictions on non-strategic trade with China. One month earlier, China had cancelled its annual wheat order, which had amounted to 32% of all wheat exported by Australia since 1960. The Chinese had decided to buy wheat from Canada, which recognized the PRC government.

New Zealand and China. On May 13 Sir Keith Holyoake, Prime Minister of New Zealand, said that his government would welcome talks with China aimed at improving relations between the two countries.

Thailand and China. On May 14 Foreign Minister Thanat Khoman of Thailand disclosed that his government was seeking to improve relations with China through mediation by an unnamed third country.

China Builds Own Jets. On May 16 *The New York Times* reported that China was manufacturing a jet fighter of its own design. Designated the F-9 by analysts, the plane was roughly based on the Soviet MiG-19.

Austria Recognizes PRC. On May 27 Austria established diplomatic relations with the People's Republic of China. The joint communiqué issued on the occasion made no reference to Taiwan, but Austria had never had relations with Taiwan.

New U.S. Position on U.N. On June 1 President Nixon announced that "a significant change has taken place among the members of the United Nations on the issue of admission of mainland China," and that the U.S. was "analyzing the situation." The administration, said Nixon, would announce its position at the fall session of the U.N. *(See Aug. 2, 1971)*

U.S. Ends Embargo. On June 10 the U.S. ended its 21-year embargo on trade with China with the announcement by the White House that it was further relaxing the restrictions on that trade. *(See April 14)* At the same time, a list of goods that could be traded with China was issued. *(See Dec. 8, 1950)*

China's exports to the U.S. would now be on the same status as that of the Soviet Union and Eastern Europe. *(See Feb. 14, 1972)*

Pentagon Papers Appear. On June 13 *The New York Times* published the first installment of the "Pentagon Papers," which sent shock waves through the administration.

Henry Kissinger later said that he felt that such revelations could undo the three most important projects then under way in the White House, all of them secret: the opening to China; the strategic arms talks with Russia; and, the talks with North Vietnam about ending the war.

The publication of the Pentagon Papers is usually cited as the primary reason for the formation of the "plumbers," a White House organization which was charged with plugging leaks of information.

The 47-volume study, which covers the period from the end of World War II to mid-1968, had been classified as top secret. Its formal title was "History of U.S. Decision-Making Processes on Vietnam."

Moscow Proposes Conference. On June 15, during the 24th Congress of the Communist Party of the Soviet Union, Moscow invited the four other nuclear powers to hold a conference on nuclear disarmament.

Okinawa Treaty Signed. On June 17 the U.S. and Japan signed a treaty whereby the Ryukyu and Daito Islands, captured by the U.S. from Japan during World War II, would revert to Japan. Okinawa is the largest of the islands. On Nov. 10 the Senate ratified the treaty by an 84-6 roll-call vote.

The reversion of Okinawa was a key part of better relations between the U.S. and Japan, an important part of the Nixon doctrine. *(See July 19, 1971)*

China and Taiwan protested the treaty's inclusion of Senkaku Island, which both Chinas claimed as sovereign Chinese territory.

Nixon on China Trade. On July 6, speaking to midwestern news media executives in Kansas City, President Nixon said that the "Chinese are going to be, inevitably, an enormous economic power." *(Text, p. 322)*

Kissinger to China. On July 9 Henry Kissinger, presidential adviser on national security, left Islamabad, Pakistan, on a secret flight to China, the result of over two years of secret White House efforts. Kissinger stayed in Peking three days, returning to Pakistan on July 11.

During his stay, Kissinger met with Chinese premier Chou En-lai. During the talks, the two leaders laid the groundwork for future Sino-American relations by reaching understandings in three areas: (1) that Taiwan was part of China; (2) that the political future of South Vietnam should be decided by the Vietnamese, and (3) that all Asian disputes should be settled by peaceful means.

In addition, Chou invited President Nixon to come to China, and Kissinger accepted the invitation for him. *(See July 15, below)*

Nixon Says He Will Go To China. On July 15 President Nixon announced on national television that Henry Kissinger had just returned from China, and that he would be going to China in the near future. The announcement, which was also released in Peking at the same time, surprised almost everyone.

In an effort to reassure Taiwan, Nixon said that "our action in seeking a new relationship with the People's Republic of China will not be at the expense of our old friends."

China, U.S.S.R. on Nixon. On July 16 the Peking *People's Daily* published an editorial explaining the Nixon visit. The article said "The meeting between the leaders of China and the United States is to seek normalization of relations between the two countries and also to exchange views on questions of concern to the two sides."

On July 16 the Soviet government newspaper *Izvestia* published a terse report on the Chinese invitation to President Nixon without comment. Western diplomats in Moscow said that Soviet officials had reacted with stunned surprise to the news. In the following weeks, the Soviet press was content merely to reprint those articles from various East European newspapers critical of the trip without any comment of their own.

Chou's Conditions. On July 19, during an interview in Peking with members of the Committee of Concerned Asian Scholars, a visiting group of U.S. graduate students, Chinese Premier Chou En-lai set the terms for improving Sino-American relations. Chou told the group that the U.S. must recognize Peking as the sole legitimate government of China and acknowledge that Taiwan was part of China. In addition, the U.S. must withdraw its troops from Taiwan, and abrogate its 1954 mutual defense treaty with that country.

Marcos on Nixon Doctrine. On July 19 Philippine President Ferdinand E. Marcos, commenting on the Nixon doctrine, said: "I am certain that this alteration and change in the policy of the United States will mean that every Asian nation and leader must review the basis for all agreements between the United States and their respective countries."

Chou En-lai on Normalization. On July 19 Chinese Premier Chou En-lai, speaking in Peking, stated that U.S. withdrawal of troops from Indochina must take precedence over other efforts to improve Sino-American relations.

This represented a modification of earlier Chinese statements stressing U.S. withdrawal from Taiwan as the most important requirement for the improvement of Sino-American relations.

Okinawa's A-bombs. On July 19, U.S. government officials announced that atomic weapons which had been located on Okinawa, and which had to be moved under the terms of the June 17 agreement with Japan, would not be moved closer to the Chinese mainland. The spokesman said that a proposal had been submitted to President Nixon in June, calling for the transfer of the weapons to Taiwan, South Korea, and the Philippines. That proposal would now be rejected.

Japanese Reaction. On July 21 Japanese Prime Minister Eisaku Sato sharply criticized President Nixon for so abruptly notifying Japan of his plans for visiting China. The announcement had triggered intense debate within Japan about Tokyo's relationship to Peking. Sato responded to this by noting that he would go to China to improve relations "when I decide circumstances permit."

Leadership Struggles

The 9th Congress of the Chinese Communist Party, which signalled the victory of the Cultural Revolution, also marked the rise to power of Lin Piao, the Minister of Defense. The first chapter of the Party constitution, passed by the congress on April 14, 1969, stated:

"Comrade Lin Piao has consistently held high the great red banner of Mao Tse-tung's Thought and he has most loyally and resolutely carried out and defended Comrade Mao Tse-tung's proletarian revolutionary line. Comrade Lin Piao is Comrade Mao Tse-tung's closest comrade-in-arms and successor."

Not quite four and a half years later, on August 29, 1973, the communiqué of the 10th Party Congress "indignantly denounced the Lin Piao anti-Party clique for its crimes," and expelled Lin, "the bourgeois careerist, conspirator, counter-revolutionary double-dealer, renegade and traitor from the Party once and for all."

The transformation did not really take that long; it was effected mostly during the autumn of 1971, when, according to Peking, Lin launched an abortive coup against Mao Tse-tung.

During the Cultural Revolution, when Mao tried to destroy and then rebuild the Communist Party, which he felt had betrayed him, the chairman had been forced to rely on Lin Piao and the army. But the "victory" of the Cultural Revolution proved to be far less than complete.

Starting with the 9th Congress, Lin began issuing calls for new mass mobilization campaigns modeled after those of the late 1950s. The earlier failure of these campaigns, particularly the Great Leap Forward, had produced the swing to the "right" which the Cultural Revolution was to have reversed. Despite the purges, however, too many leaders still remembered the campaigns' failures to allow their resurrection. Opposition to Lin's proposals sprang up everywhere.

According to Lin and the left, China should put "politics in command," and use slogans and revolutionary fervor to motivate the masses of China. Any material incentives given to the workers and peasants should reward correct political behavior, not harder work.

Opposed to this were the moderates who, although officially purged, still held significant power through the support of Premier Chou En-lai, the one man whom the Cultural Revolution had been unable to dislodge. This group argued that material incentives should be provided to those who worked hardest. During the 1960s Liu Shao-ch'i and Deng Xiaoping, both purged during the Cultural Revolution, had fostered the creation of "private plots," whereby each peasant was given a small piece of land apart from the larger communal holding and allowed to dispose of its produce as he wished. To the radicals, this was revolutionary heresy, and earned Deng the epithet of "capitalist roader."

In 1969-1970, when Lin Piao again raised the notion of "politics in command," memories of the earlier period were still fresh. Strong opposition also came from within the army: Xu Shiyou, commander of the Nanjing Military Region, one of the most powerful military men in China, stated that "peasants have the right to raise chickens and ducks for their own consumption!"

Lin Piao's Decline

With so tenuous a following, Lin allegedly joined some of his loyal commanders to launch a coup against Mao and the moderates in September 1971. According to Peking's version, the attempt was thwarted and Lin was killed while trying to flee to the Soviet Union.

The death of Lin Piao made the purge of his supporters much easier, and efforts began to end the de facto military government of China.

But the demise of Lin Piao did not signal a complete victory by the moderates. Despite the subsequent "rehabilitation" of Deng Xiaoping, the radicals still controlled the media and propaganda organs and, most importantly, Mao himself. Although the situation in Peking was far from clear, some foreign visitors to China reported that by 1974, Mao's health was extremely precarious and his speech seriously impaired. Thus, because Mao could not speak for himself, power devolved to his wife, Jiang Qing, a leading radical who purported to speak for Mao.

With these weapons, the radicals were able to subvert the campaign to criticize Lin Piao and Confucius into a campaign against Deng Xiaoping, purged again in early 1976. At the same time, the radicals mounted new campaigns, reminiscent of the Cultural Revolution, against "bourgeois influences" in culture.

But the radicals' position was never as strong as it appeared. Although they were able to prevent Deng from succeeding Chou En-lai as premier after the latter's death, the death of Mao in September 1976 left them without any allies at the center. On Oct. 6 Hua Guofeng led a coalition which arrested and jailed the most important radicals.

Following the coup, Hua moved quickly to put distance between himself and what he now labeled the "gang of four" (Jiang Qing, Yao Wenyuan, Zhang Chunqiao and Wang Hongwen), who were made the scapegoats for every problem China had suffered since the early 1960s. (The campaign against the four was still under way in 1980.)

At the same time, Hua again "rehabilitated" Deng Xiaoping as well as scores of other moderates who had been purged during the Cultural Revolution. This group quickly moved to restore stability in China. The key aspect of this new effort was the removal of many bans on cultural expression and a renewed emphasis on traditional Chinese culture.

In the economic sphere, the new leadership restored the incentives so hated by the radicals, and moved to resurrect regular economic planning. Hua announced that the new regime's goal was a modern China by the year 2000.

In foreign policy, which Chou En-lai had protected from radical influence, Deng launched new efforts to assert China's moderate foreign policy, particularly the link with the United States which had lapsed since 1973. This led to U.S. recognition of China in 1979. Meanwhile, however, the "moderate" regime of Deng Xiaoping and Hua Guofeng launched the invasion of Vietnam and a crackdown on dissidents in China.

Japan had been a firm supporter of previous U.S. position on China.

Moscow's Response to China Opening. On July 25 *Pravda* published an article warning the U.S. that "any schemes to use the contacts between Peking and Washington for some 'pressure' on the Soviet Union . . . are nothing but the result of a loss of touch with reality."

U.S. Spying Suspended. On July 28 the U.S. government announced it was suspending American intelligence-gathering missions over China by SR-71 reconnaissance planes and unmanned drones.

China's Response. On July 31 China refused to attend Moscow's proposed conference on nuclear disbandment and took the occasion to restate its position on disarmament. *(See Oct. 16, 1964)* China went on to condemn again the 1963 Nonproliferation Treaty and the current SALT talks.

On Nov. 24 the Chinese delegation to the U.N. used much the same terms to reject another Russian proposal for a disarmament conference.

China On Relations With U.S. On Aug. 1 the Peking *People's Daily* published an editorial commenting on the success of China's more moderate foreign policy: "The friendly contacts between the Chinese people and the people of other countries, including the American people, are rapidly expanding. . . . The U.S. imperialist policy of blockading and isolating China has failed completely. . . . We have friends all over the world."

U.S. Position on China in U.N. On Aug. 2 Secretary of State William Rogers announced that the U.S. would end its 20-year opposition to the seating of the People's Republic of China in the United Nations, saying that the U.S. would "support action . . . calling for seating the People's Republic of China." At the same time, Rogers also repeated the U.S. position opposing any move aimed at expelling the Republic of China. On the subject of which government should have China's seat on the Security Council, Rogers said that the U.S. would abide by the majority decision of the United Nations.

The announcement produced strong reactions in both Peking *(see Aug. 5, 1971)* and Taipei *(see Aug. 3, 1971)*.

China Explains Its Foreign Policy. On Aug. 2 the Chinese Communist theoretical journal *Hongqi* published an important explanation of China's recent opening to the U.S., which had always been treated as the primary enemy of Peking. Entitled "A Powerful Weapon to Unite the People and Defeat the Enemy," the article compared the situation in 1971 to that in 1940. In 1940 Chairman Mao Tse-tung had decided to join any group (even anti-communist) in order to oppose Japan, China's greatest enemy at that time. Today, said the article, China must again distinguish "between the primary enemy and the secondary enemy." Thus China would ally itself with the secondary enemy, the U.S., in order to "isolate and strike at" the primary enemy, the Soviet Union. In addition to the U.S., China would ally with any and all countries opposed to the Soviet Union, forming a united front against Moscow.

Taiwan's Reaction. On Aug. 3, the foreign ministry of the Republic of China issued a strong condemnation of America's proposed two-China policy, and termed the proposal a "gross insult to the U.N. charter."

China's Relations with Turkey. On Aug. 4 China and Turkey announced that they were opening full diplomatic relations. Turkey was another of the countries which had consistently opposed Chinese admission to the United Nations.

Chou Interview. On Aug. 5 Chinese Premier Chou En-lai, in a wide-ranging interview with James Reston of *The New York Times,* seemed to downplay the importance of Taiwan as a barrier to improving Sino-American relations: "At present, the most urgent problem is still Vietnam." Later in the interview, Chou said that first "the question of Vietnam and Indochina should be solved, and not the question of Taiwan or other questions."

On a related question, Chou criticized the "Nixon Doctrine" as contradictory. Reiterating traditional fears of a remilitarized Japan, Chou said that he felt that although certain actions taken by Nixon had eased tensions in the Pacific, the U.S. decision to urge Japan to assume more of its defense burden only increased tensions with China.

Finally, asked about the U.S. intention to work for a two-China policy in the United Nations, Chou said that China would flatly refuse to enter the U.N. so long as the Nationalist Chinese were represented in that body.

China's Reaction. On Aug. 5 China responded angrily to U.S. Secretary of State William Rogers' announcement that the U.S. would support a two-China policy in the United Nations. An editorial in the *People's Daily* strongly condemned any version of a two-China policy, and reiterated China's position that the settlement of the Taiwan issue was China's internal affair.

On Aug. 17 the Chinese foreign ministry issued an even stronger denunciation of Rogers' proposal.

Burma-China Relations. On Aug. 6 Burmese leader General Ne Win arrived in Peking for a seven-day visit designed to heal the four-year rupture in Sino-Burmese relations. *(See June 26, 1967)* He was received by both Mao Tse-tung and Chou En-lai. No joint communiqué was issued, and Chinese Premier Chou could only state that the situation had "developed."

India-Soviet Pact. On Aug. 9, Soviet Foreign Minister Andrei Gromyko arrived in New Dehli to sign a 20-year treaty of peace, friendship, and cooperation with India. The two countries were both in the midst of disputes with China, and the treaty was clearly aimed at limiting China's ability to take on one or the other unilaterally. According to *The New York Times,* Indian officials interpreted the treaty as meaning that the Soviet Union would come to India's defense in the event of an attack by Pakistan, a close ally of China. *(See Dec. 3, 1971)*

U.S. Suspends Convertibility. On Aug. 15 President Nixon sent shock waves through world markets by announcing that the U.S. dollar would no longer be automatically convertible to gold. The U.S.' guarantee to convert foreign-held dollars to gold at $36 per ounce had been the linchpin of the international economic system of the non-communist world, and dated from agreements signed in 1944 at Bretton Woods. Nixon's decision was prompted by the fact that the dollar was no longer "as good as gold," because foreign holdings of dollars amounted to more than three times the amount of gold held in the U.S. The move was also prompted by the worsening balance of payments picture, as well as Japanese and European refusals to help ease the problem. The decision to suspend the convertibility of the dollar meant an end to the postwar economic system as it had been known.

China's Relations with Iran. On Aug. 16 China and Iran opened full diplomatic relations. Iran had previously voted against Chinese admission to the United Nations.

U.S. Resolutions in U.N. On Aug. 17 the U.S. representative to the United Nations, George Bush, submitted two U.S. resolutions dealing with the seating of a Chinese delegation in the United Nations. One called for the General Assembly to agree that any move to expel the Republic of China be considered an "important question," thus requiring a 2/3 majority vote. The second recommended that the People's Republic of China be admitted as a member of the Security Council, but noted that the ROC had continued rights of representation in the General Assembly.

Soviet Attacks Escalate. On Aug. 20 the Soviet Union began another extensive press attack on China. The newspaper *Pravda* said that China was using the threat of a Soviet invasion as a pretext to improve relations with the West and to erect "fortifications along the whole length of the border with the Soviet Union."

Chinese Party Rebuilt. On Aug. 26 Peking announced that the last of the provincial level Communist Party committees had been formed, and that the rebuilding of the party, effectively destroyed during the Cultural Revolution, had been completed. The new party committees took the place of the revolutionary committees (revcoms) which had been established as a temporary measure in 1968 and 1969.

Brezhnev Tolerant. On Aug. 28 Soviet party leader Leonid Brezhnev said that he did not blame China for the fact that the border talks were "going slowly," that Moscow was not "losing hope" and that the Soviets would "continue to display a constructive and patient approach."

Lin Piao Dies. On Sept. 13 a Chinese plane crashed at Undar Khan in Mongolia, killing all nine people aboard. These included Lin Piao, Chinese Minister of Defense (and designated heir to Mao Tse-tung), his wife, and his son, who was deputy commander of the Chinese Air Force. On the same day, the Chief of the General Staff, the Commander of the Air Force, the Director of the Army Logistics Department, and the Political Commissar of the Navy were arrested, and have not been seen since. These events are as mysterious now as they were at the time. The Chinese insist that Lin was fleeing to the Soviet Union following an unsuccessful coup, but this has never been confirmed. Lin's death followed reports that he had fallen out of favor with Mao as well as with his subordinate military commanders. Recent reports have questioned whether Lin was even on the plane, or whether there was a plane crash at all.

The chief beneficiary of Lin's death was Chou En-lai, with whom Lin had long been at odds. With Lin dead and Liu Shao-ch'i purged, Chou became the second most powerful man in China after Mao.

The other major beneficiary was President Richard Nixon, whose policy of U.S. rapprochement with China had been opposed by Lin, and whose diplomatic initiatives may have influenced the outcome of the power struggle between Chou and Lin. Lin's defeat meant that what might have been a major obstacle to normalization on the Chinese side — the opposition of the radicals — had been defused, at least for the time being.

Nixon and Two-China Policy. On Sept. 16 President Nixon, in an unscheduled news conference, declared that the U.S. would support the admission of the People's Republic of China to the Security Council because it "reflects the realities of the situation." On the question of Taiwan, Nixon said that "we will vote against the expulsion of the Republic of China and we will work as effectively as we can to accomplish that goal."

U.N. Resolution on China. On Sept. 21, opening day of the U.N. General Assembly's 26th session, the Japanese majority party, the Liberal Democratic Party, announced its decision to have Japan co-sponsor the American two-China resolution in the United Nations. The decision came after intense debate which threatened to split the party.

U.S. Procedural Defeat in U.N. On Sept. 22 the U.N. General Assembly's General Committee voted to put an Albanian proposal on the seating of the People's Republic of China ahead of the U.S. proposals. The Albanian motion, submitted July 15, called for the admission of the PRC and the expulsion of the Republic of China.

China on U.N. Membership. On Sept. 25 the Xinhua news agency announced that the Chinese government would refuse to join the United Nations if the Nationalist Government on Taiwan were allowed to continue its membership.

Rogers on U.N. On Oct. 4 Secretary of State William Rogers, addressing the U.N. General Assembly, warned that the expulsion of the Republic of China from the U.N. might endanger the membership of other nations, and weaken the U.N. as a whole.

Kissinger's Trip to China. On Oct. 20 national security adviser Henry Kissinger arrived in China for what was scheduled to be a five-day visit. The visit was later extended, so that Kissinger was in Peking during the United Nations vote on the admission of China. Sources at the U.N. attributed the defeat of the U.S. position to Kissinger's presence in Peking.

On Oct. 27, one day after his return to the U.S., Kissinger announced that President Nixon would go to China in early 1972.

Moscow on Two-China Policy. On Oct. 20 the Soviet delegate to the United Nations Yakov A. Malik said that the U.S. argument against the expulsion of Nationalist China from the U.N. was an effort "to frighten the members" of the U.N. and amounted to "absurd inventions and ridiculous fairy tales composed for children of preschool age." Malik insisted that Taiwan was not a state but a "province of China."

PRC Admitted to U.N. On Oct. 25, following a week of intense debate, the U.N. General Assembly passed the Albanian resolution to admit the People's Republic of China and to expel the Republic of China. The vote was 76-35 with 17 abstentions. Prior to the vote, the U.S. resolution to declare the expulsion of Taiwan an "important question" requiring a two-thirds majority, was defeated 59-55 with 15 abstentions. The U.S. resolution for dual representation of China never came to a vote, due to the adoption of the Albanian resolution. *(Votes, pp. 365-366)*

Belgium Recognizes PRC. On Oct. 25 Belgium established diplomatic relations with the PRC.

Taiwan's Reaction to Expulsion. On Oct. 26 Chinese Nationalist President Chiang Kai-shek declared that his government would never recognize the "illegal action" by which his government had been expelled from the United Nations.

Countries That Have Recognized the PRC

1949:	Union of Soviet Socialist Republics		Switzerland	1964:	Tunisia		Iceland		Niger
	Bulgaria		Netherlands		France		Cyprus		Brazil
	Rumania		Indonesia		Congo (Brazzaville)				Gambia
	Hungary	1955:	Nepal		Central African Republic	1972:	Argentina		
	Czechoslovakia				Zambia		Mexico	1975:	Botswana
	Democratic People's Republic of Korea (North Korea)	1956:	United Arab Republic (Egypt)		Dahomey*		Malta		Philippines
			Syria	1965:	Mauritania		Mauritius		Mozambique
	Poland		Yemen				Greece		Bangladesh
	Yugoslavia	1958:	Cambodia	1968:	South Yemen		Guyana		Thailand
	Mongolia		Iraq				Togo		Sao Tome
	German Democratic Republic (East Germany)		Morocco	1970:	Canada		Japan		Fiji
					Equatorial Guinea		German Federal Republic (West Germany)		Western Samoa
	Albania	1959:	Sudan		Italy				Comoros
	Burma				Ethiopia		Maldives	1976:	Cape Verde
	India	1960:	Ghana		Chile		Malagasy		Surinam
			Cuba				Luxembourg		Seychelles
1950:	Pakistan		Mali	1971:	Nigeria		Zaire		Papua New Guinea
	United Kingdom		Somalia		Kuwait		Chad		
	Ceylon				Cameroon		Australia	1977:	Liberia
	Norway	1961:	Senegal		Austria		New Zealand		Barbados
	Denmark		Tanzania		Sierra Leone	1973:	Spain		Jordan
	Israel				Turkey		Upper Volta	1978:	Oman
	Afghanistan	1962:	Laos		Iran				Libya
	Finland		Algeria		Belgium	1974:	Guinea Bissau		
	Sweden		Uganda		Peru		Gabon	1979:	United States
	Democratic Republic of Vietnam (North Vietnam)	1963:	Kenya		Lebanon		Malaysia		Djibouti
			Burundi		Rwanda		Trinidad and Tobago		Portugal
					Senegal		Venezuela		Ireland

*Relations broken in 1966; Dahomey switched recognition to Taiwan.

Source: James R. Townsend (comp.), *The People's Republic of China: A Basic Handbook,* New York: The China Council of the Asia Society, Council on International and Public Affairs, 1979. For the 1949-1964 period, adapted from A. M. Halpern, *Policies Toward China: Views from Six Continents,* New York: McGraw-Hill, 1965, pp. 496-497. For later years, issues of *China Quarterly* and *Peking Review.*

Senate Reaction to U.N. Vote. On Oct. 29 the U.S. Senate, angered over the expulsion of Taiwan from the United Nations, voted 21-47 to defeat the 1972 foreign aid bill, which contained $141 million for the United Nations.

Earlier the same day, the Senate voted not to repeal the Formosa Resolution. *(See p. 13)*

Sino-Italian Trade Pact. On Oct. 29 China and Italy signed a three-year trade treaty. The agreement was the first of its kind between China and a member of the Common Market.

Peking to Support Pakistan. On Nov. 7, following a three-day meeting with a Pakistani delegation headed by former Foreign Minister Zulfikar Ali Bhutto, China pledged to "resolutely support" Pakistan should it "be subjected to foreign aggression."

Chinese Delegation to U.N. On Nov. 8 six members of the Chinese delegation to the United Nations arrived in New York. Underlining the importance placed by Peking on U.N. membership, the delegation was headed by Deputy Foreign Minister Qiao Guanhua. Huang Hua, former ambassador to Canada and China's most prominent diplomat, was to be the permanent delegate. The remainder of the delegation arrived on Nov. 11.

China's First U.N. Speech. On Nov. 15, in his first statement at the United Nations, Peking's chief delegate, Qiao Guanhua, declared that the organization must be run by all member countries and must not be "manipulated and monopolized by the great powers, particularly the U.S. and Soviet Russia."

India Invades Pakistan. On Dec. 3, fortified by Soviet military aid and a new 20-year treaty of friendship, India invaded East Pakistan in support of the Bangladesh rebels who had been defeated by Pakistan in April. The larger Indian armies enjoyed great success against the smaller Pakistani units, and cleared the area within two weeks. On Dec. 17, India ordered a cease-fire.

The Pakistani defeat was also a defeat for the Chinese, who had supported Pakistan, in the first of the Sino-Soviet "proxy" wars.

Former national security adviser Henry Kissinger later claimed that the U.S. had told Moscow of its opposition to Soviet support for the Indian move, thus siding with China.

Sino-Soviet Accusations. On Dec. 7, during the debate in the United Nations over a cease-fire in the Indo-Pakistani War, the Chinese and Soviet delegates exchanged accusations about the causes of the conflict. Chinese delegate Qiao Guanhua declared that "The Soviet Government is the boss behind the Indian aggressors. The Indian expansionists usually do not have much guts. Why have they become so flagrant now?" Qiao said that the reason was that the Soviets were "backing them up."

On the same day, the Soviet chief delegate Yakov A. Malik charged that Peking was employing the U.N. as a

1972

forum for "slander and anti-Sovietism," which he denounced as "sordid."

More Accusations. On Dec. 9 the Soviet Communist Party newspaper *Pravda* charged that the Chinese had provoked the Indo-Pakistani War by providing Pakistan with arms, inviting Pakistani leaders to Peking, and trying to "fan the Indian-Pakistan conflict."

On Dec. 12 the Xinhua news agency charged that Moscow was trying to dominate India with the military and economic aid it was providing to New Delhi. The statement also declared that the Soviet friendship treaty with India had encouraged India to challenge China and had led India to "launch armed attack on Pakistan."

U.S. Prisoner Freed. On Dec. 12 China released Richard Fecteau, a prisoner in China since 1952, when he was captured following a plane crash during the Korean War. The Defense Department had always stated that he and John T. Downey were "authorized passengers on a routine flight from Seoul, South Korea, to Japan."

At the same time, the Chinese released Mary Harbert, who had been detained in 1968 in Chinese territorial waters near Hong Kong. The Chinese also reported that Downey had committed suicide while in prison.

On Jan. 13, 1973, President Nixon, speaking at a news conference, said that the release of Downey would be more difficult because he was a CIA employee. This was the first U.S. admission of that fact. *(See March 9, 1973)*

U.S. Dollar Devalued. On Dec. 18 President Nixon announced that an agreement had been reached by the Group of Ten finance ministers, meeting in Washington, to devalue the dollar, and to revalue some other major currencies.

Secretary of the Treasury John Connally estimated that the overall effect of the agreement meant an effective devaluation of the dollar by 12 percent.

Khan Resigns. On Dec. 20 Yahya Khan, Pakistani chief of state, resigned after Pakistan's defeat in its war with India. Khan had been the major conduit by which President Nixon had his first contacts with Chinese leaders in 1969.

KMT to Hold Elections. On Dec. 23 it was announced in Taipei that the ruling Kuomintang would hold its first elections since 1947 during the next year. Nationalist President Chiang Kai-shek had always refused to hold elections in the past, insisting that they would take place after Taiwan had recovered the mainland.

U.S. Resumes Bombing of North. On Dec. 26, faced with a massive North Vietnamese buildup, which seemed to indicate an impending invasion of South Vietnam, U.S. planes struck at targets in Laos, Cambodia, and parts of North Vietnam. The attacks continued for five days.

This was the first major U.S. air action in Indochina since 1968.

Soviet Reaction to Bombing. On Dec. 28 the Soviet Union reacted strongly to the U.S. decision to resume the bombing of North Vietnam, and termed the move a violation of the 1968 U.S. commitment to halt such activity. At the same time, the Soviets also directed criticism at Peking, which was accused of keeping "silent, evidently not wishing in any way to darken President Nixon's forthcoming visit to Peking."

On Dec. 29 the Chinese foreign ministry expressed its "utmost indignation" at the bombing raids.

More Trade Restrictions Eased — Nixon in China — Shanghai Communiqué — U.S. Reassures Taiwan — Paris Set for Sino-U.S. Talks — China-Japan Trade Talks — Sino-British Diplomatic Ties — North Vietnam Invades South — U.S. Resumes Bombing North — Chinese Pingpong Players in U.S. — China Gives Pandas to U.S. — Soviet-China Border Tension — U.S. Mines Haiphong — Okinawa Returned to Japan — China-Holland Ties — Nixon in Moscow — SALT Treaty Signed — Greece Recognizes PRC — Watergate Burglary — Kissinger Again in Peking — McGovern Democratic Nominee — Last U.S. Combat Troops in Vietnam Withdrawn — Nixon Renominated — China Buys 707s — China to Buy U.S. Wheat — Tanaka-Chou Communiqué — West Germany Recognizes PRC — Kissinger says Vietnam "peace is at hand" — Nixon Re-elected — U.S. Resumes Vietnam Bombing — Australia Recognizes PRC

Nixon-Sato Talks. On Jan. 7 President Nixon and Japanese Prime Minister Eisaku Sato concluded summit talks and issued a joint communiqué setting final terms for the return of Okinawa to Japan. The communiqué made no reference to Nixon's China initiatives, over which the two countries continued to disagree.

Peking Pushes EEC. On Jan. 26 the Chinese news agency Xinhua commented favorably on the admission of Great Britain and two other countries into the Common Market. This was the first time that a Chinese commentary on the EEC had not been critical of the organization.

Moscow on Nixon Visit. On Jan. 28 Soviet Foreign Minister Andrei Gromyko issued a cautious statement concerning President Nixon's upcoming visit to China. Speaking at a news conference in Tokyo, Gromyko told reporters that "The Soviet Union desires that other countries have friendly relations with China," but on the condition that these relations did not "affect adversely the safety and interest of the Soviet Union."

Chinese Satellite Installation. On Feb. 14 a new communication satellite, Intelsat 4, which would broadcast reports of President Nixon's visit to China, went into operation. At the same time, a temporary receiving station in Peking, built by the Hughes Tool Company, was reported to have been leased to the Chinese government.

On Feb. 15 RCA Global Communications, Inc. announced that it was installing a permanent station in Shanghai which would be purchased by China for $2.9 million. *(See Aug. 18, 1972)*

Trade Bans Eased Further. On Feb. 14 White House press secretary Ron Ziegler announced that President Nixon had ordered further relaxations of restrictions on trade with China. The result was that all U.S. trade with China would henceforth be on the same basis as trade with the Soviet Union and most Soviet bloc nations.

Following the June 1971 easing of trade bans, China had imported very little from the U.S., and had exported only $5 million worth of goods, mostly via Hong Kong. *(See June 10, 1971)*

U.S. Must Reassess Policy. On Feb. 17 Adm. Thomas H. Moorer, chairman of the Joint Chiefs of Staff, told Congress that the emergence of China as a nuclear power meant that the U.S. had to reassess its military strategies about nuclear war.

Laird on China's Missiles. On Feb. 17 Defense Secretary Melvin R. Laird released the fiscal 1973 defense posture statement. On the subject of China, the report said that it was difficult to assess "either the strategic nuclear threat . . . or how that threat will evolve through the 1970s." Laird did say that it would be mid-1976 before the Chinese would be able to deploy 10 to 20 missiles capable of reaching the U.S.

Taiwan on Nixon Trip. On Feb. 17 the Nationalist Chinese foreign ministry issued a statement on President Nixon's upcoming trip to China. Taiwan declared that "it will consider null and void any agreement . . . which may be reached between the United States and the Chinese Communist regime as a result of that visit." *(Text, p. 322)*

U.S. Communist Party Scores Visit. On Feb. 18 Gus Hall, secretary general of the U.S. Communist Party, condemned President Nixon's upcoming trip to China as "an attempt to use the policies of Mao to divide the Socialist countries from the national liberation movements."

Peking Accuses Tokyo. On Feb. 20 Peking accused Japanese Prime Minister Eisaku Sato and other Japanese of plotting to establish a pro-Japanese puppet regime in Taiwan that would demand independence for the island.

Nixon Arrives in China. On Feb. 21 President Nixon arrived in China for a historic seven-day visit. It was the first time an American head of state had ever visited China, and capped two years of U.S. and Chinese efforts to end the 23-year hostility between the two nations.

At a banquet given that evening, Chinese Premier Chou En-lai said that the "great differences" which exist between the U.S. and China "should not hinder" the two countries "from establishing normal diplomatic relations."

In response, President Nixon said that although China and the U.S. "in the past have been enemies," now "there is no reason for us to be enemies." *(Texts, p. 323)*

During the visit, President Nixon, Secretary of State William Rogers, and national security adviser Henry Kissinger held a series of meetings with ranking Chinese leaders, including Chairman Mao Tse-tung.

Shanghai Communiqué Issued. On Feb. 27 President Nixon met with Chinese Premier Chou En-lai in Shanghai just prior to Nixon's return to the U.S. following his historic visit to China. At the conclusion of the talks, the two governments issued a joint communiqué which pledged both sides to work for a "normalization" of relations between the two countries.

The communiqué was a compromise consisting mostly of a statement of the areas of disagreement between the two countries, and their agreement to disagree. For its part, the U.S. "acknowledged" that there was but one China and that Taiwan was part of China. In this vein, the U.S. pledged to withdraw all its military forces from the island. *(Text, p. 323)*

It was later learned that Nixon had promised the Chinese that the U.S. would open full diplomatic relations with Peking during his second term. But the Watergate crisis interfered. *(Box, p. 212)*

The U.S. and China also reached an "agreement in principle" on the issues of debts and frozen assets.

Nixon Returns to U.S. On Feb. 28 President Nixon returned to the U.S. from China. Speaking at Andrews Air Force Base, the president said that although many differences still separated the U.S. and China, "We . . . [are] building a bridge across that gulf." Nixon stated that "the primary goal of this trip was to reestablish communication with the People's Republic of China. . . . We have accomplished that goal." *(Text, p. 325)*

China in the U.N. On March 1 a letter from China's chief delegate to the United Nations, Huang Hua, noted that his government would pay a $3-million first installment on dues to the U.N., but would not pay for items regarded as "hostile to the Chinese people" (e.g., the upkeep of the U.N. cemetery in Korea), and would not assume any of the debt owed by the Chinese Nationalists.

U.S. Reassures Taiwan. On March 2 James C. T. Shen, Nationalist Chinese ambassador to the U.S., said that Secretary of State William Rogers had assured him of the U.S. commitment to the mutual defense treaty with the Republic of China. Shen, who had gone to a special briefing on President Nixon's visit to China at Rogers' request, remarked, "I understand a little more now, but I have no comment on my personal feelings."

Paris to Be Contact Point. On March 10 the White House announced that China and the U.S. had decided to make their respective ambassadors in Paris the diplomatic channel for continuing contacts between the two countries.

On March 13 Huang Zhen, Chinese ambassador to France, and Arthur K. Watson, U.S. ambassador to France, held their first meeting.

Paris had now supplanted Warsaw as the primary contact point between Washington and Peking. French officials said they were pleased that Paris could be host to the talks, even though the French had not been consulted about it beforehand.

Chinese Trade Mission to Japan. On March 10 the first trade mission from China to visit Japan in six years (since the beginning of the Cultural Revolution) arrived in Tokyo.

On March 11 the Japan International Trade Association disclosed that two-way trade between China and Japan had totaled $93 million in January, a 15.4 percent gain from January 1971, and the third highest total for any month since trade was resumed in 1963.

Britain-China Relations. On March 13 the British and Chinese agreed to exchange ambassadors, thus regularizing their relations, which had been only partial since 1950. *(See Jan. 6, 1950)*

In the joint communiqué, Britain said that it was "acknowledging the position of the Chinese Government that Taiwan is a province of the People's Republic of China."

This peculiar wording, now known as the "British solution" to the problem of Taiwan, would be adopted by most other Western nations, including the U.S. It replaced the locution devised by Canada when it resumed relations with China. *(See Oct. 13, 1970)*

Britain had been one of the first nations to recognize China, in 1950, but the opening of full relations had been delayed by the British insistence that the status of Taiwan was "undetermined."

North Vietnam Invades South. On March 30 North Vietnam crossed the DMZ and invaded the South with four full divisions, supported by Soviet heavy tanks and covered by long range artillery. Despite the fact that the attack following a long buildup which had been monitored by the

U.S., the scale and timing of the attack came as a surprise. *(See Dec. 26, 1971)* In the fighting, the troops of South Vietnam bore the brunt of the attack, and did not fare well.

By April 2 the attack had widened to the point where 12 of North Vietnam's 13 ground combat divisions were in action. The situation worsened steadily.

Chinese to High U.N. Post. On April 5 United Nations Secretary General Kurt Waldheim announced the appointment of Tang Mingchao as Under Secretary General for Political Affairs and Decolonization.

U.S. Resumes Bombing. On April 6, faced with a full-scale invasion of South Vietnam by Hanoi, the U.S. resumed massive air strikes against North Vietnam.

On April 10, B-52s were sent against targets in North Vietnam for the first time since 1968. *(See April 16)*

Chinese Pingpong Team to U.S. On April 12 the Chinese national table tennis team arrived in the U.S. for a two-week tour. During their visit, they were received by President Nixon at the White House. The group returned to China on April 30. *(Details, p. 8)*

B-52's Bomb Hanoi and Haiphong. On April 16, with South Vietnamese troops still faring poorly against the invasion from the North, the U.S. began using B-52s to bomb the major cities of North Vietnam, especially Hanoi and Haiphong. Despite this, the North Vietnamese troops continued to advance. *(See May 9, 1972)*

Panda-plomacy. On April 16, two giant pandas, a gift from China to the U.S., arrived at the Washington, D.C. zoo. Zoos throughout the U.S. had vied for the pandas, but President Nixon gave them to the Washington zoo because Chinese Premier Chou En-lai had given them to the "American people." On April 9 the U.S. had given two musk oxen to China, but they were reported to be ailing.

Congressional Leaders to China. On April 19 Senate Majority Leader Mike Mansfield, D-Mont., and Minority Leader Hugh Scott, R-Pa., arrived in China for a two-week visit.

Soviet Buildup on Chinese Border. On May 2 the Institute for Strategic Studies, an independent research group located in London, published its annual report, which said that over one-fourth of the Soviet army was now located along or near its 7000-mile boundary with China. The report also stated that the Soviets had increased the number of divisions there from 30 to 44 during 1971.

U.S. Mines Haiphong. On May 9 President Nixon, faced with an ever-worsening situation in South Vietnam, ordered the mining of all the harbors of North Vietnam. The move risked a direct confrontation with both China and the Soviet Union, whose ships were supplying Hanoi. The mining was done to stop supplies to the North Vietnamese invasion of the South, which required massive amounts of supplies for the tanks and artillery in use.

Although it is not clear if it was due to the mining or the earlier *(see April 16)* bombing of the North, the invasion halted at about this time, and South Vietnamese forces began to counterattack with some success.

Despite the fact that the attack had resulted in massive North Vietnamese casualties and a real military victory for South Vietnam, the battle was counted as a psychological victory for Hanoi, which had demonstrated that the South Vietnamese troops were not capable of fighting unassisted, despite U.S. claims.

The confrontation with Moscow and Peking threatened by the mining never materialized, due in large part to prior U.S. efforts to relieve tension with the two nations.

Okinawa Reverts to Japan. On May 15 the Ryukyu Islands, including Okinawa, were returned to Japanese rule after 27 years of U.S. occupation, removing a troublespot in U.S.-Japanese relations. Vice President Spiro Agnew represented the U.S. at the ceremonies. *(See June 17, 1971)*

Netherlands Normalizes Relations. On May 18 the Netherlands raised its office in Peking to the status of embassy, thus opening official relations with the PRC.

Nixon to Moscow. On May 22 President Nixon arrived in Moscow for a summit meeting with Soviet leaders. It had been feared that the Russians would cancel the summit as a protest against the U.S. mining of Haiphong harbor, but they did not, indicating their commitment to détente with the U.S.

SALT Treaty Signed. On May 26 President Nixon and Soviet Party leader Leonid Brezhnev signed the first Strategic Arms Limitation Treaty (SALT I), a keystone of détente and the first successful effort to limit the nuclear arms race between the two super powers. On the same day, Brezhnev is reported to have assured Nixon that he would press the North Vietnamese to settle the war in Vietnam.

Nixon Returns to U.S. On June 2 President Nixon returned to the U.S. following the Moscow summit. He told a joint session of Congress that the trip had been "part of a great journey for peace."

Greece Recognizes PRC. On June 5 Greece opened diplomatic relations with the People's Republic of China.

Chinese Arms to Pakistan. On June 1 China was reported to have delivered large quantities of new military equipment to Pakistan under the terms of an aid agreement signed in February. Diplomatic sources in Islamabad said that the supplies were part of a $300-million economic-military deal, and include 60 MiG-19 jet fighters manufactured in China, 100 tanks and an unspecified amount of small arms.

China Blames U.S. On June 10, at the World Conference on the Human Environment in Stockholm, China denounced the U.S. and other "imperialist superpowers" as the major perpetrators of global environmental problems and demanded that under-developed countries be compensated for pollution of their environments by the developed countries.

U.S. to Inform Japan. On June 11, national security adviser Henry Kissinger assured Japanese Foreign Minister Takeo Fukuda that the U.S. would not undertake major negotiations with China without consulting Japan.

Incentives Restored. On June 12, the Peking *People's Daily* announced that material incentives for increased production were to be restored throughout China. The decision represented a significant victory for the moderates in the Chinese leadership who had always supported such incentives, and a significant defeat for the radicals, who had worked to eliminate all such "capitalist vestiges" during the Cultural Revolution.

Watergate Break-in. On June 17 five men broke into the offices of the Democratic National Committee, located in the Watergate in Washington, D.C. *(See July 24, 1974)*

Kissinger Back in Peking. On June 19 national security adviser Henry Kissinger arrived in Peking for a six-day visit. On June 24 a joint communiqué was issued stating that the meetings were held "to promote normalization."

Congressional Leaders to China. On June 23, House Majority Leader Hale Boggs, D-La., and Minority Leader Gerald R. Ford, R-Mich., arrived in China for a two-week visit.

China's Military Reorganized. On July 1 it was reported that China's militia was being rearmed and that new emphasis was being placed on the training of the regular army. The new program represented a shift from the previous stress on political indoctrination of the armed forces as advocated by former Minister of Defense Lin Piao to a policy of professionalism in the country's armed forces.

"Little Red Book" Criticized. On July 6 the Peking *People's Daily* demanded that all members of the Chinese Communist Party and government officials start to study Maoism thoroughly. It was made clear that this was not to be limited to a reading of extracts and quotations, but rather of complete texts.

The new campaign marked the repudiation of the so-called "Little Red Book" of quotations from Party Chairman Mao Tse-tung, first prepared by Defense Minister Lin Piao in the 1960s and distributed widely during the Cultural Revolution, when tens of thousands of Red Guards were often seen waving the books over their heads during the mass demonstrations of that era. *(Text, p. 306)*

Later articles revealed that this change was part of a general relaxation in cultural policy and a reduction in the cult of Mao Tse-tung.

Ford Reports on China. On July 8 House Minority Leader Gerald R. Ford, R-Mich., reported on his recent trip to China, and said that Chinese officials "don't want the United States to withdraw from the Pacific or other points. They believe our presence is important for the stability of the world, now and in the future."

Shortly afterward, this was "categorically denied" by Peking. *(See Aug. 24, 1976)*

McGovern Nominated. On July 12, Democratic Sen. George McGovern was nominated for the presidency.

The Democratic platform planks on foreign policy marked a significant departure from those of years past. While endorsing the concept of a strong national defense, the platform devoted more attention to peace in Indochina, improved relations with communist nations, and less help for non-communist totalitarian regimes.

Newsmen Exchanges. On July 30 the Associated Press and the Xinhua news agency agreed to exchange news and photographs. This was the first regular news contact between the U.S. and China since December 1949.

China's First Veto. On Aug. 1 China cast its first veto in the Security Council of the United Nations, refusing to allow Bangladesh to be admitted to U.N. membership. The veto followed a bitter attack by the Chinese on both the Soviet Union and India. China explained the veto by stating that Bangladesh had refused to "implement . . . United Nations' resolutions" concerning the withdrawal of Indian troops from the country.

U.N. Deletes Taiwan Mention. On Aug. 6 the United Nations decided to omit any mention of Taiwan in its documents and publications, including the *Statistical Yearbook.* The action was taken at the insistence of Peking.

Unrest in Canton. On Aug. 12 *The New York Times* reported an upsurge in crime in Canton with increased resistance to the "down to the countryside" movement. The report quoted refugees and travelers who said that mass trials had been held in Canton and other provincial cities, and estimated that 3,000 refugees had arrived in Hong Kong in July, the highest monthly total in ten years.

Peking Starts New Foreign Department. On Aug. 12 the Xinhua news agency announced that the Chinese foreign ministry had established a new department to deal with U.S. and Pacific affairs.

Last U.S. Combat Troops Out. On Aug. 12 the last U.S. combat troops left Vietnam. From this point forward, the U.S. would rely on air strikes and negotiations to try to settle the war.

Waldheim Lauds Rapprochement. On Aug. 13 the United Nations released Secretary General Kurt Waldheim's annual report to the General Assembly. It praised improved relations between the U.S. and China but warned against acceptance of the idea that peace could be maintained through a concert of great powers, a notion sometimes attributed to Henry Kissinger.

Satellite Installations Expanded. On Aug. 18 *The Wall Street Journal* reported the announcement by RCA Global Communications, Inc. that it had signed a $5.7-million contract with the China National Machinery Import & Export Corp. to install a new satellite communications earth station in Peking and to expand the one already in operation in Shanghai.

Nixon Renominated. On Aug. 23 Richard M. Nixon was renominated as the Republican candidate for the presidency. Only one dissenting vote was cast.

The Republican platform planks on foreign policy consisted of endorsements for Nixon's policies.

Nixon-Tanaka Summit. On Sept. 1 President Nixon and Japanese Prime Minister Kakuei Tanaka ended two days of summit talks in Hawaii and issued a joint communiqué. The statement said that both leaders shared the hope that Tanaka's upcoming trip to Peking would "serve to further the trend for the relaxation of tension in Asia." It also reaffirmed that the U.S. and Japan would maintain their treaty of mutual defense and security, but omitted a reaffirmation of the applicability of the treaty to Taiwan. (In 1969 former Prime Minister Eisaku Sato, in summit talks with Nixon, had linked the defense of Taiwan to Japanese security.) *(See Nov. 28, 1969)*

Soviets Continue Buildup. On Sept. 9, "well-placed officials" in Washington were quoted as reporting that three Soviet mechanized divisions recently had been added to the troops on the Sino-Soviet border. This brought the total number of Soviet divisions in the area to 49 — nearly one-third of the Soviet army.

China Buys 707s. On Sept. 9 China signed an agreement with Boeing Aircraft to purchase ten Boeing 707s worth about $150 million. The agreement also called for training the crews and supplying spare parts. Export licenses for the sale were issued by the U.S. in July 1972.

China to Buy U.S. Wheat. On Sept. 14 it was confirmed that the Louis Dreyfus Corporation in New York had agreed to sell more than half a million tons of U.S. wheat to China.

Japanese Envoy to Taiwan. On Sept. 19 a special envoy sent to Taipei by Japanese Prime Minister Kakuei Tanaka ended a three-day visit with no apparent success in his efforts to persuade the government on Taiwan to soften its opposition to Japan's plan to recognize the People's Republic of China.

Tanaka-Chou Communiqué. On Sept. 29, during Japanese Prime Minister Kakuei Tanaka's visit to Peking, Japan and China released a joint communiqué whereby Japan recognized the People's Republic of China as the sole legitimate government of China, thus opening full diplomatic relations between the two countries.

The communiqué also pledged that the two nations would work toward the signing of a peace and friendship treaty.

Invitation to Taiwan. On Oct. 1 Chinese Defense Minister Ye Jianying invited his "Taiwan compatriots" to tour the mainland and visit relatives. Stressing patriotic sentiments among Chinese on both sides of the Taiwan Strait, Ye declared that all Chinese belong to "one big family" and that no distinction would be drawn between "those who come forward first and those later." Ye assured Nationalist officials that even "those with wrongdoings in the past" were welcome to join the patriotic family.

McGovern's Promise. On Oct. 5 Democratic presidential candidate George McGovern announced that he would extend full diplomatic recognition to China if elected.

Chou En-lai Interview. On Oct. 9, in an interview with U.S. newsmen in Peking, Chinese Premier Chou En-lai indicated that after Chairman Mao Tse-tung died, the country would probably be governed by a collective leadership. "With such a big country and the problems facing us, how can you only have one successor?"

West Germany Recognizes PRC. On Oct. 11 West Germany established diplomatic relations with the People's Republic of China. In the joint communiqué there was no mention of Taiwan.

Kissinger Says Peace Is Near. On Oct. 26 national security adviser Henry Kissinger announced at a press conference that "peace is at hand" in Vietnam. The statement proved to be premature. *(See Dec. 18)*

On Oct. 23 the U.S. had suspended the bombing of North Vietnam, citing progress in the talks.

Nixon Elected. On Nov. 7 Richard M. Nixon easily defeated Democrat George McGovern for the presidency. Despite Nixon's landslide vote, there was no significant Republican gain in Congress or the statehouses.

Nixon Lifts Travel Ban. On Nov. 22 President Nixon lifted the ban on travel to China by U.S. ships and aircraft, ending a 22-year restriction.

On the same day, the U.S. Commerce Department announced that World Airways and Trans International Airlines, both charter firms, had been given permission by the department to fly to China.

The "Japanese Solution." On Dec. 1 Japan opened a Japan Interchange Association in Taipei, and the Nationalist Chinese opened an Association of East Asian Relations in Tokyo. The creation of these offices, which were similar to legations, represented the Japanese solution to the

---

Acupuncture

Western medicine's resistence to the exotic has given way slowly in the case of acupuncture, the ancient Chinese practice of piercing patients with long thin needles to anesthetize them or relieve pain. The western world's rediscovery of acupuncture dates from President Nixon's trip to China in 1972. One of the earliest visitors to China after Nixon reopened communications was James Reston of *The New York Times,* who reported to the newspaper's readers his personal experience with acupuncture. He had to undergo emergency surgery and received acupuncture rather than a drug anesthetic.

Other prominent Americans who have received acupuncture treatment for relief of pain include former Gov. George C. Wallace of Alabama and pro football quarterback Roman Gabriel, who said it improved his sore passing arm.

American doctors have come to accept the possibility that acupuncture may serve as a suppressant of pain. They could report to their colleagues at home that it "worked" although they had no pure scientific understanding as to why it did.

A team of scientists touring Chinese medical facilities in 1979 reported seeing operations for brain surgery and thyroid removal with no other anesthetic than acupuncture. After surgery, "the thyroid patient, neatly sutured, smiled. . ., indicated that she was feeling fine and was rolled away. . . . When [the brain patient's] face was uncovered, he looked up at us with a big smile and began waving, talking, posing for our cameras and signaling that he had come through the surgery successfully."

Despite numerous such reports, skepticism among American physicians persists. A professor of anesthesiology at the University of Virginia, Harold Carron, calls acupuncture "highly overrated and it is not being used in this country . . . highly unreliable and probably requires a strong cultural background to be effective."

A professor more sympathetic to acupuncture, David J. Mayer of the Medical College of Virginia, nevertheless believes acupuncture — while "it has an economic value in a country that has to provide medical care to a billion people" — "probably won't be used much in the West . . . except in special cases where a general anesthetic can't be used."

Source: *Science News,* Oct. 27, 1979.

---

problem of how to maintain unofficial relations with Taiwan after recognizing the People's Republic of China. The offices were staffed by regular diplomats who were on "temporary" leaves of absence.

This diplomatic innovation — *de facto* ties between two nations which no longer recognized each other — came to be known as the "Japanese solution," and was widely copied until 1979, with the U.S. opening of the American Institute in Taiwan, which operated at the consular level.

Kennedy Praises Nixon. On Dec. 11 President Nixon drew praise from one of his critics, Sen. Edward Kennedy, D-Mass. Kennedy lauded Nixon for having "on two of the most important matters of our time — China and the national economy" shown "his willingness to set aside a prior course and to launch an imaginative different course." Both initiatives, said Kennedy, were correct.

U.S. Again Resumes Bombing. On Dec. 18, U.S. B-52s again resumed the bombing of North Vietnam as the peace talks, which had seemed on the verge of conclusion, were broken off. This bombing, the heaviest of the war, provoked a tremendous public outcry in the U.S., and was labeled as "terror bombing" by its critics.

On Dec. 30, citing new progress in the peace talks, the White House announced a halt to the raids. *(See Jan. 13, 1973)*

Brezhnev Accuses China. On Dec. 21 Soviet party leader Leonid Brezhnev accused China of laying claim to what he said was Soviet territory, of sabotaging East-West détente, and of attempting to "split" the world communist movement.

Australia Recognizes PRC. On Dec. 21 Australia recognized the People's Republic of China and opened diplomatic relations with Peking. New Zealand recognized China on the same day.

In their joint communiqués, both countries adopted the so-called "British solution" to the problem of the status of Taiwan, whereby they "acknowledge" (not "recognized") that "Taiwan is a province of China." *(See March 13, 1972)*

Taiwan Hold Elections. On Dec. 23 Nationalist China held the first national elections since 1947. At stake were about 50 new seats in the Legislative Yuan and the National Assembly, as well as the entire provincial assembly, four mayoral posts, and 16 country magistrates. The ruling Kuomintang won most of the seats, but non- and anti-KMT candidates gained significant ground at all levels.

1973

Vietnam-U.S. Agreement — Bombing Halt — Paris Peace Treaty — Watergate Probe — Kissinger in Peking — China-U.S. Liaison — China Builds ICBM — China-Japan Trade Eased — Sino-Soviet Talks Stalled — Spain Recognizes PRC — Last U.S. Prisoners in China Released — North Vietnam Releases Last POWs — Nixon Aides Fired — Senate Watergate Hearings — Confucius Attacked — Tenth China Party Congress — Chou on European Unity — Agnew Resigns — Ford New Vice President — Trudeau to China — "Saturday Night Massacre" — War Powers Act — U.S. Troops Withdrawn from Taiwan — Brezhnev in India

U.S. and North Vietnam Agree. On Jan. 13 national security adviser Henry Kissinger and chief North Vietnamese negotiator Le Duc Tho settled the fundamental problems which had blocked a peace settlement in Vietnam. *(See Jan. 27, 1973)*

The agreement came after the heaviest bombings of the war by U.S. planes. *(See Dec. 18, 1972)*

Nixon Orders Total Offensive Halt. On Jan. 15, following the agreement in Paris *(see Jan. 13)*, the president ordered a complete halt to all U.S. offensive military actions against North Vietnam, including air strikes and mining of harbors.

Peace Agreements Signed. On Jan. 27, representatives of the U.S., North Vietnam, South Vietnam, and the Viet Cong signed a peace agreement in Paris. Although the agreement called for a ceasefire in Vietnam, it did not end the fighting in Laos or Cambodia. *(See March 5, 1975)*

China on Paris Agreements. On Jan. 27 a spokesman for the Chinese government reacted very favorably to the announcement of the Paris agreements and stated that they "will have a positive influence on reducing tension in Asia and the world." For the past decade, the U.S. military presence in Vietnam had been the greatest source of tension between the U.S. and China.

U.S.-Vietnamese Normalization. On Feb. 1, in an hour-long televised interview, U.S. national security adviser Henry Kissinger declared that he would try to pave the way for "normalization" of relations between the U.S. and Vietnam.

Watergate Committee Formed. On Feb. 7 the Senate voted unanimously to establish a bipartisan selected committee to investigate the entire range of activities known as "Watergate."

On May 17 the committee began public televised hearings which captivated the nation.

Second Dollar Devaluation. On Feb. 12 at a late night news conference, Treasury Secretary George P. Shultz announced that President Nixon would ask Congress to authorize a formal 10 percent reduction in the dollar's par value (its value in gold). The move was prompted by much speculative selling of the dollar in the world market.

This was the first change in the value of the dollar since 1971. *(See Aug. 15, 1971)*

On Sept. 7 Congress passed the appropriate legislation.

Kissinger to Peking. On Feb. 15 national security adviser Henry Kissinger arrived in Peking for a five-day visit. During his meetings with Chinese leaders, Kissinger concluded plans for China and the U.S. to open liaison offices, *(see Feb. 22)*, and negotiated the release of the last three U.S. prisoners still held in China. *(See March 9)*

Peking on Laos Ceasefire. On Feb. 21 the Peking *People's Daily* praised the ceasefire in Laos and said that the U.S. "must scrupulously carry out and observe the 1962 Geneva Agreement," as well as the latest ceasefire agreement, which called for withdrawal of all foreign military personnel from Laos. The article made no reference to the Chinese troops guarding roads in northwestern Laos.

Liaison Offices to Be Established. On Feb.22, following national security adviser Henry A. Kissinger's trip to Peking, the U.S. and China issued a joint communiqué announcing their agreement to establish "liaison offices" in each others' capitals. The communiqué stated that the offices would be concerned with expanding trade as well as scientific and cultural exchanges. The two countries agreed verbally to grant to the liaison offices' staffs, on a reciprocal basis, diplomatic privileges and immunities. *(Text, p. 328)*

The Senate on April 13 and the House on April 17 passed and sent to the president a bill (PL 93-22) extending diplomatic immunities and privileges to the liaison office of the People's Republic of China, which would open in Washington in May. *(See May 1, 1973)*

ROC on Liaison Offices. On Feb. 22, the Nationalist Chinese Foreign Ministry strongly criticized the U.S. decision to open liaison offices with China. It stated that the agreement "completely contravenes the wishes of" the Republic of China and that Taipei would "consider null and void any agreement which had been reached between the USA and the Chinese communist regime."

Sino-U.S. Negotiations. On Feb. 25 Secretary of State William Rogers and Chinese Foreign Minister Ji Pengfei began private conferences in Paris. The purpose of the meetings was to discuss each country's financial claims against the other. *(See May 11, 1979)*

Peking Asks for Talks. On Feb. 28 the Chinese government hosted a conference for ex-members of the Chinese Nationalist Party who lived on the mainland. The conference concluded with a public appeal to the government on Taiwan to begin negotiations aimed at the reunification of China. Appealing to Chinese nationalism, the statement said: "We are all Chinese. Why couldn't we talk for the sacred cause of unifying the motherland?" This type of appeal had not been used since the 1950s, and would be replaced by a tougher Chinese line in 1974, only to appear once again in 1975. *(See Jan. 13, 1975)*

On March 3 the government in Taipei rejected the offer as "not worthy of comment."

Tanaka's Proposal to Moscow. On March 3 Japanese Prime Minister Kakuei Tanaka sent a letter to Soviet party leader Leonid Brezhnev proposing the renewal of peace talks aimed at formally ending World War II. Tanaka also expressed renewed Japanese interest in the joint economic development of Siberia's resources. *(See Oct. 10, 1973)*

Japan and the Soviet Union had held inconclusive talks on these issues in October 1972.

China Building ICBM. On March 4 *The New York Times* reported that China was developing a three-stage liquid fuel intercontinental missile that would be 20 percent larger than the SS-9, the largest Soviet missile. The new weapon was expected to have a range of 5,000 to 7,000 miles. The *Times* also said that China had already deployed some 500 missiles with a range of 600 to 3,500 miles in "soft sites" above ground.

China Eases Trade with Japan. On March 7 China was reported to have removed a number of trade restrictions against Japan which had been in effect since April 1970. Known as "the four principles of Chou En-lai," the trade bans had prohibited Chinese trade with any Japanese firm trading with South Vietnam, South Korea, Taiwan or the Philippines, or which was owned by a U.S. firm.

Sino-Soviet Negotiations Falter. On March 8 the Xinhua news agency reported that China and the Soviet Union had failed to reach an accord on navigation in rivers along their common boundary, and had concluded the talks.

Spain Recognizes PRC. On March 9 Spain established diplomatic relations with the People's Republic of China.

Last U.S. Prisoners to Be Released. On March 9 the White House announced that the last three Americans still held prisoner in China were to be released. The prisoners issue had been one of the trouble spots in the normalization of Sino-American relations, and dated from 1952.

On March 12 Richard Downey, a CIA employee, was released at the Hong Kong border. He had been held since 1952.

On March 15 Maj. Philip E. Smith and Lt. Cmdr. Robert J. Flynn were released at the Hong Kong border. The two pilots had been held since 1965 and 1967, respectively, when their planes had gone down inside China.

Pro-CCP Groups Arrested. On March 15 the Nationalist government on Taiwan announced that two pro-Chinese Communist groups at two universities had been arrested, although none of the students would be prosecuted, because they had "confessed their errors."

U.S. Out of Vietnam. On March 29 North Vietnam released the final 67 American prisoners of war, and the U.S. withdrew its remaining 2,500 troops from South Vietnam, thus officially ending American military involvement in Vietnam. *(See April 29, 1975)*

Trade Unions Revived. On March 31 it was reported that trade unions, discredited during the Cultural Revolution, were being revived in China.

U.S. Officials Arrive in China. On April 5 the first officials of the U.S. Liaison Office in China arrived in Peking, headed by Deputy Chief Alfred Jenkins.

On May 14 the Chief of the Liaison Office, David Bruce, arrived in Peking.

In both cases, the U.S. officials had arrived prior to their Chinese counterparts, an indication of the eagerness of American interests in establishing relations.

Japan and China Begin Relations. On April 5, Chinese and Japanese ambassadors presented their credentials in the capitals of the two nations and formally opened diplomatic relations.

Telegraph Link to China. On April 17 Western Union International, Inc. announced that it had reached an agreement with China to set up a direct satellite telegraph link between Peking and New York.

Chinese Officials Arrive in U.S. On April 18 the first Chinese officials of the Chinese Liaison Office in the U.S., headed by Deputy Chief Han Xu, arrived in Washington.

On May 29 the Chief of the Liaison Office, Huang Zhen, arrived.

Vatican Initiative. On April 18 the Vatican issued a missionary bulletin which asked for a "dialogue" with Peking, and stated that the Roman Catholic church recognized that aspects of Maoist doctrine reflected "modern social Christian teaching."

Chinese Denounce U.S. On April 20 the Peking *People's Daily* severely criticized increased U.S. bombing of Cambodia. The article claimed the bombings "seriously violated" the Paris agreements. *(See July 1, 1973)*

China to Sign Nuclear Pact. On April 22, during the visit of Mexican President Luis Echeverria Alvarez to China, the two countries signed a one-year commercial treaty. During the visit, China also agreed to sign the second protocol to the Treaty of Tlatelolco, which banned nuclear weapons from Latin America. *(See Aug. 21, 1973)*

White House Reshuffle. On April 30, with increasing criticism causing partial paralysis in the White House, President Nixon announced the resignations of four men implicated in the Watergate cover-up: H. R. Haldeman, White House chief of staff; John D. Ehrlichman, chief adviser for domestic affairs; John W. Dean, III, presidential counsel; and Attorney General Richard G. Kleindienst.

Liaison Offices Open. On May 1 the U.S. and the People's Republic of China opened liaison offices in each national capital. The offices were a unique solution to the problem of facilitating relations between the two countries during the period prior to full diplomatic relations.

The establishment of the offices — which were embassies in fact, if not in name — represented a major concession by the Chinese, who had always insisted that they would never establish a diplomatic mission in a country which recognized the Republic of China on Taiwan.

Peking Protests Ads. On May 16 the Chinese government called on *The New York Times* to reject political advertisements from Nationalist Chinese or pro-Taiwan groups in the U.S. The complaint followed publication of several such ads protesting the establishment of liaison offices in Peking and Washington. The Chinese went on to say that if the *Times* continued to accept such ads, they would not be allowed to open an office in Peking. The newspaper refused to accede to the demands citing constitutional guarantees of free speech.

Tourists Still Banned. On June 9 it was reported that eight visiting U.S. congressmen had been told by Peking officials that China would continue to exclude nearly all U.S. tourists and would grant visas only to Americans with special skills, with few exceptions.

Brezhnev to U.S. for Summit. On June 16 Soviet party leader Leonid Brezhnev arrived in Washington for talks with President Nixon. During the summit, the two leaders signed agreements concerning cooperation on the development of atomic energy as well as the exchange of information on agriculture, transportation, oceanography and commerce. The two also set the end of 1974 as a target date for the completion of SALT II.

The summit, which should have been a foreign policy triumph for Nixon and national security adviser Henry Kissinger, was overshadowed by the Watergate investigations. *(Box, p. 212)*

Out of deference to the president, the Senate had announced earlier that it would suspend the Watergate hearings for the duration of the Brezhnev visit. The next witness was to be John Dean.

Illegal Meat to U.S. On June 17 Rep. John Melcher, D-Mont., made public the result of an internal investigation made by the Department of Agriculture of its meat and poultry inspection service. The report said that illegal meat products from China were being admitted in the U.S. without inspection.

Nuclear War Agreement. On June 22 President Nixon and Soviet party leader Leonid Brezhnev signed an agreement aimed at preventing nuclear war. It called for "urgent consultations" whenever the relations between themselves or another country "appear to involve the risk of nuclear conflict."

Dean Testifies. On June 25 John W. Dean III, formerly President Nixon's special counsel, began testifying before the Watergate committee. During his five days of testimony, Dean made and substantiated the most serious charges yet made against President Nixon.

Kissinger Reassures Huang. On June 26 *The New York Times* reported that national security adviser Henry Kissinger had met with Huang Zhen, the head of the Chinese Liaison Office in Washington, to allay Chinese fears that the U.S.-Soviet accords — especially the pledge to avoid nuclear war — constituted a superpower alliance against other countries.

On the same day, Secretary of State William Rogers made a similar disclaimer.

Youth League Congresses Held. Beginning June 26, the Chinese Communist Party Youth League held provincial congresses throughout China. On July 17 an official

announcement said the organization, which had ceased functioning during the Cultural Revolution, had completed its basic reorganization.

Chinese Nuclear Test. On June 27 China conducted an aboveground test of a hydrogen bomb at its Lop Nor test site in Xinjiang. The next day, protests were filed by Australia, New Zealand, Japan, Indonesia, and the Soviet Union.

Cambodian Bombing Ban. On July 1 President Nixon signed a supplemental appropiations bill (H J Res 636) which set an Aug. 15 cutoff date for all U.S. combat activities in or over Cambodia, Laos, North Vietnam, and South Vietnam. The final bill was the result of a compromise between Congress and the president, who had vetoed a stronger bill earlier in the year.

The U.S. had already terminated combat operations in all of the areas mentioned in the bill except Cambodia. Thus Congress gave Nixon six weeks to settle the war in Cambodia. *(See Nov. 7, 1973)*

Chase Manhattan and China. On July 4 David Rockefeller, chairman of Chase Manhattan Bank, announced at a news conference that he had just returned from China, where he had concluded an agreement with the Bank of China establishing a corresponding relationship between the two banks. It was the first time a U.S. bank had represented a Chinese bank in the West since 1949.

U.S. Mail to China. On July 8 the U.S. Postal Service announced the beginning of parcel post delivery service between the U.S. and China.

Soviet Envoy Recalled. On July 19 the chief Soviet negotiator at the Sino-Soviet border talks was recalled to Moscow for "official duties." He would not return for a year. The recall followed reports that the Chinese had rebuffed a new Soviet proposal aimed at ending their border conflict.

Nixon-Tanaka Summit. On Aug. 1, following two days of meetings, President Nixon and Japanese Prime Minister Kakuei Tanaka issued a joint communiqué listing 18 points of agreement on a broad range of issues which had been troubling relations between the two countries. For its part, the U.S. pledged to support Japanese admission to the United Nations Security Council and to maintain "an adequate level of deterrent forces" in Asia. Japan promised further reductions in its trade imbalance with the U.S. and strong support for Nixon's Atlantic Alliance. Both sides agreed to share oil in emergencies, and to assist in the "rehabilitation" of Indochina.

Campaign Attacks Confucius. On Aug. 7 the Peking *People's Daily* published an article that marked the beginning of a campaign to attack Confucius. Shortly thereafter, the campaign would widen to an attack on Lin Piao, the former Chinese defense minister. *(See Feb. 3, 1974)*

The campaign, which would last until the 4th National People's Congress, has been seen as an effort to reestablish party control of the army and to check accelerating trends toward regionalization in China.

China Signs A-bomb Ban. On Aug. 21 China signed the second protocol to the Treaty of Tlatelolco, which banned the spread of nuclear weapons to Latin America, in Mexico City.

Kissinger Named Secretary of State. On Aug. 22 Henry A. Kissinger, national security adviser, was named secretary of state by President Nixon. The Senate confirmed the appointment on Sept. 21.

Two years earlier, Sen. Stuart Symington, D-Mo., had echoed a common view in a Senate speech on March 2, 1971, when he said: "Kissinger is the secretary of state in everything but title."

Kissinger became the first foreign-born secretary of state in U.S. history.

Tenth CCP Congress. On Aug. 24 the Tenth Congress of the Chinese Communist Party opened in Peking. The major task of the congress was to institutionalize the changes in leadership dating from the death of Lin Piao and the purge of his followers in the military. The rise in status of Chou En-lai was confirmed by the congress, which saw the return of Deng Xiaoping and other of his supporters who had been purged during the Cultural Revolution. At the same time, however, the congress also saw the rise to power of the "gang of four," who had been a major force behind the Cultural Revolution.

Chou, a moderate, was now number two, next to Mao Tse-tung, while Wang Hongwen, a radical, was raised to number three, indicating the split. Mao, who had not left his office since January 1972, presided over the congress, but did not speak.

Despite the congress' claim to be a continuation of the Ninth Congress and thus committed to moderation, the period after the congress adjourned saw the launching of new campaigns similar to those of the Cultural Revolution.

In the area of foreign policy, the congress heard two reports which for the first time in history allowed disputes within the leadership to be aired publicly. Premier Chou En-lai strongly defended his policy of rapprochement with the U.S. and stated his belief that Moscow was a much greater threat to world peace than Washington.

Wang Hongwen, on the other hand, enunciated the radicals' position that both superpowers were equally hostile to China, and that "We must without fail prepare well against any war of aggression and guard against surprise attack" by either of the two.

The Congress closed on Oct. 28, making it the shortest ever held.

More Chinese Accusations. On Aug. 26 China accused the Soviet Union of acting like "new tsars," and claimed that Moscow had dismembered Romania and subjugated Bulgaria.

Sino-Japanese Trade Agreement. On Aug. 30 Japan and China concluded two weeks of talks on trade between the two countries and approved a three-year trade pact. The agreement provided for the exchange of most-favored nation treatment in tariffs and customs. China was reported to have rejected a full trade, commerce and navigation treaty as sought by the Japanese.

The agreement was signed the next year. *(See Jan. 5, 1974)*

Chou Supports European Unity. On Sept. 11, during a visit to China by French President Georges Pompidou, Chinese Premier Chou En-lai told him: "We ... support the people of European countries in unifying themselves to safeguard their independence."

The Chinese continue to believe that a strong Europe is an important deterrent against Soviet action against China in Asia.

Chinese Attack Détente. On Oct. 2 Chinese Deputy Foreign Minister Qiao Guanhua attacked the U.S. and the Soviet Union before the United Nations General Assembly. Qiao criticized the notion of détente, asserting that the two superpowers sought to divide the world into spheres of influence, and were fearful and mistrustful of each other. He was especially critical of Moscow, calling for the Soviets to withdraw their troops from Czechoslovakia and Mongolia. Qiao also accused the Soviets of reviving "the long-ignored trash known as the Asian collective security system," which he likened to a Russian version of the security pacts engineered by the late U.S. Secretary of State John Foster Dulles.

Agnew Resigns. On Oct. 10 Spiro T. Agnew resigned as vice president of the United States. Earlier in the day, Agnew had pleaded *nolo contendere* (no contest) to federal income tax evasion.

Nixon Names Ford. On Oct. 12, following the resignation of Spiro Agnew, President Nixon named House Minority Leader Gerald R. Ford, R-Mich., to be vice president of the U.S.

Trudeau to China. On Oct. 13 Canadian Prime Minister Pierre Trudeau told a press conference following his three-day visit to China that Canada was beginning to move toward expanded relations with China. During his stay in Peking, Trudeau had concluded agreements on trade, medical and technical exchanges, and the establishment of consulates general in the two capitals.

Saturday Night Massacre. On Oct. 20, Attorney General Elliot L. Richardson and Deputy Attorney General William D. Ruckelshaus resigned rather than fire Watergate special prosecutor Archibald Cox, as President Nixon had ordered. Solicitor General Robert H. Bork became acting attorney general and fired Cox. The president's prestige, which had been slipping, plummeted.

Faced with the public outcry, Nixon on Oct. 23 agreed to turn over the tapes of White House conversation that had been subpoenaed by the special prosecutor.

Tanaka-Brezhnev Summit. On Oct. 10 Japanese Prime Minister Kakuei Tanaka left the Soviet Union after three days of talks that reportedly ended without a major accord. Tanaka had sought, as part of a peace treaty formally ending World War II, return of the four islands at the southern end of the Kurile chain which had been seized by Russia in 1945. Russia evidently agreed only to return two. The joint communiqué was unclear on the future of the $2-billion credit the Soviets had sought from Japan to build a pipeline from the oil fields of western Siberia to the Pacific Ocean. Observers reported that the Soviet stance on oil exports had stiffened as a result of renewed war in the Middle East. Japan remained heavily dependent on Middle Eastern oil.

Chinese Criticize Ceasefire. On Oct. 24 China charged that the Middle East ceasefire was an attempt by the U.S. and the Soviet Union to "put out the blazing fire of this just war," and blamed the two superpowers for "imposing a new 'no-war, no-peace' situation on the people of the Arab countries." China went on to restate its support of the Arab cause.

China to Increase Militia. On Oct. 27 *The New York Times* reported that China had launched a major effort to increase the size and number of militia units in China. Chinese press and radio reports explained that it was necessary to arm industrial workers to counter a possible attack by "Soviet revisionist social imperialism." The

Watergate and U.S. Foreign Policy

Following the June 1973 summit meeting between President Nixon and Soviet party leader Leonid Brezhnev in Washington, national security adviser Henry Kissinger commented:

"If the summit had occurred the way it was designed, that is, two or three months after the withdrawal of the last American troops from Indochina, it would have been seen by many as the beginning of an era of peace. When it occurred a week before the John Dean testimony, it was seen by many as an attempt by the Administration to use foreign policy to escape from domestic difficulties."

Source: Marvin and Bernard Kalb, *Kissinger* (Boston: Little, Brown & Co., 1974) p. 442.

militia force could also be used to rally the people in domestic and ideological struggles, according to Peking.

War Powers Act. On Nov. 7 Congress dealt President Nixon a stunning setback when it voted to override his veto of legislation limiting the president's powers to commit U.S. forces abroad without congressional approval. Presidential press secretary Ron L. Ziegler said the president felt "the action seriously undermines this nation's ability to act decisively and convincingly in a crisis."

Called the War Powers Act, the bill (H J Res 542) set a 60-day limit on any presidential commitment of U.S. troops abroad without specific congressional authorization.

Kissinger to Peking. On Nov. 11 Secretary of State Henry Kissinger arrived in Peking for a five-day visit. Afterward, Kissinger stated that the Watergate crisis was having no impact on Sino-American relations.

More U.S. Troop Withdrawals. On Nov. 15 the U.S. announced it would begin withdrawing 3,000 of the remaining 8,000 air force personnel still on Taiwan.

Brezhnev to New Delhi. On Nov. 26 Soviet Premier Brezhnev arrived in New Delhi for talks with Indian officials.

Vice President Ford. On Dec. 6, an hour after the House of Representatives voted 387-35 to confirm him, Gerald R. Ford became the 40th vice president of the U.S. The Senate had approved the nomination Nov. 27 by a 92-3 vote.

1974

Chinese Army Power Broken — Sino-Japan Trade Pact — 4th People's Congress — China-Vietnam Clash — Japanese-Chinese Oil Deal — Western Culture Attacked — Nixon Impeachment Moves — Spratly Islands Claim — New Chinese Foreign Policy — India Nuclear Bomb — Malaysia Recognizes PRC — Nixon Resigns — Brazil Recognizes PRC — China Denounces India — Ford Pardons Nixon — Formosa Resolution Repealed — Kissinger in Peking — SALT II Talks Begin — Sino-Soviet Border Talks Stalled

New Soviet Criticisms. On Jan. 1 the Soviet Union charged that China had accepted the *de facto* independence of Taiwan in order to curry favor with the U.S.

Army's Local Power Broken. On Jan. 4 the Xinhua news agency reported that the Chinese government had carried out a major shakeup of its top military command and that eight of 11 regional commanders had been removed and reassigned to other areas. The action had the effect of reducing the power and importance of the military hierarchy and bringing it under closer civilian control.

Sino-Japanese Trade Pact. On Jan. 5 Japanese Foreign Minister Masayoshi Ohira, in Peking for a four-day visit, signed a three-year trade agreement with China which had been negotiated the year before. The agreement was the first since the two countries had exchanged ambassadors in 1972, and granted both countries most-favored-nation status. *(See Aug. 30, 1973)*

Sino-Vietnamese Fighting. On Jan. 19 China and South Vietnam began a two-day war over possession of the uninhabited Paracel (Xisha) Islands, claimed by both nations. On Jan. 20 China ousted the Vietnamese forces and took possession of the islands. Despite Vietnamese pleas for international assistance, no other nations intervened. The islands were believed to be rich in oil. *(See Jan. 31, 1974) (Map, p. 115)*

Soviet Diplomats Expelled. On Jan. 19 China expelled three Soviet diplomats and two of their wives after charging them with espionage and subversion. On Jan. 21 the Soviet Union retaliated by expelling a Chinese diplomat from Moscow.

Soviets Level New Criticisms. On Jan. 21 the Soviet Union charged that China was trying to lure Japan into anti-Soviet policies with promises of oil exports.

Italian Film Attacked. On Jan. 30 the Peking *People's Daily* assailed Michelangelo Antonioni, the Italian movie director, for his documentary "China," which he had filmed in 1972. The article called the film a "serious anti-Chinese event" and "a wild provocation against the Chinese people." The *People's Daily* published a second editorial condemning the film on Feb. 6.

Japanese Oil Agreement. On Jan. 30 Japan and South Korea signed an agreement in Seoul to develop jointly seabed petroleum reserves in the East China Sea. Prior to the agreement, much of the area had been under dispute between the two countries.

On Feb. 5 China charged that the action infringed on Chinese sovereignty in the East China Sea.

Spratly Islands Dispute. On Jan. 31, following their defeat in the Paracel Islands, the South Vietnamese moved to occupy many of the Spratly (Nansha) Islands. China protested verbally but sent no troops. On Feb. 4 the South Vietnamese landed more troops, and both China and Taiwan lodged protests. By this time, in addition to the islands held by South Vietnam, the Philippines were believed to occupy three of the islands, and Taiwan had troops on one. *(See Jan. 19, 1974)*

New Ideological Campaign. On Feb. 3 China formally launched a new campaign to criticize Confucius and Lin Piao. The Peking *People's Daily* said that it involved "consolidating and carrying to a higher stage" the gains of the Cultural Revolution. The new campaign would also continue the policy of criticizing most ancient Chinese and imported Western culture. *(See Aug. 7, 1973)*

Spratly Islands Claims. On Feb. 5 the Vietnamese foreign ministry replied to a Chinese foreign ministry statement that China would not tolerate South Vietnam's presence on the Spratly (Nansha) Islands, and reaffirmed South Vietnam's claim to the islands.

On the same day, the Philippine government also laid claim to the islands.

Impeachment Proceedings Begin. On Feb. 6 the House passed H Res 803 by a 410-4 vote, formally granting the Judiciary Committee power to investigate the conduct of President Nixon to determine whether there were grounds for impeachment.

On Feb. 19 the Senate Watergate Committee ended public hearings.

Western Book Attacked. On Feb. 6 *Jonathon Livingston Seagull,* the book by American author Richard Bach, was assailed by the Shanghai magazine *Study and Criticism.* It said of the story's principal character: "All his elitist, idealistic claptrap about finding a nobler purpose for living through the perfection of flight is simply an illusion disseminated by the bourgeoisie to distract the working class from its true goal of social revolution."

Prior to this, the book had been highly praised by Nationalist Chinese President Chiang Kai-shek as an example of how the will to succeed could triumph over material limitations.

Western Music Attacked. On Feb. 14 the Xinhua news agency published several articles criticizing Ottorino Respighi's "Pines of Rome" as one of many "bourgeois works of music." The piece had been performed by American conductor Eugene Ormandy during a visit to Peking in September 1973. A Chinese critic at that time hailed the work as "brilliant." Later analysts of the music said it was "weird and bizarre" and reflected "the nasty, rotten life and decadent sentiments" of the West.

The music of Beethoven and Schubert also was classified as "foreign things" that deserved criticism.

Radicals Attack Chou En-lai. On Feb. 20 the Hong Kong Communist Party newspaper, *Dagongbao,* reprinted a Chinese article criticizing Confucius for only "pretending" to be loyal to the king and for being "very good at adapting to changed circumstances." Analysts in Hong Kong commented that unlike previous criticism of Confucius which was actually aimed at Lin Piao, this article was very clearly directed at Chinese Premier Chou En-lai.

New Ambassador to ROC. On Feb. 21 President Nixon appointed Leonard Unger, a career foreign service officer, as U.S. ambassador to the Republic of China. It had been expected by some that the president would leave the position vacant, thus downgrading relations with Taiwan and easing the way for normalization of relations with mainland China.

Unger was confirmed by the Senate on March 13 and held the post until the U.S. broke relations with the ROC in 1979.

Schlesinger's Testimony. On Feb. 28 Defense Secretary James Schlesinger, testifying before the House Appropriations Defense Subcommittee, said U.S. troop strength in Asia would remain at present levels until at least 1977. Schlesinger noted that "political" reasons were behind the U.S. decision to keep Asian troop levels at 185,000 men. He suggested that the Chinese, fearful of Soviet intentions, were not interested in the U.S.' leaving the area. The secretary also testified that he expected Japan to increase its military spending levels and join China in opposition to

the Soviet Union: "You will see the Japanese rethink their entire self defense program." This last contention was sharply attacked by other administration sources.

French Film Protested. On Feb. 28 *The Times* of London reported that the Chinese embassy in Paris had protested the release of a new French film comedy "Les Chinois à Paris" by Jean Yanne, which it said provides "an unacceptable parallel between a socialist China and a fascist Germany."

Material Incentives Debated. On March 5 reports from Hong Kong told of a renewal of attacks on "economism," a Marxist heresy which concerned itself with the immediate welfare of the workers rather than the long-term success of the revolution. Analysts in Hong Kong described the attacks as a reaffirmation of the Cultural Revolution. It was also reported that wall posters had appeared in factories denouncing the "evil tendency" to offer workers overtime payments and other incentives to spur production, policies associated with the former chief of state Liu Shao-ch'i and current Vice Premier Deng Xiaoping.

Sino-Soviet Dispute Heats Up. On March 15 the Chinese captured a Russian helicopter and its three-man crew, claiming they were spies. On the same day Moscow claimed that the helicopter had accidentally strayed over the Chinese border. *(See April 29, 1975)*

New Chinese Foreign Policy. On April 10 Chinese Vice Premier Deng Xiaoping, in a major address to a special session of the United Nations General Assembly, outlined the basis of a new Chinese foreign policy. According to Deng, Russia's decision to act more like a superpower than a socialist state meant that "the socialist camp . . . is no longer in existence." At the same time, the anti-communist "imperialist bloc, too, is disintegrating." Thus, the previous "two bloc" theory was no longer valid.

Deng went on to state that "the world today consists of three parts, or three worlds." The first world is comprised of the two superpowers, Russia and America. The second world is comprised of all the other developed nations. The third world is made up of all the remaining, undeveloped nations. Deng offered China as the leader of the third world, as Chou En-lai had in 1954. *(Text, p. 326)*

The speech marked the first formal enunciation of a shift toward moderation in Chinese foreign policy, and a rejection of the confrontation politics which China had used from 1958 to 1969.

The new policy would be elaborated more fully in 1977. *(See Nov. 1, 1977)*

Sino-Japanese Agreement. On April 20, after 16 months of difficult negotiations, China and Japan signed a civil air agreement. Flights began on Sept. 29. Despite this, progress toward agreements on fishing rights and shipping remained slow, while no progress was being made toward the signing of a peace treaty.

House Opens Impeachment Hearings. On May 9 the House Judiciary Committee formally opened its impeachment hearings against President Nixon.

Sino-Soviet Trade Agreement. On May 15, despite an increase in the verbal hostility between the Soviet Union and China, the two nations signed a trade agreement which called for a 12% increase in trade for 1974.

India's A-Bomb. On May 16 India detonated its first nuclear weapon, which was described as "peaceful."

Malaysia Recognizes PRC. On May 31 China and Malaysia issued a joint communiqué announcing the opening of formal diplomatic relations between the two countries. Malaysia was the first ASEAN (Association of Southeast Asian Nations) country to recognize the PRC.

Another Chinese Test. On June 17 China conducted a nuclear weapon test in the atmosphere. According to the U.S. Atomic Energy Commission, it was in the range of 200 kilotons. The test was the 16th in a series which began in 1964, all but one of which had been exploded in the atmosphere.

New Zealand, Australia, India and Japan filed protests.

Jackson on Normalization. On July 8, following a seven-day visit to China, Sen. Henry Jackson, D-Wash., said that during his trip he had told Chinese leaders that China and America were developing a "real" détente, and that, unlike the "untrustworthy Russians," Americans keep their word.

Supreme Court Rules Against Nixon. On July 24 the Supreme Court unanimously upheld a lower court order that President Nixon must turn over 64 White House tapes subpoenaed earlier by Watergate special prosecutor Leon Jaworski. Included was the famous "smoking gun" tape of June 23, 1972, when Nixon ordered the FBI to obstruct the investigation of the Watergate break-in, which had occurred six days before.

Anti-Americanism in China. On July 27 the Chinese Xinhua news agency reported a marked resurgence of anti-American polemics in China. The report hailed the American people's resistance to "decadent culture" which tried to "poison the people's souls" with displays of sex and violence on television and in movies and magazines. Analysts noted that during 1974 the campaign to oppose Confucius and Lin Piao had spilled over into harsh attacks on Western music, films and other cultural exchanges with the U.S. This criticism is attributed to the radical "gang of four" which controlled most of the media and propaganda organs in China.

U.S. Marines Withdrawn. On July 31 the U.S. State Department confirmed that the last of a six-man marine unit had been withdrawn from China in late June. The withdrawal followed a Chinese protest on May 24 demanding the U.S. remove the marines, who were "the only recognizable foreign military unit in China," and were guilty of indecorous behavior. The marines, who were acting as a guard unit attached to the U.S. liaison office in Peking, were later replaced by a four-man plainclothes unit.

Nixon Resigns. On Aug. 8 President Nixon, in a televised address, resigned from the presidency. The resignation became effective the next day, at which time Vice President Gerald R. Ford was sworn in as the 38th president.

Nixon resigned rather than face almost certain impeachment by the House of Representatives because of his involvement in the Watergate cover-up.

Brazil Recognizes PRC. On Aug. 15 China and Brazil issued a joint communiqué in Brasilia, announcing their decision to begin formal diplomatic relations.

Ford on China. On Aug. 30 President Ford said he looked forward to "new peaceful relationships, not only with the Soviet Union and the People's Republic of China, but with all peoples and every nation if we possibly can." Ford renewed his pledge for "continuity in our foreign policy and continued realism in our self-defense."

China Denounces India. On Sept. 3 the Peking *People's Daily* published an editorial attacking India's recent annexation of Sikkim, which had been a buffer between the two Asian powers. The article termed the action a "flagrant act of colonial expansion."

On Sept. 11 the Chinese foreign ministry announced that China would not recognize the annexation. Sino-Indian relations, already strained, worsened.

Taiwan Has A-Bomb Potential. On Sept. 4 the CIA prepared a classified report that said that Taiwan could build a nuclear weapon by 1979. The report was not made public until 1978.

Soviet Pilot Defects. On Sept. 6 a lieutenant of the Soviet Air Force flew his MiG-25 to Japan and asked for political asylum. Many analysts date the deterioration of Soviet-Japanese relations from this event. *(See Jan. 8, 1978)*

Ford Pardons Nixon. On Sept. 8 President Ford granted former President Nixon a "full, free and absolute pardon . . . for all offenses against the United States which he has committed or may have committed" during his years as president. The pardon raised a storm of controversy, and ended the month-long "honeymoon" Ford had enjoyed with Congress and the press.

Fissionable Materials Ban. On Sept. 24 *The New York Times* reported that the major exporters of nuclear materials, including the U.S., the Soviet Union and Great Britain, had compiled a list of equipment they agreed they would supply to other nations only under assurances that it would not be diverted for explosive use. China and France refused to agree to the ban.

China Calls for Unity. On Oct. 1 the Peking *People's Daily* published a joint editorial commemorating the 25th anniversary of the founding of the People's Republic of China. The editorial repeated earlier calls for unity, claiming that it is "imperative to strengthen the Party's centralized leadership and the great revolutionary unity of the whole Party." *(See Oct. 25, 1974)*

Soviet Criticisms. On Oct. 1, China's National Day, the Soviet Presidium, the Supreme Soviet and the Council of Ministers sent their greetings and best wishes to the "Chinese people." The message stressed that normalization and restoration of friendship should be achieved through a non-aggression treaty. A commentary in *Pravda* the same day noted the aid that the Soviet Union had rendered China in the past and charged China's present leadership with ideological heresy and with siding with reactionaries.

Peking Lauds Arabs. On Oct. 2 Chinese Deputy Foreign Minister Qiao Guanhua told the United Nations General Assembly that the Arab Nations' use of oil as a political weapon was a "historic pioneering action" in the Third World's struggle against imperialism. In a clear reply to President Ford and Secretary of State Henry Kissinger, who had recently criticized high oil prices and hinted at possible U.S. reprisals against exporting countries, Qiao declared: "To fly in a rage is futile, to bluff is also futile."

Chinese Compromise. On Oct. 3 Chinese Vice Premier Deng Xiaoping told Japanese visitors in Peking that China continued to hope for the conclusion of a Sino-Japanese peace and friendship treaty and that, in this regard, China was willing "to shelve the territorial problems involving the disputed Senakaku Islands." Similar remarks were made by Deng on Nov. 10.

Chinese Views Reported. On Oct. 5 the *Toronto Globe and Mail,* citing an unnamed Chinese official said to be "close to the latest thinking on the problem," reported that the official had told Canadian visitors to China in early October that China's leaders discounted "the possibility of the Soviet Union launching an immediate attack against us. We hold that the strategic emphasis of the Soviet Union at the moment is in Europe and they would not dare to launch a war against China until they have control of Europe and the Middle East."

On the question of Taiwan, the Chinese went on record as supporting a much milder line than had been the case earlier. The officials said that there was little likelihood of a settlement of the Taiwan issue as long as Chiang Kai-shek and Chiang Ching-kuo were alive, but this was not an urgent matter. "The people of our generation hope that it will be solved in our lifetime; if it isn't it will be solved by the next."

Kuomintang Member to China. On Oct. 10 Shang Chen, formerly an important Nationalist Chinese official, was received by Chinese Minister of Defense Ye Jianying during his visit to China in October.

Formosa Resolution Repealed. On Oct. 11 Congress repealed the January 1955 Formosa Resolution, which had given the president the power to intervene in the Taiwan Strait in order to defend Taiwan. Passed during the height of the Cold War, the resolution had long since had only symbolic value. The administration had been pushing repeal since 1971, as part of the effort to normalize relations with China. *(Text, p. 311)*

China's Foreign Trade. On Oct. 11 the *Peking Review* published an article by Wang Yaoding, chairman of the China Council for the Promotion of International Trade, that summarized the latest situation in China's foreign trade. Wang reported that China had trade relations with 150 countries and regions and had signed trade agreements or protocols with more than 50 countries. The article also claimed that China's trade volume in 1974 was two and a half times what it had been in 1965, and that "The change from importing to exporting crude oil and oil products and increase in oil exports have provided China with a greater possibility of further developing her foreign trade." Although Wang gave lip service to the official Chinese policy of "self-reliance," he said that China would have to continue to increase its foreign trade in the future.

China Encourages European Unity. On Oct. 18 Poul Hartling, prime minister of Denmark, arrived in China for a nine-day visit. During his stay, the Chinese took the opportunity to underline their support for European unity in the face of what they claimed was a Soviet threat, and praised Denmark for its policy that "maintains vigilance against superpowers' coercion" and "common defense with other European countries." Chinese Vice Premier Deng Xiaoping told the Danish leader, "we shall be gratified to see Europe grow strong."

Bush Arrives in China. On Oct. 21 George H. W. Bush, the newly appointed head of the Liaison Office, arrived in Peking and held talks with Chinese Vice Premier Deng Xiaoping on Nov. 2.

Japanese Oil Deals with China. On Oct. 23 the London *Daily Telegraph* reported that China had agreed to sell eight million tons of oil to Japan in 1975. But a *Kyodo* report later said that Japanese importers had had to cancel arrangements to take delivery of the remaining 900,000 tons of the 4.9 million tons of Chinese crude oil they had originally contracted for 1974. The Japanese economic recession had reduced demand, and Chinese oil cost $.90 more per barrel than Indonesian oil. It was reported that price revision talks were scheduled for January 1975. *(See Feb. 20, 1975)*

China Calls for Struggle. On Oct. 25 the *Peking Review* published an article which seemed to take issue with the recent calls for unity by the Chinese leadership: "Denying the existence of contradictions among the people and stressing unity alone ... will of course harm the revolutionary cause."

Leaders Encouraged to Work. On Oct. 31 the Peking *People's Daily* published a front-page report that leaders of the Inner Mongolia Regional Party Committee had helped to unload railroad cars. This was followed by nation-wide reports of top Chinese leaders from party, state and army organizations participating in similar examples of manual labor. The drive appeared to be linked to the campaign to criticize Lin Piao and Confucius, since in the reports references were made to Lin's belittlement of manual labor.

Kosygin on Sino-Soviet Relations. On Nov. 3 Soviet Premier Aleksei Kosygin, speaking in Frunze, the capital of Kirgizskaya, which borders China, blamed the lack of improvement in Sino-Soviet relations on the present Chinese leadership and expressed his belief that the two countries eventually would achieve an understanding, but not while that leadership remained in power in Peking.

Chinese Propose Talks. On Nov. 7 Peking radio broadcast in Russian a message from the National People's Congress and the State Council to the Presidium and Council of Ministers of the Soviet Union on the anniversary of the October Revolution. The message called for an agreement on mutual non-aggression and on military withdrawal from all disputed areas on the border. *(See Nov. 26)*

Mansfield to China. On Nov. 12 U.S. Sen. Mike Mansfield, D-Mont., arrived in China. On the same day, he met with Premier Chou En-lai in the hospital. He later met with Vice Premier Deng Xiaoping and Foreign Minister Qiao Guanhua.

Sino-Japanese Agreements. On Nov. 13, following long and strenuous negotiations, China and Japan finally signed a shipping agreement in Tokyo. At the same time, it was also agreed to establish new consulates in Shanghai and Osaka during 1975.

Peking Calls for Army Obedience. On Nov. 13 the Peking *People's Daily* warned the army to submit unconditionally to the authority of the Chinese Communist Party: "We absolutely must not permit the army to become an instrument in the hands of the careerists." The statement followed reports that the campaign to criticize Lin Piao had evoked negative reactions within the high command.

China's New Foreign Minister. On Nov. 15 Qiao Guanhua replaced Ji Pengfei as Chinese foreign minister. Ji was reported to be in poor health.

New Strategic Arms Agreement. On Nov. 25 President Ford and Soviet party leader Leonid Brezhnev, meeting in Vladivostok, signed a joint communiqué agreeing, tentatively, to limit the number of all U.S. and U.S.S.R. offensive nuclear weapons through 1985. The details were to be worked out in Geneva in 1975.

Kissinger to Peking. On Nov. 25 U.S. Secretary of State Henry Kissinger arrived in China direct from the summit talks with Soviet leaders at Vladivostok. It was his first discussion with Chinese leaders in 12 months. Kissinger held lengthy talks with Qiao Guanhua, Chou En-lai, and Deng Xiaoping, but did not meet with Mao Tse-tung. The atmosphere seemed less cordial than on previous visits, although progress was made on the issue of frozen assets and claims, one of the sticking points in the process of normalization.

Kissinger briefed the Chinese on the summit, and agreed that President Ford would go to China in 1975.

Chinese Oil to Japan. On Nov. 25 the vice president of the Japanese Bridgestone Liquified Gas Company, Katsuro Yamamoto, said in Peking that he had agreed to extend technical assistance to China for the liquefaction of petroleum gas, and that if this were begun in 1975, Japan could begin to import liquified petroleum gas from China three years later.

Russia Rejects Chinese Offer. On Nov. 26 Soviet Party President Leonid Brezhnev, speaking at a rally in Ulan Bator, decisively rejected the Chinese offer to negotiate the Sino-Soviet border dispute. Brezhnev objected to the Chinese demand that the Soviet Union should withdraw its troops prior to talks, and said that he wanted negotiations without pre-conditions. *(See Nov. 7, 1974)*

Following closely the Soviet-American summit at Vladivostok and coinciding with U.S. Secretary of State Kissinger's visit to China, the Soviet rejection dissipated any Chinese hopes that it could use its better relations with the U.S. as a lever against the Soviet Union.

China Criticizes SALT. On Nov. 27 the Peking *People's Daily* printed a detailed criticism of the latest SALT agreement between the U.S. and the Soviet Union, claiming that it was only "new emulation rules for their next round of [the] nuclear arms race."

1975

Fourth Chinese Congress — Modernization Sought — Sino-Japanese Oil Deal — North Vietnam Offensive — Chiang Kai-shek Dies — China Buys Canadian Wheat — Cambodia Falls — China-North Korea Pact — South Vietnam Falls — Deng Xiaoping in France — Mayaguez Seized — U.S. Troops Leave Thailand — China-Philippines Announce Ties — China-Thailand Accord — Helsinki Agreement — China-Japan Agreement — Communist Takeover in Laos — China Begins EEC Talks — Agriculture Modernization Program — China Recognizes Bangladesh — Schlesinger Fired — Ford in China — "Pacific Doctrine" — China-Britain Trade Deal

Fourth Chinese Congress. On Jan. 13 the 4th National People's Congress, the first since 1964, met in Peking. The congress passed a new constitution, replacing that of 1954, and tended to confirm the leadership group already in office, thus continuing the balance between the radical "gang of four" and the moderates led by Deng Xiaoping and Chou En-lai. Ye Jianying was formally named Minister

of Defense, a post he had been holding since the fall of Lin Piao in 1971.

Chou En-lai called for the "comprehensive modernization of agriculture, industry, national defense, and science and technology before the end of the century." Chou added that the State Council would draw up a ten-year plan, to begin in 1980, to accomplish this goal.

The congress seemed to mark the end of the campaign to criticize Confucius and Lin Piao and can thus be considered as marking the end of the reconsolidation following the chaos of the Cultural Revolution.

In the area of foreign policy Chou called on his "fellow-countrymen in Taiwan" to work together with the people of the entire country to bring about Taiwan's liberation. This moderate appeal, which played down any army role in the liberation, marked a retreat from the hardline, radical policies of 1974, and a return to the more moderate stance of 1973. *(See Feb. 28, 1973)*

Chairman Mao Tse-tung did not attend the congress, and this was taken as further indication that he had retired from active political life. This impression was confirmed by the reports of a number of foreign visitors to Peking.

New Campaign Against Incentives. On Feb. 9 the Peking *People's Daily* published an editorial marking the beginning of a new campaign against the use of material incentives or "private plots" to spur the output of the Chinese workers and peasants. The article called such notions "bourgeois" and "capitalist" and stated that "some of our comrades . . . have got muddled ideas" about this, "and even regard capitalist stuff as socialist." The article revealed that the power of the Cultural Revolution radicals was still strong, and that they were determined to continue to oppose the policies of the recently-rehabilitated Deng Xiaoping, who had been purged during the Cultural Revolution because he supported such incentives.

Sino-Soviet Talks Resume. On Feb. 12 the Soviet news agency Tass reported the departure of Deputy Foreign Minister Leonid Ilyichev for Peking to resume the long-suspended border talks between the two countries.

Ilyichev was greeted in Peking by Chinese Vice Minister of Foreign Affairs Han Nianlong, his counterpart in the negotiations. Secret talks on the border question opened on Feb. 15.

Sino-Japanese Oil Trade. On Feb. 20 the *Financial Times* of London reported that China had agreed to reduce the price of its oil sold to Japan. This led the way for the signing in March of new oil contracts between the two countries. The grand total contracted for 1975 (including 900,000 tons carried over from 1974) would reach 7.8 million tons, or nearly double the four million tons shipped in 1974. Earlier in February, China had agreed to conduct some of its trade with Japan in U.S. dollars.

China Will Not Buy U.S. Wheat. On Feb. 27 the U.S. Department of Agriculture announced that the Chinese government had canceled an order for 382,000 metric tons of wheat contracted from U.S. exporters. This cancellation, and an earlier cancellation in January, represented the total amount of wheat originally ordered in 1974 by China from the U.S. *(See April 7, 1975)*

Kissinger on Southeast Asia. On March 3, after conferring with Secretary of State Henry Kissinger, a State Department official reported that Kissinger believed there was little use in any new major diplomatic efforts to settle the Cambodian and South Vietnamese conflicts.

Costs of U.S. Involvement in Vietnam: 1960-75

| Year | Troop Levels[1] | Casualties | | | | | POWs | MIAs[6] | War Costs Since FY 1965[7] |
| | | Killed Hostile | Killed Non-hostile | Wounded | | | | | |
				H[4]	NH[5]				
1960	900	0	0	0	0	0	0	$
1961	3,200	11	2	2	1	0	0	
1962	11,300	31	21	41	37	0	0	
1963	16,300	78	36	218	193	0	0	
1964	23,300	147	48	522	517	3	4	
1965	184,300	1,369	359	3,308	2,806	74	54	700,000,000
1966	385,300	5,008	1,045	16,526	13,567	97	204	15,119,000,000
1967	485,600	9,377	1,680	32,369	29,654	179	226	17,161,000,000
1968	536,100	14,589	1,919	46,796	46,021	95	294	19,278,000,000
1969	475,200	9,414	2,113	32,940	37,276	13	176	19,762,000,000
1970	334,600	4,221	1,844	15,211	15,432	12	86	14,401,000,000
1971	156,800	1,381	968	4,767	4,169	11	79	9,570,000,000
1972	24,200	300	251	587	634	105	209	6,982,000,000
1973	0	237[3]	34	24	36	2	2	5,171,000,000
1974	0	207[3]	19	0	0	0	0	1,290,000,000
1975	0	113	47	18	32	0	0	1,281,000,000
Total:	202,846[2]	46,483	10,386	153,329	150,375	591	1,334	$110,715,000,000

[1] As of Dec. 31 of each year.
[2] Average troop strength, 1960-72.
[3] All but 12 deaths in 1973 and all in 1974 were changes in status of persons previously listed as missing in action.
[4] Required hospital care.
[5] Did not require hospital care.
[6] The Defense Department listed 728 men missing in action (MIAs) as of Dec. 31, 1976. The discrepancy between this figure and the year-by-year total was attributed by the Pentagon to changes in status of persons originally listed as missing and later declared dead or returned from captivity.
[7] Estimates by fiscal year. Includes only expenditures that would not otherwise have been spent on national defense.

Source: Department of Defense

North Vietnamese Offensive. On March 5, North Vietnamese forces launched a major offensive in the central highlands of South Vietnam. By March 17 South Vietnam had begun abandoning provinces as the defeat turned into a rout.

Yao Against Incentives. On March 7 the *Peking Review* published another article in the campaign against incentives for workers in China. Written by Yao Wenyuan, one of the "gang of four" and a leader of the Cultural Revolution, the article called on local party leaders to explain the dangers of material incentives to the workers, and called for the removal of such "bourgeois rights" from China's socialist society. (*See March 31, 1975*)

China Asks U.S. to Stop Aid. On March 9 the Peking *People's Daily* published a government statement calling on the U.S. to terminate immediately its support of the Lon Nol government in Cambodia.

Singapore and China. On March 12 S. Rajaratnam, the Foreign Minister of Singapore, arrived in China for a ten-day official visit, the first ever made by an official of the government of that country. The visit had no immediate result; Singapore remained the one Pacific nation withholding recognition of the PRC.

War Criminals Released. On March 19 the Chinese Supreme People's Court granted a special amnesty to all "war criminals" in custody. Of the 293 released, 290 were referred to as supporters of Chiang Kai-shek. It was announced that those who wished to go to Taiwan would be allowed to do so.

The release was seen as a Chinese signal indicating desire to settle the Taiwan issue and move forward on normalization of relations with the U.S.

On Dec. 23 China released the 70 remaining Nationalists.

Zhang Attacks Incentives. On March 31 the Xinhua news agency published an article by Vice Premier Zhang Chunqiao, one of the leading members of the "radical" group and a member of the "gang of four," that was sharply critical of using material incentives to spur production. In addition, he wrote that China had still not completely rid itself of private ownership, "which still exists in parts of industry, agriculture as well as commerce." Zhang referred to such trends as an "evil wind" and criticized those who "are permeated with bourgeois ideas; they scramble for fame and gain and feel proud instead of ashamed for this." According to Zhang, workers should be spurred by ideology, not material rewards. The man most identified with the opposing viewpoint was Vice Premier Deng Xiaoping.

Chinese Visit Canceled. On April 4 *The New York Times* reported that a Chinese singing troupe scheduled to visit the U.S. from March 29 to April 27 had been "postponed indefinitely" by the State Department because the troupe would not drop from its repertoire a song calling for the liberation of Taiwan. Peking protested this as a violation of the Shanghai Communiqué.

Chiang Kai-shek Dies. On April 5 Chiang Kai-shek, President of the Republic of China and the last of World War II's major leaders, died of a heart attack in Taipei. Long a symbol of the U.S. policy of opposition to dealing with the Chinese Communists on the mainland, Chiang was succeeded as president by the former vice president, Yen Chia-kan (Yan Jiagan).

Chiang's death signalled no immediate change in Sino-American relations, nor did it lead to a change in Taiwan's refusal to negotiate with the mainland.

China to Buy Canadian Wheat. On April 7 it was reported that China had agreed to purchase 42 million bushels of wheat from Canada. The announcement followed Chinese cancellations of all wheat orders from the U.S. *(See Feb. 27, 1975)*

Ford on China. On April 10 President Ford underlined U.S. commitment to the Shanghai Communiqué, but promised no new moves toward recognition of Peking. *(Text, p. 328)*

Spratly Islands Dispute. Between April 11 and 29 the South Vietnamese "Liberation Navy" attacked and occupied six islands in the Spratly Archipelago (Nansha); on May 6 the Ministry of Defense in Taiwan averred it still held the small islands, which are claimed by Vietnam, China and the Philippines. *(Map, p. 115)*

Cambodia Falls. On April 16 the Cambodian government in Phnom Penh surrendered to the insurgent Communist-led Khmer Rouge.

President Lon Nol had left the country on April 1.

On the same day, U.S. officials in Saigon began to organize the withdrawal of all American citizens from Vietnam.

China and Cambodia. On April 18 the Peking *People's Daily* heralded the recent victory of the Khmer Rouge in Cambodia, announcing it as a victory for Mao Tse-tung's concept of people's war, and a defeat for the U.S. In addition, claimed the article, it showed up the Soviet Union as a "political gambler," and an unsuccessful one at that, for having "staked all on the treacherous Lon Nol clique."

China and Pakistan. On April 20 Chinese Vice Premier Li Xiannian arrived in Pakistan for a six-day visit. During his stay, Li reaffirmed Chinese support for Pakistan, praised the government of Premier Ali Bhutto, and voiced opposition to Indian expansion. During the visit, it was announced that China had offered to supply Pakistan with a wide range of textile machinery and a cement-making plant on extremely good terms.

On May 25 Dong Lin, an official of the Chinese Central Broadcasting Administration and the leader of a Chinese radio and television delegation visiting Pakistan, said in a speech that "In the event of another conflict the people of Pakistan will find their Chinese friends even closer than they were during the 1965 and 1971 wars."

China and Cambodia. On April 25 the recently installed Khmer Rouge's Royal Cambodian Government of National Union announced that Prince Norodom Sihanouk, who had been living in exile in China for five years, was to be the chief of state for life. The news seemed to indicate success for China in wooing the Cambodians.

China and North Korea. On April 26 China and North Korea signed a joint communiqué at the end of the visit of President Kim Il Sung to China. The communiqué affirmed Chinese support for the Koreans, and repeated demands for the withdrawal of U.S. forces from the south. Unlike earlier statements by Kim himself, the communiqué called for the peaceful unification of Korea, which reflected the Chinese position.

Chiang Ching-kuo to Chairman. On April 28 Nationalist Premier Chiang Ching-kuo, long-time heir apparent to his father, Chiang Kai-shek, was elected chairman of the ruling Nationalist Party on Taiwan.

China Denounces India. On April 29 the Chinese government denounced India's decision to annex the small state of Sikkim, located along the border between the two countries: "China absolutely does not recognize India's illegal annexation"; Peking accused India of indulging in the "fond dream of a great Indian empire" and of subjecting its neighbors to 20 years of "control, interference, subversion and bullying."

Americans Evacuated. On April 29 President Ford announced that the evacuation of all U.S. personnel from Vietnam had been completed. Ford said: "This action closes a chapter in the American experience" and asked "all Americans to close ranks" and "avoid recriminations."

South Vietnam Falls. On April 30 South Vietnamese President Duong Van Minh ("Big Minh") announced the unconditional surrender of the Saigon government and its armed forces to the Vietcong. Communist troops took over Saigon the same day.

Chinese Celebrate Vietnam Victory. On May 2 Peking staged a rally, attended by most major Chinese leaders, celebrating the victory of the communists in Vietnam. Minister of Defense Ye Jianying called the victory a blow against "imperialism, colonialism, and hegemonism." The South Vietnamese representative, Tran Binh, said that the victory had been helped by the support and sympathy of the people of China, "other socialist countries," and others "including the progressive people of the U.S."

Evacuations in Cambodia. On May 5 the U.S. State Department said that the Cambodian Communists had forcibly evacuated the entire population of Phnom Penh, Kompong Chang, and Siem Reap.

On June 12 *The New York Times* reported that the "long march" of nearly 2 million people from the cities to the countryside had ended.

Chinese Attacks on Moscow. On May 9 the Peking *People's Daily* published a lead editorial that accused the Kremlin of having "accomplished what Hitler wanted but failed to carry out." Moscow, it said, had used its role as a liberator in the Second World War "to perpetuate its dominance of Eastern Europe." Other Chinese commentary accused the Soviet Union of trying to bully its way to control of Pacific fishing, of seeking worldwide maritime dominance through worldwide naval exercises, and of trying to cover up its economic failure with massive loans from the West.

Deng to France. On May 12 Chinese Vice Premier Deng Xiaoping and Foreign Minister Qiao Guanhua arrived in France for a seven-day official visit. On the orders of French President Giscard d'Estaing, Deng was treated with the protocol normally reserved for a head of state. This reflected France's pleasure as being the first Western nation ever visited by a senior PRC official.

Although the Chinese leaders' speeches offered no new departures, they created an uproar, particularly from the French Communists, who were enraged at Chinese criticism of the Soviet Union.

For their part, the Chinese saw France as a possible obstacle to the West European unity they felt was necessary for successful opposition to the Soviets. Commenting privately, the French said they did not share China's view of Western Europe as some kind of "war-machine" against the Soviet Union.

No communiqué was issued, but several measures were taken to insure continued Sino-French high level contacts.

Mayagüez Seized. On May 12, Cambodian soldiers boarded and seized an American merchant ship, the *Mayagüez,* in the Gulf of Siam and took the 39-man crew captive.

On May 14, 200 U.S. marines landed on Koh Tang Island and effected the release of the captive crew. U.S. war planes also launched raids against Cambodian military installations at the same time.

ASEAN Nations Meet. On May 15 the foreign ministers of the five member-nations of the Association of Southeast Asian Nations (ASEAN) ended their meeting in Kuala Lumpur, Malaysia. The nations failed to complete their treaty of amity and cooperation, and decided to postpone the signing of a treaty.

Soviet Attack on Peking. On May 26 the Soviet journal *Sovietskaya Rossiya* accused Chinese Party Chairman Mao Tse-tung and his group of wanting to preserve the American presence in Southeast Asia and of believing that war is a good thing. In other articles, China was attacked for maintaining close relations with the Chilean military junta.

Deng on U.S. Policy. On June 3 *The Times* of London reported that Chinese Vice Premier Deng Xiaoping told a group of visiting American newspaper editors that China acknowledged the difficulty of the U.S.' pulling out of Taiwan. Still, said Deng, the U.S. eventually must break diplomatic relations with Taiwan, end the defense treaty, and withdraw all its forces. China recognized that the U.S. troops could not be withdrawn from Japan. As for Korea, Deng said that China's support for North Korea was really a buffer against the South. As for a possible American-Taiwan connection, Deng explained his preference for the "Japanese solution" by which an American representative ostensibly would handle only commercial and consular affairs. Deng rejected the notion of replacing the Taipei embassy with a liaison office. On a global scale, Deng called for stronger American reaction to the Soviet threat.

China and the Olympics. On June 3 the Chinese Xinhua news agency reported a speech by the leader of the PRC's All China Sports Federation protesting the refusal of the International Olympic Committee to admit the ACSF as the sole legitimate representative of China. The committee wanted to admit the Taiwan delegation as well as the PRC athletes.

U.S. Troops to Leave Thailand. On June 7 the U.S. and Thailand issued a joint statement making public the timetable for withdrawal of American troops and planes from Thailand. All U.S. forces were scheduled to leave by March 1976.

The announcement followed a request from Premier Kukrit Pramoj on March 17 that all 25,000 U.S. troops and 350 U.S. planes be withdrawn within a year.

Last Jets Leave Taiwan. On June 7 the U.S. State Department disclosed that the last squadron of 18 F-4 Phantom jet fighter-bombers had been removed from Taiwan in May, with 450 support personnel departing at the same time. The statement also announced that the U.S. planned to reduce the remaining U.S. personnel on the island by 30 percent — to 2,800 — by the end of June.

Philippines and China. On June 7, Philippine President Ferdinand E. Marcos arrived in China for a five-day official visit. Accompanied by his wife and daughters, he was met by Chou En-lai and Deng Xiaoping.

On June 9 the two governments signed a joint communiqué which announced the establishment of diplomatic relations. No reference was made by either side to their conflicting claims to some of the Spratly (Nansha) Islands.

On the same day, the two nations also signed a trade agreement.

Northrop Investigation. On June 9 and 10, officials of the Northrop Corp., testifying before the Senate Foreign Relations Subcommittee on Multinational Corporations, described the formation of a Swiss company designed to win contracts abroad by the use of influential foreigners in Taiwan, among other countries. The officials said the company was formed on a no-questions-asked basis to allow prominent foreigners to earn lucrative commissions for helping Northrop without being identified with the company.

Joint Venture Dropped. On June 12, Japanese trading sources were quoted as saying that the joint development of the Tyumen oil field in the eastern Soviet Union had been abandoned because of its link with the second railroad from Tyumen to the Pacific coast. The line would have to run close to the Chinese border, and the Chinese had expressed apprehension about it.

Deng on World Politics. On June 30 the prime minister of Thailand, Kukrit Pramoj arrived in China for an official visit. At a welcoming banquet Chinese Vice Premier Deng Xiaoping said that although one of the "superpowers" (the U.S.) had just suffered a defeat and had been forced to withdraw from Indochina, "the other superpower [the U.S.S.R.] with wild ambitions has extended its tentacles far and wide. It insatiably seeks new military bases in Southeast Asia and sends its naval vessels" there. "The spectre of its expansionism haunts Southeast Asia, as it hankers for converting this region into its sphere of influence some day."

Sino-Thai Relations. On July 1 China established diplomatic relations with Thailand. The two governments issued a joint communiqué in Peking, providing for the settlement of disputes by peaceful means, the renunciation of subversion and aggression, and opposition to hegemony or spheres of influence.

Sino-Soviet Split Heats Up. On July 3 the battle of words between China and the Soviet Union moved to a new level as the Chinese Xinhua news agency published a long commentary that accused the Soviet leadership of following in Hitler's footsteps. Like Hitler, Soviet party leader Leonid Brezhnev was accused of making a lot of noise about peace and disarmament while preparing for war and militarizing the economy. Like Hitler, Brezhnev was accused of invading other countries on the basis of absurd pretexts and, like Hitler, was said to feint to the east in order to attack the west. *(See Aug. 20, 1975)*

Chinese Army in the Factories. On July 19, regular Chinese army units were sent into factories in the Hangzhou area to maintain production in the face of more outbreaks of violence.

Call for End to SEATO. On July 24 Thailand Prime Minister Kukrit Pramoj and Philippine President Ferdinand E. Marcos, meeting in Manila, issued a joint communiqué calling for the gradual phasing out of the Southeast Asia Treaty Organization.

Helsinki Agreement. On Aug. 1, following a three-day conference in Helsinki, Finland, the representatives of 35 nations signed a 30,000-word "final act" of the Conference on Security and Cooperation in Europe. The pact, pacific in tone, constituted recognition of the present, post-World War II borders of the European states and contained strong statements on human rights.

Japanese Reaffirm Treaty. On Aug. 5 Japanese Prime Minister Takeo Miki arrived in the U.S. for two days of talks with President Ford. In a joint communiqué, the two countries reaffirmed support of their treaty of mutual cooperation and security. Peking reacted favorably.

Congressmen to China. Between Aug. 6 and Aug. 29, two separate congressional delegations visited China. Both groups were received by Vice Premier Deng Xiaoping. The Americans were given the impression that China accepted and attached importance to the role of the U.S. as a Pacific power, and did not favor further withdrawal from the region in the near future, with the exception of Taiwan.

Sino-Japanese Agreement. On Aug. 15, after two years of negotiation, China and Japan signed a fishery agreement in Tokyo. Although the agreement was a real step forward in relations between the two countries, the two sides remained blocked in their efforts to conclude a treaty of friendship due to Chinese insistence on a clause condemning "hegemony" (i.e., the Soviet Union).

Coup in Bangladesh. On Aug. 15 Bangladesh President Sheik Mujibar Rahman was overthrown and killed. The new leadership led the country away from its close ties to India and aligned it more closely with Pakistan and other Islamic states. China, which originally opposed the secession movement in 1971, began to make diplomatic initiatives toward the new leaders. *(See Oct. 4, 1975)*

Soviet Response. On Aug. 20 the Soviet Communist Party theoretical journal *Kommunist* published a 10,000-word editorial attack on what it identified as "Maoism," accusing China of "increasing world tension, not stopping at the unleashing of a new world war. . . . In our days," the editorial claimed, "Maoism carries a danger for the people of all states, regardless of their social systems." All "true communists" were called upon to "smash Maoism." The editorial made clear that there was no possibility of reconciliation with a regime headed by Mao.

Communist Takeover in Laos. On Aug. 23 Vientiane radio proclaimed the complete takeover of the country by the communist-led Pathet Lao.

On Aug. 26, leaders of the Pathet Lao issued a proclamation of intentions which recognized King Savang Vatthana and Premier Souvanna Phouma as well as the coalition government's National Political Council.

On Aug. 28 acting Foreign Minister Phoune Sipraseuth announced the replacement of 185 American advisers with 1,500 Soviet technicians.

Sihanouk to Cambodia. On Sept. 9 Prince Norodom Sihanouk, nominal chief of state of the new Cambodian Government *(see April 25, 1975)* arrived in Phnom Penh, where he was greeted by government leaders. On Sept. 28 Sihanouk left Cambodia, returning to Peking on Oct. 12. Sihanouk later stated that the Khmer Rouge leaders wanted him only as a figurehead. This appeared to be enough, however, for Chinese leaders, who had signed an economic and technical cooperation agreement with Cambodia on Aug. 18.

On Sept. 13 *Le Monde* reported that China was extending nearly $1 billion without interest in economic and military aid to Cambodia over five to six years. This was the most aid ever given to any one country by China, in an effort to offset growing Vietnamese and Soviet presence in Indochina.

China and the EEC. On Sept. 15 China opened formal relations with the Common Market when Li Lianbi, then Chinese ambassador to Belgium, presented his credentials to the president of the EEC Council of Ministers.

The Soviet Union does not have relations with the Common Market.

Modernization of Agriculture. On Sept. 15 the National Conference on Learning from Dazhai opened in Peking. Attended by 7,000 leaders from all over China, the month-long conference discussed the modernization of China's agriculture and laid plans for its implementation. A summary was given by Vice Premier Hua Guofeng, who announced that China would extend farm mechanization to the rest of China by 1980, "pushing the national economy forward so that China will be advancing in the front rank of the world before the end of this century." The model for the move would be the commune of Dazhai, in Shanxi Province, noted for its self-reliance, modernization of production and raising of grain under severe conditions. *(See Dec. 24, 1976)*

China Frees More Prisoners. On Sept. 22 the Xinhua news agency announced the release of 144 imprisoned infiltrators from Taiwan. The men had been captured between September 1962, and September 1965.

SEATO to Be Dissolved. On Sept. 24 the foreign ministers of the Southeast Asian Treaty Organization (SEATO), meeting in New York, agreed that because of the end of the war in Indochina, the organization should be phased out "in an orderly and systematic manner." *(See June 30, 1977)*

U.S. Mayors' Visit Canceled. On Sept. 26 the *Peking Review* reported that the visit of 14 U.S. mayors who were supposed to visit China in September had been canceled at the last minute. The difficulty was the inclusion among the mayors of Carlos Romero Barcelo, mayor of San Juan in Puerto Rico and a supporter of statehood within the U.S. for Puerto Rico. The Chinese, who supported independence for Puerto Rico, said that it was "inappropriate" for Barcelo to visit and "inconvenient" to receive him.

Qiao on Chinese Foreign Policy. On Sept. 26 China Foreign Minister Qiao Guanhua made a major address to the U.N. General Assembly in New York in which he offered a general survey of international affairs as seen from China.

Qiao stated that the two superpowers were still the fundamental cause of unrest in the world. Although they could sometimes reach such agreements as SALT or the Helsinki accords, these were only a facade behind which they continued their antagonism. Qiao specifically attacked the renewed Soviet insistence on an Asian Collective Security System, which he said was motivated by a desire to "fill the vacuum" left by the Americans.

Qiao firmly supported various Third World proposals to change the terms of international trade and to help development.

China Recognizes Bangladesh. In another departure from customary policy, China on Oct. 4 opened diplomatic relations with Bangladesh. China had supported Pakistan's efforts in 1971 to prevent the emergence of the new nation, which formerly had been part of Pakistan. *(See Aug. 15, 1975)*

Chinese Protest. On Oct. 14 China accused the U.S. of "undisguised interference in China's internal affairs" by supporting Tibetans who sought restoration of the exiled Dalai Lama to power in Tibet. The U.S. rejected the complaint.

The problem had arisen over the opening of an "Office of Tibet" in New York City, which published news letters about Tibetan affairs. The office was registered with the U.S. State Department as an agent of the Dalai Lama, the Tibetan spiritual leader who had fled Tibet in 1959 following Chinese occupation of the area.

Peking's protest coincided with the scheduled arrival in the U.S. later in October of a Tibetan song and dance ensemble. On Aug. 8 the Chinese liaison office had asked the State Department to ban the troupe, but the U.S. rejected the request on Sept. 24.

Kissinger to Peking. On Oct. 19 U.S. Secretary of State Henry Kissinger arrived in China for a four-day visit. The exchanges at the welcoming banquet were more restrained than in the past, with Chinese Foreign Minister Qiao Guanhua stating only that "on the whole, Sino-U.S. relations have moved forward in the last few years." Qiao went on to warn Kissinger that "to base oneself on illusions" about the Soviet Union "will only alert the ambitions of expansionism." Kissinger replied that the U.S. would resist hegemony, but it "will also make every effort to avoid needless confrontations when it can do so without threatening the security of a third country."

No joint communiqué was issued after the visit.

Chinese Critical of Firing. On Nov. 7 the Xinhua news agency, while offering no comment of its own, carried U.S. and other foreign comments critical of the firing of Defense Secretary James Schlesinger. Because Peking usually ignores such cabinet changes, analysts felt that this was the Chinese way of registering disapproval of the move. Because the Chinese saw Schlesinger as strongly anti-Soviet, they felt his firing was part of President Ford's decision to speed up détente with Moscow.

To underline their view, Xinhua, at about the same time, also carried articles about the failure of appeasement prior to World War II. *(See Sept. 6, 1976)*

Controls Relaxed in China. On Nov. 20 *The Times* of London reported a relaxation of government controls over culture in China and noted the reappearance of works of composers, poets and authors who had been outlawed during the Cultural Revolution. The report linked the relaxation to the apparent loss of power by Jiang Qing, wife of Chinese Party Chairman Mao Tse-tung and a major leader of the Cultural Revolution.

South China Sea Islands Dispute. On Nov. 25 the Peking *People's Daily* published an article that spelled out in full Chinese claims to the Spratly, Paracel and other islands in the South China Sea. No reference was made to the fact that Vietnam and the Philippines garrisoned some of the islands and have also claimed them. The article claimed that China's exclusive sovereignty "is widely recognized by various countries." *(Map, p. 115)*

Ford to China. On Dec. 1 President Gerald Ford arrived in China for a five-day visit. Although the visit took place in a cordial atmosphere, no joint communiqué was issued and no obvious results ensued. A meeting with Communist Party Chairman Mao Tse-tung gave Ford's visit the official stamp of approval, but Mao's age and the illness of Premier Chou En-lai, who died soon after on Jan. 7, 1976, left further Sino-American developments unclear.

Chinese Vice Premier Deng Xiaoping later claimed, in 1977, that Ford had agreed to the three Chinese demands for normalization, and had promised to recognize Peking during his second term.

The Pacific Doctrine. On Dec. 7 President Ford stopped in Honolulu on his return from Asia and announced the "Pacific Doctrine," which officials later explained was a continuation of the Nixon Doctrine, first announced in 1969. The key elements of the doctrine, according to Ford, were a stable balance of power based on continued American strength; close partnership with Japan as a "pillar" of U.S. strategy; normalization of relations with China; resolution of the outstanding Southeast Asian and Korean problems; and the creation of economic cooperation in Asia.

Peking Changes Stance. On Dec. 12 the Peking *People's Daily* published an article which called the Soviet Union "the most dangerous source of war." Previous articles had not said which of the two superpowers — the U.S.S.R. or the U.S. — was more likely to cause a war.

The article was preceded by a spate of articles by the Chinese news agency Xinhua in December that reviewed U.S. efforts to achieve détente with the Russians and argued the futility of trying to limit Moscow with "scrap paper." Xinhua said that the Soviets had close the "gap" in the nuclear arms race, and were in a superior position in conventional arms.

Sino-British Trade. On Dec. 13 Rolls Royce of Great Britain and the China National Technical Import Corporation signed a $160 million agreement for the supply and construction in China of Spey jet engines, the engine which powers the McDonnell-Douglas Phantom fighter-bomber of the RAF and Royal Navy. It was suspected that China would use the engines to build their own supersonic fighter bombers.

Chinese Release Soviet Helicopter. On Dec. 27, in a surprise move, the Chinese government announced that it was releasing the Russian helicopter and its three crewmen, detained since March 1974. *(See March 15, 1974)* The move did not seem to indicate any reduction in Sino-Soviet tensions, and the Soviet ambassador in Peking was quoted as describing the Chinese action as a "complete mystery."

Eisenhowers to China. On Dec. 29 David and Julie Eisenhower arrived in China for a five-day visit. Newsmen noted that they were greeted with a rare warmth, and were able to meet with Chinese Party Chairman Mao Tse-tung. Some analysts felt the Eisenhower visit signaled the return to a softer line on the U.S. by Peking.

1976

Deng Xiaoping Criticized — Chou En-lai Dies — Japan Imports More Chinese Oil — 18th China A-Test — Hua Guofeng Becomes Premier — Nixon Returns to Peking — ASEAN Meets — Peking Riots — China-India Accord — China-Egypt Trade Agreements — Carter on Sino-U.S. Relations — Vietnam Unified — Carter Nominated — Korean Skirmish — Ford Nominated — Schlesinger in China — Mao Dies — Chinese Government Shakeup — Coup in Thailand — Carter Elected — Sino-Soviet Border Talks — Chinese Radicals Purged — Baoding Riots

Growing Criticism of Deng Xiaoping. On Jan. 1 and again on Feb. 6 the Peking *People's Daily* published editorials critical of Chinese Vice Premier Deng Xiaoping and his supporters. Without naming Deng, the articles criticized those who said that "stability and unity" were more important than "class struggle" and claimed that "revisionists" were trying to "reverse the dictates" of the Cultural Revolution. The last statement referred to the relaxation of bans on culture put into effect during the summer and fall of 1975. *(See Nov. 20, 1975)*

U.S. Congresswomen to China. On Jan. 2 Chinese Vice Premier Deng Xiaoping met with a delegation of U.S. congresswomen visiting China. In one of his last public engagements prior to his purge *(see April 7, 1976)*, Deng lectured on the dangers of the U.S.-Soviet détente. He asserted that détente had not brought about disarmament or achieved any of its stated goals. He doubted that the U.S. was properly alert to the scale of the increased Soviet arms production and its threat to world peace. Deng was specifically quoted as having referred to "the failure of détente and the naiveté with which the United States has pursued it as an end in itself."

Mao's Poems Published. On Jan. 1 the Peking *People's Daily* published two poems written by Chinese Party Chairman Mao Tse-tung in 1965 which attacked Soviet "revisionism."

Kampuchea Established. On Jan. 3, "the State of Democratic Kampuchea" was proclaimed, replacing "Cambodia" in official usage.

Chou En-lai Dies. On Jan. 8, Chinese Premier Chou En-lai died in Peking at 82. He had been suffering from cancer since 1972. Surprisingly, Vice Premier Deng Xiaoping not only did not succeed him as premier, but was widely attacked in a furious press campaign which began in the following weeks.

Chinese Oil Reserves. On Jan. 8 *The New York Times* reported that a November 1975 CIA study had concluded that China would be unlikely to achieve a major role as an oil exporter within the next decade. This study contradicted an earlier 1975 analysis produced by non-governmental China experts that concluded that China would achieve the 1974 export levels of Saudi Arabia by 1988. *(See July 1, 1977)*

Japan to Increase Oil Imports. On Jan. 22, Japanese Prime Minister Takeo Fukuda announced that Japan planned to increase the volume of imported oil from China.

By this time, Japan was importing 3 percent of its oil from China.

China Explodes Another Bomb. On Jan. 23, China successfully conducted its 18th nuclear test. The Xinhua news agency announcement the following day repeated the statements usually made on such occasions — that these "necessary and limited" tests were conducted to break the nuclear monopoly of the superpowers and with the "ultimate aim of abolishing nuclear weapons." China's "no first use" pledge was reiterated, as well as its determination to work with others to achieve the eventual total prohibition and destruction of nuclear weapons.

South Sea Islands Dispute. On Jan. 25 *The New York Times* reported that Chinese ships had greatly expanded their naval exercises in the South China Sea since autumn 1975, moving further south and showing more assertiveness.

The Philippines, which also claimed islands in the area, was reported to have built an airfield on one of the islands under its control.

The Vietnamese army newspaper warned that Hanoi's armed forces were ready to "go as far as the . . . sea islands to maintain the security of the fatherland."

Taiwan authorities were scheduled to send a small convoy guarded by a destroyer to resupply their garrison on the one island held by them. *(Map, p. 115)*

Hua Guofeng Becomes Premier. On Feb. 7 it was announced in Peking that Hua Guofeng, minister of security and a vice premier, had been named acting premier, succeeding Chou En-lai, who died Jan. 8. Deng Xiaoping, the senior vice premier, had been acting for Chou during the latter's year-long illness.

More Criticism of Deng. On Feb. 10 a 45-page wall poster appeared at Peking University that was sharply critical of Chinese Vice Premier Deng Xiaoping, accusing him of being a "capitalist roader who formed cliques around himself" and denigrated ideology in favor of economic progress. Although the poster did not refer to Deng by name, it quoted his famous statement, made during the 1960s, that "I do not care whether a cat is black or white; the important thing is whether it catches mice," which suggests Deng's more pragmatic, moderate approach to politics.

Sino-Soviet Clash. On Feb. 12 the Chinese Xinhua news agency reported a border clash between Chinese and Soviet troops in northwest Xinjiang.

Nixon to China. On Feb. 21 former President Richard Nixon arrived in Peking for a nine-day visit. The Chinese supplied a plane for both legs of the visit. Ostensibly the visit was timed to correspond with the four-year anniversary of the signing of the Shanghai communiqué. Coincidentally, Nixon became the first westerner of note to spend much time with the new acting premier, Hua Guofeng. Nixon also met with Chinese Communist Party Chairman Mao Tse-tung. Few details of the talks were released.

The visit generated controversy in the U.S. and was hardly calculated to please the Ford administration, coming as it did on the eve of the New Hampshire primary. President Ford's campaign advisers feared it would hurt his chances there by reminding voters of Ford's pardon of Nixon.

After Nixon's return, Ford let it be known that neither he nor Secretary of State Henry Kissinger had any plans to "debrief" him, although "in time" President Ford might talk to him. Nixon was expected to turn in a written report of his visit to the State Department. *(See March 3, 1976)*

Analysts have noted that the Chinese purpose in inviting Nixon was to indicate to the U.S. that the recent leadership changes would not jeopardize the recent Sino-American rapprochement.

ASEAN Meets. On Feb. 23 the members of the Association of Southeast Asian Nations (ASEAN) held their first summit meeting in eight years at Denpasar, Indonesia. After the meeting, the leaders issued a call for economic cooperation.

Goldwater and China. On Feb. 25 Sen. Barry Goldwater, R-Ariz., sharply criticized former President Nixon's trip to China and suggested that Nixon could do the U.S. a favor by staying in China. Goldwater also accused Nixon of breaking the law by making statements on U.S. foreign policy in Peking.

On March 21 the Chinese Xinhua news agency published a sharp attack on Goldwater and his comments, the first such statement by Xinhua in several years.

Nixon's Report. On March 3 White House press secretary Ron Nessen disclosed that Secretary of State Henry Kissinger, without the prior knowledge of President Ford, had arranged for former President Nixon to provide a written report on his February trip to China. *(See Feb. 21, 1976)*

On March 22 Nessen reported that Ford had received Nixon's report the week before and had found it "very interesting and useful."

China Lauds ASEAN. On March 5 the *Peking Review* published an article commenting favorably on the first summit meeting of ASEAN, held from Feb. 23 to 24. The article stated that "as a result of the meeting, unity and cooperation among the ASEAN nations have been strengthened while the 'Asian collective security system' hawked by the Soviet Union has been spurned."

More Troop Reductions. On March 11, the *Boston Globe* reported that the U.S. would continue to reduce the number of troops it maintained on Taiwan, a force of 2,500. The article also revealed that the reduction was the result of a promise made by President Ford to the Chinese during his December 1975 visit. This latter report was unconfirmed.

Gates to China. On March 19 President Ford named former U.S. Secretary of Defense Thomas S. Gates to head the U.S. Liaison Office in China, succeeding George Bush.

U.S. to Withdraw Thailand Troops. On March 20 the government of Thailand asked the U.S. to remove all but 270 military personnel by July 4, 1976. The U.S. had hoped to leave 3,000 troops in Thailand to man various installations.

On March 21, the U.S. military ceased all operations in Thailand in preparation for its final withdrawal. *(See July 20, 1976)*

Deng Criticized. On May 15 the Xinhua news agency, marking the closing of Canton's semi-annual trade fair, criticized Chinese Vice Premier Deng Xiaoping as a "slavish comprador" for his trade policy, and gave unusual stress to the primary importance of "self-reliance." A similar criticism was published the following day.

Rioting in Peking. On April 5 a mass demonstration at the Tiananmen Square in Peking in memory of Chou En-lai erupted into violence as supporters of Deng Xiaoping fought with supporters of the "gang of four."

Wall posters which appeared in Peking in 1978 said that Deng Xiaoping was purged by Mao because of the demonstrations. *(See April 7, 1976)*

Hua Guofeng to the Top. On April 7 the Central Committee of the Chinese Communist Party formally named Hua Guofeng to succeed the recently deceased Chou En-lai as premier, and to replace the radical Wang Hongwen as first vice chairman of the party (under Mao Tse-tung). With Mao seriously ill, Hua had become the most powerful man in China.

On the same day, the Central Committee passed a resolution which stripped Deng Xiaoping, who had been Chou's heir-apparent, of all his positions, and reduced him to merely a member of the party.

Demonstrations in Peking. On April 9 Chinese Foreign Minister Qiao Guanhua and other government officials led demonstrations of more than 100,000 persons in Peking supporting the dismissal of Deng Xiaoping.

China and India to Resume Relations. On April 15 Indian External Affairs Minister Y. B. Chavan announced that for the first time in 15 years, India would send an ambassador to China. China was expected to reciprocate. *(See July 24, 1976)*

On the same day, India signed a five-year trade agreement with the Soviet Union.

South Sea Islands Dispute. On April 17 China issued a strongly worded statement repeating its claim to sovereignty over the Spratly (Nansha) Islands and indicating that the Swedish and Philippines consortium for exploring oil there was an encroachment on Chinese territory.

On May 28 the ministry of foreign affairs on Taiwan issued a statement claiming sovereignty over both the Spratly and Paracel (Xisha) Islands, saying that no country had the right to enter into contracts for oil on the Reed Bank.

On June 5 South Vietnam reaffirmed its claims over the islands, as did the Philippines on June 16. *(Map, p.115)*

Egypt and China. On April 18 Egyptian Vice President Hosni Mubarak arrived in China for a seven-day official visit. The trip followed Chinese acclamation of Egypt's abrogation of its treaty of friendship with the Soviet Union and China's statement of its readiness to send military supplies to Egypt.

On April 21 Cairo radio reported that China had agreed to sell MiG parts to Egypt. Various trade agreements were also signed. Several comments were made to the effect that the new Sino-Egyptian relationship represented China's "first foothold in the Middle East," a notion which was dismissed as nonsense by the Egyptians.

On April 21 U.S. Air Force officials said China apparently would supply spare parts for Egypt's MiG-21s, in addition to MiG-17s and MiG-19s.

On March 17 India had confirmed that it had rejected Egyptian requests for spare parts for MiG-21s.

South Africa Recognizes Taiwan. On April 26 the government of South Africa established full diplomatic relations with the Republic of China on Taiwan.

Bomb Explodes in Peking. On April 29 the Soviet news agency Tass reported that a bomb had exploded at the entrance of the Soviet embassy in Peking, reportedly killing two Chinese guards.

China's Armed Strength

China's military and missile capability in the late 1970s was far behind those of other major countries and military alliances — essentially a defensive system. According to *Jane's Weapon Systems,* "The Chinese now have a capability for nuclear strikes by missiles and bombers all around the periphery of the PRC. The Chinese have no present capability to attack the Continental United States directly and are unlikely to obtain one for at least several years. . . ."[1]

The estimates of Chinese military strength below were compiled by the International Institute for Strategic Studies.[2]

TROOPS

Total regular forces	4,325,000
Army	3,625,000
Navy	300,000
Air Force	400,000

Paramilitary Forces

Public security force and a civilian militia with various elements: the Armed Militia, up to 7 million, organized into about 75 divisions and an unknown number of regiments; the Urban Militia, of several million; the Civilian Production and Construction Corps, about 4 million; and the Ordinary and Basic Militia, 75-100 million, who receive some basic training but are generally unarmed.

LAND WEAPONS AND VEHICLES

Tanks (Soviet IS-2 hy, T-34 and Chinese-produced Type-59/-63 med, Type-60 (PT-76) amph and Type-62 lt)	10,000
Armored personnel carriers (M-1967, K-63)	3,500
Guns and howitzers (122 mm, 130 mm, 152 mm, incl. SU-76, SU-85, SU-100 and ISU-122 sp. art'y)	18,000
Mortar (82, 90, 120, and 160 mm), **rocket launchers** (132 and 140 mm), **recoilless rifles** (57, 75 and 82 mm), **antitank guns** (57, 85 and 100 mm) and **anti-aircraft guns** (37, 57, 85 and 100 mm)	20,000

SHIPS AND SUBMARINES

Major surface combat ships	23
Han-class nuclear-powered submarine	1
G-class submarine with missile tubes	1
Fleet submarines (incl. 50 Soviet R-,21 W, 2 *Ming*-class)	73
Luta-class destroyers with *Styx* surface-to-surface missiles (SSM) (more building)	7
Ex-Soviet *Gordy*-class destroyers with *Styx* SSM	4
Frigates (4 *Riga*-type with *Styx* SSM)	12
Patrol escorts	14
Sub chasers (20 *Kronstadt*-, 19 *Hainan*-class)	39
Fast patrol boats, guided missile (70 *Osa*- and 70 *Hoku/Komar*-type, more building)	140
Motor torpedo boats (P-4/-6 class)	140
Hu Chwan hydrofoils	105
Motor gunboats (*Shanghai, Swatow, Whampoa* classes)	440
Minesweepers (18 Soviet T-43 types)	30
Landing craft (15 LST, 14 LSM, 15 infantry landers)	ca. 450
Coast and river defense vessels	300

AIRCRAFT (naval, shore-based) — 700

Medium and light bombers (130 Il-28, Tu-2 lt and Tu-16 mid)	130
Fighters (MiG-17, MiG-19/F-6, some F-9, a few maritime reconnaissance aircraft)	500
Mi-4 *Hound* helicopters and light transport aircraft)	50

AIRCRAFT (air force) — 5,000

Medium bombers (Tu-16 *Badger*, a few Tu-4 med.)	80
Light bombers (300 Il-28 *Beagle*, 100 Tu-2 *Bat*)	100
Fighter-bombers (MiG-15, F-9 *Fantan*)	500
Fighters (4,000 MiG-17/-19, 80 MiG-21, some F-9)	ca. 4,100
Fixed-wing transport aircraft (300 An-2, 100 Li-2, 50 Il-14 and Il-18, some An-12/-24/-26 and Trident)	450
Helicopter (Mi-4, Mi-8 and *Super Frelon*)	350

AIR DEFENSE SYSTEM

The system is capable of providing a limited defense of key urban and industrial areas, military installations and weapon complexes. Up to 4,000 naval and air force fighters are assigned to this role, also about 100 CSA-1 (SA-2) SAM and over 10,000 AA guns.

STRATEGIC FORCES

Intermediate-range ballistic missiles (CSS-2)	30-40
Medium-range ballistic missiles (CSS-1)	30-40
Aircraft (Tu-16 medium bombers)	ca. 80

"By mid-1978 China had conducted 23 nuclear tests, including tower releases, aircraft drops, missile firings, and underground detonations. It is estimated that the Chinese stockpile consists of several hundred warheads with yields ranging from 20 kilotons to three megatons. In the related field of space technology it has launched eight satellites."[3]

---

[1] R. T. Pretty (ed.), *Jane's Weapon Systems,* London: Paulton House, 1977.

[2] The International Institute for Strategic Studies, *The Military Balance, 1978-1979,* London, 1978, pp. 56-57.

[3] P. R. Chari, "China's Nuclear Posture," *Asian Survey,* August 1978, p. 819.

Sino-Indian Trade Resumed. On May 20 *The Financial Times* reported that China and India had resumed trade with the signing of a $1.7-million trade agreement.

Sino-American Cooperation. On May 22 *The Times* of London reported that the U.S. had recently "leaked" to Peking the names of known and suspected Soviet spy ships operating in East Asia.

China and the Olympics. On May 28 the Canadian government decided to refuse to allow athletes from Taiwan to compete in the Olympics under the Republic of China banner. The decision, reported on July 1, was made under pressure from Peking. *(See July 15, 1976)*

Carter on China. On June 23 Democratic presidential candidate Jimmy Carter said he favored improving relations between the U.S. and China and, after consulting Japan, a phased reduction of U.S. ground forces in Korea. In a question-and-answer session following the speech, Carter recommended full diplomatic relations with China and strong trade relations with Taiwan.

U.S. Withdraws from Offshore Islands. On June 24 the White House announced that the U.S. had withdrawn its small military advisory teams from the Chinese Nationalist-controlled islands of Quemoy and Matsu, just off the coast of China.

Vietnam Unified. On July 2 Hanoi radio reported the formal unification of Vietnam. On the same day, leaders of the Socialist Republic of Vietnam were elected by members of the National Assembly.

On July 3 Hanoi radio announced the composition of the new leadership. Most of the 30 cabinet ministers were men who had held high positions in the North Vietnamese government.

Scott to China. On July 10 Hugh Scott, R-Pa., Senate Minority Leader, arrived in China for a two-week visit. He was quoted as saying that there would be no change in U.S.' China policy until a new administration took office.

On his return to the U.S., Scott said that there was growing Chinese impatience over normalization, a view which contrasted with the administration position.

Japanese Warning. On July 12 Japanese Foreign Minister Miyazawa Kiichi warned Senate Majority Leader Mike Mansfield, D-Mont., that the U.S. should not cancel its security treaty with Taiwan or make any sudden changes in Sino-American relations.

U.S. to Participate in Olympics. On July 15 the U.S. announced that it would compete in the Olympic games in Montreal after Canada offered to allow athletes from Taiwan to compete under their own flag and anthem, although they could not call themselves the Republic of China. China had demanded that Canada "prohibit totally the participation of the Taiwanese athletes under any circumstances."

On July 16, Taiwan withdrew from the games.

Carter Nominated. On July 15 the Democratic Party nominated Jimmy Carter for the presidency.

The Democratic platform, adopted earlier, criticized the foreign policy of the past eight years and, without naming him, criticized Secretary of State Henry Kissinger for his use of "balance-of-power diplomacy suited better to the last century than to this one." On the question of China, the platform promised "movement."

U.S. Troops Out of Thailand. On July 20 the last American soldier left Thailand. Approximately 250 U.S. military advisers remained, reportedly at the government's request. *(See March 20, 1976)*

The U.S. had closed its last two bases in Thailand on June 20.

Kissinger on Korea. On July 22 Secretary of State Henry Kissinger suggested that the U.S., China, North Korea and South Korea meet to "discuss ways of preserving the [1953 Korean] armistice agreement and of reducing tensions in Korea." The North Korean government rejected the proposal on July 23, but Kissinger continued to work toward a four-power conference during the remainder of 1976.

India and China Reestablish Relations. On July 24 K. R. Narayanan, the Indian ambassador to China, presented his credentials in Peking, thus reopening relations between Asia's two largest states. India and China had broken off relations in 1962.

On Sept. 20 the Chinese Ambassador to India, Chen Zhaoyuan, presented his credentials in New Delhi.

Earthquake in China. On July 28 a massive earthquake occurred at Tangshan, in Hebei Province, north China. The principal shock wave measured 8.2 on the Richter scale. Sixteen hours later, a second quake, measuring 7.9 on the Richter scale, hit Peking. Although no details were available, the extent of the disaster could be gauged by the enormous and unprecedented relief effort mounted by the Chinese government. Premier Hua Guofeng was placed in charge of the effort.

The United Nations offered assistance, but was refused.

The Chinese later claimed that it was the largest earthquake to hit China in more than 400 years; 655,000 people were reported dead in the quake.

Fighting in Korea. On Aug. 18 North Korean troops opened fire on U.S. and South Korean soldiers who were trimming tree branches in the demilitarized zone near Panmunjom. Two American officers were killed, and four men were wounded. Five South Korean soldiers were also wounded.

On Aug. 20 Secretary of State Henry Kissinger stated that the U.S. "absolutely cannot and will not accept" what he termed a "premeditated act of murder." Kissinger demanded "explanations and reparations" for the incident. *(See Aug. 22, 1976)*

Ford Nominated. On Aug. 19 the Republican Party nominated President Gerald Ford for president. The Republican platform stated that improvements in the relations between the U.S. and China "cannot realistically proceed at a forced or incautious pace."

North Korea's Apology. On Aug. 22 North Korean President Kim Il Sung told the U.S. government the Aug. 18 slaying of two American officers was "regretful" *(sic)* and called on both sides to take steps to prevent a recurrence of such incidents.

On Aug. 23 the U.S. State Department termed Kim's note "a positive step."

New Chinese Position on Taiwan. On Aug. 24 Chinese Vice Premier Geng Biao announced a new Chinese position on the question of Taiwan, stating that it was no longer Peking's "most pressing concern.... In today's world situation, it is Soviet social-imperialism, the No. 1

enemy, that should be dealt with first; all other problems are of secondary importance." Thus, Geng said, Peking was willing for the present to "let the United States defend" Taiwan, but "when we feel the time is right, we will candidly say: 'Please Uncle Sam, pack your bags and go.'" In the interim, concluded Geng: "We can still wait."

Geng defended his argument by noting that in some places in the world the presence of U.S. troops was beneficial to China, as they worked to deter Soviet aggression: "We agree that U.S. troops should remain stationed in some areas." Geng was speaking not just of Europe, but of certain parts of Asia as well.

Taiwan Reprocessing Plutonium. On Aug. 29, confirming a series of CIA reports, U.S. officials noted that Taiwan had begun to reprocess spent nuclear reactor fuel to acquire a stockpile of plutonium that could be used to make nuclear weapons.

Schlesinger to China. On Sept. 6 former U.S. Secretary of Defense James Schlesinger arrived in China at the head of an impressive delegation of U.S. military and intelligence experts. He had talks with many of China's leaders and visited defense installations and militia forces throughout China, including Xinjiang and Inner Mongolia.

Before leaving for Tokyo on Jan. 29, Schlesinger was quoted as having said that China's military equipment was not good enough to resist Soviet armor or aircraft. He also offered the opinion that the Soviet Union could seize large parts of China without much difficulty.

It was later reported that Schlesinger's trip was made over the objections of U.S. Secretary of State Henry Kissinger, who had blocked two earlier attempts by Schlesinger to go to China, despite Chinese invitations. *(See Nov. 7, 1975)*

Mao Tse-tung Dies. On Sept. 9 Chinese Communist Party Chairman Mao Tse-tung died at 82. The official announcement did not list a cause of death, but speculation has concentrated on either advanced Parkinson's disease or cerebral arteriosclerosis.

Mao's death followed reports that he had been *non compos mentis* for at least three years before his death.

Soviet Condolences. On Sept. 9 the Soviet Communist Party sent a telegram to the Chinese Communist Party — its first in more than a decade — expressing its "deep condolences" over the death of Chairman Mao Tse-tung.

On Sept. 14 Peking rejected the telegram.

Peking Indicates Policy Shift. On Sept. 12, Sept. 13 and Sept. 23 the official Chinese news agency Xinhua indicated a shift in the Chinese policy of rapprochement with the U.S. as it reprinted strong anti-American statements made by the late Chinese Party Chairman Mao Tsetung during the earlier period of Sino-American hostility. Such statements were not repeated.

Analysts have suggested that the statements were sponsored by the radical group which was ousted in the October 6 coup. *(See below)*

Taiwan to Halt Reprocessing. On Sept. 14 Nationalist Chinese Premier Chiang Ching-kuo told U.S. Ambassador to the ROC Leonard Unger that his government would halt all activities relating to the reprocessing of nuclear fuel.

Soviet Initiative. On Oct. 1 the Soviet party newspaper *Pravda* indicated official Soviet willingness to improve relations with Peking: "The fundamental interests of the Soviet and Chinese peoples do not clash but coincide."

New Leadership in Peking. On Oct. 6 a coalition led by Hua Guofeng, Ye Jianying and Wang Dongxing arrested nearly 30 high-ranking party and government officials, including four Politburo members, Wang Hongwen, Zhang Chunqiao, Jiang Qing and Yao Wenyuan, who would later be known as the "gang of four" and who had wielded the bulk of the power in China during the period of Mao's illness before his death on Sept. 9.

News of the arrests was kept secret for three days. On Oct. 10, the first rumors of the arrests began circulating in Peking and were confirmed in a series of mass rallies held throughout China on Oct. 21. On Oct. 24 a million soldiers and citizens held a rally at Tiananmen Square in Peking, where Wu De, Politburo member and first secretary of the Peking municipal committee, provided the first official account of the events of the past month.

The rise to power of Hua Guofeng, a virtual unknown, stunned observers both in and outside of China. Already premier, he was now elevated to chairman of the Chinese Communist Party and chairman of the military commission; it was the first time one man had ever held all three of China's top three posts.

Ford, Carter Debate on China. On Oct. 6 President Gerald Ford and Jimmy Carter met in the second of their televised debates. When asked about China, Ford stressed U.S. obligations to Taiwan and restated his contention that improvement in Sino-American relations should not be hurried.

In response, Carter said that the "great opportunity" opened by President Nixon in 1972 "pretty well has been frittered away under Mr. Ford."

Coup in Thailand. On Oct. 6, right-wing anti-Communist military leaders took control of the government of Thailand. Defense Minister Admiral Sa-ngad Chaloryu abolished the 1974 constitution and declared himself head of the administrative reform committee, which would rule the country. The takeover followed bloody battles between police and university students in which 30 people were reported killed and 1,700 students arrested. The universities were closed.

Attacks on Moscow Escalate. On Oct. 10 the Peking *People's Daily* published a long article strongly reaffirming the anti-Soviet credentials of the new Chinese leadership. Entitled "Resolutely Combat Soviet Modern Revisionism," the article was especially emphatic in stating that China had an inescapable, enduring obligation to oppose the massive "crimes" of the Brezhnev leadership. The article also made it clear that Peking's "protracted struggle" to wipe Soviet revisionism "from the face of the earth" was not merely an ideological conflict but would involve strong Chinese opposition to Soviet foreign policy: "It is necessary to oppose the acts of aggression and expansion of Soviet social imperialism."

Economic Continuity. On Oct. 25 the Peking *People's Daily* published an editorial stating that the new government of China would carry out the economic development program of the late Premier Chou En-lai.

American Plants Open. On Oct. 25 Pullman-Kellogg, a division of Pullman Inc., said that two of its ammonia-urea fertilizer complexes had begun operations in China and that a third was imminent. Built under a contract signed in 1973, the plan called for the construction of eight plants by early 1977.

Computers to China. On Oct. 28, acting on the advice of Secretary of State Henry Kissinger, President Ford allowed an affiliate of the Control Data Corporation to sell two Cyber 172 computers to China. The computer has military usefulness and is able to make calculations on nuclear tests. The transaction fell through when the Carter administration took no action on the sale.

Carter Elected. On Nov. 2 Democrat Jimmy Carter was elected as the 39th President of the U.S. by a small margin. Despite a large turnover in the Congress, the Democrats kept their large majority.

Trade with Japan. On Nov. 10 *The Financial Times* of London reported the sale of three large computers to China, one of which would be the largest and most advanced to be sent to China. This was the first instance of a Japanese sale of computers to China.

U.S. Veto. On Nov. 12 the U.S. used its 18th veto in the United Nations Security Council to block Vietnam from membership in the U.N.

China to Increase Trade. On Nov. 13, in one of the first signs of changes under the new leadership, the *International Herald Tribune* reported Chinese Vice Premier Li Xiannian had predicted that China's foreign trade, always sluggish, would be "flourishing 3 years from now." In his talks with a visiting French delegation, Li said China wanted petrochemical technology, oil and mineral exploration equipment, steel-making and power generating equipment. Li noted, however, that "one needs foreign currency to buy all these things."

On Nov. 22, the Peking *People's Daily* more clearly announced the new policy by redefining the principle of "self-reliance" which had meant that China refused to import much in the way of Western technology. The article stated that: "Self-reliance does not mean . . . a closed door policy on imports. We learn from the good experience and advanced science and technology of other countries and absorb them for our own use."

Peking Denies Softening. On Nov. 15 Chinese Vice Premier Li Xiannian strongly denied any warming of relations with the Soviet Union and accused Moscow of creating "false impressions" of a relaxation of Sino-Soviet tensions in order to "confuse" world opinion. Li also stated that Moscow was engaged in "wishful thinking and daydreaming" about a Sino-Soviet reconciliation. This theme was picked up and repeated by other Chinese leaders during November and December.

KMT Official to China. On Nov. 16 a veteran Kuomintang official and former member of the Executive Yuan in the ROC government on Taiwan, Miao Yun-tai, arrived in China from the U.S. for a ten-day visit. He was received by Politburo member Wu De.

Earlier, ROC Premier Chiang Ching-kuo had claimed that a report that Taiwan was negotiating with China was "an utterly groundless lie."

Chinese Nuclear Test. On Nov. 17 China exploded its fourth nuclear bomb of 1976. Yielding more than four megatons, it was the largest test ever conducted by the Chinese. Chinese nuclear testing in 1976, all of it conducted in the atmosphere, was later blamed for the first increase in worldwide atmospheric radioactivity in four years.

Troops Move in China. On Nov. 25 Fujian radio reported that army troops had been sent into Fujian Province to establish order. Fujian is the province directly opposite Taiwan.

Sino-Soviet Border Talks Resume. On Nov. 28 Leonid Ilyichev, Soviet Deputy Foreign Minister, arrived in Peking to resume the Sino-Soviet border talks, which had been suspended for 18 months. There were indications that the positions of both sides had hardened in the interval.

China's New Foreign Minister. On Dec. 2 Huang Hua replaced Qiao Guanhua as Foreign Minister of China.

On the same day, in an announcement by the Central Committee of the Chinese Communist Party, it was stated that Mao Tse-tung's policies on international relations would be followed by the new leadership. The announcement also restated China's position on almost all major foreign policy issues, and continued to assert that it would use the Five Principles of Peaceful Coexistence *(see June 28, 1954)* as its guide in the establishment of diplomatic relations with other nations.

During the next few weeks, China sent messages to all of its allies reaffirming its earlier foreign policy positions.

Political Prisoners on Taiwan. On Dec. 12 Chiang Ching-kuo, Premier of the Republic of China, reported that the government was holding 254 people in jail for seditious activities.

China to Mechanize Agriculture. On Dec. 24 the Second National Conference on Learning from Dazhai in Agriculture, meeting in Peking, reaffirmed 1980 as the target date of the mechanization of agriculture. *(See Sept. 15, 1975)*

Hua Guofeng Speech. On Dec. 25 Chinese Communist Party Chairman Hua Guofeng made his first major policy speech, in which he confirmed his intention to "uphold" the policies of Mao Tse-tung and to oppose the supporters of the "gang of four." On the subject of the economy, Hua said that people must "be both red and expert," a reference to the debate that had racked China for the past decade. By using the word "expert" at all, Hua signalled that there would be increased emphasis on ability over revolutionary zeal.

Radicals to Be Purged. On Dec. 28 Premier Hua Guofeng said in Peking that government and party workers who had come to power because of the "gang of four" would be purged by the end of 1976.

Rioting in China. On Dec. 29 it was reported from China that government troops had been sent to Baoding, a city 100 miles south of Peking, to put down rioting by supporters of the "gang of four."

On Dec. 30 a Chinese government official said that the rioting, which had begun Dec. 20, was being put down.

1977

Agriculture Reform — Carter on Normalization — Peking on Normalization — Army Modernization Drive — Sino-Soviet Talks Halted — Nixon Promise Reported — U.S., China Resume Talks — Beethoven, Shakespeare Restored — U.S. To Withdraw Troops from Korea — Vance on China Relations — SEATO Dissolved — Sino-U.S. Normalization Delayed — Albania-China Rift — New Chinese Leadership — Vance to China — Tito in China — Pol Pot to China — Huang at U.N. — Modernization Urged — Sino-Soviet Agreement — Dalai Lama Barred — China Buys British Planes — Prisoners Released

China's Goals. On Jan. 1 the Peking *People's Daily* published an editorial outlining China's main tasks for 1977. It called for the creation of "a completely new situation in which there are political liveliness and economic prosperity, and in which a hundred schools of thought contend and a hundred flowers blossom in science and culture, and the people's livelihood steadily improves."

China and Bangladesh. On Jan. 2 Major General Ziaur Rahman, the chief martial law administrator and chief of army staff of Bangladesh, arrived in Peking for a five-day visit. It was the first contact between leaders of the two countries. Trade and economic cooperation agreements were signed.

Vance Backs Normalization. On Jan. 8 Secretary of State-designate Cyrus Vance endorsed the Nixon-Ford policy of normalizing relations with Peking and said he probably would travel to China. At a meeting with Secretary of State Henry Kissinger and Chinese liaison officer Huang Zhen, Vance also said that Sino-American relations "will continue to be guided by the Shanghai Communiqué" of 1972.

Oksenberg on China. On Jan. 31 the *Washington Star* published an article reviewing the views of Michael C. Oksenberg, a University of Michigan professor recently hired by national security adviser Zbigniew Brzezinski to help formulate China policy. The article concluded that Oksenberg, a noted expert on internal Chinese politics, would push hard for recognition of Peking and the breaking of diplomatic relations with Taiwan.

Private Plots Return. On Feb. 2 the Chinese Communist Party theoretical journal *Hongqi* expressed its approval of selective private production, largely in the fields of agriculture and handicrafts. Such private production had been in disrepute since the onset of the Cultural Revolution ten years before.

The article also called for increased production of consumer goods such as bicycles, sugar and salt.

Carter on Normalization. President Carter, meeting on Feb. 8 in Washington with Chinese liaison officer Huang Zhen, expressed a desire for closer Sino-U.S. relations and reaffirmed the Shanghai Communiqué. The White House said "important progress" had been made at the meeting.

Peking Pushes for Normalization. On Feb. 16 *The New York Times* reported that Chinese leaders had told David Rockefeller of Chase Manhattan Bank that they wished to settle the outstanding dispute concerning the frozen Chinese assets in the U.S. (valued unofficially at $76.5 million) and the private and corporate American claims regarding property seized in 1949 (valued at $196.9 million). *(See May 1)*

Exemptions to Fishing Limits. On Feb. 21 President Carter signed legislation (H J Res 240) exempting Nationalist China and some other countries from the U.S.' 200-mile fishing limit to be imposed starting March 1.

Army Modernization Drive. On Feb. 26 the Chinese news agency Xinhua reported that Chinese Party Chairman Hua Guofeng had ordered a new drive to improve the efficiency of the Chinese army and to end the practice of putting politics ahead of know-how in running the military.

Sino-Soviet Talks Break Off. On Feb. 28 Soviet deputy foreign minister and chief Russian negotiator at the Sino-Soviet border talks, Leonid Ilyichev, left Peking on "official business" and returned to Moscow. The departure marked the end of three months of negotiations, which had followed an 18-month suspension of talks. There had been no progress. Shortly thereafter, the Soviets resumed their temporarily suspended public criticisms of the Chinese.

Aid to Taiwan. On March 10 Richard C. Holbrooke, assistant secretary of state-designate for East Asian and Pacific Affairs, testified before the House Subcommittee on Asian and Pacific Affairs that the U.S. was "in the process of phasing out" military aid to Taiwan, and that the administration was requesting only $25 million in credits for Taiwan and a small grant for training.

Chinese-Korean Trade Agreement. On March 12 China and North Korea signed a long-term trade agreement in Peking for 1977-1981.

Beethoven Restored. On March 26 it was announced in Peking that the ban on the works of Beethoven had been lifted.

Li Xiannian Interview. On March 27 the *Sunday Times* of London published an interview which Chinese Vice Premier and Politburo member Li Xiannian had given to the editor-in-chief of the Times newspapers, Denis Hamilton. On the question of Taiwan, Li reiterated the Chinese position that it was an internal affair of China, but went on to say that "The Chinese are patient. We cannot do otherwise in the case of Taiwan. China has other priorities and there are more urgent things to be done on the mainland."

Li said of Japan that "We would not be worried about some rearmament of Japan provided it was for self-defense. For a country as large as Japan they cannot do without adequate defense forces."

Peking Downplays Taiwan Issue. On March 31 *The New York Times* reported that columnist William Safire had been told by Chinese officials that "in terms of the magnitude of issues, the international situation is more important [than the rapid solution of the Taiwan problem]."

Nixon's Promise. On April 11 *The New York Times* reported that former President Nixon had promised Chinese Premier Chou En-lai in February 1972 that if re-elected that November he (Nixon) would normalize relations later in his second term.

Peking on U.S. Policy. On April 29 *The Guardian* of London reported that an unidentified "senior Chinese official" had expressed concern about the U.S. failure to react strongly enough to growing Soviet influence in places like Africa. The official was quoted as saying "The Soviet Union behaves like a thief, so if you cry out 'stop thief,' it will not be so easy to steal things. But you people in the U.S. say there is no thief."

The Washington Post quoted the same official as expressing dissatisfaction with the Carter administration's failure to make progress on the normalization of Sino-American relations: "We have not found any sign . . . of a decision being taken by the United States to resolve the problem."

U.S. and China Resume Talks. On May 1 U.S. officials disclosed that the U.S. and China had resumed talks in Washington in April regarding the settlement of their outstanding financial claims. Similar discussions had taken place from 1973 to 1975, but had ended in deadlock.

Analysts saw the claims issue as an important block to increasing Sino-American trade and the opening of full diplomatic relations. *(See March 2, 1979)*

Carter on Sino-American Relations. At a May 12 press conference, President Carter seemed to indicate a slowing of the process of normalization of relations with the People's Republic of China. Carter made three points: (1) while the Shanghai Communiqué had stated that there was only one China, it did not state who was the representative of that China; (2) there was no set schedule or deadline for normalization; and (3) the U.S. was unwilling to see the people of Taiwan pressured or attacked by mainland China. On the last point Carter said "we don't want to see the Taiwan people punished or attacked and if we can resolve this major difficulty, I would move expeditiously to normalizing relations with China."

Peking Answers Carter. On May 15 Chinese Vice Premier Ji Dengkui replied to President Carter's statement about Sino-American relations *(see above)*, in an interview published in *Yomiuri Shimbun* in Japan. Ji said: "To liberate Taiwan in a peaceful way or by armed force — this is China's domestic affair, and I even think that armed force may be the only way to liberate Taiwan." But Ji went on to acknowledge domestic U.S. opposition to the abandonment of Taiwan without a "peaceful assurance."

Singlaub Fired. On May 21 President Carter removed Major General John K. Singlaub as chief of staff of American forces in South Korea after Singlaub publicly criticized Carter's plan to withdraw U.S. troops from Korea. Singlaub had said on May 19 that the withdrawal would lead to war.

Carter later halted the withdrawal. *(See June 5, 1977)*

Carter Calls for New Foreign Policy. On May 22 President Carter called for a new, broader American foreign policy to respond to "a politically awakening world." Speaking at the commencement exercises at the University of Notre Dame, Carter listed five "cardinal premises" that should guide foreign policy, including the promotion of human rights and an end to the arms race. Carter also made it clear that improved relations with the Soviet Union and China remained a key component of American foreign policy, and that China was "a key force for global peace." *(Text, p. 328)*

Shakespeare Restored. On May 25 it was announced in Peking that the ban on the works of Shakespeare had been lifted.

Soviets Renew Criticism of China. On May 30 the Soviet government news agency Tass announced the end of a six-month moratorium on Soviet attacks on China imposed after the death of Mao Tse-tung: "The methods of the new Peking leadership have dashed hopes that the death of Mao Tse-tung would bring positive changes in China."

China's attacks on the Soviet Union had not been interrupted by Mao's death.

U.S. to Withdraw from Korea. On June 5, U.S. officials informed the governments of Japan and South Korea that 6,000 American soldiers would be withdrawn from South Korea by the end of 1978. This was to be the first stage of a withdrawal of 33,000 U.S. ground forces.

Brezhnev Blames Peking. On June 6, in an interview with the Japanese *Asahi Shimbun*, Soviet party leader Leonid Brezhnev attacked the new Chinese leadership for the failure to improve Sino-Soviet relations.

U.S. to "Challenge" Moscow. On June 10 President Carter told the Magazine Publishers Association that he was inclined "to aggressively challenge, in a peaceful way, of course, the Soviet Union and others for influence in areas of the world we feel are crucial to us now or potentially crucial 15 or 20 years from now." He referred specifically to Vietnam, Iraq, Somalia, Algeria, China and "even Cuba."

Sino-Soviet War Predicted. On June 10 Lt. Gen. Donn A. Starry, speaking at a high school commencement ceremony in West Germany, told the audience that a Sino-Soviet war was inevitable in "your lifetime," and that it was "likely" that the U.S. would become involved "once it became apparent that one or the other of the antagonists was about to win and gain absolute control of the Eurasian land mass."

On June 17 Starry received an official reprimand for not having cleared the speech in advance, but U.S. officials did not disavow his opinions.

Administration Debate. On June 24 the Baltimore *Sun* reported that a major policy debate was taking place within the administration over the conclusions expressed in a secret policy paper, Policy Review Memorandum No. 24. First prepared in April, the paper discussed many aspects of normalization of relations with China, including the problems of arms sales to both Taipei and Peking. After initial approval, further review in June and July triggered intense debate; a proposal to seek a specific commitment from Peking not to use force to seize Taiwan after normalization was achieved was now dropped. *(See Feb. 9, 1979)*

In addition, a warning that the sale of U.S. military technology to China would provoke a "fundamental reassessment" of Soviet policy towards Washington was finally rejected by those who wanted to use "the China card" to put increased pressure on Moscow. *(See Nov. 3, 1978)*

Vance on Sino-American Relations. On June 29, in a speech to the Asia Society, Secretary of State Cyrus Vance outlined the terms on which the U.S. hoped to normalize relations with China. *(Text, p. 330)* This was supplemented by a presidential press conference the following day. The U.S. said it was willing to recognize that there was only one China, that China's government was located in Peking, that Taiwan was a province of China, and that the U.S. would sever diplomatic and treaty ties with the Republic of China on Taiwan. At the same time, however, the U.S. stressed the importance of a peaceful settlement of the Taiwan question by the Chinese themselves, and insisted on guarantees from Peking that it would not use military force against Taiwan.

More Exchanges Rebuffed. On June 29 *The New York Times* reported that China had recently refused any expansion of scholarly exchanges with the U.S. until progress had been made in the normalization of relations.

SEATO Dissolved. On June 30 the Southeast Asian Treaty Organization (SEATO) was dissolved. Originally established in 1954 at the insistence of then-U.S. Secretary of State John Foster Dulles, the eight signatories had pledged to cooperate in resisting communist aggression and to support South Vietnam, Laos and Cambodia against such aggression. The fall of these three governments rendered the treaty virtually meaningless, as had the U.S. decision to encourage Asian nations to depend less on the U.S. for support. The termination of the treaty marked the end of the longest lasting of Dulles' efforts to surround and isolate China. *(Map, p. 190)*

Economic and Military Aid to Indochina: 1953-1980

(In millions — by fiscal year)

	CAMBODIA		LAOS		SOUTH VIETNAM		THAILAND	
	Military[1]	Economic	Military[2]	Economic	Military[3]	Economic	Military[4]	Economic
1953-61	$ 73.4	$219.9	$ 112.9	$267.1	$ 571.7	$1,544.9	$ 318.6	$257.2
1962-65	26.4	57.5	156.8	161.8	1,022.6	851.6	267.6	112.9
1966	——	*	69.1	57.6	686.2	736.5	53.2	46.7
1967	——	*	83.9	57.8	662.5	568.1	69.6	55.9
1968	——	*	85.0	64.4	1,243.4	536.7	89.8	49.3
1969	——	*	99.4	52.2	1,534.0	413.5	96.5	37.4
1970	8.6	*	144.6	53.8	1,577.3	476.7	110.2	29.0
1971	201.4	76.8	204.8	49.5	1,945.6	575.7	100.2	24.3
1972	197.9	57.6	290.7	52.2	2,602.6	454.6	122.7	34.0
1973	176.1	93.1	383.5	50.8	3,349.4	501.7	63.7	39.1
1974	420.1	275.5	76.0	39.5	941.9	654.3	37.2	15.1
1975	256.0	149.0	19.9	26.5	625.1	240.9	42.5	6.7
1976	——	——	——	——	——	2.5	103.5	17.3
1977	——	——	——	——	——	——	47.2	17.7
1978	——	——	——	——	——	——	38.6	7.5
1979	——	——	——	——	——	——	32.1	24.5
1980 (est.)	——	——	——	——	——	——	26.2	26.1
Totals[5]	$1,352.5	$876.1	$1,727.6	$905.5	$16,490.5	$7,097.8	$1,618.6	$719.8

* Less than $50,000.

[1] Military assistance to Cambodia almost exclusively was part of the foreign aid program.

[2] From fiscal 1968 through fiscal 1974, military aid to Laos was included in defense appropriations. Before then, almost all military assistance came from the regular foreign aid program. Military aid was returned to the regular foreign aid budget beginning with fiscal 1975.

[3] Beginning in fiscal 1967, military aid to South Vietnam was included in defense appropriations rather than in the regular foreign aid program. The transition from the foreign aid budget was begun in fiscal 1963.

[4] From fiscal 1968 through fiscal 1972, military aid to Thailand was included in defense appropriations. Before 1968 almost all military assistance came from the regular foreign aid program. Military aid was returned to the regular foreign aid budget beginning with fiscal 1973.

[5] Totals given are not equal to the sum of the figures for the individual years. Adjustments have been made in the totals for loans which were cancelled, decreased or sold to a non-U.S. government purchaser; such reductions are not reflected in the annual data.

Source: Agency for International Development

SEATO was supplanted by the Association of Southeast Asian Nations (ASEAN), comprised only of nations in the Southeast Asian area and primarily concerned with economic rather than security issues. *(See Aug. 8, 1967)*

Chinese Oil Controversy. On July 1 *The New York Times* reported that a new CIA study of China's oil reserves had concluded that China's onshore oil reserves were comparable with remaining reserves in the U.S., but that its key northern fields would likely be exhausted within 10 years. The report estimated China's reserves at 33 billion barrels.

This estimate provoked further controversy about oil in China. Chinese Vice Premier Deng Xiaoping had earlier claimed that China had reserves of more than 400 billion barrels, and other U.S. analysts had offered figures higher than the CIA estimate.

Zumwalt to China. On July 4 Chinese Vice Premier Li Xiannian told Adm. Elmo Zumwalt, retired chief of naval operations, that the Chinese desired normal relations with the U.S. but would not abandon its right to use force in resolving the Taiwan issue. Li also took the opportunity to restate the three Chinese conditions for normalization: the severance of diplomatic relations with Taiwan; the withdrawal of all U.S. troops from Taiwan; and the abrogation of the U.S.-Taiwan mutual defense treaty. Finally, Zumwalt quoted Li as saying that there was a strong motivation for improving Sino-American relations, and that the two countries "must use joint efforts in dealing with the [Soviet] polar bear."

Normalization to Be Delayed. On July 7 *The Washington Star,* quoting sources within the Carter administration, reported that Carter had decided to delay full normalization of relations with China at least until 1978. According to the report, the major reason for the delay was White House concern over a series of legislative battles expected in the fall. These sources said the president was not anxious to confront congressional critics at the same time over ending longstanding Taiwan commitments.

Chinese Pilot Defects. On July 7 a Chinese air force squadron commander defected to Taiwan by flying his MiG-19 to a Nationalist Chinese airfield near Taipei. This was the fourth such defection, but the first since 1965.

Albania Breaks with China. On July 8 the Albanian Party newspaper *Zeni I Popullit* published an editorial attacking China's "Three Worlds" theory and the practice of adopting the principle "my enemy's enemy is my friend." The editorial was the first public indication of the impact which the new moderate trends in China had had on relations with Albania, which had been China's closest ally during China's more radical phase.

Mao on Modernization. On July 8, China's *Peking Review* published a major policy statement which tried to demonstrate that the late Communist Party Chairman Mao Tse-tung had always supported the use of foreign technology to serve China's needs. Quoting extensively from Mao's writings, the article downplayed the old Chinese principle of total "self-reliance," first espoused by Mao in 1957. Now, self-reliance only meant that, when importing foreign ideas, "we must not copy indiscriminately." Arguing that China needed new technology in order to progress, the article concluded that China must absorb "the good experience and techniques from abroad for our own use so as to enhance our self-reliance capabilities and build China into a powerful, modern socialist country before the end of the century."

Taiwan Rapprochement with Russia? On July 14 Taiwan's English language *China News* carried an article by its Hong Kong correspondent offering the possibility of a Soviet-Taiwanese rapprochement.

During July and August, various other newspapers on Taiwan hinted that if the U.S. were to break with Taiwan, it would then be forced to look to Moscow for protection. This press campaign effort was seen as an effort by Taiwan to slow normalization between the U.S. and mainland China, but — because of Taiwan's firm anti-Communist ideology — was considered unlikely by U.S. officials. The campaign ended later that year.

More Chinese Criticism of Moscow. On July 15 the *Peking Review* published a major assessment of Soviet foreign policy; the article asserted that Moscow's main target was still Western Europe, while Soviet penetration of Asia and Africa were flanking movements. Entitled "Soviet Social-Imperialism — Most Dangerous Source of World War," the article claimed that starting from a position of inferiority in the early 1960s, by 1975 the Soviet Union had surpassed the U.S. in nearly all military capabilities. Drawing on historical parallels, the article recounted how both of the two world wars had been "started by late-coming imperialist countries" that wanted a "redivision of the world. . . . [M]ore and more people in the world now realize that any accommodation or concession to Soviet social-imperialism is dangerous and the lesson of the appeasement policy pursued on the eve of World War II must not be forgotten."

China's New Leadership. From July 16 to July 21, the third plenary session of the 10th Central Committee of the Chinese Communist Party met in Peking. The meeting confirmed the position of Hua Guofeng as chairman of the Central Committee and the Military Affairs Commission, the two highest posts in China. Deng Xiaoping, who had been purged from all his posts in April 1976, also was restored as vice chairman of the party, vice chairman of the military commission, and vice premier. China's "return to normalcy" is often dated from this meeting. *(See Aug. 12)*

Soviet Response to Peking Charges. On July 17 Moscow's English-language *Soviet News* published a major article charging that the new Chinese leadership still pursued "the old great power line, notable for its expansionist ambitions and enmity towards the process of easing international tensions." Taking issue with many Western analysts, the article averred that "no substantial signs of de-Maoization have so far been observed in China." On the contrary, there is an effort "to rescue, preserve and strengthen the regime created as a result of the 'cultural revolution' while rectifying to some extent Mao's most odious directives."

Sino-Soviet Trade. On July 21 Chinese Deputy Minister of Foreign Trade Chen Jie went to Moscow, where he signed a trade agreement for 1977. It was revealed that the value of the trade for 1976 had been $421 million, an increase of $152 million over 1975. Thus, despite the recent increase in polemics between the two parties, trade relations remained relatively normal.

China Goes Metric. On July 24 the Chinese news agency Xinhua announced that the State Council had recently promulgated a set of regulations calling for national adoption of the metric system and the gradual phasing out of the traditional systems.

Killings in Cambodia. On July 26, in testimony before a House International Relations subcommittee, Assistant Secretary of State Richard Holbrooke reported that more than a million people had been killed in Cambodia since the communist takeover in 1975.

Huang Hua's Promise. On July 30 Chinese Foreign Minister Huang Hua, in a secret speech to Chinese Communist Party leaders, told them of the government's decision to renounce the use of force in the "liberation" of Taiwan: "We need to let the U.S. government know that, even when China-U.S. relations are normalized, the U.S.-Taiwan mutual defense treaty is invalidated, and U.S. forces are withdrawn from Taiwan, we will not, within the next decade, use force to liberate Taiwan."

The reason for this, said Huang, was that "It is necessary to win over the United States in order to focus our strength to cope with the No. 1 enemy — Soviet revisionist social-imperialism."

This message was conveyed to U.S. leaders later in the year. *(See Aug. 22, 1977)*

Peking Calls for Talks. On Aug. 11 a spokesman for the Chinese ministry of foreign affairs stated that at China's request talks with the Soviets on the navigation of the Ussuri and Heilong (Amur) Rivers were to be held at the border town of Heihe. The last such talks had been held in February 1974. *(See Oct. 6, 1977)*

11th CCP Congress. On Aug. 12 the long-awaited 11th National Congress of the Chinese Communist Party opened in Peking. The congress confirmed the new collective leadership of Hua Guofeng, Deng Xiaoping, Wang Dongxing and Ye Jianying, and adopted a new party constitution, replacing that of 1973. The new constitution affirmed the policy of the "four modernizations" and was much stricter concerning party membership. In a four-hour report to the congress, Chairman Hua Guofeng tried to strike a balance between the philosophical principles of communism and the political and economic realities of China.

Reflecting China's more moderate foreign policy, Hua stated that although China "supports" the revolutionary struggles of all peoples, "all communist parties are independent and make their own decisions. . . . Revolution cannot be exported." Hua also asserted that Mao's thesis of the "three worlds," set forth in 1974, was "correct." *(See Nov. 1, 1977)*

The congress, which closed Aug. 18, also ratified a complete change in the provincial party leadership which institutionalized the end of local support for the recently purged "gang of four." *(List of Leaders, p. 291)*

U.S. Debate on Taiwan. On Aug. 15 Sen. Edward M. Kennedy, D-Mass., stated that it was imperative to move forward to full normalization of relations with China, and claimed that the "Taiwan issue is one for the Chinese themselves to resolve. The United States has, and should have, no other fundamental interest than that this resolution be a peaceful one." Kennedy went on to outline a five-point program whereby normalization might be achieved.

Vance to China. On Aug. 22 Secretary of State Cyrus Vance arrived in China for a five-day visit. Vance met with the ranking Chinese leaders, but would only term the talks "useful." After briefings, President Carter went further, calling the talks a "very important step" toward normalization.

On Aug. 20 *The New York Times* had reported that a State Department spokesman said no major progress was expected.

Vance's Visit Upgraded. On Aug. 23 Chinese Party Chairman Hua Guofeng affirmed for the first time his commitment to continued relations with the U.S. to counter the Soviet threat. In a speech published in the Peking *People's Daily*, Hua repeated Lenin's advice to take "advantage of every, even the smallest, opportunity of gaining a mass ally, even though this ally may be temporary, vacillating, unstable, unreliable and conditional."

This was followed the same day by a significant upgrading of Secretary Vance's trip to Peking with an announcement that he would meet with Vice Premier Deng Xiaoping. Previously, Vance had met only with Foreign Minister Huang Hua, who was not a member of the ruling Politburo.

Chinese Ambassador Returns. On Aug. 29 Wang Youping, a former ambassador to Malaysia, arrived in Moscow to fill the top Chinese diplomatic post there; it had been vacant for more than a year.

Tito to China. On Aug. 30 Yugoslav President Tito arrived in Peking to one of the most enthusiastic welcomes ever given a foreign leader. For years, Tito had been excoriated by the Chinese for his alleged abandonment of communism, for his "revisionism," and for his independence from the international communist movement. After the Soviet Union, Yugoslavia had been the most severely criticized of the communist states. Now that China had decided to modify its foreign policy, however, Tito became more a friend than an enemy. Although no joint communiqué was issued, the talks were warm and cordial, and seemed to promise closer ties between the two nations.

Deng's Views on Talks. On Sept. 6 Chinese Vice Premier Deng Xiaoping sharply contradicted U.S. accounts of Secretary of State Cyrus Vance's recent trip to China. *(See Aug. 22)* Deng said reports of progress were wrong; rather, the talks represented a setback in the effort to normalize relations between the two countries. Speaking with a delegation of Associated Press executives in Peking, Deng allowed no direct quotation, and no transcript of the interview was made. Concerning reports that China had made concessions on the Taiwan question, Deng denied

that the Chinese had made any promises about relinquishing the use of force. *(See Sept. 20, 1977)*

Four days later, Deng repeated these statements in talks with visiting Japanese parliamentarians. He again said that the Vance visit was a "step backwards" and complained that "the United States is playing with two cards [China and Taiwan]," something which Peking could not tolerate.

Panama Canal Treaties Signed. On Sept. 7 President Carter and Panamanian President Omar Torrijos Herrera signed two treaties that will transfer control of the canal to Panama by the year 2000.

The treaties were ratified by the Senate on March 16 and April 18, 1978, by identical 68-32 votes.

U.S. Denial on Liaison Offices. On Sept. 7 *The New York Times* reported that the U.S. Liaison Office in Peking had denied that Secretary of State Cyrus Vance during his recent visit to Peking had suggested the establishment of a liaison office in Taipei to replace the U.S. Embassy there.

Chinese Renew Korea Charges. On Sept. 7 the Peking *People's Daily* accused the U.S. of "interference and destruction of the Korean people's just cause of reunification."

Vance Meets Shen. On Sept. 10 the Nationalist Chinese ambassador to the U.S., James C. T. Shen, met with Secretary of State Cyrus Vance to discuss Sino-American relations. The first time in several years that the ambassador had had official talks with an American secretary of state, the meeting underscored U.S. unhappiness with the results of Vance's recent visit to Peking.

More China Hearings. On Sept. 20 the House Subcommittee on Asian and Pacific Affairs opened six days of hearing on the "practical implications" of the proposed U.S. decision to recognize the People's Republic of China. Unlike earlier China debates, there was little dispute over the decision to normalize relations with Peking. The debate was over how this was to be accomplished. Specifically, the hearings addressed the question of how to recognize Peking while maintaining relations, formal or informal, with Taipei. The hearings laid the groundwork for legislation Congress would pass in 1979.

China specialist A. Doak Barnett told the committee the Chinese were disappointed by Secretary of State Vance's trip to Peking, and by what the Chinese saw as a slowdown in U.S. moves toward normalization of relations. According to Barnett, the Chinese had seen the "whole process grind to a halt [in 1973-1975] because of a series of developments — Watergate in the United States, the collapse of Vietnam, [and] political problems in China." After the election of President Carter, Barnett said, the Chinese had "begun to wonder" if the U.S. was "moving backward." Barnett claimed that the Chinese "are prodding us to get on with the process."

Deng on Sino-Soviet Relations. On Sept. 25 Chinese Vice Premier Deng Xiaoping, playing down recent signs of improvement in Sino-Soviet relations, told the chairman of the defense committee of the West German Parliament that a Sino-Soviet rapprochement was "out of the question for the next generation." Deng said he was certain he would not see it in his lifetime, and he doubted whether Chairman Hua Guofeng would see it either.

Pol Pot to China. On Sept. 28 Pol Pot, premier and secretary of the Communist Party of Cambodia, arrived in

The Film Industry and China

Popular fiction and movies have both shaped and reflected Americans' view of China through the years. The widely read novels of prolific Nobel-prizewinning author Pearl Buck for several decades depicted — albeit somewhat romantically — a stoic, nobly suffering peasantry in such books as *The Good Earth.* Later, other authors including John Hersey *(A Single Pebble)* and Theodore H. White *(The Mountain Road)* drew on personal experience for fictional accounts of China. And translations of Andre Malraux' China novel, *Man's Fate,* have had enormous influence among American students and intellectuals.

But it is the movies that have probably most influenced the way Americans perceive China and the Chinese. Usually enacted by such unlikely and glamorous occidentals as Katharine Hepburn or Marlene Dietrich, the portrayals have ranged from the heroic to the sinister.

Historical China was dealt with in such films as *The Adventures of Marco Polo* (1937), with Gary Cooper discovering 13th century China; *55 Days at Peking* (1963), which dramatized the Boxer Rebellion of 1900; and *The Sand Pebbles* (1966), an unusually thoughtful account of U.S. "gunboat diplomacy" that was also a thinly veiled indictment of America's presence in Vietnam.

More or less straightforward Hollywood versions of Chinese peasant life could be seen in films adapted from Pearl Buck novels such as *The Good Earth* (1937) and *Dragon Seed* (1944). *Keys of the Kingdom* (1944) and *The Inn of the Sixth Happiness* (1956) were popular stories about western missionaries in China.

But, predictably, it was an exotic fantasy view of China that inspired the more imaginative efforts, featuring the Chinese at their most inscrutable, usually with an occidental heroine threatened with a fate worse than death by vicious Chinese warlords. Among the more memorable films in this genre were *Shanghai Express* (1932), *The Bitter Tea of General Yen* (1933), *The General Died at Dawn* (1936), *Shanghai Gesture* (1941), *The Left Hand of God* (1956), *Five Gates to Hell* (1957) and *Seven Women* (1965). Then there was the unsavory criminal mastermind Fu Manchu, featured in a series of low-budget thrillers.

With the advent of World War II, movies about China began to take on a more propagandistic tone. China was featured as a western ally victimized by brutal Japanese conquest in *China Sky* (1945), *China's Little Devils* (1944), *30 Seconds Over Tokyo* (1944) and *God is My Co-Pilot* (1945).

The Cold War and the Korean conflict brought a new villainy to the Chinese in Hollywood's interpretation of the scheming, insidious Oriental, embodied a decade earlier in the Japanese stereotype. This approach was perhaps most vividly realized in *The Manchurian Candidate* (1962), wherein an American POW in Korea is brainwashed by Chinese captors and programmed to assassinate an American presidential candidate.

Chinese-Americans, generally placed in smoky, seamy Chinatown settings, have been a staple of Hollywood melodrama from D. W. Griffith (*Broken Blossoms,* 1916) to Roman Polanski (*Chinatown,* 1972).

The most popular fictional character is doubtless the affable Chinese-American sleuth Charlie Chan, who can still be seen deducing solutions to crime on local television.

Chinese Film

Like those of the Soviet Union, the quality of Chinese films has fluctuated in terms of artistry and political outspokenness at the whim of government censors.

Motion pictures were introduced in China in 1913. But, according to Chinese playwright Xia Yan, "they do not have a long tradition or a unique national style. . . . It was only after the founding of the People's Republic in 1949 that the film industry began to develop." [1]

But that burgeoning development ran afoul of the Cultural Revolution. As the *Beijing* (Peking) *Review* noted, Lin Piao and the "gang of four," "who decked themselves out as the most revolutionary of revolutionaries, completely negated the achievements of the film industry after liberation. Many experienced scenarists, directors and actors and actresses were persecuted and their works were branded as poisonous weeds. In a matter of seven or eight years, all the studio grounds in the country fell into disrepair, not a single film was made, and many film workers were compelled to turn to other professions." [2]

One Chinese film, *Lin Tse-hsu* ("The Opium War"), directed by Chen Chunli, was suppressed for 15 years by Jiang Qing (Mme. Mao Tse-tung) because it did not deal with a revolutionary theme. When exhibited in Europe and the United States in 1978, the film was widely praised. A Chinese ballet film, *The White-Haired Girl,* was shown by the American Film Institute in Washington in 1973.

Unlike the Soviets, however, the Chinese otherwise have never had a film industry that produced movies widely shown in the West, nor boasted of artists of the caliber of Russian directors Eisenstein and Dovzhenko.

Recently, China has begun to allow the exhibition of U.S. movies. Among the first were Charlie Chaplin's classic *Modern Times* (1936), and the unremarkable science-fiction film, *Futureworld* (1976). And in May 1979 Zhang Hong, head of the China Film Bureau, was in the United States to arrange for exhibition of "everything from *Gone with the Wind* to *Star Wars.*"

Television

Television is in its infancy in China. There are only about 2 million sets for China's 900 million people; of these, only some 20,000 are in color. Programming for Chinese audiences, who gather in clusters around the relatively few TV sets, has been almost exclusively for government-controlled propaganda messages.

With the 1979 China-U.S. breakthrough, however, Chinese viewers have begun to see U.S. documentaries and feature films, including the 1961 version of *The Hunchback of Notre Dame.*

---

[1] *Beijing* (Peking) *Review,* April 6, 1979, p. 8.
[2] Id.

China for a month-long visit. He was met at the airport by Chinese Party Chairman and Premier Hua Guofeng as well as most of the party's vice chairmen. At his banquet speech, Pol Pot went to great lengths to express his party's commitment to the Thought of Mao Tse-tung.

Huang at the U.N. On Sept. 29 Chinese Foreign Minister Huang Hua, addressing the United Nations General Assembly, repeated the well-known Chinese view that "the continuation of fierce contention between the two superpowers is bound to lead to a world war some day." But Huang went on to defend the view: "Some people say that in repeatedly stressing the danger of a world war, China is raising a false alarm and that it is warlike and wants to provoke a war. This is vile slander. All we have done is to call a spade a spade, so that people would be on the alert."

Deng on Overseas Chinese. On Sept. 29 Chinese Vice Premier Deng Xiaoping, speaking to overseas Chinese who had returned to China for the National Day celebrations, expressed the hope "that they will continue to live in friendship with the people of their resident countries" and abide by their laws. Deng went on to say that Peking was concerned about the welfare of ethnic Chinese in other Asian countries and their right to be granted naturalized citizenship in the host countries.

Peking Calls for Modernization. On Oct. 1 a Peking *People's Daily* editorial urged the speeding-up of construction in order to run the country well and to fulfill production plans. The editorial urged people to be both "red and expert" and said "We must also study science conscientiously, learn technique and acquire . . . proficiency." Only then, concluded the article, can China achieve the four modernizations advocated by Chou En-lai and detailed by Hua Guofeng on Feb. 26, 1978.

Peking on Arms Sales to Taiwan. On Oct. 4 *The Wall Street Journal* published an interview with Chinese Vice Premier Li Xiannian in which he repeated his country's view that the shipment of arms to Taiwan by the U.S. or other countries after a normalization of relations with mainland China by the U.S. would be "manifest interference in China's internal problems." Li warned that "if the U.S. is to issue statements saying that Taiwan should be liberated peacefully, then we will issue a statement saying whether we liberate it peacefully or by force is an issue a foreign power can't interfere with."

Sino-Soviet Agreement. On Oct. 6 the Chinese news agency Xinhua announced that an agreement had been reached with the Soviet Union on navigation rights in a channel at the confluence of the Amur (Heilong) and Ussuri rivers. The matter had been under discussion for eight years, and was one of the first signs of movement in the Sino-Soviet border dispute. *(See April 26, 1978)*

Cultural Rejuvenations. On Oct. 16 the Chinese news agency Xinhua reported a general easing of restrictions on cultural activity, and the reprinting of Chinese and foreign works that had been banned in recent years. Included among the foreign works were those by Shakespeare, Heine, Gogol, Balzac and Hugo, piano compositions by Beethoven, Chopin and Bach, and drawings by Rembrandt. The report stated that the relaxation was in line with the principle of "making the past serve the present" and "making foreign things serve China."

New Education Policies. On Oct. 20 the Chinese news agency Xinhua reported the need for specialists to implement the modernization program and for the teaching programs necessary to produce such specialists. The report blamed the "gang of four" for their opposition to entrance examinations and stated that under their control the Chinese school system had declined in quality year by year.

Entrance Exams Restored. On Oct. 21 the Xinhua news agency announced that academic entrance examinations would be reintroduced. The exams had been suspended as elitist during the Cultural Revolution. It was also announced that some students would be allowed to go directly from high school to college, obviating the previous requirement that they first spend several years working in the countryside.

Pol Pot Returns to Cambodia. On Oct. 22 Pol Pot, Cambodian premier and Communist Party secretary, returned home after a month-long visit to China. During his stay he traveled widely in China and was greeted by prominent leaders at all stops. *(See Sept. 28, 1977)*

Dalai Lama Not Welcome. On Oct. 23 *The New York Times* reported that the State Department, unwilling to irritate China, was quietly blocking a proposed American visit by the Dalai Lama, the exiled religious and temporal leader of Tibet. *(See Sept. 3, 1979)*

Deng on European Communists. On Oct. 24 Chinese Vice Premier Deng Xiaoping was reported to have said in an interview with *Agence France-Presse* that China "would not like to see the communist parties of France, Italy and Spain come to power or even to participate in government" because they would carry out "a policy of appeasement" towards the Soviet Union.

Deng on Terrorism. On Oct. 26 Chinese Vice Premier Deng Xiaoping told French newspaper editors visiting Peking that terrorism, cut off as it was from the masses, had nothing to do with revolution, and he "categorically condemned terrorism as anti-revolutionary and anti-Marxist-Leninist."

China's New Foreign Policy. On Nov. 1 the Peking *People's Daily* published a major theoretical account of the "three worlds" theory *(see April 10, 1974)*, entitled "Chairman Mao's Theory of the Differentiation of the Three Worlds is a Major Contribution to Marxism-Leninism." Offered as a defense against critics of the new Chinese foreign policy as "revisionist" (i.e. seeking peace with the West), the article cited various precedents in the writings of Marx, Engels, and Lenin to justify recent Chinese foreign policy. The article was important because it underscored Chinese efforts at reconciliation with the second world to acquire the technology necessary to modernize.

China to Buy British Planes. On Nov. 5 *The Times* of London reported that Chinese Vice Premier Wang Zhen had told a British trade mission visiting China that Peking would like to purchase British Harrier vertical take-off aircraft. The British press said the Chinese were ready to place orders for at least 48 Harriers, perhaps as many as 300.

On November 28 the Soviet party newspaper *Pravda* expressed alarm over the reports. Because the Harriers use some U.S.-made parts, their sale required U.S. approval. *(See Nov. 3, 1978, Jan. 5, 1979)*

Sino-Cambodian Relations. On Nov. 10 Cambodia and China signed a protocol on the opening of telecommunication links between the two countries.

Chinese Oil Exports. On Nov. 15 Chinese Vice Premier Gu Mu told Japanese congressmen visiting Peking that China would be able to export more than 10 million tons of oil a year to Japan by 1982.

China and Vietnam. On Nov. 20 Vietnamese party leader Le Duan arrived in Peking for a six-day visit. Although he was met at the airport by Chinese Premier and party leader Hua Guofeng, observers termed his reception as "cool."

Correspondent Expelled. On Nov. 26 Ross Munro, the Peking correspondent for the *Toronto Globe and Mail,* was expelled from China for what the Chinese said were "obvious reasons." Munro had just completed a series of articles on human rights in China.

Chinese Delegation to Cambodia. On Dec. 3 Chinese Vice Premier Chen Yonggui arrived in Cambodia for a two-week visit. Chen was accompanied on a tour of the country by Cambodian Premier and party leader Pol Pot. During the visit, Chen said he had learned at first hand the determination of Cambodia to preserve its "independence, sovereignty and territorial integrity."

Chinese Language Reform. On Dec. 20 the Peking *People's Daily* published the second draft of the simplification of Chinese characters. Prepared with the approval of the State Council, the plan listed 853 simplified characters, 248 of which were already in wide use. Reports indicated that the new plan had been offered in May 1975 but rejected by the "gang of four," who were also accused of opposing the use of the phonetic alphabet and even the teaching of language in the universities.

Prisoners Released. On Dec. 20 the Indonesian government reported that it had released 10,000 political prisoners, some of whom had been held for 12 years without trial for their role in an attempted Chinese-Communist-backed coup in 1965.

1978

Southeast Asia War Grows — China Buys Egyptian Weapons — China-France Trade — Peking Raps Hanoi — China-Japan Trade — China EEC Pact — Fifth Congress Convenes — Chiang Ching-kuo New ROC Head — U.S. Wheat to China — China-Vietnam Skirmishes — U.S. to Reduce Korea Troops — Afghanistan Coup — Soviet Border Crossing - Brzezinski to China — China-Ex-Im Bank Exemption Denied — Vietnam Offensive — Sino-U.S. Scientific Exchange — New China Trade Policy — Sino-Vietnam Talks — Sino-Japanese Treaty — Hua to Romania, Yugoslavia, Iran — Sino-Soviet Pact Abrogated — Camp David Middle East Accord — Sino-Soviet Border Tension — Congressional Treaty Consultation — Hua Seeks Modernization — Soviet-Vietnam Accord — China Backs Cambodia — Deng Warns Thailand — U.S.-China Oil Deal — U.S. Invites Deng — U.S. Recognizes PRC — Taiwan Reaction — Coca-Cola to China — Vietnam in Cambodia — ROC Embassy Sold — Goldwater Sues Carter — Congress to Protect Taiwan — Deng to Visit U.S. — China Taiwan Offer

War in Southeast Asia. On Jan. 1, after Cambodia broke off diplomatic relations with Vietnam the day before, Vietnamese officials accused Cambodia of attacking and occupying Vietnamese territory along their joint border in Vietnam's Tay Ninh Province (the Parrot's Beak). Vietnam reportedly had nearly 60,000 troops in the Cambodian province of Svay Rieng.

On Jan. 2 Vietnam was reported to have captured the Parrot's Beak area.

Brzezinski on Indochinese War. On Jan. 8 national security adviser Zbigniew Brzezinski said in a televised interview that the border conflict between Cambodia and Vietnam was really a "proxy war" between China and the Soviet Union, with Vietnam receiving support from Moscow, and Cambodia receiving aid from Peking.

Soviet-Japanese Relations Worsen. On Jan. 8 Japanese Foreign Minister Sunao Sonoda arrived in Moscow for negotiations over four islands disputed by the two countries. The Russians took the opportunity to renege on a 1972 agreement over the islands and insist that "there remains no question unsettled." This was followed by large-scale military exercises off the coast of Japan. The result was to push the Japanese further toward agreements with China. *(See Feb. 16, 1978)*

China Buys Plane from Egypt. On Jan. 18, according to Japanese reports, China purchased a MiG-23 from Egypt, and would obtain SAM missiles, MAT anti-tank missiles, and T-62 tanks in the future.

China to Trade with France. On Jan. 19 French Premier Raymond Barre arrived in China for a six-day visit. He was accompanied by the heads of the most important industrial groups in France concerned with power engineering, nuclear power, chemicals and oil. Towards the end of the visit, Barre declared French readiness to help China build nuclear power stations provided that China accept "normal international safeguards."

On Jan. 23 China and France signed a scientific and technological "framework" agreement, the first of its kind between China and a Western power. The agreement dealt with joint studies and projects in several areas of advanced technology.

War in Southeast Asia. On Jan. 20 Hanoi radio broadcast an editorial stating that "We cannot help but to resort to legitimate self-defense" if Cambodian raids on Vietnam continue.

On Jan. 28, Cambodian forces continued their attack on Tay Ninh Province (the Parrot's Beak) in Vietnam.

On Jan. 30 Phnom Penh radio reported that all invading Vietnamese troops had been driven from Cambodian territory.

Peking Criticizes Hanoi. On Jan. 22 China said it regarded Cambodia as a victim of "Vietnamese aggression." It was believed that this was the first instance of Peking accusing Hanoi directly.

China Supports Sadat. On Feb. 4 Chinese Communist Party Chairman Hua Guofeng met with Egyptian President Anwar Sadat's special envoy in Peking and publicly affirmed China's support for Egypt's peace initiative with Israel. Hua described Sadat's stand as "just" and he commented that it "conforms to the interests of the Egyptian, Palestinian, and other Arab peoples."

Sino-Japanese Trade Agreement. On Feb. 16 China and Japan signed an eight-year trade agreement in Peking calling for exchanges of goods worth $10 billion during the life of the treaty. China would export coal and oil to Japan in return for technology and finished goods. *(See Sept. 11, 1978)*

Chinese Agreement with EEC. On Feb. 16 China signed a five-year trade agreement with the Common Market granting China most-favored-nation status.

U.S. Commitment to Asia. On Feb. 20 U.S. Defense Secretary Harold Brown stated that the U.S. would strengthen its strategic forces in Asia because of growing Soviet strength in the region.

Soviet Offer to China. On Feb. 24 the Soviet Union sent a private message to Peking suggesting that the two countries issue a joint statement to the effect that their mutual relations would be based on peaceful coexistence. This overture was rejected by China on March 9. In their reply, the Chinese again demanded withdrawal of Soviet troops from Mongolia and, for the first time, Soviet withdrawal from the entire length of the Sino-Soviet border.

On March 31, China made the entire exchange public.

Fifth Congress Convenes. On Feb. 26 the Fifth National People's Congress convened in Peking. The congress saw the participation of many top leaders who had been purged during the Cultural Revolution, and represented an almost complete reversal of internal Chinese policies dating from 1965. The congress adopted a new constitution, more moderate than that of 1975 but less so than that of 1954. *(Text, p. 335)* The congress saw the final consolidation in the leadership of the new post-Mao elite, begun at the 11th party congress of 1977. *(List of leaders, p. 291)*

On Feb. 26 Premier Hua Guofeng delivered a three-and-a-half hour address to the congress entitled "Unite and Strive to Build a Modern, Powerful Socialist Country." Hua traced the power struggles of recent years and detailed the defeat of the "gang of four." He stated that although this campaign against the "gang" must be continued, it was now time to look ahead and to "speed up" the modernization of the country. In the third part of the speech, Hua outlined the main features of the "four modernizations" concept for the development of the national economy advocated by Chou En-lai at the fourth congress in 1975. Specifically, Hua said, "The ten years from 1976 to 1985 are crucial for accomplishing these tasks," and submitted a draft outline of a ten-year plan. The draft called for huge increases in agricultural yield and industrial production, as well as major increases in virtually all aspects of China's economy, setting specific goals in some areas. *(Text, p. 332)*

Although not apparent at the time, Hua's announced goals touched off a major debate within the Chinese leadership as to whether they could be attained. The result was that in 1979 the goals were downgraded significantly or, in some cases, dropped altogether. *(See June 18, 1979)*

Graduate Schools Reopen. On Feb. 28 the Chinese government announced that graduate schools in a number of non-technical fields would reopen for the first time since the Cultural Revolution. The restored fields of study included history, law, religion, philosophy, literature and economics.

Religious Activity Permitted. On March 10 *The New York Times* reported sources inside China saying that religious activity, banned outright since the Cultural Revolution, was reappearing in China.

South Sea Islands Dispute. On March 11 the Philippines occupied another of the Spratly (Nansha) Islands in the South China Sea. *(Map, p. 115)* This brought the number of islands held by the Philippines to seven. Nation-alist China occupied one, the largest. Vietnam occupied three, including Spratly Island itself. China, which also claimed the islands, occupied none.

Chiang ROC President. On March 21 the National Assembly of the Republic of China, on Taiwan, elected Chiang Ching-kuo, son of former Nationalist leader Chiang Kai-shek, as president.

Brezhnev Tours Border. On March 28 Soviet President Leonid Brezhnev began an unusual 13-day tour of Siberia and the Sino-Soviet border. He was accompanied by Defense Minister Dmitri F. Ustinov.

Vietnamese Attacks. On April 7 it was reported that Vietnam had attacked across the border and into Cambodian territory. Among the conflicting reports following this latest outbreak, Cambodia claimed to have repulsed the attack on April 12.

U.S. Wheat to China. On April 10 the U.S. Department of Agriculture announced the sale of 600,000 tons of wheat to China, the first such sale since 1974. On April 18 it was announced that an additional 400,000 tons were to be sold.

Carter's Affirmation. On April 11 President Carter reiterated his hope that the U.S. and China eventually would establish full diplomatic relations. Answering questions after a speech to the American Society of Newpaper Editors in Washington, Carter said, "Our hope is that over a period of months . . . we will completely realize the hopes expressed in the Shanghai Communiqué."

China-Japan Incident. On April 13 about a hundred Chinese fishing boats were seen in and around the territorial waters to the northwest of the Senkaku Islands. The islands are claimed by both China and Japan. The fishing dispute had been shelved in the hope the two nations might sign a peace treaty. The Japanese protested the incident the next day, and within four days the ships had all been withdrawn. *(Map, p. 105)*

On April 15 Chinese Vice Premier Geng Biao termed the incident "accidental" and the Japanese later accepted this explanation.

U.S. Monitors Chinese A-Tests. On April 17 Indian Prime Minister Morarji R. Desai told Parliament that with the full knowledge of the Indian government a joint Indian-U.S. intelligence team had planted a nuclear-powered spy device in the Himalayan Mountains 12 years earlier. Reports of the mission had first appeared in a U.S. publication, *Outsider*, earlier in the month. The device was placed to monitor Chinese nuclear testing at the Lop Nor test site.

China and Vietnam Fight. On April 18 the quarrel between China and Vietnam heated up further with reports of fighting along the border, including Vietnamese tank attacks.

U.S. to Reduce Troops in Korea. On April 21 President Carter announced that the U.S. would withdraw one combat battalion from South Korea in 1978, and that two other battalions formerly scheduled to be withdrawn would remain until 1979.

Carter on Cambodia. On April 21 President Carter said the Cambodian government of Pol Pot was the "worst violator of human rights in the world today."

Negotiator Returns. On April 26 Leonid Ilyichev, Soviet deputy minister for foreign affairs and chief of the

Soviet delegation negotiating Sino-Soviet frontier questions, returned to Peking after an absence of 18 months.

Coup in Afghanistan. On April 27 a military coup occurred in Afghanistan. President Mohammed Daoud, a neutralist, was killed and his government replaced by one headed by Noor Mohammed Taraki, a Marxist.

On April 30 the Soviet Union officially recognized the new regime.

"Expert" vs. "Red." On April 30, in a reversal of Maoist policy during the Cultural Revolution, Vice Premier Deng Xiaoping called on schools, factories and offices to "recruit only those who are outstanding," and stressed that the primary responsibility of students was to study. *(See Oct. 22, 1979)*

Soviet Border Crossing. On the night of May 8-9, a force of some 30 Soviet border guards crossed the Ussuri River and penetrated about 2-1/2 miles into Chinese territory. Peking promptly filed a note of protest.

By May 12, at a meeting of Chinese and Soviet negotiators, the incident appeared to have been overlooked.

Brzezenski to China. On May 20 the president's national security adviser, Zbigniew Brzezinski, arrived in China with officials from the departments of State and Defense and the National Security Council. Speaking at a welcoming banquet, Chinese Foreign Minister Huang Hua called for all the peoples of the world to "adopt a . . . policy to upset the hegemonists' [Russians] strategic deployment." In reply, Brzezinski declared that the American commitment to friendship with China was based on a "long-term strategic view" and was not "a tactical expedient." Brzezinski agreed that the U.S. also had resolved to "resist the efforts of any nation which seeks to establish global or regional hegemony."

No discernible progress was made toward the normalization of Sino-American relations, but the Chinese were clearly pleased that Brzezinski's visit coincided with the inauguration of Chiang Ching-kuo as president of the Republic of China on Taiwan. The Nationalists considered the timing of the visit a deliberate insult.

It was learned later that two significant breakthroughs had occurred. First, Brzezinski informed the Chinese that the U.S. would not oppose the sale of arms to Peking by Europeans. More importantly, Brzezinski told Chinese leader Hua Guofeng that Leonard Woodcock, head of the U.S. Liaison Office in Peking, was prepared to start serious discussions about the remaining issues separating the two countries. These talks, to begin in July, were to deal with the U.S. demand that it be allowed to continue to sell arms to Taiwan after normalization. Those talks led directly to the December agreement. *(See Dec. 15, 1978)*

No Exemption for China. On June 2 the House of Representatives refused to exempt China from legislation requiring presidential approval before the Export-Import Bank could do business with a communist country. The vote was 179-138.

Deng on Mao. On June 3 it was reported that Chinese Vice Premier Deng Xiaoping, speaking at a conference of army political commissars, had said that former Chairman Mao Tse-tung's ideas should not be interpreted literally. "We must integrate them with reality, analyze and study actual conditions and solve practical problems."

U.S. Equipment to China. On June 9, amid increasing signs of an American "tilt" toward Peking, it was

reported that the U.S. had agreed to sell to China advanced airborne equipment for geological exploration and earthquake detection that also had potential military use. This reversed an earlier administration decision, made in May, to bar the sale. The ban on the sale of such equipment to the Soviet Union remained in effect.

Vietnamese Offensive. On June 28, diplomatic sources in Southeast Asia reported that a major Vietnamese offensive against Cambodia had begun two weeks earlier.

Vietnam into COMECON. On June 29 Vietnam was formally inducted into the Council for Mutual Economic Assistance (COMECON), the Soviet-led combine in which the only other non-European members were Cuba and the Mongolian People's Republic. *(See July 3, 1978)*

No Jets to Taiwan. On June 30 the U.S. announced that it had decided not to sell 60 F-4 fighter bombers to Nationalist China. Taiwan had been asking for the planes for three years and had stated that its current planes would be obsolete by the end of the decade. *(See July 6, 1978)*

Democracy in China. On July 1 China celebrated the 57th anniversary of the founding of the Chinese Communist Party by reprinting Chairman Mao Tse-tung's 1962 "Talk at an Enlarged Working Conference Convened by the Central Committee." The decision to print the piece and the accompanying commentary both suggested an easing of censorship.

On July 2 the Peking *People's Daily* published an editorial on the subject which said that contradictions among the people should be solved by democratic methods and not by dictatorship. The editorial also noted the need for criticism, as long as it did not come from anti-Party elements.

Western reporters soon noticed an increase in wall posters critical of the regime.

Vietnam and China to Talk. On July 2 Hanoi radio reported that Vietnam was willing to talk with representatives of the Chinese government about the problem of ethnic Chinese in Vietnam.

On July 19 Peking offered to hold high-level talks with Vietnamese officials to resolve the problem. *(See Aug. 8, 1978)*

China Cuts Aid to Vietnam. On July 3 the Chinese government issued a note to Vietnam stating that it had been compelled to recall its experts and stop technical and economic aid because the Vietnamese had "created a foul atmosphere of vilifying and inciting antagonism against China."

On the same day, the Peking *People's Daily* denied that China had any claim over persons of Chinese nationality living abroad, or that it was responsible for their actions. At the same time, the article restated that China did have the right to defend these people if they were attacked by their adopted nations.

Over the past twenty years, China had given Vietnam nearly $10 billion in economic assistance.

Taiwan Rejects Kfirs. On July 6 Nationalist China rejected a proposed purchase of 50-60 Kfir jets from Israel. The Carter administration, whose approval was required because the Kfirs used American engines, had okayed the sale on July 4. Taiwan had rejected the offer rather than offend Saudi Arabia, an important ally and the source of most of Taiwan's oil. *(See Nov. 6, 1978)*

U.S. Treaties with Taiwan

The greatest obstacle to U.S. normalization of relations with the People's Republic of China was the problem of what to do with Taiwan. On Dec. 15, when President Carter announced that the U.S. would open diplomatic relations with Peking on Jan. 1, 1979, the U.S. "acknowledged" that there was but one China, and that Taiwan was part of China.

This would seem to indicate that the U.S. recognized Peking as sovereign over the island. The reality was quite different. In fact, and despite the official statements, U.S. relations with Taiwan continued to be, for the most part, no different from U.S. relations with any other sovereign power. On April 10, when Carter signed the Taiwan Relations Act (PL 96-8), this policy became law. *(Text, p. 343)*

By the provisions of this act, all the laws, treaties, and agreements which were in effect prior to Dec. 31, 1978, would remain in effect after recognition of Peking on Jan. 1, 1979. The sole exception was the mutual defense treaty of 1954, which would be terminated within the terms of the treaty on Jan. 1, 1980. On Nov. 8, 1979, Deputy Secretary of State Warren Christopher said that of the remaining 57 Taiwan treaties and agreements, five "require current attention" and need to be renegotiated; 29 agreements can remain in effect with no change; seven military agreements, including the mutual defense treaty, will be terminated at the end of 1979; two other agreements have been rendered moot by the break-off of diplomatic relations; and 14 agreements are inactive or no longer needed. *(Complete list of all treaties and agreements, p. 348)*

Agricultural commodities	7
Other trade agreements	5
Atomic energy	2
Civil aviation	2
Economic and technical cooperation	7*
Educational and cultural exchange	2
Maritime matters	2
Postal matters	4
Customs, visas and extraterritoriality	3
Miscellaneous	5
Lapsed or supplanted	18**
Total	57

The fact that all these agreements were still in effect in December 1978, and that the U.S. would deal with Taipei and not Peking on all these matters, meant that despite its official recognition of Peking, the U.S. would continue to act as if Taiwan were a sovereign state. *(Details, p. 48)*

* Includes agreements on foreign investments in Taiwan.
** Includes 1954 mutual defense treaty.

Sino-American Scientific Exchanges. On July 7 a science and technology delegation led by Frank Press, science and technology adviser to President Carter, arrived in Peking. At the welcoming banquet, Vice Premier Fang Yi, minister in charge of the State Scientific and Technological Commission, told the delegation that: "If the obstacle of the lack of normalization . . . is removed, vast vistas will open up for the expansion of scientific and technical exchanges and cooperation between our two countries."

In response, Press told the Chinese that President Carter believed the PRC "plays a central role in the maintenance of the global equilibrium. He recognizes that a strong and secure China is in America's interest."

The visit saw the official opening of some channels for civilian scientific and technological exchange between the two countries. The communist press in Hong Kong called the visit "the most significant since Nixon."

China's New Policy on Foreign Trade. On July 8 the Peking *People's Daily* published an article stating "the need to emancipate the mind in developing foreign trade," and extolled the advantages of commercial exchanges overseas.

The article represented formal recognition by China of its need for foreign technology in order to modernize, and its abandonment of the previous policy of "self-reliance."

China to Accept Foreign Capital. On July 13, in another reversal of policy, Chinese Vice Premier Li Xiannian told a visiting Mitsui delegation in Peking that China was willing to accept foreign funds to finance its modernization programs. Li was reported to have admitted that China would require a large amount of funds in the near future, the first public acknowledgement by the Chinese of such a need.

China Cuts Aid to Albania. On July 13 the Chinese Ministry of Foreign Affairs announced that China was terminating all economic and military aid to Albania, complaining that Albania had been following an "anti-China course." The cutoff marked a further erosion of relations between the two countries, which had been extremely cordial during China's radical phase of the late 1960s.

Congress Demands Consultation. On July 25 the Senate, by a 94-0 roll-call vote, amended the 1979 military aid authorization bill, calling on President Carter to consult with Congress before taking any action affecting the 1954 mutual defense treaty between the U.S. and the Republic of China. *(See pp. 39-42)*

Sino-Vietnamese Negotiations. On Aug. 8, representatives from Vietnam and China met in Peking to try to work out plans to accommodate the one million ethnic Chinese living in Vietnam. Thousands of Chinese had already fled the country, and tens of thousands more wanted to.

On Aug. 28 the negotiations were broken off.

Sino-Japanese Treaty. On Aug. 12, after three years of intermittent negotiations, China and Japan signed a treaty of peace and friendship in Tokyo. Conclusion of the treaty had been forestalled by Chinese insistence on a clause condemning "hegemonism" (a Chinese code word for the Soviet Union). The Japanese, who wanted good relations with both Peking and Moscow, had resisted signing a treaty that Russia might see as directed against Moscow.

The successful conclusion of the treaty had begun with talks between Chinese Vice Foreign Minister Han Nianlong and Japanese Ambassador Shoji Sato during the last week of July. They were concluded by the two foreign ministers, Huang Hua and Sunao Sonoda.

The final draft stated that both China and Japan were "opposed to efforts by any other country or group of countries to establish" hegemony in the Pacific or anywhere else, a statement which was vague enough for the Japanese to insist was not aimed against the Soviet Union, but which still used the word "hegemony." *(Text, p. 340)*

On Aug. 12 the Soviet news agency Tass said that the recent Sino-Japanese treaty endangered détente and threatened security in Asia.

Hua to Romania. On Aug. 16 Chinese Communist Party Chairman Hua Guofeng arrived in Romania for an unofficial visit. The visit drew worldwide attention and was generally seen as a significant challenge to Soviet claims of exclusive influence in this part of Eastern Europe.

Romanian leaders, aware of Soviet opposition, confined their comments to expressions of the need for bilateral relations, but Hua spoke on the need to oppose "hegemonism" and the "big powers that try to rule the earth."

Several agreements were signed, including scientific and cultural exchanges.

Hua to Yugoslavia. On Aug. 21 Chinese Party Chairman and Premier Hua Guofeng arrived in Yugoslavia for an unprecedented nine-day visit. China had long opposed Yugoslavia's decision, made during the 1950s, to move away from the Warsaw Pact and maintain neutrality in East-West relations. China's new foreign policy had caused Peking to reevaluate Yugoslavia's stance, however, and during his visit Hua supported Yugoslavia's independence in developing its own form of socialism "without the imposition of any models or prescriptions." Hua concluded his visit on Aug. 28 and went on to Iran. *(See Aug. 29, 1978)*

McGovern on Cambodia. On Aug. 21 Sen. George McGovern, D-S.D., a long-time opponent of U.S. military intervention in Southeast Asia, called for international military intervention in Cambodia to halt what he called "a clear case of genocide" by invading Vietnamese forces.

On Aug. 22 the State Department formally rejected McGovern's suggestion that U.S. troops participate in such an action.

Chinese Accusations. On Aug. 22 the Chinese government accused the Soviet Union of planning to build a "nuclear base" close to China's border near Japan. *(See Sept. 18, 1978)*

Congressmen to Southeast Asia. On Aug. 23 Vietnamese Premier Pham Van Dong told an eight-man congressional delegation visiting Hanoi that his country was eager for full relations with the U.S. Dong again said his government had dropped demands that the U.S. pay Vietnam $3 billion in war reparations.

On Aug. 27 the delegation called for the normalization of relations between the U.S. and Vietnam.

Both Chinas Attend Conference. On Aug. 24 representatives from both Taiwan and China attended the 19th International Conference on High-Energy Physics in Tokyo. This was the first time that delegates from both countries had attended the same meeting.

Moscow Attacks Peking. On Aug. 24 *Pravda* printed violent attacks on the signing of the Sino-Japanese peace treaty and Hua Guofeng's visit to Romania. China was denounced as a country "in the grip of military hysteria" in which 40 percent of the budget was spent on military purposes. China's leaders were accused of "preaching hatred and hostility among peoples" and inciting a new war.

The articles also criticized "short-sighted Western politicians" for having "flaunted recently the 'Chinese Card.' " Moscow warned that Peking did not look upon them as other than temporary allies.

Hua to Iran. On Aug. 29 Chinese Communist Party Chairman Hua Guofeng arrived in Iran for a four-day visit. Although an agreement on cultural cooperation was signed, no joint communiqué was issued.

This was the first visit by a ranking Chinese leader to a non-socialist country.

Soviet Advisers to Vietnam. On Sept. 2 it was reported that the Soviet Union had completed an airlift of Soviet technicians and military equipment to Vietnam to replace the Chinese technicians withdrawn from Vietnam during the summer.

China to End Treaty with Russia. On Sept. 6 Chinese Vice Premier Deng Xiaoping told Japanese newsmen visiting China that his country intended to terminate officially its alliance treaty with the Soviet Union before next April; it had already ceased to exist in practice. *(See April 3, 1979)*

Foreign Contact Bans Eased. On Sept. 9 it was reported that the Chinese government had abolished the long-standing bans prohibiting contacts between Chinese citizens and foreigners in China.

Sino-Japanese Trade to Increase. On Sept. 11 the ministers of international trade of China and Japan, Li Qiang and Toshio Komoto, agreed to expand trade under the long-term agreement signed in February. The period covered by the agreement was extended five years, from 1985 to 1990. *(See March 19, 1979)*

U.S. Embargo Against Vietnam. On Sept. 12 the *Federal Register* published a notice stating that President Carter was extending the U.S. trade embargo against Vietnam.

Camp David Agreements. On Sept. 17 the leaders of Egypt and Israel concluded 13 days of negotiations at Camp David. In a televised address, President Carter announced that two pacts had been signed that offered a framework for a "durable settlement" of Middle East problems.

It was later reported that following the announcement of the agreements in mid-October, Carter decided to use the goodwill generated by the success at Camp David to push for the full normalization of relations with China. It was at this time that he apparently imposed a Jan. 1, 1979, deadline for this to be achieved. *(See Nov. 4, 1978)*

Soviet Buildup on Border. On Sept. 18 the London *Daily Telegraph* reported that a recent CIA study had detailed a new Soviet buildup on its border with China. Included among the more recently deployed weapons were the newest Soviet tanks, newer aircraft, and up to 30 of the SS-20 mobile ICBMs with MIRVs.

Carter's Three Points. On Sept. 19 Chai Zemin, head of the Chinese Liaison Office in Washington, met with President Carter. It was reported that Carter listed three points on which the U.S. would insist prior to the opening of full diplomatic relations: (1) the U.S. must continue its current commercial and cultural ties with Taiwan; (2) the U.S. believed that the China-Taiwan dispute must be resolved peacefully; and, (3) the U.S. should be allowed to continue to sell defensive arms to Taiwan after normalization of Sino-American relations.

Force Reductions in South Korea. On Sept. 19 the Defense Department announced that the army had in recent months reduced its forces in South Korea by some 2,000 men.

Chinese Buildup on Vietnam Border. On Sept. 25 Hanoi's official army newspaper charged that China had sent troops to the border area between the two countries.

Congress Wants to Consult. On Sept. 26 President Carter signed the 1979 security aid authorization bill (PL 95-384). Attached to the bill was an amendment stating that any proposed policy changes affecting the 1954 mutual defense treaty between the U.S. and the Republic of China were a matter for prior consultation with Congress. *(See p. 40)*

Hua Pushes Modernization. On Oct. 1 Chinese Communist Party Chairman Hua Guofeng spoke at the celebration of the 29th anniversary of the founding of the People's Republic. In his remarks, Hua called for a speed-up of the measures designed to achieve modernization and said it could be achieved by the end of the century. Hua blamed the recent failures of the Chinese economy on Lin Piao and the "gang of four" and called for the transformation of the economy through the application of modern science and technology.

Mao Invoked on Modernization. On Oct. 6 the Chinese Communist Party theoretical journal *Hongqi* published an editorial calling for the application of modern science to the Chinese economy and made several references to the late Chairman Mao Tse-tung's views on the need for progress. This seems to have been an effort to underline a continuity in approach between Mao and the current leadership.

Moscow Opposes Arms Sales to China. On Oct. 11 the Soviet government news agency Tass, commenting on repeated rumors that various Western governments were contemplating arms sales to China, claimed that such sales would "encourage the aggressive militarism of the Maoists"; it cautioned Britain that although such a policy was ostensibly aimed at counterbalancing the Soviet Union, it could endanger Britain's own security and cast a shadow over the SALT talks.

China to Buy French Weapons. On Oct. 20 it was announced in Paris that China had agreed to purchase antiaircraft and antitank missiles from France at a cost of $700 million.

Trade Credits for China. On Oct. 21 President Carter signed an agricultural exports bill (PL 95-501) that contained a provision allowing the Commodity Credit Corporation to extend short-term (up to three years) credit to the People's Republic of China. Previously, China had been ineligible for such credit under the provisions of the Jackson-Vanik amendment to the 1974 Trade Act; the ban on the Soviet Union remained in effect.

Soviet Treaty with Vietnam. On Nov. 3 the Soviet Union signed a treaty of friendship and cooperation with Vietnam in Moscow. Observers saw the treaty as a Soviet approval of Vietnam's actions in Cambodia, and as a means of pressuring China in the south.

Vance on Arms Sales to China. On Nov. 3 Secretary of State Cyrus Vance told the press that Washington would not sell arms to either Moscow or China but that it would not oppose nor approve allied arms sales to China, provided that they were defensive in nature and did not constitute a threat to Taiwan. Vance said that "in so far as other nations are concerned, this is a matter which each of them must decide for itself." *(See May 20, 1978)*

U.S. Draft Proposal. On Nov. 4 the U.S. secretly sent to Peking the draft of a proposal on the opening of full diplomatic relations between the two countries.

The president himself reportedly wrote in the target date: Jan. 1, 1979. *(See Sept. 17, 1978)*

China Backs Cambodia. On Nov. 5 Chinese Party Vice Chairman Wang Dongxing led a delegation to Cambodia for a two-day visit. During his stay Wang said that China backed the Cambodian people's "just struggle in defense of their independence."

Chinese Fallout. On Nov. 5 the U.S. Department of Energy reported that the first increase in worldwide radioactive fallout in four years had occurred in 1977, due mainly to the large Chinese nuclear test in November 1976. China continued to test in the atmosphere.

U.S. Planes to Taiwan. On Nov. 6 U.S. State Department spokeswoman Jill Schuker announced that Taiwan's request to purchase advanced jet fighter planes had been denied but that the U.S. would supply Taiwan with 48 F-5Es, which were considered to be more defensive in nature.

Taiwan again rejected an offer of Israeli Kfir jets. *(See July 6, 1978)*

Deng Warns Thailand. On Nov. 6 Chinese Vice Premier Deng Xiaoping, visiting Thailand during a tour of Southeast Asia, warned Thai officials against Soviet "expansionist activities" in the region.

Chinese Delegation to Britain. On Nov. 7 Chinese Vice Premier Wang Zhen, on a ten-day visit to Great Britain, stated that he had come "for concrete discussions with the aim of introducing [Britain's] advanced technology and equipment in various sectors of industry in China." On Nov. 9 the entire delegation watched demonstrations of various British fighter aircraft. On Nov. 15 the first Sino-British scientific and technological exchange agreement was signed. It was agreed that trade between the two should be quadrupled to reach a total of about $10 billion within the next seven years. Britain also promised to consider the sale of Harrier jump jets to China.

U.S. Cuts Troops. On Nov. 7 *The Washington Post* reported that the Carter administration had cut the number of American military personnel on Taiwan by half during the past year, leaving only 750 on the island.

Deng on Moscow-Hanoi Relationships. On Nov. 8 Chinese Vice Premier Deng Xiaoping, speaking at a press conference in Bangkok, reacted sharply to Vietnam's signing of a treaty with Russia. Responding to comments that the treaty meant the encirclement of China, Deng said that "China fears no encirclement." *(Map, p. 191)*

U.S. Firm to Build Hotels in China. On Nov. 9 Reynolds Burgund, vice president of Intercontinental Hotels Corporation, a subsidiary of Pan American World Airways, announced in Hong Kong that his firm had reached an agreement with the Chinese government to build and operate a chain of hotels in China's major cities. Construction costs were estimated at $500 million.

China on ASEAN. On Nov. 9 Chinese Vice Premier Deng Xiaoping, speaking in Malaysia, announced that

China would "support the ASEAN [Association of Southeast Asian Nations] countries in their just struggle in defense of their independence and sovereignty against outside control and interference."

U.S. Troops in Japan. On Nov. 9 U.S. Secretary of Defense Harold Brown met with Japanese Prime Minister Takeo Fukuda and Foreign Minister Sunao Sonoda in Tokyo for talks on maintaining U.S. troops in Japan. The Japanese apparently agreed to increase their financial support of the U.S. presence to about $700 million a year.

Speaking at a news conference the same day, Brown pointed to new Russian buildups in the Pacific and along the Chinese border.

More Rehabilitations. On Nov. 15 the Peking *People's Daily* published an editorial calling for the rehabilitation of those who had been purged prior to the Cultural Revolution, including those "who were classified ... as rightists in 1957." Stating that there were "some innocent people wrongly charged," the editorial blamed all the errors on Lin Piao and the "gang of four."

Vietnamese Offensive. On Nov. 18 it was reported that the Vietnamese had begun a major offensive against Cambodia. *(See Dec. 21, 1978)*

U.S. to Buy Chinese Oil. On Nov. 21 the Houston-based Coastal States Gas Corporation announced that it had signed an agreement with China to import 3.6 million barrels of crude oil starting in early 1979.

Soviet Comments on Sino-Western Rapprochement. On Nov. 24, the *Manchester Guardian* carried the comments of the influential G. Arbatov, director of the U.S.A. Institute in Moscow, warning against Western nations allying with China only in order to oppose the Soviet Union: "If such an axis is built on an anti-Soviet basis then there is no place for détente, even in a narrow sense."

The gravity of the Soviet concern was underlined by personal letters sent to the leaders of Britain, France and West Germany by Soviet President Brezhnev in late November.

Deng's Signal. On Nov. 25 Chinese Vice Premier Deng Xiaoping stated publicly that he hoped to visit Washington, a remark regarded by the White House as a signal by the Chinese that they were anxious for an agreement on the opening of full relations.

Deng on Hua. On Nov. 27 Chinese Vice Premier Deng Xiaoping told a U.S. reporter that he and Chinese Premier and Communist Party Chairman Hua Guofeng had "always been in complete agreement over everything." The statement followed reports of discord between the two top Chinese leaders.

Peking's Promise. On Dec. 3 Chinese Vice Premier Deng Xiaoping stated in an interview with U.S. reporters that the U.S. could "keep its economic interests in Taiwan." In an announcement aimed at calming the fears of American businessmen who feared that normalization would mean large financial losses for their companies, Deng added that the U.S. "can continue its investment. China has no intention of bringing down Taiwan's living standards."

Fighting in Cambodia. On Dec. 3 Hanoi radio announced the formation of the Kampuchean United Front for National Salvation in what was called a "liberated zone" of Cambodia. The front called for the people of Cambodia "to rise up for the struggle to overthrow the Pol Pot and Ieng Sary clique." The formation of the front followed reports of Cambodian defeats at the hands of Vietnamese forces invading the country.

China, Japan Open Offices. On Dec. 3, it was announced in Tokyo that the Chinese government would permit Japanese firms to open offices in Peking and that Chinese companies would be permitted to open offices in Tokyo.

Chinese Draft Proposal. On Dec. 4 the Chinese secretly sent the draft of a proposed joint communiqué between the two countries to Washington, responding to an earlier U.S. proposal. *(See Nov. 4, 1978)*

Sino-French Trade Agreement. On Dec. 4 French Foreign Trade Minister Jean-François Deniau and Chinese Foreign Trade Minister Li Qiang signed a long-term trade agreement between the two nations.

U.S. Concerned about Cambodia. On Dec. 5 the U.S. State Department issued a statement expressing concern over the "growing conflicts" between Vietnam and Cambodia and suggesting that the growing Soviet-Vietnamese relationship might hinder normalization of relations between the U.S. and Vietnam.

Japanese Equipment to China. On Dec. 5 the Japanese Nippon Steel Corporation agreed to sell China $2.03 billion worth of equipment to build a steel mill near Shanghai.

British Loan to China. On Dec. 6 it was announced in London that 10 British banks had agreed to extend industrial development credits of $1.2 billion to China at 7.25 percent interest for five years.

U.S. Invites Deng. On Dec. 11, as agreement between China and the U.S. on the opening of diplomatic relations seemed near, national security adviser Zbigniew Brzezinski secretly informed Chai Zemin, head of the Chinese Liaison Office in Washington, that an invitation was being extended to Vice Premier Deng Xiaoping to visit the U.S.

The White House received word the next day that Deng had accepted the invitation and that China had approved the final wording of the joint communiqué to be issued by the two countries.

China Detonates Nuclear Weapon. On Dec. 14 the Department of Energy announced that China had detonated a nuclear device at its Lop Nor test site in northwestern China. It was reported that the yield was less than 20 kilotons.

U.S. Restates Terms. On Dec. 14, in an effort to avoid possible misunderstandings, the U.S. secretly sent to Leonard Woodcock, chief of the U.S. Liaison Office in Peking, a restatement of the U.S. commitment to continue to sell defensive arms to Taiwan after negotiation. *The New York Times* later reported that this statement, when conveyed to the Chinese, threatened to disrupt the agreement. National security adviser Zbigniew Brzezinski was called at home by an aide who informed him that the entire arrangement was threatening to unravel. Without calling President Carter, Brzezinski immediately contacted Chai Zemin, chief of the Chinese Liaison Office in Washington, who was still objecting to the U.S. right to sell defensive arms to Taiwan after normalization. Finally, the two sides agreed to disagree, and the arms sales were not mentioned in the joint communiqué.

The U.S. later issued a "clarification" that told of the U.S. commitment to sell arms to Taiwan. In Peking, Chinese Party Chairman Hua Guofeng told a news conference that "the two sides have differing views" on the matter.

U.S. Recognizes PRC. On Dec. 15, in an unexpected move, the governments of China and the U.S. issued a joint communiqué announcing the establishment of diplomatic relations between them as of Jan. 1, 1979. The exchange of ambassadors was to follow on March 1. *(Texts, p. 341)*

The main terms of the agreement were that the U.S. recognized the People's Republic of China as the sole legitimate government of China; that the U.S. "acknowledged" Peking's position that Taiwan was part of China, and that the U.S. would end all official governmental relations with Taiwan and withdraw its troops from the island within four months. At the same time, the U.S. still could maintain and develop its existing non-governmental relations with Taiwan on a "people to people" basis.

The final agreement involved concessions by both sides. The U.S. was allowed to end its Mutual Defense Treaty with the Republic of China within the terms of the treaty, which required one year's advance notice. Second, Peking did not contradict the unilateral statement by Washington that the U.S. "expects" the Taiwan issue to be resolved peacefully. Third, despite its objections, Peking proceeded with normalization despite the U.S.' announced intentions to continue to supply Taiwan with "defensive" weapons.

For its part, Washington basically accepted Peking's terms for normalization without any formal assurance that China would not use force to take over Taiwan.

The Reaction in Taipei. On Dec. 15 at 2 a.m. local time, U.S. Ambassador to the Republic of China Leonard Unger informed ROC President Chiang Ching-kuo that the U.S. would announce its recognition of Peking later that day. Chiang convened an emergency meeting of the central committee of the Nationalist Party. A communiqué issued after the meeting said that the U.S. move would have a "tremendous adverse impact upon the free world."

In a statement of his own, President Chiang recalled promises made to Taiwan by the U.S. in recent years, and spoke contemptuously of "broken assurances." He repeated his own pledge never to deal with Peking. *(Text, p. 342)*

In a televised address Dec. 16, Chiang moderated his tone somewhat: "I want to thank all those friends in America who have supported us. From now on the Republic of China will continue to strengthen the friendship and mutual interests of the two people."

The announcement came in the midst of campaigning for Taiwan's most open elections to date, scheduled for Dec. 23, which were subsequently cancelled.

Chinese Reaction. On Dec. 16 *The Washington Post* reported that Peking had begun an intensive campaign to inform the Chinese people of the new move and to win thir support for it. The Peking *People's Daily* distributed a million copies of a special edition. Chinese Chairman Hua Guofeng held a nationally televised press conference, and Chinese television broadcast a special one-hour program explaining the decision. The Chinese press also published favorable reaction from the U.S. and the rest of the world.

Soviet Reaction. On one hand, Moscow approved the Sino-U.S. accord as "natural." On the other, the Soviets expressed concern about the possibility of Sino-American

economic and military cooperation aimed at the Soviet Union.

On Dec. 19 Soviet party leader Leonid Brezhnev sent a note to President Carter which Carter characterized as "very positive in tone." On Dec. 21 the Soviet news agency Tass disputed Carter's interpretation, revealing that Moscow had deep reservations about normalization, and particularly about the inclusion of a phrase condemning "hegemony," a code word used by the Chinese to criticize the Soviet Union.

U.S. to Maintain Ties with Taiwan. On Dec. 17 U.S. State Department chief legal adviser Herbert Hansell said that all "existing agreements with Taiwan, cultural, commercial and others, will continue in effect except for . . . the defense treaty." *(Box, p. 238; complete list, p. 348)*

China to Modernize. On Dec. 18 the 11th Central Committee of the Chinese Communist Party held its third plenary session in Peking. Because the effort to purge the supporters of Lin Piao and the "gang of four" had been largely successful, the party now began to emphasize modernization in 1979. The meeting thus formalized China's commitment to the "four modernizations." *(See Feb. 26, 1978)*

The plenum then adopted economic plans for 1979 and 1980.

China Buys U.S. Planes. On Dec. 19 the Boeing Company announced that China had purchased three Boeing 747SP jumbo jets costing $156 million, to be delivered in 1980.

Coca-Cola to China. On Dec. 19 the Coca-Cola Company announced that it would begin selling Coca-Cola in China in January 1979.

Vietnamese Advance into Cambodia. On Dec. 21 it was reported from Bangkok that Vietnamese troops had driven 70 miles inside Cambodia. On Dec. 25 Cambodia said the Vietnamese had begun a new offensive.

ROC Embassy Sold. On Dec. 22, in an effort to prevent Peking's acquisition of the property, the Republic of China sold its embassy and chancery for $10 to the Friends of Free China, a private, Washington-based group. The property was valued at more than $3 million. *(Box, p. 50)*

Goldwater Sues Carter. On Dec. 22 Sen. Barry Goldwater, R-Ariz., and other congressmen from both houses filed suit in U.S. District Court asking that President Carter's decision, announced Dec. 15, to abrogate the U.S.' mutual defense treaty with Taiwan be declared unconstitutional and invalid. The suit claimed that the Senate must ratify not only treaties but their termination. *(Details, p. 40)*

Christopher in Taiwan. On Dec. 27 angry Chinese pelted the motorcade of Deputy Secretary of State Warren Christopher with vegetables and paint shortly after his arrival in Taipei. The demonstration — tolerated, if not sponsored, by the government — was a protest against the U.S. decision to sever diplomatic relations with Taiwan. Following a stiff U.S. protest, there were no further incidents, although demonstrations continued.

On Dec. 29 Christopher concluded talks and returned to Washington. Tensions between the two countries had not been eased.

Congress to Protect Taiwan. On Dec. 28 House International Relations Chairman Clement J. Zablocki, D-Wis., said there was little that Congress could do to block President Carter's new China policy and suggested that under the circumstances Congress should concentrate on doing the best they could for Taiwan. Zablocki's comments followed an announcement by Sen. Frank Church, D-Utah, incoming chairman of the Senate Foreign Relations Committee, that he supported Carter's move.

Deng to Visit U.S. On Dec. 30 the chief of the U.S. Liaison Office in Peking, Leonard Woodcock, announced that Chinese Vice Premier Deng Xiaoping would visit the U.S. beginning Jan. 29, 1979.

Chinese Offer to Taiwan. On Dec. 31 the Standing Committee of the National People's Congress in Peking appealed to the government on Taiwan to begin direct trade and postal service between the two countries.

1979

China, U.S. Open Relations — China Supports Cambodia — Phnom Penh Falls — Woodcock to China — Carter Pledge to Taiwan — Deng in U.S. — China Invades Vietnam — U.S. Claims Settled — Sino-British Trade Agreement — China Ends Invasion — Taiwan Relations Act Cleared — China Trade Act — Vietnam Refugee Crisis — SALT II Hearings — Korea Troop Withdrawal Slowed — Air Travel to China — Vatican Seeks China Ties — Mondale in China — Nixon Returns to Peking — More China-U.S.S.R. Strife — Hua Guofeng in Europe — China Tries Dissidents — Iran Militants Seize U.S. Embassy — China Elections — Peking Backs U.S. on Iran — China Into Olympics — Goldwater Loses Suit — South Korea Coup — Soviets Invade Afghanistan.

Bombardment Ended. On Jan. 1 the Chinese government ceased its bombardment of the Nationalist Chinese islands of Quemoy and Matsu and proposed talks with the authorities on Taiwan to end the military confrontation and the "artificial tension" it caused.

On the same day, Leonard Woodcock, chief of the American Liaison Office in Peking, reported that the Chinese had been moving troops away from the area opposite Taiwan in response both to increasing tensions along the Sino-Soviet and Sino-Vietnamese borders and to the easing of tension in the Taiwan Strait area.

China, U.S. Open Relations. On Jan. 1, in ceremonies at the Chinese Liaison Office in Washington and the American Liaison Office in Peking, full diplomatic relations between the U.S. and China were established.

Treaty to Be Abrogated. On Jan. 1 the U.S. State Department formally notified the Republic of China that, under article X of their 1954 mutual defense treaty, the U.S. was abrogating the treaty, effective Jan. 1, 1980. The abrogation was challenged in Congress and in the courts. *(See Dec. 22, 1978 and June 6, 1979)*

Romanization Changes. On Jan. 1 the Chinese government began using the *pinyin* system of romanization in press dispatches and government announcements. U.S. wire services, newspapers and periodicals followed Peking's lead, as one after the other switched to the system during the spring and summer.

Castro on Rapprochement. On Jan. 1 Cuban Premier Fidel Castro said that "despite the current grand treason of China" in opening relations with the U.S., "the world will keep changing" toward communism. Castro went on to say that "Cuba cannot be bought or bribed" because "Cuba is not China or Egypt."

With Treasury Secretary Michael Blumenthal watching, diplomatic personnel lower flag that had flown over the U.S. Liaison Office in Peking and replace it with a new banner, at ceremony marking the beginning of full diplomatic relations with the PRC, March 1, 1979.

Intellectuals in China. On Jan. 4 the Peking *People's Daily* published an article by "Commentator" — indicating high-level approval — calling for an end to campaigns against China's intellectuals. The article said that during the Cultural Revolution such campaigns had gone too far and that all intellectuals were not necessarily evil. After noting that Marx, Lenin and Mao were all intellectuals, the article concluded by declaring that China needed its intellectuals for modernization.

British Planes to China. On Jan. 5, while attending the four-power allied summit conference at Guadeloupe, British Prime Minister James Callaghan announced that Britain had agreed to sell Harrier fighter planes to China as part of a $2-billion package. The Harrier was considered to be valuable to China in its defense of the border with Russia.

Deng on Cambodia. On Jan. 5 Chinese Vice Premier Deng Xiaoping told U.S. reporters in Peking that China would not send troops to Cambodia to assist the Pol Pot government.

Chinese Support for Cambodia. On Jan. 6 Prince Norodom Sihanouk arrived in Peking for a short stay en route to New York. He and his delegation were met by Vice Premier Deng Xiaoping, who declared: "The Chinese government and people firmly support Kampuchea [Cambodia] in its just struggle against Vietnamese aggression." On the following day, the Chinese government issued a statement denouncing Vietnam's "massive war of aggression" against Cambodia.

Phnom Penh Captured. On Jan. 7 Hanoi radio announced that Vietnamese troops had captured the Cambodian capital of Phnom Penh, as well as Kompong Som, the nation's major seaport.

New Government in Cambodia. On Jan. 8 the Vietnamese-sponsored National United Front for the National Salvation announced the formation of a People's Revolutionary government for Cambodia, with Heng Samrin to serve as president of the Revolutionary Council.

Moscow Hails New Government. On Jan. 9 Soviet President Leonid I. Brezhnev stated that the Cambodian rebels had overthrown a "political system of the Chinese model." He termed Pol Pot's deposed government "a hateful regime and a tyranny imposed from the outside."

On the same day, Prince Norodom Sihanouk arrived in New York to request United Nations help for the deposed government. *(See Jan. 15, 1979)*

Deng on Taiwan. On Jan. 9 Chinese Vice Premier Deng Xiaoping met with U.S. Senator Sam Nunn, D-Ga., and three other senators in Peking. Deng told the group that as long as Taiwan acknowledged Chinese sovereignty it could have full autonomy and keep its own armed forces as well as its private-enterprise economy.

Deng added that he felt the possibility of Peking's using force against Taiwan was likely only if there were "an indefinite refusal by Taiwan to enter into negotiations" or "an attempt by the Soviet Union to interfere in Taiwanese affairs."

Peking on Cambodia Invasion. On Jan. 10 the Peking *People's Daily* declared that Vietnam's invasion of Cambodia was "an important part of the 'global strategy' pushed by Moscow for world hegemony." The article went on to say that the "seizure of Indochina is only the Kremlin's first step in its expansionist pursuits in Southeast Asia."

China Trade with Taiwan. On Jan. 11 a spokesman for the Chinese Ministry of Foreign Trade said trade with Taiwan would be encouraged. This followed an announcement that China would no longer levy customs duties on goods moving to and from Taiwan.

On Jan. 25 a spokesman for the same ministry identified specific articles the two nations might trade, noting that payment could be made in mutually acceptable currencies. Residents of Taiwan were invited to the Canton Trade Fair.

Taiwan Rejects Unification. On Jan. 11, Y. S. Sun, premier of the Republic of China on Taiwan, rejected the most recent Chinese proposal for reunification of Taiwan with the mainland.

China Support for SWAPO. On Jan. 11 Chinese Vice Premier Li Xiannian, on a 20-day tour of Africa, met with leaders of the Patriotic Front and SWAPO (Southwest Africa People's Association), and was said to have pledged to send further arms and military advisors to help train Rhodesian rebels under Robert Mugabe.

Arms Sale Moratorium. On Jan. 12 *The Washington Post* reported that the Carter administration had agreed to place a one-year moratorium on arms sales to Taiwan. The temporary halt had not been disclosed earlier, and administration officials claimed that the omission was inadvertent. At the same time, the U.S. confirmed that U.S. deliveries of material already contracted for would continue on schedule. It was estimated that the cost of such U.S. weapons was $720 million, with delivery slated over the next three years. *(See Jan. 3, 1980)*

Peking Pledges Support. On Jan. 14 the Chinese government "solemnly reiterated" its support for the Cambodian government of Pol Pot, and added that the Vietnamese-supported government of Heng Samrin is "only a hastily rigged-up puppet and tool of Vietnam and the Soviet Union."

Carter Administration Still Split. On Jan. 15, speeches by Secretary of State Cyrus Vance and national security adviser Zbigniew Brzezinski revealed that the Carter administration was still deeply split over U.S. relations with the Soviet Union. In his speech Vance expressed his concern lest Moscow regard the new Sino-American relationship as directed against it, and stressed that the U.S. wanted to keep relations with the Soviet Union and China as "evenhanded" as possible.

Brzezinski took a much harder line toward the Soviets, underlining the strategic advantages that would accrue to the U.S. from its rapprochement with Peking.

Administration officials denied there was any split, and said that the two speeches, both cleared by President Carter, complemented each other.

Soviet Veto. On Jan. 15 the Soviet Union used its 111th veto to block a U.N. Security Council resolution that had sought the withdrawal of Vietnamese forces from Cambodia. *(See Nov. 14, 1979)*

Carter Names Woodcock to China. On Jan. 15 President Carter named Leonard Woodcock U.S. Ambassador to China, the first regular ambassador to that country since 1949. The Senate confirmed the appointment on Feb. 26 with little opposition, despite fears that conservatives might try to block the appointment as a protest against Carter's China policies. *(Box, p. 43)*

Japan Refuses to Help. On Jan. 16 Chinese Ambassador to Japan Fu Hao asked Japanese Foreign Minister Sunao Sonoda for joint Sino-Japanese support for Cambodia against Vietnamese aggression, the first invocation of the anti-hegemony clause of the Sino-Japanese Treaty of Peace and Amity. Sonoda refused, saying that Japan preferred unilateral diplomacy as a way of easing tensions. Japan was one of the very few non-communist nations to enjoy good relations with Hanoi.

Carter on Taiwan Pledge. On Jan. 17 President Carter said at a news conference that the U.S. had asked Peking to provide a binding, written pledge that China would not try to take Taiwan by force, but "this was not possible to achieve."

On Feb. 9 *The Washington Post* reported that officials at the State Department had contradicted Carter's statement that this request had been refused. The officials now said that the U.S. interest in such a pledge had been "implicit," and that Peking had never been specifically pressed for such an assurance.

Peking on Vietnam Refugees. On Jan. 20 *People's Daily* claimed that since the campaign against China had begun earlier in 1978, "the Vietnamese authorities have expelled over 170,000 Chinese residents, Vietnamese citizens of Chinese origin, and Vietnamese people to China."

Diplomat Recalled. On Jan. 23 the Nationalist Chinese government on Taiwan recalled Loh I-cheng, director of the China Information Service in New York City. According to unconfirmed reports, the recall followed a U.S. State Department request made to Taipei around Jan. 19 after Loh's organization conducted a letter-writing campaign designed to pressure U.S. congressmen to guarantee the security of Taiwan following normalization.

Seized Property to Be Restored. On Jan. 25, the Xinhua news agency announced that the property which had been expropriated from those labeled as "capitalist roaders" during the Cultural Revolution would be returned to them. This announcement came amidst more and more "rehabilitations" of those purged during the late 1960s.

On Jan. 29 the news agency reported that " 'citizens' rights" would be restored to those who had been termed landlords, wealthy peasants, and counterrevolutionaries.

Carter Pledge to Taiwan. On Jan. 26 President Carter told reporters he was committed to a "strong and prosperous and a free people" on Taiwan. Carter went on to say, however, that he would veto any legislation "that would violate the agreements we have concluded with the People's Republic of China."

Deng in U.S. On Jan. 28 Chinese Vice Premier Deng Xiaoping arrived in the U.S. for a nine-day visit, the first ever by a senior Chinese Communist leader.

The next day, Carter hosted a White House dinner for Deng and his wife. Former President Richard M. Nixon was a guest. Carter announced that he had accepted an invitation to visit China, and that his invitation to have Chinese Communist Party Chairman and Premier Hua Guofeng visit the U.S. had been accepted.

Soviet Buildup Reported. On Jan. 30 the Japanese defense ministry reported that the Soviet Union had increased its troop strength and was building bases on the southernmost Kurile Islands, adjacent to the northernmost Japanese island of Hokkaido. The Kurile Islands are claimed by both countries. (*Map, p. 191*)

China-Vietnam Border Buildup. On Jan. 30, U.S. intelligence sources in Washington reported that Vietnam had built up troop strength along its border with China and that China had increased its troop strength in the same area to 100,000 troops, several hundred tanks, and about 150 warplanes.

Deng Assails Soviet Union. On Jan. 30 *Time* magazine published an interview with Chinese Vice Premier Deng Xiaoping in which Deng called the Soviet Union "a hotbed of war" and warned the U.S. to be wary in limiting U.S. arms development.

Sino-U.S. Agreements. On Jan. 31 Chinese Vice Premier Deng Xiaoping and President Carter signed a series of agreements that Carter said would provide a framework for "a new and irreversible course" in Sino-American relations. Deng said the agreements were not "the end, only the beginning." Included among the agreements were: an interim consular agreement, providing for American consulates in Canton and Shanghai, and Chinese consulates in Houston and San Francisco; an overall science and technology agreement, and a separate energy accord providing for U.S. aid in building a 50-billion electron-volt nuclear accelerator in China; a separate space technology agreement entitling China to buy the services of NASA for launching a civilian communications satellite; a cultural exchange agreement; and a science agreement providing for student exchanges.

In addition to these agreements, China also agreed in principle to allow the establishment of American news bureaus in China, with details to be worked out later.

Deng Warns Vietnam. On Jan. 31 Chinese Vice Premier Deng Xiaoping told U.S. reporters that unity among the U.S., China, Japan, Western Europe and other countries was needed "to deal with Soviet hegemonism." Deng referred specifically to Vietnam's "massive armed aggression" against Cambodia "with the full backing of the Soviet Union." Vietnam had been provoking the Chinese along their border, "But as to actions to take, we will have to wait and see. I can only say two things: one, that for us Chinese, we mean what we say, and second, we Chinese do not act rashly."

China-U.S. Communiqué. On Feb. 1 Chinese Vice Premier Deng Xiaoping concluded his talks with U.S. leaders. The two sides issued a joint communiqué which acknowledged that there were areas where their interests and ideas were similar, and areas where they were not.

China and the U.S. agreed to conclude trade, aviation and shipping agreements which were to be discussed during the forthcoming visits to China by Secretary of the Treasury Michael Blumenthal and Secretary of Commerce Juanita Kreps. President Carter formally accepted an invitation to visit China at a convenient time and said Premier Hua Guofeng had accepted Carter's offer to visit the U.S.

The statement went on the "reaffirm that they are opposed to efforts by any country or group of countries to establish hegemony or domination over others."

U.S. Polled on China Views. On Feb. 2 *The New York Times* reported the results of a recent *New York Times*/CBS poll that revealed a major change in the views of the American people toward China and the Soviet Union. Of the sample, 15 percent said that they held a favorable view of the Soviet Union, while 41 percent said their view was unfavorable. Asked about mainland China, 26 percent had a favorable view, while only 24 percent had an unfavorable one. The results contrasted sharply with a 1976 poll in which respondents had rated the two countries about equally.

Deng on Cambodian Invasion. On Feb. 7 Chinese Vice Premier Deng Xiaoping, on a three-day visit to Japan, told Premier Masayoshi Ohira in Tokyo that Vietnam must be punished for its action against Cambodia.

Vietnam Claims Chinese Border Violations. On Feb. 7 Vietnamese Foreign Minister Nguyen Duy Trinh told a French correspondent in Hanoi that the Vietnamese had agreed with China in 1957-58 to maintain the border agreements established in treaties of 1887 and 1895, but that the Chinese had violated the border and provoked incidents increasingly since 1974.

No Funding for Institute. On Feb. 9 Sen. Ernest Hollings, D-S.C., chairman of the appropriations subcommittee which oversees the State Department budget, said he would not approve a transfer of State Department funds to pay for the operation of the American Institute in Taiwan, set to replace the American Embassy there on March 1, unless Congress passed enabling legislation. The White House termed Hollings' action "irresponsible." The result was that the 5,000 Americans on Taiwan were left with no link to the U.S. until April 10. Hollings' action was a protest against Carter's China policy. *(Box, p. 44)*

Carter Toughens Stand. On Feb. 9 President Carter told a news conference that the U.S. retained the option of using the 7th Fleet or even going to war to protect Taiwan against any future threat from China. This was the toughest language ever used by Carter about Taiwan and appeared to be directed at U.S. congressmen who were demanding a specific American pledge to Taiwan to replace the mutual defense treaty.

Moscow Reacts to Deng. On Feb. 9 Soviet Premier Aleksei Kosygin told Frank Press, science and technology adviser to President Carter, that the remarks made by Chinese Vice Premier Deng Xiaoping while in the U.S. were "outrageous" and should have been "refuted" by President Carter.

U.S. Warns China. On Feb. 9 a spokesman for the U.S. State Department said that the U.S. "would be seriously concerned over a Chinese attack on Vietnam."

Modernization Slows. On Feb. 9 the Peking *People's Daily* declared that China's modernization program would not begin immediately, but that a two-three year period of preparation would be required to lay the groundwork for the planned "four modernizations."

India and China. On Feb. 12 Indian Foreign Minister A. B. Vajpayee arrived in Peking. On Feb. 14 he told Chinese Vice Premier Deng Xiaoping that the border dispute was still the primary obstacle to good relations between the two countries. The official Chinese report quoted Deng as responding that this could be solved "through peaceful consultations."

Vajpayee cut his visit short as a protest against the Feb. 17 Chinese invasion of Vietnam.

U.N. to Aid China. On Feb. 13 the United Nations approved a $15-million aid program for China.

Taiwan Agrees. On Feb. 13 *The Washington Post* reported that Taiwan had finally acceded to U.S. pressure and would accept continued relations between the two

countries on a non-official basis. The administration position prevailed despite a vigorous lobbying campaign by Taiwan to win support in the Congress for some kind of continuing governnmental tie.

Vietnam on Refugees. On Feb. 14 the Vietnamese Ministry of Foreign Affairs released a memorandum declaring that on the question of the so-called Hoa (Chinese) people in Vietnam, China had "enticed or coerced" hundreds of thousands of Hoa people to go to China in order to cause disorder in Vietnam. The memorandum claimed that this had begun in early 1968. The report estimated the number of refugees at 170,000, the figure used earlier by the Chinese. *(See Jan. 20, 1979)*

Taiwan Creates Agency for Ties. On Feb. 15 James Soong, chief of the government information office on Taiwan, said that Taiwan was creating the Coordination Council for North American Affairs to act as the "counterpart to the American Institute in Taiwan" as of March 1. Soong also said that the new relationship, although non-governmental, would "have the qualities of officiality." The council would have an office in Washington and eight branches in other parts of the U.S. Nationalist China had formerly maintained 14 consular offices in America.

China Invades Vietnam. On Feb. 17, Chinese troops began an invasion of Vietnam. The Xinhua news agency called the move a "counterattack," brought on by repeated Vietnamese border incursions. *(Texts, p. 351)*

Washington Asks Withdrawal. On Feb. 17 U.S. State Department spokesman Hodding Carter III said the U.S. was calling for "immediate withdrawal of Vietnamese troops from Cambodia and Chinese troops from Vietnam."

On Feb. 18 a spokesman for the State Department said Washington was in contact with the Soviet Union, pursuing efforts to limit the conflict.

Spy Base to Stay. On Feb. 18 *The Washington Post* reported that despite President Carter's pledge to withdraw all U.S. military personnel from Taiwan by May 1, the super-secret listening post at Shulinkou would stay, still manned by some American personnel. The article said the U.S. had refused comment except to say that "no U.S. personnel are to be permanently stationed on Taiwan" after April 30.

Moscow Demands Chinese Withdrawal. On Feb. 18 the Soviet government issued a statement demanding the withdrawal of Chinese troops from Vietnam.

U.S. Non-involvement. On Feb. 18, U.S. administration sources said the U.S. would avoid any involvement in the war between China and Vietnam.

Vietnam-Cambodia Treaty. On Feb. 20 Vietnamese Premier Pham Van Dong and Cambodian Premier Heng Samrin signed a "treaty of peace and friendship" in Phnom Penh. The treaty contained a clause which gave Vietnam the right to maintain "advisers" in Cambodia to "preserve the territorial integrity."

Deng on Vietnam Invasion. On Feb. 23 Chinese Vice Premier Deng Xiaoping reportedly told Roy Jenkins, president of the European Common Market, that China needed to "punish" Vietnam, and had "carefully and soberly calculated" the risks involved.

Sino-American Shipping Agreement. On Feb. 23 the American Lykes Brothers Steamship Company signed a private agreement with the the China Ocean Shipping Company (operated by the Chinese government). The agreement opened U.S. and Chinese ports to one another's ships for the first time in 30 years.

China's Modernization Slows. On Feb. 24 the Peking *People's Daily* published an editorial significantly downgrading earlier Chinese modernization goals. Amid numerous reports of Chinese refusal to complete work on various trade agreements already signed with foreign corporations, the editorial admitted that earlier goals, especially those set by Chinese Premier Hua Guofeng at the Fifth National People's Congress, had been too high. *(See Feb. 26, 1978)* The article went on to criticize such goals, stating: "Setting some plan figures too high . . . gives rise to boasting, empty talk, and fabricated figures and reports."

The reference to "fabricated reports" recalled the situation during the Great Leap Forward in 1958 when local leaders, faced with impossible production figures set by the government, submitted reports which indicated that the quotas has been met, despite their failure.

The slowdown in modernization was taken as a further indication of the increasing power of Deng Xiaoping, leader of the moderate group, as more and more of his former subordinates, purged earlier, were returned to power. Almost all of these were economic planners who tended to favor slow, steady growth over convulsive leaps.

China on Vietnam War. On Feb. 25 Chinese Vice Premier Wang Zhen announced that China had "no intention" of moving into the Vietnamese flatland: "We are still in the process of teaching Vietnam a good lesson. . . . Our action will be limited in scope and duration."

Deng on Vietnam Invasion. On Feb. 26 Chinese Vice Premier Deng Xiaoping told a senior Japanese journalist that China would not make Vietnamese withdrawal from Cambodia a condition for Chinese withdrawal from Vietnam. He offered the opinion that the "punitive action" would end in less than the 33 days that had been needed to settle the Indian border problem in 1962.

China Cancels Japanese Contracts. On Feb. 26 China abruptly called off $2.5 billion in contracts that had been signed with Japanese manufacturers of plant equipment. No official reason was given for the move. *(See June 12)*

Carter's Letter to China. On Feb. 27 U.S. Treasury Secretary Michael Blumenthal delivered a letter from President Carter to Chinese Vice Premier Deng Xiaoping which called for the withdrawal of Chinese troops from Vietnam "as quickly as possible" because the invasion "ran risks that were unwarranted."

Chinese Call for Peace. On Feb. 27 the Peking *People's Daily* called for peace negotiations aimed at ending the fighting in Vietnam. Hanoi radio rejected the offer the next day, stating that "no nation with any self-respect would agree to hold talks under the pressure of tanks and bullets."

China Again Proposes Talks. On March 1 the Chinese foreign ministry proposed to the Vietnamese Embassy that the two sides meet at the level of deputy foreign minister to negotiate the end of the border conflict.

The Vietnamese foreign ministry replied the next day that they were ready to hold talks once the Chinese "immediately, completely, and unconditionally withdrew their troops."

U.S. and China Begin Relations. On March 1, reciprocal embassies were opened in Washington and Peking, and Ambassador Chai Zemin presented his credentials to President Carter.

The U.S. broke relations with the Republic of China the same day.

On March 7 Ambassador Leonard Woodcock presented his credentials in Peking.

Vietnam to Negotiate. On March 2 a spokesman for the Vietnamese foreign ministry stated that the government was willing to negotiate a peace settlement with China once Chinese forces were withdrawn from Vietnam.

Claims Settled. On March 2 U.S. Treasury Secretary Michael Blumenthal and Chinese Finance Minister Zhang Jingfu initialled an agreement in Peking whereby claims by U.S. citizens would be settled at 41 cents on the dollar. China would thus pay $80 million to the United States Treasury in settlement of U.S. claims totaling $197 million. The U.S. agreed to release, on Oct. 1, $80 million of Chinese assets that were frozen during the Korean War.

The agreement ended a 30-year deadlock and enabled Chinese trade with the U.S. to proceed without fear of seizure of goods. *(See May 11)*

Sino-British Trade Agreement. On March 3 Britain and China signed an agreement on economic cooperation in which the two countries set a target of $14 billion in trade and exchanges between 1979 and 1985. The agreement also contained a $5 billion credit line which the British would extend to China for investment in economic construction.

Chinese End Vietnam Invasion. On March 5, with the announced capture of the Vietnamese provincial capital of Lang Son, the Chinese stated that they would commence withdrawal of their troops.

Vietnam Mobilizes. On March 6, confronted by a Chinese invasion, the government of Vietnam issued an order for general mobilization.

Laos Accuses China. On March 6 Laos issued a statement charging that China was massing troops on her border; a day later Laos cut off all Chinese aid activities in Laos. China denied the charges flatly and "counselled" the Lao government to refrain from further hostile acts.

Senate Debate on Taiwan. On March 8 the House and Senate barely defeated amendments to the Taiwan bill that would have made the U.S. commitment to the island's defense stronger and more formal.

Charles Percy, R-Ill, sponsor of the Senate amendments, stated: "We must not lead the Chinese to miscalculate or underestimate our interests in Taiwan." In reply, Senate Foreign Relations Chairman Frank Church, D-Idaho, argued that China was incapable of attacking Taiwan and was not even anxious to do so. "The China we see today is not a China teetering on its coastline, ready to leap on that island for the purpose of subjugating its people." *(See April 10)*

Liberalization Slows. On March 15 the Peking *People's Daily* sharply criticized "certain young comrades" who would "beg the support of imperialism [the United States]" in their campaign for human rights. The article said this showed a "lack of patriotism." It was also noted that despite President Carter's statements on human rights, America was still a land of "privileges" and a "mercenary slave system of unemployment, police persecution, suicides, prostitution and so on."

The Future of Taiwan

Despite pessimistic predictions by Taiwan supporters, the first year since the U.S. decision to derecognize the Republic of China on Taiwan provoked no disaster in that island nation. Some analysts even stated that Taiwan's loss of the last major power with which it had relations had provoked a constructive reworking of its foreign policy that should have begun 15 years before.

Economically, Taiwan continued to have one of the world's highest GNP growth rates, and foreign investment again increased in 1979. Unlike 1971, when President Nixon's announcement of his intention to visit Peking was revealed, there was no slump in the real estate market and no measurable flight of investment capital. In the seven years since the Nixon breakthrough, Taiwan prepared for what was seen as the inevitable break with the United States that occurred with President Carter's Dec. 15, 1978, announcement of his new China policy.

Carter's announcement forced the cancellation of Taiwan elections and a new crackdown on dissidents but, as the government gained confidence, President Chiang Ching-kuo's liberalization program was reinstituted and then, according to reports in late 1979, accelerated so that Taiwan could compare even more favorably with Peking.

Militarily, however, government leaders on Taiwan feared that if mainland China made good on its modernization plans, Taiwan could find itslf at a military disadvantage with Peking within a decade. Few observers believed that China's antiquated armed forces were capable in 1979 of crossing the 100 miles of water separating Taiwan from the mainland; to do so, China would have to win control of the air, a feat believed impossible against Taiwan's modern air defense system. But some government officials in Taipei feared that if the U.S. failed to live up to its promise to sell Taiwan defensive weapons — particularly modern aircraft and surface-to-air missiles — Taiwan's advantage could disappear.

The same officials spoke of Taiwan's building its own planes, but noted that the enormous cost would mean a slowdown in other modernization schemes.

At the same time, some Western commentators pointed out that although Taiwan may have lost political recognition, it still had the "economic recognition" of many large and powerful nations like the U.S. and Japan, which had invested billions of dollars in Taiwan's booming economy. These analysts concluded that the world's banks were unlikely to treat a Chinese military threat to Taiwan lightly, and could form a nucleus for a new and even more powerful "China lobby" in Washington and other capitals.

China Withdraws from Vietnam. On March 16 Chinese Foreign Minister Huang Hua announced that Chinese forces, "after attaining their set goals," had completed their withdrawal from Vietnam that day. Huang went on to claim that the Chinese had captured more than 20 cities, towns and strategic points.

Although the campaign was obviously modeled after China's 1962 border war with India, it appeared that the Vietnamese troops fought well and that the result may have been less decisive than the Chinese hoped.

Huang Hua on U.S. Congress. On March 16 Chinese Foreign Minister Huang Hua told U.S. Ambassador to China Leonard Woodcock that the Chinese government regarded amendments to the Taiwan Relations Act added by Congress as "contravening" the Sino-U.S. agreement on establishing diplomatic relations.

Huang did not indicate any action to be taken by Peking in response to the bill. *(See April 10)*

Sino-Japanese Trade to Increase. On March 19 China and Japan agreed to more than double the trade target for their 13-year trade agreement, from $20 billion to between $40 billion and $60 billion. Specific targets were not agreed upon, however, amid conflicting signs that China wished to check its trade imbalance with Japan.

Vietnam Charges China. On March 22 a spokesman for the Vietnamese foreign ministry stated that Chinese troops still occupied 18 areas in Vietnam. *(See March 16)*

Maclehose to China. On March 24 Sir Murray Maclehose, governor of Hong Kong, arrived in Canton; it was the first visit to China by a Hong Kong governor since 1949.

Middle East Peace Treaty. On March 26 Egyptian President Anwar Sadat and Israeli Prime Minister Menachem Begin signed a formal peace treaty in a televised ceremony at the White House.

Taiwan Relations Act Cleared. On March 29 Congress cleared and sent to the president legislation (HR 2479) establishing informal relations with Taiwan. *(See April 10)*

Wall Posters Banned. On March 31 the Peking *People's Daily* published an announcement forbidding wall posters and the publication of any anti-communist material.

China Accuses Vietnam. On March 31 a spokesman for the Chinese foreign ministry accused Vietnam of delaying the opening of peace negotiations between the two countries.

Liberalization of Culture. On March 31 a play by Berthold Brecht, *The Life of Galileo*, opened in Peking. This was the first foreign play performed in China since the beginning of the Cultural Revolution in 1966.

China to End Treaty. On April 3 the Xinhua news agency reported that the Chinese government would not renew its 1950 treaty of friendship with the Soviet Union when it expired in 1980. The treaty had been a dead letter since 1961.

At the same time the Chinese also called for talks with Moscow aimed at ending the tensions between the two communist giants. *(See Sept. 23)*

War in Cambodia. On April 5 Hanoi radio reported that Cambodian Premier Heng Samrin's troops had captured the headquarters of former Cambodian leader Pol Pot.

On April 14 there were continued reports of fighting along the Cambodian border with Thailand between Cambodian forces, supported by Vietnam, and troops loyal to Pol Pot.

China and Laos. On April 5 the 497 Chinese technicians building a Chinese-supported road in Laos were recalled following a Laotian request. Relations between the two countries deteriorated further following Chinese charges that the Laotian authorities had permitted the movement of a 40,000-man Vietnamese army near the border with China.

China on Olympics. On April 7 Song Zhong, secretary general of the Chinese Olympic Committee, protested the effort by the International Olympic Committee to include "two Chinas." Song reiterated Chinese demands that Peking's committee be recognized as the only one representing China, but added: "As an interim arrangement, the sports organization in Taiwan may remain in the IOC under the name of the 'Chinese Taiwan Olympic Committee,'" as long as they did not use any flags, emblems or songs of the Republic of China. *(See Nov. 26)*

Taiwan Relations Act. On April 10 President Carter signed the Taiwan Relations Act (PL 96-8), which legalized the new U.S. relationship with Taiwan. Under provisions of the bill, and despite U.S. recognition of Peking, America's relations with Taiwan would continue to be similar to those between the U.S. and other sovereign powers. All U.S. treaties and agreements would remain in effect *(Box, p. 238)*; all property and investment rights would remain the same; and due to a series of exemptions written into the bill, Taiwan would have status apart from Peking on matters relating to immigration and nuclear energy.

The law also provided for relations between the two countries to be conducted, on the part of the U.S., by a non-profit corporation called the American Institute in Taiwan, which would be staffed by U.S. government personnel on temporary "leave of absence." The institute was empowered to conduct all normal consular functions for U.S. citizens on Taiwan. *(Text, p. 343)*

This arrangement went much further than the "Japanese solution" by which other countries had recognized Peking but maintained unofficial ties with Taiwan. The continuation of the treaties and, in particular, the ability to perform consular functions, led other nations to follow the U.S. example and expand the scope of their relations with Taiwan.

The bill marked a significant new departure in U.S. foreign policy and international law. Despite the fact that both China and the U.S. recognized Taiwan as sovereign Chinese territory, the U.S. would continue to treat it as an independent nation, sell it arms, lend it money, recognize its passports and grant its diplomats immunity from U.S. law.

No Spy Bases in China. On April 14 *The Washington Star* reported that senior administration officials had quashed the notion of installing spy bases within China to monitor any new SALT agreements with the Soviet Union. According to the report, the idea had been circulating at lower levels for some time, but senior officials felt China would be unwilling to accede to a U.S. request for such bases. *(See April 19)*

Peace Talks Begin. On April 18, peace talks between Vietnam and China began in Hanoi. *(See June 25)*

China Offers Spy Bases. On April 19 *The Washington Post* reported that Chinese Vice Premier Deng Xiaoping told U.S. congressmen visiting China that Peking would be willing to use American equipment on Chinese soil to monitor Soviet compliance with the proposed new SALT agreements. According to Sen. Frank Church, D-Idaho, Deng flatly refused to allow the establishment of U.S. bases in China but — if the U.S. wished to supply the technology and train the Chinese to use it — China would operate the stations and share the results with Washington.

On April 21 *The Washington Star* reported that U.S. officials in Washington had denied that the congressmen had been authorized to raise the question, and that there was no possibility of using the Chinese to monitor SALT compliance. The officials went on to say that Deng's response had been misinterpreted by the *Post* story; it actually had been a very polite refusal of the congressional offer.

Cross to Taiwan. On April 21 the American Institute in Taiwan, which replaced the U.S. Embassy there when the U.S. broke relations with the Republic of China, named retired foreign service officer Charles T. Cross to head its Taiwan office.

Peking Criticizes Moscow. On April 25 Peking radio charged that "the Soviet Union has intensified its infiltration and expansion into the West Asian region. It has been airlifting weapons to Afghanistan on a crash basis and sending large numbers of military advisers there."

Moscow replied by accusing China of aiding the Moslem guerrillas who were fighting against the Soviet-backed regime in Afghanistan.

Waldheim to Hanoi. On April 26 U.N. Secretary General Kurt Waldheim arrived in Hanoi in an attempt to negotiate a settlement between Vietnam and China over the disputed territory along their mutual border. On April 29 Waldheim went to China for talks with Chinese leaders; on May 1 he met with Chinese Vice Premier Deng Xiaoping and Party Chairman and Premier Hua Guofeng.

Chinese Casualties. On May 2 Chinese Deputy Chief of Staff Wu Xiuquan said that 20,000 Chinese soldiers had been killed or wounded in the recent invasion of Vietnam and that the Vietnamese had suffered 50,000 casualites.

India Refuses Soviet Aid. On May 2 Sher Singh, Indian minister of state for atomic energy, told the parliament that a Soviet offer to build a large atomic power plant in India had been refused.

U.S.-Japanese Joint Communiqué. On May 2 Japanese Prime Minister Masayoshi Ohira and President Carter issued a joint communiqué in Washington following talks between the two leaders. The statement called for the settlement of trade issues and "a more harmonious pattern of international trade and payment."

Claims Agreement Signed. On May 11 U.S. Commerce Secretary Juanita Kreps and Chinese Finance Minister Zhang Jingfu signed an agreement in Peking settling the claims and frozen assets question that had been initialed earlier. *(See March 2, 1979)*

Sino-American Trade Agreement. On May 14 Chinese Minister for Foreign Trade Li Qiang and U.S. Commerce Secretary Juanita Kreps initialed a bilateral trade agreement in Peking after ten days of intense negotiation. *(See July 7)* Following the recent settlement of the claims issue *(see March 2)*, the trade agreement established the framework for normal commercial relations between the two countries, ending a 30-year hiatus. The agreement also paved the way for the U.S. to grant China most-favored-nation status, which would reduce tariffs on Chinese goods imported into the U.S. by up to 75 percent. The agreement was described as the longest and most complicated the Chinese had ever signed with any nation; the U.S. reportedly had to change 75-80 percent of the draft Kreps had brought to Peking. On May 8 Kreps had signed four other agreements with the Chinese concerning scientific and technological exchanges.

The trade agreement required approval by the U.S. Congress. *(Text, p. 352)*

U.S. to Impose Quotas on China. On May 31 the U.S. Commerce Department announced that the U.S. would impose quotas on Chinese textile imports into the U.S. The announcement followed the failure of President Carter's special trade negotiator, Robert Strauss, to negotiate an agreement with China to limit Chinese sales of five categories of textiles. *(See Oct. 30)*

The Chinese, suffering from a trade imbalance with the U.S., had been anxious to increase exports, especially textiles, to America.

Prisoner Exchanges. On June 5, in the third of five exchanges, China released 487 Vietnamese prisoners while Vietnam released 55 Chinese captured during their recent border war.

Chinese Arms to Egypt. On June 5 Egyptian President Anwar Sadat announced that China had agreed to supply his country with military arms. No details were given.

On June 22 it was reported that China had sent 40 Shenyang F-6 fighter planes to Egypt, and that negotiations were underway for the purchase of additional planes.

Russia and China to Negotiate. On June 5 the Soviet news agency Tass reported that Foreign Minister Andrei Gromyko had told Chinese officials that the Soviet Union was prepared to begin negotiations on normalizing relations between the two countries. *(See Sept. 23)*

Goldwater Suit Stalled. On June 6 the lawsuit by Sen. Barry Goldwater, R-Ariz., to block President Carter's abrogation of the mutual defense treaty between Taiwan and the U.S. received a setback in federal district court. Judge Oliver Gasch ruled that the suit, which sought to have Carter's action declared illegal, had no "standing" because legislation concerning the termination was still pending in the Senate.

Within hours the Senate acted to preserve its prerogatives, insisting that the president obtain Senate approval before ending mutual defense treaties with other countries. By a 59-35 vote the Senate amended S Res 15 to restore the stronger language to that effect which had been removed by the Senate Foreign Relations Committee.

On June 12 Goldwater again filed suit, claiming the subsequent Senate action barring unilateral presidential termination of treaties gave the court authority to block Carter's Taiwan decision. *(Details, pp. 40-42; see also Oct. 17, 1979)*

Contracts Revived. On June 12 China announced that it had agreed to revive the 21 contracts with Japan that China had cancelled earlier in the year. *(See Feb. 26)* Analysts traced the decision to the May 15 agreement between China and Japan whereby the Japanese Export-Import Bank would provide $1.7 billion in yen credits to China for the development of its oil and petroleum resources.

Chinese Refugees to China. On June 16 State Department sources revealed that Richard Holbrooke, the assis-

tant secretary of state for East Asian and Pacific affairs, recently asked Chinese officials to accept more ethnic Chinese refugees from Vietnam. China had already accepted about 200,000.

Congress Opens. On June 18 the second session of the 5th National People's Congress opened in Peking, only 16 months after the first session. The congress took further steps toward regularizing the Chinese government, including adoption of a criminal code, China's first, and the abolition of the revolutionary committees (revcoms), a stop-gap measure adopted in the early 1970s.

The congress also continued the rehabilitation of those purged during earlier power struggles, and saw the return of three of Vice Premier Deng Xiaoping's former supporters.

Hua Revises Goals. On June 18, during his address to the National People's Congress in Peking, Chinese Premier and Communist Party Chairman Hua Guofeng said the economic goals which he had proposed in 1978 were too ambitious. *(See Feb. 26, 1978.)* Hua noted that China's economic problems were still severe, and that prior to launching a program of rapid modernization, a three-year period of consolidation and preparation, beginning in 1979, would be necessary. The revised plan was presented to the congress on June 21 by Vice Premier Yu Qiuli.

China Defense Budget Up. During his speech to the congress, Chinese Finance Minister Zhang Jinfu announced that China's military budget for 1979 would be $2.1 billion more than 1978's.

SALT II Signed. On June 18 President Carter and Soviet President Leonid Brezhnev signed the second strategic arms limitation treaty (SALT II), which required Senate ratification.

Chinese Protest. On June 21 the Xinhua news agency reported that Chinese Deputy Foreign Minister Han Nianlong had lodged an official protest with the Soviet Union. The move followed Soviet charges that Peking was aiding the Moslem rebels in Afghanistan, a charge that the Chinese had repeatedly and forcefully denied.

At the same time, it was reported by the London *Daily News* that Pakistan had permitted the Chinese to establish a string of military camps along Pakistan's border with Afghanistan.

Chinese Budget Deficit. On June 22 *The New York Times* reported that Chinese Vice Premier Li Xiannian had recently admitted that China suffered a $6.5-billion budget deficit in 1978. Unlike the U.S., China did not normally run deficits, and some analysts attributed the 1979 modernization slowdown to the deficit problem.

China-Vietnam Peace Talks. On June 25 a delegation from Vietnam arrived in Peking for the second round of talks with China on the border issue.

U.S. to Accept More Refugees. On June 28 President Carter announced in Tokyo that the U.S. would increase its admittance of Indochinese refugees from 7,000 to 14,000 a month for the next 12 months.

Wall Posters. On June 30, wall posters appeared in Peking accusing two members of the Politburo, Wang Dongxing and Chen Xilian, of embezzling state funds for their private use.

Vietnamese Leader Defects. On July 3 Hoang Van Hoan, a founding member of the Vietnamese Communist

Party and vice chairman of its standing committee, defected to China. One of the very few rifts in an otherwise cohesive leadership group, Hoang's defection raised the possibility that Vietnam's decision to pursue closer ties with Moscow was alienating those leaders who had always looked to China for support.

Sino-American Trade Pact. On July 7 U.S. Ambassador to China Leonard Woodcock and Chinese Minister of Trade Li Qiang signed the three-year trade agreement negotiated earlier by U.S. Commerce Secretary Juanita Kreps. *(See May 14)* The agreement required congressional approval for an exemption to the 1974 Trade Act, which limited most-favored-nation status to nations with free emigration policies. *(See Oct. 23; text, p. 352)*

China to Allow Joint Ventures. On July 8 the Chinese government published its first legislation on joint ventures between China and foreign companies. Under the new regulations, foreign companies would be permitted to invest in China and repatriate part of their profits. *(See Oct. 4)*

SALT Hearings Begin. On July 9 the Senate Foreign Relations Committee began hearings on the Soviet-U.S. strategic arms limitation treaty (SALT II).

Trade Pact with EEC. On July 18 China signed a five-year trade agreement with the Common Market. China was granted most-favored-nation status and, in return, agreed to limit textile exports to the member countries.

Korean Withdrawal Halted. On July 20 national security adviser Zbigniew Brzezinski stated that President Carter had temporarily suspended the withdrawal of U.S. combat forces from South Korea at least until 1981. There were 32,000 U.S. combat troops then in South Korea.

Bergland Hits Chinese Farming. On Aug. 8 Agriculture Secretary Bob Bergland told an audience in San Francisco that "by our standards, Chinese agriculture is hopelessly inefficient."

U.S. Flights to China. On Aug. 14, Chinese officials and officers from Pan American World Airways signed an agreement permitting public flights between San Francisco and Shanghai. *(See Sept. 14)*

Vatican Invites Ties. On Aug. 19 Pope John Paul II proposed resumption of diplomatic relations between the Vatican and China. The ties had been broken in 1949.

On Aug. 23 Fu Tieshan, the new Roman Catholic bishop in Peking, said he would welcome relations but stressed his independence from the Vatican, saying he was elected by "the voice of the people and the voice of God," and the pope in Rome had nothing to do with this. Fu also said relations with the Vatican would depend upon Rome's recognition of the independent status of the Chinese church.

The Vatican said it believed there were more than 4 million Christians — including 3 million Roman Catholics and 3,000 priests — in China in 1949, and estimated that there were still 500,000 to 2 million baptized Catholics and 500 native priests, most of them probably inactive.

The prospect for full relations remained dim, however, because the Vatican refused to break relations with Taiwan.

U.S. Law Firm to China. On Aug. 22 it was announced that Coudert Brothers of New York City had become the first American law firm to open an office in

---

The Stakes in Cambodia

". . .The future balance of power between Vietnam and China in Southeast Asia is being decided largely in Cambodia. If the Vietnamese can destroy the remnants of Pol Pot's guerrillas [in 1979] (as they have told their Soviet allies they will), their influence and prestige in the region will be immensely increased, and China will be humiliated. But if China can destroy Heng Samrin (the Cambodian leader backed by Vietnam), it will show up Vietnam as what Peking has said it is all along: a tiresome little country that grew too big for its boots.

"Foreign efforts to send in aid have run into difficulty because the outcome of this struggle is still uncertain, and both China's and Vietnam's Cambodian clients are so weak that they have to stand on what little dignity they have. Thus both Pol Pot and Heng Samrin insist that all aid must go exclusively to their side; anything less is seen as a threat to their legitimacy and survival. . . ."

Mark Frankland
The New Republic, Oct. 27, 1979

China since 1949. The office would handle legal affairs for U.S. firms doing business in China.

Jackson in China. On Aug. 24 Sen. Henry Jackson, D-Wash., concluded his 19-day visit to China by meeting with Chinese Vice Premier Deng Xiaoping. Jackson said that China was "unhappy" about the U.S. delay in approving the U.S.-China trade treaty signed July 7.

Mondale to China. On Aug. 24, Vice President Walter F. Mondale began an 11-day trip to China.

On Aug. 26 he met with Chinese Vice Premier Deng Xiaoping in Peking. The two leaders called for strengthened ties between the U.S. and China to "bolster stability" in the world.

On Aug. 27, speaking to a national television audience in China, Mondale told the Chinese people that a "strong and secure and modernizing China" was in the American interest, and that the U.S. was prepared to extend $2 billion in trade credits over a five-year period through the Export-Import Bank.

In an apparent warning to the Soviet Union, Mondale told the Chinese that "any nation which seeks to weaken or isolate you in world affairs assumes a stance counter to American interests."

This was the first time that any American leader directly addressed the Chinese nation on television. *(Text, p. 345)*

On Aug. 28 Mondale, ending two days of official talks with Chinese leaders, announced that the normalization of relations between the two countries was now a "concrete reality." Mondale also declared that "Sino-American friendship is not directed against anyone," and later added that "we do not have nor do we anticipate a military relationship."

On the same day, Mondale signed an expanded cultural exchange agreement and a protocol under which the U.S. would help China develop its hydroelectric power. Under the terms of the latter agreement, experts from the Army Corps of Engineers, the Tennessee Valley Authority, the Department of Energy and the Bureau of Reclamation would help China plan, design and supervise construction of some of the 20 power-generating dams which the Chinese hoped to build. The agreement put into effect the more generalized agreement signed by President Carter in January.

During the visit, Mondale also told the Chinese that the trade pact signed in July would go to the Congress without any links (i.e., not tied to similar concessions to the Soviet Union).

U.S. to End Air Pact. On Aug. 31 Vice President Mondale disclosed in Canton that the U.S. would end its civil aviation agreement with the Nationalist Chinese Government on Taiwan, despite earlier Carter administration declarations that all treaties and agreements, apart from the mutual defense treaty, would remain in force after relations were ended. *(See p. 348)*

On Sept. 1 the Baltimore *Sun* reported that a new unofficial agreement was being worked out by the American Institute in Taiwan to renegotiate all of the 60 treaties and agreements the U.S. had had with Taiwan. Robert Parker, president of the American Chamber of Commerce on Taiwan, who was accompanying Mondale, said "we will oppose the revision." Parker also said he was concerned that termination of the civil air agreement would set "a precedent for the termination of other agreements" and that "the administration's action is contrary to what was said at the time of normalization."

U.S. Checks to China. On Sept. 1 the U.S. Treasury Department began to allow U.S. government checks to be sent to China. The practice had been barred since 1949.

U.S. to Take More Refugees. On Sept. 2 Vice President Mondale announced in Hong Kong that the U.S. would take 2,000 more Vietnam refugees per month of the almost 70,000 who had found refuge in Hong Kong.

Castro Blames China and U.S. On Sept. 3, addressing the 6th Conference of Nonaligned Nations in Havana, Cuban Premier Fidel Castro said that most of world's major problems were caused by the U.S. and its "old and new allies" including China.

Dalai Lama to U.S. On Sept. 3, the exiled Dalai Lama, the Buddhist Tibetan leader and longtime antagonist of the PRC, arrived in the United States for a seven-week visit. *(See Oct. 23, 1977)*

Charter Flights to China. On Sept. 14 the Civil Aeronautics Board announced a series of public charter flights to China that authorities hoped would lead to regularly scheduled air service between the two countries. The new service would be provided by Pan American World Airways and the General Administration of Civil Aviation of China (CAAC), China's flag carrier. The two-week round-trip charters were to operate directly between San Francisco and Shanghai. Previously, only specially invited groups of Americans were allowed to fly directly to China.

Li on Foreign Policy. On Sept. 17, in an interview with Keith Fuller, president and general manager of the Associated Press, Chinese Vice Premier Li Xiannian said in Peking that China would continue to support the ousted regime of Cambodian Premier Pol Pot, despite the fact that it had been replaced by a new government backed by Vietnam.

On the question of Sino-Soviet negotiations, Li said the Chinese planned to raise the question of Soviet troops in Mongolia, with the aim of having them withdrawn by Moscow.

Nixon to China. On Sept. 17 former President Nixon returned to China for a three-day visit, his third. During his stay, Nixon said that the U.S. and China shared the "most basic common interest of all, that of national survival."

Pol Pot to Stay. On Sept. 21 the United Nations voted 71-35 with 34 abstentions to allow the representative of the ousted Cambodian regime of Pol Pot to take his seat in the General Assembly. Vietnamese and Soviet delegates wanted to seat the representative of the Vietnamese-backed government of Heng Samrin.

U.S. to Help China Reforest. On Sept. 22 a team of American forestry experts, headed by Gov. Clifford Finch of Mississippi, arrived in Peking and began talks with Chinese scientists on ways to replant huge areas of depleted Chinese forest land.

China and Russia to Talk. On Sept. 23 a ten-man Chinese negotiating team, headed by Deputy Foreign Minister Wang Youping, arrived in Moscow to begin talks aimed at easing Sino-Soviet tensions. It was the first attempt at such talks since 1964, when the Chinese went to Moscow following the ouster of Nikita Khrushchev. Analysts offered little hope of success.

The leader of the Soviet delegation to the talks was Leonid Ilyichev, who had headed the Sino-Soviet border talks, held intermittently and without success in Peking over the past nine years. *(See Dec. 6)*

China Signs Wildlife Pact. On Sept. 23, officials of the World Wildlife Fund announced in Peking that China had agreed to accede immediately to the convention on international trade in endangered species. The result was to bar further Chinese export of powdered rhinoceros horn, which the Chinese use as a sexual restorative, as well as exports of leopard and tiger skins.

New Vietnam Offensive. On Sept. 25 it was reported that about 200,000 Vietnamese troops had begun a major offensive against the remaining troops of Pol Pot in Cambodia.

New China-USSR Accusations. On Sept. 26, on the eve of talks aimed at improving the bitter relations between them, communist arch-rivals China and the Soviet Union accused each other of launching new propaganda campaigns that could jeopardize the negotiations. The Soviet news agency Tass complained that Peking media had increased their anti-Soviet polemics even as Chinese Deputy Foreign Minister Wang Youping arrived in Moscow. The statement also said that the talks "will be complex and not easy."

Soviet Troop Count. On Sept. 27 a West German parliamentary delegation was told in Peking that there were about 570,000 Soviet troops on China's northern and western borders. "China told us they learned recently that 54 divisions [about 10,600 men each] are posted" along the border. The group also reported that the Chinese told them they "know" that the talks in Moscow "will have no result."

China Attacks SALT. On Sept. 27 Chinese Deputy Foreign Minister Han Nianlong told the U.N. General Assembly that the SALT II treaty signed by the U.S. and the Soviet Union was meaningless because it called for no real limits on the nuclear arms race. Han said it was "No wonder that people have pointedly commented that the treaty has nothing in common with genuine disarmament."

Chinese Claim Rejected. On Sept. 27 the Vietnamese foreign ministry rejected China's claim to the Paracel (Xisha) Islands in the South China Sea.

Earlier in the month, the Philippines had reasserted its claims to the Spratly (Nansha) Islands, located in the same area. *(Map, p. 115)*

Another Policy Change. On Sept. 28 Chinese Vice Premier Gu Mu told a news conference in Peking that China was ready to apply to United Nations lending institutions for loans to finance its massive modernization programs.

Soviet Troop Buildup. On Sept. 28 the CIA reported there were about 10,000 Soviet troops on the Kurile Islands 40 miles north of the Japanese island of Hokkaido. The islands were in dispute between the two countries.

Ye's Criticism. On Sept. 29 Ye Jianying, senior vice chairman of the Chinese Communist Party, declared that China had made a series of errors culminating in the Cultural Revolution of the 1960s. In an apparent effort to put even more distance between the current leadership and that of an earlier decade, Ye said the Cultural Revolution "was an appalling catastrophe suffered by all our people." Ye seemed to exonerate Liu Shao-ch'i, purged during the 1960s, and to blame former Party Chairman Mao Tse-tung.

Mao Not a God. On Oct. 3 the Peking *People's Daily* said former Chairman Mao Tse-tung was not a sage or a god. In the ongoing de-Maoization of China, the article said "No political party and no individual is free of mistakes or fails to make errors in their activities."

U.S. Will Not Sell Arms to Peking. On Oct. 4 Secretary of State Cyrus Vance reaffirmed the U.S. decision not to sell arms to China. Vance made the statement in response to an Oct. 3 article in *The New York Times* that discussed a purported secret study prepared in the Defense Department advocating such sales so that China might assist the West in any future war with the Soviet Union.

On Jan. 3, 1980 the *Times* reported more details of the secret study, to be declassified in 1985. According to the report, China was as much as 15 years behind the U.S. and Russia in many areas of military development. Thus, although the authors agreed that Chinese participation on the side of the U.S. in a war with the Soviet Union would be helpful, there were major problems. It was estimated that it would cost from $41 billion to $63 billion to improve the Chinese military to the point where it would have a "confident capability" of successfully resisting a Soviet non-nuclear attack. In addition, there were serious doubts raised as to whether China could even absorb the high level of technology which these improvements would require.

Joint Venture Agreement Signed. On Oct. 4 China signed its first joint venture investment contract, with the E-S Pacific Corp. of San Francisco and Cleveland. The contract was announced at a news conference by Rong Yiren, chairman of China's new joint venture corporation, which was officially founded the same day. Previously, the Chinese had opposed such contracts as "imperialistic."

Hua on "Gang." On Oct. 7 Chinese Premier and Party Chairman Hua Guofeng, speaking at his second news conference in three years, announced that the members of the "gang of four," ousted by Hua in October 1976, would be placed on trial in 1980.

Agricultural Reforms Planned. On Oct. 7 *The Washington Post* reported that the Chinese Communist Party had published a report blaming China's agricultural problems on policies instituted by former Party Chairman Mao Tse-tung, and unveiling a new plan for massive reform of China's agricultural system.

Taiwan Aid Vote. On Oct. 9 the Senate adopted an amendment to the 1980 foreign aid bill (HR 4473) deleting a House-passed prohibition on the Asian Development Bank's use of U.S. contributions unless Taiwan remained a member of that bank. Supporters of the amendment claimed that the bank had no plans to expel Taiwan.

Administration to "Tilt." On Oct. 15 it was reported that the Carter administration planned to ask Congress to ratify the Sino-American trade agreement while delaying a bid for similar treatment of the Soviet Union. *(See Oct. 23)* The decision meant a setback for Secretary of State Cyrus Vances's effort to be "evenhanded" in dealing with the two powers.

On the same day, Rep. Charles Vanik, D-Ohio, said he would support the measure if the administration reached an agreement with Peking on limiting textile exports. The Chinese had earlier refused such a request. *(See Oct. 30)*

Hua to France. On Oct. 15 Chinese Party Chairman and Premier Hua Guofeng arrived in France on the first stop of a three-week European tour. In the first visit by a ranking Chinese leader to Western Europe, Hua said: "It has always been an important element of China's foreign policy to strengthen and develop friendly relations and cooperation with the countries of Western Europe." *(See Oct. 21)*

Soviets Attack Hua Trip. On Oct. 15 Moscow radio denounced Chinese Premier Hua Guofeng's trip to Western Europe and contrasted Hua's demands for increased European armament against the Soviet threat to the Soviets' own proposal for arms reduction in Europe.

Canton Trade Fair. On Oct. 16 the Xinhua news agency announced that the Canton (Guangzhou) Trade Fair, held biannually since 1956, would remain open permanently in order further to encourage Chinese international trade.

Dissident Convicted. On Oct. 16 China's most prominent young dissident, Wei Jingsheng, was convicted of revealing details of the Sino-Vietnamese War to a foreigner and agitating for the overthrow of the government. The trial of the 29-year-old magazine editor was the first public trial of several dissidents arrested in the spring of 1979. Wei was sentenced to 15 years in prison.

In Washington the State Department said the U.S. was "surprised and disappointed at the severity of the sentence."

Wei later appealed his conviction, but it was upheld on Nov. 7.

Surplus to Taiwan. On Oct. 16 Congress passed and sent to the president the fiscal 1980 foreign military aid authorization bill, which authorized the president to transfer war reserve material to Taiwan without cost to Taiwan.

Court Rules on Treaty. On Oct. 17 U.S. District Court Judge Oliver Gasch amended his ruling of June 7 and declared that a president does not have the power to end a treaty on his own authority and must seek approval of either two-thirds of the Senate or a majority of both the

House and the Senate. Gasch ordered the administration not to carry out plans formally to terminate the mutual defense treaty with Taiwan Jan. 1, 1980. *(See Nov. 30)*

Gasch's decision came on a suit by Sen. Barry Goldwater, R-Ariz., and 24 others seeking to overturn Carter's action. President Carter appealed the decision. *(Details, pp. 40-42)*

2nd Dissident Tried. On Oct. 17 it was announced in Peking that Fu Yueha, China's most prominent female dissident, had gone on trial charged with organizing mass disturbances and libeling a man she accused of raping her. On the same day, Chinese Vice Premier Deng Xiaoping announced that these dissidents did not "represent the genuine feelings of the people."

The trial was halted on Oct. 18. Later, on Dec. 24, Fu was sentenced to two years in prison for violating public order.

Deng Pessimistic. On Oct. 17 Chinese Vice Premier Deng Xiaoping told seven American governors visiting China that Peking had no illusions that its latest series of talks with the Soviet Union would succeed in lessening tensions between the two communist giants. But, continued Deng, "to have negotiations is better than not to have them at all."

Deputy Foreign Minister Han Nianlong had offered a similar analysis the day before, telling the governors that the two sides had not yet agreed on an agenda for the talks.

Military Alert in Thailand. On Oct. 18, following a series of border clashes with the Vietnamese troops occupying Cambodia, Thailand placed its armed forces on full military alert.

U.S. Ship to China. On Oct. 20 the *S.S. Velma Lykes* arrived in Canton; it was the first American ship to visit a south China port in 30 years.

Byrd on Court Ruling. On Oct. 20 Senate Majority Leader Robert C. Byrd, D-W.Va., said the Senate should formally back President Carter's decision to terminate the U.S.-Nationalist China defense treaty. Byrd said a simple majority vote would suffice, rather than the two-thirds Senate vote or majority vote in both houses demanded by Judge Gasch in his court ruling. *(See Oct. 17)* Otherwise, said Byrd, Gasch's ruling would leave "a very important foreign policy issue up in the air — precisely where it should not be."

Hua to Germany. On Oct. 21 Chinese Premier Hua Guofeng arrived in West Germany for an eight-day visit, the second stop on his European tour.

On Oct. 22, speaking at a welcoming banquet, Hua called for the reunification of Germany as a check against Soviet expansion in Europe. But West German leaders stressed that although they were committed to improved relations with China, they would not let that relationship hurt their ties with Moscow. Germany, China's third largest trading partner, had consistently refused to sell arms to Peking.

On Oct. 23 the two countries signed agreements expanding economic and cultural ties. Appearing at a joint news conference, German Chancellor Helmut Schmidt said his talks with Hua had revealed the existence of much "likemindedness" and had been "impressive and successful." *(See Oct. 28)*

More Religious Freedom. On Oct. 21 Chinese Catholics celebrated the first mass in Canton in 15 years.

Another Policy Change. On Oct. 22 the Peking *Worker's Daily* said Chinese party leaders should not discriminate against qualified non-communists; such people should be promoted in industry, science and economics.

This announcement marked a return to the policy that existed prior to 1957, when non-party people served at the highest levels in China. With the anti-rightist campaign of 1957, however, and during the Cultural Revolution, such people were discriminated against, harassed, persecuted and purged.

Trade Pact to Congress. On Oct. 23 President Carter sent the Sino-American trade agreement, signed July 7, to Congress. The pact would grant most-favored-nation status to China, a privilege not enjoyed by the Soviet Union. On the same day, Carter also signed a proclamation waiving the requirements of the Jackson-Vanik amendment to the 1974 Trade Act, which forbade granting MFN Status to nations in violation of U.S. free-emigration standards. *(Details, p. 71)*

In his letter of transmittal, Carter said China was moving to lift bans on emigration. *(Texts, p. 352)*

Peking into Olympics. On Oct. 25 the Executive Board of the International Olympics Committee (IOC), meeting in Nagoya, Japan, unanimously adopted a resolution naming Peking as the Chinese representative in the Olympics, replacing Taipei. Taiwan was to be allowed to participate only under the name of the "Chinese Taipei Olympic Committee." The resolution was then submitted to a vote by mail of all IOC members. *(See Nov. 27)*

Park Assassinated. On Oct. 26 South Korean President Park Chung Hee was shot to death at a dinner party by Kim Jae Kyu, head of the Korean intelligence agency, in what was alleged to be the first step of a coup attempt. Kim was promptly arrested and the country placed under martial law.

Hua to Great Britain. On Oct. 28 Chinese Premier and Party Chairman Hua Guofeng arrived in London on the third stop of his European tour. Without addressing the Soviets by name, Hua praised Prime Minister Margaret Thatcher because she had "unequivocally identified the source of war danger and called for effective countermeasures."

On Nov. 1 Thatcher informed Hua that Britain would agree to sell Harrier jets to China and that details could be worked out later. China had long expressed interest in the planes, which Peking believed especially suitable for use along the Sino-Soviet border. On the same day, the two countries signed agreements on cultural and educational ties, as well as a civil-air transport pact. *(See Nov. 3)*

Deng Restates Peking's Stand. On Oct. 28 Chinese Vice Premier Deng Xiaoping, meeting with a parliamentary delegation from Thailand, reiterated Peking's opposition to Vietnam and support for Hanoi's opponents: "The Chinese Government and people will use every appropriate means to support the struggle of Democratic Kampuchea [Cambodia] and all patriotic forces of that country against the Vietnamese aggressors. China will stand on the side of the ASEAN [Association of Southeast Asian Nations] countries if Vietnam attacks them. It will stand on the side of Thailand if Vietnam attacks it."

More Textile Quotas. On Oct. 30 the U.S. announced that it was further expanding the quotas imposed on the import of textiles exported from China. *(See May 31)*

Cultural Congress Convenes. On Oct. 30 the 4th National Congress of Writers and Artists opened in Peking, the first such meeting in 19 years.

Addressing the opening ceremony, Vice Premier Deng Xiaoping said that writers and artists should concentrate on the portrayal of "pioneers in the modernization drive." Deng also declared that all creative works should not only provide education and enlightenment for the people, but at the same time should be entertaining and aesthetically pleasing. Deng called for the artists to assimilate the best of all ages and all lands, a marked change from the restrictions imposed on cultural expression during the Cultural Revolution.

Wall Posters Attacked. On Nov. 3 the Peking *People's Daily* denounced persons placing wall posters on "Democracy Wall," saying they "have gone in for anarchism" and were turning "to foreigners for sympathy and support." *(See Dec. 6)*

Hua to Italy. On Nov. 3 Hua Guofeng arrived in Italy, the last stop on his four-nation European tour. Hua told Italian Premier Francesco Cossiga that China supported the emplacement of new missiles on the soil of NATO nations prior to any arms limitation talks with the Soviet Union.

Italy and China signed a series of agreements providing for closer scientific, technological, cultural and economic cooperation, and the establishment of consulates in Milan and Shanghai.

Hua returned to China Nov. 6, announcing at the Rome airport that his journey to Europe had been "crowned with success." Hua also restated his commitment to a "strong and united" Europe which would be "an important factor for peace and stability in the world."

Crisis in Iran. On Nov. 4, Iranian "students" seized the U.S. Embassy in Tehran and captured 61 Americans. The "students" announced that the hostages would be freed only after the deposed Shah of Iran had been returned to Iran to stand trial.

Mrs. Carter to Thailand. On Nov. 8 Rosalynn Carter arrived in Thailand for a three-day tour of Cambodian and Laotian refugee camps there. After her return to Washington, President Carter announced, on Nov. 13, an immediate airlift of food to Thailand and authorized $6 million to buy rice and other commodities.

U.N. to Help China. On Nov. 11 the United Nations signed an agreement with China to provide a $20-million grant to help resettle the more than 250,000 ethnic Chinese refugees who had been expelled from Vietnam. China had always refused such aid in the past.

U.N. Calls for Withdrawal. On Nov. 14 the U.N. General Assembly voted 91-21 (with 29 abstentions) to call for the withdrawal of all "foreign" troops from Cambodia. The resolution was aimed at Vietnam.

Congress on MFN. On Nov. 15 testimony before the Senate Finance Committee provoked sharp disagreement about the granting of most-favored-nation status to China while refusing to extend similar treatment to the Soviet Union.

Sen. Adlai Stevenson, D-Ill., opposed the move, maintaining that such a policy might increase tensions between the U.S. and the Soviet Union.

Sen. Abraham Ribicoff, D-Conn., said that while he would prefer to grant MFN status to both countries, he did not believe that ties with China should be delayed until negotiations with Moscow were completed.

Sen. Henry Jackson, D-Wash., testified that he was satisfied that China had complied with requirements of the Jackson-Vanik amendment to the 1974 Trade Act, and that Congress should move speedily to approve MFN for China.

Deputy Secretary of State Warren Christopher assured the committee that the U.S. had, in fact, received assurances from the Chinese about their free emigration policies, but declined to produce them, maintaining that to do so would be a violation of diplomatic privilege.

Election in Peking. On Nov. 15, in the first major election held in China in 25 years, the residents of Peking's East District elected a 350-member district congress containing 130 non-Communists. Using secret ballots, the election was expected to be a model for similar local elections to be held throughout China in 1980. These local congresses then select delegates to the National People's Congress, China's nominal parliament. *(Structure of party, see p. 368)*

Since 1954 all such elections had been rigidly controlled by the Communist Party, which had nominated the candidates, who then ran unopposed. In this election there were 592 candidates, of whom 242 were not members of the party.

Holbrooke on Southeast Asia. On Nov. 16 the *Far Eastern Economic Review* published an interview with U.S. Assistant Secretary of State for East Asia and Pacific Affairs Richard Holbrooke, who said that the "situation on the Thai-Cambodian border is dangerous" and has "the potential for an explosion." Holbrooke declared that "American policy towards the problem will be based on strong support for Thailand," and cited a recent transfer of $400 million in arms to Thailand as evidence of that support.

Thailand to Admit Refugees. On Nov. 18 it was reported that the Thai government had agreed to allow Cambodian refugees to cross the border into Thailand and declared that it would provide them with temporary shelter.

By the end of December, it was estimated that there were some 130,000 refugees in Thailand, while another 600,000 remained along the Thai-Cambodian border.

China to Curb Population. On Nov. 19 Chinese Vice Premier Chen Muhua announced that China was making new efforts to control the rapid growth of its population, and that its new goal was "to bring the growth to a standstill by the year 2000."

China and Vietnam. On Nov. 22 Vietnam accused China of preparing a new invasion, a charge that was confirmed by other diplomatic sources. The Vietnamese statement came at the 14th session of the deadlocked border negotiations between Hanoi and Peking.

China and Nepal. On Nov. 24 Chinese Foreign Minister Huang Hua concluded a four-day official visit to Nepal, where he signed a protocol defining the border between the two countries.

Peking Sides with U.S. On Nov. 26, following three weeks of official silence, the Chinese foreign ministry issued a statement on the crisis in Iran announcing that "the principle guiding international relations and the accepted diplomatic immunities should be universally respected." Peking also expressed its hope that "a reasonable and appropriate solution" to the crisis could be found "at an early date."

China in the Olympics

After years of dickering, the International Olympic Committee (IOC) on Nov. 27, 1979, approved China's readmittance to the Olympic Games, to be held next in Moscow in 1980. The committee decreed that Taiwan athletes could participate only if they were designated under the name "Chinese Taipei Olympic Committee" rather than the "Republic of China Olympic Committee." The IOC vote was 62-17.

Peking officials immediately started making plans to send some 330 athletes to compete in Moscow, as well as a figure skating team for the earlier Winter Olympics in Lake Placid, N.Y.

Less than two months later, however, China — having won the right to participate in the Olympics on its own terms — joined the United States and several other nations in threatening to boycott the Moscow games if Russia did not withdraw its troops from Afghanistan.

The People's Republic of China had not participated since its triumph in the Chinese civil war in 1949. It withdrew from the 1952 and 1956 games in protest of Taiwan's inclusion in the events. In 1958 it pulled out of the IOC.

In 1976 Canada refused to admit Taiwan's athletes to the Montreal Olympics because Taiwan insisted that they appear as representatives of the "Republic of China." Following U.S. recognition of mainland China in 1979, government officials asked the IOC to recognize the PRC athletes as the legitimate Chinese team, and the committee complied.

Chinese Leaders' Age. On Nov. 26 *The New York Times* reported that China was increasingly concerned with the advancing age of its senior leaders and had begun planning to force some of them to retire to make way for younger men. On Nov. 29 the Peking *People's Daily* called for more younger cadres to be promoted to replace older leaders, calling it an "urgent task."

Chinese Oil Discovery. On Nov. 26 it was reported that China had discovered more oil in the South China Sea off Hainan Island. The extent of the reserves was not indicated, although a radio broadcast said that oil and gas "in relatively large quantities" had been found.

Tokyo on Iran Crisis. On Nov. 27 Japanese Prime Minister Masayoshi Ohira, speaking before the Parliament, said that "Japan is watching" the situation in Iran "with deep concern and hopes that the situation will be solved as fast as possible." U.S. administration officials were reported to be dissatisfied with what they saw as the vagueness of the comment. *(See Dec. 10)*

China into Olympics. On Nov. 27 the International Olympic Committee announced that it had voted 62-17 to admit the People's Republic of China and expel the Republic of China from Olympic participation. The ROC would henceforth be allowed to participate in the games only under the name of the "Chinese Taipei Olympic Committee," and would be barred from using the flag, emblems or anthem of the ROC. *(Box, this page)*

Taiwan immediately challenged the decision in the Swiss courts, but their appeal was rejected in Lausanne. *(See Jan. 15, 1980)*

Chinese to be Repatriated. On Nov. 28 it was announced in Jakarta that Indonesia planned to send some 1 million Chinese holders of passports issued by Peking back to China by 1984. There were about 3.5 million Chinese living in Indonesia out of a predominantly Moslem population of 120 million. The Chinese refusal to integrate themselves into the country's culture had been the source of tension and anti-Chinese hostility.

Court Rules for Carter. On Nov. 30, following an administration appeal, the U.S. Court of Appeals reversed a lower court ruling *(see Oct. 17)* and voted 4-1 that President Carter had the power to abrogate the U.S. defense treaty with Taiwan. The court stated that "It would take an unprecedented feat of judicial construction to read into the Constitution" a requirement that Congress approve all treaty terminations. *(Text of ruling, p. 355)*

Carter was reportedly "very pleased" by the action, but Sen. Barry Goldwater, R-Ariz., who had brought the original suit, declared that he would appeal the decision to the Supreme Court. *(See Dec. 13)*

Peking Pledges Support. On Dec. 4 a Chinese military delegation to Thailand stressed China's support for Bangkok. The Thais called for the two countries to "strengthen cooperation between the two peoples and the two armies." For its part, the Chinese said that Peking would always stand on the side of Thailand.

Sino-Japanese Relations. On Dec. 5 Japanese Prime Minister Masayoshi Ohira arrived in Peking for a five-day official visit. During his stay Ohira signed an agreement with Chinese Premier and Party Chairman Hua Guofeng extending a series of low-interest loans from Japan to China. The new program, worth about $1.5 billion over the next 5-8 years, was in addition to the $4 billion Japan had already agreed to lend China.

On Dec. 6 China and Japan signed an agreement for joint exploration and exploitation of oil and natural gas in the Bohai Gulf off northern China. Japan would pay the exploration costs, and the two countries would share the development costs equally.

In response to Ohira's suggestion that Hua use Peking's influence to convince North Korea not to attack the South, Hua said that there was "no possibility" of such an invasion. Both leaders agreed to work toward a lessening of tension in Korea and eventual reunification of the country.

Chinese Forced to Move. On Dec. 5 *The New York Times* published an interview with a Cambodian refugee who stated that ethnic Chinese residents of Cambodia were being forced to leave the cities and move to more remote areas, a move which resembled similar actions taken by the Vietnamese toward their own ethnic Chinese population. It was estimated that in 1975 there were some 425,000 Chinese living in Cambodia.

Tougher Academic Standards. On Dec. 5 the Chinese news agency Xinhua announced that henceforth the hiring of all researchers and research fellows by the prestigious Chinese Academy of Social Sciences would be based on a nationwide examination. The report said that one of the goals of the test, to be given May 30-31, 1980, was to locate the many Chinese intellectuals who had fled Peking during the Cultural Revolution and dropped out of sight.

U.S. Charges Aid Blockage. On Dec. 6 the U.S. accused the governments of Vietnam and Cambodia of blocking distribution of the emergency aid being sent to Cambodia. The White House also charged that the Soviet Union, which had significant influence in the region, had "not brought any discernible influence to bear to alleviate the situation."

On Dec. 10 the Vietnamese news agency released a statement on behalf of the Cambodian government accusing President Carter of slander. (See Dec. 12)

Southeast Asian Tension. On Dec. 6 and again on Dec. 19, Vietnam claimed that China had massed some 15 divisions along its border with Vietnam preparatory to another invasion. At the same time, Hanoi claimed that there had been 1,300 "armed incidents" along the border since March. When questioned, some U.S. officials saw a renewal of the Sino-Vietnamese war as likely, while others, reported in the Dec. 20 New York Times, said they saw no evidence of the Chinese preparation for a new attack.

Democracy Wall Closed. On Dec. 6, following a resolution passed by the standing committee of the National People's Congress, the Peking municipal government announced that wall posters would no longer be allowed on "Democracy Wall," located on a main thoroughfare in downtown Peking. Henceforth such posters, often highly critical of the regime, would be allowed only on a designated wall in Yuetan Park, about three miles away in a residential area. The wall and its posters, in existence for about 13 months, had attracted much foreign media attention, which analysts saw as the reason for the move. (See Jan. 17, 1980)

London Breaks Ties. On Dec. 6 Great Britain announced that it was breaking diplomatic relations with the deposed Cambodian regime of Pol Pot. The statement went on to say that the British were not yet prepared to extend recognition to the Vietnamese-sponsored regime of Heng Samrin.

Most other non-Soviet-bloc nations continued to recognize the Pol Pot regime.

Talks Recessed. On Dec. 6 the Soviet news agency Tass reported that the first round of talks aimed at normalizing relations between the Soviet Union and China had ended that day, and noted that the next round would be held in Peking at a date to be determined later. Tass made no mention of progress in the talks, and Peking said that nothing had been accomplished. (See Jan. 19, 1980)

Riot on Taiwan. On Dec. 10 rioting broke out in the southern Taiwan port city of Kaohsiung (Gaoxiung) following efforts by 20-30 people to organize a rally celebrating the anniversary of the United Nations Universal Declaration on Human Rights. After the police refused to allow the rally, about 10,000 persons attacked the unarmed police, who used tear gas and then withdrew; 183 police were reported injured.

Later, police arrested 65 persons. Among those held were members of the Taiwan independence movement, a group which sought independence from both Nationalist and Communist rule. Some analysts feared the arrests marked an end to the government's more lenient policy toward dissidents, in effect since the spring.

Japan Criticized. On Dec. 10 the Carter administration charged that Japan had undercut U.S. efforts to put economic pressure on Iran to secure the release of the American hostages in Tehran. A high administration official said that the Japanese had rushed "with unseemly haste" to buy oil, originally intended for the U.S., which Carter had refused to buy because of the U.S. boycott. (See Dec. 14)

Other administration officials were upset by the Japanese statement on the crisis, which was termed as "ambiguous" and "wishy-washy." (See Nov. 27)

Goldwater on Taiwan. On Dec. 11 Sen. Barry Goldwater, R-Ariz., left Taiwan for the U.S. after a six-day visit. During his stay, Goldwater predicted that the People's Republic of China would be militarily unable to invade Taiwan successfully for at least the next 20 years. Goldwater said of Taiwan's military: "They're far superior to the mainland."

Coup in South Korea. On Dec. 12, troops under Gen. Chon Too Hwan arrested South Korean martial law commander Gen. Chung Sung Wah after a gunfight. Chon then installed Gen. Lee Hui Sung as the top military figure in Korea, but continued to hold actual power in his own hands. Chung was charged with involvement in the Oct. 26 murder of South Korean President Park Chung Hee.

American officials expressed alarm at the prospect of instability in South Korea and, on Dec. 15 protested that Gen. Chon had withdrawn his troops from the front lines in order to launch the coup, a violation of an agreement with the U.S. which prohibited such moves without American approval.

The situation in the South Korean military remained unstable through January 1980 as the young Chon began a purge of older officers who had supported Chung.

Japan Upset over Arms Sales. On Dec. 12 The Christian Science Monitor reported that Japanese industrialists and defense officials were dismayed over rumors that the U.S. might give China permission to build American helicopters and DC-9s in China. Such rumors had been consistently denied in Washington.

Japan was reported to be particularly alarmed because of U.S. moves to cut them out of the potentially lucrative arms sale market. Japan is barred by its U.S.-imposed constitution from selling weapons to communist countries.

Carter Gets Tough. On Dec. 12 President Carter, in a speech outlining future American defense spending plans, called for an end to the post-Vietnam era of non-use of U.S. military strength to check Soviet expansion, and seemed to signal the end of the Nixon Doctrine, which had defended such non-use.

Commenting on the crises in Iran and Southeast Asia, Carter said "we must understand that not every instance of the firm application of power is another Vietnam." Rather, U.S. "military weakness [will] inevitably make war more likely." Carter called for big increases in defense spending and the creation of a "rapid deployment force" that could be used to counter "the growing ability of the Soviet Union . . . to use its military power in Third World regions." The creation of such a force seemed to mark the end of former President Nixon's policy of eschewing the commitment of American troops in far-flung parts of the globe while insisting that these nations be made responsible for their own defense, aided only by U.S. funds and weaponry.

Specifically, Carter restressed the American commitment to its allies in East Asia, and declared that it was U.S. "military strength" that provided the "framework within which American alliances with these nations contribute to stability in the Pacific basin and the world."

Moscow Denies Aid Blockage. On Dec. 12 the Soviet Union strongly denied American charges that aid to the

Cambodian people was being blocked by the Vietnamese-sponsored Cambodian regime. *(See Dec. 6)* The statement, which appeared in the official news agency Tass, specifically denied charges raised in an article by James Reston in *The New York Times* on Dec. 12.

The Reston article was based on a report prepared by the CIA, a report which was also called inaccurate by the United Nations Cambodian relief director Henry R. Labouisse. On Dec. 13 Labouisse, who said the report "may give a false impression," blamed the aid stoppage on a shortage of transport to move the shipments. The CIA had claimed that the Cambodian government was collecting taxes on the shipments.

Renewed Fighting Possible. On Dec. 13 *The Washington Post* reported that some U.S. military officials believed another round of fighting between China and Vietnam was likely. According to the article, the source also said there was a greater chance a new war could spill over into Thailand, a U.S. ally that had accepted large numbers of Cambodian refugees, many of them soldiers in the army of the deposed Cambodian ruler Pol Pot. *(See Jan. 17, 1980)*

Goldwater Suit Rejected. On Dec. 13 the United States Supreme Court refused to hear a suit brought by Sen. Barry Goldwater, R-Ariz., challenging President Carter's authority to abrogate the U.S mutual defense treaty with Taiwan. *(See Oct. 17)*

The majority ruled that the suit be returned to the district court and that it be dismissed because it was a political question, and therefore non-justiciable.

The action meant Carter could terminate the treaty as planned effective Jan. 1, 1980.

Japan to Reduce Iran Imports. On Dec. 14 the Japanese Foreign Ministry announced that the government would impose an immediate ceiling on oil imports from Iran. The move followed strong U.S. pressure and sharp criticism from Secretary of State Cyrus Vance, who had warned Japan of possible trade retaliation if Japan did not stop buying Iranian oil, purchases the U.S. felt were undermining its efforts to apply economic pressure against Iran after the seizure of the U.S. Embassy on Nov. 4.

Travel Restrictions on Envoys. On Dec. 14 *The Washington Post* reported that the Carter administration would impose new travel restrictions on Chinese diplomats in the U.S. The new rules, which went into effect Jan. 1, required the Chinese to seek written permission 48 hours before traveling more than 25 miles from their consulates or embassy. According to official sources, the rules were imposed in retaliation for continuing restrictions on travel by U.S. officials in China.

Pol Pot Steps Down. On Dec. 15-17 the Cambodian Communist Party held a party congress which removed Pol Pot from his governmental posts in his ousted Cambodian regime. He was succeeded as premier by Khieu Samphan, but remained in charge of the guerrillas fighting against the Vietnamese-sponsored regime of Heng Samrin. The move was said to be an effort to unify all the various units, both communist and non-communist, who were fighting against the Vietnamese invaders.

Red Cross May Leave. On Dec. 15 *The Washington Post* reported that the International Committee of the Red Cross was reconsidering its leading role in providing food to Cambodia because so little of the aid was being distributed.

The Red Cross blamed the problem on political decisions of the Cambodian government, inefficiency, and shortage of transport.

Chinese Protest. On Dec. 18 the Chinese Foreign Ministry issued a formal protest charging that armed Vietnamese had raided China's Yunnan Province and killed an undisclosed number of civilians. The note, delivered to the Vietnamese Embassy in Peking, said: "In past weeks, the Vietnamese authorities, while making a hullabaloo against China, went on increasing tension in the Sino-Vietnamese border areas and carried on armed provocations."

On Dec. 19 the 15th session of the border talks between the two countries convened, with no results.

Trade Act Advances. On Dec. 18 the Senate Finance Committee approved without dissent a resolution (S Con Res 47) approving the trade agreement with China. The House Ways and Means Committee had approved the agreement (H Con Res 204) Dec. 13.

Neither house would take up the agreement — signed July 7 and submitted Oct. 23 — until late January, according to aides to both committees. *(Details, p. 69) (See Jan. 24, 1980)*

Bishop Consecrated. On Dec. 21 Monsignor Michael Fu Tieshan was consecrated as China's first Catholic bishop in 15 years. A spokesman for the Vatican had earlier called Fu's election "illegitimate" because it was done without the approval of Rome.

Korean President Inaugurated. On Dec. 21 Choi Kyu Hah was inaugurated as the fourth president of South Korea. Earlier he had appointed Shin Hyon Hwak as premier.

Southeast Asian War Threat. On Dec. 21 *The Washington Post* reported that Vietnam was preparing to launch a new offensive in Cambodia beginning that week. The U.S. State Department, although discounting the possibility of a Vietnamese invasion of Thailand, expressed fears about Vietnamese "hot pursuit" across the border. *(See Jan. 17, 1980)*

Rep. Lester Wolff, D-N.Y., said that a Vietnamese "invasion," or even "raids" across the border into Thailand, "would be of the gravest consequence for peace and stability in Asia."

Other sources reported more than 200,000 Vietnamese troops in Cambodia, of which 30,000-40,000 would be used against the remaining 20,000-30,000 Cambodian troops under Pol Pot.

Hanoi Charges. On Dec. 22 Vietnam accused Thailand of colluding with China to help Pol Pot. The statement declared that food, weapons and transportation were being sent to forces who were resisting the Vietnamese occupation of Cambodia.

Soviets into Afghanistan. On Dec. 25, after a month-long buildup, the Soviet Union began airlifting troops and supplies into Afghanistan. On Dec. 27, as about 20,000 Soviet troops crossed the border and invaded Afghanistan, Afghan President Hafizullah Amin was ousted in a coup and executed. He was succeeded by Babrak Karmal, who returned from exile in Czechoslovakia. By Dec. 31, Soviet troops, believed to number more than 30,000, were fanning out through the country to put down a rebellion by Moslem tribesman who opposed Marxist rule.

U.S. Reaction. On Dec. 28 President Carter called the Soviet intervention in Afghanistan a "blatant violation of accepted international rules of behavior."

It was also reported that Carter was considering the lifting of the ban against American military aid to Pakistan, imposed earlier in the year. *(See Jan. 4, 1980)*

Chinese Reaction. On Dec. 29 the Peking *People's Daily* reacted to the Soviet invasion of Afghanistan, with which it shares a 57-mile border, declaring: "Escalation of the Afghanistan intervention will only result in the spread of flames of armed rebellion into a conflagration and Moscow will get its fingers burned in it."

On Dec. 31 the Chinese Foreign Ministry called in the Soviet ambassador to Peking and demanded Soviet withdrawal from Afghanistan, terming the invasion "a threat to China's security" and declaring that it "cannot but arouse the grave concern of the Chinese people."

Taiwan's Trade. On Dec. 28 *The Washington Post* reported that since the American decision to break relations with the Republic of China on Taiwan on Jan. 1, 1978, Taiwan's rapid economic growth had continued unabated. Foreign investment in Taiwan, one of the key barometers of confidence, was $261 million in the first ten months of 1979, as opposed to $213 million during all of 1978. U.S. trade with the island nation had also increased: $10 billion in 1979 as against $7.3 billion in 1978.

Earlier in December, Taiwan's Council for Economic Planning and Development had announced it was setting an annual growth rate of 8 percent for the ten-year period beginning in 1980, down somewhat from the two-figure growth rates of the 1970s. The growth rate for 1979 was 8.5 percent, down sharply from 12.8 percent in 1978. But analysts noted that the lower growth rates reflected the maturation of the economy — as well as uncertainty about the availability of energy — rather than any problems deriving from U.S. de-recognition.

One of the results of Taiwan's new international status was a decision to allow direct trade between Taiwan and those communist countries that were "adjusting basic policy to democratic principles." Previously, all direct trade with communist nations had been forbidden, although Taiwan had allowed third parties to market their exports in these countries.

Under the new rules, which went into effect Dec. 1, Taiwan could trade with Poland, Yugoslavia, Hungary, Czechoslovakia and East Germany. Trade with Albania, Bulgaria, Romania, the Soviet Union, China and Vietnam was still forbidden.

Chinese Oil to Thailand. On Dec. 28 *The Washington Post* reported that China planned to sell another 10.36 million barrels of oil to Thailand at what were described as "friendship prices." Thailand had purchased 6.65 million barrels in 1979 under a five-year contract signed in 1978.

Study Calls for Closer Ties. On Dec. 28 the Rand Corp. released a report calling for closer ties between the U.S. and China. The report declared the Soviet Union would continue to be the major source of trouble in Asia, and would continue to try to encircle China. Thus, concluded the study, the U.S. should develop a "security relationship" with Peking.

U.S. Assures Pakistan. On Dec. 30 presidential national security adviser Zbigniew Brzezinski, speaking on ABC's *Issues and Answers*, reaffirmed the U.S. commitment to its 1959 mutual defense treaty with Pakistan and said President Carter had called Islamabad to inform President Mohammed Zia ul-Haq of the U.S. position.

Chinese Baseball

On Oct. 3, 1979, *The New York Times'* Fox Butterfield reported that one uniquely American institution — baseball — had caught on in mainland China.

During the Cultural Revolution the game was condemned as a "bourgeois pursuit" until it was "rehabilitated" in 1975. Butterfield suggested that much of the Chinese baseball fever stemmed from the success on the diamond of the Taiwanese, who learned the game from Japan and had won most Little League world series in the 1970s.

In addition to noting that the Chinese rallying cry is "sha" (kill), Butterfield reported other colorful aspects of the Chinese game:

"The vocabulary of the game, so cherished a part of baseball in the United States, is almost an exact translation into Chinese except for the shortstop. He is called the 'guerrilla.'

"Asked when the Chinese had begun to play baseball, Xie Chaoquan, the Deputy Secretary General of the Chinese Baseball and Softball Federation, displayed the usual Chinese sense of antiquity. 'According to unconfirmed reports, it began in the Qing Dynasty,' he said, sitting at an official's table in the stands behind home plate.

"In the late 19th century, he explained, some of the first Chinese students to venture abroad brought baseball back to China. Later some of Mao's Red Army guerrillas played it, Mr. Xie insisted. . . .

"Mr. Xie, China's equivalent to Commissioner Bowie Kuhn of the major leagues, denied that baseball players in China were actually paid for playing. According to him, they draw their regular salaries from the factories where they work, or the schools they attend.

"But they do receive a special subsidy of about $1 a day for food, a not-inconsiderable amount in China. They also attend training camps for several weeks before major contests like the National Games."

Brzezinski went on to say the treaty "is an important commitment and the United States will stand by it. I have been authorized to reaffirm that. . . ."

Defense Treaty Terminated. On Dec. 31 the U.S. terminated its 1954 mutual defense treaty with the Republic of China on Taiwan.

1980

SALT II Delayed — More Arms to Taiwan — U.S. To Aid Pakistan — Harold Brown to China — Soviets Veto Afghan Resolution — North, South Korea to Talk — U.N. Censures Russia — Wall Posters to Be Banned — Sino-Soviet Talks Terminated — Science Mission to Peking

Tourists to China. On Jan. 1 the Chinese news agency Xinhua announced that more than 800,000 tourists had visited China in 1979, an increase of 30 percent over 1978.

SALT II Pact Delayed. On Jan. 3 President Carter, acting in response to the Soviet invasion of Afghanistan, asked Senate Majority Leader Robert Byrd, D-W.Va., to "defer" debate on the SALT II agreement "so that the Congress and I the President can assess Soviet actions and intentions" in Afghanistan.

Moscow's Reason. On Jan. 3 the Soviet news agency Tass charged that the Soviet intervention in Afghanistan had followed an Afghan request for military assistance in putting down a rebellion armed and led by the CIA as well as by British and Chinese agents.

China Given Satellite Access. On Jan. 3 *The New York Times* reported that President Carter had recently approved a plan giving Peking access to a new U.S. Landsat photo — reconnaissance satellite to be launched in the early 1980s. According to the report, some of the technology involved would have military application. *(See Jan. 20)*

More Arms to Taiwan. On Jan. 3 the State Department announced the U.S. would sell $280-million worth of defensive weapons to Taiwan, thus ending the one-year moratorium on such sales. Included in the deal were land- and sea-based air defense missiles and TOW anti-tank missiles. The U.S. again refused to sell Taiwan high-performance aircraft such as the F-4, F-16, or F-18, but announced its willingness to provide more F-5s. Congress had 30 days to review the decision, but was not considered likely to oppose it.

The State Department also said Peking had been informed of the sales, which were "consistent with our intention, stated publicly at the time of normalization," to sell Taiwan "selected defensive equipment."

U.S. to Aid Pakistan. On Jan. 4 *The New York Times* reported that President Carter had requested Congress to pass emergency legislation lifting the bans against sending U.S. military aid to Pakistan. The ban — in effect since April 1979 — had been invoked because of Pakistan's refusal to halt nuclear weapons development. *(See Jan. 12)*

The Pentagon announced the same day that it would speed delivery to Pakistan of $150-million worth of military equipment previously purchased. The transaction had not been affected by the military aid cutoff because Pakistan had paid cash for the equipment.

Brown to China. On Jan. 5 U.S. Secretary of Defense Harold Brown arrived in China for an eight-day visit, the first by a ranking secretary of defense since 1949. The trip had been planned earlier, but Brown declared that the Soviet invasion of Afghanistan had given the mission "added significance."

At the welcoming banquet Jan. 6, Brown proposed that the U.S. and China respond with "complementary military action if jointly threatened," and also suggested that Peking and Washington "might facilitate wider cooperation on security matters."

On Jan. 8 Brown met with Chinese Vice Premier Deng Xiaoping and told him that the United States and China "should coordinate their policies in the face of the threat from the Soviet Union." Deng replied that "China and the United States should do something in a down-to-earth way so as to defend" against Soviet actions.

On Jan. 9 Brown declared that the two countries were "very parallel about the need to strengthen the other nations in the region [i.e. Pakistan] and each side will take appropriate action on its own towards that end."

Despite the outpouring of rhetoric, no concrete agreements were reached, and analysts in Washington noted that the results of the trip were largely "psychological" and "symbolic," although it was announced that a military delegation to be headed by Geng Biao, vice premier and secretary general of the CCP's military commission, would visit the U.S. in 1980.

Brown left China on Jan. 13, stopping off in Tokyo to brief Japanese leaders on the talks prior to his return to the U.S. *(See Jan. 13)*

It was later revealed that the Chinese had told Brown that Peking was ready to increase the covert supply of small arms to the Afghan rebels, and admitted that Chinese arms were being used to supply other Afghan rebels in Pakistan. In addition, Peking promised to help restore good relations between the U.S. and Pakistan, hurt by the 1979 aid cutoff and the burning of the U.S. Embassy in Islamabad.

It was also revealed that Brown informed Peking that the U.S. would welcome any Chinese military help in whatever form against Vietnam if Vietnamese forces were to cross over into Thailand. Officially, the U.S. had always discouraged such a Chinese intervention.

On the negative side, the Chinese rejected a U.S. proposal to establish a "hot line" between Peking and Washington, and informed the Americans that Hua Guofeng would be unable to come to the U.S. during the first half of 1980 because he was "too busy." *(See Jan. 24)*

Thailand Buys Arms. On Jan. 6 *The New York Times* reported that Thailand, alarmed over increasing tension along its border with Cambodia, was stepping up arms purchases from the U.S. In 1979 Bangkok placed orders for $400-million worth of weapons, a major increase over the $100 million ordered in 1978.

Despite the new weapons, analysts still believed that the Thai army was no match for the well-armed and battle-hardened troops of Vietnam.

Deng on Afghan Crisis. On Jan. 6 Chinese Vice Premier Deng Xiaoping said the Soviet invasion of Afghanistan was "a grave step," repeated Peking's "firm demand" that the troops be withdrawn, and declared that China would "work together with the Afghan people, and all countries and people . . . to frustrate Soviet acts of aggression and expansion."

Moscow's Charges. On Jan. 7 the Soviet news agency Tass charged that American and Chinese military officers were training Afghan rebels in Pakistan.

Soviet Warning. On Jan. 7 the Soviet government newspaper *Izvestia* warned the U.S. not to try to use China to counterbalance the Soviet Union. The article termed such a policy "shortsighted, to say the least."

Soviet Veto in U.N. On January 7 the U.N. Security Council passed a resolution by a 13-2 vote (Russia and East Germany opposed) calling on Moscow to remove its troops from Afghanistan. The Soviet Union then vetoed the resolution. Among others, China, the Philippines and Bangladesh supported the U.S. position. Following the veto, supporters of the resolution introduced it in the General Assembly, where there is no veto power. *(See Jan. 14)*

Hua on Afghan Crisis. On Jan. 8 Peking sharply increased its criticism of the Soviet invasion of Afghanistan as Chinese Party Chairman and Premier Hua Guofeng personally declared that "the Soviet Union's armed invasion of Afghanistan now constitutes direct aggression and the occupation of a nonaligned Islamic country of the Third World. Any excuses offered by the Soviet Union about the event are pointless."

Japan on Afghan Crisis. On Jan. 8, Japanese government officials declared Japan would take some action to

Cost of 'Containment': Aid to Countries Surrounding China

FOREIGN AID BY COUNTRY: JULY 1, 1945 - SEPT. 30, 1978

(U.S. Fiscal Years - Figures in Millions of Dollars)

U.S. OVERSEAS LOANS AND GRANTS - NET OBLIGATIONS AND LOAN AUTHORIZATIONS

	Total Military Assistance	Total Economic Assistance	Total Economic & Military Assistance	Export-Import Bank Long-Term Loans
NEAR EAST AND SOUTH ASIA				
Afghanistan	$ 5.6	$ 526.3	$ 531.9	$ 41.8
Bangladesh[1]	.3	1,312.3	1,312.6	3.3
India	145.6[2]	9,674.1	9,819.7	555.8
Nepal	2.1[3]	221.6	223.7	—
Pakistan[1]	713.2	4,880.2	5,593.4	320.0
TOTAL:	866.8	16,614.5	17,481.3	920.9
EAST ASIA				
Burma	88.7	96.8	185.5	3.4
Cambodia[4]	1,280.3	850.9	2,131.2	—
China, Republic of	4,360.4	2,206.9[5]	6,567.3	1,440.3
Hong Kong	—	43.8	43.8	44.1
Indochina, Undistributed[4]	731.5	825.6	1,557.1	—
Indonesia	369.0	2,348.0	2,717.0	603.6
Japan	1,239.7[6]	2,711.1	3,950.8	1,835.9
Korea, Republic of	7,275.4	5,893.9	13,169.3	2,017.6
Laos[4]	1,606.7	900.7	2,507.4	—
Malaysia	133.5	82.5	216.0	76.5
Philippines	922.4	1,948.2	2,870.6	852.4
Ryukyu Islands[7]	—	413.7	413.7	.5
Singapore	19.1	2.8	21.9	157.0
Thailand	1,596.4	693.5	2,289.9	121.4
Vietnam[4]	16,418.7	6,941.3	23,360.0	—
East Asia Regional[8]	—	337.8	337.8	
TOTAL	36,041.8	26,297.5	62,339.3	7,152.7
OCEANIA				
Australia	115.6	8.0	123.6	945.7
New Zealand	4.3	4.3	8.6	221.6
Trust Territory of the Pacific Islands	—	824.2	824.2	—
TOTAL	119.9	836.5	956.4	1,167.3
GRAND TOTALS of Selected Countries	$37,028.5	$43,748.5	$80,777.0	$9,240.9

1. Aid to Bangladesh prior to 1972 included in Pakistan data.
2. Begun in 1963.
3. Begun in 1965.
4. Aid to Indochina (Cambodia, Laos and Vietnam) before partition is shown under "Indochina, Undistributed." Aid after partition is shown under individual countries, which ended in 1975. (Aid by year, box p. 230.)
5. Includes aid to mainland China, 1945-49. Ended in 1965.
6. Excludes $540 million of material provided from Department of Defense stocks.

7. Ended in 1972 when the islands reverted to Japan.
8. East Asian Regional figures include loans of the Asian Economic Development Fund, and funds for technical assistance programs.

Sources: Adapted from *U.S. Overseas Loans and Grants*, Washington, D.C.: Agency for International Development, 1979; *Foreign Military Sales and Military Assistance Facts*, Washington, D.C.: Department of Defense, 1978.

register its disapproval of Soviet actions in Afghanistan. Foreign Minister Saburo Okita called the Soviet move "highly deplorable" and urged Moscow to "cease immediately [its] armed intervention of Afghanistan."

Peking to Halt Illegal Exodus. On Jan. 11 Peking published a list of regulations in a renewed effort to stem the flow of illegal refugees fleeing from Guangdong Province to Hong Kong and Macao. The new laws provided for a maximum 15-day prison term for first offenders, longer terms for repeaters. The Chinese move followed frequent complaints from Hong Kong that Peking was doing too little to help slow the flood of refugees into an already overpopulous Hong Kong.

U.S. Aid to Pakistan. On Jan. 12 the U.S. and Pakistan began high-level talks concerning the possibility of resuming American military aid to Islamabad. Pakistani Foreign Minister Agha Shahi met with Secretary of State Cyrus Vance in Washington for talks that were described as "very constructive." The U.S. agreed to supply $400 million in aid over the next two years, half of which would be military. In addition, the U.S. also proposed to begin sending aid to the estimated 400,000 Afghan refugees already gathered in Pakistan. (It was estimated that this number was increasing at the rate of several thousand per day.)

In Pakistan, local leaders were clearly unhappy with the amount of aid proposed by the U.S., and tended to talk about $1 billion as an acceptable minimum figure. One senior military commander portrayed his country as all but defenseless against a serious Soviet attack.

On Jan. 14 Pakistani President Mohammed Zia ul-Haq told *Newsweek* magazine that the Soviet invasion had significantly altered the situation in southern Asia, and that he was not optimistic about U.S. help: "The cornerstone is our relationship with China. . . . We have received almost $2 billion worth of aid from China since 1966."

Zia also hinted that if significant amounts of U.S. military aid were not forthcoming, his nation might be forced to seek accommodation with Moscow: "If you live in the sea . . . you have to learn to live with the whales." *(See Jan. 17)*

Korean Talks Proposed. On Jan. 12 North Korean Premier Li Chong Ok proposed to his South Korean counterpart, Premier Shin Hyon Hwak, a resumption of talks between Pyongyang and Seoul. The proposal was contained in a letter sent to Shin and 11 others, both in and outside the South Korean government. The two Koreas had conducted talks that began in spring 1972 but had been discontinued in August 1973. *(See Jan. 18)*

Li's letter followed by one day a North Korean proposal to reopen the "hot line" between the two capitals. The line had been opened in 1972 but fell into disuse after the August 1976 incident when two American soldiers were killed in the demilitarized zone. *(See Aug. 18, 1976)*

The U.S. State Department was said to have cautiously welcomed the initiatives.

U.N. Votes on Iran. On Jan. 13 the U.N. Security Council voted 10-2 (Mexico and Bangladesh abstaining; China not participating) for a U.S.-sponsored resolution to impose economic sanctions on Iran. The Soviet Union then vetoed the resolution. U.S. officials professed surprise at the Chinese refusal to vote, but Chinese Ambassador to the U.N. Chen Chu declared that Peking still hoped for a negotiated end to the hostage crisis.

U.S. Calls for Japan to Increase Defense Spending. On Jan. 13 U.S. Secretary of Defense Harold Brown urged

Japan to increase its military spending and expand the protection it affords its merchant shipping. The decision followed the recent Soviet buildups in the Pacific area. Japanese defense spending was reported to be about 0.9 percent of GNP, one of the smallest outlays among the industrialized nations.

The Kyodo news agency reported that Japanese officials were "somewhat perplexed" by Brown's request. According to a report in *The New York Times,* Japanese Prime Minister Masayoshi Ohira told Brown that Japan would make the decision on its own. *(See Jan. 23)*

China to Get MFN Soon. On Jan. 13 Rep. Charles A. Vanik, D-Ohio, announced that the Congress would extend most-favored-nation status to China "soon." The policy of treating China and the Soviet Union equally, said Vanik, "has been shelved as a result of Soviet troops moving into Afghanistan."

China's Trade Up. On Jan. 14 *The Wall Street Journal* reported that China's 1979 foreign trade had increased nearly 30 percent over that of 1978. Total trade for 1979 was put at $28.8 billion, representing a 27-percent increase in exports and a 33-percent increase in imports.

U.N. Censures Russia. On Jan. 14 the U.N. General Assembly voted 104-18 (18 abstentions and 12 absent) to demand the "immediate, unconditional and total withdrawal of the foreign troops from Afghanistan." The vote, which required a two-thirds majority for passage, followed a Soviet veto of a similar resolution in the Security Council. *(See Jan. 7)*

During four days of debate preceding the vote, numerous nations had denounced the Soviet invasion. On Jan. 10 the Chinese ambassador to the U.N., Chen Chu, declared that the invasion was part of a "global strategy" intent on "dominating the world." Chen compared the Soviet move to Hitler's invasion of Austria and Czechoslovakia on the eve of World War II.

The Japanese ambassador declared that the "international community remains clearly unconvinced of the Soviet explanation" for the invasion.

In a speech that stunned observers, the Indian ambassador on Jan. 11 professed his nation satisfied with the Soviet explanation for their actions, and declared his belief in Moscow's promise to withdraw the troops as soon as they were asked to do so by the Afghan government. The switch in the Indian position had followed new instructions to the ambassador from New Delhi, where Prime Minister-elect Indira Gandhi had ordered the change. India abstained on the final vote. *(See Jan. 16)*

Despite the overwhelming majority for the resolution, U.S. analysts saw little reason to believe that it alone would induce the Soviets to withdraw their troops, numbered at 80,000, from Afghanistan.

"Evenhanded" or "Balanced"? On Jan. 15, in an interview published in *The Wall Street Journal,* the president's national security adviser, Zbigniew Brzezinski, when asked about the fate of the previous U.S. policy of "evenhanded" treatment for the Soviet Union and China, denied that this was American policy: "[T]he President has very deliberately used the word 'balanced'. . . . The Soviet Union does pose a strategic challenge to the United States. China does not. The Soviet Union does impose regional and strategic strain upon us through its assertive behavior, directly or through proxies. China does not. . . . We therefore cannot pursue an identical policy towards both of these two major countries."

Competition for Trade Offices. On Jan. 15 *The New York Times* reported that a number of American cities were competing fiercely for the right to have one of two planned Chinese trade offices in their area. New York and Seattle were said to have the inside track.

The two U.S. trade offices, slated for Peking and Shanghai, had not yet been opened because, said the Chinese, there was a shortage of office space. According to the original agreement *(see May 14, 1979)*, the right to open trade offices was reciprocal, so that the Chinese offices in the U.S. would not be permitted to open until the American offices in China were allowed to do so.

Lipstick to China. On Jan. 15 *The Wall Street Journal* reported that Max Factor & Co., a unit of Norton Simon, Inc., had already begun test-marketing its cosmetics in selected retail outlets in Peking.

Taiwan Suit Rejected. On Jan. 15 a Swiss court in Lausanne denied Taiwan's motion for a temporary injunction preventing the IOC from accepting Peking as the delegation from China. Anticipating the IOC's Nov. 27, 1979 decision to admit Peking, Taiwan's IOC representative Henry Hsu had filed suit in the Swiss courts Nov. 15, 1979. Because these motions would not be heard for several months, Hsu had tried to have the court block implementation of the IOC decision in the interim. Hsu was expected to appeal. The court decision cleared the way for PRC participation in the Olympics. (The future of the 1980 Moscow Olympics was in grave doubt because of threats by the U.S. and other nations to boycott the games unless Soviet troops were withdrawn from Afghanistan.)

India Reverses Position. On Jan. 16 Indian Prime Minister Indira Gandhi reversed her country's position on the Soviet invasion of Afghanistan, declaring "I don't think that any country is justified in entering another country."

Tokyo Refuses Sanctions. On Jan. 16 Japan said that it would not join the U.S. in imposing economic sanctions on either Iran or the Soviet Union, fearing a total Iranian cutoff of oil exports to Japan.

Southeast Asian War Over? On Jan. 17 Vietnamese Deputy Foreign Minister Phan Nien seemed to indicate that the long-awaited Vietnamese offensive against the remnant forces of Pol Pot in Cambodia would not take place. Phan declared that "basically, the military problem is solved already."

No More Wallposters. On Jan. 17, in a speech to a secret meeting of high-ranking party leaders, Chinese Vice Premier Deng Xiaoping announced his intention to have the Chinese constitution amended to delete the section permitting Chinese to put up wallposters critical of the regime.

Article 45, the passage in question, is a direct quotation from the late Party Chairman Mao Tse-tung, and says citizens have the right to "write big-character posters." *(Text of constitution, p. 335)*

More Border Tension. On Jan. 17 the Chinese news agency Xinhua accused Vietnam of causing another incident along its border with China, and declared that there had been 14 such incidents in the first ten days of the new year.

Zia on U.S. Aid. On Jan. 17 Pakistani President Mohammed Zia ul-Haq met with U.S. reporters and called for a U.S.-Pakistan "friendship treaty" to augment the 1959 mutual defense pact. In the same interview, Zia character-

ized the $400-million aid package proposed by the U.S. *(see Jan. 12)*, as "peanuts." On the question of re-establishing U.S. bases in Pakistan, Zia declared: "I rule it out totally."

U.S. officials promptly rejected Zia's call for a new treaty, and said the $400 million was only part of a larger aid proposal.

South Korea Agrees to Talks. On Jan. 18 South Korean President Choi Kyu Hah announced at a news conference in Seoul that his government would respond "affirmatively" to the North Korean proposal *(see Jan.12)* for reunification talks between the two regimes. No date for the talks was set.

Huang Hua to Pakistan. On Jan. 18 Chinese Foreign Minister Huang Hua arrived in Pakistan for a five-day-official visit. It was announced that the talks would center on the Soviet invasion of Afghanistan. Earlier, the Chinese denied that they planned to send any troops to Pakistan, but Peking did reaffirm its intention to continue to send aid. It was also reported that Huang briefed Pakistani leaders on the outcome of U.S. Secretary of Defense Harold Brown's trip to Peking.

On Jan. 23 Huang declared: "Our talks demonstrated that our viewpoints are unanimous or very nearly so."

Sino-Soviet Talks to End. On Jan. 19 the Chinese Foreign Ministry announced that the Sino-Soviet talks on normalization, recessed since Nov. 30, 1979, would not be resumed. The statement declared that such talks were "inappropriate" in light of the Soviet invasion of Afghanistan.

Without talks, it was expected that the 1950 Sino-Soviet friendship treaty would be allowed to expire in February.

Carter Sees Danger. On Jan. 20, speaking on NBC's *Meet The Press,* President Carter declared the Soviet invasion of Afghanistan was the "most serious threat to peace since the Second World War." Carter went on to say that the Soviets "cannot invade an innocent country with impunity. They must suffer the consequences."

Science Delegation to Peking. On Jan. 20 a delegation headed by Frank Press, presidential science adviser, arrived in Peking for a four-day visit. The visit was designed to facilitate further scientific and technological exchanges between China and the U.S.

On Jan. 24 Press signed an accord with Peking providing for the establishment of a Chinese ground-receiving station for Landsat satellites. *(See Jan. 3)*

Carter Threatens Use of Force. On Jan. 23, in his third State of the Union Address, President Carter declared to a joint session of Congress that the United States would "use any means necessary, including force" to repel any attack on the Persian Gulf region. Carter's position, which had been progressively hardening since November 1979, seemed to mark an end to the efforts at U.S.-Soviet détente which had characterized the foreign policy of the 1970s.

Famine Averted in Cambodia. On Jan. 23 a senior State Department official announced that, for the time being, famine in Cambodia had been averted, but that vast starvation might occur in the spring of 1980 unless a major international relief effort was mounted. Cambodia had been under the threat of widespread famine since 1978.

Japan to Expand Role. On Jan. 23 Japanese Foreign Minister Saburo Okita declared that Tokyo must end its passive role in foreign affairs and "embark upon an activist foreign policy" in keeping with its position as a major economic power.

Military Equipment to China. On Jan. 24 the Department of Defense announced the U.S. would sell selected military equipment to China, although the ban on weapons sales would remain in effect.

Officials said that when Secretary Harold Brown was in Peking *(see Jan. 5),* he had told Chinese leaders the U.S. "was prepared to consider, on a case-by-case basis, the sale of certain carefully selected items of support equipment also suitable for military use, e.g. trucks, communications gear, and certain types" of radar. These officials noted that no specific agreements had yet been reached. Such sales to the Soviet Union were still banned.

Rep. Lester L. Wolff, D-N.Y., chairman of the Asian and Pacific Affairs Subcommittee of the House Foreign Affairs Committee, announced that the proposal, which required congressional approval, might have rough going: "I strongly oppose this idea until such time as we know what we are going to get in return from the People's Republic of China."

Congress Approves Trade Act. On Jan. 24 Congress voted overwhelmingly to approve the Sino-American trade agreement, signed July 7, 1979. Originally, it had been expected that there would be stronger congressional opposition to the pact, which granted most-favored-nation status to China while withholding it from the Soviet Union. But the Russian invasion of Afghanistan muted the debate. The Senate vote was 74-8; the House vote was 294-88. The president's signature was not required. *(Details, pp. 69-72; text, p. 352)*

House Ways and Means Chairman Al Ullman, D-Ore., called it "an historic occasion, a turning point in our relations" with China. But Rep. Richard T. Schulze, R-Pa., warned the U.S. should not "overreact to Afghanistan by hastily playing this so-called China card."

BIOGRAPHIES

Leading Figures in Postwar China

Chiang Ching-kuo
(1909-   )

(Jiang Jingguo)

Personal Background

Chiang Ching-kuo was born in Fenghua County, Zhejiang Province, the oldest son of Chiang Kai-shek and his first wife.

After attending a series of schools in his native province and Peking, Chiang won his father's permission to study in the Soviet Union. In 1925 he entered Sun Yat-sen University, established the year before in Moscow to train young Chinese revolutionaries, both Nationalist and Communist. Chiang graduated in 1927 but, probably due to his father's purge of the Chinese Communists earlier in the year, was not allowed by the Soviets to return to China. He continued his studies in the Soviet Union, married a Russian wife in 1935, and held a number of menial jobs during the period.

In 1937, when the Communists and Nationalists agreed to reunite for the purpose of opposing Japanese aggression in China, the Russians allowed Chiang to return home.

Public Career

With the outbreak of war in 1937 Chiang began serving in a number of middle-level positions in China's rural areas, where he earned a reputation for ruthless efficiency and honesty in a Nationalist government that was crumbling under the Japanese onslaught.

During the Chinese civil war, 1946-1949, Chiang appears to have been pushed aside in the treacherous bureaucratic infighting that plagued the hopeless Kuomintang (KMT) administration. In 1949, with the defeat of the Na-

Consistent with usage elsewhere in this book, the names of Chiang Ching-kuo, Chiang Kai-shek, Chou En-lai, Lin Piao, Liu Shao-ch'i, Mao Tse-tung and all Nationalist Chinese officials are spelled in the traditional Wade-Giles system. All other names appear in the new pinyin system.

A list of sources appears on p. 282.

tionalists, Chiang followed his father to Taiwan. When the elder Chiang resumed the presidency in 1950, he appointed his son as his personal aide. In addition to his control over the political commissars who served at all levels of the army, Chiang also came to dominate the extensive secret police operating on the island, which remained under harsh martial law, through his position as head of the political department of the Ministry of National Defense.

In October 1952 Chiang was elected to the standing committee of the KMT, and was also named head of the Chinese Youth Anti-Communist National Salvation Corps, which soon had offices in all the schools on Taiwan.

Chiang continued to rise in politics and in July 1958 was named to the Cabinet as minister without portfolio. He maintained his hold on the security apparatus and also took over the management of veterans' affairs, a powerful post in a nation with a large army. In March 1964 Chiang was named vice minister of national defense and in January 1965 succeeded to the ministry.

By 1965, with the death of Ch'en Ch'eng, who had been vice chairman of the party and vice president, Chiang became the heir-apparent to the presidency.

As his father's health began to decline, Chiang's power continued to expand until May 1972, when he became premier, thus officially taking over the day-to-day administration of the government. When his father died on April 5, 1975, Chiang was elected chairman of the KMT, thus consolidating his hold over both the party and the state.

In March 1978 Chiang was elected president — unopposed — and inaugurated in May. At the same time, he turned the office of premier over to Y. S. Sun, but continued as chairman of the party.

Analysis

In all his major offices Chiang has striven to defuse and to some extent redress the most urgent political problems on Taiwan, all of which had been ignored by Chiang Kai-shek, who had always treated Taiwan as only a way-station prior to his return to the mainland and viewed the island with what sometimes seemed contempt. Chiang Ching-kuo, on the other hand, labored to turn Taiwan into an economic showplace by increasing the gross national product and improving the lives of the citizens through more schools, increased literacy (now about 97 percent), more recreation facilities, improved transportation and political liberalization. Thus the man who came to power via the security apparatus had done much to relieve the most oppressive aspects of KMT rule. According to sources on Taiwan, much of this outraged the old guard, his father's cronies and some senior military commanders. But death seriously depleted the ranks of what young Chinese disparagingly call *laotouzi* (old heads).

Even more importantly, Chiang moved to ease the tension between the "mainlanders" — those who arrived on Taiwan after 1949 — and the native Taiwanese. Without making a policy statement, Chiang — who narrowly escaped a Taiwanese assassin's bullet in 1970 — appointed Taiwanese to key government positions, including minister of the interior and vice president, and continued to press quietly for the promotion of qualified Taiwanese throughout the country.

Chiang's style of rule has been the opposite of his father's; it resembles the ward-boss politics of an earlier American era. He is frequently out among the crowds, smiling, shaking hands and kissing babies. He raises funds by a not too subtle arm-twisting of the rich, and then distributes the money on a case-by-case basis to people in need.

Chiang's eight years of rule have already eased Taiwan through the critical transition to a new generation of a younger, mostly Western-educated, leadership, replacing his father's cohorts and hangers-on.

Chiang, a diabetic, has three sons and a daughter, none of whom exhibit any political stature on Taiwan.

Chiang Kai-shek (1887-1975)

(Jiang Jieshi)

Personal Background

Chiang was born in the town of Qukou, Fenghua County, Zhejiang Province on Oct. 31, 1887. The death of his father, a prosperous salt merchant, in 1894 left the family in difficult financial straits. Chiang had a brother, two sisters, a half-brother and a half-sister.

Chiang was married twice and had two sons by his first marriage. In 1927 he married Soong Mei-ling, the younger sister of Mme. Sun Yat-sen, despite the fact that he was already married. Soong — a Methodist — induced Chiang to convert to Christianity in 1930. The two had no children.

In 1905 Chiang went to the nearby city of Ningbo to study Chinese philosophy but, like many young Chinese of the period, soon decided that China's weakness against exploitation by foreign powers stemmed from its military impotence. So Chiang in 1907 went to north China, where he enrolled in China's first modern military academy, the Paoting (Baoding) Rapid Course School, established by the imperial government and staffed by Japanese instructors. Chiang was a brilliant student and, after graduation, won a scholarship to continue his studies in Japan. He studied at a military preparatory school, Shimbu Gakko, 1908-10, and then enrolled in the Japanese military academy, Shikkan Gakko, in 1910. It was during this period that Chiang met Chang Ch'ün (Zhang Qun) and the other young Chinese with whom he would be associated for life. He joined Sun Yat-sen's secret revolutionary society, the T'ungmenghui (Tongmenghui), in 1908.

Public Career

When the Republican Revolution broke out in 1911, Chiang and his companions rushed back to China. Chiang's military successes in the Shanghai area prompted his rapid promotion to regimental commander. In 1912, with the revolution seemingly over, Chiang returned to Japan to continue his studies.

In 1913 Chiang again returned to China to participate in the so-called "second revolution," which was quickly defeated. Now an outlaw, Chiang returned to Japan. During the next three years he divided his time between study in Japan and revolutionary organizing and fighting in China. From 1918-20, Chiang was based in Shanghai, where it was rumored that he worked for the notorious "Green Gang," a secret society that controlled the Shanghai underworld. From 1920-23 Chiang was in Shanghai and Canton, helping Sun Yat-sen in his abortive efforts to establish a revolutionary base in the latter city.

In October 1922 Sun named Chiang chief-of-staff of a Cantonese army then operating in neighboring Fujian Province. This army invaded Guangdong, seized Canton and established the last of Sun's south China governments. But years of earlier failure led Sun at this point to make a number of significant new decisions. First, he decided to ally his small government with the Soviet Union, and began to accept advisers, arms and money from the Communist International in Moscow. Second, Sun decided to allow members of the small but politically significant Chinese Communist Party to join the KMT, provided they obeyed the orders of the latter. Third, upon Russian insistence, Sun announced the formation of a military academy in Canton to train the officers who would become the basis for the establishment of a true revolutionary army.

According to Sun's own account, the KMT had suffered defeat after defeat because, although the Nationalists had built a revolutionary party, they had no revolutionary army. Thus, Sun's previous efforts to unify China had depended on an uneasy coalition of warlord armies over which the KMT had but little control. In 1924 Sun established the Whampoa Military Academy outside of Canton, and in April he named Chiang Kai-shek commandant of that academy. It was a fateful decision.

During the brief period of the last Canton government, 1923-27, the city saw a gathering of virtually every important Chinese revolutionary figure of the 20th century, whether Communist, Nationalist, or third-party, all united in an effort to free China from warlord rule and foreign occupation and bring it into the modern age. Most of these men focused their attention on the military academy, which was responsible for building the instrument by which the revolutionaries hoped to attain their goals.

But despite the facade of unity, the KMT-CCP alliance was deeply troubled. When Sun Yat-sen, the only focus of that unity, died in June 1925, a full-scale power struggle broke out. Despite his low status, it was Chiang Kai-shek who emerged as the successor to Sun when, in March 1926, following an alleged Communist plot to kidnap him, Chiang struck at the CCP and seriously undermined its position in the alliance. In June, Chiang was named commander-in-chief of the National Revolutionary Army and, with the launching of the Northern Expedition in July, tried to use this position to consolidate his hold over the movement.

At the same time, however, the Communists had allied with the left wing of the KMT, and this group had come to dominate the party itself. The crisis finally came to a head in early 1927 when this latter group established a Nationalist government in Wuhan. Chiang, who had set up his army headquarters in Nanchang, challenged the legitimacy of this regime and refused to obey its orders. Wuhan promptly stripped Chiang of all his commands, but lacking sufficient force of its own was unable to enforce the firing. After a purge of Communists and leftists from his army and the region it controlled in April, Chiang mobilized his forces for an attack on Wuhan. On Aug. 1 the Communists retaliated by organizing an uprising at Chiang's old headquarters in Nanchang. Later in the month, as the two sides neared a negotiated settlement, Chiang was prevailed upon to retire and sailed for Japan in September.

In early 1928, with the Communists purged from both governments and driven underground, Chiang returned to China to pick up the remnants of his command. By the end of the year he had captured Peking, established a new Nationalist government at Nanjing, and nominally unified China. But without any party organization by which to control the KMT's disparate armies, civil war soon broke out, 1929-30. By the end of the war, Chiang found himself in actual command of only two of China's provinces, and in partial control of about four more. Using his new army, now being trained by German advisers, Chiang renewed his efforts to convert his nominal power to actual control. By 1937, on the eve of the war with Japan, Nanjing controlled virtually all of China proper. The warlord armies, except for those in the most remote parts of China, had been defeated or disbanded, or had sworn allegiance to the KMT. Chiang's modern new army had grown, and numbered about 70-80 divisions in all. In fact, many analysts have argued that it was the Nationalist success in unifying China that prompted Japan to move up its timetable of conquest, afraid that if it waited too much longer, control of China would no longer be possible.

On July 7, a minor skirmish with the Japanese at the Marco Polo Bridge (Lukouqiao) outside Peking — the latest in a series of such incidents dating back to 1928 — marked the start of the war. After a series of conferences with his senior commanders, Chiang decided that this latest indignity from Japan would be the last, and China prepared to fight.

The Japanese armies cut swiftly through the only recently centralized warlord units in north China but, when faced with Chiang's new army, the advance slowed. At Shanghai, the economic center of his regime, Chiang placed the best of his units and ordered them to "stand or die." The Japanese attacked in August and for two and a half months the Chinese armies, for the first time in history, held their ground against a modern military organization, but at a frightful cost. With no air force, navy, armor or heavy artillery, the Chinese could rely only on their numbers and their desire to defend their homeland. Finally, in late November, with all the front-line units destroyed and his reserves exhausted, Chiang ordered a retreat. It proved to be too late, and the planned withdrawal turned into a rout as warlord units that were supposed to cover the retreat fled at the sound of the first shots. This one battle saw the destruction of virtually the entire modern sector of the Chinese army, as China suffered half as many infantry casualties as the United States did during all of World War II. More importantly, perhaps, it left the future defense of China in the hands of the very warlord armies Chiang had been trying to eliminate. But Chiang had no choice; the only alternative was to surrender. Faced with almost certain defeat, the Chinese government withdrew from Nanjing to the remote and inaccessible southwestern city of

Chongqing, cut off from its armies and the great mass of the Chinese people.

At this point, Chiang Kai-shek, devastated by the enormity of the defeat, seemed to draw inward, became remote from his subordinates, and began to reign rather than rule. Power devolved to these subordinates, many of whom quickly revealed themselves as incompetent, venal and corrupt. Competent generals were pushed aside in favor of relatives and cronies, private fortunes were made and stashed in foreign banks, and the KMT's military position continued to crumble. There were even some reports that Chiang was considering surrender.

The Japanese attack on Pearl Harbor served to draw Chiang out of his lassitude. The United States, ready to use any tool available to it to defeat Japan, officially ignored the real situation in China, and declared Chiang not merely an ally but one of the Big Four Powers.

Beginning in 1942, with U.S. money and advisers, Chiang began to rebuild his army, not to fight the Japanese but the Communists. Chiang had decided that the United States would be his salvation. Not only would America oust the Japanese for him, they would also help him defeat the Communists, who were expanding rapidly behind the Japanese lines. Unfortunately for Chiang, a corrupt and inefficient government which he no longer controlled could not rebuild his old army, even with U.S. money. Although some of the worst generals were fired after U.S. pressure, real problems remained. Chiang, unable to recoup his old power, remained afloat in a vicious whirlpool of cliques and pressure groups that resembled nothing so much as the Chinese imperial courts of another era.

Finally, in August 1945, the eight years of war with Japan suddenly came to an end. But the end of hostilities found Chiang's new army only partially rebuilt and of only marginal influence. The situation resembled that of 1930, when Chiang, controlling only a small part of China, had launched a slow but steady campaign to capture the rest. This time, he could not. Possibly stirred by the heady wine of summit conferences and great power status, Chiang acted as if he did control the KMT and China, when in fact he controlled neither. In what many rank as one of the most egregious blunders in military history, Chiang tried to occupy all of China with his small force and, worse, sent the best of his units to occupy the northeastern provinces of Manchuria. Although these troops enjoyed early success against the Communist units of his old student Lin Piao, it soon turned out that other Communist guerrilla forces were able to interdict the KMT's slender line of supply almost at will. Finally, in 1948, lacking food and ammunition, these forces surrendered to the Communists. In China proper, the thinly dispersed Nationalist armies that were trying both to rule China and restore order were picked off by the Communists one by one. Finally, in early 1949, confronted by the futility of further struggle, Chiang resigned the presidency and returned to his native district. His subordinates oversaw the transfer of the government to Taiwan, and in March 1950 Chiang resumed the presidency there, a post he held until his death.

Analysis

During his early career, Chiang, although aloof and cold, was able, like Mao, to command the respect and allegiance of a remarkable group of talented and innovative subordinates. Later, he was surrounded by incompetent and corrupt sycophants who misruled China under his blind eye. Chiang, sometimes touted as one of the great men of the century, probably does not deserve the title, despite frequent appearances on the covers of American news magazines. Never enough of a statesman to succeed as the leader of a unified China, Chiang was too much of a traditionalist to really cut the ties to the past and propose the radical solutions which literate and concerned Chinese were demanding. At the same time, and despite his lifelong tenure as commander-in-chief of the KMT armies, Chiang was not a particularly remarkable tactician or strategist. In fact, his effort to serve as both chief of state and commander-in-chief probably led to the disastrous decisions of 1937 and 1945.

What Chiang offered China was a vision and — for part of his tenure — a solution. Chiang saw a strong and militant China throwing off the imperialist shackles, and he was successful in creating an army to accomplish this task. But despite his use of Western advisers, and his Christianity, Chiang remained a native traditionalist. The fundamental basis of his thought was always Confucianism, and Chiang never relinquished his commitment to the Confucian principle of "immanence," whereby a moral leader will, by example, induce his subordinates to be moral. For Chiang, China would be restored by the force of high moral standards set by himself and his hand-picked subordinates. This system worked only as long as the army was able to move against those who resisted the strength of this collective moral force. After 1938, with his army destroyed, Chiang maintained a high moral posture but his subordinates did not, and Chiang was virtually powerless to do anything about it. By comparison, Mao used the Communist Party to enforce decisions and oversee the military and government. Chiang had never placed much emphasis on the KMT, which all but withered away during his tenure. That neglect eventually led to his defeat.

Chou En-lai
(1898-1976)

(Zhou Enlai)

Personal Background

Chou was born in Shaoxing County, Zhejiang Province, in 1898. His father had passed the imperial civil service examinations but was never named to an official post. Despite this, he belonged to the local gentry and owned a small business. In addition, other of Chou's relatives were also quite prosperous, and his mother, unlike most of her contemporaries, was well-educated.

Chou married Deng Yingchao in 1925. They had no children.

Chou received his early education in the Chinese classics and in 1912, having completed primary school, went to Tianjin, where he studied at the Nankai middle school and later at Nankai University. During this period, Chou, like many contemporaries, became an ardent nationalist, and began to seek the reasons for China's fall from

greatness. He went to Japan for a brief period of study and became involved in Chinese politics, particularly the anti-traditional, anti-foreign May 4th Movement. Chou also began to write, under a pseudonym, for the numerous publications that were springing up in China. He was arrested and jailed for his efforts in 1919.

After his release from prison in 1920, Chou joined a group of students who went to France in a work-study program that also included Li Fuchun and Nie Rongzhen. While in France, Chou enrolled in no schools and did very little work. Rather, he became involved in politics, and moved steadily to the left. He first became a Marxist and then a member of the new Chinese Communist Party in 1922. For the next two years, Chou traveled through France and Germany recruiting new members for the party among Chinese students in Europe.

Public Career

Chou returned to China in 1924 and went to Canton, where the Kuomintang and the CCP had allied to accomplish the defeat of the warlords and unify China. Chou was named deputy director of the political department of the Whampoa Military Academy under Chiang Kai-shek. Because the director, Tai Chi-t'ao, was usually absent, Chou became the effective head of the department, an extremely influential position which gave him extensive contacts with the students, many of whom he recruited for CCP membership. When the much vaunted 1st Division of the Nationalist Army was organized in 1925, with Ho Ying-ch'in commanding, Chou was named political commissar.

In 1926 Chou went to Shanghai, where he worked at organizing the trade unions and other organizations to launch uprisings, two of which were crushed by the local authorities. During this period, the Nationalists were also trying to organize the city, and the infighting between the two groups was often vicious. Finally, in March 1927, with the Nationalist army at the gates of the city, the Communists launched a successful takeover, but were then crushed by the KMT troops. Chou's role in the rebellion was fictionally portrayed in André Malraux's *Man's Fate*, a highly romanticized account of the period.

In 1928 Chou went to Moscow to attend the 6th Congress of the CCP as a member of the ruling Polituro. He stayed in Moscow and studied for a brief period at Sun Yat-sen University, where he received his first formal education in Marxist-Leninism. Chou returned to China in 1929 as an important member of the central party apparatus in Shanghai, where he continued his underground and organizational work. After a major purge of the central party in 1930, Chou, one of the few prominent figures to survive, went to Mao's Jiangxi soviet.

While in Jiangxi, Chou played an integral role in the power struggle which eventually saw the ouster of Mao from real power. In fact, it was Chou who succeeded to Mao's political positions in the army. When Mao returned to power in January 1935, Chou again switched to Mao's side — where he would stay from this point forward — and accompanied Mao on the Long March, 1934-35.

Once the CCP was established in the northwest, Chou became prominent as the CCP's chief negotiator. First, Chou convinced Chang Hsueh-liang (Zhang Xueliang), then commanding the troops responsible for exterminating the Communists, to stop his attacks. Then, in December 1936, when Chang kidnapped Chiang Kai-shek, it was Chou who interceded, possibly on orders from Moscow, to save Chiang's life. Then, as negotiations between the CCP and the KMT to achieve a united front against Japan proceeded, it was Chou who traveled back and forth for discussions between the Communist and Nationalist capitals.

After the war with Japan began in July 1937, Chou remained at the Nationalist capital until 1938, acting as the chief liaison officer for the CCP. In 1940 he went to Chongqing, the new Nationalist capital, to resume his duties. While there, he also supervised CCP propaganda activities, especially those directed at Chinese intellectuals and neutralist groups. In addition, he cultivated various Western correspondents and diplomats with a view to ensuring that the Communist view was known. In this task he and his staff were so successful that the Communists were often compared favorably with the better-known ruling Nationalists. In April 1945, as the war drew to a close, Chou was elected to the ruling Secretariat of the CCP and thus became one of the six top men in the Communist hierarchy.

Later in 1945, as the U.S. tried to mediate an end to the CCP-KMT hostility, Chou was the chief Communist delegate to the talks. Later, during the George Marshall mission, 1946-47, Chou was again chief representative for the CCP.

With the Communist victory in 1949, Chou was named premier, a post he would hold until his death in 1976. In this capacity Chou became the principal administrator of Communist China's huge bureaucracy. In addition, Chou was also top CCP liaison to the numerous non-communist groups still in existence in China, whose support, or at least neutrality, was crucial to the continuation of Communist rule. Finally, he was also named foreign minister, in which post he was China's chief spokesman in the world forum.

In this latter capacity, it was Chou who tried and failed to achieve Peking's admission to the United Nations in early 1950. Later that year, he was also the chief contact by which China warned the United States — again unsuccessfully — not to escalate the war in Korea lest China be forced to enter that conflict. In 1954 he headed the Chinese delegation to the Geneva talks on Indochina which produced partial agreement on the future of that explosive area.

Beginning with the Geneva talks and the Bandung Conference the following year, it was Chou who was credited with engineering China's opening to other third-world nations, especially those of Asia and Africa, launching Chinese aid missions to these countries and settling many of China's border disputes with its neighbors.

In 1958, with the beginning of the Sino-Soviet split, Peking apparently decided to pursue a more militant foreign policy. To underline the shift, Chou was replaced as foreign minister by Chen Yi. Despite this, Chou remained in charge of Chinese foreign policy then and afterward, still the chief intermediary between Peking and foreign countries.

In 1966, with the onset of the Cultural Revolution, Chou's position at the top became very tenuous. Previously, he had ranked third in the Chinese hierarchy, behind Mao and Liu Shao-ch'i. When Lin Piao replaced Liu, and despite the fact that Chou was still the third man in the Chinese hierarchy, many analysts predicted that Chou would be swept aside by the radical excesses of the Red Guards. But Chou again shifted, and his pronouncements during the period were as radical as any emanating from the capital. At the same time, however, Chou worked to limit the impact of the movement, while never opposing it outright. In this way, he was able to protect China's weapons research, nuclear development and oil production programs, which went on as before. In addition, he was able to save

certain high-ranking economic planners, like Li Xiannian, from being ousted, and he tried hard to exempt the foreign ministry from Red Guard attacks.

This apparently earned him the enmity of the radicals, but their repeated efforts were never enough to force Chou, who still enjoyed a unique relationship with Mao, from power. After Lin Piao was killed in 1971, Chou was the man to whom Mao turned to restore China's economy, and most analysts referred to him as heir-apparent to Mao during this period. To combat the radicals, Chou had many of the moderates who had been purged "rehabilitated" — especially Deng Xiaoping, whom he appeared to be grooming as his successor.

The end of the Cultural Revolution also saw the reassertion of China's more moderate foreign policy. China again became active in international affairs and, under Chou, responded favorably to President Nixon's initiative that reopened talks with the West. During the visits of Henry Kissinger and Nixon to China, it was Chou who met them, escorted them, and negotiated with them.

In 1972 Chou learned he was terminally ill with cancer. He entered the hospital in 1973, emerging only rarely afterward. Nonetheless, he continued to receive visitors and direct affairs of state. Mao also fell ill at about the same time, so Chou and other Chinese leaders found themselves in a struggle to determine their own successors.

When Chou died in January 1976 it appeared that he had lost that effort. Deng not only did not succeed him but was actually purged, and an unknown, Hua Guofeng, was named premier. Later in the year, however, following the death of Mao, Hua moved against the radicals, arrested the leaders, and began to reinstate the moderates. Deng re-emerged as Chou's successor, and many of Chou's former protégés — including Chen Muhua, Fang Yi, Li Xiannian, Geng Biao — were named to key positions.

Analysis

The Chinese often refer to Chou as a *budaoweng*, a weighted doll that always bounces back when knocked down. On at least three occasions, Chou found himself on the "wrong" — i.e., losing — side of a major power struggle, but was always able to change sides. His success was not only a tribute to his skills as a political infighter, but to his unique and possibly unsurpassed administrative abilities, which the CCP never felt it could do without. Indeed, Chou was the only man elected to the 1927 Politburo who was still a member in 1945.

Never offered as a candidate for the top leadership position, it does not appear that Chou ever sought it. Unlike the other major political figures of Communist China, Chou seemed content to serve rather than rule, and herein lay his greatest asset to the regime, as Chou followed a long tradition of loyal Chinese ministers who faithfully served their emperors. In the West, the comparison is frequently made between Chou and Talleyrand, who successively served France under a king, a revolutionary council, and an emperor.

Chou was a foreign minister *par excellence*. Never an original thinker or natural leader, his charm and poise, combined with his ability to follow orders, made him the ideal person to represent China to the world.

During his life, Chou met more foreigners and traveled more widely than any other major Chinese leader. In the process, he made favorable and often lasting impressions on correspondents, diplomats, statesmen, and military leaders with his wit, his urbanity, and his unflappable charm.

During World War II, when the Communists were cut off behind the Japanese lines, it was Chou who presented their case to the world press. In the 1950s, when the United States was trying to isolate China and portray its leaders as bloodthirsty martinets, it was Chou who gave the lie to the American claims. Probably more than any other single individual, Chou En-lai was responsible for the world's perception of Peking.

Within China, however, Chou performed quite a different role. As China's only premier during its first 27 years, he was the number one administrator of state policy, another task that called for tact, patience and perserverence. Although a great deal is known about Chou's role in foreign policy, very little is known about this latter responsibility, which was actually more important. As the struggles of the 1960s threatened to tear China apart, Chou emerged as the indispensable man who tried to hold the tattered remnants of the government together. This all but impossible task was performed with remarkable success, and China's recent drive to modernize is a vivid testimonial to that success.

It is not uncommon for some analysts today to maintain that with the accession of the moderates, Chou's legacy was likely to be more lasting than Mao's. But such statements do a disservice to both men. They did not compete, either about policy or for power. Mao was the formulator, the thinker, while Chou was the implementor. If Chou appears to some as a moderate, it is only because, in his natural role as negotiator, he tried to ameliorate the clash between Mao, on the one side, and Deng and Liu on the other.

Deng Xiaoping
(1904-   )

(Teng Hsiao-p'ing)

Personal Background

Deng was born to a prosperous landlord family in a small village in Guangan County, Sichuan Province, on Aug. 22, 1904. After graduating from one of the modern new middle schools, Deng joined a work-study program in France in 1920. Other participants in the program included Chou En-lai and Chen Yi. It is not known where Deng studied, but he worked in a factory in Lyons. He joined the Socialist (later Communist) Youth League in 1922 and the CCP in 1924. Little is known of his political work while in Europe, but he was certainly involved in propaganda activities, and earned himself a nickname as "Ph.D. in mimeographing."

Deng left France in 1925 and went to Moscow, where he studied for several months, probably at Sun Yat-sen University. In August 1926 he returned to China with Feng Yü-hsiang (Feng Yuxiang), a deposed warlord who was trying to make a comeback supported by Soviet arms and money. Deng worked as a political instructor under Feng until mid-1927 when Feng, like Chiang Kai-shek, purged the Communists from his army.

Public Career

Deng made his way to Shanghai, where he worked in the underground for two years. In 1929 he was sent to the southwestern province of Guangxi to act as political commissar to two small soviets there. As these guerrilla bands grew in size, the local government mobilized the army and crushed them in 1930. Deng fled north to Mao's Jiangxi soviet, where he edited the army newspaper, taught in the Red Army Academy, and held various administrative posts in the local party organization. During this period Deng aligned himself with Mao in the power struggle then taking place in the base area. When Mao was pushed aside in 1933, so was Deng. When Mao won control of the party in January 1935, Deng returned to power with him, and would remain a member of Mao's group for the next three decades. After the Kuomintang succeeded in dislodging the Communists from their base area in 1934, Deng made the Long March, 1934-35, with Mao. After their arrival in the northwest, Deng was named political commissar of Peng Dehuai's 1st Corps.

With the outbreak of war with Japan in 1937, Deng was named political commissar to the 129th Division, commanded by Liu Bocheng. Both men were natives of Sichuan, and their relationship reportedly became very close. The division controlled its own base area behind the Japanese lines, and Liu's military abilities and Deng's administrative skills allowed it to expand rapidly.

During the civil war, 1946-49, the Liu-Deng units were renamed the 2nd Front Army and won several crucial battles with the KMT, including the Huai-hai battle.

After the Communist victory, the force was transferred to southwest China to establish Communist control in the area. As rapid progress was made in this remote and backward region, Deng was called to Peking and named a vice premier, 1952-66. In this post he often served as government spokesman for Premier Chou En-lai, who was frequently out of the country. Deng also served briefly (1953-54) as finance minister.

In 1954 Deng was taken out of the realm of economics and entered party politics with his appointment, in May, as secretary general of the CCP, an important post that marked Deng's arrival at the pinnacle of power. In 1955 Deng was added to the Politburo and in 1956 was elected to the all-powerful Politburo standing committee. At the same time, he was also named to the new and very powerful position of CCP general secretary, in charge of the day-to-day administration of the party.

Thus Deng, at 52, had emerged as one of the four or five most powerful men in China and the youngest member of the ruling elite.

In the late 1950s, however, the first serious rifts began to appear in what had been a remarkably cohesive leadership group. After the failure of the Great Leap Forward in 1958 and the severe economic dislocations that followed, many state and party leaders like Deng and Liu Shao-ch'i concluded that rational and systematic economic planning was more effective than spasmodic "leaps." Liu succeeded Mao as chief of state, and he and Deng set about undoing the damage and returning China to the path of steady growth it had enjoyed prior to 1958. In the process the two leaders instituted material incentives such as wage increases and private land plots to spur production, and also worked to emphasize ability, sometimes at the expense of ideology, as a criterion for advancement.

When challenged about his use of such pragmatic techniques in a Marxist state, Deng is reported to have replied that "It does not matter if a cat is black or white, only if it catches mice."

Although the situation during the early 1960s remained murky, it appears that Mao — all but excluded from policy implementation and alarmed at what he saw as an ossification of the party — struck back. In 1966 he called on China's youth, known as Red Guards, to organize a mass movement called the Cultural Revolution, 1966-69. During the period, the party and state organizations built by Liu and Deng were smashed, the cadres dispersed and Liu and Deng labeled as "capitalist roaders."

Deng and Liu, as well as their most prominent supporters, were purged of all their posts. Late in 1966, Deng was driven through the streets of Peking wearing a dunce cap. He was attacked not only for his political errors but also for his arrogance, his love of bridge, and his interest in gourmet food. Deng was reportedly assigned to do manual labor in a camp outside Peking.

The final outcome of the Cultural Revolution had been an effective military takeover of China. Although all of China's senior leaders were committed to civilian control of the army, the newly risen Red Guard leaders were simply not experienced enough to do the job, and the way was paved for Deng's return. After Lin Piao's abortive military coup in 1971, Deng was renamed vice premier in 1973 and returned to the Politburo later in the year. Working with provincial party chiefs like Wei Guoqing and Hua Guofeng, Deng was soon able to break the hold of local military commanders on their regions, and a major government reform was accomplished.

But Deng found himself in a race against time. Premier Chou was already dying of cancer, and the only question had become whether Deng could succeed in reconsolidating his power enough to succeed Chou after the latter's impending death. The radicals who had come to power during the Cultural Revolution were numerous, while most of Deng's subordinates were still out of power. In May 1974 Chou entered the hospital.

In January 1975, at the 4th National People's Congress, the moderates appeared to win. The congress ratified Chou's proposed "four modernizations," and Deng was named first vice premier, a vice chairman of the party, and chief of staff of the PLA. But Deng's immediate subordinate in all three position was his rival, the radical Zhang Chunqiao.

When Chou died in January 1976, Deng found himself locked in a desperate struggle with Zhang for the premiership, but the post went instead to the relatively unknown Hua Guofeng, a man with whom Deng had worked during 1973-75 but who was usually linked with the radicals. In early April, Deng was again purged from all his posts and fled to the southern province of Guangdong.

Little is known about Deng's activities at this point, but it has been suggested that he contacted some major military figures, including Defense Minister Ye Jianying, about the possibility of organizing a coup against the radicals. Whatever the accuracy of such speculation, Ye did join Hua and Wang Dongxing to launch a successful coup against the radical leaders after Mao's death in October 1976. Although the stage was now set for Deng's second rehabilitation, it was delayed by the negotiations over Deng's position in the government and party. Purportedly, Deng agreed never to seek the chairmanship of the CCP. In July 1977, Deng was restored to all the posts he had held in 1973.

After his political resuscitation, Deng moved rapidly to "rehabilitate" and reappoint all the members of the state bureaucracy he and Liu had built up during the 1960s who had been purged during the Cultural Revolution. With these men back in power, Deng sought to re-establish the policies of systematic modernization abandoned by the radicals. Although in 1980 Hua was still premier, chairman of the party and chairman of the military council, most analysts saw Deng as the most powerful man in China. He was effectively the premier, and his longtime subordinate, Hu Yaobang, held Deng's old post as secretary general of the party.

Deng's return saw major domestic policy changes. Material incentives were restored, central planning reinstated, and Chou's opening to the West widened. Deng worked to "de-Maoize" China: Mao's Thought was no longer treated as gospel, nor Mao as a god. At the same time, Deng was careful to cloak his policy formulations in Maoist logic and sprinkle his speeches with quotations from the late chairman.

Analysis

The secrecy and opaqueness of Chinese politics make its future unpredictable. Nonetheless, certain facts stand out that invite speculation about the future of its political configuration.

Deng was born in 1904, and most of his recently restored subordinates were even older, thus their continuing political influence was necessarily limited. One of the most important questions for the future of China was the extent to which Deng could institutionalize his policies by creating lower levels of state and party bureaucrats who would support his policies after his death.

It appeared unlikely that Deng would move to replace Hua at the top. Deng had long been known for his over-confidence and arrogance, but his two removals from power may have convinced him of the dangers of seeking nominal authority in China. Hua, with ties to both the radicals and the moderates, seemed an excellent choice as nominal leader, with Deng exercising the real power.

In the West, Deng usually has been portrayed as a moderate pragmatist with an international outlook, a suitable successor to Chou En-lai. But that somewhat misstates Deng's thinking, the two most important aspects of which have been his militant Chinese nationalism and his Marxism. Deng grew up in a China that was easy prey for exploitation by the industrialized powers. Beginning in the 19th century, literate Chinese had begun to argue that to salvage what was uniquely Chinese, some of the devices of the West would have to be adopted.

Deng, like those early modernizers, has not pursued modernization, foreign trade or foreign student exchanges for their own sake, but as means to an end — a strong and powerful China. For Chinese like Deng who lived through the Japanese invasion and occupation of China, that could not be allowed to happen again, and even imagined slights on Chinese sovereignty are sure to be met with strong words, force, and sometimes military retaliation, as in Vietnam in 1979.

At the same time, Deng has been an ardent Marxist and to some extent a Maoist. Like other latter-day Chinese leaders, he was attracted to Marxism because it seemed to offer a way out of China's dilemmas and because it offered a blueprint for the future. That perception did not change. Although he might use material incentives to spur production, Deng would hardly allow the re-creation of capitalism in China or encourage liberal democracy in the Western sense.

Hua Guofeng
(1920-   )

(Hua Kuo-feng)

Personal Background

Hua was born in Jiaocheng County, Shanxi Province. Little is known about his family or early life, although he seems to have come from a moderately prosperous peasant family.

Hua's name is said to have been taken from three of the nine characters which made up the Anti-Japanese National Salvation Vanguard unit which Hua headed during the early 1940s. His actual surname is believed to be Su.

With the beginning of the war with Japan in 1937, Hua left middle school to join a guerrilla unit in his native county, and probably joined the Communist Youth League at about this time. Not long afterward, he headed the local branch of the Anti-Japanese National Salvation Association, a group jointly sponsored by the Communists and the Nationalists. Hua joined the CCP in 1940, and rose within the local party organization.

Hua married Han Zhizun, also a native of Shanxi and chief of the political department of the National Light Industrial Products Import-Export Corporation. They had four children, surnamed Su.

Public Career

In 1945, with the end of the war, Hua was named to head his county's party committee and was also appointed political commissar to the local guerrilla unit there. He held this post until 1947, when he was transferred to Yangqu County, also in Shanxi, where he was again named local party head and political commissar, posts he held until the Communist victory in 1949.

Hua was then transferred to south China and named head of the party committee in Xiangyin County, Hunan Province, which the Communists had just captured. Because of its high concentration of large landowners, this county was picked as the "experimental point" for the local land reform, which Hua performed with speed and efficiency, if somewhat ruthlessly.

In 1951 Hua was transferred to be party chief in the larger and more complex Xiangtan County, which was also the birthplace of Mao Tse-tung. Then, in either late 1952 or early 1953, Hua received his first big promotion, as party chief of the Xiangtan Special District, which included not only Xiangtan but eight other counties. In this position Hua was responsible for a number of programs, including the establishment of rural cooperatives, ordered by Peking at that time.

There was a great deal of resistance to the program throughout China. Hunan, which still contained many former warlords and KMT officials within its government, moved slowly against significant resistance. In the Xiangtan Special District, however, Hua pushed the program forward with speed and dispatch. Hua's success, re-markable as it may have been when compared with the rest of the province, stood out all the more because his district included Mao's native home, which Mao and other officials continued to visit. In this way, Hua, unlike other middle level party leaders, came to have frequent exposure to China's highest leaders.

In 1956 Hua was again promoted, to head the province's Culture and Education Office in the provincial capital of Changsha. Although the switch involved no increase in rank, the change from the rural area to the city and, more importantly, from party to government, marked an increase in Hua's responsibilities. During 1956 he was heavily involved in the campaign, only recently launched, to eliminate illiteracy and to establish Mandarin as the national language. In late 1957 Hua was transferred to head the CCP United Front Department in Hunan, a major promotion. In this capacity he was responsible for the "Anti-rightist Campaign" in Hunan, a crucial task in a province with such a high proportion of non-CCP officials, most of whom Hua was able to purge successfully.

In 1958, with the inauguration of the Great Leap Forward, Hua assumed even more important responsibilities. He was relieved of his United Front work and elected to the Provincial Party Committee. In addition, he was named vice chairman of the Committee for the Support of the Construction of Keypoint Projects, a member of the Agricultural Tool Improvement Committee, and chairman of the Preparatory Committee for the Hunan Economic Construction Exhibition Hall. These three posts were all integrally involved with the implementation of the Great Leap Forward in Hunan and marked Hua's first extensive experience with economic affairs. In July 1958 Hua was named a vice governor of the province.

Like the cooperatives, the Great Leap Forward generated much opposition, and officials in many areas were content to ignore government directives. Hua, whose speeches during this period convey none of the rabid and frenzied support for the movement found elsewhere, did support the plan and earnestly tried to make it work. Acting as a problem-solver and troubleshooter, Hua emerged as the man who tried to break the bottlenecks of rural supply, especially with regard to coal and sweet potatoes.

During the next two years, as many of China's regional leaders expressed their scorn for the Great Leap Forward, which had failed disastrously, Hua continued publicly to support the program. In Peking, the criticism came to a head when Peng Dehuai openly challenged Mao, who had him and his supporters purged. One of the latter was the ranking party leader in Hunan, and Hua's superior. Many accounts maintain that Mao was able to defeat this challenge, and win continued support for his position, because of data supplied by Hua proving that the plan could have worked if implemented properly. (Other local leaders, of course, were supplying Mao with similar information from their areas, but probably did not enjoy Hua's access).

In August 1959 Hua was promoted over several senior officials and appointed a party secretary following the ouster of his superior. Analysts attribute the major promotion to Hua's support of Mao and the Great Leap Forward.

By March 1960 Hua had emerged as a top leader in Hunan but found himself in a very difficult position. Officially, the Great Leap Forward was a success and was being accelerated. In fact, climatic disasters had brought drought and famine to Hunan, and food supplies were critically short, a situation which all of China's leaders officially denied but were moving to remedy. As Hunan's top trouble shooter, Hua was responsible for solving this "non-existent" problem, and he immersed himself in the problems of food transport and supply. He traveled extensively through the province in an effort to minimize the most serious effects of the drought with intra-provincial food shipments. In the process he also found himself responsible for water conservation and irrigation, which came to play a key role in easing the second year of the drought.

In 1961, while still holding his positions as vice governor and party secretary, Hua returned to Xiangtan Special District to reassume his position as party chief there. This was not a demotion — throughout China, provincial officials were being asked to take charge of local problems themselves. Hua held this position until 1966. During the period, he undertook the beautification of Mao's native Shaoshan. Apart from new factories, Hua also supervised the Shaoshan irrigation project, the first such effort in Hunan and a great success. At the same Hua also worked to build Maotian County, also within his jurisdiction, into a "model" county on the order of Dazhai. Mao was able to use the case of Maotian County to argue that his policies, when implemented effectively, were correct.

In 1964, despite his continued position as head of Xiangtan, Hua returned to the provincial capital, where he quickly emerged as the effective governor of Hunan because his two nominal superiors were non-CCP officials who had remained only as figureheads.

Hua's responsibilities were further increased in 1965 as the United States began its buildup in Vietnam. The American escalation prompted preparations for what many Chinese officials feared would eventually be an invasion of China itself. Thus all the southern provinces, including Hunan, began to prepare for war. For Hua, this meant the building and training of a large militia and, because Hunan would be a rear-area province, preparation for supplying food to the front. In addition, during 1965 and 1966 Hua also emerged as Hunan's chief spokesman on foreign affairs as he sought to explain the new situation to both cadres and officials alike. Hua offered no new policy formulations, but he did expand his contacts with defense and foreign policy officials in Peking.

By any standards, Hua's advancement had been incredibly rapid — from county party secretary to provincial governor in only 15 years — and could be matched by very few others in post-1949 China. But he was to rise even more rapidly during the next decade.

In 1966, when Mao launched the Cultural Revolution, designed to remake China and produce a suitable group of revolutionary successors, Hua, although wielding exceptional power within Hunan, was still only a little-known provincial leader.

But in August 1967, following the ouster of all of Hua's superiors in the Hunan party, he and the top army officer in the province were designated by Peking to prepare the establishment of a Hunan Revolutionary Committee to replace the CCP organs destroyed by the Red Guards. In April 1968 Hua emerged as vice chairman of the newly established committee and the second ranking official in Hunan.

In April 1969 Hua was elected to the Central Committee of the CCP and, after a series of arcane and complicated power struggles within the province, emerged as undisputed party chief of Hunan in August 1970. In December, Hunan became the first province to establish a new party committee, with Hua as first secretary.

Hua was summoned to Peking in November — immediately after the attempted coup by Lin Piao. (This sparked speculation that Hua was in some way responsible for the ouster of Lin, and may also have been involved in the purge of Lin's subordinates.)

While in Peking, Hua served directly under Premier Chou En-lai, possibly as chief of staff of the State Council. He apparently took on ever more important responsibilities during this tumultuous period. Publicly, Hua's work involved agriculture and forestry, his areas of particular expertise while in Hunan. But it is also likely that Hua's non-publicized duties involved trouble shooting for Chou, just as he had done for his provincial bosses in Hunan.

In August 1973, in recognition of his abilities, Hua was elected to the ruling Politburo. As a Politburo member, Hua continued to perform a variety of duties involving culture, education, public health, science, and technology. In January 1975 he was named the sixth-ranking vice premier and minister of public security.

Hua's appointment as vice premier coincided with Chou's announcement of the "four modernizations," which were then ratified by the 4th National People's Congress. It appears that Hua's special area of responsibility was the modernization of agriculture; in September and October 1975, when the CCP convened the "Conference on Learning from Dazhai in Agriculture," Hua gave the summing-up speech. On behalf of the State Council Hua announced a plan to mechanize China's agriculture within five years.

At this point, despite his rapid rise during the Cultural Revolution, Hua appeared to come under attack from Jiang Qing and the radicals. Probably due to radical opposition, the "four modernizations," including Hua's mechanization of agriculture, were shelved.

In January 1976, Chou En-lai, who had been ill for some time, died, and the moderates and radicals found themselves locked in a desperate struggle to determine Chou's successor as premier. Apparently, neither the moderate Deng Xiaoping nor the radical Zhang Chunqiao could generate enough support, and the post went instead to the still relatively unknown Hua, who was named acting premier in February. The move stunned Western observers, who decided that Hua was a compromise, interim appointee who would be replaced once Mao died.

But the situation in Peking grew no clearer when, in April, Deng was purged and forced to flee Peking altogether. Hua was then confirmed as premier and also named ranking vice chairman of the party, second only to Mao himself.

In July 1976 the largest earthquake in 400 years occurred at Tangshan, Hebei Province. As premier, Hua took charge of the enormous and vastly complicated relief effort. His success in this endeavor appears to have convinced skeptical leaders of his abilities and may have prompted the remark, attributed to Mao, "With you in charge, I am at ease."

Mao died in October, and a full-scale power struggle broke out as the radicals tried to have Jiang Qing named to succeed her husband as party chairman.

In a process that is still far from clear, Hua was able to build an alliance between himself, Minister of Defense Ye Jianying, and Mao's bodyguard Wang Dongxing. On the night of October 6 this group struck. Using Wang's elite security force as a vanguard, they arrested the 30-odd top radical leaders and put them in prison. Hua had himself declared not only premier but also chairman of the Central Committee of the CCP (succeeding Mao) and chairman of the Military Commission, the first man in history to fill all three positions. Hua was officially confirmed in the latter two positions in July 1977.

Analysis

The extent of Hua's power has been difficult to gauge accurately. Although he appeared to be the most powerful man in China, it seemed that the actual power was in the hands of Deng, Hu Yaobang and Li Xiannian, all of whom had more prestige in the party than Hua, the newcomer. In addition, Hua had no power base of his own, either in the party or state apparatus, and his ties to the army seemed to depend on the fragile health of the 82-year-old Ye Jianying. Unlike Mao, whom he succeeded, Hua was not a theorist or policy originator. His entire career involved policy implementation, a task now in the hands of his subordinates.

At the same time, Hua had a long history of success in management and problem-solving, skills that behooved Peking's image as it sought to modernize. Moreover, Hua had experience in a variety of areas, unlike most other top leaders who had only one area of expertise. Hua's long tenure in Hunan forced him to deal with a host of problems, providing him with a background that the top economic planners lacked. Finally, as a local official, Hua had long been on the implementation end of campaigns, plans and projects drawn up in Peking.

This experience was expected to be important as Peking began what may be its most ambitious campaign of all — the modernization of China by the year 2000.

Thus it appeared that China had chosen a party chairman who was clearly different from Mao and whose ideology would be subordinated to economic progress. Hua was a longtime supporter of Mao, and many analysts felt that he remained at least partially committed to a Maoist vision of China. If that is true, more tension could arise between Hua and Deng.

There was also some question about Hua's lack of experience at the center of government. Hua was still a local party figure at the time when the men who became his subordinates were already running China. China's future stability could depend on Hua's learning enough to smooth the transition after the deaths of China's elderly top leadership.

Although analysts first saw Hua as an interim or compromise candidate, his youth seemed to belie this assessment, and it is possible that his power could grow to match his prestige in the next decade.

Lin Piao
(1908-1971)

(Lin Biao)

Personal Background

Lin was born in Huangan County, Hubei Province, the son of the owner of a small handicraft factory. After attending a local primary school, Lin left home at the age of 10 to pursue his studies at Wuchang. He soon came into contact with the revolutionary ideas sweeping China and joined the Socialist (later Communist) Youth League in 1925. Later that year, Lin went south and enrolled in Chiang Kai-shek's Whampoa Military Academy at Canton. While there, he came to the attention of Chou En-lai, then a political instructor in the school. Lin graduated in the fourth class in 1926 and was assigned to a unit in the Kuomintang army as a cadet officer. He participated in the first phase of the Northern Expedition, rose to the rank of company commander, and joined the CCP in 1927.

Lin was married in 1937, and is reported to have had one son and one daughter. His wife, Ye Chun, remained an obscure figure until the Cultural Revolution when, like Mme. Mao, she emerged to hold powerful political positions. She was a member of "Mao's Proletarian Headquarters" and the PLA Cultural Revolution Group, and in 1969 was elected to the ruling Politburo. She was purged with the rest of Lin's supporters in 1971.

Public Career

On Aug. 1, 1927, Lin's unit joined the forces of He Long in the Nanchang Uprising, which the Communists hail as the birth of the Red Army. This insurrection was quickly quelled, however, and Lin fled south with the army remnants and linked up with the forces of Zhu De. Zhu quickly developed a high opinion of the young Lin, and thereafter took an active interest in his career. When Zhu was named commander of the 1st Army Group in 1930, he named Lin to succeed him as commander of the 4th Army. Lin continued to rise very quickly in Mao's Jiangxi soviet area, and also served as the commandant of the Red Army Academy until 1933. When Zhu was promoted to commander-in-chief of all the Chinese Communist armies, Lin succeeded him as commander of the 1st Army Group, at the age of 25.

Lin accompanied Mao and Zhu on the Long March, 1934-35, and was reappointed commandant of the Communists' military academy after their arrival in the northwest. With the outbreak of the war with Japan in 1937, Lin was named commander of the 115th Division of Zhu's 8th Route Army. In September, in one of the very few full-scale battles fought between the Communists and the Japanese, Lin won a decisive victory at Pingxing Pass. Seriously wounded in 1938, Lin traveled to the Soviet Union for medical treatment. He stayed there for three years, and some reports insist that he also received advanced military training at this time. Lin returned to China in 1942, and served as a Communist liaison to the Nationalists in Chongqing. He was recalled to Yanan in 1943 as deputy director of the party school there.

With the sudden end of the war in August 1945, Lin was given overall command of the 100,000-man force sent by the Communists to secure the vital northeastern region of Manchuria and link up with the Soviet Army occupying the area. Aided by the United States, the Nationalists also rushed most of their best units to the same area, and the Chinese civil war began there in late 1945. In the early stages of the war, the Kuomintang was successful, forcing Lin's troops to retreat steadily northward. Finally, in the summer of 1947, resupplied by captured Japanese war matériel turned over by the Russians and reinforced by troops from Korea, Lin succeeded in a forced crossing of the Sungari River and launched a brilliant campaign to drive the Nationalists out of the northeast altogether by November 1948. Perhaps more than any other, it was this campaign that sealed the Nationalists' fate.

Lin's forces were then reorganized as the 4th Front Army and transferred south of the Great Wall into China proper, where he seized the politically crucial Peking-Tianjin region in January 1949.

After the Communist victory later that year, Lin was named commander of the Central China military district and first secretary of the local party bureau. The next year, 1950, he became commander of the entire Central-South military region, including six major provinces. In the fall, units of his 4th Front Army formed the vanguard for the Chinese intervention in Korea, although Lin himself was not in command.

In September 1954, when the government was reorganized, Lin was named a vice premier. The next year he was added to the Politburo, and in May 1958 was elected a vice chairman of the CCP and a member of the all-powerful standing committee of the Politburo. At this point, Lin ranked sixth in the party hierarchy. In September 1959, following the ouster of Peng Dehuai, he was named minister of defense. As China's top military man, Lin began an intense campaign to indoctrinate China's armed forces in the "Thought of Chairman Mao."

With the onset of the Cultural Revolution, Lin rose very rapidly. The use of Mao's Thought and the "Little Red Book" — edited by Lin — to motivate the Red Guards were methods pioneered by Lin in the army. In the 1966 Politburo reshuffle, Lin was named the second-ranking member, replacing Liu Shao-ch'i as heir-apparent to Mao. He was also named to "Mao's Proletarian Headquarters," one of the two ad hoc groups directing the Cultural Revolution. Most important, however, was Lin's position as head of the Military Affairs Committee of the CCP, which — with the destruction of the regular party organs during the purges — came to replace the party in many areas. In August 1966 Lin was officially identified as Mao's "closest comrade-in-arms," replacing Liu Shao-ch'i as holder of that designation.

Lin's power increased still further in 1967 with the January order to the army to intervene in the internal fighting then dividing China. By the end of the year, China found itself under effective, if de facto, military control.

Lin's power was confirmed at the 9th Congress of the CCP in April 1969. He was formally named Mao's successor and confirmed in his position as number-two man in the party. More importantly, the new Politburo elected by the congress was stacked with his supporters and subordinate military commanders, giving him a clear majority. In an unprecedented move, China had seemingly rejected one of its most fundamental dicta: "The Party controls the gun."

Despite his new position, however, Lin's toehold on the top rung proved tenuous. Allied with the civilian radicals who had directed the Cultural Revolution, Lin appeared to be on the verge of launching a new wave of mass campaigns designed to lead China further toward his version of revolutionary utopia. But the opposition, although purged, was still active, and seemed to spring up everywhere, even within the top echelons of the army itself. At this point, in 1971, Lin reportedly allied with some of his loyal commanders to launch a coup, either against his enemies or, as is now claimed, against Mao himself. When this failed, Lin allegedly tried to flee to the Soviet Union, but his plane crashed in Mongolia and Lin was killed. With Lin's death, the remainder of his supporters were purged, and civilian control over the army had been restored by 1974.

Analysis

China's fabled government secrecy makes it difficult to arrive at definite conclusions about Lin, although some theories may be advanced. It would appear that China's participation in the Korean War had markedly different impacts on China's two most prominent military commanders. Peng Dehuai, who actually commanded the Chinese forces, came away convinced that the superiority of Chinese troop strength was no match for the superior firepower and advanced weaponry of the Americans. With the Sino-Soviet split and the termination of Soviet aid, however, there was no source of supply for such ordnance and technology, and Peng was purged in 1959.

When Lin succeeded Peng, he immediately set about restructuring the army into a force that fought with revolutionary spirit and élan, while downgrading weaponry and technical expertise. At the same time, he advocated the notion of "people's wars," which avoided direct confrontations between underarmed communist forces and well-armed Western armies. Thus, although he supported the North Vietnamese in their struggles with the United States, he resolutely opposed direct Chinese intervention in the conflict.

After Nixon's opening to China, however, as the acquisition of foreign technical expertise again appeared to be possible, Lin's emphasis on ideological purity over military sophistication became irrelevant. After his ouster, he was replaced by Ye Jianying who, like Peng Dehuai, felt that firepower was more important than polemics. A systematic program of military modernization, including efforts to build and acquire modern weaponry, was launched. During the period of China's most xenophobic bellicosity, 1959-1971, Lin was the logical choice for minister of defense. Before and after that time, however, China opted for more conventional military leaders.

Liu Shao-ch'i (1898-1969?)

(Liu Shaoqi)

Personal Background

Liu Shao-ch'i was born in the village of Yinshan, Ningxiang County, Hunan Province, in 1898, the youngest of nine children of a prosperous peasant. After receiving his early education in the Chinese classics, Liu went to the provincial capital of Changsha to pursue his studies at the same school attended by Mao Tse-tung and other early Communist leaders.

Liu was married five times. One marriage ended in the death of his spouse and three in divorce. He married his last wife, Wang Guangmei, in the 1940s. She was imprisoned during the Cultural Revolution, but freed in December 1978. In 1979 she was elected to the People's Political Consultative Conference. Liu had three sons and four daughters.

Public Career

In 1920 Liu joined the Socialist (later Communist) Youth League, and was one of the young Chinese selected for further study in Moscow, at the University for Toilers of the East (later Sun Yat-sen University). In 1921 Liu joined the CCP in Moscow, and returned to China in 1922, when he began his career as a labor organizer in Shanghai.

For the next several years Liu devoted himself almost exclusively to such work, and became one of the very few labor organizers who rose to power after the Communist shift to the countryside. Liu instituted a series of strikes in Shanghai, Hunan, Hubei and elsewhere, all of which were swiftly and brutally suppressed. Finally, in 1932, with the trade union movement all but completely destroyed, Liu made his way with the rest of the central party apparatus to Mao's Jiangxi soviet. While there, he organized rural workers and was named chairman of the All-China Federation of Labor the following year. He was elected to the ruling Politburo in 1934.

Liu began the Long March, 1934-35, with Mao, but soon went to north China, an area only nominally controlled by the Kuomintang, to organize students and intellectuals to oppose Chiang Kai-shek's policy of delaying war with Japan. With Peng Zhen, Liu was extremely successful in this effort, and in 1937, when the Japanese overran the area, Liu was able to funnel many of these people directly into the CCP. Liu remained behind the lines and continued to expand CCP power there, serving successively as head of the north China, central plains, and central China party bureaus.

In July 1939 Liu published his famous "How To Be a Good Communist," the first such political work published under his own name. Because he argued that it was the individual's social background, not his class background, that determined class outlook, it became an important part of the emerging doctrine of Maoism. In a country that was overwhelmingly rural, it was of little value to define the CCP's dictatorship of the proletariat in such a way as to limit it to workers only. Thus Liu's formulation, which allowed peasants to be called proletariat too, represented an important part of the Sinification of Marxism.

In January 1941, Liu was named political commissar of the New 4th Army, with Chen Yi taking over actual command. The success of these two men in expanding the base area controlled by the unit caused the party to recall Liu to the CCP headquarters at Yanan in 1942. In 1943 Liu was named head of the party Secretariat, putting him directly in charge of the day-to-day affairs of the party and marking his arrival at the top of the Communist hierarchy. Liu held this post until 1956, when he was succeeded by Deng Xiaoping. In 1945 he became the third-ranking member of the party after Mao and Zhu De and was also elected a vice chairman. By this time Liu had emerged as the ranking authority on party organization and structure. Following the Communist victory in 1949, Liu emerged as the third-ranking government official as well. In 1954 Liu became chairman of the standing committee of the National People's Congress, China's nominal parliament, and number-two man in the party hierarchy, second only to Mao.

After Mao announced in 1958 that he was stepping down as chief of state, Liu was named to succeed him in April 1959. At the same time, Liu was officially hailed as Mao's "closest comrade-in-arms," and had emerged as Mao's designated successor.

For the next several years, with Mao in partial retirement, Liu and his counterpart in the party, Deng Xiaoping, effectively ran China. After the disastrous Great Leap Forward in 1958, it devolved upon these two men to resurrect the Chinese economy and return it to its path of slow, steady growth, albeit without the Soviet aid program of the 1950s. In the process, the two leaders apparently downplayed emphasis on ideology and adopted a variety of more pragmatic methods to spur China's growth. Liu and Deng made promotions on the basis of ability and, more importantly, instituted material incentives such as wage increases to spur production. In the agricultural area, they allowed the peasants to set aside some land for their own use — called "private plots."

According to Mao's later account, Liu and Deng in this period treated him "like a dead relative at his own funeral," and never consulted him.

Whether angered at his lack of real power or, as seems more likely, upset over the direction in which Liu was leading China, Mao launched a mass campaign — the Great Proletarian Cultural Revolution — designed to purge Liu, Deng and their followers and restore revolutionary vigor to China's officials. In 1966 Liu was branded as the "supreme leader of the black gang," "China's Khrushchev," and "the Number 1 Party person in authority taking the capitalist road." (Deng was named Number 2). Liu was forced to make a series of confessions, as was his wife, who also came in for criticism. In October 1968 Liu was officially denounced as "a renegade, traitor and scab hiding in the Party, a lackey of imperialism, modern revisionism, and the KMT reactionary who has committed innumerable crimes." Liu was dismissed from all his posts and expelled from the CCP at the same time.

Liu's subsequent fate is unknown, although it was confirmed in early 1979 that he had died some time earlier. Many reports state that he died of pneumonia in 1969, while others insist that he was still alive in late 1978.

In the years after his purge, and despite the "rehabilitation" of most of his former subordinates, Liu remained a target for abuse and a model to be avoided. In the late 1970s, however, there were signs that Liu's status might change. 1979 saw a new series of posthumous "rehabilitations," and Deng Xiaoping, since returning to power, had moved to reinstitute most of Liu's old policies.

Analysis

The policies originally devised by Liu and Deng during the 1960s were resurrected under Deng's influence. Thus, to the extent that Mao and Liu fought over genuine policy differences, Mao's view seems to have lost. The modernizing China of 1979 seemed much closer to Liu's vision than to Mao's.

Mao Tse-tung
(1893-1976)

(Mao Zedong)

Personal Background

Mao was born in the village of Shaoshan, Xiangtan County, Hunan Province, on Dec. 26, 1893. His father was a prosperous peasant, his mother illiterate and superstitious.

Mao began to work in the fields at the age of six, and studied the Chinese classics in a local school.

Mao was one of four children — three sons and a daughter. All of the children became Communists, and all except Mao met violent deaths.

By the age of ten, Mao was also keeping the family accounts. By his own recollection, Mao's relationship with his father was often stormy. Once, when his father denounced the young Mao as lazy and useless before a group of guests, Mao ran to the edge of a pond and threatened to commit suicide. His father yielded, and Mao supposedly said that "I learned that when I defended my rights by open rebellion my father relented, but when I remained meek and submissive he only cursed and beat me the more."

Mao left home at the age of 16 to pursue his studies at a middle school about 20 miles away. It was at this time that Mao first discovered the revolutionary ideas which were sweeping imperial China at the time.

In 1911, when the revolution broke out, Mao rushed to Changsha, the provincial capital, to participate, and joined a student volunteer unit there. In 1912, the revolution over, he returned to his studies. He dropped out of school after only six months, however, convinced that he could learn more by studying on his own.

Mao began reading Western and Japanese authors in translations then beginning to appear throughout China. Like other ardent nationalists, Mao sought an explanation for China's weakness in comparison with Western nations. In 1917 he wrote his first article, arguing that the way to Chinese greatness lay in physical education and military heroism.

Mao was married three times — four if one counts an unconsummated childhood wedding arranged by Mao's family. His first wife, Yang Kaihui, was executed by the KMT in 1930. His second wife was He Zizhen, from whom he was divorced in 1937 to marry Jiang Qing. He Zizhen was a "non-person" until June 1979 when, as part of the drive to discredit Jiang Qing, she was elected to the People's Political Consultative Conference. This move followed recent moves stressing Yang's role as a martyr of the revolution. Mao had several children, including a son who died in the Korean War, another son who studied in the Soviet Union and became a translator, and at least one daughter. Some biographers say there was a third son, about whom nothing is known.

Public Career

In 1918, influenced by one of his teachers (Yang Chenchi, who would become his father-in-law), Mao moved to Peking to join what is now called the May Fourth Movement, a literary and cultural renaissance that sought to free China from its past and lead the way to glory. Mao managed to secure a post as a clerk in the library of Peking University, where he met many of the most outspoken critics of the time as well as the future founders of the Chinese Communist Party: Li Ta-chao (Li Dazhao) and Ch'en Tu-hsiu (Chen Duxiu). During his sojourn in Peking Mao continued to write on the themes of China's weakness and the evils of Western imperialism.

In 1921, now in Hunan, Mao established a branch of the Socialist Youth Corps in Changsha. In July he went to Shanghai, where he represented Hunan in the founding meeting of the CCP. Mao then returned to Changsha, where he began to organize a local chapter of the party. But local authorities moved quickly to suppress the movement, and Mao fled to Canton in 1923.

By 1926 Mao was director of the Peasant Movement Training Institute, established in 1924 to train students to work among the peasantry. In February 1927, after surveying conditions in his native Hunan, Mao wrote his "Report of an Investigation into the Peasant Movement in Hunan," in which he predicted that China's peasants "will rise like a tornado or tempest — a force so extraordinarily violent that no power, however great, will be able to suppress it." The report prefigured much of Mao's later emphasis on the Chinese peasant as a revolutionary force.

In 1927, after the campaign to unify China had begun, the KMT and CCP split, and Mao and other Communist leaders went underground, acccmpanied by whatever small armies were still intact. After a series of abortive uprisings, Mao's ragtag army linked up with an equally weak force led by Zhu De in the Jinggan mountains in southern China. The Zhu-Mao partnership, with Zhu as military commander and Mao as political commissar, was an important one, and the two men retained their partnership into the 1950s. Mao had recruited his first important subordinate.

At the same time, the KMT had completed its invasion of north China, displaced the warlords and established a new government at Nanjing in 1928. The CCP had established headquarters in Shanghai, with branches in other major Chinese cities. But as the KMT continued to consolidate its power, it was able to smash these urban organizations one after another so that by 1932 the remaining leaders of the central party, including Chou En-lai, were forced to flee Shanghai and retreat to the countryside. When they arrived in south Jiangxi, they encountered the forces of Zhu and Mao, no longer small guerrilla bands but a regular army, 100,000 men strong and ruling an area with a population of about 2 million.

This tenfold increase in size had allowed the Jiangxi soviet, as it was called, successfully to repulse several Nationalist attacks. Thus, although the newly arrived CCP leaders were nominally in charge, they soon found that Mao actually held all the power. From 1932 to 1933, the party's leaders, assisted by a small group of handpicked cadres educated in Moscow, succeeded in forcing Mao from power within the soviet.

But in October 1934 Chiang Kai-shek smashed the Jiangxi soviet. Mao and other leaders gathered their remaining forces and fled westward. During the next year, the Communists traveled 6,000 miles and lost more than two-thirds of their strength. The Long March, as it is known, ended in October 1935 when the remaining units staggered into Shaanxi, in remote northwestern China.

During the march, however, Mao succeeded in wresting control of the CCP from the central party leadership, the first communist anywhere to do so without the direct support of Moscow, and began his reign as the leader of the Chinese Communists until his death in 1976.

Mao's career between 1935 and 1949 is also the history of the CCP. Relying on the small nucleus that survived the Long March, Mao began to rebuild the party in his own image in the remote and inhospitable areas of northwest China. Far removed from both the KMT and the Japanese, the CCP enjoyed an important respite during which they could regroup and build.

During this period, as Japanese aggression against China began to provoke more and more criticism of Chiang Kai-shek, the Communists found the issue for which they had been looking. Chiang had decided earlier that the young Chinese armies he was building were simply no match for those of an industrialized Japan. Thus he had concluded that war must be delayed and that Japanese insults must be swallowed in order to buy time. But the Japanese activities had further galvanized an already highly nationalistic and aroused populace, and 1935-1937 saw the formation of numerous groups demanding that Chiang lead his armies against the Japanese and defend China's honor. Secure in the northwest, the Communists vigorously seized on this issue. They sent cadres throughout China to organize and protest, and were quickly successful in promoting themselves as the only force in China that was not "appeasing" Japan. Faced with this rising clamor, Chiang's resolve stiffened, and war with Japan broke out in 1937.

During the first year of the war, the Japanese almost completely destroyed Chiang's young armies, sank his navy, annihilated his air force, and seized most of China proper. The Nationalists retreated to the remote southwestern city of Chongqing, where they were cut off from both China and the outside world.

Under Mao, the Communists refused to contest the Japanese advance and were content to fill the power vacuum left behind the Japanese lines by the Nationalist retreat. In these "base areas," the Communists took over the local governments one by one until they had created a political entity that covered almost all of north China.

During this critical period, it was Mao who held the disparate areas together, who formulated policy and laid down administration guidelines. Leaving the actual administration in the hands of subordinates, Mao made the fundamental decisions guiding the rapidly burgeoning bases. In this effort, Mao produced some of his most famous and significant writings. In 1938 he wrote "On Protracted War," which predicted that the war with Japan would be long and that the Communist goal should not be victory, but stalemate; that Japan would never be able actually to conquer China; and that the CCP should outwait them. Thus, unlike the Nationalists, who had tried to meet the Japanese head-on, the Communists would bide their time and husband their strength. In 1940 Mao wrote "On the New Democracy," which explained to the Communist cadres that, for the time being, the dream of a socialist China would have to be postponed. The war against Japan (and the KMT) required that the CCP take allies where it could find them, without undue emphasis on their class background. This "national-democratic" stage of the revolution would later be followed by the "socialist" stage. In these and other writings, Mao performed an essential function. He explained to the average party member his role in the revolution, and shared with him the major policy decisions that were being made at the center. As a result, morale in the CCP was high from top to bottom.

When the war ended in 1945, these efforts bore fruit. The Nationalists, discredited and demoralized by their inability to defeat the Japanese, fought poorly against the Communists. Although the Communist armies still were not especially well-equipped or trained, they were able to hold together while the Nationalists disintegrated. Shattered by the Japanese military the Nationalists proved no match for the Communists, who had husbanded their strength in anticipation of the ultimate goal — control of China. On October 1, 1949, the People's Republic of China was established at Peking with Party Chairman Mao as chief of state.

The organizational techniques developed in the base areas stood the CCP in good stead after 1949. Mao remained as the source of policy while most of the actual administration was left in the hands of highly skilled subordinates. With Soviet aid and advisers, China's first ten years showed an impressive record of growth and achievement.

In 1958, however, Mao stumbled. Whether provoked by the beginnings of the Sino-Soviet split or made overconfident by China's early success, Mao discarded the Soviet model of development for one of his own — the Great Leap Forward. Mao claimed China could catch up with the industrialized nations by the end of the century. The disastrous results undid much of what China had accomplished up to that point. Mao then resigned as chief of state, and turned the post over to Liu Shao-ch'i, who moved quickly to dismantle the program and re-establish more conventional economic planning.

In 1965, Mao struck back. Claiming that the Liu-led leadership had betrayed socialism, Mao mobilized China's youth to purge those who he said were "taking the capitalist road." The activities of the Red Guards plunged China into chaos, cut it off from the outside world, and all but destroyed its economy. Although Mao succeeded in removing Liu and his supporters, he did so only after the army took over the government, an occurrence which made Defense Minister Lin Piao the most powerful man in China. Following an alleged coup attempt in 1971, Lin was killed while fleeing China.

By that time, the radicals who had led the Cultural Revolution were the only people with access to Mao, now in failing health. Ruling in his name, they seemed ready to launch another Cultural Revolution when Mao died in 1976. The old leadership, which had been awaiting its chance, quickly moved to arrest the radicals and retake power. Since then, China, so long dominated by one man, has been ruled by a collective leadership which worked to restore more normalized government.

Analysis

Mao Tse-tung always seemed larger than life, and death has not diminished his stature, as the Chinese leaders who succeeded him continue to rule in his name. He was clearly one of the "great men" of the century. He sustained a revolutionary movement for more than 15 years and ruled the world's most populous nation for almost three decades.

There are many reasons for his success. First, as a revolutionary and as a leader, Mao was able to command the loyalty of extremely intelligent, talented and diverse men. Second, Mao was successful in formulating an ideology which articulate Chinese could see as an expression of their own aspirations for China. Under Mao's direction, the program of the CCP came to represent the hopes of a generation of Chinese who were tired of Western humiliations and Chinese weakness. Inability to do this was Chiang Kaishek's greatest failure; Mao's greatest success — after a series of unsuccessful governments, when some Chinese began to despair of ever reunifying China — was in finding the key to that unity. In the process Mao "Sinicized" Marxism, applying it to a China whose peasant population had remained inert and ignored, for centuries.

Following the accession of Hua Guofeng and his moderate allies, it seemed to some that Peking's new leadership was determined to undo the Maoist legacy and take China down an entirely different path. But despite the appearances of de-Maoization, the reality was much more complex. His successors continued to rule in Mao's name and use his formulations, and any deviation from what might be seen as "pure Maoism" was not likely to be significant in the near future. Even after death, Mao remained the central figure in Chinese politics, policy and government.

Communist Chinese Leaders

Bo Yibo (1907-   )

(Po I-po)

Born in Dingxiang County, Shanghai, Bo was educated at Peking University, where he participated in the student movement. He joined the CCP secretly in 1926 and continued to do undercover work in the north. He was arrested and jailed in 1933. In 1936 he was released from prison and continued working as an organizer for various communist-front organizations.

During the war against Japan and the civil war, 1937-49, Bo performed various organizational and political tasks behind the lines. After the Communist victory in 1949, Bo served in positions related to finance and economic planning. He served as minister of finance, 1951-53, and chairman of the State Construction Commission, 1954-56, where he worked closely with the Soviet aid mission. From 1956-66 he served concurrently as a vice premier, chairman of the Scientific Planning Commission and an alternate member of the ruling Politburo.

In June 1966, with the onset of the Cultural Revolution, Bo, like most of the important economic planners, was purged as a "big renegade" and a "counterrevolutionary revisionist."

Bo was "rehabilitated" in late 1978, named a vice premier in July 1979 and re-elected to the CCP Central Committee in September. After his return he again became involved with high-level national economic planning.

Chai Zemin (1915-   )

(Ch'ai Tse-min)

Born in Wenxi County, Shanxi Province, Chai became a local district party leader behind the Japanese lines during the war, 1937-1945, and went to work in the Peking municipal government after the CCP victory in 1949. In 1953 Chai began working in the field of foreign affairs, and was appointed ambassador to Hungary, 1961-64. In 1964 he was appointed ambassador to Guinea, but was recalled during the Cultural Revolution, 1966-67, and reappointed in 1970. In May 1978 he was named chief of the Chinese Liaison Office in Washington and, with the opening of full diplomatic relations in 1979, Communist China's first ambassador to the United States.

Chen Boda (1904-   )

(Ch'en Po-ta)

Born in Huian County, Fujian Province, Chen began his career as a clerk in a local warlord army. He secretly joined the CCP, was arrested by the government, and spent several years in prison before going to Moscow, where he studied at Sun Yat-sen University. He returned to China in 1931 and joined the Communist underground in north China while teaching in Peking. During this period Chen wrote extensively on the problem of the applicability of Marxist-Leninism to the situation in China.

When war broke out in 1937, Chen went to CCP headquarters at Yanan, where he met Mao Tse-tung and became his secretary. During the ensuing years, the two men collaborated on producing the theories and arguments necessary to make Marxism relevant to China. Some analysts give Chen more credit for these writings than Mao, under whose name they appeared. Chen continued writing and in 1958 became editor-in-chief of *Hongqi*, the CCP's most authoritative and prestigious theoretical journal; in its pages Chen soon began to extol the "Thought of Chairman Mao." Chen had also been named an alternate member of the Politburo in 1956.

The beginning of the Cultural Revolution in 1966 accelerated Chen's rise. He was named head of the powerful Cultural Revolution Group, one of two ad hoc bodies directing the movement, and was promoted to regular membership in the Politburo. In 1969, with the rise of Lin Piao as second-ranking CCP leader, Chen was elected to the all-powerful standing committee of the Politburo, but was purged the next year. In 1971 Chen was accused of being a co-conspirator with Lin Piao in the latter's alleged coup attempt against Mao. Chen thereafter disappeared from public view.

Chen Muhua (1922-   )

(Ch'en Mu-hua)

Originally a protégé of Chou En-lai, Chen succeeded Fang Yi as chairman of the Commission for Economic Relations with Foreign Countries in January 1977, and was elected an alternate member of the ruling Politburo in August of that year. In February 1978 she was named a vice premier, the only woman to hold the post, and was confirmed in her commission chairmanship at the same time. In August 1979 Chen came under a brief wall-poster attack for abuse of her privileges, but appeared to have emerged unscathed. By the end of the year she seemed slated to play a leading role in China's birth control effort. Chen's origins and earlier career are obscure.

Chen Xilian (1913-   )

(Ch'en Hsi-lien)

Born in Huangan County, Hubei Province, Chen was recruited into the CCP in 1926 after participating in a peasant uprising. He graduated from the Red Army Academy in 1931 and rose quickly in the ranks of the army. During the war with Japan, 1937-45, he served as a regimental commander under Zhu De's 8th Route Army and commanded a corps during the civil war, 1945-49. After the CCP victory in 1949, Chen was sent to southwest China to mop up the Kuomintang forces still active there. In 1951 he led troops in Korea and was named commander of artillery in 1952. In 1959 Chen became commander of the Shenyang military region, in northeast China, a post he would hold from 1959 to 1973.

With the onset of the Cultural Revolution and the subsequent breakdown of regular civilian power, it was important military commanders like Chen who profited most. In 1969, at the peak of the army's power, he was elected to the ruling Politburo and seems to have been one of the commanders who did not participate in Lin Piao's abortive coup attempt of 1971. He was re-elected to the Politburo in 1973, then transferred to command of the even more important Peking military region, where the radical Wu De was mayor. In January 1975 he was named a vice premier. At this point, many Western analysts listed Chen as one of the five men most likely to succeed Mao after the latter's death.

Following Hua Guofeng's coup in 1976, however, both Chen and Wu found their power seriously curtailed. Despite his re-election to the Politburo in August 1977, and as a vice premier in February 1978, it was reported that Chen was removed from his Peking command in late 1978.

The sources used in compiling these biographies include: Howard L. Boorman (ed.), *Biographical Dictionary of Republican China,* 4 vols., New York: Columbia University Press, 1967-71; Donald W. Klein and Anne B. Clark, *Biographic Dictionary of Chinese Communism,* 2 vols., Cambridge: Harvard University Press, 1971; Union Research Institute (ed.), *Who's Who in Communist China,* 2 vols., 2nd ed., Hong Kong: Union Research Institute, 1969-70; *The China Quarterly,* London; *Issues and Studies,* Taipei; *The New York Times; Who's Who in American Politics; Current Biography; Who's Who in America.*

In addition, individual biographies provided material on Chiang Kai-shek (Emily Hahn, *Chiang Kai-shek: An Unauthorized Biography,* New York: Doubleday and Co., 1955; Pichon P. Y. Loh, *The Early Chiang Kai-shek: A Study of His Personality and Politics, 1887-1924,* New York: Columbia University Press, 1971; Hollington K. Tong, *Chiang Kai-shek,* Taipei: China Publishing Company, 1953).

Chou En-lai (Hsu Kai-yu, *Chou En-lai: China's Gray Eminence,* New York: Doubleday and Co., 1968; Li Tien-min, *Chou En-lai,* Taipei: Institute of International Relations, 1970);

Deng Xiaoping (Richard C. Bush, *Teng Hsiao-p'ing Comes to Washington: The Man and His Mission,* New York: The China Council of the Asia Society, 1979);

Hua Guofeng (Ting Wang, "A Concise Biography of Hua Kuo-feng," *Chinese Law and Government,* Spring 1978, pp. 3-71; Michael Oksenberg and Sai-cheung Yeung, "Hua Kuo-feng's Precultural Revolution Hunan Years, 1949-66: The Making of a Political Generalist," *The China Quarterly,* No. 69, March 1977, pp. 3-53; "Hua Kuo-feng," *Issues and Studies,* Vol. XII, No. 3 (March 1976), pp. 80-88);

Liu Shao-ch'i (Lowell Dittmer, *Liu Shao-ch'i and the Cultural Revolution,* Berkeley and Los Angeles: University of California Press, 1974);

Mao Tse-tung (Jerome Ch'en, *Mao and the Chinese Revolution,* London: Oxford University Press, 1965; Stuart Schram, *Mao Tse-tung,* New York: Simon & Schuster, 1966; Edgar Snow, *Red Star Over China,* New York: Random House, 1938; Dick Wilson (ed.), *Mao Tse-tung in the Scales of History,* Cambridge: Cambridge University Press, 1977).

A wall poster campaign begun in 1978 and expanded in 1979 accused Chen of a variety of crimes, of which the most important was that he used his troops to break up the Tiananmen demonstrations in favor of Deng Xiaoping in 1976, just before the coup. In June 1979, new posters accused him of having embezzled state funds. Although he still held his seat on the Politburo, it was highly unlikely that he had any real power in 1980.

Chen Yi (1901-1972)

(Ch'en I)

Chen was born in Leshan County, Sichuan Province, to a prosperous and well-educated family. In 1919 he won a scholarship to study in France, where he joined the Socialist Youth Corps. He was expelled from the country in 1921 for his revolutionary activities. He returned to China, joined both the CCP and the Kuomintang in 1923, and continued his studies in Peking.

In 1925 he went to Canton, where he worked as a political instructor under Chou En-lai at the Whampoa Military Academy. When the KMT and CCP split in 1927, Chen accompanied Zhu De southward to link up with Communist forces under Mao Tse-tung. Chen quickly became a fervent supporter of Mao, and sided with him during several important internal disputes. He participated in the Long March, 1934-35, as a corps commander, and held several major military commands during the war against Japan, 1937-45, and the civil war, 1946-49.

After the Communist victory in 1949 Chen served as the military commander of the important East China region, as well as mayor of Shanghai, 1954-1958. In 1956 he was elected to the ruling Politburo and in 1958 succeeded Chou En-lai as foreign minister, a post he held until his death in 1972.

During the Cultural Revolution Chen's brusque style of speaking and his refusal to use rigid Marxist formulations made him an early target of the Red Guards, who attacked him both verbally and physically, but Chou never ceased defending him, and Chen was never purged.

Possibly China's most brilliant tactical military commander, Chen served as foreign minister in sharp contrast to the urbane and sophisticated Chou. But Chen's more outspoken style was clearly suitable for the bellicose foreign policy adopted by China at the time of his accession to the post in 1958.

Chen Yonggui (1916-   )

(Ch'en Yung-kuei)

Chen was born in Xiyang County, Shanxi Province, to poor peasants. Little is known about his early life, but in 1956 he was selected as a "model peasant," and Peking declared that his efforts were to be emulated throughout China. In 1957 he was named secretary of the party branch of the Dazhai production brigade, Dazhai commune, in his native Xiyang. Under his leadership, the brigade enjoyed remarkable success, and in February 1964 Mao Tse-tung called on all of China: "In agriculture, learn from Dazhai." During the Cultural Revolution, the "learn from Dazhai" movement was expanded, Chen's reputation enhanced, and his ties to the radicals cemented. In April 1969 he was elected to the Central Committee and in February 1971 was named Shanxi provincial party chief. The "learn from Dazhai" campaign was again revived in 1973, and in August Chen was elected to the ruling Politburo. In 1975 he was named a vice premier.

The accession of the moderates in 1976 saw a significant downgrading of Chen's position, although he was re-elected to the Politburo in 1977, and in 1978 reappointed as a vice premier. By the end of 1979, although he still held these posts, he had not been seen in public for some time.

Chen Yun (1905-)

(Ch'en Yün)

Born in Jingbu County, Jiangsu Province, Chen had very little formal education, possibly less than six years in primary school. After working in a Shanghai printing firm, he began his career as a labor organizer under Liu Shao-ch'i. First elected to the Communist Party Central Committee in 1931, and to the Politburo in 1934, Chen participated in the Long March, 1934-35, and filled a number of economic posts behind the Japanese lines during World War II, 1937-1945.

At the end of the war, Chen was one of a handpicked CCP group that also included Li Fuchun and Peng Zhen who were sent to Manchuria with the armies of Lin Piao. Their success in the northeast was crucial to the eventual Communist victory.

After 1949 Chen held a number of key cabinet posts related to economic planning, development, and construction of heavy industry. He was one of the officials most responsible for the success of the First Five-Year Plan (1953-57), which brought him into extensive contact with the Soviet Union.

In 1956 Chen was elected to the seven-man standing committee of the Politburo and as a vice chairman of the party.

With the Great Leap Forward, which he opposed, and the split with the Soviet Union, Chen's stature dropped markedly, although he was never formally purged. In January 1967 he was attacked by Peking newspapers and wall posters as a "capitalist roader" and disappeared from public life in October 1969.

Chen reappeared in August 1972, still listed as a vice premier, but with only nominal power. As more and more such "rehabilitations" took place, Chen was re-elected as a vice chairman of the party in December 1978 and added to the all-powerful standing committee of the Politburo, ranking fifth.

Despite his lack of schooling, Chen remained one of China's most important economic planners, a position he probably owed as much to hard work as to theoretical training. Chen was always associated with the moderate group in Chinese politics, particularly Liu Shao-ch'i. Despite his age, his restoration was seen as significant because of what analysts saw as his commitment to the use of foreign assistance and central planning in the modernization of China's economy.

On July 1, 1979, he was named minister in charge of the State Financial and Economic Commission, a position that evidently put him in sole charge of China's modernization and marked him as the second most powerful man in the state government, behind Deng Xiaoping.

Deng Yingchao (1903-)

(Teng Ying-ch'ao)

Born in Xinyang, Henan Province, Deng was already an active member of the CCP when she met and married Chou En-lai in 1925. A university graduate who was one of the few women to survive the Long March, 1934-35, she served in a number of important posts involving women's activities during her career. In late 1976, following the death of her husband and Hua Guofeng's successful coup against the radicals, Deng was given more prominent positions in the government as the regime sought to use her as a symbol of their perpetuation of Chou's policies. In December 1976 she was elected a vice chairman of the National People's Congress, and in December 1978 was elected to the ruling Politburo. Despite her new status, Deng was not believed to wield significant power in Peking.

Dong Biwu (1886-1975)

(Tung Pi-wu)

Born in Huangan County, Hubei Province, to an educated but impoverished family, Dong received his early education in the Chinese classics and passed the examination for the lowest of the imperial degrees, the *shengyuan,*in 1901. He continued his studies, became a teacher and came into contact with the radical doctrines which were sweeping China at the time. Dong participated in the 1911 Revolution and joined Sun Yat-sen's T'ungmenghui (Tongmenghui). With the failure of the revolution, Dong fled to Japan, where he completed work on a law degree. He returned to China in 1920 and continued his teaching and revolutionary activities. In 1921 he attended the founding congress of the CCP. Of those present, only he and Mao would survive to assume high-ranking positions after 1949.

After the Kuomintang-Chinese Communist split in 1927, Dong fled to Japan and the Soviet Union, returning to China in 1932, when he joined Mao in the Jiangxi soviet. He participated in the Long March, 1934-35, and between 1936-45 served as a liaison between the CCP and the KMT.

In 1945 Dong was named to the ruling Politburo as the seventh ranking member of the CCP. He participated as a CCP representative at the U.S.-sponsored talks — 1945-47 — aimed at ending the civil war.

After the CCP victory in 1949 Dong was named as one of four vice premiers and in 1954 as president of the Supreme People's Court, a position he held until April 1959, when he was named vice chief of state of China under Liu Shao-ch'i. After Liu was purged during the Cultural Revolution, Dong served as acting chief of state, a largely honorary position, until the post was abolished in January 1975.

Fang Yi (1910-)

(Fang I)

Born in Fujian Province, Fang joined the CCP as a teen-ager during the 1930s in Jiangxi Province. He participated in the Long March, 1934-35, and performed middle-level administrative and financial tasks during the war with Japan and the civil war, 1937-49. After the Communist victory in 1949, Fang was sent back to his native Fujian as an administrator and economic expert. Fang served as the vice minister of finance, 1953-54, and as the Chinese trade representative in Hanoi, 1956-60. During the late 1960s Fang — fluent in Japanese, German, English and Russian — was chairman of the Commission for Economic Relations with Foreign Countries, and traveled widely.

One of the few economic experts not purged during the Cultural Revolution, Fang was succeeded by Chen Muhua in early 1977 and elected to the ruling Politburo in August 1977. In February 1978 he was named a vice premier and minister in charge of the State Scientific and Technological Commission. Fang was the second-ranking member of the Chinese group that visited the United States with Deng Xiaoping in 1979.

In July 1979 Fang became president of the Chinese Academy of Sciences, and was named to Chen Yun's powerful State Financial and Economic Commission at the same time.

Geng Biao (1903-   )

(Keng Piao)

Born in Liling County, Hunan Province, Geng's early life is obscure. By 1934 he had risen to command a regiment in Mao's Jiangxi soviet and accompanied Mao on the Long March, 1934-35. Geng continued to rise during the war with Japan and the civil war, and also served as a military representative to the U.S.-sponsored truce talks between the Communists and Nationalists in 1946.

After the Communist victory, Geng was named China's ambassador to the Scandinavian countries: Sweden, 1950-56; Denmark, 1950-55; and Finland, 1951-54. He was then appointed ambassador to Pakistan, 1956-59. In 1960 Geng was recalled to Peking and named a vice minister of foreign affairs under Chen Yi, then ambassador to Burma, 1963-67. With the onset of the Cultural Revolution, all of China's ambassadors were called home, including Geng, but in May 1969 he was appointed ambassador to Albania — the first Chinese emissary to be sent out after the Cultural Revolution had ended.

In August 1977 Geng was elected to the ruling Politburo and became a vice premier in February 1978. In early 1979 Geng stepped down as head of the CCP's international liaison department and took over as secretary general of the CCP's Military Affairs Commission. Because of Defense Minister Xu Xiangqian's poor health, it was Geng who met most frequently with Secretary of Defense Harold Brown during the latter's trip to China in January 1980. Geng was slated to head a Chinese military delegation to the U.S. later in 1980.

Gu Mu (1915-   )

(Ku Mu)

Little is known about Gu, who was mayor of Jinan from 1950-52. He was called to Peking in 1954, where he held a number of key positions related to economic planning, finally emerging as the chairman of the State Capital Construction Commission, a cabinet-level position, 1965-67.

With the outbreak of the Cultural Revolution, Gu was attacked as a "counterrevolutionary revisionist" and purged in 1967. He was later "rehabilitated" and renamed to head the commission in 1973, a post he still held in 1980. He was named a vice premier in January 1975 and appeared to be an important member of China's top economic planning group.

Guo Moruo (1892-1978)

(Kuo Mo-jo)

Born in Sichuan to a landlord-merchant family, Guo received a traditional Chinese education before going to Japan, where he received his M.D. and began to write poetry. From 1914-37 Guo spent most of his time in Japan, writing poetry and translating Western works; this soon established him as one of China's leading intellectuals. A Marxist-Leninist, Guo never joined the CCP; although an avowed leftist, he worked for the Kuomintang during the war with Japan, writing anti-Japanese propaganda. With the Communist victory in 1949, Guo stayed on the mainland and was named chairman of the All-China Federation of Writers and Artists and president of the Academy of Sciences. Guo came under criticism during the Cultural Revolution but was able to weather the attacks by confessing his "errors." He still held his positions at the time of his death in 1978.

He Long (1896-1969)

(Ho Lung)

Born in Hunan Province, He was the son of an impoverished officer in the imperial army. Young He received little formal education, and began his career as a bandit chieftain in his native district. In the 1920s, he was induced to join the Kuomintang; the political officer who was sent to indoctrinate his troops was a Communist with whom he developed a close relationship. When the KMT and CCP split in 1927, He, now a corps commander, joined the Communists. After a succession of defeats at the hands of the KMT, He returned to his native Hunan to organize a new force. Defeated again, He made his own Long March in 1935 and eventually linked up with Mao in 1936. During the war with Japan, 1937-45, He was a division commander with Zhu De's 8th Route Army. During the civil war, he was the overall commander for northwest China.

After the CCP victory in 1949, He was sent to southwest China with Deng Xiaoping and Liu Bocheng to consolidate Communist control. In 1954 He became a vice premier and was elected to the ruling Politburo in 1956. He was most active, however, as head of the National Physical Culture and Sports Commission, a cabinet-level position to which he was named in 1952. The commission was devoted to the organization and promotion of all sports in China, and was a great success.

With the onset of the Cultural Revolution He, already ranking vice chairman of the Military Affairs Committee under Lin Piao, was named head of the PLA's Cultural Revolution Group, from which posts he was able to obstruct the more excessive aspects of the purges in the armed forces. This led to his ouster in 1967 from all his posts. The same year, he was also subjected to a "trial" by Red Guard leaders.

He was posthumously "rehabilitated" in the late 1970s.

Hu Yaobang (ca. 1915-   )

(Hu Yao-pang)

Born in Hunan Province, Hu joined the CCP in 1933 and worked as an organizer and leader of the Communist Youth League. During the war with Japan, 1937-45, Hu became a political commissar and organizer in the 2nd Front Army as a protégé of Deng Xiaoping. When Deng was sent to Sichuan in 1949, Hu accompanied him. In 1952, when Deng was called to Peking, Hu went with him and was named head of the Communist Youth League, 1953-57. In 1956 he was elected to the Central Committee. When Deng was named secretary general of the CCP in 1956, Hu served under him. In 1967, when Deng was purged by the Cultural

Revolution, so was Hu. They were both "rehabilitated" in 1973 and purged again in 1976.

In late 1977, with Deng again at the top, Hu was named head of the CCP's organization department. In December 1978 he was added to the ruling Politburo. In January 1979 he was named secretary general of the CCP, a powerful post that had not existed since Deng was purged from it in 1967. With such a power base, Hu was expected to exert influence in the party for some time.

Huang Hua (1915-   )

Born to a wealthy and well-educated family in Zi County, Hebei Province, Huang received a local primary education before going to Peking, where he entered an Episcopal high school. After graduation, he studied at Yenching (Yanjing) University, where he developed a close relationship with its president, John Leighton Stuart, and became fluent in English.

While at the university, Huang came in contact with the CCP, began organizing students in north China under Peng Zhen, and joined the CCP himself at about this time. After leading a series of demonstrations, Huang's activities were exposed, and he fled to Yanan, the CCP headquarters.

During the war with Japan, while serving as a Xinhua correspondent in Chongqing, Huang maintained extensive contacts with Western correspondents and diplomats and, under the direction of Chou En-lai, became a spokesman for the CCP. He also served as a mid-level Communist representative to the U.S.-sponsored negotiations between the CCP and the Kuomintang, 1945-47.

After the Communist victory in 1949, Huang was named director of the Overseas Chinese Affairs Administration. In 1954 he accompanied Chou En-lai to the Geneva talks, where he served as spokesman for the Chinese delegation. He continued to rise within the foreign ministry and was named China's first ambassador to Ghana, 1960-65, and ambassador to the UAR in 1966. When China established diplomatic relations with Canada in 1970, Huang was named China's first ambassador to Ottawa. The next year, when China entered the United Nations, Huang was named ambassador and permanent representative. He served in this post for five years, 1971-76, and became China's most prominent diplomat. Following Hua Guofeng's successful coup against the radicals, Huang was recalled to Peking and named minister of foreign affairs in December 1976.

Huang Zhen (1909-   )

(Huang Chen)

Born in Tongcheng County, Anhui Province, Huang's early career was spent as a military commander under Mao in the Jiangxi soviet. He participated in the Long March, 1934-35, and continued to rise in the military as a commander and political commissar under Deng Xiaoping. After the CCP victory in 1949, Huang was named ambassador to Hungary, 1950-54, and ambassador to Indonesia, 1954-61. In 1961 he was recalled to Peking and named a vice minister of foreign affairs under Chen Yi. Following the establishment of diplomatic relations with France in 1964, Huang became China's first ambassador there. Recalled during the Cultural Revolution, Huang was reappointed in March 1969. In 1972-73, he served as a conduit for messages between Washington and Peking.

'The Gang of Four'

Beginning in October 1976, when Hua Guofeng arrested the most prominent radicals and had himself declared China's supreme ruler, Peking took long strides to disassociate itself from the leaders and policies of the prior decade, 1966-76. In order to do this, a vast propaganda campaign was mounted that centered the blame for the excesses of the Cultural Revolution on four individuals: Jiang Qing, Zhang Chunqiao, Wang Hongwen and Yao Wenyuan. *(See biographies, these pages.)*

Termed "the gang of four," these leaders, all of them members of China's ruling Politburo, were prominent during the Cultural Revolution. But they were neither the most important nor the most powerful of the radicals, nor were they even particularly unified as a group. Clearly, the initiative for the Cultural Revolution came not from these leaders, but from Mao himself. But because Mao's name remained sacrosanct in China after the Cultural Revolution, the "gang" was made the scapegoat of the moderates' political purge. Indeed, some of the more cynical Chinese, when asked about the period, verbally blame it on the "gang of four," but hold up five fingers, indicating that Mao should be included.

Apart from these five, however, several other figures should be included in any list of leaders of the Cultural Revolution — Lin Piao, Chen Boda and Kang Sheng, all of whom played critical roles during the period. Thus, while placing the blame on the "gang" has been an effective propaganda tool for the Chinese, it is a singularly inaccurate analytical tool for Western analysts.

In October 1979 Hua Guofeng accelerated the purge by announcing that the "gang" would be tried in 1980 under China's new criminal code.

With the establishment of reciprocal liaison offices by the U.S. and China in 1973, Huang was named the first chief of the Chinese Liaison Office in Washington. He was recalled to Peking in late 1977 and named minister of culture and deputy director of the party's propaganda department, positions he still held in early 1980.

Ji Dengkui (ca. 1923-   )

(Chi Teng-k'ui)

Little is known about Ji, whose career seems to have taken place solely within the Henan Province local party apparatus during the late 1950s and early 1960s. With the advent of the Cultural Revolution, however, Ji rose very rapidly, and by 1968 he was provincial party chief of Henan. In 1969 he was elected to alternate membership of the ruling Politburo and in 1973 was elected to regular membership. Seemingly allied with the radicals, Ji was then named political commissar of the key Peking military region. Despite the fall of the radicals in 1976, Ji was re-elected to the Politburo in 1977 and renamed a vice premier in 1978. In 1979 Ji was accused in a wall poster campaign of responsibility for the sad state of China's agriculture. He later was stripped of his position as Peking political commissar and was seldom seen in public thereafter.

Ji Pengfei (1910-)

(Chi P'eng-fei)

Born in Yongji County, Shaanxi Province, Ji graduated from a military medical college and spent his early career in the army of warlord Feng Yü-hsiang (Feng Yuxiang). In 1931 two divisions of this force revolted and joined the Communists in Jiangxi Province. Ji continued his medical duties there. After the Long March, 1934-35, Ji rose to become a high-ranking political commissar in the Communist army.

After the CCP victory in 1949, Ji was sent to East Germany as head of the Chinese diplomatic mission, 1950-53, and was then named ambassador to East Berlin, 1953-55. In 1955 he was recalled to Peking and named a vice minister of foreign affairs under Chou En-lai. When Chen Yi fell ill during the late 1960s, Ji became acting foreign minister and was formally named to the post after Chen's death in January 1972.

Ji was succeeded by Qiao Guanhua in November 1974, and was then named secretary general of the NPC standing committee in January 1975, a post he held until November 1979, when he was succeeded by Peng Zhen. In early 1979 Ji was named head of the CCP's international liaison department, and in September of that year was named a vice premier.

Jiang Qing (1914?-)

(Chiang Ch'ing)
(Stage name: Lan Ping)

Born in Zhucheng, Shandong Province, Jiang, raised by her grandparents, was a student in the provincial capital of Jinan until 1929, when she was reportedly kidnapped and sold into a theatrical troupe. She later received some formal dramatic training and from 1934-37 made several films in Shanghai, starring in two of them. When the Japanese invaded China in 1937 Jiang followed the government as it retreated westward, but in 1938 she left Chongqing and made her way to Yanan, the Communist capital behind the Japanese lines. She became a drama instructor, met Mao Tse-tung and became his mistress. Jiang joined the CCP the following year. After Mao had sent his current wife to Moscow for "medical treatment," Mao and Jiang were married in the early 1940s.

After the Communist victory in 1949, Jiang was active in Chinese cultural circles, but had little power or influence. This changed in 1965, however, with the beginning of the Cultural Revolution. Jiang soon became one of its most powerful leaders and vocal spokesmen as vice chairman of the Cultural Revolution Group. In 1967 she was elected to the Central Committee, her first non-cultural position, and later to the ruling Politburo. Despite these titles, Jiang's power continued to stem from her relationship with Mao, especially as his health declined. During the 1970s she remained an implacable foe of the moderates, especially Deng Xiaoping, and is said to have blocked an attempt to have him succeed Chou En-lai after the latter's death.

Following Mao's death in 1976, Hua Guofeng arrested the radicals, including Jiang, and labeled her a member of the "gang of four" which was accused of attempting its own coup designed to install Jiang as "empress of China." She was slated to be tried during 1980.

Assessments of Jiang are often contradictory. For some she was a selfless idealist who sought only to purify China's culture and raise its ideological and revolutionary content. For others, she was a second-rate actress who, resentful of those who had denied her success in the 1930s, had found a way to exact revenge and, in the process, all but destroyed the traditional culture of the world's oldest civilization.

Jiang's marriage to Mao was her third, and she also had at least two other lovers. She and Mao had two daughters.

Kang Sheng (1899-1975)

(K'ang Sheng)

Kang was born in Zhucheng, Shandong Province, the son of a prosperous landowner. After receiving a middle school education, Kang joined the CCP in 1924 and began underground organizing in Shanghai. In 1933 Kang went to the Soviet Union to study security and intelligence techniques.

Kang returned to China in 1937 and performed security and intelligence work in the organization department under Chen Yun. He was elected to the Politburo in 1945. In 1949 Kang was named to the Government Council and became governor of his native Shandong. After the government reorganization of 1954 Kang became less prominent in government affairs and was relegated to alternate membership in the Politburo in 1956.

With the beginning of the Cultural Revolution, Kang was returned to the Politburo in 1966 and came to be ranked seventh in the party. He was named to the standing committee of the Politburo and became a vice chairman of the party in 1973 despite the ouster of his two closest associates, Lin Piao and Chen Boda.

Kang Shi'en (1910?-)

(K'ang Shih-en)

Born into a landlord family in Chahar Province (now the Nei Mongol A.R.), Kang was recruited into the CCP while a middle school student in Peking during the 1930s by the student movement directed by Liu Shao-ch'i and Peng Zhen. In 1936 he was admitted to Jinghua University, but when the war broke out in 1937, he went to Yanan to receive political training before being named a political commissar under He Long.

In 1950 Kang was transferred to the northeast, where he directed work on the area's oil resources. In 1953 he was recalled to Peking to do similar work. In 1956 he was named vice minister of the petroleum industry, serving under Yu Qiuli from 1958 on. When Yu was transferred in 1965, Kang became acting minister.

Kang came under severe attack during the Cultural Revolution as a supporter of Liu Shao-ch'i and Deng Xiaoping, and was purged from his posts in March 1967. He was "rehabilitated" in 1971, and named minister of petroleum and chemical industries, 1973-78. In February 1978 Kang was named a vice premier and minister in charge of the State Economic Commission, an important planning board. In May 1979 Kang headed a large and important delegation to the United States, where he met President Carter. The two men discussed the possibilities of future Sino-American cooperation in the development of China's energy resources. With Yu, Kang was in 1980 one of the most important of the "second generation" of central economic planners.

Li Desheng (1916-   )

(Li Teh-sheng)

Born to a peasant family in Hubei Province, Li received only a limited education before joining the Red Army in 1935. He rose rapidly, and had become a division commander by 1949. In March 1951 Li's division was ordered to combat in Korea, and he was later named commander of the XII Corps, 1959-67.

With the beginning of the Cultural Revolution, Li began a rapid rise that led in June 1967 to his appointment as director of the Anhui Province Military Control Committee. His willingness to commit his forces to "support the left," as ordered by the leaders of the Cultural Revolution, brought him promotion to commander of the Anhui military district in April 1968. In April 1969 he was elected to alternate membership on the ruling Politburo. In September 1970 he was named director of the General Political Department of the People's Liberation Army (PLA), making him the third-ranking military man in China.

One of the few major commanders not associated with Lin Piao, Li continued to do well even after Lin's death. In August 1973 he was elected to the standing committee of the Politburo and as one of the five vice chairmen of the CCP. By this time, Western analysts were listing him as one of the most likely of the younger leaders to move up after Mao and Chou had died.

But in late 1973, as China moved to restore civilian control over the army, all the regional commanders were reshuffled, and Li was named to command of the Shenyang military region in Manchuria. He lost his vice chairmanship and his seat on the standing committee, as well as his directorship of the PLA's political department, although he still maintained membership in the Politburo, to which he was re-elected in August 1977.

Li Fuchun (ca. 1900-1975)

(Li Fu-ch'un)

Little is known of Li's early life. Born in Changsha, Hunan Province, he received a local education and went to France in 1919 on the same work-study program as Chou En-lai. He joined the CCP in 1922 and returned to China in 1925. He immediately went to Canton, where he worked under Chou as a political instructor at the Whampoa Military Academy. After the KMT-CCP split in 1927, Li did underground work in Shanghai. When the CCP organizations were suppressed by the KMT, he fled to Mao's Jiangxi soviet to work in the army's political department. He participated in the Long March, 1934-35, and during the war against Japan, 1937-45, served under Chen Yun in various financial and organizational posts. During the civil war, Li worked in Manchuria.

After the Communist victory in 1949, Li was named minister of heavy industry, 1950-52, and worked closely with the Soviet aid mission. He was named a vice premier in 1954 and also placed in charge of the State Planning Commission. In 1956 he was elected to the Politburo and in November 1966 to the standing committee of that body. Purged near the end of the Cultural Revolution in 1969, Li reappeared in August 1972, still listed as a vice premier.

With Chen Yun and Li Xiannian, Li was considered one of the most important economic planners of the Communist regime.

Li Qiang (1906-   )

(Li Ch'iang)

Born in Anhui Province, Li studied telecommunications in Moscow, returned to China and worked in the Ministry of Post and Telecommunications, 1949-52. He was then named vice minister of foreign trade, 1952-73, and traveled extensively in this post. He was elected to the Central Committee in August 1973 and in October was named minister of foreign trade, a post he still held in early 1980.

Li Xiannian (1905-   )

(Li Hsien-nien)

Born to a working-class family in Huangan County, Hubei Province, Li — about whose early life little is known — had by the 1930s become a military commander in the Henan-Hubei-Anhui (Eyuwan) soviet under Zhang Guotao, who later split with Mao, and Xu Xiangqian. During the war with Japan, 1937-45, Li was a guerrilla commander in Hubei and rose to deputy commander of the 4th Front Army under Lin Piao in 1949. After 1949, Li's primary responsibility was the consolidation of Communist power in the critical Central-South region, where he served as mayor of the major industrial city of Wuhan, 1952-54. In 1954 Li was transferred to Peking to become minister of finance, succeeding Deng Xiaoping. A few months later he was named a vice premier. In September 1956 Li was elected to the ruling Politburo.

Protected by Chou En-lai, Li was one of the very few high-ranking economic planners not purged during the Cultural Revolution. He became the senior economic specialist in China and was still a vice premier in 1980. In August 1977 he was also elected as one of the vice chairmen of the party and named to the all-powerful standing committee of the Politburo.

Liu Bocheng (1892-   )

(Liu Po-ch'eng)

Born in Kai County, Sichuan Province, Liu was the son of a traveling musician. After receiving his early education in the Chinese classics, Liu entered a military school, from which he graduated in 1911. His career in the military began with his participation in the 1911 republican revolution, and continued in the relatively progressive warlord units of southern China.

During this period his eye was removed after a wound. From this point on he was known as the "one-eyed dragon." In 1926 he joined the CCP, participated in the Northern Expedition, and took part in the Nanchang Uprising. After this was suppressed he fled to the Soviet Union, where he studied in Soviet military academies, 1927-30. After his return to China he made his way to Mao's Jiangxi soviet area and became an instructor in the Red Army Academy there, one of the few military men with both military experience and formal training. He participated in the Long March, 1934-35, and during the war with Japan, 1937-45, commanded the 129th Division of Zhu De's 8th Route Army. During the civil war he commanded the 2nd Front Army, 1948-49, and became famous for his mastery of mobile warfare.

With the Communist victory in 1949 Liu was sent back to his native southwest to consolidate Communist control of the region. He was also commandant of the People's Revolutionary Military Academy, 1951-58. He was elected to the ruling Politburo in 1956, and still retained his membership in 1980, although ill health prevented him from fully exercising it.

Lu Dingyi (1904-   )

(Lu Ting-i)

Born in Wuxi, Jiangsu Province, Lu graduated from a university in Shanghai and studied in the U.S. and the Soviet Union. A CCP member by 1924, Lu began his career doing propaganda work for the central party leadership in Shanghai. When this was broken up by the government in 1931 Lu made his way to the Jiangxi soviet where he joined Mao Tse-tung and edited the party newspaper. Lu participated in the Long March, 1934-35, and served as propaganda director for Zhu De's 8th Route Army during the war with Japan, 1937-45.

After the Communist victory in 1949, Lu was named director of the propaganda department of the CCP, and was elected an alternate member of the ruling Politburo in 1956. He was named a vice premier in 1959 and, in 1965, minister of culture.

With the onset of the Cultural Revolution, Lu's monopoly on propaganda and culture made him the first target of the radicals, who needed control of these organs to prosecute their campaign. Branded a "counterrevolutionary revisionist," Lu was stripped of all his posts in 1966 and placed on public trial in 1967. He was "rehabilitated" in 1979 and re-elected to the Central Committee of the CCP in September of that year.

Luo Reiqing (1906-1978)

(Lo Jui-ch'ing)

Born to a landlord family in Sichuan Province, Luo graduated from a branch of the Whampoa Military Academy and received police and intelligence training at the Sun Yat-sen University in Moscow. He returned to China in 1930 and joined Mao Tse-tung and Zhu De in Jiangxi as political commissar to an army division. He participated in the Long March, 1934-35, and was named deputy commandant of the Red Army Military Academy under Lin Piao in 1936. During the war against Japan and the civil war, 1937-49, he was a high-ranking military commissar to a number of Communist units.

From 1949-58 Luo served as minister of public security, in charge of all secret police functions in China. In this capacity he conducted the mass purges of 1951, 1952 and 1956. He was elected to the Central Committee in 1956 and, in 1959, with the purge of Peng Dehuai and the accession of Lin Piao, was named vice premier, vice minister of national defense, and chief of staff of the People's Liberation Army.

Luo's power and influence continued to increase until 1966, when he was purged, probably after a dispute with Lin Piao over China's reaction to the American buildup in Vietnam. Luo was viciously attacked as a follower of Peng Dehuai during the Cultural Revolution, and reportedly tried to commit suicide in 1967. "Rehabilitated" in 1977, Luo was re-elected to the Central Committee.

Ni Zhifu (1933-   )

(Ni Chih-fu)

Born in Shanghai in 1933, Ni received only three years of primary education before going to work in a kerosene fac-

tory there. In 1949, after receiving some technical education, he was transferred to a machinery factory in Peking. During the next several years, Ni became moderately well-known for a host of technical improvements and inventions, especially a high-speed drill which came to be named after him. He joined the CCP in 1958 and began part-time university study.

Despite his prominence, Ni was not one of the workers catapulted to the top of the political heap during the Cultural Revolution; he was, in fact, purged from his municipal and trade union positions, probably because of his ties with Peng Zhen. In April 1969 Ni was elected to the CCP Central Committee, and in 1971 to the standing committee of the Peking Municipal Party Committee. In August 1973 he was elected to alternate Politburo membership and as secretary of the Peking Municipal Party Committee. In April 1976 the worker groups under him refused to join those supporting the "gang of four" to suppress the Tiananmen riots in favor of the moderate Deng Xiaoping. In October 1976, after Hua Guofeng's arrest of the "gang," Ni was named second secretary of the Shanghai Revolutionary Committee under Su Zhenhua. The two men were charged with bringing the city back under the control of Peking. In August 1977, he was elected to the ruling Politburo.

Nie Rongzhen (1899-   )

(Nieh Jung-chen)

Born to a prosperous farming family in Sichuan Province, Nie graduated from middle school before going to France as a member of a work-study group that also included Deng Xiaoping. Nie studied chemical engineering and joined the CCP there in 1922. He went to Moscow for futher study in 1924 and returned to China in 1925, when he became a political instructor under Chou En-lai at the Whampoa Military Academy. After the Kuomintang-CCP split in 1927, Nie eventually made his way to Mao's Jiangxi soviet. In 1932 he was named political commissar to the 1st Army Group, commanded by Lin Piao, a post he held until 1937. He participated in the Long March, 1934-35, and after war with Japan began, was sent to organize his own guerrillas behind the Japanese lines. By the end of the war in 1945, Nie's force numbered more than 150,000 men.

During the civil war, 1945-49, he was sent to Inner Mongolia (now called Nei Mongol A.R.). After Peking fell to the Communists, Nie was named to the critical post of garrison commander, 1949-55, and also served as mayor, 1949-51. In 1950 he was named acting chief of staff of the People's Liberation Army. In October 1956 he was named a vice premier and, the next year, director of the Scientific Planning Commission. When this was reorganized as the Scientific and Technological Commission in 1958, Nie was still the director, a cabinet-level post from which he oversaw the national production of armaments as well as weapons research. By this time he had become the regime's top planner in the field of science and technology, and was in charge of nuclear weapons and missile development.

With the onset of the Cultural Revolution, Nie was named to the ruling Politburo in 1966 but soon came under attack and was removed. After the accession to power of the moderates in 1976, Nie was re-elected to the Politburo in August 1977, and as a vice chairman of the Standing Committee of the NPC. He resumed responsibilities for scientific and technical development of China's armed forces.

Peng Chong (1910-   )

(P'eng Ch'ung)

Born in Fujian Province, Peng is reported to have served as a political commissar during World War II, and in 1950 was named to the party committee of his native province. In 1954 he was sent to Nanjing, where he served as deputy mayor, 1954-57; mayor, 1957-59; and municipal party chief, 1958-68. During this period, he also served as secretary of the Jiangsu Province party committee, 1965-68.

Peng was one of the very few local party leaders during the Cultural Revolution who did not come under attack by the Red Guards and, in 1968, rose to vice chairman of the Jiangsu Revolutionary Committee. In April 1969 he was elected to alternate membership on the Central Committee and later was named Jiangsu party chief, a post he held until October 1976 when, following Hua Guofeng's coup against the radicals, he was sent to Shanghai to help bring the city back under central control. In August 1977 he was elected to the ruling Politburo. In early 1979 he was promoted to Shanghai municipal party chief.

Peng Dehuai (1898-1974)

(P'eng Teh-huai)

Born in Xiangtan County, Hunan Province, Peng received little formal education before joining a local warlord army in 1918. When his commander began a purge of communists in 1927, Peng led his forces southward to form his own army. He joined the CCP in 1928 and later worked in concert with Mao Tse-tung and Zhu De in southern China. Peng's relations with Mao were often troubled, however, and he continued to demand considerable autonomy for his units. Peng participated in the Long March, 1934-35, and later rose to deputy commander-in-chief of the Communist armies under Zhu during the war against Japan, 1937-45.

During the Korean War, 1950-53, Peng commanded the Chinese armies that invaded Korea. He was named minister of defense in 1954, succeeding Zhu as overall commander of the army. During his tenure, Peng advocated military modernization and professionalism. He was purged in 1959 after sharply criticizing Mao's Great Leap Forward. He continued to be the subject of public criticism, and was arrested during the Cultural Revolution. He was posthumously "rehabilitated" in 1978.

Peng Zhen (1902-   )

(P'eng Chen)

Born to a poor peasant family in Chuwu, Shanxi Province, Peng received a traditional education until he left home in his early twenties. He soon became involved in labor organizing, and probably joined the CCP in 1926. He was arrested for his efforts in 1929, and released in 1936. Peng then joined Liu Shao-ch'i in organizing students in north China. During the war, 1937-45, Peng continued his organizing activities behind the Japanese lines. In 1942 he was called to the CCP headquarters at Yanan and named head of the Central Party School. He thus played a key role in the 1942-44 "rectification campaign" by which Mao either purged or re-educated the newer members of the rapidly expanding CCP.

During the civil war, Peng was the ranking party official with Lin Piao in Manchuria, 1946-48, and was then named deputy director of the CCP's organization department under Liu. With the Communist victory in 1949, Peng was named mayor of Peking, 1951-66, and also concurrent chairman of the Peking municipal party committee, 1955-66. He was elected to the ruling Politburo in 1951, and in 1956 also became the second-ranking member of the party Secretariat under Deng Xiaoping.

By the mid-1960s, when Liu had replaced Mao as chief of state, many Western analysts included Peng's name among those listed as the most likely to succeed Mao. But on June 3, 1966, Peng was stripped of all his posts, the first major victim of the Cultural Revolution which would also consume his two important mentors, Deng and Liu.

In early 1966, when it appeared that the Cultural Revolution would be limited only to a purge of cultural figures, Peng was named chief of the "Group of Five" which was heading the campaign. His efforts to limit the purge, and to protect Deng and Liu, soon brought him under attack by the radicals, however, who saw his removal as the key to control of the capital and of the Cultural Revolution itself. After his purge, Peng was accused by the Red Guards of plotting a coup in February 1966, and was castigated as the chief of the Peking "black gang."

Peng was "rehabilitated" in late 1978, and in early 1979 was renamed to his post as chairman of the Peking municipal party committee, replacing the radical Wu De, who had succeeded Peng in 1966. In February 1979 Peng was named chairman of China's new legal commission, charged with overseeing the proposed new law and criminal codes instituted in early 1980. In July Peng was named a vice chairman of the standing committee of the National People's Congress (NPC) and in September was restored to his place on the ruling Politburo. In November he succeeded Ji Pengfei as acting secretary general of the standing committee of the NPC.

Peng's administrative abilities and organizational talents, as well as his close relationship with Deng Xiaoping and other moderate leaders, seemed to indicate that he might assume even more important functions in Peking in the future.

Rong Yiren (ca. 1916-   )

(Jung I-jen)

The son of a wealthy owner of a nation-wide flour business, Rong graduated from St. John's University in Shanghai and gradually came to manage and expand his father's business. After the Communist victory in 1949 Rong moved to support the new regime. Already a multi-millionaire, Rong was paid handsomely for his business when it was taken over during the 1950s. In 1956 he was named a deputy mayor of Shanghai and in 1959 was called to Peking and named vice minister of textiles. During the Cultural Revolution Rong came under heavy attack, his house was sacked, and he and his wife were beaten by Red Guards.

Rong was later "rehabilitated," and in the summer of 1979 was named to head the newly-formed China International Trust and Investment Co. (CITIC), designed to administer China's drive to attract foreign capital and oversee Chinese joint ventures with foreign companies.

Qiao Guanhua (1908-   )

(Ch'iao Kuan-hua)

Born in Yancheng, Jiangsu Province, Qiao graduated from Jinghua University and also studied in Germany. He returned to China in 1937 and worked for the *New China*

Daily News in the Nationalist capital of Chongqing during the war, 1937-45. After V-J Day he went to Hong Kong, where he became the director of the south China branch of the Xinhua news agency.

After the CCP victory in 1949, Qiao returned to Peking and worked in the foreign ministry while editing and writing for several communist publications.

In 1964 Qiao was named a vice minister of foreign affairs under Chen Yi, and was promoted to foreign minister in November 1974. Removed from his position in December 1976, he has been attacked repeatedly in the news media since then for his alleged association with the radical "gang of four" during and after the Cultural Revolution. Although Qiao himself was a protégé of Chou En-lai, his wife was apparently a close friend of Jiang Qing. In February 1978 he was reported under detention.

Seypidin (1916-   )

(Saifudin)

Born into a Uygur merchant family in Xinjiang Province, Seypidin received his early education there before going to the Soviet Union to study law and politics at Tashkent University, where he joined the Russian Communist Party. He returned to Xinjiang and participated in the Uygur autonomy movement of the 1930s. When this was suppressed, he fled to the Soviet Union, then lived for several years in Afghanistan. He returned home in 1944 and participated in further autonomy movements at that time. During the civil war, 1945-49, the province had become effectively independent.

After the Communist victory in 1949, Seypidin was one of the members of the delegation from previously autonomous Xinjiang that travelled to both Peking and Moscow to negotiate the best deal for the province's new status. He joined the CCP at this time and was named vice chairman of the province in 1954. In 1955, when it was renamed the Xinjiang Uygur Autonomous Region, Seypidin was elected chairman of its government. In August 1973 he was elected to alternate membership in the ruling Politburo and was reelected in 1977. In 1974 Seypidin was also named Xinjiang party chief and political commissar of the military units stationed there. In early 1978, however, it was reported that he had been stripped of all posts except for his largely honorary Politburo membership.

Song Qingling (1892-   )

(Soong Ch'ing-ling)

Born in Shanghai, Song graduated from Wesleyan College for Women in Macon, Georgia, in 1913. Returning to China, she married Sun Yat-sen in 1914. Her sister later married Chiang Kai-shek. When Sun died in 1925, Mme. Sun entered political life and was elected to the Central Committee of the KMT. She was associated with the leftists in the party who were purged in 1927.

Song resumed the use of her maiden name during World War II; in 1949, when the Nationalists fled to Taiwan, she remained on the mainland. Since that time she has held a number of high but largely honorary positions in the Chinese Communist Party, including vice chairman of the standing committee of the NPC. Nonetheless, she remained important to the Communists in their efforts to persuade others that they, and not the Nationalists, are the true heirs of China's most important revolutionary symbol, Sun Yat-sen.

Ulanhu (1903-   )

(Ulanfu)

Born in Inner Mongolia (Nei Mongol A.R.), Ulanhu is a Tumet Mongol, a small but relatively Sinocentric group of Mongols in northwest China. Ulanhu went to Peking to study during the 1920s, and soon became active in radical politics and the Communist Youth League. He was sent to Sun Yat-sen University in Moscow in 1925 and joined the CCP there in 1927. He returned home in 1929 and began organizing pro-communist, anti-Japanese movements in the northwest. During the war with Japan, 1937-45, Ulanhu made his way to Communist headquarters at Yanan, his first direct contact with the central party leadership apparatus. During the war he remained in Yanan, where he organized and trained other Mongolian cadres for the day when they could return home. During the civil war, 1945-49, Ulanhu was active in Inner Mongolia, where units loyal to him coordinated with Communist troops to fight against both the Kuomintang and Mongol autonomists. After the CCP victory in 1949 it was Ulanhu who was made responsible for bringing the area under Peking's control, a process that had been virtually completed by 1952, when he was named governor. Ulanhu continued to dominate the politics of the region and, in 1956, was elected to alternate membership on the ruling Politburo. In 1967, during the height of the Cultural Revolution, Ulanhu was attacked and stripped of all his posts. He was "rehabilitated" in 1973 and elected to regular membership in the Politburo in August 1977.

Wang Dongxing (1906-   )

(Wang Tung-hsing)

Born to a poor peasant family in Jiangxi Province, Wang lost both parents while he was still young, and he received little if any formal education. After joining a Red Army unit in Jiangxi, in 1933 he was made Mao Tse-tung's personal bodyguard, a post he would continue to hold with unquestioning devotion until Mao's death.

In addition to protecting Mao, who taught him to read, Wang was also Mao's valet, cook and, when the Chinese leader was ill, his nurse. As Mao's power grew, so did that of Wang, who was given responsibility for the security of all the major Communist leaders. By the 1950s he was not only vice minister of public security, but also commander of the "8341" unit, a code name for a 10,000-man security detail that also was used by Mao to spy on the Communist leaders it was supposed to protect. During the 1960s, Wang again became vice minister of public security, where he greatly expanded his power under a weak minister, Xie Fuzhi.

Because of his unswerving loyalty to Mao, Wang was an important supporter of the Cultural Revolution, which greatly increased his power. In 1966 he was named director of the General Office of the Central Committee, which replaced the Secretariat under the purged Deng Xiaoping and gave Wang almost undisputed control of the day-to-day workings of the party. As more and more leaders were purged, it was Wang's "8341" unit that carried out the arrests.

In 1969 Wang was elected an alternate member of the ruling Politburo, and in 1973 was elected to full membership. At some point during this period Wang became disenchanted with the radicals whom he had served in the Cultural Revolution. Whether this was because he felt that they could not win in the long run or because he feared that

China's Political Leaders

Chinese Communist Party
(Elected August 1977)

Chairman, Central Committee
Hua Guofeng

Vice Chairmen (5)
Chen Yun [1]
Deng Xiaoping

Li Xiannian
Wang Dongxing [3]
Ye Jianying

Politburo of the Central Committee (30)

Standing Committee (6)
Chen Yun [1]
Deng Xiaoping
Hua Guofeng

Li Xiannian
Wang Dongxing [3]
Ye Jianying

Regular Members (22)
Chen Xilian [3]
Chen Yonggui [3]
Deng Yingchao [1]
Fang Yi
Geng Biao
Hu Yaobang [1]
Ji Dengkui [3]
Li Desheng
Liu Bocheng [3]
Ni Zhifu
Nie Rongzhen

Peng Chong
Peng Zhen [2]
Ulanhu
Wang Zhen [1]
Wei Guoqing
Wu De [3]
Xu Xiangqian
Xu Shiyou
Yu Qiuli
Zhang Tingfa
Zhao Ziyang [2]

Alternate Members (2)
Chen Muhua [4]

Seypidin [3]

National People's Congress
(Elected February 1978)

Chairman, Standing Committee [6]
Ye Jianying

Chinese Government
State Council
(Appointed February 1978)

Premier
Hua Guofeng

Vice Premiers (18)
Bo Yibo [2]
Chen Muhua [4]
Chen Xilian [3]
Chen Yonggui [3]
Chen Yun [2]
Deng Xiaoping
Fang Yi
Geng Piao
Gu Mu

Ji Dengkui [3]
Ji Pengfei [2]
Kang Shi'en
Li Xiannian
Wang Zhen
Wang Renzhong [2]
Xu Xiangqian
Yao Yilin [2]
Yu Qiuli

Prominent Ministers [5]
Xu Xiangqian (National Defense)
Huang Hua (Foreign Affairs)
Jiang Nanxiang [2] (Education)
Huang Zhen (Culture)
Yao Yilin [1] (Communications)
Li Qiang (Foreign Trade)
Wu Bo (Finance)
Chen Muhua [4] (Economic Relations with Foreign Countries)

Chen Yun [2] (State Financial and Economic Commission)
Wang Renzhong [2] (State Agricultural Commission)
Gu Mu (State Capital Construction Commission)
Kang Shi'en (State Economic Commission)
Yu Qiuli (State Planning Commission)
Fang Yi (State Scientific and Technological Commission)

---

[1] *Added 1978*
[2] *Added 1979*
[3] *Inactive*

[4] *Female*
[5] *There are 38 ministries and 10 commissions in all.*
[6] *There are 21 vice chairmen.*

---

they were denying him access to Mao, Wang began to disassociate himself from them.

After the death of Mao in October 1976, it was Wang's use of the "8341" unit that arrested the so-called "gang of four" and brought Hua Guofeng to power. As a reward for his services, he was elected one of four vice chairmen of the party in 1977, as well as to the standing committee of the Politburo, making him the fifth ranking party member after Hua.

But a wall poster campaign was launched against him in late 1978. In December it was reported that he had been removed as head of the party's General Office, which was then disbanded, and as commander of the "8341" unit. In 1979 a new wall poster campaign charged him with embezzling state funds and identified him as a leader of the so-called "whateverist faction," a group which was accused of doing whatever Mao ordered. Although he had not been purged from the Politburo as of early 1980, Wang had not

been seen publicly for some time, and probably had lost all power within the government.

Due to the secretive nature of his work, reports of Wang's private life are all but non-existent.

Wang Hongwen (ca. 1936-)

(Wang Hung-wen)

Wang was probably born in Jilin Province. Accounts of his early life are sketchy, although he may have had a university education.

At the beginning of the Cultural Revolution in 1966, Wang was a local party leader in a Shanghai cotton mill. On June 12 he and six others put up a wall poster critical of the factory's managers and local Shanghai leaders. After the rebellious workers were suppressed, Wang took his case to Peking, where he was encouraged in his efforts by Jiang

Qing and Chen Boda, then the leaders of the Cultural Revolution. Wang returned to Shanghai and organized the "Shanghai Workers' Revolutionary Rebel General Headquarters." This group linked up with other, similar organizations and seized power in Shanghai in early 1967. When the Shanghai revolutionary committee was established in February, Wang was named deputy chairman under Zhang Chunqiao. Wang's organizational talents and his loyalty to Zhang led, in April 1969, to his election to the Central Committee of the CCP. In January 1971 he was named third-ranking member of the revived Shanghai Municipal Party Committee where, due to the prolonged absence of his superiors Yao Wenyuan and Zhang in Peking, Wang was responsible for the day-to-day administration of the world's most populous city. In September 1972 Wang was called to Peking, where he was frequently linked with Mao. In September 1972 Wang made an even more incredible advance when he was elected second vice chairman of the CCP, ranking below only Mao and Chou En-lai. The move stunned observers, who were still divided seven years later over the reasons for what must have been Mao's personal intervention in Wang's behalf.

In August 1973 Wang's career continued to rise, and he was elected to the standing committee of the Politburo. By this time, analysts often listed Wang as a likely successor to Mao.

In October 1976, however, following Mao's death and Hua Guofeng's coup against the radicals, Wang found himself under arrest and identified as one of the "gang of four," a group which was being blamed for virtually every ill which China had suffered during the past decade. It has been reported that Wang and the other members of the "gang" would be placed on public trial in 1980.

Wang Renzhong (1906-)

(Wang Jen-chung)

Little is known about Wang's early life. Born in Hebei Province, in 1934 he entered a Communist-sponsored school in Shaanxi Province and later worked behind the Japanese lines under Li Xiannian.

In 1949 Wang was named deputy governor under Li of Hubei Province, where he performed administrative and fiscal duties. In October 1952 he was transferred to Wuhan as deputy mayor, and in 1954 was named Wuhan party chief and acting mayor. He then was selected as Hubei provincial party leader, 1955-68, and was later named second secretary, 1961-66, and then first secretary of the Central-South party bureau, 1966-67.

With the advent of the Cultural Revolution Wang, like many local party leaders, at first expressed strong support for the new campaign. He was thus named to the Cultural Revolution Group and promoted to the ruling Politburo in August 1966. But Wang soon came under Red Guard attack and, despite organizing his own force to fight the radicals, was purged of all his posts in 1967.

After Hua Guofeng's coup against the radicals in 1976, Wang was "rehabilitated," and soon became second party secretary of Shaanxi. Following the ouster of his superior, who had been identified with the "gang of four," Wang was named Shaanxi party chief in late 1978. In December of that year he was elected to the CCP Central Committee.

In February 1979 Wang was also named a vice premier and minister in charge of the State Agriculture Commission, which oversees China's entire agricultural sector.

Wang Zhen (1909-)

(Wang Chen)

Born to a poor peasant family in Liuyang County, Hunan Province, Wang received only three years of schooling before leaving home at the age of 12. He went to work as a railroad worker in Changsha and joined the union there in 1924. He participated in the strikes led by CCP organizers, became an officer in the union, and joined the CCP in 1927. At this point, with the unions crushed, he returned to his native Liuyang to organize guerrilla forces. He participated with He Long in the Long March, 1935, and served as a military commander under He during the war with Japan, 1937-45, and under Li Xiannian during the civil war, 1946-49.

After the CCP victory in 1949, Wang was sent to the northwest, where he was named deputy (under Peng Dehuai) and then commander of the Xinjiang military region. With the government reorganization of 1954 Wang was recalled to Peking, where he was named commander and political commissar of the PLA's railroad corps. In 1956 he was named minister of state farms and land reclamation. During the Cultural Revolution, Wang came under Red Guard attack and was purged in 1967.

After the resurgence of the moderates, Wang was named a vice premier in January 1975 and elected to the ruling Politburo in December 1978. In July 1979 he was named a member of Chen Yun's powerful State Financial and Economic Commission which has authority over China's modernization effort.

Wang, married four times, reportedly has had one daughter and three sons.

Wei Guoqing (1906-)

(Wei Kuo-ch'ing)

Born in Donglan County, Guangxi Province, Wei is not Chinese but is of Zhuang nationality. After receiving a secondary education, Wei joined a warlord army in south China. In 1929 he participated in a communist uprising within this force and then served as a regimental commander under Deng Xiaoping in Deng's Guangxi soviet. When this group was suppressed in 1931, Wei made his way to Mao's Jiangxi soviet, where he served under Peng Dehuai. Wei participated in the Long March, 1934-35, and continued to rise in the military during the war with Japan and the civil war, 1937-49, finally emerging as a corps commander.

In 1950 Wei became deputy mayor of Fuzhou, but was transferred to his native Guangxi to work in the local party there in 1953. In 1955 he was named to the top government post in Guangxi, and in 1961 was also named provincial party chief.

When the Cultural Revolution broke out in 1966, Wei organized his own groups to oppose the Red Guards, and serious fighting broke out all over the area. One of the most important results was the blocking of Soviet arms shipments to Vietnam as both sides looted trains for weapons. Unlike most other local leaders, however, and despite Peking's intervention, Wei was able to hold onto his posts.

In August 1973 Wei was elected to the ruling Politburo, and in October 1975 was transferred to Canton as Guangdong Province party chief, succeeding another supporter of Deng Xiaoping, Zhao Ziyang. Wei was re-elected to the Politburo in 1977, and in September of that year was called to Peking, where he was named director of the General Political Department of the PLA, a post which had been vacant since the ouster of the radical Zhang Chunqiao the year before.

The close ties between Wei and the moderates, particularly Deng, seemed to indicate that he would continue to exert influence in the future.

Wu De (1914-   )

(Wu Teh)

Born in Fengrun County, Hebei Province, Wu joined the CCP while a university student in Peking and performed organizational work for the Communists in north China during the 1930s. During the war with Japan, 1937-45, Wu served in the army as a political commissar. After the CCP victory in 1949, Wu remained in north China and rose in the party bureaucracy. He was mayor of Tianjin, 1953-55, and first secretary of the Jilin Provincial Party Committee, 1956-66. In July 1966 he was appointed deputy mayor of Peking and became mayor after the ouster of Peng Zhen by the radicals. In March 1967 he became concurrent chairman of the Peking Party Committee and later was named chairman of the Peking Revolutionary Committee.

Wu continued to rise after the Cultural Revolution, and was elected to the ruling Politburo in 1973. In 1976, following the death of Zhu De, Wu replaced him as acting chairman of the standing committee of the National People's Congress. When the radicals were ousted in October, Wu tried to switch sides, despite his earlier opposition to the moderates and Deng Xiaoping. His bid failed, however, and his power began to decline in 1977, when a wall poster campaign named him as a leader of the "wind faction" — a group of leaders said to be trying to shift with the wind. In October 1978 he was stripped of all his posts except his Politburo membership. As of early 1980, he had not been seen in public for some time.

Xu Shiyou (1906-   )

(Hsü Shih-yu)

Born to a poor peasant family in Huangan County, Hubei Province, Xu received little formal education but studied Chinese martial arts for a short time. He began his military career with a warlord army, but rebelled in 1927 and linked up with the CCP. During the 1930s he served under Zhang Guotao and Xu Xiangqian in the Eyuwan soviet, where he rose to become regimental commander. After the Long March, Xu was a divisional and then a corps commander. During the war with Japan, Xu served as a brigade commander under Liu Bocheng in Shandong. Xu's units stayed there during the civil war and, in 1949, he was named commander of the Shandong military district.

In early 1955 Xu was transferred to command of the important Nanjing military region and elected an alternate member of the Central Committee the following year. In 1959 he was appointed vice minister of national defense under Lin Piao. In March 1968 he left Peking and was named secretary of the Jiangsu revolutionary committee. With the increase in importance of the army following its intervention in the Cultural Revolution, Xu also profited: he was elected to the ruling Politburo in April 1969. At this point, he controlled all the top army, party and government posts in Jiangsu.

In August 1973, despite the ouster of most military commanders following the attempted coup by Lin Piao, Xu was neither fired nor transferred, and was re-elected to the Politburo. In early 1977, he was transferred to Canton, although the significance of the move was not clear. In August of that year he was re-elected to the Politburo; he continued to command the Canton military region.

Xu Xiangqian (1902-   )

(Hsü Hsiang-ch'ien)

Xu was born in Wutai, Shanxi Province, received an education in the Chinese classics, and became a teacher in his native town. In 1924 he joined the Kuomintang and went to Canton, where he graduated in the famous first class of the Whampoa Military Academy.

After participating in various Nationalist military expeditions, Xu joined the CCP in 1927 and helped lead several uprisings. After these were crushed he fled to Shanghai and then made his way to the Eyuwan soviet area, where he became the ranking military leader under the political commissar Zhang Guotao. After the KMT defeated his armies, he and Zhang made their own Long March, separate from that of Mao Tse-tung and Zhu De. The two forces linked up in the summer of 1935, but Mao and Zhang soon fell out over leadership of the reunited CCP, and Xu withdrew his units to establish a base of his own. This was soon destroyed by the KMT. Zhang fled from China, and Xu made his way to Yanan in 1937. During the war with Japan, 1937-45, Xu held a number of important military commands in the Communist army.

After the CCP victory in 1949, Xu held few positions of real importance, although he continued to appear on ceremonial occasions. In 1955 he was one of ten former military commanders named as marshals of the PRC.

In 1966, Xu came out of semi-retirement to head the Cultural Revolution Group in the People's Liberation Army, but soon ran afoul of Jiang Qing, and was purged from his new posts.

Xu enjoyed a second renaissance in the 1970s when he took over as minister of defense in 1976. In 1977, he was re-elected to the Politburo and was named a vice premier in 1978.

Despite his apparent position as one of the most powerful men in China, Xu's age and ill health seemed to indicate that his power was more apparent than real.

Yao Wenyuan (ca. 1920-   )

An obscure literary critic from Shanghai, Yao was of little significance until 1965, when he emerged as the chief spokesman and propagandist for the Cultural Revolution. Closely tied to Jiang Qing, Yao was elected to the Politburo in 1969, but was purged of all his posts and named a member of the "gang of four" in 1976.

Yao Yilin (1911-   )

(Yao I-lin)

Born in Jiangxi Province, Yao began his career as a student organizer for the CCP in north China during the mid-1930s. With the Communist victory in 1949, Yao was named vice minister of trade, 1949-52, vice minister of commerce, 1952-58, then minister of commerce, 1960-67. With the onset of the Cultural Revolution, Yao was accused of being a "counterrevolutionary revisionist" and stripped of all his posts in 1967.

After the radicals were driven from power in 1976, Yao was "rehabilitated" and reappointed minister of commerce in August 1978. In July 1979 he was named a vice premier and also placed on Chen Yun's powerful State Financial and Economic Commission, the overseer of China's modernization effort.

Ye Jianying (1898-   )

(Yeh Chien-ying)

Born in Mei County, Guangdong Province, Ye received a traditional education and later traveled with his father through Southeast Asia in preparation for a career in business. Ye rejected this prospect, however, and enrolled in the Yunnan Military Institute, a revolutionary hotbed which also produced Zhu De. After graduation in 1919, Ye joined the forces of Sun Yat-sen in 1923 and in 1924 was named deputy director of instruction at Chiang Kai-shek's Whampoa Military Academy at Canton, a post equal in rank to that of Chou En-lai at the time. Although possibly already a member of the CCP, Ye participated in the Northern Expedition, serving directly under Chiang. When the CCP and the Kuomintang split in 1927, Ye went with the Communists and helped organize several uprisings which were defeated. Ye then fled to the Soviet Union, where he studied for several years.

He returned to China in 1931 and made his way to the Jiangxi soviet, where he joined Zhu and Mao Tse-tung. During the 1930s he served as commandant of the Red Army Academy and chief of staff of the Red Army, under Zhu De. He participated in the Long March, 1934-35, again as chief of staff, a post he also held under Zhu during the war with Japan and the civil war, 1937-49; he participated in the truce talks with the KMT in 1946.

After the Communist victory in 1949, Ye was sent to his native Guangdong to finish the military campaigns against remnant KMT forces and bring the area under the control of Peking. During this period, he held virtually undisputed power in south China. In 1954, when the government reorganized, Ye was called to Peking, where he was named director of the inspection department of the People's Liberation Army and a vice chairman of the National Defense Council.

In 1966, at the beginning of the Cultural Revolution, Ye was named to the CCP Secretariat, to the ruling Politburo, and as a vice chairman of the Military Affairs Commission. Following the death of Lin Piao in 1971, Ye took over administration of China's military, became a vice chairman of the party in 1973, and was formally named minister of defense in 1975.

In 1976 Ye played a crucial role in the success of Hua Guofeng's coup against the radicals and emerged — with Hua and Wang Dongxing — as one of the triumverate ruling China after that date. It has been surmised that Ye was instrumental in securing support of the army for the coup.

Ye was one of five men elected to the standing committee of the Politburo in August 1977. He relinquished his defense ministry at about this time, succeeded by Xu Xiangqian. He was named to the important position as chairman of the standing committee of the National People's Congress, China's nominal parliament, in February 1978, effectively making him chief of state. Despite his age and poor health, Ye continued to be one of the three key members of the leadership group ruling China in 1980.

Like many other Chinese Communist leaders, little is known about Ye's personal life. It is generally believed that he opposed such Maoist excesses as the Great Leap Forward, 1958, and the Cultural Revolution. He is also thought to be a firm supporter of a modernization, regularization,

and systematic upgrading of China's army — policies which had been opposed by Lin Piao and supported by the re-emerging economic planners under Deng Xiaoping.

Reportedly, Ye was married twice. His first wife was the daughter of a wealthy Chinese merchant from Malaya. He married again in 1935. He has had two sons and two daughters.

Yu Qiuli (1914-   )

(Yü Ch'iu-li)

Born in Sichuan Province, Yu — of whose early life little is known — apparently began his career in 1934 as a bodyguard for a Communist corps commander then in Sichuan. During the war with Japan and the civil war, 1937-49, Yu served as a middle-ranking political commissar in the army under He Long. During the Korean War, Yu served as a political commissar under Peng Dehuai. In 1954 he was transferred to directorship of the political department, Lanzhou military region. In 1956 he was named director of the finance department of the army, a post he held for one year. In 1958 he retired from the army and was named minister of the petroleum industry. In this post, and with the assistance of his deputy, Kang Shi'en, he was responsible for developing the Daqing oil fields, still China's most productive internal oil source. In November 1965 he was named vice chairman of the State Planning Commission, while Kang took over as acting oil minister.

During the Cultural Revolution, Yu came under severe Red Guard criticism and suffered a heart attack. Nonetheless, he was never purged due to Chou En-lai's protection — one of three cases in which Chou intervened. In April 1969 Yu was elected to the Central Committee and in October 1972 was named chairman of the extremely important State Planning Commission, a post he still held in 1980. In January 1975 Yu was named a vice premier, and in August 1977 was elected to the ruling Politburo, two other posts he still held in 1980.

One of the youngest of the central economic planners, Yu's jobs are extremely important to China's modernization plans.

Zhang Chungiao (ca. 1912-   )

(Chang Ch'un-ch'iao)

Zhang did propaganda work for the Communists behind the Japanese lines during World War II. After the Communist victory in 1949, he was sent to Shanghai, where he rose to head the *Liberation Daily* in 1954. In 1966, Zhang — an ardent supporter of Mao Tse-tung — was named chief of the Cultural Revolution Group, one of two ad hoc bodies directing the movement. In 1967 he became head of the Shanghai municipal administration. He was added to the Politburo in 1969 and the standing committee in 1973.

In January 1976 Zhang found himself locked in a bitter struggle with moderate Deng Xiaoping to succeed Chou En-lai, but the post went to Hua Guofeng, who then purged Zhang and the other radicals in the "gang of four."

Zhang Tingfa (ca. 1909-   )

(Chang T'ing-fa)

Almost nothing is known in the West about Zhang, who apparently began his career serving in the 1st Field Army under He Long. In 1956 he was reported to be serving as deputy chief of staff of the air force, and was later promoted to chief of staff. In February 1964 he was named deputy commander of the air force but was purged in 1967 as Lin Piao tightened his hold over the service. Zhang was restored to his post in 1973 and, in April 1977, was promoted to commander of the air force. In August 1977 Zhang was elected to the ruling Politburo, a post he still held in 1980.

Zhao Ziyang (1919-)

(Chao Tzu-yang)

Born to a landlord family in Henan Province, Zhao received only a middle school education. Little is known about his early career, but in 1948 he was reported holding a mid-level party post in Guangdong Province. After the Great Leap Forward in 1958, he apparently sided with Liu Shao-ch'i and Deng Xiaoping in restructuring the economy and instituting material incentives in Guangdong. In 1965 he was promoted to first secretary of the Guangdong party committee and secretary of the South China party bureau.

With the outbreak of the Cultural Revolution in 1966, Zhao came under severe attack from the Red Guards. There was fierce fighting in Canton, provincial capital of Guangdong, and in January 1967 Zhao was ousted from his posts as the fighting continued.

In May 1971 Zhao was "rehabilitated," but sent to Inner Mongolia (Nei Mongol A.R.) to work in the party office there. He returned to Guangdong the following year to help wrest control of the local party organization from the followers of Lin Piao. In 1974, following the breakup of military control over the party, Zhao was renamed first secretary of the Guangdong Party Committee and chairman of the revolutionary committee.

In October 1975 Zhao was succeeded by another supporter of Deng Xiaoping, Wei Guoqing, and transferred to become party chief of Deng's native Sichuan Province. In August 1977 he was elected an alternate member of the ruling Politburo. In September 1979 he was elevated to regular membership, a position he still held in 1980 in addition to his jobs in Sichuan.

Besides his loyalty to Deng and his policies, Zhao's relative youth and his demonstrated abilities appeared to mark him as an important leader for the future.

Zhu De (1886-1976)

(Chu Teh)

Born in Yilong County, Sichuan Province, Zhu began his career in the warlord armies of southern China, where he also became an opium smoker. In 1921, after meeting Sun Yat-sen and Ch'en Tu-hsiu, the founder of the CCP, Zhu decided to start anew. He broke his opium habit and went to Europe for study. There he met Chou En-lai and spent a year studying in Germany, where he joined the CCP. After participating in several strikes and demonstrations, he was expelled from Germany in 1926. He returned to China and joined the Nationalist army, concealing his party membership.

On Aug. 1, 1927, Zhu, already a general, participated in a Communist attempt to seize Nanchang, the capital of Jiangxi Province. The Nanchang Uprising, now celebrated as the birth of the Red Army, was defeated, and Zhu fled southward with his remnant units. In April 1928 he joined the forces of Mao Tse-tung, with Zhu as commander and Mao as political commissar. It was a propitious union, and the two retained their division of authority well into the 1950s. In 1930 Zhu was named commander-in-chief of all the Chinese Communist armies, a post he held until 1954.

During the war years, 1937-49, Zhu was the number-two man in the party under Mao.

In 1949 Zhu was elected senior vice chairman of the new Communist government at Peking. In 1954, with the promulgation of China's first constitution, the army was placed under the Ministry of Defense, headed by Peng Dehuai, and Zhu lost his position as commander-in-chief. At the same time, he was elected vice chairman of the People's Republic of China. In 1958, when Mao resigned as chairman of the government, some analysts expected that Zhu would succeed him, but the post went instead to Liu Shao-ch'i (Liu Shaoqi) in 1959. Zhu remained as a senior stateman of the party until his death in 1976.

Zhu was married four times, two marriages ending in the death of his spouse and one in separation. He married for the last time in 1929.

Among the many remarkable commanders who served under Mao prior to 1949, Zhu was undoubtedly the most important. With Mao, he mapped and implemented the essential strategies which allowed the small Communist armies to perform so successfully until their victory in 1949.

Nationalist Chinese Leaders

Chang Ch'ün (1899-)

(Zhang Qun)

Born in Huayang, Sichuan Province, Chang was a longtime friend and supporter of Nationalist President Chiang Kai-shek. Although his early training was in the military, Chang served most of his life in political posts, including Nationalist minister of foreign affairs, 1935-37, and secretary general of the National Defense Council, 1938-42. After the Communist takeover of the mainland, Chang went to Taiwan, where he was appointed secretary general of the president's office in 1954. After Chiang's death in 1975, Chang continued to be a powerful, if unseen, force in politics on Taiwan as one of the last two representatives (with Ho Ying-ch'in) of Chiang Kai-shek's "old guard."

Ch'en Ch'eng (1897-1965)

(Chen Cheng)

Born in Qingtian County, Zhejiang Province, Ch'en was one of the most important Nationalist military commanders under Chiang Kai-shek. First joining Chiang in 1923, Ch'en rose so rapidly despite average talents that his contemporaries joked that he was actually Chiang's illegitimate son. With the Nationalist defeat in 1949, Ch'en went to Taiwan, where he was put in charge of the massive land reform project there. After its successful completion in 1953, Ch'en was elected vice president in 1954 and deputy party leader in 1957. By then, he was Chiang's heir-apparent. By the time of his death in 1965, Ch'en's position was being challenged by Chiang's son, Chiang Ching-kuo.

Ho Ying-ch'in (1890-   )

(He Yingqin)

Born in Xingyi, Guizhou Province, Ho was educated in military schools in China and Japan. In 1924 he joined Chiang Kai-shek and soon became Chiang's most important military subordinate. In 1944, under criticism from the United States, Ho was removed as minister of war because of his inefficiency, but Chiang renamed him to the post in 1948. Ho accompanied the Nationalists to Taiwan in 1949, but has held no regular governmental posts since then. Despite that, he continued to be one of the most powerful behind-the-scenes spokesmen for Chiang's conservative "old guard" on Taiwan.

Wellington Koo (1887-   )

(Gu Weijun)

Born in Jiading, Jiangsu Province, Koo was educated in Western schools in China, then went to the United States, where he received a doctorate in political science from Columbia University in 1912. Koo began his diplomatic career in 1915, representing the new Republic of China as minister to Mexico, Cuba and the United States. Afterwards, he served as ambassador for and foreign minister to a succession of governments in Peking, and was Chinese representative to the League of Nations, 1920-22. In 1932 Koo made peace with the Nationalists, who had ousted the warlords, and returned to the League of Nations until 1939. Koo also served as Nationalist ambassador to France, 1936-40; to Great Britain, 1941-46; to the United States, 1946-56; and to The Hague, 1958-67. Koo's long and effective career made him perhaps the only truly international diplomatic figure produced by China in modern times.

Soong Mei-ling (1897-   )

(Song Meiling)

Born in Shanghai, Soong received much of her early education in the United States and graduated from Wellesley College in 1917, by which time her elder sister — Song Qingling — had already married Sun Yat-sen. Soong married Chiang Kai-shek in 1927, and accompanied him on his various military campaigns, serving as his secretary and English language interpreter.

During World War II she traveled frequently to America where she was said to "have taken the country by charm." In 1943 she became the first Chinese and only the second woman to address a joint session of Congress. In 1948 she returned to the U.S. to plead for more American aid for the fast-disintegrating Nationalists, but had no success. Nonetheless, she was included on American lists of the ten most admired women in the world until 1967. By the late 1970s Soong — gravely ill — had taken up permanent residence in the U.S.

T. V. Soong (1894-1971)

(Song Ziwen)

Born in Shanghai, Soong was the younger brother of Mme. Sun Yat-sen (Song Qingling) and the elder brother of Mme. Chiang Kai-shek (Soong Mei-ling). Soong received a B.A. in economics from Harvard and did graduate work at Columbia University before 1923, when Sun Yat-sen re-cruited him to do financial work for his fledgling government in Canton. Soong made substantial contributions to economic management of the new regime, and continued to serve in a number of important financial, political and diplomatic posts in Nationalist China until 1950. When the government moved to Taiwan, Soong, discredited by his failure to halt the disastrous hyperinflation that wracked China, 1946-49, took up residence in New York, where he became a prominent figure in the so-called "China lobby." Despite his failures in the late 1940s, Soong continued to be regarded as one of the most capable officials of Nationalist China.

Sun Fo (1891-1973)

(Sun Ke)

Born in Xiangshan (Zhongshan) County, Guangdong Province, Sun received his early education in Honolulu, and later graduated from the University of California in 1916. He received an M.A. in economics from Columbia University in 1917. Sun held a number of positions under the Nationalists, including presidency of the Legislative Yuan from 1932 to 1948.

Sun was usually associated with the liberal wing of the Kuomintang, but lacked the leadership and ability to mount an effective challenge to Chiang Kai-shek despite several efforts. After the Nationalist defeat in 1949, Sun lived for a time in France and then in the United States. In 1964 he went to Taiwan, where he was given a sinecure.

T. F. Tsiang (1895-1965)

(Jiang Tingfu)

Born in Shaoyang County, Hunan Province, Tsiang studied the Chinese classics, then went to America, where he graduated from Oberlin College in 1918. He received a Ph.D. in British political history from Columbia University in 1923. Tsiang then returned to China, where he taught history and did research until 1935, when Chiang Kai-shek persuaded him to leave academic life. He was appointed Chinese ambassador to the Soviet Union in 1936, and served the Nationalists in a number of other political and diplomatic posts until 1947, when he was named China's permanent representative to the United Nations. In this capacity, Tsiang successfully blocked several Soviet-sponsored efforts to unseat his government and replace it with that of Peking. He was named Chinese ambassador to the United States in 1961, and served until 1965. He died in New York City later that year.

George K. C. Yeh (1904-   )

(Ye Gongchao)

Born in Canton, Yeh was educated in China until 1919, when he went to the United States and studied at Amherst College, where he became a favorite of poet Robert Frost. He graduated *magna cum laude* in 1924. In 1926 he received his M.A. from England's Cambridge University. For the next 12 years he taught in China.

During the war against Japan, Yeh entered public service. In 1950, when Ch'en Ch'eng formed his first Cabinet on Taiwan, Yeh was named minister of foreign affairs and played a major role in the negotiation of the mutual defense treaty with the United States in 1954. He was then appointed ambassador to the United States, 1958-61.

U.S. Policymakers

Dean Acheson (1893-1971)

After a career in the State Department, Acheson was named secretary of state by President Truman, 1949-53. One of the chief architects of the post-World War II American policy of containment of the Soviet Union, he helped formulate the Marshall Plan, the Truman Doctrine, NATO and the U.S. response to the invasion of Korea. Due to his refusal to allow the U.S. to become involved in the Chinese civil war by committing U.S. troops in support of Chiang Kai-shek, Acheson came under attack from congressional Republicans who labeled him the "Red Dean."

John Moore Allison (1905-)

A career foreign service officer who had considerable East Asian experience, Allison was named assistant secretary of state for Far Eastern affairs, 1952-53. He later served as ambassador to Japan, 1953-55; to Indonesia, 1955-57; and Czechoslovakia, 1958.

Jacob Beam (1908-)

A career diplomat, Beam was U.S. ambassador to Poland, 1957-1961, during which time he was the main contact between the U.S. and China, via the Chinese ambassador to Warsaw. Beam later served as U.S. ambassador to Czechoslovakia, 1966-69, and to the Soviet Union, 1969-73.

David K. E. Bruce (1898-1977)

A career foreign service officer, Bruce served as ambassador to France, 1949-52; West Germany, 1957-59; and Great Britain, 1961-69. From 1970-71 he was the chief U.S. representative to the Vietnam peace talks in Paris. With the establishment of liaison offices in China and the U.S. in May 1973, President Nixon named Bruce head of the U.S. Liaison Office in Peking, and he held this post until 1974, when he was named ambassador to NATO.

Zbigniew Brzezinski (1928-)

Born in Poland, Brzezinski was raised and educated in Canada before graduating with a Ph.D. from Harvard University in 1953. After teaching at Harvard and Columbia Universities, he became a State Department adviser in 1966, as well as a member of various "think tanks." In 1977 President Carter named him national security adviser. Brzezinski is considered somewhat of a hard-liner on the Soviet Union, and favors using China to check Soviet power.

William P. Bundy (1917-)

After working for several years with the CIA, Bundy served as assistant secretary of state for East Asian and Pacific Affairs, 1964-69. He was named the editor of *Foreign Affairs* magazine in 1972.

George Bush (1924-)

A U.S. representative from Texas, 1967-71, and ambassador to the United Nations, Bush was later named chief of the U.S. Liaison Office in Peking, 1974-75. He was then recalled to Washington and named director of the CIA, 1976-77, and was a Republican presidential candidate in 1979-80.

James F. Byrnes (1879-1972)

A conservative, Byrnes served in the U.S. House of Representatives, 1911-25, the Senate 1931-41, and on the Supreme Court, 1943-45. Byrnes was then named secretary of state, 1945-47. In this post, he played a major role in Sino-American and Soviet-American relations. He was succeeded by George Marshall.

John Moors Cabot (1901-)

A career foreign service officer with some experience in East Asia, Cabot served as U.S. ambassador to Pakistan, 1952-53, Colombia, 1957-59, Brazil, 1959-61, and Poland, 1962-65. In the latter post, Cabot's talks with the Chinese ambassador to Warsaw were the only official contact between the U.S. and China during the period.

Charles T. Cross (1922-)

Born in China, Cross entered the foreign service in 1949 and served extensively in East Asia. He was named U.S. ambassador to Singapore, 1969-72, and chief of the new American Institute in Taiwan in 1979.

John Foster Dulles (1888-1959

Involved with foreign affairs since 1907, Dulles was named secretary of state by President Eisenhower, 1953-59. During his tenure, Dulles tried to surround and isolate China with a network of bilateral and multilateral alliances and by use of America's military might. This policy remained essentially unchanged until the late 1960s.

Thomas S. Gates (1906-)

A successful lawyer, Gates served as secretary of the Navy, 1957-59, and secretary of defense, 1959-61. He then became a director of several insurance companies until President Ford named him chief of the U.S. Liaison Office in Peking, 1976-77.

Marshall Green (1916-)

After a long career in East Asia, Green was named ambassador to Indonesia, 1965-69, assistant secretary of state for East Asian and Pacific affairs, 1969-73, and U.S. ambassador to Australia, 1973-75.

Jacob A. Gronouski (1919-)

A Ph.D. in economics, Gronouski served as postmaster general, 1963-65, and was then named U.S. ambassador to Poland, 1965-68, where he became the main contact for Sino-American relations in Warsaw.

Philip C. Habib (1920-)

A Ph.D. and career foreign service officer, Habib served as ambassador to South Korea, 1971-74, and assistant secretary of state for East Asian and Pacific affairs, 1974-76.

W. Averell Harriman (1891-   )

During his long career, Harriman served as U.S. ambassador to the Soviet Union, 1943-46, ambassador to Great Britain, 1946, secretary of commerce, 1946-49, and governor of New York, 1955-58. President Kennedy named him assistant secretary of state for Far Eastern affairs in 1961. Harriman reorganized and rejuvenated the office, which had been moribund since Sen. Joseph McCarthy's attacks on it during the 1950s.

Roger Hilsman (1919-   )

After serving with "Merrill's Marauders" in Burma during World War II, Hilsman later worked for the OSS and the CIA. A Ph.D., he was named director of the Bureau of Intelligence Research of the State Department by President Kennedy, 1961-63, and later became assistant secretary of state for Far Eastern affairs, 1963-64. In the latter two capacities, Hilsman played an important role in advocating a more open approach to China and an end to the isolation policy of the 1950s. In 1964 he became a professor of government at Columbia University.

Richard Holbrooke (1941-   )

After joining the foreign service in 1962, Holbrooke left to become the managing editor of *Foreign Policy* magazine, 1972-77. He returned to the State Department in 1977 as assistant secretary of state for East Asian and Pacific affairs.

Patrick J. Hurley (1883-1963)

A major general, Hurley served as secretary of war, 1929-33, and as President Roosevelt's personal representative to the Soviet Union, Afghanistan, India and China, 1942-43. He returned to China in 1944 with the rank of ambassador to ease the deadlocked KMT-CCP negotiations. Named ambassador to China, 1944-45, Hurley ultimately failed to bring about a truce, but his effort was continued by George Marshall. Hurley later blamed the breakdown on his betrayal by subordinate foreign service officers, and blamed Secretary of State Dean Acheson for "appeasement" of communism in Asia.

U. Alexis Johnson (1908-   )

A career foreign service officer with extensive experience in East Asia, Johnson served as U.S. ambassador to Czechoslovakia, 1953-58, during which time he held frequent meetings with the Chinese ambassador to Poland in Geneva. This was the only official point of contact between the two countries during the period. Johnson later served as ambassador to Thailand, 1958-61, ambassador to Japan, 1966-69, under secretary of state, 1969-73, and ambassador-at-large and chief of the U.S. delegation to the SALT talks, 1973-77.

Henry A. Kissinger (1923-   )

Born in Germany, Kissinger emigrated to the U.S. in 1938. He received his Ph.D. from Harvard University in 1954. After 1956 he became a leading authority on international relations and national defense policy. After Kissinger served as adviser to a series of presidents, Richard Nixon named him national security adviser in 1968. In this post, he and Nixon worked to put an end to the confrontation politics of the Cold War era and establish an environment in which nations could negotiate their differences. Kissinger used controversial means to end the war in Vietnam, instituted détente with the Soviets, and tried to settle the Middle East conflict and to end the U.S. isolation of China. He was named secretary of state in 1973, the first non-native American to hold the post. Kissinger has written extensively on foreign policy and defense issues, and was awarded the Nobel Peace Prize in 1973.

George C. Marshall (1880-1959)

A career army officer, Marshall served as chief of staff of the army during World War II and was sent to China by President Truman in 1946 to mediate between the CCP and the KMT. After his mission failed and full-scale civil war broke out, Marshall was recalled to Washington and named secretary of state, 1947-49, and secretary of defense, 1950-51. In 1953 he was awarded the Nobel Peace Prize for his efforts to aid war-ravaged Europe, called the Marshall Plan.

Walter S. Robertson (1893-1970)

After long experience in East Asian affairs, Robertson was named assistant secretary of state for Far Eastern affairs, 1953-59, serving under Secretary of State John Foster Dulles. He played an important role in implementing Dulles' policy of isolating China and was a firm supporter of the Nationalist Chinese on Taiwan.

William P. Rogers (1913-   )

A longtime friend and adviser of Richard Nixon, Rogers was named secretary of state by Nixon in January 1969. Although lacking significant background in foreign affairs, Rogers was well known for his skills as a negotiator. He was succeeded by the man many analysts were already calling the "real" secretary of state, Henry A. Kissinger, in 1973.

Dean Rusk (1909-   )

After serving in the China-Burma-India Theater during World War II, 1943-45, Rusk worked in the State Department, 1946-52, where he had an important role in shaping East Asia policy, serving as assistant secretary of state for Far Eastern affairs, 1950-51. After a stint as head of the Rockefeller Foundation, 1952-61, Rusk was named secretary of state by President John F. Kennedy and retained by Lyndon Johnson, 1961-68.

Walter J. Stoessel Jr. (1920-   )

A career foreign service officer, Stoessel was named U.S. ambassador to Poland, 1968-72. In this post, Stoessel served for a brief period as the official contact between Peking and Washington, before the talks were shifted to Paris. He was named U.S. ambassador to the Soviet Union, 1974-76, and to West Germany in 1977.

John Leighton Stuart (1876-1962)

An American missionary who first went to China in 1905, Stuart later served as president of Yenching (Yanjing) University in Peking, 1919-46, where he met and befriended many of contemporary China's leaders and intellectuals. As America tried to mediate an end to the Chinese civil war, Stuart served as U.S. ambassador to China, 1946-49, and fled the mainland after the Communist takeover.

Leonard Unger (1917-)

A longtime foreign service officer, Unger was U.S. ambassador to Laos, 1962-64; Thailand, 1967-73; and the Republic of China, 1974-78, the last man to hold the post prior to derecognition of the ROC in 1978.

Cyrus R. Vance (1917-)

A lawyer, Vance was named secretary of the Army, 1962-64, and served a number of presidents in a variety of trouble-shooting roles. He was named secretary of state in 1977, and traveled to China that year. He has been known for his advocacy of "evenhandedness" in dealing with the Soviet Union and China.

Arthur K. Watson (1919-1974)

President, 1954-63, and board chairman, 1963-70, of IBM, Watson was named U.S. ambassador to France, 1970-72. While in Paris, Watson became the contact for the ongoing conversations between Peking and Washington which had previously been conducted in Warsaw.

Leonard Woodcock (1911-)

A longtime officer of the United Auto Workers, Woodcock was elected president of the union in 1970 and held that post until 1977, when President Carter named him chief of the U.S. Liaison Office in Peking. When the U.S. established formal relations with China in 1979, Woodcock was named America's first ambassador.

TEXTS AND DOCUMENTS

Texts and Documents Relating to U.S.-China Relations

Truman Policy Statement

Following is the text of a statement made by President Truman on U.S. policy toward China on Dec. 15, 1945, on the eve of the mission to China by Gen. George C. Marshall:

The Government of the United States holds that peace and prosperity of the world in this new and unexplored era ahead depend upon the ability of the sovereign nations to combine for collective security in the United Nations organization.

It is the firm belief of this Government that a strong, united and democratic China is of the utmost importance to the success of this United Nations organization and for world peace. A China disorganized and divided either by foreign aggression, such as that undertaken by the Japanese, or by violent internal strife, is an undermining influence to world stability and peace, now and in the future. The United States Government has long subscribed to the principle that the management of internal affairs is the responsibility of the peoples of the sovereign nations. Events of this century, however, would indicate that a breach of peace anywhere in the world threatens the peace of the entire world. It is thus in the most vital interest of the United States and all the United Nations that the people of China overlook no opportunity to adjust their internal differences promptly by means of peaceful negotiation.

The Government of the United States believes it essential:

(1) That a cessation of hostilities be arranged between the armies of the National Government and the Chinese Communists and other dissident Chinese armed forces for the purpose of completing the return of all China to effective Chinese control, including the immediate evacuation of the Japanese forces.

(2) That a national conference of representatives of major political elements be arranged to develop an early solution to the present internal strife — a solution which will bring about the unification of China.

The United States and the other United Nations have recognized the present National Government of the Republic of China as the only legal government in China. It is the proper instrument to achieve the objective of a unified China.

The United States and the United Kingdom by the Cairo Declaration in 1943 and the Union of Soviet Socialist Republics by adhering to the Potsdam Declaration of last July and by the Sino-Soviet Treaty and Agreements of August 1945, are all committed to the liberation of China, including the return of Manchuria [Dongbei] to Chinese control. These agreements are made with the National Government of the Republic of China.

In continuation of the constant and close collaboration with the National Government of the Republic of China in the prosecution of this war, in consonance with the Potsdam Declaration, and to remove possibility of Japanese influence remaining in China, the United States has assumed a definite obligation in the disarmament and evacuation of the Japanese troops. Accordingly, the United States has been assisting and will continue to assist the National Government of the Republic of China in effecting the disarmament and evacuation of Japanese troops in the liberated areas. The United States Marines are in North China for that purpose.

The United States recognizes and will continue to recognize the National Government of China and cooperate with it in international affairs and specifically in eliminating Japanese influence from China. The United States is convinced that a prompt arrangement for a cessation of hostilities is essential to the effective achievement of this end. United States support will not extend to United States military intervention to influence the course of any Chinese internal strife.

The United States has already been compelled to pay a great price to restore the peace which was first broken by Japanese aggression in Manchuria. The maintenance of peace in the Pacific may be jeopardized, if not frustrated, unless Japanese influence in China is wholly removed and unless China takes her place as a unified, democratic and peaceful nation. This is the purpose of the maintenance for the time being of United States military and naval forces in China.

The United States is cognizant that the present National Government of China is a "one-party government" and believes that peace, unity and democratic reform in China will be furthered if the basis of this Government is broadened to include other political elements in the country. Hence, the United States strongly advocates that the national conference of representatives of major political elements in the country agree upon arrangements which would give those elements a fair and effective representation in the Chinese National Government. It is recognized that this would require modification of the one-party "political tutelage" established as an interim arrangement in the progress of the nation toward democracy by the father of the Chinese Republic, Doctor Sun Yat-sen [Sun Zhongshan].

The existence of autonomous armies such as that of the Communist army is inconsistent with, and actually makes impossible, political unity in China. With the institution of a broadly representative government, autonomous armies should be eliminated as such and all armed forces in China integrated effectively into the Chinese National Army.

In line with its often expressed views regarding self-determination, the United States Government considers that the detailed steps necessary to the achievement of political unity in China must be worked out by the Chinese themselves and that intervention by any foreign government in these matters would be inappropriate. The United States Government feels, however, that China has a clear responsibility to the other United Nations to eliminate armed conflict within its territory as constituting a threat to world stability and peace — a responsibility which is shared by the National Government and all Chinese political and military groups.

As China moves toward peace and unity along the lines described above, the United States would be prepared to assist the National Government in every reasonable way to rehabilitate the country, improve the agrarian and industrial economy, and establish a military organization capable of discharging China's national and international responsibilities for the maintenance of peace and order. In furtherance of such assistance, it would be prepared to give favorable consideration to Chinese requests for credits and loans under reasonable conditions for projects which would contribute toward the development of a healthy economy throughout China and healthy trade relations between China and the United States.

China Aid Act of 1948

Following is the text of Title IV of PL 80-472, the Foreign Assistance Act of 1948, authorizing $463 million for aid to China — $338 million for economic aid and $125 million for military aid. President Truman had requested $570 million in economic aid only. The bill was signed by President Truman on April 3, 1948.

Sec. 401. This title may be cited as the "China Aid Act of 1948."

Sec. 402. Recognizing the intimate economic and other relationships between the United States and China, and recognizing that disruption following in the wake of war is not contained by national frontiers, the Congress finds that the existing situation in China endangers the establishment of a lasting peace, the general welfare and national interest of the United States, and the attainment of the objectives of the United Nations. It is the sense of the Congress that the further evolution in China of Principles of individual liberty, free institutions, and genuine independence rests largely upon the continuing development of a strong and democratic national government as the basis for the establishment of sound economic conditions and for stable international economic relationships. Mindful of the advantages which the United States has enjoyed through the existence of a large domestic market with no internal trade barriers, and believing that similar advantages can accrue to China, it is declared to be the policy of the people of the United States to encourage the Republic of China and its people to exert sustained common efforts which will speedily achieve the internal peace and economic stability in China which are essential for lasting peace and prosperity in the world. It is further declared to be the policy of the people of the United States to encourage the Republic of China in its efforts to maintain the genuine independence and the administrative integrity of China, and to sustain and strengthen principles of individual liberty and free institutions in China through a program of assistance based on self-help and cooperation: *Provided,* That no assistance to China herein contemplated shall seriously impair the economic stability of the United States. It is further declared to be the policy of the United States that assistance provided by the United States under this title should at all times be dependent upon cooperation by the Republic of China and its people in furthering the program: *Provided further,* That assistance furnished under this title shall not be construed as an express or implied assumption by the United States of any responsibility for policies, acts, or undertakings of the Republic of China or for conditions which may prevail in China at any time.

Sec. 403. Aid provided under this title shall be provided under the applicable provisions of the Economic Cooperation Act of 1948 which are consistent with the purposes of this title. It is not the purpose of this title that China, in order to receive aid hereunder, shall adhere to a joint program for European recovery.

Sec. 404. (a) In order to carry out the purposes of this title, there is hereby authorized to be appropriated to the President for aid to China a sum not to exceed $338,000,000 to remain available for obligation for the period of one year following the date of enactment of this Act.

(b) There is also hereby authorized to be appropriated to the President a sum not to exceed $125,000,000 for additional aid to China through grants, on such terms as the President may determine and without regard to the provisions of the Economic Cooperation Act of 1948, to remain available for obligation for the period of one year following the date of enactment of this Act.

Sec. 405. An agreement shall be entered into between China and the United States containing those undertakings by China which the Secretary of State, after consultation with the Administrator for Economic Cooperation, may deem necessary to carry out the purpose of this title and to improve commercial relations with China.

Sec. 406. Notwithstanding the provisions of any other law, the Reconstruction Finance Corporation is authorized and directed, until such time as an appropriation is made pursuant to section 404, to make advances, not to exceed in the aggregate $50,000,000, to carry out the provisions of this title in such manner and in such amounts as the President shall determine. From appropriations authorized under section 404, there shall be repaid without interest to the Reconstruction Finance Corporation the advances made by it under the authority contained herein. No interest shall be charged on advances made by the Treasury to the Reconstruction Finance Corporation in implementation of this section.

Sec. 407. (a) The Secretary of State, after consultation with the Administrator, is hereby authorized to conclude an agreement with China establishing a Joint Commission on Rural Reconstruction in China, to be composed of two citizens of the United States appointed by the President of the United States and three citizens of China appointed by the President of China. Such Commission shall, subject to the direction and control of the Administrator, formulate and carry out a program for reconstruction in rural areas of China, which shall include such research and training activities as may be necessary to appropriate for such reconstruction: *Provided,* That assistance furnished under this section shall not be construed as an express or implied assumption by the United States of any responsibility for making any further contributions to carry out the purposes of this section.

(b) Insofar as practicable, an amount equal to not more than 10 per centum of the funds made available under subsection (a) of section 404 shall be used to carry out the purposes of subsection (a) of this section. Such amount may be in United States dollars, proceeds in Chinese currency from the sale of commodities made available to China with funds authorized under subsection (a) of section 404, or both.

Approved April 3, 1948.

Acheson States Policy in 1950

Following is the text of a speech made by Secretary of State Dean Acheson before the National Press Club on Jan. 12, 1950. In its publication of basic foreign policy documents, the State Department characterized the speech as "The basic position of the United States — review of the position as of 1950."

Foundations of Policy

This afternoon I should like to discuss with you the relations between the peoples of the United States and the peoples of Asia, and I used the words "relations of the peoples of the United States and the peoples of Asia" advisedly. I am not talking about governments or nations because it seems to me what I want to discuss with you is this feeling of mine that the relations depend upon the attitudes of the people; that there are fundamental attitudes, fundamental interests, fundamental purposes of the people of the United States, 150 million of them, and of the peoples of Asia, unnumbered millions, which determine and out of which grow the relations of our countries and the policies of our governments. Out of these attitudes and interests and purposes grow what we do from day to day.

Now, let's dispose of one idea right at the start and not bother with it any more. That is that the policies of the United States are determined out of abstract principles in the Department of State or in the White House or in the Congress. That is not the case. If these policies are going to be good, they must grow out of the fundamental attitudes of our people on both sides. If they are to be effective, they must become articulate through all the institutions of our national life, of which this is one of the greatest — through the press, through the radio, through the churches, through the labor unions, through the business organizations, through all the groupings of our national life, there must become articulate the attitudes of our people and the policies which we propose to follow. It seems to me that understanding is the beginning of wisdom and therefore, we shall begin by trying to understand before we announce what we are going to do, and that is a proposition so heretical in this town that I advance it with some hesitation.

Now, let's consider some of the basic factors which go into the making of the attitudes of the peoples on both sides. I am frequently asked: Has the State Department got an Asian policy? And it seems to me that that discloses such a depth of ignorance that it is very hard to begin to deal with it. The peoples of Asia are so incredibly diverse and their problems are so incredibly diverse that how could anyone, even the most utter charlatan believe that he had a uniform policy which would deal with all of them. On the other hand, there are very important similarities in ideas and in problems among the peoples of Asia and so what we come to, after we understand these diversities and these common attitudes of mind, is the fact that there must be certain similarities of approach, and there must be very great dissimilarities in action.

To illustrate this only a moment: If you will consider as an example of the differences in Asia the subcontinent of India and Pakistan, you will find there an area which is roughly comparable in size and population to Europe. You will find that the different states and provinces of that subcontinent are roughly comparable in size to the nations of Europe and yet you will find such differences in race, in ideas, in languages, and religion, and culture, that compared to that subcontinent, Europe is almost one homogeneous people.

Or take the difference, for instance, between the people and problems of Japan and Indonesia, both in the same Asian area. In Japan, you have a people far advanced in the complexities of industrial civilization, a people whose problems grow out of overpopulation on small islands and the necessity of finding raw materials to bring in and finding markets for the finished goods which they produce. In Indonesia, you find something wholly different — a people on the very threshold of their experience with these complexities and a people who live in an area which possesses vast resources which are awaiting development. Now, those are illustrations of complexities.

Emerging Independence

Let's come now to the matters which Asia has in common. there is in this vast area what we might call a developing Asian consciousness, and a developing pattern, and this, I think, is based upon two factors which are pretty nearly common to the entire experience of all these Asian people.

One of these factors is a revulsion against the acceptance of misery and poverty as the normal condition of life. Throughout all of this vast area, you have that fundamental revolutionary aspect in mind and belief. The other common aspect that they have is the revulsion against foreign domination. Whether that foreign domination takes the form of colonialism or whether it takes the form of imperialism, they are through with it. They have had enough of it, and they want no more.

These two basic ideas which are held so broadly and commonly in Asia tend to fuse in the minds of many Asian peoples and many of them tend to believe that if you could get rid of foreign domination, if you could gain independence, then the relief from poverty and misery would follow almost in course. It is easy to point out that that is not true, and of course, they are discovering that it is not true. But underneath that belief, there was a very profound understanding of a basic truth and it is the basic truth which underlies all our democratic belief and all our democratic concept. That truth is that just as no man and no government is wise enough or disinterested enough to direct the thinking and the action of another individual, so no nation and no people are wise enough and disinterested enough very long to assume the responsibility for another people or to control another people's opportunities.

That great truth they have sensed, and on that great truth they are acting. They say and they believe that from now on they are on their own. They will make their own decisions. They will attempt to better their own lot, and on occasion they will make their own mistakes. But it will be their mistakes, and they are not going to have their mistakes dictated to them by anybody else.

The symbol of these concepts has become nationalism. National independence has become the symbol both of freedom from foreign domination and freedom from the tyranny of poverty and misery.

Since the end of the war in Asia, we have seen over 500 million people gain their independence and over seven new nations come into existence in this area.

We have the Philippines with 20 million citizens. We have Pakistan, India, Ceylon, and Burma with 400 million citizens, southern Korea with 20 million, and within the last few weeks, the United States of Indonesia with 75 million.[1]

This is the outward and visible sign of the internal ferment of Asia. But this ferment and change is not restricted to these countries which are just gaining their independence. It is the common idea and the common pattern of Asia, and as I tried to suggest a moment ago, it is not based on purely political conceptions. It is not based purely on ideological conceptions. It is based on a fundamental and an earthy and a deeply individual realization of the problems of their own daily lives. This new sense of nationalism means that they are going to deal with those daily problems — the problems of the relation of man to the soil, the problem of how much can be exacted from them by the tax collectors of the state. It is rooted in those ideas. With those ideas they are going forward. Resignation is no longer the typical emotion of Asia. It has given way to hope, to a sense of effort, and in many cases, to a real sense of anger.

Recent Developments in China

Now, may I suggest to you that much of the bewilderment which has seized the minds of many of us about recent developments in China comes from a failure to understand this basic revolutionary force which is loose in Asia. The reasons for the fall of the Nationalist Government in China are preoccupying many people. All sorts of reasons have been attributed to it. Most commonly, it is said in various speeches and publications that it is the result of American bungling, that we are incompetent, that we did not understand, that American aid was too little, that we did the wrong things at the wrong time. Other people go on and say: "No, it is not quite that, but that an American general did not like Chiang Kai-shek and out of all that relationship grows the real trouble." And they say: "Well you have to add to that there are a lot of women fooling around in politics in China."

Nobody, I think, says that the Nationalist Government fell because it was confronted by overwhelming military force which it could not resist. Certainly no one in his right mind suggests that. Now, what I ask you to do is to stop looking for a moment under the bed and under the chair and under the rug to find out these reasons, but rather to look at the broad picture and see whether something doesn't suggest itself.

The broad picture is that after the war, Chiang Kai-shek emerged as the undisputed leader of the Chinese people. Only one faction, the Communists, up in the hills, ill-equipped, ragged, a very small military force, was determinedly opposed to his position. He had overwhelming military power, greater military power than any ruler had ever had in the entire history of China. He had tremendous economic and military support and backing from the United States. He had the acceptance of all other foreign countries, whether sincerely or insincerely in the case of the Soviet Union is not really material to this matter. Here he was in this position, and 4 years later what do we find? We find that his armies have melted away. His support in the country has melted away. His support largely outside the country has melted away, and he is a refugee on a small island off the coast of China with the remnants of his forces.

As I said, no one says that vast armies moved out of the hills and defeated him. To attribute this to the inadequacy of American aid is only to point out the depth and power of the forces which were miscalculated or ignored. What has happened in my judgment is that the almost inexhaustible patience of the Chinese people in their misery ended. They did not bother to overthrow this government. There was really nothing to overthrow. They simply ignored it throughout the country. They took the solution of their

Selections From the 'Little Red Book'...

The "Little Red Book" — quotations from Chairman Mao Tse-tung — was carried and read by millions of Chinese students, peasants, workers, Red Guards, etc. during the Cultural Revolution. The pages, about 3-1/2 by 5 inches in size, were bound by a bright red plastic cover with the title embossed in it. With a red ribbon attached as a marker, the 311-page booklet closely resembles a common prayer book or missal.

I. THE COMMUNIST PARTY

The force at the core leading our cause forward is the Chinese Communist Party.

The theoretical basis guiding our thinking is Marxism-Leninism.

> Opening address at the First Session of the First National People's Congress of the People's Republic of China (September 15, 1954).

If there is to be revolution, there must be a revolutionary party. Without a revolutionary party, without a party built on the Marxist-Leninist revolutionary theory and in the Marxist-Leninist revolutionary style, it is impossible to lead the working class and the broad masses of the people in defeating imperialism and its running dogs.

> "Revolutionary Forces of the World Unite, Fight Against Imperialist Aggression!" (November 1948), *Selected Works*, Vol. IV, p. 284.

Without the efforts of the Chinese Communist Party, without the Chinese Communists as the mainstay of the Chinese people, China can never achieve independence and liberation, or industrialization and the modernization of her agriculture.

> "On Coalition Government" (April 24, 1945), *Selected Works, Vol. III, p. 318.*

The Chinese Communist Party is the core of leadership of the whole Chinese people. Without this core, the cause of socialism cannot be victorious.

> Talk at the general reception for the delegates to the Third National Congress of the New-Democratic Youth League of China (May 25, 1957).

A well-disciplined Party armed with the theory of Marxism-Leninism, using the method of self-criticism and linked with the masses of the people; an army under the leadership of such a Party; a united front of all revolutionary classes and all revolutionary groups under the leadership of such a Party — these are the three main weapons with which we have defeated the enemy.

> "On the People's Democratic Dictatorship" (June 30, 1949), *Selected Works*, Vol. IV, p. 422.

We must have faith in the masses and we must have faith in the Party. These are two cardinal principles. If we doubt these principles, we shall accomplish nothing.

> *On the Question of Agricultural Cooperation* (July 31, 1955), 3rd ed., p. 7.

Armed with Marxist-Leninist theory and ideology, the Communist Party of China has brought a new style of work to the Chinese people, a style of work which essentially entails integrating theory with practice, forging close links with the masses and practicing self-criticism.

> "On Coalition Government" (April 24, 1945), *Selected Works*, Vol. III, p. 314.

No political party can possibly lead a great revolutionary movement to victory unless it possesses revolutionary theory and a knowledge of history and has a profound grasp of the practical movement.

> "The Role of the Chinese Communist Party in the National War" (October 1938), *Selected Works*, Vol. II, p. 208.

As we used to say, the rectification movement is "a widespread movement of Marxist education". Rectification means the whole Party studying Marxism through criticism and self-criticism. We can certainly learn more about Marxism in the course of the rectification movement.

> *Speech at the Chinese Communist Party's National Conference on Propaganda Work* (March 12, 1957), 1st pocket ed., p. 14.

It is an arduous task to ensure a better life for the several hundred million people of China and to build our economically and culturally backward country into a prosperous and powerful one with a high level of culture. And it is precisely in order to be able to shoulder this task more competently and work better together with all non-Party people who are actuated by high ideals and determined to institute reforms that we must conduct rectification movements both now and in the future, and constantly rid ourselves of whatever is wrong.

> *Ibid.*, pp. 15-16.

Policy is the starting-point of all the practical actions of a revolutionary party and manifests itself in the process and the end-result of that party's actions. A revolutionary party is carrying out a policy whenever it takes any action. If it is not carrying out a correct policy, it is carrying out a wrong policy; if it is not carrying out a given policy consciously, it is doing so blindly. What we call experience is the process and the end-result of carrying out a policy. Only through the practice of the people, that is, through experience, can we verify whether a policy is correct or wrong and determine to what extent it is correct or wrong. But people's practice, especially the practice of a revolutionary party and the revolutionary masses, cannot but be bound up with one policy or another. Therefore, before any action is taken, we must explain the policy, which we have formulated in the light of the given circumstances, to Party members and to the masses. Otherwise, Party members and the masses will depart from the guidance of our policy, act blindly and carry out a wrong policy.

> "On the Policy Concerning Industry and Commerce" (February 27, 1948), *Selected Works*, Vol. IV, pp. 204-05.

Our Party has laid down the general line and general policy of the Chinese revolution as well as various specific lines for work and specific policies. However, while many comrades remember our Party's specific lines for work and specific policies, they often forget its general line and general policy. If we actually forget the Party's general line and general policy, then we shall be blind, half-baked, muddle-headed revolutionaries, and when we carry out a specific line for work and a specific policy, we shall lose our bearings and vacillate now to the left and now to the right, and the work will suffer.

> "Speech at a Conference of Cadres in the Shansi-Suiyuan Liberated Area" (April 1, 1948), *Selected Works*, Vol. IV, p. 238.

Policy and tactics are the life of the Party; leading comrades at all levels must give them full attention and must never on any account be negligent.

> "A Circular on the Situation" (March 20, 1948), *Selected Works*, Vol. IV, p. 220.

II. CLASSES AND CLASS STRUGGLE

Classes struggle, some classes triumph, others are eliminated. Such is history, such is the history of civilization for thousands of years. To interpret history from this viewpoint is historical materialism; standing in opposition to this viewpoint is historical idealism.

> "Cast Away Illusions. Prepare for Struggle" (August 14, 1949), *Selected Works*, Vol. IV, p. 428.

. . . Of Chairman Mao Tse-tung's Quotations

In class society everyone lives as a member of a particular class, and every kind of thinking, without exception, is stamped with the brand of a class.

"On Practice" (July 1937), *Selected Works*, Vol. I, p. 296.

Changes in society are due chiefly to the development of the internal contradictions in society, that is, the contradiction between the productive forces and the relations of production, the contradiction between classes and the contradiction between the old and the new; it is the development of these contradictions that pushes society forward and gives the impetus for the supersession of the old society by the new.

"On Contradiction" (August 1937), *Selected Works*, Vol. I, p. 314.

The ruthless economic exploitation and political oppression of the peasants by the landlord class forced them into numerous uprisings against its rule. . . . It was the class struggles of the peasants, the peasant uprisings and peasant wars that constituted the real motive force of historical development in Chinese feudal society.

"The Chinese Revolution and the Chinese Communist Party" (December 1939), *Selected Works*, Vol. II, p. 308.

In the final analysis, national struggle is a matter of class struggle. Among the whites in the United States it is only the reactionary ruling circles who oppress the black people. They can in no way represent the workers, farmers, revolutionary intellectuals and other enlightened persons who comprise the overwhelming majority of the white people.

"Statement Supporting the American Negroes in Their Just Struggle Against Racial Discrimination by U.S. Imperialism" (August 8, 1963), *People of the World, Unite and Defeat the U.S. Aggressors and All Their Lackeys*, 2nd ed., pp. 3-4.

It is up to us to organize the people. As for the reactionaries in China, it is up to us to organize the people to overthrow them. Everything reactionary is the same; if you don't hit it, it won't fall. This is also like sweeping the floor; as a rule, where the broom does not reach, the dust will not vanish of itself.

"The Situation and Our Policy After the Victory in the War of Resistance Against Japan" (August 13, 1945), *Selected Works*, Vol. IV, p. 19.

The enemy will not perish of himself. Neither the Chinese reactionaries nor the aggressive forces of U.S. imperialism in China will step down from the stage of history of their own accord.

"Carry the Revolution Through to the End" (December 30, 1948), *Selected Works*, Vol. IV, p. 301.

A revolution is not a dinner party, or writing an essay, or painting a picture, or doing embroidery; it cannot be so refined, so leisurely and gentle, so temperate, kind, courteous, restrained and magnanimous. A revolution is an insurrection, an act of violence by which one class overthrows another.

"Report on an Investigation of the Peasant Movement in Hunan" (March 1927), *Selected Works*, Vol. I, p. 28.

Chiang Kai-shek always tries to wrest every ounce of power and every ounce of gain from the people. And we? Our policy is to give him tit for tat and to fight for every inch of land. We act after his fashion. He always tries to impose war on the people, one sword in his left hand and another in his right. We take up swords, too, following his example. . . . As Chiang Kai-shek is now sharpening his swords, we must sharpen ours too.

"The Situation and Our Policy After the Victory in the War of Resistance Against Japan" (August 13, 1945), *Selected Works*, Vol. IV, pp. 14-15.

Who are our enemies? Who are our friends? This is a question of the first importance for the revolution. The basic reason why all previous revolutionary struggles in China achieved so little was their failure to unite with real friends in order to attack real enemies. A revolutionary party is the guide of the masses, and no revolution ever succeeds when the revolutionary party leads them astray. To ensure that we will definitely achieve success in our revolution and will not lead the masses astray, we must pay attention to uniting with our real friends in order to attack our real enemies. To distinguish real friends from real enemies, we must make a general analysis of the economic status of the various classes in Chinese society and of their respective attitudes towards the revolution.

"Analysis of the Classes in Chinese Society" (March 1926), *Selected Works*, Vol. I, p. 13.

Our enemies are all those in league with imperialism — the warlords, the bureaucrats, the comprador class, the big landlord class and the reactionary section of the intelligentsia attached to them. The leading force in our revolution is the industrial proletariat. Our closest friends are the entire semi-proletariat and petty bourgeoisie. As for the vacillating middle bourgeoisie, their right-wing may become our enemy and their left-wing may become our friend — but we must be constantly on our guard and not let them create confusion within our ranks.

Ibid., p. 19.

Whoever sides with the revolutionary people is a revolutionary. Whoever sides with imperialism, feudalism and bureaucrat-capitalism is a counter-revolutionary. Whoever sides with the revolutionary people in words only but acts otherwise is a revolutionary in speech. Whoever sides with the revolutionary people in deed as well as in word is a revolutionary in the full sense.

Closing speech at the Second Session of the First National Committee of the Chinese People's Political Consultative Conference (June 23, 1950).

I hold that it is bad as far as we are concerned if a person, a political party, an army or a school is not attacked by the enemy, for in that case it would definitely mean that we have sunk to the level of the enemy. It is good if we are attacked by the enemy, since it proves that we have drawn a clear line of demarcation between the enemy and ourselves. It is still better if the enemy attacks us wildly and paints us as utterly black and without a single virtue; it demonstrates that we have not only drawn a clear line of demarcation between the enemy and ouselves but achieved a great deal in our work.

To Be Attacked by the Enemy Is Not a Bad Thing but a Good Thing (May 26, 1939), 1st pocket ed., p. 2.

We should support whatever the enemy opposes and oppose whatever the enemy supports.

"Interview with Three Correspondents from the Central News Agency, the *Sao Tang Pao* and the *Hsin Min Pao*" (September 16, 1939), *Selected Works*, Vol. II, p. 272.

Our stand is that of the proletariat and of the masses. For members of the Communist Party, this means keeping to the stand of the Party, keeping to Party spirit and Party policy.

"Talks at the Yenan Forum on Literature and Art" (May 1942), *Selected Works*, Vol. III, p. 70.

After the enemies with guns have been wiped out, there will still be enemies without guns; they are bound to struggle desperately against us, and we must never regard these enemies lightly. If we do not now raise and understand the problem in this way, we shall commit the gravest mistakes.

"Report to the Second Plenary Session of the Seventh Central Committee of the Communist Party of China" (March 5, 1949), *Selected Works*, Vol. IV, p. 364.

immediate village problems into their own hands. If there was any trouble or interference with the representatives of the government, they simply brushed them aside. They completely withdrew their support from this government, and when that support was withdrawn, the whole military establishment disintegrated. Added to the grossest incompetence ever experienced by any military command was this total lack of support both in the armies and in the country, and so the whole matter just simply disintegrated.

The Communists did not create this. The Communists did not create this condition. They did not create this revolutionary spirit. They did not create a great force which moved out from under Chiang Kai-shek. But they were shrewd and cunning to mount it, to ride this thing into victory and into power.

That, I suggest to you, is an explanation which has certain roots in realism and which does not require all this examination of intricate and perhaps irrelevant details. So much for the attitudes of the peoples of Asia.

U.S. Attitude Toward Asia

Let's consider for a moment another important factor in this relationship. That is the attitude of our own people to Asia. What is that fundamental attitude out of which our policy has grown? What is the history of it? Because history is very important, and history furnishes the belief on the one side in the reality and truth of the attitude.

What has our attitude been toward the peoples of Asia? It has been, I submit to you, that we are interested — that Americans as individuals are interested in the peoples of Asia. We are not interested in them as pawns or as subjects for exploitation but just as people.

For 100 years some Americans have gone to Asia to bring in what they thought was the most valuable thing they had — their faith. They wanted to tell them what they thought about the nature and relationship of man to God. Others went to them to bring to them what they knew of learning. Others went to them to bring them healing for their bodies. Others and perhaps fewer went to them to learn the depth and beauty of their own cultures, and some went to them to trade with them. But this trade was a very small part of American interest in the Far East, and it was a very small part of American interest in trade. It was a valid interest; it was a good interest. There was nothing wrong about it, but out of the total sum of the interests of the American people in Asia, it was a comparatively small part.

Through all this period of time also, we had, and still have, great interests in Asia. But let me point out to you one very important factor about our interests in Asia. That is that our interests have been parallel to the interests of the people of Asia. For 50 years, it has been the fundamental belief of the American people — and I am not talking about announcements of government but I mean a belief of people in little towns and villages and churches and missionary forces and labor unions throughout the United States — it has been their profound belief that the control of China by a foreign power was contrary to American interests. The interesting part about that is it was not contrary to the interests of the people of China. There was no conflict but parallelism in that interest. And so from the time of the announcement of the open door policy[2] through the 9-power treaty[3] to the very latest resolution of the General Assembly of the United Nations[4] we have stated that principle and we believe it. And similarly in all the rest of Asia — in the Philippines, in India, in Pakistan and Indonesia, and in Korea — for years and years and years, the interests of Americans throughout this country have been in favor of their independence. This is where their independence societies, and their patriotic groups have come for funds and sympathy. The whole policy of our government insofar as we have responsibility in the Philippines was to bring about the accomplishment of this independence and our sympathy and help. The very real help which we have given other nations in Asia has been in that direction, and it is still in that direction.

The Factor of Communism

Now, I stress this, which you may think is a platitude, because of a very important fact: I hear almost every day someone say that the real interest of the United States is to stop the spread of communism. Nothing seems to me to put the cart before the horse more completely than that. Of course we are interested in stopping the spread of communism. But we are interested for a far deeper reason than any conflict between the Soviet Union and the United States. We are interested in stopping the spread of communism because communism is a doctrine that we don't happen to like. Communism is the most subtle instrument of Soviet foreign policy that has ever been devised, and it is really the spearhead of Russian imperialism which would, if it could, take from these people what they have won, what we want them to keep and develop, which is their own national independence, their own individual independence, their own development of their own resources for their own good and not as mere tributary states to this great Soviet Union.

Now, it is fortunate that this point that I made does not represent any real conflict. It is an important point because people will do more damage and create more misrepresentation in the Far East by saying our interest is merely to stop the spread of communism than any other way. Our real interest is in those people as people. It is because communism is hostile to that interest that we want to stop it. But it happens that the best way of doing both things is to do just exactly what the peoples of Asia want to do and what we want to help them to do, which is to develop a soundness of administration of these new governments and to develop their resources and their technical skills so that they are not subject to penetration either through ignorance, or because they believe these false promises, or because there is real distress in their areas. If we can help that development, if we can go forward with it, then we have brought about the best way that anyone knows of stopping this spread of communism.

It is important to take this attitude not as a mere negative reaction to communism but as the most positive affirmation of the most affirmative truth that we hold, which is in the dignity and right of every nation, of every people, and of every individual to develop in their own way, making their own mistakes, reaching their own triumphs but acting under their own responsibility. That is what we are pressing for in the Far East, and that is what we must affirm and not get mixed up with purely negative and inconsequential statements.

Soviet Attitude

Now, let me come to another underlying and important factor which determines our relations and, in turn, our policy with the peoples of Asia. That is the attitude of the Soviet Union toward Asia, and particularly towards those parts of Asia which are contiguous to the Soviet Union, and with great particularity this afternoon, to north China.

The attitude and interest of the Russians in north China, and in these other areas as well, long antedates communism. This is not something that has come out of communism at all. It long antedates it. But the Communist regime has added new methods, new skills, and new concepts to the thrust of Russian imperialism. [These] Communistic concept[s] and techniques have armed Russian imperialism with a new and most insidious weapon of penetration. Armed with these new powers, what is happening in China is that the Soviet Union is detaching the northern provinces [areas] of China from China and is attaching them to the Soviet Union. This process is complete in Outer Mongolia. It is nearly complete in Manchuria [Dongbei], and I am sure that in inner Mongolia [Nei Mongol] and in Sinkiang [Xinjiang] there are very happy reports coming from Soviet agents to Moscow. This is what is going on. It is the detachment of these whole areas, vast areas — populated by Chinese — the detachment of these areas from China and their attachment to the Soviet Union.

I wish to state this and perhaps sin against my doctrine of nondogmatism, but I should like to suggest at any rate that this fact that the Soviet Union is taking the four northern provinces of China is the single most significant, most important fact, in the relation of any foreign power with Asia.[5]

Two Rules of U.S. Policy

What does that mean for us? It means something very, very significant. It means that nothing that we do and nothing that we say must be allowed to obscure the reality of this fact. All the efforts of propaganda will not be able to obscure it. The only thing that can obscure it is the folly of ill-conceived adventures on our part which easily could do so, and I urge all who are thinking about these foolish adventures to remember that we must not seize the unenviable position which the Russians have carved out for themselves. We must not undertake to deflect from the Russians to ourselves the righteous anger, and the wrath, and the hatred of the Chinese people which must develop. It would be folly to deflect it to ourselves. We must take the position we have always taken — that anyone who violates the integrity of China is the enemy of China and is acting contrary to our own interest. That, I suggest to you this afternoon, is the first and the greatest rule in regard to the formulation of American policy towards Asia.

I suggest that the second rule is very like the first. That is to keep our own purposes perfectly straight, perfectly pure, and perfectly aboveboard and do not get them mixed-up with legal quibbles or the attempt to do one thing and really achieve another.

The consequences of this Russian attitude and this Russian action in China are perfectly enormous. They are saddling all those in China who are proclaiming their loyalty to Moscow, and who are allowing themselves to be used as puppets of Moscow, with the most awful responsibility which they must pay for. Furthermore, these actions of the Russians are making plainer than any speech, or any utterance, or any legislation can make throughout all of Asia, what the true purposes of the Soviet Union are and what the true function of communism as an agent of Russian imperialism is. These I suggest to you are the fundamental factors, fundamental realities of the attitude out of which our relations and policies must grow.

Military Security in The Pacific

Now, let's in the light of that consider some of these policies. First of all, let's deal with the question of military security. I deal with it first because it is important and because, having stated our policy in that regard, we must clearly understand that the military menace is not the most immediate.

What is the situation in regard to the military security of the Pacific area, and what is our policy in regard to it?

In the first place, the defeat and the disarmament of Japan has placed upon the United States the necessity of assuming the military defense of Japan so long as that is required, both in the interest of our own security and in the interests of the security of the entire Pacific area and, in all honor, in the interest of Japanese security. We have American — and there are Australian — troops in Japan. I am not in a position to speak for the Australians, but I can assure you that there is no intention of any sort of abandoning or weakening the defenses of Japan and that whatever arrangements are to be made either through permanent settlement or otherwise, that defense must and shall be maintained.

This defensive perimeter runs along the Aleutians to Japan and then goes to the Ryukyus. We hold important defense positions in the Ryukyu Islands, and those we will continue to hold. In the interest of the population of the Ryukyu Islands, we will at an appropriate time offer to hold these islands under trusteeship of the United Nations. But they are essential parts of the defensive perimeter of the Pacific, and they must and will be held.

The defensive perimeter runs from the Ryukyus to the Philippine Islands. Our relations, our defensive relations with the Philippines are contained in agreements between us. Those agreements are being loyally carried out and will be loyally carried out. Both peoples have learned by bitter experience the vital connections between our mutual defense requirements. We are in no doubt about that, and it is hardly necessary for me to say an attack on the Philippines could not and would not be tolerated by the United States. But I hasten to add that no one perceives the imminence of any such attack.

So far as the military security of other areas in the Pacific is concerned, it must be clear that no person can guarantee these areas against military attack. But it must also be clear that such a guarantee is hardly sensible or necessary within the realm of practical relationship.

Should such an attack occur — one hesitates to say where such an armed attack could come from — the initial reliance must be on the people attacked to resist it and then upon the commitments of the entire civilized world under the Charter of the United Nations which so far has not proved a weak reed to lean on by any people who are determined to protect their independence against outside aggression. But it is a mistake, I think, in considering Pacific and Far Eastern problems to become obsessed with military considerations. Important as they are, there are other problems that press, and these other problems are not capable of solution through military means. These other problems arise out of the susceptibility of many areas, and many countries in the Pacific area, to subversion and penetration. That cannot be stopped by military means.

Susceptibility To Penetration

The susceptibility to penetration arises because in many areas there are new governments which have little experience in governmental administration and have not become firmly established or perhaps firmly accepted in their countries. They grow, in part, from very serious economic problems, some of them growing out directly from the last war, others growing indirectly out of the last war because of the disruptions of trade with other parts of the world, with the disruption of arrangements which furnished credit and management to these areas for many years. That has resulted in dislocation of economic effort and in a good deal of suffering among the peoples concerned. In part this susceptibility to penetration comes from the great social upheaval about which I have been speaking, an upheaval which was carried on and confused a great deal by the Japanese occupation and by the propaganda which has gone on from Soviet sources since the war.

Here, then, are the problems in these other areas which require some policy on our part, and I should like to point out two facts to you and then discuss in more detail some of these areas.

The first fact is the great difference between our responsibility and our opportunities in the northern part of the Pacific area and in the southern part of the Pacific area. In the north, we have direct responsibility in Japan and we have direct opportunity to act. The same thing to a lesser degree is true in Korea. There we had direct responsibility, and there we did act, and there we have a greater opportunity to be effective than we have in the more southerly part.

In the southerly part of the area, we are one of many nations who can do no more than help. The direct responsibility lies with the peoples concerned. They are proud of their new national responsibility. You can not sit around in Washington, or London, or Paris, or The Hague, and determine what the policies are going to be in those areas. You can be willing to help, and you can help only when the conditions are right for help to be effective.

Limitations of U.S. Assistance

That leads me to the other thing that I wanted to point out, and that is the limitation of effective American assistance. American assistance can be effective when it is the missing component in a situation which might otherwise be solved. The United States cannot furnish all these components to solve the question. It can not furnish determination, it can not furnish the will, and it can not furnish the loyalty of a people to its government. But if the will and if the determination exists and if the people are behind their government, then, and not always then, is there a very good chance. In that situation, American help can be effective and it can lead to an accomplishment which could not otherwise be achieved.

Japan. — Now, with that statement, let's deal very briefly — because the time is going on and I am almost equaling my performance in the Senate and House — let's deal very briefly with some of the problems. Let's take the situation in Japan for a moment. There are three great factors to be faced. The security matter I have dealt with. Aside from that, there are the economic questions and the political questions. In the political field, General MacArthur has been very successful and the Japanese are hammering out with some backsliding, and regaining and backsliding again of progress, a political system which is based on nonmilitaristic institutions.

In the economic field, we have not been so successful. That is in very large part due to the inherent difficulty of the problem. The problem arises with the necessity of Japan being able to buy raw materials and sell goods. The former connections of Japan with the mainland and with some of the islands have been disrupted. That has produced difficulties. The willingness of other countries to receive Japanese goods has very much contracted since the war.

Difficulties of currency have added to those problems. But those matters have got to be faced and have got to be solved. Whether they are solved under a treaty or if the procedural difficulties of that are too great under some other mechanism, they must be solved along lines which permit the Japanese greater freedom — complete freedom if possible — to buy what they need in the world and to sell what they have to offer on the mainland of Asia, in southeast Asia, and in other parts of the world. That is the nature of the problem and it is a very tough one. It is one on which the occupation authorities, the Japanese government, ourselves, and others are working. There can be no magic solution to it.

Korea. — In Korea, we have taken great steps which have ended our military occupation, and in cooperation with the United Nations, have established an independent and sovereign country recognized by nearly all the rest of the world.[6] We have given that nation great help in getting itself established. We are asking the Congress to continue that help until it is firmly established, and that legislation is now pending before the Congress.[7] The idea that we should scrap all of that, that we should stop half way through the achievement of the establishment of this country, seems to me to be the most utter defeatism and utter madness in our interests in Asia. But there our responsibilities are more direct and our opportunities more clear. When you move to the south, you find that our opportunity is much slighter and that our responsibilities, except in the Philippines and there indirectly, are very small. Those problems are very confusing.

Philippines. — In the Philippines, we acted with vigor and speed to set up an independent sovereign nation which we have done.[8] We have given the Philippines a billion dollars of direct economic aid since the war. We have spent another billion dollars in such matters as veterans' benefits and other payments in the Philippines. Much of that money has not been used as wisely as we wish it had been used, but here again, we come up against the matter of responsibility. It is the Philippine Government which is responsible. It is the Philippine Government which must make its own mistakes. What we can do is advise and urge, and if help continues to be misused, to stop giving the help. We cannot direct, we should not direct, we have not the slightest desire to direct. I believe that there are indications that the Philippines may be facing serious economic difficulties. With energetic, determined action, they can perhaps be avoided or certainly minimized. Whether that will be true or not, I can not say, but it does not rest within the power of the American Government to determine that. We are always ready to help and to advise. That is all we can and all we should do.

Asia. — Elsewhere in southeast Asia, the limits of what we can do are to help where we are wanted. We are organizing the machinery through which we can make effective help possible. The western powers are all interested. We all know the techniques. We have all had experiences which can be useful to those governments which are newly starting out if they want it. It cannot be useful if they don't want it. We know techniques of administration. We know techniques of organizing school districts, and road districts, and taxation districts. We know agricultural and industrial techniques, all of which can be helpful, and those we are preparing to make available if they are wanted, where they are wanted, and under circumstances where they have a fighting chance to be successful. We will not do these things for the mere purpose of being active. They will not be done for the mere purpose of running around and doing good, but for the purpose of moving in where we are wanted to a situation where we have the missing component which, if put into the rest of the picture, will spell success.

The situation in the different countries of southeast Asia is difficult. It is highly confused in Burma where five different factions have utterly disrupted the immediate government of the country. Progress is being made in Indochina where the French, although moving slowly, are moving. There are noticeable signs of progress in transferring responsibility to a local administration and getting the adherence of the population to this local administration. We hope that the situation will be such that the French can make further progress and make it quickly, but I know full well the difficulties which are faced by the Foreign Minister of France and my admiration and respect for him are so great that I would not want one word I say to add a feather to the burden that he carries.

In Malaya, the British have and are discharging their responsibility harmoniously with the people of Malaya and are making progress.

Indonesia. — In Indonesia, a great success has been achieved within the last few weeks and over a period of months. The round table conferences at The Hague in which great statesmanship and restraint were displayed, both on the Dutch and the Indonesian side, have resulted in this new government being formed.[9] Relations of this government with the Dutch will be very good, and the Dutch can furnish them great help and advice, and we will be willing to stand by to give whatever help we can rightly and profitably give. That situation is one which is full of encouragement although it is full of difficulty also.

India and Pakistan. — As one goes to the end of this semicircle and comes to India and Pakistan, we find really grave troubles facing the world and facing these two countries there, both with respect to Kashmir, and to the utter difficulties — economic difficulties growing out of the differences in devaluation, settlement of monetary plans back and forth, et cetera. We know that they have assured one another, and they have assured the world, that as stubborn as these difficulties may be and difficult as they may be of solution, they are not going to resort to war to solve them. We are glad to hear those assurances and the whole world is glad to hear it, but we know also that the problems are in such a situation and in such an area that they are most inflammable, and we believe that in addition to these most desirable assurances there should be some accommodation of wills to bring about a result as soon as possible.

In India and in Pakistan we are willing to be of such help as we can be. Again, the responsibility is not ours. Again we can only be helpful friends. Again the responsibility lies with people who have won their freedom and who are very proud of it.

The New Day For Asia

So after this survey, what we conclude, I believe, is that there is a new day which has dawned in Asia. It is a day in which the Asian peoples are on their own, and know it, and intend to continue on their own. It is a day in which the old relationships between east and west are gone, relationships which at their worst were exploitation, and which at their best were paternalism. That relationship is over, and the relationship of east and west must now be in the Far East one of mutual respect and mutual helpfulness. We are their friends. Others are their friends. We and those others are willing to help, but we can help only where we are wanted and only where the conditions of help are really sensible and possible. So what we can see is that this new day in Asia, this new day which is dawning, may go on to a glorious noon or it may darken and it may drizzle out. But that decision lies within the countries of Asia and within the power of the Asian people. It is not a decision which a friend or even an enemy from the outside can decide for them.

---

[1] *The Philippine Republic achieved full independence, July 4, 1946; Pakistan and India became separate dominions in the British Commonwealth, Aug. 15, 1947, India becoming a sovereign republic, Jan. 26, 1950; Ceylon was accorded dominion status in the British Commonwealth, Feb. 4, 1948; Burma became independent, Jan. 4, 1948; the Republic of Korea was proclaimed, Aug. 15, 1948; and Indonesia achieved its independence, Dec. 28, 1948.*

[2] See Secretary Hay's instructions of Sept. 6, 1899, and Mar. 20, 1900; United States Relations with China, with Special Reference to the Period 1944-1949 *(Department of State publication 3573; 1949), pp. 414-416.*

[3] *Treaty of Feb. 6, 1922;* Ibid.,*pp. 438-442.*

[4] *Res 291 (IV), Dec. 8, 1949; A Decade of American Foreign Policy, pp. 726-727.*

[5] *For background material regarding Soviet penetration of northern areas of China, see Department of State Bulletin, Feb. 6, 1950, pp. 218-219. See also Secretary Acheson's statement of Mar. 31, 1950, regarding Sinkiang: ibid., Apr. 10, 1950, p. 568.*
[6] *The independence of Korea was proclaimed Aug. 15, 1948. For the resolution of the U.N. General Assembly relating to Korean independence, see Res. 122 (ll), Nov. 14, 1947; A Decade of American Foreign Policy, pp. 677-678.*

[7] *See infra, pp. 2527-2528.*
[8] *The independence of the Philippine Republic was proclaimed July 4, 1946, by the President of the United States; see A Decade of American Foreign Policy, pp. 860-861.*
[9] *The independence of Indonesia was effected Dec. 28, 1949; see ibid., pp. 802-804.*

Mutual Defense Treaty

The United States and the Republic of China signed a mutual defense treaty Dec. 2, 1954. The Senate approved ratification of the treaty Feb. 9, 1955, by a 65-6 roll-call vote. The United States terminated the agreement Dec. 31, 1979.

The following articles contain the treaty provisions regarding the use of armed force:

Art. 2. In order more effectively to achieve the objective of this treaty, the parties separately and jointly, by self-help and mutual aid, will maintain and develop their individual and collective capacity to resist armed attack and Communist subversive activities directed from without against their territorial integrity and political stability.

Art. 5. Each party recognizes that an armed attack in the West Pacific area directed against the territories of either of the parties would be dangerous to its own peace and safety, and declares that it would act to meet the common danger in accordance with its constitutional processes. Any such armed attack, and all measures taken as a result thereof, shall be immediately reported to the UN Security Council. Such measures shall be terminated when the Security Council has taken the measures necessary to restore and maintain international peace and security.

Art. 6. For the purposes of Articles 2 and 5, the terms 'territorial' and 'territories' shall mean, in respect of the Republic of China, Taiwan and the Pescadores [Penghu]; and in respect of the United States, the island territories in the West Pacific under its jurisdiction. The provisions of Articles 2 and 5 will be applicable to such other territories as may be determined by mutual agreement.

1955 Formosa Resolution

The joint resolution (H J Res 159, S J Res 28), authorizing the president's use of armed force to defend Taiwan and the Pescadores Islands, cleared the House Jan. 25, 1955, by a 410-3 roll-call vote and the Senate Jan. 28, 1955, by an 85-3 roll-call vote. It was

repealed Oct. 11, 1974. The following is the full text:

"Whereas the primary purpose of the United States, in its relations with all other nations, is to develop and sustain a just and enduring peace for all; and

"Whereas certain territories in the West Pacific under the jurisdiction of the Republic of China are now under armed attack, and threats and declarations have been made and are being made by the Chinese Communists that such armed attack is in aid of and in preparation for armed attack on Formosa [Taiwan] and the Pescadores [Penghu]; and

"Whereas such armed attack if continued would gravely endanger the peace and security of the West Pacific area and particularly of Formosa and the Pescadores; and

"Whereas the secure possession by friendly governments of the western Pacific island chain, of which Formosa is a part, is essential to the vital interests of the United States and all friendly nations in or bordering upon the Pacific Ocean; and

"Whereas the President of the United States on Jan. 6, 1955, submitted to the Senate for its advice and consent to ratification a mutual defense treaty between the United States of America and the Republic of China, which recognizes that an armed attack in the west Pacific area directed against territories therein described in the region of Formosa and the Pescadores, would be dangerous to the peace and safety of the parties to the treaty: Therefore be it

"Resolved, [etc.,] That the President of the United States be and he hereby is authorized to employ the armed forces of the United States as he deems necessary for the specific purpose of securing and protecting Formosa and the Pescadores against armed attack, this authority to include the securing and protection of such related positions and territories of that area now in friendly hands and the taking of such other measures as he judges to be required or appropriate in assuring the defense of Formosa and the Pescadores.

"This resolution shall expire when the President shall determine that the peace and security of the area is reasonably assured by international conditions, created by action of the United Nations or otherwise, and shall so report to Congress."

Dulles States U.S. Policy on Asia in 1955

Following are excerpts, of a speech made by Secretary of State John Foster Dulles on Feb. 16, 1955, before the Foreign Policy Association in New York. The State Department cited this speech as a "review of [the basic U.S. Far East and Southeast Asia] positions as of 1955."

I am glad to be again with the Foreign Policy Association. I first spoke before you 35 years ago. So this is, in a sense, an anniversary. I know well of your work. It is good work, and I am glad that it is going on, bringing to our citizenry a better knowledge of our foreign policy.

The broad goal of our foreign policy is to enable the people of the United States to enjoy, in peace, the blessings of liberty. Under present world conditions we cannot achieve that goal by thinking just of ourselves. We must help other peoples to be free. Thus,

enlightened self-interest combines with high principle to lead us to do for others what, if conditions were reversed, we would want them to do for us.

Our task is not an easy one, nor one that can be discharged without sacrifice and risk. Stormy winds blow from Moscow and Peiping [Peking].

In Moscow Foreign Minister Molotov pours 17,000 words of abuse upon the Western powers. In Peiping Foreign Minister Chou [Chou En-lai] bitterly attacks the United States and threatens to use all the force at his command to capture Formosa [Taiwan].

A heavy responsibility devolves upon the President daily, and upon the Congress, in making delicate decisions which may spell the difference between peace and war.

All of us would like to see peace permanently assured. We long for some simple and especially some certain formula which would relieve us of the present anxious tasks. But perhaps we are learning a needed lesson, that there is no easy way to win peace.

Twice in our generation efforts have been made to secure peace by broad agreements to abolish war. The Pact of Paris of 1928 binds over 60 nations to renounce war as an instrument of international policy. But shortly after it was made, the nations fought in Europe, Asia, and Africa.

The United Nations Charter of 1945 binds 60 nations to refrain in their international relations from the threat or use of force. But there has been armed aggression in Korea which was promoted by Soviet Russia, and later Communist China was found guilty of armed aggression there.

It is good that mankind should by great pronouncements demonstrate its hatred of war and its determination to outlaw war. Idealism is indispensable. But it would be dangerous to assume that treaties or pledges alone would relieve us of the burdensome tasks we undertake in the struggle for peace.

Treaty pledges, no matter how solemn, will never restrain powerful and ambitious rulers who do not accept the restraints of moral law and who are not responsive to the will of the people. As against such despots there must be other and further restraints.

Thus the struggle goes on. We dare not relax, because the moment of relaxation is the moment of peril. Treaty declarations must be backed by a purpose that is ever sustained, by an intelligence that is ever alert, and by power which is ever ready and able to punish aggressors so that aggression will not pay.

Whenever the advocates of peace seem to lack these qualities, then peace is in jeopardy. On the other hand, so long as those qualities are manifestly present, then we can have good hope that the battle for peace will be won.

That hope is the more justified because modern weapons possess such immense destructive power. That fact is frightening. But the very fact that it is frightening means that even the most reckless will pause before taking action which would bring modern weapons into play.

During these days the Soviet and Chinese Communists are probing deeply the intentions of the free nations. But we need not feel worried or despondent, for what the despots will discover from their probing ought to restrain them.

In Europe there seems no retreat from the basic resolve to create the Western European Union and so to end the disunity of Western Europe. To replace that disunity and weakness with unity and strength will be the greatest single contribution which could be made to the cause of peace.

In Western Europe there are over 200 million highly civilized people. They possess in the aggregate the intellectual and material resources to be both prosperous and safe — provided only that they are united in spirit and properly organized to work together. When this unity is achieved, great things will come about. Western Europe will not only have the strength to solve its own internal and external problems but will be a mighty force to preserve world peace.

Far East Security Treaties

In the Far East the United States has responded to the desire of others that we join with them to assure their security. During the last 4 years, the United States has become party to security treaties with Korea, Japan, the Republic of China on Formosa the Philippines, Australia, and New Zealand. Also we have joined the eight-power Manila Pact [SEATO] for the security of Southeast Asia.

The total of these treaties is a mutual security system which, starting from the Aleutian Islands in the North, runs in a great arc to the South Pacific. This constitutes a defensive bulwark for freedom in that part of the world.

What has thus been done by many nations is important. Also important is the manner in which the United States has played its part, particularly during recent days.

When the Congress convened last January, it was organized by the Democratic Party. So when the Manila Pact and the China treaty were submitted, they were submitted by a Republican President to a Democrat-controlled body. The same was true of President Eisenhower's request for congressional authority to use the Armed Forces of the United States in the Formosa area.

Nevertheless, the two treaties were ratified and the congressional authority was granted. This was done promptly and with virtual unanimity.*

These events demonstrate a national unity and capacity for action which is needed in the world today. Too often representative processes lead to such partisanship and such consequent delays that hostile forces are encouraged to believe that democracies are inherently ineffective. The Government of the United States has shown the contrary. Partisanship was wholly subordinated to the national good, so that action of great importance could be taken with deliberation, but with decisiveness.

For this the Nation can be grateful to the leadership and to the general membership of both parties in the Congress. I know that they would expect me to pay special tribute to Walter F. George, who, as Chairman of the Senate Foreign Relations Committee, carried the heaviest aggregate burden of responsibility in relation to the three acts to which I refer.

We can all take pride, as Americans, in this demonstration of national unity and capacity. Because of it, free men throughout the world can face the future with better hope and new confidence.

Despotic Disarray in Moscow

While the capacity of the representative form of government has been recently demonstrated in the United States, there has been occurring in Moscow an extraordinary demonstration of despotic disarray. The Prime Minister of the Soviet State was peremptorily summoned to a high Soviet session in the Kremlin and subjected to the public humiliation of hearing another read his resignation and his confession of "my guilt."

With that Communist verdict we need not quarrel. But the full significance of what has occurred is still obscure and perhaps the last act of the drama has not yet been played.

Undoubtedly, we see an elemental, personal struggle for power. But also one can perceive the outlines of a basic policy difference. There must be those who are primarily concerned with the welfare, security, and greatness of the Soviet Union and its people. There are others who would have the Soviet Union and its power serve primarily as a tool of international communism and as a means of achieving its worldwide ambitions. These two ends, the one symbolized by the State, the other by the Party, do not always coincide.

To us, the Party and the State in Russia usually seem indistinguishable, because many individuals serve in dual capacities. But Lenin and Stalin constantly emphasized the distinction between the two. "The Party," said Stalin, "is not and cannot be identified with the State power."

We should keep that distinction in mind. The time may come — I believe it will come — when Russians of stature will patriotically put first their national security and the welfare of their people. They will be unwilling to have that security and that welfare subordinated to the worldwide ambitions of international communism. If their point of view should prevail, then indeed there could be a basis for worthwhile negotiation and practical agreements between the United States and the new Russia. Then there might be reactivated the historic friendship between our countries and our peoples.

Mutual Defense Treaty With China

Let me turn now to deal with some of the substantive problems which arise out of the two Far Eastern treaties to which I have referred — the China treaty and the Manila Pact.

The United States is firmly committed to the defense of Formosa and the Pescadores [Penghu]. These islands became part of the Japanese Empire in 1895. They continued as such for half a century, until they were relinquished by Japan as a result of her defeat in war — a defeat principally wrought by the efforts and sacrifices of the United States.

These islands form an important part of the Western Pacific defense system which I have described. The people of the islands eagerly seek our help.

Thus Formosa and the Pescadores have been properly a matter of concern to the United States.

In 1945 our long-time ally, the Republic of China, was entrusted with authority over these islands. In 1950, when the aggression against Korea occurred, President Truman ordered our Pacific Fleet to defend Formosa against possible Chinese Communist attack. Now that determination has been converted into our Mutual Defense Treaty with the Republic of China.

It is important to note that the treaty, except as it relates to United States territories, covers only the islands of Formosa and the Pescadores, and an armed attack directed against those islands. The congressional authority is to secure and protect Formosa and the Pescadores against armed attack, and to make secure and to protect "related positions and territories" as the President judges this would be "required or appropriate in assuring the defense of Formosa and the Pescadores."

The President did not use our Armed Forces to help the Chinese Nationalists to hold the Tachen [Dachen] Islands and Yushan and Pishan, lying some 200 miles north of Formosa. These islands were virtually unrelated to the defense of Formosa and the Pescadores. We helped the Chinese Nationalists to evacuate these islands and regroup their forces, so as to avoid a bloody and wasteful battle which would have inflamed public emotions. Thus, Nationalist China and the United States have made an important contribution to the cause of peace.

It has been suggested that Nationalist China should go further and surrender to the Chinese Communists the coastal positions which the Communists need to stage their announced attack on Formosa. It is doubtful that this would serve either the cause of peace or the cause of freedom.

The Chinese Communists have been the initiators of violence in this area. They have already formally declared their intention to take Formosa by force. If the Chinese Nationalists now oblige by making it easier for the Chinese Communists to conquer Formosa will they be less apt to do so? I doubt it.

The United States has no commitment and no purpose to defend the coastal positions as such. The basic purpose is to assure that Formosa and the Pescadores will not be forcibly taken over by the Chinese Communists. However, Foreign Minister Chou says they will use all their force to take Formosa and they treat the coastal islands as means to that end. When the Nationalists voluntarily evacuated the Tachen [Dachen] Islands, the Chinese Communists' comment was: "The liberation of these islands has created favorable conditions for our People's Liberation Army in the liberation of Formosa." Thus the Chinese Communists have linked the coastal positions to the defense of Formosa . That is the fact which, as President Eisenhower said in his message to Congress about Formosa, "compels us to take into account closely related localities." Accordingly, we shall be alert to subsequent Chinese Communist actions, rejecting for ourselves any initiative of warlike deeds.

It is hardly to be expected that the Chinese Communists will renounce their ambitions. However, might they not renounce their efforts to realize their goals by force?

Such renunciation of force is one of the basic principles of the United Nations, and the United States had hoped, and still hopes, that the United Nations may be able to effect a cessation of the present hostilities. President Eisenhower, in his message to Congress dealing with this matter, made clear that the United States would welcome action by the United Nations which might bring an end to the active hostilities in the area. The Government of New Zealand has brought this situation before the Security Council, and the United States, in the interest of peace, went to the length of voting to invite the Chinese Communists to come to the Security Council to discuss the matter.

In 1950 the Chinese Communists had accepted a Security Council invitation in relation to Korea. However, this time the Chinese Communists contemptuously rejected the invitation.

We sincerely hope that this decision of the Chinese Communists is not irrevocable and that they will abide by the principles of the United Nations rather than challenge by force the defensive

---

"Let A Hundred Flowers Blossom. . . A Hundred Schools of Thought Contend!"

The text of the speech by Mao Tse-tung to the Supreme State Conference on May 2, 1956, in which he was believed to have set forth this slogan, was not published. Lu Dingyi, director of the Propaganda Department of the Central Committee of the Chinese Communist Party, referred to Mao Tse-tung's speech when Lu spoke on May 26, 1956, to a group of scientists, social scientists, doctors, writers and others in Peking. His speech appeared in the *People's Daily* on June 13, 1956. The following is an excerpt of his remarks:

> To artists and writers, we say "Let a hundred flowers blossom." To scientists, we say "Let a hundred schools of thought contend." This is the policy of the Chinese Communist Party. It was announced by Chairman Mao Tse-tung at the Supreme State Conference.
>
> In applying this policy we have gained some experience, but it is still far too scanty. Furthermore, what I am saying is merely my own personal understanding of this policy. . . .

---

obligations of this country. In any event, we believe that their attitude toward the United Nations Security Council has not ended the responsibility of that body, which, by the charter, has the "primary responsibility for the maintenance of international peace and security."

It should not, moreover, be carelessly assumed that peace and security will be promoted merely by the non-Communist nations indefinitely granting one-sided concessions to the Communist nations.

A great danger in Asia is the fear of many non-Communist peoples that the United States has no real intention of standing firmly behind them. Already that fear has mounted to the danger point. We accepted in Korea an armistice which the Chinese Communists boisterously misrepresent as a "victory" for them. We acquiesced in an Indochina armistice which reflected the defeat of the French Union forces at Dien-Bien-Phu. We aided the Tachen evacuation. The reasons were compelling; nevertheless the result added a few square miles to the Communist domain.

If the non-Communist Asians ever come to feel that their Western allies are disposed to retreat whenever communism threatens the peace, then the entire area could quickly become indefensible.

As the situation now exists, neither the cause of freedom, nor United States security, nor world peace and security would be promoted by undermining the faith of the free Asian peoples in our strength and in our willingness to use that strength to restrain those who violently menace liberty. The American people have, through the Congress, made their own resolution clear. That is a verdict which the Government accepts as sound and which it will soberly execute.

Security of Southeast Asia

Let me turn now to Southeast Asia. In a few hours I shall be going to Bangkok to attend the first meeting of the Council created under the Manila Pact for the security of Southeast Asia.

We shall at Bangkok deal with the problem of organizing the Treaty Council. Also we shall begin to deal with the three substantive problems assigned to the Council, namely military security, security against subversion directed from without, and economic welfare. I cannot anticipate what the decisions will be, but I am confident that our gathering will show the advantages of cooperation between the East and the West.

Some Asians retain a fear, derived from past colonial relationships, that close ties with the Western powers will lead to their being dominated by the Western powers. It is essential that that fear should be dispelled.

An important step in that direction was taken at Manila when, at the inspiration of President Magsaysay, the eight powers there signed the Pacific Charter. Thereby we dedicated ourselves to promoting self-government and to securing independence for all countries whose peoples desire it and are able to undertake its responsibilities. Also, we agreed to cooperate in the economic, social, and cultural fields in order to promote higher living standards, economic progress, and social well-being.

However, words alone are not enough. It is necessary to infuse these words with the breath of life. That, I hope, will be done at Bangkok. Those who gather there will meet as equals. We shall, I think, find ways to diminish the risk of armed attack against the treaty area and the danger of subversion from without. Also we shall begin to study economic problems. These are not capable of any dramatic and spectacular solution, but they do respond to steady, painstaking, and sympathetic efforts.

The first task is to deal with fundamentals. That we are already doing, particularly in the basic realm of education. United States universities and colleges are cooperating with Asian institutions in Thailand, the Philippines, and Pakistan. Many United States technicians are serving in Asia in economic, educational, and health tasks, and the number is being increased. Our cooperation is already beginning to show results in better food and better health, and we are together taking the first steps to expand trade, to increase private investment, and to raise standards of living.

In such ways, we can justify man's faith in freedom.

There should indeed be no cleavage between the Western and Asian nations. Our concept of the nature of man had its beginning in Asia, where East and West met. We believe that all men are the creation and concern of a universal God and that He has endowed every person with a right to develop in accordance with the dictates of his individual reason and conscience.

That religious faith, politically translated into the Magna Carta, the French Declaration of the Rights of Man, and our own Declaration of Independence, was, as Lincoln said of our Declaration, nothing exclusive but designed to provide "liberty, not alone to the people of this country, but hope for the world for all future time."

We also realize that, if human liberty is to be a reality, there must be an economic as well as a political foundation. The impoverished and the destitute cannot be truly free. So we recognize that economic values are essential to give reality to the moral and political values that we cherish.

Such a philosophy is indeed very different from that of Soviet communism.

Soviet communism denies the principle of human equality and instead substitutes the principle of class rule.

It denies that men are capable of self-government and substitutes the principle of dictatorship, the so-called dictatorship of the proletariat.

It denies nationalism, except as it can be used as a slogan to drive a wedge between East and West and prepare the way for an absorption of the peoples by international communism.

It preaches a new doctrine of segregation. The peoples of Asia, it is said, must be segregated from the peoples of the West. The new nations of Asia must be segregated from association with others.

The guile behind this is obvious. The Soviet and Chinese Communists know that their combined power can dominate the Eurasian Continent. If the other nations of Europe and Asia stand alone, they will be unable to resist the iron embrace of international communism.

At the Berlin Conference last year, Mr. Molotov denounced NATO and proposed a European security system which would exclude the United States. Now the Soviet and Chinese Communists denounce the Manila Pact, because it may bring to Southeast Asia the strength needed to resist Communist aggression.

The Bangkok Conference will enable the free nations of the West and of the East to begin a vital demonstration. They can show that, through association as sovereign equals, they can each help the other to independence, security, and well-being.

That result accords with the high ideals with which our Nation was founded. It is in keeping with what our people have sought throughout their history. So our delegation goes to Bangkok with confidence, because we know that our mission is sustained by national faith and national purpose.

*Department of State Bulletin EDITOR'S NOTE. Following is a summary of congressional action on the Manila Pact, the Mutual Defense Treaty between the United States and the Republic of China, and the resolution relating to the defense of Formosa:

Manila Pact: Transmitted to the Senate on November 10, 1954; advice and consent to ratification given on February 1 by a vote of 82 to 1.

Treaty with China: Transmitted to the Senate on January 6; advice and consent to ratification given on February 9 by a vote of 64 to 6.

Formosa resolution: President's message requesting congressional action transmitted on January 24; H. J. Res. 159 introduced on January 24; resolution adopted by the House of Representatives on January 25, 409 to 3, and by the Senate on January 28, 85 to 3.

Tonkin Gulf Resolution

Following is the complete text of the Southeast Asia Resolution (H J Res 1145) enacted Aug. 7, 1964 and repealed Jan. 2, 1971.

Whereas naval units of the Communist regime in Viet Nam, in violation of the principles of the Charter of the United Nations and of international law, have deliberately and repeatedly attacked United States naval vessels lawfully present in international waters, and have thereby created a serious threat to international peace;

Whereas these attacks are part of a deliberate and systematic campaign of aggression that the Communist regime in North Viet Nam has been waging against its neighbors and the nations joined with them in the collective defense of their freedom;

Whereas the United States is assisting the peoples of southeast Asia to protect their freedom and has no territorial, military or political ambitions in that area, but desires only that these peoples should be left in peace to work out their own destinies in their own way: Now, therefore, be it

Resolved by the Senate and House of Representatives of the United States of America in Congress assembled.

SEC. 1. The Congress approves and supports the determination of the President, as Commander-in-Chief, to take all necessary measures to repel any armed attack against the forces of the United States and to prevent further aggression.

SEC. 2. The United States regards as vital to its national interest and to world peace the maintenance of international peace and security in southeast Asia. Consonant with the Constitution of the United States and the Charter of the United Nations and in accordance with its obligations under the Southeast Asia Collective Defense Treaty, the United States is, therefore, prepared, as the President determines, to take all necessary steps, including the use of armed force, to assist any member or protocol state of the Southeast Asia Collective Defense Treaty requesting assistance in defense of its freedom.

SEC. 3. This resolution shall expire when the President shall determine that the peace and security of the area is reasonably assured by international conditions created by action of the United Nations or otherwise, except that it may be terminated earlier by concurrent resolution of the Congress.

Rusk 1966 China Policy Text

Following is the statement made by Secretary of State Dean Rusk on U.S. policy toward China, March 16, 1966, before the Far East and the Pacific Subcommittee of the House Foreign Affairs Committee:

Mr. Chairman, during the last month and a half this distinguished committee and its corresponding members in the other house have heard testimony on Communist China from a number of prominent scholars and distinguished experts on Asia.

I welcome these hearings. For Communist China's policies and intentions, in all their aspects, need to be examined — and reexamined continually.

China Specialists in Government

The Department of State and other agencies of the Government do collect, study, and analyze continually with the greatest care all the information obtainable on Communist China in order to make — and, when the facts warrant, revise — judgments of Peiping's [Beijing] intentions and objectives. Highly trained Chinese-language officers here in Washington and overseas — men who specialize in Chinese history and communism — are working full time analyzing and appraising Peiping's moves. Numerous private scholars, some of whom have appeared before this committee in recent weeks, are consulted by the Department of State. And there are, of course, many specialists on Communist China in other agencies of the Government. These capable individuals — in and out of Government — systematically interchange and cross-check their analyses and estimates to provide what I believe is the most complete and most accurate picture of Communist China, its leaders, and its policies, available to any non-Communist government in the world.

Three Caveats

Before going further, I would like to enter three caveats:

First, the experts do not always agree, especially in their estimates of Chinese Communist intentions.

Second, the leaders we are discussing are both Chinese and Communist. Some of their words and acts can perhaps be best understood in terms of Chinese background — Chinese traits or historic Chinese ambitions. Others can perhaps be better understood in terms of their beliefs and ambitions as Communists. They are deeply committed to a body of Communist doctrine developed by Mao Tse-tung. Still other words and acts may be consistent with both the Chinese and doctrinaire Communist factors.

We have faced a similar problem over the years with respect to the Soviet leadership. Some of their words and acts could be explained chiefly in terms of historic Russian imperial ambitions or Russian traits or practices. Others have been clearly attributable to Marxist-Leninist doctrine, or to interpretations of that doctrine by Stalin and more recent leaders. Some sovietologists put more emphasis on the traditional nationalist or imperial factors, others put more on the Marxist-Leninist factors. There is no way to determine the exact weight which ought to be given to each of these two influences.

Likewise, with regard to the Chinese Communists, there has been considerable disagreement over the respective dimensions of the two streams of influence: Chinese and Marxist-Leninist-Maoist. Over the years some of the experts on China may not have appreciated adequately Marxist-Leninist-Maoist doctrine. Likewise, some of the experts on Chinese Communist doctrine may tend to underestimate the Chinese factors in the behavior and intentions of the Peiping regime.

The third caveat is this: Predicting what the Chinese Communists will do next may be even more hazardous than usual at this juncture. They themselves appear to be taking stock. We know that some high-level talks have been going on and that they have called some of their ambassadors back for consultation.

Chinese Communist Setbacks

We know — the whole world knows — that the Chinese Communists have suffered some severe setbacks internationally during the past 14 months. They were unable to persuade the Afro-Asians to accept their substantive views on the Second Bandung Conference. They have found themselves in difficulty in several African countries. Their diplomatic missions have been expelled from Burundi, Dahomey, and the Central African Republic. Their technicians have been expelled from Ghana. The Governments of Kenya and Tunisia have warned them against promoting revolution in Africa.

During the fighting between India and Pakistan, the Chinese Communists marched up hill and down again. They have been disappointed by the Tashkent agreement and the steps taken in accord with it. They were strongly opposed to the agreement between Japan and the Republic of Korea, which was ratified by both countries. They have suffered a major setback in Indonesia — the Indonesian Communist Party has been decimated.

Generally, in their struggle with Moscow for leadership of the world Communist movement, the Chinese Communists appear to have lost ground. Even their relations with Castro's Cuba have sunk to the level of mudslinging.

And, probably most important of all, Peiping sees the power of the United States committed in Southeast Asia to repel an aggression supported — and actively promoted — by Peiping.

Will the Chinese Communist reaction to all these setbacks be a wild lashing out? Or will it be a sober decision to draw back and even to move toward peaceful coexistence?

We, of course, hope it will be the latter. But we cannot be sure what Peiping intends to do. We do not expect the worst but we must be prepared for it.

U.S. Relations With Peking

I will not try here today to review in detail the record of our relations with the Peiping regime. In the months after the Chinese Communist takeover in 1949 we watched to see whether the initial demonstration of intense hostility toward the United States and toward Americans who were still resident in China was momentary, or reflected a basic Peiping policy. Then came the aggression against the Republic of Korea, to which, at a second stage, the Chinese Communists committed large forces, thus coming into direct conflict with the United Nations and the United States.

We have searched year after year for some sign that Communist China was ready to renounce the use of force to resolve disputes. We have also searched for some indication that it was ready to abandon its premise that the United States is its prime enemy.

The Chinese Communist attitudes and actions have been hostile and rigid. But a democracy, such as ours, does not accept rigidity. It seeks solutions to problems, however intractable they may seem.

Sino-United States Ambassadorial Talks

We have discussed various problems with the Chinese Communists at international conferences such as the Geneva conferences of 1954 and 1962.

In 1955 we began with them a series of bilateral conversations at the level of ambassadors, first in Geneva and later in Warsaw. It was our hope that by direct, systematic communication we might be able to reduce the sharpness of the conflict between us. There now have been 129 of these meetings, the latest of which took place in Warsaw today.

These exchanges have ranged widely, covering many subjects affecting our two countries. At first there was a little progress in dealing with small specific issues, such as the release of Americans being held in Communist China. Although an understanding was reached in this limited area, Peiping refused to fulfill its commitment to release all the Americans.

I think it is accurate to say that no other non-Communist nation has had such extensive conversations with the Peiping regime as we have had. The problem is not lack of contact between Peiping and Washington. It is what, with contact, the Peiping regime itself says and does.

Although they have produced almost no tangible results, these conversations have served and still serve useful purposes. They permit us to clarify the numerous points of difference between us. They enable us to communicate in private during periods of crisis. They provide an opening through which, hopefully, light might one day penetrate. But the talks have, so far, given no evidence of a shift or easing in Peiping's hostility toward the United States and its bellicose doctrines of world revolution. Indeed, the Chinese Communists have consistently demanded, privately as well as publicly, that we let them have Taiwan. And when we say that we will not abandon the 12 or 13 million people on Taiwan, against their will, they say that, until we change our minds about that, no improvement in relations is possible.

Today we and Peiping are as far apart on matters of fundamental policy as we were 17 years ago.

The Basic Issues

In assessing Peiping's policies and actions, and the problems they present to American foreign policy and to the free peoples of the world, we must ask ourselves certain key questions.

What does Peiping want, and how does it pursue its objectives?

How successful has it been, and how successful is it likely to be in the future?

Is it on a collision course with the United States?

What are the prospects for change in its policies?

What policies should the United States adopt, or work toward, in dealing with Communist China?

What Does Peking Want?

First, the Chinese Communist leaders seek to bring China on the world stage as a great power. They hold that China's history, size, and geographic position entitle it to great-power status. They seek to overcome the humiliation of 150 years of economic, cultural, and political domination by outside powers.

Our concern is with the way they are pursuing their quest for power and influence in the world. And it is not only our concern but that of many other countries, including in recent years the Soviet Union.

Peiping is aware that it still lacks many of the attributes of great-power status, and it chafes bitterly under this realization.

Arming To Become a "Great Power"

The Chinese Communists are determined to rectify this situation. They already have one of the largest armies in the world. They are now developing nuclear weapons and missile delivery systems. They are pouring a disproportionately large proportion of their industrial and scientific effort into military and military-related fields.

What is all this military power for? Some believe it to be for defensive purposes alone:

To erect a token "deterrent" nuclear capability against the United States or the U.S.S.R.;

To demonstrate symbolically that "China must be reckoned with";

To react to an imaginary, almost pathological, notion that the United States and other countries around its borders are seeking an opportunity to invade mainland China and destroy the Peiping regime.

But such weapons need not serve a defensive role. They can be used directly by Peiping to try to intimidate its neighbors, or in efforts to blackmail Asian countries into breaking defense alliances with the United States, or in an attempt to create a nuclear

"balance" in Asia in which Peiping's potentially almost unlimited conventional forces might be used with increased effect.

These weapons can ultimately be employed to attack Peiping's Asian neighbors and, in time, even the United States or the Soviet Union. This would be mad and suicidal, as Peiping must know, despite cavalier statements that mainland China can survive nuclear war. Nevertheless, a potential nuclear capability, on top of enormous conventional forces, represents a new factor in the equilibrium of power in Asia that this country and its friends and allies cannot ignore.

Peiping's use of power is closely related to what I believe are its second and third objectives: dominance within Asia and leadership of the Communist world revolution, employing Maoist tactics. Peiping is striving to restore traditional Chinese influence or dominance in South, Southeast, and East Asia. Its concept of influence is exclusive. Foreign Minister Ch'en Yi [Chen Yi] reportedly told Prince Sihanouk recently that his country's "friendship" with Cambodia would be incompatible with Cambodian ties with the United States. Peiping has tried to alienate North Viet Nam and North Korea from the Soviet Union. It has had uneven success in such maneuvers. But it has not abandoned this objective. Where Peiping is present, it seeks to exclude all others. And this is not only true in its relations with its neighbors but in the Communist world as well.

Direct Aggression

Peiping has not refrained from the use of force to pursue its objectives. Following Korea, there were Tibet and the attacks on the offshore islands in the Taiwan Straits. There have been the attacks on India. It is true that, since Korea, Peiping has moved only against weaker foes and has carefully avoided situations which might bring it face to face with the United States. It has probed for weaknesses around its frontier but drawn back when the possibility of a wider conflict loomed.

While the massive and direct use of Chinese Communist troops in overt aggression cannot be ruled out, Peiping's behavior up to now suggests it would approach any such decision with caution.

If the costs and risks of a greater use of force were reduced by, for example, our unilateral withdrawal from the region, Peiping might well feel freer to use its power to intimidate or overwhelm a recalcitrant opponent or to aid directly insurgent forces.

Mao's Doctrine of World Revolution

As I have said, the Chinese Communist leaders are dedicated to a fanatical and bellicose Marxist-Leninist-Maoist doctrine of world revolution. Last fall, Lin Piao, the Chinese Communist Minister of Defense, recapitulated in a long article Peiping's strategy of violence for achieving Communist domination of the world. This strategy involves the mobilization of the underdeveloped areas of the world — which the Chinese Communists compare to the "rural areas" — against the industrialized or "urban" areas. It involves the relentless prosecution of what they call "people's wars." The final stage of all this violence is to be what they frankly describe as "wars of annihilation."

It is true that this doctrine calls for revolution by the natives of each country. In that sense it may be considered a "do-it-yourself kit." But Peiping is prepared to train and indoctrinate the leaders of these revolutions and to support them with funds, arms, and propaganda, as well as politically. It is even prepared to manufacture these revolutionary movements out of whole cloth.

Peiping has encouraged and assisted — with arms and other means — the aggressions of the North Vietnamese Communists in Laos and against South Viet Nam. It has publicly declared its support for so-called national liberation forces in Thailand, and there are already terrorist attacks in the remote rural areas of northeast Thailand. There is talk in Peiping that Malaysia is next on the list. The basic tactics of these "wars of liberation" have been set forth by Mao and his disciples, including General Giap, the North Vietnamese Communist Minister of Defense. They progress from the undermining of independent governments and the economic and social fabrics of society by terror and assassination, through guerrilla warfare, to large-scale military action.

Peiping has sought to promote Communist coups and "wars of liberation" against independent governments in Africa and Latin America as well as in Asia.

Words Versus Actions

Some say we should ignore what the Chinese Communist leaders say and judge them only by what they do. It is true that they have been more cautious in action than in words — more cautious in what they do themselves than in what they have urged the Soviet Union to do. Undoubtedly, they recognize that their power is limited. They have shown, in many ways, that they have a healthy respect for the power of the United States.

But it does not follow that we should disregard the intentions and plans for the future which they have proclaimed. To do so would be to repeat the catastrophic miscalculation that so many people made about the ambitions of Hitler — and that many have made at various times in appraising the intentions of the Soviet leaders.

I have noted criticism of the so-called analogy between Hitler and Mao Tse-tung. I am perfectly aware of the important differences between these two and the countries in which they have exercised power. The seizure of Manchuria by Japanese militarists, of Ethiopia by Mussolini, and of the Rhineland, Austria, and Czechoslovakia by Hitler, were laboratory experiments in the anatomy and physiology of aggression. How to deal with the phenomenon of aggression was the principal problem faced in drafting the United Nations Charter, and the answer was: collective action. We do ourselves no service by insisting that each source of aggression or each instance of aggression is unique. My own view is that we have learned a good deal about this phenomenon and its potentiality for leading into catastrophe if the problem is not met in a timely fashion.

The bellicosity of the Chinese Communists has created problems within the Communist world as well as between Peiping and the non-Communist world.

Recently a leading official of a Communist state said to me that the most serious problem in the world today is how to get Peiping to move to a policy of "peaceful coexistence."

Chinese Communist Fear of Attack

At times the Communist Chinese leaders seem to be obsessed with the notion that they are being threatened and encircled. We have told them both publicly and privately, and I believe have demonstrated in our actions in times of crisis and even under grave provocation, that we want no war with Communist China. The President restated this only last month in New York. We do not seek the overthrow by force of the Peiping regime; we do object to its attempt to overthrow other regimes by force.

How much Peiping's "fear" of the United States is genuine and how much it is artificially induced for domestic political purposes only the Chinese Communist leaders themselves know. I am convinced, however, that their desire to expel our influence and activity from the western Pacific and Southeast Asia is not motivated by fears that we are threatening them.

I wish I could believe that Communist China seeks merely a guarantee of friendly states around its borders, as some commentators have suggested. If it was as simple as this, they would have only to abandon their policies which cause their neighbors to seek help from the United States.

The trouble is that Peiping's leaders want neighboring countries to accept subordination to Chinese power. They want them to become political and economic dependencies of Peiping. If the United States can be driven from Asia, this goal will be in their grasp. The "influence," therefore, that Peiping's present leaders seek in Asia is indeed far reaching.

Dominance in the Communist Movement

I had the privilege almost exactly a year ago of commenting at some length before this committee on the Sino-Soviet dispute. The essential nature of this conflict has not changed in this year. It has, if anything, intensified and widened. Its Russo-Chinese national aspects have become more conspicuous. Both sides have clearly given increased thought to the implications of a wider war in Southeast Asia for their mutual treaty obligations. I don't know what the Soviets would actually do with respect to their treaty with Communist China, but Peiping does not seem to be counting on Soviet support.

One of Peiping's most fundamental differences with Moscow centers on its desire to maintain the sharpest possible polarization between the Communist world and the United States. Peiping argues that we are the "enemy of all the people in the world." Its national interests in Asia are served by maximizing Communist [and world] pressure on us and by attempting to "isolate" us. For this reason alone the Chinese would probably have opposed any Soviet attempts to reach understandings with us. In addition there are ideological and psychological reasons for Sino-Soviet rivalry:

The intense and deadly antagonisms that have always characterized schisms in the Marxist world;

Mao's belief that after Stalin's death the mantle of world Communist leadership should rightfully have passed to him and the Chinese Communist party;

Peiping's obsession, also held or professed by the leaders of the Soviet Union during the 30 years after the Bolshevik revolution, with a fear of being threatened and encircled;

The mixture of the psychology of the veterans of the long march and Chinese traditional attitudes which has led Peiping's leaders to believe that through a combination of patience, struggle, and "right thinking" all obstacles can be conquered; and

Peiping's professed belief that the Soviets are joining with the United States in keeping China in a position of inferiority and subordination.

All these have merged to give the Sino-Soviet dispute a flavor and an intensity which rival even the current Chinese Communist antagonism for the United States itself.

We can see that the Communist Chinese have set vast goals for themselves, both internally and externally. The disastrous results of the so-called great leap forward have forced them to acknowledge that it will take them generations to achieve their goals.

They have wrought considerable changes on the mainland of China. Perhaps their greatest feat has been to establish their complete political authority throughout the country. They have made some progress in industrialization, education, and public health — although at the expense of human freedom, originality, and creativity. But their efforts to improve agriculture and to mold the Chinese people into a uniform Marxist pattern have been far less successful.

The economic, political, and social problems still confronting the Chinese Communist leaders today are staggering.

Economic Problems

Peiping's economic power will almost certainly increase over the coming years. But even with relatively effective birth control programs the population of mainland China may reach 1 billion by 1985.

Where is the food to come from? Where are the resources for investment to come from? Can the rapidly increasing military and economic costs of great-power status be carried by Chinese society at the same time that other economic tasks vital to China's economic survival are carried out? I do not denigrate in the slightest native Chinese ingenuity and capacity for incredibly hard work when I suggest that the solutions to these problems are in the gravest doubt.

Internal Political Problems

Even more important to Peiping's leaders than these economic problems, however, are the will and morale of their own people. The current leaders — Mao, Liu Shao-ch'i [Liu Shaoqi], Chou En-lai [Zhou Enlai], and others — are an intensely committed group of men whose entire lives symbolize their willingness to postpone the satisfactions of the present for the promised glory of the future.

Every generation is suspicious that the youth of today is not what it was in the good old days. But this has become another obsession of Peiping's old men. Their comments to visitors, as well as the reports of refugees, have all emphasized their distrust of the youth of the country. They fear that their grand designs and goals — both domestic and foreign — will not be pursued with zeal by the next generation.

I believe their concern may be both genuine and warranted. How pleased can young college graduates be to be sent off to rural China for years for ideological hardening? How attractive is it to the Chinese peasant and worker to be called on for years of sacrifice to bring revolution to Africa or Latin America? Will Chinese scientists accept the dogma that scientific truth can be found only in the pages of Mao Tse-tung's writings? How can professional Chinese Communist army officers and soldiers be persuaded that the words of Mao represent a "spiritual atomic bomb" more powerful than any material weapon?

I am unaware of any new revolution brewing on the Chinese mainland. I have no evidence that the current regime does not, in practical terms, control effectively all of mainland China. But there is evidence of a growing psychological weariness that in years to come could produce a significant shift in the policies of a new generation of leaders.

The dramatic succession of foreign policy failures during the last year, both in the Communist and non-Communist world, must be having some effect on the confidence of the people in the wisdom of their leaders and even on the leaders themselves.

I do not predict any quick changes in China. Nor are there simple solutions. Peiping's present state of mind is a combination of aggressive arrogance and obsessions of its own making. There are doubtless many reasons, cultural, historical, political, for this state of mind. Psychologists have struggled for years in an effort to characterize what is a normal personality. The definition of what a normal state personality might be is beyond my abilities. I would be inclined, however, to advance the view that a country whose behavior is as violent, irascible, unyielding, and hostile as that of Communist China is led by leaders whose view of the world and of life itself is unreal. It is said that we have isolated them. But to me they have isolated themselves — both in the non-Communist and Communist world.

We have little hope of changing the outlook of these leaders. They are products of their entire lives. They seem to be immune to agreement or persuasion by anyone, including their own allies.

It is of no help in formulating policy to describe Peiping's behavior as neurotic. Its present policies pose grave and immediate problems for the United States and other countries. These must be dealt with now. The weapons and advisers that Peiping exports to promote and assist insurrections in other countries cannot be met by psychoanalysis. At the present time there is a need for a counterweight of real power to Chinese Communist pressures. This has had to be supplied primarily by the United States and our allies.

We should be under no illusion that by yielding to Peiping's bellicose demands today we would in some way ease the path toward peace in Asia. If Peiping reaps success from its current policies, not only its present leaders but those who follow will be emboldened to continue them. This is the path to increased tension and even greater dangers to world peace in the years ahead.

China as a Great Power

We expect China to become some day a great world power. Communist China is a major Asian power today. In the ordinary course of events, a peaceful China would be expected to have close relations — political, cultural, and economic — with the countries around its borders and with the United States.

It is no part of the policy of the United States to block the peaceful attainment of these objectives.

More than any other Western people, we have had close and warm ties with the Chinese people. We opposed the staking out of spheres of influence in China. We used our share of the Boxer indemnity to establish scholarships for Chinese students in the United States. We welcomed the revolution of Sun Yat-sen. We took the lead in relinquishing Western extraterritorial privileges in

China. We refused to recognize the puppet regime established by Japan in Manchuria. And it was our refusal to accept or endorse, even by implication, Japan's imperial conquests and further designs in China that made it impossible for us to achieve a *modus vivendi* with Japan in 1940-41.

We look forward hopefully — and confidently — to a time in the future when the government of mainland China will permit the restoration of the historic ties of friendship between the people of mainland China and ourselves.

Elements of Future Policy

What should be the main elements in our policy toward Communist China?

We must take care to do nothing which encourages Peiping — or anyone else — to believe that it can reap gains from its aggressive actions and designs. It is just as essential to "contain" Communist aggression in Asia as it was, and is, to "contain" Communist aggression in Europe.

At the same time, we must continue to make it plain that, if Peiping abandons its belief that force is the best way to resolve disputes and gives up its violent strategy of world revolution, we would welcome an era of good relations.

More specifically, I believe, there should be 10 elements in our policy.

First, we must remain firm in our determination to help those Allied nations which seek our help to resist the direct or indirect use or threat of force against their territory by Peiping.

Second, we must continue to assist the countries of Asia in building broadly based effective governments, devoted to progressive economic and social policies, which can better withstand Asian Communist pressures and maintain the security of their people.

Third, we must honor our commitments to the Republic of China and to the people on Taiwan, who do not want to live under communism. We will continue to assist in their defense and to try to persuade the Chinese Communists to join with us in renouncing the use of force in the area of Taiwan.

Fourth, we will continue our efforts to prevent the expulsion of the Republic of China from the United Nations or its agencies. So long as Peiping follows its present course it is extremely difficult for us to see how it can be held to fulfill the requirements set forth in the charter for membership, and the United States opposes its membership. It is worth recalling that the Chinese Communists have set forth some interesting conditions which must be fulfilled before they are even willing to consider membership:

- The United Nations resolution of 1950 condemning Chinese Communist aggression in Korea must be rescinded;
- There must be a new United Nations resolution condemning U.S. "aggression";
- The United Nations must be reorganized;
- The Republic of China must be expelled;
- All other "imperialist puppets" must be expelled. One can only ask whether the Chinese Communists seriously want membership, or whether they mean to destroy the United Nations. We believe the United Nations must approach this issue with the utmost caution and deliberation.

Fifth, we should continue our efforts to reassure Peiping that the United States does not intend to attack mainland China. There are, of course, risks of war with China. This was true in 1950. It was true in the Taiwan Straits crises of 1955 and 1958. It was true in the Chinese Communist drive into Indian territory in 1962. It is true today in Viet Nam. But we do not want war. We do not intend to provoke war. There is no fatal inevitability of war with Communist China. The Chinese Communists have, as I have already said, acted with caution when they foresaw a collision with the United States. We have acted with restraint and care in the past and we are doing so today. I hope that they will realize this and guide their actions accordingly.

Sixth, we must keep firmly in our minds that there is nothing eternal about the policies and attitudes of Communist China. We must avoid assuming the existence of an unending and inevitable state of hostility between ourselves and the rulers of mainland China.

Seventh, when it can be done without jeopardizing other U.S. interests, we should continue to enlarge the possibilities for unofficial contacts between Communist China and ourselves — contacts which may gradually assist in altering Peiping's picture of the United States.

In this connection, we have gradually expanded the categories of American citizens who may travel to Communist China. American libraries may freely purchase Chinese Communist publications. American citizens may send and receive mail from the mainland. We have in the past indicated that if the Chinese themselves were interested in purchasing grain we would consider such sales. We have indicated our willingness to allow Chinese Communist newspapermen to come to the United States. We are prepared to permit American universities to invite Chinese Communist scientists to visit their institutions.

We do not expect that for the time being the Chinese Communists will seize upon these avenues of contact or exchange. All the evidence suggests Peiping wishes to remain isolated from the United States. But we believe it is in our interests that such channels be opened and kept open. We believe contact and communication are not incompatible with a firm policy of containment.

Eighth, we should keep open our direct diplomatic contacts with Peiping in Warsaw. While these meetings frequently provide merely an opportunity for a reiteration of known positions, they play a role in enabling each side to communicate information and attitudes in times of crisis. It is our hope that they might at some time become the channel for a more fruitful dialogue.

Ninth, we are prepared to sit down with Peiping and other countries to discuss the critical problems of disarmament and non-proliferation of nuclear weapons. Peiping has rejected all suggestions and invitations to join in such talks. It has attacked the test ban treaty. It has advocated the further spread of nuclear weapons to non-nuclear countries. It is an urgent task of all countries to persuade Peiping to change its stand.

Tenth, we must continue to explore and analyze all available information on Communist China and keep our own policies up to date. We hope that Peiping's policies may one day take account of the people of Asia and her own people for peace and security. We have said, in successive administrations, that when Peiping abandons the aggressive use of force and shows that it is not irrevocably hostile to the United States, then expanded contacts and improved relations may become possible. This continues to be our position.

These, I believe, are the essential ingredients of a sound policy in regard to Communist China.

I believe that they serve the interests not only of the United States and of the free world as a whole — but of the Chinese people. We have always known of the pragmatic genius of the Chinese people, and we can see evidence of it even today. The practices and doctrines of the present Peiping regime are yielding poor returns to the Chinese people. I believe that the Chinese people, no less their neighbors and the American people, crave the opportunity to move toward the enduring goals of mankind: a better life, safety, freedom, human dignity, and peace.

Nixon's First Inaugural Address

Following are excerpts of President Nixon's Jan. 20, 1969, inaugural address, which established the basis for the "Nixon Doctrine."

...The greatest honor history can bestow is the title of peace-maker. This honor now beckons America — the chance to help lead the world at last out of the valley of turmoil and onto that high ground of peace that man has dreamed of since the dawn of civilization.

If we succeed, generations to come will say of us now living that we mastered our moment, that we helped make the world safe for mankind.

This is our summons to greatness.

I believe the American People are ready to answer this call.

The second third of this century has been a time of proud achievement. We have made enormous strides in science and industry and agriculture. We have shared our wealth more broadly than ever. We have learned at last to manage a modern economy to assure its continued growth.

We have given freedom new reach. We have begun to make its promise real for black as well as for white.

We see the hope of tomorrow in the youth of today. I know America's youth. I believe in them. We can be proud that they are better educated, more committed, more passionately driven by conscience than any generation in our history.

No people has ever been so close to the achievement of a just and abundant society, or so possessed of the will to achieve it. And because our strengths are so great, we can afford to appraise our weaknesses with candor and to approach them with hope.

Standing in this same place a third of a century ago, Franklin Delano Roosevelt addressed a nation ravaged by depression and gripped in fear. He could say in surveying the nation's troubles: "They concern, thank God, only material things."

Our crisis today is in reverse.

We have found ourselves rich in goods, but ragged in spirit; reaching with magnificent precision for the moon, but falling into raucous discord on earth.

We are caught in war, wanting peace. We are torn by division, wanting unity. We see around us empty lives, wanting fulfillment. We see tasks that need doing, waiting for hands to do them.

To a crisis of the spirit, we need an answer of the spirit.

And to find that answer, we need only look within ourselves.

When we listen to "the better angels of our nature," we find that they celebrate the simple things, the basic things — such as goodness, decency, love, kindness.

"To Lower Our Voices"

Greatness comes in simple trappings.

The simple things are the ones most needed today if we are to surmount what divides us, and cement what unites us.

To lower our voices would be a simple thing.

In these difficult years, America has suffered from a fever of words; from inflated rhetoric that promises more than it can deliver; from angry rhetoric that fans discontents into hatreds; from bombastic rhetoric that postures instead of persuading.

We cannot learn from one another until we stop shouting at one another — until we speak quietly enough so that our words can be heard as well as our voices.

For its part, government will listen. We will strive to listen in new ways — to the voices of quiet anguish, the voices that speak without words, the voices of the heart — to the injured voices, the anxious voices, the voices that have despaired of being heard.

Those who have been left out, we will try to bring in.

Those left behind, we will help to catch up.

For all of our people, we will set as our goal the decent order that makes progress possible and our lives secure.

As we reach toward our hopes, our task is to build on what has gone before — not turning away from the old, but turning toward the new.

In this past third of a century, government has passed more laws, spent more money, initiated more programs, than in all our previous history.

In pursuing our goals of full employment, better housing, excellence in education; in rebuilding our cities and improving our rural areas; in protecting our environment and enhancing the quality of life; in all these and more, we will and must press urgently forward.

We shall plan now for the day when our wealth can be transferred from the destruction of war abroad to the urgent needs of our people at home.

The American dream does not come to those who fall asleep.

Limits of Government

But we are approaching the limits of what government alone can do.

Our greatest need now is to reach beyond government, to enlist the legions of the concerned and the committed.

What has to be done, has to be done by government and people together or it will not be done at all. The lesson of past agony is that without the people we can do nothing; with the people we can do everything.

To match the magnitude of our tasks, we need the energies of our people — enlisted not only in grand enterprises, but more importantly in those small, splendid efforts that make headlines in the neighborhood newspaper instead of the national journal.

With these, we can build a great cathedral of the spirit — each of us raising it one stone at a time, as he reaches out to his neighbor, helping, caring, doing.

I do not offer a life of uninspiring ease. I do not call for a life of grim sacrifice. I ask you to join in a high adventure — one as rich as humanity itself, and exciting as the times we live in.

The essence of freedom is that each of us shares in the shaping of his own destiny.

Until he has been part of a cause larger than himself, no man is truly whole.

The way to fulfillment is in the use of our talents. We achieve nobility in the spirit that inspires that use.

As we measure what can be done, we shall promise only what we know we can produce, but as we chart our goals, we shall be lifted by our dreams.

No man can be fully free while his neighbor is not. To go forward at all is to go forward together.

This means black and white together, as one nation, not two. The laws have caught up with our conscience. What remains is to give life to what is in the law; to insure at last that as all are born equal in dignity before God, all are born equal in dignity before man.

As we learn to go forward together at home, let us also seek to go forward together with all mankind.

Let us take as our goal: where peace is unknown, make it welcome; where peace is fragile, make it strong; where peace is temporary, make it permanent.

Era of Negotiation

After a period of confrontation, we are entering an era of negotiation.

Let all nations know that during this Administration our lines of communication will be open.

We seek an open world — open to ideas, open to the exchange of goods and people, a world in which no people, great or small, will live in angry isolation.

We cannot expect to make everyone our friend, but we can try to make no one our enemy.

Those who would be our adversaries, we invite to a peaceful competition — not in conquering territory or extending dominion, but in enriching the life of man.

As we explore the reaches of space, let us go to the new worlds together — not as new worlds to be conquered, but as a new adventure to be shared.

With those who are willing to join, let us cooperate to reduce the burden of arms, to strengthen the structure of peace, to lift up the poor and the hungry.

But to all those who would be tempted by weakness, let us leave no doubt that we will be as strong as we need to be for as long as we need to be.

Over the past 20 years, since I first came to this Capital as a freshman Congressman, I have visited most of the nations of the world. I have come to know the leaders of the world, and the great forces, the hatreds, the fears that divide the world.

I know that peace does not come through wishing for it — that there is no substitute for days and even years of patient and prolonged diplomacy.

I also know the people of the world.

I have seen the hunger of a homeless child, the pain of a man wounded in battle, the grief of a mother who has lost her son. I know these have no ideology, no race.

I know America. I know the heart of America is good.

I speak from my own heart, and the heart of my country, the deep concern we have for those who suffer, and those who sorrow.

I have taken an oath today in the presence of God and my countrymen to uphold and defend the Constitution of the United States. To that oath I now add this sacred commitment: I shall consecrate my office, my energies, and all the wisdom I can summon to the cause of peace among nations.

The American Spirit

Let this message be heard by strong and weak alike:

The peace we seek — the peace we seek to win — is not victory over any other people, but the peace that comes "with healing in its wings"; with compassion for those who have suffered; with understanding for those who have opposed us; with the opportunity for all the peoples of this earth to choose their own destiny.

Only a few short weeks ago we shared the glory of man's first sight of the world as God sees it, as a single sphere reflecting light in the darkness.

As the Apollo Astronauts flew over the moon's gray surface on Christmas eve, they spoke to us of the beauty of earth — and in that voice so clear across the lunar distance, we heard them invoke God's blessing on its goodness.

In that moment, their view from the moon moved poet Archibald MacLeish to write: "To see the earth as it truly is, small and blue and beautiful in that eternal silence where it floats, is to see ourselves as riders on the Earth together, brothers in that bright loveliness in the eternal cold — brothers who know now they are truly brothers."

In that moment of surpassing technological triumph, men turned their thoughts toward home and humanity — seeing in that far perspective that man's destiny on earth is not divisible; telling us that however far we reach into the cosmos, our destiny lies not in the stars but on earth itself, in our own hands, in our own hearts.

We have endured a long night of the American spirit. But as our eyes catch the dimness of the first rays of dawn, let us not curse the remaining dark. Let us gather the light.

Our destiny offers not the cup of despair, but the chalice of opportunity. So let us seize it not in fear, but in gladness — and, "riders on the Earth together," let us go forward, firm in our faith, steadfast in our purpose, cautious of the dangers; but sustained by our confidence in the will of God and the promise of man.

The Nixon Doctrine and China

President Nixon's second annual State of the World Report, delivered Feb. 25, 1971. Excerpts below deal with his policies with regard to the People's Republic of China.

...In the last twenty years, the nature of the Communist challenge has been transformed. The Stalinist block has fragmented into competing centers of doctrine and power. One of the deepest conflicts in the world today is between Communist China and the Soviet Union. The most prevalent Communist threats now are not massive military invasions, but a more subtle mix of military, psychological and political pressures. These developments complicate the patterns of diplomacy, presenting both new problems and new prospects.

...It was in this context that at Guam in the summer of 1969, and in my November 3, 1969, address to the Nation, I laid out the elements of new partnership.

"First, the United States will keep all of its treaty commitments." We will respect the commitments we inherited — both because of their intrinsic merit, and because of the impact of sudden shifts on regional or world stability. To desert those who have come to depend on us would cause disruption and invite aggression. It is in everyone's interest, however, including those with whom we have ties, to view undertakings as a dynamic process. Maintaining the integrity of commitments requires relating their tangible expression, such as troop deployments or financial contributions, to changing conditions.

The concrete results vary. In South Korea fewer U.S. troops are required, but Korean forces must receive more modern equipment. In NATO a continuing level of U.S. forces and greater European contributions are in order. The best way of maintaining stable relationships with our allies is jointly to reach common conclusions and jointly to act on them....

"Second, we shall provide a shield if a nuclear power threatens the freedom of a nation allied with us or of a nation whose survival we consider vital to our security...."

"Third, in cases involving other types of aggression we shall furnish military and economic assistance when requested in accordance with our treaty commitments. But we shall look to the nation directly threatened to assume the primary responsibility of providing the manpower for its defense...."

The People's Republic of China faces perhaps the most severe problem of all in adjusting her policies to the realities of modern Asia. With a population eight times greater than that of Japan, and possessing a much greater resource base, Mainland China nonetheless sees the free Japanese economy producing a gross national product two and a half times that of her own. The remarkable success of the Chinese people within the free economic setting of Taiwan and Singapore, and the contributions of the overseas Chinese to growth elsewhere in Asia, stands as an eloquent rebuttal to Peking's claim of unique insight and wisdom in organizing the talents of the Chinese people.

The People's Republic of China is making a claim to leadership of the less developed portions of the world. But for that claim to be credible, and for it to be pursued effectively, Communist China must expose herself to contact with the outside world. Both require the end of the insulation of Mainland China from outside realities, and therefore from change.

The twenty-two year old hostility between ourselves and the People's Republic of China is another unresolved problem, serious indeed in view of the fact that it determines our relationship with 750 million talented and energetic people.

It is a truism that an international order cannot be secure if one of the major powers remains largely outside it and hostile toward it. In this decade, therefore, there will be no more important challenge than that of drawing the People's Republic of China into a constructive relationship with the world community, and particularly with the rest of Asia.

We recognize that China's long historical experience weighs heavily on contemporary Chinese foreign policy. China has had little experience in conducting diplomacy based on the sovereign equality of nations. For centuries China dominated its neighbors, culturally and politically. In the last 150 years it has been subjected to massive foreign interventions. Thus, China's attitude toward foreign countries retains elements of aloofness, suspicion, and hostility. Under Communism these historically shaped attitudes have been sharpened by doctrines of violence and revolution, proclaimed more often than followed as principles in foreign relations.

Another factor determining Communist Chinese conduct is the intense and dangerous conflict with the USSR. It has its roots in the historical development of the vast border areas between the two countries. It is aggravated by contemporary ideological hostility, by power rivalry and nationalist antagonisms.

A clash between these two great powers is inconsistent with the kind of stable Asian structure we seek. We, therefore, see no advantage to us in the hostility between the Soviet Union and Communist China. We do not seek any. We will do nothing to sharpen that conflict — nor to encourage it. It is absurd to believe that we could collude with one of the parties against the other. We have taken great pains to make it clear that we are not attempting to do so.

At the same time, we cannot permit either Communist China or the USSR to dictate our policies and conduct toward the other. We recognize that one effect of the Sino-Soviet conflict could be to propel both countries into poses of militancy toward the non-Communist world in order to validate their credentials as revolutionary centers. It is also possible that these two major powers, engaged in such a dangerous confrontation, might have an incentive to avoid further complications in other areas of policy. In this respect, we will have to judge China, as well as the USSR, not by its rhetoric but by its actions.

We are prepared to establish a dialogue with Peking. We cannot accept its ideological precepts, or the notion that Communist China must exercise hegemony over Asia. But neither do we wish to impose on China an international position that denies its legitimate national interests.

The evolution of our dialogue with Peking cannot be at the expense of international order or our own commitments. Our attitude is public and clear. We will continue to honor our treaty commitments to the security of our Asian allies. An honorable relationship with Peking cannot be constructed at their expense.

Among these allies is the Republic of China. We have been associated with that government since its inception in 1911, and with particular intimacy when we were World War II allies. These were among the considerations behind the American decision to assist the Government of the Republic of China on Taiwan with its defense and economic needs.

Our present commitment to the security of the Republic of China on Taiwan stems from our 1954 treaty. The purpose of the treaty is exclusively defensive, and it controls the entire range of our military relationship with the Republic of China.

Our economic assistance to the Republic of China has had gratifying results. Beginning in 1951, the U.S. provided $1.5 billion in economic assistance. Its effective and imaginative use by the Government of the Republic of China and the people of Taiwan made it possible for us to terminate the program in 1965.

I am recalling the record of friendship, assistance, and alliance between the United States and the Government of the Republic of China in order to make clear both the vitality of this relationship and the nature of our defense relationship. I do not believe that this honorable and peaceful association need constitute an obstacle to the movement toward normal relations between the United States and the People's Republic of China. As I have tried to make clear since the beginning of my Administration, while I cannot foretell the ultimate resolution of the differences between Taipei and Peking, we believe these differences must be resolved by peaceful means.

In that connection, I wish to make it clear that the United States is prepared to see the People's Republic of China play a constructive role in the family of nations. The question of its place in the United Nations is not, however, merely a question of whether it should participate. It is also a question of whether Peking should be permitted to dictate to the world the terms of its participation. For a number of years attempts have been made to deprive the Republic of China of its place as a member of the United Nations and its Specialized Agencies. We have opposed these attempts. We will continue to oppose them.

The past four years have been a period of internal turmoil and upheaval in Mainland China. A calmer mood now seems to be developing. There could be new opportunities for the People's Republic of China to explore the path of normalization of its relations with its neighbors and with the world, including our own country.

For the United States the development of a relationship with Peking embodies precisely the challenges of this decade: to deal with, and resolve, the vestiges of the postwar period that continue to influence our relationship, and to create a balanced international structure in which all nations will have a stake. We believe that such a structure should provide full scope for the influence to which China's achievements entitle it.

We continue to believe that practical measures on our part will, over time, make evident to the leaders in Peking that we are prepared for a serious dialogue. In the past year we took several steps:

● In January and February of 1970, two meetings were held between our representatives in Warsaw, thus restoring an important channel of communication. The subsequent cancelling of the scheduled May meeting was at Chinese initiative.

● In April, we authorized the selective licensing of goods for export to the People's Republic of China.

● In August, certain restrictions were lifted on American oil companies operating abroad, so that most foreign ships could use American-owned bunkering facilities on voyages to and from Mainland Chinese ports.

● During 1970, the passports of 270 Americans were validated for travel to the People's Republic of China. This brought to nearly 1,000 the number so validated. Regrettably, only three holders of such passports were permitted entry to China.

In the coming year, I will carefully examine what further steps we might take to create broader opportunities for contacts between the Chinese and American peoples, and how we might remove needless obstacles to the realization of these opportunities. We hope for, but will not be deterred by a lack of, reciprocity.

We should, however, be totally realistic about the prospects. The People's Republic of China continues to convey to its own people and to the world its determination to cast us in the devil's role. Our modest efforts to prove otherwise have not reduced Peking's doctrinaire enmity toward us. So long as this is true, so long as Peking continues to be adamant for hostility, there is little we can do by ourselves to improve the relationship. What we can do, we will. . . .

Nixon Trade Speech

Following are excerpts of a speech given by President Nixon to midwestern news media executives attending a briefing on domestic policy in Kansas City, Mo., July 6, 1971.

. . . Japan, with 100 million people, produces more than Mainland China, with 800 million people. But that should not mislead us, and it gives us, and should give none of the potential competitors in world markets of Mainland China, any sense of satisfaction that it will always be that way. Because when we see the Chinese as people — and I have seen them all over the world, and some of you have, too, whether in Hong Kong, or whether in Taiwan, or whether they are in Singapore or Bangkok, any of the great cities, Manila, where Chinese are there — they are creative, they are productive, they are one of the most capable people in the world. And 800 million Chinese are going to be, inevitably, an enormous economic power, with all that that means in terms of what they could be in other areas if they move in that direction.

That is the reason why I felt that it was essential that this Administration take the first steps toward ending the isolation of Mainland China from the world community. We had to take those steps because the Soviet Union could not, because of differences that they have that at the present time seem to be irreconcilable. We were the only other power that could take those steps.

Let me be very, shall I say, limited in what I would discuss on this particular issue, because we should not consider that more has happened than has happened. What we have done is simply opened the door — opened the door for travel, opened the door for trade.

Now the question is whether there will be other doors opened on their part. But at least the doors must be opened and the goal of U.S. policy must be, in the long term, ending the isolation of Mainland China and a normalization of our relations with Mainland China because, looking down the road — and let's just look ahead 15 to 20 years — the United States could have a perfectly effective agreement with the Soviet Union for limitation of arms; the danger of any confrontation there might have been almost totally removed.

But Mainland China, outside the world community, completely isolated, with its leaders not in communication with world leaders, would be a danger to the whole world that would be unacceptable, unacceptable to us and unacceptable to others as well.

So consequently, this step must be taken now. Others must be taken, very precisely, very deliberately, as there is reciprocation on the other side.

But now let's see how this all fits into the economic program that I mentioned a moment ago, and the economic challenge. The very success of our policy of ending the isolation of Mainland China will mean an immense escalation of their economic challenge not only to us but to others in the world.

I again come back to the fundamental point: 800 million Chinese, open to the world, with all the communication and the interchange of ideas that inevitably will occur as a result of that opening, will become an economic force in the world of enormous potential.

So, in sum, what do we see? What we see as we look ahead 5 years, 10 years, perhaps it is 15, but in any event, within our time, we see five great economic super powers: the United States, Western Europe, the Soviet Union, Mainland China, and, of course, Japan. . . .

Taiwan Disclaimer

Just a week before President Nixon embarked on his trip to Peking, the Ministry of Foreign Affairs of the Republic of China (Taiwan) on Feb. 17, 1972, issued the following statement:

"President Richard M. Nixon of the United States of America has decided to proceed to the Chinese mainland for a visit from February 21-28, 1972.

"The Government of the Republic of China hereby solemnly declares that it will consider null and void any agreement involving the rights and interests of the Government and people of the Republic of China which may be reached between the United States and the Chinese Communist regime as a result of that visit, because the regime now occupying [the Chinese mainland] has no right whatsoever to represent the Chinese people.

"The Chinese Government believes that President Nixon is cognizant of the unscrupulous nature of the Chinese Communist regime and its notorious wiliness of using negotiation as a means to carry out its intrigues of infiltration and subversion vis-a-vis free nations, and that he will not lower his guard against such intrigues. Since the announcement of his intention to visit the Chinese mainland on July 15, 1971, President Nixon has, on numerous occasions, reassured the Republic of China of his desire to maintain existing Sino-American friendship and to honor all the treaty commitments. The Chinese Government trusts that the American President will live up to the solemn assurances that he has repeatedly made.

"The fact that the Government of the Republic of China has been prevented from exercising its jurisdiction over all of its territory is mainly due to the Communist armed rebellion. This is a situation which is totally different from that of some other nations brought about by international agreements. Insofar as the Republic of China is concerned, the so-called question of unification is a question as to how to destroy the Chinese Communist rebel regime and thus enable our people on the mainland to regain their freedom. On this point, there is absolutely no room for compromise or negotiation. Under no circumstances will the basic national policy of the Government of the Republic of China to recover the Chinese mainland brook any change."

Chou En-lai, Nixon Toasts

The following toasts were exchanged in Peking, Feb. 21, 1972, during Nixon's visit.

Chou En-lai. *Mr. President and Mrs. Nixon, ladies and gentlemen, comrades and friends:*

First of all, I have the pleasure on behalf of Chairman Mao Tse-tung and the Chinese Government to extend our welcome to Mr. President and Mrs. Nixon and to our other American guests. I also wish to take this opportunity to extend on behalf of the Chinese people cordial greetings to the American people on the other side of the great ocean.

President Nixon's visit to our country at the invitation of the Chinese Government provides the leaders of the two countries with an opportunity of meeting in person to seek the normalization of relations between the two countries and also to exchange views on questions of concern to the two sides. This is a positive move in conformity with the desire of the Chinese and American peoples and an event unprecedented in the history of the relations between China and the United States.

The American people are a great people. The Chinese people are a great people. The peoples of our two countries have always been friendly to each other. But owing to reasons known to all, contacts between the two peoples were suspended for over 20 years. Now, through the common efforts of China and the United States, the gate to friendly contacts has finally been opened. At the present time it has become a strong desire of the Chinese and American peoples to promote the normalization of relations between the two countries and work for the relaxation of tension. The people, and the people alone, are the motive force in the making of world history. We are confident that the day will surely come when this common desire of our two peoples will be realized.

The social systems of China and the United States are fundamentally different, and there exist great differences between the Chinese Government and the United States Government. However, these differences should not hinder China and the United States from establishing normal state relations on the basis of the Five Principles of mutual respect for sovereignty and territorial integrity, mutual nonaggression, non-interference in each other's internal affairs, equality and mutual benefit, and peaceful coexistence; still less should they lead to war. As early as 1955 the Chinese Government publicly stated that the Chinese people do not want to have a war with the United States and that the Chinese Government is willing to sit down and enter into negotiations with the United States Government.

This is a policy which we have pursued consistently. We have taken note of the fact that in his speech before setting out for China President Nixon on his part said that "what we must do is to find a way to see that we can have differences without being enemies in war." We hope that, through a frank exchange of views between our two sides to gain a clearer notion of our differences and make efforts to find common ground, a new start can be made in the relations between our two countries.

President Nixon. *Mr. Prime Minister and all of your distinguished guests this evening:*

Mr. Prime Minister, I wish to thank you for your very gracious and eloquent remarks. At this very moment, through the wonder of tele-communications, more people are seeing and hearing what we say than on any other such occasion in the whole history of the world. Yet, what we say here will not be long remembered. What we do here can change the world.

As you said in your toast, the Chinese people are a great people, the American people are a great people. If our two people are enemies the future of this world we share together is dark indeed. But if we can find common ground to work together, the chance for world peace is immeasurably increased.

In the spirit of frankness which I hope will characterize our talks this week, let us recognize at the outset these points: We have at times in the past been enemies. We have great differences today. What brings us together is that we have common interests which transcend those differences. As we discuss our differences, neither of us will compromise our principles. But while we cannot close the gulf between us, we can try to bridge it so that we may be able to talk across it.

So, let us, in these next 5 days, start a long march together, not in lockstep, but on different roads leading to the same goal, the goal of building a world structure of peace and justice in which all may stand together with equal dignity and in which each nation, large or small, has a right to determine its own form of government, free of outside interference or domination. The world watches. The world listens. The world waits to see what we will do. What is the world? In a personal sense, I think of my eldest daughter whose birthday is today. As I think of her, I think of all the children in the world, in Asia, in Africa, in Europe, in the Americas, most of whom were born since the date of the foundation of the People's Republic of China.

What legacy shall we leave our children? Are they destined to die for the hatreds which have plagued the old world, or are they destined to live because we have the vision to build a new world?

There is no reason for us to be enemies. Neither of us seeks the territory of the other; neither of us seeks domination over the other; neither of us seeks to stretch out our hands and rule the world.

Chairman Mao has written, "So many deeds cry out to be done, and always urgently. The world rolls on. Time passes. Ten thousands years are too long. Seize the day, seize the hour."

This is the hour. This is the day for our two peoples to rise to the heights of greatness which can build a new and a better world.

In that spirit, I ask all of you present to join me in raising your glasses to Chairman Mao, to Prime Minister Chou, and to the friendship of the Chinese and American people which can lead to friendship and peace for all people in the world.

1972 Shanghai Communiqué

Following is the joint U.S.-China communiqué issued at Shanghai, Feb. 27, 1972, at the conclusion of President Nixon's trip to the People's Republic of China:

President Richard Nixon of the United States of America visited the People's Republic of China at the invitation of Premier Chou En-lai of the People's Republic of China from February 21 to February 28, 1972. Accompanying the President were Mrs. Nixon, U.S. Secretary of State William Rogers, Assistant to the President Dr. Henry Kissinger, and other American officials.

President Nixon met with Chairman Mao Tse-tung of the Communist Party of China on February 21. The two leaders had a serious and frank exchange of views on Sino-U.S. relations and world affairs.

During the visit, extensive, earnest and frank discussions were held between President Nixon and Premier Chou En-lai on the normalization of relations between the United States of America and the People's Republic of China, as well as on other matters of interest to both sides. In addition, Secretary of State William Rogers and Foreign Minister Chi Peng-fei [Ji Pengfei] held talks in the same spirit.

President Nixon and his party visited Peking and viewed cultural, industrial and agricultural sites, and they also toured Hangchow [Hangzhou] and Shanghai where, continuing discussions with Chinese leaders, they viewed similar places of interest.

The leaders of the People's Republic of China and the United States of America found it beneficial to have this opportunity, after so many years without contact, to present candidly to one another their views on a variety of issues. They reviewed the international situation in which important changes and great upheavals are taking place and expounded their respective positions and attitudes.

The U.S. side stated: Peace in Asia and peace in the world requires efforts both to reduce immediate tensions and to eliminate the basic causes of conflict. The United States will work for a just and secure peace; just, because it fulfills the aspirations of peoples and nations for freedom and progress; secure, because it removes the danger of foreign aggression. The United States supports individual freedom and social progress for all the peoples of the world, free of outside pressure or intervention. The United States believes that the effort to reduce tensions is served by improving communication between countries that have different ideologies so as to lessen the risks of confrontation through accident, miscalculation or misunderstanding. Countries should treat each other with mutual respect and be willing to compete peacefully, letting performance be the ultimate judge. No country should claim infallibility and each country should be prepared to re-examine its own attitudes for the common good. The United States stressed that the peoples of Indochina should be allowed to determine their destiny without outside intervention; its constant primary objective has been a negotiated solution; the eight-point proposal put forward by the Republic of Vietnam and the United States on January 27, 1972 represents a basis for the attainment of that objective; in the absence of a negotiated settlement the United States envisages the ultimate withdrawal of all U.S. forces from the region consistent with the aim of self-determination for each country of Indochina. The United States will maintain its close ties with and support for the Republic of Korea; the United States will support efforts of the Republic of Korea to seek a relaxation of tension and increased communication in the Korean peninsula. The United States places the highest value on its friendly relations with Japan; it will continue to develop the existing close bonds. Consistent with the United Nations Security Council Resolution of December 21, 1971, the United States favors the continuation of the ceasefire between India and Pakistan and the withdrawal of all military forces to within their own territories and to their own sides of the ceasefire line in Jammu and Kashmir; the United States supports the right of the peoples of South Asia to shape their own future in peace, free of military threat, and without having the area become the subject of great power rivalry.

The Chinese side stated: Wherever there is oppression, there is resistance. Countries want independence, nations want liberation and the people want revolution — this has become the irresistible trend of history. All nations, big or small, should be equal; big nations should not bully the small and strong nations should not bully the weak. China will never be a superpower and it opposes hegemony and power politics of any kind. The Chinese side stated that it firmly supports the struggles of all the oppressed people and nations for freedom and liberation and that the people of all countries have the right to choose their social systems according to their own wishes and the right to safeguard the independence, sovereignty and territorial integrity of their own countries and oppose foreign aggression, interference, control and subversion. All foreign troops should be withdrawn to their own countries.

The Chinese side expressed its firm support to the peoples of Vietnam, Laos and Cambodia in their efforts for the attainment of their goal and its firm support to the seven-point proposal of the Provisional Revolutionary Government of the Republic of South Vietnam and the elaboration of February this year on the two key problems in the proposal, and to the Joint Declaration of the Summit Conference of the Indochinese Peoples. It firmly supports the eight-point program for the peaceful unification of Korea put forward by the Government of the Democratic People's Republic of Korea on April 12, 1971, and the stand for the abolition of the "U.N. Commission for the Unification and Rehabilitation of Korea." It firmly opposes the revival and outward expansion of Japanese militarism and firmly supports the Japanese people's desire to build an independent, democratic, peaceful and neutral Japan. It firmly maintains that India and Pakistan should, in accordance with the United Nations resolutions on the India-Pakistan question, immediately withdraw all their forces to their respective territories and to their own sides of the ceasefire line in Jammu and Kashmir and firmly supports the Pakistan Government and people in their struggle to preserve their independence

and sovereignty and the people of Jammu and Kashmir in their struggle for the right of self-determination.

There are essential differences between China and the United States in their social systems and foreign policies. However, the two sides agreed that countries, regardless of their social systems, should conduct their relations on the principles of respect for the sovereignty and territorial integrity of all states, non-aggression against other states, non-interference in the internal affairs of other states, equality and mutual benefit, and peaceful coexistence. International disputes should be settled on this basis, without resorting to the use or threat of force. The United States and the People's Republic of China are prepared to apply these principles to their mutual relations.

With these principles of international relations in mind the two sides stated that:

● progress toward the normalization of relations between China and the United States is in the interests of all countries;

● both wish to reduce the danger of international military conflict;

● neither should seek hegemony in the Asia-Pacific region and each is opposed to efforts by any other country or group of countries to establish such hegemony; and

● neither is prepared to negotiate on behalf of any third party or to enter into agreements or understandings with the other directed at other states.

Both sides are of the view that it would be against the interests of the peoples of the world for any major country to collude with another against other countries, or for major countries to divide up the world into spheres of interest.

The two sides reviewed the long-standing serious disputes between China and the United States. The Chinese reaffirms its position: The Taiwan question is the crucial question obstructing the normalization of relations between China and the United States; the Government of the People's Republic of China is the sole legal government of China; Taiwan is a province of China which has long been returned to the motherland; the liberation of Taiwan is China's internal affair in which no other country has the right to interfere; and all U.S. forces and military installations must be withdrawn from Taiwan. The Chinese Government firmly opposes any activities which aim at the creation of "one China, one Taiwan," "one China, two governments," "two Chinas," an "independent Taiwan" or advocate that "the status of Taiwan remains to be determined."

The U.S. side declared: The United States acknowledges that all Chinese on either side of the Taiwan Strait maintain there is but one China and that Taiwan is a part of China. The United States Government does not challenge that position. It reaffirms its interest in a peaceful settlement of the Taiwan question by the Chinese themselves. With this prospect in mind, it affirms the ultimate objective of the withdrawal of all U.S. forces and military installations from Taiwan. In the meantime, it will progressively reduce its forces and military installations on Taiwan as the tension in the area diminishes.

The two sides agreed that it is desirable to broaden the understanding between the two peoples. To this end, they discussed specific areas in such fields as science, technology, culture, sports and journalism, in which people-to-people contacts and exchanges would be mutually beneficial. Each side undertakes to facilitate the further development of such contacts and exchanges.

Both sides view bilateral trade as another area from which mutual benefit can be derived, and agreed that economic relations based on equality and mutual benefit are in the interest of the peoples of the two countries. They agree to facilitate the progressive development of trade between their two countries.

The two sides agreed that they will stay in contact through various channels, including the sending of a senior U.S. representative to Peking from time to time for concrete consultations to further the normalization of relations between the two countries and continue to exchange views on issues of common interest.

The two sides expressed the hope that the gains achieved during this visit would open up new prospects for the relations between the two countries. They believe that the normalization of relations between the two countries is not only in the interest of the

Chinese and American peoples but also contributes to the relaxation of tension in Asia and the world.

President Nixon, Mrs. Nixon and the American party expressed their appreciation for the gracious hospitality shown them by the Government and people of the People's Republic of China.

Nixon on China Talks

Excerpts from President Nixon's remarks made at Andrews Air Force Base, Washington, D.C., on his return from Peking, Feb. 28, 1972:

...When I announced this trip last July, I described it as a journey for peace. In the last 30 years, Americans have in three different wars gone off by the hundreds of thousands to fight, and some to die, in Asia and in the Pacific. One of the central motives behind my journey to China was to prevent that from happening a fourth time to another generation of Americans.

As I have often said, peace means more than the mere absence of war. In a technical sense, we were at peace with the People's Republic of China before this trip, but a gulf of almost 12,000 miles and 22 years of noncommunication and hostility separated the United States of America from the 750 million people who live in the People's Republic of China, and that is one-fourth of all the people in the world.

As a result of this trip, we have started the long process of building a bridge across that gulf, and even now we have something better than the mere absence of war. Not only have we completed a week of intensive talks at the highest levels, we have set up a procedure whereby we can continue to have discussions in the future. We have demonstrated that nations with very deep and fundamental differences can learn to discuss those differences calmly, rationally, and frankly, without compromising their principles. This is the basis of a structure for peace, where we can talk about differences rather than fight about them.

The primary goal of this trip was to reestablish communication with the People's Republic of China after a generation of hostility. We achieved that goal. Let me turn now to our joint communiqué.

We did not bring back any written or unwritten agreements that will guarantee peace in our time. We did not bring home any magic formula which will make unnecessary the efforts of the American people to continue to maintain the strength so that we can continue to be free.

We made some necessary and important beginnings, however, in several areas. We entered into agreements to expand cultural, educational, and journalistic contacts between the Chinese and the American people. We agreed to work to begin and broaden trade between our two countries. We have agreed that the communications that have now been established between our governments will be strengthened and expanded.

Most important, we have agreed on some rules of international conduct which will reduce the risk of confrontation and war in Asia and in the Pacific.

We agreed that we are opposed to domination of the Pacific area by any one power. We agreed that international disputes should be settled without the use of the threat of force and we agreed that we are prepared to apply this principle to our mutual relations.

With respect to Taiwan, we stated our established policy that our forces overseas will be reduced gradually as tensions ease, and that our ultimate objective is to withdraw our forces as a peaceful settlement is achieved.

We have agreed that we will not negotiate the fate of other nations behind their backs, and we did not do so at Peking. There were no secret deals of any kind. We have done all this without giving up any United States commitment to any other country.

In our talks, the talks that I had with the leaders of the People's Republic and that the Secretary of State had with the office of the Government of the People's Republic in the foreign affairs area, we both realized that a bridge of understanding that spans almost 12,000 miles and 22 years of hostility can't be built in one week of discussions. But we have agreed to begin to build that bridge, recognizing that our work will require years of patient effort. We made no attempt to pretend that major differences did not exist between our two governments, because they do exist.

This communique was unique in honestly setting forth differences rather than trying to cover them up with diplomatic doubletalk.

One of the gifts that we left behind in Hangchow [Hangzhou] was a planted sapling of the American redwood tree. As all Californians know, and as most Americans know, redwoods grow from saplings into the giants of the forest. But the process is not one of days or even years; it is a process of centuries.

Just as we hope that those saplings, those tiny saplings that we left in China, will grow one day into mighty redwoods, so we hope, too, that the seeds planted on this journey for peace will grow and prosper into a more enduring structure for peace and security in the Western Pacific.

But peace is too urgent to wait for centuries. We must seize the moment to move toward that goal now, and this is what we have done on this journey.

As I am sure you realize, it was a great experience for us to see the timeless wonders of ancient China, the changes that are being made in modern China. And one fact stands out, among many others, from my talks with the Chinese leaders. It is their total belief, their total dedication, to their system of government. That is their right, just as it is the right of any country to choose the kind of government it wants.

But as I return from this trip, just as has been the case on my return from other trips abroad which have taken me to over 80 countries, I come back to America with an even stronger faith in our system of government.

As I flew across America today, all the way from Alaska, over the Rockies, the Plains, and then on to Washington, I thought of the greatness of our country and, most of all, I thought of the freedom, the opportunity, the progress that 200 million Americans are privileged to enjoy. I realized again this is a beautiful country. And tonight my prayer and my hope is that as a result of this trip, our children will have a better chance to grow up in a peaceful world....

"Kunming Documents"

"Reference Materials Concerning Education on Situations," usually referred to as the "Kunming Documents," were secret guidelines used by Chinese propagandists as an apologia for Chairman Mao Tse-tung's decision to invite President Nixon to China in 1972. The following — translated in Issues and Studies *(Taipei: Vol. 10, June 1974) — is from lesson three: "The Great Victory of Chairman Mao's Revolutionary Line."*

...It was primarily for the sake of the people that Chairman Mao invited Nixon to visit China. Chairman Mao pointed out that we established diplomatic relations with many countries "basically by relying on the people of these countries, rather than by relying on the governments of these countries." In our diplomatic work and in our activities in foreign countries, we consider the people as a major target. It is for the sake of making the people of the United States a major target of ours that we invited Nixon to visit China.

Some people may ask: Since it is all for the sake of the people, why then should Nixon be allowed to come for a visit? This question was already answered clearly by Chairman Mao while talking to Edgar Snow. Chairman Mao said, "The people of the United States — the Leftists, the intermediate elements, the Rightists — must all be permitted to come." He added, "In seeking a solution of problems, the intermediate elements and the Leftists can do nothing. It is necessary to have problems settled with Nixon, temporarily." By "temporarily," we mean making a transitional solution with a transitional personage. Nixon holds the baton of power. To solve problems, we must have talks with him. Nixon is a man of transition, through whom we settle the Sino-U.S. relations and get in touch with the people of the United States. If you do not talk to him, it is impossible for you to get in; nor is it possible to have your influences brought into the United States;

much less is there the possibility of doing a good job in the work with the people and in publicizing Marxism-Leninism.

Chairman Mao's wise decision to invite Nixon to visit China has thrown open the gate of contacts between us and the people of the United States. It has had an influence on the people of the United States. In the past, U.S. imperialism had adopted a policy of isolating, blockading, and containing our country, thus isolating us from the American people for over twenty years. There were very few contacts between people of the two countries, and the U.S. government described us as being very bad. Nixon's seven-day visit to China was made known to the world through the media's use of satellites. Originally he [Nixon] was attempting to make publicity for himself, without noticing that the true state of affairs in China was thus made known to people of all countries in the world. Especially noteworthy was the tremendous impact resulting therefrom when people in the United States, West Europe, and North America saw the spiritual aspects and the actual situation of the people of our country. Thus, the past U.S. lies slandering China were all shattered by facts, and our international influence was expanded.

Before and after Nixon's visit to China, newspapers and journals in the United States devoted whole pages to introductions of the situation in China, specifically publicizing Chairman Mao, reprinting Chairman Mao's poems and "Quotations from Chairman Mao," and reporting how the Chinese books were warmly welcomed. In many bookstores and libraries, the books concerning China were either bought up or loaned out at once. The number of students studying the Chinese language in various universities of the United States increased rapidly and tremendously. In some universities, the number of students studying the Chinese language increased by three to four times. This explains that China and Chairman Mao have had an influence on the people of the United States.

The visit of Nixon to China led to the announcing of a Sino-U.S. joint communiqué, in which both sides agreed to expand understanding between the two countries, to establish people-to-people contacts and exchanges in science, technology, culture, sports, and the press. This is a matter of profound significance in going one step further to open up the gate of contacts between the people of China and the United States. In the days to come, the people of the United States may come to our country, and we may also go to the United States. Since the visit of Nixon to China, many American people have come to China. These people have had a deep impression of China. They went back to write articles making publicity for China. Didn't the American columnist Alsop visit Yunnan not long ago? He went home and wrote many good articles on the changes in Yunnan and Kunming, saying that the city of Kunming was neat and clean, that the spiritual aspect of the people was excellent. By making use of the established channels of friendly contacts with the American people, our country has sent out to the United States ping-pong teams, acrobatic troupes, and delegations of scientific workers to show our work methods to the American people and to promote understanding and friendship between the people of China and the United States. Chairman Mao once said, "The salvoes of the October Revolution brought us Marxism-Leninism." When Marxism-Leninism is integrated with the revolutionary practices of China, the Chinese revolution puts on a new look. Now our influences have reached the United States. If only we work with patience and enthusiasm, Marxism-Leninism-Mao Tse-tung Thought will definitely be integrated with the practices of the revolutionary movement in the United States, thereby speeding up the process of revolution in the United States. Chairman Mao also said, "Hope is pinned on the people of the United States." Revolution has already triumphed in China. If revolution triumphs also in the United States, it will create a tremendous impact on the whole world.

Theory of the Three Worlds

Speech by Chinese Vice Premier Deng Xiaoping to a special session of the U.N. General Assembly, April 10, 1979. Printed in the Peking Review, *April 19, 1979, pp. 6–11.*

At present, the international situation is most favorable to the developing countries and the peoples of the world. More and more, the old order based on colonialism, imperialism and hegemonism is being undermined and shaken to its foundations. International relations are changing drastically. The whole world is in turbulence and unrest. The situation is one of "great disorder under heaven," as we Chinese put it. This "disorder" is a manifestation of the sharpening of all the basic contradictions in the contemporary world. It is accelerating the disintegration and decline of the decadent reactionary forces and stimulating the awakening and growth of the new emerging forces of the people.

In this situation of "great disorder under heaven," all the political forces in the world have undergone drastic division and realignment through prolonged trials of strength and struggle. A large number of Asian, African and Latin American countries have achieved independence one after another and they are playing an ever greater role in international affairs. As a result of the emergence of social-imperialism, the socialist camp which existed for a time after World War II is no longer in existence. Owing to the law of the uneven development of capitalism, the Western imperialist bloc, too, is disintegrating. Judging from the changes in international relations, the world today actually consists of three parts, or three worlds, that are both interconnected and in contradiction to one another. The United States and the Soviet Union make up the First World. The developing countries in Asia, Africa, Latin America and other regions make up the Third World. The developed countries between the two make up the Second World.

The two superpowers, the United States and the Soviet Union, are vainly seeking world hegemony. Each in its own way attempts to bring the developing countries of Asia, Africa and Latin America under its control and, at the same time, to bully the developed countries that are not their match in strength.

The two superpowers are the biggest international exploiters and oppressors of today. They are the source of a new world war. They both possess large numbers of nuclear weapons. They carry on a keenly contested arms race, station massive forces abroad and set up military bases everywhere, threatening the independence and security of all nations. They both keep subjecting other countries to their control, subversion, interference or aggression. They both exploit other countries economically, plundering their wealth and grabbing their resources. In bullying others, the superpower which flaunts the label of socialism is especially vicious. It has dispatched its armed forces to occupy its "ally" Czechoslovakia and instigated the war to dismember Pakistan. It does not honor its words and is perfidious; it is self-seeking and unscrupulous.

The case of the developed countries in between the superpowers and the developing countries is a complicated one. Some of them still retain colonialist relations of one form or another with Third World countries, and a country like Portugal even continues with its barbarous colonial rule. An end must be put to this state of affairs. At the same time, all these developed countries are in varying degrees controlled, threatened or bullied by the one superpower or the other. Some of them have in fact been reduced by a superpower to the position of dependencies under the signboard of its so-called "family." In varying degrees, all these countries have the desire of shaking off superpower enslavement or control and safeguarding their national independence and the integrity of their sovereignty.

The numerous developing countries have long suffered from colonialist and imperialist oppression and exploitation. They have won political independence, yet all of them still face the historic task of clearing out the remnant forces of colonialism, developing the national economy and consolidating national independence.

These countries cover vast territories, encompass a large population and abound in natural resources. Having suffered the heaviest oppression, they have the strongest desire to oppose oppression and seek liberation and development. In the struggle for national liberation and independence, they have demonstrated immense power and continually won splendid victories. They constitute a revolutionary motive force propelling the wheel of world history and are the main force combating colonialism, imperialism, and particularly the superpowers.

Since the two superpowers are contending for world hegemony, the contradiction between them is irreconcilable; one either overpowers the other, or is overpowered. Their compromise and collusion can only be partial, temporary and relative, while their contention is all-embracing, permanent and absolute. In the final analysis, the so-called "balanced reduction of forces" and "strategic arms limitation" are nothing but empty talk, for in fact there is no "balance," nor can there possibly be "limitation." They may reach certain agreements, but their agreements are only a facade and a deception. At bottom, they are aiming at greater and fiercer contention. The contention between the superpowers extends over the entire globe. Strategically, Europe is the focus of their contention, where they are in constant tense confrontation. They are intensifying their rivalry in the Middle East, the Mediterranean, the Persian Gulf, the Indian Ocean and the Pacific. Every day, they talk about disarmament but are actually engaged in arms expansion. Everyday, they talk about "detente" but are actually creating tension. Wherever they contend, turbulence occurs.

So long as imperialism and social-imperialism exist, there definitely will be no tranquility in the world, nor will there be "lasting peace." Either they will fight each other, or the people will rise in revolution. It is as Chairman Mao Tse-tung has said: "The danger of a new world war still exists, and the people of all countries must get prepared. But revolution is the main trend in the world today."

The two superpowers have created their own antithesis. Acting in the way of the big bullying the small, the strong domineering over the weak and the rich oppressing the poor, they have aroused strong resistance among the Third World and the people of the whole world. The people of Asia, Africa and Latin America have been winning new victories in their struggles against colonialism, imperialism, and particularly hegemonism.

...The hegemonism and power politics of the two superpowers have also aroused strong dissatisfaction among the developed countries of the Second World. The struggles of these countries against superpower control, interference, intimidation, exploitation and shifting of economic crises are growing day by day. Their struggles also have a significant impact on the development of the international situation.

Innumerable facts show that all views that overestimate the strength of the two hegemonic powers and underestimate the strength of the people are groundless. It is not the one or two superpowers that are really powerful; the really powerful are the Third World and the people of all countries uniting together and daring to fight and daring to win. Since numerous Third World countries and people were able to achieve political independence through protracted struggle, certainly they will also be able, on this basis, to bring about through sustained struggle a thorough change in the international economic relations which are based on inequality, control and exploitation and thus create essential conditions for the independent development of their national economy by strengthening their unity and allying themselves with other countries subjected to superpower bullying as well as with the people of the whole world, including the people of the United States and the Soviet Union.

...The Third World countries strongly demand that the present extremely unequal international economic relations be changed, and they have made many rational proposals of reform. The Chinese Government and people warmly endorse and firmly support all just propositions made by Third World countries.

We hold that in both political and economic relations, countries should base themselves on the Five Principles of mutual respect for sovereignty and territorial integrity, mutual non-aggression, non-interference in each other's internal affairs, equality and mutual benefit, and peaceful coexistence. We are opposed to the establishment of hegemony and spheres of influence by any country in any part of the world in violation of these principles.

We hold that the affairs of each country should be managed by its own people. The people of the developing countries have the right to choose and decide on their own social and economic systems. We support the permanent sovereignty of the developing countries over their own natural resources as well as their exercise of it. We support the actions of the developing countries to bring all foreign capital, and particularly transnational corporations, under their control and management, up to and including nationalization. We support the position of the developing countries for the development of their national economy through "individual and collective self-reliance."

We hold that all countries, big or small, rich or poor, should be equal, and that international economic affairs should be jointly managed by all the countries of the world instead of being monopolized by the one or two superpowers. We support the full right of the developing countries, which comprise the great majority of the world's population, to take part in all decision-making on international trade, monetary, shipping and other matters.

We hold that international trade should be based on the principles of equality, mutual benefit and the exchange of needed goods. We support the urgent demand of the developing countries to improve trading terms for their raw materials, primary products and semi-manufactured and manufactured goods, to expand their market and to fix equitable and favorable prices. We support the developing countries in establishing various organizations of raw material exporting countries for a united struggle against colonialism, imperialism and hegemonism.

We hold that economic aid to the developing countries must strictly respect the sovereignty of the recipient countries and must not be accompanied by any political or military conditions and the extortion of any special privileges or excessive profits. Loans to the developing countries should be interest-free or low-interest and allow for delayed repayment of capital and interest, or even reduction and cancellation of debts in case of necessity. We are opposed to the exploitation of developing countries by usury or blackmail in the name of aid.

We hold that technology transferred to the developing countries must be practical, efficient, economical and convenient for use. The experts and other personnel dispatched to the recipient countries have the obligation to pass on conscientiously technical know-how to the people there and to respect the laws and national customs of the countries concerned. They must not make special demands or ask for special amenities, let alone engage in illegal activities.

...China is a socialist country, and a developing country as well. China belongs to the Third World. Consistently following Chairman Mao's teachings, the Chinese Government and people firmly support all oppressed peoples and oppressed nations in their struggle to win or defend national independence, develop the national economy and oppose colonialism, imperialism and hegemonism. This is our bounden internationalist duty. China is not a superpower, nor will she ever seek to be one. What is a superpower? A superpower is an imperialist country which everywhere subjects other countries to its aggression, interference, control, subversion or plunder and strives for world hegemony. If capitalism is restored in a big socialist country, it will inevitably become a superpower. The Great Proletarian Cultural Revolution, which has been carried out in China in recent years, and the campaign of criticizing Lin Piao and Confucius now under way throughout China, are both aimed at preventing capitalist restoration and ensuring that socialist China will never change her color and will always stand by the oppressed peoples and oppressed nations. If one day China should change her color and turn into a superpower, if she too should play the tyrant in the world, and everywhere subject others to her bullying, aggression and exploitation, the people of the world should identify her as social-imperialism, expose it, oppose it and work together with the Chinese people to overthrow it.

...History develops in struggle, and the world advances amidst turbulence. The imperialists, and the superpowers in particular, are beset with troubles and are on the decline. Countries want independence, nations want liberation and the people want revolution — this is the irresistible trend of history. We are convinced that, so long as the Third World countries and people strengthen their unity, ally themselves with all forces that can be allied with and persist in a protracted struggle, they are sure to win continuous new victories.

Liaison Office Statement

Following is the text, as made available by the White House Feb. 22, 1973, of a communiqúe between the United States and the People's Republic of China.

Dr. Henry A. Kissinger, Assistant to the U.S. President for National Security Affairs, visited the People's Republic of China from February 15 to February 19, 1973. He was accompanied by Herbert G. Klein, Alfred Le S. Jenkins, Richard T. Kennedy, John H. Holdridge, Winston Lord, Jonathan T. Howe, Richard Solomon, and Peter W. Rodman.

Chairman Mao Tse-tung received Dr. Kissinger. Dr. Kissinger [and] members of his party held wide-ranging conversations with Premier Chou En-lai, Foreign Minister Chi Peng-fei [Ji Pengfei], Vice Foreign Minister Chiao Kuan-hua [Qiao Guanhua], and other Chinese officials. Mr. Jenkins held parallel talks on technical subjects with Assistant Foreign Minister Chang Wen-chin [Zhang Wenjin]. All these talks were conducted in an unconstrained atmosphere and were earnest, frank and constructive.

The two sides reviewed the development of relations between the two countries in the year that has passed since President Nixon's visit to the People's Republic of China and other issues of mutual concern. They reaffirmed the principles of the Joint Communiqué issued at Shanghai in February 1972 and their joint commitment to bring about a normalization of relations. They held that the progress that has been made during this period is beneficial to the people of their two countries.

The two sides agreed that the time was appropriate for accelerating the normalization of relations. To this end, they undertook to broaden their contacts in all fields. They agreed on a concrete program of expanding trade as well as scientific, cultural and other exchanges.

To facilitate this process and to improve communications, it was agreed that in the near future each side will establish a liaison office in the capital of the other. Details will be worked out through existing channels.

The two sides agreed that normalization of relations between the United States and the People's Republic of China will contribute to the relaxation of tension in Asia and in the world.

Dr. Kissinger and his party expressed their deep appreciation for the warm hospitality extended to them.

Blueprint for U.S.-China Ties

President Ford's remarks on China on April 10, 1975, in a foreign policy address to Congress.

With the People's Republic of China, we are firmly fixed on the course set forth in the Shanghai communiqué. Stability in Asia and the world require our constructive relations with one-fourth of the human race. After two decades of mutual isolation and hostility, we have, in recent years, built a promising foundation. Deep differences in our philosophy and social systems will endure, but so should our mutual long-term interests and the goals to which our countries have jointly subscribed in Shanghai. I will visit China later this year to reaffirm these interests and to accelerate the improvement in our relations, and I was glad to welcome the distinguished Speaker and the distinguished minority leader of the House back today from their constructive visit to the People's Republic of China.

Carter Foreign Policy Address

Following are excerpts from a commencement speech by President Jimmy Carter at the University of Notre Dame, South Bend, Ind., May 22, 1977.

. . .I want to speak to you today about the strands that connect our actions overseas with our essential character as a nation. I believe we can have a foreign policy that is democratic, that is based on fundamental values, and that uses power and influence, which we have, for humane purposes. We can also have a foreign policy that the American people both support and, for a change, know about and understand.

I have a quiet confidence in our own political system. Because we know that democracy works, we can reject the arguments of those rulers who deny human rights to their people.

We are confident that democracy's example will be compelling, and so we seek to bring that example closer to those from whom in the past few years we have been separated and who are not yet convinced about the advantages of our kind of life.

We are confident that democratic methods are the most effective, and so we are not tempted to employ improper tactics here at home or abroad.

We are confident of our own strength, so we can seek substantial mutual reductions in the nuclear arms race.

And we are confident of the good sense of American people, and so we let them share in the process of making foreign policy decisions. We can thus speak with the voices of 215 million, and not just of an isolated handful.

Democracy's great recent successes — in India, Portugal, Spain, Greece — show that our confidence in this system is not misplaced. Being confident of our own future, we are now free of that inordinate fear of communism which once led us to embrace any dictator who joined us in that fear. I'm glad that that's being changed.

For too many years, we've been willing to adopt the flawed and erroneous principles and tactics of our adversaries, sometimes abandoning our own values for theirs. We've fought fire with fire, never thinking that fire is better quenched with water. This approach failed, with Vietnam the best example of its intellectual and moral poverty. But through failure, we have now found our way back to our own principles and values, and we have regained our lost confidence.

By the measure of history, our Nation's 200 years are very brief, and our rise to world eminence is briefer still. It dates from 1945 when Europe and the old international order lay in ruins. Before then America was largely on the periphery of world affairs, but since then we have inescapably been at the center of world affairs.

Our policy during this period was guided by two principles: a belief that Soviet expansion was almost inevitable but that it must be contained, and the corresponding belief in the importance of an almost exclusive alliance among non-Communist nations on both sides of the Atlantic. That system could not last forever unchanged. Historical trends have weakened its foundation. The unifying threat of conflict with the Soviet Union has become less intensive even though the competition has become more extensive.

The Vietnamese war produced a profound moral crisis sapping worldwide faith in our own policy and our system of life, a crisis of confidence made even more grave by the covert pessimism of some of our leaders.

In less than a generation, we've seen the world change dramatically. The daily lives and aspirations of most human beings have been transformed. Colonialism is nearly gone. A new sense of national identity now exists in almost 100 new countries that have been formed in the last generation. Knowledge has become more widespread; aspirations are higher. As more people have been freed from traditional constraints, more have been determined to achieve for the first time in their lives social justice.

The world is still divided by ideological disputes, dominated by regional conflicts, and threatened by danger that we will not resolve the differences of race and wealth without violence or without drawing into combat the major military powers. We can no longer separate the traditional issues of war and peace from the new global questions of justice, equity, and human rights.

It is a new world — but America should not fear it. It is a new world — and we should help to shape it. It is a new world that calls for a new American foreign policy — a policy based on constant decency in its values and on optimism in our historical vision.

We can no longer have a policy solely for the industrial nations as the foundation of global stability, but we must respond to the new reality of a politically awakening world.

We can no longer expect that the other 150 nations will follow the dictates of the powerful, but we must continue — confidently — our efforts to inspire, to persuade, and to lead.

Our policy must reflect our belief that the world can hope for more than simple survival and our belief that dignity and freedom are fundamental spiritual requirements. Our policy must shape an international system that will last longer than secret deals.

We cannot make this kind of policy by manipulation. Our policy must be open; it must be candid; it must be one of constructive global involvement, resting on five cardinal principles.

I've tried to make these premises clear to the American people since last January. Let me review what we have been doing and discuss what we intend to do.

First, we have reaffirmed America's commitment to human rights as a fundamental tenet of our foreign policy. In ancestry, religion, color, place of origin, and cultural background, we Americans are as diverse a nation as the world has ever seen. No common mystique of blood or soil unites us. What draws us together, perhaps more than anything else, is a belief in human freedom.

We want the world to know that our Nation stands for more than financial prosperity. This does not mean that we can conduct our foreign policy by rigid moral maxims. We live in a world that is imperfect and which will always be imperfect — a world that is complex and confused and which will always be complex and more confused.

I understand fully the limits of moral suasion. We have no illusion that changes will come easily or soon. But I also believe that it is a mistake to undervalue the power of words and of the ideas that words embody. In our own history, that power has ranged from Thomas Paine's "Common Sense" to Martin Luther King, Jr.'s "I have a Dream."

In the life of the human spirit, words are action, much more so than many of us may realize who live in countries where freedom of expression is taken for granted. The leaders of totalitarian nations understand this very well. The proof is that words are precisely the action for which dissidents in those countries are being persecuted.

Nonetheless, we can already see dramatic, worldwide advances in the protection of the individual from the arbitrary power of the state. For us to ignore this trend would be to lose influence and moral authority in the world. To lead it will be to regain the moral stature that we once had.

The great democracies are not free because we are strong and prosperous. I believe we are strong and influential and prosperous because we are free.

Throughout the world today, in free nations and in totalitarian countries as well, there is a preoccupation with the subject of human freedom, human rights. And I believe it is incumbent on us in this country to keep that discussion, that debate, that contention alive. No other country is as well-qualified as we to set an example. We have our own shortcomings and faults, and we should strive constantly and with courage to make sure that we are legitimately proud of what we have.

Second, we've moved deliberately to reinforce the bonds among our democracies. In our recent meetings in London, we agreed to widen our economic cooperation, to promote free trade, to strengthen the world's monetary system, to seek ways of avoiding nuclear proliferation. We prepared constructive proposals for the forthcoming meetings on North-South problems of poverty,

development, and global well-being, and we agreed on joint efforts to reinforce and to modernize our common defense.

You may be interested in knowing that at this NATO meeting, for the first time in more than 25 years, all members are democracies. Even more important, all of us reaffirmed our basic optimism in the future of the democratic system. Our spirit of confidence is spreading. Together, our democracies can help to shape the wider architecture of global cooperation.

Third, we've moved to engage the Soviet Union in a joint effort to halt the strategic arms race. This race is not only dangerous, it's morally deplorable. We must put an end to it.

I know it will not be easy to reach agreements. Our goal is to be fair to both sides, to produce reciprocal stability, parity, and security. We desire a freeze on further modernization and production of weapons and a continuing, substantial reduction of strategic nuclear weapons as well. We want a comprehensive ban on all nuclear testing, a prohibition against all chemical warfare, no attack capability against space satellites, and arms limitations in the Indian Ocean.

We hope that we can take joint steps with all nations toward a final agreement eliminating nuclear weapons completely from our arsenals of death. We will persist in this effort.

Now, I believe in détente with the Soviet Union. To me, it means progress toward peace. But the effects of détente should not be limited to our own two countries alone. We hope to persuade the Soviet Union that one country cannot impose its system of society upon another, either through direct military intervention or through the use of a client state's military force, as was the case with Cuban intervention in Angola.

Cooperation also implies obligation. We hope that the Soviet Union will join with us and other nations in playing a larger role in aiding the developing world, for common aid efforts will help us build a bridge of mutual confidence in one another.

Fourth, we are taking deliberate steps to improve the chances of lasting peace in the Middle East. Through wide-ranging consultation with leaders of the countries involved — Israel, Syria, Jordan, and Egypt — we have found some areas of agreement and some movement toward consensus. The negotiations must continue.

Through my own public comments, I've also tried to suggest a more flexible framework for the discussion of the three key issues which have so far been so intractable: the nature of a comprehensive peace — What is peace? What does it mean to the Israelis? What does it mean to their Arab neighbors? Secondly, the relationship between security and borders — How can the dispute over border delineations be established and settled with a feeling of security on both sides? And the issue of the Palestinian homeland.

The historic friendship that the United States has with Israel is not dependent on domestic politics in either nation; it's derived from our common respect for human freedom and from a common search for permanent peace.

We will continue to promote a settlement which all of us need. Our own policy will not be affected by changes in leadership in any of the countries in the Middle East. Therefore, we expect Israel and her neighbors to continue to be bound by United Nations Resolutions 242 and 338, which they have previously accepted.

This may be the most propitious time for a genuine settlement since the beginning of the Arab-Israeli conflict almost 30 years ago. To let this opportunity pass could mean disaster not only for the Middle East but, perhaps, for the international political and economic order as well.

And fifth, we are attempting, even at the risk of some friction with our friends, to reduce the danger of nuclear proliferation and the worldwide spread of conventional weapons.

At the recent summit, we set in motion an international effort to determine the best ways of harnessing nuclear energy for peaceful use while reducing the risks that its products will be diverted to the making of explosives.

We've already completed a comprehensive review of our own policy on arms transfers. Competition in arms sales is inimical to peace and destructive of the economic development of the poorer countries.

We will, as a matter of national policy now in our country, seek to reduce the annual dollar volume of arms sales, to restrict the transfer of advanced weapons, and to reduce the extent of our coproduction arrangements about weapons with foreign states. And, just as important, we are trying to get other nations, both free and otherwise, to join us in this effort.

But all of this that I've described is just the beginning. It's a beginning aimed towards a clear goal: to create a wider framework of international cooperation suited to the new and rapidly changing historical circumstances.

We will cooperate more closely with the newly influential countries in Latin America, Africa, and Asia. We need their friendship and cooperation in a common effort as the structure of world power changes.

More than 100 years ago, Abraham Lincoln said that our Nation could not exist half slave and half free. We know a peaceful world cannot long exist one-third rich and two-thirds hungry.

Most nations share our faith that in the long run, expanded and equitable trade will best help the developing countries to help themselves. But the immediate problems of hunger, disease, illiteracy, and repression are here now.

The Western democracies, the OPEC nations, and the developed Communist countries can cooperate through existing international institutions in providing more effective aid. This is an excellent alternative to war.

We have a special need for cooperation and consultation with other nations in this hemisphere — to the north and to the south. We do not need another slogan. Although these are our close friends and neighbors, our links with them are the same links of equality that we forge for the rest of the world. We will be dealing with them as part of a new, worldwide mosaic of global, regional, and bilateral relations.

It's important that we make progress toward normalizing relations with the People's Republic of China. We see the American and Chinese relationship as a central element of our global policy, and China as a key force for global peace. We wish to cooperate closely with the creative Chinese people on the problems that confront all mankind, and we hope to find a formula which can bridge some of the difficulties that still separate us.

Finally, let me say that we are committed to a peaceful resolution of the crisis in southern Africa. The time has come for the principle of majority rule to be the basis for political order, recognizing that in a democratic system the rights of the minority must also be protected.

To be peaceful, change must come promptly. The United States is determined to work together with our European allies and with the concerned African States to shape a congenial international framework for the rapid and progressive transformation of southern African society and to help protect it from unwarranted outside interference.

Let me conclude by summarizing: Our policy is based on an historical vision of America's role. Our policy is derived from a larger view of global change. Our policy is rooted in our moral values, which never change. Our policy is reinforced by our material wealth and by our military power. Our policy is designed to serve mankind. And it is a policy that I hope will make you proud to be Americans. . . .

Vance on Asia Policy

Following is the partial text of a speech by Secretary of State Cyrus Vance to the Asia Society in New York City, June 29, 1977.

. . .I should like to advance the basic proposition that our prospects for sustaining and developing effective relationships with the countries of East Asia are more promising than at any time since World War II. The fundamental challenges facing the Administration are to consolidate the positive developments of the past few years — the emergence of an even closer partnership with Japan, a promising "opening" with China, the growing prosperity of the Pacific Basin economy, the emerging cohesion of the ASEAN [Association of Southeast Asian Nations] grouping — and to prevent or mitigate adverse trends which could strain the presently favorable regional environment. High stakes hang on our ability to meet this challenge, for our interests in Asia are enduring and they are substantial.

I hope to leave you with these understandings:

• First, the United States is and will remain an Asian and Pacific power.

• Second, the United States will continue its key role in contributing to peace and stability in Asia and the Pacific.

• Third, the United States seeks normal and friendly relations with the countries in the area on the basis of reciprocity and mutual respect.

• Fourth, the United States will pursue mutual expansion of trade and investment across the Pacific, recognizing the growing interdependence of the economies of the United States and the region. And

• Fifth, we will use our influence to improve the human condition of the peoples of Asia.

In all of this, there can be no doubt of the enduring vitality of our country's relationships with the peoples of Asia and the Pacific.

To the people of Asia I say tonight without qualification that our nation has recovered its self-confidence at home. And we have not abandoned our interest in Asia.

We are and will remain a Pacific nation, by virtue of our geography, our history, our commerce, and our interests. Roughly one-quarter of all our trade is now with East Asia and the Pacific; last year we sold $22 billion worth of our products in the region. For the last five years, more of our trade has been with that region than with any other, including the European Community.

To be able to speak of peace and stability in Asia is a welcome change. But serious problems persist. Our tasks are to help consolidate the emerging peaceful balance in Asia and to promote economic growth that offers promise to its people.

The United States will pursue its relations with the nations of Asia with an open mind. We will continue to work closely with allies and friends. And we hope to normalize relations on a mutually constructive basis with those who have been adversaries.

The United States recognizes the importance of its continuing contribution to Asian security. We will remain a strong military presence in the area.

Japan

Of our allies and old friends, none is more important than Japan. Our mutual security treaty is a cornerstone of peace in East Asia. Japan's democratic institutions are firmly rooted, no people anywhere enjoy greater political freedom. Its dedication to peace is unquestioned. Twenty-five years ago, even though Japan had recovered from the devastation of war, its economic advance was just beginning. Today Japan's per capita gross national product is almost $5,000. In 1953 it was only about $700 in current value, less than that in many developing countries today.

Japan's growth has been an indispensable ingredient in the economic advance of the less-developed countries in the region. Its aid has been important in contributing to the well-being of these countries; we welcome its commitment to double its assistance within the next five years.

Japan's great achievements have brought with them corresponding responsibilities. Its actions, like ours, are bound to have an impact far beyond its own borders. An enlarged Japanese market for the manufactured products of other countries would make an important contribution to a healthier world economic equilibrium, as would high rates of expansion in order to stimulate the economies of other countries.

The United States and Japan must proceed in close consultation. Above all, we must settle any issue between us in a spirit of true friendship and understanding.

People's Republic of China

Turning to China, after 25 years of confrontation we are carrying on a constructive dialogue with the People's Republic of China.

Vast differences in culture, social systems, ideology, and foreign policy still separate our two countries. But the Chinese and American people no longer face each other with the hostility, misunderstanding, and virtually complete separation that existed for two decades.

We consider friendly relations with China to be a central part of our foreign policy. China's role in maintaining world peace is vital. A constructive relationship with China is important, not only regionally, but also for global equilibrium. Such a relationship will threaten no one. It will serve only peace.

The involvement of a fourth of mankind in the search for the solution of global issues is important.

In structuring our relationship with the Chinese, we will not enter into any agreements with others that are directed against the People's Republic of China. We recognize and respect China's strong commitments to independence, unity, and self-reliance.

Our policy toward China will continue to be guided by the principles of the Shanghai Communiqué, and on that basis we shall seek to move toward full normalization of relations. We acknowledge the view expressed in the Shanghai Communiqué that there is but one China. We also place importance on the peaceful settlement of the Taiwan question by the Chinese themselves.

In seven weeks, I shall be in Peking to talk with the leaders of China. A broad range of world issues demands our attention. And we want to explore ways to normalize further our bilateral relationship with the People's Republic of China. Mutual and reciprocal efforts in this regard are essential.

As we prepare to go to Peking, we recognize that progress may not be easy or immediately evident. But this Administration is committed to the process, and we are approaching the talks in Peking with that in mind.

Across Asia we have close and historic ties with many other nations, and we intend to seek new ways to strengthen them.

Republic of Korea

The Republic of Korea has made good use of the opportunities provided by peace on the peninsula to become increasingly self-reliant and self-sufficient. The standard of living of its people has improved significantly over the past decade. Its trade has grown enormously. Its agriculture has been revolutionized.

Our security commitment to the Republic of Korea and our determination to maintain it are essential to the preservation of peace in Northeast Asia.

South Korea's growth and strength are the basis for President Carter's decision to proceed with a carefully phased withdrawal of American ground troops. This will be done in a way that will not endanger the security of South Korea. We will also seek, with the concurrence of the Congress, to strengthen South Korea's defense capabilities.

Furthermore:

● Our ground troops constitute only about five percent of the total ground troops committed to the defense of South Korea.

● The gradual withdrawal of these troops over four to five years will be offset by the growing strength and self-confidence of the South Korean armed forces.

● Our air, naval, and other supporting elements will remain.

● We are working closely with the Koreans to help them increase their own defense capabilities.

The United States and the Republic of Korea share a strong desire to establish a durable framework for maintaining peace and stability on the peninsula.

● We support the entry of North and South Korea into the United Nations without prejudice to ultimate reunification.

● We are prepared to move toward improved relations with North Korea, provided North Korea's allies take steps to improve relations with South Korea.

● We have proposed negotiations to replace the existing armistice with more permanent arrangements.

● We have offered to meet for this purpose with South and North Korea and the People's Republic of China, as the parties most immediately concerned, and to explore with them the possibilities for a larger conference with Korea's other neighbors, including the Soviet Union. We will enter any negotiations over the future of the peninsula only with the participation of the Republic of Korea.

Association of Southeast Asian Nations

Ten years ago, even while war raged in Indochina, five Southeast Asian countries created a new instrument for peace — the Association of Southeast Asian Nations or ASEAN. Our ties with one of its members, the Philippines, are rooted in our shared history. The strength of these ties is reinforced by our mutual defense treaty. Each of ASEAN's other four members — Thailand, Indonesia, Malaysia, and Singapore — is an old and valued friend.

Our economic ties with the ASEAN countries have become increasingly important. From the ASEAN area we obtain one-tenth of our crude oil imports and a much higher percentage of our rubber, tin, cocoa, bauxite, and other important raw materials. These five countries, with a population larger than all of South America, bought $3.7 billion worth of American goods in 1976.

We will maintain close bilateral relations with each ASEAN country. And we welcome the opportunity to deal with them through their organization when this is their wish. We are especially pleased that the first formal U.S.-ASEAN consultation will be held within a very few months, in Manila. These talks will, we hope, form the basis for stronger American support of Southeast Asian regional efforts.

Australia and New Zealand

Close relations between the United States, Australia, and New Zealand long antedate our formal alliance in ANZUS. Only last week, the President welcomed Australian Prime Minister Malcolm Fraser to Washington. In their wide-ranging talks, particular attention was paid to the Asian region. The contribution Australia and New Zealand make to the region is vital, and we will consult closely with them on all matters of common interest.

Socialist Republic of Vietnam

While we work with traditional friends, we have begun the process of normalizing relations with the Socialist Republic of Vietnam.

Our old friends in Southeast Asia and the Pacific have been kept fully informed of our talks with the Vietnamese. They agree that the interests of all would be served by the establishment of normal relations between Vietnam and the United States.

The scars of war still exist on both sides. Both sides retain a residue of bitterness that must be overcome. But there is some progress:

● Together with the Vietnamese, we have devised a system for identifying and returning the remains of Americans missing in action in Vietnam. Soon the remains of 20 more American pilots will be returned from the land where they died — some as long as a decade ago — to the land they served so honorably and so well.

● We have lifted restrictions on travel to Vietnam and taken other positive steps to assist in the process of reconciliation.

● We have offered to lift the trade embargo as we establish diplomatic relations. And

● We will no longer oppose Vietnam's membership in the United Nations. I expect to see its delegation seated there at the next General Assembly session.

These steps make clear that we seek to move forward in building a new relationship. Remembering the lessons of the past, neither side should be obsessed by them or draw the wrong conclusions. We cannot accept an interpretation of the past that imposes unfounded obligations on us.

Meanwhile, a new flow of Indochinese refugees commands the world's urgent humanitarian concern. Their numbers are growing at a rate of 1,500 a month. A few countries — including Thailand, France, Canada, Australia, and most recently Israel — have done much to help these unfortunate people. Some nations, however, have turned their backs, leaving an increasing number of refugees to perish by drowning or disease.

I urge that shelter and aid be offered to these refugees, until more permanent resettlement can be arranged.

Today, as we look across the vast Pacific, we see the web of relationships that links us together. In Korea, we see the obvious interaction of the interests of the Koreans, the Chinese, the Japanese, the Soviets, and ourselves. Elsewhere, the web is even more intricate and complex.

Economic Progress and Problems

Peace has freed the United States and Asia to focus attention on economic growth, which has been such a striking fact about modern Asia.

Japan's economic miracle is well known, but the remarkable economic record of other countries in Asia has received less attention. Over the past five years, for example, the economy of the Republic of Korea expanded by 11 percent, the economies of Singapore, Indonesia, and Malaysia by roughly 8 percent, the economy of the Philippines by almost 7 percent.

Continuation of these gains cannot be taken for granted. We must adopt policies to insure that economic progress is not reversed and that the benefits are more widely spread.

President Carter's pledges at the London Summit [May 7-8] are as relevant to Asia as they are to other parts of the world.

- We will continue to fight inflation.
- We will continue to seek ways of developing new energy resources and to insure stable and equitable fuel prices.
- We will resist protectionist trends and support a liberal trading system.
- We will support the establishment of price stabilizing commodity agreements and buffer stocks for selected commodities, financed by producers and consumers and supported by a common fund.

In addition, our policies in Asia will be tailored to the economic problems and opportunities of the region. The role of the Asian Development Bank is of particular importance.

Human Needs and Rights

In the field of development, the United States has recently taken the lead in calling for a concerted international effort to act on an agenda of basic human needs.

In Asia and elsewhere in the developing world, our human needs agenda must include the following essential elements which I outlined last week at the OECD ministerial meetings in Paris:

- Development of the Third World's rural areas where the great majority of the poorest people live;
- An integrated strategy for increased food production and better nutrition in these areas;

- An emphasis on preventive medicine, family planning, and prenatal care at minimal cost;
- Expanded programs of primary and secondary education and on-the-job technical training;
- Renewed efforts to involve women in the process of development.

To all of these efforts the United States pledges its strong support. But in many countries rapid population growth poses a threat to economic development. While pressures of population on the land are already threatening East Asia's natural environment, some East Asian countries will double their 1970 population by the end of the century.

I believe the United States must help countries coping with these difficult problems.

We must be equally concerned with other aspects of human rights — the right to live under a rule of law that protects against cruel, arbitrary, and degrading treatment, to participate in government and its decisions, to voice opinions freely, to seek peaceful change.

We understand cultural differences. Our tradition stresses the individual's rights and welfare; some Asian traditions stress the rights and welfare of the group. We applaud the determination of Asian countries to preserve the ability, won at great cost, to determine their own policies and establish their own institutions.

But we believe strongly that there are new and greater opportunities for improving the human condition in the Asia I have described today — a continent at peace, the home of gifted and capable people secure in their national independence.

With vigilance and determination, with friendship and understanding, we encourage our Asian friends to grasp their opportunities to promote the human rights of their peoples.

To do so will not weaken any nation. On the contrary, strength of a deeper sort — the strength that comes from the full participation of all the people — will be the long-term result of dedication to the improvement of the human condition.

Those countries in Asia which have already embarked on this course will be the stronger for it, and we shall be able to work more closely with them.

I began tonight by speaking of the welcome promise of peace, and of peaceful change, that is taking hold across the region. I want to close by stressing my deep hope for a new sense of community in Asia and the Pacific. We seek:

- To build on our relationships of mutual respect;
- To consolidate the fragile stability already achieved;
- To bring greater freedom and greater respect for human rights; and
- To erase the divisions that persist.

Toward this I pledge the best efforts of the Administration; for this I ask the support of our friends in Asia and of the American people.

The Four Modernizations

The "four modernizations" were outlined in a speech by Chinese Premier Hua Guofeng to the Fifth National People's Congress on Feb. 26, 1978. The excerpts below are from a section of the speech entitled "Speed Up Socialist Economic Construction," as translated in the Peking Review, *No. 10, March 10, 1978.*

In order to make China a modern, powerful socialist country by the end of the century, we must work and fight hard in the political, economic, cultural, military and diplomatic spheres, but in the final analysis what is of decisive importance is the rapid development of our socialist economy.

At the Third National People's Congress and again at the Fourth,[1] Premier Chou, acting on Chairman Mao's instructions, put forward a grand concept for the development of our national economy which calls for the all-round modernization of agriculture, industry, national defense and science and technology by the end of the century so that our economy can take its place in the front

ranks of the world. By the end of this century, the output per unit of major agricultural products is expected to reach or surpass advanced world levels and the output of major industrial products to approach, equal or outstrip that of the most developed capitalist countries. In agricultural production, the highest possible degree of mechanization, electrification and irrigation will be achieved. There will be automation in the main industrial processes, a major increase in rapid transport and communications services and a considerable rise in labor productivity. We must apply the results of modern science and technology on a broad scale, make extensive use of new materials and sources of energy, and modernize our major products and the processes of production. Our economic and technical norms must approach, equal or surpass advanced world levels. As our social productive forces become highly developed, our socialist relations of production will be further improved and perfected, the dictatorship of the proletariat in our country consolidated, our national defense strengthened, and our people's material well-being and cultural life substantially enriched. By then, China will have a new look and stand unshakably in the East as a modern, powerful socialist country.

The ten years from 1976 to 1985 are crucial for accomplishing these gigantic tasks. In the summary of 1975, the State Council held a meeting to exchange views on a prospective long-term plan. On the basis of a mass of material furnished by investigation and study, it worked out a draft outline of a ten-year plan for the development of our economy. The outline was discussed and approved by the Political Bureau. The "gang of four"[2] attacked the State Council meeting as "the source of the Right deviationist wind" and labelled the outline a "revisionist document." This was just plain slander and vilification. After the gang's downfall, the State Council revised and supplemented the outline in the light of China's fine political and economic situation and in accordance with the ardent desire of the whole nation to accelerate the four modernizations. The draft outline of the plan is now submitted to you for consideration.

According to the plan, in the space of ten years we are to lay a solid foundation for agriculture, achieve at least 85 percent mechanization in all major processes of farmwork, see to it that for each member of the rural population there is one mu^3 of farmland with guaranteed stable high yields irrespective of drought or waterlogging and attain a relatively high level in agriculture, forestry, animal husbandry, sideline production and fisheries. The plan calls for the growth of light industry, which should turn out an abundance of first-rate, attractive and reasonably priced goods with a considerable increase in per capita consumption. Construction of an advanced heavy industry is envisaged, with the metallurgical, fuel, power and machine-building industries to be further developed through the adoption of new techniques, with iron and steel, coal, crude oil and electricity in the world's front ranks in terms of output, and with much more developed petrochemical, electronics and other new industries. We will build transport and communications and postal and telecommunications networks big enough to meet growing industrial and agricultural needs, with most of our locomotives electrified or dieselized and with road, inland water and air transport and ocean shipping very much expanded. With the completion of an independent and fairly comprehensive industrial complex and economic system for the whole country, we shall in the main have built up a regional economic system in each of the six major regions, that is, the southwest, the northwest, the central south, the east, the north and northeast China, and turned our interior into a powerful, strategic rear base.

According to the ten-year plan, by 1985, we are to produce 400 billion kilograms of grain (440 million tons) and 60 million tons of steel. In each of the eight years from 1978 to 1985, the value of agricultural output is to increase by 4 to 5 percent and of industrial output by over 10 percent. The increase in our country's output of major industrial products in the eight years will far exceed that in the past 28 years. In these eight years, state revenues and investments budgeted for capital construction will both be equivalent to the total for the past 28 years. As fellow Deputies have reviewed the various economic targets in the ten-year plan, there is no need to list them now. The accomplishment of the ten-year plan will bring about tremendous economic and technological changes and provide the country with a much more solid material base, and, given another period of hard work over three more five-year plans, the stage will be set for China to take its place in the front ranks of the world economy.

The tasks set in the ten-year plan and the envisaged development over 23 years are gigantic, but the job can be done. We have a socialist system with its advantages which can ensure a rapid growth of the productive forces. Since the Cultural Revolution, and especially since the great struggle to expose and criticize the "gang of four," Chairman Mao's revolutionary line is better understood by the broadest masses, who are filled with a growing enthusiasm for socialism. We have a large population and abundant natural resources, and after 20-odd years of construction we have established a fairly solid material base and accumulated a rich store of experience, negative as well as positive. We have all the preconditions for speeding up economic growth. Of course, there will be difficulties ahead and arduous efforts are needed to surmount

them. But there is no reason at all to be apathetic — to underestimate the favorable conditions, be pessimistic and think that this or that is impossible. In the 11 years from 1966 to 1976, despite serious interference and sabotage by Liu Shao-chi [Liu Shaoqi], Lin Piao [Lin Biao] and particularly the "gang of four," grain output still registered an annual increase of over 4.3 percent in a third of the provinces, municipalities and autonomous regions, with a maximum of 5.5 percent, and the value of industrial output went up annually by more than 12 percent likewise in a third of the provinces, municipalities and autonomous regions, with a maximum of 18.5 percent. With the smashing of the "gang of four," we believe that it is entirely possible for all the provinces, municipalities and autonomous regions to attain or exceed these rates of increase through their efforts. We are sure this splendid plan of ours can be fulfilled. . . .

To turn the plan into reality, we must also adopt effective measures and strive to solve a number of problems bearing on our whole economy.

First. Mobilize the Whole Nation and Go in for Agriculture in a Big Way.

Agriculture is the foundation of the national economy. If agriculture does not develop faster, there will be no upswing in our industry and economy as a whole, and even if there is a temporary upswing, a decline will follow, and there will be really serious trouble in the event of major natural calamities. We must have a clear understanding of this. Predominantly agricultural provinces must make an effort to develop agriculture, and predominantly industrial provinces must make still greater efforts. All trades and professions must do their best to support and serve agriculture. . . .

Second. Speed Up the Development of the Basic Industries and Give Full Scope to the Leading Role of Industry.

As the economy becomes modernized, the leading role of industry, and especially that of the basic industries, becomes more and more prominent. We must take steel as the key link, strengthen the basic industries and exert a special effort to step up the development of the power, fuel and raw and semi-finished materials industries and transport and communications. Only thus can we give strong support to agriculture, rapidly expand light industry and substantially strengthen the national defense industries.

In developing the basic industries, we must endeavor to strengthen our work in geology and in the opening up of new mines so that geological surveying and the mining industry will meet the needs of high-speed economic construction.

In developing the basic industries, we must be good at tapping the potential of the existing enterprises and at renovating and transforming them as well as at integrating this task with the building of new enterprises. In the next eight years, and especially in the next three years, our existing enterprises must be the foundation for the growth of production. We must make full use of existing equipment, make sure that complete sets of equipment are available, introduce technical transformation in a planned way and carry out extensive co-ordination between specialized departments. This will gain us time and speed and will save on investment. Meanwhile, the state plans to build or complete 120 large-scale projects, including ten iron and steel complexes, nine nonferrous metal complexes, eight coal mines, ten oil and gas fields, 30 power stations, six new trunk railways and five key harbors. The completion of these projects added to the existing industrial foundation will provide China with 14 fairly strong and fairly rationally located industrial bases. This will be decisive in changing the backward state of our basic industries. . . .

Third. Do a Good Job in Commerce and Develop Foreign Trade.

Socialist commerce is a bridge that links industry with agriculture, urban areas with rural areas and production with consumption. It is essential to make a success of commerce, for it promotes the rapid growth of the economy, consolidates the worker-peasant alliance and serves to meet the people's daily needs. . . . We should organize the exchange of industrial goods with agricultural products well, stimulate the interchange of urban and rural products, provide the markets with adequate supplies, appropriately expand commercial networks or centers, increase the variety of goods on the market, and improve the quality of service to customers. We should tighten price and market controls and deal resolute blows to speculation and profiteering.

There should be a big increase in foreign trade. In our export trade, attention should be given both to bulk exports and exports in small quantities. While expanding the export of agricultural and sideline products, we should raise the ratio of industrial and mineral products in our exports. We should build a number of bases for supplying industrial and mineral products and agricultural and sideline products for export. We should earnestly sum up our experience in foreign trade and, in accordance with the principle of equality and mutual benefit, handle our business transactions flexibly and successfully.

Fourth. Encourage Socialist Labor Emulation and Be Active in Technical Innovation and Technical Revolution.

The masses have a vast reservoir of enthusiasm for socialism. Socialist labor emulation is a good and important method of bringing the initiative and creativeness of the people into full play and of achieving greater, faster, better and more economical results in developing the economy. Each and every locality, trade, enterprise, establishment and rural commune and production brigade should fully mobilize the masses and bring about an upsurge in emulating, learning from, catching up with and overtaking the advanced units, and helping the less advanced units....

For our economy to develop at high speed, we must break free from conventions and use advanced techniques as much as possible. The broad masses have inexhaustible creative power and are fully capable of making a great leap forward in science and technology by relying on their own strength. Our workers, peasants and intellectuals should be creative and dauntless; they should dare to think, dare to speak out and dare to act and should unfold a widespread movement for technical innovation and technical revolution in urban and rural areas, coming up with new and better ways to do things and turning their talents to full account. All localities and departments must keep abreast of current developments in technology at home and abroad, work out plans and measures for employing and popularizing new techniques, strive to learn advanced science and technology, domestic and foreign, and must not get struck in a groove and rest content with old practices. We must increase technical exchanges and fight against the rotten bourgeois style of refusing to share information. Commendations and proper awards should be given to those units that have achieved marked successes in adopting new techniques, developing new technologies and turning out new products as well as to those collectives and individuals who have made inventions.

Fifth. Strengthen Unified Planning and Give Full Play to the Initiative of Both the Central and the Local Authorities.

Planned economy is a basic feature of the socialist economy. We must resolutely put an end to the anarchy resulting from the interference and sabotage of the "gang of four" and bring all economic undertakings into the orbit of planned, proportionate development. In formulating plans, we must follow the mass line, and both the central departments and the localities should do more investigation and study, endeavor to strike an overall balance, make the plans bold as well as sound and allocate manpower, material and money where they are most needed so that the various branches of the economy develop in coordination. A strict system of personal responsibility must be set up at all levels, from the departments under the State Council to the provinces, municipalities and autonomous regions right down to the grass-roots units, so that each leading cadre has his clear-cut responsibilities and nothing is neglected. Fulfillment of the state plan will thus be effectively ensured. We must check up regularly on how the localities, departments and grass-roots units are carrying out their plans. We shall commend those who fulfill their plans satisfactorily and shall hold the leading cadres responsible where the plan is not fulfilled because of their poor work and bureaucracy. In the case of serious failures necessary disciplinary action will be taken....

Sixth. Uphold the Principle of "From Each According to His Ability, to Each According to His Work" and Steadily Improve the Livelihood of the People.

Throughout the historical period of socialism, we must uphold the principles of "He who does not work, neither shall he eat" and "from each according to his ability, to each according to his work." In applying them we must firmly put proletarian politics in command, strengthen ideological and political work and teach and encourage everybody to cultivate the communist attitude towards labor and to serve the people wholeheartedly. With regard to distribution, while we should avoid a wide wage spread, we must also oppose equalitarianism and apply the principle of more pay for more work and less pay for less work. The enthusiasm of the masses cannot be aroused if no distinction is made between those who do more work and those who do less, between those who do a good job and those who do a poor one, and between those who work and those who don't. All people's communes and production brigades must seriously apply the system of fixed production quotas and calculation of work-points on the basis of work done and must enforce the principle of equal pay for equal work irrespective of sex. The staff and workers of state enterprises should be paid primarily on a time-rate basis with piecework playing a secondary role, and with additional bonuses. There should be pecuniary allowances for jobs requiring higher labor intensity or performed under worse working conditions. In socialist labor emulation, moral encouragement and material reward must go hand in hand, with emphasis on the former. As regards the reform of the wage system, the relevant departments under the State Council should, together with the local authorities, make conscientious investigation and study, sum up experience, canvass the opinions of the masses and then submit a draft plan based on overall consideration to the central authorities for approval before it is gradually implemented....

We are not yet acquainted with many of the problems that crop up in economic construction. In particular, in many respects modern production remains an unknown kingdom of necessity to us. In acccordance with Chairman Mao's instructions, the leading cadres at all levels must use their brains and assiduously study Marxism-Leninism, economics, production management and science and technology so as to "become expert in political and economic work on the basis of a higher level of Marxism-Leninism." We must study hard and work well, sum up experience, attain a better grasp of the laws governing socialist economic construction, master the art of guiding and organizing modern production, raise the level of economic management and do our economic work in an ever more meticulous, thoroughgoing, practical and scientific way, thus propelling the national economy forward at high speed....

[1] *Dec. 21, 1964, to Jan. 5, 1965, and Jan. 13-17, 1974.*
[2] *Zhang Chunqiao, Yao Wenyuan, Jiang Qing, and Wang Hongwen. (See biography p. 285)*
[3] *One-third of an acre.*

Chinese Constitution

Meeting in Peking Feb. 26-March 5, 1978, the National People's Congress, China's nominal parliament, adopted a new constitution for the People's Republic. The constitution, which replaced a charter adopted in 1975, was based largely on the 1954 constitution, China's first as a communist state.

Preamble

After more than a century of heroic struggle the Chinese people, led by the Communist Party of China headed by our great leader and teacher Chairman Mao Tse-tung, finally overthrew the reactionary rule of imperialism, feudalism and bureaucrat-capitalism by means of people's revolutionary war, winning complete victory in the new democratic revolution, and in 1949 founded the People's Republic of China.

The founding of the People's Republic of China marked the beginning of the historical period of socialism in our country. Since then, under the leadership of Chairman Mao and the Chinese Communist Party, the people of all our nationalities have carried out Chairman Mao's proletarian revolutionary line in the political, economic, cultural and military fields and in foreign affairs and have won great victories in socialist revolution and socialist construction through repeated struggles against enemies both at home and abroad and through the Great Proletarian Cultural Revolution. The dictatorship of the proletariat in our country has been consolidated and strengthened, and China has become a socialist country with the beginnings of prosperity.

Chairman Mao Tse-tung was the founder of the People's Republic of China. All our victories in revolution and construction have been won under the guidance of Marxism-Leninism-Mao Tse-tung Thought. The fundamental guarantee that the people of all our nationalities will struggle in unity and carry the proletarian revolution through to the end is always to hold high and staunchly to defend the great banner of Chairman Mao.

The triumphant conclusion of the first Great Proletarian Cultural Revolution has ushered in a new period of development in China's socialist revolution and socialist construction. In accordance with the basic line of the Chinese Communist Party for the entire historical period of socialism, the general task for the people of the whole country in this new period is: To persevere in continuing the revolution under the dictatorship of the proletariat, carry forward the three great revolutionary movements of class struggle, the struggle for production and scientific experiment, and make China a great and powerful socialist country with modern agriculture, industry, national defense and science and technology by the end of the century.

We must persevere in the struggle of the proletariat against the bourgeoisie and in the struggle for the socialist road against the capitalist road. We must oppose revisionism and prevent the restoration of capitalism. We must be prepared to deal with subversion and aggression against our country by social-imperialism and imperialism.

We should consolidate and expand the revolutionary united front which is led by the working class and based on the worker-peasant alliance, and which unites the large numbers of intellectuals and other working people, patriotic democratic parties, patriotic personages, our compatriots in Taiwan, Hongkong and Macao, and our countrymen residing abroad. We should enhance the great unity of all the nationalities in our country. We should correctly distinguish and handle the contradictions among the people and those between ourselves and the enemy. We should endeavor to create among the people of the whole country a political situation in which there are both centralism and democracy, both discipline and freedom, both unity of will and personal ease of mind and liveliness, so as to help bring all positive factors into play, overcome all difficulties, better consolidate the proletarian dictatorship and build up our country more rapidly.

Taiwan is China's sacred territory. We are determined to liberate Taiwan and accomplish the great cause of unifying our motherland.

In international affairs, we should establish and develop relations with other countries on the basis of the Five Principles of mutual respect for sovereignty and territorial integrity, mutual non-aggression, non-interference in each other's internal affairs, equality and mutual benefit, and peaceful coexistence. Our country will never seek hegemony, or strive to be a superpower. We should uphold proletarian internationalism. In accordance with the theory of the three worlds, we should strengthen our unity with the proletariat and the oppressed people and nations throughout the world, the socialist countries, and the third world countries, and we should unite with all countries subjected to aggression, subversion, interference, control and bullying by the social- imperialist and imperialist superpowers to form the broadest possible international united front against the hegemonism of the superpowers and against a new world war, and strive for the progress and emancipation of humanity.

Chapter One: General Principles

Article 1

The People's Republic of China is a socialist state of the dictatorship of the proletariat led by the working class and based on the alliance of workers and peasants.

Article 2

The Communist Party of China is the core of leadership of the whole Chinese people. The working class exercises leadership over the state through its vanguard, the Communist Party of China.

The guiding ideology of the People's Republic of China is Marxism-Leninism-Mao Tse-tung Thought.

Article 3

All power in the People's Republic of China belongs to the people. The organs through which the people exercise state power are the National People's Congress and the local people's congresses at various levels.

The National People's Congress, the local people's congresses at various levels and all other organs of state practice democratic centralism.

Article 4

The People's Republic of China is a unitary multi-national state.

All the nationalities are equal. There should be unity and fraternal love among the nationalities and they should help and learn from each other. Discrimination against, or oppression of, any nationality, and acts which undermine the unity of the nationalities are prohibited. Big-nationality chauvinism and local-nationality chauvinism must be opposed.

All the nationalities have the freedom to use and develop their own spoken and written languages, and to preserve or reform their own customs and ways.

Regional autonomy applies in an area where a minority nationality lives in a compact community. All the national autonomous areas are inalienable parts of the People's Republic of China.

Article 5

There are mainly two kinds of ownership of the means of production in the People's Republic of China at the present stage: socialist ownership by the whole people and socialist collective ownership by the working people.

The state allows non-agricultural individual laborers to engage in individual labor involving no exploitation of others, within the limits permitted by law and under unified arrangement and management by organizations at the basic level in cities and towns or in rural areas. At the same time, it guides these individual laborers step by step onto the road of socialist collectivization.

Article 6

The state sector of the economy, that is, the socialist sector owned by the whole people, is the leading force in the national economy.

Mineral resources, waters and those forests, undeveloped lands and other marine and land resources owned by the state are the property of the whole people.

The state may requisition by purchase, take over for use, or nationalize land under conditions prescribed by law.

Article 7

The rural people's commune sector of the economy is a socialist sector collectively owned by the masses of working people. At present, it generally takes the form of three-level ownership, that is, ownership by the commune, the production brigade and the production team, with the production team as the basic accounting unit. A production brigade may become the basic accounting unit when its conditions are ripe.

Provided that the absolute predominance of the collective economy of the people's commune is ensured, commune members may farm small plots of land for personal needs, engage in limited household side-line production, and in pastoral areas they may also keep a limited number of livestock for personal needs.

Article 8

Socialist public property shall be inviolable. The state ensures the consolidation and development of the socialist sector of the economy owned by the whole people and of the socialist sector collectively owned by the masses of working people.

The state prohibits any person from using any means whatsoever to disrupt the economic order of the society, undermine the economic plans of the state, encroach upon or squander state and collective property, or injure the public interest.

Article 9

The state protects the right of citizens to own lawfully earned income, savings, houses and other means of livelihood.

Article 10

The state applies the socialist principles: "He who does not work, neither shall he eat" and "from each according to his ability, to each according to his work."

Work is an honorable duty for every citizen able to work. The state promotes socialist labor emulation, and, putting proletarian politics in command, it applies the policy of combining moral encouragement with material reward, with the stress on the former, in order to heighten the citizens' socialist enthusiasm and creativeness in work.

Article 11

The state adheres to the general line of going all out, aiming high and achieving greater, faster, better and more economical results in building socialism, it undertakes the planned, proportionate and high-speed development of the national economy, and it continuously develops the productive forces, so as to consolidate the country's independence and security and improve the people's material and cultural life step by step.

In developing the national economy, the state adheres to the principle of building our country independently, with the initiative in our own hands and through self-reliance, hard struggle, diligence and thrift, it adheres to the principle of taking agriculture as the foundation and industry as the leading factor, and it adheres to the principle of bringing the initiative of both the central and local

authorities into full play under the unified leadership of the central authorities.

The state protects the environment and natural resources and prevents and eliminates pollution and other hazards to the public.

Article 12

The state devotes major efforts to developing science, expands scientific research. promotes technical innovation and technical revolution and adopts advanced techniques wherever possible in all departments of the national economy. In scientific and technological work we must follow the practice of combining professional contingents with the masses, and combining learning from others with our own creative efforts.

Article 13

The state devotes major efforts to developing education in order to raise the cultural and scientific level of the whole nation. Education must serve proletarian politics and be combined with productive labor and must enable everyone who receives an education to develop morally, intellectually and physically and become a worker with both socialist consciousness and culture.

Article 14

The state upholds the leading position of Marxism-Leninism-Mao Tse-tung Thought in all spheres of ideology and culture. All cultural undertakings must serve the workers, peasants and soldiers and serve socialism.

The state applies the policy of "letting a hundred flowers blossom and a hundred schools of thought contend" so as to promote the development of the arts and sciences and bring about a flourishing socialist culture.

Article 15

All organs of state must constantly maintain close contact with the masses of the people, rely on them, heed their opinions, be concerned for their weal and woe, streamline administration, practice economy, raise efficiency and combat bureaucracy.

The leading personnel of state organs at all levels must conform to the requirements for successors in the proletarian revolutionary cause and their composition must conform to the principle of the three-in-one combination of the old, the middle-aged and the young.

Article 16

The personnel of organs of state must earnestly study Marxism-Leninism-Mao Tse-tung Thought, wholeheartedly serve the people, endeavor to perfect their professional competence, take an active part in collective productive labor, accept supervision by the masses, be models in observing the Constitution and the law, correctly implement the policies of the state, seek the truth from facts, and must not have recourse to deception or exploit their position and power to seek personal gain.

Article 17

The state adheres to the principle of socialist democracy, and ensures to the people the right to participate in the management of state affairs and of all economic and cultural undertakings, and the right to supervise the organs of state and their personnel.

Article 18

The state safeguards the socialist system, suppresses all treasonable and counter-revolutionary activities, punishes all traitors and counter-revolutionaries, and punishes new-born bourgeois elements and other bad elements.

The state deprives of political rights, as prescribed by law, those landlords, rich peasants and reactionary capitalists who have not yet been reformed, and at the same time it provides them with the opportunity to earn a living so that they may be reformed through labor and become law-abiding citizens supporting themselves by their own labor.

Article 19

The Chairman of the Central Committee of the Communist Party of China commands the armed forces of the People's Republic of China.

The Chinese People's Liberation Army is the workers' and peasants' own armed force led by the Communist Party of China; it is the pillar of the dictatorship of the proletariat. The state devotes major efforts to the revolutionization and modernization of the Chinese People's Liberation Army, strengthens the building of the militia and adopts a system under which our armed forces are a combination of the field armies, the regional forces and the militia.

The fundamental task of the armed forces of the People's Republic of China is: To safeguard the socialist revolution and socialist construction, to defend the sovereignty, territorial integrity and security of the state, and to guard against subversion and aggression by social-imperialism, imperialism and their lackeys.

Chapter Two: The Structure of the State

SECTION I: THE NATIONAL PEOPLE'S CONGRESS

Article 20

The National People's Congress is the highest organ of state power.

Article 21

The National People's Congress is composed of deputies elected by the people's congresses of the provinces, autonomous regions, and municipalities directly under the Central Government, and by the People's Liberation Army. The deputies should be elected by secret ballot after democratic consultation.

The National People's Congress is elected for a term of five years. Under special circumstances, its term of office may be extended or the succeeding National People's Congress may be convened before its due date.

The National People's Congress holds one session each year. When necessary, the session may be advanced or postponed.

Article 22

The National People's Congress exercises the following functions and powers:

(1) to amend the Constitution;

(2) to make laws;

(3) to supervise the enforcement of the Constitution and the law;

(4) to decide on the choice of the Premier of the State Council upon the recommendation of the Central Committee of the Communist Party of China;

(5) to decide on the choice of other members of the State Council upon the recommendation of the Premier of the State Council;

(6) to elect the President of the Supreme People's Court and the Chief Procurator of the Supreme People's Procuratorate;

(7) to examine and approve the national economic plan, the state budget and the final state accounts;

(8) to confirm the following administrative divisions: provinces, autonomous regions, and municipalities directly under the Central Government;

(9) to decide on questions of war and peace; and

(10) to exercise such other functions and powers as the National People's Congress deems necessary.

Article 23

The National People's Congress has the power to remove from office the members of the State Council, the President of the Supreme People's Court and the Chief Procurator of the Supreme People's Procuratorate.

Article 24

The Standing Committee of the National People's Congress is the permanent organ of the National People's Congress. It is responsible and accountable to the National People's Congress.

The Standing Committee of the National People's Congress is composed of the following members:

the Chairman;

the Vice-Chairmen;

the Secretary-General; and

other members.

The National People's Congress elects the Standing Committee of the National People's Congress and has the power to recall its members.

Article 25

The Standing Committee of the National People's Congress exercises the following functions and powers:

(1) to conduct the election of deputies to the National People's Congress;

(2) to convene the sessions of the National People's Congress;

(3) to interpret the Constitution and laws and to enact decrees;

(4) to supervise the work of the State Council, the Supreme People's Court and the Supreme People's Procuratorate;

(5) to change and annul inappropriate decisions adopted by the organs of state power of provinces, autonomous regions, and municipalities directly under the Central Government;

(6) to decide on the appointment and removal of individual members of the State Council upon the recommendation of the Premier of the State Council when the National People's Congress is not in session;

(7) to appoint and remove Vice-Presidents of the Supreme People's Court and Deputy Chief Procurators of the Supreme People's Procuratorate;

(8) to decide on the appointment and removal of plenipotentiary representatives abroad;

(9) to decide on the ratification and abrogation of treaties concluded with foreign states;

(10) to institute state titles of honor and decide on their conferment;

(11) to decide on the granting of pardons;

(12) to decide on the proclamation of a state of war in the event of armed attack on the country when the National People's Congress is not in session; and

(13) to exercise such other functions and powers as are vested in it by the National People's Congress.

Article 26

The Chairman of the Standing Committee of the National People's Congress presides over the work of the Standing Committee; receives foreign diplomatic envoys; and in accordance with the decisions of the National People's Congress or its Standing Committee promulgates laws and decrees, dispatches and recalls plenipotentiary representatives abroad, ratifies treaties concluded with foreign states and confers state titles of honor.

The Vice-Chairmen of the Standing Committee of the National People's Congress assist the Chairman in his work and may exercise part of the Chairman's functions and powers on his behalf.

Article 27

The National People's Congress and its Standing Committee may establish special committees as deemed necessary.

Article 28

Deputies to the National People's Congress have the right to address inquiries to the State Council, the Supreme People's Court, the Supreme People's Procuratorate, and the ministries and commissions of the State Council, which are all under obligation to answer.

Article 29

Deputies to the National People's Congress are subject to supervision by the units which elect them. These electoral units have the power to replace at any time the deputies they elect, as prescribed by law.

SECTION II: THE STATE COUNCIL

Article 30

The State Council is the Central People's Government and the executive organ of the highest organ of state power; it is the highest organ of state administration.

The State Council is responsible and accountable to the National People's Congress, or, when the National People's Congress is not in session, to its Standing Committee.

Article 31

The State Council is composed of the following members:
the Premier;
the Vice-Premiers;
the ministers; and
the ministers heading the commissions.
The Premier presides over the work of the State Council and the Vice-Premiers assist the Premier in his work.

Article 32

The State Council exercises the following functions and powers:

(1) to formulate administrative measures, issue decisions and orders and verify their execution, in accordance with the Constitution, laws and decrees;

(2) to submit proposals on laws and other matters to the National People's Congress or its Standing Committee;

(3) to exercise unified leadership over the work of the ministries and commissions and other organizations under it;

(4) to exercise unified leadership over the work of local organs of state administration at various levels throughout the country;

(5) to draw up and put into effect the national economic plan and the state budget;

(6) to protect the interests of the state, maintain public order and safeguard the rights of citizens;

(7) to confirm the following administrative divisions: autonomous prefectures, counties, autonomous counties, and cities;

(8) to appoint and remove administrative personnel according to the provisions of the law; and

(9) to exercise such other functions and powers as are vested in it by the National People's Congress or its Standing Committee.

SECTION III:THE LOCAL PEOPLE'S CONGRESSES AND THE LOCAL REVOLUTIONARY COMMITTEES AT VARIOUS LEVELS

Article 33

The administrative division of the People's Republic of China is as follows:

(1) The country is divided into provinces, autonomous regions, and municipalities directly under the Central Government;

(2) Provinces and autonomous regions are divided into autonomous prefectures, counties, autonomous counties, and cities; and

(3) Counties and autonomous counties are divided into people's communes and towns.

Municipalities directly under the Central Government and other large cities are divided into districts and counties. Autonomous prefectures are divided into counties, autonomous counties, and cities.

Autonomous regions, autonomous prefectures and autonomous counties are all national autonomous areas.

Article 34

People's congresses and revolutionary committees are established in provinces, municipalities directly under the Central Government, counties, cities, municipal districts, people's communes and towns.

People's congresses and revolutionary committees of the people's communes are organizations of political power at the grassroots level, and are also leading organs of collective economy.

Revolutionary committees at the provincial level may establish administrative offices as their agencies in prefectures.

Organs of self-government are established in autonomous regions, autonomous prefectures and autonomous counties.

Article 35

Local people's congresses at various levels are local organs of state power.

Deputies to the people's congresses of provinces, municipalities directly under the Central Government, counties, and cities divided into districts are elected by people's congresses at the next lower level by secret ballot after democratic consultation; deputies to the people's congresses of cities not divided into districts, and of municipal districts, people's communes and towns are directly elected by the voters by secret ballot after democratic consultation.

The people's congresses of provinces and municipalities directly under the Central Government are elected for a term of five years. The people's congresses of counties, cities and municipal districts are elected for a term of three years. The people's congresses of people's communes and towns are elected for a term of two years.

Local people's congresses at various levels hold at least one session each year which is to be convened by revolutionary committees at the corresponding levels.

The units and electorates which elect the deputies to the local people's congresses at various levels have the power to supervise, remove and replace their deputies at any time according to the provisions of the law.

Article 36

Local people's congresses at various levels, in their respective administrative areas, ensure the observance and enforcement of the Constitution, laws and decrees; ensure the implementation of the state plan; make plans for local economic and cultural development and for public utilities; examine and approve local economic plans, budgets and final accounts; protect public property; maintain public order; safeguard the rights of citizens and the equal rights of minority nationalities; and promote the development of socialist revolution and socialist construction.

Local people's congresses may adopt and issue decisions within the limits of their authority as prescribed by law.

Local people's congresses elect, and have the power to recall, members of revolutionary committees at the corresponding levels. People's congresses at county level and above elect, and have the power to recall, the presidents of the people's courts and the chief procurators of the people's procuratorates at the corresponding levels.

Deputies to local people's congresses at various levels have the right to address inquiries to the revolutionary committees, people's courts, people's procuratorates and organs under the revolutionary committees at the corresponding levels, which are all under obligation to answer.

Article 37

Local revolutionary committees at various levels, that is, local people's governments, are the executive organs of local people's congresses at the corresponding levels and they are also local organs of state administration.

A local revolutionary committee is composed of a chairman, vice-chairmen and other members.

Local revolutionary committees carry out the decisions of people's congresses at the corresponding levels as well as the decisions and orders of the organs of state administration at higher levels, direct the administrative work of their respective areas, and issue decisions and orders within the limits of their authority as prescribed by law. Revolutionary committees at county level and above appoint or remove the personnel of organs of state according to the provisions of the law.

Local revolutionary committees are responsible and accountable to people's congresses at the corresponding levels and to the organs of state administration at the next higher level, and work under the unified leadership of the State Council.

SECTION IV: THE ORGANS OF SELF-GOVERNMENT OF NATIONAL AUTONOMOUS AREAS

Article 38

The organs of self-government of autonomous regions, autonomous prefectures and autonomous counties are people's congresses and revolutionary committees.

The election of the people's congresses and revolutionary committees of national autonomous areas, their terms of office, their functions and powers and also the establishment of their agencies should conform to the basic principles governing the organization of local organs of state as specified in Section III, Chapter Two, of the Constitution.

In autonomous areas where a number of nationalities live together, each nationality is entitled to appropriate representation in the organs of self-government.

Article 39

The organs of self-government of national autonomous areas exercise autonomy within the limits of their authority as prescribed by law, in addition to exercising the functions and powers of local organs of state as specified by the Constitution.

The organs of self-government of national autonomous areas may, in the light of the political, economic and cultural characteristics of the nationality or nationalities in a given area, make regulations on the exercise of autonomy and also specific regulations and submit them to the Standing Committee of the National People's Congress for approval.

In performing their functions, the organs of self-government of national autonomous areas employ the spoken and written language or languages commonly used by the nationality or nationalities in the locality.

Article 40

The higher organs of state shall fully safeguard the exercise of autonomy by the organs of self-government of national autonomous areas, take into full consideration the characteristics and needs of the various minority nationalities, make a major effort to train cadres of the minority nationalities, and actively support and assist all the minority nationalities in their socialist revolution and construction and thus advance their socialist economic and cultural development.

SECTION V: THE PEOPLE'S COURTS AND THE PEOPLE'S PROCURATORATES

Article 41

The Supreme People's Court, local people's courts at various levels and special people's courts exercise judicial authority. The people's courts are formed as prescribed by law.

In accordance with law, the people's courts apply the system whereby representatives of the masses participate as assessors in administering justice. With regard to major counter-revolutionary or criminal cases, the masses should be drawn in for discussion and suggestions.

All cases in the people's courts are heard in public except those involving special circumstances as prescribed by law. The accused has the right to defense.

Article 42

The Supreme People's Court is the highest judicial organ.

The Supreme People's Court supervises the administration of justice by local people's courts at various levels and by special people's courts; people's courts at the higher levels supervise the administration of justice by people's courts at the lower levels.

The Supreme People's Court is responsible and accountable to the National People's Congress and its Standing Committee. Local people's courts at various levels are responsible and accountable to local people's congresses at the corresponding levels.

Article 43

The Supreme People's Procuratorate exercises procuratorial authority to ensure observance of the Constitution and the law by all the departments under the State Council, the local organs of state at various levels, the personnel of organs of state and the citizens. Local people's procuratorates and special people's procuratorates exercise procuratorial authority within the limits prescribed by law. The people's procuratorates are formed as prescribed by law.

The Supreme People's Procuratorate supervises the work of local people's procuratorates at various levels and of special people's procuratorates; people's procuratorates at the higher levels supervise the work of those at the lower levels.

The Supreme People's Procuratorate is responsible and accountable to the National People's Congress and its Standing Committee. Local people's procuratorates at various levels are responsible and accountable to people's congresses at the corresponding levels.

Chapter Three: The Fundamental Rights and Duties of Citizens

Article 44

All citizens who have reached the age of eighteen have the right to vote and to stand for election, with the exception of persons deprived of these rights by law.

Article 45

Citizens enjoy freedom of speech, correspondence, the press, assembly, association, procession, demonstration and the freedom to strike, and have the right to "speak out freely, air their views fully, hold great debates and write big-character posters."

Article 46

Citizens enjoy freedom to believe in religion and freedom not to believe in religion and to propagate atheism.

Article 47

The citizens' freedom of person and their homes are inviolable.
No citizen may be arrested except by decision of a people's court or with the sanction of a people's procuratorate, and the arrest must be made by a public security organ.

Article 48

Citizens have the right to work. To ensure that citizens enjoy this right, the state provides employment in accordance with the principle of overall consideration, and, on the basis of increased production, the state gradually increases payment for labor, improves working conditions, strengthens labor protection and expands collective welfare.

Article 49

Working people have the right to rest. To ensure that working people enjoy this right, the state prescribes working hours and systems of vacations and gradually expands material facilities for the working people to rest and recuperate.

Article 50

Working people have the right to material assistance in old age, and in case of illness or disability. To ensure that working people enjoy this right, the state gradually expands social insurance, social assistance, public health services, co-operative medical services, and other services.
The state cares for and ensures the livelihood of disabled revolutionary armymen and the families of revolutionary martyrs.

Article 51

Citizens have the right to education. To ensure that citizens enjoy this right, the state gradually increases the number of schools of various types and of other cultural and educational institutions and popularizes education.
The state pays special attention to the healthy development of young people and children.

Article 52

Citizens have the freedom to engage in scientific research, literary and artistic creation and other cultural activities. The state encourages and assists the creative endeavors of citizens engaged in science, education, literature, art, journalism, publishing, public health, sports and other cultural work.

Article 53

Women enjoy equal rights with men in all spheres of political, economic, cultural, social and family life. Men and women enjoy equal pay for equal work.
Men and women shall marry of their own free will. The state protects marriage, the family, and the mother and child.
The state advocates and encourages family planning.

Article 54

The state protects the just rights and interests of overseas Chinese and their relatives.

Article 55

Citizens have the right to lodge complaints with organs of state at any level against any person working in an organ of state, enterprise or institution for transgression of law or neglect of duty. Citizens have the right to appeal to organs of state at any level against any infringement of their rights. No one shall suppress such complaints and appeals or retaliate against persons making them.

Article 56

Citizens must support the leadership of the Communist Party of China, support the socialist system, safeguard the unification of the motherland and the unity of all nationalities in our country and abide by the Constitution and the law.

Article 57

Citizens must take care of and protect public property, observe labor discipline, observe public order, respect social ethics and safeguard state secrets.

Article 58

It is the lofty duty of every citizen to defend the motherland and resist aggression.
It is the honorable obligation of citizens to perform military service and to join the militia according to the law.

Article 59

The People's Republic of China grants the right of residence to any foreign national persecuted for supporting a just cause, for taking part in revolutionary movements or for engaging in scientific work.

Chapter Four: The National Flag, The National Emblem and the Capital

Article 60

The national flag of the People's Republic of China has five stars on a field of red.
The national emblem of the People's Republic of China is: Tien An Men in the centre, illuminated by five stars and encircled by ears of grain and a cogwheel.
The capital of the People's Republic of China is Peking.

China-Japan Peace Treaty

Following is the text (unofficial translation) of the peace treaty signed Aug. 12, 1978, by representatives of Japan and the People's Republic of China:

Japan and the People's Republic of China,
Recalling with satisfaction that since the government of Japan and the government of the People's Republic of China issued a joint communiqué in [Peking] on September 29, 1972, the friendly relations between the two governments and the peoples of the two countries have developed greatly on a new basis,
Confirming that the above-mentioned joint communiqué constitutes the basis of the relations of peace and friendship between the two countries and that the principles enunciated in the joint communiqué should be strictly observed,
Confirming that the principles of the charter of the United Nations should be fully respected,
Hoping to contribute to peace and stability in Asia and in the world,
For the purpose of solidifying and developing the relations of peace and friendship between the two countries,

Have resolved to conclude a treaty of peace and friendship and for that purpose have appointed as their plenipotentiaries:

Japan: Minister for Foreign Affairs Sunao Sonoda

People's Republic of China: Minister of Foreign Affairs Huang Hua

Who, having communicated to each other their full powers, found to be in good and due form, have agreed as follows:

Article I

1. The contracting parties shall develop relations of perpetual peace and friendship between the two countries on the basis of the principles of mutual respect for sovereignty and territorial integrity, mutual non-aggression, non-interference in each other's internal affairs, equality and mutual benefit and peaceful co-existence.

2. The contracting parties confirm that, in conformity with the foregoing principles and the principles of the charter of the United Nations, they shall in their mutual relations settle all disputes by peaceful means and shall refrain from the use or threat of force.

Article II

The contracting parties declare that neither of them should seek hegemony in the Asia-Pacific region or in any other region and that each is opposed to efforts by any other country or group of countries to establish such hegemony.

Article III

The contracting parties shall, in the good-neighborly and friendly spirit and in conformity with the principles of equality and mutual benefit and non-interference in each other's internal affairs, endeavor to further develop economic and cultural relations between the two countries and to promote exchanges between the peoples of the two countries.

Article IV

The present treaty shall not affect the position of either contracting party regarding its relations with third countries.

Article V

1. The present treaty shall be ratified and shall enter into force on the date of the exchange of instruments of ratification which shall take place at Tokyo. The present treaty shall remain in force for ten years and thereafter shall continue to be in force until terminated in accordance with the provisions of paragraph 2.

2. Either contracting party may, by giving one year's written notice to the other contracting party, terminate the present treaty at the end of the initial ten-year period or at any time thereafter ...

Normalization of Relations

Following are the texts of President Carter's Dec. 15, 1978, address, as delivered, announcing establishment of full diplomatic relations between the United States and the People's Republic of China; a United States statement released Dec. 15; a People's Republic of China statement read by Chairman Hua Guofeng Dec. 15; and an unofficial translation of a statement by Nationalist Chinese President Chiang Ching-kuo Dec. 16:

Carter's Speech

Good evening.

I would like to read a joint communiqué which is being simultaneously issued in Peking at this very moment by the leaders of the People's Republic of China:

"Joint Communiqué on the Establishment of Diplomatic Relations Between the United States of America and the People's Republic of China, January 1, 1979:

"The United States of America and the People's Republic of China have agreed to recognize each other and to establish diplomatic relations as of January 1st, 1979.

"The United States recognizes the Government of the People's Republic of China as the sole legal government of China. Within this context, the people of the United States will maintain cultural, commercial and other unofficial relations with the people of Taiwan.

"The United States of America and the People's Republic of China reaffirm the principles agreed on by the two sides in the Shanghai Communiqué of 1972 and emphasize once again that:

"—Both sides wish to reduce the danger of international military conflict.

"—Neither should seek hegemony [that is, a dominance of one nation over the other] in the Asia-Pacific region or in any other region of the world and each is opposed to efforts by any other country or group of countries to establish such hegemony.

"—Neither is prepared to negotiate on behalf of any other third party or to enter into agreements or understandings with the other directed at other states.

"—The Government of the United States of America acknowledges the Chinese position that there is but one China and Taiwan is part of China.

"—Both believe that normalization of Sino-American relations is not only in the interest of the Chinese and American peoples but also contributes to the cause of peace in Asia and in the world.

"—The United States of America and the People's Republic of China will exchange Ambassadors and establish embassies on March 1, 1979."

Yesterday, our country and the People's Republic of China reached this final historic agreement.

On January 1, 1979, a little more than two weeks from now, our two governments will implement full normalization of diplomatic relations.

As a nation of gifted people who comprise about one-fourth of the total population of the earth, China plays, already, an important role in world affairs — a role that can only grow more important in the years ahead.

We do not undertake this important step for transient tactical or expedient reasons. In recognizing the People's Republic of China, that it is the single government of China, we are recognizing simple reality. But far more is involved in this decision than just recognition of a fact.

Before the estrangement of recent decades, the American and the Chinese people had a long history of friendship. We have already begun to rebuild some of those previous ties. Now, our rapidly expanding relationship requires the kind of structure that only full diplomatic relations will make possible.

The change that I am announcing tonight will be of great long-term benefit to the peoples of both our country and China — and, I believe, to all the peoples of the world.

Normalization — and the expanded commercial and cultural relations that it will bring — will contribute to the well-being of our own Nation, to our own national interest, and it will also enhance the stability of Asia.

These more positive relations with China can beneficially affect the world in which we live and the world in which our children will live.

We have already begun to inform our allies and other nations and the members of the Congress of the details of our intended action. But I wish also tonight to convey a special message to the people of Taiwan — I have already communicated with the leaders in Taiwan — with whom the American people have had and will have extensive, close and friendly relations.

This is important between our two peoples.

As the United States asserted in the Shanghai Communiqué of 1972, issued on President Nixon's historic visit, we will continue to have an interest in the peaceful resolution of the Taiwan issue.

I have paid special attention to ensuring that normalization of relations between our country and the People's Republic will not jeopardize the well-being of the people of Taiwan.

The people of our country will maintain our current commercial, cultural, trade and other relations with Taiwan through nongovernmental means. Many other countries in the world are already successfully doing this.

These decisions and these actions open a new and important chapter in our country's history, and also in world affairs.

To strengthen and to expedite the benefits of this new relationship between China and the United States, I am pleased to announce that Vice Premier Teng [Deng Xiaoping] has accepted my invitation and will visit Washington at the end of January. His visit will give our governments the opportunity to consult with each other on global issues and to begin working together to enhance the cause of world peace.

These events are the final result of long and serious negotiations begun by President Nixon in 1972, and continued under the leadership of President Ford. The results bear witness to the steady, determined and bipartisan effort of our country to build a world in which peace will be the goal and the responsibility of all nations.

The normalization of relations between the United States and China has no other purpose than this — the advancement of peace.

It is in this spirit, at this season of peace, that I take special pride in sharing this good news with you tonight.

United States Statement

As of January 1, 1979, the United States of America recognizes the People's Republic of China as the sole legal Government of China. On the same date, the People's Republic of China accords similar recognition to the United States of America. The United States thereby establishes diplomatic relations with the People's Republic of China.

On that same date, January 1, 1979, the United States of America will notify Taiwan that it is terminating diplomatic relations and that the Mutual Defense Treaty between the United States and the Republic of China is being terminated in accordance with the provisions of the Treaty. The United States also states that it will be withdrawing its remaining military personnel from Taiwan within four months.

In the future, the American people and the people of Taiwan will maintain commercial, cultural, and other relations without official Government representation and without diplomatic relations.

The Administration will seek adjustments to our laws and regulations to permit the maintenance of commercial, cultural, and other nongovernmental relationships in the new circumstances that will exist after normalization.

The United States is confident that the people of Taiwan face a peaceful and prosperous future. The United States continues to have an interest in the peaceful resolution of the Taiwan issue and expects that the Taiwan issue will be settled peacefully by the Chinese themselves.

The United States believes that the establishment of diplomatic relations with the People's Republic will contribute to the welfare of the American people, to the stability of Asia where the United States has major security and economic interests and to the peace of the entire world.

People's Republic of China Statement

As of January 1, 1979, the People's Republic of China and the United States of America recognize each other and establish diplomatic relations, thereby ending the prolonged abnormal relationship between them. This is an historic event in Sino-United States relations.

As is known to all, the Government of the People's Republic of China is the sole legal Government of China and Taiwan is a part of China. The question of Taiwan was the crucial issue obstructing the normalization of relations between China and the United States. It has now been resolved between the two countries in the spirit of the Shanghai Communiqué and through their joint efforts, thus enabling the normalization of relations so ardently desired by the people of the two countries.

As for the way of bringing Taiwan back to the embrace of the motherland and reunifying the country, it is entirely China's internal affair.

At the invitation of the U.S. Government, Teng Hsiao-ping [Deng Xiaoping], Deputy [Premier] of the State Council of the People's Republic of China, will pay an official visit to the United States in January 1979, with a view to further promoting the friendship between the two peoples and good relations between the two countries.

Taiwan Statement

The decision by the United States to establish diplomatic relations with the Chinese Communist regime has not only seriously damaged the rights and interests of the Government and the people of the Republic of China, but has also had a tremendously adverse impact upon the entire free world. For all the consequences that might arise as a result of this move, the United States Government alone should bear full responsibility.

In the past few years, the United States Government has repeatedly reaffirmed its intention to maintain diplomatic relations with the Republic of China and to honor its treaty commitments. Now that it has broken the assurances and abrogated the treaty, the United States Government cannot be expected to have the confidence of any free nation in the future.

The United States, by extending diplomatic recognition to the Chinese Communist regime, which owes its very existence to terror and suppression, is not in conformity with its professed position of safeguarding human rights and strengthening the capability of democratic nations to resist the totalitarian dictatorship.

The move is tantamount to denying the hundreds of millions of enslaved peoples on the Chinese mainland of their hope for an early restoration of freedom. Viewed from whatever aspect, the move by the United States constitutes a great setback to human freedom and democratic institutions. It will be condemned by all freedomloving and peaceloving peoples all over the world.

Recent international events have proven that the United States' pursuance of the "normalization" process with the Chinese Communist regime did not protect the security of free Asian nations, has further encouraged Communist subversion and aggressive activities and hastened the fall of Indochina into Communist hands. The Government and the people of the Republic of China firmly believe lasting international peace and security can never be established on an unstable foundation of expediency.

Regardless of how the international situation may develop, the Republic of China, as a sovereign nation will, with her glorious tradition, unite all her people, civilian and military, at home and abroad, to continue her endeavors toward progress in the social, economic and political fields. The Chinese Government and the people, faithful to the national objectives and their international responsibilities, have full confidence in the future of the Republic of China.

The late President Chiang Kai-shek repeatedly instructed the Chinese people to be firm with dignity and to complete the task of national recovery and reconstruction. The Government and the people of the Republic of China have the determination and the faith, which they will exert their utmost, to work together with other free peoples in democratic countries to conquer Communist tyrannical rule and its aggressive policy. Henceforth, we shall be calm and firm, positive and hardworking. It is urged that all citizens cooperate fully with the Government, with one heart and one soul, united and determined to fight at this difficult moment.

Under whatever circumstances, the Republic of China shall neither negotiate with the Communist Chinese regime, nor compromise with Communism, and it shall never give up its sacred task of recovering the mainland and delivering the compatriots there. This firm position shall remain unchanged.

Taiwan Relations Act of 1979

On March 29, 1979, Congress passed a bill (HR 2479) establishing a new relationship with Taiwan following U.S. recognition of the People's Republic of China. President Carter signed the bill (PL 96-8) into law on April 10. Major provisions are listed below.

• • •

FINDINGS AND DECLARATION OF POLICY

Sec. 2. (a) The President having terminated governmental relations between the United States and the governing authorities on Taiwan recognized by the United States as the Republic of China prior to January 1, 1979, the Congress finds that the enactment of this Act is necessary —

(1) to help maintain peace, security, and stability in the Western Pacific; and

(2) to promote the foreign policy of the United States by authorizing the continuation of commercial, cultural, and other relations between the people of the United States and the people on Taiwan.

(b) It is the policy of the United States—

(1) to preserve and promote extensive, close, and friendly commercial, cultural, and other relations between the people of the United States and the people on Taiwan, as well as the people on the China mainland and all other peoples of the Western Pacific area;

(2) to declare that peace and stability in the area are in the political, security, and economic interests of the United States, and are matters of international concern;

(3) to make clear that the United States decision to establish diplomatic relations with the People's Republic of China rests upon the expectation that the future of Taiwan will be determined by peaceful means;

(4) to consider any effort to determine the future of Taiwan by other than peaceful means, including by boycotts or embargoes, a threat to the peace and security of the Western Pacific area and of grave concern to the United States;

(5) to provide Taiwan with arms of a defensive character; and

(6) to maintain the capacity of the United States to resist any resort to force or other forms of coercion that would jeopardize the security, or the social or economic system, of the people on Taiwan.

(c) Nothing contained in this Act shall contravene the interest of the United States in human rights, especially with respect to the human rights of all the approximately eighteen million inhabitants of Taiwan. The preservation and enhancement of the human rights of all the people on Taiwan are hereby reaffirmed as objectives of the United States.

IMPLEMENTATION OF UNITED STATES POLICY WITH REGARD TO TAIWAN

Sec. 3. (a) In furtherance of the policy set forth in section 2 of this Act, the United States will make available to Taiwan such defense articles and defense services in such quantity as may be necessary to enable Taiwan to maintain a sufficient self-defense capability.

(b) The President and the Congress shall determine the nature and quantity of such defense articles and services based solely upon their judgment of the needs of Taiwan, in accordance with procedures established by law. Such determination of Taiwan's defense needs shall include review by United States military authorities in connection with recommendations to the President and the Congress.

(c) The President is directed to inform the Congress promptly of any threat to the security or the social or economic system of the people on Taiwan and any danger to the interests of the United States arising therefrom. The President and the Congress shall determine, in accordance with constitutional processes, appropriate action by the United States in response to any such danger.

APPLICATION OF LAWS; INTERNATIONAL AGREEMENTS

Sec. 4. (a) The absence of diplomatic relations or recognition shall not affect the application of the laws of the United States with respect to Taiwan, and the laws of the United States shall apply with respect to Taiwan in the manner that the laws of the United States applied with respect to Taiwan prior to January 1, 1979.

(b) The application of subsection (a) of this section shall include, but shall not be limited to, the following:

(1) Whenever the laws of the United States refer or relate to foreign countries, nations, states, governments, or similar entities, such terms shall include and such laws shall apply with respect to Taiwan.

(2) Whenever authorized by or pursuant to the laws of the United States to conduct or carry out programs, transactions, or other relations with respect to foreign countries, nations, states, governments, or similar entities, the President or any agency of the United States Government is authorized to conduct and carry out, in accordance with section 6 of this Act, such programs, transactions, and other relations with respect to Taiwan (including, but not limited to, the performance of services for the United States through contracts with commercial entities on Taiwan), in accordance with the applicable laws of the United States.

(3)(A) The absence of diplomatic relations and recognition with respect to Taiwan shall not abrogate, infringe, modify, deny, or otherwise affect in any way any rights or obligations (including but not limited to those involving contracts, debts, or property interests of any kind) under the laws of the United States heretofore or hereafter acquired by or with respect to Taiwan.

(B) For all purposes under the laws of the United States, including actions in any court in the United States, recognition of the People's Republic of China shall not affect in any way the ownership of or other rights or interests in properties, tangible and intangible, and other things of value, owned or held on or prior to December 31, 1978, or thereafter acquired or earned by the governing authorities on Taiwan.

(4) Whenever the application of the laws of the United States depends upon the law that is or was applicable on Taiwan or compliance therewith, the law applied by the people on Taiwan shall be considered the applicable law for that purpose.

(5) Nothing in this Act, nor the facts of the President's action in extending diplomatic recognition to the People's Republic of China, the absence of diplomatic relations between the people on Taiwan and the United States, or the lack of recognition by the United States, and attendant circumstances thereto, shall be construed in any administrative or judicial proceeding as a basis for any United States Government agency, commission, or department to make a finding of fact or determination of law, under the Atomic Energy Act of 1954 and the Nuclear Non-Proliferation Act of 1978, to deny an export license application or to revoke an existing export license for nuclear exports to Taiwan.

(6) For purposes of the Immigration and Nationality Act, Taiwan may be treated in the manner specified in the first sentence of section 202(b) of that Act.

(7) The capacity of Taiwan to sue and be sued in courts in the United States, in accordance with the laws of the United States, shall not be abrogated, infringed, modified, denied, or otherwise affected in any way by the absence of diplomatic relations or recognition.

(8) No requirement, whether expressed or implied, under the laws of the United States with respect to maintenance of diplomatic relations or recognition shall be applicable with respect to Taiwan.

(c) For all purposes, including actions in any court in the United States, the Congress approves the continuation in force of all treaties and other international agreements, including multilateral conventions, entered into by the United States and the governing authorities on Taiwan recognized by the United States as the Republic of China prior to January 1, 1979, and in force between them on December 31, 1978, unless and until terminated in accordance with law.

(d) Nothing in this Act may be construed as a basis for supporting the exclusion or expulsion of Taiwan from continued membership in any international financial institution or any other international organization.

OVERSEAS PRIVATE INVESTMENT CORPORATION

Sec. 5. (a) During the three-year period beginning on the date of enactment of this Act, the $1,000 per capita income restriction in clause (2) of the second undesignated paragraph of section 231 of the Foreign Assistance Act of 1961 shall not restrict the activities of the Overseas Private Investment Corporation in determining whether to provide any insurance, reinsurance, loans, or guaranties with respect to investment projects on Taiwan.

(b) Except as provided in subsection (a) of this section, in issuing insurance, reinsurance, loans, or guaranties with respect to investment projects on Taiwan, the Overseas Private Investment Corporation shall apply the same criteria as those applicable in other parts of the world.

THE AMERICAN INSTITUTE IN TAIWAN

Sec. 6. (a) Programs, transactions, and other relations conducted or carried out by the President or any agency of the United States Government with respect to Taiwan shall, in the manner and to the extent directed by the President, be conducted and carried out by or through—

(1) The American Institute in Taiwan, a nonprofit corporation incorporated under the laws of the District of Columbia, or

(2) such comparable successor nongovernmental entity as the President may designate,

(hereafter in this Act referred to as the "Institute").

(b) Whenever the President or any agency of the United States Government is authorized or required by or pursuant to the laws of the United States to enter into, perform, enforce, or have in force an agreement or transaction relative to Taiwan, such agreement or transaction shall be entered into, performed, and enforced, in the

manner and to the extent directed by the President, by or through the Institute.

(c) To the extent that any law, rule, regulation, or ordinance of the District of Columbia, or of any State or political subdivision thereof in which the Institute is incorporated or doing business, impedes or otherwise interferes with the performance of the functions of the Institute pursuant to this Act, such law, rule, regulation, or ordinance shall be deemed to be prempted by this Act.

SERVICES BY THE INSTITUTE TO UNITED STATES CITIZENS ON TAIWAN

Sec. 7. (a) The Institute may authorize any of its employees on Taiwan—

(1) to administer to or take from any person an oath, affirmation, affidavit, or deposition, and to perform any notarial act which any notary public is required or authorized by law to perform within the United States;

(2) To act as provisional conservator of the personal estates of deceased United States citizens; and

(3) to assist and protect the interests of United States persons by performing other acts such as are authorized to be performed outside the United States for consular purposes by such laws of the United States as the President may specify.

(b) Acts performed by authorized employees of the Institute under this section shall be valid, and of like force and effect within the United States, as if performed by any other person authorized under the laws of the United States to perform such acts.

TAX EXEMPT STATUS OF THE INSTITUTE

SEC. 8. (a) The Institute, its property, and its income are exempt from all taxation now or hereafter imposed by the United States (except to the extent that section 11(a)(3) of this Act requires the imposition of taxes imposed under chapter 21 of the Internal Revenue Code of 1954, relating to the Federal Insurance Contributions Act) or by any State or local taxing authority of the United States.

(b) For purposes of the Internal Revenue Code of 1954, the Institute shall be treated as an organization described in sections 170(b)(l)(A), 170(c), 2055(a), 2106(a)(2)(A), 2522(a), and 2522(b).

• • •

TAIWAN INSTRUMENTALITY

Sec. 10. (a) Whenever the President or any agency of the United States Government is authorized or required by or pursuant to the laws of the United States to render or provide to or to receive or accept from Taiwan, any performance, communication, assurance, undertaking, or other action, such action shall, in the manner and to the extent directed by the President, be rendered or provided to, or received or accepted from, an instrumentality established by Taiwan which the President determines has the necessary authority under the laws applied by the people on Taiwan to provide assurances and take other actions on behalf of Taiwan in accordance with this Act.

(b) The President is requested to extend to the instrumentality established by Taiwan the same number of offices and complement of personnel as were previously operated in the United States by the governing authorities on Taiwan recognized as the Republic of China prior to January 1, 1979.

(c) Upon the granting by Taiwan of comparable privileges and immunities with respect to the Institute and its appropriate personnel, the President is authorized to extend with respect to the Taiwan instrumentality and its appropriate personnel, such privileges and immunities (subject to appropriate conditions and obligations) as may be necessary for the effective performance of their functions.

SEPARATION OF GOVERNMENT PERSONNEL FOR EMPLOYMENT WITH THE INSTITUTE

Sec. 11. (a)(1) Under such terms and conditions as the President may direct, any agency of the United States Government may separate from Government service for a specified period any officer or employee of that agency who accepts employment with the Institute.

(2) An officer or employee separated by an agency under paragraph (1) of this subsection for employment with the Institute shall be entitled upon termination of such employment to reemployment or reinstatement with such agency (or a successor agency) in an appropriate position with the attendant rights, privileges, and benefits which the officer or employees would have had or acquired had he or she not been so separated, subject to such time period and other conditions as the President may prescribe.

REPORTING REQUIREMENT

SEC. 12. (a) The Secretary of State shall transmit to the Congress the text of any agreement to which the Institute is a party. However, any such agreement the immediate public disclosure of which would, in the opinion of the President, be prejudicial to the national security of the United States shall not be so transmitted to the Congress but shall be transmitted to the Committee on Foreign Relations of the Senate and the Committee on Foreign Affairs of the House of Representatives under an appropriate injunction of secrecy to be removed only upon due notice from the President.

(b) For purposes of subsection (a), the term "agreement" includes—

(1) any agreement entered into between the Institute and the governing authorities on Taiwan or the instrumentality established by Taiwan; and

(2) any agreement entered into between the Institute and an agency of the United States Government.

(c) Agreements and transactions made or to be made by or through the Institute shall be subject to the same congressional notification, review, and approval requirements and procedures as if such agreements and transactions were made by or through the agency of the United States Government on behalf of which the Institute is acting.

(d) During the two-year period beginning on the effective date of this Act, the Secretary of State shall transmit to the Speaker of the House of Representatives and the Committee on Foreign Relations of the Senate, every six months, a report describing and reviewing economic relations between the United States and Taiwan, noting any interference with normal commercial relations.

RULES AND REGULATIONS

Sec. 13. The President is authorized to prescribe such rules and regulations as he may deem appropriate to carry out the purposes of this Act. During the three-year period beginning on the effective date of this Act, such rules and regulations shall be transmitted promptly to the Speaker of the House of Representatives and to the Committee on Foreign Relations of the Senate. Such action shall not, however, relieve the Institute of the responsibilities placed upon it by this Act.

CONGRESSIONAL OVERSIGHT

Sec. 14. (a) The Committee on Foreign Affairs of the House of Representatives, the Committee on Foreign Relations of the Senate, and other appropriate committees of the Congress shall monitor —

(1) the implementation of the provisions of this Act;

(2) the operation and procedures of the Institute;

(3) the legal and technical aspects of the continuing relationship between the United States and Taiwan; and

(4) the implementation of the policies of the United States concerning security and cooperation in East Asia.

(b) Such committees shall report, as appropriate, to their respective Houses on the results of their monitoring.

DEFINITIONS

SEC. 15. For purposes of this Act —

(1) the term "laws of the United States" includes any statute, rule, regulation, ordinance, order, or judicial rule of decision of the United States or any political subdivision thereof; and

(2) the term "Taiwan" includes, as the context may require, the islands of Taiwan and the Pescadores [Penghu], the people on those islands, corporations and other entities and associations created or organized under the laws applied on those islands, and the governing authorities on Taiwan recognized by the United States as the Republic of China prior to January 1, 1979, and any successor governing authorities (including political subdivisions, agencies, and instrumentalities thereof).

AUTHORIZATION OF APPROPRIATIONS

Sec. 16. In addition to funds otherwise available to carry out the provisions of this Act, there are authorized to be appropriated to the Secretary of State for the fiscal year 1980 such funds as may be necessary to carry out such provisions. Such funds are authorized to remain available until expended.

SEVERABILITY OF PROVISIONS

Sec. 17. If any provision of this Act or the application thereof to any person or circumstance is held invalid, the remainder of the Act and the application of such provision to any other person or circumstance shall not be affected thereby.

EFFECTIVE DATE

Sec. 18. This Act shall be effective as of January 1, 1979.

Mondale's Peking Address

Following is the text of a speech by Vice President Walter F. Mondale at Peking University, Aug. 27, 1979, and televised nationally. The speech was delivered at 3:40 p.m. local Peking time.

I am honored to appear before you. And I bring you the warm greetings and the friendship of the President of the United States and the American people.

For an American of my generation to visit the People's Republic of China is to touch the pulse of modern political history. For nearly three decades our nations stood separate and apart. But the ancient hunger for community unites humanity. It urges us to find common ground.

As one of your poets wrote over a thousand years ago, "We widen our view three hundred miles by ascending one flight of stairs." We are ascending that flight of stairs together.

Each day we take another step. This afternoon, I am privileged to be the first American political figure to speak directly to the citizens of the People's Republic of China.

And no setting for that speech could be more symbolic of our relationship than this place of new beginnings. The history of modern China is crystallized in the story of Beijing University [Peking University] and the other distinguished institutions you represent. At virtually every turning point in 20th century China, Bei-da [Peking University] has been the fulcrum.

Sixty years ago, it was at Bei-da that the May 4th movement began, launching an era of unprecedented intellectual ferment. It inaugurated an effort to modernize Chinese culture and society. It established a new meeting ground for Eastern and Western cultures. And its framework of mutual respect sustains our own cultural cooperation today.

Forty-four years ago, Bei-da was where the December 9th movement galvanized a student generation to resist external aggression. And its message of sovereignty and nonaggression underpins our own political cooperation today.

As China looks to the future, once again it is Bei-da and your other research centers which are leading the drive toward "the four modernizations," and the closeness of your development goals to our own interests will provide the basis for our continuing economic cooperation.

Today, we find our two nations at a pivotal moment. We have normalized our relations. The curtain has parted; the mystery is being dispelled. We are eager to know more about one another, to share the texture of our daily lives, to forge the human bonds of friendship.

That is a rich beginning. But it is only a beginning.

A modern China taking its place in the family of nations is engaged in a search not only for friendship, but also for security and development. An America deepening its relations with China does so not only out of genuine sentiment, and not only out of natural curiosity. It does so out of the same combination of principle and self-interest that is the engine of mature relations among all modern states.

Our job today is to establish the basis for an enduring relationship tomorrow. We could not have set that task without our friendship. But we cannot accomplish it with friendship alone.

On behalf of President Carter, this is the message I carry to the people of China — a message about America, its purposes in the world, and our hopes for our relations with you.

The Americans are historically confident people. Our politics are rooted in our values. We cherish our fundamental beliefs in human rights, and compassion, and social justice. We believe that our democratic system institutionalizes those values. The opportunities available to our citizens are incomparable. Our debates are vigorous and open. And the differences we air among ourselves — whether on strategic nuclear policy or on energy — are signs of our society's enduring strength.

My country is blessed with unsurpassed natural resources. Moreover, we also have unparalleled human resources — workers and farmers and scientists and engineers and industrialists and financiers. With their genius we are able to transform our natural assets into abundance — not only for ourselves, but for the world.

Of course we face unsolved problems. But the high goals we set for ourselves — and our determination to meet them — are measures of our national spirit. In that striving, in that restless pursuit of a better life, we feel a special affinity for the people of modern China.

In the world community, the United States seeks international stability and peace. But we have no illusions about the obstacles we face. We know that we live in a dangerous world. And we are determined to remain militarily prepared. We are fashioning our defenses from the most advanced technology anywhere. We have forged alliances in Europe and Asia which grow stronger every year. Together with our Japanese and Western allies, we will ensure that our investment in security is equal to the task of ensuring peace — as we have for thirty years.

But we want to be more than a firm and reliable partner in world affairs. We also believe in a world of diversity.

For Sino-American relations, that means that we respect the distinctive qualities which the great Chinese people contribute to

our relationship. And despite the sometimes profound differences between our two systems, we are committed to joining with you to advance our many parallel strategic and bilateral interests.

Thus any nation which seeks to weaken or isolate you in world affairs assumes a stance counter to American interests. This is why the United States normalized relations with your country, and that is why we must work to broaden and strengthen our new friendship.

We must press forward now to widen and give specificity to our relations. The fundamental challenges we face are to build concrete political ties in the context of mutual security . . . to establish broad cultural relations in a framework of genuine equality . . . and to forge practical economic bonds with the goal of common benefit.

As we give substance to our shared interests, we are investing in the future of our relationship. The more effectively we advance our agenda, the more bonds we build between us — the more confident we can be that our relationship will endure.

And so what we accomplish today lays the groundwork for the decade ahead. The 1980s can find us working together — and working with other nations — to meet world problems. Enriching the global economy, containing international conflicts, protecting the independence of nations: these goals must also be pursued from the perspective of our bilateral relationship. The deeper the relationship, the more successful that worldwide pursuit will be.

That is the agenda President Carter has asked me to come to the People's Republic of China to pursue. That is the principal message President Carter has asked me to bring to you. It is the agenda we share for the future.

In the eight months since normalization, we have witnessed the rapid expansion of Sino-American relations.

We have reached a settlement on claims/assets and signed the trade agreement. Trade between our countries is expanding. American oil companies are helping you explore China's offshore oil reserves. Joint commissions on Sino-American economic relations and on scientific and technical exchange have been established. We have exchanged numerous governmental delegations, including the visits of many heads of our respective ministries and departments. And the flow of people between our two countries is reaching new heights.

We have gained a cooperative momentum. Together let us sustain and strengthen it.

For a strong and secure and modernizing China is also in the American interest in the decade ahead.

In agriculture, your continued development not only provides a better life for the Chinese people, it also serves our interests — for your gains in agriculture will increase limited world food supplies.

In trade, our interests are served by your expanding exports of natural resources and industrial products. And at the same time your interests are served by the purchases you can finance through those exports.

As you industrialize, you provide a higher standard of living for your people. And at the same time our interests are served — for this will increase the flow of trade, narrow the wealth gap between the developed and the developing world, and thus help alleviate a major source of global instability.

Above all, both our political interests are served by your growing strength in all fields — for it helps deter others who might seek to impose themselves on you.

Efforts in the 1920s and 30s to keep China weak destabilized the entire world. For many years, China was a flash point of great power competition. But a confident China can contribute to the maintenance of peace in the region. Today, the unprecedented and friendly relations among China, Japan, and the United States bring international stability to northeast Asia.

That is why deepening our economic, cultural, and political relations is so strategically important — not only for your security, but for the peace of the world community.

We are taking crucial steps to advance our economic relationship.

First, before the end of the year, President Carter will submit for the approval of the U.S. Congress the trade agreement we reached with you. This agreement will extend "most favored nation" treatment to China. And its submission is not linked to any other issue.

Second, I will be signing an agreement on development of hydroelectric energy in the People's Republic of China. U.S. government agencies are now ready to help develop China's hydroelectric power on a compensatory basis.

Third, the U.S. is prepared to establish export-import bank credit arrangements for the PRC on a case-by-case basis, up to a total of $2 billion over a five-year period. If the pace of development warrants it, we are prepared to consider additional credit arrangements. We have begun discussions toward this end.

Fourth, the Carter administration this year will seek congressional authority to encourage American businesses to invest in China — by providing the guarantees and insurance of the Overseas Private Investment Corporation.

We also stand ready to work with the Chinese government to reach textile, maritime, and civil aviation agreements in the shortest possible time.

As we advance our cultural relationship, universities will again be a crucial meeting-ground between Chinese and Americans, just as they were in an earlier era.

Today, gifted Chinese scholars study in America, and American scholars — many of whom I am delighted to see here today — study in China. That exchange inherits a distinguished tradition. On campuses all across the United States, Americans who lectured and studied in China in the 1930s and 40s today are invigorating our own intellectual life — none of them with greater distinction than Professor John K. Fairbank, who honors us by joining my travelling party. At the same time, we are proud that Chinese scholars who study American agronomy, engineering, and medicine have been able to contribute the skills they gained in our country to the progress of Chinese society.

It is a mutual relationship — a true reciprocity — we are now engaged in building. From us, you will learn aspects of science and technology. Our anthropologists and archaeologists have tools to share with you as you explore your own past. American and Chinese social scientists and humanists have insights to offer each other — a fuller understanding of our respective institutions and values.

And so with your help, we intend to broaden our horizons. Chinese researchers pioneer in key areas, from medical burn therapy to earthquake prediction — and we want to learn these skills from you. Where the progress of science requires global cooperation — in astronomy, in oceanography, in meteorology — our common efforts can benefit the world. And our social scientists and humanists have hardly begun to share your understanding of history of social change, and of human potential.

Strong bilateral relations serve our strategic interests. Through them, both of us can foster the world community we seek — a world that respects diversity and welcomes constructive change.

Today, there are 162 nations in the world, most of them poor. Eighty percent of the world's population live in developing countries. Every day, people in these nations are lifting their heads to demand independence and justice. Every day, efforts by rulers to oppress their people are meeting increasing resistance. Governments are coming to understand not only the necessity, but also the fundamental wisdom and decency of protecting the rights of their people through law.

When political power is more equitably shared within nations; when that power shifts from the few to the many among nations; when an era of colonialism gives way to a more just international order — these changes deserve world-wide support.

In the last few years, as the preeminent military and economic power in the world, the United States faced a fundamental choice. Were we to resist those winds of change, attaining our national security by defending the status quo? Were we to collude with a few other countries in an effort to dominate the world? Or were we to welcome change, to make the necessary adjustments, and to help shape a more just world order?

Let there be no doubt about the choice my country has made. The United States believes that any effort by one country to dominate another is doomed to failure. Neither by relying exclusively on an increasing stock of arms, nor by direct or indirect military intervention, can any nation hope to attain lasting security. On the contrary, nations which embark on that course will find themselves increasingly isolated and vulnerable.

And nothing more vividly demonstrates our belief in those principles than the normalization of Sino-American relations. Normalization signals our understanding that American security in the years ahead will be attained not by maintaining the status quo; not by colluding for purposes of domination; but by fostering a world of independent nations with whom we can build positive relations.

That is the world community we seek. It is a vision of diversity, of constructive ties — and above all, of peace.

In a world that hopes to find new energy sources, peace is essential. In a world that aims to eliminate hunger and disparities in wealth, global equilibrium is vital. In a world that is working to eradicate communicable diseases and to safeguard our environment, international cooperation is crucial.

To secure that peace, to maintain that equilibrium, to promote that cooperation — the United States is totally committed.

During the visit to the United States by Vice Premier Deng and Madame Zhuo in January, President Carter said this:

"We've not entered this new relationship for any short-term gains. We have a long-term commitment to a world community of diverse . . . and independent nations. We believe that a strong and secure China will play a cooperative part in developing that type of world community."

I would like to underscore that point. Anyone who seeks to understand America is invariably drawn back to the idea of diversity. The United States is a nation of immigrants, all of whom contribute to our society their distinct talents and traditions.

The American people find their common heritage not in a single bloodline, not in thousands of years shared national history, but in their shared ideals. And we have a profound faith in the very diversity that shapes us. We value tolerance and pluralism and mutual respect.

We aim to honor those same principles in the conduct of our foreign policy in the decade of the 80s. For Sino-American relations, that does not mean we will always agree.

But in a world that respects diversity, countries as different as the United States and China can work side by side toward common goals. Together, we can enrich our two cultures, strengthen our two economies, build better lives for both our peoples. And together, we can help stabilize the world community — fostering respect for diversity, and standing firmly opposed to intolerance and domination.

Last month, China and the United States joined many other nations in Geneva to confront the agony of the Indo-Chinese refugees. The enormity of their human tragedy defies the imagination. In a world that seeks to alleviate such suffering — suffering that transcends national boundaries — the way of conscience is the way of common cause.

Today the world watches us. In a sense, we are testing whether a developed nation and a developing nation — each with different traditions, each with different systems — can build a broad, enduring, constructive relationship. Certainly there will be serious barriers to overcome. But if we can work together, future generations will thank us. If we fail, not only will our children suffer; the entire world will feel the consequences.

Diversity and stability are not new themes in Sino-American relations. President [Theodore] Roosevelt once said this:

"It is to the advantage — and not to the disadvantage — of other nations, when any nation becomes stable and prosperous; able to keep the peace within its own borders, and strong enough not to invite aggression from without. We heartily hope for the progress of China. And so far as by peaceable and legitimate means we are able, we will do our part toward furthering that progress."

It was a bright vision three generations ago — and subsequent events only postponed the fulfillment of its promise. As we look to the future, let us resolve to rekindle the light of its insight.

U.S. Treaties in Force with
Taiwan, 1979

Agricultural Commodities

Agricultural commodities agreement, with exchange of notes. Signed at Taipei April 27, 1962; entered into force April 27, 1962.
13 UST 461; TIAS 5010; 436 UNTS 25.
Amendments:
May 25, 1962 (13 UST 1264; TIAS 5074; 459 UNTS 328).
June 9, 1962 (13 UST 1264; TIAS 5074; 459 UNTS 333).
Agricultural commodities agreement, with exchange of notes. Signed at Taipei August 31, 1962; entered into force August 31, 1962.
13 UST 1930; TIAS 5151; 460 UNTS 247.
Amendments:
January 15, 1963 (14 UST 131; TIAS 5282; 473 UNTS 380).
June 3, 1964 (15 UST 667; TIAS 5588; 526 UNTS 330).
Agricultural commodites agreement, with exchange of notes. Signed at Taipei November 19, 1962; entered into force November 19, 1962.
13 UST 2528; TIAS 5219; 459 UNTS 263.
Amendment:
January 24, 1963 (14 UST 139; TIAS 5285; 473 UNTS 372).
Agricultural commodities agreement, with exchange of notes. Signed at Taipei June 3, 1964; entered into force June 3, 1964.
15 UST 678; TIAS 5589; 526 UNTS 257.
Agricultural commodities agreement with exchange of notes. Signed at Taipei December 31, 1964; entered into force December 31, 1964.
15 UST 2272; TIAS 5717; 532 UNTS 29.
Amendment:
February 11, 1966 (17 UST 64; TIAS 5959; 579 UNTS 294).
Agricultural commodities agreement with exchange of notes. Signed at Taipei December 31, 1964; entered into force December 31, 1964.
15 UST 2295; TIAS 5718; 532 UNTS 59.
Amendment:
February 11, 1966 (17 UST 59; TIAS 5958; 579 UNTS 303).
Agricultural commodities agreement with related agreement and exchange of notes. Signed at Taipei December 12, 1967; entered into force December 12, 1967.
18 UST 3015; TIAS 6395; 701 UNTS 213.
Related amendments:
January 14, 1971 (22 UST 299; TIAS 7062; 792 UNTS 43).
April 12, 1972 (23 UST 299; TIAS 7311).

Atomic Energy

Agreement providing for a grant for the acquisition of nuclear research and training equipment and materials. Exchange of notes at Washington October 16 and December 2, 1959; entered into force December 2, 1959.
10 UST 2023; TIAS 4371; 361 UNTS 115.
Agreement for cooperation concerning civil uses of atomic energy. Signed at Washington April 4, 1972; entered into force June 22, 1972.
23 UST 945; TIAS 7364.
Extension and amendment:
March 15, 1974 (25 UST 913; TIAS 7834).

Aviation

Air transport agreement and exchange of notes. Signed at Nanking December 20, 1946; entered into force December 20, 1946.
61 Stat. 2799; TIAS 1609; 6 Bevans 787; 22 UNTS 87.
Extension and amendment:
October 22, 1969 (20 UST 2985; TIAS 6773; 726 UNTS 320).

Memorandum of agreement relating to the provision of flight inspection services. Signed at Washington and Taipei August 21 and October 1, 1978; entered into force October 1, 1978.
TIAS

Claims

Agreement relating to claims resulting from activities of United States military forces in China. Exchange of notes at Nanking October 13, 1947 and March 17, 1948; entered into force March 17, 1948.
62 Stat. 2116; TIAS 1776; 6 Bevans 823; 76 UNTS 157.

Customs

Arrangement relating to reciprocal free-entry privileges for consular officers of articles imported for their personal use during official residence. Exchange of notes at Washington September 29 and December 16, 1930; entered into force December 16, 1930.
6 Bevans 727.

Defense (See also Mutual Security)

Agreement relating to the presence of United States armed forces in China. Exchange of notes at Nanking August 29 and September 3, 1947; entered into force September 3, 1947.
61 Stat. 3755; TIAS 1715; 6 Bevans 800; 9 UNTS 91.
Agreement relating to the furnishing of certain military material to China for the defense of Taiwan. Exchange of notes at Taipei January 30 and February 9, 1951; entered into force February 9, 1951.
2 UST 1499; TIAS 2293; 132 UNTS 273.
Agreement relating to the assistance furnished by China to the United States Military Assistance Advisory Group under the agreement of January 30 and February 9, 1951. Exchange of notes at Taipei October 23 and November 1, 1952; entered into force November 1, 1952.
3 UST 5166; TIAS 2712; 184 UNTS 348.
Agreement providing for the disposition of equipment and materials furnished by the United States under the agreement of January 30 and February 9, 1951. Exchange of notes at Taipei April 3, 1956; entered into force April 3, 1956.
7 UST 893; TIAS 3571; 268 UNTS 315.
Amendment:
June 3, 1964 (15 UST 1383; TIAS 5607; 530 UNTS 355).
Agreement to facilitate construction of defense facilities as provided in agreements of January 30 and February 9, 1951, and October 23 and November 1, 1962. Exchange of notes at Taipei November 21, 1956; entered into force November 21, 1956.
7 UST 3411; TIAS 3713; 265 UNTS 241.
Mutual defense treaty.[1] Signed at Washington December 2, 1954; entered into force March 3, 1955; and exchange of notes at Washington December 10, 1954.[1]
6 UST 433; TIAS 3178; 248 UNTS 213.
Agreement relating to the construction of a scatter wave radio facility on Taiwan. Exchange of notes at Taipei August 6, 1958; entered into force August 6, 1958.
13 UST 2136; TIAS 5175; 462 UNTS 3.
Understanding relating to a communications facility in the vicinity of Kaohsiung. Exchange of notes at Taipei April 15, 1960; entered into force April 15, 1960.
13 UST 2155; TIAS 5176; 462 UNTS 19.
Agreement relating to the construction of a scatter wave control facility in the vicinity of Yangmingshan. Exchange of notes at Taipei February 28, 1962; entered into force February 28, 1962.
13 UST 2158; TIAS 5177; 462 UNTS 25.
Agreement relating to the status of United States armed forces in China. Signed at Taipei August 31, 1965; entered into force April 12, 1966.
17 UST 373; TIAS 5986; 572 UNTS 3.

Agreement relating to the deposit by China of ten percent of the value of grant military assistance and excess defense articles furnished by the United States. Exchange of notes at Taipei April 18, 1972; entered into force April 18, 1972; effective February 7, 1972.

23 UST 630; TIAS 7325.

[1] *Notice of termination delivered by the United States on December 23, 1978, effective as of January 1, 1979. The treaty was terminated on January 1, 1980.*

Economic and Technical Cooperation

Agreement concerning the United States relief assistance to the Chinese people, and exchange of notes. Signed at Nanking October 27, 1947; entered into force October 27, 1947.

61 Stat. 3374; TIAS 1674; 6 Bevans 802; 12 UNTS 11.

Economic aid agreement, exchange of notes, and exchange of aid memoire. Signed at Nanking July 3, 1948 (aide memoire dated July 27 and 28, 1948); entered into force July 3, 1948.

62 Stat. 2945; TIAS 1837; 17 UNTS 119 and 45 UNTS 326; 6 Bevans 827.

Amendments:

March 26 and 31, 1949 (63 Stat. 2425; TIAS 1923; 6 Bevans 851; 76 UNTS 245).

January 21 and 31, 1950 (5 UST 2154; TIAS 3077; 235 UNTS 354).

August 11, 1965 (16 UST 1650; TIAS 5888; 573 UNTS 291).

Agreement establishing a joint commission on rural reconstruction in China. Exchange of notes at Nanking August 5, 1948; entered into force August 5, 1948.

62 Stat. 3139; TIAS 1848; 6 Bevans 841; 82 UNTS 109.

Extension:

June 27, 1949 (63 Stat. 2702; TIAS 1975; 6 Bevans 853; 82 UNTS 126).

Agreement concerning disposition of the New Taiwan dollars generated as a consequence of economic assistance furnished to China. Exchange of notes at Taipei April 9, 1965; entered into force July 1, 1965.

16 UST 583; TIAS 5782; 546 UNTS 81.

Extension and amendments:

February 2, 1968 (19 UST 4629; TIAS 6451; 697 UNTS 321).

June 30, 1970 (21 UST 1478; TIAS 6906; 753 UNTS 397).

June 30, 1975 (26 UST 2692; TIAS 8184).

Agreement on technological advancement in connection with water resources, land utilization and various fields of irrigated agriculture. Signed at Taipei May 12, 1972; entered into force May 12, 1972.

23 UST 1135; TIAS 7374.

Education

Agreement for financing certain educational and cultural exchange programs. Signed at Taipei April 23, 1964; entered into force April 23, 1964.

15 UST 408; TIAS 5572; 524 UNTS 141.

Extraterritoriality

Treaty for the relinquishment of extraterritorial rights in China and the regulation of related matters, and accompanying exchange of notes. Signed at Washington January 11, 1943; entered into force May 20, 1943.

57 Stat. 767; TS 984; 6 Bevans 739; 10 UNTS 261.

Finance

Agreement regarding the ownership and use of local currency repayments made by China to the Development Loan Fund.

Exchange of notes at Taipei December 24, 1958; entered into force December 24, 1958.

10 UST 16; TIAS 4162; 340 UNTS 251.

Fisheries

Agreement concerning fisheries off the coasts of the United States, with annexes and agreed minutes. Signed at Washington September 15, 1976; entered into force February 28, 1977.

28 UST 1903; TIAS 8529.

Health and Sanitation

Agreement relating to the establishment and operation in Taipei of a United States Navy Medical Research Unit. Exchanges of notes at Taipei March 30, April 26, and October 14, 1955; entered into force October 14, 1955.

7 UST 173; TIAS 3493; 268 UNTS 165.

Extension and amendment:

December 27, 1956 (7 UST 3453; TIAS 3720; 268 UNTS 177).

October 3 and 14, 1978.

Investment Guaranties

Agreement relating to guaranties for projects in Taiwan proposed by nationals of the United States. Exchange of notes at Taipei June 25, 1952; entered into force June 25, 1952.

3 UST 4846; TIAS 2657; 136 UNTS 229.

Amendment:

December 30, 1963 (14 UST 2222; TIAS 5509; 505 UNTS 308).

Language and Area Studies School

Agreement concerning the status of the American Embassy School of Chinese Language and Area Studies at Taichung and its personnel and of Chinese Embassy personnel studying in the Washington area. Exchange of notes at Taipei July 15 and August 22, 1969; entered into force August 22, 1969.

20 UST 2856; TIAS 6759; 723 UNTS 209.

Lend-Lease

Preliminary agreement regarding principles applying to mutual aid in the prosecution of the war against aggression. Signed at Washington June 2, 1942; entered into force June 2, 1942.

56 Stat. 1494; EAS 251; 6 Bevans 735; 14 UNTS 343.

Agreement under section 3 (c) of the Lend-Lease Act. Signed at Washington June 28, 1946; entered into force June 28, 1946.

61 Stat. 3895; TIAS 1746; 6 Bevans 758; 34 UNTS 121.

Agreement on the disposition of lend-lease supplies in inventory or procurement in the United States. Signed at Washington June 14, 1946; operative September 2, 1945.

60 Stat. 1760; TIAS 1533; 6 Bevans 753; 4 UNTS 253.

Maritime Matters

Agreement relating to the loan of small naval craft to China. Exchange of notes at Taipei May 14, 1954; entered into force May 14, 1954.

5 UST 892; TIAS 2979; 231 UNTS 165.

Extensions and amendments:

March 22 and 31, 1955 (6 UST 750; TIAS 3215; 251 UNTS 399).

June 18, 1955 (6 UST 2973; TIAS 3346; 265 UNTS 406).

May 16, 1957 (8 UST 787; TIAS 3837; 284 UNTS 380).

October 12, 1960 (11 UST 2233; TIAS 4597; 393 UNTS 320).
August 15, 1962 (13 UST 1924; TIAS 5150; 460 UNTS 237).
February 23, 1965 (16 UST 126; TIAS 5771; 542 UNTS 361).
December 16, 1970 and January 14, 1971 (22 UST 12; TIAS 7037; 776 UNTS 334).

Agreement for the loan of small craft to China. Exchange of notes at Taipei July 8, 1959; entered into force July 8, 1958.
   10 UST 1306; TIAS 4274; 354 UNTS 47.

Agreement relating to the transfer of the USS GERONIMO to the Navy of China. Exchange of notes at Taipei December 12 and 16, 1968; entered into force December 16, 1968.
   19 UST 7857; TIAS 6623; 714 UNTS 25.

Mutual Security

Agreement relating to assurances required by the Mutual Security Act of 1951. Exchange of notes at Taipei December 29, 1951 and January 2, 1952; entered into force January 2, 1952.
   3 UST 4543; TIAS 2604; 181 UNTS 161.

Narcotic Drugs

Arrangement for the direct exchange of certain information regarding the traffic in narcotic drugs. Exchanges of notes at Nanking March 12, June 21, July 28, and August 30, 1947; entered into force August 30, 1947.
   6 Bevans 797.

Pacific Settlement of Disputes

Treaty looking to the advancement of the cause of general peace. Signed at Washington September 15, 1914; entered into force October 22, 1915. Exchange of notes signed May 11 and 19, 1916.
   39 Stat. 1642; TS 619 and 619-A; 6 Bevans 711.
Treaty of arbitration. Signed at Washington June 27, 1930; entered into force December 15, 1932.
   47 Stat. 2213; TS 857; 6 Bevans 724; 140 LNTS 183.

Postal Matters

Agreement for the exchange of international money orders. Signed at Taipei October 8 and at Washington November 14, 1957; operative October 1, 1957.
   9 UST 223; TIAS 3995; 304 UNTS 241.
Parcel post convention. Signed at Peking May 29, 1916, and at Washington July 11, 1916; entered into force August 1, 1916.
   39 Stat. 1665; Post Office Department print.
Agreement for exchange of insured parcel post and regulations of execution. Signed at Taipei July 30 and at Washington August 19, 1957; entered into force November 1, 1957.
   8 UST 2031; TIAS 3941; 300 UNTS 61.
International express mail agreement, with detailed regulations. Signed at Taipei and Washington September 11 and November 10, 1978; entered into force December 30, 1978.
   TIAS

Relief Supplies and Packages

Agreement relating to duty-free entry of relief goods and relief packages and to the defrayment of transportation charges on such shipments. Exchange of notes at Nanking November 5 and 18, 1948; entered into force November 18, 1948.
   3 UST 5462; TIAS 2749; 198 UNTS 287.
Amendments:
   October 20 and December 12, 1952 (3 UST 5462; TIAS 2749; 198 UNTS 294).

July 12 and October 26, 1954 (5 UST 2930; TIAS 3151; 237 UNTS 337).

Scientific Cooperation

Agreement relating to cooperation in science and technology. Exchange of notes at Taipei January 23, 1969; entered into force January 23, 1969.
   20 UST 374; TIAS 6639; 714 UNTS 139.
Extension:
   January 21, 1975 (26 UST 107; TIAS 8013).

Surplus Property

Agreement relating to the sale of United States excess property in Taiwan by the Armed Forces of the United States, and memorandum of understanding. Signed at Taipei July 22, 1959; entered into force July 22, 1959.
   10 UST 1643; TIAS 4312; 357 UNTS 293.

Taxation

Agreement for the relief from double taxation on earnings from operation of ships and aircraft. Exchange of notes at Taipei February 8 and 26, 1972; entered into force February 26, 1972.
   23 UST 129; TIAS 7282; 829 UNTS 287.

Trade and Commerce

Treaty of friendship, commerce, and navigation with accompanying protocol. Signed at Nanking November 4, 1946; entered into force November 30, 1948.
   63 Stat. 1299; TIAS 1871; 6 Bevans 761; 25 UNTS 69.
Agreement relating to trade in textiles with letter dated April 10, 1974. Exchange of letters at Washington April 11, 1974; entered into force April 11, 1974.[1]
   25 UST 720; TIAS 7821.
Agreement relating to the export of non-rubber footwear from the Republic of China, with annexes, agreed minutes, and related notes. Exchange of notes at Washington June 14, 1977; entered into force June 14, 1977; effective June 28, 1977.
   TIAS 8884.
Agreement relating to trade in cotton, wool and man-made fiber textiles and textile products, with annexes. Exchange of notes at Washington June 8, 1978; entered into force June 8, 1978; effective January 1, 1978.
   TIAS
Amendments:
   July 25 and 28, 1978.
   November 1, 1978.

Visas

Agreement prescribing nonimmigrant visa fees and validity of nonimmigrant visas. Exchange of notes at Taipei December 20, 1955 and February 20, 1956; entered into force February 20, 1956; operative April 1, 1956.
   7 UST 585; TIAS 3539; 275 UNTS 73.
Amendments:
   July 11, October 17 and December 7, 1956 (18 UST 3167; TIAS 6410; 697 UNTS 256).
   May 8, June 9 and 15, 1970 (21 UST 2213; TIAS 6972; 776 UNTS 344).

[1] *Exchange of letters dated April 11, 1974 terminated January 1, 1975. Letter dated April 10, 1974 remains in force.*

Hanoi and Peking Statements

Following are the texts — as printed in The New York Times *— of the Chinese government statement on the border conflict with Vietnam, as provided by Xinhua, the Chinese press agency, and relayed from Hong Kong by Reuters, and of a broadcast by Radio Hanoi as monitored and translated by the United States government, Feb. 18, 1979. Words in parentheses were indistinct in Hanoi's broadcast:*

China's Text

Ignoring China's repeated warnings, the Vietnamese authorities have of late continually sent armed forces to encroach on Chinese territory and attack Chinese frontier guards and inhabitants, causing a rapid deterioration of the situation and seriously threatening the peace and security of China's frontiers. Driven beyond forbearance, Chinese frontier troops have been forced to rise in counterattack.

While recklessly pushing an anti-China and anti-Chinese policy, the Vietnamese authorities have in the past two years carried out incessant armed provocations and hostile activities in China's border areas. Treasuring the friendship between the Chinese and Vietnamese peoples and exercising restraint and forbearance, the Chinese side has repeatedly given advice and served warning to the Vietnamese authorities with a view to avoiding a worsening of the situation. But the Vietnamese authorities, emboldened by the support of the Soviet Union and mistaking China's restraint and desire for peace as a sign of weakness, have become more and more unscrupulous and kept escalating their armed incursions into China's border areas.

They have concentrated massive armed forces along the Sino-Vietnamese border and repeatedly encroached on China's territory. They have flagrantly laid mines and built defense works on Chinese territory, willfully opened up with rifles and guns to destroy Chinese villages and kill Chinese soldiers and civilians, plundered Chinese properties and attacked Chinese trains, thus causing grave incidents of bloodshed. In the past six months alone, the Vietnamese have made armed provocations on more than 700 occasions and killed or wounded more than 300 Chinese frontier guards and inhabitants. By such rampant acts of aggression the Vietnamese authorities have meant to provoke military conflicts and heighten tension along China's southern border and disrupt China's socialist modernization program. Such acts of aggression, if allowed to go unchecked, will no doubt endanger the peace and stability of Southeast Asia and even those of the whole of Asia.

It is the consistent position of the Chinese Government and people that "we will not attack unless we are attacked — if we are attacked, we will certainly counterattack." The Chinese frontier troops are fully justified to rise in counterattack when they are driven beyond forbearance. We want to build up our country and need a peaceful international environment. We would not like to fight. We do not want a single inch of Vietnamese territory, but neither will we tolerate wanton incursions into Chinese territory. All we want is a peaceful and stable border. After counterattacking the Vietnamese aggressors as they deserve, the Chinese frontier troops will strictly keep to defending the border of their own country. We believe this Chinese position will enjoy the sympathy and support of all the countries and people who love peace and uphold justice.

The Chinese and Vietnamese peoples, sympathizing with and supporting each other in their long revolutionary struggles, have forged a profound friendship. Today's grave armed conflict between China and Vietnam is wholly the making of the Vietnamese authorities acting contrary to the will of the Chinese and Vietnamese peoples. The Chinese Government and people treasure and uphold the friendship between the two peoples. They have done so and will continue to do so in the future.

Demands of the Chinese. The Chinese Government solemnly demands that the Vietnamese authorities at once stop armed incursions and all acts of provocation and sabotage in Chinese border areas, withdraw all their armed personnel from the Chinese territory they have illegally occupied and respect China's sovereignty and territorial integrity.

The Chinese Government has always stood for a fair and reasonable settlement of the disputes between the two countries through peaceful negotiations. Past negotiations have all failed because of lack of good faith on the Vietnamese side. The Chinese Government now proposes again that the two sides speedily hold negotiations at any mutually agreed place between representatives of an appropriate level to discuss the restoration of peace and tranquillity along the border between the two countries and proceed to settle the disputes concerning the boundary and territory. The Chinese Government is prepared to enter into concrete negotiations on any constructive measures that can insure peace and tranquillity along the border between the two countries.

At this time, when Chinese frontier troops are forced to repulse Vietnamese armed incursions, the Chinese Government appeals to the Vietnamese authorities to stop on the precipice, retract from the wrong path and do not go any farther.

Vietnam's Text

China has launched an aggressive war all along the border of our country. Early in the morning of 17 February 1979, the Chinese powerholders mobilized a large armed force composed of infantry, artillery and armored forces to launch an aggressive offensive on our territory all along the frontier from Phong Tho and Lai Chau to Mong Cai town in Quang Ninh Province. They used long-range artillery pieces to wantonly fire on the cities, towns, densely populated areas and villages in order to open the road for the armored and infantry forces to launch attacks deep inside our territory.

In Lang Son they used infantry, armored and artillery forces to attack the outposts of our armed public security forces and the key positions of our (guerrilla) and militia forces in (Ban Chap,) Dinh Lap, (Chi Ma,) Nhon Sat, Loc Binh, Ba Son, Cao Loc, Dong Dang town and Van Thanh and (words indistinct) villages.

The local armed forces fiercely counterattacked, annihilating many of the enemy and setting afire and destroying many enemy tanks.

In Hoang Lien Son, the enemy used his infantry and armored forces supported by artillery to attack Muong Khuong town and used artillery to wantonly shell Lao Cai city, the power plant and Pho Moi railway station. The enemy also used his infantry force to attack and occupy the key positions of our military force at (Ban Qua,) Bat Sat district, where many of the enemy were annihilated and many (tanks) set ablaze.

Vietnamese Response. In Cao Bang, the enemy infantry attacked the military positions at Quang Hoa, Ha Quang and Trung Khanh.

In Lai Chau, the enemy attacked Ma Li Pho, Cao Son Trai and west of Route 12.

In Quang Ninh, the enemy's heavy artillery wantonly shelled Mong Cai town and his infantry force attacked (Hoanh Mai) and (Binh Duong.)

According to initial reports, the local armed forces and people in border areas fought very valiantly, exterminating many Chinese aggressors, destroying and setting ablaze many tanks. Just in (Ban Quang) area, Bat Sat district, Hoang Lien Son province, our armed forces and people annihilated 250 enemy troops and set afire four tanks.

In the Huu Nghi gate area, eight enemy tanks were set ablaze.

The struggle against the Chinese aggressors in the northern border of the fatherland has begun. The armed forces and people of various nationalities in border areas are upholding the heroic determined-to-fight-and-win tradition, resolutely dealing punitive blows to the Chinese aggressors right in the initial battle on the front line of the country.

1979 China-U.S. Trade Agreement

Following is the text of the China-U.S. Trade Relations Agreement signed by the two countries on July 7, 1979, sent to Congress Oct. 23, 1979, and approved Jan. 24, 1980, along with accompanying presidential proclamations and memoranda.

Letter to Congress

Dear Mr. Speaker: (Dear Mr. President:)

In accordance with section 407 of the Trade Act of 1974, I am transmitting a copy of a proclamation extending nondiscriminatory treatment to the products of the People's Republic of China. I also enclose the text of the Agreement on Trade Relations between the United States of America and the People's Republic of China, which was signed on July 7, 1979, and which is included as an annex to the proclamation.

The Agreement on Trade Relations will provide a nondiscriminatory framework for our bilateral trade relations, and thus strengthen both economic and political relations between the United States and the People's Republic of China. Conclusion of this agreement is the most important step we can take to provide greater economic benefits to both countries from this relationship. It will also give further impetus to the progress we have made in our overall relationship since normalization of our diplomatic relations earlier this year.

I believe that the Agreement on Trade Relations is consistent with both the letter and the spirit of the Trade Act of 1974. It provides for mutual extension of most-favored-nation tariff treatment, while seeking to ensure overall reciprocity of economic benefits. It includes safeguard arrangements to ensure that our trade with the People's Republic of China will grow without injury to domestic firms or loss of jobs for American workers.

The Agreement also confirms for American businessmen certain basic rights and facilities in establishing operations and conducting business in the P.R.C. Other provisions include those dealing with settlement of commercial disputes; financial transactions; government commercial offices; and protection for industrial property rights, industrial processes, and copyrights.

I am also enclosing a copy of my report to the Congress pursuant to section 402 (c) (2) of the Trade Act of 1974. I shall issue today an Executive order waiving the application of subsections (a) and (b) of section 402.

In the past year and a half, Chinese leaders on several occasions have called for facilitating family reunification and for simplifying the procedure for getting permission to enter or leave China. During this period we have noted a marked relaxation of Chinese emigration procedures. Processing time has been reduced for most cases and numbers of emigrants have jumped dramatically. We have recently had discussions with senior Chinese officials and firmly believe that Chinese statements and the marked increase in emigration reflect a policy of the Government of China favoring freer emigration.

I have reviewed the circumstances of Emigration from the People's Republic of China in light of all these factors, and have determined that a waiver of the application of subsections (a) and (b) of section 402 of the Trade Act of 1974 will substantially promote the objectives of that section.

I urge that Congress act as soon as possible to approve the Agreement on Trade Relations.

Sincerely,
JIMMY CARTER

NOTE: This is the text of identical letters addressed to Thomas P. O'Neill, Jr., Speaker of the House of Representatives, and Walter F. Mondale, President of the Senate.

Presidential Proclamation

As President of the United States of America, acting through my representatives, I entered into the negotiation of an agreement on trade relations between the United States of America and the People's Republic of China with representatives of the People's Republic of China;

The negotiations were conducted in accordance with the requirements of the Trade Act of 1974 (P.L. 93-618, January 3, 1975; 88 Stat. 1978) ("the Act");

An "Agreement on Trade Relations between the United States of America and the People's Republic of China", in English and Chinese, was signed on July 7, 1979, by representatives of the two Governments, and is annexed to this Proclamation;

The Agreement conforms to the requirements relating to bilateral commercial agreements specified in section 405 (b) of the Act;

Article X of the Agreement provides that it shall come into force on the date on which the Contracting Parties have exchanged notifications that each has completed the legal procedures necessary for this purpose; and

Section 405(c) of the Act provides that a bilateral commercial agreement and a proclamation implementing such agreement shall take effect only if approved by the Congress;

NOW, THEREFORE, I, JIMMY CARTER, President of the United States of America, proclaim as follows:

(1) This Proclamation shall become effective, said Agreement shall enter into force according to its terms, and nondiscriminatory treatment shall be extended to the products of the People's Republic of China in accordance with the terms of the said Agreement, on the date on which the Contracting Parties have exchanged notifications that each has completed the legal procedures necessary for this purpose in accordance with Article X of the said Agreement.

(2) General Headnote 3(e) of the Tariff Schedules of the United States is amended by deleting therefrom "China (any part of which may be under Communist domination or control)" and "Tibet" as of the effective date of this proclamation and a notice thereof shall be published in the *Federal Register* promptly thereafter.

IN WITNESS WHEREOF, I have hereunto set my hand this twenty-third day of October, in the year of our Lord nineteen hundred and seventy-nine, and of the Independence of the United States of America the two hundred and fourth.

Jimmy Carter

Text of the Agreement

AGREEMENT ON TRADE RELATIONS
BETWEEN
THE UNITED STATES OF AMERICA
AND
THE PEOPLE'S REPUBLIC OF CHINA

The Government of the United States of America and the Government of the People's Republic of China;

Acting in the spirit of the Joint Communiqué on the Establishment of Diplomatic Relations between the United States of America and the People's Republic of China;

Desiring to enhance friendship between both peoples;

Wishing to develop further economic and trade relations between both countries on the basis of the principles of equality and mutual benefit as well as nondiscriminatory treatment;

Have agreed as follows:

ARTICLE I

1. The Contracting Parties undertake to adopt all appropriate measures to create the most favorable conditions for strengthening, in all aspects, economic and trade relations between the two countries so as to promote the continuous, long-term development of trade between the two countries.

2. In order to strive for a balance in their economic interests, the Contracting Parties shall make every effort to foster the mutual expansion of their reciprocal trade and to contribute, each by its

own means, to attaining the harmonious development of such trade.

3. Commercial transactions will be effected on the basis of contracts between firms, companies and corporations, and trading organizations of the two countries. They will be concluded on the basis of customary international trade practice and commercial considerations such as price, quality, delivery and terms of payment.

ARTICLE II

1. With a view to establishing their trade relations on a nondiscriminatory basis, the Contracting Parties shall accord each other most-favored-nation treatment with respect to products originating in or destined for the other Contracting Party, i.e., any advantage, favor, privilege, or immunity they grant to like products originating in or destined for any other country or region, in all matters regarding:

(A) Customs duties and charges of all kinds applied to the import, export, re-export or transit of products, including the rules, formalities and procedures for collection of such duties and charges;

(B) Rules, formalities and procedures concerning customs clearance, transit, warehousing and transshipment of imported and exported products;

(C) Taxes and other internal charges levied directly or indirectly on imported or exported products or services;

(D) All laws, regulations and requirements affecting all aspects of internal sale, purchase, transportation, distribution or use of imported products; and

(E) Administrative formalities for the issuance of import and export licenses.

2. In the event either Contracting Party applies quantitative restrictions to certain products originating in or exported to any third country or region, it shall afford to all like products originating in or exported to the other country treatment which is equitable to that afforded to such third country or region.

3. The Contracting Parties note, and shall take into consideration in the handling of their bilateral trade relations, that, at its current state of economic development, China is a developing country.

4. The principles of Paragraph 1 of this Article will be applied by the Contracting Parties in the same way as they are applied under similar circumstances under any multilateral trade agreement to which either Contracting Party is a party on the date of entry into force of this Agreement.

5. The Contracting Parties agree to reciprocate satisfactorily concessions with regard to trade and services, particularly tariff and non-tariff barriers to trade, during the term of this Agreement.

ARTICLE III

For the purpose of promoting economic and trade relations between their two countries, the Contracting Parties agree to:

A. Accord firms, companies and corporations, and trading organizations of the other Party treatment no less favorable than is afforded to any third country or region;

B. Promote visits by personnel, groups and delegations from economic, trade and industrial circles; encourage commercial exchanges and contacts; and support the holding of fairs, exhibitions and technical seminars in each others country;

C. Permit and facilitate, subject to their respective laws and regulations and in accordance with physical possibilities, the stationing of representatives, or the establishment of business offices, by firms, companies and corporations, and trading organizations of the other Party in its own territory; and

D. Subject to their respective laws and regulations and physical possibilities, further support trade promotions and improve all conveniences, facilities and related services for the favorable conduct of business activities by firms, companies and corporations, and trading organizations of the two countries, including various facilities in respect of office space and residential housing, telecommunications, visa issuance, internal business travel, customs formalities for entry and re-export of personal effects, office articles and commercial samples, and observance of contracts.

ARTICLE IV

The Contracting Parties affirm that government trade offices contribute importantly to the development of their trade and economic relations. They agree to encourage and support the trade promotion activities of these offices. Each Party undertakes to provide facilities as favorable as possible for the operation of these offices in accordance with their respective physical possibilities.

ARTICLE V

1. Payments for transactions between the United States of America and the People's Republic of China shall either be effected in freely convertible currencies mutually accepted by firms, companies and corporations, and trading organizations of the two countries, or made otherwise in accordance with agreements signed by and between the two parties to the transaction. Neither Contracting Party may impose restrictions on such payments except in time of declared national emergency.

2. The Contracting Parties agree, in accordance with their respective laws, regulations and procedures, to facilitate the availability of official export credits on the most favorable terms appropriate under the circumstances for transactions in support of economic and technological projects and products between firms, companies and corporations, and trading organizations of the two countries. Such credits will be the subject of separate arrangments by the concerned authorities of the two Contracting Parties.

3. Each Contracting Party shall provide, on the basis of most-favored-nation treatment, and subject to its respective laws and regulations, all necessary facilities for financial, currency and banking transactions by nationals, firms, companies and corporations, and trading organizations of the other Contracting Party on terms as favorable as possible. Such facilities shall include all required authorizations for international payments, remittances and transfers, and uniform application of rates of exchange.

4. Each Contracting Party will look with favor towards participation by financial institutions of the other country in appropriate aspects of banking services related to international trade and financial relations. Each Contracting Party will permit those financial institutions of the other country established in its territory to provide such services on a basis no less favorable than that accorded to financial institutions of other countries.

ARTICLE VI

1. Both Contracting Parties in their trade relations recognize the importance of effective protection of patents, trademarks and copyrights.

2. Both Contracting Parties agree that on the basis of reciprocity legal or natural persons of either Party may apply for registration of trademarks and acquire exclusive rights thereto in the territory of the other Party in accordance with its laws and regulations.

3. Both Contracting Parties agree that each Party shall seek, under its laws and with due regard to international practice, to ensure to legal or natural persons of the other Party protection of patents and trademarks equivalent to the patent and trademark protection correspondingly accorded by the other Party.

4. Both Contracting Parties shall permit and facilitate enforcement of provisions concerning protection of industrial property in contracts between firms, companies and corporations, and trading organizations of their respective countries, and shall provide means, in accordance with their respective laws, to restrict unfair competition involving unauthorized use of such rights.

5. Both Contracting Parties agree that each Party shall take appropriate measures, under its laws and regulations and with due regard to international practice, to ensure to legal or natural persons of the other Party protection of copyrights equivalent to the copyright protection correspondingly accorded by the other Party.

ARTICLE VII

1. The Contracting Parties shall exchange information on any problems that may arise from their bilateral trade, and shall promptly hold friendly consultations to seek mutually satisfactory solutions to such problems. No action shall be taken by either Contracting Party before such consultations are held.

2. However, if consultations do not result in a mutually satisfactory solution within a reasonable period of time, either Contracting Party may take such measures as it deems appropriate. In an exceptional case where a situation does not admit any delay, either Contracting Party may take preventive or remedial action provisionally, on the condition that consultation shall be effected immediately after taking such action.

3. When either Contracting Party takes measures under this Article, it shall ensure that the general objectives of this Agreement are not prejudiced.

ARTICLE VIII

1. The Contracting Parties encourage the prompt and equitable settlement of any disputes arising from or in relation to contracts between their respective firms, companies and corporations, and trading organizations, through friendly consultations, conciliation or other mutually acceptable means.

2. If such disputes cannot be settled promptly by any one of the above-mentioned means, the parties to the dispute may have recourse to arbitration for settlement in accordance with provisions specified in their contracts or other agreements to submit to arbitration. Such arbitration may be conducted by an arbitration institution in the People's Republic of China, the United States of America, or a third country. The arbitration rules of procedure of the relevant arbitration institution are applicable, and the arbitration rules of the United Nations Commission on International Trade Law recommended by the United Nations, or other international arbitration rules, may also be used where acceptable to the parties to the dispute and to the arbitration institution.

3. Each Contracting Party shall seek to ensure that arbitration awards are recognized and enforced by their competent authorities where enforcement is sought, in accordance with applicable laws and regulations.

ARTICLE IX

The provisions of this Agreement shall not limit the right of either Contracting Party to take any action for the protection of its security interests.

ARTICLE X

1. This Agreement shall come into force on the date on which the Contracting Parties have exchanged notifications that each has completed the legal procedures necessary for this purpose, and shall remain in force for three years.

2. This Agreement shall be extended for successive terms of three years if neither Contracting Party notifies the other of its intent to terminate this Agreement at least 30 days before the end of a term.

3. If either Contracting Party does not have domestic legal authority to carry out its obligations under this Agreement, either Contracting Party may suspend application of this Agreement, or, with the agreement of the other Contracting Party, any part of this Agreement. In that event, the Parties will seek, to the fullest extent practicable in accordance with domestic law, to minimize unfavorable effects on existing trade relations between the two countries.

4. The Contracting Parties agree to consult at the request of either Contracting Party to review the operation of this Agreement and other relevant aspects of the relations between the two Parties.

IN WITNESS WHEREOF, the authorized representatives of the Contracting Parties have signed this Agreement.

Done at Beijing (Peking) in two original copies this seventh day of July, 1979, in English and Chinese, both texts being equally authentic.

LEONARD WOODCOCK
For the United States of America
LI QIANG
For the People's Republic of China

Presidential Memoranda

Memorandum for the Secretary of State
Subject: Determination under Section 402(c) (2) (A) of the Trade Act of 1974 — People's Republic of China

Pursuant to section 402(c) (2) (A) of the Trade Act of 1974 (Public Law 93-618, January 3, 1975; 88 Stat. 1978) ("the Act") I determine that a waiver of subsections (a) and (b) of section 402 of the Act with respect to the People's Republic of China will substantially promote the objectives of section 402.

On my behalf, please transmit this determination to the Speaker of the House of Representatives and the President of the Senate.

This determination shall be published in the *Federal Register*.
JIMMY CARTER

Memorandum for the Secretary of State
Subject: Determination under Section 405(a) of the Trade Act of 1974 — People's Republic of China

Pursuant to the authority vested in me under the Trade Act of 1974 (Public Law 93-618, January 3, 1975; 88 Stat. 1978) ("the Act"), I determine, pursuant to section 405(a) of the Act, that the Agreement on Trade Relations between the United States of America and the People's Republic of China will promote the purposes of the Act and is in the national interest.

On my behalf, please transmit this determination to the Speaker of the House of Representatives and to the President of the Senate.

This determination shall be published in the *Federal Register*.
JIMMY CARTER

Message to the Congress

To the Congress of the United States:
Pursuant to section 402(c) (2) of the Trade Act of 1974, (hereinafter, "the Act") I shall issue only an Executive Order waiving the application of subsections (a) and (b) of section 402 of the Act with respect to the People's Republic of China.

I wish to report to the Congress that I have determined that the requirements of section 402(c) (2) (A) and (B) of the Act have been satisfied.

JIMMY CARTER

Executive Order

WAIVER UNDER THE TRADE ACT OF 1974
WITH RESPECT TO THE PEOPLE'S
REPUBLIC OF CHINA

By virtue of the authority vested in me as President of the United States of America by section 402(c) (2) of the Trade Act of 1974 (Public Law 93-618, January 3, 1975; 88 Stat. 1978), which continues to apply to the People's Republic of China pursuant to section 402(d), and having made the report to the Congress required by section 402(c) (2), I waive the application of subsections (a) and (b) of section 402 of said Act with respect to the People's Republic of China.

JIMMY CARTER

Taiwan Treaty Court Decision

Following is the text of the decision by the United States Court of Appeals for the District of Columbia Circuit in the case brought by Sen. Barry Goldwater, R-Ariz., and others against President Carter for terminating treaty arrangements with Taiwan without approval of Congress. The court upheld the president's power to terminate the treaty on his own authority. Its action reversed an earlier decision by a U.S. District Court holding that the president did not have this power.

The Supreme Court on Dec. 13, 1979, ordered the case returned to district court for dismissal — in effect upholding the court of appeals decision. The defense treaty was terminated Jan. 1, 1980, as scheduled.

The appeals court's decision was announced Nov. 30, 1979. Omitted from the text below are footnotes and additional opinions filed by some of the judges.

PER CURIAM: The court *en banc* has before it for review the judgment of the District Court that the notice of termination given by the President pursuant to the terms of the Mutual Defense Treaty with the Republic of China is ineffective absent either (1) a manifestation of the consent of the Senate to such termination by a two-thirds vote or (2) an approving majority vote therefor by both houses of Congress. The preliminary questions we confront are, first, whether the District Court was without jurisdiction because appellees lacked standing, and, second, whether it should in any event have declined to exercise jurisdiction by reason of the political nature of the question it was called upon to decide. Since a majority of the court does not exist to dispose of the appeal on either of these bases, we reach the merits and reverse.

In doing so, however, we think it important at the outset to stress that the Treaty, as it was presented to the Senate in 1954 and consented to by it, contained an explicit provision for termination by either party on one year's notice. The Senate, in the course of giving its consent, exhibited no purpose and took no action to reserve a role for itself — by amendment, reservation, or condition — in the effectuation of this provision.

Neither has the Senate, since the giving of the notice of termination, purported to take any final or decisive action with respect to it, either by way of approval or disapproval. The constitutional issue we face, therefore, is solely and simply the one of whether the President in these precise circumstances is, on behalf of the United States, empowered to terminate the Treaty in accordance with its terms. It is our view that he is, and that the limitations which the District Court purported to place on his action in this regard have no foundation in the Constitution.

Background

In the aftermath of the Chinese Revolution and the Korean War, the United States and the Republic of China (ROC) negotiated a Mutual Defense Treaty, primarily directed against the perceived threat from the People's Republic of China (PRC). The Treaty was signed by representatives of both nations on December 2, 1954. It was approved by the Senate, and finally signed by the President on February 11, 1955. Article V of the Treaty provided that, in the event of an attack on Taiwan, the Pescadores, or United States territories in the western Pacific, each nation "would act to meet the common danger in accordance with its constitutional processes." Article X of the Treaty provided that it would remain in force "indefinitely," but said that "[e]ither Party may terminate it one year after notice has been given to the other Party."

At that time both the ROC and PRC claimed — and still claim — to be the sole legitimate government of China; both considered Taiwan a part of China. Since then over 100 nations, including all of our NATO allies and Japan, have officially recognized the PRC as the sole government of China, breaking off relations with Taiwan. In 1971 the United Nations admitted delegates from the PRC to the seats reserved for China in the General Assembly and Security Council, and expelled those from the ROC.

In the early 1970's the United States began to pursue a policy of closer relations with the PRC. The early stage of this effort culminated in President Nixon's visit to the mainland of China, during which the two nations released the "Shanghai Communiqué," declaring the goal of "normalization of relations between China and the United States." The PRC stipulated that full mutual diplomatic recognition was preconditioned on United States agreement to cease all diplomatic and other official relations with the ROC, to withdraw United States military units from Taiwan, and to terminate the Mutual Defense Treaty with the ROC.

In September 1978 Congress passed and the President signed the International Security Assistance Act of 1978, Pub. L. No. 95-384, 92 Stat. 746. Section 26 of that Act, called the "Dole-Stone Amendment," provided:

It is the sense of the Congress that there should be prior consultation between the Congress and the executive branch on any proposed policy changes affecting the continuation in force of the Mutual Defense Treaty of 1954.

On December 15, 1978, President Carter announced that the United States would recognize the PRC as the sole government of China, effective January 1, 1979, and would simultaneously withdraw recognition from the ROC. In addition, the United States announced that the ROC would be notified that "the Mutual Defense Treaty is being terminated in accordance with the provisions of the Treaty." On December 23, 1978, the State Department formally notified the ROC that the Treaty would terminate on January 1, 1980.

While severing all official ties with the ROC, the United States has sought to preserve "extensive, close, and friendly commercial, cultural, and other relations between the people of the United States and the people on Taiwan." The Taiwan Relations Act, Pub. L. No. 96-8, 93 Stat. 14, signed into law on April 10, 1979, established the statutory framework for such relations. It provided:

For all purposes, including actions in any court in the United States, the Congress approves the continuation in force of all treaties and other international agreements, including multilateral conventions, entered into by the United States and the governing authorities on Taiwan recognized by the United States as the Republic of China prior to January 1, 1979, and in force between them on December 31, 1978, unless and until terminated in accordance with law.

Id. § 4(c).

On December 22, 1978, plaintiffs-appellees filed this suit in District Court, seeking declaratory and injunctive relief to prevent termination of the Treaty without senatorial or congressional consent. The complaint alleged that the President violated his sworn duty to uphold the laws, including the treaties, of the United States. It asserted that the President has no unilateral power under the Constitution to abrogate treaties, and that the United States, not the President, is the party invested by Article X of the Treaty with the power of termination.

On June 6, 1979, the District Court dismissed the suit, without prejudice, for lack of standing. The court observed that three resolutions then pending in the Senate might resolve the controversy without need for judicial intervention. The court concluded:

If the Congress approves the President's action, the issue presently before the Court would be moot. If the Senate or the Congress takes action, the result of which falls short of approving the President's termination effort, then the controversy will be ripe for a judicial declaration. . . .

JA 631-632.

Within hours of the District Court order the Senate called up Senate Resolution 15 which, as amended by the Foreign Relations Committee, would have recognized some fourteen grounds that would justify unilateral action by the President to terminate treaty obligations of the United States. By a vote of 59 to 35 the Senate substituted for its consideration an amendment drafted by Senator Harry Byrd, Jr.:

That it is the sense of the Senate that approval of the United States Senate is required to terminate any mutual defense treaty between the United States and another nation.

125 Cong. Rec. S7015, S7038-S7039 (daily ed. June 6, 1979). Later that day, during the course of debate on the amended resolution, a dispute arose among the Senators over whether the resolution would have retrospective, or merely prospective, effect. No final vote was ever taken on the resolution, and the Majority Leader returned the resolution to the calendar.

On June 12, 1979, after the Byrd amendment was voted on, the plaintiffs-appellees filed a motion in District Court for alteration or amendment of the June 6 order of dismissal. They contended that the Senate's action on the Byrd amendment satisfied the court's stated criteria for creating a justiciable controversy. On October 17, 1979, the District Court granted this motion, ruling that the plaintiffs had suffered the requisite injury in fact because of the denial of their right to be consulted and to vote on treaty termination. The court also ruled that the case did not present a nonjusticiable political question. Reaching the constitutional question, the court granted plaintiffs' cross-motion for summary judgment. This appeal followed.

I

For purposes of the standing issue, we accept, as we must, appellees' pleaded theories as valid. A majority of the court is of the view that, at least as their principal theory has evolved — that the Senate has a constitutional right to vote on the President's proposed treaty termination and to block such termination with a one-third plus one vote — the appellee Senators have standing.

If there is merit to their allegations, such Senators have suffered injury in fact from the President's action terminating the Treaty without Senate consent. This action has deprived the Senate of the opportunity — which appellees assert to be constitutionally prescribed — to vote whether to prevent the termination of this treaty. By excluding the Senate from the treaty termination process, the President has deprived each individual Senator of his alleged right to cast a vote that will have binding effect on whether the Treaty can be terminated. The President has thus nullified the right that each appellee Senator claims under the Constitution to be able to block the termination of this treaty by voting, in conjunction with one-third of his colleagues, against it.

In our decisions on congressional standing this court has carefully drawn a distinction between (1) a diminution in congressional influence resulting from an Executive action that nullifies a specific congressional vote or opportunity to vote, in an objectively verifiable manner — which, we have found, constitutes injury in fact; and (2) a diminution in a legislator's effectiveness, subjectively judged by him or her, resulting from Executive action withholding information or failing to obey a statute enacted through the legislator's vote, where the plaintiff-legislator still has power to act through the legislative process to remedy the alleged abuses — in which situations we do not find injury in fact. To be cognizable for standing purposes, the alleged diminution in congressional influence must amount to a disenfranchisement, a complete nullification or withdrawal of a voting opportunity; and the plaintiff must point to an objective standard in the Constitution, statutes or congressional house rules, by which disenfranchisement can be shown.

In the present case, appellees plead an objective standard in the Constitution as giving them a right to vote on treaty termination. They further allege disenfranchisement in the context of a specific measure, *i.e.*, the proposed termination of the Mutual Defense Treaty. Whether the President's action amounts to a complete disenfranchisement depends on whether appellees have left to them any legislative means to vote in the way they claim is their right. In other words, do they have effective power to block the termination of this treaty despite the President's action? This is the crucial issue, and the focus of our disagreement with the concurring opinion.

The crucial fact is that, on the record before us, there is no conceivable senatorial action that could likely prevent termination of the Treaty. A congressional resolution or statute might at most have persuasive effect with the President; it could not block termination if he persisted in his present interpretation of the Constitution giving him unilateral power to terminate. That appellee Senators have no power to enact a remedy is especially clear in light of the nature of their constitutional claim. They claim the right to block termination with only one-third plus one of their colleagues. There is no way that such a minority can even force a resolution to the floor, let alone pass it. To pretend that effective remedies are open to appellees is to ignore that, first, their alleged right would enable them to block termination with a minority, and, second, that even if they could muster a majority, any legislative action they might take under the present circumstances could well be futile. The only way the Senate can effectively vote on treaty termination, with the burden on termination proponents to secure a two-thirds majority, is for the President to submit the proposed treaty termination to the Senate as he would a proposed treaty. This is the concrete remedy appellees seek. For the court to require of them some other legislative action before allowing them standing to pursue this claim would be to require a useless act.

Since the President has not afforded an opportunity for an up-or-down vote as appellees request, we do not know whether the Senate would actually block the President's action if given the opportunity. Yet courts consistently vindicate the right to vote without first demanding that the votes when cast will achieve their intended end. A live controversy exists in appellees' claim of an opportunity to cast a binding vote. The President's action has deprived them of this opportunity completely, in the sense that they have no legislative power to exercise an equivalent voting opportunity. Therefore, appellee Senators have standing.

II

Various considerations enter into our determination that the President's notice of termination will be effective on January 1, 1980. The result we reach draws upon their totality, but in listing them hereinafter we neither assign them hierarchical values nor imply that any one factor or combination of factors is determinative.

1. We turn first to the argument, embraced by the District Court, drawn from the language of Article II, § 2, of the Constitution. It is that, since the President clearly cannot enter into a treaty without the consent of the Senate, the inference is inescapable that he must in all circumstances seek the same senatorial consent to terminate that treaty. As a matter of language alone, however, the same inference would appear automatically to obtain with respect to the termination by the President of officers appointed by him under the same clause of the Constitution and subject to Senate confirmation. But the Supreme Court has read that clause as not having such an inevitable effect in any and all circumstances. *Compare Myers* v. *United States,* 272 U.S. 52 (1926) *with* In Re *Humphrey's Executor* v. *United States,* 295 U.S. 602 (1935). In the area of foreign relations in particular, where the constitutional commitment of powers to the President is notably comprehensive, it has never been suggested that the services of Ambassadors — appointed by the President, confirmed by the Senate, and of critical importance as they are to the successful conduct of our foreign relations — may not be terminated by the President without the prior authorization of that body.

Expansion of the language of the Constitution by sequential linguistic projection is a tricky business at best. Virtually all constitutional principles have unique elements and can be distinguished from one another. As the Supreme Court has recognized with respect to the clause in question, it is not abstract logic or sterile symmetry that controls, but a sensible and realistic ascertainment of the meaning of the Constitution in the context of the specific action taken.

2. The District Court's declaration, in the alternative, that the necessary authority in this instance may be granted by a majority of each house of Congress presumably has its source in the Supremacy Clause of Article VI. The argument is that a treaty, being a part of the "supreme Law of the Land," can only be terminated at the least by a subsequent federal statute.

The central purpose of the Supremacy Clause has been accepted to be that of causing each of the designated supreme laws — Constitution, statute, and treaty — to prevail, for purposes of domestic law, over state law in any form. Article VI speaks explicitly to the judges to assure that this is so. But these three types of supreme law are not necessarily the same in their other characteristics, any more than are the circumstances and terms of their creation the same. Certainly the Constitution is silent on the matter of treaty termination. And the fact that it speaks to the common characteristic of supremacy over state law does not provide any basis for concluding that a treaty must be unmade either by (1) the same process by which it was made, or (2) the alternative means by which a statute is made or terminated.

3. The constitutional institution of advice and consent of the Senate, provided two-thirds of the Senators concur, is a special and extraordinary condition of the exercise by the President of certain specified powers under Article II. It is not lightly to be extended in instances not set forth in the Constitution. Such an extension by implication is not proper unless that implication is unmistakably clear.

The District Court's absolutist extension of this limitation to termination of treaties, irrespective of the particular circumstances involved, is not sound. The making of a treaty has the consequences of an entangling alliance for the nation. Similarly, the amending of a treaty merely continues such entangling alliances, changing only their character, and therefore also requires the advice and consent of the Senate. It does not follow, however, that a constitutional provision for a special concurrence (two-thirds of the Senators) prior to entry into an entangling alliance necessarily applies to its termination in accordance with its terms.

4. The Constitution specifically confers no power of treaty termination on either the Congress or the Executive. We note, however, that the powers conferred upon Congress in Article I of the Constitution are specific, detailed, and limited, while the powers conferred upon the President by Article II are generalized in a manner that bespeaks no such limitation upon foreign affairs powers. "Section 1. The executive Power shall be vested in a President. . . ." Although specific powers are listed in Section 2 and Section 3, these are in many instances not powers necessary to an Executive, while "The executive Power" referred to in Section 1 is nowhere defined. There is no required two-thirds vote of the Senate conditioning the exercise of any power in Section 1.

In some instances this difference is reflective of the origin of the particular power in question. In general, the powers of the federal government arise out of specific grants of authority delegated by the states — hence the enumerated powers of Congress in Article I, Section 8. The foreign affairs powers, however, proceed directly from the sovereignty of the Union. "[I]f they had never been mentioned in the Constitution, [they] would have vested in the federal government as necessary concomitants of nationality." *United States* v. *Curtiss-Wright Export Corp.,* 299 U.S. 304, 318 (1936).

The President is the constitutional representative of the United States with respect to external affairs. It is significant that the treaty power appears in Article II of the Constitution, relating to the executive branch, and not in Article I, setting forth the powers of the legislative branch. It is the President as Chief Executive who is given the constitutional authority to enter into a treaty; and even after he has obtained the consent of the Senate it is for him to decide whether to ratify a treaty and put it into effect. Senatorial confirmation of a treaty concededly does not obligate the President to go forward with a treaty if he concludes that it is not in the public interest to do so.

Thus, in contrast to the lawmaking power, the constitutional initiative in the treaty-making field is in the President, not Congress. It would take an unprecedented feat of judicial construction to read into the Constitution an absolute condition precedent of congressional or Senate approval for termination of all treaties, similar to the specific one relating to initial approval. And it would unalterably affect the balance of power between the two Branches laid down in Articles I and II.

5. Ultimately, what must be recognized is that a treaty is *sui generis.* It is not just another law. It is an international compact, a solemn obligation of the United States and a "supreme Law" that supersedes state policies and prior federal laws. For clarity of analysis, it is thus well to distinguish between treaty-making as an international act and the consequences which flow domestically from such act. In one realm the Constitution has conferred the primary role upon the President; in the other, Congress retains its primary

role as lawmaker. The fact that the Constitution, statutes, and treaties are all listed in the Supremacy Clause as being superior to any form of state law does not mean that the making and unmaking of treaties can be analogized to the making and unmaking of domestic statutes any more than it can be analogized to the making or unmaking of a constitutional amendment.

The recognized powers of Congress to implement (or fail to implement) a treaty by an appropriation or other law essential to its effectuation, or to supersede for all practical purposes the effect of a treaty on domestic law, are legislative powers, not treaty-making or treaty termination powers. The issue here, however, is not Congress' legislative powers to supersede or affect the domestic impact of a treaty; the issue is whether the Senate (or Congress) must in this case give its prior consent to discontinue a treaty which the President thinks it desirable to terminate in the national interest and pursuant to a provision in the treaty itself. The existence, in practical terms, of one power does not imply the existence, in constitutional terms, of the other.

6. If we were to hold that under the Constitution a treaty could only be terminated by exactly the same process by which it was made, we would be locking the United States into all of its international obligations, even if the President and two-thirds of the Senate minus one firmly believed that the proper course for the United States was to terminate a treaty. Many of our treaties in force, such as mutual defense treaties, carry potentially dangerous obligations. These obligations are terminable under international law upon breach by the other party or change in circumstances that frustrates the purpose of the treaty. In many of these situations the President must take immediate action. The creation of a constitutionally obligatory role in all cases for a two-thirds consent by the Senate would give to one-third plus one of the Senate the power to deny the President the authority necessary to conduct our foreign policy in a rational and effective manner.

7. Even as to the formal termination of treaties, as the District Court pointed out, "a variety of means have been used to terminate treaties." There is much debate among the historians and scholars as to whether in some instances the legislature has been involved at all; they are agreed that, when involved, that involvement with the President has taken many different forms. It appears moreover that the Senate may wish to continue to determine the nature of its involvement on a case by case basis. 125 Cong. Rec. S16683-S16692 (daily ed. Nov. 15, 1979).

The District Court concluded that the diversity of historical precedents left an inconclusive basis on which to decide the issue of whether the President's power to terminate a treaty must always be "shared" in some way by the Senate or Congress. We agree. Yet we think it is not without significance that out of all the historical precedents brought to our attention, in no situation has a treaty been continued in force over the opposition of the President.

There is on the other hand widespread agreement that the President has the power as Chief Executive under many circumstances to exercise functions regarding treaties which have the effect of either terminating or continuing their vitality. Prominent among these is the authority of the President as Chief Executive (1) to determine whether a treaty has terminated because of a breach, *Charlton* v. *Kelly,* 229 U.S. 447, 473-476 (1913); and (2) to determine whether a treaty is at an end due to changed circumstances.

In short, the determination of the conduct of the United States in regard to treaties is an instance of what has broadly been called the "foreign affairs power" of the President. We have no occasion to define that term, but we do take account of its vitality. The *Curtiss-Wright* opinion, written by a Justice who had served in the United States Senate, declares in oft-repeated language that the President is "the sole organ of the federal government in the field of international relations." That status is not confined to the service of the President as a channel of communication, as the District Court suggested, but embraces an active policy determination as to the conduct of the United States in regard to a treaty in response to numerous problems and circumstances as they arise.

8. How the vital functions of the President in implementing treaties and in deciding on their viability in response to changing events can or should interact with Congress' legitimate concerns and powers in relating to foreign affairs is an area into which we

should not and do not prematurely intrude. History shows us that there are too many variables to lay down any hard and fast constitutional rules.

We cannot find an implied role in the Constitution for the Senate in treaty termination for some but not all treaties in terms of their relative importance. There is no judicially ascertainable and manageable method of making any distinction among treaties on the basis of their substance, the magnitude of the risk involved, the degree of controversy which their termination would engender, or by any other standards. We know of no standards to apply in making such distinctions. The facts on which such distinctions might be drawn may be difficult of ascertainment; and the resolution of such inevitable disputes between the two Branches would be an improper and unnecessary role for the courts. To decide whether there was a breach or changed circumstances, for example, would involve a court in making fundamental decisions of foreign policy and would create insuperable problems of evidentiary proof. This is beyond the acceptable judicial role. All we decide today is that two-thirds Senate consent or majority consent in both houses is not necessary to terminate this treaty in the circumstances before us now.

9. The circumstances involved in the termination of the Mutual Defense Treaty with the Republic of China include a number of material and unique elements. Prominent is assertion by the officials of both the Republic of China and the People's Republic of China that each of them is the government of China, intending the term China to comprehend both the mainland of China and the island of Taiwan. In the 1972 Shanghai Communiqué, the United States acknowledged that position and did not challenge it. It is in this context that the recent Joint Communiqué set forth as of January 1, 1979 that the United States recognizes the People's Republic of China as "the sole legal government of China." This action made reference to "the people of Taiwan," stating that the peoples of the United States and Taiwan "will maintain cultural, commercial and other unofficial relations." This formulation was confirmed by the Taiwan Relations Act.

It is undisputed that the Constitution gave the President full constitutional authority to recognize the PRC and to derecognize the ROC. What the United States has evolved for Taiwan is a novel and somewhat indefinite relationship, namely, of unofficial relations with the people of Taiwan. The subtleties involved in maintaining amorphous relationships are often the very stuff of diplomacy — a field in which the President, not Congress, has responsibility under our Constitution. The President makes a responsible claim that he has authority as Chief Executive to determine that there is no meaningful vitality to a mutual defense treaty when there is no recognized state. That is not to say that the recognition power automatically gives the President authority to take any action that is required or requested by the state being recognized. We do not need to reach this question. Nevertheless, it remains an important ingredient in the case at bar that the President has determined that circumstances have changed so as to preclude continuation of the Mutual Defense Treaty with the ROC; diplomatic recognition of the ROC came to an end on January 1, 1979, and now there exist only "cultural, commercial and other unofficial relations" with the "people on Taiwan."

10. Finally, and of central significance, the treaty here at issue contains a termination clause. The existence of Article X of the ROC treaty, permitting termination by either party on one year's notice, is an overarching factor in this case, which in effect enables all of the other considerations to be knit together.

Without derogating from the executive power of the President to decide to act contrary to the wording of a treaty — for example, because of a breach by the other party (*Charlton* v. *Kelly, supra*),

or because of a doctrine of fundamental change of circumstances (*rebus sic stantibus*) — the President's authority as Chief Executive is at its zenith when the Senate has consented to a treaty that expressly provides for termination on one year's notice, and the President's action is the giving of notice of termination.

As already noted, we have no occasion to decide whether this factor would be determinative in a case lacking other factors identified above, *e.g.*, under a notice of withdrawal from the NATO treaty unaccompanied by derecognition of the other signatories. No specific restriction or condition on the President's action is found within the Constitution or this treaty itself. The termination clause is without conditions and without designation as to who shall act to terminate it. No specific role is spelled out in either the Constitution or this treaty for the Senate or the Congress as a whole. That power consequently devolves upon the President, and there is no basis for a court to imply a restriction on the President's power to terminate not contained in the Constitution, in this treaty, or in any other authoritative source.

While under the termination clause of this and similar treaties the power of the President to terminate may appear theoretically absolute, to think that this is so would be to ignore all historical practices in treaty termination and past and current reciprocal relationships between the Chief Executive and Congress. The wide variety of roles played by the Executive and the Congress (or the Senate alone) in the past termination of treaties teaches us nothing conclusive as to constitutional theory, but it instructs us as to what may fairly be contemplated as to the President's future exercise of the treaty termination power. Treaty termination is a political act, but political acts are not customarily taken without political support. Even if formal advice and consent is not constitutionally required as a prerequisite to termination, it might be sought. If the Congress is completely ignored, it has its arsenal of weapons, as previous Chief Executives have on occasion been sharply reminded.

Thus, the court is not to be taken as minimizing the role of the legislature in foreign affairs. The legislature's powers, including prominently its dominant status in the provision of funds, and its authority to investigate the Executive's functioning, establish authority for appropriate legislative participation in foreign affairs. The question of whether the Senate may be able to reserve to itself in particular treaties, at the time of their original submission, a specific role in their termination is not presented by the record in this appeal and we decide nothing with respect to it. The matter before us is solely one of whether the Constitution nullifies the procedure followed by the President in this instance. We find the President did not exceed his authority when he took action to withdraw from the ROC treaty, by giving notice under Article X of the Treaty, without the consent of the Senate or other legislative concurrences.

III

In our holding in this case we do not ignore the question of justiciability. We regard the only issue here to be whether the constitutional allocation of governmental power between two branches requires prior legislative consent to the termination of this treaty under the circumstances presented by this record. Viewing the issue before us so narrowly and in the circumstances of this treaty and its history to date, we see no reason which we could in good conscience invoke to refrain from judgment, and conclude that it is the duty of the court to confront and decide that issue.

Reversed

APPENDIX

A Guide to Spelling and Pronunciation

In 1978, the State Council of the People's Republic of China announced that it had decided to use the Chinese phonetic alphabet, called *pinyin*, to standardize the romanization of the names of people and places in China. The change went into effect on Jan. 1, 1979, and was subsequently adopted by most publications in the West.

Despite its obvious improvements over the previous system (Wade-Giles), the new system, too, poses problems for the reader unfamiliar with Chinese pronunciation. In addition, Chinese pronunciation, even by the Chinese themselves, is far from standardized, and can vary much more widely than is the case with English. Thus, those who use this pronunciation guide are cautioned that it represents, in many cases, only an approximation of the correct rendering of the actual sound.

The decision to change the system of romanization creates many problems for students of Chinese history, because so much has already been written about China using the old system of transliteration. Thus, a reader who might want to do further research on, say, the Taiwan Strait crisis of 1958, would search through recent literature in vain for any reference to an island named Quemoy, which is now rendered as "Jinmen" in the *pinyin* system.

Proper Names

The familiar older spelling has been retained in this book for several major historical figures: Chiang Kai-shek; Chou En-lai; Mao Tse-Tung; Lin Piao; and Liu Shao-ch'i.

But for current Chinese leaders, the new *pinyin* system was adopted. *(For a more complete list of current leaders, see p. 291)*

Old	New
Chairman of the Central Committee	
Hua Kuo-feng	Hua Guofeng
Vice Chairmen	
Ch'en Yun	Chen Yun
Li Hsien-nien	Li Xiannian
Teng Hsiao-p'ing	Deng Xiaoping
Wang Tung-hsing	Wang Dongxing
Yeh Chien-ying	Ye Jianying
Members of the Politburo	
Chang T'ing-fa	Zhang Tingfa
Ch'en Hsi-lien	Chen Xilian
Ch'en Yun	Chen Yun
Ch'en Yung-kuei	Chen Yonggui
Chi Teng-k'uei	Ji Dengkui
Fang Yi	Fang Yi
Hsu Hsiang-ch'ien	Xu Xiangqian
Hsu Shih-yu	Xu Shiyou

Old	New
Hu Yao-pang	Hu Yaobang
Hua Kuo-feng	Hua Guofeng
Keng Piao	Geng Biao
Li Hsien-nien	Li Xiannian
Li Teh-sheng	Li Desheng
Liu Po-ch'eng	Liu Bocheng
Ni Chih-fu	Ni Zhifu
Nieh Jung-chen	Nie Rongzhen
P'eng Chen	Peng Zhen
P'eng Ch'ung	Peng Chong
Teng Hsiao-p'ing	Deng Xiaoping
Teng Ying-ch'ao	Deng Yingchao
Ulanfu	Ulanhu
Wang Chen	Wang Zhen
Wang Tung-hsing	Wang Dongxing
Wei Kuo-ch'ing	Wei Guoqing
Wu Teh	Wu De
Yeh Chien-ying	Ye Jianying
Yü Ch'iu-li	Yu Qiuli

Alternate Members

Chao Tzu-yang	Zhao Ziyang
Ch'en Mu-hua	Chen Muhua
Saifudin	Seypidin

Place Names

Similarly, traditional spelling was used for most familiar Chinese geographical names: Peking, Canton, Hong Kong, Macao, Manchuria, Tibet and Quemoy. Others — Taiwan and Shanghai, for example — retain their old spelling in the *pinyin* system.

Old	New
Anhwei	Anhui
Amoy	Xiamen
Anshan	Anshan
Changchun	Changchun
Changsha	Changsha
Chekiang	Zhejiang
Chengchow	Zhengzhou
Chengtu	Chengdu
Chinghai	Qinghai
Chungking	Chongqing
Dairen	Dalian
Hangchow	Hangzhou
Foochow	Fuzhou
Fukien	Fujian
Harbin	Harbin
Heilungkiang	Heilongjiang
Hofei	Hefei
Honan	Henan
Hopei	Hebei
Hsining	Xining
Huhehot	Hohhot
Hunan	Hunan
Hupeh	Hubei

Old	New
Kaifeng	Kaifeng
Kansu	Gansu
Kiangsi	Jiangxi
Kiangsu	Jiangsu
Kirin	Jilin
Kunming	Kunming
Kwangchow	Guangzhou
Kwangsi	Guangxi
Kwangtung	Guangdong
Kweichow	Guizhou
Kweilin	Guilin
Kweiyang	Guiyang
Lanchow	Lanzhou
Lhasa	Lhasa
Liaoning	Liaoning
Loyang	Luoyang
Luta	Luda
Nanchang	Nanchang
Nanking	Nanjing
Nanning	Nanning
Ningsia	Ningxia
Shanghai	Shanghai
Shansi	Shanxi
Shantung	Shandong
Shensi	Shaanxi
Shenyang	Shenyang
Shichiachuang	Shijiazhuang
Sian	Xi'an
Sinkiang	Xinjiang
Soochow	Suzhou
Swatow	Shantou
Szechwan	Sichuan
Tachai	Dazhai
Taching	Daqing
Taiwan	Taiwan
Taiyuan	Taiyuan
Tali	Tali
Tangshan	Tangshan
Tientsin	Tianjin
Tsinan	Jinan
Tsingtao	Qingdao
Tsitsihar	Qiqihar
Tsunyi	Zunyi
Urumchi	Urumqi
Wuhan	Wuhan
Wuhsi	Wuxi
Yenan	Yanan
Yentai	Yindai
Yinchuan	Yinchuan
Yunnan	Yunnan

Pronunciation Guide

Most Chinese words consist of an "initial" and a "final." The initial is the consonant or pair of consonants at the beginning of a word. The final is the remainder of the word, beginning with the first vowel. Some words begin with vowels and have no initial — only a final.

To use this chart, look up the initial and final in their respective lists, and combine them. For example:

Shanghai: initial "Sh" + final "ang"
                 initial "h" + final "ai"

Deng Xiaoping: initial "D" + final "eng"
                  initial "X" + final "iao"
                  initial "p" + final "ing"

Initials

b	bay		p	pay
c	hats		q	cheer
ch	church		r	leisure
d	day		s	say
f	fair		sh	shirt
g	gay		t	take
h	hay		w	way
j	jeep		x	she
k	kay		y	yea
l	lay		z	reads
m	may		zh	judge
n	nay			

Finals

a	father		iong	y + woman + ng
ai	eye		iu	yeoman
an	on		o	wall
ang	German Gang		ong	woman + ng
ao	now		ou	old
e	her		u	rule
ei	eight		ü	few, French tu
en	nun		ua	quality
eng	sung		uai	wife
er	sir		uan	quandary
i	see		üan	u + tonsil
ia	Asia		uang	quality + ng
iao	yowl		üe	sweat
ian	yen		ueng	swung
iang	Yonkers		ui	way
ie	yes		un	won
in	in		ün	French une
ing	sing		uo	wall

Conversion Table

Traditional to Pinyin

Trad.	Pinyin	Trad.	Pinyin	Trad.	Pinyin	Trad.	Pinyin	Trad.	Pinyin	Trad.	Pinyin
a	a	ch'ang	chang	chiang	jiang	ch'ing	qing	chua	zhua	ch'ui	chui
ai	ai	chao	zhao	ch'iang	qiang	chiu	jiu	ch'ua	chua	chun	zhun
an	an	ch'ao	chao	chiao	jiao	ch'iu	qiu	chuai	zhuai	ch'un	chun
ang	ang	che	zhe	ch'iao	qiao	chiung	jiong	ch'uai	chuai	chün	jun
ao	ao	ch'e	che	chieh	jie	ch'iung	qiong	chuan	zhuan	ch'ün	qun
		chen	zhen	ch'ieh	qie	cho	zhuo	chüan	juan	chung	zhong
cha	zha	ch'en	chen	chien	jian	ch'o	chuo	ch'üan	quan	ch'ung	chong
ch'a	cha	cheng	zheng	ch'ien	qian	chou	zhou	chuang	zhuang		
chai	zhai	ch'eng	cheng	chih	zhi	ch'ou	chou	ch'uang	chuang	ei	ei
ch'ai	chai	chi	ji	ch'ih	chi	chu	zhu	chüeh	jue	en	en
chan	zhan	ch'i	qi	chin	jin	ch'u	chu	ch'üeh	que	eng	eng
ch'an	chan	chia	jia	ch'in	qin	chü	ju	chui	zhui	erh	er
chang	zhang	ch'ia	qia	ching	jing	ch'ü	qu				

362

Trad.	Pinyin	Trad.	Pinyin	Trad.	Pinyin	Trad.	Pinyin	Trad.	Pinyin	Trad.	Pinyin
fa	fa	jui	rui	lin	lin	o	e	shua	shua	ts'e	ce
fan	fan	jun	run	ling	ling	ou	ou	shuai	shuai	tsei	zei
fang	fang	jung	rong	liu	liu			shuan	shuan	tsen	zen
fei	fei			lo	luo	pa	ba	shuang	shuang	ts'en	cen
fen	fen	ka	ga	lou	lou	p'a	pa	shui	shui	tseng	zeng
feng	feng	k'a	ka	lu	lu	pai	bai	shun	shun	ts'eng	ceng
fo	fo	kai	gai	lü	lü	p'ai	pai	shuo	shuo	tso	zuo
fou	fou	k'ai	kai	luan	luan	pan	ban	so	suo	ts'o	cuo
fu	fu	kan	gan	lüan	lüan	p'an	pan	sou	sou	tsou	zou
		k'an	kan	lüeh	lüe	pang	bang	ssu	si	ts'ou	cou
ha	ha	kang	gang	lun	lun	p'ang	pang	su	su	tsu	zu
hai	hai	k'ang	kang	lung	long	pao	bao	suan	suan	ts'u	cu
han	han	kao	gao			p'ao	pao	sui	sui	tsuan	zuan
hang	hang	k'ao	kao			pei	bei	sun	sun	ts'uan	cuan
hao	hao	kei	gei	ma	ma	p'ei	pei	sung	song	tsui	zui
hei	hei	k'ei	kei	mai	mai	pen	ben			ts'ui	cui
hen	hen	ken	gen	man	man	p'en	pen	ta	da	tsun	zun
heng	heng	k'en	ken	mang	mang	peng	beng	t'a	ta	ts'un	cun
ho	he	keng	geng	mao	mao	p'eng	peng	tai	dai	tsung	zong
hou	hou	k'eng	keng	mei	mei	pi	bi	t'ai	tai	ts'ung	cong
hsi	xi	ko	ge	men	men	p'i	pi	tan	dan	tu	du
hsia	xia	k'o	ke	meng	meng	piao	biao	t'an	tan	t'u	tu
hsiang	xiang	kou	gou	mi	mi	p'iao	piao	tang	dang	tuan	duan
hsiao	xiao	k'ou	kou	miao	miao	pieh	bie	t'ang	tang	t'uan	tuan
hsieh	xie	ku	gu	mieh	mie	p'ieh	pie	tao	dao	tui	dui
hsien	xian	k'u	ku	mien	mian	pien	bian	t'ao	tao	t'ui	tui
hsin	xin	kua	gua	min	min	p'ien	pian	te	de	tun	dun
hsing	xing	k'ua	kua	ming	ming	pin	bin	t'e	te	t'un	tun
hsiu	xiu	kuai	guai	miu	miu	p'in	pin	tei	dei	tung	dong
hsiung	xiong	k'uai	kuai	mo	mo	ping	bing	teng	deng	t'ung	tong
hsü	xu	kuan	guan	mou	mou	p'ing	ping	t'eng	teng	tzu	zi
hsüan	xuan	k'uan	kuan	mu	mu	po	bo	ti	di	tz'u	ci
hsüeh	xue	kuang	guang			p'o	po	t'i	ti		
hsün	xun	k'uang	kuang	na	na	pou	bou	tiao	diao	wa	wa
hu	hu	kuei	gui	nai	nai	p'ou	pou	t'iao	tiao	wai	wai
hua	hua	k'uei	kui	nan	nan	pu	bu	tieh	die	wan	wan
huai	huai	kun	gun	nang	nang	p'u	pu	t'ieh	tie	wang	wang
huan	huan	k'un	kun	nao	nao			tien	dian	wei	wei
huang	huang	kung	gong	ne	ne	sa	sa	t'ien	tian	wen	wen
hui	hui	k'ung	kong	nei	nei	sai	sai	ting	ding	weng	weng
hun	hun	kuo	guo	nen	nen	san	san	t'ing	ting	wo	wo
hung	hong	k'uo	kuo	neng	neng	sang	sang	tiu	diu	wu	wu
huo	huo			ni	ni	sao	sao	to	duo		
		la	la	niang	niang	se	se	t'o	tuo	ya	ya
i	yi	lai	lai	niao	niao	sen	sen	tou	dou	yai	yai
		lan	lan	nieh	nie	seng	seng	t'ou	tou	yang	yang
jan	ran	lang	lang	nien	nian	sha	sha	tsa	za	yao	yao
jang	rang	lao	lao	nin	nin	shai	shai	ts'a	ca	yeh	ye
jao	rao	le	le	ning	ning	shan	shan	tsai	zai	yen	yan
je	re	lei	lei	niu	niu	shang	shang	ts'ai	cai	yin	yin
jen	ren	leng	leng	no	nuo	shao	shao	tsan	zan	ying	ying
jeng	reng	li	li	nou	nou	she	she	ts'an	can	yu	you
jih	ri	lia	lia	nu	nu	shen	shen	tsang	zang	yü	yu
jo	ruo	liang	liang	nü	nü	sheng	sheng	ts'ang	cang	yüan	yuan
jou	rou	liao	liao	nuan	nuan	shih	shi	tsao	zao	yüeh	yue
ju	ru	lieh	lie	nüeh	nüe	shou	shou	ts'ao	cao	yün	yun
juan	ruan	lien	lian	nung	nong	shu	shu	tse	ze	yung	yong

Pinyin to Traditional

Pinyin	Trad.	Pinyin	Trad.	Pinyin	Trad.	Pinyin	Trad.	Pinyin	Trad.	Pinyin	Trad.
a	a	bai	pai	bi	pi	bou	pou	cao	ts'ao	chang	ch'ang
ai	ai	ban	pan	bian	pien	bu	pu	ce	ts'e	chao	ch'ao
an	an	bang	pang	biao	piao			cen	ts'en	che	ch'e
ang	ang	bao	pao	bie	pieh	ca	ts'a	ceng	ts'eng	chen	ch'en
ao	ao	bei	pei	bin	pin	cai	ts'ai	cha	ch'a	cheng	ch'eng
		ben	pen	bing	ping	can	ts'an	chai	ch'ai	chi	ch'ih
ba	pa	beng	peng	bo	po	cang	ts'ang	chan	ch'an	chong	ch'ung

Pinyin	Trad.
chou	ch'ou
chu	ch'u
chua	ch'ua
chuai	ch'uai
chuan	ch'uan
chuang	ch'uang
chui	ch'ui
chun	ch'un
chuo	ch'o
ci	tz'u
cong	ts'ung
cou	ts'ou
cu	ts'u
cuan	ts'uan
cui	ts'ui
cun	ts'un
cuo	ts'o
da	ta
dai	tai
dan	tan
dang	tang
dao	tao
de	te
dei	tei
deng	teng
di	ti
dian	tien
diao	tiao
die	tieh
ding	ting
diu	tiu
dong	tung
dou	tou
du	tu
duan	tuan
dui	tui
dun	tun
duo	to
e	e,o
ei	ei
en	en
eng	eng
er	erh
fa	fa
fan	fan
fang	fang
fei	fei
fen	fen
feng	feng
fo	fo
fou	fou
fu	fu
ga	ka
gai	kai
gan	kan
gang	kang
gao	kao
ge	ke,ko
gei	kei
gen	ken
geng	keng
gong	kung
gou	kou
gu	ku
gua	kua
guai	kuai
guan	kuan
guang	kuang
gui	kuei
gun	kun
guo	kuo
ha	ha
hai	hai
han	han
hang	hang
hao	hao
he	he, ho
hei	hei
hen	hen
heng	heng
hong	hung
hou	hou
hu	hu
hua	hua
huai	huai
huan	huan
huang	huang
hui	hui
hun	hun
huo	huo
ji	chi
jia	chia
jian	chien
jiang	chiang
jiao	chiao
jie	chieh
jin	chin
jing	ching
jiong	chiung
jiu	chiu
ju	chü
juan	chüan
jue	chüeh
jun	chün
ka	k'a
kai	k'ai
kan	k'an
kang	k'ang
kao	k'ao
ke	k'e, k'o
kei	k'ei
ken	k'en
keng	k'eng
kong	k'ung
kou	k'ou
ku	k'u
kua	k'ua
kuai	k'uai
kuan	k'uan
kuang	k'uang
kui	k'uei
kun	k'un
kun	k'un
la	la
lai	lai
lan	lan
lang	lang
lao	lao
le	le
lei	lei
leng	leng
li	li
lia	lia
lian	lien
liang	liang
liao	liao
lie	lieh
lin	lin
ling	ling
liu	liu
long	lung
lou	lou
lu	lu
lü	lü
luan	luan
lüan	lüan
lüe	lüeh
lun	lun
luo	lo
ma	ma
mai	mai
man	man
mang	mang
mao	mao
mei	mei
men	men
meng	meng
mi	mi
mian	mien
miao	miao
mie	mieh
min	min
ming	ming
miu	miu
mo	mo
mou	mou
mu	mu
na	na
nai	nai
nan	nan
nang	nang
nao	nao
ne	ne
nei	nei
nen	nen
neng	neng
ni	ni
nian	nien
niang	niang
niao	niao
nie	nieh
nin	nin
ning	ning
niu	niu
nong	nung
nou	nou
nu	nu
nü	nü
nuan	nuan
nüe	nüeh
nuo	no
ou	ou
pa	p'a
pai	p'ai
pan	p'an
pang	p'ang
pao	p'ao
pei	p'ei
pen	p'en
peng	p'eng
pi	p'i
pian	p'ien
piao	p'iao
pie	p'ieh
pin	p'in
ping	p'ing
po	p'o
pou	p'ou
pu	p'u
qi	ch'i
qia	ch'ia
qian	ch'ien
qiang	ch'iang
qiao	ch'iao
qie	ch'ieh
qin	ch'in
qing	ch'ing
qiong	ch'iung
qiu	ch'iu
qu	ch'ü
quan	ch'üan
que	ch'üeh
qun	ch'ün
ran	jan
rang	jang
rao	jao
re	je
ren	jen
reng	jeng
ri	jih
rong	jung
rou	jou
ru	ju
ruan	juan
rui	jui
run	jun
ruo	jo
sa	sa
sai	sai
san	san
sang	sang
sao	sao
se	se
sen	sen
seng	seng
sha	sha
shai	shai
shan	shan
shang	shang
shao	shao
she	she
shen	shen
sheng	sheng
shi	shih
shou	shou
shu	shu
shua	shua
shuai	shuai
shuan	shuan
shuang	shuang
shui	shui
shun	shun
shuo	shuo
si	szu,ssu
song	sung
sou	sou
su	su
suan	suan
sui	sui
sun	sun
suo	so
ta	t'a
tai	t'ai
tan	t'an
tang	t'ang
tao	t'ao
te	t'e
teng	t'eng
ti	t'i
tian	t'ien
tiao	t'iao
tie	t'ieh
ting	t'ing
tong	t'ung
tou	t'ou
tu	t'u
tuan	t'uan
tui	t'ui
tun	t'un
tuo	t'o
wa	wa
wai	wai
wan	wan
wang	wang
wei	wei
wen	wen
weng	weng
wo	wo
wu	wu
xi	hsi
xia	hsia
xian	hsien
xiang	hsiang
xiao	hsiao
xie	hsieh
xin	hsin
xing	hsing
xiong	hsiung
xiu	hsiu
xu	hsü
xuan	hsüan
xue	hsüeh
xun	hsün
ya	ya
yai	yai
yan	yen
yang	yang
yao	yao
ye	yeh
yi	i
yin	yin
ying	ying
yong	yung
you	yu
yu	yü
yuan	yüan
yue	yüeh
yun	yün
za	tsa
zai	tsai
zan	tsan
zang	tsang
zao	tsao
ze	tse
zei	tsei
zen	tsen
zeng	tseng
zha	cha
zhai	chai
zhan	chan
zhang	chang
zhao	chao
zhe	che
zhen	chen
zheng	cheng
zhi	chih
zhong	chung
zhou	chou
zhu	chu
zhua	chua
zhuai	chuai
zhuan	chuan
zhuang	chuang
zhui	chui
zhun	chun
zhuo	cho
zi	tzu
zong	tsung
zou	tsou
zu	tsu
zuan	tsuan
zui	tsui
zun	tsun
zuo	tso

United Nations Votes on Chinese Representation

The following table indicates the relative strength of the move for representation of the People's Republic of China (PRC) and the removal of the Republic of China (Nationalists) in the U.N. General Assembly during the years 1950-1971: The China question was on the provisional agenda for the 1964 session but did not come to a vote because of the U.N. stalemate over peacekeeping assessments.

The votes on the issue:

Year			For	Against	Abstentions
1950	(a) Indian resolution to seat PRC	Rejected	16	32	10
	(b) USSR resolution to unseat Nationalists	Rejected	10	38	8
1951	Moratorium (U.S. resolution not to consider any changes in Chinese representation)	Adopted	37	11	4
1952	Moratorium	Adopted	42	7	11
1953	Moratorium	Adopted	44	10	2
1954	Moratorium	Adopted	43	11	6
1955	Moratorium	Adopted	42	12	6
1956	Moratorium	Adopted	47	24	8
1957	Moratorium	Adopted	48	27	6
1958	Moratorium	Adopted	44	28	9
1959	Moratorium	Adopted	44	29	9
1960	Moratorium	Adopted	42	34	22
1961	(a) Five-power resolution (United States, Australia, Colombia, Italy and Japan) making any proposal to change the representation of China an "important question" requiring a two-thirds majority for approval	Adopted	61	34	7
	(b) USSR resolution to oust Nationalists and seat the PRC	Rejected	37	48	19*
1962	USSR resolution to oust Nationalists and seat PRC	Rejected	42	56	12*
1963	Albanian resolution to oust Nationalists and seat PRC	Rejected	41	57	12
1965	(a) 11-power resolution (U.S., Australia, Brazil, Colombia, Madagascar, Nicaragua, Gabon, Italy, Japan, Philippines, Thailand) declaring 1961 vote on "important question" still in force	Approved	56	49	11
	(b) 12-power resolution (Albania, Algeria, Cambodia, Congo-Brazzaville, Cuba, Ghana, Guinea, Mali, Pakistan, Romania, Somalia, Syria) to oust Nationalists and seat PRC	Rejected	47	47	20*
1966	(a) 15-power resolution (U.S., Australia, Belgium, Bolivia, Brazil, Colombia, Gabon, Italy, Japan, Malagasy Republic, New Zealand, Nicaragua, Philippines, Thailand, Togo) declaring China entry motion an "important question"	Approved	66	48	7
	(b) 10-power resolution (Albania, Algeria, Cambodia, Congo-Brazzaville, Cuba, Guinea, Mali, Pakistan, Romania, Syria) to oust Nationalists and seat PRC	Rejected	46	57	17*
	(c) Italian proposal (with Belgium, Bolivia, Brazil, Chile, Trinidad, Tobago) to appoint special committee to investigate PRC's position vis-a-vis U.N. membership and report to Assembly by July 1967	Rejected	34	62	25*
1967	(a) 15-power resolution (U.S., Australia, Belgium, Bolivia, Brazil, Colombia, Gabon, Italy, Japan, Malagasy Republic, New Zealand, Nicaragua, Philippines, Thailand, Togo) declaring China entry motion an "important question"	Approved	69	48	4
	(b) 11-power resolution (Albania, Algeria, Cambodia, Congo-Brazzaville, Cuba, Guinea, Mali, Mauritania, Pakistan, Romania, Syria — Sudan later became the 12th cosponsor) to seat PRC	Rejected	45	58	17*
	(c) Italian proposal with Belgium, Chile, Luxembourg, Netherlands) to appoint special committee to investigate PRC's position vis-a-vis U.N. membership and report to Assembly during 1968 session (also made an "important question" under Article 18)	Rejected	32	57	30
1968	(a) 13-power resolution (U.S., Australia, Bolivia, Brazil, Colombia, Gabon, Japan, Malagasy Republic, New Zealand, Nicaragua, Philippines, Thailand, Togo — Italy later became 14th cosponsor) declaring China entry motion an "important question"	Approved	73	47	5
	(b) 15-power resolution to oust Nationalists and seat PRC	Rejected	44	58	23*
	(c) Italian proposal (with Belgium, Chile, Iceland, Luxembourg) to appoint special committee to investigate PRC's position vis-a-vis U.N. membership and report to Assembly during next session (made an "important question")	Rejected	30	67	27
1969	(a) 18-power resolution declaring China entry motion an "important question"	Approved	71	48	4
	(b) 17-power resolution to oust Nationalists and seat PRC	Rejected	48	56	21*
1970	(a) 18-power resolution declaring China entry question an "important question"	Approved	66	52	7
	(b) 18-power resolution to oust Nationalists and seat PRC	Rejected	51	49	25*
1971	(a) 19-power resolution declaring China entry question an "important question"	Rejected	55	59	15
	(b) 21-power resolution to oust Nationalists and seat PRC	Approved	76	35	17

Two-thirds majority required for adoption.

1971 United Nations Roll Calls on China

On Two-Thirds Requirement

Resolution declaring the expulsion of the Republic of China an "important matter" and thus requiring a two-thirds vote rather than a simple majority for passage.

IN FAVOR—55

Argentina
Australia
Bahrain
Barbados
Bolivia
Brazil
Cambodia
Cent. Afr. Rep.
Chad
China (Taiwan)
Colombia
Congo (Kinsh.)
Costa Rica
Dahomey
Dominican Rep.
El Salvador
Fiji
Gabon
Gambia
Ghana
Greece
Guatemala
Haiti
Honduras
Indonesia
Israel
Ivory Coast
Jamaica
Japan
Jordan
Lebanon
Lesotho
Liberia
Luxembourg
Madagascar
Malawi
Mauritius
Mexico
New Zealand
Nicaragua
Niger
Panama
Paraguay
Philippines
Portugal
Rwanda
Saudi Arabia
South Africa
Spain
Swaziland
Thailand
United States
Upper Volta
Uruguay
Venezuela

OPPOSED—59

Afghanistan
Albania
Algeria
Bhutan
Britain
Bulgaria
Burma
Burundi
Byelorussia
Cameroon
Canada
Ceylon
Chile
Congo (Brazza.)
Cuba
Czechoslovakia
Denmark
Ecuador
Egypt
Eq. Guinea
Ethiopia
Finland
France
Guinea
Guyana
Hungary
Iceland
India
Iraq
Ireland
Kenya
Kuwait
Libya
Malaysia
Mali
Mauritania
Mongolia
Nepal
Nigeria
Norway
Pakistan
Peru
Poland
Romania
Sierra Leone
Singapore
Somalia
So. Yemen
Soviet Union
Sudan
Sweden
Syria
Tanzania
Trinidad-Tobago
Uganda
Ukraine
Yemen
Yugoslavia
Zambia

ABSTENTIONS—15

Austria
Belgium
Botswana
Cyprus
Iran
Italy
Laos
Malta
Morocco
Netherlands
Qatar
Senegal
Togo
Tunisia
Turkey

Absent—Maldives, Oman.

On Seating Peking

Resolution to seat People's Republic of China and expel the Republic of China (*UN votes on China question 1950-1971, p. 365*)

IN FAVOR—76

Afghanistan
Albania
Algeria
Austria
Belgium
Bhutan
Botswana
Britain
Bulgaria
Burma
Burundi
Byelorussia
Cameroon
Canada
Ceylon
Chile
Congo (Brazza.)
Cuba
Czechoslovakia
Denmark
Ecuador
Egypt
Eq. Guinea
Ethiopia
Finland
France
Ghana
Guinea
Guyana
Hungary
Iceland
India
Iran
Iraq
Ireland
Israel
Italy
Kenya
Kuwait
Laos
Libya
Malaysia
Mali
Mauritania
Mexico
Mongolia
Morocco
Nepal
Netherlands
Nigeria
Norway
Pakistan
Peru
Poland
Portugal
Romania
Rwanda
Senegal
Sierra Leone
Singapore
Somalia
So. Yemen
Soviet Union
Sudan
Sweden
Syria
Tanzania
Togo
Trinidad-Tobago
Tunisia
Turkey
Uganda
Ukraine
Yemen
Yugoslavia
Zambia

OPPOSED—35

Australia
Bolivia
Brazil
Cambodia
Cent. Afr. Rep.
Chad
Congo (Kinsh.)
Costa Rica
Dahomey
Dominican Rep.
El Salvador
Gabon
Gambia
Guatemala
Haiti
Honduras
Ivory Coast
Japan
Lesotho
Liberia
Madagascar
Malawi
Malta
New Zealand
Nicaragua
Niger
Paraguay
Philippines
Saudi Arabia
South Africa
Swaziland
United States
Upper Volta
Uruguay
Venezuela

ABSTENTIONS—17

Argentina
Bahrain
Barbados
Colombia
Cyprus
Fiji
Greece
Indonesia
Jamaica
Jordan
Lebanon
Luxembourg
Mauritius
Panama
Qatar
Spain
Thailand

Absent—China, Maldives, Oman.

Estimated and Projected Population

	Total	Under 15	15-64	Over 64	Natural Increase	Births	Deaths
	Thousand Persons				**Vital Rates per 1,000**		
1949	537,918	200,105	322,751	15,062	12.0	45.4	33.4
1950	547,364	205,809	326,229	15,326	13.5	45.4	31.9
1951	558,096	211,518	330,393	16,185	15.1	45.3	30.2
1952	569,904	218,273	335,104	16,527	18.0	45.2	27.2
1953	582,603	225,237	340,102	17,264	22.5	45.0	22.5
1954	596,064	232,571	345,559	17,934	23.1	44.1	21.0
1955	610,201	240,344	351,185	18,672	23.8	43.1	19.4
1956	625,004	248,608	356,940	19,456	24.2	42.6	18.5
1957	640,024	256,961	362,799	20,264	23.3	41.3	18.0
1958	654,727	264,902	368,747	21,078	22.1	40.2	18.1
1959	668,930	272,385	374,679	21,866	20.8	40.1	19.3
1960	682,091	279,088	380,427	22,576	18.2	39.9	21.7
1961	693,624	284,439	386,003	23,182	15.4	39.1	23.7
1962	705,486	289,460	392,192	23,834	18.5	37.7	19.2
1963	719,301	295,219	399,458	24,624	20.3	37.6	17.4
1964	734,359	301,061	407,812	25,486	21.2	37.2	16.0
1965	750,394	306,725	417,258	26,411	22.0	36.5	14.4
1966	766,946	312,174	427,403	27,369	21.6	36.2	14.6
1967	784,017	317,451	438,222	28,344	22.4	36.2	13.8
1968	801,983	322,723	449,907	29,353	22.9	36.3	13.4
1969	820,733	328,124	462,221	30,388	23.3	36.3	12.9
1970	840,148	333,851	474,837	31,460	23.4	35.7	12.3
1971	859,927	339,626	487,741	32,560	23.1	34.9	11.8
1972	879,520	345,184	500,654	33,682	22.0	33.5	11.6
1973	898,695	350,551	513,305	34,839	21.2	32.0	10.8
1974	917,256	355,291	525,933	36,032	19.7	30.0	10.2
1975	934,626	358,735	538,642	37,249	17.8	27.6	9.8
1976	950,744	360,794	551,453	38,497	16.4	25.5	9.1
1977	965,937	361,569	564,586	39,782	15.3	24.1	8.8
1978	980,417	360,967	578,361	41,089	14.4	23.0	8.6
1979	994,332	359,136	592,782	42,414	13.7	22.1	8.4
1980	1,007,858	356,497	607,601	43,760	13.3	21.5	8.2
1985	1,075,999	335,887	689,213	50,899	13.2	21.1	7.9
1990	1,151,665	320,873	771,480	59,312	14.0	21.9	7.9
1995	1,237,029	340,759	827,122	69,148	14.5	22.7	8.1
2000	1,328,645	375,343	872,993	80,309	13.7	22.0	8.3

Source: CIA, National Foreign Assessment Center, *China: Economic Indicators* (ER77-10508, October 1977), p. 8. Estimates prepared by the U.S. Department of Commerce, Bureau of Economic Analysis, Foreign Demographic Analysis Division.

Provincial-Level Units: Area and Population

Unit	Capital City	Area* (1970)	Population (In Thousands) 1976	1965	1953
Provinces					
Anhui	Hefei	54	45,000	37,442	30,663
Fujian	Fuzhou	48	24,000	17,823	13,143
Gansu	Lanzhou	190	19,795	15,200	11,291
Guangdong	Canton	83	54,100	42,684	34,770
Guizhou	Guiyang	67	24,000	19,302	15,037
Hebei	Shijiazhuang	75	55,193	41,428	33,181
Heilongjiang	Harbin	280	32,000	21,320	12,681
Henan	Zhengzhou	65	67,468	54,829	43,911
Hubei	Wuchang	72	43,848	35,221	27,790
Hunan	Changsha	81	49,018	40,563	33,227
Jiangsu	Nanjing	40	61,504	48,523	38,329
Jiangxi	Nanchang	64	29,400	22,271	16,773
Jilin	Changchun	110	23,000	17,177	12,609
Liaoning	Shenyang	90	44,474	32,403	22,269
Qinghai	Xining	280	3,858	2,664	1,677
Shaanxi	Xi'an	76	26,000	20,800	15,881
Shandong	Jinan	60	78,478	63,257	50,134
Shanxi	Taiyuan	61	23,000	18,349	14,314
Sichuan	Chengdu	220	100,080	81,634	65,685
Yunnan	Kunming	168	28,000	22,120	17,473
Zhejiang	Hangzhou	39	36,000	28,918	22,866

Autonomous Regions:

Guangxi Zhuang	Nanning	91	31,300	24,776	19,561
Inner Mongolia	Hohhot	225	8,500	5,778	3,532
Ningxia Hui	Yinchuan	40	3,000	2,253	1,637
Tibet	Lhasa	470	1,700	1,458	1,274
Xinjiang Uygur	Urumqi	640	10,000	7,119	4,874

Centrally Administered Cities:

Peking		.66	8,490	7,730	4,591
Shanghai		.22	12,312	10,966	8,808
Tianjin		.12	7,226	6,386	4,622
TOTAL		3,700	950,744	750,394	582,603

*In thousands of square miles.

Sources: 1970 area figures adapted from Theodore Shabad, *China's Changing Map*, New York: Praeger, 1972, p. 34; population figures from CIA, National Foreign Assessment Center, *China: Economic Indicators* (ER77--10508, October 1977), p. 9; in James R. Townsend (comp.), *The People's Republic of China: A Basic Handbook*, New York: China Council of the Asia Society, 1979, p. 21.

Growth of Chinese Communist Party

Period and Year	Number of Members	Years Covered	Average Annual Increase
United Front Period			
1921 (1st Congress)	57	—	—
1922 (2nd Congress)	123	1	66
1923 (3rd Congress)	432	1	309
1925 (4th Congress)	950	2	259
1927 (5th Congress)	57,967	2	28,508
1927 (after KMT purge)	10,000	—	—
Jiangxi Soviet Period			
1928 (6th Congress)	40,000	1	30,000
1930	122,318	2	41,159
1933	300,000	3	59,227
1937 (after the Long March)	40,000	4	−65,000
World War II			
1940	800,000	3	253,333
1941	763,447	1	−36,533
1942	736,151	1	−27,296
1944	853,420	2	58,635
1945 (7th Congress)	1,211,128	1	357,708
Civil War			
1946	1,348,320	1	137,192
1947	2,759,456	1	1,411,136
1948	3,065,533	1	306,077
1949	4,488,080	1	1,422,547
Under the PRC			
1950	5,821,604	1	1,333,524
1951	5,762,293	1	−59,311
1952	6,001,698	1	239,405
1953	6,612,254	1	610,556
1954	7,859,473	1	1,247,219
1955	9,393,394	1	1,533,921
1956 (8th Congress)	10,734,384	1	1,340,990
1957	12,720,000	1	1,985,616
1958	13,960,000	2	620,000
1961	17,000,000	2	1,520,000
1973 (10th Congress)	28,000,000	12	916,666
1977 (11th Congress)	35,000,000	4	1,750,000

Sources: Figures for the years 1921-61 adapted from John W. Lewis, *Leadership in Communist China*, Ithaca: Cornell University Press, 1963; the 1973 figure, from Chou En-lai's "Report" to the CCP 10th Congress of August 1973 in the *10th National Congress of the Communist China (Documents)*, Peking: Foreign Languages Press, 1973, p. 8; and the 1977 figure, from *Peking Review*, No. 35, August 26, 1977, p. 6; in James R. Townsend (comp.), *The People's Republic of China: A Basic Handbook*, New York: China Council of the Asia Society, 1979, p. 50.

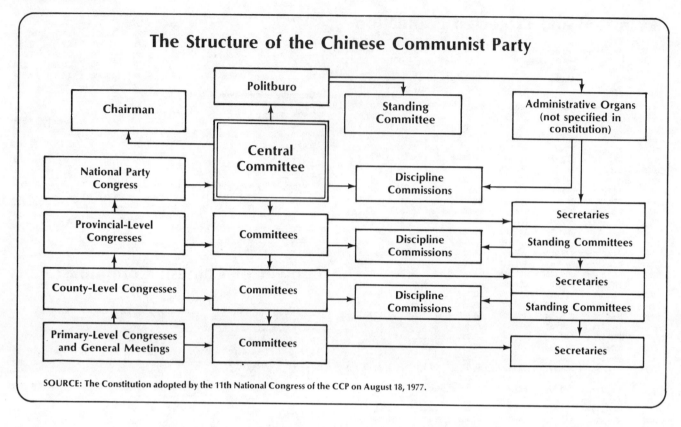

The Structure of the Chinese Communist Party

SOURCE: The Constitution adopted by the 11th National Congress of the CCP on August 18, 1977.

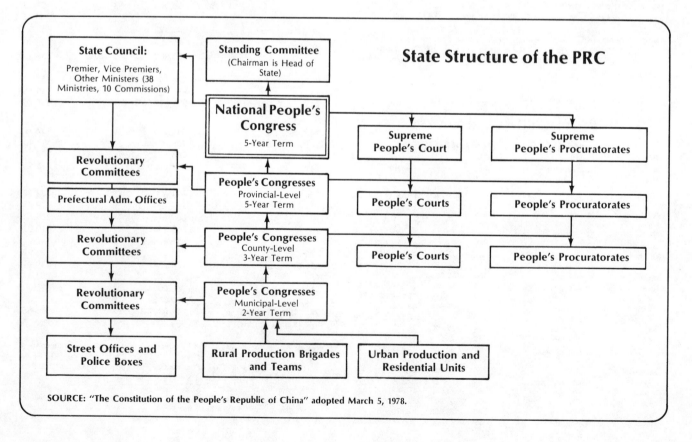

State Structure of the PRC

SOURCE: "The Constitution of the People's Republic of China" adopted March 5, 1978.

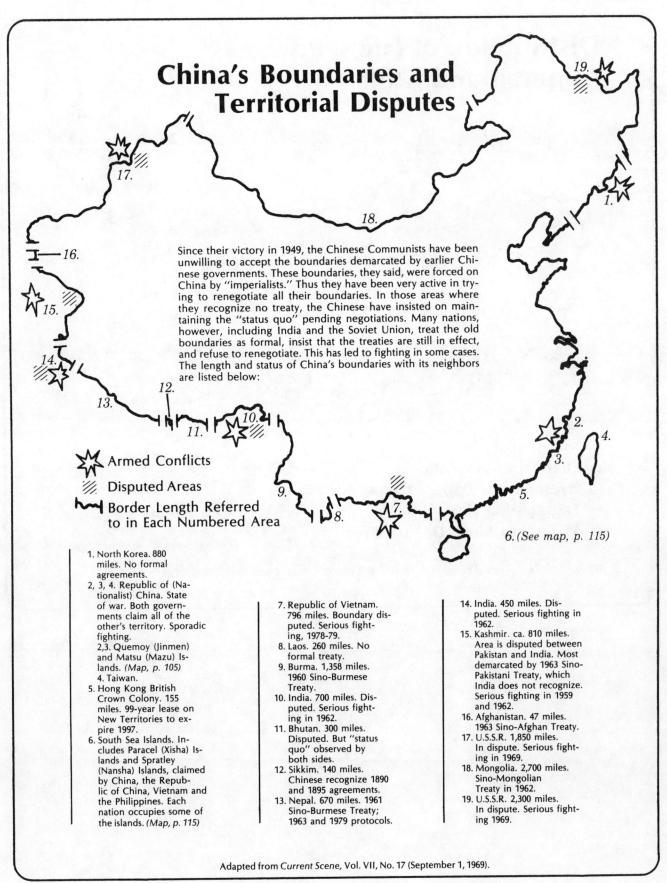

China's Boundaries and Territorial Disputes

19.

17.

18.

16.

15.

1.

14.

13.

12.

11.

10.

Since their victory in 1949, the Chinese Communists have been unwilling to accept the boundaries demarcated by earlier Chinese governments. These boundaries, they said, were forced on China by "imperialists." Thus they have been very active in trying to renegotiate all their boundaries. In those areas where they recognize no treaty, the Chinese have insisted on maintaining the "status quo" pending negotiations. Many nations, however, including India and the Soviet Union, treat the old boundaries as formal, insist that the treaties are still in effect, and refuse to renegotiate. This has led to fighting in some cases. The length and status of China's boundaries with its neighbors are listed below:

2.

4.

3.

✦ **Armed Conflicts**

▨ **Disputed Areas**

〜 **Border Length Referred to in Each Numbered Area**

9.

8.

7.

5.

6. (See map, p. 115)

1. North Korea. 880 miles. No formal agreements.
2, 3, 4. Republic of (Nationalist) China. State of war. Both governments claim all of the other's territory. Sporadic fighting.
2,3. Quemoy (Jinmen) and Matsu (Mazu) Islands. *(Map, p. 105)*
4. Taiwan.
5. Hong Kong British Crown Colony. 155 miles. 99-year lease on New Territories to expire 1997.
6. South Sea Islands. Includes Paracel (Xisha) Islands and Spratley (Nansha) Islands, claimed by China, the Republic of China, Vietnam and the Philippines. Each nation occupies some of the islands. *(Map, p. 115)*

7. Republic of Vietnam. 796 miles. Boundary disputed. Serious fighting, 1978-79.
8. Laos. 260 miles. No formal treaty.
9. Burma. 1,358 miles. 1960 Sino-Burmese Treaty.
10. India. 700 miles. Disputed. Serious fighting in 1962.
11. Bhutan. 300 miles. Disputed. But "status quo" observed by both sides.
12. Sikkim. 140 miles. Chinese recognize 1890 and 1895 agreements.
13. Nepal. 670 miles. 1961 Sino-Burmese Treaty; 1963 and 1979 protocols.

14. India. 450 miles. Disputed. Serious fighting in 1962.
15. Kashmir. ca. 810 miles. Area is disputed between Pakistan and India. Most demarcated by 1963 Sino-Pakistani Treaty, which India does not recognize. Serious fighting in 1959 and 1962.
16. Afghanistan. 47 miles. 1963 Sino-Afghan Treaty.
17. U.S.S.R. 1,850 miles. In dispute. Serious fighting in 1969.
18. Mongolia. 2,700 miles. Sino-Mongolian Treaty in 1962.
19. U.S.S.R. 2,300 miles. In dispute. Serious fighting 1969.

Adapted from *Current Scene*, Vol. VII, No. 17 (September 1, 1969).

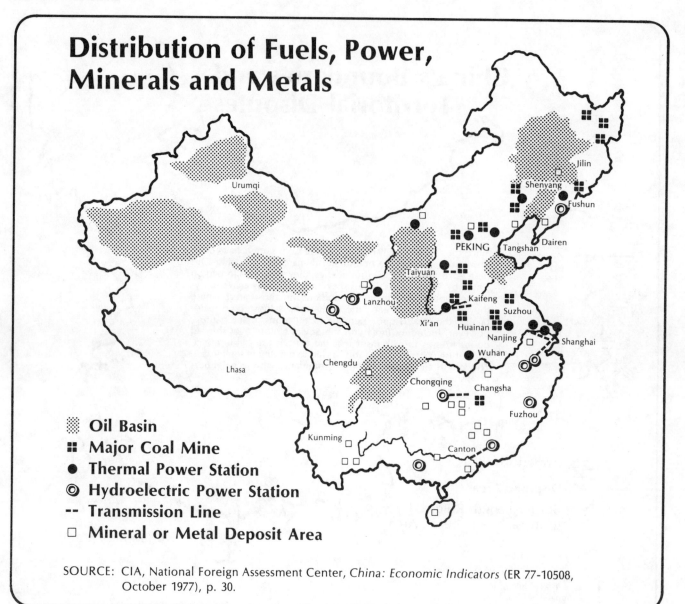

Distribution of Fuels, Power, Minerals and Metals

Oil Basin
Major Coal Mine
Thermal Power Station
Hydroelectric Power Station
Transmission Line
Mineral or Metal Deposit Area

SOURCE: CIA, National Foreign Assessment Center, *China: Economic Indicators* (ER 77-10508, October 1977), p. 30.

Selected Bibliography on China

For the reader who would like to explore certain aspects of China or China-American relations further, the following bibliography is divided topically.

Biography

(See biography section, p. 282)

Current Events

Asian Survey. Berkeley (monthly).
Beijing (formerly *Peking*) *Review.* Peking (weekly).
The China Quarterly. London (quarterly).
(a more complete list of periodicals appears on p. 75)

Economics

Eckstein, Alexander. *China's Economic Revolution.* Cambridge: Cambridge University Press, 1977.
Gurley, John G. *China's Economy and the Maoist Strategy.* New York: Basic Books, Inc., 1978.
The China Business Review. Washington, D.C. (bimonthly).
The Far Eastern Economic Review. Hong Kong (weekly).

General Introduction and History

Clubb, O. Edmund. *20th Century China.* New York: Columbia University Press, 1964.
Fairbank, John K. *The United States and China,* 3rd ed. Cambridge: Harvard University Press, 1971.
Fairbank, John K.; Reischauer, Edwin O.; and Craig, Albert M. *East Asia: The Modern Transformation.* Boston: Houghton Mifflin, 1965.
Hinton, Harold. *The People's Republic of China: A Handbook.* Boulder: Westview Press, 1978.
Michael, Franz H. and Taylor, George E. *The Far East in Modern Times,* 3rd ed. New York: Holt, Rinehart and Winston, 1975.
Snow, Edgar. *Red Star over China,* rev. ed. New York: Grove Press, Inc., 1968.
Townsend, James R., comp. *The People's Republic of China: A Basic Handbook.* New York: China Council of the Asia Society, 1979.
Wu Yuan-li. *China: A Handbook.* New York: Praeger Publishers, 1973.

Geography, Population, and Daily Life

An Illustrated Atlas of China. New York: Rand McNally, 1972.
Chen, Jack. *A Year in Upper Felicity: Life in a Chinese Village During the Cultural Revolution.* New York: Macmillan, 1973.
Crozier, Ralph C., ed. *China's Cultural Legacy and Communism.* New York: Praeger Publishers, 1970.
Kessen, William, ed. *Childhood in China.* New Haven: Yale University Press, 1975.
Leys, Simon. *Chinese Shadows.* New York: Viking, 1977.
Orleans, Leo A. *Every Fifth Child: The Population of China.* Stanford: Stanford University Press, 1973.
Shabad, Theodore. *China's Changing Map: National and Regional Development, 1949-71.* New York: Praeger Publishers, 1972.
Terrill, Ross. *Flowers on an Iron Tree: Five Cities of China.* Boston: Little, Brown and Company, 1975.

Politics in China

Domes, Jurgen. *China after the Cultural Revolution.* Berkeley and Los Angeles: University of California Press, 1977.
Guillermaz, Jacques. *The Chinese Communist Party in Power, 1949-1976.* Boulder: Westview Press, 1976.
Hinton, Harold. *An Introduction to Chinese Politics,* 2nd ed. Huntington, N.Y.: R.E. Krieger Publishing Company, 1978.

Sino-American Relations and Chinese Foreign Policy

Backrack, Stanley. *The Committee of One Million: The China Lobby and U.S. Policy, 1953-1972.* New York: Columbia University Press, 1976.
Barnett, A. Doak. *China and the Major Powers in East Asia.* Washington, D.C.: The Brookings Institution, 1977.
Blum, Robert. *The United States and China in World Affairs.* New York: McGraw-Hill Book Company, 1966.
Bueler, William M. *U.S. China Policy and the Problem of Taiwan.* Boulder: Colorado Associated University Press, 1971.
Chai, Winberg, ed. *The Foreign Relations of the People's Republic of China.* New York: G. P. Putnam's Sons, 1972.
Chen, King C., ed. *China and the Three Worlds: A Foreign Policy Reader.* Boulder: Westview Press, 1978.
Dulles, Foster Rhea. *American Policy toward Communist China: The Historical Record, 1949-1969.* New York: Thomas Y. Crowell Company, 1972.
Fairbank, John K. *China: The People's Middle Kingdom and the U.S.A.* Cambridge: Harvard University Press, 1967.
Fairbank, John K. *China Perceived: Images and Policies in Chinese-American Relations.* New York: Alfred A. Knopf, 1974.
Feis, Herbert. *China Tangle.* Princeton: Princeton University Press, 1953.
Gittings, John. *The World and China, 1922-1972.* New York: Harper and Row Publishers, 1974.
Griswold, A. Whitney. *The Far Eastern Policy of the United States.* New York: Harcourt Brace, 1938.

Hinton, Harold. *Communist China in World Politics.* Boston: Houghton Mifflin Company, 1966.

Hsiao, Gene, ed. *Sino-American Detente and Its Policy Implications.* New York: Praeger Publishers, 1974.

Hsueh, Chun-tu, ed. *Dimensions of China's Foreign Relations.* New York: Praeger Publishers, 1977.

Maxwell, Neville. *India's China War.* Garden City: Anchor Books, Doubleday and Company, 1972.

Mehnert, Klaus. *Peking and the New Left: At Home and Abroad.* Berkeley: University of California Center for Chinese Studies, 1969.

Schaller, Michael. *The U.S. Crusade in China, 1938-1945.* New York: Columbia University Press, 1979.

Schwartz, Harry. *Tsars, Mandarins and Commissars: A History of Chinese-Russian Relations.* Garden City: Anchor Books, Doubleday and Company, 1973.

Spanier, John W. *The Truman-MacArthur Controversy and the Korean War.* New York: W.W. Norton and Company, 1965.

Steele, A. T. *The American People and China.* New York: McGraw-Hill Book Company, 1966.

Sutter, Robert G. *Chinese Foreign Policy after the Cultural Revolution, 1966-1977.* Boulder: Westview Press, 1978.

Thornton, Richard C. *China, the Struggle for Power, 1917-1972.* Bloomington: Indiana University Press, 1973.

Tierney, John Jr., ed. *About Face: The China Decision and Its Consequences.* New Rochelle: Arlington House Publishers, 1979.

Tsou, Tang. *America's Failure in China, 1941-1950.* 2 vols. Chicago: University of Chicago Press, 1963.

Whiting, Allen. *China Crosses the Yalu: The Decision to Enter the Korean War.* Stanford: Stanford University Press, 1960.

Young, Kenneth T. *Negotiating with the Chinese Communists: The United States' Experience, 1953-1967.* New York: McGraw-Hill Book Company, 1968.

Zagoria, Donald S. *The Sino-Soviet Conflict, 1956-1961.* Princeton: Princeton University Press, 1962.

Teaching Materials

Howe, Christopher, ed. *Studying China: A Source Book for Teachers in Schools and Colleges.* London: Extramural Division, School of Oriental and African Studies, 1979.

Posner, Arlene and deKeijzer, Arne J., eds. *China: A Resource and Curriculum Guide.* 2nd ed. Chicago: University of Chicago Press, 1976.

Newsletters

The following colleges and universities publish newsletters with information about local programs and resources dealing with China: University of Arizona, Columbia University, Harvard University, University of Virginia, Princeton University, University of Hawaii at Manoa, University of Washington, Amherst College, University of Chicago, University of Michigan, University of California at Berkeley, University of Texas at Austin, Duke University, University of Southern California at Los Angeles, and Yale University.

Index